...tin Strokestown
...martin Strokestown
...artin Strokestown
...llyfeeny Strokestown
...yfeeney Strokestown
...feeney Strokestown
...yfeeney Strokestown
...eney Strokestown
...llyfeeney Strokestown
...llyfeeney Strokestown
...ffeeney Strokestown
...Ballyfeeny Strokestown
...ey Strokestown
...feeny Strokestown
...yfeeney Strokestown
...lass Strokestown
...lass Strokestown
...ane Kelglass stown
...ane Kelglass stown
...ane Kelglass stown
...ane Kelglass stown

(24)

<!-- Right column -->
Kilgarve. Ruskey.
Kilgarve. Ruskey.
Kilgarve Ruskey.
...or. Kilgarve Ruskey.
...kell Ruskey
...Cloonkell Ruskey
...Cloonkell Ruskey.
...Cloonkell Ruskey
...Cloonkell Ruskey.
...Cloonkell Ruskey
...Cloonkell Ruskey.
...Cloonkell Ruskey.
...Cloonkell Ruskey.
...Cloon Mullagh Ruskey.
...Mullagh Ruskey.
...Mullagh Ruskey.
...Mullagh Ruskey.
...le Mullagh Ruskey.
...Knockhall Ruskey.
...Knock Hall Rooskey.
...Tulehie Ruskey.

They Put The Flag a-Flyin'

They Put The Flag a-Flyin'

The Roscommon Volunteers *1916-1923*

KATHLEEN HEGARTY THORNE

Kathleen Hegarty Thorne

Generation Organization
Eugene, Oregon USA
2005

Copyright © 2005 by Kathleen Hegarty Thorne
ISBN 0-9633565-3-4 or 978-0-9633565-3-6
Library of Congress Control Number: 2005925147

Book Design: *Gwen Thomsen Rhoads Eugene, Oregon USA*
Front Cover Illustration: *Roland Byrne Knockthomas, Nurney, County Carlow, Ireland*
Editor: *Michael Lennon Dublin, Ireland*

The images on the front endsheets are handwritten copy of the names of Volunteers in the Kilglass Company. The tombstone images on the back endsheets are courtesy of Lew Thorne.

Published by:
Generation Organization
P.O. Box 5414
Eugene, Oregon 97405 USA
www.generationpublishing.com

SALUTE

Lew Thorne and Kathleen Hegarty Thorne.
KEVIN CLARK *THE REGISTER GUARD*

A grand twenty-one-gun salute is due my husband, Lew, without whose constant support I could never have written this book. Lew stood behind me all the way, serving as financier, chauffeur, photographer, photo restorer, computer expert, and perpetual cheerleader. He was a marvel at all those jobs!

FOR THE
LOVE OF IRELAND

Modern Ireland was not born in a warm snug nursery, but in a cold damp bog near Ballagh, Roscommon; not in the hallways of a secure, well furnished, ascendancy mansion, but in the alleyways of busy Dublin; not on the glorious rolling fields south of the Boyne, but in the deep glens of Cork and Kerry. Kathleen O'Houlighan's midwives were not middle-aged women with skill and know-how about birthing pains, but rather young men fired by passion, consumed by an ideal, with pains of their own. The real parents of this young nation were not the well educated members of a privileged landlord class, but rather the sons and daughters of shop-keepers, hewers of wood, and tillers of the soil. They waited for delivery not in a clean and cozy room, but rather in a dark, consumptive dugout that was frigid to the bone, with stagnant water oozing into their worn-out boots. Celebrations were short-lived, and feasting was unknown to the men whose rumblings of hunger punctuated the silent air. This makeshift hideout was not their lively ramblin' house, but rather their underground battle station — for a night, perhaps for several days, and, in some cases, for many months.

Who were the men who frequented this self-constructed prison? Who were these men of Roscommon who, through their faith in the future and belief in their ideals, harassed authorities, and jeopardised their families, homes, and, many times, their lives? Who were the women who supported, fed, sheltered, and nurtured them, and, at times, sacrificed their security to defend them? To these people of Roscommon, Ireland owes a debt.

The contribution made by these people to the 1916-1923 quest for Irish freedom is oft overshadowed by stories and exploits which took place in more-populous counties. Yet the blood of these Volunteers was just as red, and their lives were just as dear.

This is their tribute — the story of common people doing uncommon things with a courage and dedication which consumed their energies, their youth, and sometimes their lives. To these people who risked it all, 'tis altogether fitting that their names and deeds be recorded for future generations to honour.

County Roscommon
Battalions
1916-1921

Ballyfarnon Arigna
Keadue
Crossna
4N
Cootehall
Boyle
1N 5N Carrick-on-Shannon
East Mayo
Brigade
Croghan
Ballaghaderreen
Frenchpark
2N Kilmore
Loughglynn Elphin
3N
1S Castlerea Ruskey
Strokestown
Tarmonbarry
Castleplunkett
Ballinlough
2S
Ballinaheglish
3S
Roscommon
town
Fuerty
Athleague
Lecarrow
Knockcroghery
4S
Kiltoom
Dysart
Athlone
Brigade
Drum

NOTES TO
THE READER

**This book is not a recipe for the present or future.
It is a tribute to the past.**

The methodology of the Volunteers in the years 1916-23 has fallen into disfavour with the dawn of the twenty-first century. As with many other facets of life, weighing actions that occurred more than eighty years ago is oftentimes coloured by present day tastes and values. As a writer, I had to bear in mind that the Roscommon men of 1920 were not pondering the political ramifications of warfare years hence, but rather were dealing with the here and the now and determining what methods and weapons they had available for the task. Those men did not know that within twenty years Britain would be on her knees as a result of "total and terrible war" inflicted on her by Germany. Those men did not dare to dream that negotiations with Britain might, in some future decade, result in an independent nation. They knew only that for seven hundred years the English had been in command in Ireland. They knew only that millions of their grandparents' generation had starved and shriveled into skeletons in mud cabins during a ghastly famine that had been ignored by Westminster and perpetuated by an apathetic government policy. They knew only that each generation since 1798 had risen up against injustice, but had been crushed. They felt deep within their being that this moment in time was theirs — this was the hour to rise, to challenge, and to accept only victory. This was their Excalibur — Ireland would be free, or they would gladly give their lives in an attempt to make it so.

As the author I determined that the first part of this book would read as an unfolding story. I did not want to analyse, overlay charts and graphs, or philosophise. I intentionally chose not to author an academic study of the times. I wanted the flavour and the whisperings of the Volunteers themselves to be embedded within the story. To aid me in my quest, I examined the words of the Volunteers as preserved in the Volunteer Witness Statements and in the private papers of the North and South Roscommon Commanders. The time line of most of these records, however, stopped at the Truce; thus, I had to piece together the story of the Civil War from material found in the Military Archives. The perceptions of the participants, however, are not in evidence in those sorts of records. How the Volunteers might have felt about the situations was extrapolated from interviews which I conducted with participants and their descendants, from notes and pension letters written by Roscommon Volunteers found in the Commanders' papers, and from the works of Volunteers in other parts of the country (*No Other Law* by Florrie O'Donoghue, *When Youth Was Mine* by Jeremiah Murphy, *My Stand for Freedom* by Joe Baker, etc.). Most of those works took an Anti-Treaty stance. As a writer, I chose to mirror the sentiment I encountered in so many sources. I carried this theme through to the end of the book. This was a conscious choice. The men's motives (which they expressed so strongly and eloquently in their interviews, notes, letters, and novels) needed to be interlaced with the mix and mash of sterile facts. What people do, coupled with why they do it, are the crucial ingredients of a truly great story.

On the other hand, the absence of perceptions of the average soldier in the National Army (most of whom were ex-Volunteers) reflects more a lack of material uncovered rather than a dismissal by this author of those soldiers' sincere and heartfelt motives. They no doubt felt that "half a loaf was better than none," and that by working to consolidate power into Irish hands, they could, in due time, deal with sour-tasting allegiances and the severed North. They perhaps might even have felt betrayed by the repeated attacks by their former comrades.

Indicative of the cross purposes and contradictions of the time is a correspondence I received in 2004 from the son of a Ballaghaderreen Volunteer, John McPhillips, who had joined the Free State army:

"The loss of the stories is a tragic feature of the Ireland I grew up in. The secular history was deliberately silenced and all focus was on the role of the Church. My father and Joe Kelly [Anti-Treatyite from Ballaghaderreen], though often in conflict, did their best to keep the story of the struggle for independence alive and to honour those who gave their youth to it. Joe was a supporter of the rebirth of the IRA in the forties and fifties, while my father saw the 1921 Treaty as the final military effort."*

John McPhillips and Joe Kelly personify post-Civil War Ireland — united in devotion to a free Ireland, divergent in methods used to achieve it.

The chronology placed in the centre of the book was assembled over a period of years. As records of events, attacks, or even attempted operations were found, the dates were dovetailed into the running factual history of Roscommon and its surrounding areas. Many of the dates were derived from intelligence papers in the archives, which reveal the date on which the report was written and not necessarily the exact date on which the event occurred. This is particularly true for the Civil War period. As for the War for Independence (Black and Tan War), the reader can see the buildup of activities from 1920 through mid-1921. This crescendo of events no doubt was duplicated throughout all of Ireland. The country was indeed bubbling with "civil disobedience" which the British government agents in Dublin Castle and London reluctantly deemed uncontrollable. Thus followed a Truce.

The next portion of this book is dedicated to the men and women who participated in Ireland's struggle. Not wanting to just present a listing of names, I tried to identify these men and women with particular facts, anecdotal stories, and sometimes words written by others about them. Effort was made to include a photo of the person (when one was available). Although the listing was originally limited to people within Roscommon's borders, I expanded it to include those officers from the Westmeath part of the Athlone Brigade and officers from the East Mayo Brigade. A few from Sligo, Galway, and Leitrim found their way into the litany as well.

On the final pages of this book, I included a Surrounding Volunteers section. In it I placed the IRA command structure of Galway, Leitrim, and Mayo, a partial listing of Longford and Sligo, and a complete listing of Westmeath personnel in the Athlone Brigade who were incarcerated during the Civil War. Interesting snippets of information about various men and women from each of the counties were also included. These surrounding areas were incorporated within this book as a remembrance of those men and women who fought with Roscommon Volunteers within and without her borders. It was intended as a starting point for future historians who might choose to take up the gauntlet and record the war effort of their own county.

As to presenting the whole truth and nothing but the truth, I have failed. Although painstaking effort was made to accurately record, cross-check, and determine whether old faded papers criss-crossed with creases contained words with one "t" or two, I was not able to get everything correct. Every thread of this story was impossible to unravel with total accuracy. Scores of Roscommon people stepped forward to tell me the local lore in their community; but many of the ins and outs of warfare were not known beyond the small circle of men who were involved, and each person interpreted events in a slightly different light. For example, in the 1950s, the Bureau of Military History asked Volunteers from all over Ireland to record their remembrances of the War for Independence in their area. A certain format was suggested, but the Volunteers were free to write their own version of events as they saw them. These Volunteer Witness Statements only recently became available to the public. Because the Statements were penned more than thirty years after the events took place, there are discrepancies. Some remember an event occurring in October, another recalls the action taking place in February. One man may recall sixteen men taking on the job, another claims only ten. I have attempted to sort out those discrepancies and note them either within the text itself or in subsequent endnotes.

I close with an invitation: Come join me on a journey — to a place of remembrance of those who now lie silent. Somehow their footsteps still echo today, and their spirit can be seen in the flutter of the flag they put a flyin'.

* William McPhillips, son of John McPhillips, correspondence 25 September 2004.

THANK YOUS

Thank you to **Michael Lennon** of Dublin, contributing editor of *Roscommon Life*, who served not only as my editor, but constantly e-mailed countless leads and clues, photos, book sections, and items of interest that he thought might help make this story more complete.

The size of this book would be a great deal thinner and the text a great deal less accurate were it not for the efforts of **Tony Conboy** of Boyle, who gave me a treasure trove of local material relating to the War for Independence in Roscommon.

Thanks to **Paraic Brennan** of Ballytrasna, Boyle, for allowing me to copy and transport his grandfather's private papers.

Thanks to **Pauline Garvey** of Glenamaddy, who posted to me her father's Volunteer Witness Statement and records from the 2nd Battalion South area.

Thanks to the late **Pat Vaughan** of Boston, Massachusetts, who welcomed me into his living room for an entire day while my husband oversaw a professionally taped six-hour television interview with him.

Thanks to the late **Eamonn Duffy** of Ennis, Clare, who also allowed me to photocopy his father's Volunteer Witness Statement and take it to Oregon for further study.

Thanks to **Dermott Mullooly** and his family, who supplied his father's diary, photos, and a tad of great poteen to two weary travellers.

Michael Lennon.

Thanks to **Frank Beattie** of Rahara, who shared the knowledge passed down to him by his father, Patrick Beattie.

Thanks to **Henry Owens**, who painstakingly read through the Volunteer List and noted all my omissions. He then provided material that helped complete the picture of the 3rd Battalions North and South.

Thanks to **John Greene**, son of Michael Greene, who gave me the original handwritten copy of the Kilglass Volunteers that his father had scripted so many years ago.

Thanks to **Tom Egan**, who provided the listing of the Bealnamullia Volunteers.

Thanks to **Sister Clare Feely**, who transcribed the audio tape of her uncle, Denis Mannion, and gave me a copy.

Thanks to **Sheila Bergin** of Nenagh, Tipperary, half-sister of Sean Bergin, who fed us tea on a cold night and allowed us to photograph pictures of her late brother.

Thanks to **Commandant Joe McGrath** of the Connolly Barracks in Longford, who located a picture of Sean Connolly and allowed us to photograph it. He also forwarded a lesser known picture of Sean that he deemed a more accurate portrait.

Thanks to **Eamonn Campion** of Ballindrimley, Castlerea, who dutifully guarded the private papers of Gerald O'Connor for decades.

Thanks to **Johnny Kilcline**, who provided pictures and, most important, directions to "the house of fourteen bends."

Identification of various men in pictures was greatly aided by the efforts of **Tom Maloney** of Loughglynn, **Barry Feely** of Boyle, **Joe and Kathleen Hevican** of Carrowbehy, Castlerea, and **Eileen Banahan** of Ballagh.

Tony Conboy.

Thanks to the late **Mary Breheny** of Sandfield, Knockcroghery, who had kept Mass cards of Volunteers who had passed away, and bequeathed them to her son, Michael, who most graciously shared them with me.

Thanks to **Tom Harney** of Kiltoom, who pointed the way to many local people in south Roscommon who could help me fill in the picture of that area's activities and whose gentle interrogation techniques in interviews were a marvel to behold.

I am grateful for the letter of Rory O'Connor to the Editor of *The Irish Independent* of 30 April 1922, which was forwarded to me by **Patrick Murray** of Athlone.

Dave Derby.

Sean Raftery of Valeview, Lisalway, was a fountain of information, and a gracious guide to cottages, secret hideouts, neglected graveyards, and knowledgeable local people in the Castleplunkett/Castlerea area. Through his efforts, many pictures of men in the 2nd Battalion South appear in this book.

The story of the Westmeath Volunteers (Athlone Brigade) is much more complete thanks to the efforts of **Joe Tormey**, who took hours away from his scheduled work to guide us around the Westmeath area.

Thanks to **Seamus Nelson**, who was a party to this book from its inception, and who supplied me with endless corrections and additions regarding men in the Ballinaheglish area.

Thanks to **Edward Egan** of Milltown, Kiltoom, for mailing the photo and information about James McNeill, a bachelor, whose contribution would have gone unnoticed and undocumented save for Egan's efforts.

David Derby, grandson of Tom Derby of Boyle, deserves thanks for his fine work in restoring many of the old photos for this book. Also special thanks to **John Moore** of Eugene, Oregon, whose computer skills helped keep this complex undertaking on track.

A special thank you to **Cormac O'Malley**, who kindly mailed a dramatic and powerful picture of his father, Ernie O'Malley, for use in this book.

Thanks to **Frankie Watson** of Cootehall, who shared the fruits of her own research about the Arigna area.

Thanks to **Paddy Tiernan** and **Billy Donlon** of Strokestown for allowing me to copy the Tommy Loughran manuscript.

Eamonn Dowling, son of Edward Dowling, most graciously mailed to me the Athlone Brigade information, including the Volunteer Witness Statements from the men residing in County Westmeath.

Thanks to **Margaret McManus** of Arigna, who patiently guided me through the Cull family history in the Republican movement.

Joan O'Brien of Athlone shared an afternoon of tea, stories, and treasures hidden in her mother's old trunk.

Many thanks to **Declan Griffin** of Ballykeeran, Athlone, for sending numerous photos of men of the Athlone Brigade, as well as pictures and diaries of members of his family who were involved in the Rising.

Thank you to **Albert Siggins**, former curator of the Roscommon Museum, who was ever patient and gracious in lending me photos, photocopying material, checking my information with local sources, and leading me to various exhibits of interest.

Thanks to **Tom Nolan** of Athlone, who forwarded to me RIC police reports so I could cross-check my research.

An intriguing afternoon of antiques was complete at the Derryglad Folk Museum in Curraghboy, Athlone, when **Charlie Finneran** allowed us to photograph old pictures and Sinn Féin buttons.

Thanks to **Peter Hegarty** of Oakland, California, who forwarded to me a copy of Joe Baker's book, *My Stand for Freedom*.

Edward Egan of the Drum Heritage Group deserves thanks for sharing pictures, information, and treks through fields to locate former hideouts of the men of the Athlone Brigade.

Thanks to **Seamus Helferty** of University College Dublin Archives, who made certain I had access to all pertinent material.

Thank you to **Commandants P.B. Brennan** and **Victor Laing**, **Alan Manning**, and **Dermot O'Connor** of the Military Archives in Dublin, who provided my husband and me with wonderful old boxes of research material and equally wonderful fresh cookies and tea.

Many thanks are due to **Everett and Barbara Thorne**, whose support and financial assistance helped make the production of this book possible.

And a very special thank you to **Michael Fitzmaurice** of Dublin, former editor of the *Roscommon Association Yearbook*, without whose original suggestion to embark on this project and continued encouragement, this venture might never have gotten off the ground.

Michael Fitzmaurice.

CONTENTS

Chapter Four: Building an Organisation   *31*

Chapter Five: The Fighting Intensifies   *67*

Part II

Chronology 177

National and Roscommon events prior to and during the War for Independence, and activities in and around Roscommon during the Civil War.

Part III

Roscommon Volunteers 199

An alphabetical listing of Roscommon men and women who fought in the War for Independence and in the Civil War. The listing includes their name, Company, and Battalion. Many entries include a short biographical sketch complete with their war-time activities. Some listings include a photograph with their personal data.

Part IV

Surrounding Volunteers 453

A listing of the IRA command structure of counties surrounding Roscommon, including Galway, Leitrim, Longford, Mayo, Sligo, and Westmeath (Athlone Brigade). Each county listing also includes snippets of information about selected individuals and events in those counties. A partial listing of Civil War internees accompanies Counties Galway, Leitrim, Mayo, and Westmeath.

THE STORY BEHIND THE STORY

They spoke of him in quiet terms. Neighbours retold the local lore about a small man in stature who paced his fields with thumbs tucked under his suspenders, head bent low, seemingly weighted with the sorrows of Ireland. To and fro he retraced the course of events from 1916 to 1923, when his beloved country had been split asunder. His head would shake, his eyes would narrow as he gazed off into the distance, only to focus on another stone wall, another obstacle in his field of dreams.

Edward "Ned" Hegarty had lived his entire life in Ballinaheglish. The last son of a family of ten, he had not known his older brothers who were forced to board the boats to America. Nor had he known some of his older sisters who were doomed to an early grave by the suffocating spectre of tuberculosis. Ned revelled in the companionship of Mary and Greta, sisters nearer his age, and was bowed by the responsibility of caring for elderly parents who had tilled the land in Farragher. Not having the comforts of wife or joys of children, he became consumed by national fever. He loved only one woman — Lady Ireland.

"Chief" had been his lifelong nickname. "Chief" — a title of responsibility left over from the days of Sinn Féin Courts of 1919-22 when Ned had acted as the Chief of the Republican Police. It was a title of respect as well as fear.

Local lads in the 1950s and 60s listened attentively as their parents had whispered of this man's deeds. They were warned not to steal his apples as he had guns and was not afraid to use them. They were warned that, although slight of build, this man was a determined and strong-willed giant to be reckoned with. The youngsters had avoided him — carefully watching for the absence of his bicycle from the front stoop before creeping into the orchard to pluck the forbidden fruit. Parents of the boys had deemed Ned an isolated figure, a solitary man — alone in his thoughts, alone with his sorrows, alone with his unfulfilled life's work.

Born in the early 1890s, he had been a man of learning. Schooled at the local Franciscan monastery and serving as a monitor until he was twenty-two, he well knew the history of his country and the injustice it had suffered under British rule. That knowledge helped cement in his mind the seemingly random ideas of land reform, illegitimate landlords, indifferent administrators during famine times, and the brutality doled out to the 1916 rebel leaders in Dublin who dared to challenge the might of Britannia. When Volunteer Companies were formed throughout the county in 1917, Ned had been one of the first to join the Roscommon 2nd Battalion. He had been its first Adjutant, a position he was later to relinquish when he took over the responsibility of the Republican Police. Ned had a firm grasp of the righteousness of the cause. He needed only to be bonded to like-minded patriots. In the Volunteer movement, he found them.

Ballinaheglish was an isolated spot. Seven miles from Roscommon town, no lorries routinely came whizzing down its lanes. It was quiet, away from prying eyes of authorities. It served as a perfect meeting place for the South Roscommon Brigade staff. Jack Brennan (the first Brigade Commander), Dan O'Rourke (2nd Brigade Commander), Pat Beattie (Captain of Rahara Company), Jim Breheny (Vice Brigade Commander), Jim Quigley (Captain of the 2nd Battalion South),

Edward "Ned" Hegarty,
Chief of the Republican Police,
South Roscommon Brigade.

PHOTO COURTESY OF MICK CONCANNON,
BALLINAHEGLISH

Matt Davis (Quartermaster) — in fact all the Brigade staff would frequently make their way to the small Naughton cottage for discussions, planning sessions, and rip-roaring tirades about foiled plans, tattle-tale spies, and incompetent commanders. The walls of the Ballinaheglish cottage once resounded with voices for challenge and change. They stand now in quiet testament to brave people who helped free Ireland.

In 1992, my husband Lew and I visited the Emerald Isle for the first time to locate kin, trace our heritage, and connect with distant family members. We found instead a lonely, unattended gravesite in the old Ballinderry Cemetery bearing the lead-filled inscriptions—Michael 1920, Catherine 1930, Michael 1906, Ellen 1894, Catherine 1896, Mary 1881. We had travelled so far, yet were left with only the image of a decaying cottage and a stone marker bearing no names or dates for the last three Hegarty children. Where did they lie, where were their names inscribed?

On that visit we returned from the countryside to Roscommon town and were directed to Eight Til Late, a newsagent in the town square, where a newly reprinted book about the War for Independence in County Roscommon could be purchased. Returning to my room in Gleeson's Guest House, I reclined on the bed and devoured the entire book. No mention of Ned — only a short sentence indicating that Brigade meetings were held somewhere in Ballinaheglish. Another blank page in the chapter of the Hegarty clan.

How could the summation of a person's life be so totally ignored and unrecorded? How could one who, according to neighbours, had given his soul to Ireland not be recognised in ever so slight a way? How many other men's hopes and aspirations had been overlooked, how many other men's exploits had gone unsung, how many other simple folk had challenged the might of England yet been overlooked by the writers of history? These were the questions that crowded into my mind as the bus pulled away from the town square and rumbled down Main Street. On that November morning, this questioning great-niece of Ned Hegarty gazed out the window and beheld the reflection of her own face etched with tears. I felt a deep sorrow at leaving this small town I had only recently come to know. Little did I suspect that as the wheels of the bus whirled down the Athlone Road, my journey was just beginning.

When I boarded the Aer Lingus flight that would propel me thousands of miles away from this island of mysteries, I had no inkling of Roscommon's place in the country's history. I had no idea of the cause or cost of this War for Independence, and no family member to help guide me. Paving the pathway to understanding would be painstaking.

In the ensuing years, scores of books were purchased in bookshops throughout Ireland and toted back to the west of America. My library was supplemented by periodic shipments of hand-picked books selected by Des Kenny of Kenny's Bookstore in Galway. Biographies, surveys of Irish history, classic war novels such as *On Another Man's Wounds* by Ernie O'Malley and *When Youth Was Mine* by Jeremiah Murphy were perused. Articles from Roscommon journals were scoured for relevant facts. O'Donovan Rossa's tale of a hard life in an English prison (*Irish Rebels in English Jails*) was consumed in the comfort of an easy chair. Michael Davitt's plucking oakum in his cold damp gaol (jail) cell presented a diametrically opposing silhouette to that of my reading his life story while basking in the warm rays of Oregon summer sunshine amid towering pine trees in my backyard. Such dichotomies — and where, amidst all this seemingly jumbled and disconnected body of information, lay the heart of the matter for my great-uncle and his two sisters who had put their lives on the line during Ireland's fight for independence?

Every year my husband, who is also of Irish descent, drove the byways and highways of Roscommon to help me piece together the mosaic — following pathways leading to abandoned monuments of fallen men, plodding through cemeteries to ascertain precise dates, and locating cottages where we interviewed participants and their descendants and photographed mass cards, old wedding

pictures, IRA reunion dinners —
any photo that might help fill in the
features of so many as-yet faceless
Volunteers.

The rat-a-tat-tat of my wheeled
suitcase skimming over the pebbles
of the University College Dublin
walkways echoed through the empty
catacombs of time — the resting
place for the remains of so many
forgotten men. The search led to the
archives where the words of the
Volunteers began to speak to me.
War records were examined in the
Military Archives and the National
Archives in Dublin as were the North
and South Roscommon Brigade
Commanders Papers. We flew to
Boston, Massachusetts, and hired a professional television crew to film an
interview with Patrick Vaughan, whose brother had been killed in Cloonsuck in
June 1921. Letters to London to retrieve photographs and notes to Australia to
determine exact dates were but a fraction of the price tag of an accurate account.
And ever with me was the presence of those men whose names and faces lined the
walls and filled the filing cabinets in my office. They were forever beckoning me
to pursue the project, to complete the story, to speak to the present and future
generations about the magnificent efforts they put forth to create a free Ireland.

Why write such a tome? Why spend years accumulating data about men long
since dead, events long since crumpled into time's deep chasm?

The author's only answer is "the spirit of the men." What motives they had for
doing such work — whether they were selfless patriotism, devotion to duty, belief
in a just cause, or less exemplary notions of adventure, release from boredom,
imitation of their older brother's feats — these were the heavy cables that pulled
me through the mire of material that oftentimes engulfed me. Documentation
of what these men and women did for Ireland proved far more worthy of my
attention than the pursuit of modern-day frou-frou. Those Volunteer voices of
nearly a century ago held fast my inquiring mind and, more important, my heart
strings. They wouldn't let go until their song was recorded.

Kathleen Hegarty Thorne
October 2005

Naughton's Cottage in Ballinaheglish,
home of Dominick Rogers during the War,
meeting place for the South Roscommon
Brigade staff.

PART I

THE STORY

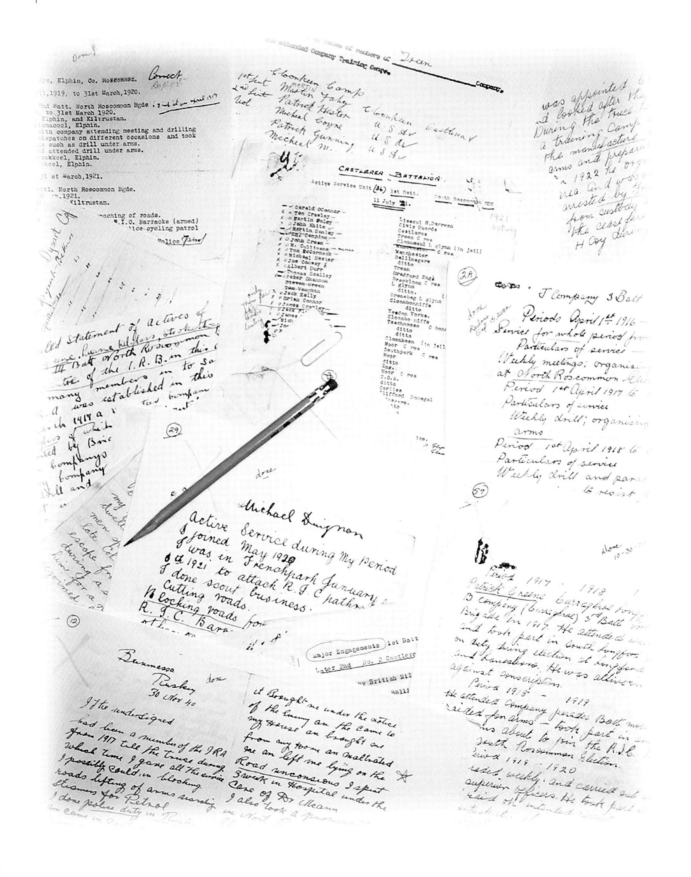

ONE

THE AWAKENING

A STONE BUILDING erected near the quays of Dubh Linn eight hundred years ago stands as an imposing monument to the days of British rule. The Castle — the word conjures up visions of magnificence, elegance, steadfastness, an imposing structure situated high on a hill surrounded by rolling acres of lush land, once the home of powerful and, perhaps, great men and women. A castle in Dublin, the Irish capital — all the more so — a bastion of the best and most glorious of the centuries between the first and second millennium. Yet while these are the romantic notions to which our imagination pivots, the swirling realities of Dublin Castle were quite, quite different.

The castle was founded by King John in 1204, and its construction is credited to Henry de Loundres, Archbishop of Dublin. Twenty years later an inventory of the King's stores in the Castle makes mention of "the chamber, the chamber beyond the Sherriff's chamber, the Alm's Hall, the workshop, pantry, the kitchen, the butlery, also one new rope for the well, one great chain to guard the prisoners and another for the bridge."[1] Were an inventory to be recorded in the first decades of the twentieth century, there would be a great deal more ropes and chains for prisoners and no mention of any alms room for the poor. Torture rooms, archives where intelligence files were stored, cubbyholes where spies cowered before receiving their £5 note — these "chambers" would have figured prominently in a list of important rooms in His Majesty's edifice in 1920.

Dublin Castle, the seat of British rule in Ireland for seven centuries.

PHOTO COURTESY OF LEW THORNE

Dublin Castle over the centuries became the nerve centre for British rule in Ireland. Persons who frequented its premises were seldom the fashionably clad members of Ireland's elite but rather administrative officers, soldiers, G men, and informers — all manner of controlling agents who walked its passageways and held its secrets.

At the beginning of the third millennium, the imposing St. Patrick's Hall, the Bermingham Tower Room, the Wedgewood and the Throne Room, and George's Hall all present a picture of refinement and beauty that beguiles the unsuspecting tourist. But behind the facade of eighteenth century Venetian artist Giambattista Bellucci's roundels or the paintings of Giovanni Paolo Panini (1692-1765) lies the essence of a building whose iron gridwork symbolises the steely control of England over Ireland for seven hundred years.

John Blake Dillon Man of Vision from Ballaghaderreen

Under an imposing elm tree in the Phoenix Park, John Blake Dillon and Thomas Davis met in 1842 to discuss the founding of a new type of Dublin newspaper. Sir Charles Gavan Duffy had solicited the two men to act as editors for the proposed literary venture titled the *Nation*. Both men were less than thirty years old when they accepted their first journalistic challenge.

Dillon was later to be described by Duffy in his book *Young Ireland* as "tall and strikingly handsome, with eyes like a thoughtful woman's and the clear olive complexion and stately bearing of a Spanish noble....He was neither morose nor cynical, but had one instinct in common with [Jonathan] Swift, the villainies of mankind made his blood boil." Such was the depiction of the Roscommon cook who shared kitchen detail with Thomas Davis, took charge of the Irish stew pot, sprinkled nationalistic flavourings into the brew, and saw to it that the fire was always blazing under the concoction.

Luke, father of John, had been "a tenant farmer on the Waldron estate, holding approximately 150 Irish acres at Blenaghbane in the townland of Lissiane..." He had held views sympathetic with the United Irishmen. Unable or unwilling to meet his rental payment, he lost his land in 1812 and moved into the town of Ballaghaderreen a few miles away. There he established a mercantile business which eventually afforded the wherewithal for his son, John Blake, to acquire a university education—first at Maynooth, then transferring to Trinity College where he met Thomas Davis and succeeded him as auditor of the Historical Society. Several

months after their meeting in the Phoenix Park with Duffy, the first edition of the *Nation* appeared.

Devoted to rekindling Irish nationalism by means of literature, revival of the language, and political proddings, the paper's young leaders astonished the readers of the country with the calibre and depth of their coverage. At the time, there was not a monument to a single Irishman in the Dublin metropolis, streets bore the names of long-forgotten English soldiers, Irish history and biography were strictly forbidden in the state-sponsored national schools, and the *Annals of the Four Masters*, the great storehouse of early Irish history, had yet to be translated from the Irish. Such were the depths of the doldrums of Irish national pride.

Dillon and Davis joined with O'Connell in agitating for the repeal of the Union, religiously covered his great mass meetings (including the Clontarf fiasco which led to O'Connell's arrest) and the trial proceedings that ensued. By December 1843 the *Nation* had the highest circulation of any Irish journal.

Many of the Young Irelanders were arrested as a result of an ill-fated uprising in 1848. Dillon escaped to France, then sailed for New York where he went into law partnership with Richard O'Gorman for a time. He returned to Ireland in 1855, was elected to Parliament for Tipperary in 1865, but died the following year. He left behind a rich literary legacy in the *Nation*, a rebel spirit which he bequeathed to his son, John (who became politically prominent in the early years of the twentieth century), and a vast array of quality friends with whom he had attempted to awaken the Irish nation to its destiny.

Although the Crown rule had generally held sway since the thirteenth century, officially Ireland had not been joined in marriage to England until 1800 when the Irish Parliament voted itself out of existence. Parliament may have cast its ballots (having been bribed and lured with promises of titles, land, and position), but many Irish people, including many in Roscommon, saw nothing but treachery and destruction of their country by the cursed absorption into the United Kingdom of Great Britain and Ireland. Other Irish, however, saw a financial opportunity.

To the ruling class of England, Ireland was to be used as the garden of the isles. Education (a national school system for the poor was established in 1831), social welfare, and respect for the customs and traditions of the inhabitants of the island were not at the top of the political agenda of Westminster. In the mid-1800s this abhorrence with anything Irish, this imperial snobbery culminated in the "Great Hunger," a catastrophe totally avoidable yet allowed to cripple the Irish nation. To some Irish men and women, the issue was clear. The bond with England must be broken.

In 1848 (The Young Irelanders) and again in 1867, rebellions broke out in Ireland. John Blake Dillon of Ballaghaderreen had been a highly visible proponent of social change in the Young Irelanders' attempt of 1848. Ned Duffy from Loughglynn played a significant role in the Fenian Rebellion of '67. Yet in each of the proposed risings against British rule, lack of sufficient arms as well as zealous informers played key roles in helping

authorities nip the outrage in the bud and imprison, transport, or execute the ringleaders. At the dawn of the twentieth century, however, a star-studded lineup of athletes assembled on the field of Irish history tackling, skirting, dodging, passing, and pounding out a new game with new rules. The boundary lines were expanded, the former rules ignored, and the goal post of "Home Rule" was broadened and replaced by a "Republic."

Birthing a Nation

Modern Ireland may have been born in 1916, but it had been conceived eleven years earlier by a lone male. In 17 Fownes Street, Dublin, toiled "a small man, modest in appearance and in demeanour, unobtrusive, not remarkable until he looked full at you, and then you forgot everything save that powerful head, those hard, steadfast balancing eyes. Here was power, intellect, and determination, and above all and behind all a sturdy commonsense..."[2] Arthur Griffith viewed his country's future through spectacles that had spent a great deal of time searching the past. He reasoned that all the former uprisings and rebellions had eventually failed due not

Michael Collins and Arthur Griffith.

only to lack of arms but because they were focused on a single leader — militant ones such as Wolfe Tone (1798), Robert Emmet (1803), and James Stephens (1867) as well as parliamentary leaders including Daniel O'Connell in the first decades of the nineteenth century and Charles Stuart Parnell in its final years. When the leader was executed or had otherwise vanished from the political scene, the spirit of the revolution he had tried to enliven died with him. Griffith wanted Ireland's future to be based on sound political policies, not on specific personalities. He did not see himself as the great saviour of the Irish people. His humble opinion of himself was limited to "the man who has a formula for substantial change in Ireland without violent upheaval." As recorded in Padraic Colum's *Ourselves Alone! The Story of Arthur Griffith and the Origins of the Irish Free State*, Griffith consulted with John O'Leary, the great American Fenian, as to its appeal.

O'Leary warned, "You have too lofty an opinion of the people's fibre, Mr. Griffith. They have been too long in slavery to exhibit the moral courage your policy demands."

Griffith replied, "I have great faith in the innate strength of the people's soul, sir."

O'Leary continued, "Don't you think it cannot appeal to a crowd; it touches no chord of patriotism or spirituality in contemporary life."

Griffith's response burst from the depths of his soul: "I am not concerned about today. Tomorrow will be ours...."[3]

Born in Dublin and educated by the Christian Brothers of St. Mary's Place and Great Strand St., Arthur Griffith had not the opportunity or funds for university training. Although his feet walked away from institutional schooling at the beginning of his teenage years, a love of learning never abandoned his eager mind, a book seldom left his hands. He became an avid reader, participated in debating societies, attended historical lectures. With his friend William Rooney, he established the journal, the *United Irishman*, whose office was a small space on the upper floors of 17 Fownes St.

Personally, Griffith was the antithesis of many modern-day heroes. He was not a good public speaker, nor was he a man driven to personal gratification or glory. His dress was plain, his demeanour not the least debonair, his interaction with people not contaminated by joviality. He more resembled a rock, a steadfast anchor to which Ireland could lash herself amid the upcoming storm. Filled with thoughtfulness, steadfastness, and above all, character, he gave to his country what was needed — a vision. Griffith's single greatest gift to the Irish people was the Sinn Féin legacy — a political framework which he founded in 1905, a framework within which to work for Ireland's independence and continuing self-government.

His quarters in 1868 were cramped and cold— very cold—frigid to the bone. A table, a stool, and several tin cans comprised the entire array of furniture in the place. Opportunity for exercise was tightly controlled. What sparse amount of food came his way was mostly gruel, and terribly untasty at that. A fragile constitution, however, was his worst enemy.

He lay on his board bed at Millbank Prison reviewing in his mind's eye the evening that he and O'Donovan Rossa had plodded through the bogland in the triangle of Boyle, Ballymote, and Ballaghaderreen. A meeting had been scheduled that night — a gathering of local men interested in joining the ranks of the Irish Republican Brotherhood. He and Rossa were to address the men's questions and concerns:

"What about the Ribbonmen?"

"Should we force them into our movement, or simply try a little friendly persuasion?"

"Will we be ready for a Rising later this year? Stephens has promised us one in late '65!"

They had talked until midnight, weighing the courses of action, firing the men with enthusiasm for the cause. Their success rate on that occasion, however, had peaked at fifty percent, for, unbeknownst to them at the time, half the prospective volunteers had been misdirected to another location and had missed the meeting entirely. He smiled to himself. Such were the ironies of the job, such were the trials of an Irish nationalist attempting to organise resistance to the English yoke.*

His father had died during the wretchedness of the Famine. As a young boy he had been apprenticed as a draper, first in Castlerea, then in Dublin. After his appointment by James Stephens as chief organiser for Connaught, he re-crossed the Shannon and laboured unceasingly to swell the ranks of the Fenian movement.

Upon hearing of the proposed uprising, the British squelched the movement by imprisoning its leaders. He had been captured in November of '65 at Fairfield House, Sandymount along with James Stephens, Charles J. Kickham, and Hugh Brophy. Although released due to his health, he did not curb his Fenian activities. On a visit to County Roscommon, he was recaptured in Boyle on 5 March 1867 at O'Leary's Hotel. Duffy was sentenced to fifteen years.

Thus his last year had been spent inching toward death in a sterile English prison cell. His twenty-seven-year-old human frame was fast succumbing to the evil clutches of deprivation, malnutrition, and isolation. All these maladies were attacking his frail constitution, and as he lay on his rigid pallet this evening, he knew that they were soon to overtake him. He closed his eyes for a final prayer, and thus did the spirit of the great Fenian Ned Duffy slip the earthly bonds of pain and sorrow.

Irish Rebels in English Prisons by O'Donovan Rossa, p. 187-188.

Whereas the pikes of former uprisings had been the chief implements for demonstrating dissatisfaction, Griffith presented a tool that could not be confiscated, a contraband not necessary to import. An idea expressed at the ballot box is a powerful commodity — difficult to seize and control.

The name Sinn Féin was chosen by Griffith, the meaning of which is "Ourselves Alone!" According to Padraic Colum, author of *Ourselves Alone! The Story of Arthur Griffith and the Origins of the Irish Free State*, William Rooney had first written to his friend Arthur in South Africa that "Sinn Féin must be our motto". The two words had also been published in a Belfast nationalistic journal called *The Shan Van Vocht*. They were incorporated in a poem written by Roscommon author and first President of Ireland, Douglas Hyde:

"It is time for every fool to have knowledge that there is no watchcry worth any heed but one — Sinn Féin amháin — Ourselves Alone!"

Griffith's view of the body politic was simply stated: "If we realise this conception of citizenship in Ireland — if we place our duty to our country before our personal interests, and live not each for himself but each for all, the might of England cannot prevent our ultimate victory."[4] Time has proven him correct. The success of the Easter Rising of 1916 was not a military victory, but rather a moral one. Within a three-year time span, the establishment of an independent parliament and the machinery with which to govern the country in the form of Republican Courts and a Republican Police Force, coupled with the deadly accuracy of the bullets of the Irish Republican Army, sent the British packing. The ideas that Arthur Griffith spent so many years formulating gave his country a foundation on which to build a modern state.

Formation of the Irish Volunteers

The year 1913 concluded with yet another rejection of the Home Rule Bill by the British House of Lords, the establishment of the Irish Citizen Army in Dublin to protect the strikers of the Irish Transport and General Workers Union, and the founding of the Ulster Volunteers in the North. The Ulster men signed, some in their own blood, their commitment to separate from any government established in Dublin. To counter this ultra-unionism, a meeting in the Rotunda in November resulted in the formation of the Irish Volunteers, who pledged to uphold the Dublin government and fight against her enemies. According to a plaque that now hangs on the wall of Wynn's Hotel in Dublin, the men who initially met there on 11 November to discuss the formation of such a group were Eoin MacNeill, Bulmer Hobson, The O'Rahilly, Padraig Pearse, Sean MacDiarmada, Eamonn

Ceannt (born in Ballymoe on the Roscommon-Galway border), and Piaras Beaslai.

Following the national lead, Volunteer groups were quick to form in County Roscommon. Beginning on 9 February 1914, the Boyle chapter led the parade under the direction of Charlie Devine (by 1916 P. J. Delahunty headed the Company).[5] The men drilled openly but, alas, with wooden rifles.[6] Soon to follow were other small local Companies:

> Castlerea 15 February 1914
> Athlone 11 April 1914
> Ballaghaderreen 30 May 1914
> Roscommon town 12 June 1914
> Knockcroghery 25 June 1914
> Elphin and Creeve 8 July 1914
> Tisrara 11 July 1914
> Frenchpark 18 July 1914
> Ballinameen 22 July 1914
> Fairymount 2 August 1914
> Volunteers established a training camp at Athlone on 4 September 1914
> Volunteer County Board formed on 10 September 1914

Meanwhile, north of Belfast in Larne Harbour on 24 April, a ship's hold was thrown open. Out of it came 10,000 Manlicher rifles, 9,100 Mauser rifles, and 2 million rounds of ammunition for the arming of the Ulster Volunteers. English authorities simply turned their heads away. In May of 1914 the Home Rule Bill was passed by the House of Commons for the third time. It was scheduled to become the law of the land. The assassination of Archduke Ferdinand in Saravejo, however, provided the kindling for a conflagration that ignited Europe. Nations aligned with other nations; battle lines were drawn. There was no time to implement the Home Rule law in Ireland. That would have to wait until after the hostilities ceased. The British Prime Minister allowed Edward Carson, leader of the Unionist party in Ulster, and his followers to vote Ulster out of any arrangement resulting in a Dublin government for a period of six years. Carson demanded that the whole of Ulster province be permanently excluded. Thus, even before the first salvo of World War I, the scene was being set for the partition of Ireland.

Two years later, in May of 1916 when both John Redmond, leader of the Irish Parliamentary Party, and Carson received proposals for the Home Rule Act, Carson's packet of material included a telling note from the Prime Minister of England:

> Whitehall Place
> May 29th, 1916
>
> My dear Carson,
> I enclose Greer's draft propositions.
> We must make it clear that at the end of the provisional period Ulster does not, whether she wills it or not, merge in the rest of Ireland.
>
> Ever sincerely,
> D. Lloyd George
>
> P.S. Will you show it to Craig?[7]

Lloyd George, the Grey Fox, was again conducting diplomacy on the sly. Carson was privately satisfied that his part of Ireland would be allowed to become

Written by Ormonde Winter in A Report of the Intelligence Branch of the Chief of Police, Dublin Castle from May 1920 to July 1921:

"Two things tend to make this rebellious movement remarkable: one is that it has, up to the present, produced no great man, and the other is that, for the first time in history, the Irishman has not succumbed to the temptation of gold."

O'Donovan Rossa's funeral in 1915.

a separate entity aligned with England within the United Kingdom. John Redmond, on the other hand, leader of the Irish Parliamentary Party, whose goal was to weasel out of Westminster a quasi-independent legislative body for all of Ireland, placed all his political eggs in the Home Rule basket. He was soon to lose his lease on the farm.

Redmond made a fatal mistake. The Irish Volunteers had originally been founded in Dublin as a response to the formation of and arming of Unionists in the north of the country. The intent was that force be used to defend the mother country. In a speech given at Woodenbridge in County Wicklow on 20 September 1914, John Redmond suggested that the Volunteers not only be utilised to *defend* the country, but go "wherever the firing line extends in defence of the right of freedom and of religion in this war." In simple terms, his oration boiled down to enlisting and exporting Irish men to France to help England win the war against Germany!

Marching off to fight on the continent was not the original intention of the founders, nor did it bode well for Redmond to suggest otherwise. A difference of opinion resulted in a split in the movement. Of the original 180,000 Volunteers, only 13,000 remained loyal to Eoin MacNeill, the head of the Volunteers in Dublin. The group that trailed John Redmond to the enlistment booths called themselves the Irish National Volunteers. More than 70,000 Irishmen volunteered for service in the War during the first year. By the signing of the armistice, an estimated 50,000 of them had fallen on French soil. The Dublin group simply retained the title Irish Volunteers and devised battle plans closer to home.

The militant men of the old Fenian tradition had not been sitting idle by the fireside during this time. Founded in 1858, the Irish Republican Brotherhood (IRB) had been a staple of Irish politics for nearly sixty years. The Brotherhood was a highly secretive organisation whose tradition of physical force to oust England had deep roots. Not a few of the contemporary IRB men envisioned making England's war with Germany their national opportunity. The IRB published leaflets and pamphlets urging men *NOT* to join the British armed forces. Marches to Bodenstown (Wolfe Tone's gravesite) were occasions for a show of defiance. The funeral of O'Donovan Rossa in August of 1915 proved to be a huge show of solidarity for the Brotherhood.

Rossa had been banished from Ireland for his part in the Fenian Uprising of 1867. His gaol tortures were well known and his resilience well respected. When he died on 29 June, the Brotherhood decided to plan a funeral the likes of which Dublin had not seen for many a year. The Crown Forces wisely withdrew from view and allowed the Volunteers in uniform to direct traffic and form an honour guard to Glasnevin Cemetery. Padraig Pearse presented a tribute which included words that have been etched in Irish history: "The fools, the fools, the fools — they have left us our Fenian dead, and while Ireland holds these graves, Ireland unfree shall never be at peace." More prophetic words have never been spoken on Irish soil.

A small but highly devoted cadre of patriots, the Supreme Council of the Brotherhood, decided to strike at England sometime during the World War. They organised their followers, infiltrated the national organisations of the Gaelic League, the Gaelic Athletic Association as well as the Irish Volunteers, and waited. ∎

1. *Dublin Castle* Historical background and Guide, p. 4.
2. *The Victory of Sinn Fein*, by P. S. O'Hegarty, p. 93.
3. *Ourselves Alone! The Story of Arthur Griffith and the Origins of the Irish Free State*, by Padraic Colum, p. 62.
4. *Ourselves Alone! The Story of Arthur Griffith and the Origins of the Irish Free State*, by Padraic Colum, p. 125.
5. Company members included: James Feely, James Turbitt, James P. Dodd, James Haran, Michael Larkin, John Sherrin, Pat Sheeran, Joseph Sherrin, John Scanlon, Jim McGarry, James Stephen Brennan, Pat Brennan, Martin Killelea, P. Wynn, and Pat Spellman.
6. *North Roscommon — its people and past*, by Cyril Mattimoe, p. 190.
7. *Michael Collins*, by Tim Pat Coogan, p. 61.

TWO

THE REBELLION

T HE IRISH REPUBLICAN BROTHERHOOD were the gardeners
who planted the seeds of The Rebellion of 1916. In August of 1914,
the Supreme Council of the Brotherhood met in Dublin and decided
to strike for Ireland's freedom and stage an uprising. In the following months,

"they financed it. They used in its furtherance the organisation of the Irish Volunteers without the knowledge of the Volunteers' Executive.... They decided its date, and its manner."[1] Joseph Plunkett, who had spent months devising the military strategy, submitted a plan to the Supreme Council in May of 1915. That plan, almost in its entirety, was implemented in April 1916.[2]

The day of the scheduled Rising was a confusing time of silence and misinformation. Due to the sudden cancellation of the Easter Sunday show of force by Eoin McNeill, Volunteers throughout the country were at a loss as to what direction to take. In Roscommon, "Easter Week and the Rebellion found this part of the country (around Strokestown) unorganised (militarily) or any preparation made and so no incidents took place around here......"[3] The only knowledge the townspeople had that anything of significance had occurred in Dublin was the scant supply of mail that arrived. Ordinarily, the horse-drawn mail car would arrive from Longford with letters and newspapers. Not on Easter Tuesday! The mail carrier informed the disappointed customers that "the Sinn Féiners had occupied Dublin and that the railroad was cut between Dublin and Mullingar."[4]

In the Castlerea area, "the Rising in 1916 came upon [them] and found [them] in a completely unprepared state of action. There were no arms amongst [the] members except some few small arms and no concrete military organisation. This, coupled with the confusion brought about by orders and countermanding orders and finally no orders, all left [them] in a state of bewilderment, with the result that nothing was attempted and the Rising was over in Dublin before we could think logically and make an estimation of the situation."[5]

In the northern part of the county, Alec McCabe, the IRB Commandant from Sligo and member of the Supreme Council, had travelled to Boyle the Sunday

"The appearance of O'Connell St. and G.P.O. — what was left of it — was an unforgettable sight. From the G.P.O. to O'Connell Bridge on both sides of the street the buildings were mostly burned out; a number of them were still smouldering, also a good portion of Lower and Middle Abbey St. The bodies of some civilians shot during the week were lying about — also a few horses about O'Connell Bridge. The heart of the city presented a picture of utter desolation."

AS RECORDED BY JACK SHOULDICE, FROM BALLAGHADERREEN, WHO PARTICIPATED IN THE RISING

THE IRISH HISTORICAL PICTURE COMPANY

Another photo of The Rising: Noblett Corner-Lower Sackville Street, Dublin 1916.

The Flag of the Republic

The 1848 revolution in France had a profound effect on the minds of the rebels in Ireland at that time, men known as the Young Irelanders. William Smith O'Brien, Thomas Francis Meagher, Richard O'Gorman, and Roscommon's own John Blake Dillon travelled to France in March of 1848 to gain an audience with the head of the French government, Lamartine. They were disappointed by his reluctance to recognise Ireland's plea for assistance with regard to a show of resistance to British rule. When the delegation returned to Dublin, Meagher carried with him a gift which had been presented by a committee of Frenchwomen — a tricolour flag. Meagher brought the flag to a meeting of Young Irelanders. That flag proved to be the banner under which the 1916 Rising in Dublin was fought. To Irishmen the tricolour symbolises the two traditions of the island — green for the Catholic inhabitants, orange for the Protestant residents, and, most important of all, white signifying peace between them.* Its triple-hued stripes rippled in the breeze over the General Post Office throughout the entire siege in 1916 and was a poignant symbol viewed by the surrendering rebels as they were marched up O'Connell Street en route to their English prisons.

*Irish Songster of the American Civil War by Derek Warfield, p. 9.

before Easter and mobilised the IRB circle there. He told the men to expect arms from Kerry and Donegal and to be ready for a fight. (McCabe had formerly obtained maps of the Sligo coastline in order to determine a suitable landing place for arms. He had chosen Aughries.) Upon reading in the local newspaper about Roger Casement's arrest, he journeyed to Dublin where, on Easter Saturday night, he met with Joseph Plunkett, Padraig Pearse, Tom Clarke, James Connolly, and Sean MacDiarmada in a house on the corner of Hardwicke Place. Here McCabe was told that despite the countermanding order of MacNeill, the Rising would proceed on Monday. He was ordered back to Sligo.[6]

On Easter Saturday night, McCabe stayed in a house in Mountjoy Square with Michael Collins, Martin Conlon, P. Donoghue, J. J. Walsh, and several others.[7] Next morning he boarded a train for the West, disembarked in Granard where he contacted John Cawley, the IRB Centre for Longford. He then obtained a car and headed to Carrick-on-Shannon, where he failed to make connections with any men he knew. He then proceeded to Boyle and joined up with James Feely who, unfortunately, had no arms to lend to any spontaneous uprising. Continuing on to Ballaghaderreen, McCabe contacted John Coleman. Again, no guns available! McCabe's driver now refused to go any farther, so McCabe and Joe O'Kelly (Adjutant 4th Batt. East Mayo Brigade) were forced by circumstances to break into a garage and take a car and head towards Tubbercurry. They had driven only a few miles before the car broke down. O'Kelly and McCabe parted company — O'Kelly returning to Roscommon and McCabe eventually reaching Keash, County Sligo. Throughout the coming days, no arms arrived, and no mobilisation took place in north Roscommon.[8]

In the extreme south of the county, the plans for the uprising included assembling men from the Coosan and Athlone areas, marching to Shannonbridge where they were to hold their ground until Roger Casement's rifles arrived and men sent by Liam Mellows would bring further orders. Zero hour: 6 p.m. Sunday night. Halfway to Shannonbridge, the countermanding orders came. The men returned to Coosan and attended a dance. A few of the Volunteers had remained behind to cut the railway, telegraph, and telephone wires outside Athlone at Cloonbonny and Glanworth.[9] For several days afterwards, some men maintained their state of readiness while others returned to work in Athlone.[10]

Volunteers around Tubbercurry had attended the local football match after which they assembled and marched together to the Town Hall. There they received a message from a courier from Ballaghaderreen that the Rising had been called off by Eoin MacNeill (who knew nothing about plans for a Rising until a few days before its projected date). Later that evening a member of the IRB met with Volunteers in a house urging them to proceed with assault plans; but question marks dueled with exclamation points and won out. The most auspicious day in Irish history (at least for the previous seven hundred years) passed without incident in and around County Roscommon.

The politicians of the county, however, lost little time in disassociating themselves from the melee in Dublin. On 18 May 1916 the Roscommon County Council passed a vote of condemnation against the Rising and all who had taken part in it.[11] The Council pledged its support for the Irish Parliamentary Party of John Redmond and John Dillon. The official voice of the county had made a statement, but the ring of Republican rhetoric was yet to resound o'er the fields of Roscommon.

Emily and Eilis Elliott, patriots in the uprising of 1916 from Tonagh, Tubberclair, Glasson, Athlone.

PHOTO COURTESY OF JOAN O'BRIEN, ATHLONE, RESTORED BY LEW THORNE

Excerpts from the obituary of
Emily Elliott Ledwith, *Westmeath Independent*
(21 April 1983)

Emily went to live in Dublin in 1910 and there she joined the Gaelic League and later became a founding member of Cumann na mBan. During the Easter Week Rising in 1916...she worked tirelessly in the Four Courts and in the Father Mathew Hall attending the wounded. She assisted a well known Capuchin priest, Fr. Augustine, while he administered the last rites to the many wounded and dying.

Fr. Augustine wrote of her..."one of the men she went with me to attend in our Four Courts was poor Thomas Allen. As I lay stretched on the floor near the window through which he had been shot by a sniper, she held up his head while I anointed him. She seemed to be oblivious and reckless of danger and I remember well, she was in a kneeling attitude opposite the window through which the bullet had come. I had to insist on her lying down, less she might be shot. Of the many brave girls I met during that memorable week, I have no hesitation in saying that she impressed me as the most fearless."

Excerpt from the Diary of Eilis Elliott O'Brien:

Report at the G. P. O. This I did without delay. I picked up two others on my way down. On arriving at P. O., Sean McDermott and P. H. Pearse were inside the door near the telephone box. In the rear of the building James Connolly lay with his leg in a cage (wounded).

Our work all night was to carry food and arms over the St. to Rease's Chambers at the corner of Abbey St. At the top of this building Fergus O'Connor had a wireless school.

Early next morning Capt. Wafer the O/C gave me a letter to deliver to his wife who lived at N. C. Rd. This order I carried out making my way through barricades, being halted and searched. When I arrived back, I was just in time to see Capt. Wafer's dead body being taken off the St.

About noon on Tuesday I volunteered for service at the Four Courts in answer to an urgent phone call for help. I made a Red Cross armlet from a piece of red blind I got in the Hibernian Bank. At Church bridge I met Barney Mellows and Peter Ledwith. They brought me through a hole in the wall of Hand's Fruit Shop. Capt. Frank Fahy was in charge here. He ordered myself and two others to the Fr. Mathew Hall in Church St., a suitable place for a hospital. In the hall we had twenty improvised beds. We carried food and arms to the different posts in the area for the rest of the week, as well as taking in the wounded for treatment.

From Comdt. Ned Daly I brought the dispatch to Denny O'Callaghan to evacuate...........

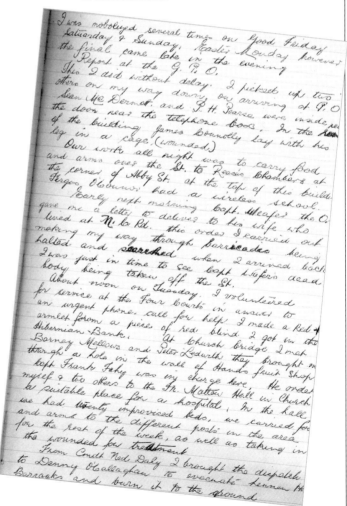

Priests of the Rebellion

Solace in the Mountains....Father Dominic O'Connor

Kilmainham Gaol was cold in January of 1921. The glares of the three judges of the Field Marshall Courtmartial were even icier.

Father Dominic O'Connor was charged with making seditious statements "likely to cause disaffection to His Majesty." He pleaded innocent (or at least failed to recognise the jurisdiction of the court), but truly he was indeed guilty of harbouring private feelings of disgust, disagreement, and disassociation from England.

Father Dominic had been the ministering priest to Terence MacSwiney, Lord Mayor the Cork. He had written down in his private notebook the musings of the man who lay dying in Brixton Prison on a self-imposed hunger strike. Father Dominic had kept the notebook after MacSwiney's death. That book was confiscated in a raid at the Church Street Friary in Dublin and had been used as evidence against him.

Trained in the University of Louvain as an historian, Cork-born Father Dominic had no wish to discard a piece of valuable Irish history, nor did he have any wish to divorce himself from the sentiments within. He tended MacSwiney to his dying day out of a sense of rightness for the cause of Ireland's freedom. His reward — five years penal servitude with two years remitted. His tour of duty began at Kilmainham, proceeding to Mountjoy, Wormwood Scrubs in England, and finally to Parkhurst Prison on the Isle of Wight. His incarceration was cut short by the general amnesty of 1922 when he returned to Ireland.

In February of 1922, Father Dominic was given the Freedom of the City of Cork award — the second of three Capuchins so honoured. When Civil War engulfed the countryside, he again marched to the battle lines administering to both Republicans and Free State troopers alike. Father Dominic remained with the garrison in the Four Courts during its bombardment in April 1922. But by August of

PHOTO COURTESY OF THE CAPUCHIN MONASTERY, ROCHESTOWN, CO. CORK. RESTORATION BY LEW THORNE

Fr. Albert Bibby and Fr. Dominic O'Connor

1922, when the Pro-Treaty government troops invaded Cork, his superiors thought it best to remove him from harm's way. Having challenged the Provisional government as well as the official Maynooth dictums, he was a marked man! Consequently, Father Dominic was propelled halfway around the globe to a tiny hamlet at the bend of an Oregon river.

The diocese to which he was jettisoned was "larger than the states of Maine, Vermont, New Hampshire, Connecticut, New York and New Jersey."* Baker City Diocese encompassed a vast area of Oregon from the Idaho border, west to The Dalles, south to Klamath Falls, and back east to Burns and Baker. Father Dominic's uncle, Father Luke Sheehan, was the pastor of the frontier parish which had been founded in 1910 on Franklin Street in the town of Bend, a village on the high plateau that sidled the Cascade mountains. Father Sheehan had been solicited to come to this remote place on the map by Father McGrath (later Bishop McGrath), who had visited Cork and pleaded with the Capuchins to send priests to aid in conversion and administration of the scattered faithful sprinkled over the near-empty spaces of eastern Oregon. Father Sheehan had responded to the call, and he, in turn, beckoned Father Dominic to a home away from home, a haven in which to work and serve the Lord. It was, geographically speaking, the complete antithesis of Ireland.

Sagebrush and sandy soil stretched for miles, peppered only with a few human settlements. Father Dominic's first assignment placed him in Hermiston, Oregon, where this author's grandfather-in-law helped mix the concrete Father Dominic used to stabilize his first altar in the church there. Father Dominic later became pastor of the Baker Cathedral, and finally was assigned to St. Francis of Assisi in Bend. During his tenure in the far west of America, Father Dominic wrote an invaluable early history of the diocese. It was here too, in this remote setting, that the great Father Dominic was to come to terms with God and His eternal plan.

After the Rising, the English moved quickly to extract the troublemakers from the populace. Considering the statistics of the country as a whole, Roscommon County included "the fifth-highest number of arrests in the months after the rebellion."[12] Twenty-two men from the county were arrested and housed in several of England's "holiday inns". The guest list included:

Michael Brennan of Carrowkeel, Fuerty (**Glasgow Prison, Reading Jail, and Frongoch**);
Peter O'Rourke of Abbeytown, Boyle (**Wandsworth Prison**);
Eddie and John James Doorley of Roscommon town; Alfred McCrann, Pat Smith of Ballyboughan, Roscommon; Jack Brennan of Carrowkeel, Fuerty; George Geraghty of Roscommon town (**Wakefield Jail and Frongoch**)

He was beloved by his parishioners. One young boy was particularly touched by the holy man. He recorded his sentiments in "Stories For Paulette," a copy of which is in the Baker, Oregon, Diocese archives. His own words cannot be improved upon:

".....Irishmen used to escape death in death. It was a grim life they led in the days of the sad songs and happy wars. Strangers patrolled them. Cold Britannia controlled them. The world ignored them. The Pope, to whom they bowed, demeaned them. They were harried off their own land, forbidden to educate their children or vote. For years, to worship their God, they had to rendezvous with 'hedge priests' on the run from the Redcoats. To see a future they had to see over the hedge. Over the hedge to where God was. Over their grim life to where the sky was blue, the green land was theirs and only blood was red. That's why Irish wakes are happy.

"I met the man who told me all this when I was very young. In those days on the back side of Oregon was like the back side of the moon. If you wanted to be lost, that was the place. But there was a ranch there that was like heaven to a small boy. Horses roamed, sheep grazed and cattle still watched for cowboys.

"Some dawns would see bands of them thundering down on the ranch, rebel yelling above the hoofbeats to be met with a 'step down and eat,' from a smiling priest. At night, sometimes, just behind their sunset, came silent Umatillas, or perhaps Nez Perces (local Indian tribes) — unshod horses barely stirring the dust. Lodge poles dragging trails that I can show you yet. All going from God knows where. All going to God knows where, slipping into history. For my little bearded exile from the misty, green Isle of Innisfree it was not a hell, but a Calvary, a place to work and wait for death. He had picked up his cross in the time of the 'Troubles' in Ireland. A man named MacSwiney was Lord Mayor of Cork and he took his stand against the British. He was not a violent man, so he didn't resort to arms, but he said: 'I will die for Ireland; I will starve.' And a world watched as he did. In his last days no one was allowed to see him. But at the very last the British relented; they allowed him to call for confessor to shrive his soul.

"He came to the English gaol, my little brown Leprechaun of a man, to save a soul and make a legend.........MacSwiney had the hero's role. He died and quickly was enshrined in the Irish Pantheon.

"My little priest had a tougher row to hoe. He had to live. For when he came to make a legend he also came to condemn himself. Condemnation to a place among alien, silent mountains where only his memories, or a little boy could find him. We knew the trail — me and his memories. It was a grand feast when we all got together. Forever branded and exiled by the British for the last rites he gave a

Celtic crosses mark the graves of Frs. Dominic and Albert in the cemetery in Rochestown, County Cork.

LEW THORNE PHOTO

self-doomed, perhaps misguided man, he crossed an ocean and a continent carrying his cross to Oregon. He served out his life and ministry there. He had not chosen his Gethsemane; it found him.....

"Throughout the rest of his life he heard confessions from ranchers, farmers, sheepherders, cowboys, Indians, whores below the redline and occasionally a youngster who didn't know then that he was kneeling before a giant. But never again a MacSwiney......"**

In September of 1934 Father Dominic was seriously injured in an automobile accident in Portland, Oregon. A year later he appeared to have suffered a slight stroke and was anointed by his uncle, Father Luke Sheehan. Father Dominic died a few days later on 17 October 1935 — only two years after he had passed the half-century mark.

Following his funeral Mass which was large and his eulogies which were poignant and heartfelt, he was buried in Pilot Butte Cemetery over which was eventually placed a towering Celtic cross; but that was not to be his final resting place. A man with the soul of this Irishman could not find peace in any other soil save Ireland's. His remains were returned to his native land in June of 1958 and buried in Rochestown, County Cork. He sleeps alongside Father Albert Bibby and at the foot of Father Augustine O.F.M. Cap., chaplains of Easter Week. As the bugler on the hillside sounded the last post, the spirits of the men who swore their allegiance to God and country were finally reunited with both.

A Brief History of the Diocese of Baker City by Father Dominic O'Connor O. M. Cap., p. 2.
**Quoted from *A Cross in the Middle of Nowhere* by Msgr. William S. Stone, p. 142-143.

John Joe Coleman, B. J. Flannery, James Cunniffe, Thomas McCormack, Bartley O'Gara, T. F. O'Hara, Joe Trimble, Patrick J. Ryan (Head Centre for the IRB), Joseph O'Kelly, Bertie Shouldice, John F. Morley all of Ballaghaderreen **(Lewes Jail)**;
Frank Shouldice of Ballaghaderreen **(Stafford Detention Barracks)**;
Jack Shouldice of Ballaghaderreen, Paddy Moran **(Kilmainham Jail, Mountjoy, and Dartmoor)**.
Athlone Brigade:
George Amos (Athlone), John Elliott (Tubberclair), Gilbert Hughes (Coosan), Sean Hurley (Athlone), Michael McCormack (Drumraney), Edward Martin (Athlone), Peadar Melinn (Athlone), Sean Mullaney (Athlone), Peter Murray (Athlone), Seamus O'Brien (Athlone), Owen Sweeny (Clonbrusk) and John Blaney (Coosan).

He Abides in Faith....Father Albert Bibby

The San Inez Valley is as beautiful an exile post as a man could wish for. Mountains shield the land from the cool breezes of the Pacific, the earth is warm, and the surrounding soil, through the modern methods of irrigation, has made for abundant crops. The valley at the dawn of the twenty-first century is known for its excellent grapes which are sold to some of California's most prestigious wineries. Yet the natural loveliness of this distant land did not comfort the soul of Father Albert Bibby (1877-1925), for he was a dying man. Having arrived at the mission near Santa Barbara, California, on 20 November 1924, he stayed a mere three months before dying of cancer at St. Francis Hospital in the town of Santa Barbara.

What had brought this Irish priest to a land so far from Dublin? Padraic O'Farrell's book, *Who's Who in the Irish War of Independence and Civil War 1916-1923*, lists Father Albert's name, along with Father Aloysius and Father Augustine as Capuchins who "attended to the spiritual needs of Irish Volunteers in Easter Week Rebellion and to Ceannt, Mallin, Colbert, Heuston, W. Pearse, O'h-Annrachain and Plunkett before executions." Need we say more?

Father Albert had followed his convictions. Yet those deeds became mileposts on a long, long road that led to exile and an early death in a former Spanish mission not far from the shores of a great aquamarine ocean — one not familiar to Father Albert's boyhood wanderings.

His youth was spent in Kilkenny where his father had an interest in the woollen trade and his parents owned a clothing store. His early education was facilitated by the Irish Christian Brothers. He later attended the academy at Rochestown near Cork City, where he received the Novice's habit on 7 July 1894. Eight years later he was ordained a priest. In May of 1902 he was transferred to the Kilkenny Friary, where he served as a Lector of Philosophy. Father Albert set about learning the Irish language, and became so proficient that he often travelled to the Irish-speaking districts to give retreats and hear confessions in the native tongue. He even appealed to his fellow Capuchin, Father Augustine, to script phrases which had relevance to hurling and which the players of the ancient game might use on the field.

He was remembered as a "frail, delicate man with brown eyes of extraordinary brightness, erect in carriage, of sallow countenance with jet black hair and high cheekbones. Quick in his walk and movements, earnest and eager, he yet was full of good humour, and when the time for recreation came along he was the life and soul of the Community."*

In 1907 Father Albert was transferred back to Rochestown, where he remained for six years until he was assigned to Dublin. That relocation proved prophetic, for it placed Father Albert in the eye of the hurricane that was soon to strike the capital and sweep the country.

Father Albert was devoted to all things Irish — language, gaiety, independence! He saw the strangulation of Irish culture and the dire poverty in the streets as a direct correlation to British rule coupled with the overly abundant luxury of the ascendancy. Clearly Lady Justice must be summoned to alleviate this discrepancy between the very wealthy and the long-suffering poor. When the Home Rule bill was shelved at the start of World War I, resulting in the Easter Rising, Father Albert accepted his role as spiritual minister to the souls of the doomed signers of the Proclamation and to the other leaders who were executed by the British. He wrote an account of Easter Week for *The Catholic Bulletin*, but, due to the censor's red ink, his rendition never appeared in print. In December of 1920 he was arrested along with Father Dominic and sent to Dublin Castle. Upon his release, his movements were observed by the authorities; in order to shield himself from this nerve-racking scrutiny, he "went on the run" and sojourned in England during 1921. A friend brought Father Albert to meet with the Irish delegates who were in London negotiating the Treaty.

The results of the signing of that document and the split in the Republican ranks weighed heavily on Father Albert's shoulders.

As a result of the unsuccessful rebellion, countrywide 2,519 men were arrested and sent to prisons. After a few weeks, however, nearly 650 were released. The rest were served with internment orders under the Defense of the Realm Act (DORA). Many of them ended up in Merionethshire in North Wales. What had once been an internment camp for German prisoners of war became "The Irish University" — Frongoch. The international complications of detaining Irish prisoners for an extended time convinced 10 Downing Street that a humanitarian gesture would pay dividends abroad — especially in America. Many of the prisoners were released by Christmas of 1916. But during those months of incarceration, the students of revolution mixed, matched, studied, bonded, solidified, and eventually graduated to bloody mayhem.

Sinn Féin Demonstrates Political Power

The death of J. J. O'Kelly provided an opportunity for this upstart Sinn Féin party to flex its muscle, enter the political arena, attract the public's attention, and win a bout. For thirty years O'Kelly had been the voice of North Roscommon in the British Parliament. He had often proved to be a staunch supporter of Michael Davitt and Land League agitation. Now he was dead. With only three weeks before voting time, a committee heavy with Sinn Féin supporters met at the Central Hotel in Boyle. Presided over by Father Michael O'Flanagan, the committee members discussed conscription, the necessity of growing more food, and possible candidates for the upcoming election. George Noble Plunkett, Papal Count and father of one of the executed signers of the Declaration of the Irish

He tried to negotiate a truce between the warring sides, but alas, to no avail. Near the stroke of midnight on 27 June 1922, Father Albert was awakened in the Friary at Church Street in Dublin and asked to accompany the Republican officers back to the Four Courts where an attack was deemed imminent. Father Albert and Father Dominic were present when the Free State artillery smashed into the walls of the hallowed building, demolishing not only stone, flesh and blood, but countless historic documents.

When the Civil War ended with Frank Aiken's order to dump arms, Father Bibby's fight was not yet over. Because of his Republican sentiments, Father Albert was stripped of his priestly functions, and was "banished" to Rochestown, where he spent ten miserable months. News of his compatriot's transfer to America (Father Dominic O'Connor left in November 1922) tolled the knell of parting day for Albert in Ireland.

The following year his superiors did indeed decide to send him to America, his first assignment being at the Capuchin Retreat House in Abbotstown, Pennsylvania. Two years later, as his health began to visibly decline, he was reassigned to the warmer climate of southern California.

The Solvang Mission was lovely, impressive in its own way, yet alien to this Irishman whose deep sense of duty and history had thrust him through the massive wooden doors onto the stone-tiled floor surrounded by strange stucco walls decorated with ornate Spanish-style religious artwork. Oh, where were the green fields of Ireland and the chilly mists that had enveloped him since his earliest recollections? They were soon to embrace him.

The funeral procession for Fathers Bibby and O'Connor in Cork City.
PHOTO COURTESY OF CAPUCHIN MONASTERY, ROCHESTOWN, CO. CORK

On the north side of the mission is a small cemetery, one dedicated to parishioners and priests who served the community. Beside the great building stand five small crosses, one of which bears the name Albert Bibby. The grave marker is there, but not the body or the soul of this Capuchin who gave so much to the cause of Irish Freedom. In 1958 his remains were returned to Rochestown to rest with his fellow friars.

Thousands of admirers were joined by Sean T. O'Kelly, President of Ireland, and Eamon de Valera, who welcomed home the bodies of Fathers Bibby and O'Connor. Several bishops and heads of religious orders, accompanied by members of the Irish Senate and Dáil, came to pay their respects to the patriot priests who had administered to Ireland's founding fathers, yet whose earthly reward had been exile. On that day, the 14th of June, forty-two years after the first burst of gunfire in the Easter Rising, there was an air of rejoicing, for Ireland was able, at last, to claim her own. "...may Erin's soil lie lightly on their mortal remains which have travelled so far to rest with their brothers in Rochestown."**

*Excerpted from correspondence with Father Bertram Mulligan, Historian for the Capuchin Order, 2 March 1999.
**Excerpted from the graveside oration given 14 June 1958 by Very Reverend Father Hilary, Vicar-Provincial.

Republic, had previously agreed to put his name forward for consideration. He became the Sinn Féin candidate.

The victory in the North Roscommon bye-election became a prized plum. The results were the first in the country to demonstrate that Sinn Féin could win, and could provide a political platform on which to stand against British rule. That victory would have proved impossible without the diligence and pluck of Roscommon curate, Fr. Michael O'Flanagan. Sinn Féin volunteers canvassed the highways and byways while invited Dublin dignitaries (Arthur Griffith, Michael Collins, Rory O'Connor, Darrell Figgis, Joe McGrath, William O'Brien) travelled the length and breadth of the northern section of the county to stump for the new candidate. Winter, however, had dumped several feet of snow on the region. Some areas recorded drifts as high as ten feet. Rail traffic to the towns of Boyle and Ballaghaderreen managed to continue, but for the candidate and entourage to speak to the villagers, some roads had to be cleared. Fr. O'Flanagan organised work parties from Ballaghaderreen to Frenchpark, Frenchpark to Elphin, and Elphin to Strokestown. They shovelled pathways for motor cars through the towering drifts. On election day, 3 February, Fr. O'Flanagan also saw to it that local youths carried aged voters on their backs to the polling stations in order for the true voice of the people to be heard. This outspoken priest had the vision to seek Plunkett as a candidate, the personal magnitude to rally the forces of the local people, and the perseverance to overcome opposition in order to achieve a goal that his conscience knew to be right for Ireland. He was the "man of the hour" for that momentous milestone in the Irish electoral process. When the clamour had died away, Count Plunkett was proclaimed

Ironic Prophesy

When the major figures of Sinn Féin attended Count Plunkett's victory rally in Boyle, their signatures were collected by two sisters who helped their mother run a newsagency and bookstore across the street from the Central Hotel: Eva McDonagh (later Mrs. Feely) of Greatmeadow and Lena McDonagh (later Mrs. Kennedy). At the centerfold of that autograph book, which is currently owned by Barry Feely, nephew of Eva, are written the words:

"England, damn your concessions; we will have our country."

Penned by Ruaidhri O'Concubhair (Rory O'Connor), one of the leaders of the Anti-Treaty forces who was hanged in Mountjoy, not by the British, but by the Irish Free State government.

Two years later additional autographs were collected, one of which was penned by James E. Feely of Boyle and dated April 1919:

"Forget not the field where they perished.
The truest, the last of the brave
All gone — and the bright hopes we cherished
Gone with them and quenched in the grave.
Far dearer the grave or the prison
Illumed by one patriot's name
Than the trophies of all who have risen
On liberty's ruin to fame."

Captain Thompson also contributed to the book. His entry is dated 2 September 1921:

Come England with your legions
and with your mighty fleet,
and fight us half trained Irishmen
in Dublin's narrow street.
Bring all your famed artillery,
shell brick and mortar down,
and how you guard small nations
we'll tell in Dublin town.

the winner: Plunkett 3,022; Devine (Parliamentary Party nominee) 1,708; Tully (proprietor and editor of the *Roscommon Herald* from Boyle), 687.

Count Plunkett walked outside Boyle Courthouse and stepped before his constituency to formally declare a policy that was to have monumental consequences for the Irish nation:

"My place henceforth will be beside you in your own country for it is in Ireland, with the people of Ireland, that the battle for Irish liberty will be fought. I recognise no Parliament in existence as having a right over the people of Ireland, just as I deny the right of England to one inch of the soil of Ireland. I do not think I will go further than the Old House in College Green to represent you. I am sent by Ireland to represent you in Ireland; to stand by you and to win Ireland's freedom upon her own soil."[13]

Thus Plunkett became the first elected official to announce his intention *not* to go to the British Parliament. Representation by Irishmen on Irish soil had been the dream of patriots throughout the nineteenth century...Robert Emmet, Daniel O'Connell, the Young Irelanders, the Fenians, the Land Leaguers.

The final derailment of the Irish Parliamentary Party and the beginning of republicanism at the ballot box were accomplished by the voters in North Roscommon, whose pencil marks on election ballots signalled the writing of a new chapter of Irish history — Chapter 20 (twentieth century) — "Home Rule — Sinn Féin Style."

Land Agitation in Roscommon

Aside from the political considerations that were clamouring to be voiced throughout the county, land issues were vying for people's attention as well. Despite the policies of the Congested District Board to break up the large ranches and distribute the land to the smaller farmers, "the great plains of Roscommon, more than nine hundred miles square, remained in the hands of grazers or ranchers, who, due to the war conditions, had made large profits from their herds of bullocks and flocks of sheep".[14] These holders of the land were in no great hurry to divide up their estates. The small farmers, however, living on the very edge of poverty on tiny unproductive plots, needed immediate solutions to their economic ills. The establishment of Sinn Féin Clubs helped channel some of the local enthusiasm for land reform into a demand for Irish independence.

The formation of Volunteer Companies drilling with hurleys as well as shotguns and the success of the bye-election fostered the hopes of farmers in the Arigna area. The 100 acres around the defunct Iron Works farm was the best land in the valley. Owned by Lord Kingston and vested in three trustees, the acreage promised added income to struggling small farmers. Arigna Volunteers met and discussed the viability of a joint Volunteer-farmer march to the land which would be led by George Plunkett, son of the recently elected Count.

On a March day, about 300 men tramped down from the mountainsides, armed with digging implements. They assembled at the bridge and proceeded to the disputed acreage. Serving as a barrier between hungry farmers and rich farmland were several hundred police who had been summoned from surrounding areas to challenge this menace. With a signal from George Plunkett, the farmers and Volunteers climbed over the fence and started digging. The familiar baton charge resulted. The farmers withdrew and within the week George Plunkett had been arrested, taken to Boyle, and sentenced to a jail term.

Other demonstrations were directed at holdings in Warren, on the east side of the town, Mockmoyne, and the Tinacarra estates, where the Volunteers and local farmers were again met with a baton charge.

The hunger for land was not limited to the north of the county. The Frenchpark area near Erritt and Carrowbehy was the target of an illegal cattle drive in which local people took part. A number of arrests were made that day by the Royal Irish Constabulary (RIC). The prisoners were tried in Loughglynn and sentenced. Another raid at Southpark, Castlerea, also proved to be a flash point for conflict.[15]

The Formation of Active Volunteer Companies in the County

Although Volunteer Companies had officially formed around the county in 1914, those groups of men had disintegrated and their organisation faded to atrophy after the split in the Volunteer movement precipitated by John Redmond and the World War I recruitment policy of the Parliamentary Party. The IRB, however, had not become comatose. They knew guerilla war was coming, and they made plans to prepare for it. "Armies of liberation, or any other sort, do not, as American politician William Jennings Bryan asserted, 'spring full panoplied from the soil.' They must be built up carefully and with patience. Fear, humiliation, pain, defeat and disappointment must be overcome. Men must be indoctrinated with the idea that they are better than the enemy, and rebels must learn that their enemies' uniform is made of penetrable fabric, not armoured steel."[16] The IRB made certain that its members headed many of the Companies and that its men were placed in key positions in the Volunteer movement to ensure control of policy.

Thus, recruitment for Volunteers began again in earnest in 1917. In the northern area, Companies began organising around the Boyle area in the early months of that year. The North Roscommon Brigade structure eventually became organised with Seamus Ryan of Strokestown being appointed O/C and Andy Nevin, Brigade Adjutant.

In mid-Roscommon, Sean Hyde had come to the county in 1917 as an instructor under the Department of Agriculture. He had worked in the 2nd Battalion South area and spent much of his time recruiting for the Volunteers. (Sean Hyde remained with the Republican cause until the end, when, on 10 April 1923, he helped a dying Liam Lynch over the bare exposed shoulder of the Knockmealdown mountains — the last hill Lynch was to climb in his short life.) In that same area, Jim Quigley had assembled more than fifty men for a parade at Ballymoe, which was reviewed by Hyde. After that assembly, individual units began to form in the Battalion vicinity. That pattern of small units was replicated throughout the county.

The 3rd Battalion North Companies were begun in early 1917 when Joe McGuinness, under the guise of campaigning for election, came to Roscommon and inducted men into the Volunteers. Sworn in at Ruskey, Sean Leavy returned to his native Scramogue and started a Company, as did other men who organised small units in Strokestown, Cloonfree, Carniska, Curraghroe, Tarmonbarry, Kiltrustan, and Northyard.

In the south of the county, Sean Hurley from Athlone town gathered together a group of men in the summer of 1917 who became the kernel (about twelve members) of the Knockcroghery Company.[17] Patrick Kelly served as its first Captain with John Breheny of Sandfield the 1st Lieutenant.

On the Brigade level, in the Roscommon town area, the South Roscommon Brigade was formed in 1917 with Jack Brennan of Carrowkeel serving as Brigade O/C. Jim Breheny of Portrunny was the Vice O/C. Matt Davis served as O/C of the 3rd Battalion (a position he relinquished to Pat Madden when Davis took over as Quartermaster and Madden returned from prison). Adjutants of the Brigade included Henry J. Finlay, soon to be followed by Ned Hegarty of Ballinaheglish, who in turn relinquished that position when he was appointed Chief of the Republican Police.[18]

Cam membership badge from Thomas Ashe Sinn Féin Club.

COURTESY OF CHARLIE FINNERAN OF DERRYGLAD FOLK MUSEUM CURRAGHBOY ATHLONE
PHOTO RESTORATION BY LEW THORNE

1. *The Victory of Sinn Féin*, by P. S. O'Hegarty, p. 10.
2. *The Victory of Sinn Féin*, by P. S. O'Hegarty, p. 11.
3. Patrick Mullooly Volunteer Witness Statement to the Bureau of Military History 1913-21, p. 2.
4. *An Old Soldier's Memories*, by Tommy Loughran, p. 129.
5. Andrew Keavney Volunteer Witness Statement to the Bureau of Military History 1913-21, p. 1.
6. Alec McCabe Volunteer Witness Statement to the Bureau of Military History 1913-21, p. 3-4.
7. Alec McCabe Volunteer Witness Statement to the Bureau of Military History 1913-21, p. 4.
8. James Feely Volunteer Witness Statement to the Bureau of Military History 1913-21, p. 2.
9. Henry O'Brien Volunteer Witness Statement to the Bureau of Military History 1913-1921, p. 2.
10. Frank O'Connor Volunteer Witness Statement to the Bureau of Military History 1913-1921, p. 2.
11. *Drum and its Hinterlands*, (Edward Egan, editor) p. 287.
12. *County Longford and the Irish Revolution*, by Marie Coleman, p. 51.
13. *For Ireland and Freedom*, by Micheál O'Callaghan, p. 8.
14. *They have fooled you again*, by Denis Carroll, p. 109.
15. *For Ireland and Freedom*, by Micheál O'Callaghan, p. 31.
16. *An Old Soldier's Memories*, by Tommy Loughran, p. 171.
17. Tom Kelly Witness Statement to the Bureau of Military History 1913-21, p. 1.
18. According to the Volunteer Witness Statement of Matt Davis, Henry Finlay of Roscommon town was appointed by GHQ as Brigade Adjutant in 1917. According to the Volunteer Witness Statement of Tom Kelly of Knockcroghery, Ned Hegarty was the Adjutant by the 1918 general meeting in Roscommon town.
19. *Drum and its Hinterland*, (Edward Egan, editor) p. 288.
20. *A Parish of Kilglass, Slatta, and Ruskey*, by Liam Coyle, p. 136-137.

A year later, due to inactivity in the area, a review of personnel and activities was deemed necessary. A Brigade Council meeting was held in Smith's Hotel in Roscommon town. Michael Staines, who attended as the representative for GHQ (General Headquarters in Dublin), presided over the meeting that selected Dan O'Rourke as O/C, with Jack Brennan serving as Vice O/C. Other officers were elected from the various Companies.

The Formation of Sinn Féin Clubs

Sinn Féin Clubs began springing up all across the county. For all intents and purposes, the Sinn Féin Clubs and the Irish Volunteers were one and the same — although some of the male members never took an active part in the actual fighting, and most of the women who joined the clubs never held a gun. The focus of both groups, however, was the same (ridding Ireland of British control), and the cross-blending of personnel was well understood by all concerned. Volunteers often worked for Sinn Féin (as in the general election of 1918).

Leadership of these clubs was spread across the social borders — from farmer to cleric, from shopkeeper to lawyer. Father Michael O'Flanagan acted as president of the Sinn Féin Club in Crossna while Father Martin O'Beirne held the position of vice president.

In the south of the county, atop Glynn's Hill in Crannaghmore, Drum, a group of young men gathered to listen to Bernard Gaffey, who had just returned from a meeting in Athlone where the establishment of Sinn Féin Clubs was touted. As a result of such encouragement, The O'Rahilly Club of Roscommon was formed. Meetings were held, foot drill, marching, and training were begun, weapons instruction by James Tormey and George Adamson from County Westmeath was initiated. Because there was much interaction between the Coosan unit of Westmeath and the newly formed Summerhill Club (they were both part of the Athlone Brigade), what few weapons were available were shared for drilling. If no guns could be obtained, then pikes would have to do (they were quietly made at Willie John Byrne's forge in Athlone).[19]

In the Kilglass area, a Sinn Féin Club, under the leadership of Michael Thomas Kavanagh, met in Thomas Cox's unused building every Sunday after the 11 o'clock Mass. By 1917 two Sinn Féin Clubs in Kilglass parish had been established — one Thomas McDonagh Club with Thomas Flanagan acting as president. At the beginning of 1918, a third one blossomed forth — The Joseph Mary Plunkett Club with John Daly serving as president. A Sinn Féin Club in Ruskey was titled the Michael Davitt Club (in honour of the man who helped lead the Land League Wars of the 1880s). St. Enda's Sinn Féin Club had been established in Kiltrustan shortly after Count Plunkett's election in 1917, with Father Patrick McGowan of Strokestown assisting in its formation. These clubs elected officers, and began the serious business of acting upon and reacting to items on the political agenda.

To entice the seemingly disinterested, a concert would be scheduled — complete with rousing patriotic tunes and recitations. When the fever pitch of enthusiasm was reached, a recruitment form for a new Sinn Féin Club would be passed out, along with particulars about the time and place of the first meeting. At the Sinn Féin meeting, a signed petition demanding complete independence was circulated, which every family was to complete. Canvassers were appointed who visited every household in their respective parishes.

Oftentimes the clubs elected to hold concerts and dances in order to raise money for the Volunteers. Concern for the prisoners was exhibited by passing various resolutions to support their cry for political rather than criminal status. During the 1918 general election, club members were instructed to "beat the bushes" and get the vote out. The Kilglass Joseph Mary Plunkett Club even passed a resolution "to pay no more rents, rates or taxes to the British Government, or to any British Government Body as a protest against the continued imprisonment of our chosen leaders..."[20] ■

THREE

THE TROUBLE TIMES

The Longford Election
"Vote Early and Vote Often"

Following the success of the Count Plunkett election in North Roscommon, national leaders devised a plan whereby an IRB prisoner would be nominated as a Sinn Féin candidate for election in the various counties. The IRB's policy was usually to nominate more "academic moderates like Eoin MacNeill or Eamon de Valera to front the movement, while the IRB controlled things in the background."[1] That deliberate policy of placing IRB men in key positions (military and political) was implemented in County Roscommon as well. "The politicians were trying to get a controlling hold on the movement and this was Mick Collins' method for seeing that they did not, and an effective one it was."[2] In neighbouring County Longford, a game plan was drawn up.

The Joe McGuinness candidacy was the brainchild of Collins, who gripped the notion with his teeth, clamped his jaw, and would not let go. Against the warnings of the prisoners incarcerated with McGuinness as well as the candidate himself[3] coupled with the misgivings of de Valera (who feared that if McGuinness were defeated, the movement would suffer a setback)[4], the young prisoner in Lewes Jail was nominated and ultimately elected on 16 May 1917. His winning slogan: "Put Him in to Get Him Out!"

Roscommon Volunteers played no small part in that victory. They crossed the border to support their Tarmonbarry-born county man and became actively engaged in the election by canvassing, protecting and guarding the speakers at meetings and in their hotel rooms, and overseeing the ballot boxes.

The Organisation of the Athlone Brigade

Although a scattering of Volunteers existed in the Athlone area prior to 1917, they were not officially organised by the time of the Longford election. A party of them did, however, travel to Ballymahon and participate in the McGuinness campaign by encouraging the people to go to the polling booths. At the end of May or early June 1917, Sean Hurley reorganised the Volunteers in the vicinity of Athlone. Seven section leaders were appointed and authorised to return to their own area and recruit members. Sean Scanlon, Frank O'Connor, and John Blaney were assigned the Coosan area. Seamus O'Brien, Thomas Cummins, Brian Martin, and Seamus O'Meara were directed to canvass Athlone town.

Classes were held by Hurley for the officers and section leaders who in turn trained their own men. O'Meara's section numbered around twenty-two. Some recruitment was done under the guise of "The Sean Costellos," a football team.

Volunteers had opportunities to display their resolve publicly. In March 1918, when Arthur Griffith came to Athlone, the Volunteers policed the town. The men paraded at Tullamore, where de Valera reviewed the troops. They even marched farther afield to Mullingar on 17 March, where a huge show of force greeted them — a force that combined all the Longford Volunteer Companies.

Previously, in September 1917, the demise of Thomas Ashe (killed from force feeding while in gaol) had provided an opportunity for Volunteers to join in a

> "The ferocity of response which this provoked indicated the quality of opposition to the {Treaty.} Just as a republic had been fought for, so the British crown was what had been fought against. The republic embodied all that was desired; the crown represented all that was detested. To fight for the former and end up owing allegiance to the latter was unthinkable to many in 1922."
>
> Charles Murphy
> *Heritage of Ireland* p. 108

> "Your information was correct. I was opposed to your policy. You have destroyed the {Redmonite} Party I revered. You have wrecked the Home Rule that I have worked for all my life. I didn't agree with your ideas or with your methods, but, by God, you are backing your ideas with your lives and that is enough for me."
>
> Michael Brennan
> *War in Clare* p. 83
> (spoken to Michael Brennan's Clare Flying Column by Mr. George Walsh, ardent Unionist, during the Black and Tan War)

national event. Some Roscommon members travelled to Dublin to attend his funeral. Ashe's coffin was escorted by twelve uniformed riflemen followed by a strong body of Volunteers. All totalled, 30,000 marched in the funeral cortege, while hundreds of thousands of onlookers lined the streets and laneways and perched in second-story windows to get a glimpse of this historic parade. Those in Athlone who did not make the trip to the capital, paraded publicly through the town and halted at the Dispensary, where Sean Hurley addressed them.

By April of 1918, a Battalion had been organised in County Westmeath. Sean Hurley became the O/C with Seamus O'Meara serving as Vice O/C. Sean O'Farrell served as Adjutant, with Thomas Noonan acting as Battalion Quartermaster. This Battalion was known as the Athlone Battalion and included the town of Athlone (membership 80), with much smaller contingents in Summerhill, Drumraney, Moate, and Bealnamullia. When Sean Hurley was arrested shortly afterwards, O'Meara became the commanding officer. One of his first official duties was to order all guns previously kept in Athlone town to be moved to a dump in the Coosan area because he felt they would be much safer away from the garrisoned town.

O'Meara organised Companies in Clonown, Taughmaconnell, Drum, Moore, and Curraghboy and, at that time, these became part of the Athlone Battalion. (Curraghboy would later be incorporated in the 4th Battalion South Roscommon at the end of 1918.)

In late April or early May at a meeting in Moate, with Diarmuid O'Hegarty representing GHQ, a Brigade was formed with Seamus O'Meara being appointed the O/C; John McCormack, Vice O/C; George Manning, Adjutant; and Peter Melinn, Quartermaster. The Battalion commanders were: Athlone — David Daly; Mullingar — M. J. Kennedy; Drumraney — Dick Bertles; Shannonbridge — Thomas Dolan. Nearly all of the officers of the Brigade were IRB men. (See the beginning of the Roscommon Volunteer Listing for a complete account of the evolution of the officers' roster.)

By July or August of 1920 another change in the Brigade structure was implemented. In the future, Mullingar Battalion would receive its orders directly from GHQ, while the Shannonbridge Battalion was transferred to the Offaly Brigade.

The Rockingham Raid

A soldier without arms is a contender sparring in a boxing ring with mittens. Revolvers, rifles, or any sort of weaponry were in scarce supply when the Volunteers first formed. Promises from "higher-ups" never materialised, and the men of Boyle became frustrated. They decided to go after some arms on their own.

The first arms raid in County Roscommon took place at Sir Thomas Stafford-King's impressive home known as Rockingham House near Boyle. (The King family who owned the structure were descended from Sir John King, whose association with the county began after the Battle of the Curlieus in 1599, when he was awarded a lease of the Boyle Abbey lands by Queen Elizabeth I.) While the residents of Rockingham were absent, a group of IRB men[5] (under the leadership of Alec McCabe) descended upon the house on or about 19 February 1918. The men were carrying revolvers supplied by McCabe. They were split into two groups — one going around to the back of the house, the other approaching the front entrance. James Feely and James Turbitt went up to the door, knocked, and, when the butler answered, they dragged him out of the house and tied him up. The rest of the men entered the house — most from the kitchen entrance where they found the servants engaged in a grand game of cards. After herding them into a single room and holding them under guard, the Volunteers headed for the gun room (the location of which they knew about because of information supplied by James Flanagan) and made off with two rifles, eight shotguns, and about 3,000 rounds of ammunition.[6] (James Feely claimed that there were about six rifles, ten or twelve shotguns, two revolvers, and an assortment of ammunition to suit each of the guns.) All the confiscated arms, however, did not enrich the coffers of the

Roscommon Volunteers. Alec McCabe took every gun, loaded it into a car he had brought from Ballymote for that purpose, and headed north. The local men never saw the arms again.[7]

The Founding of Cumann na mBan

Irish women were not oblivious to the national distress. They too saw the need and seized the opportunity for change. The national Cumann na mBan movement had been founded on 2 April 1914. Although the women's group was established as an auxiliary to the Volunteers, it was not controlled by the Volunteer Executive, but rather organised by

Rockingham House, Sir Thomas Stafford-King's mansion near Boyle.

THE IRISH HISTORICAL PICTURE COMPANY

districts and formed into its own Companies. Duties included first aid, staffing field hospitals, and becoming acquainted with general equipment. Some members fought side by side with their male counterparts in the Rising. Others were in charge of securing and hiding guns, some were instructed in the use of firearms (the Curraghroe bog in Roscommon was used as a training area for such purposes), while others acted as couriers for money transfers.

Many Roscommon women would eventually risk life and limb nursing wounded Volunteers in their homes, in dugouts, and on Incheneagh and Quaker Islands in Lough Ree. Aside from their nursing duties, many acted as cooks and lookouts while their family members or strangers rested in their safe houses. Some harboured men on the run, while others served as messengers carrying dispatches to Volunteers in the area, notifying them of upcoming engagements, suspected raids, and scheduled meetings. Some of their tactics were quite ingenious. Cumann na mBan women from the Ballinaheglish area would hide dispatches in the steel tubing of their bicycles.[8] A person wielding a wrench at the other end of the journey would loosen the screws, take off the bicycle seat, and extract the writings. Other women in the Boyle area would slice the inner tube of their bicycle tire, hide the dispatch inside the deflated inner tube, then proceed to have the tire repaired for the expected trip.[9] Others, who had less time or less access to air pumps, simply slit open the hem of their skirt, slid the dispatch into the lining, then sewed the hem back up. Women in the Ballagh area carried the messages in their shoe.[10]

Rita Leneghan of Hillstreet was ordered by Martin Fallon (O/C of the 3rd Battalion Flying Column) to be the delivery girl. For what? For the £350 payment to Corporal Meadlarklan of Boyle Barracks for his part in the escape of Michael Dockery from the barracks in June 1921. She had travelled to a house on The Crescent, Boyle, and was waiting for further instructions when her host shouted that the military were coming her way looking for strangers in town. She shot out the door and ran to the station, where a goods train was just coming in. She boarded the train and disembarked at Dromod, where she found Martin Fallon, Sean Leavy, and Michael Duignan waiting for her (interestingly, with cash in hand). She received the payout from them and proceeded to convey the money to the assigned meeting place, where she handed over the "fee."[11]

Some women in Roscommon became directly involved with firearms. Maisie McGarry of Ballymagrine near Tarmonbarry brought a supply of guns by cart from Ruskey. Girls attending Mass in Ballagh in May 1921 were called to do some quick thinking when the Tans invaded the service and Father Thomas Hurley led an impromptu procession down the main aisle and out into the churchyard. The Volunteers who had been attending Mass, having discreetly dropped their revolvers and ammunition belts on the floor of the church before proceeding outside, were delighted later to find that the girls had presence of mind to hide their weaponry in the confessional. (Forgive them, Father!)

During the Civil War, Rosie Cox of Green St., Boyle served as guide to sections of Active Service Units coming from other areas. Bridie Murray acted not only as nurse and courier in the Battle of Boyle in July 1922, but transferred some of the arms on her own person during the conflict.

At times the women served as lookouts. Crown troop movements were noted and signals sent to local Volunteers. A sheet draped over the hedge might designate an upcoming raid. Flickering torches by night might alert the Volunteers standing guard that Tan lorries were on the way. A more enjoyable aspect of their work was the raising of funds by means of dances or concerts.

Had any of these women been caught transporting Irish Republican Army (IRA) dispatches, tending to wounded men, or hiding guns, they would have become well acquainted with the stench and dampness of a prison cell.

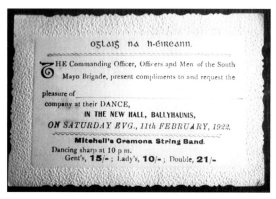

Dance programs from a few of many dance parties, often important fundraising events for the Volunteers.

GERALD O'CONNOR PAPERS

Conscription Crisis

All throughout the First World War, rumblings of conscription were felt in Ireland, but during the final year of the conflict, the low resonance became much more high pitched. Sinn Féin spoke out vehemently against the Act of Conscription. Members throughout the counties began to ask these questions:

*Why should Irish men fight for a country that was presently occupying Irish territory with thousands of troops?

*Why should Irish men fight for a country that had allowed the men's grandparents to starve to death in a ghastly famine?

*Why should Irish men fight for a country that had confiscated their ancestors' land and sent the native people "to hell or to Connaught"?

Eamon de Valera (Sinn Féin) and John Dillon (Parliamentary Party) came to the Market Square in Ballaghaderreen on 5 May 1918 to address those very queries. The two parties had put forth their strongest candidates to face one another in the general election. When de Valera called upon the sea of faces that surrounded him "to voice their resolve that they would die fighting at home sooner than yield, a cry went up in response" — a roar so loud it was heard on the other side of the Irish Sea.

According to T. Ryle Dwyer, author of *Tans, Terror and Troubles*, "it was not — as has often been supposed — the executions following the Easter Rising that drove the Irish people into the arms of Sinn Féin, but the introduction of the bill to establish compulsory military service in Ireland in April 1918."[12] That same sentiment is echoed throughout many books and Volunteer Witness Statements. Implementation of The Conscription Act was postponed to 1 May, and finally indefinitely. The threat of enforcement, however, acted as a flash point for countless nationalists who went to the polls and voted the Irish Parliamentary Party out of existence.

On the local level, the threat of having to march off to war on the Continent prodded previously silent men to raise their voices and join the chorus of Sinn Féin. In the 2nd Battalion South area alone, conscription swelled the ranks from one hundred to more than four hundred.[13] Likewise, when the threat subsided, so too did the commitment of many. Sean Leavy, O/C of the 3rd Battalion North, agrees. "When the conscription scare started, our companies expanded rapidly and soon some of them had a strength of seventy to eighty men. Most of this expansion faded out again when the crisis was over."[14] In the Knockcroghery area, the Company, which had formerly numbered in the twenties, increased its membership to over eighty.[15] Again, when the threat subsided, so too did enthusiasm for the cause. In the far south of the county, the same story is replicated: conscription flooded the ranks, and when the crisis was over, the vast majority of men became inactive.[16]

Not every area of Roscommon was likewise affected. Martin Fallon of the Curraghroe Company stated that their numbers did not significantly increase during the crisis. "This could be put down to our discretion in being selective of the men we took on..."[17] In the Athlone area, Con Costello, the Vice O/C of the Brigade, stated "there was not a huge influx of recruits into the Volunteers as took place in other areas. We were rather careful of the type of man we took into our organisation."[18]

In the Kilmore area of north Roscommon, the numbers significantly increased during the crisis but remained at the higher level with little or no dropoff. Early in 1919, when the Volunteers were put under the jurisdiction of the Dáil, the Company numbers remained constant. "Quality rather than quantity was our objective and to keep what we had and keep them active."[19]

In response to the threat of conscription, nonetheless, first aid supplies were collected in all areas. Some officers and men conducted a census of all available foodstuffs in the locale, while others targeted bridges and culverts for destruction in case the British lorries began hauling men off to the front lines. Others focused their energies on underground activities.

De Valera at the debate in Ballaghaderreen on 5 May 1918. The conscription of Irishmen to serve in the British military was protested.

PHOTO COURTESY OF JOAN O'BRIEN, ATHLONE

Dugouts

By 1918 Britain's war with Germany had become a death struggle. Men fought over insignificant pieces of real estate — back and forth over no-man's land, soldiers on both sides would thrust then retreat, grimace and then die — and die by the thousands. Britain needed more manpower. Westminster diplomats began to court this ripe ingénue named Ireland. The lady, however, was repulsed by the old men's foolish notions.

Young men of County Roscommon began to grow seriously concerned. "It was understood that the British would establish camps in areas throughout the country to enforce conscription and comb the districts for the young men."[20] In preparation for the expected roundup of enlistment men, Volunteers grabbed their shovels, found a safe place, and constructed dugouts. "It was intended to take up our abode in these if conscription was enforced."[21] For every two villages, a dugout was carved in the face of hills or turf banks, or sometimes underground. Oftentimes these hideouts had to be moved because the persistent plodding boots of Crown Forces came too close too frequently. A dugout at Tuam near Ballagh, for instance, was moved to Cornashinnagh, Fourmilehouse, because there was less foot traffic in that townland.

Dugouts varied in size. One constructed at Cloonshee near Ballagh Church could hold up to twenty men. Some were boarded on the sides, but oftentimes water seeped through and dripped down the walls. Some were furnished with bedding from disused mansions in the area. Eleven dugouts were constructed around the Knockcroghery Company area by work parties of Volunteers who made the dugouts on flat ground and covered them over with corrugated iron.

Many men used these hideaways temporarily for a few days or a week while the British Forces were saturating the area. Pat Tiernan of "E" Coy. in the 3rd Battalion

South spent countless days and nights in the dugout in Tuam townland near Ballagh. The hideout was roofed by timber and galvanised steel, covered in bog mud, and then topped with sod. Secret entrances kept the surface from being disturbed in any way. Another man in the Castlerea Battalion, Tom Crawley, lived for over a year in the Breanabeg Bog dugout that was used as Battalion headquarters.

There were two dugouts near Scramogue where men hid out for days at a time. Constructed over a deep drain, one dugout had a wooden bottom, a stack of hay on top, and was entered via a tunnel. Light was provided by a long pole with a candle at the end. Because the dugout was constructed above the water line, the men could sleep on straw. That place served as a safe haven for several years.[22]

In the 2nd Battalion South Roscommon area, dugouts had also been constructed to meet the threat of conscription, but these were not frequently used until the beginning of 1920 when enemy activity increased. In the Athlone area, however, no dugouts were constructed at all.[23]

Sean Hyde and Ernie O'Malley

When the prisoners from the Rising were released after the amnesties of 1916 and 1917, they returned to a country that was somewhat divided in its allegiances. Some of the people liked the British presence because its troops were good customers and paid hard cash. Some of the populace were apathetic — after all, Irish freedom was indeed a long-sought dream, but just that — a dream. Others, however, geared up for a future fight.

A secret volunteer force had been training to carry out assaults on the British Forces, and local leaders had stepped forward to command them. To sharpen and add precision to the county Companies, Michael Collins sent Ernie O'Malley in June, July, and August of 1918 to recruit and organise the countryside.

O'Malley spent a good deal of time in Roscommon. He visited every Company in the 2nd Battalion North, spending a week in each area.[24] In the Strokestown area, O'Malley met local Volunteers at the Sinn Féin Hall and prodded the men to contact other members and begin to organise and drill with serious intent. A parade was ordered in a hillside field on the east shore of Kilglass Lake.

When he was based in the Kilteevan area at Matt Davis' house, he slept during the day at Henry Brennan's of Cloontogher (in order to avoid detection by the authorities). At night, however, O'Malley was an energetic organiser constantly on the move. His recruitment efforts spilled over into Leitrim — on which travels he was guarded by Sean Birmingham of Strokestown. In the far south, O'Malley gave instructions to officers at Rahara each evening for some weeks. The 4th Battalion South was mobilised at various times in order to engage in sham battles at Lysterfield, Churchboro (Knockcroghery), Taughmaconnell, and Scregg. Some of the men had to travel twenty miles to attend those practice sessions.

In O'Malley's words, "A long barn smelling of oats and horse harness might be our classroom or a school house. Seated at the desks the boys and men noted my diagrams and chalk headings from the blackboard. On the roads our scouts were placed; they held bicycle lamps with red and green glass. A red flash meant something strange or uncertain; a succession of red, enemy drawing near."[25]

O'Malley sought able and inspired men to head the local Companies and train the recruits. While he was in Kiltrustan, staying at Pat Mullooly's house, Mullooly remarked to him that the Volunteer organisation should be oath bound. O'Malley couldn't have disagreed more. Typical of O'Malley's pointed and astute observations was his reply: "If men are no good without an oath, they will be no good with it."

Weaponry

The 3rd Battalion South was formed prior to the general election of 1918. The men were long on enthusiasm but short on arms. The original arsenal consisted of two old-pattern service rifles — one long-barrelled Lee Enfield and the other a carbine or cavalry type Lee Enfield,[26] some shotguns, and a good .44 sporting rifle,

"You murderer! You murderer! Do you think you will get pardon from God trying to overthrow the British Empire? You Irish, fed on potatoes and buttermilk, can never do that!"

Spoken by the priest of Lincoln Jail in England to Patrick Hegarty, imprisoned officer of the North Mayo Battalion, as recorded in Hegarty's Volunteer Witness Statement p 24.

"It was to this unique geographical predicament —- too far from Britain to be assimilated, too near to be allowed to be separate —- that so many of Ireland's anomalies and miseries could be traced."

Thomas Pakenham
The Year of Liberty p. 25

"Unfed and unread these rebels had a national spirit which fired the torches of freedom."

Quoting from John Hester, County Roscommon native, and author of *Living to Ninety — And On*

The Colonel said, "There is no hope of your beating the British Empire" to which Bertles replied, "Wait and see!"

Spoken by Dick Bertles (O/C of the 2nd Battalion Athlone Brigade) when confronted by the powerful landlord Colonel King-Harman in the Colonel's study (as recorded in Anthony McCormack's Volunteer Witness Statement p. 5)

thanks to Father Ryan of Lanesboro.[27] Guns could be purchased for the men in Dublin for nearly five pounds apiece, but money was the stumbling block. There was never enough. Oftentimes even if there were enough coins, the Volunteers from Roscommon who travelled to the capital could not get supplies.

The 3rd Battalion North area reflected this same image. A few shotguns and a revolver or two comprised their entire arsenal.[28] In the 2nd Battalion North area, there were three service rifles, a number of shotguns, a few revolvers, and sparse ammunition.[29] The 2nd Battalion South had the same problem. At the formation of the Battalion in 1918, there were a few shotguns and perhaps a revolver or two. To remedy this shortfall, at the end of 1919 a GHQ directive was issued for the entire country — raid for arms! As a consequence, the 2nd Battalion carried out a few operations which resulted in their collecting a large amount of shotguns and cartridges and a few .22 rifles. No prize service rifles, however, were confiscated. No trouble was given to the Volunteers during this raiding. The collected guns, however, were of little value, as many of them were inoperable.[30] They were deposited in local dumps.

In the far north near Ballyfarnon, raids were conducted, but few serviceable arms were collected. A small number of shotguns, some cartridges, and a few small-calibre revolvers with little ammunition were assembled and stored in a large wooden box and placed in the lakeshore at Alderford.[31]

In the extreme south of the county in the Summerhill, Drum area, rifles were sometimes borrowed from men in Westmeath, but generally the Volunteers had to raid for them. "The arms collected were placed in wooden boxes and buried in the sandpit as being the driest place that could be found..."[32] Arms dumps were not usually buildings because they proved too easy a target for British troop raids. In the town of Athlone, rifles were occasionally purchased from British soldiers garrisoned there. Liam Mellows, the man who would later be executed by the Free State, also brought arms into the Athlone area.[33]

Ingenuity oftentimes triumphed over lack of matériel. When rifles were scarce but some sort of weapon was deemed desirable, a group of men in the Coosan area of County Westmeath collected a large number of springs from cars and vans that had been dumped at Coosan. They took this specially tempered steel to the local blacksmiths, who moulded it into pikeheads. "Ash handles were prepared for the pikes, but were not fitted to them, to facilitate storage."[34]

The vast amount of arms that found their way into the hands of Volunteers, however, was seized from local people. Raiding individual houses and mansions was a constant sideline to the work of the Volunteers and took up much of their energy and guile. In the Knockcroghery/St. John's area, raids were conducted on local Unionists, ex-RIC men, landlords — anyone who might have a weapon. Sixteen raids were conducted on private houses,[35] yielding about the same number of shotguns. The men were assigned to sections and, on one occasion, raided the homes only hours before the RIC came calling at the same houses for the same guns. On another occasion, one of the raids was conducted in broad daylight with the houses having to be approached by boat on Lough Ree. In Curraghboy, twenty raids were carried out in the immediate area, while another fifteen were staged outside the Company area in conjunction with other Companies of the Battalion.[36] Volunteers were careful to confiscate not only the guns but also the ammunition that went with them. One without the other proved useless.

While most encounters came off peacefully, some turned quite ugly. In south Roscommon, Joe Kearney was seriously wounded on a raid of Feehily's house in the St. John's area. On another raid in the Knockcroghery area, Volunteers John Kelly and Edward Foley were both wounded slightly during an encounter.

To augment local Volunteer funds for arms purchase and maintenance, the Dáil floated a loan to which the country people contributed generously. In the 3rd Battalion South area, the monies were lodged with Father John Finan of Kilteevan. Towards the end of 1919 or early 1920, that Battalion solved its

"Did it really mean that it was all over? That there would be no more five o'clock curfew and that one could walk that night as late as one pleased without being shot? That one could sleep in one's own bed? That it really represented the end of seven hundred years of military occupation, the triumph of the imagination over material power, the impossible become law?"

Frank O'Connor's
An Only Child p. 209

(Observations of a young man on July 11, 1921 while watching the English troops withdraw into Cork Barracks.)

"..... it was not the oath, as such, that caused the main problem for Republicans in the 1920s, but what it stood for — British sovereignty over Ireland and the right to rule in any part of Ireland."

Nollaig O'Gadhra's
Civil War in Connaught p. 92

"I had not expected anything but death to end my part in the struggle; we had seen the grey face of death too often not to be able to know his shadow as we wandered. We did not expect to live through the war; there were too many risks to be taken, but we did feel that our cause would win."

Ernie O'Malley's *On Another Man' Wound* p. 239

dilemma by placing a levy on property owners and others to raise the needed funds. Charges were based on the Poor Law valuation (a shilling or one and six-pence in the pound).[37] The collected funds were lodged with the Brigade O/C.

In each Company area, men were appointed to collect this levy. In the Knockcroghery Company area, fourteen men were assigned this duty. In St. John's area, only nine did the work.

The northern part of the county mirrored the rest of Roscommon in contributing mightily to this fund. In the Drumlion area alone, more than £200 was collected, most of which was in £1 and £5 notes. "...it was extraordinary how the people subscribed to the fund and handed over without any compulsion their hard-earned savings."[38]

The Fight is On

The opening punches of the War for Independence were delivered during the spring and summer of 1918. For Kerry folks, the attack led by Tom McEllistrim and Jack Cronin on the Gortatlea Barracks on 13 April was the first official action of the war.[39] John Browne and Richard Laide lost their lives in that attack. Years later McEllistrim admitted that the impetus for his action was the introduction of the bill in the House of Commons that established compulsory military service for Ireland.[40]

Three months later on July 7 at Beal a' Ghleanna ("the Mouth of the Glen"), which is near Ballingeary, another incident occurred which Cork inhabitants claim was their initiation to the War for Independence. While observing two policemen stiffly seated in their jaunting car on their way to Ballyvourney, Mrs. Jack Lynch (wife of the local Company Captain of the Volunteers) mused aloud one morning on her way to Mass, "Isn't it a great pity without someone coming before them in the Glen in the evening!" Her husband pondered her casual observation. The capture of four weapons at the His Majesty's expense? Absolutely no shooting so no one would get permanently injured! With seven men against two, it could be done!

Lynch gathered six other men (Tadhg and Liam Twomey, Dan Thady McSweeney, Jamie Moynihan, Jeremiah O'Shea and Neilus O'Reilly) and laid in wait that evening for the two armed RIC officers. A fight ensued, but the two carbines and two revolvers formerly owned by the "peelers" became the first weapons paid for by the British government to be used against its own troops in later fights.[41]

The first ambush distinction is often credited to the Soloheadbeg incident in County Tipperary which occurred six months later, a clash in which Dan Breen and Sean Treacy shot and killed two armed policemen transporting gelignite. (Ironically, the site of the Soloheadbeg ambush is on the same plain where Brian Boru and his brother Mahon fought their first great battle with the Danes almost a thousand years before.)

Attempted Disarming of Guards at Carrick-on-Shannon Rail Station

On very rare occasions attack plans glide smoothly through troubled waters. More often than not a single slip-up or a lone unsuspected occurrence scuttles a project on the shoals. In the case of the attempted ambush of guards at the Carrick-on-Shannon Rail Station on 28 September 1918, however, the amount of bumbles surpassed the number of waves lapping ashore on nearby Lough Corry.

Mick McLoughlin, Vice O/C of the 5th Battalion North, worked as a porter in the station. At a meeting in Drumlion with Ernie O'Malley, Pat Mullooly, Michael Dockery, and nine others, McLoughlin suggested a plan for disarming the twenty-two military guards positioned at the station. O'Malley, who at the time was staying at Pat Mullooly's home in Kiltrustan, refined the plan and details began to take shape:

1. Eleven Carrick-on-Shannon Volunteers would board a cattle train some distance from the station. Some of the men would cover the engineer until the train rumbled into the station, then all the Volunteers would jump off and disarm the military guards.

2. In the meantime, Michael Dockery and Pat Mullooly, dressed in RIC uniforms, would proceed along the rail line and engage the sentries in conversation and subsequently disarm them.

With the waters charted, the Volunteers set sail. Firstly the RIC uniforms were to be borrowed from the Strokestown dramatic society who had them in their costume stash. The problem was that the uniforms were so musty and dirty that they would not have fooled a blind man. The disguise ruse was quickly abandoned.

Secondly, when Pat Mullooly cycled to Lisadorn, he found only Tom Mulick (from Aughrim) Barney Gannon (provider of horse and side car), Michael Dockery, and Ernie O'Malley — no Carrick Volunteers. O'Malley reported that Captain Murphy of the Carrick Company had called the whole thing off because his informers had sent word of unusual activity in the area. The assumption was that the British Forces knew the Volunteers were coming. Having travelled all this way, however, members of the 2nd and 3rd Battalion[42] were not quite ready to concede defeat. Dockery entered the town to scout it out and went into the station to meet with Mick McLoughlin. Sure enough, no Carrick Volunteers were around, and the operation was impossible without them. The whole affair had to be cancelled, which produced a rage in O'Malley who "had had his time in Roscommon extended by Collins in order to bring off this stunt."[43]

Cautiousness and musty clothes were not the only culprits of the night. Lady Luck had abandoned ship. When Mullooly met with McLoughlin the next day, McLoughlin informed him that all the young soldiers who had formerly composed the guard had been drafted off to France and were replaced by old veterans who had received their pay the day before and spent their earnings on Guinness and girls, and were in no fit shape to resist the wind, let alone an assault by the Volunteers.

The General Election of 1918 in South Roscommon

With the Sinn Féin success of Count Plunkett's election in Roscommon in 1917 and Joe McGuinness' win in Longford, the sweet smell of victory was in the air. Roscommon inhaled deeply. Sinn Féin wanted to put forth a strong candidate and in Harry Boland, whose family originated from Cams near Cloverhill, it found its champion. Boland became the Sinn Féin standard bearer for South Roscommon. Optimism abounded when Boland delivered this speech, as reported by the *Roscommon Herald* in its 30 November issue:

"We were in the Gaelic League and in the GAA, in the Irish industrial movement and all the time we were planning our Irish Republic. We believe in new times, new men, new ideas. In 1914 there was only one Republic in Europe; today there are thirty-two. When we spoke of the Republic we were called rainbow chasers. Well, the people of Europe have caught the rainbow and Ireland will catch it too — at the peace conference."

Hundreds of Roscommon Volunteers played a huge part in that election. They canvassed for voters, guarded meetings, acquired transport, and were on hand at the polling places overseeing the ballot boxes and escorting the ballot boxes to the counting centre where they stood with vigilance as their companion during the actual tabulation of votes.

Most areas of the county experienced no trouble during the election proceedings. A few scuffles were reported in isolated polling booths, but the major confrontation occurred in Athlone, where a large number of "separation women"

Pearse thought "The Rising could not fail as a noble example, and even if it was defeated militarily, it would provide the groundwork for a later movement which would triumph. It was an audacious supposition, all the more extraordinary because it proved to be correct."

Kenneth Griffith and Timothy O'Grady's *Curious Journey — An Oral History of Ireland's Unfinished Revolution* p. 48

(same source, p. 83)

..."these executions demonstrated to the country the quality of the men.....it wasn't death, it was the call to freedom which captivated us."

(spoken by Maire Comerford, octogenarian interviewed by the authors in the early 1980s)

"The guerrillas thought of themselves as sovereign. They had organised and armed themselves and paid their own way. They had brought the republic into being and nobody else had a right to give it away."

Peter Hart's *The I.R.A. & Its Enemies* p. 269

1918 Sinn Féin meeting. Count Plunkett and Harry Boland seated in centre middle row. Banners read, "Major McBride Sinn Féin Club, Kilgefin" and "Sean McDiarmada Sinn Féin Club, Roscommon."

(wives who received monies from the British government due to their husbands serving in the army) created quite a ruckus. According to Con Costello, Vice O/C of the Athlone Brigade, "jam jars and bottles were the usual missiles used by these people. On one occasion when we were proceeding into Athlone for a meeting, the Franciscan priests had to take us into the town by a circuitous route in order to avoid a clash with those people, who, we were told, had quite a large store of such weapons waiting for us."[44]

On voting day itself there were hundreds more ballots to count than in previous elections. Not from fraud but from law! The Representation of the People Act of 1918 greatly increased the number of voters — extending the franchise to take in a large number of youthful citizens, including, for the first time, women of property over the age of 30, who were inclined towards the new Sinn Féin policies.

The Republican Courts and their Police

What exactly were Republican Courts and Police? What were their duties and from whom did they receive their authority? In order to replace the British agents of control, Republican Courts and Police were set up by the Dáil. Courts were set up on the parish as well as the district level. Parish courts considered minor cases, while appeals from the parish level ended up in district courts. The jurisdiction of the district court was far broader. "They could hear reasonably substantial damage claims (up to £100) and adjudicate in land title disputes, trade union rights, and claims for compensation by workmen."[45] Court sessions were held in abandoned or even occupied houses. "No lengthy or legal technicalities were indulged in and the litigants seemed satisfied with the settlement of their differences, just as well as if some English judge with a wig and an impressive show of jurisprudence had done the job."[46] Volunteers acted as summons servers and court clerks. Oftentimes the man appointed Judge was not a man of classical Latin scholarship, but a person abundantly supplied with good common sense. He may not have been a Volunteer but a member of Sinn Féin who heard evidence to determine the guilt or innocence of men/women brought before him. "When things became hot, these courts really became military courts, as the civilian Sinn Féin judges and other personnel became inactive and the Volunteers had perforce to carry on."[47] Implementation of the sentencing, however, fell to the Police.

After the burning of the smaller barracks on Easter weekend 1920, the job of policing the territory fell to the Volunteers. According to Jim Quigley, O/C of the 2nd Battalion South, "the duty of policing the county now developed on the Volunteers and this entailed an enormous amount of work. Prisoners arrested by them had to be kept in temporary jails which came to be known as 'Unknown destinations' so called because the public or the British authorities did not know their location. Unknown destinations were generally unused houses or outoffices belonging to some house.[48] In the 2nd Battalion South area, a building in Cloverhill was used,

In the early years of the twentieth century, it was seditious to promote anti-English feelings. This author's great-uncle, Ned Hegarty of Ballinaheglish, taught his nephew Johnny Dowd and a neighbour boy, John Hester, a member of Fianna Éireann (the national Boy Scouts), about English occupation by singing a sprightly tune whose innocent words shrouded the true meaning of the hated British presence.

DORA*

A lovely young lady has landed here lately below at the lovely North Wall.
She came here among us to kiss us and hug us and know how she cuddles us all.
Her two eyes are beaming like bright bayonets gleaming
She brought a supply of the same.
If ever she'd leave us how sorely t'would grieve us, and now I will tell you her name.

DORA.... DORA
how can I worship my DORA?
She came here to teach our young men how to live, how to forget and how to forgive.
It's my DORA...never displease her in eye.
She'll treat you quite well in a first-class hotel, with the beautiful name of Mountjoy.

*DORA is an acronym for Defense of the Realm Act

while in the 2nd Battalion North area, the prisoners were kept at Kilcloghan near Elphin. In the Boyle area, Knockarush, nicknamed "Brixton," was used as a place of detention. Southward in the county, guilty parties were kept in a house in Clonown and in the Sinn Féin Hall in Summerhill.[49] Constant guards, both on the prisoners and the places, had to be maintained while they were in use.[50] Food had to be collected from local farmers, and, at times, bought with Volunteer funds.[51] Prisoners were moved frequently, according to Jim Dorr, O/C of the 5th Battalion North, "so that they could not get to know their whereabouts or the men who were dealing with them."[52]

The Police were also responsible for guarding the court sessions and afterwards for carrying out the prescribed sentences, which at times included warnings to instantly abandon the area, a fine, or confinement for a designated arrest period. At other times the sentences were more severe. A Brigade Police Officer was to control all police actions in his Brigade area.

An example of the seriousness with which these verdicts were taken can be cited in the Coosan area. Two men were tried and convicted of robbery. Their sentence included deportation to Scotland for five years, "and they did not return till the five years were up."[53] Another example which exemplifies the fairness of these homemade courts can be found in the 3rd Battalion North Roscommon area. Two cousins were disputing the division of a farm. "One wanted the best of the farm as well as a right of way through the half he proposed the other man should get. The decision of the court was that he should divide the farm as he thought it should be divided and then give his cousin choice of which half he would take."[54]

David Daly, of Faheran, Moate, describes the workings of the Courts in the Athlone vicinity: "Some big land disputes were dealt with by the Courts in this area, and the litigants in such cases had to deposit large sums of money before the cases were heard as a guarantee that they would abide by the decisions of the Court. In all cases the decision of the Courts was carried out to the full. The Courts were inexpensive and easily accessible to the people and 'red tape' was cut out completely."[55]

Procedure for arrests was outlined in a 3 March 1920 communiqué from GHQ: If an arrest takes place, report to the Battalion Police Officer in the area of arrest (report on such form as attached below). If the Battalion Police Officer agrees to the arrest, he shall sign the committal form marked B addressed to the Committee Officer at the Prison Centre. The prisoner must then be escorted to "jail," whereupon the arresting officer submits the form to the accepting officer.[56]

Another procedure followed by the Volunteers was one of trial by jury. When a non-sympathiser (or spy) was suspected of foul play, a trial was held and members of a particular Company along with their commanding officer(s) would hear evidence and pronounce judgment. The local Republican Police were responsible for carrying out the sentence.

Each area had designated Policemen who arrested and guarded prisoners. Sometimes they watched over persons from other areas of the county. On one specific occasion, a person who had been tried and convicted of shooting and wounding a Volunteer in the Knockcroghery area was transported to Cloverhill in the 2nd Battalion area and guarded for several weeks before being returned to his family. He was also fined for his indiscretion — a fine collected by the Republican Police in Knockcroghery.

The first mention of operative Republican Police was made in the bye-election of 1917[57] in north Roscommon. There was little press about them in public papers until 1920. The General Order of May 1920 first proclaimed them to be the appropriate instrument to deal with civil matters.[58]

In South Roscommon, Ned Hegarty of Ballinaheglish was appointed Chief of this force. In the north of the county, Hugh Keegan of Lackan, Strokestown, J. Tanner,[59] and James Turbitt of Boyle served in this position.

Intelligence Work

Every Battalion had its own intelligence system. An officer in each Company would be responsible for accumulating data that might prove useful to the Volunteers. Watching, tabulating the timing and strength of enemy patrols, noting suspicious behaviour of civilians who might suddenly come into money or who paid uncalled-for visits to the military, were all part of the assignment. In certain areas of Roscommon this system worked very well. In the 2nd Battalion North area, "if one wanted a report on any person in the area it could be procured without delay."[60]

The post office held a wealth of intelligence information. Through that office passed the coded messages that arrived from Dublin Castle for the local garrisons. The post office in Roscommon town was tapped, and through the furtive work of Messrs. Monaghan, McNamara, William Kilmartin and Tommy Farrell, those messages from Dublin Castle were intercepted and interpreted.[61] Sometimes those intercepted messages were sent back to IRA Headquarters in Dublin for decoding, but at other times local men, such as Michael Duignan (who was the North Roscommon Brigade Intelligence Officer) could decipher the code and get the information to the Volunteers sometimes before the intended recipients even read it.

A favourite method used by local intelligence officers was the raiding of mails. If suspicious letters were found, even without a return address, the Volunteers might take the handwriting sample into the local shops where a file was kept of orders for merchandise. The handwriting was compared to the file notes, and a match was made. Then the information was forwarded to the Battalion Intelligence Officer, who in turn passed it along to the Battalion staff for a decision.

Obtaining information from inside the RIC proved highly valuable. A Constable Campbell in Elphin would occasionally give the Volunteers tips, as did Sgts. Harte and Duffy in Roscommon town. Sgt. Galligan from Kiltoom had frequent communication with the local Volunteers. Constable William Potter of the RIC in Kiltoom was in touch with GHQ in Dublin, but he was mistakenly ambushed by local Volunteers and killed.

Men working on the railway proved to be an invaluable asset in intelligence gathering and disseminating. They carried dispatches to and from Dublin under great risk. And closer to home, the women of Roscommon in the Cumann na mBan travelled over the pathways and through the fields with dispatches that helped knit together the communication network that made the attacks possible and kept the Volunteers safer.

A Brigade Intelligence Officer had to synthesise intelligence from the Companies, the Battalions, and the Active Service Units. His reports to the Brigade Commander and to GHQ included: enemy posts and strengths (military, RIC, Auxiliaries, Black and Tans); types of troops at each post (mounted, artillery); means of transport; names of officers; distance from one enemy position to another; names of suspected spies; conditions of the roads; history of operations carried out by both sides; details about IRA failures; sniping possibilities; the workings of the enemy dispatch system; location and names of friendly officers at the post office; number of wires (telephone and telegraph); friendly telephone operators; location of Brigade headquarters and the name of the owner of the land; conditions of the railroads and staff and description of their jobs; friendly operators of barges or motor boats; names of friendly hotel personnel; important bridges in the area (their construction and possible means of destruction); and the location of fords and ferries.[62]

Election Results Fuel the National Fires

As a result of the general election of late 1918 which literally swept the Irish Parliamentary Party out of the House of Commons, the first Dáil that assembled in Dublin was heavily loaded with ardent nationalists who had just been elected on the Sinn Féin platform — separation from England. With little debate about its international ramifications, Dáil Éireann proclaimed an Irish Republic on 21 January 1919. Ireland was hitherto thought of as a separate entity (at least by many in Ireland) whose people began to establish their own government, courts, and police. It was Arthur Griffith's roadmap to independence that was followed by the Dublin legislative body. Statesmen in England, however, viewed it as a road to hell. England at that time was the centre of a worldwide empire. To have its nearest colony decide to withdraw from this mighty unit was utterly unacceptable. London meant for Ireland to pay for this bout of obstinacy, and pay dearly. ■

> "How often had we vowed, as we sat around the turf fires, or as we tramped with squelching feet, the rain dripping into our boots, that we in our generation would finish the fight?"
>
> Ernie O'Malley's
> The Singing Flame p. 45

1. *Tans, Terror and Troubles*, by T. Ryle Dwyer, p. 118.
2. Sean Leavy (O/C of the 3rd Battalion North) Volunteer Witness Statement to the Bureau of Military History 1913-21, p. 3.
3. *County Longford and the Irish Revolution*, by Marie Coleman. p. 48.
4. *Tans, Terror and Troubles*, by T. Ryle Dwyer, p. 114.
5. According to Micheál O'Callaghan's book, *For Ireland and Freedom*, the **Rockingham Raid** group included James Stephen Brennan, Alec McCabe, James Hanagan, James Dodd, James Feely, John and Patrick Sheerin, Pat Delahunty, Patrick Spellman, Martin Killalea, James Turbitt, Batt Keaney of Keash and Michael (John) McGuire of Ballymote, and James Haran. The papers of Pat Brennan indicate that James Flanagan was also a participant. (Flanagan was actually a herdsman for the estate who supplied the men with information.)
6. Pat Brennan Papers, personal diary.
7. James Feely Volunteer Witness Statement to the Bureau of Military History 1913-21, p. 3.
8. John Hester, interview by author, Roscommon town, 27 August 1994.
9. "Sis" Murray, interview by author, 21 August 1995, Dublin.
10. Eileen Banahan, interview by author, 20 November 2000, Ballagh, Roscommon.
11. Rita Leneghan written statement, Pat Brennan Papers, private collection.
12. p. 127.
13. Jim Quigley Volunteer Witness Statement to the Bureau of Military History 1913-21, p. 2.
14. Sean Leavy Volunteer Witness Statement to the Bureau of Military History 1913-21, p. 2.
15. Tom Kelly Volunteer Witness Statement to the Bureau of Military History 1913-21, p. 2.
16. Patrick Lennon Volunteer Witness Statement to the Bureau of Military History 1913-21, p. 2.
17. Martin Fallon Volunteer Witness Statement to the Bureau of Military History 1913-21, p. 2.
18. Con Costello Volunteer Witness Statement to the Bureau of Military History 1913-21, p. 2.
19. Jim Dorr Volunteer Witness Statement to the Bureau of Military History 1913-21, p. 2.
20. Frank Simons Volunteer Witness Statement to the Bureau of Military History 1913-21, p. 2.
21. Luke Duffy Volunteer Witness Statement (Vice O/C of the 3rd Battalion South Roscommon) to the Bureau of Military History 1913-21, p. 1.
22. Ciaran Leavy, son of Sean Leavy, interview by author, 27 June 2002, Roscommon town.
23. Con Costello Volunteer Witness Statement to the Bureau of Military History 1913-21, p. 2.
24. Tom Brady Volunteer Witness Statement to the Bureau of Military History 1913-21, p. 6.
25. *On Another Man's Wounds*, by Ernie O'Malley, p. 80.
26. Luke Duffy Volunteer Witness Statement to the Bureau of Military History 1913-21, p. 1.
27. Jim Quigley (O/C of the 2nd Battalion South Roscommon.) Volunteer Witness Statement to the Bureau of Military History 1913-21. p. 2.
28. Sean Leavy Volunteer Witness Statement to the Bureau of Military History 1913-21, p. 2.
29. Tom Brady Volunteer Witness Statement to the Bureau of Military History 1913-21, p. 4.
30. Sean Leavy Volunteer Witness Statement to the Bureau of Military History 1913-21, p. 5.
31. Tommy Lavin Volunteer Witness Statement to the Bureau of Military History 1913-21, p. 5.
32. Patrick Lennon Volunteer Witness Statement to the Bureau of Military History 1913-21, p. 5.
33. Anthony McCormack Volunteer Witness Statement to the Bureau of Military History 1913-21, p. 6
34. Frank O'Connor Volunteer Witness Statement to the Bureau of Military History 1913-21, p. 6.
35. Particulars of pre-Truce Activities of Curraghboy Company, 4th Battalion, South Roscommon Brigade, p. 11.
36. Particulars of pre-Truce Activities of Curraghboy Company, 4th Battalion, South Roscommon Brigade, p. 3.
37. Matt Davis Volunteer Witness Statement to the Bureau of Military History 1913-21, p. 7.
38. Jack Glancy Volunteer Witness Statement to the Bureau of Military History 1913-21, p. 6.
39. *In the Name of the Game*, by J. J. Barrett p. 55. On page 115 Barrett also identifies 10 April as the fateful day.
40. *The Kerryman*, article on Tom McEllistrim by Ryle Dwyer. 19 August 1994.
41. *Green Tears for Hecuba*, by Patrick J. Twohig, p. 27-32.

42. Participants in **Carrick-on-Shannon attempted attack** included: James Kelly, Joseph Leyland, Tom Mulick, Barney Gannon, — Gilchrist from Kilmore, Michael Mahon, Pat Mullooly, Michael Dockery, Mick McLoughlin, Ernie O'Malley.
43. Patrick Mullooly Volunteer Witness Statement to the Bureau of Military History 1913-21, p. 8.
44. Con Costello Volunteer Witness Statement to the Bureau of Military History 1913-1921, p. 4.
45. *County Longford and the Irish Revolution*, by Marie Coleman, p. 102.
46. *When Youth Was Mine — A Memoir of Kerry 1902-1925*, by Jeremiah Murphy, p.156.
47. Frank Simons Volunteer Witness Statement to the Bureau of Military History 1913-1921, p. 5.
48. Jim Quigley Volunteer Witness Statement to the Bureau of Military History 1913-1921, p. 4.
49. Patrick Lennon Volunteer Statement to the Bureau of Military History 1913-1921, p. 6.
50. Jim Quigley Volunteer Witness Statement to the Bureau of Military History 1913-1921, p. 4.
51. James Feely Volunteer Witness Statement to the Bureau of Military History 1913-1921, p. 8.
52. Jim Dorr Volunteer Witness Statement to the Bureau of Military History 1913-1921, p. 3.
53. Frank O'Connor Volunteer Witness Statement to the Bureau of Military History 1913-1921, p. 15.
54. Sean Leavy Volunteer Witness Statement to the Bureau of Military History 1913-1921, p. 5.
55. David Daly Volunteer Witness Statement to the Bureau of Military History 1913-1921, p. 10.
56. Mulcahy Papers, A/49, dated March 3, 1920.
57. *From Public Defiance to Guerilla Warfare*, by Joost Augusteijn, p. 99.
58. *From Public Defiance to Guerilla Warfare*, by Joost Augusteijn, p. 99.
59. *I.R.A. in the Fight for Freedom 1919 to the Truce*, published by *The Kerryman*, Tralee 1955, p. 24.
60. Tom Brady Volunteer Witness Statement to the Bureau of Military History 1913-1921, p. 4.
61. Frank Simons Volunteer Witness Statement to the Bureau of Military History 1913-1921, p. 38.
62. Charles Pinkman Volunteer Witness Statement to the Bureau of Military History 1913-1921, p. 4-5.

BUILDING AN ORGANISATION

Throughout the previous two years, Volunteer Companies had been formed in the county, men had drilled, been assigned election duties, collected funds for the IRA; some involved themselves in land agitation, some raided for arms. Little, however, had prepared the men for the paralysis of fear that would seize them when they actually came under enemy fire. That experience was lying in their future.

The year 1919 did, however, offer a few opportunities to test the mettle of local Companies. In January the ideology of the Volunteers intersected with the battle cry of the old Land League — "Irish land for Irish people." The site for conflict: Clooneenhartland, Strokestown.

A four hundred acre tract of land, once owned by Marcus McCausland, had been purchased by the Land Commission. There was, however, no effort by the Commission to divide the land (perhaps because the sitting lessee had friends in high places). The acreage was now rented by William Walpole, an Orangeman and Justice of the Peace, who lived at Castlenode, about a mile on the Longford side of Strokestown. One rainy evening, members of the Kilglass Company broke down a few fences and drove Mr. Walpole's cattle out onto the road — not intending to scatter them, but simply to make a point. The landlord dutifully reported the incident to the police who, upon arriving at the crime scene, found the local herd(er), Pat Carlos, had already retrieved the cattle and was mending the fence.

A few weeks later, the same Kilglass Company members decided to try again, and this time determined to be of more than nuisance value. Volunteers scouted the roads all the day preceding the projected cattle drive. No unusual British military activity was observed. Unarmed (except for a pistol carried by Tommy Loughran's brother, Jack), they entered Clooneenhartland just west of Gillstown Bridge and proceeded diagonally away from the road in search of cattle. Their line of movement brought them around the bullpark (a stonewall enclosure which held a Hereford bull). When they were about thirty yards from the bullpark, a voice bellowed, "If you move, you're dead men."[1] Immediately every Volunteer wheeled around and ran towards the road with guns blazing behind them. As Jack Loughran was climbing over the roadside wall, he was grazed by a bullet in his back but got up and ran again. James Hanley was about one hundred yards down the road strolling along, seemingly oblivious to the melee surrounding him. The Tans soon caught up with him, roughed him up, and took him away. He was held until his court appearance, at which time he was sentenced to two months imprisonment at hard labour. His sentence was suspended and he was bound to the peace for two years (which essentially gave Walpole a reprieve too, for any further action taken against his land would have resulted in Hanley being imprisoned).

The whole affair, while not of great military value, had a beneficial effect on the local Company "...even though they broke and ran when it happened. They had been fired upon, six or seven of them had been slightly wounded...and none of them had been killed. The result was a much steadier unit..."[2]

Little had prepared the men for the paralysis of fear that would seize them when they actually came under enemy fire.

Sniping at Ballymoe Barracks

General Headquarters in Dublin was most eager to eliminate the scattered RIC barracks that dotted Ireland's countryside. In 1919 an order came to local units that all barracks still occupied were to be targets. In the 2nd Battalion South area, a tempting prize loomed just across the border into Galway — Ballymoe.

In September of 1919 five men armed with shotguns[3] proceeded to take up positions outside the building. They did not meet with success, however, due to the fact that steel shutters protected the openings and shotguns were deemed totally inadequate for precision firing. A few rounds of shells were discharged before the Volunteers made a hasty retreat.

Raiding

Targeting RIC men, their barracks, and supply lines became the focus of Volunteer activity in early 1920 in County Roscommon. Raids for arms, waylaying Irish soldiers home on leave from the British army (so successful were the Volunteers that the Westminster Parliament passed a law that Irish soldiers could not transport their weapons across the Irish Sea), and targeting supplies intended for the occupying British Army became a full time operation.

About twenty members from the Athlone and Summerhill Companies in south Roscommon participated in a would-be attack on 20 February on the barracks in Ballymore, County Westmeath. They bicycled to a central meeting point near Drumraney, but the local Volunteers in charge of bringing the rifles to them never arrived. It was later learned that the Westmeath men were afraid of the reprisals that would result if an attack were staged in their area.[4] (No such fear inhibited the Longford Volunteers who attacked the Ballymahon Barracks that same night. The disappointed Athlone Volunteers could see the Verey lights shooting up from there.)[5]

Members of the 1st Battalion South devised a plan whereby they would seize some much needed arms. In April John Flanagan (later a member of the Garda Síochána, the Republic of Ireland's police force), James Crawley, James Doherty, Thomas Raftery, Tom Vaughan, Martin Foley, Peter Quinn, and John Dillon conducted a successful raid on the Castlerea Barracks. A month later on the night of 12 May, Volunteers of Drumlion Company raided the Carrick-on-Shannon Customs and Excise Office and made off with books and documents relating to income taxes. In order to alleviate fears of wanton destruction, they did, however, leave behind a note to the authorities which read:

> "Nothing taken from here save matters harmful
> to the Irish Republic."

At 11 p.m. on a May evening, six Volunteers (Seamus O'Meara, Thomas Mannion, George Manning, Brian Mulvihill, Frank O'Connor, and Michael Cunniffe)[6] held up the caretaker of the Athlone Excise Office and proceeded to dismantle the financial records of the British administration there. For four hours they destroyed records, files, documents — anything that would be helpful in the collecting of what they considered illegal charges against Irish citizens. (Frank O'Connor claims 28 June as the date of this break-in and also places Bob Ramsey, Ned Doolan, and John Doolan there. Harry O'Brien claims that the Excise Office was raided on Easter Saturday night in April and that he was present.)

Two wagonloads of two-gallon tins intended to replenish the supplies of petrol at Boyle Military Barracks were shipped in May 1920 by the British via rail to Boyle. Alerted to the fact that so much petrol sat unguarded awaiting pickup at the station, about forty Volunteers from Boyle and Doon Companies decided to help themselves. They confiscated the volatile drums from the Railway Station, then quietly consigned them to the grave, so to speak. They parked them in the unused mortuary attached to the old fever hospital. The hospital was just across the street from the station, making transfer of the contraband an easy matter.

For four hours they destroyed records, files, documents — anything that would be helpful in the collecting of what they considered illegal charges against Irish citizens.

"Each man took two tins or four gallons and passed them over the wall into the hospital grounds where another party took them and stored them in the Dead House."[7] A thorough but useless search was made by the military for miles around. They never thought to look under their very noses.

In June the 1st Battalion South intelligence scouts reported to their commanding officers that a large consignment of petrol was scheduled to be taken by rail to Ballina. Plans were made to intercept that cargo at Ballinlough Station and thus supply the Battalion area with firepower for use in future attacks. Thirty Volunteers participated in the raid which yielded several hundred gallons. Thankfully, the action did not directly engage the enemy. There were no casualties on either side.[8] Three of the Volunteers who participated, however, would later lose their lives in other engagements (Ned Shannon, Pat Glynn, and Mick Carty). The petrol taken in this raid was quickly spirited away to hiding places in the bog and potato fields around Loughglynn. The two-gallon cans were scattered in groups of "a few here" and "a few there." Patrick Vaughan of Cloonsuck was one of the persons who knew where those cans were located, and it was his job to retrieve them when upcoming operations demanded: i.e., the burning of the barracks at Loughglynn and Ballinlough and the destruction of Balfe's house in Southpark. Some of that petrol was sold in order to purchase four rifles and some hand grenades.[9]

In keeping with the thrust of arms procurement for the area, that same month two Lancers on patrol were stopped at Tarmon Cross. While Michael Egan and Dan O'Rourke kept sharp eyes out for possible danger, John Brennan and Andrew Smyth commanded the soldiers to relinquish their arms. Wise Lancers that they were, they did as ordered.[10]

On 22 June a large arms raid was carried out in the 5th Battalion North area. According to Jack Glancy, North Roscommon Brigade Adjutant, "most of the people were only too anxious to hand up the weapons to us in preference to having the R.I.C. and British Military collect them. Any raiding we did was only as a cover-up for the people in order that they could tell the R.I.C. that they had been raided by the I.R.A. and not arouse suspicion of their sympathies."[11]

The Volunteers did not restrict themselves to petrol, guns, and ammunition raids. Other types of goods and material proved enticing. A special military train conveying equipment and stores to the Lancers at Castlerea was deemed an appropriate target. Volunteers from the 1st and 2nd Battalions of South Roscommon took part in this action during June. Bicycles, horse saddles, and bridles were transferred from the train at Ballymoe Station into the hands of the Volunteers.[12] The operation turned out to be an effortless one, for the train was not guarded, but this was not known until after the action took place. The Ballymoe Station was again targeted in September when members of the Cloonboniffe, Moor, and Lisliddy Companies raided it and captured military equipment.[13]

Raiding the Mails

The postal service frequently became a target for Volunteer investigation. Information about IRA men and their activities was sent by the RIC and informers to Dublin Castle via the mails. The Castle would reverse this stream of information by issuing orders and letters of payment through the mails. Desiring to stop this free flow of spy workings, the Volunteers began to ambush local postmen and more often, the trains that carried the mail cars. Spotting an incriminating letter, however, took patience, persistence, and oftentimes a significant amount of hours and manpower.

In the Knockcroghery area, an evening train from Dublin was stopped by taking possession of the signal cabin and station a few minutes before the train's arrival. The signals were set to alert the engineer to halt at the next station (where he would not otherwise have stopped). At the railway station two men boarded the engine, while three climbed in the mail van.[14] The train was allowed to proceed slowly while the men in the mail car went through the letter bags. Some impor-

"Any raiding we did was only as a cover-up for the people in order that they could tell the R.I.C. that they had been raided by the I.R.A. and not arouse suspicion."

Jack Glancy

tant correspondence was seized in that operation, but it was soon realised that a lot more time was needed for a thorough search. Officers decided that next time the Volunteers would steal the bags off the train entirely. They succeeded in doing so at Ballymurray. Twenty bags of mail were removed to an empty house about a mile away for censoring. The searching process, however, occupied two whole nights and nearly the entire Company. Men had to sort through hundreds of pieces of correspondence while others guarded the premises and stood sentry on approaching roads.[15]

In May of 1920 Volunteers from the Athlone Battalion held up two mail trains near Fassaugh Bridge in County Westmeath. They loaded the mail bags into a motor car which was driven via Ballinahowen to the Big Bogs where the bags were transferred to a boat and taken across the Shannon to the home of Bernard Gaffey at Garrynagowna. Every evening for a solid week those letters were sorted and marked with "Passed by IRA Censor." The mail bags were then taken back across the Shannon and deposited outside Ballinahowen Post Office. Although no great espionage schemes were discovered or double agents exposed, the value of the operation lay in the planting of second thoughts in the minds of those who might otherwise be tempted to betray the Volunteers.

Sometimes the raiding of mails resulted in ironic twists of fate. In the 3rd Battalion North area, the Volunteers had intercepted a letter from Captain Peake, commanding officer of the Strokestown garrison. In a letter to his wife, he detailed his "last will and testament" as well as stated that all the "Shinners" in the area were either locked up or had left the area. He mentioned Tommy Mason, Martin Fallon, and Sean Leavy by name. Leavy, who was very much alive and living on the run in the Scramogue area, after reading this letter with his own eyes, sent the letter back to Captain Peake through the post signed with a personal notation that the Volunteers were glad to see he had his affairs settled up.[16] (Captain Peake was later to die in the Ambush at Scramogue.)

Burn Them Out!

Who were the RIC? If the political conflict was with England, why did the men of the local RIC (who were mostly Irish) take the brunt of Volunteer wrath? Did the local constable represent more than just a good-hearted man trying to keep peace in the community? Indeed he did!

The native police force of Ireland had been founded by British Home Secretary Sir Robert Peel in 1836 — thus the name "Bobbies" and "Peelers." Originally established as a subduing force, the local constables did, with varying degrees of success, become the law of the land.

Recruits were required to pass blood tests — though not of the modern variety. It was necessary for each prospective officer to have a clean bill of health with regard to Fenian blood, whether his or his father's. Records were checked at the local barracks before a man was shipped to Dublin Castle for examination. If successful in passing inspection at the Castle, a recruit was sent to the depot in the Phoenix Park for six months training. The police force operated independently of local authorities, and members could not be dismissed even by their own Inspector-General unless sanctioned by Dublin Castle. The name "Royal" was later added by Queen Victoria in gratitude for the constabulary's successful suppression of the rebellion of the Irish Republican Brotherhood (IRB) of 1867.

While images of police conjure up feelings of protection and goodwill among many who reside in communities of Europe and North America, this paternal portrayal does not accurately describe what the RIC succeeded in becoming in Ireland. Barracks were built every few miles and staffed with constables who did much more snooping into community affairs than they ever did investigating crime. Weekly reports regarding local happenings, new faces in the community, and news of suspicious meetings were sent to Dublin Castle, the heart of British intelligence in Ireland. There the information was combed through and collated. Thus a mosaic of the thirty-two counties was pieced together. Its intrigues were

While images of police conjure up feelings of protection and goodwill, this paternal portrayal does not accurately describe the RIC.

examined and scrutinised, plots (if any) were discovered, rebel leaders were closely supervised, spies were paid, informers were encouraged and rewarded. Men who diligently or unwittingly acted as the antennae for British intelligence in the provinces needed to be rendered homeless.

In the early part of 1920, Winston Churchill devised a plan (used in the Boer War) whereby the countryside would be peppered with blockhouses which could easily be defended and would supply shelter for troops who would roam the countryside and keep the IRA in check. In Ireland this type of blockhouse structure was already built — it was termed the RIC Barracks. The unoccupied buildings were to be repopulated and fortified. Little secrecy surrounded this proposal. It was printed in the daily newspapers for every member of GHQ to read.

Ever since the 1916 Easter Rising, Westminster had determined that the Irish would rise again, and do so in the capital. Every Eastertime the British positioned plenty of forces on the streets of Dublin to discourage this. It was no different in 1920. The Irish Republican Army's GHQ, however, wrote a different sort of scenario for the English audience: We strike at will, we will strike where we please. GHQ circulated a directive to all Battalions in the country. The order directed that the smaller, less protected, or vacated barracks be burned. On Easter weekend, hundreds of those structures throughout Ireland were set ablaze and rendered unfit for a return of British Forces. County Roscommon barracks which were set afire included:

Athleague
Ballintubber
Ballinameen
(members of the Boyle and Elphin Battalion helped with the burning of the barracks at Tulsk, Ballinameen and Croghan) 3 April
Ballyfarnon
Bealnamullia
Beechwood
(for the Beechwood operation, gelignite blew the gable out of the end of the barracks, thus allowing the Volunteers to set it on fire)
Carrick-on-Shannon
Castleplunkett
Croghan (burned by Drumlion Coy.)
Cootehall
Fourmilehouse
Grevisk (a fortnight later)
Hillstreet (12 May)
Kilglass
Kilmore (destroyed early in 1920)
Lecarrow Barracks
Rockfield
Scramogue

In County Westmeath, Creggan and Brawny Barracks were burned by members of the Athlone Brigade. Drumraney and Tang Companies burned Littletown Barracks.[17]
Back in Roscommon, Cloonfad and Ballinagare buildings were burned sometime in the spring/summer of that same year.
Some Volunteers claim that Hillstreet Barracks was burned 12 May 1920.
Loughglynn Barracks was burned in August by members of the Loughglynn and Ballinlough Coy.[18]
Ballinlough Barracks was burned 14 September 1920.

The Irish Republican Army's motto: We strike at will, we will strike where we please.

Pat Brennan of Ballytrasna, Boyle joined the Boyle Company of Volunteers in the spring of 1918, having been a trained Volunteer since 1914. He was appointed 1st Lieutenant two months later. He became the Boyle Company O/C in November 1920, advancing to the Battalion O/C in March 1921. One year and one month later, he was appointed the commanding officer of the 3rd Brigade in the 3rd Western Division.

His house served as a way station on the "all red route" — the pipeline for dispatches and information which ran from General Headquarters (GHQ) in Dublin to Donegal. This arrangement necessitated his rising at 2 a.m. and bicycling 10 to 12 miles to deliver the messages two or three times a week. Aside from dispatch work, his early months in the Volunteers entailed organising anti-conscription rallies and distributing leaflets.

Brennan also worked as a road foreman in Boyle — a position that allowed him access to large quantities of explosive detonators and fuses. Some of those devices were used in the assembly of the mines that exploded in front of the Elphin Barracks in 1921 and various other locations.

Raiding for arms became a must as there were precious few rifles and revolvers in the area. In the spring of 1919, he and two other comrades disarmed a soldier home on leave from the British Army. That gun proved to be a welcome addition to the small stash of weapons that would be vital in the coming years. Brennan and his cohorts also conducted raids on persons in order to prevent them from taking a law case into the British courts. Local hooligans took advantage of the disintegration of the British court system and became highwaymen of a different ilk. Robbery was their common pastime, and it was in the capacity of Battalion officer that Brennan and others tracked down the culprits and brought them to justice in the Sinn Féin Courts and subsequently carried out the sentences imposed.

A house on the outskirts of Boyle had been robbed of £100 of silver. Brennan and his subordinates carefully watched for unusual behaviour. Their suspicions were verified when a local man offered to sell a silver cup. He was arrested, forced to name his accomplice and to divulge the location of the rest of the booty (it had been stashed in four different places). It took about a week to recover it all because the robbers, who were being held in a secret and guarded

location, would give away only a portion of what they knew, thinking that each tidbit would satisfy their jailers. In the two weeks they were held in custody, the thieves also yielded up two revolvers. Their punishment: deportation.

In April of 1920, orders came from GHQ to burn the vacated barracks of small villages. Pat was present for the torching of Grevisk, Ballinameen, and Croghan RIC Barracks. One evening he and his men also quietly entered the Cootehall Income Tax office and destroyed all the records. In May 1920 Brennan participated in a raid at the Boyle Railway Station. As a result, hundreds of gallons of petrol eventually found a new home in a dump constructed a half-mile away from the train tracks. That petrol was used many times in future IRA actions.

The notion of a Belfast Boycott evolved into a mountain of work for the Volunteers. Certain firms in the North had been blacklisted, and local traders were served notice to stop doing business with them. Railway shipments had to be overseen so that these northern products did not land at the rail station nor find their way onto the shelves of the merchants in town. (Sympathetic railroad workers with access to invoices proved an invaluable assistance in this regard.)

In August of 1920 the Auxiliaries came to Boyle. Housed in the Union buildings, they proved the bane of the area. Brennan and James Feely arrested a tout (who later was unmasked as an Auxiliary) who was masquerading as an IRA man on the run from the North. After a few minutes of interrogation, their suspicions were aroused to a fever pitch. Using the ruse of pretending to reach inside his coat for documentation to prove his claims, he drew out a gun, but not quickly enough. The revolvers of Brennan and Feely, which had been pointed at him all during this altercation, found their mark. The fake Volunteer fell wounded, his arm smarting from the searing bullet holes. He was warned to clear out of town or be shot on sight. He wisely chose to leave North Roscommon behind him.

Brennan's days at his own home were numbered. His residence had been raided on numerous occasions, but in August of 1920 a more aggressive British policy took hold. After several death threats in previous days, his home was surrounded at 2 a.m. and shots were fired through the door. An awful din saturated with threatening

Balancing the scales, the barracks burnings may not have been of extreme military importance, but the psychological impact in rural Roscommon was powerful. The absence of the British paid forces from the countryside left wide swaths of territory unpatrolled and permitted much more freedom of movement by the Volunteers. The RIC were gone, their barracks burned out, and the British Forces weren't coming back! This vacuum allowed for the rise and implementation of the Sinn Féin Courts. It was the beginning of the end for British control of Ireland.

Attempted Attack on Kilmurray Military Camp

The summer of 1920 was packed with dangerous assignments for the local Volunteers. The British had positioned about one hundred soldiers near Kilmurray in order to protect a farm about which there was a dispute. At a Brigade Council meeting, a decision was made to squash these forces in the fields of Castleplunkett. "Our plan was to steal up on the Camp when the occupants would be asleep and to rush and capture the Guard. At the same time men would rush the remainder of the Camp from all directions."[19]

Scouts had been observing the movements of the Crown Forces continuously while members of the 1st, 2nd and 4th Battalion South assembled for the strike.

shouts rose to the second story bedroom window awakening the two brothers (Pat and James Stephen). Forcing their way into the house, the masked men dragged Pat outside, took him 500 yards down the road, and forced him to kneel. Threatening to shoot him, they ordered him to take an oath to quit Sinn Féin and the Volunteers. Brennan did neither. They hoisted him up against a wall and again threatened to shoot him, but tiring of this game, they eventually told him to make a run for it (planning, of course, to fill him full of lead and claim he was attempting an escape). Brennan dove into a ditch and managed to avoid all the flying bullets. His dog, who came to the aid of his master, however, was not so fortunate. Brennan's nights of sleeping in his own bed were over for many months to come.

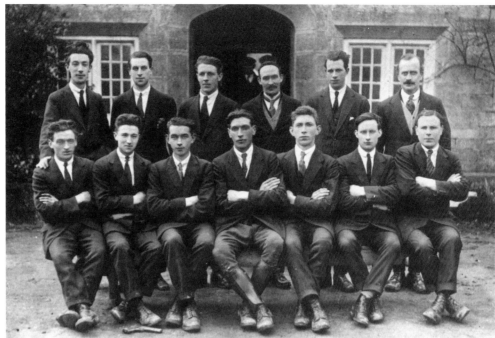

PHOTO COURTESY OF BARRY FEELY

First Battalion Council, North Roscommon Brigade, IRA, Boyle, March, 1922. Some of the men have been identified: (back row, left to right) James Feely, Patrick Cunnane, __, __, John Joe Cunnane, James Turbitt. (front row, left to right) James Stephen Brennan, Henry Feely, Phil Murray, Pat Brennan, __, __, __.

The month of September was taken up with the back-breaking work of trenching roads, raiding Boyle Post Office for information, and guarding officers and men of the Company from reprisals by the new Auxiliaries.

Much of the activity thus far was not in the nature of brilliant strikes at the enemy. The town of Boyle and its surroundings were nearly impregnable, owing to the large contingent of troops stationed there. Both Ernie O'Malley and Sean Connolly had come to this same conclusion.

Throughout all these dangerous goings-on, Brennan regularly attended IRB and Brigade Council meetings. Coming home from one such gathering in Ballinameen in March of 1921, he and his fellow Volunteers ran into a patrol of RIC and military men. The Volunteers

abandoned their bicycles, flattened into a ditch, and returned fire, and eventually crept through the darkness to safety, with no casualties.

Trouble was brewing in the area. Michael Dockery, the North Roscommon Brigade Commander, had been arrested in May and incarcerated in Boyle Barracks. The Brigade staff gave Brennan specific orders to be QUIET! No aggravating activity was to annoy the military while Dockery was in custody — a condition that was soon to change. With help from Corporal George Meadlarklan, a guard at the Barracks, both Dockery and Jim Molloy made a stunning escape by wriggling out of the washroom window. Their cell doors had been left unlocked, but they had to pass a sentry on their way to the washhouse. On 9 June, their scheduled escape date, only Molloy made it through the maze. It wasn't until the 15th that Dockery fol-

The first shot of the attack, however, was never fired. On approaching the Camp that June night, "our scouts reported that the British were on the alert and had occupied all the advantage points in the area and were apparently awaiting our attack."[20] The Volunteers, who were armed with only a few revolvers and shotguns "and all kinds of other weapons such as forks, scythes, etc."[21] deemed it foolhardy to attack a well-armed and well-positioned garrison of soldiers. In response, the men simply melted into the countryside,[22] with no loss of equipment or life. Men from the south of the county who were scheduled to participate in the offensive were notified not to head north. Another spy had done his deed!

Rebellion in India

Reverberations of shots fired for Irish Independence in the green fields of Roscommon echoed across the azure waters of the Indian Ocean and resounded over the brown plains at Jullundur, in the Punjab. There the First Battalion of the Connaught Rangers, upon hearing of the devastation and horror that was sweeping Ireland, mutinied on 28 June 1920.

Two men were shot during the melee. Sixty-nine Rangers were court-martialled, and long prison terms were liberally meted out. John Miranda died behind bars,

lowed the same modus operandi and broke for freedom. Both men waded across the waters of the Boyle River and found the assistance of Brennan and several other Volunteers who were waiting on the opposite side. They were now in the park area bounded on the south by a spiked railing and a road. In full view of the barracks square, the men proceeded with Molloy and then Dockery to a gate and from there to safekeeping.

The following month Brennan helped plan for the burning of Frenchpark Courthouse, but he personally did not attend the bonfire. Instead, he was attending IRB and Battalion meetings in which a reorganisation was being planned. In addition, social events needed tending whereby dependents of incarcerated men would be assisted. During the Truce he went to GHQ in Dublin with other Brigade officers and attended a training camp in Glenasmole House in Co. Wicklow for several weeks. He was in charge of the Brigade training camp at Mantua House for a fortnight and also the camp at the Boyle Union Buildings for six weeks. Brennan was ordered by the Brigade staff not to join the recently formed Active Service Unit because they felt his presence in Boyle was more beneficial to the cause. Heat applied to the military in Boyle would increase their chances of success elsewhere.

Upon the evacuation of British troops from Ireland, Brennan was ordered to take over the Boyle Union buildings — a place in which he lived until the Civil War broke out. In March of 1922 an army convention was held in Dublin where the military men hashed out their grievances and complaints against the newly formed Free State government. Many attendees at this meeting were men who wished to have no truck with the newly formed Free State officials and were not hesitant to say so. Brennan was there — listening.

When Michael Dockery chose to join the Free State Army, Brennan was appointed the Brigade O/C in April of 1922. After the Battle of Boyle in July 1922, Brennan ordered the Active Service Unit (ASU) to break up and for each member to go back to his own area. The Brigade ASU had included men from each of the Battalions. These men now returned to their home territory, made dugouts, and prepared for an upcoming fight. They were under the command of their own Battalion O/Cs unless otherwise required by Brigade staff for duty. Brennan himself participated in the attack on Swinford Barracks, the engagement at Killasser, the assault on Drumsna

Barracks, periodic attacks on the Free State position in Boyle, the attack on a Free State outpost at Frenchpark, the attack on the blockhouse outposts on the Boyle/Carrick-on-Shannon Road, and an ambush carried out at Lakeview, Strokestown, whereby all arms were captured.

When the new year rolled around, Brennan and other men against the Treaty attempted to disrupt the general flow of government business by raiding post offices in the Brigade area, burning the Elphin Garda Barracks, and attacking the Free State troops at Caldra on the Elphin/Boyle Road. They oftentimes worked in conjunction with the South Leitrim Flying Columns and with their North Roscommon counterparts operating out of Arigna.

The cause of the Anti-Treatyites, however, was doomed. Outgunned, out-manned, and out of hiding places, they had an increasingly difficult time just surviving. People had voted on the Treaty, approved it, and were not bent towards watching another war consume their communities. The populace that had so steadfastly aided and abetted them in the Tan War was now a divided support group. After the cease-fire was called, many Republican troops still ended up in internment camps, and those who had held onto their freedom had to survive for months in dugouts, afraid for their safety. When they did finally emerge from their hideouts, it was a slow process for the men to begin to rebuild their lives.

After the War, Pat's brother, James Stephen, emigrated to Canada — eventually crossing the border into the United States. Pat Brennan returned to farming at Ballytrasna. The military engagements of the war had consumed his youth. Middle-age pursuits were geared more towards political action. He was Chairman of the Boyle Fianna Fáil Cumann for many years and also served a term on the Co. Roscommon Committee of Agriculture. He died 7 June 1981 and is buried in Eastersnow Cemetery in Boyle, where his remains rest easy in the soil he helped to free.

*Information derived from a written statement by Pat Brennan to An Roinn Cosanta, Brainse Airgeadais, Coláiste Caoimhin, Glas Naion, Baile Átha Cliath.

By mid-1920, the RIC was a disintegrating corpse.

while eleven others died directly from mistreatment after their release from prison: Michael Kearns, Patrick J. Kelly, James Oliver, John Lynnott, William Shallow, Francis Owen Davis, Joseph Walshe, Stephen Lally, John F. Prendergast, James J. Devers, and Joseph Hawes.

Four men from Boyle were part of the defying group of Rangers: John McGowan, Paddy Scally, Michael Conlon, and Addie Hayes. All were sentenced to years behind bars but were released after the Treaty was ratified.

Only one soldier, however, was actually executed for his part in the mutiny. James Daly, who hailed from Ballymoe, just across the County Roscommon line into Galway, was the lone martyr. Today a memorial to him stands outside St. Croan's Catholic Church in Ballymoe, while another memorial to him was placed in Tyrrellspass, County Westmeath, where his parents had moved shortly after his birth.

A survivor of the infamous army insurrection rests in St. Coman's Cemetery in Roscommon town. Jack Lynch was one of seven spokesmen for the mutinous group. He was suitably dealt with by the authorities. He, as well as the rest of the men, rotted away for six months in an Indian jail, then sailed back to England in leg-irons, where they spent more months in Portland and Maidstone Prisons.

Incarceration was spent in solitary cells for twenty-three and a half hours a day. The meals of soupy porridge, near-rotten potatoes, and unsweetened black cocoa wreaked havoc on their health for years after their release in 1922.

Jack Lynch emigrated to America five years later and spent his adult life a stranger in a strange land. When Gabriel's trumpet sounded, however, Lynch wanted to be among friends. He returned to Ireland in 1965, where he died a year later. His lifelong wish was fulfilled when he was buried in his native soil, a liberated land for which he had given the fruits and blessings of his youth; but eternity stretches beyond the present for a long, long, long time, and with it extends the life force of Jack Lynch, Roscommon son.

The RIC — A Dying Breed

By mid-1920, the RIC was a disintegrating corpse. Disheartened and despised, members retired if possible, were "encouraged" to retire by the Volunteers, kept from enlisting by IRA threats, and sometimes just quietly crept away. Richard Abbot, author of *Police Casualties in Ireland 1919-1922,* agrees: "Some men simply 'walked away,' whilst others felt compelled to leave due to the situation in the country, and a number left (without giving a reason) to assist the IRA."[23] Police reports from Roscommon state the situation in even more dire terms: "The police were largely boycotted and discouraged by interference, lack of men, of transport or any adequate support. The County Inspector believes that few of his men will remain over the winter and when they have gone, or been replaced by men who know nothing, there will be no pretence of maintaining any law."[24]

The RIC position was becoming intolerable. Grievances were not met, members were prevented from communicating with each other, their circulars were seized, and they were kept in total ignorance about what was happening in other parts of the country.[25] In June of 1920, the Roscommon Volunteer leaders proclaimed a boycott of the RIC. People were instructed not to supply them with food, fuel, or transport. No one was to speak to them. The military reaction to this order was so severe that in a few weeks masked armed men were raiding houses of Sinn Féin members and threatening reprisals if this boycott were not lifted.

By mid-August the problems had spread nationwide. A secret meeting was proposed to address the concerns. Roscommon delegates to this meeting included Sgt. Galligan of Kiltoom Barracks and Sgts. P. Harte and John Duffy, who were stationed in Roscommon town. Summoned by "the Emergency Committee," delegates from throughout Ireland were asked to obtain money for travel from collections in each county, assemble in a central point in Dublin, and, most important, wear plain clothes.[26]

At the assemblage, suggestions were made to ease the tensions between the police force and the "outlaws" taking over the countryside. The Roscommon/Mayo RIC men suggested "down arms" — to go about the business of policing without arms. Some members from Kerry put forth the idea to completely disarm and do only police work. Their fear: "Police are the pawns in the game of politics." Delegates heard the dire prediction: of the 8,000 RIC throughout Ireland, 6,000 have proposed to resign.[27] Morale was low and the probability of being injured or killed was high.

The official IRA response came from a GHQ (General Headquarters) directive issued from Dublin: allow the old (retired) RIC men to assimilate into the community, assist them with employment, if possible, and contribute some funds to ease their hardship.[28] While these were noble sentiments, the reality in the small towns of Roscommon was that jobs were scarce, and what little money there was to be had was directed to arms purchase and sustaining the fighting men. And ultimately, when people's lives were on the line, the former RIC men were simply not trusted. These misgivings proved well founded; several of them were eventually killed because they were suspected of informing on the Volunteers.

A memorial for John Daly stands outside St. Croan's Catholic Church in Ballymoe.

PHOTO COURTESY OF MICHAEL LENNON

"Police are the pawns in the game of politics."

The Burning of Strokestown Courthouse

The July night had been wet. Soaked through and through, Peter Flanagan, Lt. John Hunt, Tom Dolan, Stephen Scally, Martin O'Connor, Frank Treacy, and Jimmie Beirne[29] nonetheless obeyed orders, collected petrol and paraffin at the back of John Brennan's garage, and proceeded to the Bridewell at Strokestown. A nine-foot wall surrounded the place, so they commandeered a ladder to scale it. With armfuls of hay from a nearby rick, Flanagan, Hunt, Scally, and O'Connor made their way over the wall and into the nearly solid stone building. None were familiar with petrol or its dangers. "Some of them had never even seen it before that night."[30]

They saturated the hay with the flammable liquid (which had been obtained by Willie Duffy, who worked at Brennan's garage) and scattered it around the building. Scally remained on the first floor while the other three were on the second. Then they lit a match. All were totally unprepared for what came next. The sudden combustion and loud roar took all by surprise. Confused and awed by the position in which they found themselves, the men scrambled to find a way out of the inferno. "Scally, a very calm person, made his way out of the building. He felt hurt at the time and, as soon as he caught his breath, he remembered the other three, and started back into the flames to help them."[31] The other men had wasted no time in fleeing the building, and Scally soon found himself face to face with the frightened men whose momentum carried him out of the building with them.

All the men's hands were so badly burned they proved useless in trying to climb the ladder. Willie Duffy got on top of the wall and with the other man steadying them from below, each injured man, in turn, came up the ladder and was helped onto the top of the wall, then gently lowered to the outside by Duffy.

O'Connor lived a short distance away, and he headed home immediately. Upon his arrival, his family called Dr. Dudley Forde, the local physician in Strokestown who was also known to quietly treat men of the 3rd Battalion North. Dr. Forde drove O'Connor over a hundred miles to a Dublin hospital, where O'Connor remained until further treatment was unnecessary. The other three men suffered a far worse fate.

Their homes were miles away, and they dared not travel on the roads for fear of being seen by the Black and Tans. Thus, they set out across the fields to the cottage of a cousin of John Hunt. Negotiating the ditches, each man had to be helped across by Duffy and another man, who hoisted them up one side and down the other. The one and a half mile journey to the safe house took two hours![32]

When the exhausted men arrived at the cottage, Hunt and Flanagan were placed in a settle bed, while Scally lay on a blanket on the floor. The commanding officers were notified of this disaster, but they did not call upon Dr. John Mullen, who they mistakenly did not trust. All three men had to linger for hours in intolerable pain until Dr. Dudley Forde returned from Dublin and was notified of their plight.

Dr. Forde arrived at the cottage at about six o'clock the next evening and found three men in dire circumstances. He dressed their wounds and suggested that they be taken to the Strokestown (poorhouse) Hospital. Since there was no means of conveyance, the Captain of Cloonfree Company, Michael McCoy, detailed eight sturdy men to act as stretcher-bearers, posted scouts along the roads, and transported the men to the hospital.

Alternating the load every two hundred yards, the eight men carried first Hunt (who was thought to be in the worst condition) at about 11:15 p.m. that night, then Flanagan, and finally Scally at 4:15 a.m. the next morning. Scally did not moan or show any signs of pain for, unbeknownst to the Volunteers, he was in severe shock.

Nurses Mary Bergen and Annie O'Beirne did what they could to relieve the men's pain, but it was not until later in the morning that Dr. John Mullen came upon the scene. Shocked by what he saw and wishing to be of all possible assistance, he called his son, Doctor Jack Mullen of the Dublin Hospital, and asked

None were familiar with petrol or its dangers. "Some of them had never even seen it before that night."

Stephen Scally

about the latest methods for treating severe burns. Dr. Jack arrived in Strokestown that evening and, for the next six weeks, both father and son attended the men to try and restore them to good health.

And what of the final outcome of this terrible night? Hunt, whose face was quite scarred, was quietly removed to a Dublin hospital for plastic surgery. He died a few years later. Stephen Scally was captured in December and sentenced to ten years imprisonment, O'Connor recovered sufficiently to rejoin his Company and continue through the War for Independence, and Flanagan lived to become a Civic Guard in the new Irish government. Such were the tragedies and sufferings of the men who helped put the flag a flyin'.

Ambush at Moneen

On 12 July two policemen were scheduled to cycle from Lanesboro to Roscommon to be part of a guard of honour that was to meet the Judge at the opening of the Assizes Court. The occasion presented a grand opportunity for weapons confiscation.

John O'Connor was to serve as scout — pretending to be shopping in the village of Lanesboro, yet all the while keeping a watchful eye out for the departure of the two policemen. He was to cycle ahead of them and warn the waiting Volunteers who planned not to kill but merely disarm them.

Pat Madden, his brother Dan, Luke Duffy, Henry Compton, Frank Simons, Gerald Davis, and Paddy Tiernan[33] converged on Mr. Lannon's house at Ballagh with two service revolvers, a rifle, and some shotguns. Madden had a .32 automatic pistol. (Frank Simons claimed that all had revolvers, two service rifles had been available, and the rest of the men had been armed with shotguns.)[34] They headed cross-country to the appointed ambush site at a place called Anrittabeg. Hours passed. Fatigue showed up but no police. It was a wet day for July so the men had taken shelter in an abandoned house nearby when scout O'Connor peddled up and announced the coming of the constables. The men again positioned themselves for ambush, but alas, again no policemen. Assuming the men had turned back to Lanesboro due to the inclement weather (they had actually stopped off at a pub in Ballyleague on the Roscommon side of the Shannon and indulged in some "refreshment"), the Volunteers again took refuge in the abandoned house. Soon the sounds of swishing bicycle tires ruffled their ears. Rushing out of the house, the men discovered the policemen had already passed them by. (Pat) Madden shouted for the policemen to halt and get off their bicycles. Instead of stopping, Constables Clarke and Macken peddled even faster, trying to put as much distance as possible between themselves and the Volunteers. Madden fired a shot with his revolver with no hope of hitting them but merely as a warning that his men meant serious business. The constables were unimpressed. Onward they cycled until a rifle shot rang out and Clarke fell into the ditch. The other policeman braked his cycle, grabbed his rifle, and made for shelter in a nearby house. Realising the futility of a fight with eight-to-one odds and trapped inside a house to boot, Constable Macken tied a white handkerchief to the barrel of his gun and came out onto the road. Gerald Davis took the rifle from him, and together the men marched back up the road to examine the condition of the first policeman. Clarke was dead. Henry Compton was left to guard the prisoner while the other men tended to other affairs. Macken made an attempt to seize Compton's shotgun by grabbing it by the barrel. The gun went off.[35] Macken fell to the ground, rolled over, groaned, and lay quite still. The Volunteers proceeded to collect the two carbine rifles along with about 25 rounds of .303 ammunition and the two bicycles before heading off across the field. The men shouldered the guns and took the ammunition to their dump for use in future engagements, but the bicycles were submerged in the Shannon and, when the occasion arose, were retrieved and used by members of the Column.

(Frank Simons tells a little different version of the story. He stated that when O'Connor first came along the road to warn the waiting Volunteers, the policemen were 150 yards immediately behind him. When the RIC came upon the ambush

Realising the futility of a fight with eight-to-one odds, Constable Macken tied a white handkerchief to the barrel of his gun and came out onto the road.

site, all called on them to halt. As they sprinted away on their cycles, the Volunteers ran onto the road firing first over the heads of the RIC, then at their person.)[36]

In the meantime, Father Thomas Hurley from nearby Ballagh Church, upon hearing the shooting, came to the scene and attended the dead man. While he was doing so, a lorry of Tans sped by, taking no notice of the dead constable at the side of the road or the priest administering to him.

Constable Macken bided his time. Waiting patiently until the Volunteers and the priest had departed from the area, he miraculously arose unscathed, and, instead of utilising two round bicycle tires which by now were long gone, was forced to use two flat feet and trudge back to Lanesboro.

Attempted Attacks in the 1st Battalion South Area

During that same month of July, the Battalion officers devised a plan whereby the Volunteers would have a go at a contingent of soldiers guarding the Castlerea Railway Station. Surprise was the key! Armed only with revolvers, some Volunteers boarded the train at Donamon and headed towards Castlerea, where they had planned to rush the Guard and disarm them. There was only a small number of soldiers expected there, and transport had been arranged to take the attackers and the guns away in due haste. It had been agreed that if, for some unforeseen reason, all was not well at the Castlerea Station, a signal would be given which would warn the Volunteers to make a quick exit from the train cars. Plans for the ambush were discussed with the Brigade staff.

On the appointed day, Jim Quigley (2nd Battalion), Frank Simons (3rd Battalion), Jim Breheny, Tommie Kelly of Carrigeen, John Breheny, Michael Tennant of Knockcroghery Company in the 4th Battalion, and several others boarded the train and headed to their destination, only to spot a signaller waving a red lantern warning that scores of Tans were awaiting them at the other end of the line.[37] The Volunteers made an unscheduled departure from the train — disembarking well in advance of the Castlerea Station. Pat Glynn, the Battalion O/C, had decided to abort the entire mission because it was so obvious that the British Forces were out in numbers, awaiting the arrival of the train. But how had the Tans been forewarned? The answer to that question was one with which the Battalion officers and the GHQ in Dublin had to grapple. Why were spies so well informed of Volunteer plans? The Castlerea area seemed to be infested with them despite the shooting of several in the area to discourage such conduct.

Another attempted attack, this time at Coshlieve, was also foiled that same month. Thirty-nine Volunteers from Trien, Ballinlough, and Loughglynn Companies had assembled for an ambush[38] which would most assuredly have yielded some much-needed armament had it taken place.

Athlone Brigade Strikes at Streamstown Barracks

That same month the Athlone Brigade set their sights on the Streamstown Barracks in County Westmeath. The building was not yet fortified with sandbags and wire, but it did have steel shutters to protect the military within. Selected men (about 80) from the Moate, Drumraney, and Athlone Battalions were mobilised for this venture.[39] The scheme for the capture included waylaying two members of the RIC on their way to Mass at Boher Chapel, having two Volunteers trade clothing with them, then after Mass mingling with the dismissed congregation and showing up at the door of the barracks, demanding entrance.

James Tormey and Con Costello did indeed successfully seize the RIC men and their uniforms, but from that point onward, plans went awry. When the bogus policemen neared the barracks, they found that a large contingent of Volunteers was openly drilling on the road. This, of course, had alerted the police inside the barracks, who quickly had shuttered the windows and gone to the signal cabin to phone for reinforcements. Tormey and Costello decided to stick with the original plan despite this high state of alert by the police, but when they stepped up to the barracks door, the wary RIC greeted them not with a friendly reply but a deadly

The scheme for the capture included waylaying two members of the RIC on their way to Mass at Boher Chapel, having two Volunteers trade clothing with them, then after Mass mingling with the dismissed congregation and showing up at the door of the barracks, demanding entrance.

one. Amid the flurry of shuffling feet and clicking rifles, one of the constables rolled a grenade out through a loophole on the second story. Tormey grabbed Costello by the cape and dragged him to the railway line just in time to escape the explosion.[40] The attacking party began a barrage on the building. A bomb (which failed to explode) was placed on a window sill, and sniping continued for about forty-five minutes. The whole operation resembled a rocking chair — lots of action but no progress from square one. Finally the Volunteers withdrew without injuries just before reinforcements arrived from Mullingar. The harrowed RIC were taken back to Mullingar with the newly arrived policemen, and within the next twenty-four hour period, David Daly, Battalion O/C, assembled a group of Volunteers from the Rosemount Company, who set the barracks afire.[41] IRA officers later determined that their grenades used in the attack were faulty, and they were returned to Dublin (without the Companies' compliments).

Sergeant Killed in Athlone

The raids of terror conducted by the Black and Tans were oftentimes spearheaded by local RIC who pointed out suspected men and meeting places. These local policemen were the eyes and ears of the British occupation forces, without whom the Crown troops could not have found their way around the unmarked backroads of County Roscommon or identified one "Paddy" from another. Some of these local RIC were not only vigilant in their duty, but sadistic as well. Such was the case of Thomas Craddock, who operated out of Athlone.

In the early summer of 1920, Craddock had led a group of men to Westmeath Volunteer Joseph Cunningham. Cunningham and some of his cohorts had recently ousted members of the RIC from Berry's public house in Mount Temple. Craddock and his crew meant to teach Joe and his brother a lesson. "Joe was almost beaten to death and was a wreck of a man for ever afterwards. Later on, they burned down his house."[42]

On another occasion, when the Volunteers had raided the mails, they found a letter signed by Craddock (who was on temporary duty in Mount Temple) addressed to the Head Constable in Athlone. In this correspondence, Craddock proceeded to outline his observations about the Volunteers and a plan of action against them. He was soon transferred back to Athlone where "a favourite pastime of his was to put a revolver to young men's heads who were in the movement and threaten to shoot them..."[43]

With action sanctioned by Michael Collins,[44] members of the Volunteers sought to put an end to such brutish behaviour. Volunteer patrols[45] through Athlone were increased to eight men. On four selected dates they waited in ambush position in different parts of town, but the sly Sergeant always succeeded in eluding them. On 22 August, Craddock and another policeman were spotted going into Foresters' Hall. When they exited, all guns were aimed at Craddock. He never got farther than a few steps past the doorway. The other policeman, however, was not fired upon. The Volunteers did not want to kill him "as there was nothing against him. (They) were very sorry later that (they) had let him go as he turned out to be a right villain and excelled himself in ill-treating people by beating them up..."[46]

Misplaced Zeal

On 26 August, two constables were sent by Sergeant Galligan of Kiltoom to Roscommon town. At the level-crossing near the Knockcroghery Rail Station, several Volunteers[47] were waiting for them. Amid the shower of bullets, Constable William Potter fell and did not rise again. The attack on these men resulted in a threefold tragedy. The Potter family lost one of its members, the IRA lost one of its informers, and an opportunity to capture fourteen rifles, fourteen revolvers, and a few grenades was forever gone.

This attack had not been sanctioned by GHQ, and, unbeknownst to the local Volunteers, Constable Potter "had been in touch with Mick Collins and supplying information to him."[48] Furthermore, Sergeant Galligan, the commanding officer at

These local policemen were the eyes and ears of the British occupation forces, without whom the Crown troops could not have found their way around the unmarked backroads of County Roscommon or identified one "Paddy" from another.

the Kiltoom Barracks, had contacted Brian Lenihan, O/C of the Kiltoom Company, regarding handing over the barracks to the IRA. Galligan needed a cover for such action because he would be tried and prosecuted by the British if he were perceived to be a party to such a travesty. Lenihan needed to check with his superiors, and when the matter was put to Dan O'Rourke, the commanding officer dallied. Fearing a trap, O'Rourke questioned the sincerity of the Sergeant and put off meeting with him, but Galligan was insistent, claiming that time was of the essence. Finally a meeting was arranged between the two at the priest's house in Curraghboy on Sunday morning 29 August. The murder of the policeman at Knockcroghery a few days previous, however, prompted Dublin Castle to close the barracks at Kiltoom and scatter its garrison to more-fortified stations. A golden opportunity was frittered away. According to Tom Kelly, 4th Battalion South O/C, the fourteen rifles and revolvers belonging to the RIC would have "meant a lot to our Brigade at that time and would probably have changed the whole face of our operations in south Roscommon."[49]

The Black and Tans and Auxiliaries
The RIC force was withering away. Desertions, resignations, and fear had incapacitated some units, with no sign of better fortunes to come. In answer to this situation, Britain decided to add more boots on the ground by sending in men who became notorious in Irish lore. Named for their unusual attire — a mishmash of black tunics and tan trousers, or sometimes vice versa — their name called to mind the famous pack of hounds in southern Ireland whose behaviour they mirrored. Undisciplined, sometimes sadistic, these Black and Tans left their mark on Volunteer faces, cottage doorways, and local legend. Underpaid, undertrained, and stranded in a hostile countryside, they relieved their boredom by helping themselves to the wares of local shops, raiding and sometimes demolishing homes, and bludgeoning Volunteers.

In November of 1920, another force, known as the Auxiliaries, drove into the country and aided in the attempt to subdue the Sinn Féin wave of rebellion that was sweeping the country. Mossie Harnett, author of *Victory and Woe*, described them as "the most select crowd of blackguards ever inflicted on our country."[50] An apt description!

Ambush at Ratra
It was to have been a bloodless confiscation of arms. Policemen were travelling to the Frenchpark Court from Ballaghaderreen to give testimony in a breach of licensing laws suit that was on the docket. Jim Hunt and Michael Marren of the Gurteen Battalion thought it would prove to be a perfect opportunity to trap a number of policemen in an ambush. The objective was acquisition of arms, not a bloodletting.

There were very few rifles accessible to the twenty-five Volunteers; consequently, most of the men were given shotguns, revolvers, and a few grenades with which to make a show of force. Jim Hunt was armed with a Parabellum. The operation was commanded by Hunt, with Volunteers Jimmy Dwyer, Tom McDonagh, Joe Finnegan, Thady McGowan, James Molloy, John McManmy, Tom Connolly, Paddy Connor and several others in attendance.

The men assembled the night before in a home in the half parish of Killaraght. Most were from the Sligo Battalion. Following tea and gaiety, the men stole out into the chilly night and made their way the eight miles to the ambush site. Arriving about five in the morning of 1 September, the men arranged themselves along the road and were in a high state of preparedness by 6 a.m. Jim Hunt was situated on the north side of the road, while the main body of Volunteers were directly opposite on the higher ground, and one man was positioned fifty yards from the main body armed with a shotgun. His order: let no policeman pass by you. Thomas McDonagh and Joe Finnegan were about 300 yards up the road on the Ballaghaderreen side. Finnegan had field glasses. His mission: report the number of policemen coming. At the first sighting of the police, McDonagh was to

Named for their unusual attire — a mishmash of black tunics and tan trousers, or sometimes vice versa — their name called to mind the famous pack of hounds in southern Ireland whose behaviour they mirrored.

retreat down the bye-road leading to Tibohine Church to cover any possible withdrawal of the forces in that direction.

Hunt   Dwyer
Ballaghaderreen _____Frenchpark
        McDonagh   Main Body
        Finnegan

Four hours crept by. Finally at 10 a.m. Finnegan cycled up to Hunt's position and reported: "Five armed police approaching in single file: about fifty yards separating the first three; two cycling together, one hundred yards to the rear."[51] The devil or the deep blue sea had to be faced. The ambushers were spread out along the road for only about fifty yards while the police were strung out over two hundred yards. Hunt decided to wait until another time.

His thoughts, however, did not convey themselves automatically to Dwyer, who was fifty yards down the road with orders to "let no policeman pass." Having heard no audible signal, Dwyer fired anyway at the back wheel of the policeman's bicycle. The policeman fell to the ground, feigning injury. The other policeman, instead of surrendering his arms, pointed directly at Finnegan, who by now was beside Dwyer. Simultaneous shots rang out. Finnegan's hit the mark. A third policeman who was opposite the main body of Volunteers thought better of bravado and jumped from his bicycle and surrendered. Meanwhile, at the other end of the police trail, the last two constables took cover under some bushes. McDonagh, who by now was returning up the bye-road as he heard the rifle shots, manoeuvred himself into position and fired at one of the policemen. When he aimed at the second one, his gun did not go off! The policeman's did, however, and Thomas McDonagh fell dead. The other policeman went scrambling up the road towards Ballaghaderreen as the Volunteers gathered to assess the damage. Constables McCarthy and Murphy lay dead or dying of their wounds. Someone picked up McDonagh's gun and discovered that "though Tommie's six revolver bullets were capped, some of them twice, only one was discharged."[52] McDonagh had been the victim of faulty ammunition. The men were so overwrought that they threatened to shoot the policeman who had surrendered. At this point Jim Hunt intervened. "I did happen to save him for his mother's sake,"[53] he later confessed. Hunt also related years later that the same constable who he had saved that day intentionally failed to identify Hunt when he was captured in May of 1921 and taken to Boyle Barracks.

British Raiding Party Attacked in Lough Ree
British Forces in Athlone were alerted that a suspected IRA man (Joe Kennedy) was on his way home from Longford. (He had been foolish enough to buy a gun from two supposed deserters.) One Sunday in September the RIC and Tans commandeered Coen's motorboat, which was large enough to hold a sizeable raiding party, and headed up the Shannon. (It was presumed that they were not only looking for a lone suspect, but intended to raid the islands as well.)

After 10 o'clock Mass when Seamus O'Meara, Athlone Brigade O/C, learned of this floating target, he decided to attack the British soldiers on their return voyage. He contacted Frank O'Connor of Coosan, who assembled men from his unit. David Daly, who was reviewing his local Company when he got the news, sent his men to the mouth of the river near the White Buoy to await the British Forces. In all, twenty to thirty Volunteers were mobilised.

As they idled away the minutes, they thought of various schemes they might use to stop the boat. Barbed wire strung across the river was considered, but this would have entailed the use of another boat, perhaps unwanted notice, and precious time. That idea was nixed. Instead, the commanding officers simply placed scouts on the hilltops where they could observe the river traffic. About 2:30 in the afternoon, the scouts quietly signalled the waiting Volunteers. Seamus O'Meara had

"Tommie's six revolver bullets were capped, some of them twice, only one was discharged." McDonagh had been the victim of faulty ammunition.

Micheál O'Callaghan

determined to sink the boat itself by aiming rifle fire at or below the waterline and then deal with the escaping soldiers. He did not realise that a mere rifle bullet would not be powerful enough to puncture the boat's hull[54] — especially when the bullets' thrust was being deflected by water. Frank O'Connor, however, deemed that idea ridiculous and consequently ordered his men to aim at the soldiers on board. At the first volley, three officers and four privates dropped to the deck. The Volunteers "followed the boat down the river, moving from cover to cover along the river bank to about a quarter of a mile from the town."[55] The military had a Lewis gun on board which they engaged at the first sound of rifle fire, but its trajectory was ineffective because their boat was floating too low down in the river and the firing aim was too high.[56] The whole affair lasted about twenty minutes, with the Volunteers following the boat downstream as far as they dared before calling off the engagement. The British soldiers thus escaped with relatively few injuries (six wounded, one seriously) due to the targeting by most of the attack party of the boat rather than the bodies. The encounter did give the Crown Forces pause for reflection about what might happen in the future if they were again caught as sitting ducks in the middle of the river with no escape route save the slow waters of the Shannon.

Successes and Failures by the Athlone Flying Column

Led by Seamus O'Meara, the Volunteers in Drum Company attempted to burn the barracks at Cloonark in September 1920. (Frank O'Connor claims that this attempt took place "a few nights before Tormey was killed on 2 February 1921.")[57] Guarding the building were ten to twelve well-armed Black and Tans and a sprinkling of RIC. Fifteen Volunteers assembled for the fight including Jack Kenny, Michael Naughton, Pat Lennon, and Jim McManus[58] but, alas, were disappointed by the order to cease and desist. Responsibility for the men's safety weighed heavily on O'Meara's shoulders, and he felt his chances for success were slim and the potential for slaughter great. He decided to save his manpower and fight another day.[59]

The Flying Column officers decided that perhaps the pickings were better east of the Shannon. In October, David Daly, Jim Tormey (O/C of the Flying Column), and Seamus O'Meara scouted the main Dublin to Athlone road for a possible ambush site. Armed with thirteen rifles and one shotgun and a few grenades from the Dublin factory, they took up position at Parkwood and waited. The men were not experienced in the use of rifles, so a position was chosen close to the road nearly at point blank range. As the whistle sounded for the first volley, the men opened fire on the lone lorry of Tans. That lorry was all too quickly joined by another, yet another, and still another. It seems that the Column had unwittingly attacked a convoy of Black and Tans proceeding from Gormanstown in County Meath to Galway. Realising that they had bitten off more than they could chew, the Column quickly withdrew, with no injuries, commandeered a vehicle, drove to Doon near Ballycommon, County Offaly, and arranged for a boat to transport the men across the Shannon to Garrynagowna, where they billeted for two weeks.[60]

Reprisals for this audacious act of defiance brought scores of Black and Tans to the Moate area. Several houses were burned, and many of the people stayed out in the relative safety of their fields rather than venture into their cottages.

After a well earned rest on the Roscommon side of the waters, the Column set out again. An attempted ambush on the Athlone-Ballinasloe-Galway road resulted in three days of waiting but no enemy in sight. They re-crossed the Shannon at Coosan and headed to Ballymahon where they attempted to stage an ambush on the Ballymahon/Athlone road. No suitable site could be found. They crossed the river again and marched to Garrynagowna, billeted a few more days, and set up ambush positions on the Galway road. All these actions bore no tangible results.

The commanding officers determined that it would be wise to split up the column into smaller segments, each section scouting its own prescribed area and striking when opportunity arose. Dick Bertles and Bill Casey headed to Drumraney with a small group, Harry O'Brien headed to Thomastown on the Ballinasloe/

The men opened fire on the lone lorry of Tans. That lorry was all too quickly joined by another, yet another, and still another.

Athlone Road, while Pat Macken, Seamus O'Meara, and Barney Gaffey directed their feet to the Summerhill area.

O'Meara arranged for a small ambush along the Ballinasloe road at Thomastown, under the command of Bernard "Barney" Gaffey. When the policemen did appear, the Volunteers' cartridges were damp and ineffective. Nearer to Athlone at Kielty, O'Meara's party stopped Constable Doyle on 31 October along the road and showered him with pellets. Hundreds of pellets entered his clothing, but again the cartridges were faulty. Doyle took refuge in a house, whereupon O'Meara called a halt to attempts to kill him. "He had undergone the ordeal of being ambushed at close range and Providence had saved his life and I considered he had enough."[61]

Hideout for Athlone Flying Column in Culleen.
PHOTO COURTESY OF LEW THORNE

Two days later, Dick Bertles commanded an ambush party in the Auburn area of County Westmeath on the main Athlone/Ballymahon Road. The riflemen killed the driver of the first tender "but another man, who was sitting beside the driver, showed great presence of mind and immediately took over the driver's position and drove the lorry, with all speed, through our [the Volunteers'] position..."[62] The Volunteers could not successfully disable the driver of the second vehicle either. As both tenders sped past the waiting Volunteers, they were showered with buckshot — the only weapon most of the Volunteers possessed. Three hand grenades were thrown into the tenders but failed to explode. Volunteer Seamus Finn lost his life that day. Three British soldiers were reported dead and several wounded.

North Roscommon Man Slain in Leitrim

The northern part of County Roscommon was experiencing its share of terror. Raiding parties from the barracks at Carrick-on-Shannon swooped down through the neighbouring countryside arresting, beating, and, on some occasions, killing. Two wagons containing food, clothes, and equipment had recently been stolen from the military. Crown Forces were not happy. In addition, the British raiding parties had been totally frustrated by their inability to capture Mick McLoughlin, the Vice O/C of the 5th Battalion North, whom they suspected as the chief culprit behind the theft. Patrick Gill, his sister Ann, and Mrs. Notley had the misfortune of being in the wrong place at the wrong time.

On 11 September the three were heading to a wake at Foxborough in County Leitrim. After crossing the Shannon from Corralara, they walked past the police barracks. A lorry was parked on the street, a fact they ignored to their regret. A lone shot rang out from that lorry. Patrick Gill fell in his tracks. Whether the shooting was spurred by frustration, boredom, or misidentification no one will ever know. A sham inquest was later held which returned the verdict of "killed by persons unknown."

"Pinned to the Wall with Lead"

By mid-September of 1920 the barracks of Ballinlough had been vacated by the RIC and a unit of the 9th Lancers. Volunteer plans for torching the barracks reached the ears of Henry Sampey of Willsborough, a wealthy Protestant farmer, who, although loyal to the Crown, kept quiet about local Volunteers and their activities. He had learned of the Volunteers' plan to destroy Ballinlough Barracks on 14 September, but he was also aware that the British troops had quietly reoccupied the area the night of the 13th. He sent word to Michael Glavey not to go near the barracks, but Glavey, who was suspicious of Sampey, dismissed the warning with the words, "Never mind that damn Englishman. He's trying to frighten us."[63]

Memorial in Ballinlough for the three Volunteers who lost their lives: Pat Glynn, Michael Glavey, Michael Keane.

Local Volunteers[64] assembled on the night of 14 September, and made their way to the supposedly abandoned building. To ensure complete destruction, three Volunteers armed with petrol climbed ladders to the roof. When the first flickers of flames flashed, gunfire sliced the air. The men of the Ballinlough Company, assisted by several from neighbouring Loughglynn and Clooncan, were completely taken back. The gunfire was coming from the blackness surrounding them on all sides. There was no hope of returning accurate fire, and with few available guns, the men quickly abandoned the burning business and scattered into the surrounding blackness. The silhouettes of the running Volunteers against the red/orange backdrop of the already blazing barracks proved easy targets for the concealed gunmen. When the firing ceased, three men lay dead upon the warm ground. Pat Glynn had been surprised by the whiz of bullets while he was atop the roof attempting to break a hole in it. Michael Glavey and Michael Keane had been standing in front of the barracks when the lethal barrage erupted.[65] The bodies of all three were taken to the barracks in Castlerea, where they were tossed on a heap of turf. Bloody, frigid, and lifeless, they remained there until claimed by their families for a respectable burial. Three more names were added to the ever-growing list of young Irish patriots who were robbed of a long life, yet whose sacrifice made possible the birth of a nation.

Sean Connolly Arrives from Longford

In 1920 an application was sent to General Headquarters in Dublin for an organiser to be sent to the North Roscommon area. Sean Connolly, after whom the

Sean Connolly

Connolly Barracks in Longford town is named, answered the call. He and Sean MacEoin originated from the same area in Longford, but they did not work well as a team. MacEoin was a bit of a one-man show, and thus it was decided to maximise Connolly's expertise and leadership by shipping him farther afield. He was sent to Roscommon in late September/early October to help instruct the men and plan attacks. He originally came through Hillstreet via Ruskey. Later in October he moved north to Crossna, where he reorganised the Companies of Crossna, Cootehall, and Drumlion before Christmas. These groups of men now became the 5th Battalion North Roscommon. The 4th Battalion consisted of Companies from Keadue, Ballyfarnon, and Arigna, with Jimmie O'Brien appointed as O/C. When Connelly initially came to north Roscommon, Seamus Ryan had been the O/C and Michael Dockery the Vice O/C of the Brigade. Connolly reversed the order of command. Ryan was a man of poor health who lacked the vigour and stamina for organising, recruiting, training, and planning engagements. Connolly saw in Dockery an able and eager warrior.

Connolly's first order of business was to organise the Volunteer Companies into solid and aggressive fighting units. He had no time for idle chatter or wishful thinking. He "was undoubtedly one of the great guerilla leaders that the IRA had so far produced, and his sojourn in Roscommon [had] borne good fruit."[66]

His mission was to devise and execute plans and aid in acquisition of weaponry. When he headed for Ballinameen, he brought with him twenty-five sticks of gelignite which the Roche family could incorporate into their cement mines to add punch.[67] (Jack Glancy had been sent to Fitzgerald's of Brunswick Street in Dublin to acquire "the goods." He had shipped them along with two batteries for explosive detonators to Drumsna Station.) Those ingredients were carefully measured and packed into mines by the Ballinameen Roche brothers (Jack and Michael). They were served up in the attack on Elphin Barracks on 11 February 1921.

Connolly made the Roche's home his northern headquarters and Beirnes of Carracally his alternate retreat. He helped plan the attack on Elphin dispensary and the attack on Elphin Barracks. He also envisioned several smaller operations that would irritate and, perhaps, inflict damage on the Crown Forces.

Attack on Frenchpark Barracks

Plans for an attack on Frenchpark Barracks were hatched by the South Roscommon Brigade Staff and required no small amount of coordination. Sean Bergin acted as the commanding officer for the attack. Nearly seventy men were involved in the assault, road blocking, and arms supply operation. The attack was scheduled for early Saturday morning, 2 October. The scenario for the assault included "a load of hay on a cart to be soaked in paraffin or petrol and backed up against the door of the barracks and set on fire."[68] A ring of sharp-shooters was placed around the barracks in order to confine the police, and three men armed with double-barrelled shotguns and cartridges that had been heavily slugged to be among the attackers. The Brigade staff wanted the doorways to the barracks to be covered from twenty-five yards away. A party had been detailed to climb onto the roof, break a hole in it, and pour petrol down into the barracks, forcing the RIC outside. A bomb, a stone in weight with detonator attached and a striking pin in the bottom, was supposed to be placed next to the barracks wall. Gelignite as well as scrap iron, although not much of the latter, were the chief ingredients.[69]

As the drama was being acted out, however, impromptu scenes appeared in the play. In an attempt to occupy the house across the road from the barracks, the breaking of a window pane alerted the garrison. In addition, the whole area was alive with men moving into position, and that fact was not lost on the local dog population, who howled their mistrust to the moon. The cartload of hay never made it to the door of the barracks because hand grenades were thrown out the window from that building, forcing the cart pusher to abandon his mission. A furious fire-fight ensued. The bomb was thrown into the street narrowly missing Sean Bergin, who by now was attempting to set the door of the barracks on fire himself.[70] After the Volunteers' bomb had been detonated, it became clear that no hole large enough for the attackers[71] to enter the barracks had been opened up in any wall. The party detailed to climb to the roof never got into action. The whole affair lasted less than an hour, but was called off at daybreak when it became obvious that the original plans for capture of the building would not succeed.[72]

The Reprisals

Crown Forces set out that same evening to avenge the assault on their barracks at Frenchpark. Travelling to Ballinagare, they burned the premises of Pat Martin and Michael Kelly. They proceeded to the farm of P. Hannily, where they destroyed haggards, oats, even a litter of piglets — nothing was beyond the reach of the fiery licks of their flames. Frank Flynn's home was completely scorched. The household of Dan O'Rourke was threatened. The price was high for Volunteers who exhibited such impudence as to attack a British stronghold in Ireland. Not coincidentally, all four homes threatened or destroyed belonged to Volunteers who had participated in the barracks attack: (John Joe) Martin, (James) Kelly, Brigade O/C Dan O'Rourke, and the Hanley (Hannily) brothers.

Raid at Greatmeadow

Tensions between the Volunteers and the military were rising, with Black and Tans paying more-frequent late night visits to Volunteers' homes to intimidate, beat, and sometimes shoot the occupants. In October of 1920, James Feely, O/C of the 1st Battalion North, and his brother Henry were sleeping in a shed at the back of their house. Awakened by a flashlight in his face, James jumped out of bed only to find a number of armed men in civilian clothes wearing masks crammed into the room. Henry was dropped to the floor by a rifle blow which left him unconscious. James was ordered to march down the road towards town, being shoved, kicked, and heaved along the way. Upon crossing the railway bridge, he made good his escape by vaulting the battlement and landing on the grass margin alongside the rails. It was a drop of eight or nine feet, but "was well known to [him] as [he] had often done this jump as a boy for fun."[73] He crawled into a gully, bullets

A ring of sharpshooters was placed around the barracks in order to confine the police.

whizzing around him, and lay still while the masked men ran up and down the rail line looking for him. They found nothing.

The Tans who had let Feely slip through their fingers were none too content. Revenge was the order of the day, and it had to be fulfilled. They next proceeded to the home of Pat Brennan, brother of Boyle Company Commander James Stephen Brennan. Pat suffered an horrendous beating and was left on the ground to await his destiny. Fortunately, the Tans moved on to the chemist's shop in Main Street, Boyle, where the masked men repeated their brutal performance and topped it off with a shearing of Niall Harrington's head.

Ambush at Fourmilehouse

One needs to be leery of accepting every shred of information presented, even if it is offered by reputable historians. Conflicting dates for the Fourmilehouse Ambush are given in several different books. Micheál O'Callaghan's book, *For Ireland and Freedom*, quoted the date as "October 24th 1920." Richard Abbott's *Police Casualties in Ireland 1919-1923* stated 12 October as the day of the clash. As a writer viewing the happenings from a distance of eighty years, I needed precision. And thus I sought "the horses' mouths." The papers of Jim Quigley (O/C of the 2nd Battalion South), the papers of Gerald O'Connor (O/C of the 1st Battalion South Roscommon), and the Volunteer Witness Statement of Frank Simons all indicated the day as 12 October, and so it shall be in this book.

The route between Roscommon town and Boyle had been scouted for some days previously by members of Kilbride Company to ascertain the enemy traffic pattern. Luke Duffy and Pat Madden, in order to determine the most suitable site for an ambush, had also reconnoitred the area. Ironically, the chosen spot fell within the shadow of Kilbride Church adjoining the Strokestown junction. Dan O'Rourke, Brigade Commander at the time, authorised the loan of four rifles from the Battalion's stash which were collected prior to the attack by Luke Duffy and Paddy Tiernan from Jim Quigley's house. Although most of the Kilgefin Coy. had been called into action,[74] the Company had only eight rifles (four of their own and the four picked up at Quigley's) while the rest of the raiding party were armed with shotguns and revolvers. Short on firing equipment and ammunition (about twenty rounds per rifle) but long on determination, the 3rd Battalion Volunteers stayed at a cottage in Ballagh for a few hours the night before, then slipped out into the night about 2 a.m. and stealthily made their way via New Line, Aghamuck Crossroads, and Cloonbony to Ballinderry, where they met up with the Kilbride Company. Kilbride's men were divided into three sections — one sent to occupy a position on the Roscommon side of Fourmilehouse, another section ordered to construct blockades on the Boyle Road, and a third to do the same on the Strokestown Road. A few of the Kilbride Volunteers also accompanied Madden's men to Fourmilehouse (Kilbride) Church area where they commandeered a cart and a pole from a nearby carpenter's shop. (The pole was intended to push the cart out into the road, thereby halting the lorry.) As last-minute preparations were in progress, the lookout alerted the raiding party that a lorry was due to arrive soon.[75] There was no time to secure the cart to complete the barricade.

Madden's men had been divided on either side of the road. At about 8:30 a.m., as the lorry whizzed by carrying eight occupants, it entered a murderous crossfire zone which left two constables dead at the scene (two others later died in the Strokestown police barracks). One policeman was slightly wounded, and three men were unharmed, including the driver, Constable Joyce. He was going so fast the Volunteers obstructing the roads with stones had no time to mount a viable barricade. The lorry zipped through the semi-completed blockade at Clashaganny farther along on the Roscommon/Boyle Road and took a circuitous route, winding its way to Strokestown with its macabre cargo.

Kilbride's men were divided into three sections — one sent to occupy a position on the Roscommon side of Fourmilehouse, another section ordered to construct blockades on the Boyle Road, and a third to do the same on the Strokestown Road.

Those who died at the scene included:
John Crawford, RIC, a native of Clare
Michael Kenny, RIC, a native of County Clare
Constable Francis Gallagher, a native of Strabane, died a
short time later
Martin O'Connor, a native of County Limerick
(The *Strokestown Democrat* claimed that he died at 2 p.m. the day of
the ambush.[76] He was buried at Achill, Co. Mayo on 15 October.)[77]
The other four occupants of the vehicle included:
Head Constable Conway (not injured), Sgt. Boulter (unharmed),
Constable Rahilly (injured by buckshot in his thigh and hand), and
driver William Joyce (left unscathed).

As the echo of the last shots faded over the fields and the lorry sped out of sight, the men emerged from behind their cover and gathered on the road to assess their own damage as well as that done to the Crown Forces. In a short time, a car happened by driven by RIC Inspector Hetreed dressed in plain clothes. The Inspector did not know that an ambush had just taken place. The Volunteers, at the time, had not recognised the Inspector as the civilian in the passing vehicle.[78] They allowed him to proceed on his way.

Over the ensuing years, the attack has been regarded as a great success. The immediate elation of victory, however, was dampened by the participants' realisation that although they had carried out a dangerous and effective assault, they had not succeeded in obtaining any guns or bullets from the policemen, all the while expending a goodly supply of their own precious ammunition.

The Kilgefin Company and some from Kilbride had furnished the attack men who were led by Pat and Dan Madden, as well as Luke Duffy and Frank Simons. Other men from the Kilbride Coy. acted as scouts and outposts.[79]

The wrath of the Tans was white hot. That same night the Crown Forces, in several lorries accompanying the dead constables' remains, shot up the countryside northwest of Roscommon town. Houses, cattle, and sheep were all targeted. On the following day, the Volunteers expected a big roundup in the area, with many gruesome reprisals. They didn't come, at least not for a while. In anticipation of British reprisals, Volunteers took up positions for five nights after the ambush — in houses opposite the barracks in Roscommon town, along Goff Street, in and around Harrison Hall. Some of the Volunteers from Athleague assisted in guard duty in the town, while other local Volunteers put a guard on Pat Madden's house. The 2nd Battalion also put a guard around Jim Quigley's home. All was quiet for a few days.

Within the week, however, a huge roundup involving hundreds of men descended on central Roscommon. The British Forces converged on the area where the Kilgefin Company was based. A road encircled the area and this was continually patrolled by soldiers in lorries, while men on foot combed every house and field in the area. Due to the Kilgefin Company's intelligence sources (Sgts. Duffy and Harte in Roscommon town proved helpful), the Volunteers had been alerted as to the coming swoop, and had succeeded in moving out of the collared area. Dan Madden and Patrick Farrell were not so lucky. They had been away during the previous day and were now trying to make their way back to 3rd Battalion headquarters. They were nabbed by the Tans and taken to Athlone, where they were court-martialled. Madden received ten years which he began serving in Athlone; he later was shipped to Dartmoor, where he remained until the Treaty was signed. Farrell was sent to the Curragh.

As the storm clouds gathered over the countryside and the winds of terror blew against every cottage window pane, a hint of a rainbow appeared on the horizon. Inspector Hetreed, who believed he was allowed to go free after encountering the Volunteers on the road the morning of the Fourmilehouse Ambush, saved the town of Roscommon from being burned in reprisal. (He was soon transferred and

In anticipation of British reprisals, Volunteers took up positions for five nights after the ambush.

Members of the 3rd Battalion South Flying Column at the funeral of Matt Davis in 1957. Front row: Luke Duffy (partially obscured), "Buzzer" Farrrell, Peter Collins, Paddy Tiernan (in back with cap), Dan Madden, Jimmie Devine, Michael Collins, John Brennan.

replaced by District Inspector Cole.)

The Formation of the 3rd Battalion South Flying Column

In 1917 the original Volunteer "E" Coy. consisted of Pat Madden as O/C, Dan Madden, his brother as 1st Lieutenant, and Frank Simons as the 2nd Lieutenant. Prior to the election of 1918, the local Companies were reorganised into a Battalion. Pat Madden was appointed the O/C of the 3rd Battalion with Frank Simons serving as Adjutant. By late 1920 another type of striking force was envisioned. Immediately after the Fourmilehouse Ambush, the South Roscommon 3rd Battalion South Flying Column was formed. The Active Service Unit was based at Kenny's, The Glebe, Kilrooskey, located at the foot of Slieve Bawn. Patrick Kenny had been a schoolmaster in Wexford and had purchased the house long before the Tan War. The house was large, and included a basement, ground floor, and upper rooms which made it a great meeting place and, if need be, hiding place. The house has long since been demolished.

Pat Madden was again chosen to head the group. Luke Duffy would serve as Vice O/C. Members of the Column included: the Collins brothers (Peter and Michael), John and James McDermott, Henry Compton, Dan Madden, Jim Tiernan, John and Michael Gibbons, James Cooney, Joe Fallon, and Tom Madden. The men were joined by Volunteers Stephen Murray, Tom Egan, and Tom Brennan of Kilteevan Coy. From Kilbride Coy. came Peter "Buzzer" Farrell, from Roscommon town marched Joe Finlay, "Boddins" Doorley, Tim Monaghan, Frank and Richard Simons. Pat Mulleady (Maleady) from Ballyleague joined up while a member from farther south in the county, Jack Conboy from Athleague, completed the roster.[80] At the time of its formation, the Column had only four rifles. (The others that had been used for the Fourmilehouse Ambush had been returned to the Ballinaheglish Coy.) They had only a limited supply of ammunition and precious little money to purchase any. The remaining members of the Column were armed only with a shotgun.[81]

The Volunteers had to live on the generosity of the people in order to survive. Many nights they billeted in a local sympathiser's house and kept outposts and sentinels on duty at all times.

When two men were sent to Dublin to secure more arms, they returned with only a Morris tube which was only of use for instructional purposes. Due to lack of arms and intense pressure from the Crown Forces, the Column was disbanded shortly after its formation, and each man was sent back to rejoin his own Company.

Hats Off to the Great Men

Where credit is due, let no man be reticent to give praise. According to Martin Fallon, the O/C of the 3rd Battalion North Roscommon Flying Column, "There would have been nothing in South Roscommon only for Pat Madden. Luke Duffy was a great man. The best men he had there were ex-Irish Guards who had gone to school with Madden. When they came home, the fight was on in Ireland."[82]

Leadership in South Roscommon

Richard Mulcahy, who attempted to direct Volunteer activities from GHQ in Dublin, was consistently critical of the failings of the IRA in Sligo and Roscommon.[83] Mulcahy was a lover of reports, the longer and more elaborate the better. Evidently Roscommon, North or South Brigade Adjutants, did not produce enough paperwork to impress the General.

The entire county suffered from a severe lack of arms. The southern part of the county also had the misfortune of having a Brigade Commander who exhibited a lack of military expertise at the top level. Dan O'Rourke, South Roscommon Brigade O/C, was not a member of the Irish Republican Brotherhood (IRB). He had no military training. A cautious man by nature, his expertise was in organisational work, not on the fighting field. A lot of the activity the southern Battalions undertook was never sanctioned by him. Local commanders simply did what they thought would work and informed him later. They learned early on that he would simply veto their ideas anyway.[84]

At a Brigade Council meeting at Smith's Hotel in Roscommon town in 1918, O'Rourke was chosen O/C of the Brigade — selected for his intellect and great devotion to the Irish cause. He, however, lacked the ability to guide his men in the dangerous business of war. His exceptional organisational skills, which later in his life contributed so much to the success of the Gaelic Athletic Association (GAA) and Roscommon County Council, were not the stuff of military leadership in the early years of the war. According to Gerald O'Connor, who served as the 1st Battalion South Commandant, "in mid-winter 1920-21, the (First) Battalion was completely disorganised. In January 1921 reorganisation was begun and, from the few groups of men remaining, an Active Service Unit was formed and new Battalion staff were appointed...."[85] This 1st Battalion area was O'Rourke's home territory.

Although planning for Brigade actions was supposed to have taken place at Brigade meetings, it is a fact that the most successful ambushes in the War were instigated by Pat Madden, Luke Duffy, Frank Simons, and the other devoted men in the Kilgefin Company. O'Rourke was a man of methodical planning, but he lacked the dash and daring coupled with the military know-how to win the confidence of his cohorts. Unlike Madden, who had served with the British Army and instinctively knew what it took to get things done, O'Rourke was a wary warrior.

The names inscribed on the Shankill Monument bear testament to the inadequacies of his command. A disproportionate number of those names are from the 1st Battalion South area. Many of those men did not lose their lives with a gun in their hand, but with a pillow under their head. They were victims of a spy. In all fairness to O'Rourke, however, it was discovered only too late that his Intelligence Officer, "Paddy" Egan, was a British agent conveniently planted with the Brigade staff. It was Egan who had fingered many of the local men for execution.[86]

O'Rourke was, however, an inspiring speaker. He ignited the tenders of nationalism within the hearts of his listeners. He was honest and straightforward and proved to be a good recruiter. What to do with the manpower was more problematic.

According to the Mulcahy Papers, "lack of initiative among the Brigade officers" plagued the area. "The system of dispatch work was very bad. In several cases a dispatch went through five or six different dispatch riders over a distance of seven miles."[87] It took hours for important dispatches to get to the Vice O/C and two full days to get to the Quartermaster. He lived only four miles away! Their method of communication with neighbouring Brigades was even poorer, and there was very little communication within the Brigade itself. In summation, "the main cause of general inefficiency was the non-exercise of authority by the brigadier."[88]

On 4 March 1920 a letter was sent to O'Rourke by GHQ. "You are definitely not in touch with your battalion staff. I would like to know is this so. Have a report on what each battalion is doing, what training each battalion is doing, what military work you plan for the next two months."[89] O'Rourke's reply: "I presume you are disappointed. Me too. I have been in constant touch with the Battalion staffs."[90]

JESUS, MARY, JOSEPH.

OF YOUR CHARITY
PRAY FOR THE REPOSE OF THE SOUL OF
DANIEL O'ROURKE
Ballindrimley, Castlerea,
Co. Roscommon
Who died on 4th August, 1968.
R. I. P.
— ✠ —
All I ask of you is, that wherever you may be, you will remember me at Holy Communion and at the Altar of God.

PHOTO COURTESY OF LILLIE O'ROURKE

O'Rourke was an inspiring speaker. He ignited the tenders of nationalism within the hearts of his listeners.

Instead of accepting the responsibility and changing his procedures, O'Rourke proceeded to blame others: "poor company leadership, the best of which has emigrated to England. Most of the officers have not natural ability and seemed determined not to acquire it.... Also lack of arms — as of March 1921 we can only effectively arm fifteen or twenty men."[91] We have a lot of shotguns "but I don't fancy they would be effective against such large enemy bodies as now almost invariably move through the area. The terrain of Roscommon is flat — there are few natural hiding places. The Active Service Units are hampered by arrests. P.S. Is there anybody from GHQ to give instructions in engineering? Our man for the Battalion has been arrested and cannot be helpful."[92]

The statement about being in constant contact with Battalion staff is contradicted by Martin Fallon, O/C of the 3rd Battalion North Flying Column, who lived but a few miles from the 3rd Battalion South staff area. In the Ernie O'Malley notebooks in the University College Dublin (UCD) Archives, Fallon states that O'Rourke had visited the 3rd Battalion area only once during the entire Tan War. When asked by the 3rd Battalion men as to his impression of the Fourmilehouse ambush, he stated that "it was a foolish thing to do."[93]

GHQ response to all this ambiguity was to sack O'Rourke. (According to Frank Simons, he was appointed acting Brigade O/C in March, a position he held until the Truce.)[94] In August 1921 Gerald O'Connor was appointed No. 2 Brigade Commandant in the 2nd Western Division. O'Connor, who had been the 1st Battalion South commander, began writing reports to GHQ as early as March of 1921 — several months before the Truce. There was correspondence between O'Rourke and GHQ after that date, but by that time the central command seems to have given up on a significant military action coming from his leadership.

In December of 1921 O'Rourke, as TD, had planned on voting against the Treaty. During the Christmas break, however, he changed his vote — no doubt with the understanding that when Michael Collins and the IRA got control of the Army, they would focus their rifle sights on freeing the North. With the assassination of Collins in August of that year, plans for the liberation of the northern counties never got off the drawing board.

O'Rourke, however, was a man of principle. He did attempt to stage small actions in the Castlerea area. He even participated in some of them himself. He was known by the local Crown Forces, and his Tarmon home was often visited. During the Civil War and its aftermath, when he saw the vengeance with which the new Free State government was going after the Republicans, he resigned from the Dáil, although his interest in politics never waned. He later proved instrumental in the rise of Fianna Fáil in Roscommon, serving as a local Councillor from 1928. He also served in Seanad Éireann (the Senate) from 1951-54. The Roscommon County Council (of which he was chairman for thirteen years), the championship football team of 1943 (of which he was the head coach), the GAA (of which he was the national president) and a long-running stint with Fianna Fáil as a TD all bear testimony to his skill as a great administrator. The application of sufficient pressure against the Crown Forces in South Roscommon during the years 1918-1921 does not.

Leadership in North Roscommon

In 1920 when Sean Connolly first came to Roscommon to inspire and reorganise the Companies, he found ineptitude. He approached the Brigade O/C at the time and asked if he had a gun. The Brigadier answered in the affirmative, and Connolly demanded to see it. Whereupon the Brigadier produced a twenty-five calibre automatic pistol. Connolly looked at this formidable piece of ordnance and asked, "Does it shoot?" and on being assured that it really did, he said, "Let's try it." At the latter proposal, the Brigadier expressed alarm that the shots might attract the attention of the Tan patrols. Connolly ignored this and pinned a piece of paper to the barn door to serve as a target. He then took some paces back from the door, fired and hit the target. He then handed the pistol to the Brigadier.

The Brigadier took the weapon in his right hand, aimed it at the piece of paper, turned his head to look over his LEFT shoulder, CLOSED his eyes and squeezed the trigger.[95] And thus was a new North Roscommon Brigadier appointed.

Connolly selected Michael Dockery of Elphin to command the northern Brigade. Dockery never disappointed his mentor. Many of the plans for ambushes in Elphin, Scramogue, Keadue, and Strokestown were the direct result of his input. Dockery was also present at some of those assaults.

In the early months of 1921, his name and exploits were so well known to the RIC that numerous reports sent by them to Dublin Castle lament the fact that they were unable to locate him specifically during their raids. His ribbon of luck ran out in May of 1921 when he was arrested in O'Hara's cottage in Cootehall for possession of a rifle taken off a policeman shot in the Keadue ambush. Through the efforts of numerous men in north Roscommon, he made a dashing escape from Boyle Barracks a few weeks later.

When the Treaty was signed, Dockery joined up with the Free State Army. The cursèd hex of Boyle Barracks had been broken once, but not twice in his young life. During the Civil War he was placed in charge of the Free State forces occupying Boyle workhouse. He was killed by a sniper's bullet near that same military building from whence he had made such a spectacular escape a little more than a year before.

Quoting from his obituary as printed in the *Roscommon Herald:*

The Late Brigadier Dockery
Tributes from Justices and Solicitors
(Passed by Military Censor, Dublin)

The justices and solicitors present at the last District Court in Strokestown referred in terms of regret to the tragic death of Brigadier Michael Dockery in Boyle on July the 1st, and adjourned the Court as a mark of respect. The justices present were: Messrs. Paul Egan (Chairman), Thomas Murray, P. J. McGuinness, and P. Barry.

The Chairman said the late Brigadier Dockery played a great and noble part in the fight for an Irish Republic against great odds, and his exploits and deeds were known all over County Roscommon and Leitrim. He fought the Black and Tans and Auxiliaries and the nadir minions of England with wonderful bravery, and he was the most sought-for man in the county by them. When he was captured at Cootehall through treachery, the "Tans" and Auxiliaries could not control their jubilation at such an important capture. Had he not made a sensational escape from Boyle Barracks, he would now be numbered with Kevin Barry and other Irish martyrs. It was deplorable that Brigadier Dockery should have met his death at the hands of his fellow-countrymen (but the man that shot him would yet pay the penalty). The Chairman then proposed the following resolution:

"That this District Court places on record its heartfelt regret on the death of Brigadier Michael Dockery and tenders to his bereaved relatives their deepest sympathy in their dire affliction, and that this Court do now adjourn as a small token of the regard it felt for the late lamented Brigadier."

James Feely, former O/C 1st Battalion North Roscommon, conducting a ceremony at Michael Dockery's gravesite in Ballinderry Cemetery.

PHOTO COURTESY OF BARRY FEELY

Mr. Thomas Murray, in seconding, said as one who was closely associated with the late Brigadier, he would like to refer to some of his sterling qualities. He never shirked a fight when he was up against the minions of England, and was the very personification of bravery and daring. In private life he was as harmless and inoffensive as a child, and every comrade, aye, all Roscommon, deplore his loss deeply. "Mick" Dockery's place would not be easily filled.

Mr. Gaynor on behalf of the solicitors expressed his regret at the death of the Brigadier and wished to be associated with the resolution.

Messrs. Neilan and McCormack also expressed their sympathy as did Mr. M. Gordon, Registrar, and Mr. McGrath, Organiser.

The Press representatives associated themselves with the expression of regret.

Terrible Tans Visit Ruskey

On Friday night, 15 October, Black and Tans invaded the town of Ruskey. Commandeering quarters near the barracks, they placed patrols on the roads and searched all persons leaving or entering the village. They visited specific houses known to be the homes of local Volunteers and leading Sinn Féin figures. The first item on their agenda was a visitation to John Hanley whom they dragged from his home, aimed rifles at his head, but intentionally missed their target and subsequently beat him. Next on the list of suspicious abodes was the Robinsons. Son John J. was the Captain of the Ruskey Company, and, fortunately, not at home on this evening of madness. Next came the Burke household whose one son, Joseph, was an Intelligence Officer for the 3rd Battalion North. Frustrated by the absence of the son they were really seeking, the Tans arrested the father and took him to Roscommon town, where he was released the next day. During this unannounced and uninvited stay in the village, "a large quantity of goods and valuables were taken from several shops by the armed forces."[96]

More Reprisals in Ballinagare

The Volunteers had made a real show of force when they attacked Frenchpark Barracks on 2 October. Although their assault was not completely successful due to the sound of windows breaking (which alerted the garrison) and bombs without enough punch being unable to breach the stone walls, they poured salt onto the wounded pride of the RIC and Black and Tans who called the barracks their home. The Crown Forces learned that the men who had attacked their barracks had first assembled in Ballinagare. They were determined to teach the local villagers that there was a price to be paid for aiding and abetting the IRA.

On the night of 19 October they again travelled in lorries to the town of Ballinagare. Their intelligence work had been active since the barracks assault, and they had fingered Patrick Doyle as a participant. They were right. They shot him as he exited Pat Garvey's home.

The Shooting of John Conroy

All persons in and around Fourmilehouse expected hail to rain down, gunpowder blasts, and pitchforks from hell to converge on them as a result of the Fourmilehouse ambush. Strangely enough, nothing significant happened. For the first three nights after the attack, the Volunteers posted guards who were armed only with shotguns and revolvers. The Tans bided their time, however, and quietly entered the neighbourhood on the night of 3 November. They commandeered a small lorry belonging to George Kelly from Tulsk and drove to Johnny O'Dowd's house. There they dragged him out of his house and kicked him all along the road until he pointed out the home of John Conroy. Then they kicked him back up the road as they advanced towards Conroy's homestead.

The RIC and Black and Tans were determined to teach the local villagers that there was a price to be paid for aiding and abetting the IRA.

John had recently been married or else he probably wouldn't have chanced sleeping at home. Mrs. Raftery of Castleplunkett had earlier overheard a discussion among the Tans bragging about their next victims. The names of Jim Quigley and John Conroy had been uttered. Mrs. Raftery had sent word to Quigley, who in turn warned Conroy. John, however, seemed not to have taken the warning seriously. It was a mistake which would silence his song forever, provide only blackness in place of multi-hued sunsets, and place him eternally beyond the sweet kisses of his new bride and infant child. He lies in the old Ballinderry Cemetery.

British Bonfire

In November four wagonloads of supplies were delivered at Carrick-on-Shannon Rail Station for use by the military. The wagons sat at the station unguarded. It was an oversight by the British. Jack Glancy gathered together about twenty men from the Drumlion Company, placed one man with a shotgun on the bridge over the main road, another at the gate entrance to the railway yard, and went in search of paraffin. He found sufficient supply of such at the station tank, and had his men spill it over the contents of the wagons. A single match did the rest.

Tarmon Terror

Paddy Flynn, Adjutant for the 1st Battalion South, and Dan O'Rourke were wanted men. The threat of iron manacles jingled ever louder in their ears. On the night of 21 November both were in O'Rourke's home planning to go on the run. After arrangements were hashed out, they left the house (fearing to sleep there) and headed down the road towards the Tarmon River. The rumblings of a lorry penetrated the November night-time stillness, so both men, fearing the sounds would soon converge on them, ducked under the bridge and remained in the icy waters until the noise of danger had drifted away. Frigid and fearful, they departed from their wet haven — O'Rourke heading home for warm clothes, Flynn plodding to the home of John Monaghan.

O'Rourke redressed and discussed with his wife the inadvisability of staying in his own bed that night. He no sooner had exited via the back door, when the Tans smashed in the front. They proceeded to drink what spirits would excite them, confiscate what valuables would fetch a price, then set a fire in the house.[97] O'Rourke, thankfully, was fleet of foot across the adjoining fields.

In the meantime, Paddy Flynn had entered Monaghan's house and found a welcoming dry place to rest. It proved to be only a temporary sanctuary from earthly misfortune. The Tans burst into the Monaghan home and shot Paddy Flynn several times as he lay in his bed. John Monaghan eluded their wrath by jumping from an upstairs window while his wife watched the flurry of activity with terrified eyes. Paddy Flynn, who had seen action with the Volunteers at Ballymoe several times and at Frenchpark a month earlier, would henceforth stand to on a different field of glory.

The Tans, however, were not content with the demise of only one Volunteer. Their other prey had escaped the vise and they were determined to have him crushed as well. About 10:30 a.m. the following morning, they paid a visit to Tarmon School where O'Rourke was a teacher. As Captain McKay approached the door, O'Rourke came out of the school, and, realising the seriousness of his situation, pulled a gun on the Captain. McKay grabbed for his whistle to alert the others who had assembled on the other side of the schoolhouse, but, alas, too late for the athletic and quick-thinking O'Rourke. He shoved the Captain out of way, ran toward and then hurdled the wall into Walker's field,[98] and made a successful dash to freedom.

Again the ironies of Fate present themselves. On a misty November night in 1920, one Volunteer lost his life amid a hail of bullets, while another narrowly escaped and went on to lead an active and productive life as a primary teacher, Irish language enthusiast, future President of the GAA, future Chairman of the Roscommon County Council, and member of the Dáil for the Fianna Fáil party.

The tombstone of John Conroy.
PHOTO BY LEW THORNE

It was a mistake which would silence his song forever.

Flynn's name appears on the tablets in front of the Shankhill IRA monument. O'Rourke's name appears in the annals of GAA history and County Council great leaders. Yet both men share a piece of the collective gratitude of Ireland. Both men gave what they valued most dearly — a meaningful life sacrificed for the betterment of their country.

Castlenode Confrontation

On the dark, damp night of 27 November, members of the 3rd Battalions North and South participated in a joint venture. Liam O'Doherty, O/C of the 3rd Battalion North, had devised a scheme whereby the Volunteers would commandeer the car of William Walpole, the same man whose Clooneenhartland acreage was a bone of contention in 1919. Frank Simons, Pat Madden, John Gibbons, Michael and Peter Collins, Hugh Keegan, Jim Tiernan, and Pat Mulleady (Maleady) joined forces with Liam O'Doherty[99] and his men (see footnote),[100] proceeded to Walpole's home, and announced that he had been nominated to relinquish his automobile "for the good of the cause".

The car was parked in the garage at the rear of the house on the south side. Some of O'Doherty's men went to start the automobile while two men, Collins and Gibbons, were left as sentries at the gate which was about twenty yards from the house. (Gibbons had been a sniper in World War I — a man of steady nerves and pinpoint accuracy with a rifle. It was due to his cool-headedness that this confrontation did not become a lethal clash.)

As the men continued to struggle with starting the stubborn car, the Volunteers "heard voices as if some persons were approaching the house from across the fields...Almost immediately, fire was opened by our two men we had left at the gate." A blistering barrage of bullets cut through the air. The Volunteers near the garage retreated towards Ashbrook across the Scramogue River, crossing it by footbridge at the old mill. Simons, Madden, and Pat Mulleady followed their lead, and all were reassembled safely. They headed back towards Aghadangan and on to Lismehy crossroads before holding a council of war. What had become of their two sentries? Were they to be left to the viciousness of the enemy?

The men decided to return to the Walpole house only to find a well-lighted house, a motor car parked at the front hall door that had not been there on their first visit, but no evidence of the two sentries. Some Volunteers went towards the garage to have another go at the car, while Madden, Simons and Hugh Keegan advanced towards the newcomer automobile. Suddenly gunfire was again cutting paths through the night air. The three men, who were headed for the front hall door, ran instead along the boundary wall, hurdled into a field, and amid the bleating sheep and bellowing cows managed to get away. The other Volunteers scattered as leaves in a whirlwind, and miraculously all escaped unscathed, including the sentries.[101] The lone "fatality" of the evening was the automobile that got caught in the crossfire and ended its days bearing striking resemblance to Swiss cheese. Stealing cars was tricky business.

Gunrunning

The 1916-1921 struggle for Independence was the first rebellion in Irish history whose rebels were armed with guns. Pikes had been the armament of 1798, an assortment of pitchforks and pikes had been available for the 1848 uprising. The twentieth century ushered in a new dimension of danger for all concerned.

Roscommon, being an inland county, was a difficult one to arm. Coastal landing sites were non-existent. The source for most imported guns was Dublin. Sometimes Volunteers travelled in cars to obtain a few rifles, but as there were few cars on the roads in those days, the vehicles were invariably searched.

By and large the vast amount of guns that crossed the county line came by rail. Guns were packaged in cases labelled something else. Dynamite, too, was transported in this way. Before the Rising, the Volunteers of Tubbercurry had collected money for armament. Rifles were delivered via railway to Ballymote where they were

The men decided to return to the Walpole house only to find a well-lighted house, a motor car parked at the front hall door that had not been there on their first visit, but no evidence of the two sentries.

retrieved by several Volunteers in a hired car. They drove the Short Lee Enfield rifles to just outside Tubbercurry, where they were met by another Volunteer carrying two revolvers. All proceeded into town, unloaded the rifles, and stored them in a cellar beneath the F. J. Cooke establishment to await "the moment."

Matt Davis, Quartermaster for the South Roscommon Brigade, used to take the train to Dublin and meet with Michael Staines, Quartermaster General for GHQ. Rendezvousing at Cullenswood House or Saint Enda's School in Rathfarnham, they would negotiate a trade for a few rifles or revolvers. Davis always returned to the county via train, and luckily had assistance from a railway checker named Paddy Daly who would take charge of the bags or cases and throw them off the train at the level-crossing at Corroy near Knockcroghery. There some waiting Volunteers would collect the baggage while Davis continued on to Roscommon Station.[102]

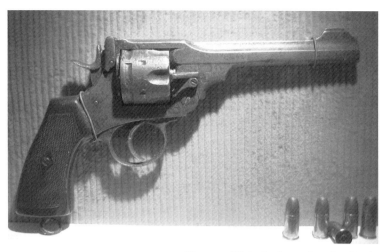

The gun of Toby Scally, 1st Battalion South Roscommon, now hangs in Hell's Kitchen pub in Castlerea.

PHOTO COURTESY OF LEW THORNE

In the northwest part of the county, a 25-pound keg of dynamite was packaged as "butter" and delivered to the Connolly Hotel in Castlerea. The keg was placed on a table in the snug where Pat Vaughan, who worked at the hotel, was to oversee its safety. Soon after its delivery, however, two policemen strolled into the snug and sat down right next to the "butter." A new plan of action popped into Pat's mind. He announced that a matchmaking transaction was due to take place shortly in that space, and would the policemen mind moving. After they vacated the room, a man with a donkey and cart arrived to retrieve the "butter" for his comrades.[103]

News of shipments of arms or "butter" arrived via dispatches. Many were verbal messages, but if any were written, they included no names, only code words. After they were read, they were destroyed. On occasion, a sympathetic rail station agent would discreetly pass the word.

Guns were, at times, transported by friendly businessmen and clergymen. The week before the Rising, Father Michael O'Flanagan, who during the early years of the second decade was stationed at Crossna, packed a rather large trunk in Dublin not with Bibles and cassocks but with sixteen shotguns and ammo. He then purchased a ticket from the capital to Sligo. He disembarked from the train at Carrick-on-Shannon, making the last leg of his journey by cart.[104]

At other times, ammunition came to the Volunteers in even more unorthodox ways. On more than one occasion a policeman in Castlerea (Keeling), who was a friend of Sean Bergin's father, passed Pat Vaughan a sling with ammunition tied at both ends. Pat would drape the sling over his bicycle handlebars and head on his way to delivery. If someone approached who might want to investigate his "luggage," Pat would toss the sling and ammunition into a field and return at a later date to retrieve it.[105] In the 2nd Battalion North area, Intelligence Officer Tom Brady acquired four boxes of shotgun cartridges which had been concealed in a sack of flour shipped from Dublin by his brother-in-law.[106] In the Frenchpark area, RIC policeman McQuinn, a native of Sligo, used to carry .303 and .45 ammunition in his uniform cap and give it to Volunteer James Haran, who in turn passed it along to James Feely of Boyle.[107]

The vast amount of guns that crossed the county line came by rail.

The Making of Ammunition

The makings of gunpowder, if a gun was available, were hard to come by. Some Volunteers spent many late nights in Raftery's Cloonboniffe blacksmith shop filling empty shell casings with sawed-off horseshoe nails. In the Strokestown area, men loaded their shot guns with "sudden deaths" (heavy slugs).[108] Other Volunteers in the Fuerty area made their own bullets by mixing a concoction of gelignite, sulphur, and charcoal. Lead sheets were melted and the liquid stirred in a saucepan, then poured into cartridges.[109] "In the Knockcroghery area, a start was made in assembling shotgun slugs. Patrick Kelly of Lecarrow, assisted by Owen Curley and Michael Cunnane, was in charge. In the months before the Truce, the St. John's Company Captain Hubert Murphy, along with Malachy Kilroy and Pat Fallon, joined Patrick Kelly of Lecarrow and concocted four pounds of powder in two nights.[110]

This gunpowder (of a sort) was "very dirty and smoky, but very powerful." A small supply of percussion caps was secured from the fog signals belonging to the railroad. Quartermaster Matt Davis and other Volunteers secured "detonators and took the mercury out of them and fitted caps into them. We removed the mercury with a steel awl which (I) afterwards learned was contrary to the right way to do it and should have caused an explosion. A wooden tool should have been used."[111]

Some units had their shotguns loaded with cartridges filled with buckshot. "It was very hard to keep the cartridges for the shotguns in condition as they were very liable to swelling from the damp unless stored under ideal conditions."[112]

During 1920 and 1921 large quantities of lead pellets about the size of a pea were made in the Knockcroghery area for use in shotguns. "The work necessitated the unloading of shot from cartridges and the procuring of lead from various places such as roofs of old houses or water pipes where such could be found...and finally the melting and making and trimming of the pellets and reloading the cartridges."[113] All guns had to be kept concealed out of doors to prevent discovery by the enemy. (If they had been stored inside a structure, they would have made a very inviting target for the British Forces.) They were sometimes put in boxes and buried in some quiet spot. "To keep these guns and cartridges safe from dampness and the guns cleaned and oiled entailed constant attention from each company quartermaster."[114]

Roadblock at Ballymurray, Roscommon.

PHOTO COURTESY GEAROID O'BRIEN, HEAD LIBRARIAN, ATHLONE LIBRARY

Road Blocking

By November "the organisation of the IRA was being perfected...the engineer's section in all Company areas was organised to make mines, bombs, to learn how to demolish bridges, and to block roads by a system of trenches."[115] These trenches were made in a section of the road that was impossible to go around and passable only by carrying planks to span the divide. After being dug, they were often camouflaged to make them undetectable to the naked eye. "These trenches were specifically designed; three cuttings were made, none fully across the road, in a zigzag fashion. On bog roads or solid surfaces it was important that the land inside the trenched road could not be used by opening gaps at either side to facilitate by-passing the cuttings."[116]

Different areas of the county used different methods. In the 2nd Battalion South area, "trenches were not cut across the roads but along the side of the road so as to catch the wheel of a vehicle and topple it over. The spoil from the trench was taken away and dumped, then the trench was covered with light timber and topped off with road material. Some hay was then shaken over the trench lightly and this was continued for a mile or so in either direction to mislead the enemy into believing that it was only a load of hay that had passed the way."[117]

Many Roscommon men simply used the less complicated method of felling trees to impede and delay Crown Forces. Before the attack on Elphin Barracks in February, the sound of busy axes echoed o'er the fields as the fighting men plodded to the ambush site. In the south of the county, seven men oftentimes took on the job of blocking the roads at Whitepark, Curraghboy, and Lysterfield during the Civil War.[118]

The Making of Bombs

A grenade factory had been started in the Dublin Brigade as early as 1918.[119] The output was estimated to be about 100 bombs per week (after a £100 startup cost and a £38.10 weekly operating budget),[120] but few of these devices ever made it inland as far as Roscommon, and those that did were a disappointment. These bombs were based on the Mills hand grenade, but were larger, heavier, and often-times 'duds' with a bad splinter effect."[121] In North Roscommon, Tommy Lavin, Vice O/C of the 4th Battalion, was experimenting with one of these Dublin demons when it prematurely exploded, and blew off his right hand. "Had the grenade segregated, as it was supposed to do, (he) would have been killed."[122]

The 3rd Battalion North Roscommon area solved the problem by building a munitions plant of their own at Muckinagh, Kilglass. Manned by Brian Connor of Sheerevagh, Ballinameen; John Murray of Gortnacloy, Mantua; and John Kelly of Muckinagh,[123] the vacated house served as sleeping quarters, factory, as well as experimental laboratory. The men who worked there often stayed for weeks at a time trying to find the right combination of gelignite (obtained from the County Council quarries) and "war flour" — a high explosive supplied by GHQ.

The men had some success with concrete mines and some bombs of cartbox type. In the north part of the county, Jack and Michael Roche of Ballinameen and William MacHenry were the chief cooks who brewed bomb blasts for the British. "Ingredients" were stored at Bessy Kelly's. Jim Dorr claims that "the bombs were cumbersome weapons and not very reliable as the fuse might not continue to burn and failures might occur in them."[124] A cartbox mine is described by Martin Fahy, the Brigade Engineer for Galway. He outlines the making of the device as such:

> "The mine was made from the box of a horse-cart, that is, the metal portion of the box at the centre of the wheel in which the axle revolves when the cart is set in motion. It was roughly twelve inches long. Inside diameter was about three inches at its wider end and about two inches at the narrower end. A blacksmith fitted a cap over each end. The caps were held in place by means of a bolt going right through the centre of the cylinder with a nut at one end to tighten the caps. Later, the practice of having the bolt run-ning through the centre of the cylinder was discarded in favour of a bolt running along the outside. This made it easier to fill with explosives."[125]

In the south of Roscommon, Patrick Breheny of Sandfield, Knockcroghery, spent many nights working with the gelignite collected from the Lecarrow quarry and devising explosives. Assisted by his brother Michael, Jim Breheny of Portrunny, and brothers William and Michael J. Fallon, Patrick Breheny became quite proficient at his job. During the Black and Tan War, Michael and Patrick Tennant, Michael Cunnane, Owen Curley, and Pat Breheny also constructed a considerable number of bombs made from tin cans and containing "a stick of gelignite which was ignited with an ordinary powder trail fuse. The cans were filled with scrap metal."[126] Unfortunately for the future Free State government, Breheny honed his expertise by fashioning bombs that blew up rail bridges at Kellybrook and Curry during the Civil War. Many of his homemade devices were exported to Westmeath and also transported north to the Kilteevan Company which used them in various locations throughout the Brigade area and beyond.

While South Roscommon enjoyed a ready supply of gelignite from the quarry at Lecarrow, Volunteers in other parts of the county found themselves in short sup-ply. The homemade grenades available to the 1st Battalion South area were filled with horseshoe nails. Those grenades would inflict a horrific amount of damage on the intended victim, but they were also capable of blowing up the builder as well. Shortly before Stephen McDermott was killed in the Woodlands of Loughglynn,

The 3rd Battalion North Roscommon area solved the problem by building a munitions plant of their own at Muckinagh, Kilglass.

Born in Cloonfower near Castlerea, educated at Summerhill and Maynooth Colleges, he journeyed across bogs and fields, urban streets and oceans, only to be drawn back to his homeland to work incessantly for her freedom. His mother Mary was an Irish speaker and bestowed a love of the native language on her son Micheál (Michael). His family roots sank deep into the small farming traditions, and the Flanagan Fenian political hue coloured the fruits of a lifetime of his labour.

He chose not to fight with a gun but with words — syllables so powerfully and energetically delivered, so infectious, that thousands responded and heeded his call. Though he spoke often from the pulpit to which he had consecrated his life, he oftentimes addressed his audiences from podiums, on street corners, in small rooms, always urging his listeners to strike a blow for liberty.

Father Michael O'Flanagan travelled extensively in America for various Irish fund-raising causes (including the cheese-making concern at Loughglynn Convent, and the Gaelic League) before being transferred to Roscommon town in 1912 as a priest on the staff at Sacred Heart parish. Politically vocal and fearless in his criticism of pronouncements he deemed unfair, his associations were not limited to ecclesiastic sects. He eventually became acting President of Sinn Féin (while de Valera was in jail), President of Sinn Féin in 1933, and Vice President of the Gaelic League.

During the first year of World War I, Fr. O'Flanagan was appointed curate at the parish of Cliffoney in Sligo. Disciplined by his bishop for making radical speeches throughout the country, he was transferred to Crossna in County Roscommon and forbidden to deliver any political addresses without church approval. The dictums of his church failed to silence him.

His leadership was invaluable during the 1917 bye-election in North Roscommon. In addition, he voiced strong opposition to conscription, the tendency of the Congested Boards to use land as bait for silent acceptance of the status quo, and England's infernal shell game of home rule for Ireland. He spoke clearly of the solution to Ireland's problems:

"The Irish question is not a question that requires much study or much thought to solve; it is quite a simple thing to solve. They don't need to gather together a carefully selected body of their own supporters and put them marking time in Trinity College for eight or nine months in order to solve this wonderful difficult Irish question. The solution is quite simple. All they have got to do is take back their French and their Shorts and their soldiers and their police and their judges and all the paraphernalia of their law and get bag and baggage out of Ireland and leave Ireland to the people for whom Almighty God made it, and whom in His Providence He caused to be born and grow up to manhood and womanhood in it."*

The cadence of his Roscommon lilt initiated the governmental rhythms of the first Dáil. In 1921 Sinn Féin sent him to America to "explain Ireland's position to people whose good will and good opinion are most important for us at the present moment." Fr. O'Flanagan did not return to Ireland until the bitter taste of Civil War was rancid in every Irish mouth. He was appalled by the state of the country — a land filled with acrimony and injustice. Nor did he shy away from criticism of the Church's role in affairs: "I would

PHOTO COURTESY OF SISTER M. O'FLANAGAN

rather go to heaven with Denis Barry (who died of hunger strike in 1923 and was barred from the sacraments) than go to hell at the head of a procession of high ecclesiastics."** Such utterances did not endear him to the Irish hierarchy. Thereafter his fiery call to arms echoed throughout the country — not a cry for insurrection but a warning against apathy, injustice, abandonment of Republican ideals.

Though politically involved all his lifetime, he often voiced opinions about other facets of the human condition. In 1915 he delivered a speech at the Maynooth Summer School on nutrition. "Food as Fashion" sounded the alarm against processed foods, white bread, alcohol and tobacco addictions. He urged Irishmen and women to "stick to the oats," maintain the natural and healthy foods that the Lord had blessed Ireland with an ability to grow. He also scolded his audiences for the slightest thought of exporting food when a threat of famine hung over the land. In later life he invented and patented watergoggles and a bed that would maintain its equilibrium no matter what outside disturbances — clearly an idea derived from many sleepless nights aboard rocking ships to and from America.

In the late 1920s, Fr. O'Flanagan was again elected to travel to America to solicit funds for Sinn Féin. De Valera's new party, Fianna Fáil, was the recipient of most monies that had formerly been earmarked for Sinn Féin. It was time to replenish the coffer. He returned to Ireland in August 1927 and commenced work translating the Ordnance Survey letters compiled by John O'Donovan in 1838. According to P.A. Sharkey, author of *The Heart of Ireland*, this work was "on par with the work done by the Four Masters..."*** Between 1928 and 1931, O'Flanagan made several trips to the United States (perhaps receiving some small funds from a lecture circuit). In 1932 the priest-scholar began yet another sizable contribution to Irish history. Written entirely in Irish, he compiled the history of various counties, his beloved Roscommon, of course, being the first on his list of completion. A ten volume series, each focused on a different county, resides in the National Library.

In 1936 Fr. O'Flanagan bid adieu to Sinn Féin. The organisation, which after the Civil War was violently opposed to any cooperation with the Free State, banned him from participating in a Radio Éireann broadcast commemorating the opening of Dáil Éireann in 1921. Fr. O'Flanagan, perhaps tiring of the isolating position of Sinn Féin or perhaps standing on his belief that a re-enactment of his part of the original opening ceremonies was harmless, did not bow to the standing committee's resolution.

Eight days short of his sixty-sixth birthday the flaming torch that had ignited the fires of nationalism throughout Ireland was extinguished. Michael O'Flanagan was buried in Glasnevin Cemetery near the Republican plot where lie many of the men and women who fought so gallantly to give birth to a Republic. He rests with kindred spirits.

*Extracted from the suppressed speech which he delivered at Ballyjamesduff in County Cavan 26 May 1918.
**Roscommon Herald 28 February 1925.
***p. 359.

he took Pat Vaughan to a quarry where he showed the sixteen-year-old how to pull the pin on one. One of those youths would soon die in a Roscommon field, the other would survive and live to be ninety-six, passing away in one of America's great cities. Such were the fortunes and ironies of war in Ireland in 1921.

Keeping the Pressure On

On 8 December Seamus O'Meara of the Athlone Brigade journeyed to Dublin with David Daly and Dick Bertles. They had been ordered by GHQ to appear in order to assess activity in their area. Meeting Michael Collins at Fleming's Hotel at 8 p.m., the men heard their leader impress upon them the absolute necessity of keeping the pressure on the British Forces. Collins informed them that "they had almost reached terms with the British Government through the intervention of Archbishop Clune, but that Galway County Council had, by their famous resolution....spiked it for the time being. The British Government had assumed we were weakening in our fight and withdrew their offers. He appealed to us to keep up the pressure and the British Government would be forced to seek peace in a short time."[127] The men returned to Roscommon with renewed determination.

That same month, Martin Fallon, James Casey, — Shiel, Patrick Moran, and Jim Lynagh entered Tarmonbarry set on attacking the enemy — any policeman who showed his face. As two Tans exited a public house, one fell wounded while the other sought refuge in the local barracks.[128]

Attack on Elphin Dispensary

It was a charade, a hoax of dramatic proportions, scripted by Patrick Connell of Corgarve, Elphin, and Sean Connolly. Connell had observed the local police for a week and knew when to strike. Connolly wanted to stage the sham attack in order to study the reactions of the garrison — their mode of defence, what reinforcements would be sent and by what route. He devised a scenario whereby the RIC would leave their centre position in the barracks and play their role of "Besieged" on the wings of the town stage.

On the evening of 13 December, two Volunteers, each hamming his part, enacted the scene. The characters were not particularly memorable — one played a drunken enthusiast of Easter Week activities, the other man the role of an ex-British soldier. They engaged in a ruckus of such proportions that twelve of the local RIC men left their barracks and followed them down the road. Unbeknownst to the policemen, however, ten other players awaited their entrance into the ambush site.

Armed only with revolvers and several cartbox mines charged with gelignite, the Volunteers attempted to engage the constables. The scene was set properly. The props, however, malfunctioned. The bombs had been hung down a wall with a cord attached to them and were held there until the enemy approached. Then they were let drop on the unsuspecting RIC. During the final moments of the production, however, unsuspecting was the adjective more descriptive of the surprised Volunteers than of the constables, for the bombs did nothing! No noise! Only the sounds of silence! The Volunteers were left to face the rifles of the RIC with revolvers that appeared smaller and more inadequate with each passing moment. In the ensuing firefight, the Volunteers made a hasty retreat, leaving behind one wounded policeman and fizzled bombs which the RIC later confiscated for inspection. The Volunteer playwrights, however, retired to their desks to devise a new plot, while the cast of characters for this production pulled down the curtain on a disappointing performance.

Death in Tibohine

Johnnie McGowan was the Captain of the Tibohine Coy. and a well known Republican figure — well known by the local people, well known by the RIC. It was dangerous for him to sleep in his own home, so as Christmas approached, he

The Attack on Elphin Dispensary

CAST:
Sean Connolly,
Michael Dockery,
John Murray,
Thomas Connor,
Sean Owens,
Patrick Connell,
Liam O'Doherty,
John Roche,
Joe Kelly (of Rathcroghan),
James Lowe,
William Cunningham,
and P. J. O'Dowd.
Tom Brady served on outpost duty.

"It was a charade, a hoax of dramatic proportions."

decided to spend the holidays with a friend, Pat Dwyer, in Rathkeery. The evening of 15 December (Roscommon RIC reports claim 15 December as do the Military Archives, while the National Graves Association claims 23 December) was to be his last.

Pat Dwyer, his son Pat, and Johnnie were the only occupants of the house. After they had retired for the evening, a party of Black and Tans broke into the house, grabbed young Dwyer, shone a light in his face so that someone outside the cottage could see. He was not the man the Tans were looking for, but they decided to give him a thrashing just the same. They next yanked Johnnie to his feet, and when he was recognised, they shot him immediately.[129] The Tans then proceeded to wreck everything in the house that was breakable. Three days later Johnnie's body was taken from the Tibohine Church and buried in the local cemetery. Despite the presence of local policemen, three shots were fired over his grave as an audible symbol of the esteem with which he was held in the quiet corners of the hearts of his people.

And thus the dreadful year of 1920 came to a close. A battle royal had been waged in the county, a struggle that would surely continue to the death in the months to come. As the Christmas bells tolled o'er the fields, "Peace on Earth" seemed but a wistful echo — a faint whispering of a beloved sentiment that was now hurling down the tumultuous tracks of time into an uncertain future. ■

1. *An Old Soldier's Memories*, by Tommy Loughran, p. 189.
2. *An Old Soldier's Memories*, by Tommy Loughran, p. 192.
3. Jim Quigley Volunteer Statement to the Bureau of Military History 1913-1921, p. 6.
4. Seamus O'Meara Volunteer Witness Statement to the Bureau of Military History 1913-21, p. 18.
5. Frank O'Connor Volunteer Witness Statement to the Bureau of Military History 1913-21, p. 10.
6. Seamus O'Meara Volunteer Witness Statement to the Bureau of Military History 1913-21, p. 23.
7. James Feely Volunteer Witness Statement to the Bureau of Military History 1913-21, p. 7.
8. Participants in the **Ballinlough Station raid** included: Martin Ganley, Thomas Crawley, Michael Carty, Edward Shannon, Michael Freyne, Patrick Glynn, John Crean, John Flanagan, James Crawley, James Doherty, Michael and William Flanagan, John Kelly, Thomas Raftery, Tom Vaughan, John Kelly (senior), Martin Foley, Brian Connor, Pat Kelly, John Flanagan, Michael Winston, Joe Fitzgerald, John Moran, John Kenny, Joe Cullen, Michael Cullen, Michael Flynn, Michael Keane, Patrick Winston, and James Wallace. Extracted from the Gerald O'Connor Papers, private collection.
9. Andy Keavney Volunteer Witness Statement to the Bureau of Military History 1913-21, p. 7.
10. Gerald O'Connor Papers, private collection.
11. Jack Glancy Volunteer Witness Statement to the Bureau of Military History 1913-21, p. 4.
12. Participants in **raid on train at Ballymoe Station:** Edward Jackson, Joseph Mullooly, James Mullooly, Andrew Finan, Patrick Dockery, Luke Raftery, James Hester, John Finan, Michael Noone, Michael Grady, William Mannion, John Ryan, Andrew Hunt, Dominick Hunt, William Kehir, Patrick Scahill, James J. Filan, Seamus Duffy, Thomas Madden, John Mannion, James Smyth, John Powell, John Beirne, Patrick Dwyer, Thomas Muldoon, Albert Kehir, John Mahon, Edward Reaney, John Ward, Frederick Tremble, Joseph Larkin, William Keaveney, John Stanley, Edward Coen, Joseph Grady, Patrick Leonard, Michael Leonard, Michael Keane, Martin Kenny, Joseph McGovern, Peter Glancy, John Conroy, Thomas Kenny, Patrick Devaney, Frank Cunnane, James Crawley, Patrick Conry, Peter Murtagh, Patrick Mulligan, Martin Foley, Patrick Flynn, Frank Flynn, Stephen Flattery, Tom Fannon, James Doherty, Patrick Dolan, Michael Flanagan, William Flanagan, Edward Kelly, John Kelly (senior), Tom Vaughan, and Richard Beatty.
13. **Ballymoe Station raid** in September. Participants: Peter Murtagh, Edward Kelly, Stephen Flattery, Patrick Mulligan, Patrick Dolan, Thomas Vaughan, William Flanagan, Richard Beatty, Francis and Pat Flynn, Michael Egan, Patrick Conry, Thomas Fannon, and Martin Foley.
Scouts: James Crawley, James Doherty, Michael Flanagan, John Kelly, and Thomas Vaughan. Extracted from the Gerald O'Connor Papers, private collection.
14. **Knockcroghery Mail Train holdup** participants: Jim Breheny, Michael Tennant, Tommie Kelly, Owen Curley, and Michael Cunnane. Three men served as scouts: Michael Feeney, Patrick Tennant, and Peter Kelly.
15. **Ballymurray Mail Train holdup** participants: Michael J. Breheny, Michael Cunnane, Michael Feeney, Thomas Naughton, William Feeney, James Geraghty, Patrick Tennant, Dan Dempsey, and John Connor. Patrick Kelly (of Sandfield) and Edward Foley served as guards at Curry Crossing. The whole operation was commanded by Tommie Kelly and Jim Breheny.
16. Sean Leavy Volunteer Witness Statement to the Bureau of Military History 1913-21, p 9.
17. Anthony McCormack Volunteer Witness Statement, Bureau of Military History, p. 8.
18. Participants: **Loughglynn Company:** Martin Ganley, Gerald O'Connor, Patrick Glynn, Michael Carty, Ned Shannon, Tom Crawley, Robert King, Pat Crawley, John Creighton, Dominick Noone, Andy Keavaney, John Crean, Michael Freyne, Patrick Beirne, John Ganley, and Robert Doherty **Ballinlough Company:** Michael Kenny, Michael Hevican, Peter Quinn, James McNulty, Charles Carroll, Michael Glavey, Thomas Coffey, Michael Crawley, Edward Dillon, Michael Hevican, Michael Scally, John Coffey.
19. Jim Quigley Volunteer Witness Statement, Bureau of Military History, p. 9.
20. Jim Quigley Volunteer Witness Statement, Bureau of Military History, p. 9.
21. Jim Quigley Volunteer Witness Statement, Bureau of Military History, p. 9.
22. Participants amassed for the **Kilmurray attack:** Martin Ganley, Pat Glynn, Mick Carty, Ned Shannon, Robert King, John Creighton, Andy Keavney, John Crean, Michael Freyne, Ned Campion, Edward Kelly, James Durr, Stephen Flattery, Peter Murtagh, Tom Satchwell, Frank and Pat Dolan, Patrick Mulligan, Pat Forde, Hubert Beatty (Betagh), Albert Durr, Michael Casserly, William Delaney, Owen Fox, Owen and John Rabbit, Joe Conway, Tom Kelly, John Hanley, James Doherty, and (another) John Hanley, Stephen McDermott, Sean Bergin, William Flanagan, Dick Beatty, Pat and Francis Flynn, Michael Egan, Michael Cullinan, Thomas McCormack, Andrew and Patrick Mulrooney, Mattie Morahan, Maurice Cunniffe, and Andrew Byron. Extracted from the Gerald O'Connor Papers, private collection. Participants also included members of the Curraghboy Coy. from

South Roscommon as stated in the *Curraghboy Coy. Summary of Pre-Truce Activities* signed by Tom Kelly. Members included: Edward Egan, Dick Mee, William Murray, Tom Bergin, John Waldron, Patrick Gallagher, Patrick Reddington, and George Fitzgerald. As stated in the *Pre-Truce Activities of Knockcroghery Coy.*, the entire company had been assembled for the attack. The St. John's Coy. members who turned out for the ambush included: Capt. Hubert Murphy, John Kilcline, Michael Murphy, John Mullaly, William Murphy, Pat Fallon, Hubert Watson, Edward Gilligan, Pat Grady, Dominick Donnelly, Thomas Donnelly, Michael Donnelly, Malachy Kilroy, Dan Kerrigan, John F. Egan, James Kelly, Frank McGuire, Pat Mullaly.

23. p. 295.
24. RIC Monthly Report written by the Inspector General to Dublin Castle, July 1920.
25. Mulcahy Papers A/40, p. 9.
26. Mulcahy Papers A/38, p. 12.
27. Mulcahy Papers A/38, p. 12.
28. Mulcahy Papers A/38, p. 18.
29. Tommy Loughran in his book *An Old Soldier's Memories* claims that Willie Duffy was also with the raiding party, p. 202.
30. Stephen Scally Volunteer Witness Statement to the Bureau of Military History 1913-21, made in 1955.
31. *An Old Soldier's Memories,* by Tommy Loughran, p. 203.
32. *An Old Soldier's Memories,* by Tommy Loughran, p. 204.
33. Luke Duffy interview, Ernie O'Malley Papers, UCD Archives No. 137.
34. Frank Simons Volunteer Witness Statement to the Bureau of Military History 1913-21, p. 8.
35. Luke Duffy Volunteer Witness Statement to the Bureau of Military History 1913-21, pp. 3-5.
36. Frank Simons Volunteer Witness Statement to the Bureau of Military History 1913-21, p. 8.
37. According to the Papers of Gerald O'Connor and Jim Quigley (O/C of the 2nd Battalion), the following men participated in the **attempted raid on the Castlerea Station:**
    4th Battalion: Michael Tennant and John Breheny of Sandfield
    3rd Battalion: Frank Simons, Gerald Davis, and Pat Conboy
    2nd Battalion: Jim Quigley
    1st Battalion: Loughglynn Coy. Martin Ganley, Pat Glynn, Tom Crawley, Gerald O'Connor; Lisliddy Coy. Dan O'Rourke, William Flanagan, Pat Flynn, Patrick Conry, Michael Egan, Thomas Fannon; Moor Coy. Sean Costello; Cloonboniffe Coy. John Flanagan, James Crawley, James Doherty, Michael Flanagan, John Kelly, Tom Raftery, Tom Vaughan, John Kelly (senior), Martin Foley, Brian Connor, Pat Kelly of Cloonelt, and another John Flanagan; Ballinlough Coy. John Moran, Joe Fitzgerald, Joe Kenny, Patrick and Michael Winston, Patrick and Thomas Lyons, John Kelly, James Wallace, Michael Keane, Gerald Fitzgerald, Peter Boyle, Peter Quinn, Michael Glavey, Michael Kenny, Michael John and Michael Thomas Hevican, Tom Hanlon, James McNulty, Joseph and Michael Cullen, Charles Carroll, Michael Scally; Ballinagare Coy. Michael Cullinan, Thomas McCormack, Andrew and Patrick Mulrooney, Mattie Moran, and Andrew Byron.
38. **Attempted ambush at Coshlieve** participants: John Moran, Joe Kenny, Joe Fitzgerald, Michael Winston, Thomas Lyons, Peter Boyle, Joseph Cullen, Patrick Lyons, James Wallace, Patrick Winston, Michael Kelly, Michael Keane, Michael Flynn, Charles Carroll, Michael Scally, James Crawley, James Doherty, Michael Flanagan, John Kelly, Thomas Raftery, Tom Vaughan, Martin Foley, Michael Mannion, Peter Coyne, John O'Brien, Michael Coyne, Martin Egan, John Grady, Terence Moran, Patrick Connolly, Thomas Page, Martin Flynn, Patrick Connor, Patrick Gunning, John White, Patrick Hester, Tom Fahy, and Michael Hester.
39. Members of Tang (County Westmeath) Company (Pat MacDermott, Peter Bannon, Anthony McCormack), and all of Faheran Coy. were involved. Also present: David Daly, Frank O'Connor, George Manning, Tom Claffey.
40. Con Costello Volunteer Witness Statement to the Bureau of Military History 1913-21, p. 11.
41. Seamus O'Meara Volunteer Witness Statement to the Bureau of Military History 1913-21, p. 26. Also Michael McCormack Volunteer Witness Statement to the Bureau of Military History 1913-21, p. 15.

42. Seamus O'Meara Volunteer Witness Statement to the Bureau of Military History 1913-21, p. 27.
43. Con Costello Volunteer Witness Statement to the Bureau of Military History 1913-21, p. 12.
44. Seamus O'Meara Volunteer Witness Statement to the Bureau of Military History 1913-21, p. 28.
45. Members of the **assault party on Sergeant Craddock** were: Seamus O'Meara, Jim Tormey, George Manning, Brian Mulvihill, and Con Costello. Derived from Seamus O'Meara Volunteer Witness Statement to the Bureau of Military History 1913-21, p. 29.
46. Con Costello Volunteer Witness Statement to the Bureau of Military History 1913-21, p. 12.
47. Participants in the **Knockcroghery Railway Station** attack were derived from the Summary of Activities by the Knockcroghery Company: Michael J. Breheny (in command), Michael Cunnane, Owen Curley, Michael Tennant, Michael Breheny of Sandfield, Patrick Tennant, and John Kelly. The Volunteer Witness Statement of Tom Kelly states that the attack was not sanctioned by the Battalion or Brigade officers.
48. Matt Davis Volunteer Witness Statement to the Bureau of Military History 1913-21, p. 7.
49. Tom Kelly Volunteer Witness Statement to the Bureau of Military History 1913-21, p. 9.
50. *Victory and Woe,* by Mossie Harnett, p. 168.
51. Jim Hunt Volunteer Witness Statement to the Bureau of Military History 1913-21, p. 8.
52. *For Ireland and Freedom,* by Micheál O'Callaghan, p. 41.
53. Jim Hunt interview, UCD Archives, Ernie O'Malley Papers, No. 133.
54. Seamus O'Meara Volunteer Witness Statement to the Bureau of Military History 1913-21, p. 31.
55. Frank O'Connor Volunteer Witness Statement to the Bureau of Military History 1913-21, p. 17.
56. Frank O'Connor Volunteer Witness Statement to the Bureau of Military History 1913-21, p. 17.
57. Frank O'Connor Volunteer Witness Statement to the Bureau of Military History 1913-21, p. 18.
58. Patrick Kenny, Drum Coy., interview by author, 24 June 2002.
59. Although this story was related to the author eighty-two years after the event supposedly took place, there is no mention of this attempted attack in the Volunteer Witness Statement of Seamus O'Meara.
60. Seamus O'Meara Volunteer Witness Statement to the Bureau of Military History 1913-21, p. 35.
61. Seamus O'Meara, Volunteer Witness Statement to the Bureau of Military History 1913-21, p. 40.
62. Michael McCormack Volunteer Witness Statement to the Bureau of Military History 1913-21, p. 18.
63. *An Old Soldier's Memories,* by Tommy Loughran, p. 200.
64. **Burning of Ballinlough Barracks.** Extracted from the Gerald O'Connor Papers, private collection. Participants: Tom Crawley, John Moran, Michael Winston, Thomas Lyons, John Kelly, Joseph Fitzgerald, Joseph Kenny, Thomas Hanlon, James Wallace, Gerald Fitzgerald, Joseph Cullen, Michael Cullen, John J. Kelly, Michael Flynn, Michael Waldron, Patrick Winston, Michael Kelly, Edward Duignan, Peter Boyle, Patrick Lyons, Andrew Judge, Michael and John Gaherty, Michael Kenny, Michael Thomas Hevican, Peter Quinn, James McNulty, Charles Carroll, Edward Dillon, Michael John Hevican, Michael Scally, Patrick Crawley, and John Coffey.
65. Pat Mullooly Papers, private collection.
66. Sean Leavy Volunteer Witness Statement to the Bureau of Military History 1913-21, p. 11.
67. Martin Fallon interview, Ernie O'Malley Papers, No. 131.
68. Tom Crawley Volunteer Witness Statement to the Bureau of Military History 1913-21, p. 9.
69. Jim Fehilly interview, Ernie O'Malley Papers, UCD Archives. No. 131.
70. Pat Mullooly Papers, private collection.
71. **Participants in the Attack on Frenchpark Barracks: 2nd Battalion:** Andrew Finan, Patrick Dockery, Luke Raftery, James Hester, John Finan, William Mannion, John Connolly, Michael Noone, Michael Grady, John Ryan, Andrew and Dominick Hunt, William Kehir, John Brennan, Andrew Smyth, Patrick Scahill, James Filan, Tom Madden, John Mannion, James Smyth, John Powell, John Beirne, John Ganley, John Rogers, Patrick

Devaney, Willie Scally, Jack and Malachy Finnegan, Patrick Moffatt, Patrick Owens, Martin Quinn, Tom Leonard, Frank Cunnane, and Jim Quigley (organisational work). Michael Egan and Alec Kenny transported Volunteers to the site.

First Battalion: Dan O'Rourke, William Flanagan, Dick Beatty, Patrick Flynn, Francis Flynn, Owen Boland, Patrick Conry, Edward Browne, Patrick Forde, Ned Campion, Joe Satchwell, Joseph Conway, Frank Dolan, Patrick Mulligan, James Doherty, John Hanley, John Hanily (Ballindrimley, Castlerea), Thomas Kelly, Patrick Kerrane, John Kerrane, Tom Satchwell, Michael Casserly, Owen Fox, Michael Cryan, Owen Rabbit, John Rabbit, Stephen Flattery, Hubert Beatty, Peter Murtagh, Edward Kelly, James P. Durr, John Shannon, Albert Durr, Thomas Waldron, William Delaney, John Flynn, Stephen McDermott, Sean Bergin, Martin Ganley, Gerald O'Connor, Tom Crawley, Ned Shannon, Mick Carty, Toby Scally, Michael Freyne, Patrick Beirne, John Crean, Michael Cullinan, Thomas McCormack, Andrew and Patrick and Michael Mulrooney, Maurice and Bernard Cunniffe, Mattie Moran (Morahan), Patrick and Andrew Byron, Edward Dockrey, Michael and Edward Kenny, James and John Joe Martin, James Glynn, Michael J. and James A. Kelly, Patrick Doyle, John and James and Peter Hanley, Patrick Cassidy, Michael J. Kenny, John Creighton, and Robert King.

Blocked roads and scouted: James Crawley, James Doherty, Michael and William and John "Sonny" Flanagan, John Kelly (senior), Thomas Raftery, John and Pat Kelly of Cloonboniffe Coy., another John Kelly of Cloonboniffe Coy., Thomas Vaughan, Brian Connor, Patrick Dolan, and Martin Foley.

72. Gerald O'Connor Papers, private collection.
73. James Feely Volunteer Witness Statement to the Bureau of Military History 1913-21, p. 9.
74. **Fourmilehouse Ambush:** Most, but not all, of the Kilgefin Company participated: Bernard Cassidy, Michael and Peter Collins, Peter Connolly, Tom and Henry Compton, James Cooney, John and Pat Corcoran, Charlie Crowley, Tom Cummins, Dominick Dempsey, Frank Donlon, James Dowling, Luke Duffy, Frank Egan, Pat and Michael Fitzpatrick, Jim and Joe and Michael Fallon, Jim Fox, John Gibbons, Michael Gibbons, Joseph Gibbons, Pat Gibbons, Willie and Paddy Hanly, Pat Hughes, Dick Hughes, Denis and Patrick Kelly, John McDermott, Jimmy McDermott, Michael McDermott, T. J. McDermott, Michael Madden, Dan Madden, Pat Madden, Tom Madden, Michael Martin, Peter Monaghan, Bill Mulligan, Martin Quinn, Michael Quinn, Dick Simons, Frank Simons, Michael Simons, Jim Tiernan, Paddy Tiernan, Pat Tiernan of Gortyleane, John Tonry, Frank Vesey, Larry Vesey, Edward Watson. Sean Bergin, John Brennan, and Liam O'Doherty were also present.
75. Luke Duffy interview, Ernie O'Malley Papers, UCD Archives P17b/No. 137.
76. *The Strokestown Democrat*, 16 October 1920, Column 1.
77. *Police Casualties in Ireland 1919-1922*, by Richard Abbott, p. 133.
78. Luke Duffy interview, Ernie O'Malley Papers, UCD Archives P17b/No. 137.
79. **Fourmilehouse** scouts and outposts compiled from the Gerald O'Connor Papers and the Pat Brennan Papers include: Jim Quigley, Michael O'Grady, Edward Naughton, Thomas Feeney, William Martin, James Curran, Edward Hegarty, Michael McDermott, Patrick Reynolds, Michael Moran, and Patrick Cummins. Thomas Smyth from the Carniska Coy. was in charge of a section blocking roads. Michael Gill and John Healy were also there.
80. Luke Duffy interview, Ernie O'Malley Papers, UCD Archives, No. 137.
81. Luke Duffy, Statement to the Bureau of Military History 1913-21, p. 6.
82. Martin Fallon interview, Ernie O'Malley Papers, UCD Archives, P17b/No. 131, p. 34.
83. *Green Against Green*, by Michael Hopkinson, p. 10.
84. Frank Simons, Adjutant of the 3rd Battalion South Roscommon, interview Ernie O'Malley Papers, UCD Archives, No. 137.
85. "History of Castlerea Battalion" by Gerald O'Connor, private collection.
86. Matt Davis Volunteer Witness Statement to the Bureau of Military History 1913-1921, p. 3.
87. Mulcahy Papers A13-23, No. 54.
88. Mulcahy Papers A13-23, No. 54.
89. Mulcahy Papers A/1-A/17, p. 7.
90. Mulcahy Papers A/1-A/17.
91. Mulcahy Papers A/1-A/17.
92. Mulcahy Papers A/1-A/17.
93. Martin Fallon interview, Ernie O'Malley Papers, P17b/No. 131.
94. Frank Simons Volunteer Witness Statement to the Bureau of Military History 1913-21, p. 36.
95. *An Old Soldier's Memories*, by Tommy Loughran, p. 214.
96. *A Parish of Kilglass, Slatta, and Ruskey*, by Liam Coyle, p. 138.
97. *Tarmon Centennial Magazine*, "Tarmon and the War for Independence" by Sister Elizabeth and Maura Flynn, p. 21.
98. *Tarmon Centennial Magazine*, "Tarmon and the War for Independence" by Sister Elizabeth and Maura Flynn, p. 21.
99. Liam O'Doherty interview, Ernie O'Malley Papers, No. 131, and Frank Simons Volunteer Witness Statement to the Bureau of Military History 1913-21, p. 16.
100. **Castlenode Confrontation** North Roscommon participants: Michael Greene, George Tanner, Sean Birmingham, William Collins, Martin Shiel, Peter Shiel, James Shiel, Michael Gill, James Hanley, and Michael Lannon. Eugene Melvin served as outpost.
101. Luke Duffy Volunteer Witness Statement to the Bureau of Military History 1913-21, p. 7.
102. Matt Davis Volunteer Witness Statement to the Bureau of Military History 1913-21, p. 8.
103. Pat Vaughan, brother of John Vaughan of Cloonsuck. Interview by author, 4 June 1996, Boston, Mass.
104. *For Ireland and Freedom*, by Micheál O'Callaghan, p. 76.
105. Pat Vaughan, brother of John Vaughan of Cloonsuck. Interview by author, 8 January 1996, Boston, Mass.
106. Tom Brady Volunteer Witness Statement to the Bureau of Military History 1913-21, p. 7.
107. James Haran Volunteer Witness Statement to the Bureau of Military History 1913-21, p. 6.
108. *An Old Soldier's Memories*, by Tommy Loughran, p. 258.
109. Michael Kilroe, Curragh, Castlecoote, dispatch rider. Interview by author 12 October 1998.
110. *Summary of Pre-Truce Activites of St. John's Company*, p. 9.
111. Matt Davis Volunteer Witness Statement to the Bureau of Military History 1913-21, p. 8.
112. Martin Fallon Volunteer Witness Statement to the Bureau of Military History 1913-21, p.6.
113. *Summary of Activities of Knockcroghery Company 1917-1923*, p. 21.
114. *Victory and Woe*, by Mossie Harnett, p. 33.
115. *Victory and Woe*, by Mossie Harnett, p. 71.
116. *Victory and Woe*, by Mossie Harnett, p. 72.
117. Jim Quigley Volunteer Witness Statement to the Bureau of Military History 1913-21, p. 6-7.
118. "Activities of Curraghboy Company January 1922 to Ceasefire," penned by George Fitzgerald. Men included: Patrick Reddington, John Waldron, Patrick Gallagher, John Monaghan, James Whelan, Patrick Kenny, and George Fitzgerald.
119. *From Public Defiance to Guerilla Warfare*, by Joost Augusteijn, p. 178.
120. Mulcahy Papers A/1-A/17.
121. Martin Fallon Volunteer Witness Statement to the Bureau of Military History 1913-21, p. 22.
122. Tommy Lavin Volunteer Witness Statement to the Bureau of Military History 1913-21, p. 12.
123. Pat Brennan Papers, private collection.
124. Jim Dorr Volunteer Witness Statement to the Bureau of Military History 1913-21, p. 4.
125. Martin Fahy Volunteer Witness Statement to the Bureau of Military History 1913-21, p. 3.
126. Tom Kelly Volunteer Witness Statement to the Bureau of Military History 1913-21, p. 9-10.
127. Seamus O'Meara Volunteer Witness Statement to the Bureau of Military History 1913-21, p. 41.
128. Martin Fallon Volunteer Witness Statement to the Bureau of Military History 1913-21, p. 6.
129. Pat Mullooly Papers, private collection.

THE FIGHTING INTENSIFIES

Formation of the Active Service Units
in the 1st and 2nd Battalion South Areas

By the beginning of 1921, the members of His Majesty's forces began to realise that Ireland was a tar baby — you could punch, you could scream, and you could kick, but the thing wouldn't release you. You merely got more mired in the goo.

As evidence of this frustration, Gerald O'Connor, the Battalion O/C for the Castlerea area, wrote a memo to GHQ in January claiming that looting shops was a common diversion for the Black and Tans and sometimes for the RIC. The next month he embellished his original statement by pointing out that the "general

The Castlerea Volunteers

PHOTO COURTESY OF SEAN BROWN
PHOTO RESTORATION BY LEW THORNE

tone and attitude of the RIC is extremely hostile towards the IRA. There is still much looting indulged in and the lack of discipline was noticeable."[1] The agitation of men cooped up in an island barracks awash in a sea of hostile countryside was equal to the aggravation of the Volunteers who were all too frequently becoming their prey. The infamous Murder Gang of Castlerea (led by Inspector King) was on the move, becoming more audacious and more persistent in its determination to ferret out these Irish "Shinners" (members of Sinn Féin). In response to this enemy activity, officers in the Castlerea area decided to form a Flying Column, a mobile group of men who were disciplined, daring, and committed.

The Active Service Unit as of the Truce included: Leaders: Sean Bergin (who was killed in April 1921), Gerald O'Connor, and Tom Crawley. Members: Martin Foley, John White, Martin Ganley, Ned Campion, John Crean, Michael Cullinan, Tom McCormack, Michael Hester, Joe Conway, Albert Durr, Toby Scally, Pete Shannon, Jack Kelly, Brian Connor, James Crawley, Jack Flanagan, James Doherty, Joe Satchwell, Michael Flanagan, Pat Kerrane, Paddy Mulligan, Pat Dolan, Francis

The World According to Lloyd George	The Volunteer Version
Brigade Officers:	
Commandant: Dan O'Rourke	True
Vice Commandant: Jack Brennan	True
Quartermaster: Matt Davis	True
Chief of the Police: Henry Joe Finlay	True, and Ned Hegarty
Director of Transport: George Geraghty	
Battalion Officers:	
Castlerea Battalion Commandant: Pat Fannon	Pat Glynn
Vice Commandant: M. Flanagan	Dick Beattie
Adjutant: John Costello	Paddy Flynn
Quartermaster: Pat Mahon	Stephen McDermott, John Flanagan, and John White
Company Captains:	
Lisliddy: James Waldron	Francis Flynn
Ballinagare: James Martin	Michael Cullinan
Loughglynn: Gerald O'Connor	Martin Ganley
Moor: Patrick Dolan	Ned Campion
Ballinlough: Bernard Lavin	Jack Moran, and Michael Winston
Trien: John Dolan	Michael Hester, and John White
Cloonboniffe: Andrew Gallagher	John and Tom Vaughan, and Martin Foley
Cloonfad	Tom Regan
Frenchpark: Michael McDermott	Michael Higgins, and Sean O'Gara

Enemy Blacklist
Whatever money the British paid for this kind of "intelligence" was too much!

Dolan, John Shannon, Tom Satchwell, Owen Fox, Maurice Cunniffe, Peter Murtagh, Tom Kelly, and the three Mulrooney brothers from Ballinagare (Michael, Patrick, Andrew).[2]

A Flying Column was also formed in the 2nd Battalion area and comprised twenty-four men under the command of Seamus McGovern.[3]

The Enemy Blacklist
Volunteer intelligence gathering was improving. Procured by the 1st Battalion South Intelligence Officer, this Crown Forces' enemy blacklist (see box at left) is a compilation of misinterpretation, miscalculation, mistakes, and miss-the-mark mumbo-jumbo. The listing is a copy of the British version of the command structure of the 1st Battalion South area.[4] A comparison of their version and the actual one is revealing.

Large-Scale Arrests in South Roscommon
Officers of Curraghboy Coy. in South Roscommon had received information regarding a man who might be relaying Volunteer information to the British authorities. The whole Company met and decided to stop the rattling tongue. Seventeen members arrested the suspected spy and his family. He and his dear ones were guarded as they were conveyed from place to place, both inside and outside the Company area, awaiting a decision about his case. The man was found guilty by court-martial and sentenced to be shot. Both Company and Battalion staff were present at the execution. Word of this killing leaked out into the community, and it wasn't long before the lorries filled with British soldiers descended on the area. Ten members of the Company[5] were arrested that 5th day of January. Most of the remainder of the Company remained free for an additional two months before they too were seized. After March the Curraghboy Company, for all intents and purposes, ceased to exist.

Multiple Assaults
As part of the Volunteers' plan for stoking the coals under the feet of British Forces, the first operation of the Flying Column in the 3rd Battalion North area was a two-prong assault. Two columns of men were dispatched in different directions on the night of 5 January. Martin Fallon and Brian Nangle led fifteen men (plus one man stationed as outpost) in an attack on the Tarmonbarry Barracks. The garrison, having been strengthened by the presence of Black and Tans, was well protected by sandbags, barbed wire, steel shutters, and a number of Lewis guns available in their armament. The Volunteers had no intention of capturing the barracks; they meant only to harass the occupiers.[6] After an hour of gunfire exchange, the Volunteers withdrew and reassembled their forces. They were certain reinforcements would come from Strokestown, so they positioned themselves along the roadside in order to ambush the Crown Forces and waited for some hours. No troops ventured out! The Volunteers[7] withdrew with no injuries.

The other portion of the Flying Column, twenty-eight Volunteers[8] (forty-two, if the figure includes claims made in the Volunteers' pension statement records) entered Strokestown with full intent to cause havoc. Their target was a particular lorry that normally went out of barracks and returned at a usual time. As the Column approached the town, the men were posted in various places. Liam O'Doherty lined up twenty-nine men (armed with rifles and shotguns) under his personal command across Church Street facing the gate to the Pakenham-Mahon mansion. Men with pistols were divided into two patrols to cover Bridge Street and Elphin Street. They were to search the public houses and shoot every Black and Tan they could find. As the patrols were moving down the side streets, an unexpected lorry loaded with Guinness, driven by Jim Gurn, rolled into the town square. O'Doherty gave the order to fire. The driver, who had served in the United States Army during World War I, reacted like a soldier. He jumped from the truck and flattened himself on the street while the lorry loaded with the precious barrels of porter became riddled with bullet holes and crashed into a store front.[9]

The gunfire alerted the British Forces, and Sergeant McArdle of the RIC emerged from the back door of Caslin's public house and ran towards the barracks. He never made it inside. Two other policemen who were trailing behind must have had guardian angels hovering over them because the gun that hit McArdle was aimed at them but jammed.[10]

Another version of these events has been recorded by various Volunteers. It seems that Sergeant Hopkins of the RIC, who was stationed in Strokestown, was a wanted man — wanted not by "the authorities" but by the IRA. He was notorious for going beyond the understood boundaries of ill treatment to prisoners. "He was wont to beat and kick them unmercifully,"[11] and there were men walking around Strokestown decades later who bore of the marks of his ill temper. He was a man about forty years of age, six feet tall, steel-grey hair and a moustache. During this operation conducted by O'Doherty, a party of men from North Roscommon entered Strokestown looking to put an end to his misbehaviour. None of those Volunteers on that mission knew the man personally. They had only a description to go by in their detective work.

In the pub next to the barracks, one of the Volunteers spotted a Sergeant matching the general description. He checked with his officers, and it was decided to attack the man as he exited the public house before he got to the barracks door. Unbeknownst to the Volunteers,[12] however, were the real whereabouts of Hopkins, for the man they had mistakenly shot was another Sergeant (McArdle), a policeman only recently transferred to Strokestown, against whom they had no grudge. The real Hopkins was never harmed and served in the force until the RIC was disbanded.

That same evening eighteen Volunteers[13] entered the town of Elphin intent on making the lives of British agents very difficult. Three members of the RIC patrol exited the barracks and walked down unknowingly to the proposed ambush site. A fourth man was just reaching the fringe area of the attack while four more members just cleared the barracks door when the shooting started. Armed with revolvers and shotguns, the IRA members succeeded in injuring two constables (Constable Sharpe seriously) but suffered no harm to their own.

To counter all this IRA activity, scores of British military fanned out into the area looting and burning homes of known Sinn Féin supporters. Three Volunteers were severely thrashed: Pat Connell of Elphin, Tom Gormley of Creeve, and Jack Beirne of Cloonroughan. A number of Volunteers were arrested, including the Elphin Battalion Adjutant Pat Beirne of Clooncunny. (Pat was later to be an important cog in the wheel of progress involving the daring escape through the Brady Tunnel at the Curragh.) One dwelling was burned down in Creeve Coy. area.

Observations for February 1921 written by a North Roscommon IRA soldier out in the field*	
Weather	Observations
4th Day very wet and cloudy. Brightening towards evening	Observed snow-drops in full bloom. Noticed catkins on the willow, and the silver beam commencing to bud.
7th Very cold and frosty	The elm buds have burst forth and are now coming into flower.
11th Dry, bracing day, frost during the night	The hyacinths are in bloom. The dead leaves are crisp beneath our feet and the sycamore laden with snow presents a ghostly appearance.
20th Damp and heavy, very dull during the day	
Pat Brennan Papers, private collection.	

Murder at the Door

Further westward in the county on 6 January, Pat Durr, William Cunnane, and Tom Leonard were resting in Leonard's house at Kennyborough, Ballintubber. Noise from outside alerted the inhabitants. Mrs. Leonard opened the door to find

Pat Madden, O/C 3rd Battalion South
Roscommon.

masked men surrounding her home. They barged through, grabbing the three Volunteers and shoved them into the kitchen. When he learned that he was to be arrested, Cunnane begged to retrieve his shoes from another room. Peering outside and finding no policemen standing guard (they had all entered the kitchen), Cunnane crawled out an open window and made a dash for darkness. Amidst the ensuing commotion, Tom Leonard took the opportunity to dive out another window and ran. The Crown Forces were livid with rage that two of their three prisoners had managed to escape. They dragged Pat Durr outside and, making certain that he would not join his comrades in the shadows, shot him three times. Durr was buried two days later in Ballintubber Cemetery.

The 6th of January was eventful not only for Volunteers within the county but also outside its borders — this time in Longford. Members of the 3rd Battalion South had crossed the Shannon in two boats about a mile south of Lanesboro. They had proceeded down the road to the village, where they waited until 1 a.m. for RIC patrols to appear. None did. The weather was abominable — cold, wet, blustery. The policemen had enough good sense to stay in out of the rain. The Volunteers were reduced to taking shelter in a hay shed until near dawn when they made their way back to the shoreline, boarded the two boats, and re-crossed the river. The wind and waves nearly swallowed them up. When they arrived on the Roscommon side, they found no comrades waiting for them. According to Luke Duffy, Vice O/C of the 3rd Battalion, their fellow Volunteers "had given up hope and having decided that we were all drowned returned to their homes."[14]

The following night, 7 January (Jack Glancy claims the 5th), Roscommon and Longford Volunteers were engaged in yet another joint venture. They had targeted the Ruskey Barracks which was an important post "as it safeguarded the crossing of the Shannon at that point which was the only one between Carrick-on-Shannon and Tarmonbarry."[15] The barracks was on the Roscommon side of the river, but Longford men were prepared to attack from across the bridge. Jim Dorr and Jack Glancy led a group of 12-15 Roscommon men (including Mick McLoughlin). They took up ambush positions and sent Carroll to scout the town (partly because Carroll had served in the British Army and was on friendly terms with the police). Carroll was captured, nonetheless, by the RIC and whisked off to their barracks. A patrol of police exited the barracks and unwittingly moved along towards the position of the Volunteers. After a quick council, the Volunteers decided not to attack the patrol, for they feared for Carroll's life if they did.[16] They withdrew without incident.

Stymied Actions

In the Castlerea area, multiple jabs had been thrust at the face of the enemy, but to no avail. As many as fifty-four men at various times had waited silently for the chance to make contact, but no opportunity presented itself. An anticipated ambush at Frenchpark on 5 January, which was a joint operation between men from the 1st Battalion South along with several from the 3rd Battalion North area, never materialised.[17]

In January an attempt was made to attack military lorries containing eighteen men in Knockcroghery. Several Battalion officers, members of the Knockcroghery

Company[18] and several from Curraghboy were on hand for the proposed event. Plans had been devised to attack the lorries which had pulled up outside the village at the priest's gate. As soon as night fell, however, the enemy moved the lorries into the lawn area close to the priest's house. Officers at the scene considered it inadvisable to attack because the priest's residence would be caught in the line of fire. As the enemy was driving away, the accidental discharge of a faulty firearm sounded the beginning of a short exchange of bullets before the lorries sped to safety.

In February "a man named McMahon came down from GHQ with information that a party of troops escorting arms was travelling by train from Dublin to the West and were to be attacked at Donamon Station."[19] The British troops would be seated in different compartments of the train. The Volunteer leaders hashed out a plan to "unhook the front carriages and let them off with the engine and then deal with the party remaining in the rear portion of the train."[20] Fifty to sixty men were assembled for action, but for some unknown reason, the assault did not take place. Volunteers disbanded, and disappointment prevailed. Clearly, change was demanded.

Luke Duffy, Vice O/C 3rd Battalion South Roscommon.

PHOTO COURTESY OF EAMONN DUFFY

Near Disaster in Loughglynn
In early 1921 GHQ decided to reorganise the Brigade staffing of South Roscommon. In addition to failed attempts at ambush, the Castlerea area had lost many men who had met their death in their own homes or the cottages of neighbours. The British military could never have found out about all those men or those out-of-the-way residences in which they took shelter without the aid of spies. Some informers had already been dealt with, but others were yet to be unveiled.

During the week of January 17th, Pat Madden, O/C of the 3rd Battalion, Luke Duffy, the Vice O/C, and Frank Simons, the Adjutant, had all travelled from the Ballagh area near Roscommon town to Loughglynn to consult with the Battalion staff there. A meeting was held in Cloonboniffe School on 21 January that was attended by fifty or so Volunteers. Their goal: reshuffling the Companies and building morale. The 3rd Battalion leaders had planned to remain in the area about ten days to help with organisational work.

Five days later a half dozen Volunteers gathered together in Martin Ganley's home in Cloonmaul. At daybreak, without warning, the place was engulfed and swarming with enemy soldiers who obviously had been tipped off about the Brigade meeting. The six men inside — Dan O'Rourke, Pat Madden, Luke Duffy, Martin Ganley, Patrick Beirne, and Michael Freyne — fled amid a hail of bullets. All escaped unscathed. Duffy and Madden were the last two out of the house, and when they found freedom, they fled in the opposite direction of the other Volunteers. Scrambling eastward for about two hundred yards, they nearly walked right into a police patrol. They dived into a ditch and made their way down to the next field (about eighty yards away). When they emerged, they were fired upon by the soldiers who were pursuing them. This hunt continued for about a mile and a half. Although Madden and Duffy were armed with revolvers, neither of them fired a shot in return. Realising the futility of openfield evasion, the two ducked into an old man's cottage and instructed him to tell the British soldiers trailing them that they had passed by a few minutes before. When the soldiers came knocking, the elderly man was as good as his word. He pointed the British in the wrong direction. After the soldiers had disappeared from sight, Madden and Duffy slipped out of the cottage and retraced their steps, only to find another party of soldiers fanning out into the countryside searching for them. They dove into a ditch and remained motionless for several hours. By 2 p.m., all seemed quiet enough. The two men darted into the nearest house. The people in that home were so poor that, although their sympathies were clearly with the famished men, they had nothing to feed them. Madden and Duffy then proceeded to another house where the residents welcomed them with warm hospitality, food, and, most happily of all, a CLEAN PAIR OF SOCKS!

After refreshing themselves, they returned to Ganley's house, only to find the place turned topsy-turvy. The Tans had torched the house. Even the cocks of hay in the haggard had been tossed. The Tans had been so infuriated by their inability to catch any of the escaping Volunteers that they stole all the bicycles and overcoats left behind by the men. Clearly it was time to return to the relative safety of Ballagh.

Madden and Duffy raided the post office that evening, taking with them three cycles (one of which they soon abandoned). They reached Ballinaheglish on Sunday morning and slipped into the house of Mrs. O'Hara. By then Sean Bergin had joined them. The lady of the house was dressed to go to Mass; however, upon seeing the bedraggled men, Mrs. O'Hara immediately took off her coat and hat and cooked up a warm breakfast. The men then fell into bed, where they slept through the entire Sabbath.[21]

This adventure was in many ways typical of the suffering and sacrifices of the age. At times the rise or fall of the nation depended on the availability of a home-cooked meal, and a lowly pair of SOCKS to warm the feet of the men who tramped o'er the fields of Ireland and won her freedom.

Roundup in Drumlion

On the night of 1 February, three lorries of RIC raided the area around Drumlion, arresting Company officers and seizing weapons. Three D13 shotguns, a number of cartridges, and one rifle were impounded. Five days later the home of the Brigade Adjutant was raided, whereupon a number of business papers were confiscated. Nothing of an incriminating nature, however, was found.

An Unlikely Comrade

Sergeant John Duffy was an unlikely ally found in an unlikely place during the war. Stationed in Athlone, Kiltoom, and Roscommon town as a constable in the Royal Irish Constabulary, this man proved to be a bonanza of espionage information. He was first placed in Athlone, where, after countless political discussions with the local physician, Dr. McDonnell, Duffy confessed that his sympathies were with the national movement and perhaps he should resign. The good doctor cautioned against such a move: "You would be only one man with us, but you would be worth a hundred men by remaining in the Force."[22] In 1917, accompanied by Dr. McDonnell, Duffy travelled to Dublin to meet Michael Collins. At that meeting Collins asked him if he could obtain the names from police records of prominent IRA men throughout the country who had come to the attention of Dublin Castle. He also asked Duffy if he could secure a key to the police cipher code. Duffy returned to Athlone where he worked officially with Dr. McDonnell, Father Michael O'Flanagan, and Willie Kilmartin, a solicitor's clerk in Roscommon town. Volunteer Thomas Farrell in Roscommon town served as an alternate contact, while oftentimes Sean Hurley in Athlone received direct messages from Sergeant Duffy.

Duffy warned local Volunteers of upcoming raids for rifles concealed in the cave at Coosan, and the reprisal raids by the RIC for the killing of Constable Potter at Knockcroghery in August 1920. When Duffy was transferred to Roscommon town, a bit of good fortune came his way. He spotted a key in the County Inspector's office, made a mental picture of it, went to McDonnell's hardware shop in town and, through a process of trial and error, made a duplicate which allowed him access to the office at any time. It was in Roscommon that Duffy obtained the list of names of prominent IRA men throughout Ireland (3,912 altogether) and passed it along to Frank Simons, Adjutant for the 3rd Battalion South. He also succeeded in getting the key to the police cipher code, which was also given to Simons. This code was used only for a three month period before being altered, but because the authorities did not suspect any subterfuge, the information gathered by the Volunteers for the next 120 days would be critical and timely. "A post office clerk named McNamara would transmit police messages to the I.R.A. for the purpose of decoding. In this way the I.R.A. knew the contents of a message even before it reached the County Inspector's office."[23]

On one occasion, Duffy was summoned with his colleagues to a meeting addressed by the District Inspector. The man told the constables that Michael Collins was coming into Roscommon town accompanied by Fr. Michael O'Flanagan. Collins was to be apprehended and shot. Alarmed by what he heard, Duffy travelled to Jack Brennan's house, where a man was always "standing-to" to receive messages. Duffy left the particulars with this man, who relayed the news that Collins was to be taken off the car as far out from Roscommon town as possible. Collins was rescued that evening and taken to Kilteevan, where he waited until after midnight when the police lorries had returned to barracks before entering the town.

Another evening Fr. O'Flanagan was scheduled to be the target of an Auxiliary assassination. Duffy dutifully warned the priest, who then made his way to Summerhill College in Sligo for safekeeping. Fr. Flanagan knew the value of good propaganda. While at Summerhill he drafted a letter which detailed the raid on his house, the destruction of vestments found within, and the lifting of a £5 note. He then sent the letter to friendly faces in America who proceeded to post the letter on the door of the British Consul's Office. The Consul's Office checked with Westminster to ascertain if there was any truth to the allegations. The British government contacted Dublin Castle, who in turn sent a convoy of twelve lorries to the Roscommon office. The County Inspector dutifully covered his tracks with the British authorities. Sgt. Duffy was not satisfied. He gained access to the Inspector's office and copied the file regarding the raid. The file ended up in Michael Collins' briefcase. Collins then sent it to America to be posted on the British Consul's doorway together with the original poster about the raid.[24]

The placement of Duffy was providential for several key men in Roscommon. He saved Pat Madden and Frank Simons from an untimely death by raising such a ruckus when the Black and Tans wanted to take the lorry out to Waterloo (where the men were supposed to be sleeping) that the District Inspector was forced to "ground" the Tans and not allow them out of barracks at night. On another occasion, when Dick Mee from Curraghboy was being held in Roscommon gaol, Duffy learned that the Tans had plans to take Mee out after all the RIC had gone to bed and shoot him. Duffy warned Mee not to leave lock-up voluntarily with anyone. Duffy spent the entire night in the dayroom making certain no unauthorised "escape" was implemented by the Tans. Mee was moved to Custume Barracks in Athlone the next day.[25]

One evening in late 1920 or early 1921, Sgt. Harte of Roscommon Barracks informed Duffy that the Auxiliaries of Longford were coming to Roscommon town to sack it and arrest all the IRA local leaders. Duffy immediately scaled the old gaol wall and found Volunteer Tom Farrell, who relayed the message to the men in the area. None of them fell victim to outrageous British Forces that night. Duffy also sent word to the Athlone and Westmeath Volunteers who were camped out on an island in Lough Ree that they should immediately vacate the area. They too were saved from a surprise and potentially deadly visit by the British military.

Duffy was a well-placed man in a well-placed time. Through his efforts, many men in Roscommon were spared capture and even death. His motivations remain

He also succeeded in getting the key to the police cipher code, which was also given to Simons. This code was used only for a three month period before being altered, but because the authorities did not suspect any subterfuge, the information gathered by the Volunteers for the next 120 days would be critical and timely.

Duffy was a well-placed man in a well-placed time. Through his efforts, many men in Roscommon were spared capture and even death. His motivations remain untold and unknown. Yet one needs to ask the question, "How would the main course of Irish Independence have been altered without a bit of Irish patriotism coupled with a dash of bravado from Sergeant John Duffy?"

untold and unknown. Yet one needs to ask the question, "How would the main course of Irish Independence have been altered without a bit of Irish patriotism coupled with a dash of bravado from Sergeant John Duffy"?

Flagwaving

By early 1921 the IRA was on the move throughout the county. If the enemy didn't venture too far from their secure settings, the Volunteers devised ways to lure them out. One seemingly innocent ploy was to hang a tricolour atop a chimney, or better still, a tree. When the agitated British soldier or Tan climbed up to rid the landscape of such objectionable fanfare, a branch halfway up the trunk would give way under his weight and send him crashing down to Mother Earth. What the soldier hadn't anticipated was the IRA having been there first, cutting several branches halfway through and concealing the cuts with dirt.[26]

Ambush at Cornafulla

Members of the Athlone Flying Column were eager for a success. On 1 February, Seamus O'Meara assembled a number of the Volunteers for an ambush on the Galway/Ballinasloe road at Mount Florence. John Lennon, a local Volunteer, was with the Column in order to identify specific RIC men. When one person did come along dressed in civilian clothes, Lennon passed word to the awaiting men that this was no policeman. Yet, moments later, Lennon levelled his rifle at him and fired a round. He missed. The policeman hightailed it around the bend in the road and succeeded in getting free of danger. The Column remained in their ambush positions for some time, but the word was out at the local Cloonark Barracks and no policemen came to investigate.

During the daylight hours of that same day (1 February), Brigade officers Ned Doolan, Brian Mulvihill, and David Daly went looking for Jim Tormey. They wanted to direct him to the Brigade O/C who was situated in Summerhill so that the two might coordinate plans. The Westmeath threesome located Tormey in the Ballycumber area of County Offaly and then proceeded to Carrick-o-Brien, arriving at dawn of 2 February. The exhausted Westmeath men were told by Tormey to rest. He and George Adamson rowed silently across the Shannon. At Carricknaughton they met up with two men, neither one of whom they would likely misname. Both were Tom Halligan (they were cousins). At the beginning of this day, an ambush plan was being refined and there were preparations to be made.

The four men travelled to Drum, skirting the railway and stopping at the Higgins house in Curryroe for a bite of food. They then proceeded on to Sarah Hughes' place at Collagorriff. As the morning sun rose higher in the sky, the foursome tramped across the fields, where they spoke with Patsy Donlon, then continued on their way to Garrynagowna. About one hundred yards behind a fence at Richard Bigley's field at Creggan,[27] the men waited for their prey. Interestingly, the spot they chose was 500 yards farther along the road from Athlone than the place where the ambush party had waited the day before.[28]

Visibility was good as the four men viewed the road to Athlone while patiently waiting for a party of police to return from that town with provisions, ammunition, and wages which they had just collected from their headquarters. About ten minutes after three, eight or ten policemen cycled past the waiting Volunteers. Tormey, realising that the party was too strong, decided not to attack but to let them go by. "After the police party had passed by, for some unknown reason, he suddenly rose up and opened fire on them. Tormey's brother had been recently murdered by the enemy in Ballykinlar Camp a few weeks previously, being shot by a sentry there for no reason, and this had upset him very seriously."[29]

The police scrambled into the roadside ditch and began to return fire. Unknown to the ambushers was a crowd of Tans and regular soldiers following the first group, and when those dozen or more soldiers became engaged in the fight, the Volunteers soon realised they were hopelessly outgunned. They determined to commence a retreating action. Tormey was the first to withdraw, followed by

Adamson. The Halligans next moved to new positions while Tormey and Adamson supplied the covering firepower. This alternate manoeuvring ensued for nearly half an hour, during which time gunshots resounded o'er the fields for several miles in all directions.

Tormey called to his fellow Volunteers to retreat while he took up a position atop Richard Bigley's plough. His vantage point was good for seeing the enemy, but unfortunately, it also made him an easy target. A single shot brought Tormey down. One of his colleagues returned to him, but Tormey was already travelling the road to eternity.

The two Halligans and Adamson dashed through the fields heading towards a place of refuge — Bernard Gaffey's house at Garrynagowna. The Tans did not pursue them, probably owing to the fact that Jack Caulfield and his sister had inadvertently driven their cart up to the ambush site. While pointing a gun at his person, the Tans ordered Caulfield to walk in the direction of the shooters. Caulfield, not willing to become a porous sponge absorbing bullets from opposing firing lines, ran for his life across the field. The Tans, fearing a ruse whereby they would be drawn out into the open field and picked off,[30] abandoned the site and kicked up dust all the way back to Athlone.

The three escapees soon met up with other Volunteers under the command of Gaffey, who had heard the commotion and had come to join the fracas. When all realised the circumstances of retreat and the unfortunate loss of Tormey, they agreed to perform a risky rescue. They did not want Tormey's body lying unattended in a field awaiting Tan mutilation. The two Halligans, Adamson, John Harney, Jimmy Lennon, brothers Michael and Edward Cunniffe, John Bohan, Mike Hunt, Mike Hogan, and Gaffey quietly returned to the ambush site unaware if any Tans were lingering about. They bore Tormey's body to a nearby stream and after one hundred yards of carrying him on their rifle-bed, someone brought over a door belonging to Michael Dunning on which his body was now transferred and taken to Tom Henry's at Togher and on to Clonown Barracks where they rested.[31] Under a blanket of darkness, Clonown Volunteers transferred Tormey's body to a pony cart, which carried his remains to the edge of the Shannon where it was loaded onto a cot (a flat-type boat used for carrying hay and turf) and floated down river to Cloonbonny. In a lonely isolated shed the body of Tormey rested.

The next day two women from Clonown ventured to Athlone where they purchased a coffin and habit. Martin Farrelly, the local undertaker, promised both discretion and silence about the purpose of their visit.[32] That evening, the Volunteers brought the coffin in a handcart to the edge of the Shannon River, where the box of death was loaded onto a cot and sailed to the Leinster side.

During that same day, members of the Clonown Cumann na mBan had ventured to the abandoned shed in order to prepare Tormey's body for burial. Washed and clothed in a habit, his remains were surrounded by lighted candles, while the dreadful silence of the day was broken by a mournful entonement of the Rosary. Then began the final leg of the journey — to a plot of ground amid the stone ruins of Ciaran's Fair City (Clonmacnoise). There, ten of his comrades bade farewell to an admired and true friend.

The Crown Forces, however, ranted and raged with revenge. Although they had not returned to the scene of the ambush, they had ascertained that one Volunteer had been killed. Where was his secret tomb? Five days after the Cornafulla clash, Tormey's fresh grave was discovered at Clonmacnoise. His remains were exhumed and brought to Athlone Barracks, where his father was ordered to identify the body. And thus the Tormey family, laden with overpowering grief, was forced once again to visit Mount Temple Cemetery, where only a few short weeks before they had buried their other young son, Joe. This was to be their price for Ireland's freedom.

Members of the Clonown Cumann na mBan had ventured to the abandoned shed in order to prepare Tormey's body for burial. Washed and clothed in a habit, his remains were surrounded by lighted candles, while the dreadful silence of the day was broken by a mournful entonement of the Rosary. Then began the final leg of the journey — to a plot of ground amid the stone ruins of Ciaran's Fair City (Clonmacnoise). There, ten of his comrades bade farewell to an admired and true friend.

Bernard Gaffey gravesite.

PHOTO COURTESY MICHAEL LENNON
RESTORATION BY LEW THORNE

Aftermath of Cornafulla

The area around Garrynagowna was rumoured to be on the hit list for the Tans as a reprisal for the Cornafulla ambush. Bernard Gaffey was the O/C of the Battalion and a prime target for vengeful and frustrated Tans. They invaded his home, dragged Bernard and his brother Paddy out of the house, and beat them unmercifully. On the way to the waiting lorry, Bernard (Barney) stumbled off the edge of a bridge over a flooded stream. He hid under the bridge and managed to gasp for breath in the few inches of airspace between the swollen waters and the under-side of the bridge. The Tans, giving him up for drowned, proceeded on their way with brother Paddy in tow. Knowing the terrain and the whereabouts of the waiting lorry, Barney struggled out of the frigid water and circled the arresting party. Suddenly he shrieked a military-like command which pierced the air and frayed the nerves of terrified Tans. Fearing a trap, the Tans abandoned Paddy and ran for their lives. The brothers were rescued from the jaws of death that night, but the Great Spectre is not easily pacified. The injuries resulting from that night's brush with Fate were to remain with Barney for months. By August, the fearsome Spectre revisited the Gaffey household, this time claiming its due. With full mili-tary honours, Bernard Gaffey was lowered into Eire's soil, there to remain with so many young men who had risked life and limb that the tree of freedom might blossom in Roscommon's fields.

Frustrating Waits

Oftentimes during the war, hours and, on occasion, days were endured waiting for something to happen or someone to appear. Attack plans seldom meshed like clockwork. There was usually a hitch, a no-show, or an unexpected turnabout. Such was the case near Tarmonbarry, where sixteen Volunteers went in search of RIC patrols.

On the night of 4 February, Martin Fallon had set his sights on a foot patrol. As was its custom, the patrol marched off towards Ruskey from Tarmonbarry, but its return route varied. Fallon "had scouted this area and had made plans selecting an assembly position from which [he] could quickly bring [his] men into ambush position on either road according to which road the patrol was returning by."[33] A local Volunteer was assigned the job of trailing the patrol and reporting back to Fallon the direction they had taken.

Fallon moved his men into assembly positions and waited for the scout's return. The scout reported that the patrol was coming back by the same road they had taken out of Tarmonbarry. The Volunteers got into position and waited. They waited, and then waited some more hours. By 2 a.m. no patrol had appeared. What had happened to the RIC men?

The answer came days later when Fallon learned that the policemen had been saved that evening by a faint-hearted local scout who deliberately misled Fallon and his men because he didn't want any action taking place near his home for fear of reprisals.[34] (That Volunteer was eventually drummed out of the movement.)

The next week Fallon and the Column revisited Tarmonbarry for another attempt at contact. Pat Mullooly, the Brigade Quartermaster, accompanied the group on this occasion. The Volunteers took over two houses on the Tarmonbarry/ Strokestown Road at 4 a.m. The occupants were herded into a third house and guarded. The men waited until 9 p.m. the next night, but again no enemy patrols came out from the barracks.

Sweep Yields Nothing

During the first week of February a huge roundup was scheduled for the Roscommon town-Ballagh area. Sgt. Duffy, from the Roscommon Barracks, claimed that there were three lorry loads of military and Tans armed with machine guns assembled for the task.[35] The Flying Column, at this time, was billeted with local people in their homes. Duffy got word to local Volunteers to stay out of harm's way. The following morning each member of the Column was awakened and alerted to head west towards Fourmilehouse. As a result of this forewarning, none of the Column was arrested, although a lot of the local people were inconvenienced. Many men and women from the Ballagh district were taken by lorry to Beechwood Barracks, where they were paraded in front of British officers and local men who were now on the British payroll. Canon Hurley from Ballagh Church was among the detainees, and by nightfall he successfully appealed to the British Commanding Officers that the women should be released. The lorries may have transported the people to the barracks, but it was a long, soggy trek home that night for many of the inhabitants of the Ballagh area.

Attack on Elphin Barracks

Days before the actual assault, the first wisp of breeze that would ultimately sweep down on Elphin Barracks and create a whirlwind blew gently. Plans for the attack had been drawn up by Sean Connolly and Michael Dockery, who had enlisted several men from the North Battalion (Martin Fallon, James Casey, Brian Nangle, and Peter Casey) to accompany five men from the South Roscommon Brigade (Pat Madden, Luke Duffy, "Buzzer" Farrell, Sean Bergin and John Gibbons). On a night in the first week of February, the men started out — some having to walk fourteen miles. As they plodded across the fields they "could hear the fellas felling trees in the frosty crisp air."[36] When they neared Elphin, they assembled at Simpson's Shop on the Black Sticks Road. Here they waited until they were summoned for the would-be attack. Carrying the heavy mines towards Elphin, they met other Volunteers from the Ballinameen area. The opening shot, however, was never fired because they were then told that the attack was postponed due to the Crown Forces prowling the town all night.

A few days later the alarm was sounded for another try. The South Roscommon men, however, did not arrive in time to get into Mrs. Lalor's house on the east side of the barracks. If the timing had been postponed until later that night, the noise

Christopher Lainge had joined the Volunteers soon after their formation. By October 1916, he was the drill instructor of a Company in Co. Cavan, but soon transferred to Clifden, County Galway, where the Marconi Signal Station was located. Lainge was suspected of being a Sinn Féiner, and thus the police kept a close watch on him. On the insistence of the RIC, Lainge was again transferred, this time to Castlerea. In County Roscommon, he served the Volunteers well.

Paddy Daly of Dublin had given Lainge three rifles which had been taken from soldiers home on leave from the French frontlines. Lainge had hidden those guns in the High Altar of Castlerea's parish church until such time as Ireland's call for freedom demanded their use. In the 1st Battalion area, he was assigned to study signalling and scouting. He also accompanied other men in his Company to the grand funeral of Thomas Ashe in Dublin.

On the plains of Roscommon, however, his duties were more mundane. Several times he was called out in the middle of the night to deliver dispatches to Castlerea. Ordered to keep an eye on the goings and comings of the RIC on the de Freyne estate, his was the job of waiting and watching and then reporting. He made a valuable contact with the police. Constable Flynn was aware of the intelligence work done by the Volunteers, and, as a result, was nervous about travelling on the roads. Lainge "played upon it [his fear] and finally assured him that I could secure his safety in return for information of raids. He agreed to supply names of 'wanted men' and particulars of raids and in consequence of information he gave the raids were fruitless."*

In November of 1917, Lainge was again moved, this time to Ballyhaunis. There, he participated in a raid on the Excise Office. He also made an intriguing trade with Pat Moylett. Moylett agreed to give the Volunteers two rifles, but on these conditions: firstly, an IOU for £10 must be issued from the Battalion O/C. The second condition was typical of the men in those times — Moylett would destroy the IOU if those rifles were used in Ireland's cause for freedom.

Two years later, Lainge returned to Roscommon, where he again engaged in intelligence work. He was appointed Intelligence Officer for the 1st Battalion South, and, later in June of 1922, for the 2nd Brigade, 2nd Western Division. During the Civil War, he captured four men at Ballinlough, and drove them under escort to Castlebar for detention. He also delivered dispatches to Michael Kilroy, O/C of the 4th Western Division, who was located at the time in Ballina. Lainge's fighting days came to an end in the signal cabin at Ballinlough in July 1922. Here, he phoned the guards at Ballyhaunis Station to warn that Free State forces were coming by road and rail — an alarm that saved them from surprise attack, but did not save Lainge from arrest by soldiers under the command of Pat Madden, the former O/C of the 3rd Battalion South. Lainge's last months of the Civil War were spent interned in Roscommon Gaol and Pump Square in Athlone.

For all the years that Lainge had silently waited for patrols to pass, for all the long hours that he had driven to gather information from friendly shopkeepers around Castlerea, for all the danger he had encountered from participating in raids and ambushes, Lainge, along with thousands of other Volunteers, was rewarded with a gaol cell in which a disheartened spirit languished.

Statement given by Christopher Lainge, Gerald O'Connor Papers, private collection.

*In Loving Memory of the young heroes who
died fighting for Ireland at Glasdrummon,
County Leitrim on 11 March 1921
(Sean Connolly was among the slain)*

On the afternoon of a bleak March day
All unprepared for the deadly fray
While machine gun on their thin ranks play:
Overmatched, outnumbered, they stand at bay,
　　Out on the hill for Erin.

There is never a murmur, no thought of flight,
Who would turn aside and the foe in sight?
They deal blow for blow in the waning light;
Though theirs an unequal, a hopeless fight.
　　They fight for the honour of Erin.

No shelter theirs, 'tis the bare hillside;
As volley to volley in rage replied;
But true as gold in the furnace tried,
They will die as their warrior fathers died,
　　Nor lower the flag of Erin.

Let cowards and weaklings for quarter cry.
We will never yield, we will never fly,
'Tis a fight to a finish; to win or die,
　　Die in the cause of Erin.

Thus the conflict rages till eve's decline —
No cravens, Erin, those sons of thine —
But though twenty to one, those Saxon swine,
Will never break through an Irish line,
　　On the heath-clad hills of Erin.

As the shades of even around them close,
While closer and closer the cordon grows,
They sink overpowered, girt round by foes,
While from many a gash the red blood flows,
　　To moisten the soil of Erin.

There is never a prisoner, all, all, are slain,
The fault is ours if they died in vain;
On the fallen flag there is never a stain,
That flag will fly on the breeze again,
　　Free as the winds of Erin.

Those soldiers of Erin sleep cold and low —
The cause they died for will live, we know —
Yet we shed no tear though we loved them so
Theirs a glorious death, with face to the foe,
　　With sword in hand for Erin.

Their sorrowing comrades laid them to rest,
to be numbered with Ireland's bravest and best,
And many a wound upon face and breast,
Better than spoken words attest
　　Their undying love for Erin.

And Leitrim is proud of her peerless sons —
Will remember while Shannon to ocean runs —
Who died like heroes facing the guns,
Nor yielding an inch to the English Huns,
　　Of the sacred soil of Erin.

by J. Mc D. Dromod, Co. Leitrim

(of breaking a window) would have alerted the policemen next door. The decision was again made to postpone.[37] Finally, by the 11th, Connolly signalled a go-ahead for the operation.

Using trees and stones, the roads were blocked as far away as the Boyle/Carrick-on-Shannon Road so that no reinforcements could come to the assistance of the Elphin garrison.[38] The attacking party was armed with rifles, shotguns, revolvers, landmines, and bombs. Connolly had gathered together a lot of cartbox mines — each with four sticks of gelignite and a fuse to ignite each one.[39] The mines had been stored under the bridge beyond Johnny Jordan's farm and were successfully transported by Brian Connor, Gerald Dalton, Thomas Brady, and John Joseph Carroll. (Jack Collins of Killina Coy. had made one of the bombs. It was of concrete type and filled with gelignite and black powder.)[40] One large mine was planted in the house next to the barracks, where it was detonated electrically in the fireplace.

All was not well with the Volunteers[41] from the initial blast. The mine did not cause the expected damage, failing to blow open a big enough hole in the gable wall. The small handmade bombs that were thrown into the cavity caused by the explosion did not catch the building on fire, nor did they force the police from their quarters. Although there were fifty IRA men engaged in blocking roads and the actual firefight, none was able to enter the barracks or set it on fire from without, for they hadn't enough petrol to ignite the monstrosity. The attack had begun at 10 p.m., and by midnight it was apparent that withdrawal was the wisest choice.[42] Connolly, who was assigned to County Leitrim shortly after this attack, promised to return to Roscommon to have another go at that confounded barracks. It was a promise he was unable to keep.

Attempted Attack on Ballaghaderreen Barracks — Oops!

Michael J. Marren, O/C of Ballymote Battalion in Sligo; Sean Corcoran, O/C of the East Mayo Brigade; and Jim Hunt, O/C of the Gurteen Battalion had met at Carracastle to draw up plans for an attack on the Ballaghaderreen Barracks. (Charles Gildea's Volunteer Witness Statement claims that he and Alec McCabe were also involved in discussions.) A total of thirty men from the Gurteen Battalion in County Sligo, East Mayo Brigade, and 1st Battalion South Roscommon were assigned to take part in the assault in February 1921. This joint venture was under the command of Alec McCabe.

A mine had been prepared at Keash Hill, Sligo, by Michael Marren (who had been a wee bit overzealous with his ingredients). The explosive device, which was scheduled to be detonated during the fight, had been delivered by McCabe and Gildea to Lyden's in Cloontia[43] (two miles northeast of Carracastle) a day previous to the attack. On the appointed night, Volunteers took up positions around the barracks, while three men took charge of the mine. A cart was used to transport the bomb. "When the cart was put close as was possible to the barracks it was to be heeled up in such a manner as to place the bomb against the barracks wall"[44] where a centre wall supported two floors.

Curfew tolled at 10 p.m., and the usual patrol exited the barracks. The policemen heard, however, suspicious whispering and promptly opened fire on the men with the cart. The Volunteers carrying the mine quickly vacated the premises, leaving the bomb behind. The other Volunteers surrounding the barracks were waiting for an explosion to cue them to commence fire. There was no noise — no explosion. Something had gone wrong. The IRA quietly withdrew from positions. The policemen captured the mine.

Thady McGowan of Sligo recorded a slightly different version in his Volunteer Witness Statement.[45] He claims about thirty men entered the town, surrounded the barracks and the approaches to it. The cart containing the mine was placed in an archway. Three men were in charge of it. When a patrol of six RIC men exited the barracks, they became suspicious of the noises and opened fire on the men near the cart. The other Volunteers, hearing the gunfire, returned fire on the barracks — an exchange that lasted twenty minutes. When it became apparent that there was no hope of getting the mine into position and no hope of outgunning the RIC, the Volunteers withdrew.

While the attack was deemed a total failure, there was a silver lining to the cloudy event. The good news for the RIC in the barracks as well as the townspeople was that the bomb had not gone off. Some weeks after the cancelled attack, it was hauled into the Aughlist bog about six miles away from the town. When it did fire, the force of the explosion shook windows four miles away. "The experts in demolition later concluded that had it exploded by the barracks, it would not only have destroyed the barracks, but half of the town as well."[46]

Spies
Like flies alighting on an infected sore, the wounded Loughglynn area seemed to attract more than its share of pesky spies. Some of the informers were known to be female. On Valentine's Day, a communication was received at GHQ from the South Roscommon Adjutant asking for a response to the question, "Have you yet decided whether capital punishment should be inflicted on women spies?" The question was posed because, as a result of a woman talking too freely with the local RIC, the Brigade staff which had met in Martin Ganley's house in January had nearly been eliminated.

The official answer from headquarters dated 4 March[47] stated that permission was given for destruction of the suspected spy's property, but questions of life and death needed to be answered by examining evidence. All information regarding women spies was to be put before a court of inquiry. The summary of such meeting would be sent to GHQ for examination and a decision.

To respond to such a dangerous situation, local leaders decided to at least address the problem of male spies head on. They knew the solution for male informers. On 6 April, W., an ex-policeman, and G., postman, who were suspected of giving information to the police in the Loughglynn area, were paid a visit by local Volunteers dressed in British uniforms.[48] Both men, unsuspecting of the true identity of their guests, were very forthcoming with names, places, and plans of the local Volunteers. The men's wagging tongues were silenced. Their lifeless bodies were later found at the gable of an old shed in the centre of the village.

Months earlier, on 23 November 1920, a Constable from Ruskey Barracks had been out cycling with a lady friend. Thought to be "a spy working in the employment of the enemy,"[49] he was kidnapped and drowned in the Shannon.

As a result of information gleaned from correspondence seized in a mail car robbery between Elphin and Castlerea, two local men (F. and H.) were targeted with death. Six Volunteers[50] broke into their homes, but, amid flying bullets, each accused man made his escape. They both scrambled to the RIC Barracks in Roscommon

The Loughglynn area seemed to attract more than its share of pesky spies. Some of the informers were known to be female. On Valentine's Day, a communication was received at GHQ from the South Roscommon Adjutant asking for a response to the question, "Have you yet decided whether capital punishment should be inflicted on women spies?"

After the Rising in 1916, Volunteers were incarcerated in a variety of prisons and camps in England. With the general release in late 1917, the work of reorganising the Volunteers began in earnest. For County Roscommon, the chief organisers were Sean Hyde (who later became the Assistant Chief of Staff of the IRA), Sean Connolly, and Ernie O'Malley.

O'Malley was an uncommon man in a time that called for uncommon courage. Idealism was his beacon, a hearty constitution and discipline his solid ship, "Republic" the shore to which he sailed through violently turbulent waters.

Ernie O'Malley had frolicked through his childhood in County Mayo; yet, some of his family roots were in Roscommon, his mother, Marion Kearney, having been born in Cloonroughan, Castlerea. At the time of Ernie's birth, his family resided in Castlebar, his father serving as managing clerk for Malachy Kelly, Crown Solicitor for County Mayo. When but a small child, his parents rented a summer house near Rosbeg, Westport, County Mayo. It proved to be the harbour which sheltered his drifting spirit and to which O'Malley would later return with his bride and attempt to anchor his family life.

PHOTO COURTESY OF CORMAC O'MALLEY   RESTORATION BY LEW THORNE

As a boy he was enraptured with the sea. The perpetual exchange of crashing waves to rocky shore and quiet receding of surf to ocean provided the contrasting rhythms which would reverberate in his writings as an adult. The lyrical descriptions of the countryside while moving secretly through those danger zones and his philosophical musings regarding the Republican struggle were all noted on a staff where the high notes of action, danger, and tension were juxtapositioned alongside sustained whole notes of solitude and reflective thinking.

He mixed not with the poorer class of Irish society, but rather contented himself with studies in Dublin at the Christian Brothers' School, North Richmond Street and Cecilia Street Medical School (opened in 1855 as the Catholic University School of Medicine and incorporated into the National University system in 1909). Nothing in his background prepared him for the volleys of Easter Week. Though not involved in the Post Office Rising, feelings of nationalism were soon to engulf him and thrust him to the forefront of the Volunteer movement. Shunned by his family for his radical views, O'Malley spent the next years of his life involved in hazardous work.

Handpicked by Michael Collins to go out into the countryside and train men for the coming struggle, O'Malley spent many rainy nights sleeping in hay ricks, befriending jacksnipes, slogging through bogland, sharing tea in Republican cottages. He was sent to Roscommon to train and organise local men into a cohesive unit. Soldiers by night, farmers by day, these

town where they remained until Truce day in July. After the hostilities, these two men wisely chose to live elsewhere. They were never seen in the area again.

Arrests in Strokestown
On 20 February 1921 a huge force of Crown troops arrived in the Strokestown area. Ten lorries of mixed RIC and Black and Tans along with infantry and cavalry units surrounded a large tract of countryside and began a systematic search. They were looking for Volunteers and their supporters. In all, about 200 people — men, women and children — were arrested (some being released soon afterwards). Liam O'Doherty, O/C 3rd Battalion North Roscommon, was one of the victims snagged in the dragnet.

Requiem for Paddy Moran
What constitutes a great man? Is it talent, good fortune, congeniality? Or something more ethereal — stamina, conviction, the willingness to put oneself last? In what packaging does greatness present itself? Beauty, physical strength, height, luxuriously clad? Greatness is an undefinable attribute which oftentimes is a matter of perspective. To many in County Roscommon, the third of eleven children born to Bartley and Bridget Moran in the ancient parish of Ardcarne symbolises the heights to which a truly great patriot can rise. To the British soldiers who hanged him in Mountjoy, he might have appeared as a likeable lad whose politics were misdirected.

country men were required to supply their own arms, attend meetings, drill (often in the demesnes of the deteriorating Big Houses to desensitise the men who formerly had held in awe the inhabitants who dwelled within), scout for enemy troops, harbour men on the run, as well as plan and execute ambushes. O'Malley's job was to teach them how to be effective.

He was a hunted man. After leaving South Roscommon and heading to the North Galway Brigade, he was cycling near the border of the two counties when he was shot in the wrist and ankle by the local police. On that evening his escape route took him through a thick hedge of thorns and brambles, the icy waters of the Suck with his bloody hand raised above the waterline to keep his revolver dry, "quaggy bog which squelched" higher than his knees, followed at daybreak by miles of countryside hobbling on a wounded ankle back to the Kilteevan area, where Joe Finlay and Matt Davis made arrangements to get him across the Shannon to Newtowncashel, County Longford. There, a car would meet him and drive him to Dublin for treatment.

Later O'Malley was to command the Second Southern Division during the Civil War. He also served as the IRA Acting Assistant Chief of Staff. Wounded during a raid on a Dublin safe house 4 November 1922, O'Malley became an unwilling witness to the grey walls of Mountjoy and Kilmainham and various military hospitals. He spent three Christmases in gaol, trying to physically and mentally survive. In Kilmainham he began a hunger strike at a time when he had not the strength to walk across the floor. Many months were spent confined to a bed where books and his own quiet thoughts fed his mind and kept hope alive within a body that had nearly succumbed to bullet wounds, constant pain, and bad food.

When the struggle ended, O'Malley travelled abroad — first to Europe, then to America. He grew away from intense Republican ideology and submerged himself in the arts — sculpture, archeology, theatre, painting, and, of course, writing. While living in Taos, New Mexico, an intellectual oasis amid the arid plateaus of south-western United States, he began, in 1929, to pen his memoirs of the Irish War of Independence and his part in it. He returned to Ireland in 1935 and eventually authored several books about his days with the Volunteers: *On Another Man's Wound*, *The Singing Flame* (edited by Frances-Mary Black), and *Raids and Rallies* (published posthumously in 1982). In his later years he also toured Ireland interviewing participants of the Black and Tan and Civil Wars while meticulously notating their responses. (His papers are preserved in the Ernie O'Malley private collection in University College Dublin Archives.)

He married an American socialite, Helen Huntington Hooker — an intelligent, artistic woman whose background and living standards were far removed from the wandering itinerant Irish soldier and poet. Their union proved stormy. Their three children were reared separately (two in the United States with Helen's family while the youngest remained in Ireland with his father).

Ernie O'Malley died in 1957, bullet fragments still buried in his back. The marks of seventeen wounds scarred his torso. Disappointment dwelt deep within his soul. Having sacrificed his youth for an ideal, he was left with an idol, a counterfeit image. Having fought for unity and peace, he was left with a divided piece of his beloved island. An adherent of Liam Lynch's belief that the "the army has to hew the way for politics to follow," O'Malley believed that if the Irish Republican Army had consulted the feelings of the people, "we would never have fired a shot. If we gave them a good strong lead, they would follow."* And lead them he did — with bravado, intelligence, and heart. Into the fields, into the demesnes, into the very crucible of fiery nationalism, this man among men, this extraordinary son of a Roscommon woman, was indeed no common man at all.

The Singing Flame by Ernie O'Malley, p. 25.

In 1999, portions of this article were published (by permission of this author) in *Living to Ninety — And On* by John Hester.

Born in 1888, Paddy Moran attended school at Cartron. In the early years of the twentieth century, schooling for persons in their mid to late teens was a privilege only the wealthy could afford. And thus Paddy was apprenticed to the grocery and bar business at O'Rourke's in Main Street, Boyle, where he laboured for three years. Work in town was tedious and, at times, a lonesome task for a boy who enjoyed the companionship of his siblings. On weekends he travelled to Crossna to be with his family. Making the trip by foot, his route often took him around the demesne at Rockingham, home of the King-Harman family. Here was an estate carved in the 1600s out of Irish land. Former occupants were scattered to the marginal fringes while the Lord of the Land claimed thousands of rich rolling acres as his birthright. To ensure the security of such a holding, RIC barracks were strategically placed around the outskirts at Boyle, Grevisk, Knockvicar, and Cootehall. As Paddy continued trudging onward to his family's small farm, which was expected to support a large brood, he mused that justice seemed to have taken a holiday, and in its place an unjust system of occupation had taken hold.

His ponderings and ramblings took him far beyond the King-Harman domain. From Boyle he was transferred to Maguire's in Mohill, County Leitrim, and then to Athy, County Kildare. By the time he was in his early 20s, he had secured a job as a barman in John Doyle's Pub in Phibsboro, Dublin. An active member of the National Union of Licensed Vintners, Grocers and Allied Trades Association, he was elected its president. This was one facet of his personality.

Paddy Moran from Crossna, Boyle

PHOTO COURTESY OF HENRY OWENS
RESTORATION BY DAVE DERBY

Paddy would gather the boys with whom he had studied his three Rs and add to their alphabet learning another R — rebellion. As a result, Crossna was one of the most steadfast Companies of Volunteers formed in the county (1916).

Another side of Paddy's consciousness was still pondering the great discrepancy between the Ascendancy and the natives. When the Volunteer movement began, Paddy saw a chance to right a wrong, to undo centuries of foreign rule, to reclaim his own inheritance.

During his visits home from Dublin, Paddy would gather the boys with whom he had studied his three Rs and add to their alphabet learning another R — rebellion. As a result, Crossna was one of the most steadfast Companies of Volunteers formed in the county (1916).[51]

When the call to arms sounded, Paddy was at his post outside Jacob's Factory in Dublin on Easter Monday 1916. When surrender was ordered, he joined his comrades on the road to English gaols — Knutsford, Wormwood Scrubbs, and most important, Frongoch. Here he met men from all over the country who had a similar ambition and similar mindset as to how to achieve it. He was released from prison in August 1916 and returned to Dublin, where he eventually began working at Lynch and O'Brien's in Dun Laoghaire. By 1920 he was manager of Magee's in Blackrock. Paddy was elected Captain of "D" Company, 2nd Battalion of the Dublin Brigade. He became more involved than ever with the work of the Volunteers.

Moran was falsely arrested following infamous Bloody Sunday. He was accused of complicity in the murder of Lieutenant Ames, one of the "Cairo Gang," a special group of intelligence men hired by Dublin Castle to locate and eliminate the IRA commanders in the capital. One of Collins' squad held a gun on a dispatch rider in an effort to give cover to the other men who actually did the killing. Moran was identified as that man. While awaiting trial, the cold realities of the hangman's noose dangled over the cell of Paddy Moran; but suddenly a hot opportunity for escape presented itself.

Two friendly soldiers in Kilmainham gaol conspired to help in the escape plans of several Volunteers. A bolt cutter was smuggled into the gaol but provided insufficient leverage for cutting through a cross bolt six feet long secured by a heavy padlock on a side gate nearest to Inchicore. The next day an extension for the bolt cutter was smuggled into the gaol, and shortly after 6 p.m. on 14 February 1921, Frank Teeling, one of the Squad, Simon Donnelly of Armagh (who would later fight in the Four Courts), and another man known as "Stewart" walked to freedom. (Stewart was really Ernie O'Malley who went on to live a daring, dangerous, and dashing life. He also produced one of the finest pieces of literature to come out of the War for Independence, *On Another Man's Wounds*.

Paddy could have gone, but refused his spot in the escaping party insisting that only a few men had any chance of successfully evading detection. He also believed that his trial would prove him innocent of the charges against him. On the night of escape, a concert in the west wing bombarded the ears of prison guards to such an extent that noises resulting from the escape were obliterated. Paddy Moran was left to face a cold stone cell wall, yet he was filled with satisfaction that the three men had gained their freedom. His fate was more uncertain.

Truth be known, Moran was nowhere near Upper Mount Street when the gun battle on Bloody Sunday ensued. According to newspapers of the time, his landlady, an official of his union, a train conductor, a passenger on the tram, and a Dublin Metropolitan Police constable all gave evidence at his trial that Moran had attended early Mass in Blackrock, returned to his boarding house for breakfast, then proceeded to board a train for Dublin in order to attend a union meeting. He did not alight from the tram until he reached Nelson's Pillar in O'Connell Street at a time when the killings had already taken place.[52] But truth and revenge waltz not on the same dance floor. Moran was known to be a Sinn Féiner, had a history of prison time as a result of the Rising, and had come under police notice for his union activities during the previous spring — those were enough sour notes to the ears of the tribunal.

The Dublin newspaper, the *Freeman's Journal*, printed articles asking for clemency on Moran's behalf. His union petitioned their M.P. in Westminster to intercede. All to no avail. As a last-ditch effort, workers in Dublin and surrounding districts were called to a general strike. An estimated 20,000 people held vigil outside Mountjoy for Moran and the other five men who were scheduled to hang with him.[53]

On the last night of his life (13 March), he wrote letters to his parents, visited with his brother Jim and three sisters, and made his peace with his Maker. Paddy Moran's greatness is not measured by a yardstick of earthly treasures but by his willingness to give up his own life that others might be free. He journeyed on this earth with purpose and faith in Ireland's future and died the next morning knowing his journey had led him ultimately to a place of peace.

P.S. His remains lay in Mountjoy for eighty years. The finale to his personal drama played out on 14 October 2001 when he and nine other men were given a state funeral. He was reinterred in Glasnevin Cemetery.

March Mayhem

The month was pockmarked by various successes and near misses throughout the county. In the list of minuses, only the attempted strike by men from Loughglynn and Moor Companies at Cloonsheever, Tibohine, can be entered. On the positive side stands a successful raid on the Boyle Post Office, an attack on an RIC patrol at Chanterland, Elphin, on 21 March; an ambush in County Westmeath conducted by the Athlone Flying Column;[54] and the well-known attacks at Keadue and Scramogue.

Attack on Keadue Police

According to Micheál O'Callaghan's *For Ireland and Freedom*, "the attack took place on the evening of March 19/20. It resulted in three policemen laying dead."[55] A different story is told by Richard Abbott, author of *Police Casualties in Ireland 1919-1922*, who claims only two policemen suffered mortal wounds and has designated 22 March as the day of ambush.[56] The Bureau of Military History Compilation of Roscommon events (dated 1954) claims that 21 March is the date of attack.[57] Sean Leavy, O/C of the 3rd Battalion North, stated that the Keadue ambush occurred three days after Scramogue, which would make the date 26 March.[58] The *Roscommon Herald* dated 4 June 1921 claims in its "Leitrim, Longford, Sligo and Mayo News" that 22 March was the decisive date. Such are the headaches of an historian who seeks accuracy yet finds mere confusion.

O'Callaghan attributes the timing to revenge for Paddy Moran's hanging in Mountjoy five days before (his assumed date for the attack). Abbott makes no claim for his assertion that the attack occurred one day before Scramogue. On logical face value, it seems unlikely that the attack would have been planned before Scramogue. Such a murderous offensive would have alerted the British Forces and perhaps stirred a spate of roundups in the area. Sean Leavy claims that Michael Dockery, Brigade O/C of North Roscommon, promised a diversionary attack *after* Scramogue in order to alleviate the expected concentration of troops on the Third Battalion areas. Also, most authors agree that young Joseph Molloy of Knockvicar was shot as a reprisal by infuriated Tans. His death occurred on 28 March, a full nine days after O'Callaghan's projected date, but only two after Sean Leavy's. This seemed the most reasonable turn of events, although warfare, and indeed life, do not always follow a precisely planned pathway. For purposes of this book, however, the author had chosen 24 March to begin the story of the Keadue attack until she visited the University College Dublin and Military Archives in the summer of 2002. There she learned that the Attack at Keadue occurred a day *before* Scramogue, making its date 22 March. In addition, in the summer of 2003, this author read the Volunteer Witness Statement of Tommy Lavin who also designates the date as 22 March. *The Strokestown Democrat* of 26 March 1921 concurs.[59]

The prelude to the Keadue ambush began a full week before the event. On the night of Paddy Moran's death, Tommy Lavin had led a party of six Volunteers into Keadue to attack a patrol, but no policemen ventured forth. The men had to settle

On the last night of his life (13 March), he wrote letters to his parents, visited with his brother Jim and three sisters, and made his peace with his Maker. Paddy Moran's greatness is not measured by a yardstick of earthly treasures but by his willingness to give up his own life that others might be free. He journeyed on this earth with purpose and faith in Ireland's future and died the next morning knowing his journey had led him ultimately to a place of peace.

The Kilronan Ambush

(Song recorded by Tom Munnelly with John Lyons, Mullalusky, Keadue. 14 June 1977. Written by Tom Munnelly.)

One old March morning as the dawn was breaking
O'er the rugged heights of the Arigna Hills,
A rebel band could be seen advancing
Down its mossy slopes and sweet rippling rills.
Brave Seamus Cull of old Arigna
Was the valiant leader who met the foe
On that cold Spring morning, near famed Lough Meelagh,
At the RIC struck a mortal blow.

Old Devereux quickly was bowled over
as on the roadway his body rolled.
And next came Dowling — his days are numbered
As the shots rang out from those rebels bold;
In wild confusion and consternation,
In headlong flight they disappeared from view,
As their comrades lay on the roadway dying,
Their cheeks now coloured red, white and blue.

The British Forces were soon contacted
As Kilronan's mountain they overran
with armoured cars and Crossley tenders,
Manned by Auxies, soldiers and Black and Tans.
Brave Cull and Gannon were quickly captured,
As on the hillside they wounded lay;
They were soon transferred to Mountjoy Prison
to await their doom on a fatal day.

God grant you glory, Brave Seamus Cull,
And open Heaven to all your men;
For the call that called you once more is calling
Adown the slopes of the Antrim glens.

for sniping at a well-defended barracks. "The garrison replied with all they had [got] and sent up numerous Verey lights. Reinforcements came from Carrick-on-Shannon, police and military, but we [the Volunteers] had cleared off before they arrived."[60] All in all, the Volunteers considered it a very unsatisfactory engagement with the British Forces.

At the next Brigade Council meeting, Michael Dockery offered £50 towards the purchase of arms to the first Battalion that successfully carried off an attack on the Crown Forces. Dockery and Jack Glancy, along with the Battalion O/C Tommy Lavin, began working on an attack plan for Keadue. When Lavin took the idea to a Battalion Council meeting, the officers determined not to wait for Brigade orders but to devise an attack of their own with what little arms they had available. A military patrol which proceeded from Drumshanbo to Drumkeerin via Arigna was to be the target. Mindful that this was Leitrim Brigade territory, arrangements were made with their officers to attack at Tarmon. Fourteen Volunteers armed with shotguns and buckshot assembled the night of 21 March only to be informed that the patrol, which was due in the early morning hours, was not going out. Unwilling to trudge home without a fight, Tommy Lavin devised a hurried plan to lure the Tans and RIC from Keadue out of their safe quarters. The ruse proved simple enough — a robbery would be staged by the Volunteers who knew full well the police would be forced to respond. Paddy McLoughlin (Captain of the Arigna Coy.), Jim and Tom Lynam (Capt. of the Ballyfarnon Coy.), and Tommy Lavin would raid the post office in Keadue at 3 a.m. The Postmaster, who was the Grand Master of the Orange Order in Connaught, was known to be very hostile to the Volunteers. He no doubt would report the burglary as soon as he discovered it the next morning.

Meanwhile the rest of the party would proceed to Kilronan and occupy ambush positions. The Volunteers[61] assembled on the roadway between Keadue and Ballyfarnon, about a mile from the village of Keadue, and chose their position wisely with good coverage of the road, clear visibility towards Keadue, and, most important, a direct line of retreat up the mountains to their rear.

After raiding the post office, Lavin and the other three men joined up with the waiting Volunteers. On route, they unexpectedly ran into Michael Dockery who, when told of the plans, agreed to accompany the others to the ambush site. All were in place by daybreak.

At a quarter to eleven in the forenoon, six policemen cycled down the road in single file to investigate the phantom robbery. The Volunteers were waiting. Lavin fired a lone shot, which was the signal to start the attack. The battle began with all policemen either falling off or jumping off their bicycles. The two constables (Devereux and Dowling) who drew their revolvers and started firing were shot dead. Sgt. O'Reilly was also wounded. (He was later to identify Glancy and Dockery when the two were incarcerated in Boyle Barracks.) "One policeman succeeded in throwing a grenade, but he threw it so far over the heads of our men [the Volunteers] that it was ineffective. One Constable Frizelle, who was the last man of the patrol, was so far behind in the line that he did not come into the ambush position and he succeeded in turning around on the road and making his escape."[62] The remaining constables surrendered, putting their hands up and shouting, "Don't fire, don't fire!" The Volunteers collected their arms and those of their fallen companions: three rifles, five revolvers, some grenades, and a small amount of ammunition.[63]

Michael Dockery claimed one of those rifles. (The gun proved incriminating when both he and Jack Glancy were captured on 10 May in O'Hara's cottage in

Cootehall.) Tommy Lavin escorted Dockery out of the area. Dockery was anxious to return to the 3rd Battalion area where an ambush at Scramogue was due to take place. Lavin and Dockery parted company in Crossna, while the rest of the men fled into the mountains where they secured and dumped the arms.

Reprisals for the Keadue offensive were swift and deadly. The whole area was scoured. The only fatality for the action was Joseph Molloy, a lad of thirteen, who was shot in a field near his home in Knockvicar for failing to halt at the Tans' command. Volunteers Owen Cull, Tom McKenna, John Cullen, Bernard Gannon, and Thomas Gaffney of Crossna were all arrested shortly afterwards, incarcerated in Boyle until 20 June, whereupon they were sent to Mountjoy where they idled their days in a prison cell, although they were never tried for the crime.

The Scramogue Ambush

Pat Mullooly and Pat Madden had often mused about the disappointment and futility of waiting for the enemy to show up on little bye roads. The Tans often avoided them because they were so vunerable to ambush. Madden and Mullooly agreed that the only place the enemy was sure to appear was on the main roads where they travelled daily.[64] Madden, Sean Connolly, Martin Fallon, and Luke Duffy had previously discussed the possibility of staging an ambush on the Strokestown/Longford Road. Sean Leavy had discussed and sanctioned a plan with his men to strike the enemy at Scramogue. A meeting was called to approve those plans and make certain that both Battalions (3rd North and 3rd South) were reading ambush plans from the same page.

Scramogue was located nearly midway between the Brigade areas. Rifles were in short supply, and most certainly rifles would be needed to keep the Crown Forces at bay while the men were retreating over open country. There were only 25 rounds of ammunition for each rifle. Even the inventory of buckshot for shotgun cartridges was low. Some of the cartridges were loaded with ball or bullets especially made for this attack.[65] Some rifles were borrowed from the Ballinaheglish Company, while a few found their way from Longford to supplement the local arms cache — eleven service rifles, a Winchester, and a sporting rifle were gathered together, two or three revolvers,[66] and an assortment of shotguns — the largest quantity of arms the men had yet beheld. (Sean Leavy claims that armament included seventeen rifles, two or three revolvers, and twenty shotguns with slugged cartridges.[67]) Volunteers from the parishes of Kilgefin, Strokestown, Kilglass, and Fourmilehouse were handpicked for the job. In the dark hours of early morning 23 March, the men quietly slipped out of their homes, trudged to prearranged gathering positions (Cooney's crossroads for the 3rd Battalion South men), then headed for Scramogue.

Other Volunteers had been alerted of the impending attack so that they could block access to the area. Some men were charged with obstructing the road between Scramogue and Tarmonbarry. The Kiltrustan Company was responsible for road blocking as well as cutting the telegraph line that ran alongside Strokestown/Elphin Road. Kilteevan Company obstructed the roads leading into the area from the Athlone side. 3rd Battalion North work parties dug trenches across the Strokestown/Tulsk Road and all roads leading from Carrick-on-Shannon, Elphin, and Kilmore. 3rd Battalion South secured the roads from Roscommon town and Lanesboro. Men from the northern end of Kilglass Company built a rough stone wall across the Strokestown/Ruskey Road at Knockhall, while the men from southern Kilglass Company made sure that any unexpected traffic on the Ballyfeeny/Scramogue Road would be unable to proceed.[68] (In point of fact, however, not all the roads to the area had been properly blocked, which is why Brian Nangle and Pat Mullooly were surrounded so quickly after the ambush by a lorryful of Black and Tans and soldiers at Farrell's public house and arrested.)[69]

Sean Leavy's parents, James Early, and Sean's sister busily prepared food for the men. When the Volunteers arrived at the ambush site several hours before daybreak, they speedily dug trenches behind the hedges in which to hide. Gaps were cut in the hedges for greater visibility and easier communication. "The ground to the east of the bend and which [was] the northern slope of Slieve Bawn gave good cover for a retreat from the position..."[70] Civilians in nearby houses were evacuated from the danger zone. John Gibbons and Buzzer Farrell, who were both excellent marksmen, were placed in the house that had been loopholed. Martin O'Connor, who had been so badly burned in the Strokestown Courthouse fire the previous June, held a shotgun in the loopholed walls of a ruined house about seventy yards in front of the main position. Pat Mullooly was in charge of a squad of shotgun men who would provide a rearguard action, if necessary.[71] When all preparations were readied, the men sat down and waited in the cold frosty air. The shooting would soon start, and who was to say which one of them would not be walking away that day?

A little after seven o'clock in the morning the sound of lorries in Strokestown revving up their motors put the men on full alert. The sight of wild duck soaring overhead brought merely groans of disappointment from the hunters crouched in the trenches below. The flying fowl would be allowed to escape this day, for the game on the ground was much more inviting but much more dangerous.

A little after seven o'clock in the morning the sound of lorries revving up their motors in Strokestown put the men on full alert. The sight of wild duck soaring overhead brought merely groans of disappointment from the hunters crouched in the trenches below. The flying fowl would be allowed to escape this day, for the game on the ground was much more inviting but much more dangerous.

Pat Madden, who was in charge of the attacking party, had commanded his men to wait until the lorries were close in order to make the buckshot from the shotguns effective. When Captain Peake of the 9th Lancers and eight other men in their Crossley tender were within thirty-five yards of the Volunteers' position, Madden ordered his best marksman to direct his fire to the driver, thus slowing the tender which had been going at a fast clip. As the tender lost momentum, it came within range of the shotguns, which poured out a blistering barrage of pellets. The driver was dead, and those who could, dived for cover. Captain Peake and Lt. Tennant, who were sitting in the front seat beside the driver, jumped from the lorry and onto the wall[72] where the driverless lorry had swerved off the road and crashed. All but one of the occupants had jumped or fallen out, most having been wounded in the first volley of fire.

The demise of Captain Peake, nephew of the Earl of Middleton, is a story riddled with conflicting testimony. Seamus Nelson, son of one of the participating Volunteers, claimed that Peake was shot in the foot or leg and began hobbling down the road towards Strokestown, but was felled by a rifleman's bullet when he was 100-150 yards from the site of the attack.[73] Tommy Loughran, in his manuscript, *An Old Soldier's Memories,* claims that during a lull in the firing when Madden had shouted, "Will ye surrender now?", Peake crawled out from behind nearby bushes "holding his hands up, palms forward and fingertips level with his shoulders....He looked towards the main ambush position, looked back towards the town and dived for the bushes. Sixteen rifles fired together and ten of them hit him."[74] Martin Fallon in his Volunteer Witness Statement claims that Peake "got over a fence into one of the fields close to the road and had fallen into the drain or dyke,"[75] where he died. Meanwhile Lieutenant Tennant, who had received a fearful wound when going over the wall, managed to crawl to a nearby house, where he died.

Another lorry filled with Black and Tans which had arrived late that morning in Strokestown for the trip to Longford was some six hundred yards behind the first vehicle seemingly stalled by engine trouble. When firing began, Pat Madden ordered the men to fire on this lorry at long range,[76] but the second lorry made a "miraculous recovery", turned quickly and sped away.

A lone machine gunner was left lying in the body of the tender. He had been hit with seven bullets and had been unable to attempt an escape. As Madden was taking the surrender, or what was left to surrender, one of the Volunteers grabbed a tin of petrol and poured the contents over the vehicle, intending to set it afire. Luke Duffy quickly jumped into the tender and scooped the gunner up in his arms and carried him to the side of the road. The man was conscious but totally incapacitated from his wounds. Fear was frozen in his eyes. Madden shouted to him, "Don't look so sharp; we are not as bad as we are painted. Nothing will happen to you here. I am in charge and Madden is my name."[77] (This same gunner failed to identify Pat Mullooly when the latter was paraded before him in the Curragh Hospital — perhaps thinking that Mullooly's face matched the voice who spared him at Scramogue.)

Surprisingly, two uninjured "civilians" were found lying under another tender. They came out with upraised arms. The Volunteers at first thought they were IRA prisoners, but the men proved to be Black and Tans headed to court-martial in Longford — one for robbing a store in Ruskey, the other for breaking the stained glass windows of Elphin Church. (The latter had been stalking Tom Brady, the Intelligence Officer for the Battalion, and was incensed that he had lost him after Brady had sneaked out the back door of the chapel.)[78]

The booty of this successful attack included guns and ammunition (two service rifles, two Webley revolvers, a Verey pistol, one Mills grenade, 227 rounds of .303),[79] a huge stock whip with short handles and an enormous thong, and a prized trophy — a Hotchkiss gun complete with 700 rounds of ammunition.[80] Madden gave all the confiscated rifles to the North Roscommon men in exchange for the Hotchkiss gun[81] (which he planned to use against the British Forces at a later date). There was, however, little time to assess the equipment or tend to the wounded. Alarm bells no doubt had been sounded at Strokestown by now — home of the Lancers. The captured Black and Tans, Evans and Buchannan, had to be taken with the escaping Volunteers.

All Volunteers headed up across the northern slope of Slieve Bawn but soon split up. Martin Fallon, Capt. James Lynagh, Pat Mullooly, Martin O'Connor, Michael Gill, and Brian Nangle took charge of one prisoner. The group headed towards Doughill. As they neared the fields in the vicinity of Farrell's public house, they halted and took cover. Cold and wet conditions prompted Mullooly and Nangle to enter the pub and get a whiskey for themselves and some for their compatriots hunkered down in a distant ditch. As they exited the public house, a lorry of Black and Tans careened around the bend in the road. Nangle and Mullooly attempted to evade capture, but they were surrounded in a neighbouring field and found themselves handcuffed and hauled off to Strokestown. The rest of their party (who were about 100 yards away) witnessed the arrests but were powerless to confront the Tans. Throughout the day, the enemy dropped men off in small groups along the Lanesboro/Scramogue Road and along the Curraghroe/ Kilrooskey Road. They searched houses along the lanes but did not venture out into the fields where Fallon and his men were hiding. The Volunteers had to remain there much of the day before heading to their dugout along the Shannon.[82] In the dark of evening, Fallon and two other Volunteers escorted the Tan (Buchannan) to the bank of the Shannon, where they intended to shoot him and dispose of his body in the river. The other two Volunteers went in search of a boat while Fallon was left to guard the prisoner. All of a sudden, Buchannan lunged at Fallon, striking him on the jaw and rendering him somewhat dazed. The Tan then bolted toward the river and hid in the branches of a sally or willow tree which bent down over the riverbank.

The Kilgefin Volunteers

Years and years have passed and gone, good and great men too,
but the memory of those Volunteers remains forever true.
Through all those years of woe and tears they bravely took this stand —
they fought against the Saxon foe to free our native land.
They proudly fought and nobly died, oh they knew not any fears.
They were from Roscommon South Battalion, the Kilgefin Volunteers.

Two miles east of Strokestown on Spy Wednesday at the dawn
these gallant men assembled 'neath the crest of ol' Sliabh Bawn.
T'was called the Scramogue Ambush where Captain Peake was shot,
but Ashbrook was the venue, right well I know the spot.
They conquered their oppressors and filled their hearts with fear.
They were from Roscommon South Battalion, the Kilgefin Volunteers.

Their Captain brave but young in years yet old in Ireland's woes,
his lifeblood he would freely give to rid Her of these foes.
The boys all followed after him o'er hillside, valley, and glen.
Well fitted was this warrior bold to command his gallant men.
He led them safe o'er bower and creek and knew not any fears.
They were from Roscommon South Battalion, the Kilgefin Volunteers.

Oh, the Black and Tans came over, and little did they care
what torture they would inflict on us. But you bet they got their share!
Rejoice, you sons of Erin's Isle, lie glad as well you may.
You fought the foe for liberty and proudly held their sway.
You drove those hirelings from our land 'mid sorrow, shame, and tears.
You were from Roscommon South Battalion, the Kilgefin Volunteers.

God rest the souls of those heroes bold! The bravest of the brave
who from those greedy ravangers our lives and homes did save.
What hardship great they did endure, those brave and fearless men.
From kindred dear they had to flee o'er mountain, bog, and glen.
Yet they always met united! So let's give three lofty cheers
to Roscommon South Battalion heroes, the Kilgefin Volunteers.

Written by Kathleen Murray of Ballyduffy, Strokestown

The most unexpected prize of the encounter, the Hotchkiss gun, a contraption unfamiliar to all the Volunteers, proved to be a weighty souvenir which had to be hauled up the slope of Slieve Bawn mountain with the retreating 3rd Battalion South men.

Fallon ran towards the returning Volunteers, jumped into their newly retrieved boat, and paddled back to where he thought Buchannan had taken refuge. They found him, shot him, and drowned him in the river.[83]

The most unexpected prize of the encounter, the Hotchkiss gun, a contraption unfamiliar to all the Volunteers, proved to be a weighty souvenir which had to be hauled up the slope of Slieve Bawn mountain with the retreating 3rd Battalion South men. (They hid it in Connolly's dugout in Fairymount.)[84] The other Tan (Evans), who was with Pat Madden's group, actually showed the men how to use the captured Hotchkiss gun[85] (no doubt hoping that he would ingratiate himself and prove to be useful to their cause). His ploy failed to save his life. He was shot in Ballagh bog.

Meanwhile, Fianna boys were scouting the mountainside, Cumann na mBan women were gathering information in the local shops about the progress and direction of British reinforcements, and local residents were bracing themselves for the expected reprisals. They never came. Only three men were captured: "Cushy" Hughes, Pat Mullooly, and Brian Nangle. Mullooly and Nangle were taken to the Lancers' Headquarters in Strokestown, then to Roscommon Barracks, and finally to Athlone, where upon their arrival they needed emergency medical attention due to their manhandling by the Lancers and RIC men of Roscommon. After a week's stay in Athlone, Mullooly and Nangle were taken to the Curragh. Following a month in the Kildare huts, they were returned to Athlone Barracks. Hughes was not with them, however, because upon his initial arrest, he had been able to produce his British military pension papers and thus was allowed to go free.

The day after the ambush, Michael, the brother of Pat Mullooly, was dragged from the Mullooly house in Kiltrustan and shot in the garden. Michael was the sole Volunteer casualty of the Scramogue Ambush.

Other Volunteers involved would later have to face tuberculosis-ridden prison cells and lifelong illnesses due to physical depravations endured for the cause of the Republic. But on that day, the Volunteers[86] (see listing in the footnotes) had won a small victory in the giant war, a victory which sustained them through many days on the wing, many nights on the run. ∎

1. Letter dated 21 February to GHQ from Gerald O'Connor, Mulcahy Papers.
2. Gerald O'Connor Papers, private collection.
3. Jim Quigley Volunteer Witness Statement to the Bureau of Military History 1913-21, p. 14.
4. Gerald O'Connor Papers, private collection.
5. Listing compiled from *Curraghboy Pre Truce Activities* and *War of Independence An Account* by Thomas Cunningham: George Fitzgerald, Patrick Reddington, William Murray, Thomas Bergin, John Waldron, John Kenny, Thomas Cunningham, Nicholas Cummins, Patrick Gallagher, Patrick Waldron.
6. Martin Fallon Volunteer Witness Statement to the Bureau of Military History 1913-21, p. 8.
7. Pat Brennan Papers, private collection: Volunteers on **Tarmonbarry patrol** included: Martin Fallon, Brian Nangle, Michael and J. Casey, James Molloy, Joe Cox, James Farrell, Patrick Murray, Michael Gunn, Peter Casey, another Peter Casey, Richard Hayden, Patrick Moran, Thomas Casey, Patrick James Gunn, Joseph Diffley, Michael and James O'Neill, Charles Noone, Thomas Goggins, James Lynagh, James Murphy, B. Gavican, Dan Hanley, Peter Shiel, Patrick Shiel, John Diffley. Pat Fallon served as the outpost. (Patrick Greene was scheduled to go but did not arrive back in time from his duty on the Republican Court to proceed with the rest of the Company.)
8. Mulcahy Papers, UCD Archives; Luke Duffy Volunteer Witness Statement to the Bureau of Military History 1913-21, p. 8; and the Pat Brennan Papers, private collection: Participants in **Strokestown attack**: Bill O'Doherty, James Molloy, Brian Kelly, Thomas Kelly, Seamus Ryan, Luke and Patrick Feeney, Pat and Thomas Greene, Sean Leavy, William Shiel, James Casey, Jim Shiel, Michael Lavery, Thomas Dillon, Willie Collins, John Murphy, Patrick Garrahan, Patrick Cox, John Casey, John Kinley, Thomas Murray, Dan Madden (of Carniska Coy.), Patrick Connor, William Collins, Michael Gibbons, Thomas Smyth, Ed Farrell, Thomas McDermott, Owen Kearns, Eugene Kearns, John Healy, John Farrell, another John Farrell, Peter Lynch, Paul Egan, Michael Gill, John Kelly (of Muckinagh), James Kelly (of Scramogue), Sean Birmingham, George Tanner, and John Gibbons of the 3rd Battalion South. Scouting duties were performed by Michael Madden, with Martin Shiel serving as outpost.
9. *An Old Soldier's Memories*, by Tommy Loughran, p. 216.
10. *An Old Soldier's Memories*, by Tommy Loughran, p. 217.
11. Martin Fallon Volunteer Witness Statement to the Bureau of Military History 1913-21, p. 12.
12. Known participants in the **Hopkins Raid**: James Stephen Brennan, Pat Glancy, Michael Dockery, James

Casey, John Breheny, and John Sheerin.

13. Compiled from the Pat Brennan Papers, private collection. Participants in the attack on **Elphin patrol:** Michael Dockery, John McGowan, John J. Conry, Paddy Joe Gannon, Pat Reynolds, Tom Gormley, Andrew Beirne, Michael Lynch, James Beirne, Luke Cox, Bernard Beirne, Pat Farrell, Willie McDermott, John Leneghan, William Cunningham, Patrick and Bernard Cullen.

14. Luke Duffy Volunteer Witness Statement to the Bureau of Military History 1913-21, p. 8.

15. Jim Dorr Volunteer Witness Statement to the Bureau of Military History 1913-21, p. 6.

16. Jack Glancy Volunteer Witness Statement to the Bureau of Military History 1913-21, p. 9.

17. Volunteers present for the **attempted attack at Frenchpark**. Information amassed from the Gerald O'Connor Papers, private collection, and the Pat Brennan Papers, private collection: John Kelly of Sheerevagh, Martin Ganley, Gerald O'Connor, Tom Crawley, John Crean, Michael Freyne, Joe Satchwell, Stephen McDermott, Sean Bergin, Ned Campion, Joe Conway, Francis and Patrick Dolan, Patrick Mulligan, John Hanily, James Doherty, John Hanley, Thomas Kelly, Patrick and John Kerrane, Tom Satchwell, Michael Casserly, Owen Fox, Michael Cryan, Owen and John Rabbit, Stephen Flattery, Hubert Beatty, Peter Murtagh, Edward Kelly, James Durr, John Shannon, Albert Durr, William Delaney, John Flynn, John Flanagan, James Crawley, James Doherty, Michael Flanagan, William Flanagan, John Kelly, Thomas Raftery, Tom Vaughan, John Kelly, Martin Foley, Brian Connor, Pat Kelly, John Flanagan, Michael Cullinan, Michael, Andrew and Patrick Mulroony, Thomas McCormack, Mattie Morahan, and Andrew Byron.

18. Extracted from the *Activities of the Knockcroghery Company* and the *Particulars of Pre-Truce Activities of Curraghboy Coy*. Participants in the **attempted ambush at Knockcroghery** include: Thomas Kelly (in command), Dick Mee, William Murphy, John Kenny, Thomas Bergin, John Breheny, Michael J. Breheny, Owen Curley, Michael Cunnane, Jim Cunnane, Patrick Fallon (senior), Paddy Fallon, Michael Quigley, William Fallon, Michael J. Fallon, Thomas Geraghty, Patrick Breheny, Michael Breheny, Michael Coyne, Thomas Rogers, Dominick Rogers, Michael Tennant, Patrick Tennant, Dan Dempsey, Patrick Breheny.

19. Jim Quigley Volunteer Witness Statement to the Bureau of Military History 1913-21, p. 8.

20. Jim Quigley Volunteer Witness Statement to the Bureau of Military History 1913-21, p. 8.

21. Luke Duffy Volunteer Witness Statement to the Bureau of Military History 1913-21, pp. 9-10.

22. Sergeant John Duffy Statement to the Bureau of Military History 1913-21, p. 1.

23. Sergeant John Duffy Statement to the Bureau of Military History 1913-21, p. 11.

24. Sergeant John Duffy Statement to the Bureau of Military History 1913-21, p. 14.

25. Sergeant John Duffy Statement to the Bureau of Military History 1913-21, p. 20.

26. *An Old Soldier's Memories*, by Tommy Loughran, p. 264.

27. *Drum and its Hinterland*, edited by Edward Egan, p. 295.

28. Seamus O'Meara Volunteer Witness Statement to the Bureau of Military History 1913-21, p. 44.

29. Seamus O'Meara Volunteer Witness Statement to the Bureau of Military History 1913-21, p. 44.

30. *Drum and its Hinterland*, edited by Edward Egan, p. 296.

31. *Clonown The History, Traditions and Culture of South Roscommon Community*, p. 76.

32. *Clonown The History, Traditions and Culture of South Roscommon Community*, p. 77.

33. Martin Fallon Volunteer Witness Statement to the Bureau of Military History 1913-21, p. 9.

34. Martin Fallon Volunteer Witness Statement to the Bureau of Military History 1913-21, p. 10.

35. Sergeant John Duffy Statement to the Bureau of Military History 1913-21, p. 16.

36. Martin Fallon interview, Ernie O'Malley Papers, UCD Archives, No. 131, p. 64.

37. John Kelly interview, Ernie O'Malley Papers, UCD Archives, No. 131.

38. Jack Glancy Volunteer Witness Statement to the Bureau of Military History 1913-21, p. 9.

39. Martin Fallon interview, Ernie O'Malley Papers, UCD Archives, No. 131, p. 64.

40. Tom Brady Volunteer Witness Statement to the Bureau of Military History 1913-21, p. 10.

41. Compiled from the Martin Fallon interview, Ernie O'Malley Papers, UCD Archives, No. 131; John Kelly (of Muckinagh) interview, Ernie O'Malley Papers, UCD Archives No. 131; and Pat Brennan Papers, private collection. Participants in **attack on Elphin Barracks:** Michael Dockery, Liam O'Doherty, Sean Owens, Sean Connolly, Joe Kelly (of Rathcroghan), John Roche (of Ballinameen), Jim Lowe of Mantua, Austin Feely, John Kelly (of Muckinagh), Pat Mullooly, John Beirne, Andrew Beirne, Brian Connor, Wilfred Feely, John Murray, Martin Dockery, Thomas Kelly, Patrick Higgins, Willie McDermott, Pat Mulvihill, Gerald Dalton, J.J. Carroll, Martin Connor, Pat Brady, Bernard Connor, Pat Reynolds, John Kelly (of Ballinameen), Michael Roddy, Eddie Carlos, Thomas Murtagh, Bernard Flanagan, David McDermott, Pat Connell, Martin Connor, James Kelly (of Ballinagare), Patrick Keenan, P. J. O'Dowd, Peter Casey (later a Sgt. in the Garda), Joseph Brennan, Michael Harrington, and Luke Roddy. Brian Nangle was in charge of the following men blocking roads between Strokestown and Elphin: Thomas Brady, Thomas Goggins, Dominick Duignan, James Beirne, John McGowan, Patrick Murray, John McKeon, Jack Glancy, Michael Duignan, and Peter Lynch. Michael Lynch scouted the town while Thomas Mulick and Michael Rushe stood guard.

42. Pat Brennan Papers, private collection.

43. Jim Hunt interview, Ernie O'Malley Papers, UCD Archives, P17b/ 133.

44. Jim Hunt Volunteer Witness Statement to the Bureau of Military History 1913-21, p. 11.

45. Thady McGowan Volunteer Witness Statement to the Bureau of Military History 1913-21.

46. Jim Hunt interview, Ernie O'Malley Papers, UCD Archives, P17b/ 133.

47. Mulcahy Papers A/1-A/17.

48. Tom Crawley Volunteer Witness Statement to the Department of Military History 1913-21, p. 14.

49. The Collins Papers, Ref.A/0535-Group VIII. Letter dated 7 March 1922 from G.O.C., 3rd Western Division.

50. Pat Brennan Papers, private collection. Men involved: Seamus Ryan, Thomas Connor, Michael Neary, Thomas Tiernan, Michael McGarry, and Joe Kelly (of Rathcroghan).

51. *For Ireland and Freedom*, by Micheál O'Callaghan, p. 75.

52. "Was Paddy Moran Judicially Murdered?" *The Irish Press* 25 March 1971, p. 11.

53. "Was Paddy Moran Judicially Murdered?" *The Irish Press* 25 March 1971, p. 11.

54. The Volunteer Witness Statements of Seamus O'Meara and Con Costello do not always agree. Costello's statement claims that he took the Column over to Westmeath after the Cornafulla Ambush, whereupon he divided it into three units. He goes on to describe actions which Seamus O'Meara claims took place in October 1920. Costello also states that Bernard Gaffey commanded one of those units, but this is unlikely as Gaffey was beaten so severely right after the Cornafulla Ambush that he died the following August. Patrick Mullooly, however, in his Witness Statement claims that Gaffey assisted him in his escape from Athlone Barracks in May 1921.

55. *For Ireland and Freedom*, by Micheál O'Callaghan, p. 86.

56. p. 212.

57. Gerald O'Connor Papers, private collection.

58. Sean Leavy in *I.R.A. in the Fight for Freedom*, p. 198.

59. "Ambush at Keadue," *The Strokestown Democrat*, p. 1.

60. Tommy Lavin Volunteer Witness Statement to the Department of Military History 1913-21, p. 8.

61. Participants in **Keadue Ambush** derived from interview with Jack Glancy, Ernie O'Malley Papers, No. 131: Michael Dockery, Seamus and Michael

Cull, Jimmie O'Brien, Tommy Lavin. Names derived from Tommy LavinVolunteer Witness Statement: Patrick McLoughlin, Jim and Tom Lynam. There are seven men unnamed who were also part of this attack, as Lavin specifies that fourteen men were engaged in the operation. Owen Cull and Bernard Gannon were arrested shortly after the ambush.

62. Tommy Lavin Volunteer Witness Statement to the Department of Military History 1913-21, p. 10.
63. Tommy Lavin Volunteer Witness Statement to the Department of Military History 1913-21, p. 10.
64. Pat Mullooly Volunteer Witness Statement to the Bureau of Military History 1913-21, p. 19.
65. Luke Duffy Volunteer Witness Statement, Department of Military History 1913-1921, pp. 10-14.
66. *I.R.A. in the Fight for Freedom,* "Scramogue Ambush did not Make for Happy Relations between Lancers and Tans," by Sean Leavy, p. 196.
67. Sean Leavy Volunteer Witness Statement to the Bureau of Military History 1913-21, p. 14.
68. *History of Kilglass, Slatta, Rooskey,* by Liam Coyle p. 139.
69. Pat Mullooly Volunteer Witness Statement to the Department of Military History 1913-21, p. 23.
70. Martin Fallon Volunteer Witness Statement to the Department of Military History 1913-21, p. 13.
71. *An Old Soldier's Memories,* by Tommy Loughran, p. 267.
72. Martin Fallon Volunteer Witness Statement to the Bureau of Military History 1913-21, p 15.
73. Seamus Nelson, resident of Ballinaheglish, interview by author, 11 October 2003, Roscommon town.
74. *An Old Soldier's Memories,* by Tommy Loughran, p. 270.
75. p. 15.
76. Frank Simons Volunteer Witness Statement to the Bureau of Military History, p. 24.
77. Pat Mullooly Volunteer Witness Statement to the Bureau of Military History 1913-21, p. 20.
78. Tom Brady Volunteer Witness Statement to the Department of Military History 1913-21, p. 5.
79. Mulcahy Papers A/38.
80. Luke Duffy Volunteer Witness Statement, Department of Military History 1913-1921, p. 13.
81. Pat Mullooly Volunteer Witness Statement to the Bureau of Military History, p. 21.
82. Martin Fallon Volunteer Witness Statement to the Bureau of Military History, p. 17.
83. Martin Fallon interview, Ernie O'Malley Papers, UCD Archives, No. 131.
84. Frank Simons Volunteer Witness Statement to the Bureau of Military History, p. 28.
85. Frank Simons interview, Ernie O'Malley Papers, UCD Archives, No. 137.
86. **Scramogue Ambush** participants: Compiled from personal interviews; Luke Duffy interview, Ernie O'Malley Papers, UCD Archives; Pat Brennan Papers, private collection; various Volunteer Witness Statements; and *Raids and Rallies* by Ernie O'Malley.

Participants named by Luke Duffy: Pat Madden, Luke Duffy, Frank Simons, John Gibbons, Jim Tiernan, Peter Collins, Tom Madden, Michael Collins, Jimmy McDermott, John McDermott, Michael Gibbons, William Hanley, Frank Egan, Paddy Tiernan, Dick Simons, Peter Connolly, Dick "Cushy" Hughes, Pat Fitzpatrick, Michael Fitzpatrick, Pat Mullooly, Peter Farrell, Martin O'Connor and Hugh Keegan.

Ernie O'Malley names Ned Cooney, Quartermaster of the Longford Brigade, as being present. (Descendants of men in the ambush, however, do not remember hearing about Cooney being with the Volunteers that day.)

Pat Brennan Papers cite these participants: Brian Nangle, John Kelly (of Muckinagh, Strokestown), Joseph and John Diffley, Eugene Kearns, Michael Greene, John J. Robinson, Michael Walsh, Luke Feeney, Dan Madden (Carniska Coy.), Michael Gunn, Henry Compton, Bill Mulligan, Peter Shiel, John Farrell, Patrick Moran, Charles Noone, Peter Casey, (another) Peter Casey, James Lynagh, Thomas Kelly, Pat Maleady (Mulleady, Martin Fallon, James Shiel, Michael Casey, Richard Hayden, James Kelly (of Scramogue), Peter Lynch, Michael and James O'Neill, William Collins, Patrick Walsh, and Michael Gill.

Men cutting communication wires and blocking roads: Pat and Michael Toolan, Patrick O'Connor, Joseph Stewart, James Hanley, Thomas Smyth, Patrick Cox, Patrick James Gunn, John Healy, Michael Madden, Dan Hanley, Patrick Greene. Hugh McDermott and Patrick Murray served as armed guards for the axemen, while Pat Fallon, Joseph Fallon, James Nelson, Thomas Casey, Michael Hunt, Peter Spalding, Frank Reilly, Thomas Dillon, John Farrell, Bernard Gavican, Francis Farrell, Michael Gearty, Michael Doorley, Tom Murray, and Martin Shiel served as outposts. According to the Volunteer Witness Statement of Sean Leavy, he was at the ambush site in the early hours but had walked back towards Longford to check on the road block. By the time he returned to the ambush site, the shooting had ceased.

Thomas Brady in his Volunteer Witness Statement claims that he, Tim Caulfield, and Michael Tiernan from Kiltrustan Company were serving as outposts on the Strokestown/Elphin Road at Cregga about six miles from Scramogue.

The Volunteer Witness Statement of Martin Fallon claims that Capt. Jack Murphy of Scramogue Company was present, as does the manuscript of Tommy Loughran, *An Old Soldier's Memories.*

Tommy Loughran's manuscript also places James Casey and James Murphy at the scene. He also claims that he and his brother Jack were involved blocking roads.

A hand-written copy of William Nugent's summary of war activities includes his claim to acting as an outpost for the Scramogue Ambush.

Post Script: Sean Leavy in I.R.A. *in the Fight for Freedom* claims that thirty nine men were present, although he does not name them. The private papers of Pat Brennan, Brigade O/C in the North during the Civil War, indicate between 40-60 men were engaged in some capacity.

SIX

THE CONFLICT
REACHES A CRESCENDO

During the months of April, May, and June, the tenor of rebellion raised to a fever pitch across the county. Assassinations, Crown Forces' reprisals, attempted ambushes, attacks on barracks, arrests, raids — all forms of civil upheaval took place on a daily basis. The common people remained as resolute as ever, the fighting spirit of the men in the field did not wane (although their supply of ammunition did), and commanders of various Volunteer units continued to aggressively challenge the enemy.

Shootings and Reprisals

In the west of the county, Seamus Mulrennan was wounded on 27 March at Lisacul while evading arresting officers. The youngest victim of the Tan War fell on 28 March. Failing to halt when ordered by the British Forces, Joseph Molloy, age 13, was shot dead at Lyonstown, Keadue. On 5 April a man from Scramogue was shot. A widower with small children, he toyed dangerously with hosting Tans in his home. The man was suspected of informing on the Volunteers in regard to an attempted ambush weeks before. He was forever silenced.

The next evening the Tans sought their own brand of vengeance. Pat Conry of Tarmon, Castlerea, was taken from his home by masked men. The next morning at early light, his family went in search of him and located his mutilated body in a nearby field. James Monds, a member of the Church of Ireland and activist in land reform, also fell victim that night. Tans invaded his home, terrorised his family, and threatened to shoot his oldest son. Reversing their decision, they seized the father and took him with them. Next morning his body, riddled with bullets, was found near his home. Monds was not a Volunteer although he clearly sympathised with their goals. He had been an outspoken critic of landlordism. It was enough "evidence" to pinpoint him as a marked man.

Curfew Notice — British Style

Restoration of Order in Ireland Regulations

Whereas several cold blooded and revolting murders have recently taken place in the vicinity of Castlerea and whereas the presence of this gang of murderers must be well known to persons residing in the District who have made no attempt to assist the Crown Forces in locating and dealing with these murderers.

Now I, Colonel T. S. Lambert C.B.,C.M.G., Colonel Commandant, 13th Infantry Brigade, Competent Military Authority, in exercise of the powers conferred on me by Section 10 of the Restoration of Order in Ireland Regulations, and all other powers (granted) me thereunto enabling,

Hereby Order that,

All licensed Premises in the town of Castlerea, in the County of Roscommon, be closed at 7 p.m. each night with effect from 21.4.1921 until further notice,

And I Order that,

The occupier of every licensed premise shall cause to be permanently exhibited in a prominent place in his premise, a copy of this Order,

And I Warn,

All and every person whatsoever who may contravene or fail to comply with any of the provisions of these Orders or the conditions or restrictions imposed thereby, that they shall be guilty of an Offence.

Signed At Athlone, this 14th day of April 1921.

(sd) T. S. Lambert Colonel
Colonel Commandant
COMPETENT MILITARY AUTHORITY

Active Service Unit Strikes in Castlerea

The Volunteers in the Castlerea area decided to enter the cooking business. As a measured response to the killing of their fellow Volunteer Pat Conry and an innocent victim, James Monds, plans were made to stir the pot, turn up the heat, and scald any unfriendly ingredients who happened to be nearby. On 7 April, ten men

Sean Bergin with his family. Sean is on the far right.

casually entered the town of Castlerea armed with two rifles, shotguns, and a few revolvers, and went in search of anyone in a British army uniform.[1] They found only one. Lance Corporal Edward Weldon of the Leicester Regiment fell victim that day. As the Volunteers[2] were withdrawing from the town, the military opened fire on them from the barracks, unfortunately killing an innocent bystander as she stood in her doorway: Mary McDonagh, wife of a publican. Peter Noone was also wounded in his right leg.[3]

An attempted ambush near Loughglynn that same month proved less successful, with twenty-six Volunteers standing ready to assault the enemy forces. The Tans and RIC did not appear. The following month eight Volunteers in the 1st Battalion South held up and disarmed two soldiers at Cloonfad,[4] but two proposed ambushes, one on an RIC patrol near Ballymoe and the other at Lisacul, proved fruitless.

The Woodlands of Loughglynn

The small village of Loughglynn was a seething hotbed of activity for the South Roscommon Brigade during the Black and Tan War. Many sons of farmers were involved with the Volunteers, and the inhabitants of many cottages opened their doors to the boys on the run — sheltering, feeding, occasionally nursing them. Such was the case with Sean Bergin.

Bergin was born in Cappamore, Co. Limerick, but moved to Nenagh, Co. Tipperary, when he was but four years old.[5] The oldest son of the family, he had been apprenticed to work in the Connolly timber yard in Castlerea. He was the sparkplug of the Battalion Flying Column and had helped in its formation. Bergin, though quite young, was not a healthy man, for he had contracted pleurisy and pneumonia while hiding in the damp fields during countless cold nights. Due to his illness, he had been taken in early January 1921 to the Cloonboniffe cottage of Micheál O'Callaghan and attended by Nurse Margaret Coll, who was home on visit from the United States. The O'Callaghan's house was a watched gathering point for Volunteers; consequently, Bergin was secretly moved to the home of Nurse Coll's parents, which was more secluded. News of his transfer found its way to the ears of the Black and Tans stationed at Castlerea. When the sounds of the lorries were heard on the pathway to the Coll's, Bergin was wrapped in blankets and placed in a heated makeshift tunnel next to Cloonboniffe Church. After the military had exited the scene, the O'Callaghans extracted Bergin from his hiding place and found him in a much worsened condition. Preparations were made to gingerly move him from safe house to safe house until he could be admitted to a hospital. After being supplied with an overcoat, Bergin was taken to Castlebar hospital, where he was registered under an assumed name. Why an overcoat? Because at that time an overcoat was well beyond the means of an average farmer, and the cloak would add a tinge of respectability to his presence and thus lessen any suspicions that might arise.

Vera McDermott in *The Woodlands of Loughglynn* and Micheál O'Callaghan in *For Ireland and Freedom* both claim that Bergin was in the hospital until March of 1921. However, Luke Duffy claims that Bergin was with him in late January in

Ballinaheglish.[6] The formal papers of Gerald O'Connor claim that Bergin was actively involved in the attack on Elphin Barracks in February 1921. Martin Fallon concurs.[7] Bergin was also cited in Gerald O'Connor's papers as being involved in the attack on the military at Castlerea in early April 1921. Whatever Bergin was doing the weeks and months prior to mid-April, we can be certain that he was with a party of men making their way o'er the fields near Loughglynn on the evening of 18 April. As the Volunteers neared the village, they left four members (Bergin, Stephen McDermott, Toby Scally, and Joe Satchwell) at Roger McDermott's cottage. As luck or ill-luck would have it, the rest of the party, including Tom Crawley, trudged on to the next townland.[8]

According to Vera McDermott's book, *The Woodlands of Loughglynn*, Bergin's return elicited a hearty meal, good humour, and gay songs from the boys and the neighbouring girls who had gathered at the cottage to greet their returning hero. Amid the hoopla and excitement, "a wild keening sound[ed] that hushed the revellers. Stephen shivered. 'Someone's walkin' over me grave,' he said, 'it sounds like the banshee.'"[9]

Another version of events is written by Roger McDermott's daughter, Mary, in the *Roscommon Herald*. She claims that the four men were "tired, hungry and bedraggled." They were fed a warm meal, knelt down to say the Rosary "but were so exhausted their beads fell out of their hands. They then tumbled into bed..."[10]

Whatever version is correct, events of the following morning are certain as death. All the lads were snugly asleep in the hidden loft when the inevitable sound of lorries thundered through the early morning air and alerted the McDermott household that danger was stampeding to their doorstep.

Roger McDermott crashed the handle of his pitchfork on the ceiling to awaken the sleeping lads who stumbled down the unsteady ladder. Half-dressed and in a heightened state of "fight or flight," Bergin cautioned Roger McDermott to keep Stephen in the house, roll up his pants, and pretend he was just an innocent boy. Young McDermott would have none of it. He followed Bergin out the door and together they headed for the north end of the field. They would never see the other side of it. Because of Bergin's weakened condition, the slow pace at which the men travelled allowed for Tans to close in on them.

During the raid, Toby Scally took a bullet in the thigh and was propelled into a ditch. The Tans assumed he was dead and moved on. Satchwell received a blow to the head from a Tan rifle, but later convinced the Tans that he was an ex-British soldier and that "he was in the house under duress...They kept him as a prisoner, however. They could not afford to let him out and let him talk."[11] But on the morning of 19 April, Bergin and McDermott bore the brunt of the Tan rage. Cornered in the woodlands, their bare feet and hands were crushed by the repeated blows of rifle butts, and they were executed under a tall elm tree that stood sentinel over their death site until a violent gale toppled it ten years later.[12]

When Sean Bergin's parents were notified of their son's death, the undertaker in their native Nenagh sent his driver, Mattie Jones, to retrieve the body from the woods. Sean was buried in the family plot in Lisboney Cemetery, but his deeds were seldom spoken of by his family.[13] Grand patriotic sentiment of "dying for the cause" was too sensitive, too near and dear for his family to face or embrace.

Sean's nephew Patrick did attend the fiftieth anniversary of the shooting in Loughglynn, where a monument had been erected in the fields behind the cottage where the two men, Bergin and McDermott, crossed to the spiritual side. And what of the other Volunteers? After the Tan War, Satchwell returned to his home. Toby Scally, who had joined the Anti-Treaty forces during the Civil War, was arrested near Castlebar and interred in Mountjoy. His gun, later smuggled to America, was returned to Castlerea and is now displayed at the Hell's Kitchen pub. He died in 1971. Satchwell passed away two years later. Bergin and McDermott, however, live on in poetry, song, spirit, and in the consciousness of

Events of the following morning are certain as death. All the lads were snugly asleep in the hidden loft when the inevitable sound of lorries thundered through the early morning air and alerted the McDermott household that danger was stampeding to their doorstep.

those who well remember the sacrifices made by very young men to free their beloved country from its long-held shackles.

No-Shows
In the spring months of 1921, several assaults on the RIC in the North Roscommon area were planned, but they never materialised. Occasionally the orders were misconstrued, but most times the enemy did not appear when or where they were scheduled. Several attempts were made in May to ambush the Crown Forces at Ardnagowna (Smithhill) just east of Elphin. Men waited for hours with boredom their constant companion.[14] On the night of 21 April, sixteen Volunteers lay in wait for a patrol on the Tarmonbarry/Ruskey Road. The enemy did not happen by that night, nor a week later on the 30th. A sixth sense, blind luck, a hotly contested card game? Who knows what reasons tempered the fingers that spun the fortune wheel on those evenings and kept the British soldiers and Black and Tans safe from the bullets of the waiting Volunteers?

Spies Executed in 3rd Battalion South Area
Informers were not limited to any single area of the county. The 3rd Battalion South area had men who were under a cloud of suspicion for some time. One worked in the post office, another had been a member of the RIC. One evening several of the Volunteers, dressed in British officer uniforms, knocked on the door of one of them. Luke Duffy positioned himself outside the house but well within hearing range of all that was to be said. After gaining admittance to his house, "the British soldiers" proceeded to extract information from this man who seemed ever so willing to tell everything he knew about the local movement — names, hideouts, arms. As the masquerading Volunteers left the house, the man asked if payment would be forthcoming — after all, his palms had been well greased the last time he supplied information.

The former RIC member was especially friendly towards the Volunteers. He often asked them to come visit him, supplying them with information about forth-coming raids and districts that were targeted for search. On one visit, he advised Frank Simons that a raid was planned by the police and that Simons should make certain all his men were moved to designated "safe" areas — townlands of Ballincurry, Ballinwully, Carrowmoneen, Aghamuck, and Fairymount. Gut instincts saved the skin of many men in the Kilgefin Company that evening. Simons did just the opposite of what the man had suggested. Sure enough, the following morning those townlands were scoured by the military, police, and Lancers from Strokestown. "There was not a bush or a crevice of any size or description that they did not fire into and they used up some thousands of rounds of ammunition in combing the area. They took everyone of military age, both male and female, and brought them to a cottage at Beechwood where they were required to parade past a window. Some local individual who knew the people of this area was apparently inside for the purpose of identification. They got none of the men they were looking for."[15]

The Battalion officers sent a memo to GHQ requesting further instructions about this man and the other suspect. Some weeks later they received their answer. The two men were to be shot. One of the informers had been passing information through a shop boy in Roscommon named McCullagh (who succeeded in getting out of the country before harm came his way). This was confirmed by the friendly Sgts. Duffy and Harte in Roscommon town. This informer also had another agent in Strokestown to whom he reported.

On the night of 8 May, the firing party was detailed to wait at Kilrooskey cross-roads. The two men were collected from their homes and marched across the fields, the two being conducted separately to their point of destiny. According to the usual IRA practice, some of the guns had been loaded with blanks while others held the live ammunition. (The Volunteers did not know which weapon they were firing.)

"There was not a bush or a crevice of any size or description that they did not fire into and they used up some thousands of rounds of ammunition in combing the area."

Frank Simons

Before the final shots were delivered, the ex-RIC man asked that his family not be harmed — a condition agreed to by the Volunteers. But most ironically, he asked that his sons be taken into the IRA if they were deemed worthy. (The man's daughter, who was also suspected of spying, was saved from deadly harm by being tied up to the gate outside Kilgefin Church, where she was found the next morning by parishioners going to the 8:30 a.m. Mass.)[16] After the order to fire had been issued and the noise had died away, signs were placed on the two bodies, which were left on the roadside as a warning — a grim reminder that freedom's price is dear for all, informer as well as combatant.

Cloontymullen

There were no fax machines in those days, no e-mail, no mobile phones; in fact, few telephones of any kind were available. Messages had to be hand delivered and were often transported by bicycle, sometimes by foot. Many times information was misdirected or, at the very least, misunderstood as to its significance. Such was the case for the mine explosion at Cloontymullen.

Michael Quinn of Fairymount, who had formerly been in the British Army, was an intelligence agent for the 3rd Battalion South. He reported to Bill Mulligan, who in turn relayed to his superior officer, Luke Duffy, that Quinn had noticed several men snooping around the Roscommon/Lanesboro Road. From the appearance of their uniforms, he recognised them as British engineers. The IRA frequently dug trenches to impede tender traffic. Quinn surmised that the engineers were seeding the trenches with their own brand of fireworks. In anticipation that the IRA would reopen this particular trench at Cloontymullen, the British Army decided to plant a Mills bomb with pin extracted and a flat stone put on the lever to keep the striker spring compressed.[17]

Luke Duffy dutifully notified the men in the area not to reopen old trenches, but to make new ones. That order was never received on the morning of 11 May, when four Volunteers commenced to reopen an old cut. Several other men were acting as scouts along the road. The trench at Beechwood they chose to reopen was located at a point in the road that was raised much higher than the land on either side of it. The soil was bog mould, and once the surface layer was removed, it was easy to re-dig the trench. The dimensions of the trench were six feet wide and six feet deep — making it impassable to any wheeled traffic.[18]

When one of their shovels disturbed the pre-planted Mills bomb, the men "heard a fizzling noise"[19] before being bombarded with an horrific explosion. Three of the men sustained incredibly gruesome wounds — Jimmy Gannon, John O'Connor, and Johnny Kelly had their mid-bodies blasted open. "Parts of their pants were driven in through their skins."[20] Only one man appeared to have cheated the devil of death — John Scally, who hadn't a wound from the knee up.[21]

With great speed and extreme secrecy, other Volunteers transported these men first to Garraghan's and then to Incheneagh Island for treatment. The Volunteer officers contacted Dr. Halloran of Lanesboro and Miss Donellan, who acted as nurse. The two went over to the island about 3 a.m. and promptly treated the patients. The nurse stayed on to tend to the men. Doctor Charles Kelly of Roscommon town visited the men to oversee their recovery, Dr. Kelly having been rowed to the island by Paddy McDermott of Annaghmore. Amazingly, the three men, despite such vicious wounds, survived the ordeal; because the attending physician was not notified that one of the Volunteers had received a slight wound in his leg, Scally died ten days later of blood poisoning. He was secretly buried in Kilteevan Cemetery with the aid of Matt Davis and his men who took "great care to conceal the new grave. Flagstones and galvanised iron sheets were placed around it. The cut sods were numbered and the surplus clay was carried away in bags, and finally the grass was raked up."[22] Such deceptions were necessary, even in death, because the British Forces were looking for a freshly opened earthen tomb, having seen the blood in the trench at Cloontymullen.

In anticipation that the IRA would reopen this particular trench at Cloontymullen, the British Army decided to plant a Mills bomb with pin extracted and a flat stone put on the lever to keep the striker spring compressed.

The other three men were transferred to Inchcleraun (Quaker) Island. Weeks later, news was received that the area around the homes of O'Connor and Gannon was scheduled to be searched. These two men were now able to return to their own area, leaving Kelly to recuperate alone. He was taken to a place called Rinnany, where he remained for a fortnight and was then moved back to Quaker Island, and finally, after the Truce, to Jervis Street Hospital in Dublin. It was not until June of 1924 that Kelly was finally released from (George V) St. Bricin's Military Hospital. A tragedy for all concerned — one man dead, one man injured so severely that it took nearly three years to heal him, and two more fortunate ones whose wounds healed more quickly yet who would forever be scarred by their experience in a trap mined trench at Cloontymullen.

Restructuring the Army

"About 1921 an idea was floated, which was accepted by (Richard) Mulcahy, much against (Michael) Collins' will, that the Army would be reorganised in terms of Divisions....up to this time there had been local companies, local battalions, and in each county, at least one or sometimes two or three brigades, depending on the strength of the population, and each brigade would have its own Active Service Unit or Flying Column, with a large number of part-time volunteers who would assemble when needed for a particular operation, and would provide intelligence and maintenance services. The system was extremely flexible, to minimise damage and worked perfectly. However, it was decided to merge larger bodies of men together and to adopt a more formal military structure..."[23]

As that regrouping related to Roscommon, for example, South Roscommon was originally divided into four Battalions — No. 1 around the Castlerea area, No. 2 the adjoining area eastwards towards Roscommon town. The 3rd Battalion centered around Roscommon town, while the 4th Battalion extended from Knockcroghery to the Shannon River and southward to Athlone. In 1920 the Athlone Brigade had been formed, grouping the areas south of the rail line between Athlone and Galway with other surrounding units of Volunteers in Westmeath. Thus that section of the county belonged to an entirely different Brigade. The northwest corner of the county around Ballaghaderreen had originally been associated with the East Mayo Brigade. (See opening pages of the Volunteer Listing for complete details of Division boundaries and Company titles.)

Bad Luck and Mis-timing

Terence McGlynn, a native of Ardcarne, had been killed in an ambush in Dublin on 9 April. Paddy Moran had been hanged in Kilmainham only a few short weeks before that. Considering the northeast section of the county to be a cauldron of Sinn Féin brew, the RIC made more and more frequent raids, hoping to catch the cooks. Jack Glancy and Michael Dockery met at Hillstreet on 16 May and then cycled to Cootehall for a meeting at which arrangements were to be made for the establishment of a Flying Column.[24] They planned to concoct an ambush, hopefully involving the Hotchkiss gun only recently captured in the Scramogue Ambush. Also of paramount importance was the construction of a dugout that would house this Column.[25]

The night was clear of clouds and the moon shone brightly on the surrounding fields as the two men headed to Paddy O'Hara's cottage. O'Hara had two sons in the movement and always welcomed other Volunteers into his cottage. If they brought a little bottle of whiskey with them, well all the better. About a mile from O'Hara's home, Dockery stopped at a public house owned by another O'Hara (William). At this late hour of the evening (11:30 p.m.), they knocked on the door and were admitted by young Joe, who proceeded to pour some whiskey into a lemonade bottle while Dockery and Glancy each ordered a bottle of beer. They had placed their guns on the table. William O'Hara was down at the barn, so when a light tap was heard at the door of the private entrance to the pub/house, Nan O'Hara opened it without any forethought of danger. It was a mistake. A wall of RIC, Tans, and Auxiliaries faced her. They tumbled into the room and recognised Dockery at once. Glancy was a stranger to them, and he played on their ignorance by claiming to be a man named Molloy. Both men were taken outside, where Dockery darted for freedom but was halted by a bullet that embedded itself in the heel of his shoe. Glancy tried to slowly shuffle off down the road as if to wander home, but was stopped by a soldier who informed him that he was going nowhere.

Meanwhile the other policemen in the O'Hara pub/house had found the two rifles — one of which was recognised as Sgt. Dowling's rifle (taken during the Keadue Ambush). How was this rifle so easily recognised? "..a piece of cord attached to the swing swivel" was the giveaway. Moving down towards the village where the soldiers planned to shoot them, Glancy and Dockery were continuously pummelled by fists and rifle butts. The policemen didn't leave them an untouched eye or nose.[26] "Shoot them now," cried one of the policemen. But Sgt. Tanning from Boyle countered, "Don't shoot them — let's have the satisfaction of hanging them."

Regan's Ford truck was commandeered. Glancy was handcuffed to Willie O'Hara and Mullaney (Mullarkey), O'Hara's workman,[27] while Dockery was bound to Joe O'Hara. The truck rumbled towards Boyle Barracks. The words of Jack Glancy best describe the journey: "The big Auxiliary who fired at us with his revolver was also one of our escort and he had very big hands, and it seemed to give him great pleasure to tear his nails down through the skin and flesh of our faces."[28] When they arrived at the Barracks, they were placed in lockup, searched, urinated on, and then soaked in liquid tossed at them from a mug, which most assuredly was not Guinness.

The next morning they were taken to the day room, then handed over to the military, brought inside the barracks, and kicked down stone steps where they were locked in solitary confinement in basement cells. Jack Glancy still bore the black and blue marks of that May thrashing when he was transferred to Mountjoy in July.[29] Glancy was not released from prison until the following January. Dockery, however, was soon to make an ingenious escape.

Dozing for the Republic

Ireland was a garrisoned country with tens of thousands of British troops and their paid snoopers, the RIC, greatly outnumbering the Volunteers. Pitched battles were suicidal. Small raids and ambushes were as close as the Volunteers could get to hassling the forces. In County Roscommon the towns were not large, the country-side even more intimate. RIC men knew many inhabitants in their district. The most dangerous place to sleep while you were a hunted man was in your own bed. In the Castlerea area, Volunteers were afraid to approach their own cottages, and in the warm evenings preceding the Truce they spent many nights sleeping under the canopy of stars. A favourite ploy was to find a field where a cow had laid down to rest and boot the bovine out of her cosy nest. The Volunteer would then snuggle into the warm patch surrounded by tall grass that kept him hidden from the prying eyes of the authorities.

Blueprint for Bombs

The construction of the bombs used in the war was not an exact science. The maker had to guess as to the amounts of explosives to be used and oftentimes had to improvise a container. There was a general formula, but frequently the builder had to approximate or sometimes substitute. Different bombs were built in various ways depending on their projected use.

Cement mines were formed in one and one half foot square cases of wood. The cement was mixed with sand, but the heart was left empty so it could contain varying amounts of gelignite. It was capped with pitch overhead. The fuse went down through the middle of the frame. An electric detonator could also ignite it, thus giving the Volunteer a choice of using battery or fuse. Some of these mines

In the warm evenings preceding the Truce they spent many nights sleeping under the canopy of stars. A favourite ploy was to find a field where a cow had laid down to rest and boot the bovine out of her cosy nest. The Volunteer would then snuggle into the warm patch surrounded by tall grass that kept him hidden from the prying eyes of the authorities.

Michael and Jack Roche of Ballinameen.

could weigh as much as six stones.[30] Horse cart box bombs could weigh in at 10 to 11 pounds, while an ass cart box was built on a smaller scale.

Another method of construction called for a few sticks of gelignite, about four in all, loosely packed. The outside circumference was clamped with bolts. A screw placed through a hole permitted the entry of the fuse. Gelignite in this type of bomb was very sensitive. It could quickly freeze in 4 to 5 hours of exposure to the cold.[31]

When Roscommon Volunteers travelled to Dublin, Diarmuid O'Hegarty would lecture them on the use and construction of explosives. Classes would include hands-on experience in throwing bottle bombs, mixing and hardening explosive substances, use of gelignite in land mines, and use of explosive mines against doorways, passageways, and stone walls.[32]

The Roche cottage of Ballinameen was home to many bomb-making sessions. Jack and Michael, both blacksmiths, constructed the devices with the assistance of their mother, Celia. The explosive mechanism used at the Elphin Barracks attack was constructed by John Murray, the Roche brothers, John Kelly, and Brian Connor at the Muckinagh munitions cottage.[33] Four electric detonators and a coil of fuse had been procured by Jack Glancy in Dublin. He had wired Feely's Monument Company in Boyle that "the Marble was on the way." Feely had contacted Jim Dorr and several other Volunteers who waited at Drumsna Station for the contraband. These devices were somewhat successful in blowing gaping holes in the barracks wall. The bomb scheduled to have been used in the attack on the barracks at Ballaghaderreen in February was composed of a barrel of concrete reinforced with scrap iron.

Attack on Ballaghaderreen Barracks from a Train

The night of 17 May was a fine one for such doings. The Volunteers implemented a plan whereby they held up a train from Ballaghaderreen to Kilfree, then went to the Mullaghroe Station where they met the Dublin/Sligo train. They disarmed two soldiers and took possession of the engine. One of the Volunteers, Richard McGough from Tuam, was an engine driver and knew how to manipulate the controls of such a large and generally unfamiliar contraption. He manoeuvred the train towards Ballaghaderreen and stopped on the railway bridge about thirty yards from the RIC barracks. The Volunteers started shooting — an exchange that lasted about ten minutes. Not wishing to push their luck any further, they backed up the engine in the direction of Kilfree. About 300 yards from Ballaghaderreen, however, they spotted six RIC constables coming from the direction of Frenchpark. The Volunteers again moved the train up to the original position on the bridge and opened fire on the six newcomers.

Inside the train, bullets from the RIC whizzed through the air, some finding their mark, slightly wounding McGough (McGoff) and — Harrington. It was time to go! When the Volunteers attempted to reverse the train for the second time, the obstinate machine would not budge. The three men darted off the train and retreated by foot to the mountains.

When they neared the hills, they decided to go to Mullaghroe, Co. Sligo. On their way they passed Peter Finn's pub at Monasteraden and stopped. Definitely a mistake! Five minutes later a contingent of police and Tans surrounded the pub, but not before the three men dashed out the back door.

Harrington made his way towards the bog, while Jim Hunt ran full bore for nearly a half hour. He tried to put as much distance between himself and the pursuing Tans. Only one man kept up the pace. Hunt occasionally fired a pot shot over his shoulder to discourage his pursuer when he got too near. The Tan, an Englishman named Little, however, finally caught up with Hunt, who attempted to shoot him. Alas, he had no bullets left.

When the other Tans reached the two front runners, they were furious. They wanted to shoot Hunt on the spot, but ironically, the Tan Little, who had chased him down the hardest, came to Hunt's defence. Had it not been for Little, Hunt "would not have survived the night."[34]

The wounded McGough was also taken prisoner that evening, but the reports made years later about the incident make no mention of Harrington. To his great relief, perhaps the bog "swallowed up his identity."

Escape from Athlone Barracks

The land was rife with attack, counterattacks, executed spies, and threatening situations. Not every inch of the county could be properly guarded by the Crown Forces, not even every inch of British military property.

While incarcerated in an underground cell in Athlone Barracks, Pat Mullooly developed a nasty case of scabies. Dr. McDonnell of Athlone spoke with the medical officer in the barracks about transferring Mullooly to the hospital ward[35] (where a rescue or break out would be more easily accomplished). When Mullooly was sent to the medical orderly, the man suggested that instead of the traditional sulphur baths to cure the rash, Mullooly should scrape between his fingers with a match box to keep the area infected; thus, his housing conditions would be safer and the possibility for escape greater — perhaps even successful enough to allow Mullooly to later tell the story of the war to his grandchildren. On the night of 24 May (more precisely the morning of 25 May), Pat Mullooly, who had been arrested after the Scramogue Ambush, was resting with both eyes open in his hospital bunk at Athlone Barracks. The chiming of the town clock at 2 a.m. alerted him that it was now his time to strike. While the sentries outside his room were being changed, he quietly opened the window and squeezed through to the window-sill, and jumped to the ground. When he landed, he jammed his back and, according to Mullooly, "immediately got an awful pain in my feet and back and could not straighten my body. I ran in a stooped position to the ladder — nearly on all fours — and climbed to the top of the wall, putting my trenchcoat which I had taken with me on the glass which covered the top."[36] He dallied not at all to partake of the fruits of British hospitality, but rather took the ladder with him and ran across the orchard to the main barrack wall. He climbed the ladder, negotiated through three strands of barbed wire, and then dropped into a plantation of laurels which proved to be the church private grounds. Scaling yet another short barricade, he ran across the roofs of low sheds and dropped into a lane at the head of Connaught St., then headed west to friendly territory.

After receiving tea at a hospitable house, he accompanied the local people on their way to the bog to cut turf. After hiding in a bog hole for part of the day, he was visited at 10 p.m. by Barney Gaffey, the O/C of the 3rd Battalion Athlone Brigade, who put Mullooly on a donkey cart and brought him to Taughmaconnell, where he was given medical treatment by Eva Fitzgerald of Athlone and Dr. McDonnell of the same town. He sheltered with the O'Connell and Flynn families for a week and was given £5 from the Battalion funds to purchase some new clothes. He was then directed to the Castlecoote Coy. and from there to Pat Madden's home in Ballagh.

It was now mid-June and Mullooly moved on to Curraghroe, from there to a dugout in Scramogue, and finally to Hillstreet, where he met (recently escaped) Michael Dockery. The two planned an ambush on Tully Hill near Kilglass, which, owing to a no-show by the enemy, proved a fruitless endeavour. Mullooly, however, was now completely free to fight another battle, plan another attack, strike another blow for an independent Ireland.

Informants

Many men during those years of strife who gave information to Crown Forces or their stooges found an early and cold grave into which an IRA bullet propelled them. Signs pinned on murdered informants announced to the local inhabitants

When Mullooly was sent to the medical orderly, the man suggested that instead of the traditional sulphur baths to cure the rash, Mullooly should scrape between his fingers with a match box to keep the area infected; thus, his housing conditions would be safer and the possibility for escape greater.

that this could be their fate if they were caught aiding and abetting the enemy. When a woman was suspected, the punishment was usually not death but some form of humiliation and isolation. Consider the case of Miss Brennan. She was thought to be carrying information to the RIC in Castlerea. Local Volunteers kidnapped her, shaved her head, and kept her under observation for six months. Surrounding residents were well aware of her predicament.

Another example of ridicule heaped upon a woman's head was the Sunday exposure. When a local lass was thought to be carrying tales to her Black and Tan boyfriend, the woman was tied up to a post outside of church on a Sunday morning. Her clothes would be secured up around her neck — in effect, exposing her. When the first churchgoers arrived for Mass, she would be "unmasked."

When circumstances demanded, punishments could be more severe. In the Loughglynn area, two women were known to be spying for the enemy. One was the wife of an RIC man. Because neither of the women made any secret of their sympathies, the Volunteers decided the area would be better off without them. The ladies found their homes set ablaze and warnings delivered to clear out of the area. They took the advice.

Even guilt by association brought scorn upon one's head. Evelyn O'Callaghan, a teacher from Nenagh, Sean Bergin's hometown, had a brother in the RIC. Although no one could prove any misdeeds on her part, the hostile attitudes of the villagers swept decisively against her after Bergin's murder. Local Volunteers would boo her as she walked down the pathways. Cold stares and glares met her on the street corners. She transferred from her position in Castlerea and endured the rest of the war behind a desk in a smaller school in Castleplunkett.

Mantua (Kilmaryal) Church Invaded by Crown Forces

On 17 May the Tans and local RIC paid a visit to the home of Father Malachy Brennan of Mantua. Fr. Brennan, who was noted for his strong stand for Irish independence, had recently been transferred from Caltra, Co. Galway, where his house had been riddled with bullets from the Crown Forces. On this May day in Mantua, the Tans took his bicycles, threatened his sister, and promised more of the same if he did not denounce "Irish savagery" from the pulpit. Typical of his spirit, Fr. Brennan informed the officers that his orders came from Maynooth, not Dublin Castle.

On the following Sunday, 22 May, Crown Forces again appeared at the Mantua Church. While Father was engaged in saying Mass, the troops were busy searching his abode for incriminating evidence. After confiscating a bottle of whiskey and a rather expensive cigarette case (which had been a present), the troops surrounded the male congregation and threatened them. The troops again targeted Father Brennan, who reiterated his stance that he would not denounce the local boycott nor would he take any orders to do so from the likes of the Inspector.

In mid-June, the soldiers paid yet another visit to Fr. Brennan, and the whole show of threats and intimidation being met with firm Irish resistance was played out. The Crown Forces decided more-drastic measures were required.

On the following Sunday, 26 June, the congregation had just been seated after the gospel when the rat-a-tat-tat of machine gun fire pounded the roof of the church. Women and children shrieked at the noise and stormed the sanctuary, where many of them clung to Father's vestments. Under Father's calming countenance, the congregation finished Mass, after which the military in the back of the church separated the men from the women. The females were ordered to one side of the church, where they were lectured on the evils of assisting the IRA and what ills would befall them personally if they were caught doing so. The men were lined up on the opposite church wall, where some were beaten and all were warned to withhold tea and sympathy from the IRA or their houses would be burned and their rights to turf cutting nullified.

As to Father Brennan, the real target of the raid, the same intimidation and oral grilling took place. Due to the familiar steadfastness of the pastor, however, no new proclamations were declared, no new rules of conduct were promised. The arrival of the Truce two weeks hence no doubt saved Father Malachy Brennan and his congregation from future interrogations or worse.

Kilrooskey Fight

Three Volunteers were involved in a trench-cutting operation on 30 May on the road from Rhatigan's pub to Beechwood. Dick Simons and James Nelson were digging while — Farrell was serving as sentry armed with a Lee Enfield rifle (taken from Constable Macken at Moneen). The two men digging had placed their shotguns nearby. Without warning, a lorry of Tans came upon them. The Volunteers quickly took flight across the fields. In the darkness surrounding the area, the Tans lost track of the work party. They fired into the dusky surroundings, only to hit Farrell's rifle — splitting it in two, flinging fragments of the gun stock into his face.[37] Farrell hurled himself across a nearby wall and waited quietly for the Tans to pursue him. Unaware that Farrell was also armed with a grenade, the policemen neared the hidden man. When they were close enough for the bomb to do its work, Farrell tossed it. Constable George Redding was killed. The remaining constables, fearing a greater number of men lay in ambush, made short work of dashing back to the lorries. Redding was abandoned by his comrades in the field until the next day when three lorries of Tans under Inspector Cole came to retrieve his body. (This version of events differs remarkably from the Roscommon RIC reports to Dublin Castle: "This fight was a good one and a force of ten police beat from 60 to 100 rebels after an hour's conflict.")[38]

Carnagh Clash

On 1 June the Volunteers engaged the RIC near Carnagh, Kiltoom. One policeman was wounded, and his fellow constables, who sought to root out the rebels from a house where the assailants were last seen, barged into the Murphy cottage. At the sound of crashing doors and angry policemen, sixty-seven-year-old Patrick Coyle of Bredagh, Kiltoom, who happened to be there doctoring a horse, attempted to run away. He was shot. He later died of his wounds in Athlone. The two Murphy brothers (Hubert and Tom), who had indeed been involved in the Carnagh conflict and who were now hiding near the house, escaped, Hubert by hiding in nettles for two hours.[39] A military inquiry into the death of Coyle found a verdict of involuntary manslaughter. The local people, however, came to a much different verdict from their own inquiries.

Castlerea Murder Gang Strikes Again

Three Volunteers had been resting in Connor's house in Aghadrestan near Loughglynn on 2 June when they were surprised by a party of armed Tans whose careful aim did not miss the body of Mick Carty, an active member of the South Roscommon Flying Column. Nor did his fellow Volunteer escape injury. Pete Shannon's body was pockmarked by eight bullets — one of which left him with permanently damaged vocal chords. For the duration of his life, Pete spoke in a hoarse whisper. Pete was taken to Athlone Hospital; later he was imprisoned in Mountjoy, where he remained until the Truce. His brother Edward (Ned) avoided the sting of bullets that day.

Lightning Strikes Twice

A thunderbolt hit the British Military the night of 15/16 June 1921.[40] (The personal diary of Pat Brennan claims the 9th or 15th of June, and the RIC Monthly Report to Dublin Castle states 15 June as the precise date.)[41] James Molloy, who had previously been arrested for his attack on a police patrol in Ballymote, had recently escaped from Boyle Barracks! Boyle Barracks — a British stronghold garrisoned by the Bedfordshire Regiment, with the RIC and a group of Black and Tans stationed in the District Headquarters beside the main gate of the barracks. All these forces were augmented by a company of Auxiliaries housed in the old

Without warning, a lorry of Tans came upon them. The Volunteers quickly took flight across the fields. In the darkness surrounding the area, the Tans lost track of the work party. They fired into the dusky surroundings...

Military barracks at Boyle, restored in 1995 by the Roscommon County Council as the King House Visitor Centre.

Boyle Workhouse. How could such an escape happen? How could such a lowly Irish peasant outfox so much military expertise? Well no matter, for it would not happen again. And yet it did!

Michael Dockery had spent several weeks behind bars. Having been caught with a rifle taken from the Keadue ambush site, Dockery had been brought to the barracks, stripped naked, and thoroughly examined for any markings or unusual characteristics. Since that crude initiation to life behind bars, he had whiled away the hours in a basement cell; but, worse yet, he was up for a murder charge and due to be taken to Dublin for trial — a sure death sentence. Dockery was the O/C for the North Roscommon Brigade, and his demise would have been a huge loss to the area. It was imperative that he be rescued.

Housing disagreeable Volunteers was not a strain on His Majesty's budget. A containment structure was supplied by the lean-to shed attached to the barracks wall which at one time had acted as a miniature firing range. Bedding consisted of a bag of straw with two threadbare blankets per man — an amenity not required in the warm summer of 1921. A trench dug along the clay floor served as a latrine. "Drinking water came from the river through which passed all the sewage of the town."[42] Breakfast consisted of a bucket of tea "with broken hard biscuit and a jam jar for each pair of men."[43] A lone dinner plate was shared among FOUR cell-mates.

Phil Murray, a prisoner who formerly served as the Adjutant to the Brigade, approached Corporal Meadlarklan, a sympathetic military policeman. Aside from "sympathy," Meadlarklan was given £300.[44] (According to Pat Mullooly, Quartermaster for the Brigade, Meadlarklan never personally received a penny.[45] Meadlarklan's daughter, B. Wickins of Leighton Buzzard, England, also denies any personal profit motive for her father's actions.[46]) Meadlarklan could have been merely the conduit through which funds were paid to other willing constables (i.e., the guard in the guard-room who controlled the keys). According to Rita Leneghan of Hillstreet, she later picked up the money from Martin Fallon and Sean Leavy and "conveyed it to the place where it was handed over."[47]

Through the pipeline between Murray and Meadlarklan flowed intelligence data regarding Dockery's placement (he was still incarcerated in a basement cell), daily schedules, and duty roosters. Joe Martin, altar boy for Masses conducted at the Barracks, aided the escape plans by transporting dispatches hidden in his knickers. The Corporal also visited the premises of Miss Margaret Judge, who operated a shop on Main Street. The store offered cigarettes, sundry items, and a convenient location for transferring information. (See "Roscommon Volunteer Section, Corporal Meadlarklan" for further details.)

Four days after Molloy's "disappearance," James Feely, Martin Killalea, Murray, and Peter Heslin again set in motion escape plans — this time to assist Dockery and Jack Glancy. Corporal Meadlarklan stole the keys out of the guardroom and opened the locks to Dockery's as well as Jack Glancy's cell. "Unfortunately, some-one had given Sergeant Buggy a message to deliver to Jim Hunt — tobacco or something — with the result that when he, the Sergeant, came down to deliver the message, he found the padlocks open and he then locked them and (our) hopes were dashed. Afterwards, that same evening, Dockery's padlock was again opened but not mine [Glancy's]."[48] Dockery, led by Corporal Meadlarklan, made his way to the washhouse, escaped through the window, and waded into the river, only to be met by the same men who had aided in Molloy's escape: Pat Brennan, Pat Delahunty, Luke Dempsey, Tom Derby, Tom Lohan, Batty Reid,[49] and Patrick Chapman.

Lightning striking once — an entree from angels — seasoned with human care-lessness! Lightning striking twice — in the same place — an unpalatable dish con-cocted by scoundrel Irish rebels — peppered with obstinacy and guile. What was needed was a new recipe in a new kitchen with hotter ovens and wily cooks — off to Sligo Gaol, Mountjoy, or, better still, the Curragh with the rest of the lot! And away they went.

A Spy is Drowned
He had been born in Lancashire, married in March of 1919, and, a year later, according to Richard Abbott in *Police Casualties in Ireland 1919-1922*, joined the Royal Irish Constabulary.[50] (Tom Crawley in his Volunteer Witness Statement claims that the man was a Black and Tan.)[51] Harold Round was stationed in the town of Castlerea. Oftentimes he was observed heading out into the countryside at night dressed in plain clothes. The Volunteers strongly suspected that his mission was spying!

On 16 June three Battalion officers, who were staying in John Farrell's house between Ballinagare and Castlerea, noticed a strange man dressed in civilian clothes cycling past. He seemed to take special note of the house they were occu-pying. One of the Volunteers followed him directly, another came shortly after (in case the first Volunteer got into trouble). The two men stopped the stranger, recognised him as Constable Round, and relieved him of his .45 Webley revolver and eighteen rounds of ammunition. Round admitted that he was on intelligence work, and, rather ironically, asked for a Catholic priest in order that he might be baptized.[52] The Volunteers procured a priest for him, and after his baptism, locked him in a nearby barn, where he was kept under constant surveillance while the men held a kangaroo court to determine his fate. The officers were well aware they could never release him, for he knew too much. They did not wish to shoot him, and consequently decided to take him to the River Suck at Donamon, where stones were placed around his neck before he was tossed into the waters.

Knockcroghery Exhales Its Final Puff
(There has been some confusion about the precise date of the burn-ing of Knockcroghery — 18 June, claimed Jack Kirwan in "Night of Terror," *Co. Roscommon Historical and Archaeological Society Journal*. F. Coyne in the same journal, Vol. III p. 28, claimed 19 June. The private papers of Gerald O'Connor, O/C of 1st Battalion South Roscommon, later the O/C of No. 2 Brigade in the 2nd Western Division, denoted 21 June. The Military Archives in Dublin state

Knockcroghery after it was burned.

the same date. Also the Roscommon RIC Monthly Report written by the District Inspector to Dublin Castle claimed that 21 June was the day.)

For centuries the little village of Knockcroghery, located six miles south of the town of Roscommon on the Athlone Road, has been a smoking establishment. Local legend claims that the first settlers to start up the pipe-making businesses were of Scottish descent who had immigrated there after the Battle of the Boyne. They were pipers (the bowl of a clay pipe is exactly the proper size needed for storing musket powder for the guns of that time) and had chosen Knockcroghery because of its proximity to Carnamaddy, St. John's, where the superior clay lent itself to moulding. Some of the descendants of those pipers became famous throughout Ireland. (The local clay had, at one time, even been shipped to the famed potteries of Belleek, Ireland.) When the nearby supply became depleted in the 1880s, a substitute had to be imported from Devonshire, England.

Several families became the principal pipers of Knockcroghery: the Curleys, the Lyons, and the Fitzgeralds. Fashioned from blocks of hardened clay into the "forty-three" style, the pipes were a family-run industry complete with delivery by horse and cart to all parts of the country.

On the evening of 21 June, however, more than just the usual puffs of pleasant pipe smoke hung in the nighttime air. Fiery fingers clawed the black sky. The houses had been set ablaze by the Black and Tans, who had brought petrol into the village and scattered it on the thatched-roof houses. After the inhabitants were herded out into the cool air, a match was struck, and all the people's possessions melted, disintegrated, and vaporised into plumes of billowy smoke.

Why was this village burned? Over the decades of the twentieth century the story had been related that the Crown Forces had been misinformed. General Lambert, Commanding Officer of the British troops in the west of Ireland, had been ambushed by members of the Tubberclair Company and killed the day before near the village of Glasson, Athlone. British intelligence mistakenly pinpointed Volunteers from Knockcroghery for the deed. (Captain Elliott of the Tubberclair Company in County Westmeath was actually in charge of the ambush that resulted in the General's death.)[53] The British decided to torch the village as a reprisal and warning to other Volunteer groups. While this version has gained credence through repetition over the years, it may not be the entire story.

Pat Madden, O/C of the 3rd Battalion South, was a determined fighter and strategic planner. In March his men had captured the Hotchkiss gun in the Scramogue Ambush. He meant to make good use of it. Madden devised a plan whereby that high-powered gun would be situated on the main road in Knockcroghery, aimed at the British Forces that travelled in tenders from Roscommon to Athlone. Lumber which was logged near Moate, County Westmeath, was routinely transported to Knockcroghery for rail shipment. On a particular mid-June day, however, the lumber was not placed near the rail station but moved around the town for defensive positions. A local man earned his £5 that day by giving this information to the Crown Forces. They were so incensed that the Volunteers would attempt so rash an attack on them that they took their vengeance out on the local people and torched the whole village.[54]

Whatever the motivation for the destruction, the innocent inhabitants were left with nothing but the clothes on their backs. They took shelter with family and friends in the district. Smouldering cinders and barren stone walls greeted them when they returned to their homes. The not-so-innocent spy, who had informed about the Volunteers' planned attack, paid for his deed with more than a charred house. He was shot!

Quiet Corners

Contrasted to all the actions cropping up all over the hills and fields of the county, the Kilmore area of North Roscommon remained unseeded. This was an intentional neglect due to the fact that the Brigade Headquarters was located around Hillstreet, and "if large enemy forces had been attracted into the area it would have restricted the movements of the staff and communications severely."[55]

The Bravest Men in Ireland

Such a lowly piece of furniture to exhibit so grandiose a claim! A gold plaque attached to its back reads: "The Bravest Men in Ireland Sat in this Chair — The Old IRA." Where did the chair come from, and by what stretch of hyperbole did the inscription come to be placed on the back of a seemingly ordinary wooden chair made in Ballyhaunis in 1916?

Patrick Vaughan's treasured chair from his family home in Cloonsuck, Castlerea.

PHOTO COURTESY OF LEW THORNE

After the War, the chair had been dismantled, placed in a shipping crate, and misdirected to several countries in Europe (Italy, France, and the Netherlands) before reaching its final destination in Boston, Massachusetts. And what a dilapidated specimen of craftsmanship it presented after reassembly — a singed crescent in the back slat coupled with a huge hole in the seat. Brave men sitting in it indeed — more than likely simple men, audacious and/or distracted individuals. What pomp, what an outlandish proclamation, and yet what profound truth.

For the chair had been one of a set of eight made for the Vaughan family of Cloonsuck. On it had rested the fighting men of the 1st Battalion South Flying Column — daring, bold, unconcerned about their own physical safety, burning with a desire to free Ireland. On this chair was seated Martin Ganley, Ned Shannon, or John Vaughan on the morning of 22 June when a thunderous explosion of crashing glass startled the men and roused them from their drowsy state. Vaughan lobbed a hand grenade into the midst of the Black and Tans who had surrounded the house. Failing to explode, it offered no protection or distraction for the men trapped inside. Grabbing the chair and holding it up in front of him to serve as a shield, one of the men attempted to deflect the ravages of bullets streaming unceasingly from the guns of the Tans. Shannon and Vaughan decided to bolt for the back door beyond which fields might provide an escape route. It was not to be. Unbeknownst to them, another squad of Tans had assembled on the west side of the house and to the rear. When Shannon and Vaughan entered the clearing, they were greeted by a barrage of lead that tore through their bodies.

North Roscommon Brigade Strength As of July 1921:		
1st Battalion	257	
2nd Battalion	142	
3rd Battalion	314	
4th Battalion	145	
Total	858	
North Roscommon 2nd Battalion Strength As of July 1921:		
"A" Coy.	27	0 interned
"B" Coy.	25	1 interned
"C" Coy.	14	4 interned
"D" Coy.	27	3 interned
"E" Coy.	11	6 interned
Aughrim	16	3 interned
Battalion Staff	5	
Total:	142[57]	

Vaughan died within minutes, Shannon a short time later after his body had been placed on a cart by the Tans and was en route to Castlerea. Fearing the worst, Mrs. Ellen Vaughan attempted to go to her son's body which lay in the field. One of the Tans struck her with a rifle butt.[56]

Ganley, who had remained behind in the house, at first hid from the soldiers. Upon a second search, however, the Tans found him and John's brother, Tom. The two men were herded out onto the road along with other family members who had been aroused from a sound sleep by the commotion. Not content with killing two men, another group of Tans climbed to the roof and attempted to set the thatch ablaze. Meanwhile inside the house, the furniture, the dishes, every item of value was heaved and tossed. The wooden chair, on which had been seated any one of the three, was but one of many items whirled into the tornado of destruction.

Martin Ganley survived that day. He was arrested, court-martialled, and sentenced to fifteen years penal servitude at Mountjoy. He was released following the Treaty. Tom Vaughan, who at the time was suffering from a recent bout of pneumonia, was beaten senseless, arrested, and taken to Athlone Barracks. A doctor ordered his release three months later due to his ill health. Tom was to suffer throughout his lifetime from the thrashing he endured that terrible day in June. And the chair, a witness to one of many battles for freedom in Ireland, what of it? It stands, complete with golden plaque, next to a fireplace in the living room of Pat Vaughan's daughter in Cape Cod, Massachusetts, where it bears stoic testimony to truly brave young men who lived not to see the birds flutter and grass bend in the late summer breeze of 1921.

North Roscommon Men Active Until the End

On 25 June, men from Ballinameen, Mantua, and Breedogue Companies assembled with the intent of ridding Frenchpark of the two most hated symbols of British rule — the barracks and the courthouse. A large part of the garrison had already moved to new quarters in the dispensary a few hundred yards away. To confine those men, some Volunteers sniped at that building. A ring was placed around the barracks, and three men with double-barrelled shotguns (with cartridges heavily slugged) covered the doorways from twenty-five yards away.[58] Other Volunteers began torching the courthouse and barracks. Planned by Pat Brennan and commanded by Sean Owens and John Kelly, the operation succeeded in setting the buildings aflame.[59]

By this time in the war, small patrols venturing out onto roads were but a memory. The IRA was active and getting deadlier all the time. British Forces sequestered themselves inside well-fortified barracks and waited until nightfall before they came out onto the lanes and main roads. When they did leave the barracks, they travelled in groups of fifteen to twenty; moreover, to confuse the watchful IRA, they did not move about with any degree of regularity. Sometimes they took this road, another time they sallied forth in the opposite direction. Their patrols did not return to barracks by any predictable route. To counter this, Martin Fallon, on Saturday 2 July, led twenty-seven Volunteers[60] towards Tarmonbarry. Rather than guess which way the patrol would return, Fallon sent a scout ahead to report on the positioning of the patrol. When Fallon learned they had gone out the Longford road, he assembled his men by the schoolhouse. It was a moonlit night — perfect for ambush.

Martin Fallon, armed only with a revolver, walked down the road towards the barracks, intent on getting near enough to throw a bomb at the patrol when it returned. His men, equipped with the rifles, were 100 yards behind him when he spotted a patrol from the Longford side suddenly descending on the barracks. Fallon fell to the ground, blasted his whistle, and ducked — trying to avoid the crossfire between the RIC patrol in front and his own men behind him. Although he managed to get a few shots off from his revolver, most of the patrol escaped into the barracks. In the ensuing fight, however, several RIC constables were wounded. The only casualty of the night was not a result of Volunteer gunfire but from a Verey light pistol which exploded in the hand of Sergeant Smith. The Volunteers suffered no injuries, and Fallon considered himself a lucky man to have survived the vise of sharpshooters pressing from both sides.[61]

Two days later Thomas McGowan was shot in Tarmonbarry by members of the IRA. McGowan was not a Volunteer, and the killing turned out to be the result of a local family feud rather than any politically motivated assassination. The men who pulled the triggers were court-martialled and sentenced to deportation. Sean Leavy, O/C of the 3rd Battalion North, went to McGowan's family, apologised, explained what happened and what action was taken in regard to the assailants.[62]

About the 10th of July, Pat Mullooly assembled a group of men for an assault on another patrol at Lavally, Strokestown. Armed with only a single rifle, two hand grenades, and some shotguns, they waited for their prey. About forty men were involved in the attempted ambush, most of them blocking roads. They made "so much noise in throwing down the stone walls and building them across the roads that they were heard in Strokestown, and instead of the RIC coming out the way we wanted them, they went instead by the Elphin road and raided (Tom) Brady's."[63]

Assistance from the Grave

Jack Farrell, a landlord who lived in the Ballinagare area, succumbed to his final trouble during the Trouble Times. He was buried in an extravagant lead coffin in the Kilcorkey Cemetery. Shortly after the last amen had been pronounced, Volunteers secretly returned to the graveyard, "resurrected" his coffin, then proceeded to melt it down and formed bullets that found their way into IRA firearms.

An American Commission

News of the atrocities of the Black and Tans travelled across the Atlantic Ocean. In 1921 an American Commission was formed whose purpose was to investigate conditions in Ireland. Through the efforts of the editors of the New York *Nation*, this commission assembled in Washington to hear first-hand accounts of the happenings in Ireland. The Commission was composed of 150 persons from a variety of backgrounds, including five state governors, eleven U. S. senators, thirteen congressmen, mayors of fifteen cities, several leading Roman Catholic clergymen, as well as seven Protestant Episcopal and four Methodist bishops. Following are a few excerpts from the Commission's final report.

Testifying witness: Father English, American citizen who resided in Whitehall, Montana, who had recently returned from a visit to his parents' home in County Limerick:

"About the date that I arrived in Ireland, a fresh correspondent there, one of the representatives of the Paris *Matin*, had an interview with Lord French, the Lieutenant Governor of Ireland. This was published in the papers over there, the English and Irish papers. He asked French what the trouble was in Ireland. French said the difficulty in Ireland was two hundred thousand young men who should have emigrated. I believe that the only possible reason and the explanation that I heard around there was that the reason for the destruction of these creameries [in Limerick] and other business houses was to throw out of employment the young men and compel them to leave the country — in addition, of course, to the auxiliary reason, the attempt to terrorise out of the minds of the people their hope for independence."[64]

He was buried in an extravagant lead coffin in the Kilcorkey Cemetery. Shortly after the last amen had been pronounced, Volunteers secretly returned to the graveyard, "resurrected" his coffin, then proceeded to melt it down to make lead shots that found their way into IRA firearms.

Moydrum Castle.

This same priest also interviewed a soldier on the train travelling from London to Hollyhead. Father English's testimony regarding that conversation:

"About the fifteenth of July I met a young man on the train who told me he was an army officer, a first lieutenant, about to be sent to take command of his company in Ireland in the County of Roscommon. He told me he had been over there before and was home on a furlough for two weeks. He said, "I wish to God I never had to go over there again." I said, "Why?" He said, "Because it is the most distasteful work I have ever done." He looked young. I asked him, "How old are you?" He said, "I am not quite twenty-two yet, and only out of the military school a short time." I said, "What is the nature of your duties in Ireland?" He said, "I command a body of about one hundred fifty men in the County of Roscommon. I am to look after that part of the country." I said, "Are you given full jurisdiction there?" He said, "Yes." I said, "How, for instance, would you act in the case of a riot or in case your men were going through the country and stones were thrown at them, or you saw people who looked suspicious?" He said, "I have the right to order my soldiers to fire."

"The reason I introduce this is to show that a young man not yet twenty-two years of age has the power of life and death in that part of the country."[65]

The Burning of Castlemaine (Moydrum Castle)

A few days after the burning of the village of Knockcroghery, local IRA commanders received orders from GHQ to destroy an equal number of homes belonging to British sympathisers. The Athlone Brigade commander, Con Costello, "did not consider it would be fair to burn those people's houses for something which was not their fault."[66] A more appropriate target was sought. Lord Castlemaine lived in Moydrum Castle (four miles on the Mullingar side of Athlone), and was a member of the British House of Lords. His was the home selected to pay the price.

On 3 July, about twenty men (thirty to forty claims Frank O'Connor) under the command of Tom "Con" Costello were mobilised for the action. British soldiers and officers from Athlone were frequent visitors to the house, and the Volunteer officers did not know whether they would encounter a group of them there that night and have a fight of it. After knocking on the main door and (of course) being refused entry, the Volunteers broke in a door panel of the castle and stated the purpose of their visit. Lady Castlemaine asked for time to gather her valuables. She was granted this request, although she was reminded that the Tans had not been as accommodating when they had recently burned homes in the Coosan area as a reprisal for General Lambert's killing. The household servants were rounded up and put in a safe place while the interior was liberally sprinkled with petrol and paraffin. Holes were "made in the floors and ceilings to give the flames ventilation."[67] After all persons had been accounted for, the castle was set afire. Lady Castlemaine remained very dignified under the circumstances and never winced. She later refused to identify any of the men involved. "She informed the military that the men who burned the Castle were gentlemen and behaved as such."[68]

The Burning of the Town of Ballaghaderreen

During the summer of 1921, Black and Tans stationed in Ballaghaderreen decided to get rid of "Shinners" from the area once and for all. Grabbing a torch, they set out on a mission of destruction. When RIC Constable Patrick O'Dowd confronted them and informed them that he was in charge, he ordered them to return to quarters. They ignored him. Out on the street, their first stop was a large shop, John Flannery and Co. Soon adjacent stores were ablaze. People jammed the street, watching in disbelief as their town and its contents went up in smoke. "And then quite mysteriously the operation was called off and no more premises were set alight. It was learned afterwards that Sergeant O'Dowd had approached the military authorities and as a result of this visit the Tans were recalled to their barracks."[69]

The town of Ballaghaderreen.
THE IRISH HISTORICAL PICTURE COMPANY

Reining in the Troops

A secret army spread throughout a country with semi-autonomous commanders is a wily and nebulous creation difficult to mould and control. Oftentimes an individual Brigadier would get what he thought was a good idea, act upon it, then write a dispatch to GHQ after the fact. (Such was the case with Dan Breen and Sean Treacy's ambush at Soloheadbeg.) The men in Dublin tirelessly attempted to provide some kind of "standard procedure" to all units. Consider the examples of neighbouring Counties Galway and Offaly.

A commandant in Galway wrote a letter to Dr. O'Malley, a local hospital administrator, threatening the personnel that "if you have not your hospital cleared of all Black and Tans within 24 hours you take the consequences." GHQ was quick to respond that "as far as hospitals and hospital staff are concerned, they must be regarded as common institutions ministering to all. The good Dr. O'Malley should be told that he can expect your protection and that the former message was a bogus one."[70] (The IRA army generals huddling around the Liffey conference table could see the wisdom and humanitarianism of leaving hospitals off limits for retaliatory strikes. If storming hospitals that were ministering to foreign troops became the order of the day, many Volunteers housed in British facilities might have had to pay a terrible price.)

In Offaly, on 19 February 1921, the Athlone train had been held up and robbed of money destined for payroll of the local RIC. GHQ was quick to point out that such actions were to be reported to the local Battalion Commander, and the money taken from such action be lodged with him so that he might forward the funds to the Minister of Finance for the Dáil, Michael Collins. An independent army engaged in mass extortion was not the vision of the men in Dublin Headquarters who struggled to hold together the divergent horses harnessed in their team. The reins of power must be tightly held so that all efforts be directed towards the same goal — an idea of noble origin but not always implementable.

Roscommon Police Casualties in the War for Independence

extracted from *Police Casualties in Ireland 1919-1922* by Richard Abbott

The following list includes only members of the RIC. It does not include men who were British soldiers or members of the Black and Tans (except where noted). The following Irish men were either born in County Roscommon and served in another county, or were killed within the county borders.

Name/ townland origin	Date of Death	Place
Peter Wallace from Co. Roscommon	14 May 1919	Kilmallock Co. Limerick
William Finn from Castlerea	9 April 1920	Lackamore Wood Newport, Co. Tipperary
Michael Horan from Co. Roscommon	25 June 1920	Co. Tipperary
Martin Foley from Castlerea	21 August 1920	Oranmore Co. Galway
Thomas M. Craddock	22 August 1920	Athlone
William J. Potter *(Micheál O'Callaghan claims that Potter was killed in November.)*[71]	26 August 1920	Knockcroghery Co. Roscommon
Edward Murphy	1 September 1920	Ratra, Frenchpark Co. Roscommon
Martin McCarthy	2 September 1920	Ratra, Frenchpark Co. Roscommon
Michael J. Hynes from Co. Roscommon	22 September 1920	Rinneen Co. Clare
Michael Kelly from Co. Roscommon	22 September 1920	Rinneen Co. Clare
Thomas Leonard from Knockcroghery	25 September 1920	Falls Road Belfast
John Crawford Francis Gallagher Michael Kenny Martin O'Connor	All died 12 October 1920	Fourmilehouse Co Roscommon
William Carroll from Roscommon	"Disappeared" 18 October 1920 after an attack at Ruan, Co. Clare. RIC records show him as being dismissed on that date. Where did Constable Carroll go? Perhaps "off with the boys"	
Michael Dennehy	Reported missing 23 November 1920	Drowned near Ruskey (as a suspected spy)
Thomas Dillon from Co. Roscommon	24 November 1920	Phoenix Park Dublin
Peter Shannon from Elphin	17 December 1920	Swanlinbar Co. Cavan
Peter J. McArdle	5 January 1921	Strokestown
Stephen Carty from Co. Roscommon	13 January 1921	Cratloe Co. Clare
Tom Satchwell from Castlerea	22 February 1921	Mount Charles Co. Donegal
John William Hughes from Roscommon	22 February 1921	Donegal town
Martin John Greer from Cootehall	23 February 1921	Dublin

Ambush at Southpark, Castlerea

News of a Unionist house in Tarmon having been destroyed by the Volunteers did not sit well with the RIC and Black and Tans of the area. They vowed revenge. Plans for reprisals reached the ears of the First Battalion South officers. Armed with shotguns (each man with only two cartridges for his gun), Volunteers from Lisliddy and Moor Companies took up positions at Southpark along the road the

Name/ townland origin	Date of Death	Place
Charles O'M. Reynolds from Co. Roscommon	16 March 1921	Clifden Co. Galway
William Devereux from Co. Roscommon	22 March 1921	Keadue Co. Roscommon
Michael Dowling	22 March 1921	Keadue Co. Roscommon
Edward L. Leslie	26 March 1921 from wounds sustained during the Scramogue ambush in Co. Roscommon. Capt. Peake of the Ninth Lancers and Lt. Tennant were killed on site. Two Black and Tans, Evans and Buchanan, met their deaths in the hours following the attack on 23 March.	
Patrick Early from Co. Roscommon	29 March 1922	Cullavill Co. Armagh
Martin Fallon from Co. Roscommon	3 May 1921	Clonakilty Co. Cork
Thomas McCormack from Co. Roscommon	4 May 1921	Rathmore Co. Kerry
Thomas Bridges from Co. Roscommon	14 May 1921	Drumcollogher Co. Limerick
Leonard Harte	16 May 1921	Accidentally shot at Carrick-on-Shannon
Francis J. Butler Co. Roscommon	19 May 1921 as a result of wounds incurred in an attack at Newport, Co. Mayo.	
George Redding	30 May 1921	Kilrooskey Co. Roscommon
Joseph Cooney from Co. Roscommon	1 June 1921	Castlemaine Co. Kerry
Martin Feeney from Co. Roscommon	2 June 1921*	Kallegbeg Cross Co. Tipperary
John Doherty from Co. Roscommon	2 June 1921	Carrowkennedy Co. Mayo
George Southgate	6 June 1921	Accidentally shot at Ballaghaderreen Barracks
Harold "Sammy" Round Co. Roscommon	Missing 16 June 1921	Frenchpark Harold Round was drowned in the Suck after being found guilty of spying against the local IRA men.
Thomas Conlon from Co. Roscommon	10 July 1921	Belfast
James King from Galway	11 July 1921	Castlerea Co. Roscommon

*The RIC Memorial in St. Paul's Cathedral in London gives 2 July 1921 as the death date.

The disbandment of the RIC began on 7 January 1922 and proceeded in batches of 200-300 men at a time. According to Richard Abbot, author of *Police Casualties in Ireland 1919-1922*, "some men simply 'walked away,' whilst others felt compelled to leave due to the situation in the country, and a number left (without giving a reason) to assist the IRA."[72]

The total number who served in the Auxiliary Division of the RIC was slightly more than 2,000. In April 1921 there were fifteen companies, one of which was located in Roscommon.

Black and Tans would likely travel. The time: dusk on 9 July. After waiting several hours, four to five cyclists appeared on the road. They were the advance guard of a unit coming from Castlerea. The Volunteers opened fire, whereupon three or four of the cyclists fell and did not move.

A strong contingent of Crown Forces (about fifty-five) soon followed, too large for the meagre amount of ammunition the Volunteers had available. The

Medical Hall of Fame

Nurse Margaret Coll (Mrs. D. Mulrennan of Cloonsuck, Castlerea) had trained for nursing in America but returned to Ireland in time to help many a Volunteer ease his "Republican itch." (Men on the run could seldom change clothes. After many days of wearing the same attire, a Volunteer's skin would begin to break down, causing a rash and resulting itch. Nurse Coll distributed many ointments and salves to the men to ease their discom-

Nurse Coll

fort.) John Vaughan would often take a wounded man to her for treatment. Most of the doctors and nurses at that time lived in the towns and were required to report any suspicious patient (gunshot wounds). She also tended Sean Bergin, who was seriously ill with pleurisy and pneumonia, shortly before his demise in the Woodlands of Loughglynn.

Nurses **Alice Fayne** of Cloonmore and **Catherine Kenny** of Blenavoher in County Longford nursed the wounded men brought to Incheneagh Island in Lough Ree.

Doctor Clarke of Loughglynn tended Toby Scally after he had been wounded in The Woodlands of Loughglynn.

Dr. Dudley Forde of Strokestown, assisted local Volunteers on numerous occasions, and travelled, at great risk to himself and his companions, to Quaker and Incheneagh Islands in Lough Ree to tend to the wounded.

Dr. Charles Kelly of Abbey Street, Roscommon, ventured numerous times to Quaker and Incheneagh Islands in Lough Ree to attend to wounded Volunteers. Among his many success stories was the treating of three of the four men who were wounded by a mine explosion on the Lanesboro/Roscommon Road at Cloontymullen.

The **Farrell family** tended wounded men brought to Quaker Island.

The **Walsh family** oversaw the care of the wounded and dying men brought to Quaker Island.

The **Connaughton**, **O'Shea**, and **Killian families** of Incheneagh Island in Lough Ree risked many dangers to tend to the injured Volunteers brought to them.

Volunteers[73] immediately began to retreat across the fields. None of the attacking party was injured. Two other men, however, who arrived late for the ambush, walked right into the Crown Forces and were apprehended, beaten, and taken to Athlone.

Later, an abandoned mask was found at the scene — an obvious indication of the Black and Tans' intentions. In the days that followed, two soldiers and one Black and Tan were reported missing from the Castlerea Barracks.

The Last Shot of the Black and Tan War

The sun hung high in the heavens. It was 11 July, almost one hour shy of noon, the appointed start of the Truce. Inspector James King of the Castlerea RIC had just stepped out the door of his home, where he took breakfast. (For his safety, he often slept in the barracks.) Normally a quick-paced and watchful walker who warily kept to the middle of the road with his hand on his revolver, he opted to ride his bicycle that morning. It was the last ride out for him. A bullet cut through him, bringing to a close the reign of terror which he had helped perpetuate. An Irishman born in County Galway, King was a hated and feared authority in the area where he had led numerous raids on the Volunteers. In those times the pathways of western Roscommon were not marked with signs. The foreign Black and Tan thugs had no clue as to how or where to find the hideaways and meeting houses of the Volunteers. King had been their guide. In addition to leading them to secret rendezvous places, he delighted in brutal beatings of the IRA men he happened to find there. His sadistic behaviour went far beyond the bounds of wartime cruelty.[74] Thus it was that within the hour before the Truce, two local Volunteers made certain that Inspector King would know no peace on earth.

Although hostilities officially ended at noon, the two were hunted until six o'clock that evening. On leaving the scene, one Volunteer's bicycle chain had broken, and the other stopped to let him climb onto the back of his bicycle. Then one of the Volunteers pushed the bicycle to the railway station, where they both abandoned the useless transport and headed off across the fields. After being pursued for several hours, the two escaped capture by rolling up their pant legs and pretending to be shepherds herding their flock.[75] The War for Independence in County Roscommon had started in February 1918 with a raid on the luxurious castle at Rockingham on the shores of Lough Key. It ended in a lowly sheep field outside of Castlerea. ∎

1. Tom Crawley Volunteer Witness Statement to the Bureau of Military History 1913-21, p. 10.
2. Gerald O'Connor Papers, private collection. Participants directly engaged in **The Attack at Castlerea:** Sean Bergin and Stephen McDermott (both of whom lost their own lives two weeks later), Joseph Conway, Tom Crawley and Martin Foley. Acting as part of a covering party a short distance from the scene: Martin Ganley, Ned Shannon, Mick Carty, John Crean, Michael Freyne, Patrick Beirne, Tom Kelly, Joe Satchwell, Albert Durr, John and Michael Flanagan, James Crawley, James Doherty, (another) John Flanagan, Brian Connor, John Kelly, Tom Raftery, Tom Vaughan, John and Pat Kelly of Cloonboniffe, William Flanagan, and Gerald O'Connor.
3. Tom Crawley Volunteer Witness Statement to the Bureau of Military History 1913-21, p. 10.
4. Extracted from the Gerald O'Connor Papers, private collection. Participants in **disarming of a Black and Tan at Cloonfad** in April were: Luke Cunningham, Tom Regan*, Edward Birmingham*, John and Tom Mullarkey*, James Moran*, John Keane*, James Kelly*, Martin Tighe, Tom Cruise, and John Green. Participants in **disarming of two British soldiers at Cloonfad** in May were: * noted above, and James Birmingham.
5. Sheila Bergin, half-sister of Sean Bergin, interview by author, 6 November 2003, Nenagh, Tipperary.
6. Luke Duffy Volunteer Witness Statement to the Bureau of Military History 1913-21, pp. 9-10.
7. Martin Fallon interview, Ernie O'Malley Papers, UCD Archives, No. 131.
8. Tom Crawley Volunteer Witness Statement to the Bureau of Military History 1913-21, p. 12.
9. *The Woodlands of Loughglynn*, by Vera McDermott, p. 51.
10. "The Woodlands of Loughglynn," *Roscommon Herald*, 12 April, 1996.
11. Tom Crawley Volunteer Witness Statement to the Bureau of Military History 1913-21, p. 12.
12. *The Woodlands of Loughglynn*, by Vera McDermott, p. 55.
13. Patrick Bergin, nephew of Sean, interview by author, 24 August 1994, Roscommon town.

14. **Smithhill attempted ambushes**. Participants: Michael Lynch, John J. Conry, John McGowan, Martin Dockery, James Beirne, and Tom Gormley. Compiled from the Pat Brennan Papers.
15. Frank Simons Volunteer Witness Statement to the Bureau of Military History 1913-21, p. 31.
16. Frank Simons Volunteer Witness Statement to the Bureau of Military History 1913-21, p. 32.
17. John Kelly Volunteer Witness Statement to the Bureau of Military History 1913-21, p. 3.
18. John Kelly Volunteer Witness Statement to the Bureau of Military History 1913-21, p. 1.
19. Luke Duffy interview, Ernie O'Malley Papers, UCD Archives, No. 137.
20. Luke Duffy interview, Ernie O'Malley Papers, UCD Archives, No. 137.
21. Luke Duffy interview, Ernie O'Malley Papers, UCD Archives, No. 137.
22. *Roscommon Association Dublin Yearbook*, 1986, "Tragedy in Cloontymullen," by Bill Mulligan, p. 43.
23. *Michael Collins and The Brotherhood*, by Vincent MacDowell, p. 85.
24. *For Ireland and Freedom*, by Micheál O'Callaghan, p. 100.
25. Jack Glancy Volunteer Witness Statement to the Bureau of Military History 1913-21, p. 12.
26. Jack Glancy interview, Ernie O'Malley Papers, UCD Archives, No. 131, p. 62.
27. "Mullaney" claims Micheál O'Callaghan in *For Ireland and Freedom*, p 100. "Mularkey" says Jack Glancy in his Volunteer Witness Statement to the Bureau of Military History 1913-21, p. 14.
28. Jack Glancy Volunteer Witness Statement to the Bureau of Military History 1913-21, p. 15.
29. Jack Glancy Volunteer Witness Statement to the Bureau of Military History 1913-21, p. 15.
30. Jim Fehilly interview, Ernie O'Malley Papers, UCD Archives, No. 131.
31. Bill O'Doherty interview, Ernie O'Malley Papers, UCD Archives, No. 131, p. 39.
32. Gerald Davis interview, Ernie O'Malley Papers, UCD Archives, No. 137.
33. John Kelly interview, Ernie O'Malley Papers, UCD Archives, No. 131.
34. Jim Hunt Volunteer Witness Statement to the Bureau of Military History, p. 16.
35. Sergeant John Duffy Statement to the Bureau of Military History 1913-21, p. 18.
36. Pat Mullooly Volunteer Witness Statement to the Bureau of Military History, p. 30.
37. Mulcahy Papers, P7 A18.
38. RIC Monthly Report written by the Inspector General to Dublin Castle, May 1921.
39. Tony Murphy, son of Hubert. Interview by author. 4 August 2004. Roscommon town.
40. Micheál O'Callaghan in his book *For Ireland and Freedom* claims the time of the escape was 21 May (p. 102).
41. The dates were derived from Pat Brennan's personal diary, p. 5, and from the RIC Monthly Report written by the District Inspector to Dublin Castle, June 1921 (718).
42. Andy Keavney Volunteer Witness Statement to the Bureau of Military History 1913-21, p. 10.
43. *Boyle Vol. 2 Its People, Its Times Past and Present*, compiled by Morlurg Writers, Boyle. p. 37.
44. Pat Brennan, Summary of Activities, private collection.
45. Pat Mullooly Statement to the Department of Military History, handwritten note on p. 34a.
46. Mrs. B. Wickins, daughter of George Meadlarklan, Leighton Buzzard, England, correspondence with author, 21 September 2004.
47. Rita Leneghan of Hillstreet, Activity Summary, Pat Brennan Papers, private collection.
48. Jack Glancy Volunteer Witness Statement to the Bureau of Military History 1913-21, p. 18.
49. *For Ireland and Freedom*, by Micheál O'Callaghan, p. 102.
50. p. 313.
51. Tom Crawley Volunteer Witness Statement to the Bureau of Military History 1913-21, p. 11.
52. Tom Crawley Volunteer Witness Statement to the Bureau of Military History 1913-21, p. 11.
53. Con Costello Volunteer Witness Statement to the Bureau of Military History 1913-21, p. 20.
54. Frank Beattie, son of Pat Beattie, Capt. of the Rahara Coy. Interview by author, 23 June 2002, Rahara, County Roscommon.
55. Jim Dorr Volunteer Witness Statement to the Bureau of Military History 1913-21, p. 8.
56. Pat Vaughan, formerly of Cloonsuck, filmed interview on 10 April 1995, Boston, Mass.
57. Pat Brennan Papers, private collection.
58. Jim Fehilly interview, Ernie O'Malley Papers, UCD Archives, No. 131, P17b.
59. Pat Brennan Papers, private collection: **Attack on Frenchpark Barracks and Courthouse** participants: John Murray of Gortnacloy, Mantua, Thomas Connor, Michael Duignan, Michael Dockery, Sean Owens, Owen Dockery, John Moran, Joe Kelly of Rathcroghan, Bernard Flanagan, John Kelly of Sheerevagh, James Kelly, Peter Dockery, Thomas Murtagh, Phil Duignan, J. J. Keenan, Pat Keenan, J. P. Beirne, James Pettit, Dominick Duignan, William Kelly, Michael Roche, Jim Fehilly, Matthew Murtagh, Tim Murtagh, Thomas F. Kelly. David McDermott brought guns from his place. Michael Rushe served as the armed outpost. Thomas Brady stood guard duty. Eddie Carlos and Jack Roche were both burned as a result of the attack.
60. Participants in **Attack on Tarmonbarry Barracks:** Martin Fallon, Patrick Cox, John and Joseph Diffley, John J. Robinson, James Kelly, Charles Noone, James Farrell, Bernard Gavican, James Molloy, Patrick Moran, John Farrell, another John Farrell, Luke Feeney, William Shiel, Thomas Green, Michael Gunn, Pat Fallon, Peter Casey, Patrick Greene, Patrick Gunn, John Casey, Peter Shiel, Dan Hanley, Michael Casey, Michael and James O'Neill, Richard Hayden, James Lynagh, and William Collins. Thomas Dillon served as an outpost.
61. Martin Fallon interview, UCD Archives, Ernie O'Malley Papers, No. 131, P/76.
62. Sean Leavy Volunteer Witness Statement to the Bureau of Military History 1913-21, p. 23.
63. Pat Mullooly Volunteer Witness Statement to the Bureau of Military History 1913-21, p. 33.

64. *Evidence on Conditions in Ireland,* transcribed and annotated by Albert Coyle, p. 65.
65. *Evidence on Conditions in Ireland,* transcribed and annotated by Albert Coyle, p. 68.
66. Con Costello Volunteer Witness Statement to the Bureau of Military History 1913-21, p. 20.
67. Henry O'Brien Volunteer Witness Statement to the Bureau of Military History 1913-21, p. 17.
68. Con Costello Volunteer Witness Statement to the Bureau of Military History 1913-21, p. 21.
69. *For Ireland and Freedom, by* Micheál O'Callaghan, pp. 129-130.
70. Mulcahy Papers P7 A/1 to A/17.
71. *For Ireland and Freedom, by* Micheál O'Callaghan, p. 125.
72. p. 295.
73. Compiled from the Gerald O'Connor Papers, private collection. **Ambush at Southpark** participants: Frank Flynn, Peter Murtagh, Edward Kelly, Stephen Flattery, Hubert Betagh, Patrick Mulligan, Michael Cryan, James Durr, John Shannon, Michael Grady, James Hester, Andrew Hunt, Dominick Hunt, Michael Hussey, William Kehir, Tom Madden, John Mannion, William Mannion, Patrick Moran, Michael Noone, John Powell, Luke Raftery, John Ryan, Patrick Scahill, James Smyth, John Beirne, Joe Conway, Patrick Dockery, Seamus Duffy, James Filan, Andy Finan, and John Finan.
74. Pat Vaughan, interview by author, 10 April 1995. Boston, Massachusetts.
75. Tom Crawley Volunteer Witness Statement to the Bureau of Military History 1913-21, p. 14.

SEVEN

THE TRUCE

Momentum, Morale, Munitions

In the early months of 1921, the increased activity of both the IRA and the Crown Forces indicated an alarming escalation of the fight. The IRA was on the move, and England well knew it. ("Chronology of Events" beginning on p. 177 will verify this.) What were the men in the field thinking when the Truce was called? While they were in training camps taking instruction in scouting, intelligence, musketry, and first aid, were they focused on a compromise which would afford them a foreign ruler? A compromise which would give up the North? Even though King George had opened the northern parliament in Belfast on 22 June, most Volunteers did not recognise that as a defining moment. Their writings resonate with hope rather than resignation. Many felt that, at best, the Truce would bring them what they had fought for, a free Ireland — and at worst, it would provide a much needed rest and opportunity for training until such time that hostilities resumed.

In the eyes of the Vice O/C of the 3rd Battalion South Roscommon, Luke Duffy, "when the Truce came, we were glad of the respite and to be able to get a decent rest. We were in a better position than ever before to have carried on the fight. Our morale was very high and gaining strength, the men were eager for a fight, and the people were supporting us by all means in their power."[1]

Last British guard in the Castle Athlone, 1922.

PHOTO COURTESY OF GEAROID O'BRIEN, HEAD LIBRARIAN, ATHLONE LIBRARY

According to Pat Mullooly, Quartermaster for the North Roscommon Brigade, "None of us believed that the Truce would last very long. The morale of our forces, speaking for the lower ranks, was very high and we were in no way over-awed by the British Forces when the Truce came. All we lacked was good armament and good leadership, both of which was severely lacking."[2]

Frank Simons (acting South Roscommon Brigade O/C at the time of the Truce) agrees. "Our morale was high and certainly on the day of the Truce, or the days preceding it, the idea of giving up the fight, or in any way conceding anything to the enemy, had never entered into any Volunteer's head."[3] Years later in 1973 when Simons was interviewed by James McCormick, his perspective had changed. "If there was no Truce, you'd be alright. But once you had a truce, you had to have peace because the Crown Forces at work...they knew everything about us."[4]

In the far south of the county, Frank O'Connor, O/C of the 1st Battalion, Athlone Brigade, stated that "the Truce found us in a fairly good position for carrying on the fight...arms of all types, of course, were still very scarce...ammunition for the weapons we had was also scarce enough, but sufficient to carry on with for the time being..."[5]

An opposing view was held by Sean Leavy, O/C of the 3rd Battalion North. "How did they ever consent to withdraw their forces from the country...there was the spick and span might of an Empire handing over its institutions to a ragged, poorly trained and, above all, very poorly armed force as ours was. I doubt if the Truce had broken that we could have continued to oppose them for very long."[6]

Martin Fallon, O/C of the Flying Column in the 3rd Battalion North area, claimed, "None of us thought that the Truce would last long or that England would concede very much. At the same time I did not see how we could very well start again and the longer it lasted the worse this became. The people would not like to undergo another period of raids, arrests, reprisals, probably more intense than previously.....It was a grave mistake, I consider, to allow the Volunteers to go into the towns and so forth and, in many cases, to associate with the British forces."[7]

The Leitrim Brigade Commander, Bernard Sweeney, who later was to fight with the men of north Roscommon during the Civil War, declared, "The armament position at the Truce was deplorable. We had lost a big portion of the rifles we had [in the attack on Selton Hill where Sean Connolly was killed] and while we lived in hope there did not seem to be any hope of replacing them. The days of surprising small parties of the enemy and disarming them had gone as they operated in much bigger formations now and with much greater strength."[8]

The Truce did, however, offer respite. When Jack Glancy was released from prison in January 1922, he walked out into a very different country. "It was now fashionable to show you had been in the movement or to pretend that you were anyway. All the same, it was great to feel free again and to be able to go around without hindrance and not to be on the alert always..."[9]

Within the bowels of the University College of Dublin lie the archives. These rooms serve as the receptacle of popularly held versions of the past as well as little-known twists and ironic turns of history. While conducting research in the summer of 2000, this author happened upon a chance comment by Liam O'Doherty (the first O/C of the 3rd Battalion North Roscommon) recorded by Ernie O'Malley in his notebooks. O'Doherty mentioned that after Christmas in 1920, Sean Connolly (organiser from Longford) went to see Mick Collins in Dublin. When Connolly returned to Roscommon, he reported that his discussion with Collins "gave us the impression ...that we wouldn't get a republic...."[10]

The juxtaposition of those two perspectives — that of the Roscommon officers in the field vs. that of Sean Connolly derived from a conversation with Collins — crystallises the dichotomy of the Civil War. On one hand, momentum was propelling the Volunteers to increased activity with more-precise results. On the other hand, the political possibilities (or perceived impossibilities) were creeping into the thinking of the leaders in Dublin.

September 1921: Escape through the Brady Tunnel
(The author wishes to credit Micheál O'Callaghan's rendition of this episode as written in *For Ireland and Freedom*. Without O'Callaghan's interview of Joe Galvin, much of this story would have forever remained unknown.)

The Brady tunnel could not have been constructed but for the grit and know-how of an Arigna man. He was ably assisted by another Roscommon Volunteer — this one from the south of the county. Together they dug, with a metal bar and knives and spoons from the prison cookhouse,[11] a tunnel which became the escape route for seventy men.

The first tunnel had promise. Jim Brady, originally from Co. Cavan, had been a coal miner in Arigna. An active union organiser who fought with the Volunteers, he found himself inactive in Hut 31 of the Curragh Internment Camp when he was first approached about the feasibility of a tunnel by the O/C of the neighbouring Hut 32, Liam Murphy, along with Todd Andrews of Dublin, Joe Galvin of Roscommon, and several other officers. Brady thought it could be done. It started as a two-foot square and was sunk four feet deep into the sandy soil. It then had angled out past the two "walls" of barbed wire surrounding the camp. The fencing was 10 feet high and 8 feet in thickness.

Begun by Jim Brady, who was assisted by Scottie Regan of Keadue and Joe Galvin of Mount Talbot, the tunnel was successfully completed and awaited only the proper moment to belch forth its contraband. At first only seven men knew of its existence, but as the date for escape arrived, more and more men were notified to be ready to take flight. One of the designated escapees managed to get a note out to GHQ that a particular night was the scheduled "time of release." Unfortunately, the British raided the Mary St. Headquarters in Dublin and found the note. The following day fully armed Scottish Borderers rushed into the Curragh and quickly located the unauthorised escape hatch. The first tunnel had been a construction success but an intelligence disaster. After nine days of being deprived of privileges and going on hunger strike, the men "settled down to be model prisoners."[12] The guise didn't last long.

A second tunnel was begun. Following the discovery of the first tunnel, the British had dug a four foot wide by four foot deep trench around the inside of the perimeter barbed-wire fence—eventually intending to flood it. They didn't think a tunnel could go deep enough to escape the seepage that would inevitably occur. Using only crude utensils, Brady, Galvin, and Regan took turns at the face of the tunnel where little air circulated. The threat of cave-in was ever present because the race against time allowed for little effort to be expended on supports beams. "The tunnel was propped at intervals by pieces of bed boards."[13] The extracted dirt was hoisted up from the underground tunnel in pillow cases. It was then distributed into jacket pockets or paper bags before being scattered in the crawl spaces beneath the huts.

Eighteen days after it was begun, the diggers thought they had gone out far enough so that when they opened their "hatch" they would be beyond the reach of the bright lights that continually fanned the compound. They opened a small outlet, but, alas, found that they were short of the mark. They worked another day but feared to dawdle any longer as it was thought that the trench surrounding the compound was to be flooded the next day.[14] It was now or never.

Brady and Galvin were the first to go through. They were given a few minutes head start in order to snip holes in the barbed-wire fencing. The men carried a pair of wire cutters which had been obtained from a party of soldiers who had come to the camp days before to install more barbed wire in the boundary fences. The soldiers had arrived with four pair of cutters, but, unbeknownst to them, had left with but three.

More than sixty men followed Brady and Galvin — squirming and wriggling their way through the underground passageway. Many were from GHQ in Dublin. A sizeable group were Roscommon men from both the North and South Brigades. More would have found freedom that evening, but one of the men insisted on carrying a suitcase on his back through the tunnel, which caused the supports to collapse.

As the Roscommon contingency assembled outside the steel-pronged boundary of the Curragh, they soon realised that a thick fog had enveloped the area and they were at a loss as to finding direction. Who better to ask than the One Who Knows All Ways? Kneeling down on the plain of Kildare, the men quietly recited the rosary. "As they finished praying they heard rooks cawing in the nearby trees. They knew that the only trees anywhere near the Camp were at the back of the grandstand on the Curragh race course."[15] When they reached the trees, they had their bearings battened down as tightly as their determination to go far and fast from this place.

When they reached a group of houses near the Hill of Allen, they decided to take a chance on a friendly face. Lady Luck smiled. They were given a meal, and

Joe Galvin,
Cloonlaughnan, Mount Talbot
Escapee through the Brady tunnel.

PHOTO COURTESY OF DERRY O'DONNELL

then the son of the owner took them across the Hill of Allen to the home of the priest in the village of Rathangan. At the pastor's home they were supplied with footwear because they had escaped through the tunnel in their stocking feet and had made the journey from the camp across some rocky, rough ground.

Their next place of rest was the Weymes Hotel in the village of Carbury, where the proprietor greeted them with open arms. He even put a big Leyland car at their disposal, and, as they all piled into it, he told the driver to "drive them as far as they want to go."[16] The Volunteers arrived near Athlone around midnight, but sent the car back because a late-night arrival of so grand a car might arouse suspicion.

In the morning, one of the Murphy brothers of Kiltoom called in a favour. He asked his friend, Mr. Fitzpatrick of Connaught St., to lend them a small lorry. Heading northward, the lorry dropped off in Kiltoom Murphy and Dick Mee (Captain of the Curraghboy Coy.), then proceeded to Pat Tennant's home in Knockcroghery. As the men rested there, a dispatch was sent to the 3rd Battalion informing the officers that some very bedraggled and weary Volunteers needed transport. Pat Madden and Frank Simons arrived shortly thereafter with two cars which took the rest of the men to their destinations. Henry Compton of Ballagh left the group in Roscommon town. Tom Moran of Crossna (the brother of Paddy), Pat Beirne of Clooncunny, Pat McNamara (Culliagh, Strokestown), Jim Farrell (Whitehall), and Pat Barry were dropped off in Strokestown and driven home by an accommodating Paddy Duffy.

What of the mastermind and his cohort? To what corner of Ireland had Jim Brady and Joe Galvin directed their feet? The pair made their way to Dublin, then on to a camp in the Dublin Mountains, and eventually found refuge in the safety of their own homes in Roscommon. But a future fracture in the IRA organisation would find these two friends, who together had courageously faced a wall of dirt and a dangerous road to Ireland's capital city, on opposing sides. Jim Brady would fight another day in the Arigna Flying Column with men opposed to the Treaty. Joe Galvin, on the other hand, would join the Free State Army.

The Irish Republican Army Roster Swells

After the Truce, which was perceived by many as a victory for the IRA, local men who had done little during the heat of the Tan War jumped on the bandwagon and proceeded to ride it down to the River of Glory. The immediate threat had passed, or at least was on hold, and the men who had truly done the dangerous work and risked their lives doing so were viewed as heroes. Suddenly membership in the Volunteer movement was chic!

The morning roll call was answered by hundreds of new voices. Training camps were set up throughout the county (mostly in anticipation of future battles to be waged), and men attended them by the hundreds. The problem of arming all these new recruits, however, was never solved.

The IRB was also reorganised. — McCormack from Tipperary came to the county for such a purpose. In addition, the active men came out from under cover. They were glad for a rest. In the words of a common soldier, like James P. Flanagan of Mantua, Elphin, "I can gladly admit to heaving a sigh of relief and taking a week's holiday when the Truce came."[17] For many, their meagre ammunition was now spent shooting ducks and geese. Men no longer on the run returned to their home quarters only to be observed ever more closely by the local police. The genie had been let out of the bottle, and stuffing it back inside would prove to be nigh impossible should hostilities resume.

Training Camps

While the politicians were scurrying around London and Dublin examining every word of every proposal, soldiers around the country were busy preparing themselves in the training camps. Sligo had sixteen camps within its borders.[18] Roscommon camps servicing the central and northwest sections of the county had been set up at Runnamoat (Ballinaheglish), Donamon Castle, Cloonkeen

---

The following is a copy of a report from the Headquarters of the 2nd Western Division. The Active Service Unit consisted of about forty men. The syllabus includes the training schedule in the Brigade Camp for the month ending 31 December 1921. Training occupied four hours each day as well as one lecture on some of the Special Services.

Daily routine:
7:30 a.m. Reveille
8:00-8:45 a.m. Physical Drill
9:00 a.m. Breakfast
10:15-11:30 a.m. Drill with Arms
11:30-12:30 p.m. Fatigue
12:30-1:00 p.m. Break
1:00-2:30 p.m. Dinner
2:30-3:30 p.m. Squad Drill
3:30-4:30 p.m. Lecture
4:30-5:30 p.m. Company Drill
5:30 p.m. Break
6:00-7:00 p.m. Tea
7:00 p.m. Mounting Guard
7:15-10:00 p.m. Recreation
10:00 p.m. Roll Call
10:30 p.m. Lights out

Lecture topics included:
Musketry
Machine gun training (stripping, assembling, etc.)
Learning how to use the Lewis and Hotchkiss guns
Bomb construction and use
Engineering
Signalling (flags, lamps, and Morse Code)
First Aid.

(Castlerea), Hermitage, Erritt and Carrowbehy (Castlerea), Swinford (Co. Mayo), Kilkerrin (Glenamaddy), Castlerea Barracks, Ballymoe, Ballinrobe (Co. Mayo). Volunteers south of Roscommon town attended the Battalion camp at Drinaun, Ballygar. Officers from that area came north to Runnamoat and Donamon for instruction.

Training camps for Battalion and Company officers in the north of the county were held at Mantua House where Brian MacNeill, son of Eoin MacNeill, and D. Corry served as instructors. The general camp for the 1st Battalion North Volunteers was held at Boyle Union Buildings. Others in the northern part of the county attended camp at the Cootehall Courthouse. Brigade and Battalion staff officers were ordered to attend a camp at Glenasmole House in County Wicklow.

Directives from GHQ included suggestions and specific subjects to be included in the training sessions: machine gun squads, first aid, musketry, engineering (including grenade making), scouting, and signalling.

A Reprisal Gone Awry

Some of the RIC policemen in Castlerea had been over-zealous in their work during the Black and Tan War. Constables Moran, John Kiely, James King, and Jameson were renowned for their driven personalities and sadistic bents. Inspector King had been dealt with on the final day of the Truce. Kiely, who had accompanied the raiding party to John Vaughan's house in Cloonsuck in June, was due for the Volunteers' attention.

Late in 1921 Pat Vaughan and several other men approached Kiely's house, which bordered a cemetery. When the firing started, Kiely made a quick exit out the back door and zigzagged his way through the tombstones. He did not join those on whom he trod that night. The only lasting shreds of evidence of the failed attack were the preponderance of pockmarks and chips that disfigured many of the markers in the graveyard.

The Belfast Boycott

The Belfast boycott was initiated by Dublin Headquarters in response to the campaign against Catholics in the north of Ireland. Notices were sent to Brigades all over the country encouraging local commanders to ban northern goods from their area and to take whatever measures deemed necessary to discourage traders from stocking such merchandise.

To stop the flow of boycotted goods, officers in each Company area that included a rail line would patrol the rail station to ascertain that no items from the North were unloaded. Volunteers would raid the mails and find inventories, order forms, and/or confirmation sheets which would lead them to a specific trader. Those merchants would be notified by typewritten note (in Boyle area the notices were transcribed by Bridie Murray) to stop their dealings with the northern firms. Volunteers, who had connections with railroad personnel, would hold up trains and take off restricted goods. Oftentimes the goods were completely destroyed.

If boycotted goods were found on shelves, Volunteers would sometimes station themselves outside the premises of said merchants and "discourage" customers from going into the store. Those merchants who had accounts in the Ulster Banks were especially targeted. A few specific examples of Volunteer enforcement of the Belfast boycott include the following:

- a number of traders in Ballymote on Fair Day in October were presented with a printed order demanding that they pay a fine for trading with the Ulster Bank. Fines ranged from £5 to £100. On their refusal to pay, the IRA put an armed guard on their premises, refusing entry to customers.
- In March the mails were held up in the Crossna area. Letters were censored, and all invoices from the Belfast firms going to W. H. Lynn in Ballyfarnon were noted. The next day the Volunteers seized and destroyed all the goods that had entered his store from Belfast.

- In the south of the county, mail trains to and from Dublin were stopped and the mail car searched for incriminating evidence. In Knockcroghery specifically, James Breheny, Patrick Kelly, Owen Curley, and Thomas Kelly were the official guardians at the railway station assigned to see that no Belfast goods were consigned there. In Curraghboy, thirteen men[19] raided the mails seven or eight times and made certain that any suspicious billings or intended orders were turned over to their officers. In the Dysart Company, Denis Gacquin, both John Gateleys, Thomas Lynch, and John McDonnell performed this duty.

Boycotts of Belfast goods were one form of restriction; boycotts of the policemen themselves were quite another. After repeated warnings, a woman in Frenchpark was not abiding by the boycott. She insisted on continuing to sell her milk to the RIC men in the barracks, which she delivered in a tankard by pony and cart. To dissuade her from further commerce, a student home on leave from University College Dublin (UCD) put three pig rings into her posterior so that she couldn't bear the pain of sitting on her cart. James Feely, O/C of the 1st Battalion North, was not amused by this prank and ordered an investigation. Other Volunteers in the locality, however, smiled rather than winced.

Overall, enforcing boycotts occupied much of the Volunteers' time. It required constant raiding of railway stores and removal and/or destruction of goods involved. What with raiding mail cars, visiting traders, and enforcing the rulings, the men were on call continually. Their efforts bore fruit. According to the Roscommon RIC Monthly Report written by the District Inspector to Dublin Castle in June 1921, "Belfast and North of Ireland goods are now rigidly boycotted all over the County. Commercial travellers for Belfast, who constituted two thirds of those coming around, are never seen now."[20]

Summary of Armament

The following is a summary of armament held by the Battalions in North Roscommon[21] as of December 1921:

	1st Battalion	2nd Battalion	3rd Battalion	4th Battalion
Rifles:				
Lee Enfield	1	2	2	0
Martins	1	0	0	0
.22	2	0	0	0
Mauser	0	0	1	0
Winchester	0	0	1	0
Miniature	0	0	2	0
Shotguns:				
Double barrelled	12	Unknown	22	18
			(17 being repaired)	
Single barrelled	12	Unknown	35	6
			(12 being repaired)	
Automatics:	2	0	7	3
Revolvers:	0	0	3	6
Grenades:	5	0	10	
Homemade bombs:	12	0	0	
Rounds of Ammo:				
for .303:	71	14	25	0
Shot gun	176	69	76	123
Automatics			50	
Revolvers	100	30	7	6

Why Didn't de Valera Go?

The most important negotiations in centuries were about to take place between English and Irish representatives. The fate of the nation, nay the very concept of nationhood, was to be decided. Why didn't Ireland's consummate politician choose to go to London? Why was Michael Collins, on whose head a price had once been posted by the British, appointed to sit across the table from Lloyd George?

According to the unpublished papers of Desmond Fitzgerald, Minister for Publicity, as cited in Padraic Colum's book *Ourselves Alone! The Story of Arthur Griffith and the Origins of the Irish Free State*,

"The general view was that de Valera should take charge of that duty. He himself totally refused...His reasoning was thus: 'Whoever goes must compromise. But even when they have compromised, no agreement may be reached. Then we must again take up the struggle. But you cannot adopt the method of war from compromise. The people, rightly or wrongly, regard me as a symbol of the fighting Republic. I want to keep myself free (in the case of failure to reach a settlement after having compromised) to rally the people to fight, not for a compromise but for an absolute claim.'"[22]

Padraic O'Farrell, author of *Sean MacEoin The Blacksmith of Ballinalee*, claims that MacEoin became a severe critic of de Valera for not joining the negotiating team because: "(a) He [de Valera] was fully aware that he would achieve little more, if not less, than what Lloyd George had already offered him in London and (b) he hoped that the personable Collins and the adroit Griffith might well negotiate something worthwhile."[23]

A book published in 1997 entitled *Michael Collins and The Brotherhood* by Vincent MacDowell claims that "of the five plenipotentiaries, only Collins was a member of the Brotherhood (the IRB). It is a fair conclusion that de Valera, skilled in intrigue as he was, ensured the result, knowing that the British would never concede a Republic and knowing also that failure on this point would destroy the one man he feared in all the Dáil."[24]

Tim Pat Coogan in his *Michael Collins* biography hints of the same sinister motivation. When de Valera first returned from America (where he had flitted around for eighteen months while the rest of Ireland was heaving and retching as a result of the Tan terror), de Valera had wanted to ship Collins out of the country. Send him to America! The single most important man capable of running and coordinating the Irish counterintelligence was to be sent to America? This scheme of de Valera's never came to pass because so many around him saw the stupidity of its implementation.

P. S. O'Hegarty, in his book *The Victory of Sinn Féin*, claims, "He [de Valera] knew when he [first] went over to see Mr. Lloyd George, that he would not be discussing independence with him, and he knew when he came back, just how far Mr. Lloyd George was likely to go. He knew; when the Plenipotentiaries went over, that they could not bring back independence, and he opposed every attempt in the Dáil to bind them to independence or to limit their powers. But in the final hour he changed. He stabbed in the back the men he had sent over to do what they had done, knowing well what was the most they could accomplish..."[25]

When the first round of pre-Truce talks began between the Irish delegation and His Majesty's government, de Valera did not even bother to take Collins with him as part of the group. Yet when serious negotiations started, Collins was forced by de Valera to go to London, where he was elected, along with Arthur Griffith, to head the delegation. Why would a person who ran the super-secret hit squads in Dublin be "advanced" to the position of chief political negotiator to determine Ireland's independence? Could it be, perhaps, (as others have suggested) that de Valera had his own political agenda? De Valera knew that nothing like Republic status was going to be gained from the Treaty, and who better than Collins would make the perfect scapegoat? The end result, as de Valera assessed it, was going to be unpopular, perhaps even extremely divisive. The agreement would surely create

Eamon de Valera

a hailstorm of protest, and de Valera wanted to be protected under an uncompromised umbrella when the thunder rolled.

Quoting from Coogan's work, "The man who had felt his place was in America during most of the Tan war felt he must stay in Dublin during the coming diplomatic offensive in London. Collins, who thought of himself as a soldier, not a politician, resisted bitterly."[26] And further, "after his lengthy tête-à-têtes with Lloyd George, Eamon de Valera knew better than any man alive how slim was the prospect of a Republic and what sort of settlement he and his colleagues were likely to get."[27]

Logic should have dictated the wisdom of keeping the head of the entire Irish intelligence network secluded from the political circle of intrigue across the Irish Sea. Logic should have suggested thrusting the craftiest negotiator out into centre ring to duel with Lloyd George, non-affectionately known as "the Grey Fox." But logic sparring with personal jealousy and self-interest is seldom the victor.

Michael Collins himself noted that when he put his name to the Treaty, he had "signed his own death warrant." De Valera's actions (whether personally or politically motivated, or both!) removed himself from harm's way. His refusal to sit at the negotiating table placed the burden and the agony squarely on the shoulders of Griffith and Collins, both of whom, for different reasons, would die a few short months, later leaving de Valera the sole "heir apparent."

A New Year's Dilemma

The Treaty was debated and passed by the Dáil on 7 January 1922 by a vote of sixty four to fifty seven. (Roscommon TDs Count Plunkett and Harry Boland voted against the Treaty, while Dan O'Rourke and Andrew Lavin voted for it.) The results were catastrophic.

All men and women had to wrestle with their own conscience to determine whether this compromise would be enough. Could they accept the stepping-stone approach which Michael Collins was promoting? Would they abide by the voting results of the Dáil? Others, loyal to the bone and fiercely independent, felt that the deal was a sham, that Collins had capitulated, and that the Republic was still a far-off illusion but worth struggling for. These two opposing viewpoints vied for dominance in the ring of public opinion and did battle in the minds and hearts of every Irish person.

The Cumann na mBan Convention

Women of Ireland met in Dublin to have their say. Members of the Cumann na mBan from all four provinces held their convention on 5 February and voted 419 to 63 against the Treaty.[28] Constance Markievicz was elected president while members in favour of the Treaty were asked to resign. They did indeed leave the main group but formed their own called Cumann na Saoirse; it never took an active military role in the upcoming Civil War. Such a resounding defeat for the Treaty demonstrated the tenacity and determination of most of the women on the fighting line.

Split of the Irish Republican Army

Support for the Treaty had been touted by newspapers throughout the country, while the clergy encouraged its acceptance from pulpits. The Supreme Council of the Brotherhood had approved it by an 11 to 4 vote. The common people were weary of the war. The army men were not quite so sure.

According to Michael Hopkinson, author of *Green Against Green*, Collins' strategy included the sentiment "my idea is that if we can get our own army we can tell the British to go to hell."[29] This, no doubt, was Collins' stepping-stone approach incarnate — accept the Treaty first, consolidate power, build a strong army and civil government system, and then eventually deal with the points of the Treaty that he found objectionable — those same points that the Anti-Treatyites abhorred NOW.

The Anti-Treaty side was summed up by Mary MacSwiney's speech during the Dáil debates: "I ask you to vote in the name of the dead [1798, 1848, and 1916] against this treaty and let us take the consequences." The lines were clear-cut, the sentiments solidly felt, compromise a doubtful conclusion.

Volunteers in the North of Ireland

On 14 January 1922, some of the Monaghan Gaelic football team were arrested in Co. Tyrone on their way to Derry to play in the final of the Ulster Championship. Prisoners included Major-General Dan Hogan, O/C of the 5th Northern Division, and a number of his IRA subordinates. Documents were found on their persons relating to plans to free three prisoners due to be executed in Derry Gaol.

As a result of the crisis which ensued, "the formation of a united IRA Northern policy by Dublin and an Ulster Council Command was established."[30] With the knowledge and consent of Michael Collins and Richard Mulcahy in Dublin, plans were devised for a cross-Border raid that would result in the kidnapping of forty-two prominent Loyalists from the north of Ireland. These men were to be used as hostages in exchange for the Monaghan footballers as well as the three IRA prisoners behind bars in Derry. Tom Ketterick, from West Mayo, was sent to Coolaney, Co. Sligo, to help organise these kidnapping raids. Ketterick did his job well. The Loyalists were captured.

In February a newly formed Ulster IRA Council planned future kidnapping raids. Winston Churchill responded by increasing the number of British troops along the Border. These disturbances in the North did not stop. An elastic band of violence stretched across the Border, with each side tugging and blaming and shooting. The number of incidents increased to such an extent that the Boyle newspaper, the *Roscommon Herald*, filled its columns in June with stories about IRA activity near the troubled Border area.[31]

Weapons Procurement

The Anti-Treatyites of the 3rd Western Division discovered a conduit for obtaining arms. No longer confined to the possibilities of arms within the county or nearby Sligo, the command structure hooked up with other commanders in various parts of the country. In one instance, members of the Division went to Birr, where they received mausers that had been landed at Waterford. Eventually about 150 of those guns found their way into the hands of Sligo and Roscommon men.[32]

The Republican Army Convention

The fabric of the country was slowly shredding apart. Seamstresses on both sides of the garment were so intent on fashioning an appropriate dress for Lady Ireland that neither glanced at the material itself and asked, "What are we doing to the essence of and integrity of the threads? Will this frayed garment be suitable to clothe Kathleen Ni Houlihan for the world's eyes, or, more importantly, for our own?"

News of a proposed gathering of Anti-Treaty officers reached the Provisional Government offices and was denounced. The Anti-Treaty men ignored the objections and attended the Army Convention in Dublin on 26 March. According to the notes of Florrie O'Donoghue, Brigade Adjutant and Intelligence Officer of the Cork No. 1 Brigade, 211 delegates attended the affair[33] (four GHQ officers and eight Divisional commandants served as ex-officio delegates). The 2nd and 3rd Western Divisions (which included North and South Roscommon) were each represented by eighteen delegates,[34] while representation for all the Western Divisions totalled sixty eight. Officers present included Liam Lynch (head of the Anti-Treaty forces), Tom Maguire (East Mayo), Liam Pilkington (affectionately known as the "Fighting Saint") from North Roscommon/Sligo, Michael Kilroy (West Mayo), as well as Oscar Traynor (Dublin Brigade), and Sean Russell (Director of Munitions).

Convention business included reaffirming allegiance to the Republic and the republican status of the army, choosing a new Army Executive, re-establishing the

We didn't see the sense of the Civil War — the people had voted...they had voted for acceptance of the treaty. Mick Collins said one night, "so and so with the Treaty, thank God, I'm not a Treatyite. But when I see an opportunity... by God, I'm goin' for it."*

Spoken to Frank Simons and Pat Madden by Michael Collins in a hotel in Dublin after the Truce.

*Taped interview with Frank Simons by James McCormick, summer 1973, Roscommon town.

112

OGLAIGH NA HEIREANN

GENERAL CONVENTION

. . TO BE HELD AT . .

MANSION HOUSE

On the 9th April, 1922, at 9.30 o'c. a.m.

Admit _____ O'Rourke

as Delegate of _____ Bde. _____ Div.

Signature _____ O'Malley

119

OGLAIGH NA HEIREANN

GENERAL CONVENTION

. . TO BE HELD AT . .

MANSION HOUSE

On the 9th April, 1922, at 9.30 o'c. a.m.

Admit _____ Gerald O'Connor

as Delegate of _____ No. II Bde. _____ 2nd West. _____ Div.

Signature _____ O'Malley

Convention passes — Gerald O'Connor Papers

Belfast boycott, designating that dog-license money be collected by the local Volunteers, and ordering that the new Civic Guard be boycotted. More ominously, Tom Maguire, commandant from Mayo, felt that fifty percent of the delegates were in support of strong action against the Provisional Government.[35] His was not a lone opinion. Eoin Neeson, in his book *The Civil War 1922-1923*, writes that a majority of the Army was opposed to accepting the Treaty.[36]

At the sessions, some members insisted that the Army Executive have full control over the IRA and that the Provisional Government's efforts to build an army of its own under Dáil control should be shunned. (Three days after the commencement of the convention, the Army Executive ordered the destruction of the *Freeman's Journal* on the grounds that it had printed some rather unflattering reports about the convention.)

The political stand of these delegates against the Provisional Government caused them much financial woe. Because the convention broke ties with GHQ, the Provisional Cabinet officially declared that only officers loyal to GHQ would receive pay. This left Anti-Treaty men without reliable and consistent funds. Due to this unanticipated drought, the stream of money to support their activities had to come from elsewhere. Orders were issued by some IRA commanders to engage in bank robberies and post office raids. The Northern Bank (the Provisional Government's bank) in Drumshanbo was relieved of thousand of pounds in May by order of the Army Executive.[37] From mid-March to mid-April nationwide statistics include 331 raids on post offices along with 319 attacks on the Great Southern and Western Railways.[38]

"Go Home"

Gerald O'Connor assembled his men on the lawn of the Clonalis House in Castlerea to issue his final orders. "Go home! Leave it to the politicians to fight it out, but we are not going to shoot fellow Irishmen." And thus, most men of the 1st and 2nd Battalions, South Roscommon Brigade, holstered their guns, rose from the grounds of the ancient O'Connor family home, and proceeded down the pathways and narrow trails that led each man to his cottage and his own private memories. Some were satisfied that they had done all they were expected to do. A few who had been informers and pocketed the English five pound notes were glad that they had survived the war without having been found out. Other men, stellar patriots who saw Ireland's galvanised forces for a united country being sucked into a Saxon black hole, shouldered a weighty burden — "A nation once again" — will we ever have it?

124 ■ THEY PUT THE FLAG A-FLYIN'

Quandary for Participants

During the early months of 1922, the IRA was a fractured organisation. Which side to take? That was the question posed to every Volunteer by his commanding officer, his friends, his conscience. Throughout the country "whole brigades and divisions went Pro-and Anti-Treaty, and sometimes were divided within themselves. The IRA was now two armies."[39] The fabric of the Roscommon Volunteers was now checkered. For example, the officers of the 3rd Battalion South — Pat Madden, Luke Duffy, Frank Simons — led their Company into the Free State Army, while Matt Davis, Brigade Quartermaster, championed the Anti-Treaty forces in South Roscommon by leading the Flying Column. Davis' ASU included men from Kilteevan, Curraghboy, Knockcroghery, and St. John's Companies along with other Volunteers from neighbouring sections of Galway and Westmeath. Men who remained in the local Companies reorganised and gave support — on-call manpower as well as material — to the Flying Columns that roamed the area.

Some individuals, who were members of the First Battalion South Roscommon, participated in attacks on Free State forces at Castlerea, Ballinagare, and Ballinrobe during July of 1922. Many Republicans (Anti-Treatyites) in the northern part of the county took to the hills and joined forces with other like-minded fighters in Sligo, Leitrim, and Mayo. There was no clear-cut line of demarcation.

Even the national command structure of the IRA was torn to shreds. The Directors of Engineering (Rory O'Connor), Chemicals, Munitions, and Purchasing were still Republicans. The commanding officers of the 1st, 2nd, and 3rd Southern Divisions, of the 2nd (Tom Maguire), 3rd (Liam Pilkington), and 4th Western (Michael Kilroy), of the 4th Northern (Frank Aiken), and of the Dublin Brigade (Oscar Traynor) all took a stand against acceptance of the Treaty.[40] "Almost all the IRA in Mayo, Sligo and West Galway had gone anti-Treaty."[41] Ireland was truly a house divided against itself and one which would surely fall.

Free State Command Areas

The Provisional Government set up five command areas for the country. The southwestern command region consisted of Clare, Limerick, Kerry, and Cork, while the southeast area included Kilkenny, Waterford, south and mid-Tipperary. The Curragh Command was headed by J.J. O'Connell, who oversaw the old 3rd Southern Division, while Sean MacEoin's headquarters in Athlone proved to be the one the Republicans (Anti-Treatyites) in the western counties had to deal with. MacEoin had been given command of the Midland Division in November of 1921 and took over Athlone Barracks from the British on 28 February 1922, a truly remarkable sight for local persons who viewed the transition with a mixture of awe and incredulity (see photo on page 474).

Shortly after the Army Convention in March, Sean MacEoin and Anti-Treaty officers faced off in Custume Barracks. MacEoin stripped Paddy Morrissey, the local IRA Brigade commander, of his Sam Browne belt and expelled him,[42] along with other Anti-Treatyites, from the barracks. The Republicans moved not far away, however, but simply set up headquarters in the Royal Hotel. George Adamson, now an officer in the Free State Army, the man from Westmeath who had done so much to train the South Roscommon Volunteers during the Tan War and had participated in the Cornafulla Ambush, was shot dead on 24 April.

Boyle Barracks

When the British Forces evacuated their former barracks throughout the country as a result of the signed and voter-approved Treaty, there was great confusion as to which side (Pro or Anti-Treaty) was to inherit the structures. The general rule of thumb seemed to be whichever forces were nearest and strongest would attempt to claim the prize. For the men involved in the Boyle Barracks take-over, the seizure resembled more a tug-of-war than a smooth-sailing transition.

North Roscommon's Martin Fallon, a former commander of the 3rd Battalion North Flying Column, had attended the IRA Army Convention and declared for

British troops leaving Athlone.

the Anti-Treaty side. The British had already handed over the barracks to the local IRA men in March. Many Volunteers from the Boyle area and its environs had actually moved into the Barracks—eating and sometimes sleeping there. Accommodations were soon to change! A few days after the Army Convention in March, Fallon met with Pro-Treaty officers in Carrick-on-Shannon, a head-to-head confrontation that resulted in his switching positions. The Anti-Treaty Divisional Staff in Sligo was not pleased, and consequently gathered as many armed men as possible who would strengthen the defending Anti-Treaty garrison at Boyle.

The ASU (also known as the Flying Column) was recalled from the Border areas, and the headquarters of the 3rd Western Division was moved from Sligo to Boyle.[43] Local men occupying the vacated buildings were ordered to hold them, by force of arms if necessary.

On 5 April a split among the forces that occupied Boyle Barracks occurred. "Republican sympathisers overcame the Free State adherents. By strategy Republicans 'turn[ed] the tables' and Free State [was] put to flight after a short engagement. They [Free State] made Strokestown their H.Q. then."[44] As a result of this division, a reorganisation of the 3rd Brigade began. New officers were appointed as others left for the Free State cause. Thus some men who had been in the ranks of the IRA during the Tan War were now promoted to officer positions in their former Companies. Others who had been Battalion officers advanced to the Brigade level. For example, Pat Brennan, who had been the acting O/C of the 1st Battalion North in 1921, now became the Brigade O/C, while Michael Dockery, the former Brigade O/C, took a commission in the Free State Army.

Each Volunteer was now forced to select a side with which to fight or at least cooperate. Not infrequently, a man switched his allegiance during the course of events. It is not unusual to read in the intelligence papers of the government or in the pension statements of the Volunteers themselves that a man joined the Free State Army, gained access to weapons and equipment, then quietly made his way out the barracks back door with hardware in tow.

Who Really Killed General George Adamson?

The following was enclosed with a letter written by Rory O'Connor, IRA Director of Publicity, Four Courts, to the Editor of *The Irish Independent* 30 April 1922:

Republican Summary of the Events of Adamson's Death:
With reference to the above shooting, **the official report from Beggar's Bush** states:

PHOTO COURTESY OF GEAROID O'BRIEN

Free State Commander George Adamson

1.) "After midnight on Monday a party of their officers left Custume Barracks, Athlone, and proceeded to the Royal Hotel outside of which they commandeered a motor car. When the party returned to Barracks, one officer was missing.

2.) A search party of three with Brigadier Adamson proceeded in the direction of Irishtown, and at Mr. Bigley's they noticed a man standing in a gate-way. He was told to put up his hands, and, as he did not comply, one of the officers accompanying the Brigadier covered him with his revolver.

3.) Suddenly there was a rush, and the party of four officers found themselves surrounded by a party of armed men. They put up their hands, and as soon as they complied with the order and were disarmed, the man in the doorway levelled his revolver at Brigadier Adamson and fired point blank into his ear. The Brigadier fell mortally wounded — the bullet passing through the skull."

The report from your special press representative states:

The house where Sean McKeon [MacEoin] is staying is almost opposite the scene of the tragedy. He was in bed at the time, and when he heard the firing he hastily dressed himself and rushed out to find the Brigadier lying in a pool of blood. Lying beside the body was the General's revolver which had apparently fallen from his pocket. All the chambers were full with live ammunition.

Evidence of Major General McKeon at the inquest:

1.) On Tuesday morning witness [Major General McKeon], while in bed at Mr. Duffy's, after having returned from Tralee, heard about four shots close to the house. He sprang out of bed, lowered the window and picked up his revolver which was on the table.

2.) Looking out he heard the sound of retreating footsteps. There was a scramble just opposite Mr. Duffy's. Witness saw one man and called on him to halt and asked "who goes there?", to which the reply was given "a friend", and witness did not see any more of him.

[**Note inserted by Rory O'Connor:** How did this man disappear? Did General McKeon fire on him when doing so after being called on to "halt"? If not, why not, considering the fact that firing had just taken place? He has done so in the daylight on other occasions when there was no previous firing. Did Major General McKeon ask any further questions from the window considering that there was a scramble? How does the last part of his statement compare with the following?]

Lieutenant O'Meara, who accompanied Brigadier Adamson on the occasion, stated at the inquest: "We put up our hands immediately and were disarmed. Immediately four or five shots went off. I noticed Brigadier Adamson fall, and the men who had covered us ran. Two of my party went down to the Barracks to report the occurrence. I remained, and shortly after Major General McKeon arrived.

The Doctor's evidence: Dr. Thomas O'Donnell stated that the deceased officer had a large wound in the left ear which was plugged with Dr. Chapman's assistance. Witness made an examination of the body after death and found two wounds—one in the back of the head high up, the entrance wound, and the exit wound in the left ear. The cap of the deceased officer had corresponding perforations, the entrance one being at the back.

Note: 1.) the report from Beggar's Bush states "the man in the doorway levelled his revolver and fired point blank into his ear."

2.) Lieutenant O'Meara, the Brigadier's comrade, states "four or five shots went off...noticed Brigadier Adamson fall and the men who had covered us ran."

3.) Dr. O'Donnell states "the entrance wound was at the back of the head high up, and the exit wound in the left ear." The Doctor's evidence goes to show that the bullet entered high at the back of the head, and came out through the left ear. This certainly shows that the direction of the bullet was downwards; consequently, it must have been fired from a fair height. When a revolver is levelled it is not held and presented so high that the shot would take such a course as that indicated in the medical evidence. The report from Beggar's Bush is proved glaringly contradictory."

Arthur Griffith in Sligo

In order to enlist support for the Treaty and rally the people behind the new Provisional Government, Arthur Griffith announced his plans to travel to Sligo town and speak on Easter Sunday. Anti-Treatyites would have none of it! Liam Pilkington, O/C of the 3rd Western Division, issued a statement that all meetings of a political nature were banned from the 3rd Western area. Griffith simply ignored the ultimatum.

On 13 April, the Thursday night preceding Easter, Pro-Treaty troops entered the town under cover of darkness and took up positions. The following evening a gathering was held at which time a message was proclaimed that ordinary citizens should refrain from political demonstrations. The upshot of the meeting was a confirmation that Griffith would indeed attend the Sunday gathering and that no riotous behaviour would be tolerated.

National troops under the command of Tony Lawlor and Ned Cooney were dispatched to the town. Anti-Treaty troops were drafted from all areas of the 3rd and parts of the 4th Western Division. Many public buildings were occupied by one side or the other. Tensions were high. The Anti-Treaty Executive issued orders that no blood-letting was to take place. According to Michael Farry, author of *The Aftermath of Revolution Sligo 1921-23,* the orders were given because a ban on public speaking throughout all of Ireland was totally unenforceable, and Liam Lynch had told Pilkington to withdraw his dictum.[45] The local Republican officers were not happy. They were spoiling for a fight or, at least, a show of strength. By having neither, morale sagged, and some officers completely left the Division.[46]

Unsanctioned Lanesboro Bank Robbery

The robbery of Lanesboro Bank in April was a totally unauthorised operation taken on by individuals who saw some advantage to grabbing free money under the guise of raiding for "the cause." When local Roscommon commanding officers in the 3rd Battalion learned of such thievery, they ordered the funds to be returned. Some monies, however, never found their way back into the bank vault.

Mount Talbot Raid

On the night of 7 April, an armed party of Republicans[47] surrounded and seized Mount Talbot House. They confronted W. J. Talbot, a fifty-year-old descendant of the Talbot family who had originally settled Mount Talbot during the Cromwellian Plantation. (He was descended from an Old English Catholic family from Malahide, Co. Dublin, who chose to come to Connaught rather than go to Hell!) Talbot was taken outside. His wife Julia was left inside to imagine the worst when she heard scuffling and several shots.

Talbot was not physically harmed, but his life was threatened by one of the Volunteers. Cool persuasion by Joe Galvin and Tommy Kelly saved Talbot's life that evening, but the following day the Talbots packed their belongings and left for Dublin. Julia admitted her husband to a nursing home (he suffered from asthma and bronchitis), and she went to check in at a local hotel. She never checked out. Julia, who was the daughter of Sir Capel Molyneux of Castle Dillon in County Armagh, died that evening, leaving behind a husband who had not only lost his wife but his secure way of life.

Mount Talbot House

While the Talbots were in turmoil in Dublin, the Volunteers were enjoying the fruits of their labour in Roscommon. They tested all the wine in the Talbot cellar, but after a few days, they were chased off the place by the local authorities, but not without a gun battle.

The stately mansion house was never the same. It soon became a barracks for National troops who were flooded out of their beds when the Anti-Treatyites blew up the huge water tanks in the towers of the castle. Later Mount Talbot's bridge was demolished. The home itself lasted a few more years. It was sold shortly after Mr. John Talbot's death, and stones were pulled down and used for construction of his former tenants' buildings[48] — yet another victim in a long enduring war against landlordism and British occupation.

Occupation of the Four Courts

On 13 April the Anti-Treaty Army Executive, anxious to set up a command centre in Dublin, chose James Gandon's imposing edifice located on the Liffey quayside. The Four Courts seemed sufficiently judicial for image's sake, spacious enough to accommodate men and supplies, and centrally located. A total of 120 men garrisoned inside the building. Later recruits to the cause were placed around the city in the Masonic Hall, Ballast Office, and even Kilmainham gaol.

Roscommon, the Jewel

During the Black and Tan War, County Roscommon had glinted like a multi-faceted gemstone. While not brilliant in the direct sunlight of military prowess, one could turn the jewel another direction and watch as it flashed with fire. In the South Roscommon Brigade, the western and mid-county region planned and successfully implemented a few engagements that caused serious damage to the enemy. In the far north of the county, no major War for Independence battles took place (due to the concentration of troops stationed in Boyle), while in the extreme south of the county, no large-scale conflicts had occurred from 1918-1921 partly due to the proximity of the British military fortress at Athlone. Only an occasional conflict in that area is remembered. But with the start of the Civil War, roles changed. The gemstone was alternately dull and brilliant, cool and undistinguished, or dancing with colour. Volunteers from the Boyle and Arigna area, who had not challenged the British directly in many key engagements during the Tan War, fought like tigers against the Free State troops. Men of western Roscommon, who had attempted several serious engagements during the Tan War, were advised by their officers to go home and not engage in any activity whatsoever. Some men disobeyed those orders. Many Volunteers in the extreme south remained neutral or joined the Flying Column commanded by Matt Davis.

In mid-Roscommon, the 3rd Battalions North and South carried off the most successful fights of the Tan War. The attacks at Fourmilehouse, Elphin patrol and barracks in February 1921, Frenchpark in June 1921, Tarmonbarry patrols in January and February 1921, and Scramogue in March all bore the fingerprints of competent planners and tenacious fighters. Yet when the Civil War came, many in the 3rd Battalion South (Athleague, Kilbride, Cloontuskert, Kilgefin, and Roscommon Companies) went to the Free State side and participated in the Civil War as men and officers of the National Army. This is not necessarily true for the 3rd Battalion North. Many of those men joined the Active Service Units (ASUs) of their local IRA Battalions.

The county boundaries became porous. Anti-Treaty men flowed west, north, and east to join up with other like-minded soldiers. There were no solid boundary lines — only friendly terrain where groups of Anti-Treaty men were harboured and sustained, or, as the Civil War wore on, hunted.

After the Battle of Boyle in the opening days of July, the Divisional ASU broke up, and each man was sent to his local area to make dugouts and be at the command of the local Battalion O/C "unless required for Brigade work and with the exception of a section attached to the Brigade Field Headquarters."[49] Thus the nugget that was Roscommon took on various hues depending on the particular time frame during each war and, especially after the split of the army, the mindset of specific commanders of each Company within the county.

The Formation of the Anti-Treaty Active Service Units in North Roscommon

With new allegiances being proclaimed as a result of the Army Convention, a realignment of forces within the IRA took place. New Brigade, Battalion, and Company officers were named, and new titles went to new men depending on which side of the Treaty line they stood. Anti-Treaty leaders in the county deemed it wise to form a Flying Column (ASU) of their own which was mobile, well armed, and stocked with dependable men. Its member roster included:[50]

> "You'll have to fight in our area if you are false to your oath ... That's where you'll meet with immediate and terrible war."
>
> Spoken by Ernie O'Malley to Ginger O'Connell, assistant Chief of Staff in the Free State Army, as quoted in *The Singing Flame* by Ernie O'Malley p. 44.

- 1st Battalion North: Pat Brennan, Patrick Chapman, Michael Chapman, Paddy "Kid" Lynch, Paddy Kellegher, Michael J. Larkin, Pat Glancy, Michael Glancy, William Dockery, Michael Dockery (not the former O/C of the Brigade but another man of the same name), Richard Murray, James Flanagan, James Brady, Owen McLoughlin, Phil Murray, Martin Killalea, John Sheeran, John Kelly (of Ballinameen), Jack Roche, Michael Roche, John Moran, Tommy Shannon, Michael Connor, Michael Harrington
- 2nd Battalion North: Sean Owens, Brian Carroll, Paddy Moran (of Clooncunny, Elphin), James Duffy, John James Conroy (Conry), Joe Kelly (of Rathcroghan), Tom Mahon, Tommy Connor, Peter Dockery, Tommy Kelly (of Cloonkerin)
- 3rd Battalion North: Brian Nangle, Frank O'Donoghue, John Nugent, Pat and Hugh Giblin, Joe Cox, Luke and Andy Feeney, Dan Hanley, Richard Hayden, James Farrell, James Kelly, Luke Cox, Michael J. McNamara, Kelly Igo, James Padian, Frank McGuinness, Peter Lynch, Patrick Walsh, and Frank Gannon
- 4th Battalion North: Pat and John McKeon (Knockroe, Croghan), Tom Lowe, John Leneghan, Mick McLoughlin of Corlara, Carrick-on-Shannon, Martin Cummins, Michael Keogh, Pat and James W. Duignan (Kilbride, Kilmore), Peter McCrann, John and Michael Healy of Kilmore, Joseph Elwood, Thomas Noone, Peter Donnelly
- 5th Battalion (South Leitrim) Battalion: Sean O'Farrell, Sean Quinn, ____ Finn, Patrick O'Rourke, John Charles Keegan, Tom Kilroy.

The Formation of the Anti-Treaty Active Service Units in South Roscommon

- Volunteers for the 1st Battalion South: Tom Crawley (O/C), Martin Foley (Vice O/C), Michael Delaney (Adjutant), James Heneghan (Capt.), John Beirne, Tim Jennings, Michael Regan (Capt.), Mark McDonagh, Joseph Kenny. (Participants in various engagements can be found in the footnotes of Chapter 8.)
- Volunteers for the 2nd Battalion South: John Ryan (Vice O/C), Michael Grady (Capt.), Pat McCormack, Patrick Reynolds, Michael Conboy, Bernie Farrell, James Cahill, William Kehir, Luke Raftery, Martin Mockler, Patrick Dockery, John Mannion, Pat McCarthy, John Hester, Thomas Kelly, Michael Leonard, James McDermott
- 3rd and 4th Battalion South: Headed by Matt Davis of Kilteevan Company, the Brigade Flying Column included: William Murray (Curry, Curraghboy), John and Patrick Waldron (Curry, Curraghboy), James Whelan (Ardmullan, Curraghboy), Martin Kelly (Ballygar, Co. Galway), Hubert Watson — Battalion Quartermaster (Kiltoom), John Monaghan (Cornalee, Curraghboy), Patrick Kenny (Curraghboy), Patrick Cunniffe (Bredagh, Dysart), William Mulrooney (Ballygar), Patrick Reddington (Rackans, Curraghboy), George Fitzgerald (Ardmullan, Curraghboy), John and Michael Breheny (Sandfield, Knockcroghery), William Fallon (Kilcash, Knockcroghery), Dan Dempsey, Patrick Gallagher (Whitepark, Curraghboy), John Joe Ennis, James Martin. Members of local Companies who helped and supported these men included: Michael J. and Edward and Tom Fallon (all of Kilcash, Knockcroghery), Pat Breheny (Battalion Engineer from Sandfield, Knockcroghery), Patrick Breheny (Portrunny), Jim Breheny (Portrunny) served as Intelligence Officer for the 3rd and 4th Battalions, Thomas Naughton (Feeragh, Ballymurray), Michael Naughton (Portrunny, Knockcroghery), Thomas Hayden, John Kilcline (4th Battalion Vice O/C), Malachy Kilroy, John Naughton, Joseph McKeon (Ballagh, Knockcroghery), Edward Costello (Corramore, Kiltoom), Laurence Butler (Curry, Curraghboy), Edward "Sonny" Egan (Curraghboy), Bernard Coyne (Lisbrock [Lisbaun], Curraghboy), Laurence Harrison (Cam, Brideswell), and John Nolan (Ballygar).[51]

Known members of the Athlone Brigade Involved in Attacks on Free State Soldiers

■ Thomas and Daniel McGiff (Drumraney), Anthony McCormack (Tang), Pat Macken (Castlepollard), Mick Pender (Athlone), James Martin (The Hill of Berries), John Galvin (Carrick), Frank O'Connor (Coosan), Brian Mulvihill (Coosan), Paddy Golden (Coosan), Thomas Berry (Tubberclair), Jack Costello (Crosswood), Jack Kelly (Mt. Temple), Paddy Fitzpatrick and his brother (Cornamaddy), Bertie Gaynor (Tullywood), Harry O'Brien (Athlone), James Fox (Athlone), Ned Dowling (Athlone), Simon Mulvihill (Coosan). They were assisted by Michael Finneran (Glasson), James Casey (Killenure), Tim McCann (Portlick), Pat Killian (Glasson), Paddy Cunningham (Killenure), Ned Flynn (Kilkenny West), Michael Tinn (Tonagh), Tom Heslin (Littletown), L. Corrigan (Kilfaughney), Pat Keegan (Tubberclair), and Willie Keegan of Tubberclair

Joint IRA Offensives

Northern clashes were stepped up during the months of April, May, and June. Michael Collins and Liam Lynch were involved in a scheme whereby a large consignment of arms was dispatched to the North. To avoid detection, arms supplied by Britain to Collins' government were swapped with guns from Anti-Treaty units so that no guns captured along the Border from IRA men would bear British serial numbers. Volunteers to participate in such actions were requested from the southern counties.

Seamus Woods, O/C of the 3rd Northern Division, pointed out the inadvisability of mounting an attack in Belfast where the Catholic community would be so exposed to reprisals. A police raid on the Belfast IRA liaison office at St. Mary's Hall revealed the names of nearly every officer in the Division. One month later, 350 IRA and Sinn Féin members were arrested.[52]

Attack on the Four Courts in Dublin

By summertime 1922 the Anti-Treaty forces had occupied the Four Courts for more than two months. Communication between the Anti-Treatyites and the Provisional Government had been frequent and somewhat friendly. According to a letter penned by Rory O'Connor, "we were never requested to evacuate the Four Courts. On the contrary, at one meeting of the Coalition Army Council, at which Mulcahy, O'Duffy, [Liam] Mellows, Liam Lynch and myself were present, we were only asked to evacuate the Ballast Office, the Kildare St. Club, the Masonic Hall and Lever Bros. At that stage we actually discussed coordinated military action against NE Ulster......."[53] This statement is collaborated by Ernie O'Malley in his book *The Singing Flame*. He states that on 28 June at 3:40 a.m. the

Four Courts damage
PHOTO COURTESY OF EAMONN DOWLING

Four Courts garrison was handed a message ordering them to vacate the building. "Paddy O'Brien [O/C of the garrison] ordered the guards to fall in by sections. He read the message to them and they laughed. It was the first time the Staters had ever asked us to leave the Courts."[54]

The timing of the ultimatum was determined, as usual, by events in London. On 22 June, Sir Henry Wilson, the former Chief of the Imperial General Staff, was assassinated by two IRA men, Reginald Dunne and Joseph O'Sullivan. This event was the "straw that broke the camel's back." Fed up with Collins' procrastination regarding the occupation of the Four Courts, Lloyd George ordered the Provisional Government to attack the "Irregulars" or consider the consequences of a breached Treaty.

The notice for evacuation read:
I, acting under the order of the Government, hereby order you to

evacuate the buildings of the Four Courts and to parade your men under arrest, without arms, on that portion of the Quays immediately in front of the Four Courts by 4 a.m. Failing compliance with this order, the building will be taken by me by force, and you and all concerned with you will be held responsible for any life lost or any damage done.

By order
Thomas Ennis
O/C 2nd Eastern Division

Later that same morning, the big guns loaned by the British began hammering at the walls of the Four Courts. Victims of the firing were not only Republicans along with the building's mortar and iron, but also invaluable records stored in the basement. Seven and a half hours of a blistering cacophony sounded the opening bell for this most vicious of all fights. The shelling of the Four Courts served as the preface of a very bitter and dark chapter in Irish history.

We're All in this Alone

News of the attack on the Four Courts struck the eardrums of Anti-Treaty forces in the west like a thunderclap. According to Michael Hopkinson, author of *Green Against Green,* "The night of the Four Courts a Divisional meeting was held in Sligo...[Frank] Carty was fighting on his own for destruction at once [of Free State forces scattered throughout the west] but Brian MacNeill was discussing his idea that all available men and arms should march at once on the North."[55] Tom Carney, O/C of the East Mayo Flying Column, submitted the notion that troops should advance on Athlone.[56] Such divergent views mirrored the confusion and disarray of the command structure of the Anti-Treatyites. No one had contemplated a Civil War, and surely no one had made any plans for military cooperation if one should occur. Each unit and Division was putting forth its own idea of priority and procedure. "The failure to co-ordinate policy and to communicate effectively with GHQ ended any hope of an offensive policy being adopted in the west."[57]

As recorded in Ruairí O'Bradáigh's book, *Dílseacht,* Tom Maguire, O/C of the 2nd Western Division, claimed that "there was no cohesion or military council formed between the military commanders in the West, Liam Pilkington of the Third, Michael Kilroy of the Fourth and himself. When a Western command was established in 1923 to co-ordinate action, it was too late."[58]

Aside from mixed military strategies and snafus, the political situation was entirely different than it had been one year before. During the Tan War "the British had had a big army for sure, with a compliant police force and a few spies, but [now] the Free State had an army, half the people, the British government and public opinion of their side."[59] From its very inception, the Civil War was a David and Goliath struggle. ∎

1. Luke Duffy Papers, private collection.
2. Pat Mullooly Volunteer Witness Statement to the Department of Military History 1913-21, p. 33.
3. Frank Simons Volunteer Witness Statement to the Bureau of Military History 1913-21, p. 38.
4. Frank Simons taped interview, conducted by James McCormick, summer 1973, Roscommon town.
5. Frank O'Connor Volunteer Witness Statement to the Bureau of Military History 1913-21, p. 26.
6. Sean Leavy Volunteer Witness Statement to the Bureau of Military History 1913-21, p. 23-24.
7. Martin Fallon Volunteer Witness Statement to the Bureau of Military History 1913-21, p. 20.
8. Bernard Sweeney Volunteer Witness Statement to the Bureau of Military History 1913-21, p. 17.
9. Jack Glancy Volunteer Witness Statement to the Bureau of Military History 1913-21, p. 19.
10. Liam O'Doherty interview, Ernie O'Malley Papers, P17b/131, p. 45.
11. *Dublin Made Me,* by C. S. Andrews, p. 186.
12. *For Ireland and Freedom,* by Micheál O'Callaghan, p. 83.

13. *Dublin Made Me*, by C. S. Andrews, p. 186.
14. *For Ireland and Freedom*, by Micheál O'Callaghan, p. 83.
15. *For Ireland and Freedom*, by Micheál O'Callaghan, p. 79.
16. *For Ireland and Freedom*, by Micheál O'Callaghan, p. 80.
17. James P. Flanagan statement to the Department of Defence, Pat Brennan Papers, private collection.
18. *The Aftermath of Revolution Sligo 1921-23*, by Michael Farry, p. 31.
19. *Pre-Truce Activities of Curraghboy Company* penned by George Fitzgerald. **Volunteers who raided the mails** included: Dick Mee, William Murray, John Waldron, George Fitzgerald, Thomas Bergin, Edward Egan, Patrick Gallagher, Patrick Reddington, John Kenny, Nicholas Cummins, Thomas Cunningham, John Watson, and Laurence Butler.
20. Roscommon RIC Monthly Report, June 1921, (718).
21. Pat Mullooly, Quartermaster for North Roscommon Brigade, private papers.
22. *Ourselves Alone! The Story of Arthur Griffith and the Origins of the Irish Free State*, by Padraic Colum, p. 276.
23. *Blacksmith of Ballinalee*, by Padraic O'Farrell, p. 71.
24. *Michael Collins and the Brotherhood*, by Vincent MacDowell, p. 97.
25. *Victory of Sinn Féin*, by P. S. O'Hegarty, p. 109.
26. *Michael Collins*, by Tim Pat Coogan, p. 227.
27. *Michael Collins*, by Tim Pat Coogan, p. 223.
28. *The Irish Civil War An Illustrated History*, by Helen Litton, p. 88.
29. p. 37.
30. *The Aftermath of Revolution Sligo 1921-23*, by Michael Farry, p. 52.
31. *Roscommon Herald*, 3 June 1922.
32. Tom Scanlon interview, Ernie O'Malley Papers, UCD Archives, P17b/133.
33. *No Other Law*, by Florence O'Donoghue, p. 219.
34. *No Other Law*, by Florence O'Donoghue, p. 335.
35. *Green Against Green*, by Michael Hopkinson, p. 68.
36. p. 95.
37. *Green Against Green*, by Michael Hopkinson, p. 90.
38. *Green Against Green*, by Michael Hopkinson, p. 90.
39. *The Civil War*, by Eoin Neeson, p. 91.
40. *The Singing Flame*, by Ernie O'Malley, p. 49.
41. *Green against Green*, by Michael Hopkinson, p. 158.
42. *Who's Who in the Irish War of Independence and Civil War 1916-1923*, by Padraic O'Farrell, p. 179.
43. *The Aftermath of Revolution Sligo 1921-23*, by Michael Farry, p. 55.
44. Pat Brennan personal diary, p. 7. Pat Brennan Papers, private collection.
45. p. 60.
46. Jack Brennan interview, UCD Archives, Ernie O'Malley Papers, p17b/137.
47. Patrick Fitzmaurice correspondence, Oranmore, Co. Galway, 27 December 2002.
48. The Crofton Papers, National Library, Dublin, MS 22,825 and MS 23,022.
49. Pat Brennan Papers, private collection.
50. Pat Brennan Papers, private collection.
51. Extracted from the 4th Battalion Company Commanders' Papers, private collection.
52. *Green Against Green*, by Michael Hopkinson, p. 84-85.
53. Rory O'Connor letter sent from Mountjoy Prison, Dublin, August 1922. Cited in *Civil War in Connaught 1922-1923*, by Nollaig O Gadhra, p. 18.
54. p. 95.
55. p. 158.
56. *The Aftermath of Revolution Sligo 1921-23*, by Michael Farry, p. 76.
57. *Green Against Green*, by Michael Hopkinson cites as his sources the report of Ernie O'Malley to Liam Lynch, and various dispatches from western commanders found in the Mulcahy Papers in UCD Archives.
58. p. 19.
59. *When Youth Was Mine — A Memoir of Kerry 1902-1925*, by Jeremiah Murphy, p. 203.

EIGHT

CIVIL WAR
IN CONNAUGHT

The Civil War in Ireland was an acrimonious conflict. Unlike most wars where true believers stake out a principle, join up with other like-minded patriots, and fight for the duration, Ireland's civil strife was a result of ruptured trust and shattered dreams. The Volunteers all began on the same side with the same goal — separation from England. They pooled their meagre resources and cooperated with each other to challenge Britain's claim. When the momentum of that battle began to shift against the Crown Forces and seriously threaten England's hold on her colony, Lloyd George called a Truce. As the guns of war were laid to rest, the words of divisional politics reared their ugly heads.

After breezy discussion had been exhausted and the winds of war whipped viciously o'er the land, men found themselves wrenched from the very friendships that had sustained them only a few short months earlier. Former colleagues, with whom they had traversed the fields and laid in silent ambush for the dreaded enemy, now found themselves to be the enemy for whom their former colleagues were now waiting. It was a bitter, bitter experience.

> "I believe it was all a matter of lust for power by the top notch politicians at the time."
>
> Spoken by Frank Simons (acting O/C South Roscommon Brigade at the time of the Truce), interview with James McCormick, summer of 1973, Roscommon town.

Sligo

At the time of the bombardment of the Four Courts in June, Sean MacEoin, the National Army's O/C of the Western Command, was in Sligo town having just returned from his honeymoon in Donegal. At a glance he could spot the formidable old military barracks with its thick walls perched atop the hill. He knew it to be garrisoned by the Anti-Treatyites, as were Numbers 1 and 2 barracks. The Treaty supporters had managed to hold onto the county gaol.

On Friday 30 June a large contingent of government soldiers unloaded barbed wire in front of the courthouse. Although the local Anti-Treaty forces had been joined by several Flying Columns from the west of Mayo,[1] it became obvious that the National Army numbers were growing as quickly as the Anti-Treaty supplies were dwindling. Rather than be boxed into an inescapable cage, the Anti-Treaty (Republican) forces decided to torch and clear out. Around midnight, a huge fire engulfed No. 1 barracks as well as the adjoining recreation hall; the blaze was extinguished by soldiers with MacEoin acting as fire marshal. The Republicans had burned the old fortress rather than relinquish it to the Free Staters. Most of the IRA left town — many heading for the Collooney area, where they proceeded to cut the rail lines. The next day Sligo town buzzed with activity as National soldiers frisked all civilians passing the courthouse. Later that night Republicans with rifles searched all who passed outside the National Bank. The town was a replica of much of Ireland — opposing forces staring down a gun barrel at each other while ordinary civilians were balancing on a tightrope between them trying to buy a loaf of bread.

The day after the Four Courts assault, the forces under Commandant Joe Sweeney in Donegal had launched an attack on Finner Camp, just south of Ballyshannon. MacEoin knew, however, that he must secure counties Sligo and Leitrim if he were going to maintain control of the northern areas. Aside from

Athlone and a small garrison at Roscommon town, there was no base west of the Shannon available to him. Boyle was his gateway to Sligo. He meant to secure it. It was not going to be easy!

The Battle for Boyle

All four IRA commanders of the Western Divisions had taken the Anti-Treaty stand. Their forces had moved in to occupy the local barracks. Boyle was no exception. Active Service Units of the Republican Army had thrown out the Free State adherents in April, but by the 1st of June the government troops occupied the Union Building. On 29 June all Shannon bridges and the Railway Bridge were demolished in preparation for the main attack on Boyle Barracks. On the first day of July, the gunfire sounded.

In the months before, Liam Pilkington (Commandant of the 3rd Western Division), who had been very reluctant to start a Civil War within his domain, had sent many of his men to the North to snipe across the Border at the B-Specials (the British paid auxiliary police force). But in the opening days of July, policy changed, attitudes hardened, men were recalled. The Republicans were ordered to attack the Free State forces wherever they found them.

In Boyle the workhouse and adjacent buildings were held by Free State soldiers commanded by Michael Dockery. After securing positions in houses overlooking the workhouse and cutting communication lines, Republican forces attacked the Pro-Treaty men. Among the many combatants were members of the East Mayo Flying Column who headed for the workhouse which was surrounded by walls.[2]

The government forces had been warned of the coming foray — Anti-Treaty troops had amassed, bridges had been destroyed, communication lines had been severed. It was a firefight of vicious intensity. The wall of lead was solid, and it was not until near daybreak that the East Mayo Column could safely re-scale the walls and withdraw from the interior grounds of the workhouse. All the East Mayo men made the retreat safely save one — Knox Roughneen from Kiltimagh, Mayo, who was taken prisoner. The Battle for Boyle ended tragically for one Free State officer who was permanently disabled, and for Michael Dockery, former O/C of the North Roscommon Brigade, the man who had planned the attack on Elphin Barracks, participated in the Keadue ambush, then made such a daring escape from Boyle Barracks only one year before. Now he lay dead, shot by a storming party on that sad day.

Throughout the fierce engagement some members of the Cumann na mBan of Boyle were quite busy supporting their fighting men. Bridie Murray, sister of Josie, was one of those brave women on duty at First Aid Stations set up. She distributed food, bandages, and lotions to the Anti-Treaty troops in town as well as those stationed as outposts, where she also checked for casualties. On occasion she transported arms under fire.

All throughout the next day (Sunday) sniping continued, roads remained block-aded, bridges were made impassable, telegraph lines and instruments were disman-tled, and all communication was cut off. The town was isolated from the outside world. Late in the evening, Free State reinforcements arrived along with the armoured car, *Ballinalee*, and, more ominous, at least three machine guns.[3] The savagery of the fight within Boyle was such that the Anti-Treaty men decided to evacuate the barracks. When they left, they mined it lest it be of use to the com-ing Free State troops. Decidedly overpowered by arms, the Republicans also left the workhouse area, but seized other outlying positions which they desperately tried to hold for the next four days. At one of those positions (Ballytrasna), eight Anti-Treaty men were taken prisoner and one Free State trooper, Sgt. Frank Balfe, lost his life.[4]

The Anti-Treatyites took up ambush positions at Ardeash, Croghan Road, but the two Free State lorries they were seeking did not pass that way. Another rail-way bridge at Hollymount was destroyed, and communication lines were severed. The original strength of the Anti-Treaty forces was sizably diminished due to the order that sent all men back to their own Brigade areas. The sixteen Boyle area Republicans[5] who remained in the vicinity successfully evaded capture at Ardcarne, where they were billeted. They soon made their way to Ballinameen, where they got very little food or rest before another big roundup by troops from Strokestown began combing the area.

Back to Sligo

By 5 July the town of Boyle rested safely in the hands of the Free State troops under Alec McCabe. Bidding farewell to the *Ballinalee*, the residents watched as the armoured curiosity made its way northward to Sligo town, where it proved to be an equally intriguing spectacle.

The next day the *Ballinalee* took part in an attack on the Wine Street Barracks which was still held by Republican forces. Afterwards it was driven south to the area near Collooney, where it loomed as a prized trophy for the Anti-Treatyites who had set up an ambush. Leaving Markree Castle about six on the morning of 13 July, the company of government soldiers approached Dooney Rock on the shore of Lough Gill only to be halted by a roadblock manned by Frank Carty's Column. Shots rang out. Four National troopers fell dead (Patrick O'Callaghan, Pro-Treaty officer in charge; John Sweeney; John Farrell of Longford; and Sean Adair). The *Ballinalee* changed hands.

The day before, Alec McCabe, moving north from Boyle, had fought a two-hour battle with Anti-Treatyites who had occupied the barracks, courthouse, and other command positions in the town of Ballymote. Commander McCabe's troops routed the Republicans amid the leaping flames from the abandoned burning barracks.

On 14 July, Anti-Treatyites used the *Ballinalee* to attack government troops in Sligo town. An ultimatum of surrender was sent to the courthouse where the Free State soldiers had taken refuge. It was dutifully declined. The Bishop of Elphin personally tried to intervene by negotiation, but when that effort failed, he positioned himself inside the courthouse. "Not wishing to expose the Bishop to danger and realising the propaganda the enemy would make of it if the Bishop was either killed or wounded by our attack we [the Anti-Treatyites] left the town with all the men."[6]

The north Roscommon-Collooney-Ballymote area was threatening to become a springboard from which the Republican forces could dive into the surrounding area. MacEoin decided to dry gulch it. On the evening of the 13th, a contingent of 120 soldiers from Athlone, led by MacEoin, boarded a train headed east. At Mullingar, the train was halted; MacEoin disembarked along with other officers who cut the telegraph wires and switched the rail lines so that the troop train would head for Collooney via Boyle.[7] Next morning the Provisional forces, who had been joined by Commandant Lawlor's soldiers, positioned themselves in and around Collooney and were accompanied by an old 18-pounder artillery piece secluded in the sawmill. MacEoin sent messages to the Catholic and Protestant ministers instructing them to lead their parishioners out of town a safe distance. When civilians were cleared, MacEoin's soldiers and those of the Republican forces did battle.

Overwhelmed by superior firing power, the Republicans decided to withdraw to the southwest. Unbeknownst to them, Free State Commandant Matt O'Farrelly, dressed as a civilian, had left his troops on the southwest side of town and walked to MacEoin to check on the progress of the fighting. MacEoin ordered O'Farrelly back to his own area, and while retracing his steps O'Farrelly encountered Republicans attempting to slip out of town. "He thought he was finished but his wits were quick. He looked like one of them. 'Come on', he shouted. 'You'll have me waiting for you all day. At the double.'" Under the guise of being the men's rightful commander, O'Farrelly led the Republicans through the town, hustling through the streets at quick pace, until he ordered a halt directly in front of MacEoin.

'Good God Almighty!' came a disbelieving voice. 'We've been captured by one man.'"[8]

By nightfall, the Provisional troops were in charge. The following morning Frank O'Beirne, Vice O/C of the IRA Battalion, was made a prisoner along with twenty-two other men who had been taking sanctuary in a house near the railway station. Scores of Republicans were captured.[9]

After the loss of Collooney in mid-July, Republicans felt their efforts would be better directed to hit and run operations. They abandoned the towns and concentrated their forces on the tips of a triangle. Liam Pilkington, 3rd Western Divisional Commander, and Seamus Devins, O/C of Grange Battalion, both based at O'Rahilly House in north Sligo (estimated strength 100 men, 90 rifles), were responsible for helter-skelter in that area. Frank Carty (O/C of Tubbercurry Battalion) and his group (estimated to be 40-60 men strong) were "based along the Ox Mountains between Coolaney and Curry."[10] The Arigna/Sligo Columns headed by Ned Bofin, Harold McBrien, and Seamus Cull along with a group in Boyle harassed the Free State forces in north Roscommon, Leitrim, and east Mayo.

Mayo, Northwest Roscommon, and Leitrim

County Mayo presented a problem to the Dublin command centre. Michael Kilroy had a disciplined force in west Mayo which used the areas of Buckagh, Treenlaur, and Skirdagh near Newport as its base. His and Frank Carty's Columns "were among the largest and most active Republican forces in the Twenty-six counties during the early phases of the war."[11] Oftentimes the men criss-crossed back and forth over the county borders to augment forces for the other Column. (Such was the case in early July when members of the West Mayo ASU were ordered to Castlebar and from thence to Sligo to serve under Frank Carty.)[12] Tom Maguire's Column operated in the Ballinrobe area and, at times, added support personnel to Frank Carty's men on the other side of the Ox Mountains. The Pro-Treaty commanders were determined to counter this activity.

In Westport on 24 July the Provisional Government landed 400 men, 600 rifles, one eighteen-pound gun, one armoured car, and 150 bicycles.[13] This force proceeded eastward and added reinforcements to Free State troops, some of whom occupied Castlebar (which was secured on 25 July) and others who had already swept through northwest Roscommon.

The Anti-Treatyites had laid siege around Castlerea[14] for the previous weeks. On Friday morning 21 July, Clonalis House was the scene of fighting where about sixty Anti-Treatyites were arrested and a large store of looted goods was found in surrounding buildings. In Ballaghaderreen, the Republicans had held the town for three weeks prior to the National troops arriving. They had used John Dillon's residence as their headquarters. For all those weeks, business had been suspended, and interaction with surrounding counties had been kept to a minimum. To secure their hold on the town, the Anti-Treaty forces had placed mines opposite Dillon's home at Flannery's corner, the courthouse, and other centres. They had destroyed four bridges which spanned the river adjacent to the town. Their stranglehold on the town was successfully broken on Wednesday evening 26 July.[15]

A skirmish took place in Ballinagare during the latter part of July. Twenty-five Anti-Treaty men[16] fought off the advancing Free State troops; but, overwhelmed by numbers and firepower, the men retreated to safe ground. The Anti-Treatyites had cut telephone wires and damaged a railway bridge at Castlerea, but the National troops successfully dislodged them on 28 July. Others[17] did battle with advancing government troops in Ballinlough.

Mayhem ruled the day as hundreds of men, Pro and Anti-Treaty, attacked each other. To the west of Roscommon, machine gun fire resounded in the town of Ballina for more than an hour. On that same day to the east in County Leitrim, rail lines were torn up between Manorhamilton and Dromahair, and armed men refused to allow them to be repaired. At Dromore, Co. Sligo, the Anti-Treaty forces abandoned the barracks, but they continued to hold the Workhouse as their headquarters. Communication with the outside world was difficult because the nearby bridge at Farnaharpy Skreen connecting them with Sligo had been destroyed.

"I Will Fight No More Forever" *quoted from Chief Joseph, American Nez Perce Indian*

The start of the Civil War rent a gut wrenching cry from all corners of Ireland. So too in Roscommon. Men wrestled with their dark side and with demons far greater for answers. Some participants continued in the struggle against the new Free State forces; others, following the lead of Michael Collins in Dublin, joined the new National (Free State) Army, hoping that this interim period might prove to be the pathway to independence. Others, no matter what the desired outcome, could not quarter a war against their own. Following is a letter of resignation that typifies the sentiment of the last group:

OGLAIG NA H-EIREANN

Headquarters
No. 2 Brigade
2nd Western Division
Castlerea
July 8th, 1922

To: G. O'Connor
Officer Commanding, No. 2 Brigade

A Chara,

I wish to be relieved of my duties as Brigade Adjutant, also to inform you that I will not participate in the present struggles under existing circumstances.

Ever since the Army split I have hoped for a settlement. With the enemy still in the country, it seems incredible that responsible persons could not knit the Army for the one common purpose.

Apart from the general aspect, the position here in our own area is not very encouraging. Since hostilities began there has been no definite plan of action.

The only operations so far are the blockading of roads and the interruption of train service.

From a military standpoint I cannot see the advantage of such tactics. We are not only endangering our own supply, but the supplies of the people. While admitting that the peoples' verdict in the present issue has not the force of honesty behind it, yet I think their apparent hostility is pretty justifiable.

Concluding I can only say that I joined the Volunteers five years ago, and feel I have done nothing dishonourable since, and can console myself with the thought of having no responsibility for the present regrettable situation.

I still remain Republican, and have no intention of joining what I consider the domestic enemy. I feel optimistic also that we have not long to wait until we have to band ourselves together again for the common enemy.

I take full responsibility for the action I am now taking, and trust you will accept my resignation in the spirit with which it is tendered.

Mise,
Do Chara
Sean Costello[18]

Sean Costello in later years.
PHOTO COURTESY OF SEAN COSTELLO

The views expressed in this resignation were endorsed by the Brigade O/C who discussed the situation with Adjutant Costello before he drafted the letter. It was then submitted to IRA Divisional Commandant Tom Maguire on 10 July 1922. A few days later by arrangement with the Divisional O/C, a special Brigade Council meeting was held to consider the matter, at which the Divisional O/C presided. After a full and frank discussion, several Brigade and Battalion Officers resigned rather than participate in fratricide.[19]

Strength of the IRA in South and North Roscommon

Oftentimes writers downplay the size and scope of the Volunteer movement, especially in areas outside Munster. By examining the private papers of Gerald O'Connor, Commandant of No. 2 Brigade in the 2nd Western Division and Pat Brennan, Commandant of No. 3 Brigade in the 3rd Western Division during the Civil War, we get a different view. O'Connor's figures indicate strength on a Battalion level, while Brennan's represent numbers of Volunteers on a Brigade level. Both men's calculations include the entire strength of their command after the new Divisional system was implemented. Those Divisions went beyond the Roscommon County borders and included parts of neighbouring counties.

1st Battalion South Roscommon

Company	Former Strength 1 July '21	Fallen Away*	Actual Strength 1 July '22
Loughglynn	24	4	20
Ballinagare	30	2	28
Moor	31	11	20
Cloonboniffe	29	19	10
Trien	60	40	20
Cloonfad	49	14	35
Ballinlough	44	28	16
Castlerea	42	20	22
Galway Coys.:			
Granlahan	34	9	25
Gorthaganny	40	25	15

Total strength of the Battalion: 211

North Roscommon Brigade

Battalion	Former Strength 1 July '21	Actual Strength 1 July '22
1st Battalion North	257	176
2nd Battalion North	142	103
3rd Battalion North	314	125
4th Battalion North	145	67
5th Battalion (includes parts of other counties)		314
6th Battalion (includes parts of other counties)		406

Total strength of the Brigade: 1191**

*Fallen Away refers not only to those whose interest had waned, but also to those who joined the Free State Army or emigrated.

** The decrease in numbers (from July 1921 to July 1922) does not necessarily represent Volunteer disinterest. At the time of the outbreak of the Civil War, seventeen members of the 2nd Battalion North alone were incarcerated.

North Roscommon Men Attack in the West

In order to obtain a little shuteye and escape from the constant sweeps by National troops around Boyle, members of North Roscommon's ASU had moved to Mayo by late July. After a week's rest, they, in conjunction with the East Mayo men, participated in the attack on Swinford Barracks on 4 August 1922. Plans were prepared by Joe Sheehy, who had been arrested in Ballina but mistakenly released by the Free State troops.[20] For over an hour the gunfire rang out until the barracks was finally captured and all guns and ammunition distributed to the attackers.[21] One Anti-Treaty man was killed (Joseph Traynor). After the Swinford success, the men immediately faced off with Tony Lawlor's troops at nearby Killasser. Soon after, the North Roscommon men trudged home, only to prepare for an attack on Drumsna Barracks on 24 August.[22] Armed with rifles and revolvers, they had mined the door and barged into the barracks before the Free State troopers realised what had happened. They made off with five Lee Enfield rifles and 180 rounds of .303 ammunition.[23] (Pat Brennan, Commandant of the Brigade, states that seven rifles were procured with 300 rounds of .303 ammunition.)[24] The twenty-five attackers withdrew westward into Co. Roscommon, where they were spotted by Free State intelligence officers at Croghan in early September.[25]

The Arigna Flying Column

The Arigna Flying Column had formed during harvest time of 1921. Grouped with the 3rd Western Division, its members included men from Crossna and the Arigna valley. When the Divisional structure was implemented, all of South Leitrim was joined to the 3rd Brigade, with Sean O'Farrell from Dromod serving as Battalion O/C. The Crossna Battalion (which had formerly been the 4th Battalion North Roscommon) was transferred to the 2nd Brigade, 3rd Western Division.

Known Members of the Arigna Flying Column

Many men from the North Roscommon Active Service Unit fought with the Arigna Column (see Chapter 7, page 130). Others included:

Officer — Ball

Frank Barlow of Keadue, arrested on 3 February 1923

Thomas Beirne of Greaghrevaugh, Arigna, captured 4 September 1923

Officer W. Beirne

Ned Bofin, Column leader, arrested 25 March 1923

Paul Bofin, brother of Ned

James Callery, arrested 14 November 1922, held in Stone Park, and not released until December of 1923

The Cull Brothers: Michael, Seamus, and Owen (Michael was killed on 6 January, Seamus on 27 February 1923)

John Cullen

Seamus Devins, killed on Benbullben on 20 September 1922

James Doyle of Crossna, captured 20 May 1923

John Doyle, Quartermaster of Crossna Coy., captured 3 February 1923 by a cycling column

Patrick Doyle of Derreenaseer, Knockvicar, brother of James and John, arrested 8 September 1922 and sent to Athlone two months later

Charles Duignan, 1st Lieut. of Keadue Coy.

Francis and Patrick Duignan of Derreenavoggy, Arigna

Jack, James, and Patrick Duignan (Corgullon, Kilbride, Kilmore)

John Duignan of Ballyfarnon

Pat Duignan, Kilfaughna, Knockvicar, 1st Lieut. of Crossna Coy.

Officer Tom Duignan of Sligo, captured in June 1923, released in December 1923

Officer Stephen Flynn

The Gaffney brothers from Keadue: Thomas Bartley, Patrick and Michael

Seamus Gaffney, former Vice O/C of the 4th Battalion North Roscommon, was an officer

Bernard Gannon of Drumlion Company

Michael Gilhooley, Quartermaster of Arigna

Patrick Gilhooley, arrested, sent to Athlone

Owen Gilroy, arrested in September 1923

Thomas Gilroy of Jamestown, County

Leitrim, of the South Leitrim ASU, captured on 29 May 1923

Thomas Gilboy of Ballure, Kiltimagh, County Mayo — part of the 2nd Sligo unit

— Guihens from Arigna

James Kelly of Boyle

Joe Kennedy of Cloonglooney, Carrick-on-Shannon

Joseph Leyland of Cloonfad, Cootehall, Boyle

Thomas Leyland from Leitrim section, (emigrated to New York)

J. McBreen

Harold McBrien, Officer

Michael McBrien of Carrigallen, captured in the spring of 1923

Joe McDevitt (McDavitt) headed a Flying Column in Mayo and occasionally fought with North Roscommon men

Peter McGearty of Arigna, Carrick-on-Shannon, arrested 3 February 1923

The following two listings could be one and the same man:

J. McLoughlin, captured at Drumsna 4 September 1923

Joseph McLoughlin of Ballyfarnon, deserted from Boyle Barracks in September 1922

Tom McKenna from Keadue

Frank Manning from (Tomisky, near Ruskey, Co. Leitrim) Barnacoola Coy., 5th Battalion, No. 3 Brigade, 3rd Western Division

"May" Mannion, captured 20 May 1923

Thomas Martin, Vice O/C of the 4th Battalion North, from Fostra, Crossna, Boyle

Jim Moran, brother of Paddy, of Crossna, arrested 3 February 1923

Francis Mulherin, captured 4 September 1923

James Mulligan of Ballinamore, Leitrim, captured in September 1922

Officer Jimmie O'Brien: O/C of the 4th Battalion North Roscommon

Stephen O'Connor of Sligo

Officer Vincent Ryans

Father Ryans, brother of Vincent. Six days after the capture of Ned Bofin, Father was arrested at Knockranny House in Keadue

Tom Shanley of Dromod, captured in March 1923 after attack on Ruskey Barracks

Thomas Treacy of Cootehall, arrested 3 February 1923

Pat Tymon of Arigna, killed 27 February 1923

Stephen Flynn originally headed the Flying Column but was replaced by Seamus Cull after Flynn was arrested. Ned Bofin was the Adjutant for the Column while

Pat Gaffney from Arigna served as the Quartermaster. Gaffney had his work cut out for him.

In the autumn of 1921 there had been precious little armament within the Brigade area: only four Lee Enfield rifles, a few shotguns, an assortment of revolvers, and twelve Mausers.[26] After the acceptance by the people of the Treaty and the resulting split in the Republican movement in March, war clouds hung heavy in the sky. The Arigna Column (which numbered over 100) was determined to augment their meagre arms supply. In July 1922 they captured seventeen rifles from Riverstown Barracks in Co. Sligo.

Intelligence

A lesson learned well from the British: ascertain what your opponent is doing, where he has been, what arms he possesses, where he is going, and what his intentions are once he gets there. This kind of information is accumulated in the small villages and towns and sent to a central command, where a pattern can be discerned and information cross-checked. In late July, the former acting O/C of the South Roscommon Brigade, Frank Simons, was put in charge of organising this system for the Free State Army. His original bailiwick included operation setups in Galway and south Roscommon. (North Roscommon, Sligo, Sligo town, Ballymote, and Boyle already had intelligence officers.) Men on the government payroll from Simon's appointed area would funnel information to him, and he, in turn, would send in reports to Athlone via the Midland Western Railway.

National trooper Dolan in Manorhamilton had linked up with Captain Pinkman of Carrick-on-Shannon. Reports were coming in from the areas of Drumsna, Elphin, Keadue, and Drumshanbo. The Longford region was generally thought to be free of Anti-Treatyites except for the Glasson-Westmeath, Athlone area.[27]

Peace Feelers

Was there no way out? Were there no cooler heads who could disengage the opposing Irish forces and seek some kind of compromise? These persistent questions throbbed in the minds of Anti-Treaty commanders who decided to send out peace feelers. Father James Roddy, CC, of Geevagh, County Sligo, acted as a go-between. A lone Republican hoisting a white flag approached a government outpost in Ballyfarnon requesting a meeting with a Free State officer from Boyle, Commandant Mitchell. The topic to be discussed: terms of surrender. Mitchell refused to participate in any talks,[28] but Commandant Lavin travelled from Boyle and attended the meeting. It was decided to hold another conference the following Sunday, 6 August, in Ballyfarnon. Ned Bofin, Harold McBrien, Fr. Roddy, and Commandants Mitchell and Lavin were present, but they solved nothing except to postpone hostilities for No. 2 Brigade area from Sunday 6 August at 6 p.m. to Wednesday 9 August at 8 p.m.[29]

The next day Tom Duignan and several other members of the Arigna Column, under the mistaken impression that a surrender had been negotiated, approached the Boyle Barracks, where they were disarmed and arrested. When Commandant General O'Farrelly (Free State) arrived from Athlone, he explained that no general truce was binding, except for the No. 2 Brigade area, and only for a very limited time. He subsequently released the prisoners. The final sentences of the intelligence report relating to this bear quoting: "This incident of the arrest of the prisoners has had the effect of hardening up those Irregulars who were wavering. This also applies to the North Roscommon Column so that now there is very little hope of being able to influence either of these Columns to surrender to National troops."[30]

"May the Hand That Shot Him Wither"

Word of Michael Collins' demise on 22 August spread like a wildfire over the plains of Ireland. Typical of the Roscommon man's reaction to the news were the words spoken by Tommy McGreevy. During that August afternoon he was working in his Ballinaheglish field deftly tossing the dried grass with his hayfork when a messenger brought the horrifying details. McGreevy put down his fork, sighed, and with quivering cheeks moistened by tears from his sad eyes uttered the words, "May the hand that shot him wither."

Today, in the opening decade of the twentieth-first century, no one is certain that McGreevy's mild curse ever came to pass. Despite written volumes of speculation and TV documentaries, no one really knows whether Collins was shot by one of his own men, Emmet Dalton, or, as theorised by Vincent MacDowell in *Michael Collins and The Brotherhood*, the substitute driver, M. B. Corry, or whether Collins was felled by the bullet from a rifle held by a fellow Irishman who was part of an ambush party of "Irregulars" in Collins' home territory. Was Collins really killed by an isolated party who happened to stake out his return trip through the narrow "Mouth of Blossoms"? Was Collins really deemed a loose cannon with regard to his scheme to supply the IRA in the North with men and material for further confrontation with the Unionists — a position which the British could not abide? Was Collins really on a peace mission in Cork with the possibility of stopping the Civil War within his grasp? Did British Intelligence really desire Collins' death because they felt the Provisional Government officials would prove more pliable to their desires? Was an IRA ambush simply a cover for an assassination of this Irish rogue that the English couldn't control?

Meda Ryan's book *The Day Michael Collins Was Shot* and Patrick J. Twohig's *The Dark Secret of Bealnabláth* offer some convincing evidence of the supposed killers at the ambush scene. John Pinkman, in his book *In the Legion of the Vanguard*, puts forth the theory that Collins was killed by a British Intelligence Officer (no name). But no one really knows who was responsible for Collins' death. Various authors disagree as to entrance and exit wounds and possible motives. No one knows why a guerilla fighter of the calibre of Collins would have "stepped from behind cover" to fire into unseen targets in the hills. No one knows why de Valera was but a few miles away when the ambush took place. No documents exist which aptly describe the post mortem — a procedure that would have answered the question of wound size, proximity to the murder weapon, perhaps even the size of the bullet which ended his life — and could have ruled out a rifle bullet or a short-ranged Mauser pistol cartridge as the deadly culprit. No one knows why de Valera would not allow a tombstone on Collins' grave until nearly twenty years had passed (a certificate of authorisation was finally signed by de Valera himself on July 31, 1939).[31] No one knows what great things "the Big Fellow" might have accomplished had the bullet at Béal na mBláth not been so deadly accurate. The only certainty resulting from the question,

Michael Collins at the funeral of Arthur Griffith, who died on 12 August 1922 of natural causes.

PHOTO COURTESY OF THE IRISH HISTORICAL PICTURE COMPANY

> "Who had the most to gain by Collins' death?"
> is the counter
> "Who had the most to lose?"
> T'was Ireland!

The death of both Captains, Arthur Griffith on 12 August from natural causes and Collins on 22 August, severed the small ship of state from its moorings. Without the vision of Griffith, the vessel lost its celestial bearings. Without the hand of Collins to rein in the raging tempers on both sides, storm clouds converged and poured down acid rain on the green fields of Ireland.

National Army Reorganisation and Anti-Treaty Strength

Small groups of men travelling at will over the Irish countryside were a very common sight during those trying times — a common sight, yet a very difficult target for an army with a rigid chain of command. MacEoin had only 2,100 men stationed in all his Western Command.[32] In August it was decided to break up those forces into smaller columns of men of about 150 to counter the offensive actions of the Anti-Treaty Flying Columns in and near Roscommon. Estimates of those Republican Columns included:[33]

Roscommon	Officers	Men	Ammo.	Officers' Names
Ballinameen	3	30	little	Pat Brennan O/C
				James Stephen Brennan
				Michael Larkin Q/M
Ballyfarnon	3	10	100 rds.	John Sherrin
				Martin Killalea
Arigna	4	150	1200 rds.	Harold McBrien
				Ned Bofin Adjutant,
				but often acting O/C
Westmeath				
Coosan	4	30	600 rds.	Paddy Morrissey O/C
				Pat Macken Q/M
				James Martin
				Christopher "Kit" McKeon
Mayo				
Castlebar				Michael Kilroy
Ballinrobe	20	300	Mausers rifles shotguns bombs	Tom Maguire
				P. J. Ruttledge IO
Charlestown	3	30-40		Tom Maguire
East Mayo		48		

A Snapshot of August Activities in and around Roscommon

- 7 August: Under the command of Harold McBrien, a portion of the Arigna Column raided a train at Glenfarne on the Leitrim-Cavan border. This group was also active in blocking roads around Manorhamilton. National troops from Sligo were on their trail.
- The Drumraney Column in Co. Westmeath ambushed National troops at Tang on 8 August. Four Anti-Treaty officers were arrested: Daniel McGiff, —Moran, —Canells, and —McLynn.
- 10 August: James Pilkington, brother of Liam, was arrested in Galway.
- 11 August: National troops captured three ex-British Army personnel fighting with the Arigna Column — Captain Coulter, Captain Cole, and Private McAllister. Thirty Republicans were arrested near Kiltimagh, including Henry Deignan, —Fitzpatrick, and James Groarke. In Charlestown, fifty Anti-Treaty men from Frank Carty's Column entered the town at 9 p.m. and commandeered Murphy's lorry.
- The strength of the East Mayo Flying Column was estimated to be about forty-eight men, soon to be augmented by about thirty Volunteers from Sligo.
- Hungry and worn, the Anti-Treaty forces raided O'Hara's in Cootehall for foodstuffs and drink on 12 August.
- On 13 August the Crossna Flying Column arranged an ambush at Crossna Chapel. They locked the people inside the church for safekeeping, took over Golden's house, and bored holes in the wall. Ned Bofin was in charge of this operation.[34] Anti-Treaty men also stole 120 tons of petrol from Carrick-on-Shannon and transported it to Charlestown.

- East Mayo Volunteers travelled to Boyle in order to engage the National troops there. Commanders felt that activity in north Roscommon would help relieve the pressure the East Mayo Column was feeling from the Free State pressing from the West.
- On 14 August, twenty men from the North Roscommon Flying Column attempted to blow up the Boyle Railroad junction. They succeeded in partially demolishing two bridges — at Knockvicar and Cootehall.[35]
- In the south part of the county, a train was robbed at Kiltoom on 18 August[36] — bacon, flour, and tobacco found their way into boats that headed across Lough Ree. Another party lifted portions of train track 100 yards from the station. The engine was unhooked from the wagons and sent at full speed towards Knockcroghery. When it reached the torn up track, it rammed through sleepers and came to a standstill, blocking the line.[37]
- On Friday 18 August, six engineers from Belfast travelled by train to Ballaghaderreen. Nine others were expected soon afterwards. Special effort by the National troops was made to arrest Liam Forde of Lisacul, who was suspected of collaborating with them. Forde, however, was in Dublin and not to be found. Stakeouts for individual Volunteers were proving difficult because the Anti-Treaty soldiers were patrolling the town.
- Several days later twenty Mayo men were observed crossing the fields heading in the direction of Ballinameen. The local men there were poorly armed, possessing only a few shotguns and four rifles.
- 22 August saw the capture of thirty men from the Arigna Flying Column and a field hospital, including four nurses. Also on that date, petrol was seized in Leitrim by the Anti-Treatyites and conveyed to Curry, Co. Sligo.
- Three days later Ballaghaderreen was the site of a clash between the National troops under Alec McCabe and a Column of Anti-Treaty men. O/C of the East Mayo Column, Tom Carney, was captured along with Brigade Adjutant Joe O'Kelly of Ballaghaderreen, Battalion Adjutant Edward "Ned" Mullen, and the Brigade chemist, Michael Larkin of Boyle.
- Further south, the Coosan Column spent 18 August sniping at Athlone Barracks. They also succeeded in aiding a few escaped prisoners. Headed by O/C Paddy Morrissey, the three officers and twenty men endeavored to disrupt the movement and communication of the Free State forces by blocking roads and cutting communication wires. They even tried to destroy a bridge across the Shannon and also the Shannon viaduct.[38] The Column mounted an ambush near Glasson, Athlone, on 25 August.[39] Free State Lieutenant Sean McCormack of Castle Barracks in Athlone, who was a native of Moate, was shot dead while attending to wounded officer Rhatigan, who hailed from Tullamore. Patrick Murtagh, a civilian, was also shot while innocently passing by the scene.
- Within the Ballygar Company of County Galway, there were three members with the last name Hannon, one of whom helped plan the attack on Mount Talbot in August. The grand home was being garrisoned by twenty National troopers under the command of Henry Compton (a former member of Pat Madden's Flying Column). A large number of Republicans (200, say the military intelligence reports)[40] participated in a gun battle in which one Anti-Treaty man was killed, one wounded, and one taken prisoner.
- Saturday morning 26 August twenty Republicans were observed leaving Ballaghaderreen with five officers from North Roscommon. Their destination: Boyle. That evening they attacked the town patrol, sniped at the barracks and fired on the outposts on the Boyle Railway Bridge.[41] The Anti-Treaty men were armed with rifles, revolvers, and a Thompson machine gun.
- By the end of August, IRA officers Pat Brennan, Jim Brady, and Mick McLoughlin had left Ballinameen and headed back west to Ballaghaderreen. They left behind a Column consisting of roughly thirty men, three officers, five rifles, very little ammo, but, interestingly enough, a motor car.[42] The automo-

PHOTO COURTESY OF FRANK SIMONS

"There was little or no Civil War down here in Roscommon. I arranged here with some of the fellas on the opposite side that I wouldn't attack them nor they wouldn't attack us. ...that arrangement...Ken O'Donnell was witness of that...came along and attacked Mount Talbot and they nearly blew it up. Well, they planned to blow it up anyway. That's what started the Civil War in Roscommon."

Spoken by Frank Simons in an interview conducted by James McCormick, summer of 1973, in Roscommon town.

bile had been stolen from the British by Pat Brennan, his brother James Stephen, and Michael Larkin. For lack of fuel, however, it proved to be of little use to them. Eventually the old contraption rusted away in Brennan's front yard in the following decades.[43]

- On 31 August a small group of Anti-Treaty men had raided Martin and Lynn's establishment in Ballyfarnon and commandeered boots, socks, and drinks.[44] This group, headed by Harold McBrien of Collooney, was estimated to be about fifty men strong, with nine officers who had access to thirty rifles. They even had several Thompson submachine guns, according to intelligence reports. To contradict this first observation, another subsequent report stated that the Column totalled closer to a 150 men, with access to sixty rifles, 1,2000 rounds of ammo, fifty shotguns, and two machine guns. The report also noted that although McBrien was the official O/C, Ned Bofin was the man who lit the fire under the men. He compelled them to go to bed at 8 p.m. so they could rise at 2 a.m. and be on the move. Some of his men were more afraid of him than they were of the Free State troops.[45]

- On the 6th day of the new month of September, dawn had greeted the Free State garrison of Drumshanbo with the sight of Seamus Cull leading an attack party. The Anti-Treatyites rushed the building and seized it in five minutes. The yield: 32 rifles.[46] On 9 September the Manorhamilton Garrison was also attacked.

Time Out!
In early September, Ned Bofin's Flying Column was spending a great deal of time between Geevagh and Highwood district of County Sligo. Intelligence officers for the Free State sent memoranda to the Western Command stating that they suspected that Bofin's men had succeeded in smuggling arms from Germany via a submarine that landed at Belmullet, Co. Mayo.[47] But by mid-September, Bofin's Column was still lingering in the same area. Why so? War issues aside, Bofin had taken time out to court his sweetheart who lived in the area. (He married her a few months later.) His soldiers were billeted in the houses of Conlon, Donagher, and McManus who lived on the mountain side near a place called Keogh's Lodge.

Accurate Intelligence
In a 4 September communiqué from Boyle to Athlone, an Intelligence Report noted that the "irregulars pass almost every day from Ballaghaderreen to Frenchpark. They call and stay in a house — Miss Gallagher of the Gate house. She is the I.O. [Intelligence Officer] for them in the Frenchpark area."[48] Another example of the detail which was noted by the National Intelligence Officers was found in a report from the 2nd Western Division area dated in early September. On Monday evening six Anti-Treatyites were seen passing through Derrane from Fourmilehouse, headed to Matt Davis' place in Kilteevan. Davis' absence of four hours from his home on the following Wednesday night was noted, along with an aside stating that Hennigan's house nearby had been raided that same night.

Members of the Flying Column centered around Ballinameen were oftentimes seen crossing the border to the East Mayo Brigade area and vice versa. Intelligence reports from this period note the ease with which the men poured across county lines in all directions. It was mentioned in one report that "townspeople it appears are mostly afraid to go to work in the country and the country people are mostly engaged in both sides of this struggle."[49]

Another example of keen reporting came into the Western Command in August 1922. "The movements of Bofin's Flying Column [Arigna] are reported on daily. Their sleeping quarters are known nightly." Interestingly, a note scribbled in the margin of the Intelligence Report is indicative of the frustration of Sean MacEoin's command: "WHAT IS BEING DONE?"[50]

The Free State had a reasonably good grasp of who was involved in Anti-Treaty operations, where they were, and how much armament the group had accumulated. The Free State's problems stemmed mostly from having an inadequate number of *trained* personnel. True, they were recruiting vast numbers of young men, many of whom had been teenagers during the war with Britain. Some were unseasoned troops, some had no particular heart attachment to their cause, some were fighting for an as-yet untried government established in Dublin. Others, however, were totally committed to subduing the Anti-Treatyites because they felt the Treaty was Ireland's best chance for a true break with England. The National Army's intelligence system, while reasonably accurate, could not be put to maximum use simply because

National Army Brigade Staff in Athlone, 1922.

PHOTO COURTESY OF GEAROID O'BRIEN, HEAD LIBRARIAN, ATHLONE LIBRARY

the number of troops stationed in the various towns of Roscommon was inadequate to cope with the large number of roving bands of men. The Anti-Treatyites, on the other hand, were on very familiar ground, and most were vitally invested in the ideal of a Republic. Unfortunately for Ireland, both sides were locked in a death struggle.

The Struggling Free State Military Situation
To counter all this civil disobedience and place significant troop strength in the field, Sean MacEoin disbursed his troops within County Roscommon as follows:[51]

Place	Officers	Soldiers
Carrick-on-Shannon	2	36
Castlerea	1	45
Roscommon town	2	48
Boyle	3	96

By December of 1922, troop deployment had changed somewhat:[52]

Carrick-on-Shannon	2	38
Castlerea	3	46
Roscommon town	4	49
Boyle	23	100
Custume Barracks (Athlone)	46	602

Civil War in the Neighbouring Counties
In early September, Frank Carty obtained the armoured car *Ballinalee* from north Sligo and used it in an attempt to capture Tubbercurry Barracks. Although Carty seized some food, clothes and footwear, his men failed to secure the building. (The attack failed owing to the tenacity of the Free State commanding officer who refused to give up.)[53]

The armoured car was then taken by Joe Baker and Michael Kilroy (of the West Mayo Flying Column) to be used in an attack on Ballina. The twelfth day of September was the date chosen for the attempt. The Anti-Treaty men cleared the Bunree Bridge and captured the Moy Hotel, which was being used as a garrison for the Free State troops. With little food and less sleep but a plentiful supply of guns and ammunition, the victorious Republicans divided into two groups — one headed into the Ox mountains, the other travelled along the North Coast Road. Free State soldiers under Tony Lawlor arrived the next day, secured the town, and then, with the armoured vehicle *The Big Fella* (named after Michael Collins) in their midst, proceeded to split their forces and track the two groups of Anti-Treaty men. A half mile outside Bonnyconlan, the Republicans, situated on both sides of the road, ambushed the National troops — an action in which Free State Brigadier Joe Ring was fatally shot and Lawlor wounded along with five other rank and file. After advancing to the hill and capturing fifteen prisoners, the National troops encountered the *Ballinalee*, the armoured car commanded by the Republicans. The first driver of *The Big Fella* (Ingham) was killed, and a second driver, Stephen McGinny, took over the wheel. The *Ballinalee* retreated in the direction of Tubbercurry, doubled back and took a bye-road in the direction of Cloonacool.[54] With this huge swoop in progress, the retreating Republicans separated from each other and, in small groups, melted through the cordon. The *Ballinalee* inadvertently took a horseshoe-shaped road at the base of Benbulben Mountain. National troops closed in. The Anti-Treatyites who manned the car, realising the futility of trying to escape with their prize intact, abandoned the metal albatross. The driver, Alfie McGlynn, stuffed a mattress down the tower and ignited it with petrol in an attempt to make it unusable to the Free State troops.[55] The Republicans set out with the Vickers gun and headed up over the crest of the mountain. They never reached the other side.

It was during this operation that Brian MacNeill, son of Eoin MacNeill, the man who had issued the countermanding order for the Easter Rising and who was a minister in the Provisional Government, was captured and killed. He along with Seamus Devins, a Brigadier General from Sligo, Patrick O'Carroll, and Joe Banks were trapped on the mountain on 20 September. They had surrendered and been disarmed, and then they were shot. (MacNeill had been a trainer in Mantua House in County Roscommon during the winter of 1921-22.) As twists of fate would have it, the abandoned armoured car was turned over to Free State Commander Luke Duffy, Pat Madden's former Vice O/C for the 3rd Battalion South Roscommon Brigade.[56] The following day, Duffy took half of the government troops and proceeded to Manorhamilton, Glenfarne, Kiltyclogher, and on to Ballintrillick, Co. Sligo.[57]

War Activity in Galway

Men from southeast Galway had joined up with south Roscommon men to form a Flying Column. Together they had held Ballygar Barracks until a show of force by the National troops routed them. According to Nollaig O'Gadhra in *Civil War in Connaught*, on 20 September "a large force of Republicans made a lightning attack on the town of Tuam. It was calculated that there had been three or four hundred of them, supposedly under the leadership of Commanders Maguire and Powell."[58] Another raid was carried out on Tuam by Commandant Tom Maguire on 7 October during which he posted notices informing citizens that if they were were foolhardy enough to attempt to fix the bridges just blown up by the Republicans, they would be fired upon. Maguire's days of freedom were numbered, however, as he was captured with some of his men a few weeks later.[59]

Longford

A small Flying Column operating out of the Lanesboro, Longford area comprised about fifteen men and two officers. This group made Incheneagh Island in Lough Ree their headquarters and were purported to be among the culprits in the train robbery at Kiltoom on 18 August. The Ballymahon Column was not considered particularly active, although they were suspected of aiding and abetting escaped prisoners from Ballymahon Barracks.

The Prize of Boyle

The garrison at Boyle and all that it commanded was a trophy sparred for more than once during the Civil War fight. In September, two Free State soldiers deserted their post — Joseph McLoughlin of Ballyfarnon and Owen McLoughlin of Rockingham. On 6 September an evening attack on the Free State outpost took place. The Anti-Treatyites won the day (or rather night) as the government troops were forced to withdraw into the barracks. During the week of 9 September those same National soldiers threatened to "ground their arms" if they were not paid.

At 10:15 p.m. on the night of 16 September, a group of twenty-five men was seen making their way in the direction of the cemetery. The government soldiers feared an attack on the Railway Bridge and sent reinforcements toward that position. An hour later the first shot echoed. Rifle and Thompson machine gun fire then buffeted the Free State troops, but they held their ground and answered with an equally intense barrage. The Anti-Treatyites withdrew momentarily but came back four different times that night to punish the defenders of the bridge. By 5:30 a.m. nothing had been altered since the night before — no casualties, no bridge, no surrender.

Members of the Arigna Column continued their own harassment by sniping at a column of National troops operating from Boyle under Commandant Lavin. As a result of this action, one Anti-Treaty man was captured — James Mulligan of Ballinamore, Leitrim.

Raiding

The Anti-Treaty soldiers did not limit their attention to guns, infrastructure, and military convoys. They were wanted men who had no home base, yet had to feed, clothe, and arm themselves. Often they would confiscate goods from local merchants (a fact which did not usually endear them to the local shopkeepers). Sometimes their thievery took on an air of farce more than one of tragedy. On Monday night 28 August, Paddy Devaney, William Kellegher, and John Ryan of the 2nd Battalion South broke into shops in Frenchpark and commandeered boots, whiskey, and cigarettes. On 18 September the village of Dysart was raided and food stuffs, drink, clothing and £70 were confiscated. A few weeks earlier Ned Bofin's Column had raided a train in Dromahair, Leitrim, and commandeered *eggs!*

Mayo

In the early part of September, Castlebar reverberated with the boom of bombs and machine gun fire ricocheting off the walls of the town buildings. Ballina Castle was scorched and rendered into ashes. The loss was in excess of £100,000 and included antique furniture and 350 paintings. Wires were cut between Ballyhaunis and Ballinlough. In the vicinity of Irishtown, noise of machine gun fire alerted the townspeople that a large number of Anti-Treaty men were staying at Ballinvilla and had fortified the place.

During the last week of September, banks in Ballina town were raided and relieved of £25,000. One hundred rifles and 200 rounds of ammunition were also lifted from the town barracks. On 27 September yet another attack took place on Swinford Barracks.

Diversions

Even dedicated soldiers, though, needed an occasional break. On 11 September a traveller going to Sligo from Ballina was held up outside Dromore West and compelled to buy drinks for about twenty Republicans. He knew three of the leaders: — Collery, Tom Ruane, and — McCawley. On that same date, J. O'Donnell, a reporter for the *Roscommon Herald*, was confronted in Ballaghaderreen by Tom Foley, Al Kelly (brother of Joe), and Seamus Mulrennan.

In the Leitrim area, a gang of thieves were operating under the name of the IRA but were basically filling their war chest with goods from unauthorised heists.

Chests wouldn't hold all the booty the men had stolen, so they had constructed a secret dugout in which to store it. When the O/C of the South Leitrim Brigade, Bernard Sweeney, discovered the shenanigans, he had the men followed and arrested and then paraded at Cloone Chapel at Mass time for all the parishioners to see. To fully display the extent of their crime, the O/C had the thieves laden with as many stolen articles as possible heaped on their backs as they plodded down the main aisle.[60] Needless to say, their burglary days were over.

September Gaol Breaks and Captures

Out: Frank O'Beirne, Dominick Benson and Vice O/C of the Sligo Brigade Henry Brehony escaped from Athlone Barracks, while Tom Scanlon absconded from Longford.

In: Joe McDevitt (leader of a Flying Column) was captured in Irishtown, Tom and Bernard Martin from Athlone (Bernard escaped in October), Edward Dowling, Michael Finneran (Glasson), William and Denis Mannion (The Hill of Berries), and Hugh and Patrick Giblin from Ruskey. In an ambush on the road at Lisavalley between Mountbellew and Tuam, Con Fogarty, O/C of the Galway Brigade, was captured (according to Nollaig O'Gadhra's account in *Civil War in Connacht*).[61] Ex-Quartermaster Pat Macken and John Shortle of Baylin, Athlone were also arrested.

Northeast Roscommon Activity

In September, men from the North Roscommon Flying Column made contact with sympathetic Free State soldiers inside the barracks at Carrick-on-Shannon. They formulated a plan whereby the barracks would be handed over to the Anti-Treaty faction. But plans for the surrender of the barracks fell through when the Anti-Treaty men were unable to surprise an enemy outpost on the Shannon Bridge.[62]

Dromahair was handed over to the Republicans because the National troops were disheartened about not having been paid.[63] A large quantity of material was transferred to the Anti-Treatyites: a Lewis gun, twenty rifles, and a number of revolvers. These alternating thrusts of attack and counter-attack continued throughout the area, when two days later Free State troops from Carrick-on-Shannon and Mohill converged on the Republicans at Derrycarne House, Dromod — an action that resulted in the capture of three Anti-Treatyites.

On 16 September four Free State soldiers left Boyle headed towards Cootehall. On their return trip they were ambushed one and a half miles from Cootehall by a dozen or so Anti-Treaty men. Two National soldiers were wounded.

October

The brisk winds of October swept o'er the plains bringing not the warmth of a turf fire but a chilling reality. Two new dugouts were constructed and equipped in the Boyle area which proved to be the nerve centre for the 3rd Western Division. From this command post, efforts were made to consolidate and coordinate movements against the National troops and infrastructure.

In the northwest corner of the county, on 2 October, more than a hundred Anti-Treatyites were seen in the Ballaghaderreen area. Strengthened by forty men from Belfast who were armed with a Lewis gun, this Column engaged in sniping at various points around town and attacked the National troops; one government soldier was wounded. Free State troops, when they tried to counter this "lawlessness," were ambushed on the roads leading to and from the town.

Twin Tribulations

There are several examples in Roscommon's war history of brothers dying within a short time of each other. In the first weeks of 1921, Joe and James Tormey (Cornafulla Ambush) fell within a three-week period. Two Cull brothers from

Arigna (Michael and Seamus) died within a two month period. Another example of a family's double tragedy can be pinpointed in the Ballaghaderreen area. The Mulrennan brothers of Lisacul were also struck down within one month of each other. Patrick was killed while a prisoner at Pump Square Athlone Gaol on 6 October or 3 November (see footnote).[64] On 14 October, his brother Seamus had been leading an Anti-Treaty Column which encountered the Free State troopers under Commandant Mitchell. As the government patrol was returning from Ballina to Boyle, they came in contact with Mulrennan's men near Ballaghaderreen. In the firefight that ensued, Seamus was killed, another of his men, Tom Foley, was wounded, and the rest of his men captured. Two rifles, seven shotguns, a Colt automatic, and a large quantity of .303 ammunition were also seized by the government troops, who suffered no casualties.[65] The local community mourned the death of their fallen hero. The following notice was sent to the nearby schools:

The Mulrennan brothers, James (Seamus) and Pat, died of battle wounds within one month of each other.

PHOTO COURTESY OF LEW THORNE

> To/ The Principals
> Lisacul School (Boys)
>
> From/ The Competent Military Authority
> Ballaghaderreen
>
> You are hereby ordered
> to close your schools
> for today, being the
> occasion of the funeral
> of Comdt. Seumas Mulrennan, IRA,
> who was murdered by
> Free State Forces on the 14th.
>
> Ballaghaderreen
> 17 October 1922

    Throughout the area, both inside and on the fringes of the county, various actions by Flying Columns kept the populace and the Free State troops on edge. Mohill Barracks was attacked on 3 October — a fifteen-minute firefight that resulted in no injuries. Geoghegan Barracks in Castletowngeoghegan, County Westmeath, was burned by a Column of forty Anti-Treaty men on the 9th. Two days before, a Free State sentry had been wounded at Boyle.
    On 20 October the Arigna Column attacked the Drumshanbo Barracks — a place they regularly visited in small batches of six to seven men. This day, however, nearly fifty assembled in the town and barricaded the streets. Sometimes the sheer anger of the moment erupted, as was the case with a spontaneous attack on a carload of Free State officers on the Ardcarne/Boyle Road on 28 October.

The Irish Free State
In the fall of 1922, the constitution of the Irish Free State became law. Military courts began to operate from 15 October onward. To add to the Republican woes, on Sunday, 22 October, a pastoral letter was read from every pulpit in Ireland whose terms excommunicated those men in arms against the government.

Pro-Treaty Casualties of the War in and around County Roscommon Extracted from Padraic O'Farrell's *Who's Who in the Irish War for Independence and Civil War 1916-1923*		
Name	Place of Death	Date
Officers:		
Sean Adair	Dooney Rock, Sligo	13 July 1922
George Adamson	Athlone	24 April 1922*
John Boyle	Dooney Rock, Sligo	14 November 1922
Patrick O'Callaghan	Dooney Rock, Sligo	13 July 1922
Patrick Columb	Mullingar	27 April 1922
Patrick Coyle	Brosna, Co. Offaly	27 January 1923
Matthew Cullen	Tullamore, Co. Offaly	28 August 1922
Michael Dockery	Boyle	2 July 1922*
T. Healy	Glenamoy, Co. Mayo	16 September 1922
S. Higgins	Glenamoy, Co. Mayo	16 September 1922
Patrick Kilkelly	Claremorris, Co. Mayo	18 February 1923
Sean McCormack	Glasson, Athlone	25 August 1922
J. McLoughlin	Gowel, Co. Leitrim	1 June 1922
P. Moran	Ballina, Co. Mayo	18 August 1922
Joe Ring	Bonnyconlan, Co. Mayo	12 September 1922*
Capt. Skelly	Boyle	2 July 1922
Michael Skelly	Swinford, Co. Mayo	21 August 1922
Michael Walshe	Westport, Co. Mayo	24 November 1922
NCOs and Men:		
Frank Balfe	Boyle	Early in Week of July 2 1922*
Michael Bannon	Tubbercurry, Co. Sligo	25 August 1922
James Beirne	Sligo	3 July 1922
James Blackhall	Swinford, Co. Mayo	10 February 1923
John Blaney	Ferbane, Co. Offaly	4 July 1922*
Andrew Callaghan	Boyle/Carrick-on-Shannon Road*	20 February 1923
John Carter	Leenane, Co. Galway	3 December 1922
John Carter	Mayo	3 December 1922
John Carty	Headford, Co. Galway	9 April 1923
James Clarke	Powelsborough, Co. Sligo	30 November 1922
William Collins	Srahmore, Co. Mayo	19 February 1923
Thomas Connelly	Clifden, Co. Galway	October 1922
Patrick Coyle	Castlebar, Co. Mayo	7 March 1923
Edward Crabbe	Erris. Co. Mayo	16 September 1922
John Deasy	Newport, Co. Mayo	28 July 1922
Stephen Diviney	Athenry, Co. Galway	1 October 1922
William Doherty	Claremorris, Co. Mayo	21 August 1922
Joseph Dolan	Drumshanbo, Co. Leitrim	6 September 1922
James Duffy	Castlebar, Co. Mayo	13 August 1922

John Blaney of Athlone was killed in battle on 4 July 1922

As Dan Breen, the author of *My Fight for Irish Freedom*, stated, "The Civil War was bad, but it saved us this much — it saved us from the government of Maynooth. The people were split on the issue of the Treaty but the Hierarchy went out and attacked the Republic, threw bell, book, and candle at it in nearly every pulpit in the country. And they drove one half of the people against them..."[66] Every Anti-Treatyite faced the possibility of death if he were so unfortunate as to be caught in the cross hairs of the Free State rifles: but, equally weighing, was the possibility of facing eternity without the solace of the sacraments of his Church.

This situation represents the very worst nightmare a statesman could conjure up. Dublin government enactments cemented with Church pronouncements presented a daunting monolith of power to the lone Republican out in the field struggling for an ideal. The media portrayed the Republican as an "Irregular" renegade, a title stinging in its bite, because it was thrust upon the very man who had helped bring about the existence of the State that was now an anathema to him.

"What's Good Enough for Collins....."

While the Anti-Treaty faction might have felt great sting and resentment in the actions of the Dublin government, the National soldiers had their own version of tragedy in this Irish production. During the War for Independence, many IRA Companies throughout the country had been headed by IRB men. When the time to vote for or against the Treaty came upon them, many chose to put their trust in Collins. Sean Leavy, O/C of the 3rd Battalion North Roscommon, thought that if "the Treaty was good enough for Michael Collins, it was good enough for me." Leavy confessed to having no hope of getting the British out of Ireland entirely. He viewed the Treaty as the best opportunity for Irish men to take over the functions of government, rule the country, and work together to bring the other six counties back into the fold.[67]

Woes of the Western Command

The area of the Western Command was large. The closest sizable military base was located at Athlone, in the middle of the country. For massive troop movements, train transport was needed; yet once government soldiers got to designated towns, they were forced to eat the local food and plod the roads just like their Republican adversaries.

There were numerous complaints of no pay for Free State soldiers for as long as four months. An officer in Sligo lamented that he hadn't sufficient ammunition, rifles, or transport to pursue Frank Carty's Column. Pro-Treaty troops handed over the Charlestown barracks to Republicans because "the garrison said there was no use in fighting for those who don't care to look after us."[68] Some of the National troops had neither proper underwear nor adequate outer clothing for an Irish winter swoop through the rainy and cold hills. In fact, many of them had no uniforms at all and were reduced to soldiering in civilian attire.[69] An intelligence report dated 31 October noted that "a much more liberal supply of rifles, revolvers, ammunition, grenades, field glasses, in fact all military equipment should be afforded us as supplies of these are up to the present not at all satisfactory."[70] Shopkeepers grumbled about unpaid items commandeered by Pro-Treaty troops.[71]

The ability of some of the commanders was also a frequent cause of concern to GHQ. On 19 October Mulcahy sent a message to MacEoin pointing out "personally, I cannot sense that there is any solid administration or organisation over the area pressing back the forces of disorder there — I am afraid that I begin to find this, namely, that the people of the area feel that no impression at all is being made on the situation, and that they are beginning to whisper to themselves that they have no confidence in Sean McKeon (MacEoin)."[72]

Worse yet was the position of second in command, Tony Lawlor. Father Thomas Brett, CC, Kilmaine, Co. Mayo, wrote of Lawlor's harsh treatment of his charges "recounting that a Longford contingent had arrived in Ballinrobe after a long march with only two hours sleep."[73] Lawlor's comments about strict Prussian discipline and shooting men to maintain it provide insight into a frustrated commander.

Lawlor was struggling with trying to rein in the wild mustangs of Republicanism roaming the area. In December he wrote to the Western Command Headquarters in Athlone pleading for more ammunition and some horses. Mounted infantry was deemed the most efficient method of flushing the Republicans out of the treacherous mountains: "Get me the Curragh horses or give me permission to buy up a hundred mountain ponies. I must have flying columns in earnest."[74] He also begged for additional ammunition for his men: "You have to keep me full of .303 (ammunition). I am using it unstintingly." On one occasion, he did bend the rules

Pro-Treaty Casualties of the War in and around County Roscommon *continued*

Name	Place of Death	Date
C. Falley	Ballyhaunis, Co. Mayo	6 September 1922
John Farrell	Dooney Rock, Co. Sligo	13 July 1922
Michael Finnegan	WIA at Claremorris, Co. Mayo	5 January 1924
Edward Fitzgerald	Ballinamuck, Co. Longford	22 March 1923
Timothy Hanniffy	Renmore Hospital, Galway	20 July 1922
Thomas Hartigan	Ballinasloe, Co. Galway	19 July 1922
Alfred Hayes	Glasson, Athlone	22 August 1922
(An ambush by the Flying Column occurred on 25 August.)		
Michael Hogan	Castlebar Infirmary, Co. Mayo	31 August 1923
Thomas Ingham	Bonnyconlan, Co. Mayo	14 August 1922*
William Joyce	Kilmulkin, Co. Offaly	2 December 1922
Thomas Keane	Headford Barracks, Co. Galway	8 April 1923
James Lyons	Renmore Hospital, Co. Galway	9 April 1923
Hugh McCaffrey	Tubbercurry, Co. Sligo	no date
Patrick McEllin	Shanmore, Newport, Co. Mayo	23 November 1922
Michael McGrade	Claremorris, Co. Mayo	29 November 1922
Michael McManus	Dowra Barracks	6 January 1922*
(The Arigna Column attacked Dowra Barracks on 25 January 1923. It is, perhaps, not the same incident.)		
Matthew McNamara	Meelick Tower, Co. Mayo	10 October 1922
Thomas Moore	Castlebar, Co. Mayo	17 August 1922
John Moyles	Ballyhaunis, Co. Mayo	5 December 1922
John Mulligan	Longford	8 May 1922
Patrick Murphy	Newport, Co. Mayo	24 November 1922
John Murray	Athlone	10 October 1922
Frank Neary	Swinford, Co. Mayo	2 September 1922
William Newcomber	Athlone	6 March 1923
Gerald O'Connor	Gort, Co. Galway	8 July 1922
Thomas Rawl	Glenamoy, Co. Mayo	16 September 1922
Henry Richards	Sligo Courthouse	29 June 1923
James Skeffington	Town Hall, Sligo	8 November 1922
Charles Sullivan	Newport, Co. Mayo	28 August 1922
John Sweeney	Dooney Rock, Sligo	13 July 1922
Thomas Tiernan	Ballyhaunis, Co. Mayo	26 August 1922
Joseph Traynor	Swinford, Co. Mayo	4 August 1922
Michael Walshe	Barnaderg, Co. Galway	1 September 1922
Patrick Walshe	Galway	8 July 1922
Austin Woods	Sea View, Newport	24 November 1922

*indicates this author's dates or place of injury differ with O'Farrell

Commandant Tony Lawlor leads men into Custume Barracks.

to provide comfort for his soldiers. After fording a frigid river under fire on 24 November, his 250 men were wet to the waist, most to the armpits. It was raining, and there were few beds; consequently, he commandeered some whiskey, gave each man a glass of it, a quarter loaf of bread, and a half tin of Bully Beef, and, best of all, made huge fires. According to Lawlor, the men "suffered little as a result of their hardships."[75]

Heavy Armament

Aside from the see-saw action of Republicans and Free State troops who alternated between capturing *The Big Fella* and *Ballinalee* armoured vehicles only to have them repossessed by the opposing side, news leaked out from the Atlantic seaboard that Republicans had their own version of a motorised vehicle. And indeed they did! The steel boiler from Mulranny Hotel in Newport was mounted on a chassis with wheels and included a powerful motor. Known as "the Queen of the West," the vehicle sported small openings in the sides of the cylinder which had been set up in a horizontal position for protected firing positions. It played its part commendably in the attack on Clifden Barracks on 29 October.[76]

A Region at War with Itself

The area around Drumshanbo and Dromahair was crawling with activity throughout November. The Republicans were in position around Dowra by 13 November, and seven days later they were still seen assembling between Drumsna and Dowra. An attack on Dromahair Barracks was led by Seamus Cull. Combining intrigue with bravado, the commanders devised a plan whereby they sent two pretty local girls to pass by the barracks to distract and lure the soldiers away. The ruse didn't work. The Free State soldiers simply insulted the women, but to no ultimate avail. The Arigna Column captured the armament in the barracks anyway — a sizeable haul of thirty-one rifles and a Lewis gun![77]

Roads between Carrick-on-Shannon and Boyle were often blocked. Heavy trenching took place on 10 November, just two days before an attempt to capture the bridge at Boyle, where a sentry was held up, disarmed, and taken away. On the 14th another attempt to capture the bridge was made. This time Republicans, dressed in Free State uniforms, crept up in bare feet and overpowered the sentry.

Elsewhere around the northern area, two Free State soldiers from the Carrick-on-Shannon Barracks deserted their posts and brought with them a Lewis gun.[78] The Ballinameen Column (which numbered about sixty) kept busy blocking roads, cutting wires, and raiding mails, robbing National troops of their greatcoats, and disrupting the communications between Dublin, Sligo, and Ballymote.[79] In mid-November Anti-Treaty men near Manorhamilton held up a train and took goods valued at £10-15. They tore up roads and blew up bridges within a radius of five miles of the barracks. Heavy sniping occurred at Mohill Barracks on 14 November. By the end of the month, more than sixty Anti-Treaty men were seen to pass between Cloone and Mohill on their way to yet another attack on Mohill Barracks. North into Sligo, spies were shot (5 November), the printing works of *Connaught Men* were raided the week of 9 November, while other Republicans were tearing up the rails of the GS&WR line near Coolloney.

In the southern part of County Roscommon, similar activity occurred. National troops raided Kiltoom on 5 November and captured three Republicans.

Curraghboy was also hit at the same time. The railway bridge between Kiltoom and Knockcroghery was mined and the train held up and robbed a week later. Guards on the canal boats in the Shannon were frequently attacked. On 9, 15, and again on 25 November, boats near Quaker Island were robbed. Booty included salt, flour, and the ever-welcome barrels of porter.

On 19 October, government troops boarded a canal steamer and sailed up to Quaker Island. Here they docked and quietly made their way up to a hideout used by the Anti-Treaty men. They surrounded the house, and captured nine prisoners, three Mauser pistols, three service rifles, and a supply of ammunition. They also discovered a large cache of foodstuffs believed to have been taken from the derailed train at Kiltoom. The Free State troops also beheld the saddening sight of "four beds, the pillows of which were saturated with iodine. Presumably they had been lately used by wounded men."[80] Government troops returned to the island again on 22 November where they captured Matt Davis, the O/C of the South Roscommon Flying Column, and Thomas Walshe. Brigade papers relating to the 4th Brigade, 2nd Western Division, were also seized.[81]

In the town of Strokestown, Anti-Treaty men had stopped Capt. Murphy and taken his revolver. On 9 November, Free State troopers entered the town in an attempt to capture those responsible for the theft, but the Republicans cleared out of town before the government troops arrived. In mid-November Republicans slipped into Ruskey — some looting shops while others, in the northwestern part of the county, cut wires along the line near Kilfree in south Sligo.

On 24 November, the road between Roscommon town and Donamon was finally cleared, having been blocked for days previously. National troops were sent to patrol the roadway to make certain it remained open to traffic. In the western part of County Roscommon, seventeen men[82] from the former First Battalion South Roscommon attacked a train at Clooncundra. A party of six Republicans called at the Civic Guard Station in Loughglynn on 17 November and gave the guards notice to "clear out within 24 hours!"

On the last day of November, a party of thirty-eight National troops proceeded from Williamstown and came within two miles of Castlerea. They were met by Republicans whose plan was to snipe at patrols and the barracks while another group raided the post office, bank, and local shops.[83] The plan failed because the Free State soldiers met them in Patrick Street and wouldn't back away. Five Ballaghaderreen men were wounded in the exchange. (—Fallon of South Mayo was one of three arrested.)[84]

On the morning of 2 December, a small patrol of National troops consisting of eight men and an officer were ambushed on the road to Ballintubber within a mile of town. The guns blasted away across a fifteen-yard divide and wounded two Free State soldiers. The National troopers chased the attackers to the Corner House Frenchpark. Altogether the fight lasted five hours until the Anti-Treatyites withdrew. Three Republicans were injured, including Tommy Neary; he was seriously wounded and removed to Athlone Hospital.

Government-ordered Executions

The killing of selected prisoners began on 17 November with several relatively unknown men in the Republican movement (Richard Twohig, Peter Cassidy, James Fisher, and John Gaffney). Seven days later Erskine Childers was arrested at his cousin Robert Barton's home in County Wicklow. (Childers had been the supplier of arms to the Volunteers before the Easter Rising, the man whose yacht resided at the close of the twentieth century in the yard at Kilmainham gaol.) He was executed for possession of a pistol — a gun given him by Michael Collins! The death of this Director of Propaganda for the Republican forces was meant to set an example to the rebellious men in the countryside that government officials meant business. The men in the provinces got the message. The following day, Liam Lynch, Chief of the Republican resistance, addressed a letter to the Speaker of the Dáil threatening all those who voted for such draconian measures.

According to Michael Hopkinson, author of *Green Against Green*, "henceforward the war had the character of a vendetta on a national scale."[85]

Chaos Engulfs the County/Country

Ideologies were clashing on a daily basis in all parts of Roscommon (see the Chronology section of this book). On 28 December, the barracks at Dowra on the Leitrim-Cavan border was a target of thirty members of the Arigna Column led by Seamus Cull and Ned Bofin. The barracks was attacked at 4 a.m., with firing lasting only ten minutes. All the while a Thompson sub-machine gun[86] was rat-a-tat-tatting against the building's stone walls. Cutting telegraph wires (Ballymote/Sligo and Boyle/Kilfree 5 December), attacking couriers (Castlerea 7 December), raiding post offices (Drumsna 14 December and Drumshanbo on the 20th), destroying signal boxes (Carrick-on-Shannon, Dromod, and Drumsna on 10 December and again on the 27th), raiding mail cars (Leitrim to Ballyfarnon car hit on 16 and 19 December, Carrick-on-Shannon/Drumshanbo on the 20th), even directing traffic at the Ballyfarnon Fair — all manner of civil disobedience was directed against the struggling government forces. On 6 December the mail train was raided at Ballaghaderreen — the second time in a week!

Southward, Flying Columns conducted numerous raids on boats that sailed past Quaker Island. Trains and bridges often fell victim to the guile and demolition expertise of the Anti-Treaty men. In Westmeath, the Tang Bridge on the Athlone/Ballymahon Road was blown up on 12 December. Thirty armed men held up the train at Streamstown, boarded it, and rode to Castletowngeoghegan Station, where they raided the goods store and the Station Master's office.[87] Four days later the Athlone Bridges between mileposts 73 and 76 were mined. The Kilgarvan Bridge proved passable, but the Fawcett Bridge between Moate and Athlone was badly damaged. Denis Fitzgerald, the O/C of Offaly Brigade, was captured. Areas of the 1st Midland Division — Moate, Ballycumber, Ballymore — were alive with Anti-Treaty Columns. In late December, a train was waylaid at Knockcroghery with the engine being detached and sent ahead without a driver.

Central Roscommon was not without incident. On 8 December, Republicans ambushed a carload of Free State officers at Lakeview, Kilglass, near Strokestown. One officer was wounded while arms and ammunition were captured by Republicans. Five days later the clash at Ruskey[88] resulted in the death of Frank O'Donoghue, who had served as the Vice O/C of the 3rd Battalion.

County Roscommon was consumed by torment and strife on all sides. It was indeed a microcosm of the nation. On 7 December, members of Dublin No. 1 Brigade, acting upon orders, assassinated Sean Hales, a Pro-Treaty TD and brother of Tom Hales who had led the ambush party against Michael Collins at Béal na mBláth. Another man was wounded in the attack, Padraic O'Maille, the Deputy Speaker of the Dáil. Members of the Cabinet were incensed. An order was given (with Mulcahy initiating the paperwork and McGrath and Kevin O'Higgins consenting)[89] to make a show of force.

Four men, representing the four provinces of Ireland and all of whom were members of the IRB, faced a firing squad in Mountjoy prison yard — Rory O'Connor (Monkstown, Co. Dublin), Joe McKelvey, Chief of Staff of the IRA (Stewardstown, Co. Tyrone), Liam Mellows (originally from Wexford but active in Connaught), and Dick Barrett (West Cork). These men had been taken prisoner after the seizure of the Four Courts in June and had endured incarceration for six months in Mountjoy gaol. According to Joe Baker, O/C of the West Mayo IRA Brigade, "we regarded their [the Mountjoy four] deaths at the time as 'legalized murder'.....we still had supporters and friends around the countryside and if the Free State legislators thought their action was calculated to bring a quick end to the war, they were mistaken."[90]

Was this the FREE State that was being touted and fought for? Was this the

Liam Mellows

FREE state of affairs that Irish people, on both sides of the political divide, had sacrificed so much to bring about? Where were the men of solid principles on both sides of this war who examined the present situation and asked themselves the questions, "Is this the morally right thing to do? Is this the anchor with which we hope to steady our ship of state? Is this the sexton with which we choose to chart our ship's course through the troubled waters of self government? Is all this merely a shadow of that great Republic for which the fighters of 1916 and many since have given their lives?" Unfortunately for the country, the answers to these queries had no time to meander through great and stalwart minds but only to whiz through gun barrels held by National soldiers as well as by Republicans, all of whom loved Ireland dearly and were devoted to her cause. This is indeed history worthy of tears. ■

1. *My Stand for Freedom*, by Joe Baker, p. 43.
2. *Memories of an Old Man*, by John Snee, p. 9. Included in the contingent of Republicans who took part in the Battle for Boyle were members of Snee's Flying Column from East Mayo — Mick Duffy, M. McKeon, Tom Regan, M. Hunt, P. Behan, and John Snee. Mick Duffy was accidentally wounded the first night of occupation (he later died of his wounds).
3. Pat Brennan personal diary, Pat Brennan Papers, private collection.
4. Pat Brennan Papers, private collection.
5. Known Anti-Treaty participants in the **Battle of Boyle**, compiled from the Pat Brennan Papers, private collection: Tom Connor, John J. Conry, David McDermott, John Kelly (of Sheerevagh), Pat Chapman, Sean Owens, Richard Murray, Michael Greene, Joe Kelly (of Rathcroghan), James Kelly, Mick Neary, Michael Chapman, Sean Birmingham, Michael Glancy. Mardy Connor and James P. Flanagan were assigned to block roads.
6. Tom Scanlon interview, Ernie O'Malley Papers, UCD Archives, P7/B/106 as notated in *The Aftermath of Revolution* by Michael Farry, p. 225.
7. *Ireland's Civil War*, by Calton Younger, p. 363.
8. *Ireland's Civil War*, by Calton Younger, p. 366.
9. According to Michael Farry's *The Aftermath of Revolution Sligo 1921-23*, forty prisoners were taken (p. 78). Michael Hopkinson in *Green Against Green* states seventy men were seized (p. 159). Padraic O'Farrell claims in *Who's Who in the Irish War of Independence and Civil War 1916-1923* that O'Beirne was captured with twenty-three Anti-Treatyites (p. 181).
10. *The Aftermath of Revolution Sligo 1921-23*, by Michael Farry, p. 80.
11. *Green Against Green*, by Michael Hopkinson, p. 212.
12. *My Stand for Freedom*, by Joe Baker, pp. 42-43.
13. *My Stand for Freedom*, by Joe Baker, p. 160.
14. **Attack at Castlerea** known Roscommon Republican participants compiled from the Gerald O'Connor Papers: Joe Conway, Tom Regan, Gerald Fitzgerald, Joseph Cullen, Michael Cullen, and Joseph Fitzgerald.
15. Mulcahy Papers, UCD Archives, P7/B/71-90.
16. Roscommon participants in the **battle at Ballinagare** compiled from the Gerald O'Connor Papers and Pat Brennan Papers: Toby Scally, Tom Crawley, Joe Conway, Tom Kelly, Ned Campion, John Shannon, Martin Foley, Tom Vaughan, Tom Regan, Michael Jennings, William Rattigan, James Birmingham, Michael Cullinan, Thomas McCormack, Andrew and Patrick and Michael Mulrooney, Mattie Morahan, Edward Dockery, Maurice and Bernard Cunniffe, Patrick and Andrew Byron, Edward Kenny, Patrick Mulleague, and James Flanagan (of Rockingham, Boyle).
17. **Ballinlough engagement** Roscommon participants: Michael Coyne, John O'Brien, Christopher Lainge, Gerald and Joseph Fitzgerald, and Joseph Cullen.
18. Gerald O'Connor Papers, private collection.
19. Gerald O'Connor Papers, private collection.
20. Intelligence Report, Western Command, dated 2 September 1922. Military Archives.
21. Known Roscommon participants in the **attack on Swinford Barracks**: Pat Brennan, William Dockery of Elphin, James Kelly (of Ballyfarmoyle, Ardcarne, Boyle), Joe Kelly (of Rathcroghan), Pat Chapman.
22. There is some confusion as to the date of the **attack on Drumsna Barracks**. The Intelligence Report from the South Leitrim Brigade Headquarters dated 24 August 1922 claims that day for the assault. Pat Brennan's private diary claims sometime during the week ending 26 August. Another Intelligence Report in the Military Archives dated September 9 describes the military actions that took place at Drumsna.
23. Intelligence report from the South Leitrim Brigade Headquarters dated 24 August 1922.
24. Pat Brennan personal diary, Pat Brennan Papers, private collection, p. 11.
25. Intelligence Report, Western Command, dated 4 September 1922. Military Archives, Cathal Brugha Barracks, Dublin.
26. Tom Duignan interview, Ernie O'Malley Papers, UCD Archives, No. 133, p. 69.
27. Western Command Intelligence Report dated 27 July 1922.
28. Western Command Intelligence Report dated 10 August 1922, signed by Harry J. Conroy, Col. Commandant Western Command, Military Archives, Cathal Brugha Barracks.
29. Western Command Intelligence Report dated 10 August 1922, signed by Harry J. Conroy, Col.

Commandant Western Command, Military Archives, Cathal Brugha Barracks.

30. Western Command Intelligence Report dated 10 August 1922, signed by Harry J. Conroy, Col. Commandant Western Command, Military Archives, Cathal Brugha Barracks.

31. *Michael Collins*, by Tim Pat Coogan, p. 430.

32. *The Blacksmith of Ballinalee*, by Padraic O'Farrell, p. 92.

33. Intelligence Reports, Western Command, dated 8 August 1922.

34. Intelligence Reports, Western Command, dated 13 August 1922.

35. Participants in the **bridge demolition at Knockvicar and Cootehall:** Jimmie O'Brien (Crossna), Vincent Ryans (Arigna), Pat and Stephen Brennan (Boyle), John Sheerin (Lough Key, Boyle), John Coleman (Lough Key), and Michael Larkin.

36. Men who **derailed Kiltoom train:** The Flying Column of South Roscommon which included John Breheny, William Fallon, Dan Dempsey, George Fitzgerald, William Murray, James Whelan while others helped rip up railroad ties and acted as scouts. Patrick Breheny (of Sandfield, Knockcroghery) and James Martin assisted in blocking the train.

37. Intelligence Reports, Western Command, dated 18 August 1922.

38. Intelligence Reports, Western Command, dated 23 August 1922.

39. Participants include: Thomas McGiff (Drumraney), Anthony McCormack (Tang), Pat Macken (Castlepollard), Mick Pender (Athlone), James Martin (The Hill of Berries), John Galvin (Carrick), Frank O'Connor (Coosan), Brian Mulvihill (Coosan), Paddy Golden (Coosan), Thomas Berry (Tubberclair), Jack Costello (Crosswood), Jack Kelly (Mt. Temple), Paddy Fitzpatrick and his brother from Cornamaddy, Bertie Gaynor (Tullywood), Harry O'Brien (Athlone), James Fox (Athlone), Ned Dowling (Carricknaughton), Simon Mulvihill (Coosan). They were assisted by Michael Finneran (Glasson), James Casey (Killinure), Tim McCann (Portlick), Pat Killian (Glasson), Paddy Cunningham (Killinure), Ned Flynn (Kilkenny West), Michael Tinn (Tonagh), Tom Heslin (Littletown), L. Corrigan (Kilfaughney), Pat Keegan (Tubberclair), and Willie Keegan of Tubberclair.

40. Intelligence Reports, Western Command, dated 28 October 1922, written from Claremorris Command to Commandant Tony Lawlor.

41. Intelligence Reports, Western Command, dated 4 September 1922. Military Archives, Cathal Brugha Barracks, Dublin.

42. Intelligence Reports, Western Command, dated 4 September 1922. Military Archives, Cathal Brugha Barracks, Dublin.

43. Paraic Brennan, grandson of Pat Brennan, interview by author, 17 June 2002, Boyle, Roscommon.

44. Intelligence Reports, Western Command, dated 1 September 1922. Military Archives, Cathal Brugha Barracks, Dublin.

45. Intelligence Reports, Western Command, dated 4 August 1922. Military Archives, Cathal Brugha Barracks, Dublin.

46. Tom Duignan interview, Ernie O'Malley Papers, UCD Archives, No. 133, p. 69. Compiled from the Pat Brennan Papers and the interview of Tom Duignan, op. cit. Some participants in the Drumshanbo Barracks attack: Seamus Cull, Ned Bofin, Pat Tymon, one of the Gaffneys, Michael Cull, Seamus Devins, Tom Duignan, James Kelly (of Ballyfarmoyle, Boyle), Michael Mahon, Joseph Leyland. Joseph Dolan, Free State soldier, was KIA.

47. Intelligence Reports to the Western Commanded dated 15 September 1922, Bureau of Military History, Cathal Brugha Barracks, Dublin.

48. Intelligence Reports, Western Command, dated 4 September 1922.

49. Western Command Intelligence Report, dated 31 October 1922.

50. Intelligence Reports, Western Command, dated 11 August 1922.

51. Mulcahy Papers A/38.

52. Intelligence Reports, Western Command, dated 27 December 1922.

53. *My Stand for Freedom*, by Joe Baker, p. 55.

54. Intelligence Reports, written by the Free State Commander of the 2nd Western Division in Claremorris, dated 28 October 1922.

55. *The Aftermath of Revolution Sligo 1921-23*, by Michael Farry, p. 84.

56. Mulcahy Papers, UCD Archives, P7/B/73.

57. Intelligence Reports, written by the Free State Commander of the 2nd Western Division in Claremorris, dated 28 October 1922.

58. p. 42. (Tom Powell later became the Republican O/C of the prisoners held in Garrison Detention in Athlone.)

59. According to *Civil War in Connaught* by Nollaig O'Gadhra, Maguire was taken prisoner near Ballinrobe in County Mayo. According to Ruairí O'Brádaigh's book, *Dílseacht*, Maguire was captured in a dugout in the Headford area of North Galway. Both agree that the time frame was around the third week of October. Papers in the Military Archives denote 6 November as the date the two were arrested.

60. Pat Brennan personal diary, p. 13, Pat Brennan Papers, private collection.

61. p. 39.

62. Pat Brennan personal diary p. 12, Pat Brennan Papers, private collection.

63. Mulcahy Papers, UCD Archives, P7/B73.

64. Uinseann MacEoin's book *The IRA in the Twilight Years 1923-1948* states an October date, as do Intelligence Papers and Michael Hopkinson's *Green Against Green* (p. 216). Yet the inscription on Mulrennan's tombstone in Cuiltyboe Cemetery in Loughglynn indicates the date as 3 November.

65. Intelligence Papers of the Western Command, October 1922.

66. *Ireland's Civil War*, by Calton Younger, p. 483.

67. Ciaran Leavy, son of Sean, interview by author, 5 August 2004, Scramogue.

68. *Green Against Green*, by Michael Hopkinson, p. 217.

69. *My Stand for Freedom*, by Joe Baker, p. 63.

70. Intelligence Reports, Western Command, dated 31 October 1922.

71. *Green Against Green*, by Michael Hopkinson, p. 216.

72. Intelligence Papers, Western Command, dated 19 October 1922 addressed to Major General McKeon from the Office of Commander-in-Chief.

73. *Green Against Green*, by Michael Hopkinson, p. 218.

74. Western Command Intelligence Papers dated 4 December 1922, signed by Anthony O'Lawlor.

75. Western Command Intelligence Papers dated 4 December 1922, signed by Anthony O'Lawlor.

76. *My Stand For Freedom*, by Joe Baker, p. 72.

77. Tom Duignan interview, Ernie O'Malley Papers, UCD Archives, No. 133.

78. Tom Duignan interview, Ernie O'Malley Papers, UCD Archives No. 133, p. 69.

79. Intelligence Reports, Western Command, dated 2 December 1922.

80. Mulcahy Papers, UCD Archives, P7/B/71-90.

81. Intelligence Papers, Western Command, dated 22 November.

82. Derived from the Gerald O'Connor Papers, private collection. Participants in the **Burning of Train at Clooncundra**: Tom Crawley, John Crean, Toby Scally, Tom Kelly, Tom Satchwell, Patrick Mulligan, Francis and Patrick Dolan, Albert and James Durr, Stephen Flattery, Ned Campion, Peter Murtagh, Edward Kelly, John Shannon, John Rabbit, John Kerrane.

83. Intelligence Reports, Western Command, dated 5 December 1922.

84. **Attack at Castlerea** participants: Toby Scally, Tom Crawley, Jimmy Dwyer of Sligo, Patrick McCarthy, John Crean, William Delaney, Gerald Fitzgerald, Peter Murtagh, Edward Kelly, James Durr, Stephen Flattery, Albert Durr, John Shannon, Frank Dolan, Patrick Dolan, John Flynn, Michael Casserly, James Doherty, Patrick Mulligan, Tom Satchwell, Tom Kelly, Hubert Beatty, Michael Hanley, John Hanley, John Kerrane, James Moran, John Keane, James Kelly, Bernard Cunniffe, Edward and James Birmingham, John and Thomas Mullarkey, Tom Regan, Thomas McCormack, Andrew Mulrooney, James Kelly, Edward Kenny, and Maurice Cunniffe. Compiled from the Gerald O'Connor Papers, private collection.

85. *Green Against Green*, by Michael Hopkinson, p. 190.

86. Intelligence Reports, Western Command, dated 2 December 1922.

87. Intelligence Reports, Western Command, dated 12 December 1922.

88. Known participants in the **fight at Ruskey:** Brian Nangle in charge, Michael Walsh, James Farrell, Michael Greene, John J. Robinson, Richard Hayden, Pat Murray (of Tarmonbarry), James Kelly (of Scramogue), Patrick Walsh.

89. *Green Against Green*, by Michael Hopkinson, p. 191.

90. *My Stand For Freedom*, by Joe Baker, p. 94.

NINE

DREAMS TORN ASUNDER

"Forward was the Watchword"[1]

As the new year dawned, the Free State enjoyed the financial support of England, the spiritual blessing of the Catholic Church, and a reservoir of men from which to fill the ranks of its foot soldiers. The Dublin government had an intelligence system modelled on the British system and the material wherewithal to make it work. The Anti-Treatyites had none of these. Worse yet, those in the Republican movement knew that to be so, yet fought on, leaving the political strategies to the higher-ups. As their own manpower continually decreased (not necessarily due to desertion but to incarceration), the remaining soldiers had more and more responsibilities thrust upon their shoulders.

One of the most difficult choices they had to make in the field was to release the captured Free State soldiers. They had no prisons in which to confine them, and feeding them would be an extra burden on the local people. In addition, valuable man-hours would have to be expended guarding them. Thus the rule-of-thumb was simply to disarm the soldiers and send them on their way — only to find the same Free State troopers shouldering new rifles and facing them across another field, in another ditch, around another corner.

North Roscommon Men in Neighbouring Counties

On 6 January 1923, three men drove into the town of Ballyconnell, County Cavan, in a motorcar. The vehicle stopped at the post office, two men entered, disconnected the telephone, and raided the premises. They also entered Foster's shop and took £33. Upon exiting the store, the two were challenged by Captain Kellegher of the National Army. In the ensuing exchange of fire, Michael Cull of Arigna was killed and his companion escaped into the waiting car, which raced out of town towards Ballinamore, County Leitrim.

Nearly two weeks later, members of the Arigna Column destroyed the bridges at Galley (Drumshanbo), Jamestown, and Drumsna. They burned the signal boxes as well. (The signal boxes at Dromod and Drumsna had already been torched earlier, on 4 January.) Telephone lines were severed at Leitrim village, Carrick-on-Shannon, and Drumsna. Led by Seamus Cull and Paul Bofin, the Flying Column broke into Dowra Barracks, Co. Cavan, on 25 January and confiscated greatcoats, tunics and caps, boots and leggings. All items would be welcomed by men who spent a great deal of time on the run out in the harsh elements of an Irish winter.

The Arigna Column kept on the move. Mostly their actions were defensive, or of the evasive or raiding nature. At other times, however, the need for supplies prompted a bold offensive operation. Six days after the raid on the Dowra Barracks, more than 100 men travelled to County Leitrim to engage in a dangerous game. The stakes were high — a number of rifles in the barracks at Ballinamore. The opponent was a strong garrison of soldiers complete with a Black and Tan who had stayed on in Ireland to serve as a Free State gunner. Seamus Cull led the attack party. Twelve Volunteers had been left in Drumshanbo, and the runners used the train. At points along the road, the men departed and went with the Mohill lads to block roads.

Tintown Diary
The following are writings by Republican prisoners confined in gaol during the Civil War. The original diary of their notations was on loan to the Roscommon County Museum in 1997. Albert Siggins, Director of the museum at that time, obtained the book from the wife of Toni Barron, who came to live in Fuerty parish in the early 1990s. (Albert Siggins is also a member of that parish.) Toni's younger brother P. was a prisoner in Cell No. 27 wing III in Mountjoy Gaol in 1923. The soldiers' own words best describe their regard for their country, their everyday life, their internal conflicts.

It's all very fine to be pleasant
when life goes along like a song;
but the man worth the while
is the man who will smile
when everything goes deadly wrong.
Gerald Fitzgerald

Live for those who love you,
for those whose hearts are true,
for the love of God above
and the good that you may do.
Marian O'Reilly
2nd July 1923

For Freedom's battle once begun
Bequeathed from bleeding sire to son
Though baffled oft is ever won.
Briged McComgary

Far dearer the grave or the prison
Illumined by one patriot's name,
than the trophies of all who have risen
on liberty's ruin to fame.
Tomas O'Carrol
Tintown No. 3 Camp, 8 July 1923

"A gun in the hand
is worth two in the holster."

Laurence Savage
Bishopstown
Streamstown
Co. Westmeath
Tintown Camp No. 3
16th August 1923

When on a lonely road you travel
wishing a friend to see.
Turn your thoughts to Erin
and kindly remember me.

Betty Gormley

Never fear for Ireland
for She has soldiers still.

William Dandy
Hut 13
Tintown 3
Camp Curragh
5 August 1923

When years and months are gliding by
and on this page you cast your eye,
remember it was a friend sincere
that left their kind remembrance here.

W. F. Plunkett
Tintown No. 3 Camp
12 October 1923

Sure 'twas for this Lord Edward died
and Wolfe Tone sunk serene,
Because they could not bear to see
the Red above the Green.
And t'was for this that Owen fought
and Sarsfield nobly bled.
Because their eyes were hot to see
the Green above the Red.

Liam Duffy
Monastevan
(County Kildare)
No. 3 Camp Tintown Curragh
7 July 1923

What is worse than any Hun?
An Irishman with an English gun!

P. Byrne 669
Drogheda

We have walked the ring in
Mountjoy Jail
up to our knees in mud,
but what care we if old Ireland's free
if we are up to our necks in blood.

Liam Mellows

When the men arrived in Ballinamore on 31 January, sixteen ventured into town. Six men took up positions in front of the barracks, six behind the building. A local hound barked madly at the intruders but failed to arouse the garrison. When the men surveyed the barracks, they found a wire fence from the sandbagger post in front with new wire running to the eaves so that an assailant could not toss in a bomb. Clearly another alternative was needed.

The men carried a mine which had been made at the Cull house in Arigna (both brothers had worked in the coal pits before the war) and sticks of gelignite. Four men (including Tom Duignan) got into the house beside the barracks and broke through three walls. Then a whistle sounded from the garrison's head officer. By then, some of the IRA were atop the roof, proceeding to tear off some of the slates. Armed with the gelignite and five-gallon drums, they threatened to blow up the building. They shouted to the head officer to surrender and if he didn't he would bear responsibility for his men's well being (or lack thereof). The men on the roof ripped up more slates with rifle fire and made a place for the mine. They then went to an L-shaped part of the rooftop and detonated the mine. It blew down the ceiling of the room the soldiers occupied as well as the ceiling of the adjoining room. The Volunteers again called on the Free State troops inside to surrender. Seamus Cull hollered to the commanding officer, "If you don't surrender, the other mine will go off." All this action had taken several hours; it was now about 6:30 p.m.[2]

Hesitation gripped the Free State commander. Indecision was broken when the crack of a rifle shot from across the street was heard, a shot which pierced the Free State machine gunner's cheek. The game was up — it was time to fold. The Arigna Column made off with thirty-six rifles, a machine gun, and numerous revolvers, carrying the hardware on a door made into a plank. Soon, however, the escape route was blocked.

Lorries arrived, and the Column ran right into them. Cull and Deignan dove into a ditch; two machine guns ripped across the top rim. They scooted to the back of the ditch, but it afforded scant cover from the deadly fire. They squirmed their way through the oozy mud and eventually freed themselves.

Jimmie O'Brien had brought some of the Volunteers over from the Roscommon side of the Shannon which added to the Column's manpower. In the ensuing fight, the tables turned and the Anti-Treatyites captured some of the Free State men and marched them towards the Shannon. Due to an insufficient number of IRA men to guard the National troopers as prisoners, the Column members eventually let them go, but not before the soldiers had explained the reason they had been so ferocious in their attack that day: they had recently been ambushed by another IRA Flying Column, and a number of them had been killed. They had not been inclined to be merciful.

Local Executions

"...It is said that the Free State 'provincialised' its killings, both official and unofficial, by having the majority of them carried out away from Dublin...." Nollaig O'Gadhra, author of *Civil War in Connaught*, was of the opinion, "that their objective was to involve all of their senior officers in this policy, so that there would be no denying it afterwards."[3] Tuam and Athlone were among the selected sites. On 20 January, Thomas Hughes of Bogganfin, Athlone, was shot, along with four other men, at Custume Barracks in Athlone. Hughes had only recently been arrested on 21 December 1922 at Lisdonagh House, Caherlistrane, Co. Galway (two miles south of Shrule, Co. Mayo). The other executed Volunteers were:
- Martin Bourke (Burke) from Caherlistrane, Co. Galway (whose last night of freedom had been spent at Luke Raftery's house in Lisalway, Castlerea). He had been arrested on 4 January
- Stephen Joyce from Derrymore, Caherlistrane, Co. Galway
- Michael Walsh from Derrymore, Caherlistrane, Co. Galway
- Hubert Collins from Kilkeel, Headford, Co. Galway

160 • THEY PUT THE FLAG A-FLYIN'

The funeral procession of Thomas Hughes.

The following are excerpts from the final letters of Thomas Hughes written to his family the night before he died:

- "I feel very happy tonight and am prepared to die. It is not everyone who has twelve hours for same." *Letter to his sister Pearl*
- "It is now 6 p.m. We are just after being told that we are to be executed in the morning at 8 o'clock. Do not fret for me, as with God's Holy Will, I will be prepared to meet Him." *Letter to his mother*
- "The Free State officers and men are as nice as they can be to us and you must not think I am dying bearing any malice towards them. I forgave them as they are only doing what they think is their duty.. it is no crime to die in a noble cause." *Letter to his grandfather*[4]

The sixth member of the doomed group of prisoners escaped the firing squad. Tom Maguire, O/C of the Second Western Division IRA, had been captured in October, court-martialled, and sentenced to die on this day. At the time, Maguire was an elected TD for South Mayo and South Roscommon and this, no doubt, spared his life. It did not spare the life of his younger brother, Sean, who was executed at Tuam three months later.[5] (Tom Maguire escaped from Garrison Detention in Athlone in June 1923.)

Another man with Roscommon connections who met his doom at the hands of Free State government was Colm Kelly. A native of Offaly, Colm had spent happier times working in Castlerea, where he had become a member of the Roscommon team that won the 1906 Connaught Senior Hurling Championship. On 26 January 1923, he was executed in Birr, Co. Offaly.[6]

New Headquarters

During the closing months of 1922, the heat generated by the government troops around Boyle had become intense. The IRA Western Division Headquarters staff had been reduced to sharing a dugout with the 3rd Brigade centered around Ballinameen. In January two new dugouts were constructed, one of which would accommodate the Divisional staff officers.

Off on the skilly diet
when bars and bolts had bound me,
and bullets whizzing day and night.
Oh, Mountjoy Jail, confound thee!

J. J. Cunningham
C Company
Second Battalion
No. I Brigade
Third Northern Div.

I wish I could by letter
and sit by your side as of old,
One clasp of your hand
would be better
than messages written in gold.

J. Shiels
Tintown Camp
10 September 1923

In 1916 the seed was sown
for the Irish republic
and that alone.
But before that seed was fully grown
it was trampled by traitors like Sean
McKeon.

Peter Maguire
Soran
Ballinalee, Co. Longford

It's worth all bitter pangs endured
for Ireland's Holy Sake.
By manly hearts that meet the steel
though women's hearts may break.
Should weak souls grow faint and cold,
Oh never, friend, forget
the land your comrades died to save
we have still to fight for yet.

James Hartnett
Cork City
July 1923

Beware of your friend — You know
your enemy.

Patrick MacSweeney
Tintown No. 3
Late Harolds Cross Rd.
Dublin

Eire! Upon the hills the Dawn is
breaking,
Gold and crimson brightening over
the gray.
Arise! and lift thy bleeding head to
see it,
Eire! It is the dawn of Freedom's Day.

Brigid Ni Congain

One of their first concerns was to establish a reliable dispatch system. From the days of the Tan War, the Red Route which wound its way through north Roscommon and ended in Sligo/Donegal had been an efficient method of communication for the Volunteers. During the Civil War, however, the dispatch system had to be overhauled owing to the fact that many of the Free State troops knew the course of the former route and its carriers.

Leadership of National Troops

At the beginning of 1923, Free State Commanders in the Western region included:

- Alec McCabe, member of the IRB Supreme Council: Ballymote to Ballaghaderreen
- Comdt. Mitchell: Boyle to Ballyhaunis
- Luke Duffy, former Vice O/C of the 3rd Battalion South Roscommon: Claremorris to Addergoole on Lough Conn, Co. Mayo
- — Brannick: Ballinrobe to Kiltimagh
- Pat Madden, former O/C of the 3rd Battalion South Roscommon: Ballina to Swinford
- — McGouchin: Charlestown to Skeheen, Kilmovee, Co. Mayo

Area Consumed by Mischief

In County Mayo on 13 January, the road between Claremorris and Swinford was trenched and a bridge damaged. The Swinford/Ballina road was likewise trenched, and two bridges suffered damage. The Charlestown/Swinford road incurred only a single injury at a bridge site, while the Kiltimagh/Balla road saw only a small bridge targeted. Five days later a series of signal box burnings at Swinford, Kiltimagh, Ballinlough, Ballymoe, Donamon, and Knockcroghery indicated a coordinated effort to stop the functioning of the trains.

The Ballybay Bridge in south Roscommon was blown up at 1:20 a.m. on 13 January. Two days later the roads around Larkfield were blocked by felled trees. Roger's shop in Knockcroghery was looted on 23 January, and later that same week escaped prisoner Thomas Martin of The Hill of Berries made his way to safety with the assistance of local Volunteers.

On 21 January the Elphin Civic Guards were officially removed from the barracks because the building had been burned. That same day the bridges at Jamestown, Drumsna, and Galley (Drumshanbo) were again destroyed, and signal boxes too! Mohill Barracks was attacked again on 24 January, this time from three different positions.

In the Boyle area, 3rd Western Division Headquarters issued orders to raid all the post offices in the Brigade area and to destroy all official documents found within. Four prisoners (Patrick O'Connor, Chris McGlynn, Francis Scanlon, and John Johnston) escaped from the Boyle Barracks by cutting the iron bar from the window in their cell and navigating across the iron railing on the outside.

On the second day of February, the post offices at Kilrooskey, Knockcroghery, and Lecarrow were raided and old age pension money carried off. By the 8th, the Kiltoom signal cabin was gutted by fire, and roads in Kiltoom, Bealnamullia, and Lecarrow were obstructed by felled trees. Nine Free State soldiers returning to the Castlerea garrison on 7 February were attacked at Ballygar by twenty Anti-Treaty men, an encounter that resulted in a half-hour shootout.

South Roscommon Flying Column Activities

Republicans in south Roscommon were adamant about not allowing the new upstart government, with such close ties to England, to function properly. Frontal military assaults were avoided, but lessons from the past were hard to unlearn. What had worked during the Tan War became the recipe for the present one. Hit and run guerilla tactics were the order of the day.

After the IRA split in March, Matt Davis was named head of the South Roscommon Flying Column. Martin Kelly of Ballygar also served as a commanding officer. They and their men were quite prepared to resist the Treaty by any means — collecting arms, recruiting for the Republican cause, visiting homes of ex-RIC and warning them to leave the area, raiding homes where arms were likely to be found, road blocking, mining of bridges, robbing banks and post offices, and sniping at Free State soldiers — these were the tactics of choice selected by the fighting men in the field. The South Roscommon men conducted specific raids at Glennons (Corralea), the Doyle home (Liswilliam), Mannion's place in Ardmullan, and Kelly's at Cornalee, and attacked the Free States forces at Mount Talbot. The Flying Column and men in the local Companies paid unscheduled visits to the Lecarrow quarry in search of gelignite, cut telegraph wires, and escorted escaped prisoners from Athlone.

On 22 January, members of the Column mined a railway bridge at Kiltoom and tore up the rail lines. The mail train was derailed and supplies taken to Incheneagh Island. Occasionally, the Column members commandeered the local people to help block the roads. At Athlone, 100 yards of cable was maliciously cut from the local telephone circuit. On 7 February the waterworks at Athlone was sabotaged. Although the building was destroyed, the water power and supply to the town was only slightly interrupted.

Attack on the Boyle/Carrick-on-Shannon Road

Roundups in the Arigna area were becoming more frequent, more stunning, more lethal. The men on the run had to keep running. These roundups were being staged from four government-held outposts. At 4:45 a.m. on 16 February, men from the North Roscommon Flying Column attacked four Free State block-house outposts on the Boyle/Carrick-on-Shannon Road. After a three-hour gun battle, they captured three of the cabins, twelve rifles, and 500 rounds of badly needed .303 ammunition.[7] One post was manned by Free State soldier Merriman, who was wounded in the hip. Also at that post was Andrew Callaghan, who was so severely injured that he died in St. Bricin's Military Hospital, Dublin, on 20 February.

Harps carved by an inmate in Tintown No. 3.

PHOTO COURTESY OF ALBERT SIGGINS

Attack at Castlerea

In February a group of Volunteers entered the garrisoned town of Castlerea with the intent of capturing the Free State forces and their weapons. Twenty-five men assembled and were supposed to take up positions covering the front of the barracks. The scouts, however, had failed to do their homework, for as Tom Crawley and the other twenty-four Volunteers emerged from a laneway, they came face to face with an equal number of Free State soldiers. Withdrawal was impossible, and a firefight erupted in which two Free State soldiers were wounded, one Volunteer was hit by bullets, and another killed.

Trains

Keeping the locomotives running safely and smoothly was a challenge for the National government. Rail lines were quite subject to dismantling, and bridges over which the trains travelled were constantly being targeted. On 14 February five bridges were blown up in the Longford/Westmeath area: at Forgney, Co. Longford, leading to Mullingar; two bridges at Tang, Co. Westmeath; a canal bridge at Ballymahon; and the nearby Shrule bridge. Two weeks later on the 27th, the train travelling between Ballinasloe and Athlone was held up at Thomastown at 5:15 p.m. The engine was detached and sent full steam ahead to Athlone, where it collided with wagons which were being shunted, derailing them. Thankfully there were no casualties.

Armoured Lancia car of type used for railway protection in the Civil War. Photo taken 15 April 1923

PHOTO COURTESY OF EDWARD EGAN DRUM, ATHLONE

This metal bridge at Ballycumber was damaged on 24 February 1923.

PHOTO COURTESY OF EAMONN DOWLING
PHOTO RESTORATION BY LEW THORNE

Two days later, the passenger train from Roscommon was fired on and brought to a standstill at Kiltoom by twelve Anti-Treaty men. They ordered all the people out, and any suspicious person was searched. Unbeknownst to the captors was the importance of one of the passengers, Frank Simons, Head of the Free State Intelligence for Galway/Mayo/Sligo/Roscommon, who was on the train escorting a prisoner. A number of unarmed National soldiers from Claremorris were also on board. These troopers were taken some distance away from the train and deprived of their great coats and leggings before being set free. Simons, who was carrying a gun, was taken towards Curraghboy, relieved of £12 and his weapon, and released.

Other men in the attacking party uncoupled the engine from the carriage, brought it up the line a short distance, and reversed it. It hurtled back in the direction of the carriages, which it hit with terrific force, completely shattering one of them. The engine itself jumped the rails.

Meanwhile, Commandant Tony Lawlor, who had been waiting for the train in Athlone, despaired of its arrival. He sent eleven National soldiers by special train to investigate the delay. After arriving at Kiltoom and searching the area, those soldiers found no trace of the men responsible.

Occasionally train delays were caused by more-deadly sabotage. On 15 March, Lieutenant Gill, who was an Engineer at Athlone, was sent with an escort of twenty National soldiers to remove the mine from the railway bridge two miles out on the Ballinasloe line. He and his crew found twelve pounds of gelignite with fuse and detonator attached. They were too late to be of help eight days later when the bridge at Kilgarvan was blown up.

Human Courage — Daring Faithfulness

Seamus Cull and Patrick Tymon had been part of the Arigna Flying Column since its inception. In mid-February they had travelled to Cavan, where they engaged the government troops. After an encounter with soldiers on the streets of the town, they decided to retreat to what they thought was safe territory. On the night of 26 February, they left a safe house near Ballinaglera on the northwest shore of Lough Allen. Typical of February nights, the wind blew cold as the two rowed across Lough Allen and came ashore near Burchell's Wood. Wet and hungry, the men slogged to the Cull home in Tullynaha, Kilronan Parish, where they enjoyed a warm meal, dry clothes, and inquired about the local activity of the Free State troops.

Both men mentioned to the Cull sisters that they had seen a very tall woman cloaked in black standing on Cooney's Bridge. Could she be a spy or perhaps a spectre of impending death?[8] Fearful that the house might be raided, they decided to sleep in the dugout concealed in the bank of the Arigna River, where mine shafts had once been the passageways for extracting iron ore for smelting at the Arigna Iron Works. Before moving across the field to the dugout, they asked to be awakened by 9 a.m. so they could be on the move early the next day.

All the local Volunteers (Pro or Anti-Treaty) would have known of this dugout because it had been used numerous times throughout the Black and Tan War. On the morning of the 27th, Free State troops assembled outside Tymon and Cull's hideout. Sometime later the people in the valley heard an explosion. They feared the worst.

According to the *Leitrim Advertiser* of 8 March 1923, coroners Dr. McGauran and Dr. Ciaran Delaney recorded that the two men "died of shock as a result of an explosion when an officer of the National Army exploded a mine at the entrance

Tymon & Cull Memorial, Arigna.
PHOTO COURTESY OF LEW THORNE

to the cave." The inquest jury returned a verdict of "no blame" because the army officers stated that they had not known anyone was in the dugout. Yet documents in the National Army's operation report code A/89 1 March 1923 indicate that "two Irregulars found dead in dug out blown up by a party under Capt. Baxter at Arigna. Troops believing dug out occupied called on them to surrender which they refused to do."

The two versions do not match. Such was the aria of the Civil War opera — different lyrics being sung by differing tenors — words to the tunes rearranged according to the agenda of the maestro. The ultimate tragedy of that war is encapsulated in this incident. Young men, on opposite banks of the political stream of thought, viewing the River of Independence from entirely differing perspectives, yet, in the end, both wishing to ride its current to freedom from England.

Family Troubles
Soldiers in the field were not the only ones who paid a price for rebellion. In March, the intelligence officer of the North Roscommon Flying Column reported that a particular Free State soldier was in the habit of beating up women and children belonging to families of IRA members and warning off their workmen. This particular soldier also liked to imbibe. As a result of his outrageous behaviour, officers of the Flying Column ordered his favourite watering hole in Boyle to be kept under surveillance by two men posted near the entrance of the public house. The watching men had every intention of stopping this miscreant from ever bothering wives and children again. They didn't, however, get a chance. The soldier must have had an intelligence system of his own, for he failed to appear at that pub again.[9]

Strokestown Attack
At 1:30 a.m. on 6 March, the garrison at Strokestown was attacked by a group of Anti-Treaty men. As luck would have it, Captain Lavin and a strong escort were just returning from Athlone when gunfire erupted. They quickly came to the rescue of the beleaguered garrison. When the attackers saw how seriously they were out-gunned, they quietly withdrew, suffering no casualties.

Dwindling Republican Resources
Throughout the early months of 1923, the strength of the National government and its troops was ever increasing, while the numbers and resources of the Republicans fighting against it slipped downward on a steady decline. Important IRA leaders were being trapped and incarcerated, and supplies became more dangerous to confiscate. Indicative of the range and scope of arrests:
- David Daly, O/C 1st Batt., Athlone Brigade, captured on 30 January
- Jim Moran, Frank Barlow, John Doyle, Thomas Treacy, and Peter McGearty, five members of the Arigna Column, arrested by a cycling patrol from Boyle on 3 February
- Twenty-seven Anti-Treatyites surrendered at Moate, 8 February
- Francis Fitzpatrick, who formerly held the rank of Captain in the National Army, arrested 10 February
- John Loftus (a dischargee from the National Army) and two others arrested in Athlone for abetting the IRA, 12 February
- Michael O'Connell, Captain of Taughmaconnell Company, arrested on 23 February
- John (Lawrence) Kildea of Clonoghil, Taughmaconnell (in possession of a large box of candles, shotgun, caps and boots, and two bales of leather), arrested on 24 February

Arigna's Green Vale

by Steward Daly of Glankilamoy,
known in the United States as Michael Daly.
In the 1920s he published a book of verse.

High above Slieve Anierin the sun arising
Lough Allen lay smiling romantic to see,
And gallant Sinn Féiners for Erin were fighting
While war spread its wings o'er that isle in the sea.
England's murderers were shooting at random,
While dark desolation did follow their trail,
And that was the time that the Black and Tans came
To murder the boys in Arigna's green vale.

Bravely they faced them and gave them a battle
With something to think of for many a day,
For there ne'er was a foe but they ventured to tackle
And that in itself is the least they can say.
But England's resources were at their disposal
And men and munitions at length did prevail,
But though captured they proved well their devotion
To Ireland indeed Arigna's green vale.

Since Cullen, McKenna, Cull, Gannon, and Tymon
Were wounded severely and chained in a cell
Along with the Guihens, Flynn, Scanlon and Brady
For daring to love their dear Ireland so well.
But the old fighting spirit was there in its grandeur
Which sweetens each breeze the old valley exhales.
The spirit their fathers refused to surrender
When first they arrived in Arigna's green vale.

Since Cromwell of old drove them over the Shannon
Their wonderful courage did never abate.
From the time that the Frenchmen arrived in Killala
And Erin lay bleeding in dark '98
Though after Collooney the French were retreating,
And Ballinamuck saw their efforts to fail,
They yet would not leave them, although they were beaten
Those heroes of old from Arigna's green vale.

Sinn Féiners were flowers that bloomed in old Erin,
And England's red rose was out-revelled by them,
And braver ne'er grew on the banks of the Shannon
Than those that adorn Arigna's fair glen.
High o'er the mountain the moonlight is gleaming,
The valley romantic her heroes shall hail,
And joy on the face of each cailín there beaming
To meet the brave boys of Arigna's green vale.

- Michael Mulvey, Brigade Engineer of No. 3 Offaly Brigade, arrested 27 February. (He had in his possession nine detonators, one 45 dry cell battery fully charged, and documents relating to the manufacture of explosives.)
- Thomas Shanley of Dromod (O/C of the 5th Battalion of North Roscommon), arrested 5 March
- Seven Anti-Treaty men taken at Ruskey, 9 March
- May Donellan, an employee of the Ballinameen Post Office, arrested 15 March for abetting the IRA. Bridget Donellan was arrested on 21 March. Both were interned in Athlone
- Thomas Roddy of Lisacul and a Lewis gunner from Frank Carty's Column, arrested 15 March
- James Martin, Vice O/C of the Athlone Brigade, Thomas Muldoon, and Thomas Mannion (all of The Hill of Berries), arrested 26 March
- Mr. Beatty, Miss Sheila Feeney, and Miss Sally Conway arrested in Ballaghaderreen for assisting Anti-Treaty men. They were charged with carrying dispatches, 28 March
- Pat Roddy and Redmond Costello arrested in Ballaghaderreen for hiding Anti-Treaty men, 29 March
- Father Ryans arrested at Knockranny House in Keadue, 30 March
- Michael Brady (Carrick, Drumlish), John Nolan (Ballygar), William Mulrooney (Ballygar), and Martin Mulligan (Creggs), arrested 30 March

Raids by the National Troops

On 6 March, ten Free State soldiers surrounded the Three Jolly Pigeons public house on the road to Ballymahon in County Longford. In the ensuing firefight, National soldier William Newcomber was killed. A day later, Frank O'Connor, second O/C of the 1st Battalion Athlone Brigade, was trapped and arrested by a contingent of forty-six soldiers under the command of Commandant Garrahan. On 12 March, Capt. Lenehan headed a cycling patrol that entered Ruskey and found Anti-Treaty men surrounding the Civic Guard Barracks. They had the Gardaí out on the street stripped of their supplies, and the barracks had been saturated with petrol. A gun battle left one Republican wounded, and Captain Lenehan suffered a slight wound to his knee.

Unknown prisoner —
one of thousands.

Fifteen National soldiers led by Capt. Lavin raided Cootehall, Crossna, and Keadue and arrested two men on 15 March. Two deserters from Beggar's Bush Barracks in Dublin (— Walsh and — McPhillips) were captured in Ballaghaderreen. The Arigna/Riverstown area was scoured by Comdt. Mitchell, who rounded up four Anti-Treaty men (including the Arigna Column leader, Ned Bofin) on 25 March.

As the month of April came upon the land, there was an intense push to hunt and arrest Anti-Treaty men and those who aided them. On 1 April, National troops searched the congregation, but left the Leitrim village chapel undisturbed. There were no arrests. The day before, raids in the Drumsna area resulted in much Free State activity but no measurable gains — nothing incriminating was found, and no one was seized. A dance at Croghan was interrupted on 4 April, but the music played on after the National soldiers withdrew with no suspicious persons in tow. On that same day, all public houses in Ballintubber were searched, but to no avail. On 6 April, Captain Cox and seven other National soldiers proceeded to Scramogue, where rumour had suggested a raid on the post office was about to take place. No evidence found — no raid, no apparent raiders.

It was obvious that more-intensive raids needed to be conducted in order to capture "dissidents." On 5 and 6 April, troops from Castlerea, Ballaghaderreen,

Strokestown, and Carrick-on-Shannon took part in dozens of roundups. Soldiers from Carrick-on-Shannon left the barracks at 2:30 a.m. and searched the Croghan area. They found no suspicious characters. Several houses in Arigna, the glen, and crossbridge were also searched. Again no results. In the Carrick-on-Shannon area, a bag of County Down mail was discovered. Near Ballyfarnon a search by nine National soldiers yielded nothing of any worth. Twenty Free State troopers from Ballaghaderreen found zero when they scoured the Ballinameen area, and troops from Castlerea and Castleplunkett met with similar results in those areas. Frenchpark raiders also came up with no arrests. Elphin, Ballaghaderreen, and Strokestown were visited, but again the elusive Republicans were not to be found.

Republican Truce Talks

On the national scene, leaders in the Republican Executive were realising they simply could not sustain a successful military operation for many more weeks. It was decided to summon a meeting of the Army Executive and contact Eamon de Valera and invite him to be present. During the early months of 1923, it was extremely difficult to travel through the network of Free State troops and, worse yet, to attempt to assemble the entire command structure of the Republican Army under one roof. Despite the odds and the perils, most of the men did indeed assemble at James Cullinane's, Bliantas, Co. Waterford, at the base of the Monavullagh mountains south of Clonmel on 23 March.[11] At the conclusion of the meeting, which lasted three more days, a vote was taken on a proposal to bring the war to an end. That proposal was defeated by one vote. The ultimate decision to cease and desist, however, was postponed until all members of the Executive could be present. By that time, de Valera would have terms of a peace settlement to present to all parties.

Word of this gathering reached Dublin, and resulted in a huge roundup whose main objective was the capture of the Republican leaders. Across the Knockmealdown Mountains Chief of Staff Liam Lynch and a small party of followers were pursued by Free State soldiers. On 10 April a single shot from a long-range rifle brought Lynch down. His comrades Frank Aiken, Bill Quirk, and Sean Hyde (who had visited Roscommon in early 1917 and inducted men into the Volunteers) attempted to carry Lynch up across the crest of the mountain. When their slow pace became a danger to them all, Lynch insisted that they leave him there, in the heather of an Irish hilltop. And thus did the figurative head of Republican resistance part with his friends with whom he had waged a war, first against the British and subsequently against his fellow countrymen. Lynch died that evening, and with him the personification of the fighting spirit of the Republicans passed from the land.

Suspension of Offensive

The strength of the Anti-Treaty movement was being sapped. All over the country men were withdrawing deeper into the glens, farther into the vales. The death of Liam Lynch left Frank Aiken to take up the Republican banner. There was, however, little left to wave. De Valera had been trying to broker a cease-fire with the Cosgrave government, but his conditions were entirely out of the realm of possible negotiation for the Free State government:

Free State Prisoners

The Republican prisoners held during the Civil War in Sean MacEoin's military command area included 612 in Athlone, and four in Carrick-on-Shannon.

Anti-Treaty Estimated Strength in March 1923[10]

Place	Leaders	Rank and File	Arms
Longford	Casserly, Keegan and Knight	60	
Athlone	Thomas McGiff heading operations on the east bank of the Shannon	20	17 rifles 20 revolvers 5 bombs 2 motor bicycles
	Mick Pender and James Martin of The Hill of Berries leading the Republicans on the west bank	20	15 rifles 15 revolvers 4 bombs 2 mines 1 motor bicycle
Boyle	Ned and Paul Bofin, Pat Brennan and Frank Carty commanding them	140-150	

Captain Garrahan will be sent back to Athlone under close arrest i.e. in charge of an Officer of equal rank, and charged with drunkenness, disgraceful conduct, insubordination, insulting language to a superior Officer, resisting arrest, conduct calculated to give warning to the enemy of the approach of National Troops, refusing to obey orders, refusing to hand over his arms when under arrest.

Quoted from
Intelligence Papers of
the Western Command
dated 4 December 1922

1) The sovereignty of the Irish nation and the integrity of its territory are inalienable.

2) Any instrument purporting to the contrary is, to the extent of its violation of the above principle, null and void.

On 27 April, Aiken issued a proclamation announcing a suspension of offensive action by the Anti-Treaty forces. The cease-fire was to take effect Monday 30 April. Two weeks later, the Republican Cabinet decided not to continue the fight, but also chose not to surrender arms. Thus it was that the Civil War ended in no decisive victories for the Free State, no clear-cut acquiescence by the vanquished. "Dump Arms" was the order of the day — with the understanding that tomorrow those same weapons might be called upon to fire again in the name of the Republic.

The Last Official Engagement in North Roscommon

On 29 April, the last officially sanctioned conflict between Anti-Treaty men and Free State forces took place on Elphin Street in Boyle. A government patrol of seven men was ambushed by five Republicans. After an hour of rapid exchange of fire, two of the National troopers fell wounded. The rest surrendered, munitions and all. Shortly after this encounter, news of the general cease-fire order was received and subsequently obeyed by the Brigade staff in North Roscommon. The guns finally hushed. Or did they?

A Sampling of 1923 Anti-Treaty Activity after the "Dump Arms" Order

- The post office in Aughacashel, Co. Leitrim, was raided on 10 May. Money and stamps valued at £70 were taken.
- The W. E. Williams' premises in Ballyforan were raided on Friday night 11 May by unknown persons.
- Six Republican prisoners escaped from Longford on 14 May, including Seamus Duffy of Creggs, Co. Roscommon, who was the Adjutant of the 3rd Battalion No. 2 Brigade.
- A town patrol in Ballaghaderreen was sniped at on 15 May.
- The post office in Loughglynn was raided; £3-10 was found missing the next morning.
- On 18 May, the dispatch rider from Carrick-on-Shannon to Drumshanbo was fired on.
- Rate Collector James Connor of Frenchpark was stopped on 22 May by four masked men who took £3 cash and tore up his receipts.
- Clonbrook House on the Dillon estate near Ahascragh was broken into by three men on 22 May. The intruders demanded money and took £3 from the owner and a few pounds from his sister. They gave the chauffeur six days to clear out of the area. They also stole an electric lamp, three shirts, three flannel shirts, five gallons of porter, and a gold watch. In addition, they broke the telephone and tore down the British Coat of Arms.
- A car stolen from Comdt. Tony Lawlor in Ballygar was found on 24 May in the village of Castletogher, four miles from Glenamaddy. It had been concealed in a field.
- On 26 May the post office at Ballymote was raided by three men.
- A boat near Quaker Island on Lough Ree was raided on 27 May. Six quarter barrels of porter were taken along with two tins of paint and twelve planks of timber.
- Sniping occurred at Drumshanbo Barracks on 8 June.
- The greenish/blue automobile belonging to Mr. J. Sharpe of Clontuskert, Ballinasloe, valued at £300, was confiscated on 13 October.
- Kilmore Barracks in Co. Galway was raided on 17 October. Anti-Treatyites took four top coats, three bicycles, and two torch lamps.
- Pension money belonging to the old folks in the Strokestown area was taken from the post office by masked men on 27 October.

- On 8 November, Kilrooskey Post Office was raided at 10 p.m. Stamps and £6 were taken.
- In Strokestown, thirteen Anti-Treaty men held up a courier from Athlone on 8 November and took his gun and car.
- A canal boat was attacked by Anti-Treaty forces on 9 November.
- An attack by Anti-Treaty men was staged at Moate, and an ambush occurred at Glasson, Athlone, 9 November.
- On 10 November, — Gaffney, J. Higgins, and J. McBreen broke into Michael Geoghegan's house in Aughacashel, Co. Leitrim, and threatened him. He was the clerk of the local courts.
- Frank Carty and five other men visited Bunninadden, Co. Sligo, on 13 November and threatened the local postman.

Examples of 1923 Government Raids after the "Dump Arms" Order
- A Sergeant and six troopers searched the houses of — Duignan and Jack and Michael Roche on 16 May in the Ballinameen area. They suspected Anti-Treaty men were sleeping there.
- A raid on the dance hall at Kilmore in north Roscommon on 21 May resulted in the arrest of nine persons, four of whom were soon released.
- On 23 May, the Civic Guards travelled to a shebeen near Kiltoom for the purpose of raiding it. They were thwarted by women and children present, who attacked them with forks.
- In June 1923, Frank Carty's house in Bunninadden, Co. Sligo, was raided. A dance at Rossan School near Ballinamuck, Co. Longford, and houses in the Glan district near Ballyfarnon were also searched. Dugouts in Lisacul and Loughglynn were discovered.
- On 6 June, the National troops waited on the mainland opposite Quaker Island, Lough Ree, for any sign of Anti-Treaty movement.

August Sting Operations
As summer wound its way to August, sting operations were set in motion. Because it was known that the Anti-Treaty forces frequently travelled specific routes from area to area, and oftentimes on bicycles, a scheme to trap them was devised.[12] Squads of six men dressed in civilian attire were to take up positions at crossroads and interrogate all suspicious persons who were found there between the hours of midnight and 4 a.m. The men were placed a reasonable distance apart, two of each squad armed with revolvers. The halting process was to be done as quietly and thoroughly as possible because an innocent-looking townsperson could be an advance guard for men who had been on the run a long time and were wanted by the National government.

Each Battalion O/C was to send a reliable officer or NCO to be in charge of each squad. A detailed report was to reach Command HQ no later that 10 a.m. Friday morning, 3 August 1923. The operation was to commence on Thursday 2 August and repeat again on Saturday night, the 4th. The following were the crossroads targeted:
- Crossroads near the Kiltoom Station
- First crossroad on Ballymahon side of Glasson, Athlone
- Killogeenaghan crossroad between Athlone and Moate
- Bernard's crossroads near Bealnamullia, Athlone
- Curraghboy crossroads between Kiltoom/Ballygar
- Frenchpark/Ballaghaderreen crossroads near Ratra House
- Fairymount/Ballaghaderreen crossroads between Loughglynn/Frenchpark
- Cloonfower crossroads between Loughglynn/Ballinlough
- Lavin's public house near Ballyrush Bridge, Boyle
- Castlefore crossroads, Keshcarrigan/Fenagh, Co. Leitrim
- Kilclare crossroads near Leitrim village
- Crossroads midway between Keadue/Leitrim

- Carrowcrory crossroads between Boyle/Ballymote
- Rathallen crossroads near Ballinameen
- Breedogue crossroads between Frenchpark/Boyle
- Churchstreet crossroads between Frenchpark and Ballaghaderreen
- Brackloon crossroads between Ballinagare and Elphin
- Clooneyquinn crossroads between Tulsk/Elphin
- Crossroads at Ballymoe Station
- Coolteigue crossroads between Roscommon/Fourmilehouse
- Scardaun crossroads Athleague/Knockcroghery
- Carracastle on the Charlestown/Ballaghaderreen Road.

Other checkpoints in neighbouring counties included:
- Drapers Bridge between Taghshinney/Abbeyshrule, Co. Longford
- South of Killoe between Longford/Ballinalee, Co. Longford
- Leggah crossroads between Arvagh, Co. Cavan/Ballinamuck, Co. Longford
- Greagh crossroads between Cloone/Ballinamore, Co. Leitrim
- Derraghan crossroads between Lanesboro/Kenagh, Co. Longford
- Crossroads in Sligo, Offaly, and Westmeath were also targeted that weekend. The dragnet proved quite successful.

Operations by the National Army continued throughout the remaining months of 1923:
- A Lisacul dugout was found by a Lieutenant and eight troopers, and all bedding burned on 18 August
- 24 September in the Ballyfarnon District, the home of J. Duignan was searched and his son John was found. The son was active with the Anti-Treatyites.
- The Republican Court at Farnagh, Moate, was surrounded on 29 October by members of the Civic Guard from Clara, Co. Offaly. They took possession of the defendant, who was accused of beating an old man.
- On 7 November 1923, a house in Boher near Ballymore, Co. Westmeath, was raided. National troops found five sticks of gelignite, a box of detonators, and five rounds of .303 ammunition.

Partial Listing of Arrests (and Killings) in 1923 after the "Dump Arms" Order
- Relentless searches by the Free States forces of the countryside and known Republican hideouts resulted in the arrest of scores of Anti-Treaty men.
- On 11 May, Charles Gannon arrested in Ballaghaderreen
- In the District of Cartown and Kiltoghert near Carrick-on-Shannon, two prisoners, —Rourke and — Lynch, were captured on 16 May. They were both escapees from the Curragh
- — Farrelly arrested at Dromod Railway Station and taken to Boyle 23 May
- Michael O'Donnell of Castlebar, Co. Mayo, arrested 9 July in Strokestown. He was suspected of organising the Anti-Treaty movement in the Battalion area
- Captured in Longford between 11-16 July: — Boyle of Dunmore, Co. Galway; — Higgins of Dunmore, Co. Galway; — Donlon of Tuam; James Duffy of Moyne, Co. Longford; James Quinn of Killoe, Longford; and John Whelan of Granard, Co. Longford
- Jack Roche and John Kelly of Ballinameen were arrested at Rathallen crossroads at 3:30 a.m. on 3 August
- Liam Pilkington, O/C 3rd Western Division IRA, captured at Cletta crossroads on 8 August
- Thomas "Toby" Mannion, shot in action at The Hill of Berries on 14 August
- Men from afar arrested in Ballaghaderreen on 15 August: Patrick Fitzpatrick and Eamon Martin from Liverpool, and Denis Martin from Glasgow, Scotland
- James Macken of Aghagreagh, Ballinalee, Co. Longford, arrested 24 August
- Members of the Arigna Flying Column arrested on 4 September: Francis Mulherin and Thomas Beirne. A Sergeant and six National troopers sur-

Toby Mannion memorial.

The last official skirmish of the Civil War in Roscommon took place on Elphin Street, Boyle.

THE IRISH HISTORICAL PICTURE COMPANY

rounded a house at Altagowlan in Kilronan parish. Mulherin and Beirne ran out of the house and were called upon to halt. The troopers fired four shots over their heads, but the two cried back, "Never surrender!" The troopers aimed their rifles and brought down Beirne, but Mulherin thought better of trying to outrun a rifle bullet. He stopped!

- Arigna Column members Owen Gilroy and J. McLoughlin arrested in early September in Drumsna
- Near Ballinasloe, several Republicans were trapped inside a gamekeeper's cottage in mid-September, including Jack Keogh, leader of the Republicans in South Galway, and James Downey of Ahascragh
- On 26 September Michael O'Farrell, brother of Sean, the O/C of the Battalion in Drumard, Dromod, Co. Leitrim, was arrested. In his house was found a large amount of "Irregular" propaganda from the O/C of the Western Division regarding dumping arms and making dumps. Communication from Frank Aiken was also discovered
- An officer and thirteen National soldiers arrested Mick Pender of Athlone and William Jennings of The Hill of Berries in Cornalee at a dance in Fallon's house on 27 September
- Fifteen Anti-Treatyites arrested in Ballinasloe area 4 October
- Patrick Dolan of Moor Company near Castlerea arrested in Roscommon in possession of a Colt revolver on 18 October. He claimed the gun was given to him by Dick Mee, the former Captain of the Curraghboy Company
- John Downes of Ballaghaderreen, who had escaped from Longford Barracks in November 1922, was re-arrested 28 October 1923
- Thomas McGiff, O/C of the 2nd Battalion Athlone Brigade, was captured escaping from Mrs. McCormack's house in Bishopstown, Co. Westmeath. He

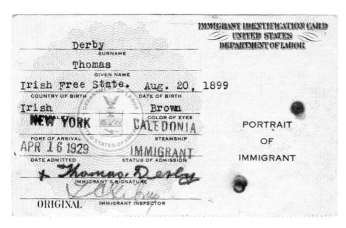

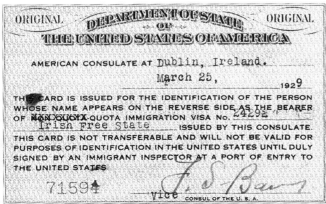

Immigration papers of Tom Derby of Boyle. After the bitter ending of the Civil War, many Irish emigrated.

1. *My Stand for Freedom*, by Joe Baker, p. 94.
2. Tom Duignan interview, Ernie O'Malley Papers, No. 133.
3. p. 142.
4. Extracted from *Civil War in Connaught 1922-1923*, by Nollaig O'Gadhra, p. 71-72.
5. *Dílseacht*, by Ruairí O'Brádaigh, p. 25.
6. *Roscommon Herald*, July 19 2000 and *Civil War in Connaught 1922-1923*, by Nollaig O'Gadhra, p. 146
7. Pat Brennan personal diary, p. 13, and Pat Brennan Papers, private collection.
8. Margaret Cull McManus interview with Frankie Watson of Cootehall, 12 August 1997.
9. Pat Brennan personal diary, p. 14.
10. Western Command Intelligence Reports, dated 8 March 1923.
11. *No Other Law*, by Florence O'Donoghue, p. 299.
12. Western Command Intelligence Reports, dated 31 July 1922.
13. p. 26.
14. *The IRA in the Twilight Years*, by Uinseann MacEoin, p. 77.
15. p. 229.
16. Pat Brennan personal diary, p. 15, and Pat Brennan Papers, private collection.
17. *When Youth Was Mine — A Memoir of Kerry 1902-1925*, by Jeremiah Murphy, p. 283.

was caught 500 yards from the house on 17 November 1923

■ National troopers raided Kiltoom area and captured three Anti-Treaty men (one wounded). Ambush at Ferbane, Co. Offaly, resulted in one National soldier killed in action and one Anti-Treaty man captured. In a raid on Curraghboy, six Anti-Treatyites were captured, while a similar raid at Mount Temple, Co. Westmeath, resulted in the arrest of two Republicans ...and the list goes on and on and on.

Here and there, in houses and at crossroads, near public houses and in abandoned outhouses, the Anti-Treaty soldiers were being picked up and were disappearing into prisons. Hunted, outgunned, with no hope of victory, these men continued the fight to the end — burdened by bitter realities that faced them.

The War was not Yet Over

The dump arms order in May was issued by the Chief of Staff (Frank Aiken), but was not necessarily agreed to by every member of the local IRA in the field; consequently, the fighting men in Roscommon may or may not have abided by its declaration. Many did not want to cave in to the Pro-Treaty troops or to what they considered to be an illegitimate government in Dublin. On the other hand, those who may have wanted to give up and go home could not do so because the Free State government did not issue an amnesty.

After the cease-fire order was issued and throughout the year of 1923, the Provisional Government ordered its thousands of troops in the provinces of Ireland to continue hunting down the Republicans. According to Ruairí O'Brádaigh in his book *Dílseacht The Story of Comdt. General Tom Maguire*, "Shoot-on-sight was still in operation and 12,000 prisoners were in jails and prison camps as the (1923) election was under way."[13] Uinseann MacEoin, in his book *The IRA in the Twilight Years*, verifies O'Brádaigh's claim: "A Public Safety [Emergency] Bill was introduced on June 15, providing for the continued detention of 12,000 Republicans.[14] It passed through the Dáil on 2 July.

Ernie O'Malley states in his book, *The Singing Flame*, that "our men who wished to avoid capture were hunted like foxes."[15] Pat Brennan, O/C of the 3rd Brigade in the 3rd Western Division, which encompassed most of North Roscommon, stated that "all our men had to continue living in their dugouts. If they ventured home, they would be immediately pounced on by the enemy, beaten up and arrested, (and perhaps shot under the plea of escaping). Most of them had to continue in this way up to July and August [of] 1924."[16]

Jeremiah Murphy, active Republican in County Kerry and author of *When Youth Was Mine*, quoted his friend Denny Reen: "When I joined the Volunteers in 1913 I never thought I would have to steal away from home by night." Yet Denny and streams of former IRA men "whose heart and soul had been given to the cause of independence...had planned and fought and suffered only to be reduced to the status of hunted criminals"[17] poured into emigrant ships and sailed away. Ireland lost thousands of devoted young men to the shores of Australia and America. Others simply returned home to pick up the pieces of their lives. ■

Final Thoughts

The account of the War for Independence and Civil War in Roscommon has been recorded; yet, the conclusion lacks a defining moment. To borrow a phrase from the American poet T. S. Eliot, the Irish Civil War ended "not with a bang but a whimper." There were no obvious victors, simply a countryside littered with walking wounded — hearts cut and spirits gashed and dashed — wounds that were years healing. Scars were still evident when this author interviewed Volunteers and the women who aided them seventy years after the events took place. Psychologically, the Civil War rent the country in two, and two it remained for decades to come.

The real story of the Roscommon Volunteers and their participation in the conflicts has been buried under the bitterness and sorrow of the Civil War period. Participants said very little to their children or others around them about those times and events. Most took their secrets to their graves. The men and women who had wrested control from England with great personal sacrifice had to live out their lives with sadness in their hearts. They had fought for one Ireland, but were left with two. Their comrades, with whom they had started the War, became their adversaries before it ended. What one man saw as a stepping-stone opportunity towards self-government, his neighbour saw as a sellout. Each person had started the War with determination and promise. Each finished it with an unfullfilled dream. Both sides had ferociously challenged the other when, if cooler heads had prevailed, perhaps an olive branch might have bridged the gap between them. All were left to ponder their prize and examine the price of the victory or defeat. All in all, it was a burden of sorrow heavy to bear.

This book has attempted to pay tribute to all soldiers, Pro and Anti-Treaty alike, who fought the good fight, gave all their energies to the cause, and who, unlike any generation before them for seven hundred years, successfully challenged foreign rule. Together they laid the cornerstone for an Irish Republic.

On Christmas Eve 1992, when Patrick Duignan of Kilfaughna, Knockvicar, Boyle, was lying on his deathbed, his son quietly went up to him and leaned over to whisper his good-byes. Patrick, who had been in a near coma and was not expected to live through the night, opened his eyes, gazed up at what he thought was one of his former comrades, and uttered his last words: "Weren't we great men!" And so they were.

Perhaps the words of ninety-three-year-old Patrick Vaughan, brother of John Vaughan of Cloonsuck, will add another perspective to the struggle and its costs. When asked by this author the question "Was it worth it?" he paused for a very long time as his mind sorted back through the years to scenes still vivid in his memory. Regret shaded his first syllables, but vanished quickly as confirmation of his life's work dawned, then mushroomed in his mind:

"That's a hard question. I had my house burned, one brother killed, and another brother beaten so badly that he suffered all through his life. But you see...we freed Ireland. We took the first step! We put the flag a-flyin'."

What more magnificent epitaph could be etched on the tombstone of a generation?

CHRONOLOGY

CHRONOLOGY

National and Roscommon events prior to and during the War for Independence, and activities in and around Roscommon during the Civil War

National Events in bold italic text
Local events in plain text

1913

***Ulster Volunteer Force formed in Belfast
31 January 1913***

***The Irish National Volunteers formed in Dublin
25 November 1913***

1914

Formation of Cumann na mBan 2 April 1914

    Irish National Volunteer Companies formed in County Roscommon:

        Boyle *9 February*

        Castlerea *15 February*

        Athlone *11 April*

        Ballaghaderreen *30 May*

        Roscommon town *12 June*

        Knockcroghery *25 June*

        Elphin and Creeve *8 July*

        Tisrara, Ballyforan *11 July*

        Frenchpark *18 July*

        Ballinameen *22 July*

        Fairymount, Castlerea *2 August*

        Volunteers establish training camp at Athlone *4 September*

        Volunteer County Board formed *10 September*

Britain declared war on Germany 4 August 1914

Home Rule Bill (excluding the nine Ulster counties) passed, but implementation suspended 15 September 1914

Split in Volunteer Movement: (Redmondites support English position in World War I and form National Volunteers; Republicans splinter off and form Irish Volunteers) 20 September 1914

1915

Irish Republican Brotherhood puts forth a plan for the Rising May 1915

Padraig Pearse reads the Proclamation for independence on 24 April, 1916
IRISH HISTORICAL PICTURE COMPANY

Republicans take over leadership of Gaelic League; Douglas Hyde stands down 29 July 1915

Padraig Pearse delivers oration at O'Donovan Rossa's funeral 1 August 1915

1916

Ireland is excluded from British Conscription Bill 5 January 1916

The Rising 24 April 1916

Fifteen leaders of the Rising executed 3 May to 10 May 1916

    Roscommon County Council passes condemnation vote against the Rising *18 May*

    Roscommon/Athlone men arrested after the Rising and sent to Wakefield, Glasgow, Wandsworth and Frongoch *23 May*

Ulster Unionist Council agrees to Home Rule if six Ulster counties are excluded 12 June 1916

1917

Volunteer Companies formed and re-formed in Roscommon *1917*

Founding of Sinn Féin Clubs throughout the county "Election in the Snows" — Count Plunkett wins Roscommon bye-election. He becomes the first Sinn Féin candidate in the country to pledge NOT to go to London to represent Ireland *3 February*

Land Agitation at the Iron Works farm in Arigna and in Warren, Mockmoyne and Tinnacarra areas around Boyle *March*

Joe McGuinness election in Longford *16 May*

Many Volunteer prisoners freed in general amnesty 18 June 1917

< Thomas Ashe, nominal head of the IRB, dies of forced feeding 25 September 1917

Eamon de Valera elected President of Sinn Féin and proclaims "an independent republic" as the party's aim 25 October 1917

Fr. Michael O'Flanagan celebrates Mass at Crossna (after a long, diocesan-induced silence) *28 October*

North and South Roscommon Volunteer Brigade Staffs have formed by the end of the year

1918

Right to vote extended to men aged 21 and over and women aged 30 and over 5 February 1918

First raid for arms in the county — Rockingham House *19 February 1918*

Arthur Griffith speaks in Athlone *March*

Lloyd George's government threatens to extend Conscription Act to Ireland April 1918

Conscription crisis swells the ranks of the Volunteers *Spring*

Athlone Brigade organised *April*

Eamon de Valera and John Dillon debate in Market Square Ballaghaderreen *5 May*

Ernie O'Malley visits County Roscommon to help organise Companies *June, July, August*

British government bans all public gatherings 5 July 1918

Police make large scale raids for arms in Roscommon *5 July*

Attempted disarming of the military guard at Carrick-on-Shannon Railway Station *28 September*

First World War ends; over 200,000 Irish had enlisted in the British Army—tens of thousands had died 11 November 1918

Sinn Féin gains 73 of 105 Irish seats in the United Kingdom General Election 14 December 1918

1919

Ambush at Soloheadbeg, Co. Tipperary — the spark plug that ignites the War for Independence 21 January 1919

Dáil Éireann established 21 January 1919

Republic of Ireland, proclaimed on Easter Monday 1916, is ratified by Decree No. 1 R. p. 16. 22 January 1919

The First Dáil assumes control of the Volunteers

Cumann na mBan branches started throughout the county

Attempted cattle raid on Walpole's land at Clooneenhartland, Strokestown *January*

Attack on policeman in Athlone *January/February*

Raid on oil depot in Athlone *Spring*

Gaelic League concert at Ballinasloe prohibited *25 May*

Dáil Éireann establishes Republican Courts 18 June 1919

Irish Volunteers become known as The Irish Republican Army 20 August 1919

Sinn Féin is banned and Dáil Éireann declared illegal by Dublin Castle 12 September 1919

General raiding for arms begins in the county

Sniping at Ballymoe RIC Barracks *September*

Income tax office in Roscommon town raided. Documents destroyed *Late 1919*

1920

Two Volunteers disarm a soldier in Strokestown *2 January*

Raid on Lecarrow quarry by Volunteers *Early months of 1920*

RIC raids Drum Church *6 February*

Athlone men attempt attack on Ballymore Barracks in County Westmeath *20 February*

Raid for 500 gallons of petrol at Boyle Station *February*

Raid on intended RIC recruits at Cloontuskert *10 March*

First Black and Tans arrive in Ireland 25 March 1920

Capture of arms at Castlerea RIC Barracks *April*

Keystone from bridge over Cross River is removed at Summerhill, Athlone *April*

Volunteers fire on RIC patrol at Kilglass Chapel. Twenty minute exchange of gunfire results in no injuries *April*

Co. Roscommon RIC Barracks burned at Athleague, Ballintubber, Ballinameen, Ballyfarnon, Bealnamullia, Beechwood, Carrick-on-Shannon, Castleplunkett, Croghan, Cootehall, Fourmilehouse, Kilglass, Kilmore, Lecarrow, Rockfield, and Scramogue — *Easter weekend April 1920*

Westmeath RIC Barracks burned at Creggan, Drumraney, Brawny (Athlone) and Tang, Co. Westmeath — *Easter weekend April 1920*

Raid on the Excise Office in Athlone *May*

Raid on Boyle Railway Station *May*

Barracks at Hillstreet burned *12 May*

Raid on Carrick-on-Shannon Customs and Excise Office *12 May*

Ballinagare Barracks burned in 1920.

Barracks at Cloonfad and Ballinagare burned in *Spring/Summer*

Barracks at Grevisk burned *May*

Raid on income tax office at Ardnanagh, Roscommon town *May*

Athlone Battalion Volunteers raid mail train near Fassaugh in Co. Westmeath *May*

Attempted attack on military camp at Kilmurray *June*

Roscommon Volunteer leaders order boycott of RIC *14 June*

Proposed attack on Tulsk Barracks. (Military vacated before attack could take place) *June*

Raid for petrol at Ballinlough Station *June*

Disarming of two soldiers at Tarmon Cross, Castlerea *June*

Members of Kilmore Coy. raid police near Drumsna *June*

Capture of enemy stores at Ballymoe *June*

General raid for arms in 5th Battalion North area *22 June*

Connaught Rangers Mutiny in India 28 June 1920

Attempted attack on Castlerea Station Guard *July*

Disarming of military at Southpark, Castlerea *July*

Athlone Volunteers strike Streamstown RIC Barracks *July*

Burning of Strokestown Bridewell *July*

Attack of RIC patrol at Drinagh, Curraghroe *July*

Ambush of RIC at Moneen, Cloontuskert on Roscommon/Lanesboro Road *12 July*

Volunteers hold up train at Drumsna and confiscate mail *20 July*

British Forces raid Dáil Éireann Commission on Industries at Carrick-on-Shannon. Arrest Col. M. Moore, Darrell Figgis, and others *21 July*

RIC damage business premises at Castlerea *2 August*

Masked men raid houses of Sinn Féin members and threaten reprisals if boycott is not lifted *18 August*

Sgt. Thomas Craddock shot in Athlone *22 August*

Burning of Loughglynn Barracks *August*

Ambush of RIC at Knockcroghery Station *26 August*

Formation of North Roscommon Flying Column *September*

Ambush at Ratra, Frenchpark *1 September*

Attempted attack on Cloonark Barracks, Drum, Athlone *September*

Sniping at Ballaghaderreen Barracks *September*

British raiding party attacked in Lough Ree *September*

Burning of Tulsk Barracks *September*

Pat Gill shot by British Forces at Drumsna *11 September*

Attempted ambush at Knockroe on the Boyle/Elphin Rd. Enemy is a no-show *September*

Burning of Ballinlough Barracks *14 September*

Attack at Carrick-on-Shannon Courthouse *September*

Sinn Féin Court in Athlone raided by Crown Forces — judges, solicitors, witnesses arrested *17 September*

RIC burn, bomb, and fire into private premises in Drumshanbo *22 September*

Uniformed men with blackened faces fire randomly in Carrick-on-Shannon *22 September*

Sean Connolly arrives in Roscommon from Longford *Late September/early October*

Mails taken from Ballyfarnon Post Office *Autumn*

Mail car raided by Roscommon Volunteers at Ballyfermoy in Leitrim *Autumn*

Athlone men ambush lorry at Parkwood in County Westmeath *October*

Attempted attack on military at Lecarrow quarry — enemy is a no-show *October*

Attempted ambush of RIC at Curraghaleen, Drum, Athlone *October*

Raid at Smithhill, Elphin *October*

Tans raid homes of Volunteer officers in 1st Battalion North *October*

Raid at Greatmeadow, Boyle *October*

Attack on Frenchpark Barracks *2 October*

Ambush at Fourmilehouse *12 October*

Formation of the Flying Column of 3rd Battalion South *October*

Reign of Terror in Ruskey *15 October*

Armed masked men in Athlone search for Volunteers wanted by the authorities *16 October*

Sacking of Ballinagare by Crown Forces who kill Pat Doyle *19 October*

RIC fire on civilians in Athlone. Michael Burke wounded *22 October*

PHOTO COURTESY OF IRISH HISTORICAL PICTURE COMPANY

< *Death of Terence MacSwiney after 74 days on hunger strike 25 October 1920* (photo of Terence above)

Attack near Kielty, Drum by Athlone Flying Column. Constable Doyle wounded *31 October*

Shopkeepers in Boyle warned to close down in observance of the funeral of Terence MacSwiney *31 October*

Kevin Barry, eighteen-year-old student, hanged in Dublin — the first official execution since 1916 1 November 1920

Burning of supply wagons at Carrick-on-Shannon *November*

British Forces fire on each other in error in Athlone. Three wounded *2 November*

Tans sack the village of Knockcroghery *November*

Attack on Tarmonbarry Barracks *November*

Tans burned Sinn Féin Hall at Crannagh, Drum, Athlone *November*

Attack by Athlone Column in Auburn, County Westmeath. Volunteer Seamus Finn killed *2 November*

John Conroy taken from his home at Rathconnor, Fourmilehouse and shot *3 November*

RIC burn premises of George Geraghty in Roscommon town and flog citizens *3 November*

British Forces burn down Athlone Printing Works — perhaps because editor McDermot Hayes came

out strongly against the Crown actions *3 November*

Jim Tormey and Harry O'Brien make escape in Mardyke St., Athlone. One RIC wounded. RIC retaliates by burning the pub of Mr. L. Maguire *4 November*

Lloyd George states he has "murder by the throat" in Ireland 9 November 1920

Attack on military at Tarmon, Castlerea *November*

RIC wreck plant of *Leitrim Observer* and attempt to destroy building by fire *9 November*

Athlone Black and Tans order all businesses to close on 11 November to honour Armistice Day *9 November*

RIC burn halls and private businesses in Drumsna *10 November*

Linda Kearns, Seamus Devins O/C of Grange Battalion in Sligo Brigade, and two other men arrested en route to Frenchpark for an expected attack on the Auxiliary headquarters *20 November*

"Bloody Sunday" — Michael Collins' squad eliminates the "Cairo Gang" (eleven British spies) in Dublin and in retaliation British soldiers open fire and kill eleven spectators in Croke Park 21 November 1920

Patrick Flynn shot in Tarmon, Castlerea *21 November*

Dan O'Rourke, O/C of South Roscommon Brigade, narrowly escapes capture at Tarmon School *22 November*

Constable "disappears" from Ruskey Barracks *23 November*

Attempt to steal William Walpole's car *27 November*

Burning of the Liverpool Docks by the IRA 28 November 1920

Mail horse van held up near Scramogue (twice!) *Late 1920*

Athlone Brigade staff meet with Michael Collins in Dublin *8 December*

Attempted ambush of patrol at Frenchpark *12 December*

Ambush of police near Elphin Dispensary *13 December*

Volunteers enter Tarmonbarry and shoot Black and Tan *December*

Johnnie McGowan of Frenchpark murdered by the Tans *15 December*

Government of Ireland Act establishes Six County Northern parliament but similar provision for the South is ignored by the Dáil 23 December 1920

Four Auxiliaries rob Strokestown Northern Bank *23 December* (They are sentenced to five years penal servitude on *12 March 1921*)

Holdup of train at Kilfree Junction, Ballaghaderreen *late December*

The GHQ papers for the years before 1921 were lost when the records were transferred from Harcourt Street. Thus information is more comprehensive from January 1921 onward.

Kilgefin Parish surrounded by Crown Forces. "A number of useless fellows arrested" *January*

Attempted ambush of military lorry in Knockcroghery *January*

Kilteevan and Curraghboy Companies attempt ambush on Roscommon/Athlone Road near Clooncraff for three consecutive days. (Enemy is a no-show) *Three days in January*

South Roscommon Brigade Vice O/C Jim Breheny and 4th Battalion South O/C Tom Kelly arrested *January*

Suspected spy executed in 4th Battalion South area resulting in arrest of ten Curraghboy Coy. Volunteers *5 January*

Attempted attack at Castlerea *5 January*

Attack on Tarmonbarry Barracks *5 January*

Volunteers engage RIC in Strokestown. Sergeant McArdle shot *5 January*

Eighteen Volunteers attack in Elphin — Constable Sharpe seriously wounded *5 January*

Attempted attack at Frenchpark. Enemy doesn't show up *5 January*

Pat Durr shot in Leonard's house at Ballintubber *6 January*

Crown Forces raid and shoot up town of Castlerea *6 January*

Crown Forces reprisal in 2nd Battalion North area — two Sinn Féin members arrested, three cows shot *6 January*

Attempted ambush of RIC in Lanesboro by 3rd Battalion South Roscommon men *6 January*

Crown Forces conduct sweep in Strokestown area specifically looking for Liam O'Doherty and Pat Madden *6 January*

Attempted attack on Ruskey patrol *7 January*

Formation of the IRA Active Service Unit in Castlerea *January*

Members of Elphin Battalion hold up the mail car but find nothing of importance *8 January*

RIC search congregation at Cootehall Church. Four Volunteers arrested *10 January*

Passenger train held up at Kilfree Junction, Ballaghadereen. All males searched by IRA *10 January*

Attempted attack at Frenchpark *12 January*

Another attempted attack at Ruskey *12 January*

Crown Forces raid District Council meeting near Castlerea *12 January*

Joe Tormey of Moate, Co. Westmeath shot by sentry at Ballykinlar Camp *14 January*

Joe McGuinness, TD, arrested in Castlerea *19 January*

Raid on post office in Castlerea area *19 January*

Attack on police patrol in 4th Battalion North area *22 January*

Ballyfarnon Courthouse burned *22 January*

Martin Ganley's house and hay burned in Loughglynn. Brigade staff barely escapes *26 January*

Crown Forces sweep 2nd Battalion North area arresting several Volunteers *27 January*

Ballyfarnon Post Office raided (two suspicious bills for goods recovered) *Late January*

Attempted attack on lorry of Tans in Ballymore, Co. Westmeath. Cancelled — due to a snow storm! *Late January*

Attempted attack on troops travelling through Donamon Station *February*

Three lorries of RIC raid Drumlion, Carrick-on-Shannon. (Nine Volunteers arrested — only three detained) *1 February*

Attack on Elphin cancelled due to all-night patrols *1 February*

Athlone Flying Column attempts ambush on Galway/Ballinasloe Road *1 February*

Huge roundup in Ballagh area. No Volunteers arrested *1st week of February*

Attempted attack on Ballaghaderreen Barracks *February*

< Ambush at Cornafulla, Drum, Athlone. James Tormey killed (left is the Tormey memorial) *2 February*

PHOTO COURTESY OF LEW THORNE

Crossna Coy. blocks roads leading to Sligo *3 February*

4th Battalion North Commandant, John J. Doyle, arrested *3 February*

Intelligence Officer of Elphin Battalion shoots and seriously wounds arresting officer. (No reports about this in the newspaper) *4 February*

Attempted ambushes at Ruskey and Tarmonbarry. Enemy is a no-show on *4 February*

Another attempt at Ruskey and Tarmonbarry the week of *7 February*

RIC raid home of Brigade Adjutant in 5th Battalion North area. (Nothing incriminating found) *6 February*

Carrick-on-Shannon Volunteers raid the mail. (Nothing important found) *6 February*

Attempted ambush in Connaught St., Athlone *7-8 February*

British military raids entire Strokestown area *8 February*

Roundup in "B" Coy. (Ballinaheglish) area of 2nd Battalion South. One Volunteer arrested *9 February*

Attack on Elphin Barracks *11 February*

Ballinlough area searched by Crown Forces. No arrests *11 February*

1st Battalion South Volunteers destroy property of women spies. Ladies are ordered to leave the area *12 February*

Military raids the entire Strokestown area AGAIN *12 February*

RIC raid Drumlion, Carrick-on-Shannon *14 February*

Mixed forces raid Elphin area looking for Michael Dockery. Yield: one rifle, twenty rounds of ammo. No Dockery! *14 February*

Youth suspected of spying on the Volunteers near Castlerea ordered to leave. He did! *16 February*

Capt. of Crossna Coy. arrested *16 February*

Spy executed in 1st Battalion South area *19 February*

Three lorries of mixed military and RIC hold up people coming from Mass at Dangan, Kilmore *20 February*

Volunteer Joe Morrissey killed at Athlone *20 February*

Attempted attack by members of Athlone Flying Column on Ballymore Barracks in Co. Westmeath *20 February*

Successful attack on Ballymahon Barracks by members of the Athlone Column *20 February*

Ten lorries of RIC, Black and Tans, and infantry calvarymen raid Strokestown area and arrest 200 people (most released) *20 February*

Crown Forces raid "B" Coy. (Ballinaheglish) area in 2nd Battalion South area AGAIN! *21 February*

Three Volunteers attack enemy patrol near Elphin *22 February*

Attempted ambush near Strokestown. (No enemy appear) *26 February*

Attempted ambush at Cloonsheever (in Fairymount parish) *March*

Narrow escape of 1st Battalion North Council at Ballinameen *March*

Kilmaryal (Mantua) Church raided. No arrests *5 March*

Croghan Church raided by RIC *5 March*

RIC raid Knockcroghery *5 March*

Strokestown mails raided *7, 9, and 12 March*

Crown Forces raid Donamon Castle and surrounding woods. No arrests made *8 March*

Houses in Carrick-on-Shannon destroyed by masked men *8 March*

Alec McCabe (of Ballymote, Co. Sligo) arrested at Carrick-on-Shannon *9 March*

Crown Forces surround and round up all men in Castleplunkett, Ballintubber, and the west end of Ballinaheglish parish. One man detained. No Volunteers arrested *9 March*

Squads lie in wait in 2nd Battalion South "B" Coy. area. Threatening notices posted on shop windows. Enemy is a no-show *Early March*

Seven Volunteers attempt to ambush patrol near Elphin. (No military appear) *10 March*

Roads blocked in Elphin area *11 March*

Two Auxiliary RIC sentenced to penal servitude for Roscommon robbery *12 March*

Mixed Crown Force commandeer Elphin locals to fill in trenched roads *13 March*

Paddy Moran of Crossna hanged in Mountjoy *14 March*

Seven Volunteers snipe at Keadue RIC Barracks *14 March*

"B" and "D" Companies (Ballinaheglish and Fuerty) in 2nd Battalion South area prepare ambush for RIC. Enemy fails to appear *14 March*

Jurors in Cloverhill area stopped from attending Assizes *14 March*

"D" Coy. (Fuerty) in 2nd Battalion South area tries to go it alone at ambush site. Still no enemy happen upon the scene *15 and 16 March*

RIC raids Rahara. Two officers and two privates arrested. Battalion Council escapes under fire *17 March*

Mails raided in Elphin area...nothing important found *18, 19, and 23 March*

Three attempts to ambush police patrol in Ballymore, Co. Westmeath. No enemy appear *March*

All mails in Crossna area held up and censored. Invoices from Belfast firms seized *18 March*

Crossna Volunteers confiscate and destroy Belfast goods going to W. H. Lynn in Ballyfarnon *19 March*

RIC raids Curraghboy — active Company members arrested *20 March*

Attack on RIC patrol at Chanterland, Elphin *21 March*

All roads from enemy bases leading to Keadue trenched by Crossna Volunteers *22 March*

Robbery of post office in Ballyfarnon *22 March*

The Kilronan Ambush (Attack at Keadue)
22 March

Ambush at Scramogue, Strokestown *23 March*

Michael Mullooly killed at his home in Kiltrustan, Strokestown *24 March*

Crown Forces engage Seamus Mulrennan's Column at Lisacul *27 March*

Joseph Molloy (age 13) shot by Crown Forces at Lyonstown, Boyle *28 March*

Belfast goods destroyed at Donamon Station. (Ten tons of it!) *28 March*

Sean Corcoran, O/C of East Mayo Brigade, and planner of attack on Ballaghaderreen Barracks, shot by RIC at Crossard, Ballyhaunis *1 April*

Jurors in 4th Battalion South area stopped from attending British Court *3 April*

RIC search congregation of Cloonboniffe Church near Castlerea. No arrests *3 April*

Charlestown, Co. Mayo bank robbed of £5000 *4 April*

Five Volunteers in enemy uniforms visit suspected informers in Loughglynn district *4 April*

Alleged spy shot near Scramogue, Strokestown *5 April*

Two spies shot in Loughglynn *5 April*

Attempted ambush near Athlone (the lorries failed to appear) *6 April*

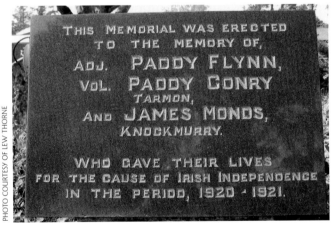

PHOTO COURTESY OF LEW THORNE

THIS MEMORIAL WAS ERECTED TO THE MEMORY OF, ADJ. PADDY FLYNN, VOL. PADDY CONRY TARMON, AND JAMES MONDS, KNOCKMURRY. WHO GAVE THEIR LIVES FOR THE CAUSE OF IRISH INDEPENDENCE IN THE PERIOD, 1920 - 1921.

< Castlerea men Patrick Conry of Tarmon and James Monds killed by Black and Tans *6 April*

Party of Volunteers enter Castlerea as a reprisal for shooting of James Monds and Patrick Conry. One soldier, one civilian wounded *7 April*

Attempted ambush at Loughglynn *7 April*

All mails raided in Strokestown area. Correspondence seized *8 April*

Small Flying Column moves to Frenchpark. Enemy is a no show *8 April*

Alleged spy shot in Castlerea *9 April*

Terence McGlynn (of Drumshinnagh, Ardcarne) killed in shootout in Dublin 9 April 1921

Loughglynn Chapel raided — all men searched
10 April

Several Volunteers captured in Carrick-on-Shannon area *10 April*

Michael J. Breheny of Knockcroghery Coy. arrested *11 April*

Spy shot at Drumshanbo *11 April*

Crown Forces conduct roundup in Loughglynn. No arrests *11 and 14 April*

Alleged spy found shot in Athlone *13 April*

Attempted ambush of police in 4th Battalion South area. (Enemy does not appear) *14 April*

Another attempted ambush near Frenchpark. No enemy appear *14 April*

Roundup in 3rd Battalion South area. Many brought from four miles away. All women questioned and searched *16 April*

Roads trenched and blocked in Boyle area *17 April*

Ballinagare Chapel raided by Crown Forces *17 April*

Twelve Volunteers attempt an attack at Frenchpark. (No enemy appeared) *18 and 21 April*

1st Battalion South Flying Column moves to East Mayo to assist in planned attack *18 April*

Attack in the Woodlands of Loughglynn *19 April*

Sixteen Volunteers from Strokestown area attempt an attack on the Tarmonbarry/Ruskey Road. (No luck) *21 and 30 April*

Attempted attack on police at Carrick-on-Shannon. (Police do not appear) *21 April*

Jurors prevented from attending Assizes in 3rd Battalion South area *21 April*

RIC attempt to serve notice on farmer in 3rd Battalion South area, but "they couldn't bring their lorries within a half a mile of the place." *21 April*

Ten Volunteers attempt an attack at Elphin. (No enemy appear) *22 and 30 April*

House of RIC Sgt. raided by Volunteers in regard to land dispute (3rd Battalion South area) *23 April*

Boyle Railway Station raided. (All boycotted goods destroyed) *24 April*

Four Volunteers arrested in reprisal raid by Crown Forces in Strokestown area *24 April*

Two houses burned in Loughglynn *24 April*

Trien Chapel (Castlerea area) raided (one girl arrested) *24 April*

Railway wires cut between Donamon and Roscommon Station *25 April*

Mail car raided between Creggs and Roscommon town *25 April*

Mails raided, correspondence seized in Crossna area *25 April*

House raided in Cloonboniffe, Castlerea by Crown Forces (one civilian arrested) *26 April*

After keeping diary of Crown Forces' numbers and movements, 3rd Battalion South Volunteers report enemy too strong to attack *26 April*

Two priests' houses in Loughglynn raided *27 April*

Roundup in two villages including woods of Runnamoat, Oran. (No arrests) *29 April*

Volunteer from Donamon Coy. arrested *30 April*

Attempted ambush at Tubbrit, Athlone, Co. Westmeath *last of April*

Several attempted ambushes of police patrol at Smithhill, Elphin *May*

Crown Forces surround Ballinaheglish Chapel — question and search all men *1 May*

All roads from Roscommon town to Lanesboro trenched. Lorry overturns and one soldier wounded *1 May*

Attempted ambush of RIC near Ballymoe *2 and 3 May*

Roads cut in Trien Coy. area (Castlerea) *3 May*

Raid for boycotted goods in Ballinlough *4 May*

Mails raided between Castleplunkett and Frenchpark *4 May*

Disarming of two British soldiers at Cloonfad *5 May*

Raid for boycotted goods in Loughglynn *5 May*

Mail car from Roscommon to Creggs raided by Fuerty Coy. *5 May*

Black and Tans raid Loughglynn Chapel *5 May*

Crown Forces burn two houses near Ballintubber (Patrick Cunnane's and Mrs. Leonard's) *6 or 7 May*

Two alleged spies in the Kilrooskey area killed *8 May*

Castlerea/Ballinlough road blocked *8 May*

Military shoots Patrick Wynne in his home at Killeenboy, Kilteevan *9 May*

Military pays a visit to Fr. Thomas Hurley in Ballagh Chapel. Orders him to denounce all this civil outrage. Fr. Hurley claims Bishop as his boss, not the Black and Tans *9 May*

IRA attacks British Forces at Emmoo, Roscommon. (Some Crown Forces wounded) *May*

Crown Forces raid the Loughglynn demesne *9 May*

Wires cut between Roscommon and Donamon by Ballintubber Coy. *10 May*

Emigration passport signed in 1st Battalion South area — (an important function because without permission from IRA, the man could be shot as a deserter) *10 May*

Half of bridge taken up in 4th Battalion South area. Police blew up the rest *10 May*

Attempted ambush of RIC at Lisacul *10-12 May*

Roads trenched. Auxiliaries place mines in them in 3rd Battalion South area *10 May*

< Mine Explosion at Cloontymullen, Kilteevan *11 May* *(Photo of memorial above.)*

Hubert Tully from Clooneyquinn, Tulsk killed at Galway Station *11 May*

O'Brien's house burned down in Milltown, Curraghboy *14 May*

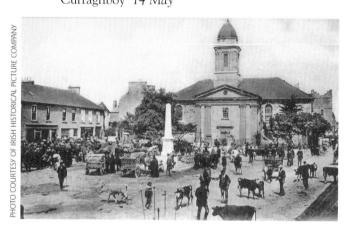

< Mixed forces raid large part of Roscommon town. All entering searched, all wishing to exit require permission. A number of men photographed with Harry Boland during 1918 election were given twelve hours to leave town *15 May*

Michael Dockery, O/C of North Roscommon Brigade, and Jack Glancy, Adjutant, arrested in Cootehall *16 May*

Attack on Ballaghaderreen Barracks from the train *17 May*

Crown Forces search Fr. Malachy Brennan's home near Mantua (Kilmaryal) Church *17 May*

Jim Molloy escapes from Boyle Barracks *21 May*

Crown Forces again search Fr. Brennan's home near Mantua Church *22 May*

Portions of Ballaghaderreen set afire by Tans *May/June*

Roads blocked near Roscommon by "A" (Cloverhill) Coy. *24 May*

Pat Mullooly escapes from Athlone Barracks *24 May*

Customs House, Dublin burned by the IRA 25 May 1921

Wires cut between Roscommon and Donamon by Ballintubber Coy. *25 May*

Attempted ambush of RIC by "E" Coy. around Tarmon, Castlerea *25-26 May* (Mulcahy Papers claim dates as 22-25 May)

Two prisoners escaped from Athlone Barracks *24 or 26 May*

Roundup of Volunteers in 2nd Battalion South area *26 May*

Military car burned in Athlone *27 May*

Flying Column for 2nd Battalion South area partially formed *29 May*

Military rifle range at Athlone burned *30 May*

Mails raided between Loughglynn and Castlerea *30 May*

Constable shot near Kilrooskey during road-cutting operation *30 May*

Attempted ambush at Drummullin, Elphin in 3rd Battalion North area *June*

Burning of Ballymore Courthouse in Co. Westmeath *June*

IRA and RIC engage at Carnagh, St. John's, Athlone *1 June*

Patrick Coyle (age 67) shot in Murphy's house in Carnagh East, St. John's by Crown Forces *1 June*

Road from Roscommon to Castlerea blocked with felled trees and loose stones *1 June*

Attack on patrol at Ruskey *June*

Spy executed in Athlone area *June*

RIC attacks Volunteers at Aghadrestan, Castlerea. Mick Carty killed *2 June* (1 June says the Military Archives)

Railway wires cut between Roscommon and Castlerea *4 June*

Castlerea/Cloonboniffe road strewn with glass *5 June*

Lineman for railroad held up and uniform taken in 2nd Battalion South area *5 June*

Loughglynn mail raided *8 June*

Belfast goods destroyed at Donamon Station *10 June*

Castlerea/Ballinlough mail raided *11 June*

Attempted ambush in 3rd Battalion South area. Enemy fails to appear *11 and 12 June*

Thomas Rush shot by British Forces at Lisacul, Ballaghaderreen for failing to halt *12 June*

Police patrol fired on in Charlestown, Co. Mayo *13 June*

Michael Dockery escapes from Boyle Barracks *15 June*

Telegraph wires between Roscommon and Castlerea put out of commission *16 June*

Harold Round, stationed in Castlerea, captured by IRA on 16 June and drowned in the River Suck on *17 June*

< Correal House, home of the Magann (McGann) family, near Four Roads destroyed by the IRA. Magann was the Resident Magistrate in Coolderry House *14 June*

Raid on railway store in 3rd Battalion South area — three picks, shovels, two rail lifters, one crowbar, and a pair of wire cutters taken *17 June*

Enemy forces raid Erritt district near Castlerea *17 June*

Attempted ambush in the 3rd Battalion South area. Enemy fails to show *20 June*

Col. Lambert dies in IRA attack on his private car near Moydrum Castle, Athlone, home of Lord Castlemaine *20 June*

Burning of Knockcroghery village *21 June*

Police patrol at Annaghmore in north Roscommon fired upon *21 June*

IRA raid Loughglynn for boycotted goods *21 June*

Ballinlough Post Office raided *21 June*

Six County Northern Ireland parliament opened by King George V 22 June 1921

Attack at the Vaughan house in Cloonsuck, Castlerea. (Ned Shannon and John Vaughan killed) *22 June*

Wires cut between Donamon/Ballymoe *22 June*

Volunteers in 3rd Battalion South area visit J. P. (who had seconded a vote of sympathy for a Black and Tan killed in the area). He was forced to apologize and promise not to sit at "British Court" again *22 June*

Frenchpark Barracks and Courthouse attacked *25-26 June*

Crown Forces fire on Mantua Church during Mass *26 June*

Raid on Cloonfad for boycotted goods *27 June*

Belfast goods destroyed including seven tons of potatoes in 2nd Battalion South area *28 June*

Four policemen killed in ambush between Galway and Milltown *28 June*

Trien, Castlerea mails raided *30 June*

Attempted ambush by Athlone Flying Column at Tubbrit on Athlone/Ferbane Road, Co. Offaly Volunteers, not wanting any action near their hide-out, blocked the road so lorries could not enter ambush zone *late June-July*

Glenamaddy workhouse destroyed *1 July*

Ned Weir, agitator for land reform, shot near Ballintubber *1 July*

RIC patrol attacked at Ballygar *1 July*

Five farmhouses at Coosan, Athlone burned by masked men *2 July*

3rd Battalion North men head for Tarmonbarry *2 July*

Creggan House, in south Roscommon, burned as a reprisal for homes destroyed in Coosan *3 July*

Constable in Ballaghaderreen fired on — no injuries *4 July*

Two Constables wounded in attack near Ruskey *5 July*

Two policemen fired on in Athlone — no injuries *6 July*

Thomas McGowan shot at Tarmonbarry by IRA men over a family dispute. It was not an army-sanctioned action *6 July*

Unionist house in Tarmon, Castlerea destroyed *9 July*

Ambush at Southpark, Castlerea *9 July*

Attempted ambush of police at Lavally, Strokestown *10 July*

The Demise of Inspector King of Castlerea *11 July*

The Truce between the IRA and British Forces is signed. Estimated fatalities during the war — 400 RIC, 150 Military, and 750 IRA and civilians 11 July 1921

Luke Killian of Crith dies *21 August*

Escape through the Brady Tunnel at the Curragh *September*

Anglo-Irish Peace Conference opens in London 11 October 1921

Training camps at Mantua, Runnamoat, Donamon, Cloonkeen, Hermitage, Erritt, Ballymoe, Castlerea, Cloonshee, Boyle Union Buildings, Cootehall Courthouse *Autumn/Winter*

Signing of Peace Treaty in London 6 December 1921

Dáil Éireann begins debate on Treaty 14 December 1921

1922

Dáil Éireann approves Treaty by 64 to 57 vote 7 January 1922

Provisional Free State Government takes over from British 16 January 1922

Sniping along the Northern Ireland border early months of 1922

National Cumann na mBan Convention (419 votes against the Treaty, 63 for the Treaty) 5 February

The Garda Síochána (Civic Guard) is established 21 February 1922

PHOTO COURTESY OF GEAROID O'BRIEN HEAD LIBRARIAN ATHLONE LIBRARY

< Takeover of Athlone Barracks by Free State forces (photo shows the British Forces leaving the barracks) *28 February*

Takeover of Boyle Barracks by the Irish Republican Army *March*

Anti-Treaty Army Convention in Dublin 26 March 1922

Split among the IRA forces in Boyle Military Barracks *5 April*

IRA men break into Mount Talbot House. Threaten W. J. Talbot *7 April*

The Carrick-on-Shannon Masonic Hall and Surgeon Parke Memorial Hall burned *April*

Unsanctioned robbery of Lanesboro bank by a few Roscommon Volunteers *April*

Reorganisation of 3rd Brigade in the new 3rd Western Division due to the split in the Army *week of 7 April*

Four Courts, Dublin occupied by Anti-Treaty forces 13 April 1922

Arthur Griffith speaks in Sligo town *16 April*

Joseph Leavy KIA in Mullingar *27 April*

Mutiny at Custume Barracks, Athlone *April*

George Adamson shot in Athlone *24 April*

Recapture of car from Republicans by the Free State forces in Strokestown *late April*

Northern Bank in Drumshanbo raided *May*

John Thomas Carley of Strokestown, shopkeeper asst. in Enniskillen, arrested *23 May*

Spy in Cootehall shot *29 May*

Eugene Kelly of Lisacul accidentally shot while occupying Boyle Barracks *3 June*

Free State General Election: Pro-Treaty parties secure 82 seats; Anti-Treaty and other parties 46 seats 16 June 1922

The Civil War Officially Begins — Free State forces attack the Four Courts 28 June 1922

Actions in and Around County Roscommon

Some of the following dates were extracted from intelligence reports in the Military Archives. They reflect the date on which the report was written not necessarily the exact date on which the incident took place

---

All Shannon bridges and the railway bridge near Boyle demolished in preparation for main attack *29 June*

Surrender of Anti-Treaty garrison at the Four Courts *30 June*

Battle of Boyle *1 July*

Siege of Sligo begins. Rail lines torn up and communications cut at Collooney, Co. Sligo *1 July*

Frank Carty's Flying Column attacks Collooney area *2 July*

Michael Dockery shot in Boyle by Republican snipers *2 July*

Gelignite and battery wires discovered at Ballinameen. Curfew called in Boyle *2 July*

Captain Skelly of the National Army killed (KIA) in Boyle *2 July*

Surrender of all Republican forces in Dublin 2 July 1922

Attack on Wine Street Barracks in Sligo *6 July*

Sgt. Frank Balfe of the Free State Army, KIA at Ballytrasna, Boyle *8 July*

Thomas Sheehan died from wounds suffered in combat Sligo *9 July*

Anti-Treatyites abandoned RIC Barracks in Tuam *early July*

Four killed at Collooney (Dooney Rock), Co. Sligo *13 July*

   Patrick O'Callaghan (Pro-Treaty officer)

   John Sweeney

   Sean Adair

   John Farrell (close associate of Sean MacEoin from their Longford days)

Battle at Ballymote, Co. Sligo *12 July*

Republicans attack Sligo town *14 July*

Ox Mountains sweep by National Army *14 July*

Pro-Treaty troops attack Collooney *15 July*

Anti-Treaty troops take over Tuam Barracks *15 July*

Surrender of Republicans at Collooney including Frank O'Beirne, O/C of Collooney Battalion, *15 July*

Pro-Treaty troops fan out from Galway City *17 July*

< Pro-Treaty troops enter Castlerea *20 July*

Attack at Clonalis House, Castlerea *21 July*

Government troops and material land at Westport *24 July*

Attacks occur on Free State forces at Castlerea and Ballinlough *week of 24 July*

Attack on Riverstown Barracks, Co. Sligo by Arigna Column *July 1922*

Three-week siege of Castlerea by Anti-Treaty forces ends. Sixty Anti-Treaty (AT) men arrested *25 July*

Free State troops march into Tuam and take over Workhouse *25 July*

Castlebar occupied by government troops *25 July*

Anti-Treaty siege of Ballaghaderreen lifted at 6 p.m. *26 July*

Edward Hegarty, Vice Brigadier of West Mayo Brigade, and brother of Patrick Hegarty, leader of the North Mayo Brigade, KIA *27 July*

National troops dislodge Republicans at Ballinagare *28 July*

Ballina occupied by government troops *28 July*

Rail lines between Manorhamilton and Dromahair torn up *28 July*

Dromore West Police Barracks abandoned by AT. They hold Workhouse as their HQ *28 July*

Battle at Balla, Co. Mayo. Machine gun fire heard for an hour. Some AT wounded *29 July*

Anti-Treaty men damage railway bridge at Castlerea *29 July*

Railway bridge at Ballymoe blown up *31 July*

Republicans offer resistance in Castlebar. Gaol and barracks burned. Post Office saved through the efforts of local people *31 July*

Train service to Ballina resumed after thirty-day suspension. Anti-Treaty men resist at Crossmolina. 1 National soldier killed *2 August*

Attack on Swinford Barracks by North Roscommon Flying Column. Joseph Traynor KIA *4 August*

Firefight at Killasser, Co. Mayo *5-6 August*

Temporary truce in No. 2 Brigade area, 3rd Western Division *6 August*

Column under Harold McBrien raids train at Glenfarne, Co. Sligo *7 August*

Raid by Republicans on Tuam *8 August*

Drumraney Column ambushes National troops at Tang, Co. Westmeath. Four Republicans arrested *8 August*

Two members of Ballyfarnon Column killed in skirmish with National troops *8 August*

Longford Barracks attacked *9 August*

National troops attacked in Granard and Drumlish *9 August*

James Pilkington, brother of Liam, arrested in Galway *10 August*

Thirty Anti-Treaty men arrested near Kiltimagh, Co. Mayo including Henry Deignan, — Fitzpatrick, and James Groarke *11 August*

Ambush near Ballina. Lewis gun rakes field where Anti-Treaty men had thrown themselves down. Five prisoners taken *11 August*

Fifty Sligo Anti-Treatyites enter Charlestown and commandeer Murphy's lorry *11 August*

Three ex-British Army men arrested for fighting with the Arigna Column *11 August*

Anti-Treaty soldiers raid O'Hara's at Cootehall *12 August*

PHOTO COURTESY OF IRISH HISTORICAL PICTURE COMPANY

< *Michael Collins lead Free State officers at funeral of Arthur Griffith 12 August 1922*

Crossna Column attempts to blow up Boyle Railway Bridge and sets up ambush at Crossna Chapel *13 August*

Cootehall and Knockvicar bridges partially destroyed *14 August*

Castlebar taken over by Anti-Treatyites. Object: allow (AT) members of the County Council to attend quarterly meeting and take possession of County Council funds (£70,000) *16 August*

Drumkeerin Barracks, Co. Leitrim attacked *17 August*

Train robbed at Kiltoom. Supplies loaded onto boats *18 August*

Special effort made to arrest Liam Forde of Lisacul who was supposed to meet engineers sent from Belfast at the train station *18 August*

Anti-Treatyites try to capture Roscommon town barracks and protection post at the old gaol. (They did not succeed) *21 August*

Ballinameen Anti-Treaty men reinforced by twenty men from Mayo *21 August*

North Roscommon men steal petrol from Carrick-on-Shannon Station *21 August*

Rail line from Foxford and Ballina Station torn up *22 August*

Michael Collins killed in ambush in Béal na mBláth 22 August 1922

Thirty Anti-Treaty men from Arigna Column captured at Arigna — also field hospital and four nurses *22 August*

Bomb attack at Custume Barracks *23 August*

Raid on Drumsna Barracks by North Roscommon men. Eleven National soldiers surrender *24 August*

Tom Carney, O/C of East Mayo Column, Joe O'Kelly of Ballaghaderreen, Edward Mullen, and Brigade Chemist Michael Larkin captured by National troops under Alec McCabe *25 August*

Ambush at Glasson near Athlone *25 August*

Attack around Tubbercurry. National Flying Column decoyed by priest working for Frank Carty *26 August*

Attack on Boyle patrol and outposts on the Boyle Railway Bridge *26 August*

Republicans ambush Ford car with National officer and five men between Boyle and Cootehall *26 August*

Lanesboro Barracks occupied by Anti-Treatyites *27 August*

Shops in Frenchpark raided by Anti-Treatyites *28 August*

Fifteen Anti-Treatyites captured in house between Claremorris and Balla. (12 rifles, 4 Mausers, and a Thompson sub-machine gun also confiscated) *28 August*

Martin and Lynn in Ballyfarnon raided by Anti-Treatyites *31 August*

Frank Carty's Column in Sligo attempts capture of Tubbercurry Barracks — *early September*

Sligo Champion office raided *1 September*

T. Lally, leader of Anti-Treaty men in Tourmakeady, Co. Mayo, captured *2 September*

Castlebar attacked by Anti-Treatyites. Bombs and machine gun fire crack through the air *2 September*

Frank Neary, KIA, Swinford Barracks, Co. Mayo *2 September*

Republicans attempt to burn Lanesboro Barracks. They did not succeed *3 September*

John Spellman, Intelligence Officer in Ballaghaderreen, arrested at Boyle Station *4 September*

Dromahair Barracks handed over to Republicans. (Free State troops not being paid) *4 September*

Monday morning gaol breaks: Frank O'Beirne of Sligo and Dominick Benson escape from Athlone. Tom Scanlon of Sligo escapes from Longford Barracks, and Vice O/C of the Sligo Brigade, Harry Brehony, finds his way to freedom *4 September*

National troops raid Saints Island in Lough Ree (Anti-Treaty men had already evacuated) *5 September*

Anti-Treaty men invade Tuam *5 September*

Ballina Castle burned to the ground. £100,000 damage. (Also Massbrook House, Crossmolina burned the same morning) *5 September*

Republicans attack Free State troops near Kinnegad, County Westmeath. (One Anti-Treatyite wounded, three captured) *5 September*

Republicans surrounded at Derrycarne House, Ruskey. No arrests on land, but three Anti-Treatyites captured trying to swim across the Shannon *6 September*

Attack on Free State outpost near Boyle *6 September*

C. Falley, Ballyhaunis, Co. Mayo, KIA *6 September*

Attack on Drumshanbo Barracks in Co. Leitrim by Arigna Column led by Seamus Cull. Joseph Dolan, Pro-Treaty soldier, KIA *6 September*

Anti-Treaty attack twenty-five National troopers near Kilkelly, Co. Mayo *6 September*

Main road between Roscommon town and Ballygar blocked by felled trees. Telegraph poles cut down *7 September*

Attempted ambush at Ballinalee, Co. Longford *7 September*

Republican (Anti-Treaty) raid on Dromahair Barracks Co. Leitrim. (Twenty-five rifles, 3000 rounds of ammunition and one Lewis gun taken) *8 September*

William Cosgrave elected Free State Government President 9 September 1922

Manorhamilton garrison attacked *9 September*

National Army ambushed near Tuam. Volunteer Walsh killed, Cooney wounded *9 September*

Free State troops in Boyle threaten to "ground arms" if not paid *week of 9 September*

Raid on Lackan (near Strokestown) Post Office *9 September*

Successful raid on Ballina by Anti-Treatyites *12 September*

Athlone Brigade QM Pat Macken and John Shortle captured *12 September*

Three Anti-Treatyites captured at Murtagh's Post Office in Tang (Arrested: David Tierney (Moate), Peter Sherton (Dublin), and Patrick Boyle (Baileboro, Co. Cavan) *12 September*

Attack at Ballymote, Co. Sligo. John Durkan KIA *13 September*

< Free State troops from Roscommon and Castlerea converged on eight Anti-Treaty men firing from Finan house in Lisalway, Castlerea (pictured above). No injuries, no arrests *13 September*

Republican Court scheduled to meet on the 15th at Johnston's Bridge Creamery, Dromod. Notice obtained by National troops on *13 September*

Free State Brigadier Joe Ring of Mayo KIA at Bonnyconlan *14 September*

Forty Anti-Treatyites rushed guards outside Drumshanbo Barracks. Captured equipment: 16 Lee Enfield with 1000 rounds of ammunition, 10 single barrel shotguns, 53 fuse bombs, and 11 Mills bombs *14 September*

Party of fifty Anti-Treatyites (Republicans) moved in groups of 3s and 4s on road one mile Longford side of Glasson. Assumed the men had come from Quaker Island *15 September*

Another attack near railway bridge in Boyle *16 September*

Four Free State troopers leave Boyle headed for Cootehall. On return trip they are ambushed by a dozen or so Anti-Treaty men one and half miles from Cootehall *16 September*

Attack at Castlebar Gaol *17 September*

Two Anti-Treatyites captured midway between Athlone and Kiltoom *17 September*

Village of Dysart raided by Anti-Treaty men *18 September*

1922 *continued*

Ned Bofin's Column frequents the district between Geevagh and Highwood in County Sligo *week of 18 September*

In county Sligo there is a movement of troops towards Glencar Mountains. Around Ballintrillick sniping continues. General MacEoin gets words that the armoured car *Ballinalee* (which is in Republican hands) is taking a horseshoe-shaped road along Benbulben Mountain. He sends in troops. The Anti-Treatyites abandon the armoured car and head up across the mountain. They never get to the other side. The clash was known as the attack at Ballintrillick/Glencar *20 September*

> Joe Banks KIA
> Henry Benson KIA
> Peter Burns KIA
> Todd Burns KIA
> Brigadier Seamus Devins KIA
> Thomas Langan KIA
> Brian MacNeill KIA
> Patrick O'Carroll KIA

300-400 Anti-Treaty troops attack Tuam *20 September*

Three Anti-Treaty men taken prisoner at Kiltyclogher, ten at Manorhamilton, and eight to ten at Cliffoney, Co. Sligo *20 September*

Raid on Anti-Treaty headquarters at O'Rahilly House in Sligo results in quick abandonment by IRA *20 September*

Republicans raid banks in Ballina, County Mayo. £25,000 taken *around 18 September*

National Army sentries on bridge at Carrick-on-Shannon fired on *21 September*

Signal box burned at Drumsna *21 September*

Anti-Treatyite John Lohan KIA in Killeen, Co. Galway *22 September*

National troops raid Kiltoom area — capture six Anti-Treaty men who had been sniping at the Athlone Barracks *23 September*

Another attack on Swinford Barracks *27 September*

Newtowncashel, Co. Longford mail car held up *28 September*

Raid by Anti-Treatyites on Tuam — commandeered goods *30 September*

Two new Brigade dugouts made near Boyle *early October*

Sniping all around Ballaghaderreen by a hundred local men and those from Swinford and Belfast. One National soldier wounded *2 October*

Attack on Mohill Barracks *3 October*

Party led by Free State Comdt. Lavin ambushed several times on route to Arigna *3 October*

Five Anti-Treatyites raid the residence of Merrick Lloyd of Croghan *3 October*

Large railway bridge across the Shannon at Drumsna damaged—seriously hampering traffic between Dublin and Sligo *4 October*

Fifteen Anti-Treaty men captured in Ballinasloe area *4 October*

Surprise raid by Republicans on Tuam *7 October*

Wires cut — small body of Anti-Treaty men seen around Kilteevan *7 October*

Engagement with military at Ballinross, Castlerea *October*

Sniping at Strokestown Barracks *October*

National trooper on sentry duty wounded in Boyle *7 October*

Geoghegan Barracks in Castletown, Co. Westmeath burned. Telegraph wires cut *9 October*

Army Powers Act passed in Dublin giving tribunals power to execute anyone arrested carrying arms or ammunition 10 October 1922

National soldier John Murray KIA in Athlone *10 October*

Peter Breslin (of Elphin) killed in Mountjoy Gaol in attempt to escape *10 October*

Members of East Mayo Column captured. Seamus Mulrennan, brother of Patrick, KIA *14 October*

Thomas Maguire.

Tom Maguire, O/C of the 2nd Western Division IRA, captured in Headford along with General Powell of Mayo and sixteen other Anti-Treaty men *mid-October*

Harassing attack on Boyle Barracks *14 October*

Government troops under Capt. Garrahan raid Incheneagh Island in the Shannon. Capture prisoners, arms and explosives *19 October*

Fifty men from the Arigna Column barricade streets in Drumshanbo *20 October*

Catholic hierarchy Pastoral Letter orders excommunication for Anti-Treatyites October 22 1922

Train on the Great Southern & Western Railway (GS&WR) held up at milepost 73. All mail bags and eight stone bags of flour taken *22 October*

Ned Bofin and his men seen in Keadue *24 October*

National troops see "suspicious men" laying mine at Lung Bridge near Ballaghaderreen *25 October*

Joe Kelly, who escaped from Sligo Gaol the previous week, seen in Ballaghaderreen. He was named the new O/C of the Flying Column *25 October*

IRA Column spotted in Elphin. Mick McLoughlin O/C of this group of twelve *25 October*

Lieut. Donnelly of Boyle garrison held up and robbed of his revolver and Sam Browne belt *25 October*

Patrol from Dowra Barracks ambushed *26 October*

Rail line between Castlebar and Westport occupied by strong Anti-Treaty force *27 October*

Attack on carload of Free State officers on Ardcarne/Boyle Road *28 October*

Ballyforan sub office raided *28 October*

Burning of signal cabin at Carrick-on-Shannon *November*

Patrick Mulrennan of Lisacul killed while a prisoner at Athlone *6 October or 3 November* (see Roscommon Volunteer listing for clarification page 393)

Road from Boyle to Carrick-on-Shannon blocked *3 November*

Dromahair Barracks, Co. Leitrim attacked by Arigna Column *Early November*

First group of Gardaí arrive in Tuam *4 November*

Two suspected Free State spies shot in Tubbercurry, Sligo *5 November*

Raid on Kiltoom (three Anti-Treaty men captured) *week of 5 November*

Ambush at Ferbane, Co. Offaly. One National trooper killed *week of 5 November*

Raid on Curraghboy *week of 5 November*

Attack on Mohill Barracks, Co. Leitrim *6 November*

Three National soldiers at Ballinameen held up and robbed of their great coats. There were no prisoners, no one killed *7 November*

Thirteen Anti-Treaty men stage an attack in Strokestown *7 November*

Twenty to twenty-five Republicans from Frank Carty's Column raid principal businesses in Charlestown *7 November*

Anti-Treaty men take two Ford motor cars and loot goods from shops in Strokestown. Free State troops enter the town attempting to capture these men who also had held up Capt. Murphy and taken his revolver. No arrests were made *9 November*

Sligo printing works of the newspaper *Connachtman* raided. "Seditious material" captured *week of 9 November*

Anti-Treaty men near Collooney, Co. Sligo tear up rails on the GS&WR lines *week of 9 November*

Post office at Drumkeerin robbed. £47 taken *9 November*

Forty-six prisoners escape from Longford Barracks *9 November*

National patrol lay in ambush near rail line at Newtownforbes. They capture six escaped prisoners from Longford Barracks *9 November*

Heavy trenching of roads between Boyle and Carrick-on-Shannon *10 November*

Forty National soldiers battle with thirty Anti-Treaty men at Jamestown, Co. Leitrim. Six Republicans captured *11 November*

17 AT captured at Claremorris *11 November*

Bridge between Kiltoom and Knockcroghery mined. Trains held up and goods taken *11 November*

Boyle Bridge piquet held up, disarmed, and taken away *12 November*

Christopher "Kit" McKeown, leader of small Flying Column, killed in action in Moate *12 November*

Anti-Treatyites in position around Dowra. Strength unknown *13 November*

Heavy sniping at Mohill Barracks — Anti-Treaty Column estimated to be fifty strong *14 November*

Charlestown Hibernian Bank set afire by Republicans *14 November*

Attempt to capture bridge at Boyle. Republicans dress in Free State uniforms and approach in bare feet *14 November*

Four East Mayo Anti-Treaty men captured at Markree Castle, Co. Sligo. (Two of them had escaped from Sligo Gaol — Joe O'Kelly from Ballaghaderreen and William McDonagh) *14 November*

Raid by Republicans near Quaker Island. £200 worth of goods stolen *15 November*

Attack on guard at Boyle Railway Bridge *16 November*

Anti-Treatyites enter Ruskey — loot shops, cut wires along the line near Kilfree *16 November*

Ballinamore Barracks attacked. Raiders take uniforms, hand cuffs, batons, whistles, and clothes *16 November*

Party of Anti-Treaty men seen in Drumshanbo *16 November*

Fight at Shannonbridge lasts thirty minutes. Thompson sub-machine gun and rifles used by Anti-Treaty men. One National soldier killed *16 November*

Free State Government begins policy of "official executions". Seventy-seven carried out over the following six months 17 November 1922

Anti-Treaty men near Manorhamilton hold up train and take goods valued at £10-15. Block roads and blow up bridges within a radius of five miles of the barracks. Two National soldiers wounded *17 November*

Party of six Republicans call at Civic Guard station at Loughglynn and give policemen twenty-four hours to clear out *17 November*

1922 *continued*

Anti-Treaty Columns (60-90 strong) blocking roads, sniping, cutting wires in Ballinameen, Cootehall, Kilmore and Boyle area *17 November*

Party of armed men seen travelling to Shrule, Co. Mayo to operate with South Roscommon Column already positioned there *17 November*

Burning of the train at Clooncundra, Castlerea *November*

Roundup of Republicans near Headford *18 November*

Free State troops ambushed on way to Galway from Tuam *18 November*

Anti-Treatyites seize fifty gallons of petrol at Ballaghaderreen from lorry hired by the Anglo-American Oil Company *18 November*

Fifty armed Anti-Treatyites seen at Quaker Island *20 November*

Republican Column in position between Drumshanbo and Dowra — strength unknown *20 November*

Bridge at Cootehall in disrepair. Road to Ballinameen blocked *21 November*

Commanders of 2nd, 3rd, and 4th Western Divisions IRA meet to discuss war plans *22 November*

Fifty Republicans assemble near Boyle — object: obtain arms for Bofin's Column *22 November*

Raid for supplies by Republicans at Tuam *22 November*

National troops raid Incheneagh and Quaker Islands. Matt Davis, O/C of the South Roscommon Flying Column, arrested along with Thomas Walshe *22 November*

Anti-Treaty men raid houses in Ballinamore, Co. Leitrim and take away goods in commandeered lorry *23 November*

Road between Roscommon town and Donamon blocked for days. Patrol sent out to "see it doesn't happen again" *24 November*

Michael Kilroy, O/C of the 4th Western Division, captured by government forces near Claremorris. Vice O/C Michael Walshe and others wounded or killed. *24 November*

Post office at Cootehall robbed of £15 *24 November*

Free State troopers repair Ballybay Bridge. Repairs on Ballyforan Bridge nearly completed *25 November*

Anti-Treaty men rob boat near Quaker Island *25 November*

Signal cabins at Donamon and Knock burned as of *27 November*

Ballybay Bridge blown up again. Road between Kilteevan and Knockcroghery broken *27 November*

Vacated Dromod Barracks burned by Anti-Treaty men a few days before *28 November*

Sixty Anti-Treaty men pass between Cloone and Mohill on their way to an attack on Mohill Barracks *30 November*

Anti-Treatyites attack patrol at Castlerea. Three (AT) prisoners taken *30 November*

Three-hour gun battle near Ballintubber. AT Tommy Neary severely wounded *2 December*

North Roscommon Flying Column again cut telegraphic communication between Dublin, Sligo, and Ballymote *2 December*

Fitzgerald's of Connaught St., Athlone raided by National troops who found a Sam Browne belt, three packages of field dressing, field glasses, and an electric torch *2 December*

Capture of Free State officers in Strokestown *December*

John Moyles, Ballyhaunis, Co. Mayo, KIA *5 December*

Republicans capture column of National troops at Drumshanbo *5 December*

Shannonbridge post attacked. Half hour gun battle. No casualties *5 December*

Attack on Castlerea by Republican forces *5 December*

Wires cut between Boyle/Kilfree *5 December*

Dennison House in Dowra, Co. Cavan raided by masked men. The son was shot, father wounded *5 December*

Republicans fell trees near Cloonfad *5 December*

Anthony McCormack, O/C of Tang Coy. in Westmeath, found in chimney of Hoares public house in Ballymore, Co. Westmeath. A gunshot wound in his leg was deemed serious *5 December*

Rail line repaired at Ballyhaunis *5 December*

Attack on patrol of eight National soldiers in Ballymore, Co. Westmeath *5 December*

Twenty-two National troops looking for Brian Mulvihill of Westmeath raid Kiltoom. In Strevens house, they find doctor's bag, ammo, field dressings, and notebook containing names of the leaders of Cumann na mBan in Co. Mayo *5 December*

Ballymote/Sligo lines cut between Boyle and Kilfree — twelve spars of wire broken *6 December*

Two advance cars of National troops fired on in Drumshanbo *6 December*

Mail train at Ballaghaderreen raided — second time this week *6 December*

Two Republican prisoners taken at Strokestown *6 December*

Attack on Free State courier at Castlerea *7 December*

Anti-Treaty men commandeer a car at Arigna to take them to Drumshanbo *7 December*

Republican forces attack Free State troopers at Lakeview, Kilglass, Strokestown. One Free State officer wounded *8 December*

Mountjoy Foursome (Rory O'Connor, Joe McKelvey, Liam Mellows and Dick Barrett) hanged 8 December 1922

Post office sub station at Leitrim raided *8 December*

Anti-Treatyites active around Drumshanbo *9 December*

National troops fired on while investigating a reported take-over of Boyle Town Hall. Anti-Treatyites positioned at the post office and passages leading to the town hall. Sgt. Skeffington shot *9 December*

Signal boxes at Carrick-on-Shannon, Dromod, and Drumsna destroyed *10 December*

Tang Bridge on the Athlone Road blown up *12 December*

Two boatloads of Anti-Treaty men from Arigna land at Faughey Point *12 December*

Boat raided near Quaker Island — porter and JAM! taken *12 December*

Thirty AT hold up train at Streamstown and ride to Castletown Station where they raided for goods and robbed the station master's office *12 December*

Anti-Treaty men patrol the streets of Ballaghaderreen on Fair and Market days *early December*

Frank O'Donoghue of Northyard, Kilglass, Strokestown, Vice O/C of the 3rd Battalion North Roscommon Flying Column, dies of wounds received at Ruskey *13 December*

Frank Carty's men hold up train between Kilfree and Ballymote. Engine unhooked and let run into Sligo town. Four National troopers disarmed *14 December*

Party of Republicans operating between Strokestown and Elphin. Strokestown Courthouse burned *14 December*

Post office at Drumsna raided *14 December*

Another raid on Quaker Island — one barrel of porter, one Firkin consigned to Carrick-on-Shannon taken *14 December*

Ned Bofin and his Column at Ballyfarnon Fair — regulating traffic! *14 December*

Column of 150 Anti-Treaty men spotted at Grange, Fourmilehouse *15 December*

Attack on Castlerea Barracks led by T. Maloney and — Burke of Mayo. Burke later died from wounds received *15 December*

Tullywood House, Tullymagawley and Glynwood House captured by National troops. Rifle, two revolvers, flashlamp, field dressings, boots and trenchcoats confiscated *15 December*

Ballinacaragy village in Longford raided by members of the Athlone Brigade *16 December*

Mail car from Leitrim to Ballyfarnon raided *16 December*

Bridges between mileposts 73-76 blown up. Kilgarvan Bridge still passable, but Fawcett Bridge

between Moate and Athlone badly damaged *16 December*

Raid by FS forces on Quaker Island. Box of jam and a barrel of porter recovered *week of 18 December*

Bridge wrecked between Ballinamuck and Drumlish, Co. Longford *week of 18 December*

Group of Anti-Treaty men (sixty strong) concentrated around Ballinameen, Cootehall, and Kilmore. AT leaders — Casey, — Duffy, and Patrick Dunleavy (O/C of the North Galway Brigade) present at Kilmore *19 December*

Small number of Mayo Anti-Treaty men raid Charlestown Post Office and several shops *19 December*

Mail car from Leitrim to Ballyfarnon raided AGAIN *19 December*

Mail car between Carrick-on-Shannon and Drumshanbo held up and not allowed to proceed to Dowra, Co. Cavan *20 December*

Drumshanbo Post Office raided — £3 taken *20 December*

Lanesboro Barracks attacked by ten men *21 December*

Post office at Gurteen, Co. Sligo raided — stamps taken *21 December*

Thomas Hughes of Bogganfin, Athlone captured in Lisdonagh House (about two miles south of Shrule, Co. Mayo) *21 December*

Anti-Treatyite Edward Kilroy killed in action at Charlestown, Co. Mayo *23 December*

Sixteen prisoners, including Con Fogarty, O/C of the North Galway Brigade during the War for Independence, escape from prison *26 December*

Carrick-on-Shannon and Drumsna signal boxes destroyed again *27 December*

Dowra garrison (Co. Cavan) overwhelmed and disarmed by thirty members of the Arigna Column led by Seamus Cull and Ned Bofin — greatcoats, tunics, caps, leggings and boots taken *28 December*

Attack on Collooney Barracks and Markree Castle in Sligo *end of December*

Train held up at Knockcroghery. Engine detached and sent ahead without driver *30 December*

Free State troopers capture seven Republicans at Queally's public house near Caherlistrane, Galway *30 December*

1923

Three prisoners escape from Pump Square in Athlone *3 January*

National troops raid Ballaghaderreen. Tom Flannery shot for sheltering AT men *3 January*

Raid on the mail and post office in Boyle *4 January*

Bye roads between Roscommon town and Ballygar blocked and small bridge blown up *4 January*

Signal boxes at Dromod and Drumsna blown up
4 January

Attack on Free State forces at Ruskey *January*

Bridge at milepost 73 between Athlone and Moate blown up a second time *4 January*

Anti-Treatyite Michael Cull of Arigna killed in Ballyconnell, Co. Cavan *6 January*

Michael McManus (Pro-Treaty soldier) killed at Dowra Barracks *6 January*

Boat raided near Quaker Island - kilns, porter, and bags of flour taken by armed men *6 January*

Martin Bourke (Burke), O/C of Flying Column in Galway, captured in Castlerea in possession of a revolver and ammo *8 January*

Raid on Banaglara district, three miles from Dowra, Co. Cavan *8 January*

One Republican arrested in Castlerea attempting to procure arms from a National trooper *8 January*

Sligo Railway Station burned to the ground by Republicans *11 January*

Main road from Carrick-on-Shannon to Drumshanbo blocked midway between Leitrim and Drumshanbo *11 January*

Four Anti-Treatyites (J. Healy, James Padian, Richard Hayden, John Farrell) arrested in Strokestown *11 January*

Wires cut between Castlerea and Frenchpark *11 January*

Mine placed under railway line at Knockcroghery. It was removed by National troops *12 January*

Civic Guard Station at Boyle burned *13 January*

Poles and wires cut in Kilkelly, Co. Mayo *13 January*

Roads blocked and bridges damaged in Swinford area of Co. Mayo *13 January*

Ballybay Bridge blown at 1:20 a.m. *13 January*

Signal boxes at Carrick-on-Shannon and Drumsna destroyed *14 January*

Bridges at Jamestown, Drumsna, and Galley blown up *14 January*

Trees felled across road at Larkfield near Athlone *15 January*

Signal boxes burned in Swinford, Kiltimagh, Ballinlough, Ballymoe, Donamon, and Knockcroghery *18 January*

Burning of Elphin Garda Barracks *20 January*

Official Executions in Athlone *20 January*

    Martin Bourke from Caherlistrane, Co. Galway

    Thomas Hughes from Bogganfin, Athlone

    Stephen Joyce from Derrymore, Caherlistrane, Co. Galway

    Michael Walsh from Derrymore, Caherlistrane, Co. Galway

    Hubert Collins from Kilkeel Headford, Co. Galway

Thomas Hannelly died from wounds in Ballaghaderreen *21 January*

100 yards of cable cut from local telephone circuit at Athlone *21 January*

Civic Guard removed from Elphin because the barracks had been burned *21 January*

Bridges at Jamestown, Galley, and Drumsna again mined *21 January*

Kiltoom bridge blown up. Tracks torn up, train derailed. Ammo and provisions taken to Incheneagh *22 January*

Mile cabin 73 at Fossa in Co. Westmeath burned *22 January*

Trees felled at Kilkenny West, Co. Westmeath. Auburn, Arnagraph and Walderstown too! *22 January*

Rogers' shop in Knockcroghery looted by seven Anti-Treatyites *23 January*

Pedestrians held up and searched by AT men in Drumshanbo *24 January*

Mohill Barracks attacked from three positions *24 January*

Another attack on Dowra Barracks by Arigna Column *25 January*

Colm Kelly, champion footballer who formerly lived in Castlerea, executed by order of military court in Birr, Co. Offaly *26 January*

Thomas Martin of The Hill of Berries escapes from Athlone *27 January*

Five Anti-Treaty men arrested between Boyle and Ballaghaderreen *28 January*

David Daly, O/C of 1st Battalion, Athlone Brigade, arrested in Moate *30 January*

James Farrell of Ballaghaderreen arrested at Castlemore by Capt. Lavin *30 January*

Arigna Column attacks Ballinamore Barracks in Leitrim *31 January*

Four prisoners escape from Boyle *1 February*

Cox's house in Cootehall raided by Free State troops; no Anti-Treatyites captured *2 February*

Post offices in Kilrooskey, Knockcroghery, and Lecarrow raided. Old age pension money carried off *2 February*

Five Anti-Treaty men captured by cycling patrol from Boyle: Frank Barlow, Jim Moran, John Doyle, Thomas Treacy, and Peter McGearty *3 February*

Anti-Treatyite James McGuinn KIA Co. Sligo *4 February*

Boats raided near Quaker Island — biscuits, fruit taken *5 February*

Carrick-on-Shannon and Drumkeerin mail car held up at Drumshanbo. Mail bag for Dowra opened and some correspondence taken *5 February*

Waterworks at Athlone blown. Building destroyed, but water power and supply to town only slightly interfered with *7 February*

Ballinamore Catholic Hall in Co. Leitrim destroyed by armed men *7 February*

National troops were attacked at Ballygar by twenty Anti-Treatyites *7 February*

Twenty-seven Anti-Treatyites surrender at Moate *8 February*

Kiltoom signal cabin burned. Roads in Kiltoom, Bealnamullia, and Lecarrow blocked *8 February*

Francis Fitzpatrick, who formerly held rank of Captain in Custume Barracks, arrested *10 February*

Three Anti-Treaty men raid the home of Michael Ward (in Moate area) whose son is a Lieutenant in the National Army *10 February*

Discharged National soldier, John Loftus, arrested for abetting the Republicans in Athlone *12 February*

Mail car from Carrick-on-Shannon to Drumkeerin held up at Leitrim *12 February*

Free State dispatch rider, Volunteer Fitzpatrick, captured at Woodlawn (between Boyle and Carrick-on-Shannon) *13 February*

Roads at Ruskey blocked *13 February*

Boats near Quaker Island raided — seven flour bags taken *14 February*

Five bridges in Longford/Westmeath blown up *14 February*

Government troops sweep through Arigna area. One National soldier dies of his wounds *15 February*

North Roscommon Flying Column attacks National troops on Boyle/Carrick-on-Shannon Road *16 February*

Harry Brehony, Vice O/C of Sligo Brigade, recent escapee from prison (Sept. 1922) KIA *16 February*

Attack on Free State troops in Castlerea *February*

Neutral IRA led by Sean O'Hegarty of Cork and others meet in Dublin and appeal for truce. Published in newspapers *17 February 1923*

Granard Civic Guard Barracks burned *17 February*

Elphin Civic Guard Barracks raided. Occupants warned to "clear out" *19 February*

Outposts at Drumsna attacked at 10 p.m. *19 February*

Eighteen Republicans captured at Cluid in Co. Galway. Six would be executed at Tuam two months later *19 February*

Roscommon/Athlone Road blocked three miles from Athlone *21 February*

Monksland Railway cabin and adjoining lamp room burned to the ground *21 February*

Lt. Swan, the paymaster, fired on between Elphin and Boyle. No injuries *22 February*

Michael O'Connell, Capt. of the Taughmaconnell Coy., arrested — supposedly in possession of seditious material *23 February*

Cornafulla Post Office raided — money valued at £5-6 and about £6 stamps taken *25 February*

Thomastown Post Office, Athlone raided *25 February*

Seamus Cull and Patrick Tymon killed in government swoop in Arigna *27 February*

Train held up and engine detached at Thomastown, Athlone at 5:15 p. m. *27 February*

Michael Mulvey, believed to be the Brigade Engineer for No. 3 Offaly, arrested at Thomastown, Athlone *27 February*

Carrick-on-Shannon Station looted — eight bags of flour, one bag of sugar, and a bag of tea missing *28 February*

National soldier — Todd accidentally wounded at Glasson. He was removed to Athlone Hospital *1 March*

Attack at Lake Forbes (just south of Ruskey) *March*

Passenger train stopped at Kiltoom — all passengers ordered off *1 March*

Thirteen Anti-Treaty men captured by National soldiers from Tuam *3 March*

Boat near Quaker Island raided *4 March*

Two Anti-Treatyites arrested in Ruskey. (One was Thomas Shanley, the O/C of the 5th Battalion North) who lived in Dromod *5 March*

Guard at Carrick-on-Shannon Station attacked at 3:45 a.m. *6 March*

National troops at Strokestown attacked at 1:30 a.m. *6 March*

Croghan Post Office raided *6 March*

Shots fired at Ballaghaderreen Barracks. After fifteen minutes, attackers withdraw *6 March*

National troops raid Three Jolly Pigeons public house on road to Ballymahon in Co. Longford. Free State soldier William Newcomber killed in ensuing firefight *6 March*

Pat Mullooly and twelve other National soldiers who were patrolling the road between Ballaghaderreen and Frenchpark arrested a man thought to have taken part in a recent robbery in Frenchpark *7 March*

Frank O'Connor, O/C of the 1st Battalion Athlone Brigade, captured *7 March*

Luke Duffy, former Vice O/C of the 3rd Battalion South Roscommon, out on cycling patrol with several other soldiers attempted to arrest Anti-Treaty men at Cootehall. The Republicans got away *9 March*

Seven Republicans arrested in Ruskey as a result of two different fights *9 March*

Fifteen Anti-Treatyites snipe at Carrick-on-Shannon Barracks *10 March*

Three Anti-Treaty men arrested between Lisacul and Ballaghaderreen — Francis Tolan, Patrick Corcoran, and Michael Fitzgerald *11 March*

National troops from Longford enter Ruskey and find Civic Guard Barracks under attack. A firefight ensues *12 March*

Athleague Post Office raided *13 March*

Martin McGuinn and Patrick Stenson (both Anti-Treaty men) KIA at Curry, Co. Sligo *13 March*

May Donellan, employee at Ballinameen Post Office, arrested for abetting the Republicans *13 March*

Carrick-on-Shannon Barracks attacked by forty Republicans armed with rifles and Thompson gun *13 March*

House of Free State Commandant Mitchell burned at Mohill *14 March*

Road between Carrick-on-Shannon and Leitrim village blocked *14 March*

Road between Castlerea and Fairymount blocked and wires cut *14 March*

Two Anti-Treaty men captured — Thomas Roddy of Lisacul and E. Colligan of Belfast (a Lewis gunner in Frank Carty's Column) *15 March*

Engineers from Athlone Barracks dismantle a mine found on the railway bridge two miles from Ballinasloe *15 March*

Captain Lavin and fifteen National troopers raid Cootehall, Crossna, and Keadue. They arrest two Republicans *15 March*

Two deserters from Beggar's Bush Barracks in Dublin arrested in Ballaghaderreen *15 March*

Attack on National troopers operating in Mount Temple/Moate area. One Republican and a civilian were killed *16 March*

Boat raided at Quaker Island. Two half barrels of porter taken *16 March*

Postman in Ballinameen held up *16 March*

Castlerea Barracks sniped at for thirty minutes *18 March*

Carrick-on-Shannon Railway Station sniped at *19 March*

Mail car between Boyle/Cootehall held up by seven Anti-Treatyites. All mail seized *20 March*

Bridget Donellan, employee of Croghan Post Office, arrested *21 March*

Commanding Officers of the Irish Republican Army (the Republican Executive) meet in Nire Valley, south of Clonmel, Co. Tipperary to vote on ending the war *23 March 1923*

National troops raid the home of Michael O'Connell in Taughmaconnell *23 March*

Kilgarvan Bridge blown up *23 March*

Republicans raid Dysart Post Office *23 March*

Curraghboy Post Office raided. Receipt given for stolen goods signed "South Roscommon Brigade, I.R.A." *24 March*

Anti-Treatyite Nicholas Corcoran KIA in Tuam *24 March*

Capture of four Arigna men in Riverstown, Co. Sligo including Column leader Ned Bofin *25 March*

Capture of Vice O/C of Athlone Brigade, James Martin, his brother Thomas, Thomas Muldoon, and Thomas Mannion (all of The Hill of Berries) *26 March*

National troops raid Lisacul. No arrests *26 March*

Three arrested in Ballaghaderreen for carrying IRA dispatches *28 March*

Raid on Castleplunkett area. No arrests *29 March*

Two men arrested in Ballaghaderreen for hiding Anti-Treaty men *29 March*

Fr. Ryans, brother of Vincent, helpful curate in the Arigna area, captured at Knockranny House in Keadue *30 March*

National troops raid Drumsna area. No arrests *31 March*

John Nolan and William Mulrooney of Ballygar and Martin Mulligan of Creggs arrested *30 March*

Attempted ambushes on National troops on Boyle/Elphin Road. No conflict resulted because troops did not appear *1st week April*

National troopers search congregation at Leitrim Chapel. No arrests *1 April*

Ballinasloe Railway Bridge attacked at 8:45 p.m. A half-hour gun battle results in one National soldier wounded *2 April*

Village of Leitrim searched by Free State troops *3 April*

Dance at Croghan raided by National soldiers. Nothing found *4 April*

All public houses in Ballintubber searched by National soldiers. Nothing found *4 April*

Multiple raids by National soldiers in the north and west of the county. No arrests were made *5/6/7 April*

Houses in Keadue searched by Free State troops *6 April*

Ballygar and Ballyforan raided. John Naughton and Denis Ennis arrested *7 April*

Pro-Treaty Sinn Féin party re-forms as Cumann na nGaedheal *8 April 1923*

A Sergeant in the National Army and sixteen men patrolling the roads near Kiltoom fired on at 12:15 a.m. *8 April*

IRA attacks Headford, Co. Galway. Dan McCormack (member of the Galway Flying Column) was badly wounded, having a part of both his leg and arm torn away by a bullet. (He died six years later on 15 August 1929 as a result of those wounds) *8 April*

Liam Lynch, Chief of Staff of the Republicans, is killed. Frank Aiken becomes new Chief of Staff 10 April 1923

Three Anti-Treaty men arrested near Drumlish, Co. Longford — (Thomas Christy, P. J. Donoghue, and M. Campbell). They were held in Mohill Barracks awaiting transfer to Longford *11 April*

Unused dugout in Ballintubber discovered *11 April*

Sean Owens of Elphin arrested. (He would, later in life, be very instrumental in helping to erect the Shankill Monument) *11 April*

Official executions in Tuam *11 April*

James O'Malley, Oughterard

Frances Cunnane, Kilcoona, Headford

John Newell, Winefort, Headford

Sean Maguire — Tom Maguire's brother — Cross, Cong

Michael Monaghan, Clooneen, Headford

Martin Moylan, Farmerstown, Annaghdown

Cloone, Leitrim searched. Also small island in Drumkeiltra Lake. Nothing found *13 April*

Pat Spellman of Ballaghaderreen arrested *15 April*

Dance in Castlerea raided *16 April*

Two Anti-Treatyites arrested in Drumraney, Co. Westmeath: Joseph Mallayne and William Cunningham *17 April*

Cease-Fire Order issued by Frank Aiken, Chief of Staff 27 April 1923

Military patrol in Boyle ambushed. Two soldiers wounded *29 April*

Official cease-fire takes effect 30 April 1923

The last official executions (Chris Quinn and William Shaughnessy) take place at Ennis, Co. Clare *2 May*

Post office in Aughacashel, Leitrim raided. Money and stamps valued at £70 taken *10 May*

National troops capture well-known Republican Martin Kyne of Caherlistrane *week of 10 May*

W. E. William's premises raided in Ballyforan *11 May*

Six Republicans escape from Longford Barracks *14 May*

Sniping at National troops on patrol in Ballaghaderreen *15 May*

Two escaped prisoners from the Curragh recaptured near Carrick-on-Shannon *16 May*

Roche home in Ballinameen searched by National troops. Nothing found *16 May*

Loughglynn Post Office raided *17 May*

Dispatch rider from Carrick-on-Shannon fired upon *18 May*

"May" Mannion and James Doyle of the Arigna Column arrested by troops from Ballyfarnon *20 May*

Raid on dance hall at Kilmore, Roscommon. Nine arrested — four released *21 May*

Clonbrook House, Ahascragh raided by Anti-Treatyites *22 May*

Rate collector from Frenchpark robbed *22 May*

Sinn Féin Courts dealt death blow — new system of justice for Ireland will henceforth be modelled on the British system 23 May 1923

— Farrelly arrested at Dromod Railway Station and taken to Boyle *23 May*

Women and children attack the Civic Guards at a shebeen on the road between Kiltoom and Kilmore, Co. Galway *23 May*

Car previously stolen from Commandant Tony Lawlor recovered near Glenamaddy, Co. Galway *24 May*

Dump Arms Order issued by Chief of Staff Frank Aiken 24 May 1923

Post office in Ballymote raided *26 May*

Boat near Quaker Island raided *27 May*

Multiple swoops by government soldiers: Frank Carty's house in Bunninadden, Co. Sligo; dances at Ballinamuck, Lisacul, and Loughglynn; and houses in Glan district *1 June*

National troops watch and wait for signs of Anti-Treaty movement on Quaker Island *6 June*

Sniping at Drumshanbo Barracks *8 June*

Tom Maguire, Commandant of the 2nd Western Division IRA and TD, and five others escape from Athlone prison *10 June*

Public Safety Bill continues detention of 12,000 Republicans 15 June 1923

Fr. Michael O'Flanagan released from prison after being charged with sedition 27 June 1923

Raid on Ballygar Barracks. Uniforms and batons stolen *1 July*

Michael O'Donnell, IRA organiser from Co. Mayo, arrested in Strokestown *9 July*

Sting operation at various crossroads in the county *2-4 August*

Jack Roche and John Kelly, North Roscommon Column members, arrested at 3:30 a.m. at Rathallen crossroads *3 August*

Liam Pilkington, O/C 3rd Western Division IRA, captured *8 August*

"Toby" Mannion shot by National soldiers at The Hill of Berries, Athlone. He died days later at Athlone Military Hospital *14 August*

Three men (two from Liverpool, one from Scotland) arrested in Ballaghaderreen *15 August*

Dugout discovered in Lisacul area *18 August*

Arigna Column members Owen Gilroy and J. McLoughlin arrested in Drumsna *early September*

Francis Mulherin and Thomas Beirne of the Arigna Column captured *4 September*

Government post at Glenamaddy evacuated. Troops re-stationed in Roscommon town *19 September*

Carrick-on-Shannon post evacuated and special infantry take charge there *20 September*

Home of J. Duignan in the Ballyfarnon district raided by National troops. John Duignan arrested *24 September*

Four Republicans escape from Athlone Military Barracks *25 September*

Three Anti-Treaty men arrested in Ballinasloe *25 September*

Michael O'Farrell, brother of Sean who was O/C of the 5th Battalion North, arrested *26 September*

Mick Pender and William Jennings of the Athlone Brigade arrested at a dance at Fallon's house at Cornalee (twelve miles from Athlone) *27 September*

Four men arrested in Athlone (Tom Keogh, — Prendergast, — Mannion, and one other *1 October*

Fifteen Anti-Treatyites arrested in Ballinasloe area *4 October*

Car belonging to Mr. J. Sharpe of Ballinasloe confiscated *13 October*

Kilmore Barracks in Co. Galway raided by Anti-Treaty men *17 October*

Patrick Dolan arrested in Roscommon town in possession of a colt revolver *18 October*

Strokestown Post Office raided *27 October*

Anti-Treatyite John Downes of Ballaghaderreen, who aided Jim Molloy in his escape from Boyle Barracks, arrested *28 October*

Republican Court in Faheran, Moate, Co. Westmeath raided by National troops and Civic Guards from Clara *29 October*

House in Boher near Ballymore in Co. Westmeath raided — gelignite and detonators found *7 November*

Kilrooskey Post Office raided by IRA *8 November*

Courier from Athlone held up at Strokestown. AT take car and gun *8 November*

Government roundups at Kiltoom and Curraghboy. Several Republicans captured *9 November*

Attack by Anti-Treatyites at Moate. One Republican killed *9 November*

Ambush at Ferbane. One National soldier killed *9 November*

Ambush at Glasson. Two National soldiers killed *9 November*

At Mount Temple two Anti-Treaty men captured *9 November*

— Gaffney, J. Higgins, and J. McBreen broke into Michael Geoghegan's house in Aughacashel Co. Leitrim and threatened him. Geoghegan was the clerk for the local courts *10 November*

Frank Carty and five other Anti-Treaty men visit Bunninadden, Co. Sligo and threaten the local postman *13 November*

Thomas McGiff, O/C of the 2nd Battalion Athlone Brigade, captured *17 November*

Col. Frank Simons of the National Army was arrested on the instructions of the General Officer in Command at Athlone. Seems that Simons had ordered a driver and Ford car to report to his office, and when the driver didn't come soon enough, Simons simply took the car himself. Maybe he just wanted to go home for Christmas! *23 December*

1924

The Army Mutiny. Roscommon Barracks robbed *9 March 1924*. When the Civil War ended, the standing Army of Ireland numbered 55,000, a staggering figure for such a small, newly independent nation to support (and control)! Many of these soldiers were given their marching papers, a large percentage being of Republican sentiment. During this Army Mutiny, when the loyalty of soldiers and specific military units was questioned, locals proceeded to lighten the armament load of Roscommon town barracks.

1925

Two Irelands.

In November of 1925 details of the Boundary Commission were leaked to the press. They stated that with few adjustments the boundary was to remain "as is". The governments of Great Britain, Northern Ireland, and the Free State all agreed that the findings of the Commission should be accepted. Violence and blood had spilled on too many roads in Ireland for any popular outpouring of sentiment to seriously challenge the Commission's findings. Why was not the entire province of Ulster included in "northern" Ireland? Why were only six of the nine counties considered for inclusion into the United Kingdom? The answer lies in demographics — political, as well as religious. Only six of the nine were firmly held by Protestant majority. Three of the Ulster counties contained a Catholic majority or a percentage too high to be considered manageable. Thus it is that County Donegal, the northernmost county in Ireland, is part of the Republic of Ireland. And thus it was that the Ireland of ancient times, an island ruled by clansmen, kings, and, later, the English governors, now became officially divided into two separate political entities — one, a nation recently born, the other an appendage of a neighbouring island. ■

THE VOLUNTEERS

'A' COY. 1st BATT. NORTH ROSCOMMON BRIGADE, I.R.A.

BOYLE - March, 1922.

Boyle Company
1st Battalion North Roscommon
Photo taken the day the British vacated Boyle Barracks in March 1922
Left to right Back row: 1. — 2. Pat Brennan 3. —
Next to last row: 1.— 2.— 3. Michael Spellman 4. — 5. — 6. John Gormley 7. James Feely 8. James Doyle 9. — 10. — 11. —
Third row from top: 1. — 2. Paddy Kellegher 3. — 4. — 5. — 6. — 7. Harry "Lewis" Christy 8. W. Brennan 9. — Hopkins 10. John McGowan
11. Tom Lohan
Fourth Row from Top: 1. John Spellman 2. John White 3. — 4. Tom Derby 5. Josie Murray 6. — 7. K. Horan 8. — 9. — 10. —
11. Phil Murray
Front Row:1. "Digger" Brennan 2. Willie Ivers 3. Tom Gormley 4. Peter Brennan 5. Patrick Chapman 6. Richard Murray 7. Henry Feely 8. James
Stephen Brennan 9. Joe Sheerin 10. Michael Glancy 11. Patrick Glancy 12. Malachy Flanagan 13. Luke Dempsey

PHOTO COURTESY OF UNA "SIS" MURRAY
PHOTO RESTORATION BY DAVE DERBY

Author's Notes

Thank You to the County of Roscommon IRA Commemorative Committee that erected the Shankill Monument at Elphin. Joe O'Kelly, former Adjutant of the 4th Battalion East Mayo Brigade from Ballaghaderreen, served as secretary to the group who worked from Easter 1949 to September of 1963 to solicit sufficient funds, engage an architect, and finally erect the structure. Other members of the organising committee included Patrick O'Connell and Patrick McKeon, joint Treasurers, Sean Owens, James "Brody" Kelly, John Kelly of Ballinameen, Michael Hanley, Patrick McCrann, Jack Leonard, and Frank O'Grady. J. F. O'Connor, a native of Fourmilehouse, Roscommon, helped spearhead the collection campaign in America. Gary Trimble of Dublin served as the designer. Commandant Tom Maguire of Mayo (commanding officer of the Second Western Division of the IRA) performed the unveiling ceremony. Michael Coen, the last survivor of the original organising committee of 1926, died at the age of ninety. He was laid to rest in the Tulsk Cemetery on 14 January 1998.

Note: Nineteen out of thirty-one names on the list in front of the monument are from the 1st and 2nd Battalion areas of South Roscommon. Volunteers from those areas comprise nearly 2/3 of the total killed during the War. Most did not fall in action, but rather were killed in their own homes or those of their neighbours.

Explanation: In 1924 a Military Pension Act was passed whereby persons with pre-Truce service in certain prescribed National organisations and those who had served in the National Army between 1 July 1922 and 1 October 1923 were awarded pensions from the Free State government. Ten years later, when de Valera's government came to power, another Pension Act was passed whereby the original guidelines were expanded to include those who had been active during Easter Week in 1916 and anyone who had continuous service from 1 April 1921 to 11 July 1921.

The onus of proof was on the person applying for the pension. Thus, many men had to return to their commanding officers to ask that their service be authenticated. From some of these papers has come the listing of men involved in certain actions.

Unfortunately, this author had no such documentation for those who joined the Free State Army. Those soldiers were automatically awarded a pension, and did not have to "prove" their participation. That is the reason such men's biographies are so devoid of specifics in this book, especially in the 3rd Battalion South area, which was so active during the Black and Tan War.

May it also be noted that perhaps a Volunteer did indeed give much service to the cause during those years but was not awarded a pension. This author found numerous examples of that, especially in the First Battalion South area, where the paper trail was most complete. The story, however, does not confine itself to Roscommon. On a national scale, 82% of those who applied for a pension under the 1924 Act were denied one. For the 1934 Act, 81% saw no monies awarded.*

Department of Defence, Finance Branch, Aras an tSaile, Renmore Galway.

I never served in the National Army. I did not apply for certificate under 1924 Act. I did not ask the Free State government for anything. I did apply under the 1932 Act. I was called before the Board, (but) was informed that my disability did not reach the required standard (of) 80%.

Excerpted from the Pension Form of George Fitzgerald of Ardmullan, Curraghboy.

THE VOLUNTEERS

"They had a great capacity for self sacrifice."

spoken on 23 October 2003 by Mary Gallagher of Ballaghaderreen,
daughter of George Murphy of Scramogue

Ireland screamed to be released of her leg irons. Alarms of the men and women of 1916 awoke a sleeping nation to its destiny. After the arrest of the Dublin rebels, news of their demise took a week to reach the far corners of the island. Eighty-one years later in 1997, ninety-four-year-old John Snee of Kilkelly, Mayo, clearly recalled tears in the eyes of the older generation as they stood in the town square, heard the news of the execution of John MacBride (one of their own) shouted by Constables Doyle and O'Donoghue, and felt again the hopelessness and despair of yet another failed rebellion. Others felt rage.

John Redmond and the Irish Parliamentary Party had been busy peddling enlistment forms to thousands of young men who would eventually spill their Gaelic blood in the trenches of Europe during World War I. Not a few young men and women thought that Ireland's chance for freedom lay not in the fields of France but the hills of Cork, the mountains of Kerry, the plains of Roscommon, the streets of Dublin.

A year after the 1916 Rising, serious effort was given to training a secret army. Why secret? Lack of weaponry, equipment, uniforms, and pay for starters. Also because a different kind of battleground was envisioned. A full-fledged pitched battle against overwhelming British firepower was deemed sheer suicide. The British would eventually be driven from Ireland not by the mass numbers of soldiers that confronted them on a battlefield but by the raw courage of men sniping from hedgerows or behind stone walls, raiding governmental offices, torching barracks buildings, trenching the roads, felling trees to hinder vehicular traffic, informing of suspicious troop movements, and not incidentally, by assassinating the network of British-paid spies of Dublin Castle. It was a concerted effort, not only of the higher ups in Dublin, but of the common people in the small villages and in the countryside. It took all the abilities of the administrators at the GHQ, the political powers in the provinces, brave soldiers who slogged through the mud and silently waited for a powerful enemy to appear, and gallant souls in the cottages who fed and housed those men, cycled their messages, and rocked away sleepless nights waiting and listening for the lorries in order to give adequate warning to their exhausted guests. It was the pluck, the determination, the grit of the small people who won for Ireland her place among nations.

Much has been written about the exploits of the men of Munster — and indeed, rightfully so. But there were others in the country whose activities caused worry to the Crown Forces. There were scores of men from Roscommon who grew all too familiar with prison walls and all too familiar with Black and Tan intimidation. According to the Gerald O'Connor Papers (the O/C of No. 2 Brigade in the 2nd Western Division in 1921), the attack on the RIC Barracks in Frenchpark took seventy men. Twenty-eight Volunteers engaged in a gun battle with a patrol in Strokestown in January of 1921. Who were these men? Why is it that few of their names are known beyond the whispers of their own families?

Perhaps the crushing disappointment of the Civil War silenced any whoop-di-lah about their participation. Perhaps the very nature of the organisation that

They were all ordinary young men, for the most part in their twenties, who enjoyed all the pleasures and amusements that rural life could give fifty years ago, but they turned their backs on all this to dedicate their young lives to the Volunteer movement and all it stood for. They were well aware of the price they might have to pay for this devotion to an ideal but they never faltered.*

*Spoken by Gerald O'Connor, No. 2 Brigade Commandant in the 2nd Western Division, at the 50th Commemoration (1970) of the eleven members of the Castlerea Battalion who lost their lives in the fight for Ireland's freedom. It is a sentiment applicable to many persons on this list.

Officers prior to and on Truce date — 11 July 1921
North Roscommon Brigade

O/C Seamus Ryan then Michael Dockery
Vice O/C Michael Dockery then Seamus Ryan
Adjutant: Andy Nevin, Andy Lavin (tended his resignation Dec. 1920
when he was sent to engineering assignment), Jack Glancy and Michael Duignan
Quartermaster: Martin Killalea, Patrick Mullooly, and Martin Fallon (after Scramogue)
Intelligence Officer: P. J. Delahunty
Brigade Chemist: John Murray
Headquarters: Hillstreet

First Battalion (Boyle area)
O/C James Feely and Pat Brennan
Vice O/C Martin Killalea and John Kelly
Adjutant: Phil Murray and Patrick Glancy
Quartermaster: John Sherran (Sherrin), Owen Dockery

Companies:
Boyle Capt. James Stephen Brennan and Luke Dempsey
Doon Capt. John Sheeran
Ballinameen Capt. John Kelly and Michael Harrington
Breedogue Capt. Edward Robinson
Frenchpark Capt. Malachy Doddy, Michael Higgins, and Sean O'Gara
Fairymount Capt. Joseph Callaghan

Second Battalion (Elphin area)
O/C Sean Owens of Ballyroddy
Vice O/C Martin Dockery
Adjutant: Pat Beirne of Clooncunny and Brian Carroll of Strokestown
Quartermaster: John Toolan of Clooneyquinn
Intelligence Officer: Tom Brady

Companies:
Mantua Capt. Edward Holmes and Thomas Connor
Killina Capt. Patrick Collins
Tulsk Capt. Mick Neary and Edward Simpson
Creeve Capt. Brian Beirne
Elphin Capt. John Pryal and Timothy Beirne
Aughrim Capt. John Leneghan and Thomas Mulick

Third Battalion (Strokestown area)
O/C Liam O'Doherty and Sean Leavy of Ashbrook
Vice O/C Sean Leavy, Brian Nangle, and Peter Casey
Adjutant: Andy Nevin, Tommie Mason, Brian Nangle, and James Murphy (after Scramogue)
Quartermaster: Patrick Cox of Ballyhubert, Scramogue, Martin Fallon, Brian Nangle, and James Casey
Intelligence Officer: Brian Dayton
Chief Engineer: Frank O'Donoghue

Companies:
Carniska Capt. Owen Kearns and James Shiel
Curraghroe Capt. Brian Nangle and James Lynagh
Scramogue Capt. Patrick Cox, Sean Leavy, John Murphy, James Lannon
*Tarmonbarry Capt. Daniel Fallon and James Farrell

required secrecy and discretion worked against self promotion. Perhaps the burden of just making a living and surviving those brutal, grinding days of poverty and disillusionment took focus and energy that might otherwise have been diverted to Veteran organisations and flag waving. For whatever reason, the Roscommon contribution to the War effort has been under-reported and, to an extent, under-appreciated.

This section of the book will attempt to right that wrong, enlighten the future generations as to their ancestors' trials and travails, and hopefully honour those great Irish people who went so far with so little to accomplish so much.

*Slatta Capt. Luke Cox
*Ruskey Capt. John J. Robinson
Kilglass Capt. Patrick McCormack and Michael Greene
Kiltrustan Capt. Patrick Mullooly, Michael Warren, Michael Fallon, Joe Conroy
Strokestown Capt. Tom Shevlin and Sean Birmingham
Cloonfree Capt. Michael McCoy, Peter Flanagan, and M. Scally (whose Company membership
 totalled fifteen, all of whom were IRB)

Fourth Battalion (Crossna area)

O/C John J. Doyle, Tom Moran and Jimmie O'Brien
Vice O/C Bernie Ryan, Thomas Martin, Seamus Gaffney, Tom Moran, Tommy Lavin
Adjutant: Seamus Cull of Arigna
Quartermaster: J. Glynn of Crossna and Patrick Gaffney of Keadue
Meetings held in Crossna and sometimes Ballyfarnon

Companies:

Arigna Capt. Patrick McLoughlin, Jim Brady
Ballyfarnon Capt. Joe Cunnane, Joseph Noone, Tommy Lavin, Thomas Lynam
Crossna Capt. Jimmie O'Brien, John Nolan
Keadue Capt. Patrick Duignan, James Lyons
Cootehall Capt. William Cox

Fifth Battalion — Carrick-on-Shannon

O/C Joe McCormack of Cortober, Jim Dorr, and Darby Meehan
Vice O/C Michael McLoughlin and William Ward
Adjutant: William Ward, Jack Glancy, and Hubert Lenehan
Quartermaster: M. Moore, Michael Noone, John Lynch of Cootehall, and Paddy McKeon

When the Divisional structure came into being, part of Leitrim became the 5th Battalion grouped with the
North Roscommon (3rd) Brigade in the 3rd Western Division. The Battalion staff included:
O/C of the 5th Battalion: Sean O'Farrell of Dromard, Dromod and Thomas Shanley of Clooneagh, Dromod,
Leitrim
Vice O/C Thomas McKeon
Adjutant: John J. Cooney of Augnaglace, Cloone, Mohill, Leitrim
Quartermaster: James Canning of Tooma, Cloone
Intelligence Officer: Patrick Joseph McGovern, who later emigrated to New York
Other Staff members included: John Charles Keegan (who later emigrated to San Francisco);
Patrick O'Rourke of Cloncowley, Drumlish, Co. Longford; Bernard Ryan of Annaghmacoolen,
Cloone, Co. Leitrim

Companies:

Kilmore Capt. Jim Dorr and Patrick Healy
Drumlion Capt. Luke Butler, Bernard Gannon, Joe McCormack, Jack Glancy, Bernard Farrell, and
Thomas Lowe
Croghan Capt. Tom Devaney, Patrick McKeon, and Joe Elwood
#Cootehall Capt. William Cox
*Drumboylan Capt. Luke Moran
#Cootehall Company was originally in the 5th Battalion. After the reorganisation into Divisions,
 General Headquarters considered it to be the 4th Battalion
*Denotes Companies referred to in the GHQ papers in the UCD Archives, but not referred to in
Micheál O'Callaghan's book *For Ireland and Freedom.*

Military Divisions

On a national scale, each of the thirty-two counties was organised into Brigades,
each Brigade being divided into Battalions. Five to eight Companies formed the
Battalion. Officers were elected by the Company, while section and squad commanders were appointed by the Captain. Brigade staff was elected by Battalion
commanding officers. The actual number of persons in each category varied from
county to county and within the same county depending on availability of personnel. (Some men were killed, others imprisoned, others went on the run.) As
vacancies in the ranks occurred, positions were filled by other men who became

Officers as of 1 July 1922
North Roscommon Brigade

O/C Pat Brennan
Vice O/C Martin Killalea of Doon
Adjutant: John Roche of Ballinameen
Quartermaster: John J. Conry of Creeve, Elphin
Director of Chemistry: Michael J. Larkin

1st Battalion: Boyle Area
O/C John Kelly of Sheervagh, Ballinameen
Vice O/C John Sheeran (Sherrin) of Doon, Boyle
Adjutant: Pat Glancy of The Place, Elphin
Intelligence Officer: Phil Murray, The Barracks, Boyle

2nd Battalion: Elphin area
O/C Sean Owens, Lismacool, Mantua
Vice O/C Martin Dockery, Drummullin, Elphin
Adjutant: Brian Carroll of Killina, Clooneyquinn
Quartermaster: Paddy Connell of Corgarve, Elphin
Intelligence Officer: Seamus Ryan of Bridge St., Strokestown

3rd Battalion: Strokestown area
O/C Brian Nangle, Scramogue
Vice O/C Frank O'Donoghue of Northyard, Scramogue
Adjutant: Joseph Cox of Scramogue (according to Pat Brennan Papers). Sean Birmingham of The Farn, Strokestown (according to the Department of Defence)
Quartermaster: Frank McGuinness (according to Pat Brennan Papers). Michael Greene of Kilglass, Strokestown (according to the Department of Defence)

4th Battalion: Kilmore area
O/C Michael Keogh of Kilbride, Drumsna
Vice O/C Luke Butler of Drumlion, Croghan
Adjutant: John Healy of Cloonglassney, Strokestown
Quartermaster: Patrick McKeon of Lecarrow, Croghan

the officers in charge. Thus the Roscommon Volunteer list on the following pages is not completely accurate, some members being active for only a few months — their positions filled by someone else who was himself arrested, while others lasted the duration of the War. Some men managed to keep their own activities and responsibilities well hidden, and we do not know their identities. The Irish Republican Army was, after all, a secret organisation, whose structure discouraged a wide range of knowledge about activities or personnel outside the local group. Consequently, some men may have felt they "did all the work," while other persons who didn't really participate in this dangerous game could later proclaim heroic deeds. From this distance, it is impossible to weigh and counterweigh the claims and personal achievements. What we can know at the dawn of this twenty-first century is that many Roscommon people were involved, many sacrificed their youth for the cause, many suffered a lifetime of ill-health resulting from the harsh conditions, many lived the years after the War with a heart full of regret and what-ifs, and some did not live to see the dawn of the next day.

In Roscommon the engine for operating Volunteer Companies was given a fuel injection by the presence of Sean Hyde, Ernie O'Malley, and Sean Connolly. Those men helped to shore up Companies and define Battalion and Brigade structures. The introduction of the Division structure did not come about until 1921. During that year the "idea was floated, which was accepted by (Richard) Mulcahy, much against (Michael) Collins' will, that the Army would be reorganised in terms of Divisions ... up to this time there had been local companies, local battalions, and in each county, at least one or sometimes two or three brigades, depending on the strength of the population, and each brigade would have its own Active Service Unit or Flying Column, with a large number of part-time volunteers who would assemble when needed for a particular operation, and would provide intelligence and maintenance services. The system was extremely flexible, to minimise damage and worked perfectly. However, it was decided to merge larger bodies of men together and to adopt a more formal military structure..."*

The decision to divisionalise the country came about for a variety of reasons. Firstly, there was fear that a British raid in Dublin would wipe out the General Headquarters Staff and paralyse the command structure. As quoted from *British Intelligence in Ireland 1920-21 The Final Reports*, "In 1921 nearly all the officers of the Dublin Brigade, I. R. A. were known, and a good percentage of them had been arrested, including the I. R. A. Director of Intelligence, the head of their secret service and four battalion IOs ... Eight of the principal departments of Dáil Éireann and I. R. A. had been raided successfully and three dumps had been taken. Twice was the G. H. Q. of the I. R. A. raided, on one occasion the Chief of Staff's personal office and plans being captured and only three days before the Truce the office of the I. R. A. police was taken."** Clearly, there was cause for concern. There was a need, therefore, to give more freedom and responsibility to commanders scattered around the country. Secondly, in order to simplify the stream of paperwork, a few Divisional commanders was deemed far easier to communicate with than scores of county Brigadiers.

As that Divisional regrouping related to Roscommon, for example, South Roscommon was originally divided into four Battalion areas — No. 1 around the Castlerea area, No. 2 the adjoining area eastwards towards Roscommon town. The 3rd Battalion centred around Roscommon town and east to the Shannon, while the 4th Battalion extended from Knockcroghery to the Shannon River and southward towards Athlone. Areas of the extreme south of the county were part of the Athlone Brigade. (See map on page vii.)

When this Divisional structure was introduced into Roscommon county in August/September of 1921, South and North Roscommon were separated from each other and grouped with surrounding areas. The 2nd Western Division included parts of east Galway, South Mayo, Castlerea, South Roscommon, and Tuam. The southern boundary of this 2nd Western Division was a line south of the railway via Craughwell, Dunsandle, Aughrim to the Suck River below Ballinasloe and along the river to the Shannon.

It was Commandant Tom Maguire's contention that the rail line between Ballinasloe and Athlone formed the southern border of the 2nd Western Division, but that certain modifications had to be made. The location of Custume Barracks had to be considered in the geography. During the Civil War, Athlone became the headquarters for the Free State's Western Command.

The 3rd Western Division included most of County Sligo, North Roscommon, parts of Leitrim, and corners of Counties Mayo, Donegal, and Fermanagh. The Divisional demarcation was a line south of Strokestown, Tulsk, Castlerea to Ballinlough, west of Swinford and Aclare along the Ox Mountains to the sea between Dromore and Skreen. Liam Pilkington served as the O/C of this Division.

Titles and groupings of men changed. For example, in the northwestern section of Roscommon, the Company of Seamus and Pat Mulrennan from Lisacul, which had formerly been referred to as part of the 4th Battalion in the East Mayo Brigade, was now known as the 3rd Coy., No.2 Brigade, 2nd Western Division. In the Castlerea area, Gerald O'Connor held the position of the 1st Battalion South Roscommon Commander. Later, when the Western Division was formed in August 1921, he became No. 2 Brigade Commandant in the 2nd Western Division. Thus, the listing of officers on the following pages is not totally accurate due to the fact that men floated in and out of positions of responsibility as necessity demanded, and their titles changed with the new Divisional structure.

Officers prior to and on Truce date — 11 July 1921
South Roscommon Brigade

O/C Jack Brennan of Carrowkeel, Dan O'Rourke of Castlerea,
Frank Simons (March 1921-Truce) and Gerald O'Connor of Lisacul, No. 2 Brigade Commandant in the 2nd Western Division
Vice O/C Paddy "Boddins" Doorly, Jack Brennan, Jim Breheny of Portrunny Knockcroghery, and Frank Simons (January-March 1921)
Quartermaster: Matt Davis of Kilteevan
Adjutant: Henry J. Finlay, Edward "Ned" Hegarty
Ned Hegarty of Ballinaheglish also served as Chief of the Republican Police
Intelligence Officer: Paddy Egan (who was later suspected of being a British agent*)
Headquarters: Paddy Naughton's cottage in Ballinaheglish (Dominick Rogers was the resident during the War). Meetings held every fortnight which all Battalion Commanders attended
*Matt Davis Volunteer Witness Statement to the Bureau of Military History 1913-21. p. 3.and
*Tom Crawley Volunteer Witness Statement to the Bureau of Military History 1913-21. p. 15.

First Battalion (Castlerea)
O/C Dan O'Rourke, Pat Glynn, Gerald O'Connor
Vice O/C Tom Crawley
Adjutant: —Beatty, Paddy Flynn, Albert Durr, and John Costello
Quartermaster: Stephen McDermott, John Flanagan, and John White

Companies:
Ballinagare Capt. Michael Cullinan
Castlerea Capt. Sean Bergin and Martin Foley
Lisliddy Capt. Francis Flynn
Moor Capt. Ned Campion
Loughglynn Capt. Pat Glynn, Martin Ganley
Ballinlough Capt. Jack Moran, Michael Winston, Joe Kenny
Cloonboniffe Capt. John Vaughan, Martin Foley, and Tom Vaughan
Trien Capt. Michael Hester and John White
Cloonfad Capt. Tom Regan

Second Battalion (Oran)
O/C Jim Quigley of Fourmilehouse
Vice O/C Pat Conboy of Castlecoote
Adjutant: Ned Hegarty of Ballinaheglish, James Kenny, and Seamus McGovern

Companies:
Cloverhill Capt. Edward Jackson
Ballinaheglish Capt. Michael O'Grady

For the purpose of this book, the author has attempted to adhere to the county groupings and identifications as they existed at the beginning of the Black and Tan War unless otherwise noted.
*Michael Collins and The Brotherhood by Vincent MacDowell, p. 85.
** British Intelligence in Ireland 1920-21 The Final Reports, edited by Peter Hart, p. 35.

The Volunteers
Successful guerilla warfare depends on meticulous planning, availability of weapons, level headedness, cool men to execute the plans and, not incidentally, a place to hide after the engagement. The terrain of north Roscommon lent itself more to this type of hit and run activity than did the undulating fields of the south separated merely by rock walls. Also the configuration of the county allows for much more space and population in the northern half than in the southern. Thus, the majority of engagements and ambushes took place north of Roscommon town. Oftentimes men from neighbouring counties assisted in a raid near the border, and though, strictly speaking were not Roscommon inhabitants, surely aided the fight for independence within her borders. These men, as much as they are known to the author, have been included in the alphabetical listing starting on page 210.

(South Roscommon Brigade continued)

Castleplunkett Capt. Jack Ryan, and Luke Raftery
Fuerty Capt. Bernie Kearney
Donamon Capt. Pat Dwyer
Ballintubber Capt. Peter Glancy, Alec Kenny, John Conry

Third Battalion (Ballagh area)

O/C Pat Madden
Vice O/C Luke Duffy
Adjutant: John Sinnott, Frank Simons
Quartermaster: Pat Treacy and John Gibbons

Companies:

Kilgefin Capt. Pat Madden, Frank "Dan" Madden, Henry Compton, and Jim Tiernan
Kilbride Capt. Tom Murray, M. Murray, and Peter Farrell
Cloontuskert Capt. John O'Connor
Kilteevan Capt. Jack Brennan
Roscommon town Capt. Tim Monaghan and John J. Doorley
Athleague Capt. John Kelly and John Conboy

Fourth Battalion (Knockcroghery area)

O/C Patrick Kelly of Lecarrow (resigned for health reasons in mid-1919) and Tom Kelly of Carrigeens (Post Truce — Michael J. Breheny and John Breheny)
Vice O/C Johnny Kilcline
Adjutant: Tom Kelly of Mount Talbot
Quartermaster: Owen Curley
Intelligence Officer: Patrick Kelly
Meetings always held at Rahara

Companies:

Four Roads Capt. Joe Galvin
Knockcroghery Capt. Patrick Kelly, Joseph Coyne, Jim Breheny, Paddy Fallon, Michael Breheny
St. John's Capt. Thomas Keogh, Patrick Grady, and Hubert Murphy
Curraghboy Capt. Lolly O'Brien, Sonny Egan, Dick Mee, and Michael Fallon
Dysart (Company incorporated in the 4th Battalion at the end of 1920) Capt. Martin McDonnell, Denis Gacquin, and John Gately
Kiltoom (Company incorporated in the 4th Battalion at the end of 1920) Capt. Brian Lenihan
Rahara Capt. Patrick Beattie
Ballygar (Company incorporated in the 4th Battalion at the end of 1920)
Ballyforan Capt. Patrick Flynn

Sinn Féin postcard published by M.J. Farrell, Roscommon,

POSTCARD COURTESY OF ALBERT SIGGINS

Athlone Brigade

The Defence Dept. records consider most of the south of the county to be in the 4th Battalion South Roscommon (Knockcroghery Coy., St. John's, Rahara, Curraghboy, Tisrara, Dysart, Kiltoom, and Ballygar, Galway). The line of demarcation between the 4th Battalion and the Athlone Brigade was determined by the southern boundary of the railroad line from Galway to Athlone.

This Brigade structure requires a little explanation. By March or April of 1918, a Battalion was organised in County Westmeath area. Known as the Athlone Battalion, it included the Athlone, Summerhill, Drumraney, Moate, and Bealnamullia areas. (The Curraghboy Company was originally included in this arrangement. At the end of 1918, however, that Company became part of the South Roscommon Brigade.) Officers at that time were:

O/C Sean Hurley
Vice O/C James Martin, Seamus O'Meara
Adjutant: Sean O'Farrell
Quartermaster: Thomas Noonan

A month later an order from GHQ arrived which promoted the idea of a Brigade in the Westmeath area. After several months of meeting with local representatives on both sides of the Shannon River, a Brigade was formed which included these officers:

O/C Seamus O'Meara (Sean Hurley was arrested in late 1917)
Vice O/C Sean Scanlon, Tom "Con" Costello
Adjutant: Sean O'Farrell, then later George Manning
Quartermaster: Robert Ramsey, Pat Macken

According to Tom "Con" Costello, the Vice O/C and later O/C of the Brigade, the Brigade was comprised of four Battalion: 1st Battalion — Athlone area; 2nd Battalion — Drumraney; 3rd Battalion — Summerhill area; 4th Battalion — Mullingar area. (Michael McCormack of Drumraney also claims that his area was in the 2nd Battalion.) Seamus O'Meara differentiates the Battalion area a little differently: he organised a Battalion on the Connaught side of the Shannon which he termed the 1st Battalion, Athlone Brigade. The town of Athlone now became the 2nd Battalion, Drumraney the 3rd Battalion, Mullingar the 4th, and Shannonbridge the 5th. Very shortly after this time, the 5th Battalion was transferred to the control of the Offaly Brigade with Thomas Dolan serving as Battalion O/C. At the end of 1920, Mullingar split off from the Athlone Brigade and received its orders directly from GHQ. James Maguire became the O/C of that Brigade. M. J. Kennedy later served in that capacity. Thus there were three Battalions that comprised the Athlone Brigade at Truce time. Using Costello's numbering system:

1st Battalion (Athlone area)

O/C David Daly and Francis O'Connor
Vice O/C James Martin of The Hill of Berries, Athlone
Adjutant: George Manning and Joe Kennedy of Athlone
Quartermaster: Frank Fitzpatrick, Brian Mulvihill of Ballykeevin

Companies:

Coosan Capt. Henry (Harry) O'Brien, Francis O'Connor
Mount Temple Capt. James Shortle
Kiltoom Capt. Brian Lenihan
Athlone Capt. James Fox
Moate Capt. Hugh Sheerin and Patrick Macken
Faheeran Capt. Tom Claffey

2nd Battalion (Drumraney)

O/C Sean (John) McCormack, Dick Bertles, Thomas John McGiff
Vice O/C Peter Ballesty
Adjutant: Michael McCormack, Brian Martin
Quartermaster: Patrick Mahon, Thomas Cuffe
Battalion Engineer: Michael Seery

Companies:

Drumraney Capt. William Moran
Tang Capt. Anthony McCormack
(First Lieutenant John Feeny with Bill Casey, an ex British army soldier, acting as drill instructor)
Ballymore Capt. Thomas Kearney and James Lynch
Tubberclair Capt. Michael Carty
Bishopstown Capt. Michael Finn
Rosemount Capt. John Dooley

(Athlone Brigade continued)

3rd Battalion (Summerhill area)

O/C Bernard (Barney) Gaffey
Vice O/C Pat Watson of Drum
Adjutant: Michael Cunniffe of Monksland
Quartermaster: Edward Cunniffe of Monksland

Companies:
"A" Company Edward Dowling
Summerhill Capt. John Harney and Tom Halligan
Bealnamullia Capt. William Fallon
Taughmaconnell Capt. Michael O'Connell
Clonown Capt. William Fallon
Drum Capt. John Killian and Pat Watson
Berries Capt. John Blaney and James Martin
Moore Capt. Patrick Flynn
Monksland Capt. Sean Bannon

Evolution of the Brigade Officers:

Brigade O/C Sean Hurley, Seamus O'Meara, Tom "Con" Costello
Vice O/C John McCormack, Tom "Con" Costello, George Adamson
Quartermaster: Peter Melinn, Robert Ramsey, replaced by Jim Tormey
Strength of the Athlone Battalion: In 1919 estimated about 1000

Flying Column organised in October 1920 and first brought together in the home of David Daly.
It numbered about 20 men
James Tormey O/C
Members known: Con Costello, Seamus O'Meara, Harry O'Brien, Pat Macken, Bernard Gaffey, Dick Bertles, George Manning, Brian Mulvihill, David Daly, George Adamson, Frank O'Connor, Tom Halligan, William Mannion, James Dalton, Ned Dowling, Tom Martin, Bernard Martin, Denis Mannion

---

East Mayo Brigade

4th Battalion (which incorporated areas of west Roscommon as well as east Mayo)

O/C of the Brigade Sean Corcoran of Kiltimagh and Tom Carney

4th Battalion

O/C Dominick Doherty of Lisacul
Vice O/C John Morley of Ballaghaderreen
Adjutant: Joe O'Kelly of Ballaghaderreen
Medical Officer: (for Anti-Treaty side during Civil War) Tom Murray

Companies:
Ballaghaderreen Capt. John Joe Coleman
Lisacul Capt. B. Madden
Brusna Capt. John Costello
Tibohine Capt. Johnnie McGowan

Officers as of 1 July 1922
South Roscommon Brigade

The South Roscommon Brigade as a unit did not participate in the Civil War, although many individual members did indeed take part in the struggle. All but a few members of the Kilgefin Company in the 3rd Battalion South joined the Free State Army. Men in the west section of the county joined Anti-Treaty Mayo men and formed Flying Columns, one of which was commanded by Seamus Mulrennan of Lisacul. Others in the northeast and mid section joined with men of the surrounding counties to attack positions in Leitrim and Cavan and Longford. South of Roscommon town, men joined a Flying Column headed by Matt Davis and roamed over areas of Galway, Westmeath, and parts of Longford.

The funeral procession for George Adamson in 1922.

PHOTO COURTESY OF GEAROID O'BRIEN, HEAD LIBRARIAN, ATHLONE LIBRARY

William Abraham (Garranlahan) his home served as the headquarters for "I" Company in the 2nd Battalion, No. 2 Brigade, 2nd Western Division during the post-Truce times

George Adamson (Moate, County Westmeath) which formed part of the Athlone Brigade of which he became the Vice O/C. An excellent athlete who was also a sure shot with a rifle. Gave weapons instruction to Volunteers in the Crannagh training base in south Roscommon. Participated in the **ambush at Parkwood** in County Westmeath in September 1920. Several months later he, along with Tom Halligan and another Volunteer, attempted to assassinate Captain Tully of the Athlone RIC. They followed him through town on several occasions — locating him once with a group of other officers. Not knowing exactly which man was Tully, the Volunteers let all the RIC pass them by. Adamson was also present at the **Cornafulla Ambush**. In the spring of 1921, he and Gerald Davis were coming back from a trip to Westmeath, when they approached a barn-yard in Carricknaughton where a couple of Black and Tans were courting two local girls. In the attempt to disarm the Tans, Adamson was shot in the chest. He was taken across the Shannon to Ballycumber, where he was nursed back to health by relatives of Con Costello.* He joined the Free State Army, and was fatally shot in the chest in Irishtown on 25 April 1922 during the dispute over the occupation of Custume Barracks. Michael Farry in his *The Aftermath of Revolution Sligo 1921-23* states that Adamson was leading a party of officers from Custume Barracks and was headed to the Royal Hotel, which was held by the Anti-Treatyites. Identity of person(s) responsible for his demise was never totally established (see page 127). Buried Mt. Temple Cemetery

Con Costello Volunteer Witness Statement to the Bureau of Military History 1913-1921, p. 24.

George Amos (Chapel Street, Athlone) imprisoned after the Rising and sent to Wandsworth Prison on 9th May

Frank Balfe (Boyle) a sergeant in the Free State Army, killed in action at Ballytrasna, Boyle 8 July 1922

Henry Banahan (Cloontuskert Coy.) 3rd Battalion South Roscommon

Patrick and Mary Anne Banahan (Cappagh) near Ballagh, ran a safe house where Sean Bergin once stayed for a week. Patrick, although not a Volunteer himself, was seized at his home and threatened with interrogation at the local barracks. His wife, Mary Anne, pleaded with the Tans to allow her husband to change his clothes, which were old and full of holes. Seems she wanted him to look nice for his "public appearance!"

Michael Bannon (Creggan, Athlone) joined the Free State Army, and was killed in Tubbercurry, Co. Sligo on 25 August 1922

Sean Bannon (Halls Bridge, Athlone) Captain of the Monksland Company in the 3rd Battalion Athlone Brigade

Thomas Bannon (Bealnamullia) 3rd Battalion Athlone Brigade. Bannon drilled with his Company, trained to use firearms, took an active part in the General Election of 1918, attended Battalion meetings, worked with the Republican Police

Sean Bannon,
Captain of Monksland Company.

PHOTO COURTESY OF MARY RAFFERTY

PHOTO RESTORATION BY LEW THORNE

force at disputed farmland in Bealnamullia and Clongowna. He was with a group of Volunteers that seized ammunition from an airplane that made a forced landing at Keelogues in 1919. Took part in the **burning of the Barracks at Bealnamullia**, mobilised for an attack on Cloonark Barracks, and **attempted an ambush at Curraghaleen** in October 1920. Near Truce time, he guarded the ASU Headquarters in the area, destroyed the bridge at Millbrook, blocked roads at Millbrook and Monksland, harboured and aided escaped prisoners. During the Truce he trained at Greenfield, Donamon, and Falty in addition to collecting funds to aid the Volunteers and attending the Arbitration Courts

Frank Barlow (Keadue) 4th Battalion North Roscommon. Fought side by side with James Kelly in the **attack on Ballinamore Barracks** in January 1923. A month later on 3 February, he found himself behind bars in Athlone

Peter Barrett (Ahascragh in Galway) a Peter Barrett was imprisoned in Athlone in 1922. In 1923 Peter of Ahascragh was attending a dance in the Drum area of south Roscommon when he was taken out of the building and shot. He had apparently been mistaken for another man. (Perhaps he was mistaken for Peter Barrett of Craughwell who participated in the Galway activities of Easter Week and had been imprisoned in Frongoch.) He is buried in Dysart Cemetery. His name is inscribed on the tablets in front of the Shankill Monument near Elphin

Paddy Barry (Barcullen, Knockvicar, Boyle) 4th Battalion North Roscommon, escapee through the Brady tunnel at Curragh Internment Camp in September 1921

James Beattie (Ballagh, Knockcroghery) a member of the Rahara Coy., 4th Battalion South Roscommon, brother of Patrick, served as the Quartermaster for the Company. James joined the Volunteers from the St. John's Coy. on arms raids — one which yielded three shotguns, another which yielded one shotgun and a quantity of cartridges. After the War he was a part time farmer and owner of a sawmill. Died 1973 and buried in St. Coman's Cemetery in Roscommon town

Patrick Beattie (Rahara Coy.) 4th Battalion South Roscommon. He not only was Captain of the Company, but also a member of the Brigade staff. He joined the IRB in 1914 along with Joe Galvin of Mount Talbot, Tom Kelly of Knockcroghery, and Joe Finlay of Roscommon town. Patrick used to travel from Rahara to Ballinaheglish riding his bicycle across the fields. But one stretch proved unnavigable, and he had to carry his bicycle on his shoulders for a mile.* Beattie served as a Judge in the local Sinn Féin Court at Culleen Hall. He participated in the **attempted ambush at Clooncraff** — an operation under the command of Pat Madden. He was also present in early January for the **attempt to ambush a lorry of Tans in Knockcroghery**. He and James Beattie used to wait in ambush positions along with Pat Madden's men on the road from Lanesboro to Roscommon town. There was never an opportunity for a fight because the military did not show up on those occasions. While attending a Battalion meeting in Lackan near Sliabh Bán on St. Patrick's Day in 1921, he and the other staff members were surrounded by a British patrol, but escaped amid a hail of bullets. A drain in the nearby field proved a perfect place to seek refuge. After the burning of Knockcroghery in June 1921, Patrick had planned to form an Active Service Unit in the south because he knew that after that incident no IRA member would be safe sleeping at home. The news of the Truce, however, halted his plans.* Beattie was never apprehended during the Tan War, and did not participate in the Civil War. He is buried in Rahara Cemetery

Frank Beattie, son of Patrick, interview by author 23 June 2002, Rahara, Co. Roscommon.

Francis Beatty (Ballaghaderreen) incarcerated during the Civil War in Athlone on 28 March 1923

James Beattie of the Rahara Coy. 4th Battalion South Roscommon.
PHOTO COURTESY OF FRANK BEATTIE

Patrick Beattie of the 4th Battalion South Roscommon.
PHOTO COURTESY OF FRANK BEATTIE

Hubert Beatty (Betagh) (Moor Coy.) 1st Battalion South Roscommon, participated in the **attempted attack on Kilmurray Military Camp** in June 1920, the **attack on Frenchpark Barracks** 2 October 1920, the **attempted ambushes at Castlerea** and **Frenchpark** in January 1921, **ambush at Southpark, Castlerea** in July 1921, and, during the Civil War, the **attack at Castlerea** in November 1922

Michael Beatty (Beatagh) (Beattie) (Lisliddy Coy.) 1st Battalion South Roscommon. During the Truce he attended the Company training camp where he specialised in intelligence, scouting, and dispatch work

Patrick Beatty (Betagh) (Beattie) (Lisliddy Cross, Castlerea) 1st Battalion South Roscommon. Was present at Pat Glynn's Memorial Service in 1970

Richard Beatty (Betagh) (Beattie) (Lisliddy) 1st Battalion South Roscommon, Company Captain. Took part in the **destruction of barracks** in 1920 as well as the **attempted attack on Kilmurray Military Camp** in June 1920. He also participated in the **capture of enemy stores at Ballymoe** that same month, the **raid and capture of military equipment at Ballymoe** in September 1920, and the **attack on Frenchpark Barracks** 2 October 1920. By July 1921 he was living in England

P. Behan a member of a Mayo Company, who became part of an Active Service Unit for the 3rd Brigade, 2nd Western Division. He, along with John Snee, Tom Regan, M. Hunt, Mick Duffy, and M. McKeon, spent the first months after the Truce sniping at B-Specials along the six-county Border. He was part of the group of Anti-Treaty men who took over the Boyle Barracks during the Civil War

Andrew Beirne a member of Creeve Coy. in the 2nd Battalion North Roscommon. Participated in the **attack on the Elphin RIC patrol** on 6 January 1921, and the **attack on Elphin Barracks** a month later. After the War he emigrated to Liverpool

Bernard Beirne (Kye, Elphin) participated in the **attack on the Elphin patrol** 5 January 1921. During the Civil War he was arrested 14 September 1922 and incarcerated in Athlone on 14 November 1922. He was released from imprisonment on 3 February 1923, whereupon he emigrated to New York

Brian Beirne (Creeve) 2nd Battalion North Roscommon. He was the first Captain of Creeve Company. His house was burned by the Tans. After the War he emigrated to New York

Brian Beirne, also in Creeve Company in the 2nd Battalion North Roscommon, who acted as Quartermaster. He later emigrated to England

Edward Beirne (Ballykilcline, Ruskey) a member of the Kilglass Company in the 3rd Battalion North Roscommon. Arrested during the Civil War 8 September 1922, and transferred to Athlone on 14 November

James Beirne (Kilclogherna, Strokestown) 2nd Battalion North Roscommon. Joined Kiltrustan Company in 1918. When that Company broke up, he joined Creeve Coy. in December 1919. Beirne was appointed 2nd Lieutenant in January 1921. Beirne attended meetings, drilled with arms, carried dispatches, collected arms, dissuaded locals from attending the British Courts, and raided the mails. He took part in the **burning of Hillstreet Barracks** in May 1920, the **attack on the Elphin patrol** 5 January 1921, served as an armed outpost (at Smithhill) for the **attack on the Elphin Barracks** 11 February, lay in wait for several ambushes at Smithhill during the month of May, smuggled explosives to Aughrim that same month, lay in wait at an ambush site at Drummullin in June, and was present at the **attempted attack at Lavally** a day before the Truce. He often carried dispatches because his home was on the border between three different Battalions. Beirne went to the Mantua training camp for two weeks during the Truce. During the Civil War he worked for the Republican side carrying arms, doing intelligence work, and removing equipment after the **Lakeview ambush** in December 1922. His health deteriorated during this time, and he eventually applied for a disability pension which was denied him

Hugh Beirne (Cloonycattan, Elphin) 2nd Battalion North Roscommon

James Beirne (Kildalloge, Strokestown) brother of Thomas, served as the Quartermaster for the Strokestown Company after it had been incorporated into the 3rd Western Division

Jimmie Beirne (Cloonfree Coy.) 3rd Battalion North Roscommon. Took part in the **attempt to burn down the Strokestown Bridewell** in July 1920

John Beirne a member of the Kilgefin Coy., 3rd Battalion South Roscommon. He later became a farmer

John Beirne (Cloonroughan, Clooneyquinn) Quartermaster of Elphin Coy,. 2nd Battalion North Roscommon. Spent his time with dispatch work, drilling, and organising the Sinn Féin Club. Participated in the **attack on Elphin Barracks** on 11 February 1921, and was beaten by the Tans in retaliation for that action. Arrested and sent to Athlone Barracks and the Curragh until his release on 11 December 1921

John Beirne (Ballyglass, Ballinagare) 1st Battalion South Roscommon. He drilled with his Company, collected funds for the Dáil loan, and served under the command of Captain Michael Cullinan. Participated in the **raid on the military train at Ballymoe** in June 1920, the **attack on Frenchpark Barracks** 2 October 1920, and the **ambush at Southpark, Castlerea** 10 July 1921. During the Civil War he became a member of the Active Service Unit of the 1st Battalion South. Later emigrated to the United States

John James Beirne (Ballykilcline, Ruskey) a member of the Kilglass Company in the 3rd Battalion North Roscommon

John P. Beirne (Carrownageeragh, Boyle) 1st Battalion North Roscommon. Took part in the **attack on Frenchpark Barracks and Courthouse** in June 1921

Michael Beirne (Grange, Fourmilehouse) 3rd Battalion South Roscommon

Pat Beirne (Clooncunny, Strokestown) Adjutant for the 2nd Battalion North Roscommon. He was one of the original members of the Killina Company. On the night of 2 January 1920, he and Tom Brady attacked a soldier and disarmed him in Strokestown. Mulcahy Papers indicate that the Battalion Adjutant (Beirne) was arrested in a swoop on 27 January 1921. Beirne was taken in retaliation for attacks on Elphin police patrols. He became a prisoner at Boyle Military Barracks, Athlone, and Curragh, from which he successfully escaped through the Brady tunnel in September 1921. Died 19 January 1977

Patrick Beirne (Byrne) (Ballyglass West, Loughglynn) 1st Battalion South Roscommon. Took part in the **destruction of vacant barracks** in 1920, and the **attack on Frenchpark Barracks** 2 October 1920. He ran for his life when Martin Ganley's house was surrounded (and burned) by the Crown Forces in January 1921. That same month he took part in an **attempted attack at Castlerea and Frenchpark**. He served in the covering party for the **attack on the military at Castlerea** on 6 April 1921, and participated in the **attempted ambush at Loughglynn** later in April. In May he lay in **ambush at Lisacul** (an action taken in conjunction with the East Mayo men). On that occasion no enemy appeared

Pat Beirne (Carrigeen, Kilglass, Strokestown) Kiltrustan Coy. in the 3rd Battalion North Roscommon

Patrick Beirne (Ballykilcline, Ruskey) a member of the Kilglass Company in the 3rd Battalion North Roscommon

Patrick Beirne 1st Lieutenant for Kilmore Company in the 5th Battalion North Roscommon. His home was a drop spot for dispatches (carried by Brian Connor of Ballinameen). After the War he emigrated to the United States

Peter Beirne (Corderryhugh, Fuerty) Fuerty Coy., 2nd Battalion South Roscommon

Thomas Beirne (Ballykilcline, Ruskey) a member of the Kilglass Company in the 3rd Battalion North Roscommon

Thomas Beirne (Kildalloge, Strokestown) brother of James, served as Quartermaster of "I" Company in the 3rd Battalion North Roscommon in the latter part of 1921. He took the Anti-Treaty side during the Civil War, and was interned in Athlone on 5 March 1923

Thomas Beirne (Greaghnaleava, Arigna) 4th Battalion North Roscommon. Beirne was active with the Arigna Flying Column during the Civil War, and was arrested on 4 September 1923 along with Frank Mulherin by the Free State troops. He was wounded in the operation

Timothy Beirne (Kilmacumsey, Elphin) 2nd Battalion North Roscommon, Captain of the Elphin Company

William Beirne (Ballyfeeny, Strokestown) a member of the Kilglass Company in the 3rd Battalion North Roscommon

Edward Bellew (Bealnamullia, Athlone) 3rd Battalion Athlone Brigade. Bellew drilled with his Company, trained to use firearms, took an active part in the General Election of 1918, attended Battalion meetings, worked with the

Republican Police force at disputed farmland in Bealnamullia and Clongowna. He was with a group of Volunteers that seized ammunition from an airplane that made a forced landing at Keelogues in 1919. Took part in **the burning of the Barracks at Bealnamullia**, mobilised for an attack on Cloonark Barracks, and **attempted an ambush at Curraghaleen** in October 1920. Near Truce time, he guarded the ASU Headquarters in the area, **destroyed the bridge at Millbrook**, blocked roads at Millbrook and Monksland, harboured and aided escaped prisoners. During the Truce he trained at Greenfield, Donamon, and Falty, in addition to collecting funds to aid the Volunteers and attending the Arbitration Courts

Joseph Belton (Toberavaddy, Athleague) a member of "D" Coy. in the 2nd Battalion South Roscommon. He, along with Pat Conboy, James Keegan, Tom Mannion, James Kenny, Seamus McGovern, and Patrick Farrell captured a Tan during the War for Independence

Sean Bergin (Moor Coy.) 1st Battalion South Roscommon. Bergin was a native of Nenagh, Tipperary. Sent by his father to Castlerea to learn about the timber business, he helped organise the Battalion Flying Column and became its O/C. Both Sean's father and his brother Patrick were incarcerated during the war.* In 1920 Bergin became very sick with pleurisy and pneumonia, and was hidden in Micheál O'Callaghan's home in Cloonboniffe before being transferred to Nurse Coll's parents' home, and then to Castlebar hospital (under an assumed name and cloaked in a borrowed overcoat to add an air of respectability). Both Vera McDermott in *The Woodlands of Loughglynn* and Micheál O'Callaghan in *For Ireland and Freedom* claim that Bergin was in the hospital until March of 1921. The private papers of Gerald O'Connor and the Volunteer Witness Statement of Frank Simons, however, place Bergin at particular battles: the **attempted attack on Kilmurray Military Camp** in June 1920, the **attack on Frenchpark Barracks** 2 October 1920, the **Fourmilehouse Ambush** on 12 October 1920, the **attempted attacks at Castlerea** in January 1921, the **attack on Elphin Barracks** 11 February 1921, the **attempted ambush at Cloonsheever** in March, and the **attack on the military at Castlerea** 7 April 1921. Wherever he spent the first months of 1921, we can be certain that he arrived at the cottage of Roger McDermott in Loughglynn on the night of 18 April. After an evening of gaiety with the local girls, he and three other Volunteers retired for the night. It was to be his last. He and his comrades were surprised the next morning by a party of Tans who had obviously been informed of the Volunteers' whereabouts. He, along with Stephen McDermott, met death in *The Woodlands of Loughglynn* 19 April 1921. Buried Lisboney cemetery

Sheila Bergin, half sister of Sean, interview by author, 6 November 2003, Nenagh, Tipperary.

Thomas Bergin (Bergen) (Carrick, Curraghboy) 4th Battalion South Roscommon. From 1917-March 1919 did organisational work, drilled, and performed scouting duties. Attended lectures and instructions given by Ernie O'Malley during his tour of the Battalion area. Performed police duty during the South Roscommon election and in conjunction with enforcement of Dáil decrees. Bergin was one of a group of Volunteers who raided the private homes of three men — two of whom had joined and one who was about to join the RIC. Not surprisingly, these men had a change of heart! He also raided for arms. About twenty raids were conducted within the Company area, and another fif-

Sean Bergin of the 1st Battalion South Roscommon.

PHOTO COURTESY OF SHEILA BERGIN

Excerpted from: Oration given by Gerald O'Connor on the 50th Anniversary Commemoration of Sean Bergin's Death
19 April 1971

I think I should mention briefly some of my personal recollections of Sean Bergin. The trait that struck one from first meeting him was his refinement — physical refinement and his refinement of thought and speech...He had a great sense of humour in every situation that arose and was always ready for a laugh.

Beneath this mask there was a complete dedication to his duties as a Volunteer Officer and a toughness that surprised one. If there was danger, he ignored it. If there were obstacles in his way, he deliberately refused to see them or be influenced by them.

Altogether he was a worthy son of the county which produced the Treacys, the Breens, the Hogans, the Robinsons and the many illustrious names that have gone into history. That, I think, is the highest compliment I can pay him and in that company we remember him today as he shall always be remembered.

teen were outside the immediate area and performed in cooperation with other Companies of the Battalion. He prevented jurors from attending the British Courts, and held periodic meetings of Dáil Courts when necessity arose. Manufactured ammunition and constructed dugouts for storage of same. Raided the mails and the premises of a court messenger to the British Courts, and seized books and documents in relation to British administration. Bergin participated in the **attempted attack on Kilmurray Camp** in June 1920, an operation that was called off the night of the intended action, the **attempted attack at Clooncraff,** and the **attempted attack on a military lorry at Knockcroghery** in January 1921. The entire Company participated in the arrest of a suspected spy. That man was tried by court-martial and eventually executed — an action which prompted the arrest of ten members of the Company on 5 January 1921 including Bergin. He was severely beaten, taken to Athlone Barracks, and incarcerated in a cell with no bed for three months. Later transferred to Mountjoy, and finally, in the last days of June, shipped across the waters to Wormwood Scrubbs and Pentonville Prisons in England. Tom Hales from Cork was his commanding officer in prison. Released 11 January 1922. After the War he emigrated to the USA

William Berry (Glasson, Co. Westmeath) part of a unit that acted in conjunction with Volunteers from the Athlone Brigade. Imprisoned in Frongoch, the "Irish University"

Dick Bertles (Walderstown, Co. Westmeath) In 1918 Bertles was appointed the Battalion commander in the Drumraney area. This was part of the Athlone Brigade. He was a member of the Athlone Flying Column. He **commanded an ambush party** in late 1920 **at Auburn** in County Westmeath in which four or five RIC were wounded and Volunteer Seamus Finn lost his life. He was also present at the **attack on Streamstown Barracks** in July 1920. He was arrested near Truce time, and his position was taken by Thomas McGiff. Bertles was killed during the Civil War in Ballymore on 22 January 1923. He is buried in Drumraney Cemetery. Before the hostilities, he had been a carpenter

Edward Birmingham (Ballinross, Cloonfad, Ballyhaunis, Co. Mayo) 1st Battalion South Roscommon. Took part in the **destruction of barracks** in 1920, the disarming of two British soldiers at Cloonfad in May 1921, and the **attack at Castlerea** in November 1922. Served as 1st Lieutenant of Cloonfad Coy., which had, in July 1922, thirty-five members. In October 1922 he and his brother and the two Mullarkey brothers engaged the **military at Ballinross.** He also took part in the **attack on Free State troops at Castlerea** on 30 November 1922

James Birmingham (Ballinross, Cloonfad, Ballyhaunis, Co. Mayo) a member of the Cloonfad Coy. in the 1st Battalion South Roscommon. Took part in the **destruction of barracks** in 1920, and the disarming of two British soldiers at Cloonfad in May 1921. During the Truce he attended the Company training camp where he specialised in intelligence, scouting, and dispatch work. In July 1922 he joined with other Anti-Treaty men in the **attack at Ballinagare.** He and his brother Edward and the two Mullarkey brothers engaged the **military at Ballinross** in October, and a month later took part in the **attack on Free State troops at Castlerea**

Sean Birmingham (Farnbeg, Strokestown) 3rd Battalion North Roscommon, was sworn into the IRB in August 1916 and the Volunteers a year later. He became an officer in 1918, and served as an armed bodyguard for Ernie O'Malley when the latter was organising the county units in June, July, and August. He raided for arms at T. McDonnells, Bridge Street; Medical Hall in Church St.; Phelim O'Neill's, Church St.; Gayners in Bawn St.; and Mount Browne House among other assorted sites (at times commanding the raiding party). Accompanied by Tommie Mason and Martin O'Connor, he held up and searched District Inspector

William Berry and Sean Costello.

Nixon and Head Constable Glancy from Strokestown, commandeered Jack Feeley's car for Battalion Commandant to convey prisoners, and raided houses of persons suspected of being loyal to the Crown. Organised destruction parties for various barracks in the Battalion area, and took part in **destruction of records in the local income tax offices and courthouse**. He assisted five members of the military forces stationed at Strokestown to desert — bringing their arms and ammunition with them, which Birmingham dutifully turned over to Captain Tom Shevlin. He served as scout at the **attack on Walpole's house at Castlenode**, and the **attack on the military at Tarmon** — both in the month of November 1920. He was part of the **assault party in Strokestown** on 6 January 1921, but was arrested thirteen days later and sentenced to two years penal servitude for being in possession of "seditious material." (Sinn Féin literature was found in the thatch of his home.) He became a guest of the British in Athlone, Mountjoy, Wormwood Scrubbs, and Wandsworth. While in prison, he participated in two different hunger strikes —one for eighteen days, the other for three weeks. He was released in January of 1922, but soon returned to his rebel ways. When he came back to his home, he reorganised the Strokestown Coy. and was appointed its Captain. He also served as the Battalion Intelligence Officer under Brian Nangle. He travelled to Boyle in June of 1922 to report for service, but was advised to return to his own Battalion area and await instructions. Birmingham was re-arrested on his way back at Elphin by his former comrade, Sean Leavy (now in the Free State forces). He was detained at Athlone until October 1922, when he was released on parole. Birmingham didn't get to enjoy the fresh air for long. He was re-arrested on 29 October. In January 1923 he obtained a doctor's release from prison. Before the War, Birmingham had been a printer with the *Strokestown Democrat*, but job opportunities were limited for Republicans after the War. When the sons of the owner were old enough to join the business, he was forced to seek employment as a temporary road ganger working eight months out of the year at distances of up to ten miles away from his home in order to support a wife and six children. Such was his sacrifice for Ireland

John Blaney, Berries Company.

John Blaney (Wolfe Tone Terrace, Athlone) Company Captain in the 3rd Battalion Athlone Brigade. The Berries Company was associated with the Coosan Company in County Westmeath. During Easter week, he was with a party of men who headed for Shannonbridge ready to defend it until Roger Casement's rifles arrived. Halfway there, the men received the countermanding order and returned to Coosan. Soon after, he was arrested and sent to Wakefield on 13 May, but was released a few weeks later. He served with the local IRA unit until the Truce, at which time he joined the Free State Army. On 4 July 1922 he was travelling with a party of soldiers between Ferbane and Ballycumber, County Offaly when they were ambushed. He was killed instantly. He had been shot in the head and "it was when they got out of the danger zone that Acting-Brigadier Adamson and his party discovered the terrible calamity that had befallen their popular comrade. He had remained in a kneeling position, his rifle tightly gripped, and his head bent down."* He is buried in Cornamagh Cemetery, Athlone

Quoted from his obituary notice in the Westmeath Independent, July 1922. (Interestingly, George Adamson had been killed in April of 1922.)

Michael Blighe (Trien Coy.) 1st Battalion South Roscommon

James Bodkin (Carniska Coy.) 3rd Battalion North Roscommon

Edward "Ned" Bofin (Arigna area) affectionately known as "The Republican DeWet," Bofin, along with Seamus Cull, headed a Flying Column during the Civil War which challenged Sean MacEoin's Free State forces many times. While a huge roundup was going on in his home territory, Bofin was busy getting married in Leitrim village. His luck ran out on 25 March 1923, however, when he and three others were captured in the Arigna mountains by the Free State troops

Paul Bofin (Arigna area) brother of Ned, 4th Battalion North Roscommon, active with the Flying Column. He had been incarcerated in Sligo Gaol from which he escaped on 17 October 1922. He was re-arrested with his brother Ned on 25 March 1923

Johnny Bohan 3rd Battalion Athlone Brigade. Johnny was a charter member of The O'Rahilly Sinn Féin Club of Summerhill in south Roscommon. In April 1920 he helped John Harney, who was a stonemason by trade, dismantle the keystone of the arch of the bridge over the Cross River at Summerhill. Unfortunately, the Tans had the damage repaired within a day

Harry Boland (of Dublin) participated in the Rising, and for his efforts was sentenced to ten years (five years remitted). In 1918 he became the Sinn Féin standard bearer for South Roscommon. Travelled with de Valera to the United States to raise money and American consciousness for Irish freedom. Later, in the Civil War, was shot by the Free State forces at the Grand Hotel in Skerries, and died at St. Vincent's Hospital in Dublin 2 August 1922 (a few weeks before his great friend Michael Collins was assassinated)

James Boland (Carrowduff) 2nd Battalion South Roscommon. Served as cook for the IRA men when they occupied Donamon Castle

Norah Boland (Fourmilehouse) member of the Cumann na mBan. Quiet, silent worker, who took in many men on the run. An Irish speaker who would teach the neighbouring children the language

Owen Boland (Southpark, Castlerea) 1st Battalion South Roscommon. Participated in the **attack on Frenchpark Barracks** 2 October 1920

Patrick Boland (Castlerea) pub proprietor and grocer, who sent out fresh meat to feed the Volunteers in a house in Caranbeg when the men were on the run. Buried in St. Joseph's Cemetery in Castlerea

Martin Bourke (Caherlistrane, Co. Galway) O/C of a Flying Column in Galway during the Civil War, spent his last night of freedom in the home of Luke Raftery of Lisalway, Castlerea.* The next morning, he figured that the Free State forces had eased up on his area, and he headed back to his own county. He was arrested in Castlerea on 8 January and subsequently executed in Athlone by the Free State on 20 January 1923

Sean Raftery, nephew of Luke, interview by author, 16 April 2004, Valeview Castlerea.

Michael Bowles (Boyle) 1st Battalion, North Roscommon Brigade, later in life the conductor of the Radio Éireann Symphony Orchestra

Matt Boylan participated in the **attack on the Carrick-on-Shannon Courthouse** in September 1920

Michael Boyle (Lisacul) 1st Battalion South Roscommon

Patrick Boyle (Athleague Coy.) 3rd Battalion South Roscommon

Peter Boyle (Ballinlough Coy.) 1st Battalion South Roscommon. Participated in the **attempted ambush at Coshlieve** in July 1920, the **attempted attack on the Castlerea Station Guard** that same month, and the **burning of the Barracks at Ballinlough** 14 September 1920. During the Truce he attended the Battalion's training camp specialising in engineering

James Brady (Killina Coy.) 2nd Battalion North Roscommon. He was one of the first members of the Company when it formed in August of 1917

Michael Brady (Killina Coy.) 2nd Battalion North Roscommon. He was one of the first members of the Company when it formed in August of 1917

Patrick Brady (Ballinameen Co.) 1st Battalion North Roscommon. Took part in the **attack on Elphin barracks** in February 1921

Peter Brady (Killina Coy.) 2nd Battalion North Roscommon. He was one of the first members of the Company when it formed in August of 1917, brother of Tom. Soon afterward he moved to Dublin

Jim Brady (Arigna) 4th Battalion North Roscommon. Although a Cavan man, he enlisted in the Volunteers when he lived at Arigna. He was a miner whose expertise was invaluable in digging the tunnel out of the Curragh in September of 1921. According to C. S. Andrews, author of *Dublin Made Me*, "Only a very expert miner and a brave and strong man could have dug that tunnel. Brady was all of these."* Starting from Hut 31, the three-foot wide by two-feet high tunnel proved to be the escape hatch through which seventy men wiggled and squirmed their way under the campgrounds and out passed the barb wires that surrounded the Curragh. Many of those men were never recaptured. During the Civil War he was a member of the Active Service Unit (Flying Column) of North Roscommon. He was the man responsible for the **destruction of bridges at Knockvicar and Cootehall**. Brady worked as a trade union organiser. After the War he moved to Tullywaltra, Druminespic, Balieboro, County Cavan

p. 186.

Thomas Brady (Drinane, Strokestown) Intelligence Officer for the 2nd Battalion North Roscommon, a founding member of the Killina Company. Joined the IRA in February of 1917. He was also a member of the IRB — taken into the organisation by Michael Dockery. He supplied the use of a house for drilling, confining prisoners, and for making bombs. (John Kelly claimed that he conveyed such bombs to **Elphin** the night of the **attack on the barracks**.) Assisted in the **burning of Ballinameen Barracks** at Easter time 1920, and the **burning of Tulsk Barracks** in September. He was appointed the IO in 1920. Brady did outpost duty the night of the **Elphin Dispensary ambush** on 13 December 1920, blocked roads the night of the **attack on Elphin Barracks**, cut the communication wires between Elphin and Strokestown the day of the **Scramogue Ambush**, and was on guard near the barracks the night the **barracks and courthouse in Frenchpark** were burned. Attended training camps during the Truce. During the Civil War John Kelly claims that Brady joined a bogus Free State Company and came away with bombs, which he promptly gave to the IRA Flying Column. Information he was able to obtain also saved the Battalion O/C from being ambushed by the Free State troops

Thomas Brady (Ballinameen Coy.) in the 1st Battalion North Roscommon

Jim Breheny (Portrunny, Ballymurray) 4th Battalion South Roscommon. The Knockcroghery Coy. formed in 1917 with Patrick Kelly of Culleen, Lecarrow as Captain and Breheny serving as the 1st Lieutenant. (He was later promoted to O/C of the Battalion which included the St. John's and Knockcroghery area when the South Roscommon Brigade was first formed in 1918.) He served as the Vice O/C of the South Roscommon Brigade. Both Breheny and Pat Kelly were delegates to Roscommon town to elect the Brigade staff. In the summer of 1918, he attended courses of instruction given to officers by Ernie O'Malley at Rahara each evening for several weeks, took a course in semaphore and Morse signalling, and commanded his men in the sham engagements at Taughmaconnell under O'Malley's watchful eye. Breheny also served as a Judge in the Sinn Féin Courts. He headed a party of Volunteers who visited homes of men in the RIC and those about to join. As a result of that visit, the potential RIC recruits decided on another line of work. Breheny participated in the 1918 election, and kept a sharp eye out for Belfast goods, making certain none were landed at Knockcroghery station. He, along with Pat Kelly, Thomas Kelly, and Owen Curley, drew up a set of rules for the opening and closing of shops and public houses — hours which were enforced by local Volunteers. He went house to house canvassing for signatures to the plebiscite for independence. He commanded the party responsible for the **burning of Lecarrow Barracks**. Breheny, along with his men, joined forces with the Kilteevan and St. John's Companies and prepared an **ambush at Clooncraff** — an operation under the command of Pat Madden. Breheny commanded numerous raids for arms. On one occasion, he raided two houses in the Rahara area in which the raiding party was fired on. (The door of the house was finally forced open and a gun and revolver and ammunition were confiscated "for the good of the cause.") On another occasion, Breheny oversaw the trial and sentencing of a man arrested for firing on a Volunteer. That man was transported by Breheny, Tommie Kelly, Owen Curley, and John Breheny to Cloverhill, where he was guarded by local Volunteers for several weeks before being returned to his family. Breheny commanded a party of Volunteers who raided the evening mail train from Dublin and censored the mail taken from it. He commanded the **attempted ambush of two RIC constables at Lecarrow**, the **attempted attack on a military lorry at Knockcroghery**, and the **guarding of the village of Knockcroghery** on 15 August 1920. He also participated in the **attempted attack at Kilmurray Camp** as well as the **proposed attack on the military guard at Castlerea Railway Station**. Breheny oversaw the **holding up of a goods train at Ballymurray** — an action in which large amounts of mail were confiscated and later censored. Four enemy soldiers at Culleen were intercepted and taken by Breheny, Luke Killian, and a few Kilteevan men to a house several miles away. The men lost not their lives but their uniforms. As chief Brigade officer in the

Jim Breheny, 4th Battalion South Roscommon.

area, Breheny oversaw the trials and sentencing of spies. In January of 1921, he and Tom Kelly of Carrigeen were sleeping in a cock of hay near Kelly's home when the all-clear signal (a sheet put out in the yard) was given for he and Kelly to enter the house for breakfast. Patrick Tennant arrived shortly afterwards with an urgent dispatch, but, before anything was done about it, two lorries arrived with troops that surrounded the house. All three men were taken. He was made a prisoner in Athlone Barracks as well as in Perth, Scotland. During the Civil War Breheny took the Anti-Treaty side and served as the Intelligence Officer for the 3rd and 4th Battalions, collected gelignite, made a variety of mines, and assisted the Flying Column with clothing, boots, and supplies. After the War Jim farmed the land. He died on 10 May 1978 and is buried in the ancient Portrunny Cemetery not twenty feet from his former back door

John Breheny (Lisdaulan, Sandfield, Knockcroghery) 4th Battalion South Roscommon, brother of Patrick, Michael, and Owen. Knockcroghery Coy. was formed in 1917 and John became its first 1st Lieutenant. Breheny paraded with the Volunteers and participated in semi-weekly drills. He attended a course of instruction for officers given by Ernie O'Malley at Rahara, and was present for the sham battles overseen by O'Malley at Taughmaconnell in the summer of 1918. Participated in the South Roscommon election of 1918. Breheny was with a party of Volunteers who called on six men who were contemplating joining the RIC. After the Volunteers' visit, the recruits all "got cold feet"! He raided many houses for arms. On one occasion, the daylight raid of an ex-RIC man succeeded in yielding a shotgun, revolver, and, best of all, an RIC uniform. On another occasion, Breheny took part in **raiding two hostile houses** in which four guns, one revolver, and a quantity of ammunition were captured. On a raid in the St. John's area, Joseph Kearney was so seriously wounded that he required treatment in a Dublin hospital. Took part in the **attempted attack at Kilmurray Camp** in June 1920 — an action that was cancelled the night of the intended assault. Breheny was also part of a group of ten Volunteers who arrested and tried a man for firing on and wounding another Volunteer. Breheny, along with Jim Breheny, Owen Curley, and Thomas Kelly transported the man to his "prison" — an abandoned building in the Cloverhill area. He was also in charge of collecting the fine for such miscreant behavior! In addition, Breheny took part in the **proposed attack on the Castlerea Station Guard** in July 1920, the **attempted ambush of two RIC constables at Lecarrow,** an **attempted attack at Clooncraff** in May 1921, an operation under the command of Pat Madden, and an **attempted attack on a military lorry at Knockcroghery**. He, along with the rest of his Company, **guarded the village of Knockcroghery** from reprisal on 15 August 1920 — a reprisal precipitated by British Forces being fired upon on Lough Ree. He was also second in command of an **attempted attack on a party of military about eighteen strong at Knockcroghery** in January 1921. On 21 March 1921, Breheny was hiding out at Jim Quigley's in Rathconnor in the 2nd Battalion area, where he had no doubt gone for a Brigade meeting. A knock was heard on the door of the main house, but Breheny, Quigley, John Gibbons, and a brother of John Conroy were sleeping in an out building. After ten minutes of flurry in the main house, the Tans left, unknowingly abandoning the four Volunteers who had been silently watching the goings-on from the safe vantage point of an adjacent building. John Breheny commanded the **attempted attack at Scrine** — an operation thwarted by the lorry taking a different route back to base. He commanded the **attack on the RIC Barracks at Ballygar** on 1 July 1921. John Breheny, along with his brother Patrick, made the mines used by the Company, devices they put to good use in **attempts to blow up two bridges** — one at **Curry** and the other at **Ballymurray**. During the Truce he was the commanding officer at the Battalion Camp at Drinaun, Ballygar, and was a delegate to Commandant Tom Maguire's review of the Brigade at Ballygar. He was also engaged in the Sinn Féin Courts, appointed to a special service unit, and served as O/C of the 4th Battalion, taking part in the **blowing up of Kellybrook and Curry Railway bridges**, collecting gelignite for the

John Breheny of the 4th Battalion South Roscommon.

A Woman Devoted to Ireland.
Mary Breheny
(Sandfield, Knockcroghery),
member of Cumann na mBan.

This woman gave four sons to the Movement. Mary ran a safe house as well as lending her field for use as a dugout.

Died 1 November 1938 and buried in Killenboy, Knockcroghery

Michael Breheny of Sandfield, Knockcroghery, 4th Battalion South Roscommon.

making of mines, and commanding a South Roscommon Flying Column, which roamed the area irrespective of county borders and fought the Free State forces where they found them. He later emigrated to the USA, but returned to Ireland, and died on 16 June 1975

Michael J. Breheny 4th Battalion South Roscommon, brother of Jim and Patrick. The Knockcroghery Company was formed in 1917 with Patrick Kelly serving as Captain. Breheny drilled with the Volunteers, and acted as a Policeman and summons server for the Sinn Féin Courts. He attended sham battles at Taughmaconnell overseen by Ernie O'Malley in the summer of 1918. Participated in the South Roscommon election of 1918, served as an armed escort for bank officials taking sums of money to fairs in Knockcroghery, acted as an enforcer of Sinn Féin rules regarding public houses, and was in charge of the party of Volunteers who **burned the Lecarrow Barracks**. He, along with some members of his Company assisted by the Battalion staff, acted in conjunction with Kilteevan Company and **attempted an ambush at Clooncraff** in January 1921, an action under the command of Pat Madden. He raided many houses for arms. On one occasion, the daylight raid of an ex-RIC man succeeded in yielding not only guns but an RIC uniform as well. On another occasion, he commanded the party that raided two houses (one RIC and the other a Unionist) that had to be approached by boat on Lough Ree. Breheny also partnered with Volunteers from St. John's Company and raided homes in their district. Took part in the **attempted attack at Kilmurray Camp** in June 1920 — an action that was cancelled the very night of the proposed assault. He, along with the rest of his Company, **guarded the village of Knockcroghery** from reprisal on 15 August 1920 — a reprisal precipitated by British Forces being fired upon on Lough Ree. Breheny **commanded the attack on two RIC men at Knockcroghery Railway Station** on 26 August 1920 — an action that cost one constable his life. Commanded the **attack on a goods train at Ballymurray** in which twenty bags of mails were taken from the train and subsequently censored by Volunteers. He was with the party of Volunteers who **attempted an attack on a party of military about eighteen strong at Knockcroghery** in January 1921, and the **attempted ambush at Scrine**. He collected the IRA levy — a fund that helped purchase arms and equipment for the local Company. He was captured on 11 April 1921 and interned. He later emigrated to the USA

Michael Breheny (Lisdulan, Sandfield, Knockcroghery) brother of John, Patrick, and Owen. Knockcroghery Company, 4th Battalion South Roscommon, was assembled for action in 1917 with Patrick Kelly serving as Captain. Breheny drilled with the Volunteers, served as a Policeman with the Sinn Féin Courts, and canvassed house to house for signatures to the plebiscite for independence. He attended practice battles at Taughmaconnell overseen by Ernie O'Malley in the summer of 1918, served as an armed escort for bank officials taking sums of money to fairs in Knockcroghery, and acted as an enforcer of Sinn Féin rules regarding public houses. He took part in the **burning of Lecarrow Barracks,** and in raids on two hostile houses in the Rahara area. Breheny was one of ten men who tried a man convicted of firing on a Volunteer. The man was subsequently taken to Cloverhill, and detained under guard for several weeks before being returned safely to his family. Participated in the **attempted attack on a military lorry in Knockcroghery**, an **ambush at Knockcroghery Railway Station** on 26 August 1920 in which one policeman lost his life, and the **attempted ambush of a party of military about eighteen strong at Knockcroghery** in January 1921. After the Truce he was appointed to a special service unit, and served as Adjutant of the Company. Breheny was involved with the making of mines, raiding for bicycles which proved useful to the Brigade Column, and supplying clothing to the Flying Column. Died 23 July 1975

Owen Breheny (Lisdaulan, Sandfield, Knockcroghery Coy.) 4th Battalion South Roscommon, brother of John, Michael, and Patrick. During the Truce Owen was assigned to a special service unit. After the War he farmed the land. Buried in Gailey Cemetery in Knockcroghery

Patrick Breheny (Glanduff, Kiltoom) St. John's Company in the 4th Battalion South Roscommon. Breheny drilled with his fellow Volunteers twice weekly, and helped in the 1918 General Election

Patrick "Paddy" Breheny (Knockcroghery Coy.) 4th Battalion South Roscommon, brother of Jim and Michael J. Knockcroghery Company was assembled for action in 1917 with Patrick Kelly serving as Captain. Breheny drilled with the Volunteers, and attended practice battles at Taughmaconnell overseen by Ernie O'Malley in the summer of 1918. He supplied the petrol to burn the **Lecarrow Barracks**. He took part in the **attempted ambush of a party of military about eighteen strong at Knockcroghery** in January 1921, the **attempted ambush at Scrine**, and assisted in the **Emmoo Ambush** in the 3rd Battalion area on 20 May 1921. Breheny's most important contribution to the war effort may have been his tending to men from the 3rd Battalion who were wounded and brought to an island in Lough Ree. He was also one of eight men entrusted with important dispatches throughout this period. During the Truce he attended the Battalion Camp at Drinaun, Ballygar, was a delegate to Commandant Maguire's review of the Brigade at Ballygar, and carried out police duties and worked in the Arbitration Courts. He was also appointed to a special service unit. He later emigrated to the USA, went into the grocery business, and died in September 1966

Patrick Breheny (Sandfield, Knockcroghery Coy.) 4th Battalion South Roscommon, brother of John, Michael, and Owen. His home was raided on numerous occasions during the Tan War. Patrick was one of the founding members of the Knockcroghery Coy. which formed in 1917 under the leadership of Captain Patrick Kelly. Breheny paraded with the Volunteers, and participated in the semi-weekly drills. He was a Policeman for the Sinn Féin Courts and, in addition, worked as a summons server. He went house to house canvassing for signatures for the plebiscite for independence. Breheny was present for the sham battles overseen by Ernie O'Malley at Taughmaconnell in the summer of 1918. Breheny and nine other members of the Company paid visits to six recruits intending to join the RIC. Those men changed their plans! Participated in the South Roscommon election of 1918, and served as an armed escort for bank officials taking sums of money to fairs in Knockcroghery. He also enforced the rules drawn up by the Republican Police which applied to public houses. Breheny cut the telegraph wires to prevent the news of the **burning of Lecarrow Barracks** from reaching Athlone. He, along with other members of his Company in conjunction with Kilteevan Company and some Battalion staff, took part in the **attempted ambush at Clooncraff**. He raided houses for arms. On one occasion, the daylight raid of an ex-RIC man succeeded in yielding a shotgun, revolver, and an ever-welcome RIC uniform, which could be put to good use at a later date. Breheny was part of a group of ten men who tried and convicted another man of firing on and wounding a Volunteer. The man was transported to Cloverhill, where he was detained by Republican Police for several weeks before being returned to his family. Breheny collected the fine imposed on him. He took part in the **attempted attack at Kilmurray Camp** in June 1920 — an action that was cancelled the very night of the intended assault, and the **attempted ambush of two RIC constables at Lecarrow**. He, along with the rest of his Company, **guarded the village of Knockcroghery** from reprisal on 15 August 1920 — a reprisal precipitated by British Forces being fired upon on Lough Ree. He also took part in the **attempted attack on a party of military about eighteen strong at Knockcroghery** in January 1921, and the **attempted ambush at Scrine**. Patrick Breheny, along with his brother John, made a considerable number of mines used by the Company. Patrick collected the gelignite and assembled the contraptions — devices utilised in the attempts to **blow up two bridges** — one at Curry and the other at Ballymurray. Patrick carried those mines from Lecarrow — a distance of about five miles. In

Patrick Breheny, Sandfield, Knockcroghery Chief Engineer for the 4th Battalion South Roscommon.

PHOTO COURTESY OF MICHAEL BREHENY

addition, he took part in the **attack on the RIC Barracks at Ballygar**, made two attempts to **blow up the railway bridge at Farnaseer** near Knockcroghery, and was one of only eight men entrusted with important dispatches in the area. During the Truce he attended the Battalion Camp at Drinaun, Ballygar, was a delegate of Commandant Tom Maguire's review of Brigade at Ballygar, in addition to carrying out police work. He was also engaged in the Sinn Féin Courts during this time, and was appointed to a special service unit. During the Civil War Breheny was promoted to the Chief Engineer for the 4th Battalion, taking part in the **blowing up of Kellybrook and Curry Railway bridges**, assisting in blocking the ballast train at Kiltoom, collecting the gelignite for the making of mines, and raiding an ex-RIC man's house and serving him notice to leave the county. He also supplied the Flying Column with clothing and boots. He was interned in the Curragh for part of the war. After the hostilities, he put his engineering skills to good use working for Hanlon Ford in Ballymurray. He died 16 March 1981

Tom Breheny (Knockcroghery) interned in Athlone 25 January 1923

Francis Brennan (St. John's Coy.) 4th Battalion South Roscommon. He drilled with his fellow Volunteers twice weekly. His father was none too fond of the idea of his son joining the IRA, and he kicked him out of the family home. Brennan emigrated to the USA and never came back to Ireland

James Stephen Brennan (Ballytrasna, Boyle) Captain of "A" Company in the 1st Battalion North Roscommon, brother of Pat. James Stephen joined the IRB in February 1915. Took part in the **Rockingham Raid**, the first arms raid in the county. Participated in the disarming of soldiers, and the **Hopkins raid**, which occurred in Strokestown in mid-February 1921. Carried dispatches on the Red Route. He was beaten by the Black and Tans at his home August 1920. Raided for arms, sat in ambush for many nights, and generally supported his brother Pat's efforts. During the split in the Army, he took the Republican side, and, according to intelligence reports, **blew up the Knockvicar and Cootehall bridges** on the 14th of August. He was arrested shortly after on 27 August, and sent to Mountjoy on 10 January 1923. After the War he emigrated to North America. Arriving in Canada, he went across the border to the United States, where he lived as an illegal immigrant. He worked in an athletic club

Jim Brennan (Kilteevan Coy.) 3rd Battalion South Roscommon. Both he and his brother Jack served in the Company. He was once threatened by the local police

John "Jack" Brennan, Vice O/C of the South Roscommon Brigade.

by having a hood placed over his head and ordered to give information about his brother Jack's whereabouts. Although he refused to divulge any pertinent facts, the Black and Tans let him go

Jim Brennan (Cootehall Coy.) 5th Battalion North Roscommon. Arrested 8 August, sent to Athlone, and finally shipped to Mountjoy on 10 January 1923

John Brennan a member of the Kilgefin Coy., 3rd Battalion South Roscommon. He later joined the Garda Síochána

John "Jack" Brennan (Carrowkeel, Fuerty) 3rd Battalion South Roscommon, brother of Michael. He had originally been the Captain of Kilteevan Company. Jack was also on the first Sinn Féin County Council. On the 2nd of June 1916, he was sent to Wakefield Prison as an "honoured guest." Later he was transferred to Frongoch, "The Irish University." In early 1917 he was present when Jim Quigley was sworn into the Volunteer movement. Brennan was appointed the first O/C of the South Roscommon Brigade. He later took the position of Vice O/C when Dan O'Rourke took overall command in late 1918. He took part in **disarming two Lancers at Tarmon Cross** in June 1920, the **attack on Frenchpark Barracks** 2 October 1920, and the **Fourmilehouse Ambush**. Ernie O'Malley stopped at Brennan's home, and received dressing for the wounds O'Malley had received in Ballymoe. Brennan's Volunteer activities aroused the suspicions of the local police and Black and Tans, who harassed his brother Jim by placing a hood over his head and threatening to shoot him.* He was arrested during the Civil War on 18 August 1922, and sent to Athlone. Brennan served on the South Roscommon Brigade staff, and was widely known and respected by the men. Long after the final salvo of the War, many who knew him regretted that Brennan had not been the permanent choice for Brigade Commandant of South Roscommon. After the hostilities, he lived in Emlagh near Castleplunkett, and finally moved to Salthill, Galway. He died in 1973 and is buried in St. Coman's Cemetery in Roscommon town

Matty Brennan, nephew of Jack, interview by author, 30 October 2003, Fuerty, Roscommon.

Joseph Brennan (Clogher, Mantua, Castlerea) participated in the **attack on Elphin Barracks** 11 February 1921

Kate Brennan (Clooncraff) welcomed many a man on the run into her home

Fr. Malachy Brennan, P.P. (a native of Cliffoney, Co. Sligo) who was transferred to Mantua in October of 1920. His devotion to the Gaelic League and his Sinn Féin sympathies were known to the RIC, and his home was often searched. Pronouncements from the altar were repeatedly scrutinised by the local officials. During Mass on 26 June 1921, his church was invaded by armed policemen and his congregation threatened. Father Brennan simply ignored the flying bullets and continued on with church service. He concluded his Mass with these words to his congregation, "You have now the grace of God in your hearts. Have no fear. God bless you" (propitious words for the struggle ahead). Fr. Brennan was a member of the National Executive of Sinn Féin, and helped establish the Republican Courts in which he sometimes acted as Judge. Interested in "all things Irish," he was active in the Gaelic League almost from its inception, and was himself a speaker of the native tongue. Father Brennan was transferred to various parishes throughout Roscommon, and he left a trail of building projects in his wake — the Sinn Féin Hall near Ballinasloe, Mantua Parish Hall, with additions or refurbishing to every school in Ahascragh Parish during his ministry there. He died in March 1967, and is buried in the cemetery adjoining Ahascragh Church

Michael Brennan (Carrowkeel, Fuerty) brother of Jack, he was arrested after the 1916 Uprising, and sent to Glasgow and Reading Prisons and finally to Frongoch, "The Irish University." Brennan campaigned extensively for Harry Boland during the 1918 election. He turned his energies towards politics, becoming Chairman of the Roscommon County Council from 1921-1934. He also served as a Deputy in the Dáil from 1927 to 1943, and became the founder and first secretary of the G.A.A. Provincial Council. In later years, when he was asked by his nephew if he had any regrets about his own actions or those of his brothers during the Wars, he firmly replied, "I do not."* Died in the 1960s, and buried in Athleague Cemetery

Matty Brennan interview, Fuerty, Roscommon, 30 October 2003.

Michael "Mick" Brennan.
PHOTO COURTESY OF TONY CONBOY

Mr. Brennan (Elphin) foreman of the snow removal crew, who laboured for several days clearing the road between Elphin and Frenchpark for Count Plunkett's visit in the 1917 bye election

Pat Brennan (Kilgefin Coy.) 3rd Battalion South Roscommon

Pat Brennan (Kiltrustan) served as Adjutant of Kiltrustan Company in the 3rd Battalion North Roscommon

Patrick Brennan (St. John's Coy.) 4th Battalion South Roscommon. When the Company first started in 1917, Brennan drilled with other Volunteers two nights a

Pat Brennan (Ballytrasna, Boyle) Commandant of No. 3 Brigade, 3rd Western Division during the Civil War. He joined the Boyle Company of Volunteers in the spring of 1918, having been a trained Volunteer since 1914. He was appointed 1st Lieutenant of Boyle Coy. two months later. His duties included dispatch work, organising anti-conscription rallies, and raiding for arms. Pat also worked as a road foreman in Boyle — a position that allowed him access to large quantities of explosive detonators and fuses. In February 1920, he participated in a **raid at the Boyle Railway Station**, resulting in seizure of hundreds of gallons of petrol. Two months later, he was present for the **burning of Grevisk**, **Ballinameen**, and **Croghan RIC Barracks**. He also destroyed the Cootehall Income Tax office records. In August of 1920, his home was surrounded at 2 a.m., and shots fired through the door. Masked men dragged Pat outside, threatening to shoot him. They ordered him to take an oath to quit Sinn Féin and the Volunteers. Brennan did neither. In the ensuing months, Brennan trenched roads, raided the Boyle Post Office, and guarded officers and men of the Company from reprisals by the new Auxiliaries. He aided in the **escape of Michael Dockery from Boyle Barracks**. Upon the evacuation of British troops from Ireland, Brennan was ordered to take over the Boyle Union Buildings — a place in which he lived until the Civil War broke out. Because Michael Dockery, the former O/C of the North Roscommon Brigade, chose to join the Free State Army, Brennan was appointed the Brigade O/C in April of 1922. Present at the **Battle of Boyle** in July 1922; the **attack on Free State outpost at Frenchpark**; the **demolition of the Knockvicar and Cootehall bridges** in August 1922; the **attack on Swinford Barracks** and at **Killasser**; assault on Drumsna Barracks; the **burning of the signal cabin at Carrick-on-Shannon**; ambush at Lakeview, Strokestown; burning of the Elphin Garda Barracks; and **the attack on Free State troops at Caldra on the Elphin/Boyle Road**. After the War Pat Brennan returned to farming at Ballytrasna. He died 7 June 1981, and is buried in Eastersnow Cemetery in Boyle

PHOTO COURTESY OF BARRY FEELY

week — Tuesdays and Thursdays. He collected gelignite several times, and was present when **O'Brien's house was burned** — an operation undertaken because the Volunteers feared it would be used by the British Forces. He later emigrated to the USA

Tom Brennan (Kilteevan Coy.) 3rd Battalion South Roscommon. A member of Pat Madden's Flying Column

Tom Brennan (Kilbride Coy.) 3rd Battalion South Roscommon

Winnie Brennan (Ballytrasna) sister of Stephen and Pat, member of the Cumann na mBan, who risked life and limb helping the fighting men

Peter Breslin of Elphin. Joined the Volunteers in 1913 in Dublin, where he was attached to the 1st Battalion. He served his unit as Quartermaster and Supplies Officer. Breslin took part in the Easter Rising. Surviving his activities during the Tan War, he fought in the Four Courts, where he, Ernie O'Malley, and the Court's Quartermaster, set fire to the heap of weapons the garrison left behind when they surrendered. He was incarcerated in Mountjoy, where he was killed on 10 October 1922 in an attempted gaol break

Roger Brock (Kilbride Coy.) 3rd Battalion South Roscommon

Michael Brocken (Knockhall, Ruskey) a member of the Kilglass Company in the 3rd Battalion North Roscommon

Jimmie Brown (Cloonboniffe) whose house was open to men on the run

John Brown (Cloontuskert Coy.) 3rd Battalion South Roscommon

Edward Browne (Castleteehan, Castlerea) 1st Battalion South Roscommon. Participated in the **attack on the Frenchpark Barracks** 2 October 1920

Mai Browne (Cloonfad) opened her home to many men on the run. The Crown Forces responded to her kindness by frequently searching her house

Peter Browne (Hodson Bay) Kiltoom Coy. in the 4th Battalion South Roscommon. After the War he became a farmer

Thomas Browne (Cloghermore, Mantua,) 2nd Battalion North Roscommon. Listed in the GHQ papers in the UCD Archives as the Second Lieutenant of Tulsk Company

Mattie Burgoyne (Roscommon Coy.) 3rd Battalion South Roscommon. Died 1971 and buried in St. Coman's Cemetery

James Burke (Kilgarve, Ruskey) a member of the Kilglass Company in the 3rd Battalion North Roscommon

John Burke a member of Cloverhill Coy. in the 2nd Battalion South Roscommon. He drilled with his Company, collected funds for the Dáil loan, and served under the command of Edward Jackson. Burke later emigrated to the United States

John Burke served as 1st Lieutenant of Kilcroan Coy. in the Glenamaddy Battalion. Although located in Co. Galway, this Battalion was incorporated into the 2nd Western Division with Gerald O'Connor, former O/C of the 1st Battalion South Roscommon, serving as Brigade Commandant. His Company consisted of fifty-two members in April of 1922

John Burke (Cloonmurly, Kilteevan) 3rd Battalion South Roscommon. After the War he served on the Roscommon County Council from 1925 to 1928 as a Sinn Féin member

Joseph Burke (Kilgarve, Ruskey) a member of the Kilglass Company in the 3rd Battalion North Roscommon. Served as an Intelligence Officer for the 3rd Battalion. His home was raided in January 1921. Four months later he was charged in Athlone with possession of documents relating to the operation of Sinn Féin Courts. He was sentenced to two years

Martin Burke was a member of "B" Coy., 2nd Battalion South Roscommon. Burke later emigrated to England

Michael Burke (Athlone) wounded when the RIC fired on a group of civilians in Athlone on 22 October 1920

Patrick Burke (Kilgarve, Ruskey, Dromod) joined the Kilglass Coy. in the 3rd Battalion North Roscommon in 1919. Raided the mails, carried dispatches, searched for arms, and kept guard at Sinn Féin Courts. He **captured** a large amount of **munitions** in July 1920 **at Lavagh, Ruskey**. Arrested 7 January 1921, and interned until the general amnesty in December of 1921

Thomas Burke (Captain) of Glinsk Coy., Glenamaddy Battalion, which was incorporated into the 2nd Western Division with Gerald O'Connor, former O/C of the 1st Battalion South Roscommon, serving as No. 2 Brigade Commander

Joseph Burns (Cortober, Carrick-on-Shannon) took the Anti-Treaty side during the Civil War. Arrested 3 August 1922, and sent to Athlone on 14 November. Transferred to Mountjoy 10 January 1923

Luke Butler (Drumlion, Croghan) When the 5th Battalion was formed at the end of 1919, Butler served as the Captain of Drumlion Company. He was arrested and interned in 1920-1921. After the Western Division was formed, he served as the Vice O/C of the 4th Battalion

William Butler (Curraghboy Coy.) 4th Battalion South Roscommon

Harry Byrne (Sallygrove) a member of the Curraghboy Coy. in the 4th Battalion South Roscommon

John Byrne (Ballyglass, Ballinagare) served as 1st Lieutenant of his Coy. in the 1st Battalion South Roscommon. Took part in the **burning of the barracks at Frenchpark** 2 October 1920

Michael Byrne (Trien Coy.) 1st Battalion South Roscommon

Laurence Butler (Curry) a member of the Curraghboy Coy. in the 4th Battalion South Roscommon. From 1917-March 1919 did organisational work, drilled, practiced scouting procedures and military exercises during the visit to the area by Sean Connolly, performed police duty during the South Roscommon election (guard duty at polling booths and escorting ballot boxes to counting centres). Helped with Dáil Courts when necessity required their convening. Butler participated in arms raids — twenty raids were conducted within the Company area, and another fifteen raids were outside the immediate area and performed in conjunction with other Companies of the Battalion. He also raided the premises of a court messenger to the British Courts and seized books and documents relating to same. Butler manufactured ammunition and constructed dugouts for its storage. Prevented jurors and litigants from attending British Courts, and raided the mails. The entire Company participated in the arrest and confinement of a suspected spy. That man was tried by court-martial and eventually executed — an action which prompted the arrest of ten members of the Company in January 1921. While his comrades were in prison, Butler raided the homes of persons sympathetic to the enemy, and took part in the preparations for an attack on Ballygar Barracks. He was arrested in March 1921, court-martialed on charges of possession of treasonable documents, but was acquitted owing to contradictory evidence presented by Crown witnesses. During the Civil War Butler took the Anti-Treaty side, and spent time blocking roads and assisting the Flying Column

William Byrne (Cornaseer) Kiltoom Coy. in the 4th Battalion South Roscommon

Willie John Byrne (Athlone) when guns were in short supply for drilling purposes in the training base near Crannagh in south Roscommon, Byrne used to fashion pikes for the men in his forge in Athlone.* He also made a mould for the construction of buckshot and homemade bombs of the canister type, which were filled with gelignite**

*_Drum and Its Hinterland_ by Edward Egan, p. 288.
**_Seamus O'Meara Volunteer Witness Statement to the Bureau of Military History_, p. 52.

Andrew Byron (Falmore, Ballinagare) 1st Battalion South Roscommon. Drilled with his fellow Volunteers, collected funds for the Dáil loan, and enforced the Belfast boycott. Took part in the **destruction of barracks** in 1920, the **attempted attack on Kilmurray Military Camp** in June, the **attempted attack on the Castlerea Station Guard** in July, the **attack on Frenchpark Barracks** 2 October 1920, and several attempted ambushes in Castlerea in January 1921. During the Truce he attended the Company and Battalion training camps. He took the Anti-Treaty side during the Civil War, and fought the Free State troops **at Ballinagare** in July 1922. Later he emigrated to England, where he died and is buried

Patrick Byron (Falmore, Ballinagare) 1st Battalion South Roscommon, brother of Andrew. He participated in the enforcement of the Belfast boycott. Patrick took part in the **destruction of barracks** in 1920, and participated in the **attack on Frenchpark Barracks** 2 October 1920. During the Truce he attended the Company training camp. In July 1922, during the Civil War, he fought against the Free State troops **at Ballinagare**

J. Cafferkey (Loughglynn Coy.) 1st Battalion South Roscommon. After the War he emigrated to the United States

Denny Cahill (Flagford, Carrick-on-Shannon) listed in the GHQ papers in the UCD Archives as the 2nd Lieutenant of Drumlion Company in the 5th Battalion North Roscommon

James Cahill When the Western Division was formed, he volunteered to serve with the Oran Battalion Flying Column

John Cahill (Athleague Coy.) 3rd Battalion South Roscommon

Patrick Cahill (Athleague Coy.) 3rd Battalion South Roscommon

Joseph Callaghan (Lisduff, Fairymount, Castlerea) Captain of "F" Company in the 1st Battalion South Roscommon

James Callery (Doogarg, Knockvicar, Boyle) arrested 28 August 1922 and sent to Athlone. He was released from Stone Park on 19 December 1923

John Callery (Cloonycattan, Elphin) a member of Creeve Coy. in the 2nd Battalion North Roscommon

Edward "Ned" Campion,
Captain of Moor Company
1st Battalion South Roscommon.

Edward "Ned" Campion (Ballindrimley) Moor Company Captain in the 1st Battalion South Roscommon, a native of Blackloon. He participated in the **destruction of barracks** in 1920, the **attempted attack on Kilmurray Military Camp** in June 1920, the **attack on the Frenchpark Barracks** 2 October 1920. He followed that up with action in the **attempted attacks at Castlerea and Frenchpark** in January 1921, the **attempted ambush at Cloonsheever** in March, the **attempted ambush at Loughglynn** in April, the **attempted ambush at Lisacul** (in conjunction with the East Mayo men) in May, and the **attempted ambush of RIC patrol near Ballymoe** that same month. Campion took an active part in the Civil War, **attacking at Ballinagare** in July 1922, and **burning the train at Clooncundra** in November. Later, in 1933, Campion joined the Free State army as a recruiting officer, retiring with the rank of Commandant. Died 25 September 1983 and is buried St. Joseph's Cemetery, Castlerea

John Carey (Ballinaheglish Coy.) 2nd Battalion South Roscommon. He drilled with his Company, collected funds for the Dáil loan, and served under the command of Michael O'Grady

John Thomas Carley (resident of Kilglass, Strokestown) worked as a shop assistant in Enniskillen. Arrested 23 May 1922. Incarcerated on a prison ship in Belfast Harbour, and later moved to Lough Larne. The American cargo ship, *Argenta*, was deemed "unseaworthy" by the US government, and promptly purchased by the Military Advisor of the Government of Northern Ireland for use as a floating gaol. The £3000 purchase price was cheap rent for the Northern Ireland government to pay. It proved to be a very dear price for the unfortunates held within its hold. Carley was released in September 1923

Dan Carlos (Clooneen, Kilglass Strokestown) a member of the Kilglass Company in the 3rd Battalion North Roscommon

Patrick Carlos (Clooneen, Kilglass Strokestown) also a member of the Kilglass Company in the 3rd Battalion North Roscommon

Tom Carney Anti-Treaty Brigadier General in Mayo, commanded the **attack at Swinford Barracks** in August 1922 which involved many North Roscommon men. He was arrested near Ballaghaderreen on 25 August by a column of Alec McCabe's Free State men

Eddie Carlos (Dooneen, Ballinameen) 1st Battalion North Roscommon. Joined the IRA in 1920. Performed dispatch work, guarded prisoners, collected guns from the area, and assisted in the smooth functioning of the Sinn Féin Courts. Participated in the **attack on Elphin Barracks** in February 1921, and was severely burned as a result of the **torching of the barracks and courthouse in Frenchpark** on 25 June 1921. Eddie served as a sentry for the bomb-making works at Roches in Ballinameen, and conveyed rifles from Lenehan's in Hillstreet to Ballinameen. During the Truce he attended the training camps specialising in engineering. When the Civil War started, he was arrested in July 1922, and interned in Boyle. Moved to Athlone on 2 September, Mountjoy on 10 January 1923, and finally Tintown (the Curragh) on 20 February. Upon his release in September of 1923, he was appointed Battalion O/C Fianna Éireann

Jimmie Carrington (Cloonshanagh) a member of the Tarmonbarry Coy. of the 3rd Battalion North Roscommon

Brian Carroll (Corracreigh, Killina, Elphin) Adjutant of the 2nd Battalion North Roscommon. He was one of the founding members of the Killina Company when it formed in 1917. Brian was a member of the Active Service Unit (Flying Column) during the Civil War formed in North Roscommon commanded by Pat Brennan. After the War he emigrated to America, but returned to live in Strokestown in 1945, where he was instrumental in the formation of the St. Patrick's Boxing Club of which he was the first president

Charles Carroll (Erritt, Tibohine, Castlerea) 1st Battalion South Roscommon. Participated in the **attempted ambush at Coshlieve** in July 1920, the **attempted attack on the Castlerea Station Guard** that same month, the **burning of the Barracks at Ballinlough** 14 September 1920, and the **burning of Loughglynn Barracks** in September 1920. He also participated in the **attempted ambush at Lisacul** (in conjunction with the East Mayo men) in May 1921. After the War he was involved in the motor business, and became an undertaker in Ballinlough

George Carroll (Ballyduff, Kiltoom) 4th Battalion South Roscommon

Gregory Carroll (Corracreigh, Killina) listed in the GHQ papers in the UCD Archives as the 2nd Lieutenant in the Killina Company, 2nd Battalion North Roscommon, brother of John Joseph and Brian

James Carroll (Ballymacurley) born in England in 1887, Carroll visited the Ballymacurley area many times as a child. He joined the British Army, and was stationed in India. He returned after World War I to Ireland and Her cause. According to the Gerald O'Connor Papers, James served as the Director of Training for No. 2 Brigade in the 2nd Western Division. After the War he farmed in the Ballymacurley area. He died on Christmas Day 1964

Jamsey Carroll (Boyle) 1st Battalion North Roscommon, a member of the Volunteers since before the Rising

John Joseph Carroll (Corracreigh, Killina) Killina Coy. in the 2nd Battalion North Roscommon, brother of Gregory. Transported and placed the mines in the **attack on Elphin Barracks** in February 1921

Joseph Carroll Quartermaster for Kilmore Company in the 5th Battalion North Roscommon

Pat Carroll (Croghan area) 5th Battalion North Roscommon

Patrick Joseph Carroll (Mountcashel) served as a scout for the Kilgefin Coy., 3rd Battalion South Roscommon. After the War he became a farmer. Died in the 1990s

William Carroll (born in Mount Talbot) was a member of the RIC in Clare, when he changed sides and fought with the IRA. He served as a Captain in West Clare. During the War he was badly wounded, and took six months to recover before returning to active duty

Frank Carty (Clooncunny, Ballinacarrow, Co. Sligo) O/C of the Tubbercurry Battalion with whom Roscommon men fought. Planned the attack on Major Percival's house in the spring of 1920. He was arrested three days later. His escapades included being rescued from Sligo Gaol, an escape from Derry Prison, a recapture in Glasgow Scotland, and an attempted rescue from a police van in that city. He obtained his freedom just before the Truce, and, in 1921, was elected to the Sligo County Council. During the Civil War he was one of the four top commanders in Sligo, who successfully challenged the Pro-Treaty troops. He remained in the IRA long after the "dump arms" order, and was arrested 4 January 1925, and conveyed to Crumlin Road Prison

James Carty (Castleplunkett Coy.) 2nd Battalion South Roscommon. He drilled with his Company, collected funds for the Dáil loan, and served under the command of Captains Jack Ryan and Luke Raftery

John Carty (Fuerty) 1st Lieutenant of Fuerty Coy. in the 2nd Battalion of South Roscommon. He drilled with his Company and collected funds for the Dáil loan. He served under the command of Bernie Kearney. Carty was placed in charge of transport for the 3rd Battalion, No. 2 Brigade when the 2nd Western Division was formed. His home served as the headquarters for "D" Company during the post-Truce times. He later emigrated to the United States

Mick Carty, Aghadrestan, Loughglynn.

Michael (Mick) Carty (Aghadrestan, Loughglynn) 1st Battalion South Roscommon. He was a member of the Flying Column. Under the leadership of Martin Ganley who served as his Captain, Carty participated in the **destruction of barracks** in 1920, the **raid for petrol at Ballinlough Station** in June 1920, the **attempted attack on Kilmurray Military Camp** that same month, and the **attack on Frenchpark Barracks** 2 October 1920. He was present at the **attempted ambush at Cloonsheever** in March 1921, and acted in the covering party for the **attack on the military at Castlerea** on 6 April 1921. He also was part of the **ambush party at Loughglynn** in April 1921, an **attack party at Lisacul** (an action taken in conjunction with the East Mayo men) in May 1921, and the **attempted ambush of an RIC patrol near Ballymoe** that same month. Shot 2 June 1921 by the Tans at the home of the O'Connors in Aghadrestan, and is buried in Cuiltyboe Cemetery. Name inscribed on the tablets in front of the Shankill Monument near Elphin

John Carty (Trien Coy.) 1st Battalion South Roscommon

John Carty (Athlone area) see Surrounding Volunteer section at the end of the Roscommon Listing

Edward "Ned" Casey (Knockhall, Ruskey) a member of the Kilglass Company in the 3rd Battalion North Roscommon

James Casey (Knockhall, Kilglass, Strokestown) Quartermaster for the 3rd Battalion North Roscommon. Took part in the **attack on the RIC patrol at Strokestown** in January 1921, and the **attempted attack on Elphin Barracks** on 4 February 1921. He later moved to Main Street, Roscommon town. James Casey was a powerfully built man. A 5'10" frame packing over 200 pounds of solid muscle, his brown hair framed a faced punctuated by blue eyes and an angelic smile. He "looked the opposite of what he really was — a high class fighting hero and dead shot"*

An Old Soldier's Memories by Tommy Loughran, p. 216.

John Casey took part in the **attack on the RIC patrol at Strokestown** in January 1921, and the **attack on the RIC Barracks at Tarmonbarry** in July 1921

Larry Casey (Roxborough, Derrane, Roscommon) a member of Kilgefin Coy., 3rd Battalion South Roscommon

Michael Casey (Derryhannee, Curraghroe) helped with the 1917 bye election. Participated in the **attack on the Tarmonbarry patrol** in January 1921, **Scramogue Ambush**, and the **attack on the Tarmonbarry Barracks** in July 1921

Peter Casey (Newtown, Tarmonbarry) joined the IRA in 1917, and became the Vice O/C of the 3rd Battalion when Sean Leavy assumed the O/C position in 1920. Participated in the **attack on the Tarmonbarry patrol** in January 1921, the **Scramogue Ambush**, and the **attack on Tarmonbarry Barracks** in July 1921. After the War he started a garage business in Roscommon town, which later grew to be "one of the most successful garage businesses in the west of Ireland." Died 1953

Peter Casey from the Tarmonbarry area, 3rd Battalion North Roscommon. He participated in the **attack on the Tarmonbarry patrol** in January 1921, **attack on Elphin Barracks** on 11 February 1921, and **Scramogue Ambush**. He was also a member of the Flying Column. After the War he became a Sergeant in the Garda Síochána, and was stationed at Tullyvin, Cootehill, Co. Cavan

Thomas Casey served as an **outpost at Scramogue**, and participated in the **Tarmonbarry patrol attack** in January 1921 armed with a shotgun. He was arrested in April 1921, and given a six months sentence. Released at the general amnesty. He later joined the Garda Síochána, stationed at Ennis, Co. Clare

Francis Caslin (Elphin Street, Strokestown) 2nd Lieutenant of Kiltrustan Company in the 3rd Battalion North Roscommon. He took over the leadership position after Pat Mullooly was arrested. After the War he became a farmer. He is buried in the Strokestown Cemetery

James Casserly (Ballinlough Coy.) 1st Battalion South Roscommon

John Casserly (Mockmoyne, Boyle) a member of Croghan Coy. in the 5th Battalion North Roscommon. After the War he joined the Garda Síochána, and was stationed in Mallow, County Cork

Michael Casserly (Tully) a member of Moor. Coy. in the 1st Battalion South Roscommon. Participated in the **attempted attack on Kilmurray Military Camp** in June 1920, the **attack on the Frenchpark Barracks** 2 October 1920, the **attempted attacks at Castlerea** and **Frenchpark** in January 1921, and, during the Civil War, the **attack at Castlerea** in November 1922

Bernard Cassidy (Corry) a member of the Kilgefin Coy., 3rd Battalion South Roscommon. Many of the members of the Kilgefin Company participated in the **Fourmilehouse Ambush** on 12 October 1920. Emigrated to the USA

Jack Cassidy (St. Patrick St., Castlerea) 1st Battalion South Roscommon. Interned for his Sinn Féin sympathies (see photo on page 400). By July 1922 Cassidy was serving as a Lieutenant in charge of engineering for No. 2 Battalion, 2nd Brigade, 2nd Western Division. He was present for Pat Glynn's Memorial Service in Loughglynn Church in 1970

Michael Cassidy (Strokestown) 3rd Battalion North Roscommon. In the aftermath of the Rising, he was sent to "The Irish University," Frongoch, in Wales

Patrick Cassidy (Ballinagare) 1st Battalion South Roscommon. Drilled with his fellow Volunteers, collected monies for the Dáil loan, and enforced the Belfast boycott. Participated in the **attack on Frenchpark Barracks** 2 October 1920

Dan Caulfield (Ballaghaderreen) took the Anti-Treaty side, and was arrested and sent to Mountjoy in January 1923. He was transferred to Tintown II on 20 February, and not released until 18 December 1923

Michael Caulfield (Trien Coy.) 1st Battalion South Roscommon

Timothy Caulfield (Largan, Strokestown) Kiltrustan Coy. in the 3rd Battalion North Roscommon. He, along with Michael Tiernan and Tom Brady, served as far outposts for the **Scramogue Ambush**

Dan Cavanagh (Derryfeacle, Ruskey) a member of the Kilglass Company in the 3rd Battalion North Roscommon

W. T. Cavanagh Republican Judge in the Kilglass area

Pat Cawley (Boyle) 1st Battalion North Roscommon, member of the Volunteers since before the Rising

Eamonn Ceannt, born in Ballymoe on the Roscommon/Galway border. Member of the IRB, Commandant of the 4th Dublin Brigade, and member of the National Council that helped plan the Easter Rising. Also a signer of the Proclamation of the Irish Republic. After his arrest, he was executed at Kilmainham on 8 May 1916. (He was ministered to before his death by Father Albert Bibby, who was later exiled to Solvang, California, where he died of cancer. This author has visited and paid her respects to both Fr. Bibby's former gravesite in California, and his permanent resting place in Rochestown, County Cork. She thanked him for all "the boys")

John Chapman (Clooncommon, Kilmore) in 1922 he was serving as the 1st Lieutenant of "A" Company in the newly formed 4th Battalion of the 3rd Western Division. Took part in the **robbery of the Dublin-Sligo mail train**. He took the Anti-Treaty side in the Civil War, and was arrested on 6 September 1922. He was sent to Athlone, where he was released two months later

Michael Chapman (Green St., Boyle) 1st Battalion North Roscommon. Joined the Volunteers in March 1917. Took part in the anti-conscription demonstrations, parades, dispatch work, raiding railway stations and searching RIC luggage, and confiscating petrol of boycotted traders. Before the Civil War, he stood guard duty at the vacated military and RIC Barracks in Boyle. When the firing started on 1 July 1922, he took part in an **attack on Free State forces on the Boyle/Frenchpark Road**, and was appointed general runner, whose job it was to connect up with different sections of the Column after they had been sent back to their Battalion areas from the Battle of Boyle. Chapman was eventually sent home by orders of Pat Duignan and Tom Carney (O/C of the East Mayo Brigade) due to a swollen stomach and feet — a condition incurred from exposure and continual dispatch work through mountain passes and down the by-roads. He was attended for three months in his neighbour's house by Doctor Leyland. When he did return home, he was arrested, and charged with shooting a Free State soldier on the Boyle/Carrick-on-Shannon Road. Chapman was shoved up next to a wall and threatened with execution, but ultimately saved by a "dying man's confession." Afterwards, he kept in contact with the ASU in their dugouts, supplying information regarding Free State troop movements

Patrick Chapman (Abbeytown, Boyle) 1st Battalion North Roscommon. Member of the Connaught Rangers, who enlisted in 1914, and fought in Iraq, Egypt, Haifa, Jerusalem, and France. Joined the IRA upon his return to Ireland in July 1919. Chapman did intelligence work. In 1919 he secured information and 100 rounds of ammo and a revolver from a friendly soldier who worked as the cook in Boyle Barracks. After returning home from an arms raid north of town in June 1920, he and two other Volunteers were surprised by a patrol of RIC, which resulted in an exchange of gunfire and one RIC policeman being wounded. From April to July, he engaged in raids for arms and Belfast goods, and held up the Boyle Post Office (which was about 300 yards from the military and RIC Barracks). A September raid on an ex-RIC Sergeant, who lived on the west side of town within 200 yards of the Tan Barracks, yielded a revolver, shotgun, and ammunition. Chapman aided in the **escape of Molloy and Dockery from Boyle Barracks** in May 1921. During the Truce he served as the musketry and drill instructor in the Battalion camps for five weeks. Before and after this period, he attended the Company camps to teach the basics. Chapman performed guard duty on the Union Buildings at Boyle before the outbreak of the Civil War. During the War Chapman served as Quartermaster for the ASU, and took an active role in the **Battle of Boyle, Swinford Barracks 4 August, Killassar, attack on Frenchpark, Drumsna Barracks** 24 August, and the **firefight at Derrycarne House** in Ruskey on 6 September. He also participated in the near constant ambushes and harassment of the Free State troops in Boyle, **attack on the outposts on the Boyle/Carrick-on-Shannon Road** in February 1923, **ambushes at Ardeash, and on Elphin Street**. He remained on the run until August 1924, living in dugouts. He was a member of Local Defence Force in 1941. Died 1974 and is buried in Ardcarne in Boyle

Harry "Lewis" Christy (Boyle) 1st Battalion North Roscommon. Later in life became a tailor. Buried in Ardcarne Cemetery in Boyle

Joe Claffey a guard on the trains that travelled through northeast Roscommon. He gave excellent service to the Volunteers by carrying dispatches and munitions

Clancy (see Glancy)

Frank Cline (Knockhall, Ruskey) a member of the Kilglass Company in the 3rd Battalion North Roscommon

Rev. Fr. Patrick J. Cline, C.C. (native of Dooan, Kilglass; curate at Elphin) active supporter of Sinn Féin candidate in the 1917 bye election, organised a work party to shovel 3-4 foot snowdrifts from the road between Frenchpark and Elphin in time for Count Plunkett's visit. Gave Sis Murray (Josie Murray's wife) her first Sinn Féin badge when she was six years old

Edward Coen (Donamon Coy.) 2nd Battalion South Roscommon. He drilled with his Company, and collected funds for the Dáil loan. Took part in the **raid on the military train at Ballymoe** in June 1920. Later emigrated to the United States

John Coen (Donamon Coy.) 2nd Battalion South Roscommon, brother of Edward. He drilled and paraded with his Company, and served under Captain Pat Dwyer

James Cofferky (Killmore, Ballaghaderreen) arrested during the Civil War, and taken to Mountjoy on 10 January 1923

Jim Coffey (Ballaghaderreen) one of the first members of the Ballaghaderreen Coy. in the East Mayo Brigade. He was the brother of Pat, Martin, and John

John Coffey (Ballaghaderreen) he was a member of the Ballaghaderreen Coy. in the East Mayo Brigade

John Coffey (Tully, Carrowbehy, Castlerea) Ballinlough Coy., 1st Battalion South Roscommon. Participated in the **burning of the Barracks at Ballinlough 14 September 1920**, and the **burning of the Loughglynn Barracks** in September 1920. During the Truce he attended the training camps at Hermitage and Erritt

Martin Coffey (Ballaghaderreen) one of the first members of the Ballaghaderreen Coy. in the East Mayo Brigade; brother of Patrick, John, and Jim. In 1919 he was appointed clerk in the Republican Court

Pat Coffey (Capel St., Ballaghaderreen) one of the first members of the Ballaghaderreen Coy. in the East Mayo Brigade. Arrested during the Civil War on 8 September 1922, and taken to Athlone two months later

Patrick Coffey (Kilteevan Coy.) 3rd Battalion South Roscommon

Thomas Coffey (Ballinlough Coy.) 1st Battalion South Roscommon. Participated in the **burning of the Ballinlough** and **Loughglynn Barracks** in September 1920

Michael Cole (Trien Coy.) 1st Battalion South Roscommon

Bernard Coleman (Bandagh, Ballaghaderreen) arrested during the Civil War in November 1922, and sent to Athlone

James "Happy" Coleman (Ballaghaderreen) one of the founding members of the Ballaghaderreen Coy. in the East Mayo Brigade. Died in the influenza epidemic of 1918, and is buried in Kilcoman Cemetery

---

Railding for Arms

Pat Chapman's account of his activities during the War:

I joined the IRA about July or August 1919 and from that until the beginning of 1920 I was put on intelligence work by the Battalion Commandant. My orders were to move about among the enemy and find out these — strength about raids to be carried out and all other matters that would be useful to us.

About the middle of November 1919 I got very friendly with a cook in the military barracks by the name of Langley being an ex-soldier myself and both of us being in France. We used to have some long talks when we met about the different battles and places resulting in I getting him to bring me out ammunition amount in all to 75 rounds — fifty .303 and twenty-five Webley also a Webley revolver which I gave him one pound for myself and John Sheerin (of Doon, Boyle) paid for it. I also got from (him) on two occasions information about the round ups of Jim Hunt, Marren (M. J. Marren of Mount Irwin, Gurteen, Co. Sligo), and a few others — especially the wanted Hunt and Marren. Those raids were carried out at the time he told me, but with no results as the information had got(ten) there hours before the start on the raids.

In February 1920 I was notified to attend a meeting about two miles outside the town (of Boyle) and at this meeting we were told by the Commandant that he had received orders to carry out an extensive campaign of raids for arms, boycott of Belfast goods, and RIC obstruction of British Courts etc.

Returning home from one of those raids which took place north of town, myself and two other lads came in contact with a town patrol of RIC under Head Constable O'Sullivan on the outskirts of town. They called on us to halt and put our hands up. We refused, then they opened fire on us. We returned the fire and after an exchange of shots for about fifteen minutes or so, we made our escape. This was June 1920.

On another occasion we received information that an ex-RIC Sgt., who lived on the west side of town within about twenty yards of the Tan's Barracks, had a revolver and shotgun; and another man that had a shotgun about 400 yards across country from this. Myself and about six others were detailed to call on them and ask them to hand over the firearms and if they refused to take them. We called at the RIC Sgt. first and demanded the firearms. He denied having any. We then demanded to have the door opened and we would search the house. He answered by firing on us from the window. We replied and after a few minutes succeeded in forcing the door and secured the revolver and shotgun with some ammunition. We then crossed the river to the other house but got nothing after searching the house and barns. Later on in 1920 we made another visit and secured his shotgun.

John Joe Coleman (The Square, Ballaghaderreen) first Company Captain in the East Mayo Brigade (which took in parts of west Roscommon), arrested after the Rising and housed in Lewes and Glasgow Jails. On Easter Monday, Coleman was contacted by Alec McCabe, who informed him that a Rising was to take place in Dublin irregardless of Eoin MacNeill's countermanding the original orders. Coleman had no men mobilised and only two rifles to offer for the cause.* Coleman served as the drill instructor of the Ballaghaderreen Company. He, along with twenty-some other Volunteers, took part in the **Ambush at Ratra** on 1 September 1920 under the command of Jim Hunt. He was arrested during the Civil War on 8 September 1922, and sent to Athlone two months later. After the War he owned a pub/restaurant in which prominent Sinn Féin members met. Died in the 1960s and is buried in Kilcolman Cemetery

Alec McCabe Volunteer Witness Statement to the Bureau of Military History 1913-21, p. 5.

John Coleman (Lough Ce, Boyle) 1st Battalion North Roscommon. Coleman took part in the **demolition of the Knockvicar and Cootehall bridges** in August 1922. He was a member of the Civil War North Roscommon Flying Column

Martin Coleman (Ballaghaderreen) one of the first members of the Ballaghaderreen Coy. in the East Mayo Brigade

John J. Colgan (Elphin) first Sinn Féin Council in Roscommon. An auctioneer by trade

John Coll (Knockmurry) 1st Battalion South Roscommon. Participated in the **attack on Frenchpark Barracks** 2 October 1920

John J. Colleran (Ballaghaderreen) interned in "the Irish University," Frongoch, after the Rising

Michael Colleran (Drum Coy.) 3rd Battalion Athlone Brigade

Andy Collins (Croghan) 1st Lieutenant of Croghan Company in the 5th Battalion North Roscommon

Annie Collins (Lisonuffy) Carniska Company area. Member of Cumann na mBan. Died 1991

Annie Collins of Lisonuffy

PHOTO COURTESY OF JOHN AND ELIZABETH GREENE

Ellie Collins with husband Jim Shiel, in later life.

PHOTO COURTESY OF JOHN AND ELIZABETH GREENE

Ellen "Ellie" Collins (Lisonuffy) 3rd Battalion North area. Member of Cumann na mBan. Her home was used as a regular meeting place because of its out-of-the-way location. Up a boreen and situated right next to a cemetery, Volunteers could show up any time and receive a welcome. Once, when a prisoner was held in Moher bog, she fed the person daily. Famous visitors to her home included Ernie O'Malley, and local commanders Luke Duffy and Martin Fallon. In 1923, she married the Company Captain, Jim Shiel. She died in 1992

Jack Collins (Killina Coy.) 2nd Battalion North Roscommon. He was one of the first members of the Company when it formed in August of 1917. He made one of the mines used in the **attack on Elphin Barracks** in February 1921

Michael Collins (Aughamuck, Kilrooskey) Kilgefin Company, 3rd Battalion South Roscommon, a member of the IRB and Pat Madden's Flying Column, brother of Peter. Present at the **Fourmilehouse Ambush** in October 1920, the **shootout at Castlenode** in November 1920, the **Scramogue Ambush** in March 1921, and the fight at **Kilrooskey**. He accompanied John Scally's body to Incheneagh Island after the **mine explosion at Cloontymullen**. He, along with nineteen other Roscommon Volunteers, crossed the Shannon in the icy cold of January 1921 to attack the barracks in Lanesboro (the attack was unfortunately cancelled). After the Truce he joined the army, and served as Quartermaster in the

West of Ireland until 1924. Two years later, he joined the Department of Posts and Telegraphs, and served as postman on the Kilrooskey route for forty years. Died 14 February 1974, and buried in the Kilgefin Cemetery

Patrick Collins (Cammoge, Clooneyquinn, Castlerea) 2nd Battalion North Roscommon. He was one of the first members of the Killina Company when it formed in 1917, serving as its first Captain. Arrested as a result of a Crown Forces sweep on 27 January 1921

Peter Collins (Ballybeg, Strokestown) Lieutenant in "E" Coy., 3rd Battalion South Roscommon, brother of Michael, also a member of the IRB and Pat Madden's Flying Column. Served as the sentry when Mr. Walpole of Castlenode was being forced to relinquish his car "for the good of the cause" in November 1920. Present at the **Fourmilehouse** and **Scramogue Ambush**. After the Truce he joined the Free State Army. Died 28 February 1977 and buried in Kilgefin Cemetery

Peter Collins served as 1st Lieutenant of Kilkerrin Coy. in the Glenamaddy Battalion. Although located in Co. Galway, this Battalion was incorporated into the 2nd Western Division with Gerald O'Connor, former O/C of the 1st Battalion South Roscommon, serving as No. 2 Brigade Commandant. His Company consisted of fifty-six members in April of 1922

Stephen Collins
Castleplunkett Coy.

Stephen Collins (Castleplunkett Coy.) 2nd Battalion South Roscommon. He and James Durr of Baslick were arrested during the Civil War while crossing the Castlerea Bridge. Before they were apprehended, they quietly let their revolvers slip into the river, thus avoiding being charged with a capital crime. After the War, Collins emigrated to New York

William Collins (Lisonuffy, Strokestown) joined the IRA in 1917, and was attached to "A" Coy., 3rd Battalion North Roscommon. He drilled with the men, raided for arms, assisted in the functioning of the Sinn Féin Courts, collected funds to resist conscription, took part in the South Longford election as well as the General Election of 1918. He participated in the **destruction of the Fourmilehouse Barracks,** the **attack at Walpole's house** in November 1920, the **Strokestown patrol** on 6 January 1921, **Scramogue Ambush**, and the **attempted ambush at Tarmonbarry.** After the War he became a farmer. Died 1991

Thomas Comack (Clooneen, Kilglass, Strokestown) a member of the Kilglass Company in the 3rd Battalion North Roscommon

Thomas Comack (Ballymartin, Strokestown) also a member of the Kilglass Company in the 3rd Battalion North Roscommon

Kathleen Comber (Athlone) violinist, who provided the merriment for dances given by the Summerhill Cumann na mBan club. Proceeds went to the IRA

Harry Compton

Patrick Commer (Athleague Coy.) 3rd Battalion South Roscommon

Henry Compton (Kilgefin) 3rd Battalion South Roscommon, a member of Pat Madden's Flying Column. Many of the members of the Kilgefin Company participated in the **Fourmilehouse Ambush** on 12 October 1920. Compton was present at **Scramogue**, and the **ambush at Moneen**. He served as Captain of Kilgefin Company, but was captured and sent to the Curragh. He escaped through the Brady tunnel in September 1921, and was never behind bars again. Compton was in front of them many times, however, as he later became Superintendent of the Garda Síochána. Moved to Blackrock, Dublin. Died 1 May 1972

Michael Collins, Aughamuck, Kilrooskey. 3rd Battalion South Roscommon.

Peter Collins of Ballybeg, Strokestown, 3rd Battalion South Roscommon.

William Collins, Lisonuffy, Strokestown. 3rd Battalion North Roscommon.

Kate Compton, sister of Henry, served as cook for "the boys"

Tom Compton (Tuam, Kilrooskey) cousin of Henry, a member of "E" Coy,. 3rd Battalion South Roscommon. Many of the members of the Kilgefin Company participated in the **Fourmilehouse Ambush** on 12 October 1920. After the War he became a small farmer. Died 17 December 1981 and is buried in Kilgefin Cemetery

Martin Conagh (Head of Signals) for the Glenamaddy Battalion. When the Divisional structure for the Army was implemented throughout the country, this Battalion became part of No. 2 Brigade, 2nd Western Division under the command of Brigade O/C Gerald O'Connor of Lisacul

Jack Conboy (Kilmore, Athleague) served with the British Army during World War I in France in a horse regiment. Jack was the Head Centre for the IRB in the Athleague area, and served as Captain of the Company. He also was part of Pat Madden's Flying Column. Died in 1986

James Conboy (Toberavaddy, Athleague) brother of Pat, a member of Fuerty Coy. in the 2nd Battalion South Roscommon. Born in 1895, he was but a young man when the charge bugle sounded for the Volunteers during the War for Independence. Died in the early 1960s

Michael Conboy (Ballinaheglish) 2nd Battalion South Roscommon. He drilled with his Company, and collected funds for the Dáil loan. When the Western Division was formed, he volunteered to serve with the Oran Battalion Flying Column. He later emigrated to England

Pat Conboy. Vice O/C of the 2nd Battalion South Roscommon.

Pat Conboy (Toberavaddy, Athleague) Vice O/C of the 2nd Battalion South Roscommon, brother of James, a prisoner in Castlerea before being shipped farther afield. Born in Passage (between Castlecoote and Athleague), he had been a prominent county footballer before the War. He, along with James Keegan, Joseph Belton, Seamus McGovern, Tom Mannion, James Kenny, and Patrick Farrell captured a Tan during the War for Independence. He fought on the Anti-Treaty side during the Civil War, and was interned. After the hostilities, he became a farmer and agricultural contractor. Died 1973 and is buried in Fuerty Cemetery

Tom Concannon (Chief of Police) for Glenamaddy Battalion, which was part of No. 2 Brigade, 2nd Western Division when the Divisions were formed. Gerald O'Connor of Lisacul was in charge of the Brigade

Edward Conlon (Ballyglass, Ballymacurley) a member of "B" Coy. in the 2nd Battalion South Roscommon

Henry Conlon (Lisnaneane, Clooneyquinn) Tulsk Coy. in the 2nd Battalion North Roscommon

Martin Conlon (Hillsgrove in the parish of Kilmore) a member of the IRB Supreme Council. Moved to Dublin as a youth, where he became a member of the Keating Branch of the Gaelic League, and a member of the IRB. He also acquired a knowledge of his native language. During Easter Week he was stationed at North King Street, and fought near the Four Courts. He visited Roscommon in 1917 after the Plunkett election along with Fr. Michael O'Flanagan to interest and enlist the local men of the Kiltrustan area in the Volunteer movement. Conlon returned in 1918 to Strokestown to organise an IRB unit there. Conlon's home in Cabra Park in Dublin was always open to men on the run. After the Truce he became a TD for Co. Roscommon as a member of the Cumann na nGaedheal party, and served from 1925-1933. (His first year of election in Roscommon he received 21,118 votes!) Five years later, he again entered politics, this time in the Seanad, where he occupied a seat until 1943. As a member of the Dáil, he introduced a bill which required all aspirants to the legal profession to pass a competency test in Irish. That requirement stands today

Michael Conlon (Boyle) Connaught Ranger, who joined the Indian Mutiny in 1920. Sentenced to ten years penal servitude in Maidstone Prison. After the hostilities were over in Ireland, he was released. He returned to Ireland, and joined the Irish Free State Army

Bernard Connaughton (Sandfield) 4th Battalion South Roscommon. Knockcroghery Coy. was formed in 1917 with Patrick Kelly serving as Captain. Connaughton drilled with the Volunteers, and attended practice battles at Taughmaconnell overseen by Ernie O'Malley in the summer of 1918. Participated in the South Roscommon election of 1918, and collected the IRA levy from the local people. He, along with the rest of his Company, **guarded the village of Knockcroghery** from reprisal on 15 August 1920 — a reprisal precipitated by British Forces being fired upon on Lough Ree. After the War he returned to farming. He died in 1956

James Connaughton (Finisolin, Kingsland, Boyle) Adjutant for "D" Breedogue Company in the 1st Battalion North Roscommon. He later emigrated to Chicago

James Connaughton (Rahara Coy.) 4th Battalion South Roscommon. He was interned in Athlone in 1920. A year later, he became a rate collector with the Roscommon County Council, a position he held for over forty years

John Connaughton (Rahara Coy.) 4th Battalion South Roscommon

John Connaughton (Aghagad, Creggs) a member of Fuerty Company in the 2nd Battalion South Roscommon

Joseph Connaughton 4th Battalion South Roscommon. Knockcroghery Coy. was formed in 1917 with Patrick Kelly serving as Captain. Connaughton drilled weekly with the Volunteers, and attended practice battles at Taughmaconnell overseen by Ernie O'Malley in the summer of 1918. He was a summons server for the Sinn Féin Courts, and participated in the South Roscommon election of 1918. He was one of ten men from the Company who arrested and tried a man for firing on a Volunteer. The accused was sentenced to weeks of confinement in Cloverhill. Joseph was a member of the Company throughout the Black and Tan conflict, but did not participate in the Civil War. He died at a young age

Patrick Connaughton 4th Battalion South Roscommon. Connaughton was one of the founding members of the Knockcroghery Coy. which was formed in 1917 with Patrick Kelly serving as Captain. Connaughton drilled with the Volunteers, and attended practice battles at Taughmaconnell overseen by Ernie O'Malley in the summer of 1918. Participated in the South Roscommon election of 1918. He, along with the rest of his Company, **guarded the village of Knockcroghery** from reprisal on 15 August 1920 — a reprisal precipitated by British Forces being fired upon on Lough Ree. During the Truce Patrick commanded the men serving as the Police Force with the Sinn Féin Courts. He later emigrated to the USA

Thomas Connaughton (Rahara Coy.) 4th Battalion South Roscommon

William Connaughton 4th Battalion South Roscommon. In 1917 the Knockcroghery Coy. was formed with Patrick Kelly serving as Captain. Connaughton drilled with the Volunteers, and also attended sham battles at Taughmaconnell overseen by Ernie O'Malley in the summer of 1918. Participated in the South Roscommon election of 1918. He blocked roads, and, during the Truce, worked as a Policeman with the Sinn Féin Courts. He later emigrated to the USA

John Joe Connell (Killina Coy.) 2nd Battalion North Roscommon. He was one of the first members of the Company when it formed in August of 1917

Michael Connery (Killina Coy.) 2nd Battalion North Roscommon. He was one of the first members of the Company when it formed in August of 1917

Patrick Connell (Corgarve, Elphin) served as the First Lieutenant for "E" Coy., 2nd Battalion North Roscommon, a member of the IRB. He devised the plan for the **attack at Elphin Dispensary** on 13 December 1920, and helped plan the **attack on Elphin Barracks** 11 February 1921. He was beaten by the Tans in retaliation for attacks on Elphin police forces. Connell's house was destroyed, and he was interned for part of the War. He served as the Quartermaster for the 2nd Battalion area during the Civil War. During that time, he participated in the **attack at Boyle** in July 1922, the **attack and capture of Boyle Railway Bridge** in November 1922, and the **ambush at Caldra**

Patrick Connery, 2nd Battalion North Roscommon, was one of the first members of the Killina Company formed in August of 1917. He served as the 2nd Lieut.

Annie Connolly (Flaherty) (Fairymount, Kilrooskey) an active member of the Cumann na mBan, who used to lecture about the Republican movement at the Fourmilehouse. She was in charge of the rifle hideout in Fairymount. A hole was dug near her house. She wrapped the rifles in sacks, placed them in the hole, then put galvanized iron over the top. A heavy layer of dirt and sod crowned the hideout on which she dutifully fed her chickens. Annie died in October 1971 and is buried in St Coman's Cemetery

Dan Connolly (Clonberne) which became part of No. 2 Brigade in the 2nd Western Division under the command of Gerald O'Connor of Lisacul. His home served as the headquarters for "H" Company during the post-Truce times

Jim Connolly (Four Roads) 4th

Annie Connolly, Fairymount, Kilrooskey

Battalion in the South Roscommon Brigade

Jim Connolly (Ballinagare Coy.) 1st Battalion South Roscommon

John Connolly (Cryanstown, Knockvicar, Boyle) 4th Battalion North Roscommon

John Connolly (Milltown, Castleplunkett) a member of "C" Coy. in the 2nd Battalion South Roscommon. He had been a soldier in the British Army during World War I, but when he returned to Roscommon, his fighting was for Lady Ireland. Participated in the **attack on Frenchpark Barracks** 2 October 1920. After the War he emigrated to Leeds, Yorkshire England

John Connolly (Connelly) (Athleague Coy.) 3rd Battalion South Roscommon

John Connolly (Trien Coy.) 1st Battalion South Roscommon

Joseph Connolly (Bally Beg) Kiltoom Coy. in the 4th Battalion South Roscommon, brother of Thomas. After the War he became a farmer. Died in the 1970s and buried in the new Kiltoom Cemetery

Michael Connolly (Kiltrustan Coy.) 3rd Battalion North Roscommon. He later joined the Garda Síochána and was stationed in Ballyjamesduff

Patrick Connolly (Trien Coy.) 1st Battalion South Roscommon. Took part in the **attempted ambush at Coshlieve** in July 1920, and the **attempted ambush of RIC patrol near Ballymoe** in May 1921. Blocked roads and scouted on the day Inspector King was shot in Castlerea. Attended the old Castlerea Barracks training camp during the Truce, where he specialised in scouting and dispatch work

Peter Connolly (Fairymount, Kilrooskey) brother of Annie, a member of "E" Coy., 3rd Battalion South Roscommon. Many of the members of the Kilgefin Company participated in the **Fourmilehouse Ambush** on 12 October 1920. Connolly was present at the **Scramogue Ambush** in March of 1921. On one occasion, he served as a lookout perched up in a tree for so long that the pains in his legs remained with him throughout his life. He did not participate in the Civil War, but rather returned to farming. He died in July 1972, and is buried in Kilgefin Cemetery

Sean Connolly (Brigade Vice-Commandant of Longford) a Volunteer organiser appointed by Michael Collins. He and Sean MacEoin (the Blacksmith of Ballinalee) re-formed the Ballinalee Volunteer force in 1917, but the two did not "pull together" well, and thus Connolly was sent to Roscommon where his talent for organising and inspiring men would shine. He earned their deepest respect. Connolly led a party in late January/early February to attack a patrol of Tans from the Ruskey Barrack. On four successive nights, the party lay in wait, but no enemy appeared.* Among his other mischiefs, he, along with Michael Dockery, participated in the **attack on the Elphin Dispensary** on 13 December 1920, and the

Sean Connolly, Brigade Vice-Commander of Longford.

attempted burning of the **Elphin Barracks** on 11 February 1921. Shortly after that attack, Connolly was sent to County Leitrim with the understanding that he would return to Roscommon and have another go at the Elphin Barracks.** He never got his chance. He was with the Leitrim Flying Column at the home of Charles Flynn at Selton Hill, Mohill on 11 March 1921, when the Column was surrounded by British military. Connolly was wounded — apparently shot while in the act of throwing a grenade from which the pin had been extracted.*** He died that night at Carrick-on-Shannon military barracks. The whereabouts of the Column had been made known to the Crown Forces by a spy. Connolly Barracks in Longford town is named in his honour

Memories of an Old Soldier by Tommy Loughran, p. 258.
**Patrick Mullooly Volunteer Witness Statement to the Bureau of Military History, p. 18.
***Charles Pinkman Volunteer Witness Statement to the Bureau of Military History, p. 13.

Thomas Connolly (Feamore) Kiltoom Coy. in the 4th Battalion South Roscommon, brother of Joseph. After the War he became a farmer. Buried in the new Kiltoom Cemetery

William Connolly (Cryanstown, Knockvicar, Boyle) 4th Battalion North Roscommon

Bernard Connor (Dooneen, Ballinameen) Quartermaster for the 1st Battalion North Roscommon. Took part in the **attack on Elphin Barracks** on 11 February 1921. In August of 1922, he became the Intelligence Officer for the Flying Column

Brian Connor (Sheerevagh, Ballinameen) 1st Battalion North Roscommon. Joined Company "C" in April 1920. Took part in collecting guns, and delivering dispatches to Lenehans and Delia Beirne's in Hillstreet, Murphys in Scramogue, and Mulloolys in Kiltrustan. He assisted the Roche brothers in making bombs for the Brigade. Conveyed some of those bombs to the house adjoining the **barracks** in preparation for the **attack on Elphin Barracks**. Served as an armed guard for Sean Connolly when he was travelling from Ballinameen to Hillstreet. Assisted in the construction of the Brigade dugout, guarded James Molloy after his escape from Boyle Barracks, and accompanied him from Ballinameen to Finigans in Clooncuney on 28 and 29 June 1921. Connor conveyed rifles from Lenehans in Ashforth, Hillstreet, and Glancy's house in Drumlin to Ballinameen. Also served as a clerk to the Republican Courts at Ballinameen and Fairymount. During the Truce he attended the engineering and first aid classes at Cootehall Courthouse taught by Andy Lavin TD. He lived and worked in the Divisional munitions factory at Muckinagh, Kilglass from October 1921 to July 1922. (He wasn't keenly aware of the ratio of gunpowder to sulfur.*) During the Civil War he joined the local Free State Company solely to serve as a spy for the Anti-Treaty forces. Connor succeeded in "smashing said company," but was arrested on 2 October 1922, and interned at Athlone on 14 November. He was released shortly afterwards. After the War he and his brothers emigrated to New York, where he worked on the trams. His brother Michael became gravely ill, and the other two boys tossed a coin to determine which of them would return to Ireland with the ailing brother.** Brian is the brother who escorted Michael back to Ireland, where Brian remained until his death in 1980. He is buried in St. Attracta's Cemetery in Ballinameen

Brian Connor (Cloonboniffe Coy.) 1st Lieutenant of Cloonboniffe Coy. in the 1st Battalion South Roscommon. He joined the Company in 1919, and participated in the **train raid at Ballinlough**, the **destruction of vacant barracks** in 1920, the **attempted attack on the Castlerea Station Guard** in July 1920, and the **attack on Frenchpark Barracks** 2 October 1920. The following year he participated in the **attempted ambush at Loughglynn**, and the **attempted ambush of an RIC patrol near Ballymoe** in April 1921. During the month of May, he joined with other Volunteers in an **attempted ambush at Lisacul** (in conjunction with the East Mayo men). During the Truce Connor worked in the training camps, and was prominent in the use of firearms. He was a member of the Flying Column. Later emigrated to Yeadon, Yorkshire England

*John Kelly, interview by author, 15 November 2003, Muckinagh, Strokestown.
**John Kelly, interview by author, 15 November 2003, Muckinagh, Strokestown.

Charlie Connor (Roscommon Coy.) 3rd Battalion South Roscommon

Frank Connor (Aghadrestan) in whose home men on the run found food and comfort. Tans surrounded his home on 2 June 1921 killing Mick Carty and wounding Pete Shannon

Jack Connor (Killina Coy.) 2nd Battalion North Roscommon. He was one of the first members of the Company when it formed in August of 1917

John Connor (Kilbride Coy.) 3rd Battalion South Roscommon

John Connor (Farm, Ballymoe) served as the 2nd Lieutenant of Williamstown Coy. in the Glenamaddy Battalion. Although located in Co. Galway, this Battalion was incorporated into the 2nd Western Division with Gerald O'Connor, former O/C of the 1st Battalion South Roscommon, serving as No. 2 Brigade Commandant

Luke Connor (Roscommon Coy.) 3rd Battalion South Roscommon

Martin "Mardy" Connor (Yambo, Mantua, Castlerea) 2nd Battalion North Roscommon, brother of Thomas. Joined the Irish Volunteers in January 1917. Took an active part in the election of Count Plunkett, and marched in anti-conscription parades. In January of 1919, he was appointed Adjutant of "A" Company, helped with Sinn Féin Courts, raided for Belfast goods, made dugouts, and took part in the **attack on Elphin Barracks** on 11 February 1921. Blocked roads in anticipation of the **attack on Boyle Barracks** July 1922. During the Civil War he carried dispatches under arms, trenched roads, transported arms to the Flying Column, and served as the Company Intelligence Officer

Michael Connor (Sheerevagh, Ballinameen, Boyle) 1st Battalion North Roscommon. He was a member of the Active Service Unit (Flying Column) during the Civil War. He was the brother of Brian. He emigrated to New York after the War, where he became gravely ill, forcing him to return to Ireland

Michael Connor (Clooneen, Kilglass, Strokestown) a member of the Kilglass Company in the 3rd Battalion North Roscommon

Michael Connor (Cuilmore, Strokestown) a member of the Strokestown Coy. in the 3rd Battalion North Roscommon

Patrick Connor (Trien Coy.) 1st Battalion South Roscommon. Took part in the **attempted ambush at Coshlieve** in July 1920, and the **attempted ambush of RIC patrol near Ballymoe** in May 1921. Blocked roads and scouted on the day Inspector King was shot in Castlerea. Attended the Cloonkeen training camp during the Truce

Thomas Connor (Yambo, Mantua, Castlerea) 2nd Battalion North Roscommon. Joined the IRA in January 1917, and was appointed Captain of "A" Company in September 1918. Drilled his Company, helped with the first election of a Republican TD, collected funds for the Dáil Loan, held court on local offenders who disobeyed IRA orders, constructed two dugouts, and raided for arms (seventeen guns and ammunition collected in about thirty raids). Participated in the **attempted ambush of a patrol at Frenchpark** 12 December 1920, and the **attack on a RIC patrol at Elphin Dispensary** the following evening, after which he was forced to go on the run. He was present at the **burning of the Frenchpark old Barracks and Courthouse** on 26 June 1921. When the Flying Column was formed, he was appointed the Adjutant. In early 1921, the Tans raided his home, and smashed to smithereens a good bit of furniture and window panes. His cattle were targets for the Tan terror as well. During the Truce he attended training camps at Mantua and Cloonshee. He was a member of the Active Service Unit (Flying Column) during the Civil War commanded by Pat Brennan. Before the Boyle Barracks were attacked on 1 July 1922, Connor was instrumental in getting the Anti-Treaty troops released from custody. He was one of the officers who commanded the **attack on the Free State troops in the Boyle Union Buildings** on 1 July 1922. Connor was arrested a week later in Elphin, and detained in Strokestown and Athlone, whereupon, due to his declining health, he was released in October of 1922. Upon his return to Roscommon, he again assisted the Anti-Treaty forces with food, safe storage of ammo, and money when necessary. He was appointed the Vice O/C of the 2nd Battalion

Patrick Connor (Clooneen, Kilglass, Strokestown) 2nd Lieutenant of Kilglass Company in the 3rd Battalion North Roscommon. Connor was one of the Volunteers guarding a Republican Court in April 1920 at Kilglass Chapel when a party of RIC from Ruskey happened by and twenty minutes worth of shots were exchanged. He also took part in the **attack on the RIC patrol at Strokestown** in January 1921, and the **attack near Ruskey village** on 5 July 1921

Peter Connor (Carrowbaun, Clooneyquinn) 2nd Battalion North Roscommon. He was one of the founding members of the Killina Company when it formed in 1917 — serving as its First Lieutenant. Arrested as a result of a Crown Forces sweep on 27 January 1921

Thomas Connor (Carniska Coy.) 3rd Battalion North Roscommon

Christy Conroy (Kilbarry) a member of the Tarmonbarry Coy. of the 3rd Battalion North Roscommon

Frank Conroy (Conry) (Moher, Ruskey) 2nd Lieutenant in Slatta Company in the 3rd Battalion North Roscommon. Served as an instructor to his Company

John Conry (Conroy) (Raveege, Ballintubber) a member of "F" Coy. in the 3rd Battalion, No. 2 Brigade, 2nd Western Division. Took part in the **raid on the military train at Ballymoe** in June 1920. He later became Captain of the Coy. After the War he farmed his land. He is buried in Ballintubber Cemetery

John Conroy (Tonlegee, Fourmilehouse) 2nd Battalion in the South Roscommon Brigade. Although not a member of the assault party, was shot on 3 November 1920 by the Tans in reprisal for the **Fourmilehouse Ambush**. "A very good man on active service."* Buried in the old Ballinderry cemetery. His name is inscribed on the tablets in front of the Shankill Monument near Elphin

Quoted from the Gerald O'Connor Papers

Patrick Conroy (Tonlegee, Fourmilehouse) 2nd Battalion in the South Roscommon Brigade, brother of John. After a meeting of the Brigade staff in Ballinaheglish in March 1921, Pat, Jim Quigley, Jim Breheny, and John Gibbons were asleep in the outbuilding of Quigley's place when a raid took place. Quigley, who was awakened by barking dogs, and watching the assembly of soldiers outside the main house, ordered all inside to be quiet. Conry, however, was much too deep in welcome sleep to hear the order, and continued to snore. He was rudely aroused from his slumber only to watch as the soldiers and RIC searched the main house but totally passed by the outhouse in which the four men had taken shelter. Later in life, Paddy became a farmer. Buried in the Ballinderry Cemetery

John James Conry (Conroy) 2nd Battalion North Roscommon. Joined Creeve Coy. in 1917 and was appointed First Lieutenant in 1919. Participated in the **burning of Hillstreet Barracks** in May 1920, **attack on Elphin patrol** on 5 January 1921, **attempted ambushes at Smithhill** in May, and several other attempted ambushes near Elphin and Strokestown. When the Western Division was formed, he was appointed assistant Brigade Quartermaster in April 1922, and volunteered for the Active Service Unit. During the Truce he trained in Mantua and Cloonshee camps. He occupied Boyle Barracks for some time after it was taken over from the British military. Conry was arrested 1 July, but escaped by diving out of a speeding car as it passed through Elphin. In November 1922, he took part in the **attack on Free State troops on Boyle Railway Bridge,** and the **attack** in February 1923 **on the Boyle/Carrick-on-Shannon Road.** All the while, he continued to be a regular attendee at the Brigade Council meetings. After the ceasefire, Conry spent many months still on the run avoiding capture. He, like so many other young men who had sided with the Anti-Treatyites, emigrated. He settled in New York

Joseph Conry (Conroy) (Kiltrustan) Captain of the Company, who mounted an attempted attack near Truce time on two Tans who regularly cycled from Ruskey to Strokestown. The plan failed because a local girl, Mary McConville, unknowingly thwarted the attempt by getting in between the Tans. The waiting Volunteers had only shotguns, and did not want to risk hurting the innocent girl. They let the patrol pass

Martin Conry (Conroy) was a student in engineering at Galway University in September 1922. He gave useful assistance to the IRA regarding bomb making in that area

Patrick T. Conry (Conroy) (Killina Coy.) in the 2nd Battalion North Roscommon. Arrested in 1920-21. He later emigrated to Brooklyn, New York

Patrick Conry (Tarmon) a member of Lisliddy Coy. in the 1st Battalion South Roscommon. Participated in the **destruction of vacant barracks** in 1920, the capture of enemy stores at **Ballymoe** in June 1920, the **attempted attack on the Castlerea Station Guard** in July 1920, the **raid and capture of military equipment at Ballymoe** September 1920, and the **attack on the Frenchpark Barracks** 2 October 1920. Taken by the Tans from his home 6 April 1921 and later found dead in a nearby field. His name is inscribed on the tablets in front of the Shankill Monument near Elphin

William Conroy (Elphin) incarcerated during the Civil War in Athlone on 18 February 1923. He was not released until the 14th of April the following year

Joseph Conway (Moor Coy.) 1st Battalion South Roscommon. Joined the Volunteers in 1918, serving as dispatch rider. He later became a member of the Active Service Unit (Flying Column). In 1920 he participated in the **destruction of various barracks**, the **attempted attack on Kilmurray Military Camp** in June 1920, and the **attack on Frenchpark Barracks** 2 October 1920. The next year he took part in the **attempted attacks on Castlerea** and **Frenchpark** in January, the **attempted ambush at Cloonsheever** in March, the **attempted ambush at Castlerea** on 6 April, and the **attempted ambush at Loughglynn** later that month. In May he was with his fellow Volunteers in the **attempted ambush at Lisacul** (an action taken in conjunction with the East Mayo men), and the **attempted ambush of an RIC patrol near Ballymoe**. The day before the Truce, he took part in the **ambush at Southpark, Castlerea**. During the Truce he gave continuous service at Brigade and Battalion headquarters and in the training camps. Conway took an active role in the Civil War — participating in the **attacks at Clonalis** in July 1922 and **Castlerea** that same month. He was captured by the Free State forces on 21 July 1922 and held at Athlone. He was transferred to Mountjoy and later to Tintown, from which he obtained his release 18 December 1923. He bade farewell to Ireland as did so many other young men and emigrated to Bradford, England

Michael Conway (Boyle) 1st Battalion North Roscommon, a member of the Volunteers since before the Rising

Paddy Conway (No. 2 Brigade Quartermaster) which was part of the 2nd Western Division commanded by Tom Maguire. In 1921 he became part of the ASU formed in the Tuam Battalion area

Sallie Conway (Carrowkey Barney Carroll, Claremorris) arrested during the Civil War, and taken to Athlone in March of 1923. She was released in April to the custody of Miss D. O'Gara of Main St., Ballaghaderreen

Edward "Ned" Cooke (Goff Street, Roscommon town) 3rd Battalion South Roscommon, secured guns from Dublin. After the War he worked in Dublin, where he became a bus driver. He is buried in Donnycarney Cemetery in north Dublin

James Cooney (Aghamuck) a member of "E" Coy., 3rd Battalion South Roscommon, and a member of Pat Madden's Flying Column. Many of the members of the Kilgefin Company participated in the **Fourmilehouse Ambush** on 12 October 1920. He later became a farmer. Died in the 1960s

John Cooney (Ballaghaderreen) interned after the Rising in Frongoch, "The Irish University"

"Lizzie" Cooney (Aghamuck) sister of James, member of Cumann na mBan. Later married Martin Cummins. Died 1958

Ned Cooney Brigade Quartermaster for Longford. According to Ernie O'Malley, Cooney took part in the **Scramogue Ambush**. (Descendants of Roscommon men who did participate do not recall their fathers ever talking about Cooney being present.) He did lead a Flying Column that harassed the British Forces around Kenagh in County Longford. Joined the Free State Army and retired in the 1940s with the rank of Major. Brother-in-law to the "Blacksmith of Ballinalee," Sean MacEoin. Died in the 1960s and is buried in Ballymacormack Cemetery, County Longford

Richard Cooney a member of "E" Coy., 3rd Battalion South Roscommon. He later emigrated to the USA

John Corcoran (Killattimoriarty) a member of "E" Coy., 3rd Battalion South Roscommon. Many of the members of the Kilgefin Company participated in the **Fourmilehouse Ambush** on 12 October 1920. After the War he became a farmer

Pat Corcoran a member of "E" Coy. 3rd Battalion South Roscommon. Many, but not all, of the members of the Kilgefin Company participated in the **Fourmilehouse Ambush** on 12 October 1920

Patrick Corcoran (Lisacul) East Mayo Brigade. Arrested on St. Patrick's Day in 1923, and sent to Stone Park, where he was incarcerated until his release in mid-December that same year

Thomas Corcoran (Kilbride Coy.) 3rd Battalion South Roscommon, served as the 1st Lieutenant of the Company. Fought against the Free State forces during the Civil War, and was arrested 25 January 1923

William Corcoran (Carrowduff) a member of "B" Coy. in the 2nd Battalion South Roscommon, who served as a Republican Judge. After the War became a farmer

Sean Corcoran (Kiltimagh) East Mayo Brigade O/C (which took in parts of west Roscommon). Arrested after the Rising, and sent to Wandsworth on 13 May 1916. Incarcerated at Dartmoor along with Eamon de Valera and sixty-four other Sinn Féiners. He was eventually transferred to Frongoch. Sean used to travel many nights with a barefooted Jim Hunt through Ballaghaderreen looking for patrols. Commanded the party that **burned the Ballacorick Barracks** at Easter time 1920. Plans for an **attack on the Ballaghaderreen Barracks** in February 1921 were hatched with Hunt at Carrick Castle. He was the commanding officer of John Snee, one of just a few men this author personally interviewed. Corcoran was killed in action at Crossard, Ballyhaunis in April of 1921. (His charge, John Snee, lived to be one hundred years old, dying in May of 2002)

Paddy Cormican (Cloghan) 4th Battalion South Roscommon, ran a safe house for men on the run near the Four Roads area

Richard Corr (Carrowndangan) a member of "B" Coy. in the 2nd Battalion South Roscommon, Republican Police. Active in the Land League, who often referred to himself as "an old wounded soldier from the landlord of the West." He drilled with his Company, collected funds for the Dáil loan, and served under Captain Michael O'Grady. After the War he became a sales representative for Castlebar Bacon factory. He took an active part in the forming of Fianna Fáil in the county, being on hand in Roscommon town to welcome de Valera on 19 June 1926. Buried in Oran Cemetery

Stephen Corrisan (Lisdeane, Ballaghaderreen) East Mayo Brigade. Arrested during the Civil War, and sent to Stone Park. Released 20 December 1923

Dan Corry During the Truce he was a trainer in the Mantua camp for members of the Roscommon Brigade. Later in life he became the Commandant of the Army Equitation School

George Cosgrave (St. Columbus Terrace, Athlone) scouted the town in August 1920 for the whereabouts of Sergeant Craddock. He was arrested during the Civil War on 30 July 1922, and sent to Athlone on 2 September. He was transferred to Mountjoy in January of 1923. After the War he worked at High Power Wireless Station in Athlone

John Cosgrave a member of Cloverhill Coy. in the 2nd Battalion South Roscommon. He drilled with his Company, collected funds for the Dáil loan, and and served under the command of Captain Edward Jackson. After the War he emigrated to England

Michael Cosgrove (Ruane, Kilglass, Strokestown) a member of the Kilglass Company in the 3rd Battalion North Roscommon

C. Costello (Loughglynn Coy.) 1st Battalion South Roscommon. After the War he emigrated to England

Edward Costello (Corramore, Kiltoom) St. John's Coy., 4th Battalion South Roscommon. When the Company first started in 1917, Costello drilled with other Volunteers two nights a week — Tuesdays and Thursdays. He worked in the 1918 election, and participated in several Company raids for arms — one of which yielded three shotguns. He was with a party of men who **raided the Kiltoom train for mail**. During the Truce he became a member of a special service unit. Costello took an active part in reorganising his Company after the split in the IRA ranks in March of 1922

James Costello (Flashagh, Dunmore) 2nd Lieutenant of the Kilterna Coy. in the Glenamaddy Battalion. Although located in Co. Galway, this Battalion was incorporated into the 2nd Western Division with Gerald O'Connor, former O/C of the

1st Battalion South Roscommon, serving as the Brigade Commandant. Costello took the Anti-Treaty side during the Civil War, and was arrested at his father's house in July 1923. He had been involved in raids in the Glenamaddy and Dunmore area. At the time of his arrest, he was in possession of a United States passport (which had not been signed). He was a prominent member of Knight's Flying Column in County Longford

John Costello (Castlerea) 4th Battalion, East Mayo Brigade (which took in parts of west Roscommon), Company Captain. He came to the attention of the authorities shortly after he and other Volunteers stopped the train from continuing its journey into the Castlerea Railway Station in July of 1920. He was arrested and sent to Mountjoy. Upon release in December 1921, he was appointed Adjutant for No. 2 Brigade, 2nd Western Division. Present at the Clonalis House when Gerald O'Connor asked the men to return to their homes and not engage in hostilities against fellow Irish. Costello resigned his position as Brigade Adjutant on 8 July 1922 rather than attack those with whom he had once fought. After the War he worked for the E. J. McDermot firm in Castlerea until his retirement. He died in Dublin 5 November 1970, and is buried in Cuiltyboe Cemetery in Loughglynn

John (Sean) Costello of Athlone. Died as the result of wounds suffered during the Easter Rising in 1916

PHOTO COURTESY OF DERRYGLAD FOLK MUSEUM CURRAGHBOY, ATHLONE

John (Sean) Costello (native of Athlone) a member of "F" Company, 1st Battalion in Dublin, who was wounded while carrying dispatches to Boland's Mills during Easter Week. He died of his wounds 26 April 1916 at Sir Patrick Dun's Hospital in Dublin. Buried in Dean's Grange, Dublin

Redmond Costello (Knockanconny, Ballaghaderreen) incarcerated during the Civil War in Athlone 31 March 1923. He was arrested for hiding Anti-Treaty men

Thomas "Con" Costello (Ballynahoun, Athlone) joined the Volunteers in early 1917 in Moate. He drilled and paraded with his men, and attended the huge Brigade mobilisation at Mullingar in 1918. Took part in the anti-conscription activities — collecting data for a census of foodstuffs and arms in the area. In 1918, Costello became a member of the IRB, taken in by Joe McCormack of Drumraney. In early 1920 when Sean Hurley was arrested, Costello was appointed Vice O/C of the Athlone Brigade under Seamus O'Meara. He, along with other men from the Athlone Battalion, participated in the **attempted capture of the Streamstown RIC Barracks** in County Westmeath in July 1920. He was saved from death during that attempt when James Tormey grabbed Costello and yanked him away from the doorway just before a grenade hurled by the RIC from a upstairs window exploded in front of them. Costello was a member of the Flying Column, and participated in the **raid on Lecarrow Barracks,** and the **holdup of a train at Fassaugh**. He also was with the party who **killed Sergeant Craddock** in Athlone on 22 August 1920. The next month he participated in the **attack on the military on the Shannon** and, in October, the **ambush at Parkwood** in County Westmeath. Costello travelled with the Flying Column in County Westmeath and Roscommon during the autumn and winter months. In early 1921, he was with the Column when they attempted an attack on a policeman in Moate. He was also with a party of Volunteers who attempted to attack a group of British officers going on a fishing trip upriver from Athlone. The first shot of that ambush was never fired because James Tormey and George Adamson got in a gun battle with two Tans in a nearby barnyard. The shooting alerted the officers on the river, and the Column quickly withdrew. In March/April of 1921, when Seamus O'Meara resigned his position as O/C of the Athlone Brigade, Costello was appointed in his stead. He was in charge of the party that **burned Castlemaine** in June of 1921. After the war years, he moved to Drogheda where he managed a grocery shop

John Coughlan (Ballygar Coy.) which was considered part of 4th Battalion South Roscommon when the Divisional structure was implemented

Michael Coughlan (Ballygar Coy.) which was considered part of 4th Battalion South Roscommon when the Divisional structure was implemented

Ciss Cox (Kilbarry) member of the Cumann na mBan, sister of Josie

Frank Cox (Ballytoohey) a member of Tarmonbarry Coy., 3rd Battalion North Roscommon

John Cox (Kilbarry) a member of the Tarmonbarry Coy. in the 3rd Battalion North Roscommon. Took part in the **attack on the RIC barracks in Tarmonbarry**

John Cox (Crunkill, Ruskey) a member of the Kilglass Company in the 3rd Battalion North Roscommon

Joseph Cox (Killinordan, Scramogue) 1st Lieutenant of Slatta Company in the 3rd Battalion North Roscommon, brother of Pat. Joseph had been arrested and incarcerated in Athlone by January 1921. During the Civil War he served as the Adjutant for the 3rd Battalion North, and was a member of the Active Service Unit. After the War he farmed the land. Died 9 March 1986

Josie Cox (Kilbarry) a member of the Tarmonbarry Coy. of the 3rd Battalion North Roscommon. Arrested before the Scramogue ambush and interned for part of the War. He became a Captain in the Free State Army

Luke Cox (Northyard, Scramogue) Captain of Slatta Company in the 3rd Battalion North Roscommon, brother of Joseph. Participated in the **attack on the Elphin patrol** 5 January 1921. He was also a member of an Active Service Unit (Flying Column) in North Roscommon. He was arrested early in the Civil War on 27 July 1922, and taken to Athlone in September. He was later transferred to Mountjoy in January of 1923, and, three months later, shipped to the Curragh from which he escaped

Michael Cox (Foxhill, Cootehall) 1st Lieutenant of Cootehall Company in the 5th Battalion North Roscommon

Owen Cox (Northyard, Scramogue) Slatta Company in the 3rd Battalion North Roscommon, brother of Luke

Patrick Cox (Killinordan, Scramogue) 3rd Battalion North Roscommon, brother of Joseph. Performed dispatch work, raided for arms and the mails. Took part in the **attack on the RIC patrol at Strokestown** in January 1921, blocked roads for the **ambush at Scramogue**, and participated in the **attack on RIC patrol at Tarmonbarry** in July 1921

Patrick Cox (Ballyhubert, Scramogue) 3rd Battalion North Roscommon. He was a member of the IRA from 1918. He presided over a local arms dump. He was captured in 1920, and made a daring attempt at escape for which he was badly beaten — so much so that his health was permanently impaired. He was imprisoned in Longford, Athlone, Mountjoy, and Perth. Released in January 1922

Rosie Cox (Green St., Boyle) Captain of the Cumann na mBan in Boyle. She attended drill lectures, carried dispatches, received and helped distribute literature regarding the Belfast boycott, organised socials, took up collections in aid of IRA prisoners and their families, and transferred arms and ammunition for the men. Her house served as the venue of an IRA training camp for five weeks during the Truce, a time during which she spent procuring and preparing food. During the Civil War she attended to casualties, and transferred arms under fire. Because the 3rd Western Division command was situated just outside of Boyle, Rosie took on the responsibilities of a great deal of dispatch work, as well as serving as guide for men coming from outside the area to headquarters who reported for meetings and interviews. She also supplied food and information to the Headquarters staff

Thomas Cox (Ruskey) 2nd Lieutenant in Ruskey Company in the 3rd Battalion North Roscommon

William Cox Captain of the Cootehall Company in the 5th Battalion North Roscommon, a Company which had about thirty-five members. After the War he emigrated to the States

Willie Cox (Cloonshannagh) a member of the Tarmonbarry Coy. of the 3rd Battalion North Roscommon. He later emigrated to Elmhurst, Long Island, New York

James Coyle (Southpark) 1st Battalion South Roscommon

Patrick Coyle (Gailey, Knockcroghery) a member of the Rahara Coy. in the 4th Battalion South Roscommon. Died 1980

Patrick Coyle (Bredagh, Kiltoom) a blacksmith by trade, who was visiting the Murphy home in St. John's to treat a sick horse when a party of Tans broke in and shot him on 1 June 1921. He later died of his wounds. He had no connection to the Volunteer movement. His name is inscribed on the IRA monument at Shankill

Bernard Coyne (Lisbaun) a member of the Curraghboy Coy., 4th Battalion South Roscommon. From 1917-March 1919 did organisational work, drilled, practiced scouting procedures and military exercises when Sean Connolly paid a visit to the area, manufactured ammunition, and constructed dugouts. Performed police duty during the South Roscommon election (guard duty at polling booths and escorting ballot boxes to counting centres). Also performed police duty in relation to enforcement of Dáil decrees. Coyne facilitated the holding of Sinn Féin Courts when necessity arose. He participated in arms raids — twenty raids were conducted within the Company area, and another fifteen raids were outside the vicinity and performed in conjunction with other Companies of the Battalion. Coyne was one of two men in the Company who were attached, for a time, to the Brigade Active Service Unit. He took part in the **attempted ambush at Clooncraff**. The entire Company participated in the arrest and confinement of a suspected spy. That man was tried by court-martial and eventually executed — an action which prompted the arrest of ten members of the Company on 5 January 1921. After that time, Coyne took part in raids on homes of persons sympathetic to the enemy, and prepared for the **attempted attack on Ballygar RIC Barracks**. He was arrested in March 1921. Released in January 1922, whereupon he returned home and rejoined his Company. He took the Anti-Treaty side in the split, and raided homes of ex-RIC men, blocked roads, and generally tried to harass the Free State troops

John Coyne (Milltown) Dysart Coy. in the 4th Battalion South Roscommon. Joined the Company in 1919 and helped with the Republican Police

John Coyne (Trien Coy.) 1st Battalion South Roscommon

Joseph Coyne (Knockcroghery Coy.) 4th Battalion South Roscommon.* Knockcroghery Company was formed in 1917 under the leadership of Patrick Kelly. Coyne drilled weekly with the other Volunteers, attended courses of instruction given by Ernie O'Malley at Rahara in the summer of 1918, took a course in semaphore and Morse signalling, and took part in the practice battles at Taughmaconnell overseen O'Malley. Participated in the South Roscommon election of 1918, served as an armed escort for bank officials taking sums of money to fairs in Knockcroghery. Coyne cut the telegraph wires in preparation for the **burning of Lecarrow Barracks**. He later emigrated to the United States of America

According to Tom Kelly, O/C of the 4th Battalion, Joseph Coyne was the first O/C of Knockcroghery Coy. (Volunteer Witness Statement to Bureau of Military History, p. 2.)

Michael Coyne (Trien Coy.) 1st Battalion South Roscommon. Took part in the **attempted ambush at Coshlieve** in July 1920, attended the Cloonkeen and Hermitage training camps during the Truce, and took over the position of Director of Training in the Castlerea RIC Barracks training centre. Took part in the **attack at Ballinlough** during the Civil War in July 1922. Later emigrated to the USA

Michael Coyne (Sandfield, Knockcroghery) 4th Battalion South Roscommon, served as Quartermaster of Knockcroghery Coy., 4th Battalion South Roscommon. The Company was formed in 1917 with Patrick Kelly serving as Captain. Coyne, along with the rest of his Company, **guarded the village of Knockcroghery** from reprisal on 15 August 1920 — a reprisal precipitated by British Forces being fired upon on Lough Ree. He also took part in the **attempted attack on a party of military eighteen strong at Knockcroghery** in January 1921. His was the job of making sure that Company weapons were distributed before engagements, collected after attacks, and cleaned and kept in working order at all times. During the Truce he was appointed to a special service unit. After the War he became a farmer. Died 1993. Buried in Gailey Cemetery

Michael Coyne (Donamon) a member of "E" Coy. in the 2nd Battalion South Roscommon. He drilled with his Company, collected funds for the Dáil loan, and served under the command of Captain Pat Dwyer

Michael Coyne, Sandfield Knockcroghery.

Patrick Coyne (Donamon) a member of "E" Coy. in the 2nd Battalion South Roscommon. He drilled with his Company, collected funds for the Dáil loan, and served under the command of Captain Pat Dwyer

Patrick Joseph Coyne (Trien Coy.) 1st Battalion South Roscommon

Peter Coyne (Clooncah, Castlerea) 1st Battalion South Roscommon, a member of Trien Coy. Participated in the **attempted ambush at Coshlieve** in July 1920, the **attempted ambush of RIC patrol near Ballymoe** in May 1921. An hour before the Truce was to take effect, he scouted and blocked roads while Inspector King was shot in Castlerea. He attended the Hermitage training camp during the Truce, where he specialised in scouting. His home served as the HQ for "E" Coy., 2nd Battalion, No. 2 Brigade in the 2nd Western Division during the post-Truce times

Tom Coyne (Trien Coy.) 1st Battalion South Roscommon. He later emigrated to the United States

Agnes Crawley (Aghalour near Loughglynn) dispatch carrier, and proprietress of a "safe house" for men on the run

James Crawley (Taghnoose, Carrowbehy, Castlerea) 1st Battalion South Roscommon. Participated in the **destruction of vacant barracks** in 1920, the **capture of arms at the Castlerea RIC Barracks** in April 1920, and the **raid for petrol at Ballinlough Station** in June 1920. He served as scout for the **capture of enemy stores at Ballymoe** in June 1920, and participated in the **attempted ambush at Coshlieve** in July 1920, the **attempted attack on the Castlerea Station Guard** in July 1920, and the **raid and capture of military equipment at Ballymoe** September 1920. He blocked roads in preparation for the **attack on Frenchpark Barracks** 2 October 1920, took part in the **attempted attacks at Castlerea and Frenchpark** in January 1921, and the **attack at Castlerea** in April 1921. During that same month, he participated in the **attempted ambush at Loughglynn,** and the **attempted ambush of an RIC patrol near Ballymoe.** In the month of May, he joined with other Volunteers in an **attempted ambush at Lisacul** (in conjunction with the East Mayo men). During the Truce he attended the Battalion training camps. He was a member of the Active Service Unit formed in January 1921

Michael Crawley 1st Battalion South Roscommon. Participated in the **burning of Ballinlough and Loughglynn Barracks** in September 1920

Patrick Crawley (Tully, Carrowbehy, Castlerea) 1st Battalion South Roscommon. Participated in the **burning of the Barracks at Ballinlough 14 September 1920,** and the **torching of Loughglynn Barracks** in that same month. He was arrested for possession of Gerald O'Connor's photograph on which was written as a tongue-in-cheek joke "*6'1" of treason/terror.*" Interned during part of the War. During the Truce he attended the training camps at Hermitage and Erritt. By April of 1922, he was serving as the 2nd Lieutenant of the Gorthaganny Coy., which was part of No. 2 Brigade, 2nd Western Division. After the War he worked for the Land Commission

Tom Crawley (Aghalour near Loughglynn), 1st Battalion South Roscommon. A member of the South Roscommon Flying Column. Joined the Volunteers in 1917 under the leadership of Pat Glynn. Drilled with his fellow Volunteers, took part in the 1918 election, and canvassed for the Dáil loan. Participated

Left to right: Pat Crawley, Ned Campion (face obscured by hat of man in front), Martin Ganley (with hat), Jack Flynn (in second row), Mick Hevican, Peter Quinn, Michael Kenny and Owen Mahon.

PHOTO COURTESY OF JOE AND KATHLEEN HEVICAN

Tom Crawley, Vice O/C of the 1st Battalion South Roscommon.

PHOTO COURTESY OF EAMONN CRAWLEY
PHOTO RESTORATION BY DAVE DERBY

in the **destruction of Ballinagare, Ballintubber, Cloonfad,** and **Ballinlough barracks** in 1920, the **petrol raid at Ballinlough Station** in June 1920, the **burning of the Loughglynn Barracks,** the **raid for petrol at Ballinlough, attempted attack on the Military Camp at Kilmurray** in June 1920, **attempted attack on British Forces at Castlerea Station** July 1920, and the **attack on Frenchpark Barracks** 2 October 1920. The next year Crawley, along with John Crean, entered the town of Castlerea in late January with the intention of attacking any suitable military target. When no other Volunteers showed up, both men grew suspicious, because they knew this to be a Company operation. They quietly withdrew from town. (They hadn't known of the Tan raid on Martin Ganley's house in Cloonmaul the day before, which had nearly wiped out the Brigade staff.) Crawley took part in some **sniping at Frenchpark Barracks** January 1921, the **attempted ambush of RIC at Cloonsheever** March 1921, the **attack on the military in Castlerea** on 6 April 1921, **attempted ambush at Loughglynn** 7 April 1921, **attempted ambush of RIC patrol at Lisacul** (in conjunction with the East Mayo Brigade) May 1921, and the **attempted ambush of RIC near Ballymoe** that same month. He and Commander Gerald O'Connor were hiding in a dugout in the Breanabeg Bog when Black and Tans tramped right over the top of their hideout. Crawley spent months living in that dugout, which was used as Battalion Headquarters. He accompanied Ned Campion when the two engaged Inspector King in Castlerea, and fired the last shots of the Black and Tan War. During the Truce he was active in the Battalion training camps including those at Runnamoat, Donamon, Cloonkeen, and Castlerea. He resigned from the IRA in July 1922, but could not stay aloof from the fight that was consuming the country. He rejoined in December, and in early spring 1923, led twenty-five men who were to take up positions covering the front of the Castlerea Barracks, which was then occupied by the Free State forces. A gun battle ensued leading to a retreat of his men. He retired from the IRA in June 1923. Crawley began with the Volunteers as Company Lieutenant, advanced to Battalion Adjutant, then to Vice O/C of the Battalion, and, after July 1921, was promoted to the rank of Battalion Commandant. Despite all of this service to the Volunteer cause, Crawley was denied an IRA pension. Years of petitioning to the government by Crawley and his commanding officers resulted in multiple denials. Following the War, Crawley became a member of the Garda Síochána, and was stationed in Ballyfarnon. After many decades of service there, he retired and moved to Clover Hill, Ballaghaderreen, where he took up gardening for a hobby. "A cool, witty man that enjoyed reading, he loved going for a glass of Guinness at the local, where he enjoyed the company of old comrades and friends."* He died 22 October 1971 and is buried in Kilcommon Cemetery, where his tombstone bears the inscription "Thomas Crawley O/C 2nd Battalion No. 2 Castlerea Brigade Old IRA"

Paddy Crawley, grand-nephew of Tom, correspondence 15 February 2004.

John Crean (Breanabeg) 1st Battalion South Roscommon, a member of John Vaughan's Cloonboniffe Company. Crean served as a member of the Battalion Active Service Unit which was formed in January 1921. Participated in the **destruction of vacant barracks** in 1920, the **raid for petrol at Ballinlough Station** in June 1920, the **attempted attack on Kilmurray Military Camp** that same month, and the **attack on Frenchpark RIC Barracks** 2 October 1920. The next year Crean, along with Tom Crawley, entered the town of Castlerea in late January with the intention of attacking any suitable military target. When no other

Volunteers showed up, both men grew suspicious and withdrew from town. (They hadn't known of the Tan raid on Martin Ganley's house in Cloonmaul the day before which had nearly wiped out the Brigade staff.) Crean also acted in the covering party for the **attack on the military at Castlerea** 7 April 1921. He participated in the **attempted ambush at Lisacul** in May 1921 in conjunction with the East Mayo men, and the **attempted ambush of RIC patrol near Ballymoe** that same month. He was constantly "on the run" from November 1920 up until the Truce. He attended the training camps during the Truce, while serving as the Captain of Loughglynn Coy. in the 1st Battalion, No. 2 Brigade of the 2nd Western Division. Crean took the Republican side during the Civil War, and in November took part in the **burning of the train at Clooncundra**, and the **attack at Castlerea**. His home served as the headquarters for "B" Company during the post-Truce times. After the War he emigrated to Northenden, Manchester England

Stephen Crean (Breanabeg) 1st Battalion South Roscommon

Michael Cregg (Tonroe, Kingsland, Boyle) 1st Lieutenant of Breedogue Company in the 1st Battalion North Roscommon

Michael Crehan (Ballygar Coy.) which was considered part of 4th Battalion South Roscommon when the Divisional structure was implemented

Patrick Crehan (Ballygar Coy.) when the Divisional structure was put in place, south Galway was grouped with parts of south Roscommon and became part of the 4th Battalion South Roscommon

Denis Creighton (Creaton) (Ballaghaderreen) first Sinn Féin Council in Roscommon, brother of Jack and Roger. As a member of Cumann na nGaedhael, he served on the Roscommon County Council in 1925 and 1928. In 1934 he served as a member of Fine Gael

Jack Creighton (Figh, Loughglynn) one of the first members of the Ballaghaderreen Coy. in the East Mayo Brigade, brother of Denis and Roger. He was a member of the South Roscommon Flying Column. With Martin Ganley serving as his Captain, Creighton participated in the **destruction of vacant barracks,** the **attempted attack on Kilmurray Military Camp** in June 1920, and the **attack on Frenchpark Barracks** 2 October 1920. Creighton also served as the Adjutant for Loughglynn Coy. He took part in the special service training (intelligence, scouting, dispatch work) during the Truce. During the Civil War he served with Seamus Mulrennan's Flying Column

Roger Creighton (Figh, Loughglynn) served as an Intelligence Officer for the Ballaghaderreen Coy. in the East Mayo Brigade, brother of Jack and Denis

James Crofton (Carrick-on-Shannon) arrested during the Civil War, and sent to Mountjoy on 10 January 1923

Hugh Croghan (Corgarve, Elphin) Tulsk Coy. in the 2nd Battalion North Roscommon

Martin Croghan (Corboghil) a member of Carniska Coy., 3rd Battalion North Roscommon. Served as an Intelligence Officer for the Company, and was the founding secretary of the first Sinn Féin Club established in Carniska in 1918. Croghan served as the secretary of the Conscription Committee (also known as the "No Tax" Committee), and as a District Court Clerk of the Republican Courts in the North Roscommon area. After the War he became the manager of the Strokestown Waterworks, a position he held for thirty-six years. Died in 1964, and is buried in Kilcooley Cemetery, Tulsk

Charlie Crowley a member of "E" Coy., 3rd Battalion South Roscommon. Many, but not all, of the members of the Kilgefin Company participated in the **Fourmilehouse Ambush** on 12 October 1920

Thomas Cruise (Altore, Ballinlough) a member of the Cloonfad Coy. in the 1st Battalion South Roscommon. Took part in the **disarming of a Black and Tan at Cloonfad** in May 1921

Jack Creighton, a member of the East Mayo Flying Column.

PHOTO COURTESY OF PATRICIA DUNN
SOUTH ORLEANS, MASSACHUSETTS

Martin Croghan, member of Carniska Coy. 3rd Battalion North Roscommon.

PHOTO COURTESY OF HENRY OWENS

John Cryan (Boyle) 1st Battalion North Roscommon, a member of the Volunteers since before the Rising

Michael Cryan (Cloonbard, Castlerea) 1st Battalion South Roscommon. Participated in the **attack on the Frenchpark Barracks** 2 October 1920, the **attempted attacks at Castlerea** and **Frenchpark** in January 1921, and the **ambush at Southpark, Castlerea** 10 July 1921. Buried in Baslick Cemetery

Michael Cryan (Gortwilliam) a member of "F" company in the 2nd Battalion, No. 2 Brigade of the 2nd Western Division

Patrick Cryan of Athenry, Galway served as a member of "F" Coy. in the 2nd Battalion, No. 2 Brigade in the 2nd Western Division

Thomas Cryan (Seefin, Cloonloo, Boyle) 1st Battalion North Roscommon. After the Rising he was sent to Wandsworth on 13 May. He was later transferred to Frongoch, "The Irish University"

James Cuddy (Castlestrange, Fuerty) a member of Fuerty Coy. in the 2nd Battalion South Roscommon, brother of John. He drilled with his Company, collected funds for the Dáil loan, and served under the command of Captain Bernie Kearney. Died before the 1940s

John Cuddy (Castlestrange, Fuerty) a member of Fuerty Coy. in the 2nd Battalion South Roscommon, brother of James

Annie Cull, sister of Seamus, Michael and Owen, member of the Cumann na mBan, who used to meet her cohorts near Duignan's in Arigna. During the period of the War for Independence and subsequent civil conflict, Annie lost her father, mother, and two brothers. Despite all that had been taken from her, this lady remained a devoted Republican throughout her lifetime. She married Harold O'Brien (one of the leaders of the Arigna Flying Column), and lived in Ballintogher, County Sligo. She died in 1964, and is buried in the local cemetery

PHOTO COURTESY OF MARGARET CULL MCMANUS
PHOTO RESTORATON BY LEW THORNE

Seamus Cull (Tullynaha, Arigna) Adjutant of the 4th Battalion North Roscommon, brother of Owen and Michael. Seamus became the Vice O/C of the Arigna Battalion when Stephen Flynn was arrested. He was also in charge of over 100 men in the Flying Column. At the time of the Truce, the Arigna area could claim only four Enfield rifles, a few shotguns and revolvers, and twelve German Mausers.* Cull meant to remedy that situation. When the Civil War broke out, his Column captured 17 rifles from the Riverstown Barracks. He and his brothers manufactured some of the mines used to destroy local barracks. His battles took him far afield — into Counties Sligo, Leitrim, and Cavan. He led a Column of men into Leitrim in September 1922, where they **captured the Drumshanbo Barracks** in a mere five minute firefight. He also led his Column in a **raid on the Dowra Barracks** on 25 January 1923, and the **attack on Ballinamore Barracks** 31 January. His men respected his abilities and the commitment he exhibited. Years later one of them recorded, "When Seamus Cull was in charge, there was no surrender."** In February of 1923, Cull and Paddy Tymon had travelled to Cavan, where they engaged the Free State forces. They returned to the Arigna area the night of 26 February in order to obtain food, warm clothing, and perhaps some short respite from the war. He was killed the next day when the Free State troopers exploded a Mills bomb at the entrance of a dugout in the riverbank in which he and Tymon were hiding. His name is inscribed on the tablets in front of the Shankill Monument. On 19 September 1999, a memorial was dedicated to Seamus and his co-patriot, Patrick Tymon. The memorial stands above the dugout where they met their deaths, and was sponsored by the Roscommon County Commemorative Committee (see photo on page 164)

*Tom Deignan (Duignan) interview, Ernie O'Malley Papers, No. 133, p. 69.
**Tom Deignan (Duignan) interview, Ernie O'Malley Papers, No. 133 p. 70.

Michael Cull (Tullynaha, Arigna) served as the 1st Lieutenant of the Arigna Company in the 4th Battalion North Roscommon, brother of Annie, Owen, and Seamus. Michael was with the attacking party at Keadue 22 March 1921. He accompanied his brother and other Anti-Treaty men when they **attacked the Drumshanbo Barracks** in September 1922. He was killed at Ballyconnell in County Cavan on 6 January 1923. Name inscribed on the tablets in front of Shankill Monument near Elphin. The name of the Cull brothers is still spoken with reverence by those who live in the Arigna area

Owen Cull (Tullynaha, Arigna) 4th Battalion North Roscommon, brother of Seamus and Michael. In March of 1921, he was arrested by the Black and Tans and charged with the murder of the RIC constables at the Keadue ambush. He was beaten, all of his teeth broken off by rifle butts,* and taken to Boyle Barracks. He was sentenced by court-martial to death, and sent to Mountjoy, but released in January 1922. Throughout his life, Owen was saddened by the results of the War, but was never regretful of his part in it. Although he had lost two brothers, he felt it was the right action, at the right time, for the right cause. In the 1940s, he became disgusted with Fianna Fáil and the politics of incarcerating IRA men. He voted for Sean McBride's new party, and lived long enough to see an Irish Republic declared. He worked as a labourer for the Roscommon County Council. Died 1966 at the age of 73. Buried beside the Arigna Church

*Margaret Cull McManus, interview by author, 17 June 2002, Arigna.

Bernard Cullen participated in the **attack on the Elphin patrol** 5 January 1921. After the War he emigrated to the USA

James Cullen (Knockhall, Ruskey) a member of the Kilglass Company in the 3rd Battalion North Roscommon

John Cullen (Knockhall, Ruskey) a member of the Kilglass Company in the 3rd Battalion North Roscommon

John Cullen (Arigna) 4th Battalion North Roscommon, arrested on charges of the murder of RIC constables at Keadue, and sent to Boyle Barracks then to Mountjoy. He was held in prison until January of 1922, though he never received a trial. Cullen was active with the Ned Bofin Flying Column during the Civil War. He, along with his other comrades, was immortalised in the poem, "Arigna's Green Vale" by American emigrant Michael Daly

Owen Cull, Tullynaha, Arigna.
4th Battalion North Roscommon.

Joseph (Josie) Cullen (Carrick, Ballinlough) 1st Battalion South Roscommon. Participated in the **raid for petrol at Ballinlough Station**, the **attempted ambush at Coshlieve** in July 1920, the attempted **attack on the Castlerea Station Guard** that same month, and the **burning of the Ballinlough Barracks** 14 September 1920. During the Truce he attended the Battalion training camp specialising in dispatch work. Josie took the Anti-Treaty side in the Civil War, and participated in the attack at **Ballinlough** and **Castlerea** in July 1922. He was arrested, and incarcerated in Mountjoy in January 1923. After the War he farmed the land. He was present in 1970 at the Memorial for Pat Glynn, who had died fifty years earlier in the burning of Ballinlough Barracks. He also had his picture taken with the Old IRA group in 1973. Died on 9 June 1976, and is buried in the Ballinlough Cemetery. Since only his two daughters survived, when Josie passed away, so too did the Cullen name in Carrick, Ballinlough

Josie Cullen with family. He is the fifth from the left.

Michael Cullen (Carrick, Ballinlough) brother of Josie, 1st Battalion South Roscommon. Michael served as the 1st Lieutenant of the Company. Participated in the **raid for petrol at Ballinlough Station** in June 1920, the **attempted attack on the Castlerea Station Guard** in July 1920, and the **burning of Ballinlough Barracks** 14 September 1920. While on the run, he was thought to be hiding in a house in Ballinlough when the place was surrounded by Black and Tans. They blew open holes in the front door with their rifle fire, thinking they were finally getting their man. When the door swung open, they discovered that they had

Michael Cullen, 1st Lieutenant of
Ballinlough Company
1st Battalion South Roscommon.

shot, instead, the innocent owner of the house.* During the Truce Cullen attended the training camps at Castlerea, Hermitage, Cloonkeen, and Kilkeerin in Galway. His home served as the headquarters for "G" Company, No. 2 Brigade, 2nd Western Division during the post-Truce times. He took the Anti-Treaty side during the Civil War, and fought against the Free State troops at **Castlerea** in July 1922. He was arrested and sent to Tintown A. Michael was released on 22 February 1923. After the War he emigrated to England, where he met his bride-to-be. They returned to Ireland briefly, then finally emigrated to Brighton, Boston, where he worked for the Boston Transport Company at Bennett Street for twenty-four years before his retirement. Died 12 August 1973, and is buried in Saint Joseph's Cemetery in West Roxboro, Boston

Gerry Cullen, nephew of Michael, correspondence with author, 21 November 2004.

Mrs. Cullen, employee of the Ruskey Post Office, who supplied copies to the local Volunteers of all telegrams coming from Dublin to Elphin and vice versa

Patrick Cullen participated in the **attack on the Elphin patrol** 5 January 1921. After the War he emigrated to the USA

Thomas Cullen (Killina Coy.) 2nd Battalion North Roscommon. He was one of the first members of the Company when it formed in August of 1917

Andrew Cullinan (Knockroe, Ballinagare) 1st Battalion South Roscommon. He emigrated to the United States

Michael Cullinan (Knockroe, Ballinagare) Company Captain in the 1st Battalion South Roscommon Brigade. Cullinan drilled his men, collected for the Dáil loan, and enforced the Belfast boycott. Took part in the **destruction of vacant barracks** in 1920, the **attempted attack on Kilmurray Military Camp** in June 1920, the **attempted attack on the Castlerea Station Guard** in July 1920, the **attack on Frenchpark Barracks** 2 October 1920, and several attempted ambushes in Castlerea in January 1921. He was a member of the Active Service Unit formed in January 1921. During the Truce he attended the Company and Battalion training camps specialising in dispatch, scouting, or intelligence work. During the Civil War Cullinan took the Anti-Treaty side, and fought the Free State troops **at Ballinagare** in July 1922. After the War he became a farmer. Buried in Ballinagare Cemetery

Martin Cummins (Killmacuagh) member of the Kilgefin Company, 3rd Battalion South Roscommon. Later became a farmer. Died 1964

Martin Cummins 4th Battalion North Roscommon. He was a member of the ASU. He later emigrated to the United States

Nicholas Cummins (Ardmullan) a member of Curraghboy Coy., 4th Battalion South Roscommon. From 1917-March 1919 did organisational work, drilled with the men, performed scout and dispatch duty, paraded with his Coy. during a visit to the area by Sean Connolly, did police duty during the South Roscommon election and in conjunction with enforcement of Dáil decrees. Cummins was with a group of Volunteers who raided the private homes of three men — two of whom had joined and one who was about to join the RIC. Not surprisingly, these men had a change of heart! There were a total of twenty arms raids conducted within the Company area, and another fifteen raids were outside the immediate vicinity and performed in conjunction with other Companies of the Battalion. Cummins took part in those actions as well as a special raid for arms in the Kiltoom area. Prevented jurors from attending the British Courts, and held periodic meetings of Dáil Courts when necessity arose. Manufactured ammunition and constructed dugouts for storage of same. Seven or eight mail cars were robbed during this time, and Cummins was part of the attacking party. He served as a scout on the night of the **attempted ambush of a military lorry at Knockcroghery** in early January 1921. The entire Company participated in the arrest and confinement of a suspected spy. That man was tried by court-martial and eventually executed — an action which prompted the arrest of ten members of the Company on 5 January 1921 including Cummins. He was severely thrashed and taken to Athlone Barracks and incarcerated in a cell with no bed for three months. Later transferred to Mountjoy, and finally, in the last days of June, he was shipped across the waters to Wormwood Scrubbs and Pentonville Prisons in England. Tom Hales from Cork was his commanding officer in prison. Released 11 January 1922

Patrick Cummins (Upper Carrowduff) a member of "B" Coy. in the 2nd Battalion South Roscommon. Present at the **Fourmilehouse Ambush**. He also served as a cook when the IRA occupied Runnamoat House

Patrick Cummins (Killina Coy.) 2nd Battalion North Roscommon. He was one of the first members of the Company when it formed in August of 1917

Tom Cummins (Kilmacuagh) a member of "E" Coy., 3rd Battalion South Roscommon. Tom had a fine singing voice. Once when the Tans stopped him, they made him kneel, and ordered him to curse de Valera. Cummins replied, "I don't know how to curse, sir," and then made good use of a sad face. Many of the members of the Kilgefin Company participated in the **Fourmilehouse Ambush** on 12 October 1920

Frank Cunnane 1st Lieutenant of Ballintubber Coy. in the 2nd Battalion South Roscommon. Cunnane took part in the **raid on the military train at Ballymoe** in June 1920, and the **attack on the Frenchpark Barracks** 2 October 1920. His house was burned by the Tans. After the War he emigrated to Philadelphia

James Cunnane (Ballyfarnon) 4th Battalion North Roscommon Brigade, brother of Joseph. Prisoner in Mountjoy in August 1921

Joseph Cunnane (Alderford House, Ballyfarnon) first Captain of the Ballyfarnon Company in the 4th Battalion North Roscommon, brother of Patrick. Although Cunnane had no previous military experience, he did all the instruction at parades. He had his men out canvassing, collecting funds, and working the polling booths during the Count Plunkett election. He assembled his men for the march on Lord Kingston's land near Arigna in March 1917 that ended in a baton charge by the RIC, but no redistribution of land. He and his two brothers were arrested after a general arms raid in 1918 and sent to Mountjoy

Jim Cunnane (Knockcroghery Coy.) 4th Battalion South Roscommon. Served as the Adjutant for the Company and later for the Battalion. The Company was formed in 1917 under the leadership of Patrick Kelly. Cunnane paraded with the Volunteers, and attended practice battles at Taughmaconnell overseen by Ernie O'Malley in the summer of 1918. Participated in the South Roscommon election of 1918, and carried a couple of tins of petrol to the **Lecarrow Barracks** before it was set afire. Took part in the **attempted attack at Kilmurray Camp** — an action that was cancelled the very night of the proposed action. Cunnane was a member of a party of Volunteers that succeeded in raiding sixteen different homes and collecting about as many shotguns. He, along with the rest of his Company, **guarded the village of Knockcroghery** from reprisal on 15 August 1920 — a reprisal precipitated by British Forces being fired upon on Lough Ree. Cunnane participated in the **attempted ambush of two RIC constables at Lecarrow,** the **attempted attack on a party of military about eighteen strong at Knockcroghery** in January 1921, and **attempted ambush at Scrine.** During the Truce he attended the Battalion Camp at Drinaun, Ballygar, the Brigade camp at Ballinaheglish, the Brigade camp at Donamon, and was a delegate to Commandant Tom Maguire's review of the Brigade at Ballygar. He was engaged in the Sinn Féin Courts during this time, and appointed to a special service unit. He later emigrated to the United States of America

Michael Cunnane (Knockcroghery Coy.) 4th Battalion South Roscommon. The Company was formed in 1917 with Patrick Kelly serving as Captain. Cunnane drilled with the Volunteers, and attended practice battles at Taughmaconnell overseen by Ernie O'Malley in the summer of 1918. Cunnane was with a group of Volunteers who visited six intended recruits to the RIC and "dissuaded" them from joining the force. He also raided an ex-RIC man's house and seized four guns, one revolver, and a quantity of ammunition. He assisted Captain Pat Kelly with the making of moulds for slugs used in shotguns. Participated in the South Roscommon election of 1918, the **burning of Lecarrow Barracks**, and the **attempted attack at Clooncraff** — an proposed action staged in conjunction with Kilteevan Company and under the command of Pat Madden. Cunnane was a member of a party of Volunteers that succeeded in raiding sixteen different homes and collecting about as many shotguns. He was also involved in a raid on two hostile houses in Rahara — raids in which the party was fired upon, slightly wounding one of the men. Took part in the **attempted attack at Kilmurray Camp** — an action that was cancelled the very night of the proposed action. He, along with the rest of his Company, **guarded the village of Knockcroghery** from reprisal on 15 August 1920 — a reprisal precipitated by British Forces being fired upon on

Lough Ree. Cunnane was one of five men involved in raiding the evening mail train to Dublin. He, Tommie Kelly, and Owen Curley broke into the mail car and pilfered the sacks, looking for incriminating letters to Dublin Castle — letters which were then sent to GHQ in Dublin instead. He also participated in the **attempted ambush of two RIC constables at Lecarrow,** the **attempted ambush of a military lorry at Knockcroghery,** the **ambush of two RIC men at Knockcroghery Railway Station** — an action in which one of the policemen lost his life. He also held up a goods trains near Ballymurray and removed twenty bags of mails for censoring. He was present at the **attempted attack on a party of military about eighteen strong at Knockcroghery** in January 1921, the **attempted ambush at Scrine,** the **attempt to blow up the Curry and Ballymurray bridges,** and the **attack on RIC Barracks at Ballygar** on 1 July 1921. Cunnane was also with the men when they **attempted to blow up the railway bridge at Farnaseer.** Cunnane made a considerable number of fuse bombs used by the Company. He was one of a few men entrusted with important dispatches during this time. During the Truce he attended the Battalion Camp at Drinaun, Ballygar. He later emigrated to the USA

Owen Cunnane (Ballyfarnon) served as the 1st Lieutenant of Ballyfarnon Company in the 4th Battalion North Roscommon

Patrick Cunnane (Alderford House, Ballyfarnon) 4th Battalion North Roscommon, brother of Joseph

Michael Keane, ___, and William Cunnane. Photo taken at Pat Glynn's Memorial Service in 1970.

William Cunnane (Ballintubber) 2nd Battalion South Roscommon, who narrowly escaped the Tans' terror at Tom Leonard's house on 6 January 1921. He later became a member of the Flying Column that trained in the Charleston area after the Truce was signed

Bernard Cunniffe (Ballinagare Coy.) 1st Battalion South Roscommon. Drilled with his fellow Volunteers, collected for the Dáil loan, and enforced the Belfast boycott. Participated in the **destruction of vacant barracks** in 1920, and the **attack on Frenchpark Barracks** 2 October 1920. During the Truce he attended the Company and Battalion training camp specialising in dispatch, scouting, and intelligence work. He took the Republican side during the Civil War and fought the Free State troops at the **attack at Ballinagare** in July 1922, and the **attack at Castlerea** in November 1922. He later emigrated to the United States

Brian Cunniffe (Captain of Kilkerrin Coy.) although located in Co. Galway, this Company was incorporated into No. 2 Brigade of the 2nd Western Division which was commanded by Gerald O'Connor, former O/C of the 1st Battalion South Roscommon Brigade. Kilkerrin Coy. was part of the Glenamaddy Battalion. During the Civil War Cunniffe became a member of an ASU formed with the Tuam Battalion

Edward "Ned" Cunniffe (Monksland) Quartermaster of his area. In 1919 he took an oath to the Republic in the presence of Rev. Fr. Keane, who was then the chaplain of Summerhill Convent. A year later he acted as lookout while the keystone in the arch of the bridge over the Cross River at Summerhill was being dismantled

Jack Cunniffe (Drum Coy.) 3rd Battalion Athlone Brigade. He took the Oath of Allegiance to the Sinn Féin Party at the Ardkeenan House, the local Volunteer gathering point*

*_Drum and Its Hinterland_ by Edward Egan, p. 301.

James Cunniffe (Ballaghaderreen) one of the first members of the Ballaghaderreen Coy. in the East Mayo Brigade. A butcher by trade, he was arrested after the Rising, and first sent to Lewes and later to Glasgow Jail. He ended his "visit" to the bigger isle by being incarcerated in Frongoch

Maurice Cunniffe (Ballinagare Coy.) 1st Battalion South Roscommon. Drilled with his Company, collected monies for the Dáil loan, and enforced the Belfast boycott. Participated in the **destruction of vacant barracks** in 1920, the **attempted attack on Kilmurray Military Camp** in June, and the **attack on Frenchpark Barracks** 2 October 1920. He was present at several attempted ambushes in Castlerea in January 1921, and became a member of the Active Service Unit formed in that month. During the Truce he attended the Company and Battalion training camps specialising in dispatch, scouting, and intelligence work. He took the Anti-Treaty side during the Civil War, and participated in the **attack at Ballinagare** in July 1922, and the **attack at Castlerea** in November 1922. Later emigrated to the United States

Michael Cunniffe (Monksland) Adjutant of the 3rd Battalion Athlone Brigade, brother of Ned. He took the oath of allegiance in 1919 with his brother in the presence of Rev. Fr. Keane. He also served as a lookout in April 1920 when the keystone in the arch of the bridge over the Cross River at Summerhill was being dismantled in order to impede the lorry traffic. Took part in the **raid on the Athlone Excise Office** in May 1920. Later in life became a farmer. Buried in the Four Roads Cemetery

Patrick Cunniffe (Bredagh) Dysart Coy., 4th Battalion South Roscommon. Joined the Company in 1917. Attended parades, received instructions under Ernie O'Malley, helped in the 1918 election. He was appointed to work with the Republican Police. Patrick worked with the members of the Curraghboy Coy. during the Civil War, raiding homes of ex-RIC men and confiscating their weapons

Thomas Cunniffe (Curracot, Mt. Talbot) Tisrara Coy., 4th Battalion South Roscommon, served as a 1st Lieutenant for the Company

Tom Cunniffe (Drum Coy.) 3rd Battalion Athlone Brigade. He took the Oath of Allegiance to the Sinn Féin Party at the Ardkeenan House, the local Volunteer gathering point*

Drum and Its Hinterland by Edward Egan, p. 301.

The Arrest of the Curraghboy Volunteers

Personal reflections as written by Thomas Cunningham of Gortfree 1978

...."we of the Curraghboy Company, numbering approximately twenty members, carried on until the 5th of January 1921 when ten of our members were arrested in the early hours of the morning about four o'clock. As the frost lay heavily on the ground, we suffered very (much) from the cold, being allowed only to half dress ourselves. I myself had to walk about a mile with my boots unlaced and, of course, we were all handcuffed. I would like to mention here that the conduct of those RIC and Black and Tans in our homes on that morning was that of ruffians and blackguards — not that of policemen. After they gained entry, the violence was indescribable, the threats and blows were countless and included a mock hanging with a rope which they seemed to have carried around with them for the purpose of terrorising the people, putting me on my knees with a gun to my head saying an Act of Contrition, they gave me three minutes to live. I was then only 19 years old. Nor do I say that comrades had it any less severe. Their bloodspattered faces and gaping wounds told their own tale. Indeed one man was almost unrecognisable. We were kept for many hours in open lorries which added to our suffering.

"On the way to Athlone Barracks, passing by a public house, those Bravadoes decided to make a call to refresh themselves after their morning's work, of course, as usual, they paid for nothing. But the good proprietor, now R.I.P. whose name was Willie Fallon of Brideswell, asked our captors if he could give the prisoners a drink and wonder of wonders they agreed. One of the Tans went around with a bottle and glass holding it up to our mouths himself because with the handcuffs you were helpless yourself. It was obvious his generosity was costing him nothing because he gave you a very large measure. May God rest the noble soul of the man who bore the cost. I feel sure it prevented some of us from pneumonia if not from death.

"Eventually (we were) taken to Athlone Barracks where we were confined in cells without any bed. After about three months, we were tried by Field General court-martial, charged with the kidnapping and disappearance of a spy or enemy agent, found guilty, and sentenced to 18 months imprisonment with hard labour. Eventually we were transferred to Mountjoy prison around the first June 1921 where we had to suffer for fourteen nights without a bed.....

"Subsequently transferred to England in the last days of June under armed escort with every two men handcuffed together as we were transferred from the boat to the train. I would like to state here that we had in our group two very distinguished IRA officers from West Cork namely Patt Harte and Tom Hales, the latter being our own commanding officer in prison. Both of those men after arrest were severely tortured being strapped down on a stretcher and then the torturers got to work with pincers and pliers crushing and removing their finger and toe nails plus beating and burning by means of cigarette ends, so when the torturers had finished Hales was unconscious and Harte was insane and had to be removed to a mental hospital where he died a few years later. Tom Hales also passed on, his life probably shortened by his sufferings and his years of service to his country. May their noble souls R.I.P. those gallant soldiers of Ireland........"*

Author's notes: Harte was incarcerated in Pentonville during the Truce, at which time Michael Collins, concerned for Harte's health, visited him.
Major Percival of the Essex Regiment was the officer responsible for the orders to beat and torture Hales and Harte. He was also the officer in charge of the raiding party that burned the home of Michael Collins in Woodfield, West Cork. Collins ordered his assassination, but various attempts failed. Percival ended his military glory days by surrendering Singapore to the Japanese in World War II.
Tom Hales became the officer in charge of the ambush party at Béal na Bláth.

Bernard Cunningham (Culleen, Lecarrow) a member of St. John' Coy. in the 4th Battalion South Roscommon. During the Truce he was appointed to a special service unit

John Cunningham (Coolatober) Dysart Coy., 4th Battalion South Roscommon. Joined the Company in 1917. Attended parades, received instructions under Ernie O'Malley, helped in the 1918 election, and raided for arms

Luke Cunningham (Kilcolgan, County Galway) a member of the Cloonfad Coy., 1st Battalion South Roscommon. Participated in the **disarming of a Black and Tan at Cloonfad** in May 1921. Served as assistant Director of Training in the camps after the Truce. He later joined the Garda Síochána

Michael J. Cunningham (Culleen, Lecarrow) a member of St. John' Coy. in the 4th Battalion South Roscommon. During the Truce, he, along with his brother, was appointed to a special service unit

Michael Cunningham (Gailey, Knockcroghery) a member of St. John' Coy. in the 4th Battalion South Roscommon. During the Truce he too was appointed to a special service unit

Thomas Cunningham (Ardmullan) a member of the Curraghboy Coy. in the 4th Battalion South Roscommon. From 1917-March 1919 did organisational work, drilled with the men, performed military exercises during a visit to the area by Sean Connolly, did police duty during the South Roscommon election and in conjunction with enforcement of Dáil decrees. Cunningham was with a group of Volunteers who raided the private homes of three men—two of whom had joined and one who was about to join the RIC. Not surprisingly, these men had a change of heart! Cunningham raided for arms. There were a total of twenty raids conducted within the Company area, and another fifteen raids outside the immediate vicinity and performed in conjunction with other Companies of the Battalion. Cunningham took part in a special raid for arms in the Kiltoom area. He prevented jurors from attending the British Courts, and held periodic meetings of Dáil Courts when necessity arose. Manufactured ammunition and constructed dugouts for storage of same. Seven or eight mail cars were robbed during this time, and Cunningham participated in those actions. He served as a scout on the night of the **attempted ambush of a military lorry at Knockcroghery** in early January 1921. The entire Company participated in the arrest and confinement of a suspected spy. That man was tried by court-martial and eventually executed — an action which prompted the arrest of ten members of the Company on 5 January 1921, including Cunningham. He was severely thrashed and taken to Athlone Barracks, and incarcerated in a cell with no bed for three months. Later transferred to Mountjoy and finally, in the last days of June, he was shipped across the waters to Wormwood Scrubbs and Pentonville Prisons in England. Tom Hales from Cork was his commanding officer in prison. Released 11 January 1922. After the War he became a farmer. Buried in Cam Cemetery

William Cunningham of the 2nd Battalion North, took part in the **attack at the Elphin Dispensary** 13 December 1920, and the **attack on the Elphin patrol** 5 January 1921. He later emigrated to England

Jack Curley (Roscommon Coy.) 3rd Battalion South Roscommon

Owen Curley (Knockcroghery Coy.) 4th Battalion South Roscommon. The Knockcroghery Company was formed in 1917 under the leadership of Patrick Kelly of Lecarrow. Curley paraded with the Volunteers, and served as a clerk with the Sinn Féin Courts. He attended courses of instruction held at Rahara by Ernie O'Malley each evening for some weeks, and took part in the practice battles at Taughmaconnell in the summer of 1918. He also took a course in semaphore and Morse signalling. Curley canvassed house to house for signatures to the plebiscite for independence. He was with a group of Volunteers who visited six intended recruits to the RIC and successfully "dissuaded" them from joining the force. Participated in the South Roscommon election of 1918, enforced the Belfast boycott, and helped write up a set of rules for shopkeepers regarding hours of operation. Assisted Patrick Kelly in making moulds for slugs for use in shotguns. He, along with his Company and in conjunction with Kilteevan Company, took part in the **attempted ambush at Clooncraff**, an operation under the command of Pat Madden. Curley raided numerous houses for arms. On one occasion, the raid of an ex-RIC man and several others "hostile to the IRA" succeeded in yielding four guns, one revolver, and a quantity of ammunition. On another occasion, he was a member of the party which raided a private house in the St. John's area — a raid which resulted in one Volunteer being seriously wounded and requiring attention in a Dublin hospital. He, along with Jim and John Breheny and Tommie Kelly, transported a local man to his "prison" — an abandoned building in Cloverhill where the man spent several weeks. His offence: firing at and wounding a Volunteer. Curley censored mail taken from a postman en route from Knockcroghery to Roscommon town, and took part in raiding the evening mail train from Dublin. Curley took part in the **attempted attack at Kilmurray Camp** — an action that was cancelled the very night of the proposed assault. He also participated in the **attempted ambush of two RIC constables at Lecarrow**, an **attempted attack on a military lorry at Knockcroghery**, and **guarding the village of Knockcroghery** from reprisal on 15 August 1920 — a reprisal precipitated by British Forces being fired upon on Lough Ree. Curley participated in the **attack on two RIC men at Knockcroghery Railway Station** on 26 August 1920. In January 1921 he was a member of the party that **attempted an attack on a group of military about eighteen strong at Knockcroghery**. He was also at **Scrine for an attempted attack**. During this time, Curley made a considerable number of fuse bombs for the Company and served as the Battalion Quartermaster. Throughout the Truce he was actively involved in the Arbitration Courts. He later emigrated to the USA

William Curley (Errick, Four Roads) 4th Battalion South Roscommon. William was a dispatch rider who, on one occasion, was delivering a message by bicycle from Willie Kilcline of St. John's Coy. to Pat Egan of Kilronan, Ballygar. Curley happened upon a checkpoint outside Beade's pub in Rahara. Quick thinking William hid the dispatch in a nearby wall, and proceeded on through the checkpoint. He waited around the area until the military had given up their surveillance, then returned to the wall, only to spend the next several hours trying to remember exactly where he had hidden his important document*

Patrick Fitzmaurice correspondence, 27 December 2002, Oranmore, Galway.

Curley's Farmhouse (Cooleen Hill in Knockcroghery) where Pat Mullooly found a welcome after his escape from the Athlone Barracks

Thomas Curran (Trien Coy.) 1st Battalion South Roscommon

Gerald Dalton (Corracreigh, Clooneyquinn) 2nd Battalion North Roscommon. Listed in the GHQ papers in UCD Archives as the Adjutant for Killina Company. Transported and placed the mines for the **attack on Elphin Barracks** in February 1921

James Curran (Farragher, Ballymacurley) 2nd Battalion South Roscommon, Intelligence Officer and dispatcher, who, in November 1920, ditched his heavy hobnailed boots and ran barefoot across the fields to warn Dan O'Rourke, O/C of South Roscommon Brigade, that Tans were headed towards Tarmon. He arrived too late! Acted as an outpost during the **Fourmilehouse Ambush**. When the 2nd Western Division was formed, Curran became the Head of Intelligence for the 3rd Battalion, No. 2 Brigade. He joined the Free State Army. Later he became a farmer. He is buried in Oran cemetery

James Dalton a member of the Athlone Flying Column commanded by James Tormey. Dalton travelled with the Column back and forth across the Shannon, attempting ambushes in both County Westmeath and County Roscommon

David Daly (Faheran, Moate) a member of the Athlone Brigade. He joined the Volunteers in 1914 and the IRB four years later. Sworn into the IRB movement by Sean McCormack of Drumraney, Daly became the Head Centre for Westmeath. The Volunteer Company that had formed in early 1914 fell apart after the split precipitated by John Redmond; thus, the Company was reorganised in 1917 with Peter Melinn and Sean Hurley serving in prominent positions. Daly and Sean McCormack formed another Company of fifteen members. In 1918 Daly was appointed the Athlone Battalion O/C. He participated in the **attack on Streamstown Barracks** in July 1920, the **ambush at Parkwood** in County Westmeath in September 1920, and the **attempted ambush of a convoy on the Athlone-Ballinasloe-Galway Road** in October. He was captured in April 1921 at the home of the McCormack brothers in Moate. Imprisoned in Athlone and the Curragh, but escaped through the Brady tunnel in September 1921. He then went to the Brigade training camp at Benown. He fought with the Anti-Treaty men during the Civil War, and was arrested in Moate on 30 January 1923, at which time he handed over his revolver, ammunition, a bomb and some gelignite

John Daly (Culleenaghmore, Slatta, Kilglass) sheltered fugitives in his cabin.

James Daly (Scramogue Coy.) 3rd Battalion North Roscommon

James Daly (Rahara Coy.) 4th Battalion South Roscommon

John Daly operated around Drumsna and worked in conjunction with Mick McLoughlin

John Daly took part in the **attack near Ruskey village** on 5 July 1921

John Daly (Culleenaghmore, Slatta, Kilglass) sheltered many men on the run. He lived in an isolated cabin where he kept the Volunteers in his loft

John Daly (Altogownan, Boyle) was arrested during the Civil War and taken to Dundalk on 12 April 1923

Joseph Daly (Carraune) served as the Adjutant for Cloverhill Coy. in the 2nd Battalion South Roscommon

Joseph "Paddy" Daly (Athlone area) a guard on the railway, who heard about the arrest of a senior officer in Roscommon, and boarded a train in Athlone and travelled to Dublin to warn Michael Collins that the officer incarcerated had handwritten instructions about an upcoming meeting in the capital of all the Brigade Commanders in Ireland. "Had it not been for Daly's action, the British would probably have made a great swoop and GHQ and all the brigade officers throughout the country would have been captured."* Paddy Daly "gave wonderful service in this respect, as well as carrying munitions.**

Seamus O'Meara Volunteer Witness Statement to the Bureau of Military History 1913-21, p. 13.
***Jack Glancy Volunteer Witness Statement to the Bureau of Military History 1913-21, p. 4.*

Henry Daly (Athleague Coy.) 3rd Battalion South Roscommon

Katy Daly (Culleenaghmore, Slatta, Kilglass) member of the Cumann na mBan. After the War she became a rate collector for the Roscommon County Council in the Kilglass area. Died in 1988 and buried in Kilglass Cemetery

Katy Daly (Cornamagh) active in Cumann na mBan

Michael Daly (Rahara Coy.) 4th Battalion South Roscommon

Peter Daly (Athleague Coy.) 3rd Battalion South Roscommon

Tom Daly aided in Jim Molloy's escape from Boyle Barracks

Katy Daly (Culleenaghmore, Slatta, Kilglass)

Tom Daly (Cloonfad Coy.) 1st Battalion South Roscommon

Denis Darcy (Killina Coy.) 2nd Battalion North Roscommon. He was one of the first members of the Company when it formed in August of 1917

Joseph Darcy (Ballaghaderreen) one of the first members of the Ballaghaderreen Coy. in the East Mayo Brigade. During the Civil War he was arrested in March of 1923, and taken to Athlone, where he was released a month later

Gerald Davis (Kilgefin Coy.) 3rd Battalion South Roscommon, inducted into the IRB by Andy Cooney. In 1918 Pat Madden came to Dublin looking for work. Davis got him into his own unit of Volunteers (Company "C"). (Both Madden and Andy Cooney were arrested in York Street for illegal drilling.) When the men returned to the Roscommon area, Davis loaned his deceased brother's rifle to Pat Madden's Company. (His brother had died in WWI in France.) Davis took part in an **ambush on the Lanesboro-Roscommon Road,** and was the first person to assist John Scally after the blowup of the mine. He also took part in **Moneen,** the **burning of Athleague Barracks,** the **attempted attack on the Castlerea Station Guard,** the **attack on Frenchpark Barracks**, and the attempted assassination of a British spy in Dublin. While in service for the Volunteers, Gerald was trained in Dublin by Diarmund O'Hegarty in explosives

Gerald Davis, 3rd Battalion South Roscommon.

and by Rory O'Connor in engineering. In March/April of 1921, he was sent by GHQ to the Athlone area to take charge of operations there. He ordered that any policeman in the town of Athlone was fair game. In the spring of 1921, he and George Adamson were coming back from a trip to Westmeath, when they approached a barnyard in Carricknaughton where two Black and Tans were courting two local girls. In the attempt to disarm the Tans, Davis was wounded in his right arm, while Adamson was shot in the chest. Davis narrowly escaped a roundup near Moate along with George Adamson and Ned Dowling. The next swoop, however, netted him. By mid-May 1921, he was a prisoner at Athlone Barracks, where he was identified by the soldier with whom he had had the scuffle in the barnyard. He was sentenced to life, and sent to Mountjoy, from which he escaped carrying smuggled guns and clothing. During the Civil War he was arrested on 16 July 1922, and sent to Dundalk. After the War he became a medical doctor, and joined the Irish National Army. In the 1950s he was interviewed by Ernie O'Malley, and his words are included in the O'Malley Papers in the UCD Archives in Dublin

James Davis (Lisnanarriagh) Cloontuskert Coy. in the 3rd Battalion South Roscommon. Tended to the wounded men brought to Incheneagh Island in Lough Ree

Larry Davis (Lisnanarriagh) a former soldier, who gave his short Lee Enfield rifle to the 3rd Battalion South Flying Column

Matt Davis (Cloontymullan, Kilteevan) 3rd Battalion South Roscommon. Davis helped to found the Irish Volunteers in County Roscommon. When the group was in its infancy in 1917 (there was really no actual unit of men to command), Davis was appointed the O/C of the 3rd Battalion South. At a later meeting, he was appointed the Quartermaster of the South Roscommon Brigade, a position he held until the Truce. His home served as the base for Ernie O'Malley when O'Malley came to Roscommon in the summer of 1918. As Quartermaster, his was the job of procuring guns and safely storing them. With the funds collected from the local people, Davis often travelled to Dublin to buy armament, but often returned to Roscommon empty handed. Even ammunition was difficult to come by. A very dirty and smoky (but very powerful) substance was manufactured in Cloonmine, Ballymurray. Davis organised a work party to dig and then conceal the grave of John Scally, who had been wounded by a mine on the Lanesboro-Roscommon Road at Cloontymullen. His was the only Company in the 3rd Battalion South to take the Anti-Treaty side in the Civil War. Davis served as the O/C of the 3rd Battalion, 2nd Western Division IRA. He headed a Flying Column which roamed over south and west Roscommon and beyond. He was captured by the government forces under the command of Captain B. Masterson after a raid on Quaker Island in Lough Ree on 22 November 1922. He was taken to Athlone, where he was sentenced to death, but was the only one of six men to be reprieved. He was transferred to Mountjoy, where he went on hunger strike for twenty-two days. Davis was released in 1924. Two years later, he was elected Chairman of the Roscommon *Comhairle Cenntair* of Fianna Fáil. Davis later served as secretary of the party's Kilteevan *Cumann* in 1928, the vice chairman of the Roscommon County Council in 1934, and the vice chairman of Fianna Fáil's Roscommon *Dail Cheanntair* in 1936-37. He became a Fianna Fáil TD for Athlone-Longford in 1937-38. Died in 1957 and is buried in Kilteevan Cemetery

Brian Dayton (Bumlin, Strokestown) 3rd Battalion North Roscommon. At Truce time Brian was an Intelligence Officer for the 3rd Battalion

Thomas Dean served as 1st Lieutenant of Frenchpark Coy. in the 2nd Battalion, 2nd Western Division. Many in his Company joined the Free State Army after the Truce

Deignan (see **Duignan**)

Patrick Delahunty (Boyle) a native of Waterford, owner of a garage at Bridge Street, where a few Sinn Féin sympathisers gathered to plan the first Sinn Féin

My uncle, James Hayden, was a member of the Fenians and had to fly from the country with some others as a result of his activities. Another uncle, Patrick Hayden, tried to follow on in the lines laid down by his brother and was a keen supporter of Parnell. I knew my Uncle Pat well. He was an out and out separatist. The R.I.C. gave him a rough time of it and on several occasions I saw the police prevent him from speaking at meetings. I always felt that it was my duty to vindicate his memory.*

*Matt Davis Volunteer Witness Statement to the Bureau of Military History 1913-21, p. 1.

Matt Davis, Quartermaster for the South Roscommon Brigade.

PHOTO COURTESY OF EMA STAUNTON

meeting in Boyle. He joined the IRB in February 1915 under Alec McCabe. Delahunty was the first O/C of the Boyle Company, which formed in 1917. He drilled his men, and organised them to take part in the Longford bye election. He took part in the **Rockingham Raid**, the first raid for arms in the county, and, as a result, was arrested and sent to Mountjoy, where he participated in the hunger strike organised by Austin Stack. Delahunty served as Intelligence Officer for the North Roscommon Brigade while servicing the Black and Tan vehicles. He also aided in Jim Molloy's **escape from Boyle Barracks**. Near the end of 1920, Patrick warned Pat Brennan, O/C of the 1st Battalion, of an upcoming raid in Ballytrasna. As a result of such warning, Brennan evaded arrest. After the Black and Tan War, Delahunty joined the Free State Army with the rank of Captain. Retired in 1928 and moved to Dublin, where he died in the 1930s

Mrs. P. J. Delahunty was a prominent member of the Boyle Cumann na mBan

Michael Delaney (Ballygar Coy.) which was considered part of 4th Battalion South Roscommon when the Divisional structure was implemented

Michael Delaney (Main Street, Castlerea) Moor Coy. in the 1st Battalion South Roscommon. When Michael first became involved with the Volunteers, he was a medical student in Dublin — a classmate of Kevin Barry. He served as the Adjutant of No. 2 Battalion in the 2nd Brigade of the 2nd Western Division. Delaney took part in the **attempted attack on Kilmurray Military Camp** in June 1920. During the Civil War he became a member of the Active Service Unit of the 1st Battalion South, and served as its Adjutant. He was arrested on 21 July 1922, and transferred to Athlone two months later. After the War he completed his medical studies, and became a Medical Officer in Arranmore Island, Burtonport, Co. Donegal. He then moved to Geevagh, Co. Sligo, and finally to Castlerea, where he ended his career. His final days were spent in a home next to his daughter in Rathcroghan, Tulsk. He died 1984 and is buried in Tulsk Cemetery

William "Paddy" Delaney (Cloonbunny, Loughglynn) 1st Battalion South Roscommon. Participated in the **attempted attack on Kilmurray Military Camp** in June 1920, **attack on Frenchpark Barracks** 2 October 1920, and the **attempted attacks on Castlerea** and **Frenchpark** in January 1921. During the Truce he attended the Company training camp. He took the Anti-Treaty side during the Civil War, and participated in the **attack at Castlerea** in November 1922. Present at Pat Glynn's Memorial Service in 1970

Dan Dempsey (Knockcroghery Coy.) 4th Battalion South Roscommon. The Company was formed in 1917 under the leadership of Patrick Kelly of Culleen, Lecarrow. He, along with the rest of his Company, **guarded the village of Knockcroghery** from reprisal on 15 August 1920 — a reprisal precipitated by British Forces being fired upon on Lough Ree. Dempsey participated in the **attempted attack on a party of military about eighteen strong at Knockcroghery** in January 1921, the **attempted ambush at Scrine**, the holding up of a **goods train at Ballymurray**, and the **burning of a large house at Milltown, Curraghboy** which was about to be taken over by the British military. During the Civil War, he was one of five men who were mainly responsible for reorganising the Knockcroghery Company. He was also one of only three men who joined the Brigade Flying Column and travelled the fields of Galway, Roscommon, Westmeath, and Longford and fought the Free State forces where they found them. He held up and **derailed the train at Kiltoom**, taking possession of necessary provisions. He was arrested on 18 August of 1922, and taken to Athlone on 2 September 1922. After the War he moved to Dublin

Dominick Dempsey (Tuam) a member of the Kilgefin Coy., 3rd Battalion South Roscommon. Many of the members of the Kilgefin Company participated in the **Fourmilehouse Ambush** on 12 October 1920

Luke Dempsey (Greatmeadow, Boyle) joined the IRA in the summer of 1918, and later, in January of 1921, was appointed the Captain of Boyle Coy. in the 1st Battalion North Roscommon. He was arrested after ordering shopkeepers in Boyle to close their stores after the death of hunger striker Terence MacSwiney. In May of 1920, he took part in a **raid on the Boyle Railway Station** in which hundreds of gallons of gasoline were seized. He also guarded prisoners who were serving sentences imposed by the Sinn Féin Courts. Luke was present for the **burning of Grevisk RIC Barracks** in May of 1920. In September he was a member of the ambush party who took up positions at Greatmeadow in Boyle. Six days of waiting resulted in nothing. The enemy failed to appear. In March of 1921, Dempsey took part in an armed **raid of the Boyle Post Office**, which resulted in the seizure of documents detailing the amount of weaponry and ammunition in the Ballaghaderreen and Keadue Barracks. He also aided in the **escape of Jim Molloy and Michael Dockery from Boyle Barracks**. During the Truce he became transport officer at the Brigade camp. In June 1922, he joined the National Army, and served for eighteen months. Later in life he became a farmer. Died in the 1980s and buried in Ardcarne Cemetery in Boyle

Margaret Dempsey (Boyle) sister of Luke, active member of the Cumann na mBan

Michael Dempsey (Trien Coy.) 1st Battalion South Roscommon

Michael Dempsey (Kanefield, Baslick) Castleplunkett Coy., 2nd Battalion South Roscommon

Michael Dempsey (Barrymore, Kiltoom) a member of the Kiltoom Coy. in the 4th Battalion South Roscommon

Tom Deraney in 1922 he served as the 1st Lieutenant for Croghan Company in North Roscommon. He later emigrated to the United States

Tom Derby (Boyle) 1st Battalion North Roscommon, aided in the **escape from Boyle Barracks** of James Molloy and Michael Dockery. After the War he went to live in America, but returned to Ireland, where he reared a family of seven. He came from a family of carpenters, and chose to earn his living in that trade. Died in October 1973 and buried in Assylin Cemetery

Jimmie Derrig (Boyle) 1st Battalion North Roscommon, a member of the Volunteers since before the Easter Rising, sentenced after **'the conacre take over'** in Boyle. The agitation was directed at holdings at Warren, on the east side of town, and at Mockmoyne and Tinnacarra on the west side

Tom Derby (on the left) with members of his family.

"He seemed a pained person who had perhaps given up on the great dream of Ireland being the Garden of Eden that everybody expected it to become."

written by his grandson David Derby in 2003

PHOTO AND RESTORATION COURTESY OF DAVE DERBY

Paddy Devaney (Raveege, Ballintubber) served as the 1st Lieutenant of "F" Company in the 2nd Battalion, No. Brigade, 2nd Western Division. Patrick was shot during an argument over land rentals by an agent of the landlord Chichester. The bullet was secretly removed by a local man. Devaney aimed his own gun sights at the **military train at Ballymoe** in June 1920, and the **Frenchpark Barracks** on 2 October 1920. During the Civil War Devaney took the Anti-Treaty side, and, along with two other cohorts, robbed shops in Frenchpark of whiskey, cigarettes, and most important for an Irish winter, BOOTS! After the War he became a farmer. Buried in Ballintubber Cemetery

Tom Devaney (Faus, Croghan) first Captain of Croghan Company in the 5th Battalion North Roscommon. During the Tan War, Tom was arrested, and while being transported to prison with a large group of men, the Tans stopped at a pub and allowed the prisoners to eat. Tom asked to go out back and "take care of business." A few minutes later, he heard the roar of the engines of the transports, ran around the side of the building only to see the Tans (who had completely forgotten about him) and his comrades (who hadn't) leaving without him. And what did he do? The War (or even prison) without the friendship of his mates was unbearable. He shouted to the withdrawing soldiers, "Wait for me! Wait for me!"* After the War he emigrated to England, married in 1926, then returned to Dublin in the 1940s and became a grocer. Died 1987 and buried in Mt. Jerome Cemetery

Maureen O'Keefe, daughter of Tom, interview, 25 November 2000, Ballinalee, Longford.

Charles Devine (Boyle) formed the first Company of Volunteers in Boyle in 1914. They drilled openly with wooden rifles

James "Jimmy" Devine (Roscommon Coy.) 3rd Battalion South Roscommon

Tom Devaney, Captain of Croghan Coy.

PHOTO COURTESY OF MAUREEN O'KEEFE

Jimmy Devine, 3rd Battalion South Roscommon

Michael Devine (Roscommon Coy.) 3rd Battalion South Roscommon

Paddy Devine (Boyle) 1st Battalion North Roscommon, a member of the Volunteers in 1915

Tom Devine (Boyle) 1st Battalion North Roscommon, a member of the Volunteers before the Rising

Tom Devine (Crunkill, Ruskey) a member of the Kilglass Company in the 3rd Battalion North Roscommon

William Devine (Creemully, Fuerty) a member of Fuerty Coy. in the 2nd Battalion South Roscommon. He drilled with his Company, collected funds for the Dáil loan, and served under the command of Captain Bernie Kearney. He died before the 1940s

Joseph Diffley (later in life resided in Lisrattigan, Edgeworthstown, Co. Longford) a member of the Curraghroe Coy. in the 3rd Battalion North Roscommon. Joined the Volunteers in 1917. Attended meetings, weekly drills, and paraded in the South Longford Election at Longford town, Killashee, and Lanesboro. He also took part in the North and South Roscommon elections. Diffley participated in the armed raid of intended RIC recruits at Cloontuskert in March of 1920. Took part in the **burning of the Scramogue Barracks,** stood guard duty in the Kilgefin area on the night of the Fourmilehouse Ambush, took part in the **attack on Tarmonbarry Barracks** in January 1921, and the **Scramogue Ambush** two months later. He served as an active member of the Flying Column, cutting roads, raiding mails, and participating in several attempted ambushes. He was present at the **attack on Tarmonbarry Barracks** on 2 July 1921

John Diffley (Derryhanee) Curraghroe Coy. in the 3rd Battalion North Roscommon. Joined the Volunteers in 1917, took an active part in the Longford election of Joe McGuinness, and was on parade with his Company at Longford town, Killashee, and Lanesboro. Collected arms at Clondra, Killashee, and Rathclyne in County Longford, drilled and paraded with his fellow Volunteers. Participated in the armed **raid of a recruitment meeting** held in Cloontuskert, the **burning** of the vacated **Scramogue Barracks**, protective duty in Kilgefin area after the Fourmilehouse Ambush, the **attack on Tarmonbarry patrol** 5 January, **Scramogue Ambush**, and the **attack on the RIC Barracks at Tarmonbarry** on 2 July 1921. He died before the end of the 1930s

Thomas Diffley (Strokestown) 3rd Battalion North Roscommon. Captain of the local Company of Volunteers. After the War he became a farmer. Died in the 1970s and buried in the new Strokestown Cemetery

Edward Dignan (see **Edward Duignan**)

Edward Dillon (Carrowbehy, Castlerea) Ballinlough Coy., 1st Battalion South Roscommon, participated in the **burning of the Barracks at Ballinlough** 14 September 1920, and the **torching of Loughglynn Barracks** in that same month. He also took part in the **attempted ambush at Lisacul** (in conjunction with the East Mayo men) in May 1921. During the Truce he attended the training camps at Hermitage, Erritt, and Runnamoat. After the War he became a carpenter. Died 17 October 1968

John Dillon (Ballinlough Coy.) 1st Battalion South Roscommon, participated in the **capture of arms at Castlerea Barracks** in April 1920

John Dillon (Cloonfree, Strokestown) 3rd Battalion North Roscommon. Joined the Volunteers in October 1916, helped with the North Roscommon election, attended weekly meetings, collected arms. Took up his post at the General Election of 1918, and transported bombs and grenades through his Battalion area. He assembled for six consecutive nights waiting to take part in the **proposed attack on Tulsk Barracks**, which was unexpectedly evacuated before the attack could take place. Assisted at the Sinn Féin Courts, transported injured Volunteers from the Strokestown Courthouse fire to hospital, and subsequently guarded them. He was arrested, and held prisoner in Strokestown, Longford, and Athlone Barracks. He was finally sent to the Curragh, where he remained until December of 1921

Patrick Dillon (Fuerty) a member of Fuerty Coy. in the 2nd Battalion South

Roscommon. After the War he emigrated to the United States

Thomas Dillon joined the IRA in 1917. He was present at the **attack in Strokestown** in January 1921, served as an outpost on the day of the **Scramogue Ambush** and for the **attack on Tarmonbarry Barracks** in July 1921. During the Civil War he participated in the destruction of military cars

Thomas Dillon (Carrowntarriff) Dysart Coy., 4th Battalion South Roscommon. Joined the Company in 1917. Attended parades, received instructions under Ernie O'Malley, and helped in the 1918 election. He was appointed to work with the Republican Police

Joseph Dixon (Athlone) was very valuable in setting up and serving in the local Sinn Féin Courts. He was the contact man for the IRA in that area

Edward Dockery (Dockrey) (Cloonsheever, Tibohine) Ballinagare Coy. in the 1st Battalion South Roscommon. Participated in the **destruction of vacant barracks** in 1920, the **attack on Frenchpark Barracks** 2 October 1920, and the **attack at Ballinagare** in July 1922. He served as the 2nd Lieutenant of Ballinagare Coy. During the Truce he attended the Company and Battalion training camps specialising in dispatch, scouting, or intelligence work. Later emigrated to the United States

James Dockery (Castleplunkett Coy.) 2nd Battalion South Roscommon

Martin F. Dockery (Drumlish, Drummullin, Elphin) brother of Michael J. Martin joined the Volunteers in 1917 and was appointed 1st Lieutenant of Creeve Coy. He spent his time drilling, raiding for arms, doing dispatch work, and "strongly encouraging" people not to attend the British Courts. In September 1919, he was appointed the Battalion Vice O/C. He was present at the Battalion staffing and Council meetings. Took part in the **burning of Hillstreet Barracks** on 12 May 1920, waited in ambush for a cycling patrol in July, made an attempt to attack a patrol in Elphin in September. On 4 February 1921, he was in charge of men trenching and blocking roads for the anticipated attack on **Elphin Barracks** (which was cancelled). On the night of the real fireworks, 11 February, Dockery was in charge of men waiting in the second house from the barracks. He was also in the **ambush party at Smithhill** in May 1921 and at **Lavally** (near Strokestown) on the day before the Truce. He attended the Roscommon training camps including Mantua Brigade camp, and Cloonshee Battalion camp. He also travelled to the officers' training camp at Glenasmole House in County Wicklow. Went to Boyle after the barracks had been taken over by the local IRA. Shortly after the outbreak of Civil War, he was arrested as an Anti-Treatyite, and detained in Athlone, where he remained until Christmas of 1923. After the War he emigrated to Brooklyn, New York, where he managed a tavern in which he kept a jar for IRA donations (see box)

Michael Dockery (Ballinameen Coy.) 1st Battalion North Roscommon. Took part in the **attack on Frenchpark Barracks and Courthouse** in June 1921. He was a member of the Active Service Unit in 1921 under Pat Brennan. After the War he joined the Garda Síochána and was stationed in Peterswell, Loughrea

Michael J. Dockery (Drumlish, Drummullin, Elphin) Creeve Coy.

Owen Dockery (Knockglass, Ballinameen) Quartermaster for the North Roscommon 1st Battalion under Pat Brennan. Took part in the

"Dad (Martin Dockery) kept a tavern, Dockery's Restaurant, at 11 West 31st Street in New York City for forty-two years before retiring in 1975 at age seventy-five. He was the vice commandant of the (2nd) Roscommon Battalion of the Irish Republican Army and was imprisoned during Ireland's fight for independence. He told me he had nothing against the English people. The guards treated him well, but the government of England was another matter. He kept a donation jar on the bar for the Saint Francis Bread Line on 35th Street and one behind the bar for the IRA."

Martin J. Dockery,
Lost in Translation Vietnam A Combat Advisor's Story,
p. 1.

Michael Dockery (Lissadorn, Elphin) was appointed the O/C of the North Roscommon Brigade in January 1921. Participated in the **attempted attack on the Carrick-on-Shannon Station Guard** in September 1918, the **attack on the Elphin Dispensary** on 13 December 1920, the **attack on Elphin Barracks** 11 February 1921 (an operation which he and Sean Connolly planned), and the **Keadue Ambush** in March of that year. Dockery was arrested in May 1921 (in possession of a rifle from the Keadue ambush) and charged with murder. He was severely beaten and taken to Boyle Barracks, where he was kicked down a flight of stone steps and kept in a basement cell. Because he was likely to be executed owing to the fact that he was charged with a capital offence, the Volunteers planned his daring escape on 15/16 June. He joined the Free State Army, and, according to Micheál O'Callaghan's *For Ireland and Freedom*, was killed by a sniper's bullet in Boyle Workhouse grounds 2 July 1922. Michael Hopkinson in his book, *Green Against Green*, concurs. The date and place differ with Padraic O'Farrell's *Who's Who in the Irish War of Independence and Civil War* which claims 7 July in County Sligo as the fateful moment. Obituary notice in the *Roscommon Herald* stated that Dockery was killed 1 July, but his tombstone is carved with the 2 July death date. He was buried in the old Ballinderry Cemetery

attack on **Frenchpark Barracks and Courthouse** in June 1921. After the War he joined the Garda Síochána, and was stationed in Rathangan, Co. Kildare, where he died in 1981

Patrick Dockery (Dockrey) (Lisalway, Castlerea) 2nd Battalion South Roscommon. Took part in the **raid on the military train at Ballymoe** in June 1920, the **attack on Frenchpark Barracks** 2 October 1920, and the **ambush at Southpark, Castlerea** 10 July 1921. After the War he returned to farming. Died 15 June 1976, and buried in Rathmoyle, Kilmurray

Peter Dockery (Peake, Ballinagare) 2nd Battalion North Roscommon. He took part in the **attack on Frenchpark Barracks and Courthouse** in June 1921. He was a member of the Active Service Unit during the Civil War, specialising in making cartbox mines. After the War he rented out his farmland and worked as an all around handyman — fixing guns, maintaining spinning wheels, etc. Local legend claims that Dockery had special powers for healing. He would lick a burn and the wound would soon heal.* He died in the early 1960s

John Martin, resident of Ballinagare, interview by author, 14 August 2004.

William Dockery (Drumlish, Drummullin, Elphin) brother of Michael and Martin. Joined the Volunteers in April 1919. Took an active part in capturing local robbers, raiding for arms and mail on trains, and **burning of Grevisk Barracks.** Arrested and beaten after ordering Boyle shopkeepers to close their doors after the death of Terence MacSwiney. He raided the Boyle Post Office for official letters, and was arrested for same on 17 March 1921. He became a prisoner at Boyle Barracks until June, then was removed to the Curragh until the general amnesty. He was a member of the ASU during the Civil War commanded by Pat Brennan. He was present for the takeover of local military and RIC barracks, the **capture of Swinford Barracks, attack on Free State forces at Killasser Co. Mayo' capture of outpost on the Boyle railroad bridge,** and the **firefight at Lakeview School.** When the cease-fire order came, he obeyed it. The Free State troops did not, however, let bygones be bygones. Dockery was forced to stay on the run until well into 1924. Emigrated to Brooklyn, New York

Patrick Dockery, Lisalway, Castlerea.

James P. Dodd (Boyle) Alec McCabe took him into the IRB in February 1915. He became a member of the IRA in 1916, during which year he paraded every day of Easter Week with his Company. He was on the original committee to place Count Plunkett's name on the ballot, took part in the **Rockingham Raid,** and became active in land agitation. He was sentenced after the **conacre takeover in Boyle,** and became a "guest" at Mountjoy. After the War he served as a member of the Roscommon County Council from 1934 to 1942. He was a grocer and auctioneer in Boyle

Malachy Doddy (Ballaghaderreen town) first Captain of the Frenchpark Company

Dominick Doherty (Lisacul) O/C of 4th Battalion East Mayo Brigade (which incorporated some Companies in west Roscommon). He, along with the Mulrennan brothers, would often go to Ballaghaderreen to encourage the men to organise and train

James Doherty (Taghnoose, Carrowbehy, Castlerea) 1st Battalion South Roscommon, served with the Cloonboniffe Coy. Participated in the **capture of arms from the Castlerea Barracks** in April 1920, and the **raid for petrol at Ballinlough Station** in June 1920. He served as scout for the **capture of enemy stores at Ballymoe** that same month. Took part in the **attempted ambush at Coshlieve** in July 1920, the **attempted attack on the Castlerea Station Guard** in July 1920, the **raid and capture of military equipment at Ballymoe** September 1920, blocked roads in preparation for the **attack on Frenchpark Barracks** 2 October 1920, and was in attendance at the **destruction of vacant barracks** in 1920. When the New Year rolled around, Doherty participated in the **attempted attacks at Castlerea** and **Frenchpark** in January 1921, and acted in the covering party for the **attack on the Castlerea** military 6 April 1921. A month later he participated in the **attempted ambush of an RIC patrol near Ballymoe,** and the **attempted ambush at Lisacul.** He was a member of the Active Service Unit which was formed in January 1921

James Doherty (Main Guard Street, Galway) a member of Moor Coy. in the 1st Battalion South Roscommon. Participated in the **attempted attack on Kilmurray**

Military Camp in June 1920, the **attack on Frenchpark RIC Barracks** 2 October 1920, the **attempted ambush at Loughglynn** in April 1921, and the **attempted ambush at Lisacul** (in conjunction with the East Mayo men) in May. During the Truce he attended the Company training camp. James held out for the Anti-Treaty side. He joined forces with other like-minded souls in the **attack at Castlerea** during the Civil War in November 1922

James Doherty (Ballinagare Coy.) 1st Battalion South Roscommon

Mick Doherty (Abbey Street, Roscommon town) a member of the 1918 Sinn Féin election committee in South Roscommon

P. Doherty (Lisalway, Castlerea) a member of "C" Coy. in the 2nd Battalion South Roscommon. He was burned during the **attack on the Frenchpark Barracks** 2 October 1920

Robert Doherty (Loughglynn Coy.) 1st Battalion South Roscommon, participated in the **destruction of vacant barracks** in 1920, and took part in the special service training (intelligence, scouting, dispatch work) during the Truce

Francis Dolan (Moor Coy.) 1st Battalion South Roscommon, brother of Patrick. Took part in the **destruction of vacant barracks** in 1920, the **attempted attack on Kilmurray Military Camp** in June 1920, the **attack on Frenchpark Barracks** 2 October 1920, and the **attempted attacks at Castlerea** and **Frenchpark** in January 1921. He was a member of the Active Service Unit formed in January of 1921. Dolan took the Anti-Treaty side during the Civil War, and participated in the **burning of the train at Clooncundra** and the **attack at Castlerea** in November 1922. After the Truce, during a melee in Castlerea, Frank took a snappy thud to the head when the Volunteers were in Hanley Hall and reacted to the British troops tearing down the tricolour. The Volunteers threw one of the Brits out a window, and Frank was cracked in the skull by the soldier's enraged comrades

J. P. Dolan (Church Street, Roscommon town) member of the 1918 Sinn Féin election committee in South Roscommon. He was a butcher by trade

James Dolan (Drum Coy.) 3rd Battalion Athlone Brigade

James Dolan of Annagh, Athlone was arrested on 18 July 1922, and sent to Athlone on 2 September 1922

John Dolan (Trien Company) 1st Battalion South Roscommon

Michael Dolan (Ballyconboy, Mantua), officer in the local Company, a member of the IRB

Patrick Dolan (Cloonslanor) Carniska Coy. in the 3rd Battalion North Roscommon. After the War he became a farmer. Died in the 1990s

Thomas Dolan In 1918 Dolan was appointed the Battalion commander in the Shannonbridge area. This was part of the Athlone Brigade. His men often crossed the Shannon River from Offaly and worked in conjunction with Roscommon Volunteers

Patrick Dolan (Moor Coy.) 1st Battalion South Roscommon, brother of Francis. Participated in the **capture of enemy stores at Ballymoe** in June 1920, the **attempted attack on Kilmurray Military Camp** in June 1920, the **raid and capture of military equipment at Ballymoe** September 1920, the **attack on Frenchpark Barracks** 2 October 1920, and the **attempted attacks at Castlerea** and **Frenchpark** in January 1921. He was a member of the Active Service Unit formed in January of 1921. During the Truce he attended the Company training camp. Dolan took the Anti-Treaty side in the Civil War, and took part in the **burning of the train at Clooncundra**, and **attack at Castlerea** in November 1922. He was captured in Roscommon town 18 October 1923 with a Colt revolver in his possession — a gun he claimed was given to him by Dick Mee, the former O/C of the Curraghboy Coy.

Tom Dolan (Cloonfree Coy.) 3rd Battalion North Roscommon. Took part in the **attempt to burn down the Bridewell at Strokestown** in July 1920

John Donaghy (Clooneybrennan, Elphin) incarcerated in Mountjoy January 1923

James Donegan (Ballyglass, Ballymacurley) a member of "B" Coy. in the 2nd Battalion South Roscommon

Michael Donegan (Trien Coy.) 1st Battalion South Roscommon

Thomas Donegan (Trien Coy.) 1st Battalion South Roscommon

Bridget Donellan (Ballinameen) who worked at the post office in Croghan, was arrested 21 March 1923, and incarcerated at Athlone. She was considered an Intelligence Officer working with the Anti-Treaty forces

May Donellan (Ballinameen) sister of Bridget, an employee of the Ballinameen Post Office, arrested 13 March 1923, and incarcerated in Athlone

Frank Donlon a member of "E" Coy., 3rd Battalion South Roscommon. Many of the members of the Kilgefin Company participated in the **Fourmilehouse Ambush** on 12 October 1920

Michael Donnellan (Castleplunkett Coy.) 2nd Battalion South Roscommon

Donnelly family (Coolderry, Four Roads) had several sons and daughters involved in the Republican movement. Maisie was a member of Cumann na mBan. Joseph served as the Quartermaster of the Tisrara Coy. He and his brothers emigrated to New York in the 1920s

Dominick Donnelly (Carrownure Upper, Kiltoom) St. John's Coy. in the 4th Battalion South Roscommon. When the Company started in 1917, Donnelly was the first Quartermaster. He drilled with other Volunteers two nights a week — Tuesdays and Thursdays, and worked with the Republican Courts. In 1918 his Company, now under the command of Patrick Grady, participated in the sham battles for training purposes under Ernie O'Malley at Lysterfield, Taughmaconnell, and Churchboro. He worked in the 1918 election, constructed dugouts, and **stopped the train in Kiltoom** in order to raid the mail cars. He, along with twelve other members of his Company, took part in the **attempted ambush at Clooncraff** under the command of Pat Madden, and the **attempted ambush at Kilmurray Military Camp** in June 1920

Joseph Donnelly (Coolderry, Four Roads) a member of the Tisrara Coy. 4th Battalion South Roscommon, served as the Quartermaster for the Company

Joseph Donnelly (Rahara Coy.) 4th Battalion South Roscommon

Luke Donnelly (Boyle) was inducted into the IRB by Alec McCabe in February 1915

Michael Donnelly (Corraclogh, Kiltoom) St. John's Coy. in the 4th Battalion South Roscommon. When the Company first started in 1917, Donnelly drilled with other Volunteers two nights a week — Tuesdays and Thursdays, and worked with the Republican Courts. In 1918 his Company, now under the command of Patrick Grady, participated in the sham battles for training purposes under Ernie O'Malley at Lysterfield, Taughmaconnell, and Churchboro. He worked in the 1918 election, constructed dugouts, took part in several raids for arms — one of which yielded three shot guns, and another raid that occurred on the same night that Volunteer Kearney was severely wounded. Donnelly **stopped the train in Kiltoom** in order to raid the mail cars. He, along with twelve other members of his Company, took part in the **attempted ambush at Clooncraff** under the command of Pat Madden, and the **attempted ambush at Kilmurray Military Camp** in June 1920. He was present when **O'Brien's house was burned** — an operation deemed necessary because the British were about to take over the residence. During the Truce he was appointed to a special service unit

Michael Donnolly (Rahara Coy.) 4th Battalion South Roscommon

Peter Donnelly (Foxwood, Kilmore) in 1922 he served as the 2nd Lieutenant for "D" Company in the newly formed 4th Battalion, 3rd Western Division. He was a member of the ASU during the Civil War

Peter Donnelly (Strokestown) was arrested during the Civil War on 6 September 1922, and taken to Athlone two months later

William Donnelly (Cornaseer, Kiltoom) first Sinn Féin County Council. After the Civil War he was elected in 1925 as a member of the Pro-Treaty party, Cumann na nGael, and served until 1928. He was a shopkeeper and farmer

William Donnelly (Rahara Coy.) 4th Battalion South Roscommon. After the War he took an active part in forming Fianna Fáil in the county. He was on hand to welcome de Valera to Roscommon town on 19 June 1926

Frank Donoghue (Northyard, Scramogue) see Frank O'Donoghue

T. Donoghue Republican Judge in the Kilglass area

John Doolan (Carricknaughton, Athlone) a member of the Athlone Battalion. Took part in the **raid on the Athlone Excise Tax office** in May 1920

Ned Doolan (Carricknaughton, Athlone) a member of the Athlone Battalion. In the winter of 1920, he, along with George Adamson and Tom Halligan, attempted to assassinate Captain Tully of the Athlone RIC. They followed him through town on several occasions — locating him once with a group of other officers. Not knowing exactly which man Tully was, the Volunteers let all the RIC pass them by. He also took part in the **raid on the Athlone Excise Tax office** in May 1920. Doolan took an active part in the Civil War on the Anti-Treaty side. He was arrested and incarcerated in Athlone 21 April 1923

The Dooley Family provided a safe house in The Hill of Berries area

Jerry Dooley (Frenchpark) 1st Battalion North Roscommon. Although a native of Kildare, Dooley served as the original 2nd Lieutenant of the Frenchpark Company when it was formed in 1919

Pat Dooley (The Hill of Berries) a member of the Kiltoom Coy. in the 4th Battalion South Roscommon

John Dooner (Aghmagree) Kilteevan Coy. in the 3rd Battalion South Roscommon

Patrick Dooner (Junior) (Derrymoylin, Ruskey, Dromod) a member of Tarmonbarry Coy. in the 3rd Battalion North Roscommon

Eddie Doorley (Lanesboro Street, Roscommon town) 3rd Battalion South Roscommon, brother of "Boddins," and John James. He was arrested after the Rising and on 13 May 1916 was sent to the British prison at Wakefield. Eddie was later transferred to an internment camp in Wales — Frongoch. He was released but again re-arrested and incarcerated in Athlone during the spring of 1921. He was a butcher by trade

Church Street in Roscommon where John James Doorley lived.

PHOTO COURTESY OF ALBERT SIGGINS

John James Doorley (Lanesboro Street, Roscommon town) 3rd Battalion South Roscommon. He was the Captain of the Roscommon Company. His two brothers, "Boddins" and Eddie, were also involved in the movement. Took part in the Rising and was subsequently arrested. He was listed as a garage owner when he sailed across the Irish Sea on 13 May to Wakefield Prison. He was later transferred to Frongoch, "The Irish University." He served as Captain of the Company. After his brother "Boddins" had received a severe thrashing, John James challenged the offending Tan to a match in the town square. Stories told eighty years later confirm that Doorley soundly trounced him. After the War he owned a shop in Roscommon town that supplied townspeople with groceries, petrol, and radios

Michael Doorley (Shroove, Strokestown) Scramogue Coy. in the 3rd Battalion North Roscommon. Served as an outpost for the **Scramogue Ambush**

Paddy "Boddins" Doorley (Lanesboro Street, Roscommon town) 3rd Battalion South Roscommon, and a member of Pat Madden's Flying Column. "Boddins" was appointed the first Vice O/C of the South Roscommon Brigade. Secured guns from Dublin. He was badly beaten by the Tans at Mote Park Demesne, and returned home in such a state, that his brother, John James, challenged the offending Tan to a one-on-one fight in the town square. (See John James bio. for outcome).

John James Doorley, Captain of Roscommon Coy.

PHOTO COURTESY OF ALBERT SIGGINS

Paddy "Boddins" Doorley.
PHOTO COURTESY OF ALBERT SIGGINS

"Boddins" was a member of the 1918 Sinn Féin election committee in South Roscommon. He emigrated to the United States, but later in life returned to Ireland. He died 6 October 1961, and is buried in St. Coman's Cemetery in Roscommon town

Brian Dorr (Ballagh, Hillstreet) 5th Battalion North Roscommon, brother of Jim and Patrick. In 1921 after attending the fair at Croghan, Brian was accosted by a group of Tans who questioned him about Volunteers and their whereabouts. After refusing to give information, Brian was forced to face a wall where the Tans proceeded to beat him with their rifle butts. The result of such blows permanently injured his spine, and left him an invalid for the rest of his life. He died on Christmas Day 1943, and is buried in Shankill Cemetery

Jim Dorr (Ballagh, Hillstreet) joined the Volunteers in August 1917 under the sponsorship of Pat Dunleavy from Mayo, who was working in Kilmore at the time. There were twelve founding members of the Company. Threat of conscription drove that number up to thirty-five. Dorr served as the first drill instructor of the unit. He helped construct dugouts, collected guns, made an inventory of foodstuffs in the area, and listed bridges to be destroyed. Although technically only the 1st Lieutenant, Door did the work of the Captain of the Company until he became the official Captain in early 1919. He raided for arms in 1920, succeeding in obtaining a dozen shotguns and a fair amount of cartridges. Took part in the **seizure of a tender loaded with rations at Drumsna Railway Station** in June 1920, and the **attempted attack on the Ruskey Police Barracks** on 7 January 1921. In early 1921 he waited at the Drumsna Rail Station for detonators and batteries which Jack Glancy was transporting from Dublin. On the night of the **attack on Elphin Barracks**, he and his men were blocking the roads leading from Kilmore and Carrick-on-Shannon to Elphin. He delivered on horseback a concrete mine and some gelignite to the Kilglass area in preparation for the **Scramogue Ambush.** By 11 July 1921, he was the Battalion O/C. Jim joined the Free State Army. Later he owned a garage in Carrick-on-Shannon. He died in March 1973, and is buried in Aughrim Cemetery in Hillstreet

Patrick Dorr (Ballagh, Hillstreet) 5th Battalion North Roscommon, brother of Jim and Brian. He was a carpenter by trade. Pat died in November 1970 and is buried in Aughrim Cemetery in Hillstreet

John Joe Dougherty served as 2nd Lieutenant of the Arigna Company in 4th Battalion North Roscommon. After the War he emigrated to the USA

Patrick Dowd (Ballygar Coy.) which was considered part of 4th Battalion South Roscommon when the Divisional structure was implemented

Brigid Dowling (Carricknaughton, Athlone) a member of The O'Rahilly branch of the Cumann na mBan, who attended weekly first aid classes, scouted and took charge of arms for the Flying Column, collected funds for clothing for the Column, and fed the men. She also carried bombs, high explosives, revolvers and ammunition, electric batteries, and assisted in getting two wounded men to safety

Christy Dowling Captain of "K" Castlerea Coy. in the Castlerea Battalion area of the 2nd Western Division. His home served as the headquarters for "K" Company during the post-Truce times

Edward "Ned" Dowling (Carricknaughton, Athlone) Dowling joined the Irish Republican Army on 1 September 1917, and was appointed Company Captain of "A" Company, Summerhill Battalion, Athlone

---

Edward Dowling Volunteer Witness Statement, 29 March 1939

"I was arrested in April 1921 and got badly beaten by the Tans. I was kicked about the abdomen. I was stripped in the cell in Athlone R.I.C. Barracks and beaten again for a long time. I was later beaten again and knocked unconscious. My face and nose was cut up and upper gum. They kept me stripped naked in the cell for two or three hours. It was after they gave me back my clothes and took me out to the lorry and threw me down off the lorry and kicked me about. My whole body was sore. I was black and bruised all over. They brought me in and washed me up and put me back in the cell. After about four hours they brought me out to the Barracks room and then took me across to Military Barracks and put me into a cell there for the night. I was left undisturbed there and the next morning I was put on identification parade. When I came back I was put into a detention room with ten or twelve others. Dr. O'Byrne, Dispensary, Ballynacargry, Co. Westmeath was a prisoner there and he examined me. He couldn't give me any treatment. A few days afterwards the stomach was very much swollen. I complained to the Military Doctor and he painted me with iodine. Dr. O'Byrne told me to stay in bed and I was in bed for a fortnight. My body remained black and bruised for about 6 or 7 weeks. I was moved from Athlone to Rath Camp about June 1921 and remained there until December of that year...."

Because of that horrendous beating in 1921, Dowling suffered from a multitude of problems which left him unable to perform hard labor. He secured employment in the later years as a doorkeeper in the G.P.O. in Dublin

Brigade in November 1920. He organised and helped train his men, collected arms and funds for the Volunteers. He took part in a **raid on the Lecarrow quarry**. He participated in the **attempted ambush at Ballymore Barracks**, raided Athlone petrol stores, and was present with his unit at Mullingar during a local government election. He served as a member of the Athlone Flying Column, and participated in the **raid on the Athlone Income Tax office** in November 1920, and was in charge of the **raid on the Athlone Railway Station**, taking material necessary for the construction of bombs. He took part in all the major conflicts between Athlone and Mullingar as well as South Roscommon until his arrest in April 1921. "On capture he was taken to Athlone RIC Barracks, stripped naked, severely beaten and kicked in the stomach and groin over a period of several hours."* He was imprisoned in Athlone and the Curragh, where he remained until Christmas of 1921. Upon his release, he returned to his unit and was appointed the Vice O/C of the Battalion. His unit took possession of Cloonark RIC Barracks, but was forced, due to lack of arms and personnel, to hand over the barracks to Free State troops. During the Civil War he fought on the Republican side in Roscommon, Offaly, and Ballygar, Galway. He participated in the **Ambush at Glasson** in August 1922. A month later, on 23 September 1922, he was taken into custody in the Kiltoom district. A party of government troops arrested Dowling, Tom and Bernard Martin, William and Denis Mannion (all members of the Athlone Flying Column). Dowling was again sent to Athlone, and finally to the Curragh (Harepark Camp). Upon his release in 1924, he returned to farming on the family land. In 1927 he married a former member of the Cumann na mBan, Annie O'Connor, and moved to Dublin. Died 1974 and buried in Clonown Cemetery (see box on page 266)

Eamonn Dowling, son of Edward, correspondence with author, 3 February 2004.

James Dowling a member of "E" Coy., 3rd Battalion South Roscommon. Many of the members of the Kilgefin Company participated in the **Fourmilehouse Ambush** on 12 October 1920

John Dowling (Carricknaughton, Athlone) Summerhill Coy., 3rd Battalion Athlone Brigade. John took part in drilling with other Company members, carrying dispatches, working in the 1918 election campaign, seizing mail, collecting shotguns, assisting in making dugouts, and performing guard duty for the Flying Column. He participated in the **seizure of telephone cables and batteries from the Athlone Railway Station** in April 1921, and **cutting the Crannagh Bridge** in May. He chose to fight on the Anti-Treaty side during the Civil War, and he took charge of high explosives that were handed over to him by members of the Cumann na mBan

Michael Dowling (Glanduff, Kiltoom) a member of the St. John's Coy. in the 4th Battalion South Roscommon. He drilled with other Volunteers two nights a week — Tuesdays and Thursdays and worked in the 1918 election

Patrick Dowling (Glanduff, Kiltoom) a member of the St. John's Coy. in the 4th Battalion South Roscommon. He also drilled with other Volunteers two nights a week and worked in the 1918 election

Jack Downes (Ballaghaderreen) a tricolour enthusiast in 1916 who, with the aid of several other Volunteers from Ballaghaderreen, used to scale the town's flagpoles and replace the Union Jack with the green/white/orange Irish banner. He became a prisoner at Boyle Barracks in May 1921, where he aided Jim Molloy's escape by pushing him through the window of the wash house and letting him down on a rope. He was an active Republican during the Civil War, being arrested and taken to Longford, from which he escaped in November 1922. He was captured again in Ballaghaderreen on 28 October 1923

Edward "Ned" Dowling, Company Captain of "A" Company, Summerhill Battalion, Athlone Brigade.

PHOTO COURTESY OF EAMONN DOWLING

Joseph Downes (Castlerea) a member of the post office staff in Castlerea, intelligence gatherer for the Volunteers. Arrested and sentenced to years of penal servitude

May Downes (Ballaghaderreen) member of the Cumann na mBan

James Downey (Ahascragh) Ballygar Coy. which was considered part of 4th Battalion South Roscommon when the Divisional structure was implemented. He fought with the South Roscommon Flying Column during the Civil War, and was arrested along with Jack Keogh in September 1923

Agnes "Aggie" Doyle (Derreenaseer, Knockvicar, Boyle) member of Cumann na mBan

Bernard Doyle (Roscommon Coy.) 3rd Battalion South Roscommon

J. Doyle (Bealnamullia Coy.) served with the Bealnamullia Coy. during the Civil War. He harassed the Free State troopers by blocking roads at Larkfield and Bealnamullia, assisting the Flying Column at blocking a road near Curraghboy, assisting prisoners to escape and join their various units, storing and transporting arms and explosives when and where required by the Flying Column, and serving as an outpost guard for the Column to ensure their safety. After the War he emigrated to the United States

James Doyle (Woodfield, Knockvicar, Boyle) brother of John Joe and Patrick. Listed in the GHQ papers in the UCD Archives as Quartermaster for Crossna Company in the 4th Battalion North Roscommon. He fought with the Arigna Flying Column during the Civil War, and was arrested with May Mannion on 20 May 1923

John J. Doyle (Derreenaseer, Knockvicar, Boyle) O/C of the 4th Battalion North Roscommon, brother of James and Patrick, arrested and detained in Boyle Barracks and Athlone Barracks in early 1921, but escaped through the Brady tunnel at the Curragh the following September. He fought with the Arigna Flying Column during the Civil War, and was arrested by Free State troops and interned on 3 February 1923. After the War he emigrated to New York, but, upon retiring, returned to Ireland and lived at his native place, Deerreenaseer, Knockvicar, Boyle

John Doyle (Runnamoat, Ballymacurley) a member of "B" Coy. in the 2nd Battalion South Roscommon. He drilled with his Company, collected funds for the Dáil loan, and served under the command of Captain Michael O'Grady

Joseph Doyle (Clongowna, Drum) 3rd Battalion Athlone Brigade. Doyle drilled with his Company, trained to use firearms, took an active part in the General Election of 1918, attended Battalion meetings, worked with the Republican Police force at disputed farmland in Bealnamullia and Clongowna. He was with a group of Volunteers that seized ammunition from an airplane that made a forced landing at Keelogues in 1919. Took part in the **burning of the Barracks at Bealnamullia**, mobilised for an attack on Cloonark Barracks, and **attempted an ambush at Curraghaleen** in October 1920. Near Truce time, he guarded the ASU Headquarters in the area, **destroyed the bridge at Millbrook**, blocked roads at Millbrook and Monksland, harboured and aided escaped prisoners. During the Truce he trained at Greenfield, Donamon, and Falty, in addition to collecting funds to aid the Volunteers and attending the Arbitration Courts. During the Civil War he took the Republican side, serving as the Company Adjutant. He harassed the Free State troopers by blocking roads at Larkfield and Bealnamullia, assisting the Flying Column at blocking a road near Curraghboy, assisting prisoners to escape and join their various units, storing and transporting arms and explosives when and where required by the Flying Column, and serving as an outpost guard for the Column to ensure their safety

May Doyle (Derreenaseer, Knockvicar, Boyle) member of Cumann na mBan, sister of John, James, and Patrick

Patrick Doyle (Derreenaseer, Knockvicar, Boyle) brother of John, May, and James, fought with the Arigna Flying Column during the Civil War, and was arrested on 8 September 1922 and incarcerated in Athlone on 14 November. After the War he moved to Dublin, where he was an agriculturist. When he died in 1959, Comdt. Pat Brennan commanded forty men who formed the honour guard that escorted Doyle to his final resting place in Ardcarne Cemetery

Patrick Doyle (Drummin) Ballinagare Coy., 1st Battalion South Roscommon. Drilled with fellow Volunteers, collected funds for the Dáil loan, enforced the Belfast boycott. Participant in **burning the Frenchpark Barracks**, 2 October. In reprisal for such an attack, he was shot by the Tans 19 October 1920 as he exited Pat Garvey's place in Ballinagare. His name is inscribed on the tablets in front of the Shankill Monument near Elphin

Patrick Doyle (Cornaseer) Kiltoom Coy. in the 4th Battalion South Roscommon

Patrick Doyle (Stonepark, Roscommon) 3rd Battalion South Roscommon

Joseph Drury (Teevnacreeva, Frenchpark) arrested during the Civil War on 19 September 1922, and taken to Athlone

Tom Duane (Strokestown Coy.) 3rd Battalion North Roscommon, captured under DORA, and sentenced to five years of British accommodations in Athlone, Mountjoy, Wormwood Scrubbs, and Wandsworth. He was not released until February of 1922

Edward "Ned" Duffy (Loughglynn) HONOURARY MEMBER, an IRB recruiter, whose tireless work and idealism inspired many men from Roscommon, but earned Ned a convict suit in Millbank Prison in England, where he died in January, 1868. Because of his efforts, the embers of Republican rebellion simmered in the county until such time as the winds of Black and Tan terror whipped them into a giant conflagration

James Duffy (Castle Street, Elphin) 2nd Battalion North Roscommon. Served as the Company Intelligence Officer. He was present at the **attack on Boyle** in July 1922. A member of the Active Service Unit of North Roscommon during the Civil War. Interned in Athlone 4 April 1923

James Duffy (Charlestown) Interned in Hare Park

John Duffy, Sergeant in the RIC, stationed in Athlone, Kiltoom, and Roscommon town. After countless political discussions, Dr. McDonnell had cautioned Duffy, who was sympathetic to the national movement, not to resign from the RIC — "You would be only one man with us, but you would be worth a hundred men by remaining in the Force."* In 1917, accompanied by Dr. McDonnell, Duffy travelled to Dublin to meet Michael Collins. At that meeting, Collins asked him if he could secure the names from police records of prominent IRA men throughout the country who had come to the attention of Dublin Castle. He also asked Duffy if he could obtain a key to the police cipher code.** Duffy returned to Athlone, where he worked with the IRA through Dr. McDonnell, Father Michael O'Flanagan, and Willie Kilmartin, a solicitor's clerk in Roscommon town. Thomas Farrell in Roscommon town served as an alternate contact, while oftentimes Sean Hurley in Athlone received direct messages from Duffy. Duffy warned local Volunteers of upcoming raids for rifles concealed in the cave at Coosan, and the reprisal raids by the RIC for the killing of Constable Potter at Knockcroghery in August 1920. When Duffy was transferred to Roscommon town, he spotted a key in the County Inspector's office, painted a mental picture of it, went to McDonnell's hardware shop in town, and made a duplicate, which allowed him access to the office at any time. It was in Roscommon that Duffy obtained the list of names of prominent IRA men throughout Ireland (there were 3,912 of them,)*** and passed it along to Frank Simons, Adjutant for the 3rd Battalion South. He also succeeded in getting the key to the police cipher code, which was also given to Simons

*Sgt. John Duffy Statement to the Bureau of Military History 1913-21, p. 1.
**Ibid. p. 5. ***Ibid. p. 10.

Luke Duffy (Clooncagh) Kilgefin Coy. Vice O/C of 3rd Battalion South Roscommon, and the first 1st Lieutenant of the Company when it was formed in March 1917. His father, who had been a member of the British Army, acted as drill instructor for Kilgefin Coy. He took part in the **Fourmilehouse Ambush, Scramogue Ambush,** and **Moneen.**

> "Good leaders make everything happen. If you have good leaders, there's always ways and means of getting something done."
>
> Spoken by Frank Simons, taped interview with James McCormick, 1973, Roscommon town

Luke Duffy, Vice O/C of 3rd Battalion South Roscommon.

PHOTO COURTESY OF EAMONN DUFFY

Luke was reputed to have been a crack shot. He, along with Pat Madden and Frank Simons, orchestrated many a daring raid in South Roscommon along with other loyal members of the Active Service Unit. After the Truce, he and many other members of the Kilgefin Company joined the National Army in which he served in the Sligo/Leitrim areas. Later in life he farmed at Clooncagh near Strokestown. He died 5 November 1971, and is buried in Lisonuffy Cemetery. His funeral oration was delivered by his fellow officer William Mulligan, Intelligence Officer of the 3rd Battalion. The last salute to a gallant soldier was rendered by a detachment of the Irish Army from Connolly Barracks in Longford. A cartridge from that final farewell resides in the Roscommon Museum

Martin Duffy (Charlestown) interned Hare Park, and released 19 December 1923

Martin Duffy (Killina Coy.) 2nd Battalion North Roscommon. He joined the Company in 1917, and drilled every Tuesday night at Ball Alley House

Mick Duffy a member of a Mayo Company near Kilkelly when he became a member of an Active Service Unit for the 3rd Western Brigade. His unit **took over Boyle Barracks** in the spring of 1922, but he was accidentally wounded and died of his wounds eighteen months later at the age of thirty-three

Paddy Duffy (Elphin) friendly impromptu chauffeur for the men recently escaped from the Curragh Prison Camp in September 1921

Patrick Duffy (Lisacul) East Mayo Brigade, was arrested during the Civil War and taken to Athlone, from which he was not released until 23 February 1923

Seamus Duffy (Oughtagh, Creggs, Galway) a member of Castleplunkett Coy. in the 2nd Battalion South Roscommon. He drilled with his Company, collected funds for the Dáil loan, and served under the command of Captains Jack Ryan and Luke Raftery. Took part in the **raid on the military train at Ballymoe** in June 1920, and the **ambush at Southpark, Castlerea** 10 July 1921. When the Western Division was formed, Seamus served as the Adjutant for the 3rd Battalion, No. 2 Brigade. He was arrested during the Civil War, but escaped from Longford on 14 May 1923. After the War he became a schoolteacher in Creggs

Joseph Duggan (Tibarney) a member of the Tisrara Company in the 4th Battalion South Roscommon. Took part in the **raid on Mt. Talbot** in April 1922. He later moved to Coolderry and finally to Farbreagues, Ballymurray

Charles Duignan (Crosshill, Arigna) 1st Lieutenant of the Keadue Company in the 4th Battalion North Roscommon. He fought with the Arigna Flying Column headed by Seamus Cull during the Civil War

Dominick Duignan (Dooneen, Ballinameen, Boyle) 1st Battalion North Roscommon. Took part in collecting funds for the Brigade and for the Dáil loan, parading, drilling, and enforcing the Belfast boycott. He was blocking roads on the night of the **Elphin Barracks attack** in February 1921, and was present at the **attack on Frenchpark Barracks and Courthouse** in June. During the Truce he attended a training camp in Boyle

Edward "Ned" Duignan (Dignan) (Deignan) (Clooncrim) Ballinlough Coy., 1st Battalion South Roscommon. He was a member of the South Roscommon Flying Column whose picture was taken in the Charlestown/Ballaghaderreen training camp during the Truce. While there, he specialised in dispatch work. Participated in the **burning of the Barracks at Ballinlough** 14 September 1920. During the Truce he attended the training camp at Swinford. He later emigrated to Yonkers, New York

Francis Duignan (Derreenavoggy, Kilronan, Boyle) a member of the 4th Battalion North Roscommon. He was active on the Anti-Treaty side, fighting with the Arigna Flying Column during the Civil War

Jack Duignan (Corgullon, Kilbride, Kilmore) brother of Patrick, James William, and Michael. Joined the IRA in 1919, and participated in attacks in County Sligo. During the Truce he served with a Volunteer detachment along the six county Border. When the Civil War broke out, he returned to his original unit and fought the Free State troops in County Sligo and North Roscommon. He was arrested in 1923, and interned at Sligo, Athlone, and the Curragh, where he participated in a forty-one day hunger strike. He was released in 1924, and emigrated to New York, where he died 1 August 1928. He is buried in Calvary Cemetery in New York City

James W. Duignan (Corgullon, Kilbride, Kilmore) 1st Lieutenant of Ruskey Company in the 3rd Battalion North Roscommon. After the split in the IRA, he joined the Free State Army only to defect with some badly needed rifles. During the Civil War he became a member of the ASU. After surviving for several years on the run from the national troops, he emigrated to the USA, where he served in the American Army during World War II in Italy, Germany (he helped free Dachau Concentration Camp), and later Japan. He left the army in 1955 with the rank of Sgt. Major. He is buried in New York.* (Interestingly, when James would come back to Ireland, he would intentionally wear his American army uniform so that the Free State troopers would not "lift him" off the street**

James Duignan, nephew of James W., correspondence with author, 7 October 2003.
** James Duignan, nephew of James W., correspondence with author, 7 October 2003.*

Joe Duignan (Thomastown Demesne, Drum) 3rd Battalion Athlone Brigade, took his oath of allegiance to the Republic at Ardkeenan House where many dances organised by the Volunteers were held

John Duignan (Ballyfarnon) Arigna Flying Column. Arrested 24 September 1923

Michael Duignan (Scurbeg, Ballinameen) 1st Battalion North Roscommon. Joined the Volunteers in May 1920. Sniped at the **Frenchpark Barracks and Courthouse** in June 1921. His house was open to men on the run. After the War he became a farmer. Died 6 May 1970 and buried in Ballinameen Cemetery

Michael Duignan (Moher, Kilglass, Strokestown) served as the North Roscommon Brigade Adjutant and Intelligence Officer at the time of the Truce. Scouted and blocked roads for the **attack on Elphin Barracks** in February 1921. He later joined the Free State Army

Michael Duignan (Roscommon Coy.) 3rd Battalion South. After the War he became a farmer in the Kilbride area. Died 1983 and buried in Aughrim Cemetery

Michael Duignan (Corgullon, Kilbride, Kilmore) brother of Patrick, Jack, and James. Michael served as the 2nd Lieutenant for "A" Company (Kilmore), 5th Battalion North Roscommon

Michael Duignan (Scurbeg, Ballinameen) 1st Battalion North Roscommon.

PHOTO COURTESY OF KATHLEEN TOOLAN

Patrick Duignan (Keadue) first Sinn Féin Council in Roscommon. After the War he became involved in politics serving as treasurer of the Fianna Fáil North Roscommon Executive in 1927

Patrick "Pappy" Duignan (Kilfaughna, Knockvicar, Boyle) 1st Lieutenant of the Crossna Company in the 4th Battalion North Roscommon. During the Tan War, Patrick brought a shipment of guns to his home to be stored for a few days before being sent off to other parts of the countryside. His mother cautioned that the guns simply could not be kept in their house, and a more suitable "dump" needed to be found. Patrick and a few other Volunteers tore up the floorboards of the local church and placed the rifles there under the watchful eye of St. Joseph. When Volunteer leaders came down from Dublin, Patrick and his brother, Michael, used to row them across the lake to a dugout on the Rockingham estate.* Duignan took an active role in the Civil War on the Anti-Treaty side, fighting with the Flying Column in Sligo and North Roscommon. He was arrested during the Civil War, and kept in Boyle Barracks for a few days until his sisters interceded for him and secured his release** (they were both quite charming and pretty). After the War he became a farmer. Died 1993, but not before finally revealing to his son the secret hiding place of the old revolver used in the Wars. Buried in Killeenan Cemetery

*Jerry Duignan, son of Patrick, interview by author, 27 September 2004, Rinn, Carrick-on-Shannon. **Ibid.*

Patrick Duignan (Derreenavoggy, Kilronan, Boyle), 4th Battalion North Roscommon. He was active with the Arigna Flying Column during the Civil War

Patrick Duignan listed in the GHQ papers at UCD Archives as Chief Engineer for the 5th Battalion North Roscommon. Took part in the **Dublin-Sligo mail train robbery**

Patrick Duignan (Corgullon, Kilbride, Kilmore) Patrick took charge of housing and feeding numerous Flying Column members. While the men were gathered at the table eating, their guns would all be piled in a corner with a lookout positioned outside listening for the sound of Tan lorries.* His father's land (complete with dugout along the Dublin-Sligo rail line) was situated where the boundaries of three Flying Columns converged (North Roscommon, Arigna, and South Leitrim). He would convey members of the Leitrim and Longford Flying Columns across the Shannon, where they were met by a key man from Annaduff — the distance by water being ten miles. In addition, he worked at the Drumsna Railway Station as a milesman — a position that allowed him to send and receive dispatches from GHQ in Dublin. He also hid Commandant Mick McLoughlin on his land after McLoughlin's escape from Carrick-on-Shannon Gaol. Arrested during the Civil War on 6 September 1922, and taken to Athlone on 14 November. After the War he became a farmer in Caramore near Cox Cross on the road to Strokestown. Buried in Kilmore Cemetery

*James Duignan, *nephew of Patrick, correspondence with author, 1 October 2003.*

Phillip Duignan (Dooneen) Ballinameen Coy. in the 1st Battalion North Roscommon, took part in the **attack on Frenchpark Barracks** in June 1921. After the War he emigrated to New Jersey

T. Duignan (Dignan) (Loughglynn Coy.) 1st Battalion South Roscommon. After the War he emigrated to the United States

Thomas Michael Duignan (Tartan, Ballinameen, Boyle) 2nd Lieutenant for "C" Company in the 1st Battalion North Roscommon

Tom Duignan (Deignan) (Sligo) Anti-Treaty Comdt. in East Sligo. Duignan was active in Sligo during the Black and Tan War. He was involved in the **attempted ambush at Five Cross Roads** in February 1921, and the **attack on Collooney Barracks** in March 1921. He joined the Arigna Flying Column at its inception in the harvest of 1921. During the Civil War, Duignan was with the Column when it attacked the **Drumshanbo Barracks** and **Ballinamore Barracks** in early 1923. He also participated in the attacks on **Keadue** and **Ballyfarnon Barracks**. He was captured in June of 1923, and sent to Sligo Gaol. He went on hunger strike, and was released at Christmas time 1924. His recollections were recorded by Ernie O'Malley in the 1950s and are part of the Ernie O'Malley Papers at UCD Archives

John Dunaphy (Elphin) interned in Tintown A at the Curragh. Released 18 December 1923

Patrick Dunleavy (Barbersfort House, Ballyglunin, Co. Galway) In 1919, Dunleavy went to Claremorris, where he was named O/C of the Battalion. In December 1920, he became the O/C of the North Galway Brigade (after Con Fogarty was arrested), and in January 1921 the O/C of the Flying Column. He had previously worked in Kilmore, County Roscommon in the summer of 1917, and took Jim Dorr into the Volunteer organisation

Thomas Dunleavy (Glenamaddy Battalion Commandant) which was part of No. 2 Brigade, 2nd Western Division, under Brigade Commander Gerald O'Connor. In 1921, he became part of the ASU formed with the Tuam Battalion

Tim Dunleavy (Captain of Barnadery Coy.) who became part of an ASU formed with the Glenamaddy Battalion which was part of No. 2 Brigade in the 2nd Western Division

Thomas Dunne (Farnbeg, Strokestown) 3rd Battalion North Roscommon. Captured in January 1921 and sentenced to two years for being in possession of "seditious material." Sinn Féin literature was found in the thatch of his home. (A man named Dunn(e) along with thirteen other Anti-Treatyites attacked the Free State troops at the Chapel Gate near the village of Ballintubber on 2 December 1922. A firefight ensued whereby the attackers were chased to Corner House, Frenchpark and captured)

Ann Dunning was a member of the Cumann na mBan of Summerhill in south Roscommon

Kathy Dunning sister of Ann, was also a member of Cumann na mBan

Kieran Dunning (Drum Coy.) a member of Father Flanagan's Sinn Féin Club

Michael Dunning (Drum Coy.) 3rd Battalion Athlone Brigade

Paddy Dunning (Drum Coy.) 3rd Battalion Athlone Brigade, a member of Father Flanagan's Sinn Féin Club

Albert Durr (Brackloon, Castlerea) 1st Battalion South Roscommon. Served as Battalion Adjutant in late 1920. Participated in the **destruction of vacant barracks** in 1920, the **attempted attack on Kilmurray Military Camp** in June 1920, and the **attack on Frenchpark Barracks** 2 October 1920. The year 1921 brought new challenges. Albert became a member of the Active Service Unit which had formed in January 1921. He took part in the **attempted attacks on Castlerea** and **Frenchpark** in January 1921, the **attempted ambush at Cloonsheever** in March 1921, served in the covering party for the **attack on the military at Castlerea** on 6 April, and was part of the **ambush party at Loughglynn** that same month. In May he participated in the **attempted ambush at Lisacul** (an action taken in conjunction with the East Mayo men), and the **attempted ambush of RIC patrol near Ballymoe**. During the Civil War he took the Anti-Treaty side, and engaged the Free State troops in the **burning of the train at Clooncundra**, and the **attack at Castlerea** in November 1922. He was arrested shortly thereafter, and sent to Athlone on 30 November 1922. After the War he emigrated to Detroit, Michigan

James Durr (Brackloon, Castlerea) 1st Battalion South Roscommon, brother of Albert. Participated in the **destruction of vacant barracks** in 1920, the **attempted attack on Kilmurray Military Camp** in June 1920, the **attack on Frenchpark Barracks** 2 October 1920, the **attempted attacks on Castlerea** and **Frenchpark** in January 1921, and the **ambush at Southpark, Castlerea** 10 July 1921. He took part in the **burning of the train at Clooncundra** and the **attack on the Free State troops in Castlerea** in November 1922. He and William Collins were arrested during the Civil War while crossing the Castlerea Bridge. Before they were apprehended, they quietly let their revolvers slip into the river, thus avoiding being charged with a capital crime

John Durr (Toberkeagh) Ballintubber Coy., 2nd Battalion South Roscommon, served as Adjutant for the Company. Later emigrated to Southport, Lancashire, England

Matt Durr (Kilteevan) 3rd Battalion South Roscommon, a distant cousin of Gerald Davis. Matt, along with the other members of Kilteevan Company, took the Anti-Treaty side in the Civil War. Their Company was the only one in the 3rd Battalion South to do so

Pat Durr (Brackloon, Castlerea) Moor Coy., 1st Battalion South Roscommon. He was present in 1970 at the reunion of Volunteers held in memory of Pat Glynn, who had died fifty years before in the burning of Ballinlough Barracks

Patrick Durr (Toberkeagh, Ballintubber) a member of "F" Coy. in the 2nd Battalion South Roscommon. He drilled with his Company, collected funds for the Dáil loan, and served under the command of Captains John Conroy and Alec Kenny. Shot by the Tans in Tom Leonard's home at Kennyborough, Ballintubber 6 January 1921. He was buried in Ballintubber Cemetery. His name is inscribed on the tablets in front of the Shankill Monument near Elphin

Patrick Durr (Baslick) parish of Tulsk, 2nd Battalion North Roscommon

Frank Dwyer (Donamon) a member of "E" Coy. in the 2nd Battalion South Roscommon.

Jimmy Dwyer (Vice O/C of Gurteen Battalion in the South Sligo Brigade) took part in the **Ambush at Ratra** on 1 September 1920, and the **attack on Free State troops at Castlerea** on 30 November 1922

Margaret (Maggie) Dwyer (Cuppanaek) sister of Jim, member of the Cumann na mBan

Patrick Dwyer (Emlagh Beg, Donamon) Captain of "E" Coy. in the 2nd Battalion South Roscommon. Took part in the **raid on the military train at Ballymoe** in June 1920. Joined the Free State Army

Patrick Dwyer (Rathkeery, Castlerea) who harboured Johnnie McGowan when the latter was on the run, and in whose house Johnnie was shot by the Tans in December 1920

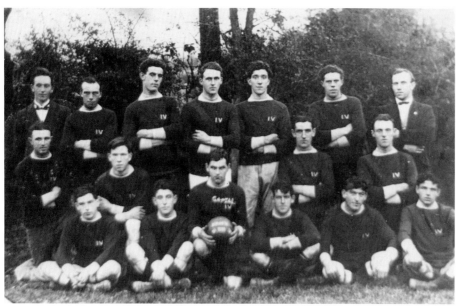

Donamon Football Team.
1918 Senior Football
Championship Winners

Back row (left to right): Martin Flannery,
Patrick Hennigan, Joseph Mullooly, Stephen
Kehir, James Reynolds, Patrick Freehilly,
Edward Jackson

Centre row: Michael Kelly, Patrick Reynolds,
Michael Harrington, Frank Conlon

Seated front row: John Lynn, Jack Hegarty,
Patrick Dwyer, Albert Kehir, Joseph Farrell,
Peter Shally

Many of these men were also involved in
the Volunteer movement. Pat Dwyer served
as Caption of Donamon Coy, while Edward
Jackson was the Captain of Cloverhill Coy.

Tommy Dwyer (Boyle) 1st Battalion North Roscommon, a member of the Volunteers since before the Easter Rising

Patrick Earley (Rathconnor) Kilbride Coy., 3rd Battalion South Roscommon

James Early (Treanacreeve, Scramogue) provided food for the Volunteers before their engagement at the **Scramogue Ambush**

Bernard Egan (Ballagh) Rahara Coy., 4th Battalion South Roscommon

Edward "Sonny" Egan (Curraghboy Coy.) the second Captain of the Curraghboy Coy. in the 4th Battalion South Roscommon. From 1917-March 1919 did organisational work, drilled, performed scouting duties, attended lectures and instruction given by Ernie O'Malley, performed police duty during the South Roscommon election and in conjunction with enforcement of Dáil decrees. Egan was one of a group of Volunteers who raided the private homes of three men — two of whom had joined and one who was about to join the RIC. Not surprisingly, these men had a change of heart! Egan raided for arms, his own closet being the first target — he gave up his own shotgun and twenty cartridges to the Company. Participated in the **attempted attack on Kilmurray Camp** in June 1920, and the **attempted ambush of a police lorry** conveying military equipment from Athlone to Ballyforan. The ambush did not take place owing to lack of time to coordinate offensive plans. Prevented jurors and litigants from attending the British Courts, manufactured ammunition, and constructed dumps for arms equipment. He was a member of a party of Volunteers who attempted to **ambush police at Clooncraff**. Raided the mails and also helped to convene the Sinn Féin Courts when they were necessary. Prepared for the attack on Ballygar RIC Barracks, but was arrested in March 1921 before the assault could take place. Egan and other members of the Company had discovered a suspected spy and charged him. It was as a result of this action that ten men from the Curraghboy Company were arrested in January and five more two months later. After March of 1921, the Curraghboy Company was decimated and became a mere outpost. The men in prison, however, continued the fight with hunger strikes. During the Civil War Egan guarded two local shopkeepers four nights who were being raided by a third party using the name IRA, and prevented the sheriff's bailiff from carrying out an eviction at Mrs. Faynes in Curraghboy. After the War he became a farmer. Died 1936 and buried in Cam Cemetery

Frank Egan (Cappagh) a member of "E" Coy., 3rd Battalion South Roscommon. Many of the members of the Kilgefin Company participated in the **Fourmilehouse Ambush** on 12 October 1920. Egan was also present at the **Scramogue Ambush** in March 1921

George Egan (Clongowna, Bealnamullia) 3rd Battalion Athlone Brigade. Egan drilled with his Company, trained to use firearms, took an active part in the General Election of 1918, attended Battalion meetings, worked with the Republican Police force at disputed farmland in Bealnamullia and Clongowna. He was with a group of Volunteers that seized ammunition from an airplane that made a forced landing at Keelogues in 1919. Took part in the **burning of the Barracks at Bealnamulla**, mobilised for an **attack on Cloonark Barracks**, and **attempted an ambush at Curraghaleen** in October 1920. Near Truce time, he guarded the ASU Headquarters in the area, **destroyed the bridge at Millbrook**, blocked roads at Millbrook and Monksland, harboured and aided escaped prisoners. During the

Truce he trained at Greenfield, Donamon, and Falty, in addition to collecting funds to aid the Volunteers and attending the Arbitration Courts. During the Civil War he took the Republican side. He harassed the Free State troopers by blocking roads at Larkfield and Bealnamullia, assisting the Flying Column at blocking a road near Curraghboy, assisting prisoners to escape and join their various units, storing and transporting arms and explosives when and where required by the Flying Column, and serving as an outpost guard for the Column to ensure their safety

James Egan (Cloonsellan) Kilteevan Coy., 3rd Battalion South Roscommon

John Egan (Trien Coy.) 1st Battalion South Roscommon

John Egan (Cloonsellan) Kilteevan Coy., 3rd Battalion South Roscommon

John Egan (Rahara Coy.) 4th Battalion South Roscommon

John F. Egan (Ballagh, Rahara) a member of St. John's Coy. in the 4th Battalion South Roscommon. Egan drilled with other Volunteers two nights a week — Tuesdays and Thursdays. He participated in several raids for arms — one in which three shotguns were secured, the other on the night that Joseph Kearney was shot (although Egan's raiding party went in the opposite direction to Kearney's). He took part in the **attempted ambush at Kilmurray Military Camp** in June 1920. He was with his Company when **O'Brien's residence was burned down** — an action deemed necessary because the house was thought to be soon taken over by the British. He collected gelignite on several occasions, and was with the party that **blew up the Ballybay Road Bridge**. During the Truce he became a member of the special service unit formed during this time, as well as worked with the Sinn Féin Court at Culleen. He died at a young age

Laurence Egan (St. John's Coy.) in the 4th Battalion South Roscommon. Egan drilled with other Volunteers two nights a week — Tuesdays and Thursdays and worked in the 1918 election. He participated with his unit in the sham battles staged at Taughmaconnell under the supervision of Ernie O'Malley in the summer of 1918. He also kept busy blocking roads and constructing dugouts. He later moved to Dublin

Martin Egan (Trien Coy.) 1st Battalion South Roscommon. Participated in the **attempted ambush at Coshlieve** in July 1920, and the **attempted ambush of RIC patrol near Ballymoe** in May 1921. Blocked roads and scouted on the day Inspector King was shot in Castlerea (11 July 1921). Attended the Cloonkeen training camp during the Truce where he specialised in scouting. Later emigrated to England

These next two may indeed be the same man!

Michael "Paddy" Egan (Tarmon, Castlerea) 1st Battalion South Roscommon. Acted as a scout at the **disarming of the Military at Tarmon Cross** in June 1920, took part in the **attempted attack on Kilmurray Military Camp**, and the **capture of enemy stores at Ballymoe**, all of which occurred in the month of June 1920. He also took part in the **attempted attack on the Castlerea Station Guard** in July 1920, the **raid and capture of military equipment at Ballymoe** September 1920, and he accompanied the cart that transported Volunteers to the **attack on Frenchpark Barracks** 2 October 1920. By July 1921 he had emigrated to the USA

"Paddy" Egan (Ballinagare Coy.) 1st Battalion South Roscommon, served as the Intelligence Officer for the Brigade but was later suspected of being a British agent. He moved out of the country

Michael Egan (Kilbride Coy.) 3rd Battalion South Roscommon, served as Quartermaster for the Company

Patrick Egan (Trien Coy.) 1st Battalion South Roscommon

Paul Egan (Ballybeg, Strokestown) Carniska Coy. in the 3rd Battalion North Roscommon. Acted as a Judge in the Sinn Féin Courts, took part in the **attack on the RIC patrol at Strokestown** in January 1921

Peter Egan (Caltragh) Cloontuskert Coy. in the 3rd Battalion South Roscommon. He was near the **explosion at Moneen**, but was not injured. After the War he lived in Portnahinch, then moved to Newtowncastle. He never married. He is buried in Cloontuskert Cemetery

Ted Egan (Rahara) in the 4th Battalion South Roscommon. He later emigrated to America

Eilis Elliott O'Brien

Emily Elliott Ledwith.

Timothy Egan (Rahara Coy.) 4th Battalion South Roscommon, served as the Adjutant for the Company

Tom Egan (Cloonsellan) Kilteevan Coy. in the 3rd Battalion South Roscommon, a member of Pat Madden's Flying Column

Edward Egerton (Castlecoote, Fuerty) 2nd Lieutenant in Fuerty Coy. in the 2nd Battalion South Roscommon. He died before the 1940s

Eilis Elliott (Tonagh House, Glasson, Co. Westmeath) founding member of Cumann na mBan. During 1915-1916, she and her comrades would collect arms and equipment for the Volunteers after the big matches in Dublin. She also made hand grenades. During the Rising, she was in the General Post Office as well as the Four Courts, where she carried food and arms to the different outposts. On Friday, she helped carry all the wounded and the dead to Father Mathew Hall, Church St., where "all waited for the end as the machine guns were up against us at this time."* She was later to marry Seamus O'Brien from Athlone. Eilis was very active in the committee to erect the IRA Monument in Athlone town. She even kept, in her old trunk, the original drawing of the statue and the amounts contributed by the townspeople for the building of the memorial

Easter Rising 1916 Miscellaneous Notes from Eilis O'Brien compiled by G. Griffin, December 2003.

Emily Elliott (Tonagh House, Glasson, Co. Westmeath) founding member of Cumann na mBan. She moved to Dublin in 1910, and participated in the Rising, where she was a member of the Four Courts garrison, and worked tirelessly in the Father Mathew Hall (the makeshift hospital area). She assisted the famous Capuchin priest, Fr. Augustine, while he administered the last rites to many of the dying soldiers.* She later married Peter Ledwith, who was also in the Four Courts that week. They lived at Lagan, Mount Temple, Moate. She died in April of 1983 and is buried in Glasnevin Cemetery

Quoted from "A Westmeath Heroine of 1916," Westmeath Independent, 21 April 1983

John J. Elliott (Athlone) arrested after the Rising, but released from custody in mid-May. He was a member of the Tubberclair Company in the Athlone Brigade. Elliott planned and executed the **ambush near Glasson, Athlone** that resulted in the death of General Lambert in June 1921

Joseph Elwood (Canbo, Croghan) served as the Adjutant for the Croghan Company in the 5th Battalion North Roscommon. He also "stepped up to the plate" and served as Captain when Tom Devaney was arrested. He was a member of the Anti-Treaty Active Service Unit (Flying Column) during the Civil War

Maurice Elwood (Ballinagare Coy.) 1st Battalion South Roscommon

Bernard English (Clooncah) Kilteevan Coy., 3rd Battalion South Roscommon

Denis Ennis (Coolatober, Ballyforan) fought with the Flying Column in South Roscommon during the Civil War. He was arrested in Ballyforan on 7 April 1923

John Joe Ennis (Coolatober, Ballyforan) fought with the Flying Column in South Roscommon during the Civil War. He held up a detective at Ballyforan and relieved him of equipment and papers, and blocked roads in preparation for the **destruction of the bridge at Ballyforan**

Martin Fahy (Ballygar Coy.) which was considered part of 4th Battalion South Roscommon when the Divisional structure was implemented

Thomas Fahy (Kilbride Coy.) 3rd Battalion South Roscommon

Tom Fahy (Cloonkeen, Castlerea) served as 1st Lieutenant in Trien Company in the 1st Battalion South Roscommon. Took part in the **attempted ambush at Coshlieve** in July 1920. Participated in the **attempted ambush of RIC patrol near Ballymoe** in May 1921. Attended the training camp at the old Castlerea Barracks during the Truce

Daniel Fallon (Corraun) Captain of "D" Company (Tarmonbarry) in the 3rd Battalion North Roscommon, which was, according to Bill Doherty as recorded in the Ernie O'Malley Papers, "an excellent Company." After the War he emigrated to England

Dominick Fallon (Ballyleague) Cloontuskert Coy., 3rd Battalion South Roscommon

Elizabeth Fallon (Clonown, Athlone) later Mrs. Wall of Boston, who travelled, along with Mary Fallon, to Athlone to secure a coffin and habit for James Tormey after he had been killed at the Cornafulla Ambush in February 1921

Edward Fallon (Kilcash, Rahara) Knockcroghery Coy. in the 4th Battalion South Roscommon, brother of Michael J., Thomas, and William. The Company was formed in 1917 under the leadership of Patrick Kelly of Culleen, Lecarrow. Fallon worked on the County Council election. During the Truce he was appointed to a special service unit. When the Civil War broke out, Edward Fallon stood with his brothers on the Anti-Treaty side. He collected gelignite along with other members of the St. John's Coy. for use in mines, which his two brothers, William and Michael J., constructed. He raided for transport for the Flying Column, and helped supply it with food and clothing

Frank Fallon (Cloontuskert Coy.) 3rd Battalion South Roscommon

Harry Fallon (Cloontuskert Coy.) 3rd Battalion South Roscommon

Jack Fallon (Newtown, Whitehall) a member of the Tarmonbarry Coy., 3rd Battalion North Roscommon. Took part in an **attempted ambush in Tarmonbarry** in 1920, and served as an outpost for the **Scramogue Ambush**. He was also good at making gunpowder!

Jim Fallon (Cappagh) a member of Kilgefin Coy., 3rd Battalion South Roscommon. Many of the members of the Kilgefin Company participated in the **Fourmilehouse Ambush** on 12 October 1920. He later became a farmer

John Fallon (Tullyneeny) Dysart Coy., 4th Battalion South Roscommon. Joined the Company in 1917. Attended parades, received instructions under Ernie O'Malley, helped in the 1918 election. He was appointed to work with the Republican Police, and performed dispatch work. Took part in raiding for arms and a raid on an RIC man's home at which time the Volunteers destroyed all the papers in the constable's possession and ordered him to quit his job

John Fallon (Bealnamullia) 3rd Battalion Athlone Brigade. Fallon drilled with his Company, trained to use firearms, took an active part in the General Election of 1918, attended Battalion meetings, worked with the Republican Police force at disputed farmland in Bealnamullia and Clongowna. He was with a group of Volunteers that seized ammunition from an airplane that made a forced landing at Keelogues in 1919. Took part in the **burning of the Barracks at Bealnamullia**, mobilised for an **attack on Cloonark Barracks**, and attempted an **ambush at Curraghaleen** in October 1920. Near Truce time, he guarded the ASU Headquarters in the area, **destroyed the bridge at Millbrook**, blocked roads at Millbrook and Monksland, harboured and aided escaped prisoners. During the Truce he trained at Greenfield, Donamon, and Falty, in addition to collecting funds to aid the Volunteers and attending the Arbitration Courts. He took the Republican side during the Civil War. He harassed the Free State troopers by blocking roads at Larkfield and Bealnamullia, assisting the Flying Column at blocking a road near Curraghboy, assisting prisoners to escape and join their various units, storing and transporting arms and explosives when and where required by the Flying Column, and serving as an outpost guard for the Column to ensure their safety

Joseph Fallon (Cappagh) a member of "E" Coy., 3rd Battalion South Roscommon, part of Pat Madden's Flying Column. Participated in the **Fourmilehouse Ambush** on 12 October 1920, and **Scramogue**. Joined the Free State Army. Later he became a small farmer at Cappagh. Died 10 October 1977 and buried in Kilgefin Cemetery

Memorial Dinner. (left to right) Peter Farrell, John Rafferty, Luke Duffy, Frank Simons, Joe Fallon, Pat Fitzpatrick, Paddy Tiernan.

PHOTO COURTESY OF EAMONN DUFFY

Martin Fallon (Doughil, Curraghroe) O/C of the 3rd Battalion Flying Column in North Roscommon, which was established in late 1920. Fallon joined the Volunteers in 1917, and became one of the founding members of the Curraghroe Company which, in the early weeks, numbered five! A year later he was appointed 2nd Lieutenant. He also became a member of the IRB, being taken into the group at Michael Green's of Kilglass. During one of the arms raids in which he participated, he, Michael Noone, and Paddy Shiel ran into shotgun pellets—but not ones fired by an enemy. They were outside the front door of a man whom they knew had a Mauser rifle and a shotgun. Noone's gun accidentally fired and his shot ricocheted off the walls of the house sending the tiny pellets into Fallon's legs and those of Paddy Shiel. Fallon and four other Volunteers (James Casey, William Shiel, Patrick Moran, and Jim Lynagh) entered Tarmonbarry in December of 1920 looking for contact with the police. They succeeded in wounding one Tan who was exiting a public house. In early 1921, Fallon was selected as Battalion Quartermaster. He took part in the **attempted attack on a Tarmonbarry patrol** in early February, the **attack on Elphin Barracks** on 4 February 1921, and, a month later, the **ambush at Scramogue**, after which Fallon's group took charge of one of the Tan prisoners. The Tan attacked Fallon from behind, fled into the bushes alongside the Shannon, was recaptured, and drowned in the river.* After Michael Dockery's arrest in May 1921, Fallon became the O/C of the North Roscommon Brigade. He was in charge of the **attack on the Tarmonbarry patrol** in early July 1921. Fallon began the Civil War in sympathy with the sentiments of the Anti-Treatyites. He changed his mind, and later attack Boyle in April '22 which was, at that time, in Anti-Treaty hands. He also held Sligo Courthouse against Anti-Treaty troops. Later in life he became a farmer at Toomona near Tulsk. He died 9 April 1977, and is buried in Cloontuskert Abbey

Martin Fallon, O/C of the 3rd Battalion Flying Column in North Roscommon.

PHOTO COURTESY OF HENRY OWENS

*Martin Fallon interview, Ernie O'Malley Papers, UCD Archives, No. 131

Mary Fallon (Clonown, Athlone) later became Mrs. Mary Moran, Ballygorry, St. John's, Knockcroghery. She, along with Elizabeth Fallon, travelled to Athlone to secure a coffin and habit for Volunteer James Tormey after he had been killed at Cornafulla in February 1921

Michael Fallon, a member of the Kilgefin Company in the 3rd Battalion South Roscommon Brigade. Many, but not all, of the Kilgefin Company were present at the **Fourmilehouse Ambush** on 12 October 1920

Michael Fallon (Largan, Strokestown) nicknamed "the Old Captain." He was the Captain of the Volunteer Company in Kiltrustan in 1921. He also had been a Volunteer in the Cork/Kerry area. He owned a quarry in the land opposite the old Kiltrustan school. He died in the 1950s and is buried in Kiltrustan Cemetery

Michael Fallon (Tryne) a member of Curraghboy Coy. in the 4th Battalion South Roscommon. From 1917-March 1919 did organisational work, drilled with the men, performed scouting duties, paraded with his Company during a visit to the area by Sean Connolly, and did police duty during the South Roscommon election and in conjunction with enforcement of Dáil decrees. Fallon raided for arms, his own closet being the first target — he gave up his own shotgun and fifteen cartridges for the Company's use. Manufactured ammunition and constructed dugouts for storage of same. The entire Company participated in the arrest and confinement of a suspected spy. That man was tried by court-martial and eventually executed — an action which prompted the arrest of ten members of the Company on 5 January 1921. Fallon escaped the dragnet. After this mass arrest of his fellow Volunteers, Fallon raided homes of persons associated with the enemy and hostile to the IRA. He participated in the preparations for an **attack on Ballygar Barracks** and was one of a few men left standing in his Company (after more arrests in March) to actually participate in the assault

Michael J. Fallon (Kilcash, Rahara) Knockcroghery Coy. in the 4th Battalion South Roscommon, brother of William, Edward, and Thomas. The Company formed in 1917 under the leadership of Patrick Kelly of Culleen, Lecarrow. Fallon paraded with the Volunteers, attended practice battles at Taughmaconnell overseen by Ernie O'Malley in the summer of 1918, participated in the South Roscommon election of 1918, and the County Council election. He served as an armed escort for bank officials taking large sums of money to fairs in Knockcroghery. He also served as a scout on the Athlone side during the **burning of Lecarrow Barracks**. Fallon was in the raiding party which descended on two hostile houses in the Rahara area. He took part in the **attempted attack at Kilmurray Camp** — an action that was cancelled the very night of the proposed action. Fallon was also with a party of Knockcroghery men who, in conjunction with Kilteevan Volunteers, **attempted an ambush at Clooncraff** — under the command of Pat Madden. He, along with the rest of his Company, **guarded the village of Knockcroghery** from reprisal on 15 August 1920 — a reprisal precipitated by British Forces being fired upon on Lough Ree. Fallon participated in the **attempted attack** on a party of military about eighteen strong **at Knockcroghery** in January 1921, and the **attempted ambush at Scrine**. He also collected the IRA levy from the local people, and took part in the **burning of O'Brien's home** in Curraghboy on 14 May 1921 — a house the local Company feared would soon be occupied by British Forces. During the Truce he resumed work in the Arbitration Courts, and was appointed to a special service unit. When the Civil War broke out, Michael J. took the Anti-Treaty side along with his brothers. He took part in the **blowing up of Kellybrook and Curry Railway bridges**, collected gelignite from Lecarrow quarry, and constructed mines which were used by the Anti-Treaty forces in the area. He was arrested and incarcerated in Tintown A at the Curragh, and finally released on 18 December 1923. He took the train from the Curragh and got off at Knockcroghery Station. While walking down the main road into the village, he was shunned by a couple, who deliberately walked on the opposite side of the street to avoid him. Denis O'Brien, owner of the local pub and a Free State advocate, brought Michael into his public house and treated him to a drink—an act of kindness not forgotten over the years

Michael Fallon (Bealnamullia) during the Black and Tan War, he had been arrested and sent to Ballykinlar Internment Camp in County Down, where he spent thirteen months in Hut 30. Following the Truce, he returned to his native place.* Fallon worked in the Athlone Railway Station and served with the Bealnamullia Coy., 3rd Battalion Athlone Brigade during the Civil War. He harassed the Free State troopers by blocking roads at Larkfield and Bealnamullia, assisting the Flying Column at blocking a road near Curraghboy, assisting prisoners to escape and join their various units, storing and transporting arms and explosives when and where required by the Flying Column, and serving as an outpost guard for the Column to ensure their safety

*_Drum and Its Hinterland_ by Edward Egan. p. 304.

Nan Fallon (Clonown, Athlone) who helped prepare the body of James Tormey for burial after he was killed at the Cornafulla Ambush

Paddy Fallon (Knockcroghery Coy.) 4th Battalion South Roscommon, served for a time as the Captain of the Coy., which was formed in 1917 under the leadership of Patrick Kelly of Culleen, Lecarrow. Fallon paraded with the Volunteers, and attended practice battles at Taughmaconnell overseen by Ernie O'Malley in the summer of 1918. Fallon commanded the Athlone side of the scouts for the **burning of the Lecarrow Barracks**. He assisted the St. John's Company on numerous raids for arms. He assembled with his Company for an **attempted ambush at Clooncraff** under the command of Pat Madden, took part in the **attempted attack at Kilmurray Camp** — an action that was cancelled the very night of the proposed action. He, along with the rest of his Company, **guarded the village of**

Knockcroghery from reprisal on 15 August 1920 — a reprisal precipitated by British Forces being fired upon on Lough Ree. Fallon participated in the **attempted attack** on a party of military about eighteen strong **at Knockcroghery** in January 1921, **attempted ambush at Scrine**, and the **attack on RIC Barracks at Ballygar**. He also collected the IRA levy from the local people, and made the mines used by the Company. He was present at the attempt to **blow up the bridges at Curry and Farnaseer** near Knockcroghery. He was also one of a few entrusted with important dispatches. During the Truce he continued to be involved with police work. He later emigrated to the USA

Patrick Fallon (Senior) (Knockcroghery Coy.) 4th Battalion South Roscommon. The Company was formed in 1917 under the leadership of Patrick Kelly of Culleen, Lecarrow. Fallon paraded with the Volunteers, and attended practice battles at Taughmaconnell overseen by Ernie O'Malley in the summer of 1918. He, along with the rest of his Company, **guarded the village of Knockcroghery** from reprisal on 15 August 1920 — a reprisal precipitated by British Forces being fired upon on Lough Ree. Fallon participated in the **attempted attack** on a party of military about eighteen strong **at Knockcroghery** in January 1921, and the **attempted ambush at Scrine**. During the Truce he attended the Battalion Camp at Drinaun, Ballygar, and became a delegate to Commandant Tom Maguire's review of the Brigade at Ballygar. All the while he continued to be engaged in the Sinn Féin Courts. He was also appointed to a special service unit. He later emigrated to the United States

Patrick Fallon (St. John's Coy.) 4th Battalion South Roscommon. When the Company first started in 1917, Fallon drilled with other Volunteers two nights a week — Tuesdays and Thursdays, and worked as a Republican Policeman with the Republican Courts. He worked in the 1918 election and constructed dugouts in the area. Fallon raided for arms on numerous occasions. He was with the other raiding party the night that Joseph Kearney was severely wounded in the stomach while at Feehily's house. Fallon worked in connection with the Belfast boycott, collected monies for the Defence Fund and IRA levy, and also collected more lethal gelignite. He, along with other twelve other members of his Company, took part in the **attempted ambush at Clooncraff** under the command of Pat Madden, and the **attempted ambush at Kilmurray Military Camp** in June 1920. He was present at the **burning of O'Brien's house** — a house thought to be soon taken over by British Forces. Fallon, along with Hubert Murphy (Company Captain), Malachy Kilroy, and Patrick Kelly (Captain of Knockcroghery Coy.) concocted two pounds of gunpowder one night only to repeat their feat the next evening. He also engaged in **blowing up the bridge at Ballymurray,** and **raided the train at Kiltoom for mail**. During the Truce he attended the Battalion Camp at Drinaun, Ballygar Co. Galway, and served as a delegate to Commandant Maguire's Army Review in Ballygar. He was also active with the Republican Courts at Culleen, and was appointed to the special service unit formed during this time. Fallon later joined the Garda Síochána

Patrick Fallon (Lurgan, Shankill, Elphin) 2nd Battalion North Roscommon

Patrick Fallon (Doughil, Curraghroe) 3rd Battalion North Roscommon, brother of Martin. He participated in an attempted ambush at Curraghroe, and served as an outpost at the **attack on the Tarmonbarry patrol** in January 1921. He also did outpost duty at **Scramogue,** and participated in the **attack on Tarmonbarry Barracks** on 2 July 1921

Peter Fallon (Lodge, Tarmon village) a member of Tarmonbarry Coy. 3rd Battalion North Roscommon

Stephen Fallon (Fairymount) served as a scout for the Kilgefin Coy., 3rd Battalion South Roscommon. After the War he became a farmer. Died 1970s

Thomas Fallon (Drum Coy.) 3rd Battalion Athlone Brigade

Thomas Fallon (Fuerty Coy.) a member of Fuerty Coy. in the 2nd Battalion South Roscommon. After the War he emigrated to the USA

Thomas Fallon (Kilcash, Rahara) member of the Knockcroghery Coy., 4th Battalion South Roscommon. The Company was formed in 1917 under the leadership of Patrick Kelly of Culleen, Lecarrow. Fallon paraded with the Volunteers, and attended practice battles at Taughmaconnell overseen by Ernie O'Malley in the summer of 1918. Tommy went house to house canvassing for signatures to the plebiscite for independence. He served as an armed escort for bank officials carrying large sums of money to and from the fairs at Knockcroghery. He was present at the **burning of Lecarrow Barracks**. He also collected the IRA levy from the local people. Tommy took the Anti-Treaty side in the Civil War, and was a member of the Company in July 1922. He raided for transport for the Brigade Flying Column of which his brother, William, was a member

Tim Fallon (Knockcroghery Coy.) 4th Battalion South Roscommon. He later emigrated to the United States

Timothy Fallon served with the Bealnamullia Coy., 3rd Battalion Athlone Brigade during the Civil War. He harassed the Free State troopers by blocking roads at Larkfield and Bealnamullia, assisting the Flying Column at blocking a road near Curraghboy, assisting prisoners to escape and join their various units, storing and transporting arms and explosives when and where required by the Flying Column, and serving as an outpost guard for the Column to ensure their safety. After the War he emigrated to the USA

William Fallon (Kilcash, Rahara) Knockcroghery Coy. in the 4th Battalion South Roscommon, brother of Michael J., Thomas, and Edward. The Company was formed in 1917 under the leadership of Patrick Kelly of Culleen, Lecarrow. Fallon paraded with the Volunteers, did house to house canvassing for signatures to the plebiscite for independence, and attended practice battles at Taughmaconnell overseen by Ernie O'Malley in the summer of 1918. Fallon was with a group of Volunteers who visited six intended recruits to the RIC and "dissuaded" them from joining the force. Participated in the South Roscommon election of 1918, and served as an armed escort for bank officials taking large sums of money to fairs in Knockcroghery. He also was in position as a scout on the Athlone side during in the **burning of Lecarrow Barracks**. Raided two hostile houses in Rahara area for arms, and took part in the arrest and trial of a man accused of firing and wounding a Volunteer. He also saw to it that the fine from such person was collected. Took part in the **attempted attack at Kilmurray Camp**. Fallon assembled, along with other members of his Company, for an **attempted attack at Clooncraff**, an action under the command of Pat Madden. He **guarded the village of Knockcroghery** from reprisal on 15 August 1920 — a reprisal precipitated by British Forces being fired upon on Lough Ree. Fallon participated in the **attempted attack** on a party of military **at Knockcroghery** in January 1921, the **attempted ambush at Scrine,** and the **attack on RIC Barracks at Ballygar** on 1 July 1921. He also collected the IRA levy from the local people, and gelignite from the local quarry for the making of bombs. He blocked roads and was present at the burning of **O'Brien's house in Curraghboy** — a residence feared to be soon taken over by the British military. During the Truce he attended the Battalion Camp at Drinaun, Ballygar, and was a delegate to Commandant Tom Maguire's review of the Brigade at Ballygar. He was also engaged in the Sinn Féin Courts during this time, appointed to a special service unit, and served as Captain of the Company. During the Civil War he took part in the **blowing up of Kellybrook and Curry Railway bridges,** made bombs, and became a member of the South Roscommon Flying Column, which roamed

William Fallon (Bealnamullia) Fallon was the 2nd Company Captain of Bealnamullia Coy. in the 3rd Battalion Athlone Brigade. He was responsible for drilling his Company, and training them in the use of firearms. He organised his men so that they could all take an active part in the General Election of 1918. Fallon attended Battalion meetings, and worked with the Republican Police force at disputed farmland in Bealnamullia and Clongowna. He was with a group of Volunteers that seized ammunition from an airplane that made a forced landing at Keelogues in 1919. He participated in the **burning of the Barracks** at **Bealnamullia**, mobilising for an **attack on Cloonark Barracks**, and **attempting an ambush at Curraghaleen** in October 1920. Near Truce time, he helped arrange for his men to guard the ASU Headquarters in the area. Fallon helped to **destroy the bridge at Millbrook**, block roads at Millbrook and Monksland, and harbour escaped prisoners. During the Truce he trained at the officers' camps at Greenfield, Donamon, and Falty, in addition to collecting funds to aid the Volunteers and making certain that the Arbitration Courts functioned smoothly. He was not a participant in the Civil War

the area irrespective of county borders and fought the Free State forces where it found them. He was arrested 24 September 1922, and sent to Athlone two months later. He was transferred to Tintown II on 20 February 1923 from which he was finally released on 18 December 1923. He died at a young age

James Fannon (Roscommon Coy.) 3rd Battalion South Roscommon

Paddy Fannon (Castlerea) 1st Battalion South Roscommon, served as the Lieutenant in charge of intelligence for the 2nd Battalion, No. 2 Brigade of the 2nd Western Division. Interned for his Sinn Féin sympathies

Tom Fannon (Lisboy, Castlerea) 1st Battalion South Roscommon. Participated in the **destruction of vacant barracks** in 1920, the **capture of enemy stores at Ballymoe** in June 1920, the **attempted attack on the Castlerea Station Guard** in July 1920, and the **raid and capture of military equipment at Ballymoe** September 1920. During the Truce he attended the Company training camp and specialised in intelligence, scouting, and dispatch work

James Farland (Curraghroe, Scramogue) during the Civil War Farland was arrested on 6 September 1922, and transferred to Athlone on 14 November

Alfred Farrell (Donamon) a member of "E" Coy. of the 2nd Battalion South Roscommon

Bernard Farrell (Carrick-on-Shannon) interned in 1920-21. In 1922 he served as the Captain of Drumlion Company in the newly formed Western Division's 4th Battalion

One of the following Bernard Farrells volunteered to serve with the Oran Battalion Flying Column when the 2nd Western Division was formed

Bernard Farrell (Fuerty) 2nd Battalion South Roscommon

Bernard Farrell (Carrowduff, Ballymacurley) 2nd Battalion South Roscommon Brigade. Served as a cook when the IRA occupied the Runnamoat House. He later emigrated to America, where he worked in the catering business. He married and returned to Ireland. The Land Commission allotted him a farm in Grange, Fourmilehouse. He is buried in the new Ballinderry Cemetery

Bryan Farrell (Ballygar Coy.) which was considered part of 4th Battalion South Roscommon when the Divisional structure was implemented

Ed Farrell (Lismehy, Strokestown) participated in the Rising, where he was a worker in Boland's Mill. He also served as a member of Carniska Coy. in the 3rd Battalion North Roscommon. Took part in the **attack on the RIC patrol at Strokestown** in January 1921. Died in the 1930s

Francis Farrell (Cloonfower, Ruskey) a member of Tarmonbarry Coy. of the 3rd Battalion North Roscommon. Served as an outpost for the **Scramogue Ambush**

James Farrell (Roscommon Coy.) 3rd Battalion South Roscommon. Company was commanded by J.J. Doorley

James Farrell (Ballygar Coy.) which was considered part of 4th Battalion South Roscommon when the Divisional structure was implemented

James Farrell (Curraghroe Coy.) 3rd Battalion North Roscommon. Served as an outpost for the **Scramogue Ambush**, and was present at the **attack on Tarmonbarry Barracks** in July 1921

James Farrell of Crunaun, Ballaghaderreen, was arrested at Castlemore on 30 January 1923 by Captain Lavin and twelve National Army soldiers

J. Farrell (Moor Coy.) 1st Battalion South Roscommon

Jim Farrell (Corramagrine, Whitehall, Tarmonbarry) was the Captain of "D" Company in the 3rd Battalion North Roscommon. He took part in the Easter Rising of 1916, where he was positioned at Jacob's Biscuit Factory. As a result of his actions, he was interned in Frongoch, the "Irish University." Upon release in December 1916, he returned to Tarmonbarry, where he helped mobilise the Tarmonbarry Company. Farrell took part in the South Longford election, held up boats on the Shannon and took ammunition off them, and assisted in the **attack on Tarmonbarry patrol** in January 1921. He was arrested in February 1921, and sent to the Curragh Prison Camp, from which he escaped through the Brady tunnel in September. He came back to the east Roscommon area, and became a member of an Active Service Unit (Flying Column) on the Anti-Treaty side during the Civil War. He was present at the **attack on Ruskey Barracks** in 1922 and 1923, and the **engagement** with Free State troopers **at Lake Forbes**. When the cease-fire came, he laid down his arms and went home

John Farrell (Brackloon, Ballinagare) his home served as the headquarters for "C" Company in the 2nd Battalion, No. 2 Brigade, 2nd Western Division during the post-Truce times

John Farrell (Tobervaddy, Athleague) a member of Fuerty Coy. in the 2nd Battalion South Roscommon

John Farrell (Stonepark, Roscommon) fought against the Free State during the Civil War, and was incarcerated in Athlone in November 1922, and transferred to Tintown II in March of 1923

John Farrell (Ruskey) 3rd Battalion North Roscommon. Joined the IRA in 1917, blocked roads, did police duty in Ruskey, helped with the North Roscommon bye election, and served as the personal agent for Joe McGuinness in the Longford election. Conveyed arms across the Shannon River, an activity which brought him to the attention of the authorities, who visited his home and beat him unconscious. A three week hospital stay was the consequence. Took part in the **attack on the Strokestown patrol** in January 1921, **Scramogue Ambush**, and the **attack on the Tarmonbarry patrol** in July 1921. During the Civil War he rescued a Republican who was wounded in the same firefight in Ruskey on 13 December 1922 that ended the life of Frank O'Donoghue

There were two John Farrells in the Curraghroe Company of the 3rd Battalion North Roscommon. One lived at Trila-Dillon, Curraghroe, Co. Roscommon; the other lived at Mt. Dillon, Curraghroe, Co. Roscommon

John Farrell (Shannon View, Ruskey) a member of Ruskey Coy. in the 3rd Battalion North Roscommon. Took part in the **attack on the Strokestown patrol** in January 1921, served as an outpost at the **Scramogue Ambush**, and participated in the **attack on the Tarmonbarry patrol** in July 1921

John Farrell (a native of Cootehall) deserted during the Civil War from the National Army stationed in Boyle Barracks on 10 October 1922, taking with him a rifle and 100 rounds of ammunition. He went to Cootehall, where he was met by Ned Bofin in Regan's public house. The next day he was observed wearing civilian clothes, but still toting a rifle

Joseph Farrell (Island, Donamon) a member of "E" Coy. of the 2nd Battalion South Roscommon. He drilled with his Company, collected funds for the Dáil loan, and served under the command of Captain Pat Dwyer

Martin Farrell (Ballaghaderreen) one of the first members of the Ballaghaderreen Coy. in the East Mayo Brigade

May Farrell (Moher) Kilgefin parish, member of the Cumann na mBan. Later married Dan Madden. Died in 1982

Michael "Wad" Farrell (Ballaghaderreen) one of the first members of the Ballaghaderreen Coy. in the East Mayo Brigade

Pat Farrell (Coosan, Co. Westmeath) Farrell used to come to The O'Rahilly Sinn Féin Club near Drum in south Roscommon and train the new recruits to the IRA. The men were instructed in foot drill and the use of arms, although oftentimes there were precious few arms with which to practice. During the Civil War he took the Anti-Treaty side. He was arrested in December 1922, and sent to Athlone. In January he was transferred to Mountjoy

Patrick Farrell (Ballyleague, Lanesboro) a member of the Active Service Unit of the 3rd Battalion South Roscommon. He was captured in the roundup after the Fourmilehouse ambush and became a guest of the British government at Athlone detention barracks and later at the Curragh. He remained incarcerated until after the Truce. Farrell emigrated to the United States of America, where he died on 23 December 1930 at the young age of 28, only one month after he had been married. He is buried in America

Patrick Farrell (Ballyleague, Lanesboro),
PHOTO COURTESY OF EILEEN BANAHAN

Patrick Farrell (Drumlish, Elphin) participated in the **attack on the Elphin patrol** 5 January 1921. He died at a young age

Patrick Farrell (Toberavaddy, Athleague) a member of Fuerty Coy. in the 2nd Battalion South Roscommon. He drilled with his Company, collected funds for the Dáil loan, and served under the command of Captain Jack Conboy. He, along with James Keegan, Joseph Belton, Seamus McGovern, Tom Mannion, James Kenny, and Pat Conboy captured a Tan during the War for Independence

Peter Farrell (Moher, Ballyleague, Lanesboro) brother of Pat, a member of the 3rd Battalion South Roscommon. After the War he too emigrated to America

Peter Farrell (Kilbride Coy.) Captain of the Kilbride Company in the 3rd Battalion South Roscommon, affectionately known as "Buzzer," a member of the Flying Column, present at the **attack on Elphin Barracks** in January 1921, and **Scramogue** two months later, where he was positioned in a house that had been loopholed. Farrell was an excellent marksman, having served in the Irish Guards in World War I. He later joined the Free State Army. Died 9 January 1966, and is buried in St. Coman's Cemetery in Roscommon town

Thomas Farrell (Roscommon Coy.) 3rd Battalion South Roscommon, served as the 1st Lieutenant of the Company. Farrell also served as the contact man with Sergeant Duffy in Roscommon town. As a result of Farrell's conscientious intelligence work, many local men were saved from capture

Thomas Farrell (Cloontuskert Coy.) 3rd Battalion South Roscommon

Thomas Joseph Farrell (Ballygar Coy.) which was considered part of 4th Battalion South Roscommon when the Divisional structure was implemented

Martin Farrelly "sympathetic shopkeeper" in Athlone

Alice Fayne from Cloonmore, Kilteevan, who nursed the four men on Incheneagh Island in Lough Ree who had been injured by the land mine explosion at Cloontymullen. For her efforts, her house was later raided by Crown Forces

John Fayne (Kilteevan Coy.) 3rd Battalion South Roscommon, brother of Alice. Served as the 1st Lieutenant of the Company

Thomas Feehily (Lieutenant) in charge of Accounts and Records for the Battalion in No. 2 Brigade, 2nd Western Division. Although located in Galway, this Battalion was incorporated into No. 2 Brigade, 2nd Western Division. The Division Commander was Tom Maguire

Emmett Feeley (The Hill of Berries, Athlone) served as a Judge in the Republican Courts. A carpenter by trade. Died 1970, buried in Kiltoom Cemetery

Thomas Feeley (Carrowphaden, Lecarrow) 4th Battalion South Roscommon

William Feeley (Barrymore) Kiltoom Coy. in the 4th Battalion South Roscommon, served as the 1st Lieutenant of the Company. He was arrested during the Civil War on 19 July 1922, and taken to Athlone. At the beginning of the new year, he was transferred to Mountjoy (10 January 1923). After the War he worked for the railroad. He also took an active part in forming Fianna Fáil in the county. He was on hand to welcome de Valera to Roscommon town on 19 June 1926. He served as secretary of Kiltoom Fianna Fáil *Cumann* in 1928. Died in Roscommon town and buried in St. Coman's Cemetery

The Feeley Cottage (Carrowphaden, St. John's) where men on the run received a hot meal and companionship. During the entire War, their house was never searched

Austin Feely (Carrigeen, Mantua, Elphin) 2nd Battalion North Roscommon. Blocked roads, collected arms, and participated in the **attack on Elphin Barracks** 11 February 1921

Henry Feely (Greatmeadow, Boyle) 1st Battalion North Roscommon. He, along with Henry Tivnan, Addie Hayes, and Willie Devine, climbed the flagpole outside the home of the local British Army recruiter in Boyle. The mischievous boys

Peter "Buzzer" Farrell, 3rd Battalion South Roscommon.

burned that Union Jack outside the door of the recruiter's home. He was never apprehended for this stunt, but his luck didn't hold out. After he joined the Volunteers in the spring of 1918, he performed dispatch work, procured arms, took part in the capture and trial of local robbers, raided a train, and captured an enemy petrol. Feely was present at the **burning of Grevisk and Ballinameen Barracks,** and enforced the Belfast boycott. He was arrested and beaten by the RIC after ordering Boyle shopkeepers to keep their doors closed

Henry Feely (on left) leading a parade of Volunteers in Boyle commemorating the 50th Anniversary of The Rising, 1966.

PHOTO COURTESY OF BARRY FEELY

after the death of hunger striker Terence MacSwiney. He was arrested in Carrick-on-Shannon in 1920 for conspiracy, and sentenced to a term of imprisonment in Mountjoy. During the Truce he attended the training camps, and took courses in engineering. He was on duty at the **take over of Boyle Barracks** from the British. During the Civil War Henry participated in the **attack on the Free State outpost at Frenchpark,** the **burning of a signal cabin at Carrick-on-Shannon, ambush at Lakeview, Strokestown** in December 1922, raiding post offices, the **burning of Elphin Garda Barracks,** and the **attack on Free State troops at Caldra** on the Elphin/Boyle Road. Re-arrested in Carrick-on-Shannon, and sentenced for conspiracy. He became a "guest" of the Free State government at Boyle Military Barracks, Mountjoy, and the Curragh. Later in life he became a stonecutter. Died 1970, and is buried in Ardcarne Cemetery in Boyle

James Feely (Greatmeadow, Boyle) brother of Henry. Feely joined the Irish Volunteers in 1914 under the leadership of Charlie Devine. A year later Alec McCabe took him into the IRB. He was on the original committee to put forth Count Plunkett's name for the North Roscommon election, and a member of the first Sinn Féin County Council. Feely was appointed by Ernie O'Malley to be the first O/C of the 1st Battalion in the North Roscommon Brigade. He took part in the **Rockingham Raid,** after which he was arrested and sent to Mountjoy, where he participated in a hunger strike organised by Austin Stack. He subsequently ate many meals at His Majesty's expense at Mountjoy, Galway Gaol, and Belfast. During 1919 he took part in various raids for arms in which a number of shotguns and a few revolvers were confiscated. In April 1920 after participating in the **burning of Grevisk Barracks,** Feely went to Cootehall where he, along with several local Volunteers, **burned the Income Tax office.** He took part in the **raid of petrol from the Boyle Railway Station.** Feely served as a Judge in the Sinn Féin Courts. His home was raided in October 1920, and he made good a daring escape by vaulting the railway bridge battlement in Boyle. He was arrested in early 1921, and incarcerated in Boyle Military Barracks, where he is often credited with helping to instigate the daring escape of Jim Molloy and Michael Dockery; however, according to his own words, he "had no part in the planning of it."* He finished the War in the Curragh, and was released with the other prisoners after the signing of the Treaty. He joined the Free State Army at its inception, and held the rank of Commandant. He later resigned, and joined the Garda Síochána. Died 1965 and buried in Assylin Cemetery in Boyle

*James Feely Volunteer Witness Statement to the Bureau of Military History 1913-21, p. 10.

Spoon carved from bone used by Henry Feely while in Mountjoy (typical of the cutlery issued to prisoners of that time).

COURTESY OF BARRY FEELY
PHOTO BY LEW THORNE

John Feely (Boyle) 1st Battalion North Roscommon, a member of the Volunteers before the Rising. Later worked as a stonemason on the Ballaghaderreen Cathedral. He moved to Belfast where he is buried

Michael Feely (Carrowcuill, Kilmore) 5th Battalion North Roscommon. The first Captain of Kilmore Company. Imprisoned in Mountjoy in 1921

Wilfred Feely (Carrigeen, Mantua, Elphin) 2nd Battalion North Roscommon. Blocked roads, collected arms, and participated in the **attack on Elphin Barracks** 11 February 1921

Andy Feeney (Mongagh, Curraghroe) 3rd Battalion North Roscommon, brother of Luke. Andy used the Curraghroe bog for weapons instruction for new Volunteers. He was a member of an Active Service Unit (Flying Column) in North Roscommon. He fought on the Anti-Treaty side, and was arrested during the Civil War on 6 September 1922, and sent to Athlone on 14 November. After the War, he emigrated to Chicago where he, along with his brother Luke, worked for the J.O. Stoll Corporation. In 1953 he became an executive for the North American Phillips Corp. Andy lived a long life, dying in 1999 in Saint Leo, Florida

Constable Feeney of Athlone, an unlikely hero, who had the "hit list" which had been posted in the barracks removed. The list contained many well known leaders of Sinn Féin, a large percentage of whom were not connected with the IRA

Gerald Feeney (Ballaghaderreen) one of the first members of the Ballaghaderreen Coy. in the East Mayo Brigade. He had an arms dumps on his land during the Civil War. He was the Intelligence Officer for the Ballaghaderreen area, but was arrested in August of 1922

Luke Feeney (Ballaghaderreen) one of the first members of the Ballaghaderreen Coy. in the East Mayo Brigade

Luke Feeney (Mongagh, Curraghroe) Captain of the Curraghroe Company in the 3rd Battalion North Roscommon. He worked as a Policeman for the Sinn Féin Courts. Took part in the **attack on the RIC patrol** at Strokestown in January 1921, **Scramogue Ambush**, and the **attack on Tarmonbarry Barracks** 2 July 1921. Attended the training camps during the Truce. He fought against the Treaty, and became a member of the Active Service Unit (Flying Column) in North Roscommon during the Civil War, and participated in the **attack on the Ruskey patrol**. After the War he emigrated to Chicago, where he worked for the J. O. Stoll Corporation along with his brother, Andy. He enlisted in the United States Army during World War II, and was wounded. In 1951 he joined the staff of the *Chicago Tribune* newspaper. Died 1964

Michael Feeney (Gortlustia, Scramogue, Strokestown) 1st Lieutenant of "C" Company in the 3rd Battalion North Roscommon

Michael Feeney (Fearagh, Ballymurray) 4th Battalion South Roscommon. Knockcroghery Coy. was formed in 1917 with Patrick Kelly serving as Captain. Feeney served as the 2nd Lieutenant of the Company. He drilled with the Volunteers, and attended practice battles at Taughmaconnell overseen by Ernie O'Malley in the summer of 1918. Participated in the South Roscommon election of 1918, and the **burning of Lecarrow Barracks.** Feeney worked as a Policeman and summons server with the Sinn Féin Courts, and served as an armed escort for bank officials taking large sums of money to fairs in Knockcroghery. He was mobilised with his Company for the **attempted attack at Kilmurray Camp** — an action that was cancelled the very night of the proposed action. He, along with the rest of his Company, **guarded the village of Knockcroghery** from reprisal on 15 August 1920 — a reprisal precipitated by British Forces being fired upon on Lough Ree. He also participated in the **attempted ambush at Clooncraff** — an operation under the command of Pat Madden. Feeney raided for arms — on one such daylight raid he had to approach several houses by boat from Lough Ree. He also assisted the St. John's Company with a number of raids. Feeney served not only as a scout for a **raid on the evening mail train to Dublin** but, after the seizure of the mails, he examined the correspondence as well. He, along with eight other men, **held up a goods train at Ballymurray Railway Station**. He also spent many hours going house to house collecting the IRA levy. He was with the Company when they attempted to blow up the **bridge at Farnaseer**, and then at the **burning of O'Brien's house** at

Curraghboy on 14 May that the Volunteers feared was about to be taken over by British Forces

Patrick Feeney took part in the **attack on the RIC patrol at Strokestown** in January 1921

Sheila Feeney of Main Street, Ballaghaderreen was arrested during the Civil War for abetting the IRA. She was taken to Athlone, but released to G. Feeney's "custody" on 7 April 1923

Tom Feeney (Ballyglass, Ballymacurley, Oran) served as Adjutant for "B" Coy. in the 2nd Battalion South Roscommon. Participated in the **Fourmilehouse Ambush**

William Feeney of Glenamaddy, Galway served as the Chief of Armour for No. 2 Brigade, 2nd Western Division

Jim Fehilly (Boyle) North Roscommon Brigade. Present at the **attack on Frenchpark Barracks and Courthouse** 25 June 1921. Helped make the arrangements for **Michael Dockery's escape from Boyle Barracks.** Fehilly was acquainted with the building of bombs, their type and specifications, and knew the people who did it well. In the 1950s he was interviewed by Ernie O'Malley regarding his wartime activities. His words are preserved in the archives of UCD in the Ernie O'Malley Papers

William Feeney (Carramore, Roscommon) 4th Battalion South Roscommon. Knockcroghery Coy. was formed in 1917 with Patrick Kelly serving as Captain. Feeney drilled with the Volunteers, and attended practice battles at Taughmaconnell overseen by Ernie O'Malley in the summer of 1918. Went house to house collecting signatures for the plebiscite for independence and participated in the South Roscommon election of 1918. He was mobilised with his Company for the **attempted attack at Kilmurray Camp** — an action that was cancelled the very night of the proposed action. He, along with the rest of his Company, **guarded the village of Knockcroghery** from reprisal on 15 August 1920 — a reprisal precipitated by British Forces being fired upon on Lough Ree. He, along with eight other men, **held up a goods train at Ballymurray Railway Station,** and he served as an outpost on the Athlone side when an attempt was made to **blow up the bridges at Curry and Ballymurray.** He was also with the Company when an attempt was made to blow up the **bridge at Farnaseer.** He helped block the roads from Athlone to Roscommon, and took part in the **burning of O'Brien's house** in Curraghboy on 14 May that the Volunteers feared was about to be taken over by British Forces

James J. Filan (Mullygollan) Castleplunkett Coy., 2nd Battalion South Roscommon. Participated in the **raid on the military train at Ballymoe** in June 1920, the **attack on Frenchpark Barracks** 2 October 1920, and the **ambush at Southpark, Castlerea** 10 July 1921. He was an officer in charge of signalling. Joined the Free State Army. After the War he emigrated to New South Wales, Australia

Andrew Finan (Lisalway) served as Adjutant of "C" Coy. (Castleplunkett) in the 2nd Battalion South Roscommon, brother of John, and cousin to this author. Participated in the **raid on the military train at Ballymoe** in June 1920, the **attack on Frenchpark Barracks** 2 October 1920, and the **ambush at Southpark, Castlerea** 10 July 1921. When the 2nd Western Division was formed, Andrew was in charge of Accounts and Records. His home served as the headquarters for "C" Company during the post-Truce times. Later in life became a farmer. Died 18 July 1966. Buried Ballintubber Cemetery

Denis Finan (Lisalway) his home served as the headquarters for "C" Company, 3rd Battalion, 2nd Western Division

Father John Finan, the curate of Kilteevan, who acted as the local agent for the loan floated by the Dáil

John Finan (Lisalway) a member of "C" Coy. in the 2nd Battalion South Roscommon, brother of Andrew, and cousin to this author. Took part in the **raid on the military train at Ballymoe** in June 1920, the **attack on Frenchpark Barrack** 2 October 1920, and the **ambush at Southpark, Castlerea** 10 July 1921. The Finan land in Lisalway was a safe haven for Republicans during the Civil War

Michael Finan (Castleplunkett Coy.) 2nd Battalion South Roscommon

Tom Finan (Castleplunkett Coy.) 2nd Battalion South Roscommon

Henry Joe Finlay (Main Street, Roscommon town) 3rd Battalion South Roscommon, a member of the Active Service Unit commanded by Pat Madden. His father was an old Fenian — thus Joe came by his politics genetically! He lived

Andrew Finan, Lisalway, Castlerea
2nd Battalion South Roscommon.

Roscommon in 1903. Finlay's shop was near where the boxes are on the road (left).

PHOTO COURTESY OF ALBERT SIGGINS

in a bungalow a short distance out of town on the Roscommon/Athlone Road. He was also a member of the 1918 Sinn Féin election committee in South Roscommon. Finlay used to meet with Pat Beattie of Rahara and Joe Galvin of Mount Talbot in a pub to discuss IRB business. He was the first South Roscommon Brigade Adjutant. After the Treaty, he joined the Free State Army, but resigned after the 1924 mutiny. In 1923 he was elected to serve as a TD for the Cumann na nGaedheal party, a position he also resigned. He was a publican, whose premises were on Main Street in Roscommon town. Died 1959 and buried in St. Coman's Cemetery

Henry Joe Finlay, Member of Pat Madden's Flying Column in the 3rd Battalion South Roscommon.

PHOTO COURTESY OF ALBERT SIGGINS

Seamus Finn (Rosemount, Co. Westmeath) see Westmeath Volunteers in Surrounding Volunteers section

__ Finn (South Leitrim Battalion) a member of the North Roscommon Active Service Unit

Tom Finn (Loughglynn) in April of 1922, Tom was serving as the 2nd Lieutenant of Loughglynn Coy. in the 1st Battalion South Roscommon. He later emigrated to England

Jack Finnegan (Toberkeagh) Ballintubber Coy., 2nd Battalion South Roscommon. He drilled with his Company, collected funds for the Dáil loan, and served under the command of Captains John Conroy and Alec Kenny. Took part in the **attack on Frenchpark Barracks** 2 October 1920. After the War he emigrated to England

James Finnegan (Finigan) (Cloonfelliv, Castlerea) Trien Coy. in the 1st Battalion South Roscommon

James Finnegan (Keadue, Boyle) arrested during the Civil War on 28 August 1922, and taken to Athlone on 2 September 1922

Joe Finnegan (Clooncunny, Co. Sligo) served as the Quartermaster of the Gurteen Battalion in South Sligo. He was the scout for the **Ambush at Ratra**. His job: to signal the number and formation of the RIC patrol. During the actual fight, he and Jimmy Dwyer became involved in a shootout with two of the constables. In late December 1920 or early 1921, Finnegan took part in an attempt to disarm two RIC constables travelling on the train that had stopped at Kilfree Junction. That same evening, he, Jim Hunt, and Michael Marren attempted to seize the arms of the Bedford Regiment members who were travelling on the train to Ballymote Station. When the three men recognised that they were totally outgunned, they settled for firing on the carriages containing the military. After the War Finnegan became a Superintendent of the Garda Síochána. Died 28 December 1941, and buried in Monasteraden Cemetery, five miles from Ballaghaderreen

Malachy Finnegan (Toberkeagh) Ballintubber Coy., 2nd Battalion South Roscommon. Along with his Company, he spent weeks drilling and collecting funds for the Dáil loan. Took part in the **attack on Frenchpark Barracks** 2 October 1920

Patrick Finnegan originally fought with the East Mayo Brigade. After the War he became a farmer, and lived around Trien. He is buried in Oran cemetery

Patrick Finnegan (Bushfield, Castleplunkett) a member of "B" Coy. in the 2nd Battalion South Roscommon

Martin Finneran (Ballygar Coy.) was considered part of 4th Battalion South Roscommon when the Divisional structure was implemented

Michael Finneran (Moyvannan) Kiltoom Coy. in the 4th Battalion South Roscommon. After the War he became a farmer. Buried in new Kiltoom Cemetery

Woody Finneran (Mount Talbot) served as a cook for the Volunteers in Mount Talbot. He later emigrated

Michael Finnerty (Midgefield, Strokestown) a member of Carniska Coy. in the 3rd Battalion North Roscommon

Frank Fitzgerald (Ballykeevin, Westmeath) served as the Quartermaster of the Athlone Battalion

George Fitzgerald (Ardmullan) 4th Battalion South Roscommon. From 1917-March 1919 did organisational work, drilled with the men, performed scouting duties, paraded with men during a visit to the area by Sean Connolly, participated in police duty during the South Roscommon election and in conjunction with enforcement of Dáil decrees. Fitzgerald served as scout for a raid on the private homes of three men — two of whom had joined and one who was about to join the RIC. Not surprisingly, those men had a change of heart! Fitzgerald raided for arms, his own closet being the first target — he gave up his own gun for the Company's use. He took part in arms raids — twenty were conducted within the Company area, and another fifteen raids were outside the immediate vicinity and performed in conjunction with other Companies of the Battalion. He took part in the **attempted attack on Kilmurray Camp** in June 1920. Prevented jurors from attending the British Courts, and held periodic meetings of Dáil Courts when necessity arose. Manufactured ammunition and constructed dugouts for storage of same. Raided the mails and the premises of a court messenger to the British Courts — whereupon books and documents were seized. Fitzgerald **held up a military dispatcher at Curraghboy** and promptly confiscated his paperwork. He served as a scout on the night of the **attempted ambush of a military lorry at Knockcroghery** in January 1921. The entire Company participated in the arrest of a suspected spy. That man was tried by court-martial and eventually executed — an action which prompted the arrest of ten members of the Company on 5 January 1921 including Fitzgerald. He was beaten and taken to Athlone Barracks and incarcerated in a cell with no bed. He remained there for three months, and was later transferred to Mountjoy, and finally, in the last days of June, he was shipped across the waters to Wormwood Scrubbs and Pentonville Prisons in England. Tom Hales of Cork was his commanding officer in prison. He spent several weeks on hunger strike, and went for months without proper clothes (protesting treatment as a criminal rather than a political prisoner). He was also held in leg irons and a shirtjacket. Released 11 January 1922, whereupon he returned to Curraghboy and rejoined his Company with the intent of resisting the Treaty. He served as the Company O/C, drilled the new recruits, and attempted to organise an ASU intended for the north of Ireland. He raided homes of ex-RIC men and ordered them to leave the country, led **an attack** on Free State forces at **Mount Talbot** in conjunction with the South Roscommon Flying Column and the south Mayo men.

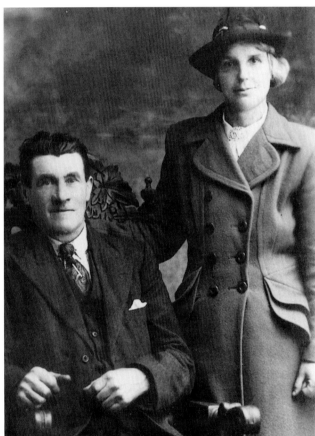

George Fitzgerald and his wife Margaret. He was in the 4th Battalion South Roscommon.

PHOTO COURTESY OF MR. AND MRS. JAMES FITZGERALD SCRINE, RAHARA

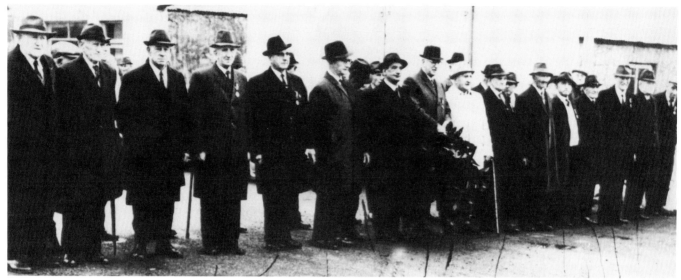

Reunion of Roscommon I. R. A. Men.
Photo taken in Castlerea May 1973
Left to right: Sean Leavy (Scramogue), Bill
Mulligan (Coolnafarna), Michael Boyle
(Lisacul), John Kilmartin (Roscommon), J.
Moran (Roscommon), Michael Keane
(Castlerea), Walter McGuire (Kilglass,
Strokestown), Pat Vaughan (Boston,
Massachusetts formerly of Cloonsuck), Dr.
Michael Delaney (in white coat)
(Castlerea), Stephen Flattery (Aghalour,
Loughglynn), T. Keane (Clooncrim,
Ballinlough), Joe Cullen (with cap in back
row) (Carrick, Ballinlough), Joe Satchwell
(Cloonkeen, Castlerea), Peter Murtagh
(Corlis, Castlerea), Ned Campion
(Ballindrimley, Castlerea) and —.

Others in the background include Peter
Coyne (Clooncagh, Castlerea), Gerald
Fitzgerald (Ballinlough), and Jack Flynn
(Cloonree, Castlerea)

PHOTO COURTESY OF MICHAEL FITZMAURICE

Fitzgerald and two others **derailed a train at Kiltoom**, blocked roads at Whitepark, Curraghboy, Lysterfield, Rahara, and Lisbaun, intending to delay troop movements, and guarded two shopkeepers' premises who were being victimized by local hooligans. Gelignite was his target in the Lecarrow quarry, and cutting telegraph wires became a common activity. During this Civil War period, Fitzgerald worked and travelled with the Anti-Treaty Flying Column in the areas of Castlerea, Galway, Tuam, Dunmore, and Ballygar. He was arrested by the Free State troopers in August 1922, and sent to Athlone on 2 September 1922. Military Archive records indicate that he was transferred to Newbridge and released on 20 December 1923. In his Specimen Pension Form, Fitzgerald claimed that he escaped shortly after his arrest and continued his work of blowing up bridges and road blocking until he was again taken into custody in November 1922. He claimed that he again escaped in January 1923, and for the following months worked with the Flying Column in south Roscommon, Westmeath, Longford, and Galway. He stated that he was finally apprehended in the fall of 1923, and released in January 1924, whereupon he held up a Garda station and was again sentenced to "seven or eight" months for refusing to give bail. Died in April 1983 and buried in St. Coman's Cemetery in Roscommon town

Gerald Fitzgerald (Ballinlough Coy.) 1st Battalion South Roscommon. Participated in the **attempted attack on the Castlerea Station Guard** in July 1920, and the **burning of Ballinlough Barracks** 14 September 1920. During the Truce he attended the Battalion's training camps at Cloonkeen and Kilkerrin specialising in intelligence and signalling work. Gerald was in charge of signalling for the 1st Battalion, No. 2 Brigade in the 2nd Western Division. An Anti-Treatyite, he took part in the **attack at Ballinlough** in July 1922, and the **attack at Castlerea** that same month during the Civil War. He was arrested on 19 July 1922, and sent to Athlone in September. He finished out his time behind bars in Mountjoy, from which he was released on 17 December 1923. He helped to start the Fianna Fáil party in Roscommon, serving as secretary of the *cumann* in Ballinlough in 1928. He was present at 1971 and 1973 reunions of IRA men

John Fitzgerald (Ballinlough Coy.) 1st Battalion South Roscommon, brother of Gerald. John took the Anti-Treaty side during the Civil War. He was captured 28 July 1922, and sent to Athlone two months later. He was transferred to Mountjoy, and finally to the Tintown A, from which he was released on 18 December 1923. He was present at the Pat Glynn Memorial Service at Loughglynn Church in 1970

John Fitzgerald (Monksland) Bealnamullia Coy. in the 3rd Battalion Athlone Brigade. Fitzgerald drilled with his Company, trained to use firearms, took an active part in the General Election of 1918, attended Battalion meetings, worked with the Republican Police force at disputed farmland in Bealnamullia and

Clongowna. He was with a group of Volunteers that seized ammunition from an airplane that made a forced landing at Keelogues in 1919. Took part in the **burning of the Barracks at Bealnamullia**, mobilised for an **attack on Cloonark Barracks,** and **attempted an ambush at Curraghaleen** in October 1920. Near Truce time, he guarded the ASU Headquarters in the area, **destroyed the bridge at Millbrook**, blocked roads at Millbrook and Monksland, harboured and aided escaped prisoners. During the Truce he trained at Greenfield, Donamon, and Falty, in addition to collecting funds to aid the Volunteers and attending the Arbitration Courts. During the Civil War he took the Republican side. He harassed the Free State troopers by blocking roads at Larkfield and Bealnamullia, assisting the Flying Column at blocking a road near Curraghboy, assisting prisoners to escape and join their various units, storing and transporting arms and explosives when and where required by the Flying Column, and serving as an outpost guard for the Column to ensure their safety

Joseph Fitzgerald (Ballinlough Coy.) 1st Battalion South Roscommon. Participated in the **raid for petrol at Ballinlough Station** in June 1920, the **attempted ambush at Coshlieve** in July 1920 and the **attempted attack on the Castlerea Station Guard** that same month, the **burning of Ballinlough Barracks** 14 September 1920, and the **attack at Ballinlough** and **Castlerea** during the Civil War in July 1922. After the War he emigrated to the United States

Michael Fitzgerald (Ballymore, Kiltoom) 4th Battalion South Roscommon. After the War he became a farmer and moved nearer to Roscommon town

__ Fitzgerald (Ballaghaderreen) a surveyor in the British Civil Service, who resigned his position, married — Jordan, and ran an Irish bookshop and newsagency in town. He was one of the first Volunteers in the Ballaghaderreen Coy. in 1915

John Fitzmaurice (Ballygar Coy.) was considered part of 4th Battalion South Roscommon when the Divisional structure was implemented

Owen Fitzmaurice (Ballygar Coy.) when the Divisional Structure was put in place, Ballygar Coy. became part of the 4th Battalion South Roscommon

Bernard Fitzpatrick (Connaught St., Athlone) loaned a small lorry to the escapees from Curragh Prison Camp in September 1921

Eva Fitzpatrick (Connaught St., Athlone) a member of Cumann na mBan

Michael Fitzpatrick (Cloonshee, Ballagh) a member of "E" Coy., 3rd Battalion South Roscommon. Many of the members of the Kilgefin Company participated in the **Fourmilehouse Ambush** on 12 October 1920. Michael was present at the **Scramogue ambush.** Died 1924

Pat Fitzpatrick (Cloonshee, Ballagh) brother of Michael, a member of "E" Coy., 3rd Battalion South Roscommon. Many of the members of the Kilgefin Company participated in the **Fourmilehouse Ambush** on 12 October 1920. Also present at the **Scramogue Ambush** in March of 1921

Dominick Flanagan (Cloonboniffe Coy., Castlerea) 1st Battalion South Roscommon. During the Truce he attended the Company training camp and specialised in intelligence, scouting, and dispatch work

Edward Flanagan (Corracreigh, Killina Coy.) 2nd Battalion North Roscommon. He was one of the first members of the Company when it formed in August of 1917

Bernard Flanagan (Dooneen, Ballinameen, Boyle) Quartermaster for "C" Company in the 1st Battalion North Roscommon. Collected funds for the Company and Brigade and delivered such monies to the Brigade Quartermaster. Present at the **attack on Elphin Barracks** in February 1921, and the **attack on Frenchpark Barracks and Courthouse** in June. He was in charge of arms and ammunition for the area, and made raids in hostile districts — an activity that brought him unwanted attention from the Tans. His house was constantly raided. During the Truce he collected and held safe in an arms dump the guns and ammunition for the Brigade area. He attended training camps at Boyle and Mantua, on which occasions he travelled with bombs and ammunition (for demonstration purposes). During the Civil War his house served as the Republican headquarters, where classes for arms use and engineering took place. He was arrested in September 1922, and held in Boyle Barracks — the first ten nights without bed or bedding. After the War he became a farmer. Died 1959 and buried in Caldra Cemetery

James Flanagan, Rockingham, Boyle

James Flanagan (Rockingham, Boyle) 1st Battalion North Roscommon. Flanagan was taken into the IRB by Alec McCabe in February 1915. He participated in the **Rockingham Raid**, and he was involved in encounters with the RIC in the demesne. Helped in the **escape of Michael Dockery from Boyle Barracks**. A member of the Anti-Treaty Active Service Unit (Flying Column) of North Roscommon during the Civil War. He was arrested on 11 October 1922, and sent to Athlone in November. After the War he continued working at the Rockingham Estate. He also became a farmer. Died 1983 buried Ardcarne Cemetery

James P. Flanagan (Cartron, Mantua, Castlerea) 2nd Battalion North Roscommon. Joined the IRA in early summer 1918, and during the following six months "did not do a lot of good, [but] at least did not do a lot of harm." He left the area in January to enroll in school in Mount Bellew. He returned to North Roscommon from Glasnevin in February, and was sworn into "A" Company in late spring 1920. Did protective duty, enforced the Belfast and RIC boycotts (under arms,) raided for arms, cleaned and transferred guns, collected the IRA levy, enforced the decisions of the Dáil Courts which was, in his own words, "a dirty thankless job." He participated in drills and parades — one of which was held during the daytime "nearly costing the arrest of all sixty men by the Aussies supported by aircraft." Arrested 12 January 1921, and held in Strokestown and Longford Barracks until 25 March. During the Truce he attended Mantua and Cloonshee camps, and was appointed Battalion officer in charge of medical services under Patrick J. O'Dowd (the Brigade Medical Officer). He attended lectures two to three times weekly, and arranged for the Company first aid stations. When the Civil War started, he helped block all the roads in the area to prevent troop movements, and billeted a Flying Column of eighteen men for five days. In October of 1922, he resigned from the IRA "because of disagreement of policy and lack of cohesion..." Flanagan ends his pension application request with the following words: "The above is the story of my activities, ..(long)..perhaps, but accurate just the same. It rests with you Gentlemen either to accept it or reject it, but you would never have got it if you hadn't told me last April or so, that I was not a person to whom the (pension) act applied."

> "..July, August, September (1919) was continuous drilling, meeting, organising, Dáil loan, Sinn Féin and so on, marching with hurleys etc., dispatch work, looking after old guns etc. and all that kind of activity, now I suppose regarded as of no consequence, but serving its purpose then....
>
> ....Reported for duty on my return home from Agricultural College Glasnevin, about February 1920 as a result of police attention following the shooting of a British agent at Hampstead Glasnevin. Why they took a fancy to me I never bothered to ascertain, and reckoning that 'a live mouse was better that a dead lion' I moved on. ..(In late 1920) ...Disrupting communication and blocking roads etc. also became fashionable during this period, and, of course, "A" Coy. had to be in fashion. As a sideline, I prepared Coy. and operational maps, kept various records, — public services, and was generally useful, but others days I regretted all the fine time and energy wasted on a lot of this codology.
>
> ...So the time passes until near the end of June 1922 and the Civil War is on the horizon and eventually breaks out. We get orders to block all the roads to prevent troop movements. We do so, Rathcroghan/Mantua to Boyle Road. Shots are exchanged and we come under indirect fire in a fair sized scrimmage around (Ballinagare). The same happens in Mantua — no one is injured but all the main roads and the intersecting ones are rendered impassable, and now, once again, starts the blessed dispatch work. T'was bad enough before the Truce, but it wouldn't — two weeks or so after the Civil War. Endeavored at start of Civil War to keep medical services and personnel intact and non-combatants, but failed, and thereafter took part with "A" Company in all its activities..."

Snippets from the statement applying for a Military Service Certificate by James P. Flanagan of Mantua

John Flanagan (Cloonelt, Castlerea) 1st Battalion South Roscommon. Joined the Volunteers in the spring or early summer of 1918. Participated in the **destruction of vacant barracks** in 1920, the **raid for petrol at Ballinlough Station** in June 1920, the **attempted attack on the Castlerea Station Guard** in July 1920, the **attack on Frenchpark Barracks 2 October 1920**, the **attempted attacks at Castlerea** and **Frenchpark** in January 1921, and served as part of the covering party for the **attack on the Castlerea military 6 April 1921**. He also participated in the **attempted ambush at Loughglynn,** and the **attempted ambush of an RIC patrol near Ballymoe** — both during the month of April. The following month he was again with the Volunteers at the **attempted ambush at Lisacul** (in conjunction with the East Mayo men)

John Flanagan (Flanaghan) "Sonny" (Taghnoose, Castlerea) Quartermaster for 1st Battalion South Roscommon, brother of Michael and William. Participated in the **destruction of vacant barracks** in 1920, the **capture of arms from the**

Castlerea Barracks in April 1920, the **raid for petrol at Ballinlough Station** in June 1920, the **attempted attack on the Castlerea Station Guard** in July 1920, blocked roads in preparation for the **attack on Frenchpark Barracks** 2 October 1920, the **attempted attacks at Castlerea** and **Frenchpark** in January 1921, and was part of the covering party for the **attack on the military at Castlerea** on 6 April 1921. Participated in the **attempted ambush at Loughglynn**, and the **attempted ambush of an RIC patrol near Ballymoe** in April 1921. During the month of May he joined with other Volunteers in an **attempted ambush at Lisacul** (in conjunction with the East Mayo men). During the Truce he attended the Battalion training camps. He was a member of the Active Service Unit formed in January 1921. After the War he joined the Garda Síochána

John Flanagan (Nadnaveigh, Strokestown) a member of the Cloonfree Coy. in the 3rd Battalion North Roscommon

Joseph Flanagan (Moher, Strokestown) a member of the Carniska Coy., 3rd Battalion North Roscommon

Matt Flanagan (Trien Coy.) 1st Battalion South Roscommon

May Flanagan (Ballaghaderreen) member of the Cumann na mBan

P. Flanagan (Loughglynn Coy.) 1st Battalion South Roscommon. After the War he emigrated to the USA

Patrick Flanagan (Trien Coy.) 1st Battalion South Roscommon

Peter Flanagan (Strokestown) Captain of Cloonfree Company in the 3rd Battalion North Roscommon. Took part in the **attempt to burn down the Bridewell at Strokestown** in July 1920, an action in which he was severely burned. After the War he served as a member of Garda Síochána

Michael Flanagan (Flanaghan) (Taghnoose, Castlerea) 1st Battalion South Roscommon, brother of John and William. Participated in the **destruction of vacant barracks** in 1920, the **raid for petrol at Ballinlough Station** in June 1920, scouted for the **capture of enemy goods at Ballymoe** that same month, the **attempted ambush at Coshlieve** in July 1920, the **attempted attack on the Castlerea Station Guard** in July 1920, the **raid and capture of military equipment at Ballymoe** September 1920, and blocked roads in preparation for the **attack on Frenchpark Barracks** 2 October 1920. The following year he did not cease his activities. He took part in the **attempted attacks at Castlerea** and **Frenchpark** in January 1921, and acted in the covering party for the **attack on the Castlerea military** 6 April 1921. Participated in the **attempted ambush at Loughglynn**, and the **attempted ambush of an RIC patrol near Ballymoe** in April. During the month of May he joined with other Volunteers in an **attempted ambush at Lisacul** (in conjunction with the East Mayo men). During the Truce he attended the Battalion training camps. He was a member of the Active Service Unit formed in January of 1921

Thomas Flanagan (Killina Coy.) 2nd Battalion North Roscommon. He was one of the first members of the Company when it formed in August of 1917

Thomas Flanagan (Ballaghaderreen) one of the first members of the Ballaghaderreen Coy. in the East Mayo Brigade

Thomas Flanagan (Trien Coy.) 1st Battalion South Roscommon

Thomas Flanagan (Ballinagare Coy.) 1st Battalion South Roscommon

William Flanagan (Flanaghan) (Taghnoose, Castlerea) 1st Battalion South Roscommon, brother of John and Michael. Participated in the **destruction of vacant barracks** in 1920, the **raid for petrol at Ballinlough Station, attempted attack on Kilmurray Camp** in June 1920, **capture of enemy stores at Ballymoe** that same month, **attempted attack on the Castlerea Station Guard** in July 1920, **raid and capture of military equipment at Ballymoe** September 1920, and blocked roads in preparation for the **attack on Frenchpark Barracks** 2 October 1920. The next year found him with other Volunteers waiting in ambush at **Castlerea** and **Frenchpark** in January. He also participated in the **attempted ambush at Loughglynn**, and the **attempted ambush of an RIC patrol near Ballymoe** in April 1921. During the month of May he joined with other Volunteers in an **attempted ambush at Lisacul** (in conjunction with the East Mayo men). During the Truce he attended the Battalion training camps. He later emigrated to England

Bernard Joseph Flannery (Ballaghaderreen) 1st Battalion South Roscommon, arrested after the Rising and sent to Lewes Jail on 20th May. Later transferred to His Majesty's accommodations in Glasgow Prison and finally to "the Irish

University," Frongoch. When he returned to Ballaghaderreen Company, he served as an officer

John Flannery (Ballaghaderreen) one of the first members of the Ballaghaderreen Coy. in the East Mayo Brigade. He was arrested during the Civil War on 8 September 1922, and sent to Athlone in November

Martin Flannery (Ballindall) a member of Cloverhill Coy. in the 2nd Battalion South Roscommon

Patrick Flannery (Ballaghaderreen) one of the first members of the Ballaghaderreen Coy. in the East Mayo Brigade

Tom Flannery (Ballaghaderreen) one of the first members of the Ballaghaderreen Coy. in the East Mayo Brigade, brother of Patrick, Joe, and John. He was killed during the Civil War for harbouring Republicans (see box below). His name is inscribed on the tablets in front of the Shankill Monument near Elphin

Stephen Flattery (Aghalour, Loughglynn) a member of Moor Coy. in the 1st Battalion South Roscommon. Participated in the **destruction of vacant barracks** in 1920, the **attempted attack on Kilmurray Military Camp** in June 1920, the **capture of enemy stores at Ballymoe** in June 1920, the **raid and capture of military equipment at Ballymoe** September 1920, the **attack on Frenchpark Barracks** 2 October 1920, the **attempted attacks on Castlerea** and **Frenchpark** in January 1921, and the **ambush at Southpark, Castlerea** 10 July 1921. During the Truce he attended the Battalion and Company training camps. He took the Anti-

---

Particulars of the arrest and subsequent death of Tom Flannery

The night of the 2nd and early in the morning of the 3rd of January 1923 was cold but bright. Brigadier P. Mullooley (Mullooly) was in charge of 25 National troops (Irish Free State troops) who were conducting house searches in Ballaghaderreen. They tried to arrest two young men in Pound Street, one of the men escaped down the back-way opposite Boherbul Road, shots were fired at him but missed. It is thought that the second man, Thomas Flannery, allowed himself to be caught as a "delaying tactic" so that the other man could escape. The first man was a senior officer of "The Irregulars" well known to the Free Staters and a big thorn in their side and someone they would dearly love to capture, so his arrest was to be prevented at all costs, even if it meant that one of his colleagues put his own life in danger, to ensure the continued freedom of this "most wanted" man. Mullooley said afterwards that Flannery had a stone about 2 lb. weight in his hand and had a round of .45 revolver ammunition and a dispatch on his person.

Two soldiers were left in charge of Tom Flannery while the searchers went on in the houses in the area. Privates William Dyer and Patrick J. McDermott were the men left in charge of the prisoner and they said that as they were passing an archway Flannery "twisted around" and ran through into a lane-way, down to what we know as "The Plantation." They shouted "Halt!" and fired shots. By now other soldiers joined them in chasing the prisoner. It is thought that because of it being a bright night that the soldiers saw a silhouette of Tom crossing a ditch. More shots were fired, one of which hit him in the right leg. They then re-arrested him. He had a very serious wound in his thigh and an exit wound. About three quarters of an hour later Brigadier Mullooley saw Tom Flannery wrapped in a blanket and been (being) taken into a house. Flannery asked for a doctor and requested Mullooley to send for Mrs. Cecilia Flannery, his mother. Mullooley said that there was no doctor available but that he would send for a chemist and a medical student. Whether either the chemist or student visited the scene, the writer does not know, but we do know that Mrs. Flannery never got Tom's message from Mullooley and (or) from any of his men.

Tom was then taken to Ballymote, where Mullooley and the National (FS) soldiers were stationed. (National troops did not take up quarters in Ballaghaderreen until the first days of February 1923.)

In Ballymote Tom complained that his leg was very heavy but the pain had eased. He got little or no treatment in Ballymote. That morning (3rd) he was taken to Boyle to be brought to Dublin by train.

Dr. B. Coughlan, Army Doctor, stationed at Boyle said that when Flannery was brought to him at 12:15 p.m. he was in a very weak condition and considered it a case for major surgery. There were no facilities in Boyle to carry out an operation so he said he dressed the wounds and put the leg in splints for his journey to Dublin. Dr. Coughlan said he sent a telegram, shortly after 2 p.m. to Army Medical H.Q. in Dublin requesting an ambulance to meet the train from Boyle to Broadstone Station. Captain L. E. O'Beirne, Boyle escorted Tom to Dublin. He was on a stretcher and had to go in the guard's van of the train.

At Army Headquarters in Dublin, Private J. McKensie A.M.C. received Dr. Coughlan's telegram at 7:10 p.m. As it didn't state in the telegram who the patient was, he assumed it was a wounded soldier. He ordered the ambulance and made arrangements with the Richmond Hospital to receive the patient. The ambulance arrived at the Broadstone (no longer used) at 7:15 p.m. and it was then he discovered that the patient was a prisoner. He cancelled the Richmond Hospital arrangement. He telephoned the Director General of Medical Services and was told to take the prisoner to Portobello Hospital. He did not get to Portobello Hospital until just after 9 p.m., one and three quarters hours after arriving in Dublin, a distance of less than two miles.

At Portobello Barracks Hospital the patient was to be seen by a Dr. Henaghan but he was in bed suffering from influenza. He was told immediately by his orderly that Mr. Flannery had arrived — yet it was after 10 p.m. before he attended to him.

Septic poisoning had by this time set in. Tom Flannery died of his wounds at 7 p.m. on Thursday 4 January 1923.*

Barry Flannery, correspondence with author, 27 November 2004.

Treaty side in the Civil War, and participated in a **sniping attack on Castlerea** Barracks in September 1922, the **attack at Castlerea** in November 1922, and the **burning of the train at Clooncundra** that same month. Stephen attended Pat Glynn's Memorial Service at Loughglynn Church in 1970, and a reunion of former IRA men in 1973. Died 27 March 1978 and buried in Baslick Cemetery

Patrick Fleming (Trien Coy.) 1st Battalion South Roscommon

Henry Flood (Knockhall, Kilglass, Ruskey) a member of the Kilglass Company in the 3rd Battalion North Roscommon

Brian Flynn (Derrinlurg, Mt. Talbot) a member of the Tisrara Company in the 4th Battalion South Roscommon

Charles Flynn (Cuilbalkeen, Ballyfarnon) 4th Battalion North Roscommon. Flynn served as the Adjutant for the Ballyfarnon Company when it was first formed in February 1917

Frank Flynn (Tarmon, Castlerea) Lisliddy Company, 1st Battalion South Roscommon. Participated in the **destruction of vacant barracks** in 1920, the **capture of enemy stores at Ballymoe**, the **attempted attack on Kilmurray Camp** in June 1920, the **raid and capture of military equipment at Ballymoe** September 1920, the **attack on Frenchpark Barracks** 2 October 1920, and the **attack at Southpark, Castlerea** 10 July 1921. Frank's house, haggard, and all his oats were burned by vengeful RIC and Tans the night of the Frenchpark Barracks attack. During the Truce he attended the Company training camp, and specialised in intelligence, scouting, and dispatch work

James Flynn (Derrycarbry) Kilteevan Coy. in the 3rd Battalion South Roscommon, brother of Michael

Jimmy Flynn (Ballyforan) 4th Battalion South Roscommon, brother of Johnny. Later in life became a farmer

John Flynn (Trien Coy.) 1st Battalion South Roscommon

John Flynn (Killina Coy.) 2nd Battalion North Roscommon. He was one of the first members of the Company when it formed in August of 1917. He served as its Quartermaster and its Intelligence Officer

John "Jack" Flynn (Cloonree, Castlerea) 1st Battalion South Roscommon. Participated in the **attack on the Frenchpark RIC Barracks** 2 October 1920, the **attempted attacks on Castlerea** and **Frenchpark** in January 1921, and, during the Civil War, the **attack at Castlerea** in November 1922. Present at Pat Glynn's Memorial Service in 1970

Johnny Flynn (Ballyforan) 4th Battalion South Roscommon. Emigrated to America (1926-1962) but returned to Ireland in his later years

Joseph Flynn is listed in the Department of Defence Records as the 2nd Lieutenant for Ruskey Company in the 3rd Battalion North Roscommon

Joseph Flynn (Coolagarry) a member of Curraghboy Coy. in the 4th Battalion South Roscommon. There were a total of twenty arms raids conducted within the Company area, and another fifteen raids were outside the immediate vicinity and performed in conjunction with other Companies of the Battalion. Flynn took part in those actions as well as a special raid on the premises of a court messenger to

(left to right) Dan O'Rourke, Martin Foley, Willie Crawley (flag bearer), Ned Campion, Jack Flynn (in back), Joe Satchwell, Gerald O'Connor.

the British Courts from which books and documents were seized. Manufactured ammunition, and constructed dugouts for storage of same. The entire Company participated in the arrest and confinement of a suspected spy. That man was tried by court-martial and eventually executed — an action which prompted the arrest of ten members of the Company on 5 January 1921. Flynn escaped that roundup and another one in March

Martin Flynn (Cloonkeen) a member of Trien Coy. in the 1st Battalion South Roscommon. Took part in the **attempted ambush at Coshlieve** in July 1920. Attended Cloonkeen training camp during the Truce, where he specialised in intelligence work

Matthew Flynn (Derrinlurg, Mt. Talbot) Tisrara Coy., 4th Battalion South Roscommon, served as Adjutant for the Company

Michael Flynn (Derrycarbry) Kilteevan Coy., 3rd Battalion South Roscommon, brother of James

Michael Flynn (Carrick, Ballinlough) 1st Battalion South Roscommon. Participated in the **raid for petrol at Ballinlough Station** in June 1920, the **attempted ambush at Coshlieve** in July 1920, and the **burning of the Ballinlough Barracks** 14 September 1920. During the Truce he attended the training camp at Hermitage. He served as the 2nd Lieutenant of Ballinlough Company in April 1922. After the War he emigrated to the United States

Patrick Flynn (Tarmon) Adjutant of the 1st Battalion South Roscommon Brigade. Participated in the **destruction of vacant barracks** in 1920, the **raid on the enemy train at Ballymoe**, and the **attempted attack on Kilmurray Camp** in June 1920, the **attempted attack on the Castlerea Station Guard** in July 1920, the **raid and capture of military equipment at Ballymoe** September 1920, and the **attack on Frenchpark Barracks** 2 October 1920. Flynn was shot in his neighbour John Monaghan's house by the Tans 21 November 1920.* Name inscribed on the Shankill IRA Monument

*_Tarmon Centennial Magazine_, "Tarmon and the War for Independence," by Sister Elizabeth and Maura Flynn, p. 21.

Patrick Flynn (Ballyforan) Captain of Moore Company in the Athlone Brigade, brother of Jimmy and Johnny. Later in life became a farmer. Buried in the Dysart Cemetery

Patrick Flynn (Deerpark, Boyle) Quartermaster for Doon Company in the 1st Battalion North Roscommon

Patrick Flynn (Ballymartin, Strokestown) a member of the Kilglass Company in the 3rd Battalion North Roscommon

Stephen Flynn (Ballyfarnon) served as an officer in the Arigna Flying Column during the Civil War. Upon his arrest, Seamus Cull stepped into his shoes

Thomas Flynn (Grange, Fourmilehouse) was arrested on 11 October 1922, and sent to Athlone a month later. He was soon released on 30 November 1922

Thomas Flynn (Ballymartin, Strokestown) a member of the Kilglass Company in the 3rd Battalion North Roscommon

Thomas Flynn (Castle Street, Roscommon town) 3rd Battalion South Roscommon, served as the 2nd Lieutenant of the Company. After the War he worked in the post office

Flynn's Cottage (Taughmaconnell) was a safe house for men on the run

Edward Foley (Corgarve, Knockcroghery) 4th Battalion South Roscommon. The Company was formed in 1917 with Patrick Kelly serving as Captain. Foley drilled with the Volunteers, and attended practice battles at Taughmaconnell overseen by

The Ballad of Paddy Flynn
by Padraig Hannelly

On a warm bed lay a Rebel sleeping
in Monaghan's house on the Tarmon Road.
T'was early morning, the sun was rising
and his weary body had shed its load.
While on the run he had little comfort
and seldom slept in a feather bed.
He dreamt of Ireland, a land of freedom,
and thoughts of comrades went through his head.

From Castlerea, the Tans and soldiers
set out in lorries to smash their foe.
With hate and vengeance and one ambition —
to raid the houses and burn them low.
They soon invaded this little cottage
and found the Rebel asleep in bed.
They drew their colts and loaded rifles
and in cold blood they shot him dead.

As Paddy Flynn lay still and bleeding,
he had no chance to make a fight.
His aged parents, brave and weeping,
sat and watched this gory sight.
Let those of us who follow after
not forget our men who died
to keep alive the spark of freedom
so that we may hold our heads with pride.

Ernie O'Malley in the summer of 1918. Participated in the South Roscommon election of 1918, and the **burning of Lecarrow Barracks**. Foley was a member of a party of Volunteers that succeeded in raiding sixteen different homes and collecting about as many shotguns. (At one of the homes, he was fired upon and wounded.) Took part in the **attempted attack at Kilmurray Camp** — an action that was cancelled the very night of the proposed action. He, along with the rest of his Company, **guarded the village of Knockcroghery** from reprisal on 15 August 1920 — a reprisal precipitated by British Forces being fired upon on Lough Ree. He also participated in the **attempted ambush of two RIC constables at Lecarrow**. Foley was one of several men who collected a fine from a man accused of shooting at another Volunteer (a potentially dangerous challenge), and was also one of a few men entrusted with important dispatches during this time. He also spent many hours going house to house collecting the IRA levy. Foley served as the outpost on the Roscommon side when an attempt was made to **blow up bridges at Curry and Ballymurray,** and as a sentry at Curry crossing when a **goods train was held up at Ballymurray Railway Station**. He also was present when the Volunteers of the Athlone Brigade **attempted to blow up the railway bridge at Farnaseer**. During the Truce he carried out police work, and was appointed to a special service unit

Martin Foley (born in Clooncoose North) a member of the 1st Battalion South Roscommon, who took over as Captain of the Cloonboniffe Coy. after John Vaughan was shot in June 1921. Participated in the **destruction of vacant barracks** in 1920, the capture of arms from the Castlerea Barracks in April 1920, the **raid for petrol at Ballinlough Station** in June 1920, **capture of enemy stores at Ballymoe** that same month, the **attempted ambush at Coshlieve** in July 1920, the **attempted attack on the Castlerea Station Guard** in July 1920, the **raid and capture of military equipment at Ballymoe** September 1920, and the **attack on Frenchpark Barracks** in October 1920. The new year brought even more action to Foley. He took part in the **attempted attacks at Castlerea** and **Frenchpark** in January 1921, and the **attack on the military at Castlerea** on 6 April 1921. He also participated in the **attempted ambush at Loughglynn**, and the **attempted ambush of an RIC patrol near Ballymoe** in April 1921. During the month of May he joined with other Volunteers in an **attempted ambush at Lisacul** (in conjunction with the East Mayo men). During the Truce he gave full time service in the training camps. When the Western Division was formed, he volunteered to serve with the Castlerea Battalion Flying Column. On 9 February 1922, Foley, along with Commandant Tom Crawley, took over the RIC Barracks at Loughglynn. During the Civil War Foley took the Anti-Treaty side, and participated in the **attack at Ballinagare** in July 1922. After the War he owned his own footwear shop in Castlerea. Foley was present at the Old IRA gathering of men at Pat Glynn's Memorial Service in 1970. He joined his comrade in death ten years later. He is buried in Mount Jerome Cemetery in Dublin

Michael Foley took part in the **attack on the Carrick-on-Shannon Courthouse** in September 1920

Thomas Foley (Ballaghaderreen) took the Anti-Treaty side and was arrested during the Civil War on 14 October 1922 after the battle that ended the life of his Column leader, Seamus Mulrennan. Foley was sent to Athlone a month later. In January of 1923, he was transferred to Mountjoy and later to Tintown II, from which he was released on 18 December 1923

Joseph Forde (Cloonfinglass, Tibohine) Quartermaster for the Fairymount Company in the 1st Battalion North Roscommon

Liam Forde (Lisacul) a native of Ballycastle, Ballina, Co. Mayo. A teacher at Lisacul National School from 1911, he served as a staff officer in the 4th Battalion East Mayo Brigade. During the Civil War he served with Seamus Mulrennan's Flying Column. Forde had an arms dump on his property. He was targeted for arrest by the Free State troopers when they noticed him waiting for engineers at

Martin Foley, 1st Battalion South Roscommon.

PHOTO COURTESY OF PEARSE FOLEY

Ballaghaderreen train station. These were no ordinary engineers — they had been sent from Belfast for mischief against the government troops. He was arrested on 30 August 1922, and taken to Wellington a month later. He was transferred to the Curragh in October, and spent three days in the "Brigadier" hospital before escaping. In 1947 he became the president of the Irish National Teachers Organisation

Pat Forde (Moor Coy.) 1st Battalion South Roscommon, interned for his Sinn Féin sympathies. Participated in the **attempted attack on Kilmurray Military Camp** in June 1920, and the **attack on the Frenchpark Barracks** 2 October 1920

Jack Forsyth (Ballaghaderreen) a member of the East Mayo Brigade, prisoner at Boyle Barracks

James Fox Captain of Athlone Company in the Athlone Battalion. During the Civil War he took the Anti-Treaty side, and participated in the **Ambush at Glasson** in August 1922

Jim Fox a member of "E" Coy., 3rd Battalion South Roscommon. Many, but not all, of the members of the Kilgefin Company participated in the **Fourmilehouse Ambush** on 12 October 1920

Owen Fox (Cloonbard) a member of Moor Coy. in the 1st Battalion South Roscommon. Served from April 1918 to April 1923. Participated in the **attempted attack on Kilmurray Military Camp** in June 1920, the **attack on Frenchpark Barracks** in October 1920, the **attempted attacks at Castlerea** and **Frenchpark** in January 1921, and the **attempted ambush of RIC patrol near Ballymoe** in May 1921. Fox was a member of the ASU from January to July 1921, and served as the 1st Lieutenant of Moor Coy. He attended the Battalion and Company training camps during the Truce. In the Civil War he took the Anti-Treaty side, and participated in the **attack on Free State forces at Castlerea** in November 1922. He later emigrated to New York

Michael Fox (Cloonsellan) a member of the Kilteevan Coy., 3rd Battalion South Roscommon

Pat Fox (Derryconny, Fourmilehouse) a member of the Kilteevan Coy. in the 3rd Battalion South Roscommon. Pat fought with the Anti-Treatyites serving under his Commanding Officer, Matt Davis. He was arrested 28 September 1922, and sent to Athlone in November. He was transferred to Mountjoy in January of 1923

Lily Frayne (Frain) (Drumman More, Ruskey) was a prominent organiser for the Cumann na mBan movement

Michael Frayne (Knockhall, Ruskey) during the Civil War he took the Anti-Treaty side, and was arrested on 8 September 1922 and sent to Athlone

Patrick Frayne (Castleard, Ballaghaderreen) during the Civil War he was arrested on 28 October 1922, and released two months later

Paddy Freehily (Highlake) a member of "B" Coy. in the 2nd Battalion South Roscommon. Before the War he had been a footballer for the county. During the early years of the struggle, he, along with his Company, drilled, collected money for the Dáil loan, assembled first aid supplies, and served under the command of Captain Michael O'Grady. After the War he became a small farmer. Died 1961 and buried in Oran Cemetery

Michael Freeman, Loughglynn, served as a Judge in the Sinn Féin Courts. A blacksmith by trade

Michael Frehill (Castleplunkett Coy.) 2nd Battalion South Roscommon. He drilled with his Company, collected funds for the Dáil loan, and served under the command of Captains Jack Ryan and Luke Raftery

A. G. French (Kilmore) 4th Battalion North Roscommon. Incarcerated during the Civil War in January 1923 at Mountjoy

Allen French (Drumsna) took the Anti-Treaty side during the Civil War, and was arrested on 3 July 1922, and transferred to Athlone in September

Michael Freyne (Cloonmaul, Loughglynn) 1st Battalion South Roscommon. Participated in the **destruction of vacant barracks** in 1920, the **raid for petrol at Ballinlough Station** in June 1920, the **attempted attack on Kilmurray Camp** later that same month, and the **attack on Frenchpark Barracks** 2 October 1920. He

Paddy Freehily, 2nd Battalion South Roscommon.

PHOTO COURTESY OF TONY CONBOY

made a narrow escape when enemy troops surrounded Martin Ganley's house in Cloonmaul, Loughglynn in January 1921. Freyne ran quickly enough and far enough to elude capture. His enthusiasm for the cause was not dampened, however, as he acted in the covering party for the **attack on the military at Castlerea** 7 April 1921, and took part in the **attempted ambush at Loughglynn** that same month. In May he took part in the **attempted ambush at Lisacul** — an action taken in conjunction with the East Mayo men, and the **attempted ambush of RIC patrol near Ballymoe** (also in May). During the Truce he attended the Battalion as well as the Company training camps. After the War he emigrated to the United States of America

Ned Freyne (Cloonmaul, Loughglynn) 1st Battalion South Roscommon. Present at Pat Glynn's Memorial Service in 1970. Buried in Cuiltyboe Cemetery

__ Freyne (Ballymurray) served as a Judge in the local Sinn Féin Court

John Fryar (Cloonybrien, Cootehall) listed in the GHQ papers in the UCD Archives as the Adjutant for Cootehall Company in the 5th Battalion North Roscommon

Michael Fullard (Goff Street, Roscommon town) a member of the Roscommon Coy., 3rd Battalion South Roscommon

Michael Gacquin (Tisrara Coy.) 4th Battalion South Roscommon, served as the Company Captain. He was born in Dysart, but reared by his aunt in Cloghnashade, Mt. Talbot. His home was often searched by the Black and Tans. After the War he emigrated to the United States

Ann Gaffey a member of the Cumann na mBan club of Summerhill

Denis Gacquin (Cornalee, Curraghboy) served as the second Captain of the Dysart Coy., 4th Battalion South Roscommon. Joined the Company in 1917. Attended parades, received instructions under Ernie O'Malley, helped in the 1918 election. He was appointed to help organise the Republican Police, and participated in the work involved in the Belfast boycott. Took part in raiding for arms, procuring ammunition and collecting gelignite for use in the Battalion area, scrutinising the letters obtained by the Curraghboy Coy. left in the Dysart Post Office, raiding the mails between Ballyforan and Four Roads/Dysart and Taughmaconnell, and making dugouts. He helped prepare for an ambush of an RIC lorry which came along the road on the 3rd of each month. That month, however, the lorry failed to appear. Took part in the **ambush at Rahara**. During the Truce he attended the training camps at Ballinaheglish and Donamon. In the Civil War, he, along with his Company, assisted the Anti-Treaty Flying Column, helped escaped prisoners, carried dispatches, and blocked roads at Dysart and Ballyforan on five different occasions

Bernard "Brian" Gaffey (Garrynagowna) 3rd Battalion Athlone Brigade Commanding Officer, charter member of The O'Rahilly Sinn Féin Club of Summerhill. In his home in May 1920, the Volunteers searched through mail that had been taken off trains at Fassaugh Bridge in County Westmeath. In late 1920 and early 1921, his home was the base for the Athlone Flying Column. Gaffey was among the Volunteers who returned to the scene of the **Cornafulla ambush** to rescue the body of James Tormey from the field. Beaten by the Tans in retaliation for that ambush in February 1921. Gaffey aided Pat Mullooly when the latter escaped from Athlone Barracks in May 1921. Gaffey suffered so severely from the Tan thrashing in February that he died of his injuries the following 17 August. He was buried with full military honours in the Old Drum Cemetery. His tombstone proudly displays his association with the Volunteer movement

Edward Gaffey (Correal, Four Roads) a member of the Tisrara Coy. in the 4th Battalion South Roscommon

Jack Gaffey (Drum Coy.) 3rd Battalion Athlone Brigade

John Gaffey (Cregganmeen, Castlerea) a member of Trien Coy., 1st Battalion South Roscommon

Joseph Gaffey (Cornaseer) Kiltoom Coy. in the 4th Battalion South Roscommon. Died in the 1930s

Mary Gaffey a member of the Cumann na mBan of Summerhill

Michael Gaffey (Cregganmeen, Castlerea) a member of Trien Coy., 1st Battalion South Roscommon

Bernard "Brian" Gaffey, Garrynagowna 3rd Battalion Athlone Brigade.

Michael Gaffey Name inscribed on the IRA Athlone Monument

Paddy Gaffey (Garrynagowna) 3rd Battalion Athlone Brigade. He took the Oath of Allegiance to the Sinn Féin Party at the Ardkeenan House, the local Volunteer gathering point.* After the Cornafulla Ambush in February of 1921, he was dragged from his home along with his brother Bernard ("Barney") and beaten senseless. Through Bernard's craftiness (yelling a military-like command from the darkness, which startled the Tans into thinking it was a trap,) Paddy was abandoned by the arresting soldiers and saved from incarceration. After the War he became a farmer. Died 1980s. Buried in Drum Cemetery

*_Drum and Its Hinterland_ by Edward Egan, p. 301.

Thomas Gaffey (Cregganmeen, Castlerea) a member of Trien Coy. in the 1st Battalion South Roscommon

Bartley Gaffney (Cartronaglogh, Keadue) fighting on the Anti-Treaty side during the Civil War, he was arrested on 23 July 1922, and taken to Athlone on 2 September 1922. He was released two months later

At least one of the Gaffney brothers of Keadue was present at the **attack on Drumshanbo Barracks** in September 1922

Michael Gaffney (Keadue) listed in the UCD Archives GHQ papers as the Adjutant for Keadue Company in the 4th Battalion North Roscommon. He was a member of the Anti-Treaty Flying Column during the Civil War. After the War he emigrated to the United States

Patrick Gaffney (Keadue) served as Quartermaster for the Company and later for the 4th Battalion North Roscommon. He was a member of the Anti-Treaty Flying Column during the Civil War. He emigrated to America

Patrick Gaffney (Geevagh, Arigna) Died 1980s. Buried in Geevagh Cemetery

Thomas Gaffney (Derreenatawy, Crossna) 4th Battalion North Roscommon, severely beaten and arrested for murder of RIC constables at Keadue, a "guest" at Boyle Barracks and Mountjoy. Released in January 1922

John T. Gaherty (Clooncrim, Ballinlough) 1st Battalion South Roscommon. Participated in the **burning of the Barracks at Ballinlough** 14 September 1920. During the Truce he attended the Battalion training camp specialising in signalling

Michael Gaherty (Clooncrim, Ballinlough)1st Battalion South Roscommon. Participated in the **burning of the Ballinlough Barracks** 14 September 1920

Miss Gallagher (Gate House, Frenchpark) acted as the intelligence officer for the Anti-Treatyites in the Frenchpark area. She sheltered the men as they travelled from Ballaghaderreen to Frenchpark

Hugh Gallagher (Cartron, Bealnamullia) 3rd Battalion Athlone Brigade. Gallagher drilled with his Company, trained to use firearms, took an active part in the General Election of 1918, attended Battalion meetings, worked with the Republican Police force at disputed farmland in Bealnamullia and Clongowna. He was with a group of Volunteers that seized ammunition from an airplane that made a forced landing at Keelogues in 1919. Took part in the **burning of the Barracks at Bealnamullia**, mobilised for an **attack on Cloonark Barracks**, and **attempted an ambush at Curraghaleen** in October 1920. Near Truce time, he guarded the ASU Headquarters in the area, **destroyed the bridge at Millbrook**, blocked roads at Millbrook and Monksland, harboured and aided escaped prisoners. During the Truce he trained at Greenfield, Donamon, and Falty, in addition to collecting funds to aid the Volunteers and attending the Arbitration Courts. Gallagher took the Anti-Treaty side in the Civil War, and was arrested 29 July 1922, and sent to Athlone on 2 September 1922

Charles Gallagher (Croghanbeg) during the Civil War he took the Anti-Treaty side, and was arrested and sent to Tintown A, where he remained until his release on 19 December 1923

James Gallagher (Kilteevan Coy.) 3rd Battalion South Roscommon

Jim Gallagher (Brusna, Ballaghaderreen) one of the first members of the Ballaghaderreen Coy. in the East Mayo Brigade. He moved to Liverpool, where he was active with the Volunteers. His was the job of procuring explosives from the mining area of St. Helen's

Martin Gallagher (Ruskey) arrested during the Civil War on 8 August 1922, and taken to Athlone on 2 September 1922

Michael Gallagher (Knockhall, Ruskey) a member of the Kilglass Company in the 3rd Battalion North Roscommon

Reilly Gallagher who harboured Toby Scally after the latter had been shot at the Woodlands of Loughglynn

Tom Gallagher (Tibohine) 1st Battalion South Roscommon. After the War he emigrated to America

Tom Gallagher (Carton, Ballaghaderreen) during the Civil War he was arrested on 14 September 1922, and sent to Athlone a month later. By 6 November he had secured his released

Joe Galvin (Cloonlaughnan, Mount Talbot) a member of the IRB, and frequent visitor to Ned Hegarty's house in Ballinaheglish for Brigade meetings. Galvin had stolen rifle ammunition from the Athlone Barracks which was used in the Scramogue Ambush.* In March of 1921, he was arrested, and held in Mount Talbot's post, Roscommon Gaol, and Athlone Barracks before being sent to the Curragh Internment Camp, where he hatched the idea of a tunnel. As recording in *Dublin Made Me*, by C. S. Andrews, "the only tools they had were a metal bar and knives and spoons from the cook-house." In September of 1921, seventy prisoners escaped through that famous "Brady" tunnel (so named because Jim Brady of Arigna was the principal digger). On 7 April 1922, he, along with Tommy Kelly and several other men, broke into Mount Talbot Castle. Galvin saved Mr. Talbot, whose life was threatened by one of the other men. Galvin later joined the Free State Army, and remained an officer until 1929, when he became a social welfare officer in Roscommon. He commanded a column of National soldiers during the Civil War operating out of Castlebar. He served as a training officer for the part time Local Defence Force during World War II. Galvin died in May 1970, and is buried in Four Roads Cemetery

For Ireland and Freedom by Micheál O'Callaghan, p. 81.

Patrick Gallagher (Whitepark) a member of Curraghboy Coy. in the 4th Battalion South Roscommon. From 1917-March 1919 did organisational work, drilled with the men, performed scouting duties, paraded during a visit to the area by Sean Connolly, performed police duty during the South Roscommon election and in conjunction with enforcement of Dáil decrees. Gallagher was one of a group of Volunteers who raided the private homes of three men — two of whom had joined and one who was about to join the RIC. Not surprisingly, these men altered their plans! Gallagher raided for arms, his own closet being the first target — he gave up his own revolver and seven rounds to the Company. Gallagher participated in arms raids — twenty raids were conducted within the Company area, and another fifteen raids were outside the immediate area and performed in conjunction with other Companies of the Battalion. He took part in a special raid for arms in the Kiltoom area. Participated in the attempted **attack on Kilmurray Camp** in June 1920, an operation that was called off the night of the intended attack. Prevented jurors from attending the British Courts, and held periodic meetings of Dáil Courts when necessity arose. Manufactured ammunition and constructed dugouts for storage of same. Raided the mails and the premises of a court messenger to the British Courts — whereupon books and documents were seized. The entire Company participated in the arrest and confinement of a suspected spy. That man was tried by court-martial and eventually executed — an action which prompted the arrest of ten members of the Company on 5 January 1921 including Gallagher. He was beaten and taken to Athlone Barracks and incarcerated in a cell with no bed for three months. Later transferred to Mountjoy and finally, in the last days of June, he was shipped across the waters to Wormwood Scrubbs and Pentonville Prisons in England. Released 11 January 1922 whereupon he returned to Curraghboy and rejoined his Company with the intent of resisting the Treaty. He blocked roads at Whitepark and Bredagh intending to delay National troop movements, guarded two shopkeepers' premises who were being victimised by local hooligans, assisted George Fitzgerald in evading arrest, and generally harassed the Pro-Treaty soldiers. Later in life he became a small farmer and postman. Died 1981 and buried in Rahara Cemetery

PHOTO COURTESY OF DERRY O'DONNELL

Joe Galvin. Cloonlaughnan, Mount Talbot. Member of the IRB.

John Galvin (Cloonlaughnan, Mount Talbot) 4th Battalion South Roscommon, dispatch carrier. In the summer of 1921, Galvin took part in the **ambush at Corofin** in County Clare. In 1927 he emigrated to London, where he worked as a registered nurse. At the time of interview with this author in 1997, John was 104 years old, and the last survivor of the South Roscommon Brigade living in Ireland. His life had nearly crossed over three centuries. He was born before the twentieth century began (15 October 1893,) and died four months before the beginning of the twenty-first (September of 1999). On a follow-up visit in the summer of 1999, John could not easily communicate with this author due to his advanced age. He did, however, utter the three words that had left so indelible a mark on his long and eventful life. The words: "Black and Tans!"

PHOTO COURTESY OF LEW THORNE

John Galvin, 4th Battalion South Roscommon.

Nellie Galvin (Summerhill, Athlone) member of Cumann na mBan

Sean Galvin (Carricknaughton) see Surrounding Volunteers (Westmeath Section) at the end of Roscommon Listing

Bill Ganley, labourer for Mr. Hand in The Hill of Berries, Athlone, arrested with Thomas "Toby" Mannion for suspicious behavior on 17 July 1922, and sent to Athlone in October

Francis Ganley (Newtown, Whitehall) a member of the Tarmonbarry Coy. in the 3rd Battalion North Roscommon. Joined the IRA in 1917, and took part in mail raids, the encounter at **Levins Gate**, the **Tarmonbarry Barracks attack** in 1920, and the **attempted ambush at Ballytoughy** in April 1921. During the Civil War he took the Republican side, and fought against the Free State forces at **Lake Forbes** in March 1923

John "Jack" Ganley (Willsgrove, Ballintubber) 2nd Battalion South Roscommon. During the early years of the struggle, he, along with his Company, drilled, collected money for the Dáil loan, and assembled first aid supplies. Took part in the **attack on the Frenchpark Barracks** 2 October 1920. After the War he farmed his land. Buried in Ballintubber Cemetery

John Ganley (Cloonmaul, Loughglynn) 1st Battalion South Roscommon. Participated in the **destruction of vacant barracks** in 1920, and the **attempted ambush at Lisacul** (in conjunction with the East Mayo men) in May 1921. Took part in the special service training (intelligence, scouting, dispatch work) during the Truce. He later emigrated to America

Martin Ganley (Cloonmaul, Loughglynn) the first 1st Lieutenant of the Company and later its Captain, 1st Battalion South Roscommon, member of the Flying Column. Participated in the **destruction of vacant barracks** in 1920, an

attack on the military at Castlerea in April 1920, the petrol **raid at Ballinlough Station** in June 1920, the **attempted attack on Kilmurray Camp** that same month, the **attempted attack on the Castlerea Station Guard** in July 1920, the **attack on Frenchpark Barracks** 2 October 1920, **attempted ambush at Castlerea** in January 1921, **attempted ambush at Cloonsheever** in March 1921, and acted in the covering party for the **attack on the military in Castlerea** on 6 April 1921. Also in April he joined his comrades in an **attempted ambush at Loughglynn**, and the **attempted ambush of RIC patrol near Ballymoe**. In May 1921 he was part of the **ambush party** laying in wait **at Lisacul** (an action taken in conjunction with the East Mayo men). In January of 1921, his home had been the meeting place for men on the Brigade staff and officers of the 3rd Battalion South, who were in the area to help reorganise the men and light a fire of enthusiasm under them. Ganley's home was surrounded by the Crown Forces, and when the Volunteers within succeeded in escaping, a frustrated group of Tans burned Ganley's house to the ground. They even tossed the hay in the haggard. Before they torched the house, the Tans were careful enough to confiscate the overcoats and bicycles the Volunteers had left behind. Martin was shot by the Tans at the Vaughan house in the village of Cloonsuck in June 1921. He was saved from being killed by an RIC sergeant who intentionally misidentified him. He was sentenced to fifteen years penal servitude and sent to Mountjoy. Ganly was released in January 1922. A stonemason by trade. Buried Kilruddane Cemetery near Loughglynn

Martin Ganly (noted by an arrow) attended a memorial service for a fallen colleague. Other Volunteers also attended, including (left to right) Ned Campion (partially obscured), Tom Waldron (in back), Joe Satchwell, Jack Flynn, and Martin Foley (in back). Others present included Thomas Roddy, and Dan O'Rourke.

PHOTO COURTESY OF JOE AND KATHLEEN HEVICAN

Bernard "Barney" "Paddy" Gannon, Captain of Drumlion Company of the 5th Battalion North Roscommon, who took Jack Glancy into the organisation in late 1917 or early 1918. The Company was small — only fourteen strong, but very secretive. Participated in the **attempted attack on the Carrick-on-Shannon Station Guard** in September 1918. He was a member of the Arigna Flying

Column, and arrested after the **Keadue Ambush** in March 1921, and taken to Boyle Barracks. Later he was transferred to Mountjoy

Charlie Gannon (East Mayo Brigade) was active with Volunteers in the Liverpool area in 1920-21. Arrested 11 May 1923 for Anti-Treaty activities

Francis Gannon (Kilbarry, Ruskey) served as the 1st Lieutenant of Tarmonbarry Company in the 3rd Battalion North Roscommon. He was a member of the ASU

The Gannons who lived at the foot of Slieve Bawn, outside the village of Ashbrook, were an example of the ordinary people's determination and sacrifice. That family fed their own pig to the lads who stayed there on the run.* It was a supreme effort on their part

Ciaran Leavy, son of Sean, interview by author, Scramogue, 29 June 2002.

John Gannon (Cloonfower) a member of the Tarmonbarry Coy. of the 3rd Battalion North Roscommon

Joseph Gannon (Rodeen, Hillstreet, Drumsna) 2nd Battalion North Roscommon. Served as the 1st Lieutenant for Aughrim Company

Jim Gannon (Cloontuskert Coy.) 3rd Battalion South Roscommon, injured in the **Lanesboro-Roscommon Landmine Operation**, and as a result was taken to Incheneagh Island in Lough Ree. His injuries were so severe that only through the dedication of Dr. Dudley Forde of Strokestown, Dr. Charles Kelly of Roscommon town, and Nurse Fayne who tended to him did Jim ever survive the explosion. Later in life he became a small farmer, and worked for the County Council. Died in the 1980s, and reportedly is buried in Ballyhaunis Cemetery

Martin Gannon (Ballintise) 2nd Lieutenant of the Dunmore Coy. in the Glenamaddy Battalion. Although located in Co. Galway, this Battalion was incorporated into No. 2 Brigade, 2nd Western Division with Gerald O'Connor, former O/C of the 1st Battalion South Roscommon, serving as Brigade Commandant. Gannon's home was used as the headquarters of "A" Company

Patrick Joseph Gannon (Carrow, Elphin) 2nd Battalion North Roscommon. Joined the IRA in 1917, did dispatch work, blocked roads in preparation for various engagements, and participated in the **attack on the Elphin police patrol** in January 1921

Frank Gardiner (Ruane, Kilglass, Strokestown) a member of the Kilglass Company in the 3rd Battalion North Roscommon

Michael Gardiner (Ruane, Kilglass, Strokestown) Kilglass Company in the 3rd Battalion North Roscommon

Thomas Gardiner (Ruane, Kilglass, Strokestown) also a member of the Kilglass Company in the 3rd Battalion North Roscommon

J. Garrahan (Lisnerfoll, Ballaghaderreen) during the Civil War he was arrested, and sent to Tintown in February 1923

(See Geoghegan)

Jim Garrahan transported to Portnahinch by sidecar the three injured Volunteers of the Lanesboro mine explosion

Joe Garrahan (Cloonbony, Fourmilehouse) 3rd Battalion South Roscommon. He later emigrated to Providence, Rhode Island

Michael Garrahan (Cloonbony, Fourmilehouse) 3rd Battalion South Roscommon. He too later emigrated to Providence, Rhode Island

Patrick Garrahan took part in the **attack on the RIC patrol at Strokestown** in January 1921

Peter Garrahan (Gortlustia, Scramogue) 2nd Lieutenant of "C" Company in the 3rd Battalion North Roscommon

Eugene Garrick (Aghagad, Fuerty) a member of "D" Coy. in the 2nd Battalion South Roscommon as of July 1922. Brother of John. He had not been a member the year before

John Garrick (Aghagad, Fuerty) a member of "D" Coy. in the 2nd Battalion South Roscommon as of July 1922. He too was a recent member of the Volunteers

Luke Garvin (Cloontogher, Kilteevan) 3rd Battalion South Roscommon

William Garvin (Cloontogher, Kilteevan) 3rd Battalion South Roscommon

John Gately (Feevagh) 4th Battalion South Roscommon. Captain of Dysart Company. Joined the Company in 1917. Attended parades, received instructions under Ernie O'Malley, helped in the 1918 election. He was appointed to work with the Republican Police, participated in the work involved in the Belfast boycott, and acted as a summons server for the Courts. Took part in raiding for arms, raided the mails between Ballyforan and Thomas Street, blocked roads between Ballyforan and Four Roads/Dysart and Taughmaconnell, made dugouts, and fashioned ammunition. He helped prepare for an ambush of an RIC lorry which came along the road on the 3rd of each month. That month, however, the lorry failed to appear. Took part in the **ambush at Rahara**. During the Truce he attended officers' training classes at Rahara three evenings a week, and the Battalion camp at Ballygar. During the Civil War, he, along with other members of his Company, assisted the Anti-Treaty Flying Column, helped escaped prisoners, carried dispatches, and blocked roads at Dysart and Ballyforan on five different occasions. After the War he became a farmer. Died in 1975 and is buried in Dysart Cemetery

John Gately (Bredagh) served as the 1st Lieutenant of Dysart Coy. in the 4th Battalion South Roscommon. Joined the Company in 1917. Attended parades, received instructions under Ernie O'Malley, helped in the 1918 election. He was appointed to work with the Republican Police, and served notice to all traders in the Company area to boycott Belfast goods. Gately raided the mails between Ballyforan and Thomas Street, blocked roads between Ballyforan and Four Roads/Dysart and Taughmaconnell, made dugouts, and fashioned ammunition. He helped prepare for an ambush of an RIC lorry which came by the road on the 3rd of each month. That month, however, the lorry failed to appear. During the Truce he attended officer training classes at Rahara three evenings a week, and the camps at Ballinaheglish and Donamon. During the Civil War, he, along with his Company, assisted the Anti-Treaty Flying Column, helped escaped prisoners, carried dispatches, and blocked roads at Dysart and Ballyforan on five different occasions

Peter Gately (Gatley) (Monksland, Athlone) during the Civil War he was arrested on 10 July 1922, and sent to Athlone in September. He was transferred to the Curragh, where he spent some time in the hospital before being released on 18 December 1923

Thomas Gately (Feevagh, Dysart) 4th Battalion South Roscommon, served as the 2nd Lieutenant for the Dysart Company, which he joined in 1917. Attended parades, received instructions under Ernie O'Malley, helped in the 1918 election. He was appointed to work with the Republican Police, took part in raiding for arms, blocked roads between Ballyforan and Four Roads/Dysart and Taughmaconnell, made dugouts, and fashioned ammunition. He also was with the ambush party of an RIC lorry which came along the road on the 3rd of each month. That month, however, plans were foiled because the lorry failed to appear. During the Truce he attended officers' training classes at Rahara three evenings a week, the Battalion training camp at Ballygar for two weeks, and the training camps at Ballinaheglish and Donamon. During the Civil War, he, along with his Company, assisted the Anti-Treaty Flying Column, helped escaped prisoners, carried dispatches, and blocked roads at Dysart and Ballyforan on several occasions. After the War he emigrated to America

Bernard Gavigan (Erra, Clondra, Co. Longford) a member of the IRA from 1917. Participated in the **attack on the Tarmonbarry patrol** on 5 January 1921, served as an outpost at **Scramogue**, and returned to **Tarmonbarry** in July for another go at the barracks

Annie Joe Gavigan (Ballylugnagon, Boyle) member of the Cumann na mBan

May Gavigan (Ballylugnagon, Boyle) sister of Annie Joe, member of the Cumann na mBan

Thomas Gavigan (Ballylugnagon, Boyle) First Battalion North Roscommon

George Gavin (Abbeytown, Roscommon) member of the 1918 Sinn Féin election committee in South Roscommon

James Gavin (Leitrim Rd., Carrick-on-Shannon) during the Civil War he was arrested on 3 August 1922, and sent to Athlone two months later

Thomas Gately, 4th Battalion South Roscommon.

PHOTO COURTESY OF MICHAEL BREHENY

John Gavin (Kiltoom Coy.) 4th Battalion South Roscommon, served as the 2nd Lieutenant of the Company

Kate Gavin (Clonown, Athlone) helped prepared the body of James Tormey for burial after he was killed at the Cornafulla Ambush

Tim Gavin (Racecourse, Ballymurray) 4th Battalion South Roscommon, a member of the Knockcroghery Company as of 11 July 1921

Matt Gaynor (Roscommon Coy.) 3rd Battalion South Roscommon

Patrick J. Gaynor (Clooneen, Kilglass, Strokestown) a member of the Kilglass Company in the 3rd Battalion North Roscommon

Michael Gearty (Corramagrine, Whitehall) a member of the Tarmonbarry Coy. 3rd Battalion North Roscommon since 1917. Took part in the **Levins Gate** encounter with the RIC, the **attempted attack in Tarmonbarry** in December 1920, served as an outpost for the **Scramogue Ambush,** and lay in ambush on several occasions

Rev. Roderick Gearty, P.P. (Strokestown) active supporter in the Count Plunkett bye election of 1917. In 1921 he made a speech in support of the Treaty from the steps of the church

William J. Gearty a member of the Tarmonbarry Coy., 3rd Battalion North Roscommon. After the War he emigrated to Chicago

Michael Genoy (Kilbride Coy.) 3rd Battalion South Roscommon

Patrick Genoy When the Western Division was formed, Patrick was a member of "B" Company, 2nd Battalion South Roscommon. He later emigrated to England

Mrs. Geoghan of the 3rd Battalion North Roscommon area, a member of Cumann na mBan

Denis Geoghegan (Derreen, Strokestown) a member of the Carniska Coy., 3rd Battalion North Roscommon

Michael Geoghegan, a member of the IRB, was the driver of the train for the **attack on Ballaghaderreen Barracks** on 17 May 1921

Patrick Geoghegan (Gerraghan) (Ballaghaderreen) arrested during the Civil War on the Anti-Treaty side, taken to Tintown 20 February 1923

John Joe Geoghegan (Carrownadurly, Thomas Street) Dysart Coy., 4th Battalion South Roscommon. Joined the Company in 1917. Attended parades, received instructions under Ernie O'Malley, helped in the 1918 election. He was appointed to work with the Republican Police. Took part in raiding for arms, and a raid on the home of an RIC man, who was warned to quit his job. The Volunteers also destroyed all of the papers in the constable's possession at that time. Geoghegan was part of an attempted ambush of an RIC lorry which came along the road on the 3rd of each month. That month, however, the lorry failed to appear. During the Truce he attended training camps at Ballinaheglish and Donamon. Throughout the months of the Civil War, he, along with his Company, assisted the Anti-Treaty Flying Column, helped escaped prisoners, carried dispatches, and blocked roads at Dysart and Ballyforan

Theobald Geoghegan (Carrownadurly, Thomas Street) Dysart Coy., 4th Battalion South Roscommon, brother of John Joe. Joined the Company in 1917. Attended parades, received instructions under Ernie O'Malley, helped in the 1918 election. He was appointed to work with the Republican Police. Geoghegan was a member of the ambush party that lay in wait for an RIC lorry which usually came along the road on the 3rd of each month. That month, however, the lorry took another route. During the Truce he attended training camps at Ballinaheglish and Donamon. Throughout the months of the Civil War, he, along with his Company, assisted the Anti-Treaty Flying Column, helped escaped prisoners, carried dispatches, and blocked roads at Dysart and Ballyforan on five different occasions

David Geraghty served as the 2nd Lieutenant of Polredmond Coy. in the Glenamaddy Battalion. Although located in Co. Galway, this Battalion was incorporated into No. 2 Brigade, 2nd Western Division with Gerald O'Connor, former O/C of the 1st Battalion South Roscommon, serving as the Brigade Commandant. Geraghty later joined the Garda Síochána, and was stationed in Gorey, Co. Wexford

George Geraghty (Goff Street, Roscommon) 3rd Battalion South Roscommon. In the aftermath of the Rising, he was sent to Wakefield Prison on the 2nd of June 1916. Later he was transferred to Frongoch internment camp in Wales, where he was elected the Provost Marshall for the south camp. He was arrested again and jailed in Usk Prison in Wales, from which he participated in a daring escape in 1919 along with Frank Shouldice of Ballaghaderreen.* On 3 November 1920, his premises were burned by the RIC. During the Civil War he followed the lead of the 3rd Battalion South commanders and joined the Free State Army, serving as an officer. He also served on the Roscommon County Council from 1920-25. Died in 1952, and buried in St. Coman's Cemetery

*<u>Frongoch</u> by Sean O'Mahony, p. 63 and 102.

Jack Geraghty (Roscommon) 3rd Batt. South Roscommon. He became a "guest" at Wakefield Prison in 1916

James Geraghty (Bracknagh, Knockcroghery) 4th Battalion South Roscommon. The Company was formed in 1917 with Patrick Kelly serving as Captain. He drilled with the Volunteers, and attended the sham battles at Taughmaconnell overseen by Ernie O'Malley in the summer of 1918. Participated in the South Roscommon election of 1918. Geraghty served as a member of the armed escort for bank officials who were taking large sums of money to the Knockcroghery fairs. He manned the barricades set up on the Roscommon/Athlone Road for the **burning of Lecarrow**

George Geraghty and his wife. Geraghty was a member of Roscommon Company in the 3rd Battalion South.

Barracks. Geraghty and others of his Company participated in an **attempted ambush at Clooncraff** — an operation under the command of Pat Madden. He, along with the rest of his Company, **guarded the village of Knockcroghery** from reprisal on 15 August 1920 — a reprisal precipitated by British Forces being fired upon on Lough Ree. He, and eight other Volunteers, **stopped a goods train at Ballymurray Railway Station** and removed over twenty bags of mail, which were subsequently censored. Geraghty and his Company attempted an **ambush at Scrine** — an action that did not take place owing to the fact that the lorry did not return by the expected route. He was present at the attempt to **blow up the Curry and Ballymurray bridges**, and the **bridge at Farnaseer**. He blocked roads, and took part in the **burning of a house in Milltown, Curraghboy** (O'Brien's) — a home the Volunteers thought was soon to be occupied by British Forces. During the Truce he was assigned to a special service unit, and also carried out police work for the Sinn Féin Courts

Michael Geraghty (Kilcash, Rahara) 4th Battalion South Roscommon. The Knockcroghery Company to which Geraghty belonged was formed in 1917 with Patrick Kelly serving as Captain. Geraghty drilled with the Volunteers, and attended the sham battles at Taughmaconnell overseen by Ernie O'Malley in the summer of 1918. Participated in the South Roscommon election of 1918. Geraghty served as a member of the armed escort for bank officials who were taking large sums of money to the Knockcroghery fairs. He, along with the rest of his Company, **guarded the village of Knockcroghery** from reprisal on 15 August 1920 — a reprisal precipitated by British Forces being fired upon on Lough Ree. He also collected the IRA levy from the local people — a fund that provided purchasing power for equipment. Michael not only collected money but gelignite as well. He **raided the Lecarrow quarry** along with William Fallon of Kilcash, Rahara, and Pat Breheny of Sandfield, who would transport the material to the manufacturing site, where Pat and his brother John Breheny joined by Pat Fallon would construct the mines

Michael Geraghty (Corramagrine, Whitehall) during the Civil War he took the Anti-Treaty side, and was arrested on 21 July 1922, and sent to Athlone in September

Tom Geraghty served as 1st Lieutenant of Clonberne Coy. in the Glenamaddy Battalion. Although located in Co. Galway, this Battalion was incorporated into No. 2 Brigade of the 2nd Western Division with Gerald O'Connor, former O/C of 1st Battalion South Roscommon, serving as Brigade Commandant. His Company consisted of forty-five members in April of 1922

Patrick Geveran (Monksland) served with the Bealnamullia Coy., 3rd Battalion Athlone Brigade during the Civil War. He harassed the Free State troopers by blocking roads at Larkfield and Bealnamullia, assisting the Flying Column at blocking a road near Curraghboy, assisting prisoners to escape and join their various units, storing and transporting arms and explosives when and where required by the Flying Column, and serving as an outpost guard for the Column to ensure their safety

Tom Geraghty (Kilcash, Rahara) 4th Battalion South Roscommon. The Knockcroghery Company to which Geraghty belonged was formed in 1917 with Patrick Kelly serving as Captain. Geraghty drilled with the Volunteers, and attended the sham battles at Taughmaconnell overseen by Ernie O'Malley in the summer of 1918. Participated in the South Roscommon election of 1918. Geraghty served as a scout on the Athlone side when the **Lecarrow Barracks** was burned. He also raided two hostile houses in Rahara in which one of the Volunteers was wounded. Took part in the **attempt on Kilmurray camp** — an action that was canceled because a spy had alerted the British garrison there. He, along with the rest of his Company, **guarded the village of Knockcroghery** from reprisal on 15 August 1920. He was present in January 1921 at the **attempted attack in Knockcroghery** on a party of military about eighteen strong. In quieter times, he blocked roads, and was part of an **attack party at Scrine** — an attack that did not occur because the lorries took another route. His Company also attempted to **blow up bridges at Curry and Ballymurray**

Anne Gibbons (Clooncagh, Strokestown) mother of Volunteers Michael and Pat. The women would assemble in the kitchen of her safe house while the lads were in the loft. One day the Tans burst into the room, and threatened her with a gun to her neck. They demanded to know where her sons were hiding. She refused to tell them. They shot the dog, and set the hay ricks on fire, but her sons were safe!

Elizabeth (Lizette) Gibbons (Clooncagh, Strokestown) sister of Michael and Pat. Dispatch carrier. She would hide the messages in her shoe or shopping bag and meet Molly Parker on the road. The Parkers' home was a ramblin' house, whose owners had no known connection with the Volunteer movement. It made a safe house for meetings! Died 13 January 1993, and buried in Kilgefin Cemetery

Helen Gibbons (Ballincurry, Kilgefin) member of Cumann na mBan. Later emigrated to the United States of America

John Gibbons (Roscommon) 3rd Battalion South Roscommon. In the aftermath of the Rising, he was sent to Wakefield Prison on the 2nd of June 1916. Later he was transferred to Frongoch internment camp in Wales. On 3 November 1920, his premises as well as those of George Geraghty were burned by the RIC

John Gibbons (Aghamuck, Ballagh) Officer in the 3rd Battalion South Roscommon, a member of Pat Madden's Flying Column, brother of Josie, and an IRB man. While attending a fair in Lanesboro, he drank a few too many Guinnesses and signed his name to a British Army enlistment form. While serving in WWI in France, he was coming across "no man's land" and found a wounded man lying at his feet. He reached down, turned him over, and picked up the person only to discover it was his brother! He returned to Ireland during the Troubles, where he served with the Kilgefin Company. Many, but not all, of the members of that Company participated in the **Fourmilehouse Ambush** on 12 October 1920. Gibbons served as the lookout when Mr. Walpole of Castlenode (a local land owner) was being forced to relinquish his car "for the good of the cause" in November 1920. Present at the **attack on Elphin Barracks** in February 1921, and the **ambush at Scramogue**, where, because he was such an excellent marksman, he was positioned in the loopholed house with a clear view of the road. Gibbons served on the Brigade Staff, which often met at Naughton's cottage in Ballinaheglish. After a meeting on 21 March 1921 (two days before Scramogue),

Elizabeth Gibbons Collins.

he, a brother of John Conroy, Jim Quigley, and John Breheny of Knockcroghery were hiding out at Jim Quigley's in Rathconnor. A knock was heard on the door of the main house, but the four men were sleeping in an out building. After ten minutes of flurry in the main house, the Tans left empty handed, unknowingly leaving behind four Volunteers who thereafter caused them many a headache. After the War, Gibbons moved to Clooneybeirne, Tulsk. Died 10 March 1978, and is buried in Kilcooley Cemetery

Joseph "Josie" Gibbons (Aghamuck, Ballagh) Kilgefin Coy., 3rd Battalion South Roscommon, a member of Pat Madden's Flying Column, and brother of John. A former British soldier, whose expertise was invaluable when he focused his gun sights on ridding Ireland of the rule of Britannia. He had been wounded in the back during World War I. Many, but not all, of the members of the Kilgefin Company participated in the **Fourmilehouse Ambush** on 12 October 1920. After the Tan War he became a farmer. Died in 1950, and buried in Kilgefin Cemetery

Michael Gibbons (Clooncagh, Strokestown) a member of "E" Coy., 3rd Battalion South Roscommon. A member of Pat Madden's Flying Column. Many, but not all, of the members of the Kilgefin Company participated in the **Fourmilehouse Ambush** on 12 October 1920. Michael took part in the **attack on the Strokestown patrol** in January 1921. Was also present at the **Scramogue Ambush**, after which he saw action near the Shannon where he handed over a prisoner to Martin Fallon. After the War he became a farmer. Died in 1 June 1957, and is buried in Kilgefin Cemetery

Pat Gibbons (Clooncagh, Strokestown) a member of "E" Coy., 3rd Battalion South Roscommon, brother of Elizabeth and Michael. Pat joined the IRA when he was sixteen years old. Many, but not all, of the members of the Kilgefin Company participated in the **Fourmilehouse Ambush** on 12 October 1920. After the **Scramogue Ambush** he hid in a stream until daybreak, when he ventured to Mrs. Carroll's safe house, where he delighted in a cup of hot tea. He later became a farmer. Pat died 13 September 1987, and is buried in Scramogue Cemetery

Tom Gibbons (Ballaghaderreen) part of the East Mayo Brigade. Fought with men from Galway

Daniel Giblin (Ballymoylin, Kilglass, Strokestown) is listed in official Department of Defence papers as the 1st Lieutenant of Kilglass Company in the 3rd Battalion North Roscommon as of 1 July 1922. Took part in the **raid on the land at Clooneenhartland** in the spring of 1919, the **encounter with an RIC patrol at Ballyfeeny School** in April 1920, and the **attack near Ruskey village** on 5 July 1921

Edward "Ned" Giblin (Knockhall, Ruskey) a member of the Kilglass Company in the 3rd Battalion North Roscommon

Hugh Giblin (Drumman Beg, Ruskey) 3rd Battalion North Roscommon. He was a member of the Active Service Unit (Flying Column) of North Roscommon. He was arrested on 13 August 1922, and sent to Athlone in November. He finally obtained his release on 18 January 1924. After the War he emigrated to the United States

Patrick Giblin (Drumman Beg, Ruskey) during the Civil War he took the Anti-Treaty side, and was arrested on 5 September 1922, and sent to Athlone two months later

William, Pat, or Michael Gilchrist from Ballycummin, Kilmore. Participated in the **attempted attack on the Carrick-on-Shannon Station Guard** *in September 1918*

Michael Gilhooly Quartermaster for Arigna Company in the 4th Battalion North Roscommon. During the Civil War he became the Captain of the Company, which took a strong Anti-Treaty stand. After the War he moved to Kilsyth, Scotland

(left to right) Michael Collins, J. Sweeney from Longford, and Michael Gibbons.

PHOTO COURTESY OF EILEEN BANAHAN
PHOTO RESTORATION BY DAVE DERBY

Patrick Gilhooly (Arigna) was arrested during the Civil War as an Anti-Treatyite, and taken to Athlone. He was released on 10 March 1923

John Gill (Corlara, Kilmore) 2nd Lieutenant of Kilmore Company in the 5th Battalion North Roscommon. Took part in the **seizure of a tender loaded with rations at Drumsna Railway Station** in June 1920. He was arrested for this mischief, but released six week later

Michael Gill (Cloonycarron More, Strokestown) a member of the Carniska Coy., 3rd Battalion North Roscommon. Joined the Volunteers in 1917, and helped with both the North Roscommon and South Longford elections. Paraded with other Volunteers, raided for arms, made dugouts, performed dispatch work, and helped enforce the Belfast boycott. Gill blocked roads for the **Fourmilehouse Ambush** in October 1920, took part in the **confrontation at Castlenode** in November 1920, the **ambush at Strokestown** on 6 January 1921, and the **Scramogue Ambush** on 23 March. After the War he became a farmer. Died 1969

Patrick Gill (Kilmore) killed by a Tan on 11 September 1920 while walking through the village of Drumsna on his way to a funeral. According to the Volunteer Witness Statement of Charles Pinkman, Intelligence Officer for Leitrim, Gill was a Volunteer.* Patrick is buried in Jamestown Cemetery. Name inscribed on the Elphin IRA monument *p. 12.

(back row) James Owens, William Collins, Jim Kearns, Redmond Hayden.
(front row) Luke Owens and Michael Gill.

PHOTO COURTESY OF HENRY OWENS
PHOTO RESTORATION BY LEW THORNE

Tom Gill (Castleplunkett Coy.) 2nd Battalion South Roscommon

Joseph Gillane (Araghty, Athleague) 3rd Battalion South Roscommon

Bernard Gilleran (Kinitty, Kilbride) 3rd Battalion South Roscommon

James Gilleran (Clooncraff, Kilteevan) 3rd Battalion South Roscommon. He was incarcerated in Mountjoy, and moved to Tintown on 20 February 1923

John Joe Gilleran (Clooncraff, Kilteevan) 3rd Battalion South Roscommon. Barges loaded with porter used to sail up the Shannon River three times a week in order to deliver the mighty spirits up the canal to Lanesboro, Tarmon, and Carrick-on-Shannon. While hiding from the Tans on Quaker Island, John Joe was lucky enough to partake of some of this refreshment. He was heard to remark, "If this be war, I hope it goes on forever!" His luck ran out, however, when, on 18 August 1922, he was arrested during the Civil War, and taken to Athlone in September

Michael Gilleran (Kinitty, Kilbride) 3rd Battalion South Roscommon

Lizzie Gillhooly (Drumagissaun, Kilglass) member of Cumann na mBan

Nellie Gillhooly (Drumagissaun, Kilglass area) member of Cumann na mBan

Edward Gilligan (Glanduff, Kiltoom) a member of St. John's Coy. in the 4th Battalion South Roscommon. Gilligan drilled with other Volunteers two nights a week — Tuesdays and Thursdays, and worked in the 1918 election. He and his Company, under the command of Captain Patrick Grady, participated in the sham battles for training purposes under Ernie O'Malley at Lysterfield, Taughmaconnell, and Churchboro. He collected monies for the Defence Fund, the IRA levy, as well as more lethal gelignite for the making of bombs. He, along with a dozen other men from the Company, took part in the **attempted ambush at Clooncraff** under the command of Pat Madden, and the **attempted ambush at Kilmurray Military Camp** in June 1920. He was involved in several raiding parties, one of which occurred the same night that Joseph Kearney was severely wounded in the stomach at Feehily's. He also raided the mails several times when trains were stopped at Kiltoom. He was with his Company when **O'Brien's residence was burned down**

Lizzie and Nellie Gillhooly.

PHOTO COURTESY OF LIAM COYLE

— an action deemed necessary because the house was thought to be soon taken over by the British

Martin Gilligan (Larkeel, Frenchpark) during the Civil War he took the Anti-Treaty side, and was arrested on 1 September 1922, and sent to Athlone

Martin Gilligan (Hazelbrook House, Ballygalda, Roscommon) a member of the Athleague Coy. in the 3rd Battalion South Roscommon. He participated in the **burning of Athleague and Beechwood Barracks** at Easter time 1920, **raided the Roscommon income tax office**, and stood guard in Roscommon town after the Fourmilehouse Ambush. He joined the National Army in March 1922 with the rank of 1st Lieutenant. He left the Army two years later because "he'd be fighting against friends." Gilligan emigrated to the United States in 1928, where he worked as a bus engine mechanic for Third Avenue Buses-Surface Transportation in New York. Died 1981

Thomas Gilligan (Kilbride Coy.) 3rd Battalion South Roscommon

John Gillooly (Crunkill, Ruskey) a member of the Kilglass Company in the 3rd Battalion North Roscommon

Patrick Gillooly (Abbey Street, Roscommon town), member of the 1918 Sinn Féin Council in South Roscommon, Secretary to the County Council, and later appointed permanent County Secretary, a position he held until 1944

"Sonny" Gillooly (Crunkill, Ruskey) a member of the Kilglass Company in the 3rd Battalion North Roscommon

Thomas Gillooly (Clooncashel Beg, Kilgefin) 3rd Battalion South Roscommon

John Gilmartin (Knockcroghery area) a former member of the British Army. Though not a Volunteer himself, he acted as drill instructor in 1917 for the Company, and taught semaphore and Morse code signalling. When the RIC began taking too much notice of his activities, he "made a graceful exit"

Patrick Gilmartin (Frenchpark) during the Civil War he took the Anti-Treaty side, and was arrested and sent to Athlone on 7 March 1923

Thomas Gilmore (Ballygar) arrested and sent to Tintown in February 1923

Owen Gilroy fought with the Arigna Flying Column during the Civil War, and was arrested in Drumsna in early September 1923

Thomas Gilroy (Jamestown, South Leitrim) participated in the **attack on the courthouse in Carrick-on-Shannon** in September 1920, and the **robbery of the Dublin-Sligo mail train**. He and Bernard Sweeney of the South Leitrim Brigade travelled by car to Strokestown in October in 1920, where they met with the Sharkey sisters, who gave them two rifles and some ammunition. Gilroy was a member of the Arigna Flying Column during the Civil War. Captured 29 May 1923

Laurence Ginnell a resident of London, formerly of Delvin, Westmeath, who ran as the Sinn Féin candidate. He was Joint Treasurer with Cosgrave of Sinn Féin in 1917. He became the Minister for Propaganda in the first Dáil 1919. The next year, he travelled to America, where he gave testimony to the American Commission on Conditions in Ireland, a panel of Congressmen and community leaders investigating the current brutality by Crown Forces in Ireland. Ginnell was a man well versed in his country's history and financial matters, who was not to be silenced by the Commission's interviewers

Jack Glancy (Drumlion) Captain of the Drumlion Coy. A member of the IRB, who also served as Adjutant of 5th Battalion (Carrick-on-Shannon) North as well as Adjutant of the North Roscommon Brigade. Glancy accompanied Sean Connolly in the autumn of 1920 when the latter came to Roscommon to organise the Companies. He was sent to Fitzgeralds of Brunswick St. in Dublin to obtain the batteries for the explosive detonators, which he shipped to Drumsna for the mines that would play a crucial role in the attack on Elphin Barracks. Participated

Patrick Gillooly.

in the **burning of wagons at Carrick-on-Shannon Railway Station** in November 1920. He also led the attack party in the **attempted assault on the Ruskey Barracks** on 7 January 1921 and again a week later. He blocked roads on the Boyle/Carrick-on-Shannon Road in preparation for the **attack on Elphin Barracks**. Arrested at Larry Joe O'Hara's cottage in Cootehall along with Michael Dockery on 16 May 1921, and charged with the murder of the policemen during the Keadue ambush (although he was not there). Glancy and Dockery were both given a terrible beating. Glancy was held prisoner at Boyle Barracks and Mountjoy. He was released in January of 1922. Glancy was interviewed by Ernie O'Malley in the 1950s, and his words are included in the O'Malley collection in the archives at University College Dublin

Michael Glancy (Chapel Street, Elphin) 2nd Battalion North Roscommon. Raided for arms, encountered and dueled with RIC patrols, and took part in the **attack on Boyle** in July 1922. He was a member of the Anti-Treaty Active Service Unit (Flying Column) of North Roscommon. He was arrested during the Civil War, and sent to Mountjoy on 10 January 1923

Patrick Glancy (Chapel Street, Elphin) listed in the GHQ papers in the UCD Archives as the Adjutant of the 1st Battalion North Roscommon under O/C Pat Brennan. He also served in that position when the Western Division was formed. Took part in the **Hopkins Raid** in Strokestown in early 1921, carried dispatches, and was involved with skirmishes with the RIC. Helped with the **escape of Michael Dockery from Boyle Barracks**. He was a member of the Active Service Unit (Flying Column) of North Roscommon during the Civil War, and participated in the **attacks at Boyle and Caldra**

Peter Glancy (a native of Corry, Aughrim, he resided at Enfield, Ballintubber) Captain of "F" Coy. in the 2nd Battalion South. Took part in the **raid on the military train at Ballymoe** in June 1920. In reprisal, the British Forces burned the thatched roof of his house. A stonemason by trade, he was the foreman on the building of the church in Ballintubber, which was completed in 1899

Peter Glancy, Enfield, Ballintubber, 2nd Battalion South Roscommon.

PHOTO COURTESY OF SEAN RAFTERY

Tom Glancy (Lisadorn, Elphin) 2nd Battalion North Roscommon. A member of the Aughrim Coy. Arrested in January 1921, and sentenced to two years for possession of arms. He was a tailor by trade. Buried in the old Aughrim Cemetery

Denis Glennon (Turlagh, Rahara) 4th Battalion South Roscommon

Michael Glavey (Clooncan, Ballinlough) 1st Battalion South Roscommon. Born in 1884, Michael was a tailor by trade before becoming interested in the national struggle. He participated in the **attempted attack on the Castlerea Station Guard** in July 1920, the **burning of the Loughglynn Barracks**, and the **burning of Ballinlough Barracks** on 14 September 1920 in which he lost his life. He is buried in the Ballyhaunis Cemetery. His name is inscribed on the tablets in front of the Shankill Monument near Elphin. The Gorthaganny GAA Club is also named after him

James Glennon When the Western Division was formed, James was a member of "B" Coy., 2nd Battalion South Roscommon. He later emigrated to England

John Glennon (Captain) of the Polredmond Company. The Company included sections of Galway, and became part of No. 2 Brigade when the 2nd Western Division was formed. Gerald O'Conner served as Brigade Commandant. Glennon joined the Free State Army

John Glennon (Turlagh, Rahara) 4th Battalion South Roscommon

Patrick Glennon (Policeman) for the Glenamaddy Battalion. When the Divisional structure for the Army was implemented throughout the country, this Battalion became part of No. 2 Brigade, 2nd Western Division under the command of Brigade O/C, Gerald O'Connor of Lisacul

Thomas Glennon Director of Training for the 1st Battalion in No. 2 Brigade in the 2nd Western Division. Although located in Galway, this Battalion was incorporated into No. 2 Brigade under the command of Gerald O'Connor. He had formerly been the Commanding Officer of the 1st Battalion South Roscommon Brigade

South Roscommon Volunteers in 1970 at the 50th Anniversary commemorating the death of Commandant Pat Glynn

Left to right: Back row: Jack Cassidy (St. Patrick's St., Castlerea), Gerald Fitzgerald (Ballinlough), Michael Keane (Castlerea), Michael Kenny (Erritt, Gortaganny), Patrick Beatty (Lisliddy Cross), John Kilmartin (Roscommon town)

Middle row: Jack Flynn (Cloonree), Stephen Flattery (Aghalour, Loughglynn), John Fitzgerald (Ballinlough), Tom Waldron (Ballindrimley, Castlerea), Martin Foley (Clooncoose North), Michael Thomas Hevican (Derrinea, Carrowbehy), Tom Fahy (Cloonkeen), Gerald O'Connor (Loughglynn), William Delaney (Cloonbunny, Loughglynn), Owen Mahon (Southpark), Ned Freyne (Cloonmaul) and —

Front row: Tom Satchwell (Cloonbard, Kilmurray), Tom Vaughan (Cloonsuck, Cloonboniffe), Pete Shannon (Aghaderry, Loughglynn), Martin Ganley (Cloonmaul), Joe Satchwell (Termon Beg), Ned Campion (Ballindrimley, Castlerea), Andy Keavney (Aghadrestan, Loughglynn), Pat Roddy (Drumnalasson, Ballaghaderreen), Peter Murtagh (Corlis, Castleplunkett), Patrick Vaughan (Boston, Mass.— formerly of Cloonsuck, Cloonboniffe)

Thomas Glennon (Milltown, Curraghboy) Bealnamulla Coy. in the 3rd Battalion Athlone Brigade. Glennon drilled with his Company, trained to use firearms, took an active part in the General Election of 1918, attended Battalion meetings, and worked with the Republican Police force at disputed farmland in Bealnamullia and Clongowna. He was with a group of Volunteers that seized ammunition from an airplane that made a forced landing at Keelogues in 1919. Took part in the **burning of the Barracks at Bealnamullia**, mobilised for **an attack on Cloonark Barracks**, and **attempted an ambush at Curraghaleen** in October 1920. Near Truce time he guarded the ASU Headquarters in the area, **destroyed the bridge at Millbrook**, blocked roads at Millbrook and Monksland, harboured and aided escaped prisoners. During the Truce he trained at Greenfield, Donamon, and Falty, in addition to collecting funds to aid the Volunteers and attending the Arbitration Courts

Ann Glynn (Aghaderry, Loughglynn) sister of Pat, who ran to summon Curate Geraghty in order to administer last rites to Stephen McDermott and Sean Bergin after the shooting in the **Woodlands of Loughglynn**

J. Glynn (Crossna) Quartermaster of the 4th Battalion North Roscommon

James Glynn (Deerpark, Ballinagare) 1st Battalion South Roscommon. Participated in the **attack on Frenchpark Barracks** 2 October 1920

Rev. John Joseph Glynn (a native of Carrigallen, Co. Leitrim) was educated at the Marist Brothers school and Summerhill College, Sligo, before going to Maynooth College. He held curacies at Scramogue (1912-1914), and Roscommon town

(1914-1915), Elphin (1915-1918), and at Drumlion in Croghan parish (1918-1922). While stationed in Drumlion, he served on the Sinn Féin executive in North Roscommon, and attended a Sinn Féin meeting in Croghan in late 1920. He was arrested, tried by court-martial, and interned in Boyle Barracks for several weeks. After the War his ministries included Lisacul (1922-1929), Castlerea (1929-1942), and Ardcarne parish Cootehall, Boyle (1942-his death in 1967)*

*Information supplied by Michael Lennon, editor

John Glynn (Trien Coy.) 1st Battalion South Roscommon

John Glynn (Castleplunkett Coy.) 2nd Battalion South Roscommon. He lived in Kilmurray. On one occasion, he was particularly sought after by the authorities, and was sheltered by Peter Dowd, cousin to this author, in Knockalegen

Pat Glynn (Ballinagare Coy.) 1st Battalion South Roscommon

Terence Glynn born at Derrygirraun, Ardcarne. Glynn entered business in Ballyfarnon and Longford before transferring to Dublin. There he became involved with the Dublin Volunteers. He was part of an ambush party that engaged the enemy in Harcourt Street. Glynn was killed by the premature explosion of a grenade on 9 April 1921, and buried Ardcarne cemetery

Tom Glynn (Castleplunkett) 2nd Battalion South Roscommon. Used to hide out in the loft of Johnny Dowd's house. Emigrated to America, but later in life returned to the Boyle area

Rev. Fr. Godwin, C.C. (curate at Arigna) active Sinn Féin supporter of the bye election of 1917, who harboured George Plunkett while the latter was recruiting for the Volunteers in Arigna

Thomas Goggins (native of Bridge Street, Strokestown) a member of Tulsk Company. Joined the Volunteers in April 1917 in the Killina unit under Captain Conry. In April 1918, he was appointed to help start a Company in Tulsk parish under Capt. Michael Neary. He raided for arms, did dispatch work, and secured accommodations for the Flying Columns who came through the area. Raided the mail car between Elphin and Castlerea several times, on one occasion capturing correspondence "going to the Castle which led to the capture of two spies, one of whom afterwards escaped and was followed and shot in Belfast."* Blocked

A childhood photo of Pat Glynn.
PHOTO COURTESY OF PATRICIA ENGLERT

Pat Glynn (Aghaderry, Loughglynn) O/C of the 1st Battalion South Roscommon. Participated in the **destruction of vacant barracks** in 1920, the **raid for petrol at Ballinlough Station** in June 1920, the **attempted attack at Kilmurray Camp** that same month, and the **attempted attack on the Castlerea Station Guard** in July 1920. Glynn was tragically killed in the **burning of Ballinlough Barracks** 14 September 1920. Buried Kilruddane cemetery. On the 50th anniversary of his death, a Memorial Service was held at Loughglynn Church, where many of the surviving members of the South Roscommon Brigade posed for a group photo (see opposite page), one of the few in existence. His war mementos were given to the Roscommon Museum in 1995 by his niece in America. Name inscribed on the tablets in front of the IRA monument at Elphin

Excerpted from a speech given by Andy Keavney on 22 November 1970 to Members of the Old IRA at Tully's Hotel in Castlerea

I knew Pat Glynn from cradle to grave. I knew him as a small boy going to school. He was a shy but very thoughtful little lad. And I remember quite well, of course, he was always the best in the class. He did not want any praise for it because he was a very retiring kind of boy — thoughtful, industrious and hardworking — a lad that liked to do everything well, and that followed him through life. No matter what he turned to, he wanted the job to be done well. And when he joined the Volunteers, he went into them heart and soul....I will just give you one instance. He called into me one night — oh, a very, very wet night it was, and he told me he was going further.

I asked him, "Was there anything in particular on? Was it a big thing?"

He said, "No." He was going to review a Company and I said, "if that is all you are doing tonight, you had better stay home and not go out in this weather."

"Well," he said, "I told them I would be there and I am going."

When he was coming back about three hours later, he called in again. He was wet to the skin, surely. As he came in he smiled and said "t'was worth it all because there was not a single one absent tonight."

Now I might mention that Company as we have some of them here still — that was Moor Company.

Pat was a kind of fellow who inspired confidence, and he did inspire every member of the Volunteers in the whole area at the time. They would follow him anywhere, they would do anything that he wanted, but he was always the first himself to do everything — that was Pat Glynn.

roads for the **attack on a police patrol in Elphin** (5 January 1921), and the **attack on Elphin Barracks** on 11 February 1921. He was arrested shortly afterwards and taken to Roscommon Barracks and Athlone, where he was incarcerated until the Truce

Thomas Groggins, pension application, p. 2. Pat Brennan Papers, private collection

John Goode (Monksland, Athlone) arrested during the Civil War on 10 July 1922, and interned in Athlone two months later

Tom Gorman (Ballaghaderreen) one of the first members of the Ballaghaderreen Coy. in the East Mayo Brigade

Johnnie Gormley (Elphin Street, Boyle) 1st Battalion North Roscommon, a member of the Volunteers since before the Rising. Joined the Free State Army. During the 1940s he was the postman in Boyle, and in 1947, the year of the great blizzard, conveniently got himself stranded in the Rushe family home in Cloonloo. After much searching, he was finally located with "tea mug in hand" sporting a Cheshire cat grin!

Tom Gormley (Carrowkeel, Elphin) 2nd Battalion North Roscommon. Joined the IRA in July 1917, and in July of 1919 was appointed the 2nd Lieutenant for his Company. Present at the **burning of Hillstreet Barracks** 12 May 1920, **ambush of police patrol** between Elphin and Strokestown in July 1920, **attempted ambush at Smithhill** in October 1920, and the **ambush at Elphin** 5 January 1921. Two days later, his father's house was set afire by the Crown Forces and badly damaged. That action did not deter him. He continued to perform police duty, assist at Sinn Féin Courts, and collect arms. Gormley used to visit the Boyle Hospital for business reasons. After the gallons of petrol were stolen from the Boyle Railway Station in May 1920 and stored in the hospital morgue, Gormley used to retrieve the petrol as needed by taking it in his cart covered by an old sack. He passed by the Auxies guard each time, but he was never suspected. He was arrested 25 January 1921, and beaten by Sergeant Forde in retaliation for attacks on police forces in Elphin. He was interned in Athlone, later incarcerated in the Curragh, and released 20 November 1921

John Gorwin (Frenchpark) during the Civil War he was sent to Tintown on 20 February 1923

James Grady a member of "B" Coy., 2nd Battalion South Roscommon. After the War he emigrated to the United States of America

James Grady (Ballaghaderreen) during the Civil War he was arrested on 8 August, and incarcerated in Athlone on 2 September 1922

James Grady (Rinnagan, St. John's, Lecarrow) 4th Battalion South Roscommon. Grady drilled with other Volunteers two nights a week — Tuesdays and Thursdays, blocked roads, and constructed dugouts

John Grady (Ballymacurley, Oran) a member of "B" Coy. in the 2nd Battalion South Roscommon

John Grady (Ballaghaderreen) one of the first members of the Ballaghaderreen Coy. in the East Mayo Brigade. In 1919 he was arrested for helping to lead the local Ballaghaderreen Company in a march on the big ranches. At the time, he operated a small printing plant. He was sent to Brixton Prison

John Grady (Trien Coy.) 1st Battalion South Roscommon. Took part in the **attempted ambush at Coshlieve** in July 1920, and in the **attempted ambush of an RIC patrol near Ballymoe** in May 1921. Attended the Hermitage and Castlerea Barracks training camps during the Truce. Later emigrated to England

Joseph Grady (Islands, Donamon) a member of "E" Coy. of the 2nd Battalion South Roscommon. Took part in the **raid on the military train at Ballymoe** in June 1920

Martin Grady a member of the Castleplunkett Coy. in the 2nd Battalion South Roscommon

Michael Grady (Ballyglass, Ballinagare) a member of "C" Coy. in the 2nd Battalion South Roscommon. Took part in the **raid on the military train at Ballymoe** in June 1920, the **attack on Frenchpark Barrack** 2 October 1920, and the **ambush at Southpark, Castlerea** 10 July 1921

Michael Grady of Ballymacurley (see O'Grady)

Patrick Grady (Rinnagan, Kiltoom) 4th Battalion South Roscommon. Served as the original 1st Lieutenant, and then was promoted to Captain of the St. John's Company. Grady drilled the Volunteers two nights a week — Tuesdays and Thursdays. He worked with the Republican Courts and in the 1918 election. He commanded his Company at the sham battles for training purposes in the summer of 1918 under Ernie O'Malley at Lysterfield, Taughmaconnell, and Churchboro. He took part in the **attempted ambush at Kilmurray Military Camp** in June 1920, and **raided the mails** when the train was stopped **at Kiltoom**. He blocked roads and constructed dugouts for Company use. Grady participated with the Knockcroghery Company and raided a Unionist home in which a bayonet and sword were seized. During the Truce he attended the Battalion training camp at Drinaun, Ballygar

Patrick Grady (Islands, Donamon) a member of "E" Coy. of the 2nd Battalion South Roscommon

Thomas Grady (Rinnagan, St. John's, Lecarrow) 4th Battalion South Roscommon. Thomas Grady drilled with the Volunteers two nights a week — Tuesdays and Thursdays. He also worked in the 1918 election, blocked roads, constructed dugouts, and collected gelignite on occasion

Thomas Grady (Trien Coy.) 1st Battalion South Roscommon

John Graham (Kilbride Coy.) 3rd Battalion South Roscommon

Joseph Graham (Kilbride Coy.) 3rd Battalion South Roscommon

John Grealy Quartermaster of Ballyhaunis Battalion in the East Mayo Brigade. Took the Anti-Treaty side in the Civil War, and initially commanded Boyle Barracks. Arrested in October 1922, and endured a hunger strike

Michael Grealy (Curraghroe, Strokestown) was killed by the Free State troops in Mullingar Barracks in 1922. His body was not released for burial until 1924. Grealy lies in Cloontuskert Cemetery. His name is inscribed on the tablets in front of the Shankill Monument near Elphin

John Green (Greene) a member of Cloonfad Coy. in the 1st Battalion South Roscommon. Took part in the **disarming of a Black and Tan at Cloonfad** in May 1921. By July 1921, he was living in England

Michael Greene (Ruane, Kilglass, Strokestown) Captain of Kilglass Company in the 3rd Battalion North Roscommon. Michael was the Head Centre of the IRB in the area long before the Kilglass Volunteer Company was formed in 1917. He worked with Ernie O'Malley when the latter came to the county to organise Companies. Seamus O'Ryan, the Brigade O/C at that time, appointed Michael to train and drill many Volunteer Companies in the surrounding area. He was a "jack-of-all-trades" within the Volunteer movement — cutting roads, raiding the mails, pilfering the Kilglass and Strokestown Post Offices, preventing men from joining the RIC by raiding their homes, raiding shops that stocked Belfast goods. He also relieved the Northern Bank of some of its funds. Due to his activities, his own home was constantly invaded by the Crown Forces, which forced him to go on the run. Michael was with a group of Volunteers who **attempted to invade Walpole's land at Clooneenhartland, Strokestown** in January 1919 and drive the cattle from it. He was also in charge of a group of men who were guarding a Republican Court in April 1920 at Kilglass Chapel when a party of RIC from Ruskey happened by and twenty minutes worth of shots were exchanged.* He took time to serve on the Roscommon County Council from 1920-25 as a member of Sinn Féin (which was a dangerous job during those times). Greene was present at the **Castlenode shootout** in November 1920, **Scramogue Ambush**, and **attack near Ruskey village** on 5 July 1921. During the Truce he attended the training camps for three months. Taking the Anti-Treaty position, he took part in the **Battle of Boyle** on 1 July 1922, the **attack at Ruskey** in January of 1923, and again two months later at the same village. From July 1922 until the cease-fire, he was on the run constantly, but continued to serve as Captain of the Kilglass Company. During that time he helped oversee the many dugouts in the Kilglass area where the ASU was safely looked after. After the War he became a farmer. He was again elected to the Roscommon County Council for Fianna Fáil in 1934 and served until 1942. Due to the irreparable damage done to his health during

Michael Greene, Kilglass Company

the course of the Wars, he died prematurely in 1943, and is buried in Kilglass graveyard

Michael Greene, written statement, private collection

Patrick Greene (Curraghroe Coy.) 3rd Battalion North Roscommon. Joined the Volunteers in 1917. He took part in the election in North Roscommon, and the election in South Longford at Longford town, Killashee, Clondra, and Lanesboro. Greene collected arms, and participated in organising the boycott of the RIC in the area — taking part in the **raid on RIC recruits at Cloontuskert** 10 March 1920. Greene was a Justice under the Republican Courts, and when on court duty, he sometimes had to walk up to twelve miles to attend. In Greene's own words, "when the parish Justices were being appointed, all appointments were made from IRA men that were on the run, and we can claim to have never let a case into the British Courts during that period."* He took part in the **burning of Scramogue Barracks**, stood guard in the Kilgefin area on the evening of the Fourmilehouse ambush, and blocked roads for the **Scramogue Ambush.** He took part in the **attack on the RIC Barracks at Tarmonbarry** on 2 July 1921

Pension statement of Patrick Greene, Pat Brennan Papers, private collection

Thomas Greene (Curraghroe Coy.) 3rd Battalion North Roscommon. Took part in the **attack on the RIC patrol at Strokestown** in January 1921, and the **attack at Tarmonbarry** 2 July 1921. He later emigrated to Uddington, South Lanarkshire, Scotland

John Greg (Trien Coy.) 1st Battalion South Roscommon

John Grenham (Cloonellan, Drum) 3rd Battalion Athlone Brigade

Thomas Griffin (Athleague Coy.) 3rd Battalion South Roscommon

Thomas Griffin (Rahara Coy.) 4th Battalion South Roscommon, served as the 2nd Lieutenant of the Company

Patrick Groarke (Carrowkeel, Rahara, Athleague) 4th Battalion South Roscommon. After the War he became the secretary of the Fianna Fáil cumann in South Roscommon in 1928

Michael Grogan (Carrowbaun, Castleplunkett) 2nd Battalion South Roscommon

Tom Grogan (Carrowbaun, Castleplunkett) 2nd Battalion South Roscommon

Pat Guckian (Carrick-on-Shannon) an officer in the South Leitrim Brigade headed by Bernard Sweeney, took part in the **attack on the courthouse in Carrick-on-Shannon** in September 1920, and **attacks at Garadice, Eslin, Fenagh** and other Leitrim localities

Guihen Brothers (Arigna) 4th Battalion North Roscommon, fought with the Arigna Flying Column during the Civil War

Michael Gunn (Tullyvarran, Curraghroe) listed in the GHQ papers in the UCD Archives as the Quartermaster of "B" Company (Curraghroe) in the 3rd Battalion North Roscommon. Took part in the **attack on the RIC patrol at Tarmonbarry** in January 1921, **Scramogue Ambush**, and the **attack on the Tarmonbarry Barracks** 2 July 1921

Patrick James Gunn (Curraghroe) 3rd Battalion North Roscommon. Joined the Volunteers in 1917. He participated in the **attack on the Tarmonbarry patrol** in January 1921, **Scramogue Ambush**, and the **attack on the Tarmonbarry Barracks** in July 1922. He was a member of the Active Service Unit

Patrick Gunning (Trien Coy.) 1st Battalion South Roscommon. He served as the 2nd Lieutenant of Trien Coy. in April 1922. Gunning participated in the **attempted ambush at Coshlieve** in July 1920, and the **attempted ambush of an RIC patrol near Ballymoe** in May 1921. He scouted and blocked roads on the day Inspector King was shot in Castlerea. Attended the Cloonkeen training camp during the Truce, where he specialised in scouting. Later emigrated to the United States of America, but he returned to Ireland and was present at an Old IRA meeting in 1971

Thomas Haire (Castlerea) in charge of signalling for No. 2 Brigade in the 2nd Western Division

Ann Halligan (Carricknaughton, Drum, Athlone) member of the Summerhill Cumann na mBan, sister of Tom

Nan Halligan, sister of Ann, also a member of Cumann na mBan

Ann Halligan, Summerhill Cumann na mBan

Tom Halligan (Bogganfin, Athlone) first Company Captain in the 3rd Battalion Athlone Brigade. In 1919 he took an oath of allegiance to the Republic at the Summerhill Convent in the presence of Rev. Fr. Keane. Halligan was a member of the party of Volunteers who trailed Captain Tully of Athlone through town on several occasions—locating him once with a group of other officers. Not knowing exactly which man was Tully, the Volunteers let all the RIC pass them by. Halligan, his cousin Tom Halligan, Jim Tormey, and George Adamson were in the ambush party at the **Cornafulla Ambush**. He was a member of the Athlone Flying Column. Halligan took the Anti-Treaty side during the Civil War, and, among other activities, blocked roads at Cranagh Mills, where he and his cohorts were surprised by Free State troopers, who opened fire on them with a machine gun. After the War he became a farmer. Died 1986, and buried in Kiltoom Cemetery

Tom Halligan (Carricknaughton, Drum, Athlone) 3rd Battalion Athlone Brigade. He also took an oath in 1919 to the Republic in the presence of Rev. Fr. Keane, the chaplain of Summerhill Convent. Present at the **Cornafulla Ambush**

James Hanagan (Henegan) (Spa, Boyle) 1st Battalion North Roscommon. A member of the IRB. Took part in the **Rockingham Raid**, the encounter with an RIC man in the demesne, and the **escape of Michael Dockery from Boyle Barracks**. He was a member of the Active Service Unit (Flying Column) during the Civil War

Dan Hanley ("Handy") (Mongagh, Scramogue) 3rd Battalion North Roscommon, joined the Curraghroe Company in 1917. Hanley was active with the Volunteers during the elections in North and South Roscommon as well as in the Longford election of 1917. He collected arms and **raided potential RIC recruits at Cloontuskert** on 10 March 1920. Hanley took part in the **burning of the Cullagh (Scramogue) Barracks**, and stood guard duty at Kilgefin on the night after the Fourmilehouse ambush, took part in the **attack on Tarmonbarry Barracks** in January 1921, and was blocking roads the morning of **Scramogue Ambush**. He also took part in the **attack on the RIC Barracks in Tarmonbarry** in July 1921. He was a member of the North Roscommon Flying Column during the War for Independence under the command of Martin Fallon

James Hanley (Hanily) (Ballinagare Coy.) 1st Battalion South Roscommon. Participated in enforcing the Belfast boycott, and the **attack on Frenchpark Barracks** 2 October 1920. After the War he emigrated to the United States, but later returned to Ireland

James Hanley (Clooneen, Kilglass, Strokestown) 3rd Battalion North Roscommon. Took part in the **Clooneenhartland cattle raid** in the spring of 1919, during which he was wounded. He was arrested, and sentenced to probation for two years. In November 1920 he participated in the **Castlenode shootout**. By March of 1921, he was cutting trees and blocking roads in preparation for the **Ambush at Scramogue**

John Hanley (Ballygar Coy.) which was considered part of 4th Battalion South Roscommon when the Divisional structure was implemented. He fought with the Anti-Treaty men during the Civil War, and was arrested on 8 July 1922, and sent to Athlone two months later

John Hanley (Captain) of Kilcroan Coy. in the Glenamaddy Battalion. Although located in Co. Galway, this Battalion was incorporated into No. 2 Brigade, 2nd Western Division with Gerald O'Connor, former O/C of the 1st Battalion South Roscommon, serving as Brigade Commandant. His Company numbered sixty-two after the Truce

John Hanley (Ruskey) a leading Sinn Féin figure, whose house was raided in October of 1920, and who was threatened with execution. The Tans gave him a severe thrashing, but spared his life through no kindness on their part. All six rifles aimed at him failed to hit their target

Tom Halligan (Bogganfin, Athlone), 3rd Battalion Athlone Brigade.

Tom Halligan (Carricknaughton, Drum, Athlone), 3rd Battalion Athlone Brigade.

ALL HALLIGAN PHOTOS COURTESY OF EDWARD EGAN, DRUM, ATHLONE

John Hanley (Hanily) (Ballinagare) 1st Battalion South Roscommon. Participated in the **attempted attack at Frenchpark** in January 1921

John Hanley (Hanily) (Ballindrimley, Castlerea) a member of Moor Coy. in the 1st Battalion South Roscommon. Participated in the **attempted attack on Kilmurray Camp** in June 1920, the **attack on Frenchpark Barracks** 2 October 1920, and the **attempted ambushes at Castlerea** and **Frenchpark** in January 1921. During the Truce he attended the Company training camp. He took the Anti-Treaty side during the Civil War, and participated in the **attack at Castlerea** in November 1922

Michael Hanley (Hanily) (moved to Main Guard Street, Galway) 1st Battalion South Roscommon. Brother of John. Participated in the **attack on Frenchpark Barracks** 2 October 1920, and the **attack at Castlerea** in November 1922. After the War he emigrated to England

Michael Hanley (Hanly) (Ballinagare) 1st Battalion South Roscommon

Michael Hanley (Ballygar Coy.) which was considered part of 4th Battalion South Roscommon when the Divisional structure was implemented

Michael Hanley (Killina Coy.) 2nd Battalion North Roscommon. He was one of the first members of the Company when it formed in August of 1917

Michael Hanley (Cloonard, Castlerea) during the Civil War he took the Anti-Treaty side, and was arrested on 21 July 1922, and sent to Athlone two months later. He was transferred to Mountjoy then finally to Tintown, where he served his time until 19 December 1923

P. Hanley (Hannily) (near Ballinagare) had his home, hay, and haggards burned by vengeful Tans on the night of the Frenchpark Barracks attack (2 October 1920)

Paddy Hanley (Hannily) 1st Battalion South Roscommon. Served as the 1st Lieutenant of the Castlerea Coy. Interned in Ballykinlar (see photo page 400)

Patrick Hanley (Hanly) (Mountcashel, Kilrooskey) 3rd Battalion South Roscommon, brother of William. Many, but not all, of the members of the Kilgefin Company participated in the **Fourmilehouse Ambush** on 12 October 1920

Patrick Hanley (Kilteevan) during the Civil War he fought on the Anti-Treaty side, and was arrested and sent to Athlone on 25 January 1923

Peter Hanley (Ballinagare) 1st Battalion South Roscommon. Drilled with his Company, collected funds for the Dáil loan, and enforced the Belfast boycott. Participated in the **destruction of vacant barracks** in 1920, and the **attack on Frenchpark Barracks** 2 October 1920. After the War he became a small farmer

Thomas Hanley (Clooneen, Kilglass, Strokestown) a member of the Kilglass Company in the 3rd Battalion North Roscommon

Tom Hanley (Fairymount) a member of the Kilgefin Coy., 3rd Battalion South Roscommon

Tommie Hanley (Kilbarry, Ruskey) a member of the Tarmonbarry Coy. of the 3rd Battalion North Roscommon. Worked as a dispatcher on the Red Route

William Hanley (Cloonmore, Whitehall) a member of Tarmonbarry Coy. in the 3rd Battalion North Roscommon

William Hanley (Hanly) (Mountcashel, Kilrooskey) member of "E" Coy., 3rd Battalion South Roscommon. Many, but not all, of the members of the Kilgefin Company participated in the **Fourmilehouse Ambush** on 12 October 1920. William was present at the **Scramogue Ambush** in March of 1921. After the War he farmed the family land

Thomas Hanlon (Carrick, Ballinlough) 1st Battalion South Roscommon, participated in the **attempted attack on the Castlerea Station Guard** in July 1920, and the **burning of the Barracks at Ballinlough** 14 September 1920. During the Truce he attended the Battalion training camp specialising in dispatch work

Frank Hannon (Gortacoosan) Kiltoom Coy. in the 4th Battalion South Roscommon. Farmer and carpenter by trade

John Hannon (East Mayo Brigade) was active with Volunteers in the Liverpool area in 1920-21

Michael Hannon (Cloverhill, Roscommon) a member of "A" Coy. in the 2nd Battalion South Roscommon

Michael Hannon (Ballygar Coy.) which was considered part of 4th Battalion South Roscommon when the Divisional structure was implemented

Patrick Hannon (Ballygar Coy.) although in Co. Galway, Ballygar Coy. was considered part of the 4th Battalion South Roscommon

Patrick Hannon (Athleague Coy.) 3rd Battalion South Roscommon

Tom Hannon (Muckanagh, near Ballygar, Galway) which was considered part of 4th Battalion South Roscommon when the Divisional structure was implemented. He organised a **raid on Mount Talbot** in August 1922. The next month, he travelled to America with his brother, who had recently been ordained a priest

James Haran (Boyle Coy.) 1st Battalion North Roscommon. He was first taken into the IRB by Alec McCabe in February 1915. Haran participated in the **Rockingham Raid**, after which he was arrested and sent to Mountjoy, where he participated in a hunger strike organised by Austin Stack. After weeks of incarceration, he was finally tried for the crime, but technicalities proved insurmountable for the Crown's case

John P. Haran (Frenchpark) born in Charlestown, County Mayo, he was apprenticed in several different towns before arriving in Frenchpark. He had previously joined the Volunteers in County Mayo, and trained under Major Sean McBride. He arrived in County Roscommon in March of 1919, and became a member of the newly organised "B" Company (Frenchpark), serving as its 1st Lieutenant. In 1919 he served as the sub-Treasurer of his Company for the Dáil loan with the Catholic curate in Breedogue acting as the Treasurer. After September of 1920, he was on the run with Mayo men, and was with Sean Corcoran the night before he was killed in April 1921. He fought in Counties Mayo and Sligo, and was a great friend of Frank Shouldice and Tom Flannery of Ballaghaderreen. After the War he moved to Limerick

and he was released. When he returned to Boyle, he found he was an unwelcome employee at his former place of business. He then went to Sligo, and later emigrated to the United States

The Hardiman household, in the bog in Drumlosh in south Roscommon, where the Volunteers used to meet. Obscure and unnoticed by the Tans, it was a perfect place to assemble. The Volunteers' guns, however, were always stored 100 yards away to ensure their safety lest a surprise raid take place*

Paddy Kenny, interview by author, 24 June 2002, Johnstown, Cornafulla.

"Mike" Hardiman, son of Jack, although small in stature (he was a dwarf), lent his weight to the cause by serving as a sharp lookout when meetings were held in his home. His safe signal echoes down through the decades— "All is clear. They'll be no war!"*

Paddy Kenny, interview by author, 24 June 2002, Johnstown, Cornafulla.

__ Hare (Boyle) 1st Battalion North Roscommon, a member of the Volunteers since before the Rising

Denis J. Harlow (Main Street, Roscommon) a member of the Roscommon Coy., 3rd Battalion South Roscommon, beaten by the Tans at Mote Park Demesne

Hubert Harlow (Corry) a member of the Kilgefin Coy., 3rd Battalion South Roscommon

James Harlow (Killeenboy, Kilteevan) 3rd Battalion South Roscommon

John Harney (Crannagh, Drum) 3rd Battalion Athlone Brigade, charter member of the The O'Rahilly Sinn Féin Club of Summerhill. He was arrested in April 1919 after the authorities found guns and rifles in his hayloft. He was sent to Mountjoy, where he began a nine day hunger strike (because the authorities would not allow him to smoke in his cell). The smoking ban was lifted, but he again participated in a hunger strike joined by his brothers Thomas and James.* He was released after three months, but returned to mischief, when a year later, he, along with other Volunteers acting as helpers and scouts, dismantled the keystone in the arch of the bridge spanning the Cross River in Summerhill

Drum and Its Hinterland by Edward Egan, p. 290.

Tom Harney, 3rd Battalion Athlone Brigade.

Michael Harrington (Tartan, Ballinameen, Boyle), 1st Battalion North Roscommon Brigade.

Michael Harney (Drum Coy.) 3rd Battalion Athlone Brigade

Patrick "Sonny" Harney (Drum Coy.) 3rd Battalion Athlone Brigade, brother of Tom. He too died in the 1980s and is buried in Drum Cemetery

Tom Harney (Drum Coy.) 3rd Battalion Athlone Brigade. Tom carried dispatches and collected guns for the Volunteers. He and his mates persuaded a local girl to stop romancing an RIC man by giving her a rather unattractive hair cut. Tom worked for the railroad. He died in the early 1980s, and is buried in Drum Cemetery

James Harrington (Monksland, Athlone) Bealnamullia Coy. in the 3rd Battalion Athlone Brigade. Harrington drilled with his Company, trained to use firearms, took an active part in the General Election of 1918, attended Battalion meetings, worked with the Republican Police force at disputed farmland in Bealnamullia and Clongowna. He was with a group of Volunteers that seized ammunition from an airplane that made a forced landing at Keelogues in 1919. Took part in the **burning of the Barracks at Bealnamullia**, mobilised for **an attack on Cloonark Barracks**, and **attempted an ambush at Curraghaleen** in October 1920. Near Truce time, he guarded the ASU Headquarters in the area, **destroyed the bridge at Millbrook**, blocked roads at Millbrook and Monksland, harboured and aided escaped prisoners. During the Truce he trained at Greenfield, Donamon, and Falty, in addition to collecting funds to aid the Volunteers and attending the Arbitration Courts

John Harrington (Kiltoom Coy.) 4th Battalion South Roscommon. A stonemason by trade. Built the rectory at Church of the Risen Christ in Kiltoom. Died at an early age

Michael Harrington (Tartan, Ballinameen, Boyle) Captain of "C" Company in the 1st Battalion North Roscommon Brigade. His Company had over sixty men listed on the books. Harrington was reported to have been an excellent shot. He took part in the **attack on Elphin Barracks** 11 February 1921, and the **burning of Frenchpark Barracks** in June. He was a member of the Anti-Treaty Active Service Unit (Flying Column) during the Civil War commanded by Pat Brennan. He spent several years hiding out in dugouts during months of conflict. After the War he became a small farmer, and worked for the County Council. Died 1 November 1954, and is buried in Frenchpark

Michael Harrington (Cloverhill Coy.) a member of "A" Coy. in the 2nd Battalion South Roscommon. He later joined the Garda Síochána

Niall Harrington (Boyle) "A" Company, 1st Battalion North Roscommon, whose father had once been Lord Mayor of Dublin. Participated in **arms raids at Boyle, Cootehall, Grange, and Ballinameen**, in addition to **burning of the barracks at Grevisk** and the **Cootehall Tax and Revenue Office** Easter 1920.* Beaten by the Tans at the chemist shop in Boyle in August 1920. Later transferred to "C" Company, 2nd Dublin Battalion. After the Truce he became a Colonel in the Irish Army, where he was in action against the Four Courts garrison

Who's Who in the Irish War of Independence and Civil War 1916-1923, by Padraic O'Farrell p. 42 and p. 162

Laurence Harrison (Cam, Brideswell) a member of Curraghboy Coy., 4th Battalion South Roscommon. Prevented jurors from attending the British Courts, manufactured ammunition and constructed dugouts for storage of same, and collected the IRA Brigade levy for arming the Volunteers. The entire Company participated in the arrest and confinement of a suspected spy. That man was tried by court-martial and eventually executed — an action which prompted the arrest of ten members of the Company on 5 January 1921. Another five were arrested in March. Harrison was not among them. After the War he became a farmer. Buried in Cam Cemetery

John Harte (Trien Coy.) 1st Battalion South Roscommon

James Hayden (Elphin Street, Strokestown) 3rd Battalion North Roscommon, shot through the lung by an RIC constable in Elphin after a football match. He eventually died of cancer of the lung

Thomas Hayden (Knockcroghery) 4th Battalion South Roscommon. Hayden was one of a dozen men who comprised the Knockcroghery Company as of July 1922. He worked with the Anti-Treaty men of the area to wreak havoc on the Free State troops. He died at a young age

Addie Hayes (Church Street, Boyle) began his demonstration against Saxon rule in his youth. As a teenage lad, he climbed the flagpole outside the local British Army recruiter's home in Boyle, claimed the Union Jack, and burned it. For that stunt he was never apprehended. Three years later, however, his stand against tyranny was more defiant. He was one of four members from Boyle who took part in the Connaught Ranger Indian Mutiny in 1920. For his efforts, he was sentenced to ten years penal servitude in Maidstone Prison. He returned to Boyle in 1923, after which he joined the Garda Síochána

Richard Hayden (Trila [Martin], Curraghroe, Strokestown) 3rd Battalion North Roscommon. Joined "B" Coy. in 1917, and attended parades, took part in the North and South Roscommon elections, collected arms, **raided the RIC recruiting meeting at Cloontuskert** in March of 1920, took part in the **burning of Scramogue Barracks**, and stood guard in the Kilgefin area in October after the Fourmilehouse Ambush. Collected arms at Clondra, Killashee in Longford, and took an active part in the **attack on Tarmonbarry Barracks** in January 1921, **Scramogue Ambush**, and the **attack on Tarmonbarry Barracks** in July 1921. During the Truce he spent time in the training camps. In the Civil War Hayden was a member of the Anti-Treaty ASU. Participated in the **attack on Ruskey Barracks** in December 1922, and the destruction of military cars at Curraghroe. The new year was not kind to him. He was arrested in January, and held in prison until September 1923

Christopher Healy (Clooneragh) a member of the Carniska Coy., 3rd Battalion North Roscommon. After the War he emigrated to America

James Healy (Lavagh, Ruskey) during the Civil War he took the Republican side, and was arrested on 6 September 1922, and sent to Athlone two months later. He was released on 13 December 1922

John Healy (Cloonglassney, Strokestown) joined the Volunteers in 1917. He took part in the North Roscommon election, drilled with his comrades, collected arms and funds to fight conscription. During 1918 he assisted in the general election, and helped to enforce the Belfast boycott. He participated in the **destruction of Ballinderry Barracks**, and attacked recruits for the RIC in Strokestown. Assisted at Sinn Féin Courts guarding prisoners. Blocked roads in preparation for the **Fourmilehouse Ambush**, and served as guard in the Kilgefin area for the expected reprisals. Participated in the **attack on the Strokestown patrol** on 6 January 1921, and was out the night before the **Scramogue Ambush** blocking roads. He was a member of the ASU in North Roscommon

John Healy (Kilmore) served as a staff officer for the 5th Battalion North Roscommon. When the 3rd Western Division was formed, he served as the Adjutant for the 4th Battalion. During the Civil War he was a member of the Active Service Unit of North Roscommon. He and his men were supplied clothing and ammunition by John J. Robinson, Capt. of Ruskey Coy.

John Healy (Lavagh, Ruskey) Kilglass Coy. in the 3rd Battalion North Roscommon

Michael Healy is listed as the 1922 Captain of Kilmore Company, which had formerly been a part of the 5th Battalion. After the reshuffling to form the 3rd Western Division, the 5th Battalion became the 4th Battalion in the 3rd Brigade. He was a member of the Flying Column. After the War he regrouped himself with flocks of emigrants headed for the United States

Patrick Healy (Cartron, Kilmore) served as the first 2nd Lieutenant of the Kilmore Company in the 5th Battalion North Roscommon Brigade. He later became the Captain of the Company. Listed in the GHQ papers in the UCD Archives as the Intelligence Officer for the 5th Battalion North Roscommon. Took part in the **robbery of the Dublin-Sligo mail train**

Patrick Healy (Lisacul, Ballaghaderreen) during the Civil War he was detained in Athlone. He obtained his release from prison in April 1923

John Heavey (Knockhall, Ruskey) a member of the Kilglass Company in the 3rd Battalion North Roscommon

Michael Hegarty, Clooncundra, Castlerea

Thomas Heavey (Knockhall, Ruskey) a member of the Kilglass Company in the 3rd Battalion North Roscommon

Edward "Ned" Hegarty (Farragher, Ballinaheglish) When Ernie O'Malley came to the area in 1918, the 2nd Battalion South was organised with Hegarty serving as its first Adjutant. At a meeting in Roscommon town in 1918, Hegarty was elected the South Roscommon Brigade Adjutant. Aside from his adjutant duties, he took time out to block roads for the **Fourmilehouse Ambush**. In 1920 he assumed the duties of Chief of the Republican Police for South Roscommon, and, for the duration of his life, was locally referred to as "Chief". His was the responsi-bility of arresting and guarding of prisoners, as well as enforcing punishment for informers and spies throughout the Brigade area. After the War, the results of which disgusted him, he refused a position with the Garda Síochána, and instead chose to work for the Land Commission. He suffered from respiratory problems in the later years of his life due to his staying out in the dugouts and damp hiding places during the War. He ran as an independent for Roscommon County Council in the June 1928 election. He remained a staunch member of the IRA until his death in 1959. His indomitable spirit proved to be the inspiration to his great-niece who is the author of this book. Buried in the old Ballinderry Cemetery

Jack Hegarty (Cloonycolgan) Officer in the 3rd Battalion South Roscommon, who joined the Free State Army. Never one to make rash decisions, Jack courted a local girl, Nellie Hughes, for fifty years! Died in January of 1973, and buried in Oran Cemetery

John Hegarty (Carrownalasson) a member of the Kilbride Coy., 3rd Battalion South Roscommon. After the War he returned to farming. Died 1983, and buried in Kilbegnet Cemetery

Maggie "Greta" Hegarty (Ballinaheglish) member of the Cumann na mBan, sister of Ned, swift and steady messenger for the South Roscommon Brigade, who car-ried dispatches in the steel tube of her bicycle. Throughout her life she never regretted the sacrifices made, only that the outcome had not been what was hoped for. She married late in life, and spent her last years in Newbridge, County Galway. She died in 1961, and is buried in Augiart Cemetery, County Galway

Mary Ann Hegarty (Ballinaheglish) member of the Cumann na mBan, who took into her home many men on the run. Dan O'Rourke spent countless days and nights in her cottage on the Farragher road. After the War she remained on the farm, serving as cook and housekeeper to her brother, Ned. Died 1951. Buried in the old Ballinderry cemetery

Michael Hegarty (Clooncundra, Castlerea) 2nd Lieutenant of the Cloonboniffe Coy. in the 1st Battalion South Roscommon. He met with an untimely death in 1935 as a result of an accident in the bog. Buried in Castlerea Cemetery

James Heneghan served as Captain of the Granlahan Coy. in 1922. The Company had formerly been associated with the Cloonboniffe Coy. of the South Roscommon Brigade. During the Civil War he became a member of the Anti-Treaty Active Service Unit

Martin Heneghan (Henehan) (Beahy, Castlerea) was incarcerated in Athlone 30 December 1922

Patrick Heneghan (Henehan) (Beahy, Castlerea) during the Civil War he fought on the Anti-Treaty side, and was incarcerated in Athlone. He was not released until 13 April 1923

Bartley Hennigan (Ballygar Coy.) which was considered part of 4th Battalion South Roscommon when the Divisional structure was implemented

Bernie Hennigan (Ballinaheglish) 2nd Battalion South Roscommon

Patrick Henry (Drum Coy.) 3rd Battalion Athlone Brigade. He served as drill master for the Company in O'Connell's field and on the lands of Mount Hussey. He had formerly been in the British Army

Michael Herney
(Nerney) Served as the 2nd Lieutenant for "E" Company (Elphin) in the 2nd Battalion North Roscommon

Peter Heslin
(Aughavas, County Leitrim), head officer at Boyle Barracks in 1920. Sentenced to three years, and moved to Mountjoy. Later emigrated to America

James Hester
(Ballyglass, Ballymacurley) 2nd Battalion South Roscommon. Participated in the **raid on the military train at Ballymoe** in June 1920, the **attack on Frenchpark Barracks** 2 October 1920, and the **ambush at Southpark, Castlerea** 10 July 1921. James often remarked to his son that belonging to the IRA was the best that he could do for his country.* After the War he became a small farmer. Died in the early 1940s, and is buried in Oran Cemetery. This author interviewed his son, John, many times in the course of writing this book

John Hester, son of James, interview by author, Lanesboro, Longford, 15 August 2004.

3rd Battalion South Roscommon Officers in front, left to right: Henry Compton, Tommie Kelly, Frank Simons, Jack Hegarty, Peter "Buzzer" Farrell and John Gibbons.

Photo taken 23 April 1922
PHOTO COURTESY OF ALBERT SIGGINS
PHOTO RESTORATION BY LEW THORNE

James Hester (Cloonbard, Castleplunkett) a member of "C" Coy. in the 2nd Battalion South Roscommon. Took part in the **attack on Frenchpark Barracks** 2 October 1920. He became a farmer after the War. Died 24 May 1967, and is buried in Rathmoyle Cemetery

John Hester (Cloonbard, Castleplunkett) a member of "C" Coy. in the 2nd Battalion South Roscommon. When the 2nd Western Division was formed, John was in charge of first aid in the 3rd Battalion, No. 2 Brigade. He also volunteered to serve with the Oran Battalion Flying Column. He later emigrated to the USA

John Hester (Trien Coy.) 1st Battalion South Roscommon

Michael Hester (Trien) Company Captain in the 1st Battalion South Roscommon. Took part in the **attempted ambush at Coshlieve** in July 1920. He became a member of the Active Service Unit in January 1921. Participated in the **attempted ambush of RIC patrol near Ballymoe** in May 1921. During the Truce he attended the training camps at Hermitage, Swinford, and Runnamoat. Later emigrated to San Francisco

Patrick Hester (Trien Coy.) 1st Battalion South Roscommon. Served as the 2nd Lieutenant in the Company. Took part in the **attempted ambush at Coshlieve** in July 1920. Participated in the **attempted ambush of RIC patrol near Ballymoe** in May 1921. Attended the Cloonkeen, Erritt, Hermitage, and Castlerea training camps during the Truce. He also emigrated to San Francisco

Inspector Vincent J. Hetreed, an unlikely hero, who believed he was allowed to go free after encountering the Volunteers on the road the morning of the **Fourmilehouse Ambush**. He is credited with later saving the town of Roscommon from being burned in reprisal. He was soon transferred and replaced by District Inspector Cole, who, according to Frank Simons as recorded in the Ernie O'Malley Papers in UCD, was termed a "Hard Egg"

James Hester (Ballyglass, Ballymacurley) 2nd Battalion South Roscommon.
PHOTO COURTESY OF JOHN HESTER

Michael John Hevican, Derrinea,
Carrowbehy, Castlerea

Michael Thomas "Mick" Hevican, Derrinea,
Carrowbehy, Castlerea

Michael John Hevican (Derrinea, Carrowbehy, Castlerea) 1st Battalion South Roscommon. Participated in the **burning of the Loughglynn Barracks**, and the **burning of the Barracks at Ballinlough** 14 September 1920. He was also a member of the party that **attempted to attack the Castlerea Station Guard**. In May of 1921 both he and his cousin, Michael Thomas Hevican, took part in the **attempted attack at Lisacul** — an operation that was planned in conjunction with the East Mayo Brigade. Michael attended the training camps at Hermitage and Erritt, where he specialised in signalling. By July 1921 he was serving as the 1st Lieutenant of Gorthaganny Coy. After the War he emigrated to England, where he resided until the early 1960s. He returned to Ireland to live with his two sisters. Died 28 January 1965, and buried in Urlour Cemetery, County Mayo

Michael Thomas Hevican (Derrinea, Carrowbehy, Castlerea) 1st Battalion South Roscommon. Took part in the **burning of the Barracks at Ballinlough** 14 September 1920 armed with a shotgun and revolver. He was present at the **burning of the Barracks at Loughglynn**, and the **attempted attack on the Castlerea Station Guard** in July 1920. On 24 January 1921 he was captured by the Black and Tans, stripped naked, beaten, and threatened with shots fired over his head. It didn't deter him! In May of 1921 both he and his cousin, Michael John, took part in the **attempted attack at Lisacul** — an operation that was planned in conjunction with the East Mayo Brigade. After the Truce Michael attended the training camps at Ballinagare, Erritt Lodge, and Cloonkeen. By July 1921 he was serving as the Captain of the Gorthaganny Coy. in the 2nd Battalion, No. 2 Brigade, 2nd Western Division. (The Gorthaganny men had previously been attached to the Cloonboniffe Coy. at Truce time. By August of 1921, they had formed a separate Company.) Hevican took part in the Civil War on the Anti-Treaty side, assisting the East Mayo Brigade, and harbouring men on the run in dugouts on his property. He was also responsible for a large arms dump (a machine gun, 100 rifles, 200 revolvers, and a large quantity of ammo)* for several months. After the War he farmed the land. He was present for the Pat Glynn Memorial Service held at Loughglynn Church in 1970. He died 10 August 1981, and is buried in Gorthaganny Cemetery

Michael Thomas Hevican, written statement, private copy

Jimmie Higgins (Boyle) sentenced after the *'conacre take over'* in Boyle. A member of the North Roscommon Sinn Féin executive, he was arrested while attending one of their meetings at Croghan. He was subsequently imprisoned in Boyle Barracks. Higgins was with Michael Cull of Arigna when Cull was shot at Ballyconnell on 6 January 1923. Higgins escaped!

John Higgins (Attyflynn, Dunmore) 1st Lieutenant of Kilterna Coy. in the Glenamaddy Battalion. Although located in Co. Galway, this Battalion was incorporated into No. 2 Brigade of the 2nd Western Division

Michael Higgins (Frenchpark) the second Captain of "B" Company in Frenchpark (as it was known then). It was disbanded after a short time and consolidated into other units

Patrick Higgins (Mantua Coy.) 2nd Battalion North Roscommon. Listed in the GHQ papers in UCD Archives as the Quartermaster for Company. Took part in the **attack on Elphin Barracks** on 11 February 1921

Thomas Higgins (Grange, Fourmilehouse) during the Civil War he was arrested on 11 October 1922, taken to Athlone a month later, released on 11 January 1923

Ann Hoban from Slatta, Kilglass taught first aid techniques to the Cumann na mBan women of the Tarmonbarry/Ruskey area

Bill Hoban (Ballyglass, Ballymacurley) a member of "B" Coy. in the 2nd Battalion South Roscommon

Johnny Hogan (Garrynagowna, Drum) a member of the Summerhill Coy., 3rd Battalion Athlone Brigade, charter member of The O'Rahilly Sinn Féin Club. In April 1920 Johnny helped John Harney, a stonemason by trade, to dismantle the keystone of the arch of the bridge over the Cross River at Summerhill in order to impede lorry traffic. Unfortunately, the Tans had the damage repaired within a day. He was dragged from his bed and beaten senseless as a reprisal for the **Cornafulla Ambush**

Michael Hogan (Garrynagowna, Drum) a member of the Summerhill Coy., 3rd Battalion Athlone Brigade, brother of Johnny, returned to the site of the Cornafulla ambush that night. His intention: he, along with other members of the Company, wanted to rescue the body of James Tormey, who had been killed that day and whose body still lay in the field

Nelly Hogan (Garrynagowna, Drum) sister of Johnny and Michael. A member of the Cumann na mBan club of Summerhill in south Roscommon

Samuel Hollis (Church St., Athlone) arrested on 18 August 1922, and incarcerated in Athlone on 2 September 1922

Edward Holmes (Ballyroddy, Elphin) 2nd Battalion North Roscommon. Captain of Mantua Company in 1916. He was one of the founding members of the Killina Company when it formed in 1917

Patrick Hopkins (Cagglekeenagh, Strokestown) a member of the Carniska Coy., 3rd Battalion North Roscommon. After the War he emigrated to the United States

Bryan Horan (Ballygar Coy.) was considered part of 4th Battalion South Roscommon when the Divisional structure was implemented

__ Hughes worked in the Drumsna Railway Station and participated in the **seizure of a tender loaded with rations at the Railway Station** in June 1920

Dick "Cushy" Hughes (Kilnalosset, Kilgefin) ex-British soldier who had been wounded in the spine in World War I. A member of "E" Coy., 3rd Battalion South Roscommon, and Pat Madden's Flying Column. Many, but not all, of the members of the Kilgefin Company participated in the **Fourmilehouse Ambush** on 12 October 1920. "Cushy" was present at the **Scramogue Ambush**, where he is reputed to have traded his shotgun for the .303 Enfield rifle of his ambush partner. He was not impressed! When shown the rifle, Cushy is reported to have exclaimed, "Damn it! Haven't you got anything better than that."* He was captured after the ambush on his way to Kilrooskey, but, because he was able to produce his British military pension papers, he was released unharmed. After the War he farmed at Kilnalosset, Kilrooskey. Died 21 April 1977, and buried in Derrane Cemetery

Luke Duffy interview, Ernie O'Malley papers, UCD Archives

Peter Shiel, Dick "Cushy" Hughes, John Corcoran, and Peter Collins.
PHOTO COURTESY OF EAMONN DUFFY

Gilbert Hughes (Coosan, Athlone) arrested after the Rising and sent to Wakefield on 13 May 1916 but released within a few days

Patrick Hughes (Kilnalosset, Kilgefin) 3rd Battalion South Roscommon, brother of Dick. Many, but not all, of the members of the Kilgefin Company participated in the **Fourmilehouse Ambush** on 12 October 1920. After the War, he emigrated to the United Kingdom

Sarah Hughes (Carricknaughton, Drum) in whose home the four men involved in the Cornafulla ambush spent the preceding night

Thomas Hughes (Caran, Ballinaheglish) 2nd Battalion South Roscommon

Thomas Hughes, executed at
Athlone in 1923.

Thomas Hughes (Bogganfin, Athlone) During the Black and Tar War, he acted as armoury officer for the IRA Brigade. Hughes was present when the British turned over Custume Barracks. He took the Republican side in the army split, and was captured by the Free State forces on 21 December 1922 at Lisdonagh House (about two miles south of Shrule). Executed in Athlone on 20 January 1923 when he was but twenty-one years old. Buried in Cornamagh Cemetery near Athlone. His name is inscribed on the tablets in front of the Shankill Monument near Elphin as well as the IRA monument in Athlone

William Hughes (Caran, Ballinaheglish) was a member of "B" Coy., 2nd Battalion South Roscommon, brother of Thomas. He later emigrated to Canada

Canon Humphries, the Protestant rector in Knockcroghery, who sheltered the Catholic priest, Father Eamon Bartley Kelly, whose home had been set ablaze on the night the Tans burned the village in June 1921

Andrew Hunt (Milltown, Castleplunkett) a member of "C" Coy. in the 2nd Battalion South Roscommon. Took part in the **raid on the military train at Ballymoe** in June 1920, and **ambush at Southpark, Castlerea** 10 July 1921. After the War he emigrated to Australia

Jim Hunt (Gurteen, Co. Sligo) joined the RIC in 1912 and trained at the depot in the Phoenix Park, after which he was sent to barracks in Co. Cork, and later to Laois. He left the RIC in 1916, and joined the Irish Volunteers. A year later he was sworn into the Irish Republican Brotherhood (IRB). When Owen Tansey died in the flu epidemic of 1918, Hunt was selected as the O/C of Gurteen Battalion. In November of 1919 he was with Patrick Hegarty of Mayo driving to Breedogue in Roscommon in order to organise a Dáil loan. On the return trip, Constable Sullivan of Boyle put a cordon on the road. When they reached the danger zone, Hunt, who was unarmed, could do nothing more that duck while the gun of Patrick Hegarty was blazing. (Dr. Doyle, who was with the two men, was slightly wounded.) Because of this escapade, Hunt was sentenced to three months in Sligo Gaol, where he met Sean MacEoin and Alec McCabe. He was released in February 1920. Upon gaining his freedom, he took part in the **raid on Major Percival's Temple House** in Ballymote. Planned by Frank Carty, the Volunteers laid in wait surrounding the residence all night, then when the residents began to stir about the house in the morning, the Volunteers rushed the house eventually seizing a number of revolvers, one Peter-the-Painter, and some shotguns. Hunt was again arrested in March 1920 for collecting money without a military permit. (It was really for the IRA arms fund.) Again he was sent to Sligo. During the Tan War, Hunt had ten to twelve men permanently under his command. He was the officer in charge at the **Ambush at Ratra** on 1 September 1920 in which twenty-five men took part. After the ambush, Hunt saved one of the captured RIC men from death. He "did happen to save him for his mother's sake."* Later when Hunt was a prisoner in Boyle Barracks, this same RIC man returned the favour by failing to identify Hunt. He also took part in the **attack on the RIC barracks at Collooney** in March 1921. Hunt was again arrested after an **attack on the Ballaghaderreen Barracks** in May 1921, transferred to Boyle Barracks, and incarcerated there until July of that year. Later transferred to Mountjoy, where he was sentenced to remain for twenty years. He was released by the terms of the Treaty in February 1922. One week into the Civil War, he was among the men watching for the Free Staters in Sligo town. *The Aftermath of Revolution Sligo 1921-23* by Michael Farry claims that Hunt was the only Sligo Battalion O/C to eventually take the Pro-Treaty side (p. 105). After the War he emigrated to the United States, and stayed for but a few years. When he returned to Ireland, he purchased a farm in Gurteen, and worked the land until his death in December 1970. He is buried in Gurteen

*Jim Hunt interview, Ernie O'Malley Papers, UCD Archives, No. 133

Dominick Hunt (Milltown, Castleplunkett) 2nd Battalion South Roscommon. Took part in the **raid on the military train at Ballymoe** in June 1920, the **attack on Frenchpark Barracks** 2 October 1920, and the **ambush at Southpark, Castlerea** 10 July 1921. After the War he became a farmer. Buried in Ballintubber Cemetery

John Hunt (Carrick-on-Shannon) fought with Sean Connolly at Selton Hill in County Leitrim, but was captured afterwards and sent to Boyle Barracks. He was there at the time of Michael Dockery's escape in June 1921

John Hunt (Cloonfree, Strokestown) 1st Lieutenant of Cloonfree Company in the 3rd Battalion North Roscommon. Took part in the **attempt to burn down the Bridewell at Strokestown** in July 1920. He was quite severely burned, and ultimately required plastic surgery in Dublin. He died a few years later

John Hunt (Milltown, Castleplunkett) a member of "C" Coy. in the 2nd Battalion South Roscommon. He, along with his Company, drilled, and collected money for the Dáil loan. After the War he moved to London

Mary Hunt (Cloonloo, Boyle) sister of Jim, member of the Cumann na mBan

Mickey Hunt (Stonepark, Co. Mayo) a member of a Mayo Company who became part of an Active Service Unit for the 2nd Western Division. He, along with John Snee, Tom Regan, P. Behan, Mick Duffy, and M. McKeon, spent the first months after the Truce sniping at B-Specials along the six-county Border. Mickey was part of the group of Anti-Treaty men who **took over the Boyle Barracks** during the Civil War

Michael Hunt (Ashbrook, Scramogue) 3rd Battalion North Roscommon. He was a postman, who lost his position due to Volunteer activities. He served as an all-night outpost for the **Scramogue Ambush**, and took an active role in the Civil War on the Anti-Treaty side. He participated in the **attempted ambush at Ruskey** in February 1922. He was also entrusted with special dispatches

Michael Hunt (Newtownflood) 3rd Battalion Athlone Brigade, a charter member of The O'Rahilly Sinn Féin Club of Summerhill. He was involved in the removal of the keystone of the arch in the bridge over the Cross River at Summerhill in April 1920. He served as a dispatch messenger while working on the railroad. He also was with the party that arrived in Cornafulla in February 1921 to take Jim Tormey's body away. Arrested on 11 June 1921, and sent to Ballykinlar Interment Camp in County Down

Tom Hunt (Summerhill) 3rd Battalion Athlone Brigade, brother of Michael, also a charter member of the local Sinn Féin Club

John Hurley (Carrandangan, Ballinaheglish) a member of "B" Coy. in the 2nd Battalion South Roscommon

Rev. Dr. Thomas Hurley (native of Corlackan, Ballymoe, Co. Galway) served as the parish priest in Ballagh from 1918-1946. Active supporter of Count Plunkett in the bye election of 1917. Rev. Hurley was a true friend of "the boys." One Sunday morning when he was conducting Mass, he looked up and saw a group of Black and Tans coming in the main door of Ballagh Church. Rev. Hurley knew that many of the parishioners that morning were Volunteers who were armed. During those years to have been arrested carrying a gun was a sure ticket to one of any number of

Sean Hurley (Excise St., Athlone) a native of Cork, was arrested after the Rising and sent to Wakefield on 2 June 1916. He was later transferred to a former German prison-of-war camp in Wales, "The Irish University," located at Frongoch. Sean did an enormous amount of work during 1917-18 in organising and recruiting men for the Volunteers. John (Sean) delivered a recruitment speech on the corner of Drum Old Cemetery in early 1917, resulting in the formation of the Summerhill and The O'Rahilly Sinn Féin Clubs. He was arrested in the spring of 1919, and interned in Wormwood Scrubbs. Sean was replaced as O/C by Seamus O'Meara who, when speaking with Michael Collins, offered to resign the commanding position in 1918 in favour of Hurley. Collins declined the offer, stating that Hurley was more useful in the Sinn Féin aspect of the movement. Hurley joined the Athlone Company as an ordinary Volunteer, and served as a Judge in the Sinn Féin Courts.* Hurley barely escaped capture when the Tans invaded his home in the fall of 1920. He succeeded in pulling himself onto the roof of his house, where he had to stay for nearly twenty-four hours before being rescued. After the War he worked on the mechanical staff of the Athlone Printing Works, Ltd.

Seamus O'Meara Volunteer Witness Statement to the Bureau of Military History 1913-21, p. 15 and 27.

"His Majesty's inns." Quick thinking saved the day! Rev. Hurley called for the two oldest men in the parish and his own young servers to carry the processional cross and candles down the main aisle. He then went to confer with the leader of the military. Assured that no harm would come to the general population, he returned to the altar, and completed Mass. He did announce that the policemen were looking for specific men who would, no doubt, be armed. At the conclusion of the final "Amen," priest and flock reverently walked down the aisle and gathered outside beyond the entranceway. The Volunteers within had sufficient opportunity to drop their guns and ammunition belts on the floor inside the church before following the congregation outside. The local girls, ever the tough and ready supporters, hid the weapons and belts inside the confessional. Even during the day-to-day battles with the British Forces, Canon Hurley was ever available to the Volunteers in matters of both material and spiritual natures. "It was quite a usual thing to find him pacing up and down the road outside the house where we were holding a meeting or having a meal."* God bless Father Hurley! He died in 1955

Frank Simons Volunteer Witness Statement to Bureau of Military History 1913-21, p. 40.

John Hussey (Kilbride Coy.) 3rd Battalion South Roscommon

Michael Hussey (Emlagh, Castleplunkett) a member of "C" Coy. in the 2nd Battalion South Roscommon. During the War years, he was arrested because he had in his possession a cart with Jack Brennan's name on it. (Brennan was highly sought by the local police.) Hussey was severely beaten and threatened with shooting. Took part in the **ambush at Southpark, Castlerea** 10 July 1921. After the War he became a farmer. Died 3 December 1967, and buried in Rathmoyle, Kilmurray

Thomas Hussey (Ballygar Coy.) was considered part of 4th Battalion South Roscommon when the Divisional structure was implemented

John Hynes (Jamestown, Ballyforan) a member of the Tisrara Coy. in the 4th Battalion South Roscommon

Martin Hynes (Jamestown, Ballyforan) brother of John, a member of Tisrara Coy., 4th Battalion South Roscommon

Michael Hynes (Drum Coy.) 3rd Battalion Athlone Brigade

William Hynes sworn into the IRA by George Fitzgerald of Ardmullan

Kelly Igoe (Northyard, Scramogue, Strokestown) Slatta Company in the 3rd Battalion North Roscommon. He was a member of the Anti-Treaty Active Service Unit during the Civil War

Martin Igoe (Lissagallen, Fuerty, Roscommon) a member of Cloverhill Coy., 2nd Battalion South Roscommon

John Irwin (Ballaghaderreen) one of the first members of the Ballaghaderreen Coy. in the East Mayo Brigade

Joseph Irwin (Anrittabeg) Cloontuskert Coy., 3rd Batt. South Roscommon

Edward Jackson (Cams, Fuerty, Roscommon) Captain of "A" Coy. in the 3rd Battalion, No. 2 Brigade of the 2nd Western Division, formerly Cloverhill Coy. of the 2nd Battalion South Roscommon. Took part in the **raid on the military train at Ballymoe** in June 1920. His home served as the headquarters of "A" Company during the post-Truce times. Twenty years after the War, he still bore a blue mark on his forehead — a testament to a narrow escape from a British bullet

John Jeffers served as 1st Lieutenant of Glenamaddy Coy. in the Glenamaddy Battalion. Although located in Co. Galway, this Company was incorporated into No. 2 Brigade in the 2nd Western Division with Gerald O'Connor, former O/C of the 1st Battalion South Roscommon, serving as Brigade Commandant. His Company consisted of twenty-five members in April of 1922

Patrick Jeffers (Lieutenant) in charge of Transport for the 1st Battalion, No. 2 Brigade in the 2nd Western Division

Michael Jennings (Cloonfad Coy.) 1st Battalion South Roscommon. Participated in the **attack at Ballinagare** in July 1922. Later emigrated to the United States

Thomas Jennings He too volunteered to serve with the Castlerea Battalion Flying Column

Tim Jennings (Pollanalty, Ballinlough) When the Western Division was formed, he volunteered to serve with the Castlerea Battalion Flying Column

William Jennings (Barrymore, The Hill of Berries) a member of the Kiltoom Coy. in the 4th Battalion South Roscommon. Took the Anti-Treaty side in the Civil War. He was active in the destruction of railways.* Captured 27 September 1923 at a dance at Fallon's house in Cornalee (twelve miles from Athlone)

Intelligence Papers of the Western Command

Benedict Jordan Adjutant for the Fairymount Company in the 1st Battalion North Roscommon. After the War he joined the Garda Síochána

Jordan's Cottage in Cartonmore whose residents welcomed Toby Scally with open arms after the latter had been wounded in The Woodlands of Loughglynn

An example of the emotional and economic impact of the War for Independence and the Civil War is found in an examination of "A" Coy. of the 2nd Battalion South Roscommon. In July 1921 that Company was comprised of fourteen men. By the 1950s only three of that original number lived in Ireland. Three had died an early death (James Shally, Thomas McDermott and John Conroy), while seven had emigrated to the United States, and one had gone to England. One member had joined the Garda Síochána (Michael Harrington), Martin Kearney resided in Salthill Galway, while one remained in Roscommon (Thomas Roarke).

Andrew Judge (Clooncrim, Ballinlough) 1st Battalion South Roscommon. Judge participated in the **burning of the Barracks at Ballinlough** on 14 September 1920. During the Truce he attended the Battalion training camp specialising in dispatch work. He later emigrated to New York

Frank Judge (Church Street, Roscommon town) member of the 1918 Sinn Féin election committee in South Roscommon. His interest in politics continued after the War. In 1925 he served as a member of the Roscommon Town Tenants Association. He also was an active participant in local amateur dramatic productions

Miss Margaret Judge (Geevagh) member of the Cumann na mBan, shopkeeper in Boyle, who provided information which aided in the **escape** of Jim Molloy and Michael Dockery **from Boyle Barracks**. She later moved to Dublin

Bernard Kane (Trien Coy.) 1st Battalion South Roscommon

Joe Kane (Carrickmore, Boyle) 1st Battalion North Roscommon, member of the Volunteers before the Rising

Rev. Fr. Michael Keane, C.C. (Killina) active supporter of Count Plunkett during the 1917 North Roscommon bye election

Rev. Bernard Keane (chaplain at Loughglynn Convent) carried messages for the local Volunteers, son of James Keane, who was the author of the poem *The Woodlands of Loughglynn*

J. J. Keane (Castleplunkett Coy.) 2nd Battalion South Roscommon

James Keane (Kilbegnet) 2nd Lieutenant of the Kilbegnet Coy. in the Glenamaddy Battalion. Although located in Co. Galway, this Battalion was incorporated into No. 2 Brigade, 2nd Western Division with Gerald O'Connor, serving as Brigade Commandant

John Keane (Cloonfad) 1st Battalion South Roscommon. Participated in the **destruction of vacant barracks** in 1920, took part in the **disarming of two British soldiers at Cloonfad** in May 1921, and the **attack at Castlerea** in November 1922. During the Truce he attended the Company training camp, where he specialised in intelligence, scouting, and dispatch work. Died 1971

John Keane (Cloonberlagh, Killashee, Co. Longford) 1st Lieutenant of the Tarmonbarry Company in the 3rd Battalion North Roscommon

Michael Keane (Clooncrim, Ballinlough) Adjutant for the Ballinlough Coy. in the 1st Battalion South Roscommon. Participated in the **raid for petrol at Ballinlough Station** in June 1920, the **attempted ambush at Coshlieve** in July 1920, and the **attempted attack on the Castlerea Station Guard** that same month. He was killed in the **burning of Ballinlough Barracks** 14 September 1920. Buried Granlahan cemetery. His name is inscribed on the tablets in front of the IRA monument near Elphin

Michael Keane (Castlerea) 1st Battalion South Roscommon. He went to America, but later in life returned to Ireland, where he became a pub proprietor (The Cosy Bar in Castlerea). Present for Pat Glynn's Memorial Service in 1970

Michael Keane (Runnamoat, Ballinaheglish) a member of "B" Coy. in the 2nd Battalion South Roscommon in 1921

Michael Keane (Emlagh More, Donamon) 2nd Battalion South Roscommon. Took part in the **raid on the military train at Ballymoe** in June 1920

Pat Keane (Runnamoat, Ballinaheglish) a member of "B" Coy. in the 2nd Battalion South Roscommon, brother of William and Michael

William Keane (Runnamoat, Ballinaheglish) a member of "B" Coy. in the 2nd Battalion South Roscommon, brother of Michael and Pat

Batty Keaney (Ballymote, Sligo) a member of the IRB. He, along with Michael (John) Maguire, drove down from Sligo with Alec McCabe in February 1918 and met Roscommon Volunteers at the first gate of the Rockingham estate on the Carrick Road. He then took part in the **Rockingham Raid**. Later he was sent to

Michael Keane (Clooncrim, Ballinlough), 1st Battalion South Roscommon.

Dartmoor as a result of being charged with the **burning of the Liverpool docks**. He joined the Free State Army, and rose to the rank of Lieut. Colonel. Moved to Dublin

Bernie Kearney (Correal, Fuerty) Captain of "D" Coy. in the 2nd Battalion South Roscommon. When cycling dispatches around the county, he hid the notes in his handlebars. After the messages were delivered, the receiver always destroyed the paper. Bernie was imprisoned after the **Fourmilehouse Ambush**. He was released after the Truce, and re-arrested for Anti-Treaty activities during the Civil War on 21 July 1922, and sent to Athlone on 2 September 1922. Later in life became a farmer, but eventually emigrated to Chestnut Hill, Massachusetts

Con Kearney (Knockcroghery Coy.) 4th Battalion South Roscommon

Cornelius Kearney (Ballinturly, Ballinaheglish) a member of "B" Coy. in the 2nd Battalion South Roscommon in 1921

Edward "Ned" Kearney (Newtown, Ballymacurley) 2nd Battalion South Roscommon, fought in the Dardenellas in World War I, and was a participant in the Battle of Ypres. He returned to Ireland, where he joined the Volunteers, and became their drill and weapons instructor. He also served as the Quartermaster of the Ballinaheglish Coy. He was a great character — prone to grand story telling. After the War he worked for the County Council

John Kearney When the Western Division was formed, John was a member of "B" Coy., 2nd Battalion South Roscommon. He, along with his Company, drilled, collected money for the Dáil loan, and served under Captain Michael O'Grady. After the War he emigrated to America

Joseph Kearney (Knockcroghery Coy.) 4th Battalion South Roscommon. Knockcroghery Company was formed in 1917 under the leadership of Patrick Kelly of Culleen, Lecarrow. Kearney drilled with his fellow Volunteers and attended the sham battles at Taughmaconnell overseen by Ernie O'Malley in the summer of 1918. Participated in the South Roscommon election of 1918, constructed dugouts, and blocked roads. Along with Michael Tennant, he stopped two enemy soldiers cycling from Athlone to Roscommon, and relieved them of their bicycles and dispatches. He raided numerous houses for arms. On one occasion, he invaded the home of an ex-RIC man and a non-sympathiser, securing four guns, one revolver, and a quantity of ammunition. He joined Hubert Murphy, Capt. of St. John's Coy., Johnny Kilcline of Corrigeen, Knockcroghery, Hubert Watson of Kiltoom, and several other Volunteers from the Knockcroghery Coy. in a raid on Feehily's house. He was shot and severely wounded in the stomach during that raid. Kearney was taken to Incheneagh and later to a Dublin hospital, where he recovered. He was arrested in September 1920 and imprisoned. After the War he joined the Garda Síochána

John Kearney (Knockcroghery Coy.) 4th Battalion South Roscommon

Martin Kearney (Salthill, Galway) a member of "A" Coy. "Cloverhill" in the 2nd Battalion South Roscommon

Michael Kearney (Correal, Fuerty) a member of "D" Coy. in the 2nd Battalion South Roscommon

Patrick Kearney When the Western Division was formed, Pat was a member of "B" Coy., 2nd Battalion South Roscommon. After the War he emigrated to Canada

Patrick Kearney (Churchboro, Knockcroghery) 4th Battalion South Roscommon. The Company was formed in 1917 with Patrick Kelly serving as Captain. During the Civil War, Kearney and three other men raided the house of an ex-policeman and ordered him to leave the county

William Kearney (Ballymacfarrane, Donamon) a member of "E" Coy. of the 2nd Battalion South Roscommon. He, along with his Company, drilled, collected money for the Dáil loan, constructed dugouts when conscription threatened

Eugene "Eodie" Kearns (Clooncagh, Strokestown) Carniska Coy. in the 3rd Battalion North Roscommon, brother of Jim. Joining the Volunteers in 1916, Kearns was appointed Company Captain at the time of reorganisation in 1918. He trained his men, and participated in the election of that year. He was present at the **attack at Strokestown** in January 1921 as well as **Scramogue** two months later, armed with a shotgun. He commanded "an excellent Company" according to Bill Doherty as recorded in the Ernie O'Malley Papers. He was also a member of Martin Fallon's Flying Column. After the War he joined the Garda Síochána, and was stationed in Limerick. He died in Ennis 25 June 1977, and is buried in Kildorrery Cemetery in Cork

Eugene "Eodie" Kearns,
Carniska Company

Francis Kearns (Smutternagh, Corrigeenroe, Boyle) was arrested for Anti-Treaty activities during the Civil War on 27 August 1922, and sent to Athlone on 2 September 1922

Jim Kearns (Clooncagh, Strokestown) a member of Carniska Coy., 3rd Battalion North Roscommon. He was arrested the same night as Luke Duffy, and spent the next three weeks in Roscommon Barracks. After the War he became a farmer. He died in 1958, and buried in Lisonuffy Cemetery

John Kearns (Aghawerriny, Kilgefin) 3rd Battalion South Roscommon. Some, but not all, of the members of Kilgefin Company took part in the **Fourmilehouse Ambush** in October 1920

Pat Kearns (Aghawerriny, Kilgefin) 3rd Battalion South Roscommon. He too may have participated in the **Fourmilehouse Ambush**

Patrick Kearns (Drumcormack, Knockvicar, Boyle) 4th Batt. North Roscommon

James Keaveney (Lieutenant) in charge of armour for the 1st Battalion, No. 2 Brigade in the 2nd Western Division. Although located in Galway, this Battalion was incorporated into No. 2 Brigade, under the command of Gerald O'Connor in the 2nd Western Division

Luke Keaveney (Cloonchambers, Castlerea) a member of Trien Coy., 1st Battalion South Roscommon. He served under Captain John White

Jim Kearns,
Clooncagh, Strokestown

Thomas Keaveney (Athlone) worked as a pawn broker's assistant. When British soldiers from the Athlone Barracks would bring their rifles in to be pawned, Keaveney would, at a later date, make certain that the local Volunteers received them. (This practice of pawning rifles did not last long for the British military)

William Keaveney (Donamon) 2nd Battalion South Roscommon. Took part in the **raid on the military train at Ballymoe** in June 1920. He became the Battalion M.O. (medical officer) when the 2nd Western Division was formed. Joined the Free State Army

Andy Keavney (Aghadrestan, Loughglynn) 1st Battalion South Roscommon. Andy was sworn into the IRB by Michael Brennan in March 1915. He was instrumental in starting the Loughglynn Volunteer Company in 1918. Participated in the **destruction of vacant barracks** in 1920, and the **attempted attack on Kilmurray Camp** in June. He was arrested in April 1921, and held in Boyle Barracks and the Curragh until Christmas 1921. Later in life he became the principal of the national school in Loughglynn. He was present at Pat Glynn's Memorial Service and the IRA Reunion Dinner in Castlerea in 1970. After retirement he moved to Dublin, and then to Ennis, Clare

Edward Keegan (Corracreigh) a member of Killina Coy., 2nd Battalion North Roscommon. He was one of the first members of the Company when it formed in August of 1917. After the conscription crisis ended, Keegan faded out of the movement. He was considered too old to be an active Volunteer. He had served under Captain Patrick Collins

Hugh Keegan (Lackan) near Strokestown. 3rd Battalion North Roscommon Brigade. He was Chief of the Republican Police in North Roscommon, and a member of Pat Madden's Flying Column. Present at the **shootout at Castlenode** in November 1920, and the **ambush at Scramogue** in March 1921. After the War he became Superintendent of the Garda Síochána, and resided in Castlecomer, Co. Kilkenny

Andy Keavney,
Aghadrestan, Loughglynn
1st Battalion South Roscommon.

James Keegan (Cremully, Castlestrange, Fuerty) a member of Fuerty Coy. in the 2nd Battalion South Roscommon. He, along with Pat Conboy, Joseph Belton, James Kenny, Tom Mannion, Seamus McGovern, and Patrick Farrell captured a Tan during the War for Independence

John Keegan (Coolroghaun) near Creggs. After the War he became a farmer. Died 1979 and buried in the new Kilbegnet Cemetery

John Charles Keegan (South Leitrim Battalion) North Roscommon Active Service Unit during the Civil War commanded by Pat Brennan. Keegan was on the staff for the 5th Battalion. He later emigrated to San Francisco

Michael Keena (Lisdillure) a stonemason in Drum parish in south Roscommon. He had his house burned by the Tans

John Keenan (Cloonshannagh, Newtown) a member of the Tarmonbarry Coy., 3rd Battalion North Roscommon

John Joseph Keenan (Knockglass, Ballinameen) 1st Batt. North Roscommon. Took part in the **attack on Frenchpark Barracks and Courthouse** in June 1921

Patrick Keenan (Ardeash, Boyle) 1st Battalion North Roscommon. Took part in the **attack on Elphin Barracks** in February 1921, and the **attack on Frenchpark Barracks and Courthouse** in June of that year. He was a member of the Anti-Treaty Active Service Unit (Flying Column) during the Civil War. He was arrested on 31 August 1922, and sent to Athlone on 2 September 1922

Albert Kehir (Keher) (Ballydooley, Oran) took part in **raid on the military train at Ballymoe** in June 1920. Served as the 2nd Lieutenant of Donamon Coy. in 2nd Battalion South area. Later joined the Free State Army

William Kehir (Keigher) (Ballyglass, Ballinagare) 1st Lieutenant of Castleplunkett Coy. in the 2nd Battalion South Roscommon. Participated in the **raid on the military train at Ballymoe** in June 1920, the **attack on Frenchpark Barracks** 2 October 1920, and the **ambush at Southpark, Castlerea** 10 July 1921. When the Western Division was formed, he volunteered to serve with the Oran Battalion Flying Column. After the War he emigrated to Brooklyn, New York, but never returned to Ireland

Dominick Kehir (Keigher) (Ballyglass, Ballinagare) a member of Castleplunkett Coy. in the 2nd Battalion South Roscommon. After the War he joined the Garda Síochána. Buried in Rathmoyle, Kilmurray

John Joseph Keigher (Ballyroddy, Elphin) a member of Aughrim Coy. in the 2nd Battalion North Roscommon. Interned from January to December of 1920

RIC Constables Keiton and McGurk, members of the constabulary stationed in Elphin, who resigned in protest after an unprovoked shooting of two citizens on Main Street. They both married sisters and later emigrated to America

Paddy Kellegher (Flannerys & Co., Boyle) 1st Batt. North Roscommon. Active Service Unit (Flying Column) of North Roscommon. Emigrated to United States

William Kellegher (Castleplunkett) On 4 September 1922, he, along with Paddy Devaney and Seamus Ryan, broke into shops in Frenchpark, and commandeered boots and whiskey — both soothing remedies for cold Irish nights!

Alfred "Alfie" Kelly (O'Kelly) (The Square, Ballaghaderreen) one of the first members of the Ballaghaderreen Coy. in the East Mayo Brigade. Arrested during the Civil War, sent to Athlone 29 Janurary 1923, released on 20 April 1923

Andrew Kelly (Toberrory, Rathcroghan) officer in the IRB

Bernard Kelly a member of Fuerty Coy. in the 2nd Battalion South Roscommon. After the War he emigrated to the United States

Bertie "Michael" Kelly (O'Kelly) (Ballaghaderreen) one of the first members of the Ballaghaderreen Coy. in the East Mayo Brigade, brother of Joe. He was a medical student in Dublin before travelling to Liverpool, where he and his brother, Joe, were active with the Volunteer movement in that city

Bessy Kelly (Scormore, Mantua) 1st Battalion North Roscommon. Stored the cart box mines used by the Volunteers

Brian Kelly took part in the **attack on the RIC at Strokestown** in January 1921

Cissie Kelly (Ballaghaderreen) member of the Cumann na mBan

Colm Kelly (a native of Offaly) who worked in Castlerea. He had been a member of the Roscommon team that won the Connaught Senior Hurling Championship title in 1906. Colm was later executed for his part in the Civil War. Execution site and date — Birr, Co. Offaly, 26 January 1923

Dan Kelly (Trien Coy.) 1st Battalion South Roscommon

Daniel Kelly (Beechwood, Tonlegee, Kilteevan) 3rd Battalion South Roscommon. He was incarcerated in Athlone on 26 November 1922 for his Anti-Treaty activities during the Civil War, and sent to Mountjoy two months later. He was then transferred to Tintown A, where he was released on 18 December 1923

Denis Kelly (Ballinwully, Kilgefin) a member of "E" Coy., 3rd Battalion South Roscommon. Many, but not all, of the members of the Kilgefin Company participated in the **Fourmilehouse Ambush** on 12 October 1920. He joined the Free State Army, and later emigrated to America, but returned to Ireland where he lived at Ballinwully. Died 11 July 1987, and buried in Kilgefin Cemetery

Denis J. Kelly (Dysart) imprisoned in Monaghan Gaol. He was a member of the first Sinn Féin County Council, and remained a member until 1925. He served as the Chairman of the Roscommon County Council in 1919-1920. Kelly actively supported Cumann na nGaedheal from 1925-28. He died as a result of a traffic accident in Dublin in 1929

Dick Kelly (Ballinwully, Kilgefin) 3rd Battalion South Roscommon

Eddie Kelly (O'Kelly) (Ballaghaderreen) was one of the founders of the Sinn Féin Club, brother of Alfred

Edward Kelly (Corlis, Castlerea) 1st Battalion South Roscommon. Kelly was a member of Moor Company under the command of Ned Campion. He participated in the **destruction of vacant barracks** in 1920, the **attempted attack on Kilmurray Military Camp** in June 1920, the **capture of enemy stores at Ballymoe** in June 1920, the **raid and capture of military equipment at Ballymoe** September 1920, the **attack on Frenchpark Barracks** 2 October 1920, the **attempted ambushes at Castlerea** and **Frenchpark** in January 1921, and the **ambush at Southpark, Castlerea** 10 July 1921. During the Truce he attended the Company training camp. Kelly took the Anti-Treaty side in the Civil War, and participated in the **burning of the train at Clooncundra**, as well as the **attack at Castlerea**, both of which occurred in November 1922

Edward Kelly (Carrigeens, Ballymurray, Roscommon) father of Tom, the O/C of the 4th Battalion. Edward was arrested in January 1921 because the Tans could not locate his son for whom they were really searching. He was taken to Roscommon town gaol, and later transferred to Athlone. When his son, Tom, was captured in late January, Edward was released

Eugene Kelly (Corracoggil North, Lisacul, Ballaghaderreen) 1st Battalion South Roscommon, accidentally shot by a companion on 3 June 1922 while occupying the Boyle Barracks after the Treaty, buried in Cuiltyboe Cemetery. Name inscribed on the tablets in front of the Shankill Monument near Elphin

Francis Kelly (Kilteevan Coy.) 3rd Battalion South Roscommon

James "Brodie" Kelly (Willsgrove, Ballintubber) a member of "F" Coy. in 3rd Battalion, No. 2 Brigade, 2nd Western Division. His home served as the headquarters for the Anti-Treaty "F" Company during the post-Truce times. Later in life he moved to Dublin, where he was the manager for Frank Colgan, an IRA veteran from County Mayo. (His father had owned the pub in Ballintubber.) Kelly was on the Organising Committee for the Shankill Monument. He is buried in Ballintubber Cemetery

James Kelly (Ballyfarmoyle, Ardcarne, Boyle) 5th Battalion North Roscommon. James joined the Volunteers in 1917. He drilled with other men, raided for arms, raided the mails, obstructed British Army recruitment meetings, and helped to establish the Republican Courts while urging citizens to boycott the British ones. He participated in the **attack on Leitrim Barracks** in May 1920, and raided the sheriff's house in Leitrim for arms in September of 1920 — an operation that yielded two shotguns and two revolvers (but not without a firefight lasting twenty-five minutes). That same month he took part in the **attempted capture of a mili-**

Eugene Kelly, Lisacul, Ballaghaderreen.

tary post at Carrick-on-Shannon, and held up the RIC on the road between Leitrim and Drumshanbo thus securing two more revolvers. In April 1921 he was on outpost duty armed with a Lee Enfield rifle during the **attack on Drumshanbo Barracks** when, in mid-battle, he was called to go into the fray and situate himself at the back of the barracks. James spent three months in the training camp at Drumharney, and afterwards joined the ASU. Present at the **attack on Boyle** 1 July, where he was positioned at the workhouse. He, along with other members of the Anti-Treaty ASU, attacked the **Barracks at Swinford** and the **Riverstown Barracks** in August, the **Drumshanbo Barracks** in September, and the **Dromahair Barracks** two months later. During 1923 he participated in the **attack on Ballinamore Barracks** on 31 January, but from then to the following January he was on the run and out of commission as a viable threat to Free State forces

James Kelly (Cordrumman, Scramogue) 3rd Battalion North Roscommon. Joined "C" Coy. of the Irish Republican Army in 1918. He attended weekly drills, collected arms, blocked roads, raided mails, and took part in the South Roscommon election. Was present at the **destruction of Cullagh vacated Barracks**. He was with the unit of men who **attacked the patrol in Strokestown** on 5 January 1921, and at the **Scramogue Ambush**. After that attack, he had to go on the run, and remained so during the Civil War, all the while supporting the Anti-Treaty cause. He took part in road cutting, felling trees, and general harassment of Free State forces, for which he was arrested and severely beaten. He took part in the **attack on Ruskey and Tarmonbarry Barracks**, and was present at the destruction of a military car at Curraghroe

James Kelly (Carrick, Kiltoom) a member of St. John's Coy. in the 4th Battalion South Roscommon. Kelly drilled with other Volunteers two nights a week — Tuesdays and Thursdays, and worked in the 1918 election. He participated in the sham battles for training purposes under Ernie O'Malley at Lysterfield, Taughmaconnell, and Churchboro in the summer of 1918. He collected gelignite as well as less dangerous commodities — monies for the Defence Fund and the IRA levy. He stopped the **train at Kiltoom** and pilfered the mails. He also held up two postmen and raided their mails for RIC letters. He took part in the **attempted ambush at Kilmurray Military Camp** in June 1920. He also kept busy blocking roads and constructing dugouts. He raided for arms — involving himself in another raiding party (in the opposite direction) the night Volunteer Joseph Kearney was seriously wounded at Feehily's home. He was with his Company when **O'Brien's residence was burned down** — an action deemed necessary because the house was thought to be soon taken over by the British. He also was with the party that **blew up the Ballybay Road Bridge**. During the Truce he became a member of the special service unit formed during this time, as well as worked with the Sinn Féin Court at Culleen

James Kelly (Gurteen, Cloonfad) 1st Battalion South Roscommon. Participated in the **destruction of vacant barracks** in 1920, and took part in the **disarming of two British soldiers at Cloonfad** in May 1921. During the Truce he attended the Company training camp, where he specialised in intelligence, scouting, and dispatch work. He took the Anti-Treaty side in the Civil War, and **attacked the Free State forces at Castlerea** in November 1922. Emigrated to Manchester England

James Kelly (Glanduff, Kiltoom) a member of St. John's Coy. in the 4th Battalion South Roscommon. Kelly drilled with other Volunteers two nights a week — Tuesdays and Thursdays

James A. Kelly (Ballinagare, Castlerea) 2nd Battalion North Roscommon, listed in the GHQ papers in the UCD Archives as the 2nd Lieutenant of Mantua Coy. Participated in the **destruction of vacant barracks** in 1920, the **attack on Frenchpark Barracks** 2 October 1920, **attack on Elphin Barracks** in February 1921, and the **attack on Frenchpark Courthouse and Barracks** in June of that year. During the Truce he served as musketry instructor. Kelly took the Republican side during the Civil War, and participated in the **attack at Castlerea** in November 1922

James Kelly (Sandfield) a member of the Knockcroghery Coy. in the 4th Battalion South Roscommon. The Company was formed in 1917 under the leadership of Patrick Kelly of Culleen, Lecarrow. Kelly drilled with the Volunteers, attended practice battles at Taughmaconnell overseen by Ernie O'Malley in the summer of 1918. Participated in the South Roscommon election of 1918, and, along with the rest of his Company, **guarded the village of Knockcroghery** from reprisal on 15 August 1920 — a reprisal precipitated by British Forces being fired upon on Lough Ree. Kelly blocked roads, made dugouts, and was one of eight men entrusted with important dispatches during this time. Died 23 April 1975, and buried in St. John's Cemetery

Joe Kelly (Rathcroghan) 2nd Battalion North Roscommon, the First Lieutenant of "A" Company (Mantua). Joined the IRB and the Volunteers in 1917. Kelly drilled, raided for arms, took part in the **burning of Tulsk Barracks** in July 1920, the **attack at the Elphin Dispensary** 13 December 1920, the **attack on Elphin Barracks** on 11 February 1921, and the **burning of Frenchpark Courthouse and Barracks** the night of 25/26 June 1921. He was appointed Vice O/C of the Active Service Unit (Flying Column) formed in North Roscommon at this time. During the Truce he spent some days in Dublin being trained in the use of a machine gun. He returned to Roscommon, and attended the Mantua and Cloonshee training camps. He was then sent to Muckinagh, Kilglass to work under John Roche in the making of bombs. When the Boyle Barracks was being taken over, he travelled to that town, and stayed in the barracks. Before he vacated the barracks during the **Battle of Boyle** on 1 July, he mined the building. Kelly took an active part in the **attack and capture of Riverstown Barracks, Swinford Barracks, Drumsna Barracks, Frenchpark Barracks**, and **the attack on out-posts on the Boyle/Carrick-on-Shannon Rd**. He was arrested about the time of the cease-fire, and detained in Athlone, Kilmainham, and the Curragh for almost a year. He emigrated to New York

John Kelly (Lisduff, Mt. Talbot) a member of the Tisrara Coy. in the 4th Battalion South Roscommon

John Kelly (Currocot, Mt. Talbot) a member of the Tisrara Coy. in the 4th Battalion South Roscommon

John "Jack" Kelly (Ararghty, Athleague) (Athleague Coy.) Company Captain, 3rd Battalion South Roscommon. He was among the IRA "occupation troops" in Mount Talbot. After the War he became a cattle dealer, and served as secretary of the Athleague Fianna Fáil cumann in 1928

John Kelly (Kilbride Coy.) 3rd Battalion South Roscommon

Joe Kelly (O'Kelly) (Ballaghaderreen) Adjutant of 4th Battalion East Mayo Brigade (which incorporated several Companies in west Roscommon), a member of the IRB. O'Kelly and Alec McCabe stole a car out of a garage in Ballaghaderreen Easter Monday 1916 and headed towards Tubbercurry in Sligo in order to muster men and gather them together for a show of force. The attempt proved futile. They had gotten only a few miles out of town when the car broke down. Seeing headlights on the road and assuming it was British transport, the two parted company, each making his way to his own home turf. O'Kelly was arrested after the Rising for his Sinn Féin sympathies, and sent to His Majesty's prison at Lewes on 20 May. He was later sent to "The Irish University," Frongoch. As part of Lloyd George's appeal to American sympathies, Kelly, along with the other internees, was released seven months after arrest. It was a decision the Crown was soon to regret. In 1917 O'Kelly was again arrested after his return from County Longford, where he had helped with the Joe McGuinness election. While walking down the street in Ballaghaderreen, two constables grabbed him and announced they were taking him to the barracks. He drew his pistol and in the ensuing scuffle, the two policemen were shot — although not seriously. Joe was sent to Dublin for trial, and from thence to Dundalk, where, at the time, hunger strikes were taking place. After three weeks on hunger strike, Joe was released, and returned "back to his old post as secretary of the Sinn Féin Club and Volunteer organiser."* Joe sailed across the Irish Sea, and became active as a gun runner in Liverpool — purchasing, storing, and shipping arms to Ireland. He participated in the **burning of the Liverpool docks** on 28 November 1920. Kelly took the Anti-Treaty side during the Civil War, and was arrested near Ballaghaderreen by troops under Alec McCabe on 25 August 1922. He was taken to Sligo Gaol, from which he escaped in mid-October. In late October, he was named O/C of the Flying Column, because Seamus Mulrennan had been killed. His leadership was short-lived. He was recaptured at Markree Castle on 14 November 1922. Four decades later he was elected chairman of the Commemorative Committee that erected the Elphin IRA monument. Died 1966

*_The Western People_, "Service in Ballaghaderreen," by John McPhillips, 19 September 1964.

John Kelly (Cootehall) listed in the GHQ papers in the UCD Archives as the Quartermaster for Cootehall Company in the 5th Battalion North Roscommon

John Kelly (Taghnarra, Cloonboniffe) 1st Battalion South Roscommon. Participated in the **destruction of vacant barracks** in 1920, the **raid for petrol at Ballinlough Station** in June 1920, the **attempted ambush at Coshlieve** in July 1920, the **attempted attack on the Castlerea Station Guard** in July 1920, the **raid and capture of military equipment at Ballymoe** September 1920, and blocked roads in preparation for the **attack on Frenchpark Barracks** 2 October 1920. He also took part in the **attempted attacks at Castlerea** and **Frenchpark** in January 1921, and served in the covering party for the **attack on the military at Castlerea** 7 April 1921. Participated in the **attempted ambush at Loughglynn**, and the **attempted ambush of an RIC patrol near Ballymoe** in April 1921. During the month of May he joined with other Volunteers in an **attempted ambush at Lisacul** (in conjunction with the East Mayo men). During the Truce he attended the Battalion training camps. He was a member of the Active Service Unit formed in January 1921. Later emigrated to Philadelphia

John Kelly (Ballinlough) 1st Battalion South Roscommon, participated in the **attempted attack on the Castlerea Station Guard** in July 1920, and the **burning of the barracks at Ballinlough** 14 September 1920. During the Truce he attended the Battalion training camp specialising in dispatch work

John Joe Kelly (Coolatinny, Ballinlough) 1st Battalion South Roscommon, participated in the **burning of the Barracks at Ballinlough** 14 September 1920. During the Truce he attended the Battalion training camp specialising in intelligence work

John Kelly (senior) (Rusheen, Castlerea) 1st Battalion South Roscommon. Participated in the **destruction of vacant barracks** in 1920, the **raid for petrol at Ballinlough Station** in June 1920, the **capture of enemy stores at Ballymoe** that same month, and the **attempted attack on the Castlerea Station Guard** in July 1920. He also blocked roads in preparation for the **attack on Frenchpark Barracks** 2 October 1920. Served in the covering party for the **attack on the Castlerea military** 6 April 1921. Participated in **attempted ambush at Loughglynn** and the **attempted ambush of an RIC patrol near Ballymoe** in April 1921. During the month of May he joined with other Volunteers in an **attempted ambush at Lisacul** (in conjunction with the East Mayo men)

John Kelly (Sheerevagh, Ballinameen, Boyle) 1st Battalion North Roscommon.

PHOTO COURTESY OF ANTHONY KELLY

John Kelly (Sheerevagh, Ballinameen, Boyle) Vice Commandant of the 1st Battalion North Roscommon. Kelly was an IRB member, and served as a centre for his area. He joined the IRA in 1914, was secretary of the local Sinn Féin Club, and collected over sixty pounds for the Dáil loan. He trenched roads, raided the mails and houses for arms, and imposed the Belfast boycott. He was present at the **attempted attack at Frenchpark** on 5 January 1921 and again in March, and was in charge of the rifle section at the **attack on Elphin Barracks** on 11 February. Kelly assisted in the **escape of the men from Boyle Barracks** in May, and the **burning of the barracks and courthouse in Frenchpark** in June. He also prepared an ambush at Elphin where he was nearly shot by one of his own men! During the Truce he attended Mantua and Boyle camps — specialising in making bombs and mines. In April of 1922, he helped to reorganise the Battalion while functioning as the District Justice on the Republican Courts. He also organised Fairymount and Grange Companies during this time. When the Civil War swept over Roscommon, he was a member of the Anti-Treaty Active Service Unit (Flying Column). Kelly was present at the **attack on Union buildings at Boyle** 1 July 1922, **raided Frenchpark Barracks** and captured arms and equipment, attacked and **captured a military outpost at Boyle Railway Station** and on the Boyle/Carrick-on-Shannon Road. Kelly sniped at Free State soldiers in late August, and disarmed a Free State officer in December. He was arrested 3 August 1923, and interned in Athlone. The prison, though, was not strong enough to hold him. He escaped two months later with other men, and was forced to go on the run for several more months. After the War Kelly served as the Chairman of Boyle Fianna Fáil *comhairle ceanntair* in 1926, and held a seat on the Roscommon County Council for over a decade. He also farmed his land at Sheerevagh, Ballinameen. Died in December 1969, and is buried in Caldra Cemetery

John Kelly (Muckinagh, Strokestown) 3rd Battalion North Roscommon, Kiltrustan Coy. Joined the IRA in May 1919 as part of "H" Coy. In that year, he carried dispatches, raided the mails, and confiscated arms. In 1920 he assisted in the Sinn Féin Courts, and the Belfast boycott. Took part in the **ambush of Strokestown patrol** on 6 January 1921, **attack on Elphin Barracks** in February, and the **ambush at Scramogue**. In addition, he was one of a few who worked in an evacuated cottage in Muckinagh to construct bombs. The two-story house belonged to Pat Holmes, and was located in a remote part of the field. (It came complete with a ghost.)* During the Civil War John assisted Republican Columns by guiding them through his area, securing board and room for them, and continuing his work in the munitions factory. He also took part in two engagements against the Free State troops during 1922. After the War he became a farmer. He died in 1984 and is buried in the new Strokestown Cemetery

Interview John Kelly, son of John, Muckinagh Strokestown 15 November 2003

John Kelly (Muckinagh, Strokestown) 3rd Battalion North Roscommon.

John Kelly (Anrittabeg, Cloontuskert) a member of the Kilgefin Coy., 3rd Battalion South Roscommon. Many, but not all, of the Kilgefin Coy. participated in the **Fourmilehouse Ambush** in October 1920. After the War he became a farmer

John Kelly (Moneen) a member of Cloontuskert Company in the 3rd Battalion South Roscommon. Joined the Volunteers in early 1919. He was injured in May 1921 in the **Lanesboro-Roscommon Landmine Operation**, and as a result was taken to Incheneagh and Quaker Islands in Lough Ree, and, after the Truce, to Jervis Street Hospital in Dublin. It was not until June 1924 that Kelly was finally released from (George V) St. Bricin's Military Hospital. After the War he lived in Moneen, and travelled to Roscommon town where he worked in social welfare. Buried in Cloontuskert Cemetery

John Kelly (Cloonmore) a member of the Tarmonbarry Coy.

Joseph Kelly (Roscommon Coy.) 3rd Battalion South Roscommon

John Kelly (Knockcroghery Company) 4th Battalion South Roscommon. The Company was formed in 1917 under the leadership of Patrick Kelly of Culleen, Lecarrow. Kelly drilled with the Volunteers, attended practice battles at Taughmaconnell overseen by Ernie O'Malley in the summer of 1918. He was one of a very few number of men entrusted with carrying GHQ dispatches. He took part in raiding six houses of RIC recruits, which resulted in those men changing their minds! Participated in the South Roscommon election of 1918, the **burning of Lecarrow Barracks**, and the **attempted attack at Kilmurray Camp**. He also was present with his Company when, in conjunction with Kilteevan Coy., the men **attempted an ambush at Clooncraff** under the command of Pat Madden. He and his Company, **guarded the village of Knockcroghery** from reprisal on 15 August 1920 — a reprisal precipitated by British Forces being fired upon on Lough Ree. Eleven days later, he, and six other Volunteers, ambushed two RIC men at Knockcroghery Railway Station — an action in which one of the constables lost his life. Kelly took part in a number of arms raids in the area. The men worked in sections and succeeded in forestalling the enemy who were also taking up shotguns at the same times — sometimes within a few hours after the Volunteer visits. Kelly, however, was wounded in one of those forays. He later joined the Garda Síochána

Joseph Kelly of Carrick, Kiltoom, participated in a raid with the St. John's Coy.

Josie Kelly (Ballaghaderreen) member of the Cumann na mBan, sister of Sean

Mark Kelly (Ballaghaderreen) one of the first members of the Ballaghaderreen Coy. in the East Mayo Brigade. He was a native of North Mayo

Martin Kelly (Ballygar Coy.) was considered part of 4th Battalion South Roscommon when the Divisional structure was implemented. He became an officer in a Flying Column that fought in south Roscommon during the Civil War

another Martin Kelly (Ballygar Coy.)

Michael Joseph Kelly (Ballinagare) 1st Battalion South Roscommon. He drilled with his Company, and enforced the Belfast boycott. Participated in the **destruction of vacant barracks** in 1920, the **burning of the Barracks at Ballinlough** on

14 September 1920, and the **attack on Frenchpark Barracks** 2 October 1920. After the War he emigrated to the United States

Michael Kelly (O'Kelly) (Ballaghaderreen) one of the first members of the Ballaghaderreen Coy. in the East Mayo Brigade

Michael Kelly's licensed premise in Ballinagare was burned to the ground as a reprisal for the attack on Frenchpark Barracks. His home served as the headquarters for "B" Company in the 2nd Battalion, No. 2 Brigade, 2nd Western Division during the post-Truce times

Michael Kelly (Ballinlough Coy.) 1st Battalion South Roscommon. Served as Adjutant for the Company. Took part in the **attempted ambush at Coshlieve** in July 1920, and in the **burning of the Barracks at Ballinlough** 14 September 1920. During the Truce he attended the training camp at Hermitage

Michael Kelly a member of "A" Coy. in the 2nd Battalion South Roscommon. After the War he emigrated to the United States

Patrick Kelly (Culleen, Lecarrow) 4th Battalion South Roscommon. The Knockcroghery Company was formed in 1917 under his direction. Kelly and Jim Breheny were the Company representatives to Roscommon town, where a Brigade staff was selected. He served as a Judge with the Sinn Féin Courts which were held monthly. He attended instructional courses given by Ernie O'Malley at Rahara each evening for several weeks during the summer of 1918, and commanded his men at the sham battles at Taughmaconnell overseen by O'Malley. Kelly went house to house canvassing for signatures to the plebiscite for independence, and compiling a list of all available foodstuffs. Kelly (along with two other Kellys — Tommie and John) was entrusted with important dispatches to Roscommon town. Kelly took part in a raid on the homes of six intended RIC recruits. After the Volunteer visit, the recruits changed their minds! Participated in the South Roscommon election of 1918, helped to set up the rules for opening and closing hours for shops in Knockcroghery, and, along with Jim Breheny, Owen Curley and Tom Kelly, **oversaw the enforcement of the Belfast boycott** in the area. Kelly also made a start in the making of moulds used for slugs for shotguns. Kelly cut the telegraph wires in preparation for the **burning of the Lecarrow Barracks.** He, along with his Company and in conjunction with Kilteevan Company, took part in the **attempted ambush at Clooncraff** under the command of Pat Madden. He raided numerous houses for arms. On one occasion two homes in Rahara were raided — an action which resulted in one Volunteer being slightly wounded, but guns and ammunition secured nonetheless. Kelly also partnered with Volunteers from St. John's Coy. and raided homes in their district. Took part in the **attempted attack at Kilmurray Camp** — an action cancelled the very night of the proposed assault. He, along with the rest of his Company, **guarded the village of Knockcroghery** from reprisal on 15 August 1920 — a reprisal precipitated by British Forces being fired upon on Lough Ree. Kelly also participated in the **attempted ambush of two RIC constables at Lecarrow**, and the **attempted attack on a military lorry at Knockcroghery**. He was captured in April 1921 and interned. During the Civil War period, Kelly took the Anti-Treaty side, and held the rank of Battalion Intelligence Officer. After the War he became a farmer and blacksmith, a trade in which his height and stoutness served him well. Died 5 August 1964, and buried in Gailey Cemetery

Michael Kelly (Trien Coy.) 1st Battalion South Roscommon

Michael Kelly (Kinnity, Fourmilehouse) a member of the Kilbride Coy. in the 3rd Battalion South Roscommon. After the War he became a tradesman and well known local musician

Michael Kelly worked as a guard on the trains that travelled through northeast Roscommon. He gave excellent service to the Volunteers by carrying dispatches and munitions

Michael Kelly (St. John's Coy.) 4th Battalion South Roscommon. He later joined the Garda Síochána

Michael Kelly (Tully, Kilglass, Strokestown) a member of the Kilglass Company in the 3rd Battalion North Roscommon

Michael Kelly (Carrowmoney, Rahara) 4th Batt. South Roscommon

P. Kelly (Beechwood, Kilteevan) 3rd Battalion South Roscommon. He was arrested during the Civil War, and sent to Mountjoy on 10 January 1923. He was transferred to the Curragh on 22 April 1923, from which he escaped

P. Kelly served as the 2nd Lieutenant of Frenchpark Coy.

Patrick Kelly (Kilteevan) Kelly was arrested during the Civil War on 28 September 1922, and sent to Athlone two months later

Patrick Kelly (Ballinwully) a member of the Kilgefin Coy. in the 3rd Battalion South Roscommon, brother of Denis. He often worked with Pat

Madden's group in the Ballagh area. Many, but not all, of the members of the Kilgefin Company participated in the **Fourmilehouse Ambush** on 12 October 1920. After the War he became a farmer. Died 24 November 1988, and buried in Kilgefin Cemetery

Patrick Kelly (Athleague Coy.) 3rd Battalion South Roscommon

Patrick Kelly (Trien Coy.) 1st Battalion South Roscommon

Patrick Kelly (Kilglass, Knockcroghery) 4th Battalion South Roscommon. The Knockcroghery Company formed in 1917 under the leadership of another Patrick Kelly (of Culleen, Lecarrow). Patrick was one of several men who arrested another person for firing on and wounding a Volunteer. The man was sentenced to weeks of confinement at Cloverhill

Patrick Kelly (Cloonelt, Castlerea) 1st Battalion South Roscommon, dispatch rider for John Vaughan's Cloonboniffe Company. Participated in the **destruction of vacant barracks** in 1920, took part in the **raid for petrol at Ballinlough** June 1920, the **attempted attack on the Castlerea Station Guard** in July 1920, blocked roads in preparation for the **attack on Frenchpark Barracks** 2 October 1920, **attempted attacks at Castlerea** and **Frenchpark** in January 1921, and served in the covering party for the **attack on the Castlerea military** 6 April 1921. Participated in the **attempted ambush at Loughglynn**, and the **attempted ambush of an RIC patrol near Ballymoe** in April 1921. During the month of May he joined with other Volunteers in an **attempted ambush at Lisacul** (in conjunction with the East Mayo men). During the Truce he attended the Battalion training camps. He joined the Free State Army. Later he emigrated to the United States

Patrick Kelly (Feevagh) Dysart Coy., 4th Battalion South Roscommon, served as Quartermaster for the Company, which he joined in 1917. Attended parades, received instructions under Ernie O'Malley, helped in the 1918 election. He was appointed to work with the Republican Police. Took part in raiding for arms, and a raid on the home of an RIC man who was warned to quit his job. The Volunteers also destroyed all of the papers in the constable's possession at that time. Kelly was part of an attempted ambush of an RIC lorry which came along the road on the 3rd of each month. That month, however, the lorry failed to appear. During the Truce he attended the officers' training camp at Rahara for three evenings a week, and the camp at Ballygar. Throughout the months of the Civil War, he, along with his Company, which took the Anti-Treaty side, assisted the escaped prisoners, carried dispatches, and blocked roads at Dysart and Ballyforan on five different occasions. After the War he emigrated to America

Patrick Kelly (Cam) a member of Curraghboy Coy. in the 4th Battalion South Roscommon

Patrick Kelly (Sandfield, Knockcroghery) 4th Battalion South Roscommon, brother of James. The Company was formed in 1917 under the leadership of Patrick Kelly of Culleen, Lecarrow. Kelly drilled with the Volunteers, attended practice battles at Taughmaconnell overseen by Ernie O'Malley in the summer of 1918. Participated in the South Roscommon election of 1918, served as an armed escort for bank officials taking large sums of money to fairs in Knockcroghery, and as a scout on the Athlone side during in the **burning of Lecarrow Barracks**. Raided for arms at two hostile houses in Rahara area, took part in the **attempted attack at Kilmurray Camp**. He, along with the rest of his Company, **guarded the village of Knockcroghery** from reprisal on 15 August 1920 — a reprisal precipitated by British Forces being fired upon on Lough Ree. Kelly served as a sentry at Curry Crossing when the goods train was held up near Ballymurray Railway Station. He also collected the IRA levy from the local people — funds which bought supplies and guns for the local Volunteers

Peter Kelly (Scregg House, Knockcroghery) 4th Battalion South Roscommon. The Company was formed in 1917 with Patrick Kelly of Culleen, Lecarrow, serving as Captain. Kelly participated in the South Roscommon election of 1918. He, along with the rest of his Company, **guarded the village of Knockcroghery** from an expected reprisal on 15 August 1920 — anticipated because British Forces had been fired upon on Lough Ree. He also acted as scout when the **evening train to Dublin was stopped** and searched for mail. He later censored items taken from that train. After the War he became a farmer. Died 1978. Buried in Gailey Cemetery

Peter Kelly, Knockcroghery.
PHOTO COURTESY OF MICHAEL BREHENY

Peter Kelly (Ballygar Coy.) was considered part of 4th Battalion South Roscommon when the Divisional structure was implemented

Rev. Fr. Kelly, C.C. (curate at Keadue) active supporter of Count Plunkett in the bye election of 1917

Roger Kelly (Tully, Kilglass, Strokestown) a member of the Kilglass Company in the 3rd Battalion North Roscommon. He served under the command of Captain Michael Greene

Thomas Kelly (Carrigeens, Ballymurray, Roscommon) a member of Curraghboy Coy. in the 4th Battalion South Roscommon. Kelly drilled with the Volunteers, and served as a Judge with the Sinn Féin Courts. He attended instructions at Rahara given by Ernie O'Malley in the summer of 1918, and took a course in semaphore and Morse signalling. He attended the Battalion mobilisations held at Scregg, and Churchboro, and the sham battles at Taughmaconnell overseen by O'Malley. He went house to house canvassing for signatures for the plebiscite for independence. Participated in the South Roscommon election of 1918, kept strict watch on local shopkeepers regarding Belfast goods, and kept Knockcroghery Station under surveillance watching for contraband. He, along with Jim Breheny, commanded the party who **burned Lecarrow Barracks**. Kelly raided for arms. On one occasion, he and six other men raided several houses (including one of a former RIC man), and confiscated four guns, a revolver, and a quantity of ammunition. On another night, two homes in Rahara fell victim to his party's surprise tactics. The door was forced open, and guns and ammunition promptly confiscated. Kelly also partnered with Volunteers from St. John's Company and raided homes in their district. He was entrusted to carry many important dispatches to Roscommon town. Took part in the **attempted attack at Kilmurray Camp** — an action that was cancelled the very night of the proposed assault. He, along with the rest of his Company, **guarded the village of Knockcroghery** from reprisal on 15 August 1920 — a reprisal precipitated by British Forces being fired upon on Lough Ree. Kelly and Jim Breheny oversaw a local trial of a man accused of shooting and wounding a Volunteer. Ten men decided the sentence: "prison for a number of weeks." Kelly, Jim and John Breheny, and Owen Curley transported the man to Cloverhill, where he was guarded for many days before being returned to his family. Participated in the **holdup of the evening mail train** from Dublin, **attempted ambush of two RIC constables at Lecarrow**, and the **proposed attack on Castlerea Railway Station**. Commanded the search operation after the **attack on a goods train at Ballymurray**, whereby twenty bags of mails were taken from the train and censored by Volunteers. Kelly also commanded the **attempted attack** on a party of military about eighteen strong **at Knockcroghery** in January 1921. Later that month, he and Jim Breheny were sleeping in a cock of hay near Kelly's home, when the all clear signal (a sheet put out in the yard) was given for he and Breheny to enter the house for breakfast. Patrick Tennant arrived shortly thereafter with an urgent dispatch, but before anything was done about it, two lorries arrived with troops that surrounded the house. All three men were taken. Kelly was incarcerated in Athlone Barracks, Mountjoy, Wormwood Scrubbs, and Pentonville Prisons. Released on Christmas Eve 1921. Tall and stout, Kelly was a self-educated man, who earned his living as a farmer. He died 12 October 1981 at the age of eighty-six

Sean Kelly (Ballaghaderreen) member of the Ballaghaderreen Coy. in the East Mayo Brigade

Thomas Kelly (Moor Coy.) in the 1st Battalion South Roscommon. Participated in the **attempted attack on Kilmurray Military Camp** in June 1920, the **attack on Frenchpark Barracks** 2 October 1920, and the **attempted ambushes at Castlerea** and **Frenchpark** in January 1921. He took part in the **attempted ambush at Cloonsheever** in March, the **attempted ambush at Loughglynn** in April, the **attempted ambush at Lisacul** (an action taken in conjunction with the East Mayo men) in May 1921, and the **attempted ambush of an RIC patrol near Ballymoe** that same month. He was a member of the Active Service Unit from January 1921 until the Truce, after which he spent much of his time in the training camps. During the Civil War Kelly took the Anti-Treaty side, and was active in the **attack at Ballinagare** in July 1922, and the **attack at Castlerea** in November 1922. Thomas also participated in the **burning of the train at Clooncundia** later that month. He later moved to Lifford, County Donegal

Thomas Kelly (Tonlagee, Kilteevan) a member of "A" Coy. in the 2nd Battalion South Roscommon

Thomas F. Kelly (Cloonkerin) Mantua Coy. in the 2nd Battalion North Roscommon. Took part in the **attack on Elphin Barracks** on 11 February 1921, and the **attack on Frenchpark Barracks and Courthouse** in June. He initially joined the Free State Army, but deserted with his rifle to participate in the **attack on Boyle Barracks** in July 1922, and firefights in Sligo and Mayo. He was a member of the Anti-

Treaty Active Service Unit formed in North Roscommon during the Civil War. He later emigrated to New Jersey

Tommy Kelly (Cam) a member of the Curraghboy Coy., 4th Battalion South Roscommon

William Kelly 2nd Battalion North Roscommon, took part in the **attack on Frenchpark Barracks and Courthouse** in June 1921

William Kelly (Castlerea) was arrested during the Civil War on 27 August 1922, and sent to Athlone a month later

Thomas Kelly (Carrowntemple, Four Roads) Adjutant for the 4th Battalion South Roscommon, joined the Volunteers when he was sixteen. After 1918 Tommie could not sleep in his house at night for fear of a raid, but his daytime hours were spent with his father in the family tailoring and outfitting business. Tommie was blessed with a good neighbour, Paddy Connell, who worked across the road from Kelly's father. Connell was a blacksmith who, when he suspected trouble or heard motorised vehicles coming his way (they were almost always carrying British troops), would alter the tone and rhythm of his anvil in order to warn Tommie of impending danger. Tommie was present at the **attack on the RIC patrol in Strokestown** in January 192 and the **Scramogue Ambush** in March 1921. He joined the National Army, and was stationed in Co. Mayo. In the 1930s he was decommissioned from the Army, and returned to civilian life. During World War II, he moved to London, where he died in 1965, and is buried in that great city

William Kelly (Carroward) a member of the Kilgefin Coy., 3rd Battalion South Roscommon. Some, but not all, of the Kilgefin Coy. took part in the **Fourmilehouse Ambush** in October 1920. After the War he joined the Garda Síochána. Died in the 1980s

William Kelly (Creggs) was arrested during the Civil War for his Anti-Treaty activities, and sent to Athlone. He was released on 30 November 1922

Frank Kennedy (High St., Athlone) arrested April 1922 for his Anti-Treaty activities, and sent to Kilmainham Gaol, where he was released on 18 July 1922

Joseph Kennedy (Carrick-on-Shannon) in 1922 he served as the Captain of "D" Company in the 4th Battalion of the newly formed 3rd Western Division

Joseph Kennedy (Athlone) served as the Adjutant of the Athlone Battalion. One afternoon he bought a Parabellum from two so-called "deserters" from the British Army. Later that evening, he was ordered to deliver some dispatches to Longford. It proved to be an assignment that saved him from a gaol cell, because the deserters were really spies sent to entrap him. His home was raided that night. After the War he emigrated to New York

Luke Kennedy (Tanseyfield, Elphin) was arrested during the Civil War on 14 September 1922 for his Anti-Treaty activities, and sent to Athlone in November. He was soon released

M. Kennedy (Donamon) "E" Coy. in the 2nd Battalion South Roscommon

Tom Kennedy (Raveege, Ballintubber) a member of "F" Coy. in the 2nd Battalion South Roscommon

The Kenny Household, known as The Glebe in Kilrooskey, former home of the Church of Ireland rectors, and, during the Black and Tan War, used as the first "home" of Pat Madden's Flying Column. The house was large and allowed for sleeping quarters on several levels. It was often used by men on the run. One of the daughters (Rose) of the schoolteacher, Pat Kenny, was a member of Cumann na mBan. She later married Pat Madden. Both Rose and Pat Madden died early in life, both in the same year — 1939

Alec Kenny (Carrowbaun, Ballintubber) Captain of Ballintubber Company in the 2nd Battalion South Roscommon, brother of Thomas. Accompanied the cart that transported the Volunteers to the **attack on Frenchpark Barracks** 2 October 1920. He replaced Peter Glancy as Captain of the Company. After the War he worked with the Roscommon County Council. He is buried in Ballintubber Cemetery

Alfred Kenny (Ballinagare Coy.) 1st Battalion South Roscommon. During the Truce he attended the Company and Battalion training camps

Bernard Kenny (Lissagallen, Fuerty) a member of "D" Coy. in the 2nd Battalion South Roscommon

E. Kenny (Cargins, Donamon) a member of "E" Coy., 2nd Battalion South Roscommon

Edward Kenny (Ballinagare Coy.) 1st Battalion South Roscommon. Drilled with his fellow Volunteers, collected funds for the Dáil loan, and enforced the Belfast boycott. Participated in the **destruction of vacant barracks** in 1920, the **attack on Frenchpark Barracks** 2 October 1920, and, during the Civil War, the **attack at Ballinagare** in July 1922, and the **attack at Castlerea** in November 1922. During the Truce he attended the Company and Battalion training camps specialising in dispatch, scouting, or intelligence work

Frank Kenny (Ballinagare Coy.) 1st Battalion South Roscommon

Jack Kenny (Drum Coy.) 3rd Battalion Athlone Brigade, a member of Father Flanagan's Sinn Féin Club who, after the War, emigrated to Boston. No one in Ireland ever heard from him again

James Kenny (Castlestrange, Fuerty) Quartermaster for Fuerty Coy. in the 2nd Battalion South Roscommon. James also served as the Quartermaster when the 2nd Western Division was formed. Kenny was on the first Sinn Féin County Council. He, along with James Keegan, Joseph Belton, Seamus McGovern, Tom Mannion, Pat Conboy, and Patrick Farrell captured a Tan during the War

John Kenny (Carrick, Ballinlough) 1st Battalion South Roscommon. Participated in the **raid for petrol at Ballinlough Station** in June 1920

John Kenny (Curraghboy Coy.) 4th Battalion South Roscommon. From 1917-March 1919 did organisational work, drilled with the men, performed scouting duties, paraded with fellow Volunteers during a visit to the area by Sean Connolly, performed police duty during the South Roscommon election and in conjunction with enforcement of Dáil decrees. Kenny was one of a group of men who raided the private homes of three men — two of whom had joined and one who was about to join the RIC. Not surprisingly, these men had a change of heart! Kenny raided for arms, his own closet being the first target — he gave up his own shotgun, revolver, and about sixty cartridges for Company use. Kenny participated in arms raids. Twenty raids were conducted within the Company area, and another fifteen raids were outside the immediate vicinity and performed in conjunction with other Companies of the Battalion. Prevented jurors from attending the British Courts, and held periodic meetings of Republican Courts when necessity arose. Manufactured ammunition and constructed dugouts for storage of same. Took part in the **attempted ambush at Clooncraff**, and the **attempted attack of a military lorry at Knockcroghery** in January 1921. Seven or eight mail cars were raided during this time, and Kenny took part in some of those actions. The entire Company participated in the arrest and confinement of a suspected spy. That man was tried by court-martial and eventually executed — an action which prompted the arrest of ten members of the Company on 5 January 1921, including Kenny. He was beaten and taken to Athlone Barracks and incarcerated in a cell with no bed for three months. Later transferred to Mountjoy and finally, in the last days of June, he was shipped across the waters to Wormwood Scrubbs and Pentonville Prisons in England. Released 11 January 1922

John Kenny (Glanduff, Kiltoom) St. John's Coy. in the 4th Battalion South Roscommon.

Joseph Kenny (Carrick, Ballinlough) Captain of the Ballinlough Coy., 1st Battalion South Roscommon. Joseph participated in the **attempted ambush at Coshlieve** in July 1920, and the **attempted attack on the Castlerea Station Guard** that same month. He also was involved in the **burning of the Barracks at Ballinlough** 14 September 1920 where three men lost there lives. At Truce time he attended the training camp at Runnamoat. During the Civil War he became a member of the Anti-Treaty Active Service Unit of the 1st Battalion South

Martin Kenny (Ardmore, Donamon) 2nd Battalion South Roscommon. Took part in the **raid on the military train at Ballymoe** in June 1920

Martin Kenny (Driney, Loughglynn) 1st Battalion South Roscommon. He took part in the **raid on Ballymoe Station** September 1920

Michael "Mick" Kenny (Ballygar Coy.) was considered part of 4th Battalion South Roscommon when the Divisional structure was implemented. He lived in Johnstown, Drum. He was a member of Father Flanagan's Sinn Féin Club. Kenny had a few narrow escapes during his days as a Volunteer. He was picked up once for a month, but released for lack of evidence. Mick worked as a driver for a trading merchant. He joined the Free State Army, and was part of the group that took over Custume Barracks in Athlone. After the War he worked as a contractor farmer and chauffeur. Died 1969, and buried in Drum Cemetery

Michael Kenny (Erritt, Gortaganny, Castlerea) Adjutant for the Ballinlough Coy., 1st Battalion South Roscommon. Participated in the **attempted attack on the Castlerea Station Guard** in July 1920, the **burning of the Barracks at Ballinlough** 14 September 1920, the **burning of Loughglynn Barracks** September 1920, and the **attack on Frenchpark Barracks** 2 October 1920. He also took part in the **attempted ambush at Lisacul** (in conjunction with the East Mayo men) in May 1921. During the Truce he attended the training camps at Hermitage and Erritt. He served as the 1st Lieutenant of the Gorthaganny Coy. in April 1922. After the War he earned his living in farming, carpentry, and as an undertaker. He was present in 1970 at the Memorial Sevice for Pat Glynn, who had died fifty years earlier in the burning of Ballinlough Barracks. Died 1980 and buried in Cuiltyboe Cemetery

Michael J. Kenny (Cashelnagole, Ballinagare) 1st Battalion South Roscommon. Drilled with his Company, enforced the Belfast boycott, took part in the **destruction of the local barracks**, and participated in the **attack on Frenchpark Barracks** 2 October 1920

Patrick Kenny (Johnstown) Drum Coy., 3rd Battalion Athlone Brigade, brother of Michael. He was attending Mass on Sunday 6 February 1920 in Drum Church when an unidentified voice interrupted the service with the words, "The Tans are coming, if anyone wants to leave, do so now."* It was an obvious cue to the assembled Volunteers to vacate the premises — pronto! And indeed the Tans did arrive and proceed to interview everyone in the chapel. Kenny's house was raided several times (his brother was an active Volunteer). In back of his home, there was a little house in the bog that served as a gathering and sleeping place for the Volunteers. When the men met together, they did not take their weapons with them, because they were afraid that in the event of a raid all would be confiscated. Instead, the guns were stacked together a few hundred yards from the house. Patrick oftentimes acted as the guardian and lookout for the older men. As a young man of eighteen, he witnessed the takeover of Custume Barracks from the British on 28 February 1922. British troops marched out along with their tanks and horses. They saluted the members of the Irish Free State Army, who were standing by (see photo page 474). Patrick was one of a few men on this list who was personally interviewed by this author (in the summer of 2002)

*_Drum and its Hinterland_ by Edward Egan, p. 302.

Patrick Kenny (Johnstown), 3rd Battalion Athlone Brigade.
PHOTO COURTESY OF PATRICK KENNY

Patrick Kenny (Corramore, Curraghboy) 4th Battalion South Roscommon. Civil War activities included raiding homes of ex-RIC and searching for arms, blocking roads at Whitepark, Curraghboy, and Lysterfield. He later emigrated to England

Patrick Kenny (St. John's Coy.) 4th Battalion South Roscommon. Kenny drilled with other Volunteers two nights a week — Tuesdays and Thursdays. Patrick **raided the mails when the train was stopped at Kiltoom**. He was with his Company when **O'Brien's residence was burned down** — an action deemed necessary because the house was thought to be soon taken over by the British. During the Truce Kenny became a member of the special service unit. After the War he joined the Garda Síochána

Patrick Kenny (Ballinagare Coy.) 1st Battalion South Roscommon. He later emigrated to the United States

Richard Kenny (Ballinagare Coy.) 1st Battalion South Roscommon

Rosie Kenny (New Glebe, Kilgefin) member of the Cumann na mBan. She later married the O/C of the 3rd Battalion, Pat Madden. Died in 1939

Tommy Kenny (Raveege, Ballintubber) 2nd Battalion South Roscommon. Took part in the **raid on the military train at Ballymoe** in June 1920. When the 2nd Western Division was formed, Thomas became a 2nd Lieutenant in the 3rd Battalion, No. 2 Brigade

Thomas Kenny (St. John's, Lecarrow) 4th Battalion South Roscommon. Kenny drilled with other Volunteers two nights a week — Tuesdays and Thursdays. He blocked roads, and **raided the mails when the train was stopped at Kiltoom**. He was with his Company when **O'Brien's residence was burned down** — an action deemed necessary because the house was thought to be soon taken over by the British. During the Truce Kenny attended the Battalion camp at Drinaun, Galway, and became a member of the special service unit. After the War he joined the Garda Síochána

Val Kenny (Roscommon) 3rd Battalion South Roscommon, beaten by the Tans at Mote Park Demesne, member of the 1918 Sinn Féin election committee

William Kenny (Cartron Coote, Kilteevan) 3rd Battalion South Roscommon. After the War he became a farmer

Johnnie Kenoy (Cloonsuck, Castlerea) harboured many men on the run

Eddie Keogh, a merchant in Church Street, Roscommon town, who came daily for several weeks in January 1921 and brought food to three prisoners in Roscommon Gaol — Jim Kearns, Tommy Loughran, and Keogh's friend, Luke Gibbons, who had been arrested by mistake

John Joe Keogh (Ballyfeeny, Kilglass, Strokestown) a member of the Kilglass Company in the 3rd Battalion North Roscommon

Michael Keogh (Kilbride, Kilmore) Quartermaster for Kilmore Company in the 5th Battalion North Roscommon. Took part in the **robbery of the Dublin-Sligo mail train**. After the 3rd Western Division was formed, he served as the O/C of the 4th Battalion. He was a member of the Anti-Treaty ASU

Tom Keogh First Captain of St. John's Company

Jim Kerrane (Ballyglass, Loughglynn) 1st Battalion South Roscommon. Arrested in Flannery's shop in Ballaghaderreen, and sent to Longford and Athlone Barracks. Jim was an Irish speaker, who emigrated to Coventry, England, where he died at a young age

John "Jack" Kerrane (Moor Coy.) 1st Battalion South Roscommon. Took part in the **attack on Frenchpark Barracks** 2 October 1920, the **attempted ambushes at Castlerea** and **Frenchpark** in January 1921, the **burning of the train at Clooncundra**, and the Anti-Treaty **attack at Castlerea** during the Civil War in November 1922. During the Truce he attended the Company training camp and specialised in intelligence, scouting, and dispatch work. After the War he became a cattleman. He is buried in Castlerea Cemetery

Patrick Kerrane (Ballindrimley, Castlerea) 1st Battalion South Roscommon. Participated in the **attack on Frenchpark Barracks** 2 October 1920, and the **attempted ambushes at Castlerea** and **Frenchpark** in January 1921. He was a member of the Active Service Unit formed in January of 1921. During the Truce he attended the Company training camp and specialised in intelligence, scouting, and dispatch work. After the War he married and moved to Bolton, Lancashire, England

Paul Kerrigan (St. John's Coy.) 4th Battalion South Roscommon. He emigrated to the United States

Larry Kesey (Kilgefin Coy.) 3rd Battalion South Roscommon

Daniel Kerrigan (Carnagh West, St. John's) 4th Battalion South Roscommon, served as the 2nd Lieutenant of the St. John's Coy. Kerrigan drilled with other Volunteers two nights a week — Tuesdays and Thursdays. He worked with the Republican Courts, and in the 1918 election. He and his Company, under the command of Captain Patrick Grady, participated in the sham battles for training purposes under Ernie O'Malley at Lysterfield, Taughmaconnell, and Churchboro. He collected monies for the Defence Fund, the IRA levy, and more lethal gelignite. He, Johnny Kilcline, and Hubert Watson stopped two postmen and raided their mails for RIC letters. He, along with a dozen other men from the Company, took part in the **attempted ambush at Clooncraff** under the command of Pat Madden, and the **attempted ambush at Kilmurray Military Camp** in June 1920. He was also on duty for the County Council Election of 1920 positioned at Taughmaconnell Station. He raided for arms — involving himself in actions which yielded three shotguns one night, a revolver another. He was with another raiding party the night Volunteer Joseph Kearney was seriously wounded at Feehily's home. He also **raided the mails when the train was stopped at Kiltoom**. He was with his Company when **O'Brien's residence was burned down** — an action deemed necessary because the house was thought to be soon taken over by the British. During the Truce he attended the officers' camp at Donamon, and served as a delegate to Commandant Tom Maguire's Review at Ballygar. Kerrigan also became a member of the special service unit formed during this time. After the War he emigrated to the United States of America

Patrick Kielty (Cleaheen, Cootehall) 5th Battalion North Roscommon Brigade

John Kilbane (Knockhall, Ruskey) a member of the Kilglass Company in the 3rd Battalion North Roscommon

Johnny Kilcline (Carrigan More, Lecarrow) St. John's Company, Vice O/C of the 4th Battalion South Roscommon. When the Company first started in 1917, Johnny was the first Adjutant. He drilled with other Volunteers two nights a week — Tuesdays and Thursdays, worked with the Republican Courts, served summons, and patrolled the public houses. In the summer of 1918, his Company, now under the command of Patrick Grady, participated in the sham battles for training purposes under Ernie O'Malley at Lysterfield, Taughmaconnell, and Churchboro. He worked in the 1918 election, and constructed dugouts in the area. Kilcline raided for arms on many occasions. He was present at the raid on Feehily's house in which Joseph Kearney was severely wounded in the stomach. Kilcline worked in connection with the Belfast boycott, collected monies for the Defence Fund and IRA levy, and also collected more lethal gelignite. He, Hubert Watson, and Dan Kerrigan stopped two postmen and raided their mails for RIC letters. He, along with other members of his Company, took part in the **attempted ambush at Clooncraff** under the command of Pat Madden, and the **attempted ambush at Kilmurray Military Camp** in June 1920. He was also on duty for the County Council Election of 1920 positioned at Dysart Station. He engaged in the **blowing up of Ballybay Road Bridge**. During the Truce he attended the Brigade training camp at Ballinaheglish at least two days each week, the officers' camp at Donamon, the Battalion camp at Drinaun, Galway, and was a delegate to Commandant Tom Maguire's Review at Ballygar. All the while, he also served in the Courts at Culleen. Kilcline also became a member of the special service unit formed during this time. Taking the Anti-Treaty side during the Civil War, he **blew up the Kellybrook and Curry Railway Bridges**, blocked ballast trains, collected gelignite, and helped assemble the heavy mines used locally, and raided for transport and arms for the Brigade Flying Column. Upon receiving a note from the Chief of Republican Police ordering the execution of a local man, Johnny ignored the order as well as the words written at the top of the note — "Burn this before you read it." The note was hidden for many years in a box in the loft of the Kilcline house until the roof of the old cottage caved in.* After the War he became a farmer, worked for the County Council, and served as Secretary to Fianna Fáil in Glanduff. He died in April 1978, and is buried in St. John's Cemetery — not a thousand yards from his former back door

Johnny Kilcline, Vice O/C of the 4th Battalion South Roscommon.

PHOTO COURTESY OF JOHN KILCLINE

John Kilcline, son of Johnny, interview by author, Lecarrow, 26 October 2003.

Malachy Kilcline (Carrigan More, Lecarrow) a member of St. John's Coy., 4th Battalion South Roscommon, brother of Johnny

Patrick Kilcline (Lecarrow, St. John's) 4th Battalion South Roscommon

Patrick Kilcommons (Lisnagavragh, Four Roads) a member of the Tisrara Coy. in the 4th Battalion South Roscommon

John Kilcourse (Ballaghaderreen town) one of the first members of the Ballaghaderreen Coy. in the East Mayo Brigade, brother of Tom and William, sons of a carpenter

Tom Kilcourse (Ballaghaderreen town) He too was one of the first members of the Ballaghaderreen Coy. in the East Mayo Brigade

William "Billy" Kilcourse (Ballaghaderreen town) along with his brothers, he became one of the first members of the Ballaghaderreen Coy. in the East Mayo Brigade

Lawrence Kildea (Clonoghil, Taughmaconnell) was incarcerated in Athlone during the Civil War on 24 February 1923 and released two months later

Edward Kilduff (Circular Road, Roscommon town) 3rd Battalion South Roscommon. After the War he worked as a County Council ganger

P. Kilgallon (Boyle) dispatch rider for Anti-Treatyites. Arrested December 1922

Thomas Kilgarrif (Dunmore Coy. in Galway) part of No. 2 Brigade, 2nd Western Division, under Brigade O/C Gerald O'Connor. He was arrested after the Rising, and, when released, helped to form the Dunmore Company of Volunteers. He also organised the Dunmore Sinn Féin Club, and was the Head Centre for the IRB circle in that area. He was a member of the North Galway Flying Column under the command of Patrick Dunleavy

Tom Kilkenny (Castleplunkett Coy.) 2nd Battalion South Roscommon

Martin Killalea (Doon, Boyle) was taken into the IRB by Alec McCabe in February 1915. Killalea was on the original committee to place Count Plunkett's name on the North Roscommon ballot. He served as the Vice O/C of the 1st Battalion North Roscommon, as well as serving as the Quartermaster of the Brigade. He took part in the **Rockingham Raid**, "guest" at Boyle Barracks, Mountjoy, and the Curragh. He was a member of the Anti-Treaty Active Service Unit (Flying Column) during the Civil War. Arrested and interned again during that time. In July 1922, when North Roscommon was wedded to Leitrim and became the 3rd Western Division, he served as the Vice O/C of the Brigade under Pat Brennan. After the War he lived in Doon overlooking Lough Key. Died in the 1960s

Edward "Ned" Killian (Mihanboy, Drum) 3rd Battalion Athlone Brigade. After the War he became a teacher and moved to Galway

James Killian (Mihanboy, Drum) first secretary of the Father Flanagan Sinn Féin Club in Drum

James Killian (Killion) (Clooncraff, Kilteevan) 3rd Battalion South Roscommon, shot and severely wounded by the Tans. After the War he returned to farming. Died 1964 and buried in Kilteevan Cemetery

John Killian (Mihanboy, Drum) Company Captain in the 3rd Battalion Athlone Brigade

John Killian (Kellybrook, Knockcroghery) a member of St. John's Coy. in the 4th Battalion South Roscommon, served as the engineer for the Company

John Killian (Mihanboy, Drum) Served as 1st Lieutenant in Drum Coy. in the 3rd Battalion Athlone Brigade. He moved to Dublin, whereupon Denis Naughton took his place. He earned his living in Dublin as a tram driver. He later returned to Drum and farmed the land. Died in the early 1970s and is buried in Drum Cemetery

James Killian, Clooncraff, Kilteevan

PHOTO COURTESY OF MICHAEL BREHENY

Luke Killian (Killion) (Cruit, Knockcroghery) 4th Battalion South Roscommon. The Knockcroghery Company was formed in 1917 under the direction of Patrick Kelly. Killian paraded with other Volunteers, and participated in the sham battles at Taughmaconnell overseen by O'Malley in the summer of 1918. Participated in the South Roscommon election of 1918. The Company, in conjunction with Kilteevan Company, took part in the **attempted ambush at Clooncraff**. Took part in the **attempted attack at Kilmurray Camp** — an action that was cancelled the very night of the proposed assault. He, along with the rest of his Company, **guarded the village of Knockcroghery** from reprisal on 15 August 1920 — a reprisal precipitated by British Forces being fired upon on Lough Ree. Killian and Jim Breheny intercepted four enemy soldiers at Culleen, and took them to a house about three miles distant. There they relieved the military men of their attire, and gave them civilian clothes. (The uniforms were later used to great advantage by the Company in trapping suspected spies.) Killian died 21 August 1921 as a result of injuries suffered in a motor bicycle accident while returning home from Volunteer duties. His name is inscribed on the tablets at the Shankill Monument near Elphin

Thomas Killian (Killion) (Cloonsellan, Kilteevan) 3rd Battalion South Roscommon

Mattie Killilea (Ballygar Coy.) was considered part of 4th Battalion South Roscommon when the Divisional structure was implemented

John Kilmartin (Roscommon) 3rd Battalion South Roscommon. Member of Roscommon Company. Present at Pat Glynn's Memorial Service at Loughglynn Church in 1970

Maudie Kilmartin was a member of the Summerhill Cumann na mBan club in Drum, South Roscommon

346 ■ THEY PUT THE FLAG A-FLYIN'

William Kilmartin (Roscommon town) intelligence gatherer for the Company

John Kilowmy (Roscommon Coy.) 3rd Battalion South Roscommon

John Kilroe (Cooly, Fuerty) brother of Michael. He was a section leader in Galway (just a mile over the Roscommon border), but participated in many skirmishes within County Roscommon. After the War he became a rate collector. He died in the 1960s, and is buried in the Athleague Cemetery

Michael Kilroe (Cooly, Fuerty) born in County Roscommon near the Galway border, he became a dispatch rider for the Fuerty Company with which his brother John was associated. After the War he turned to travelling sales for his livelihood. He is one of a few survivors of this list with whom the author spoke (in the autumn of 1998). He died the following year, but not before he shared his Irish wit, and stories about melting down lead in saucepans to fill empty cartridges

James Kilroy (Ballygar Coy.) was grouped with the 4th Battalion South Roscommon when the Divisional structure was implemented

John Kilroy (Ballygar Coy.) 2nd Lieutenant of the Company, which was considered part of 4th Battalion South Roscommon when the Divisional structure was implemented

Malachy Kilroy (Toberdan, St. John's) 4th Battalion South Roscommon. When the Company first started in 1917, Malachy drilled with other Volunteers two nights a week — Tuesdays and Thursdays, and served as a Republican Policeman with the Republican Courts. He worked in the 1918 election, and his Company, now under the command of Patrick Grady, participated in the sham battles for training purposes under Ernie O'Malley at Lysterfield, Taughmaconnell, and Churchboro. He also constructed dugouts in the area. Kilroy raided for arms on several occasions. He accompanied the other raiding party the night that Joseph Kearney was severely wounded in the stomach while raiding Feehily's house. Kilroy worked in connection with the Belfast boycott, collected monies for the Defence Fund and IRA levy, and also collected more deadly gelignite. He also helped to **stop and raid the train at Kiltoom** for mail. He, along with other twelve other members of his Company, took part in the **attempted ambush at Clooncraff** under the command of Pat Madden, and the **attempted ambush at Kilmurray Military Camp** in June 1920. He was present at the **burning of O'Brien's house** — a house thought to be soon taken over by British Forces. Kilroy, along with Hubert Murphy (Company Captain), Pat Fallon, and Patrick Kelly (Captain of Knockcroghery Coy.) concocted two pounds of gunpowder one night and then repeated their feat the next evening. He was also with the party, that **blew up the Ballybay Road Bridge**. During the Truce he was active with the Republican Courts at Culleen. He also became a member of the special service unit formed during this time. Kilroy took an active part in the Civil War on the Anti-Treaty side — **blowing up the Kellybrook Bridge**, blocking ballast trains, and collecting gelignite for use in bombs. After the War he emigrated to the United States

Tom Kilroy (Cloonboley, Drum) 3rd Battalion Athlone Brigade. He took the Oath of Allegiance to the Sinn Féin Party at the Ardkeenan House, the local Volunteer gathering point*

Drum and Its Hinterland by Edward Egan, p. 301.

Andrew King (Shankill, Elphin) 2nd Battalion North Roscommon. Listed in the GHQ papers in the UCD Archives as the Elphin Company Quartermaster. After the War he became a farmer

George King (Ballymartin, Kilglass, Strokestown) a member of the Kilglass Company in the 3rd Battalion North Roscommon

John King (Stonepark, Roscommon) 3rd Battalion South Roscommon

Robert King (Figh, Lisacul) 1st Battalion South Roscommon. Served from April 1918 to December 1921 with the Loughglynn Company. Participated in the

Michael Kilroe, Fuerty Company.
PHOTO COURTESY OF LEW THORNE

destruction of vacant barracks in 1920, the attempted attack on Kilmurray Camp in June, and the attack on Frenchpark Barracks 2 October 1920. Arrested 9 February 1921, and served sentences in Athlone and the Curragh. Released in December 1921, and, by July 1922, was serving as the 1st Lieutenant of Loughglynn Coy. He took the Anti-Treaty side during the Civil War. Robert King, Jack Creaton, Toby Scally, and Liam Forde joined Seamus Mulrennan's Active Service Unit, and were on the move throughout the area. After the War he returned to farming. Died 1968, and buried in Lisacul Cemetery

Christopher Lainge ("H" Coy.) 1st Battalion South Roscommon. He had been a member of the Cavan Volunteers since 1915, serving as a drill instructor. In October of 1916, he was transferred to Clifden, where he was under observation by the local police because the Marconi Signal Station was located there (perhaps too near to a suspicious man with questionable political views and knowledge of telegraphy). He was transferred to Castlerea, where he joined the Volunteers several weeks later. Dan O'Rourke directed him to study signalling and scouting methods. In the spring of 1918, Lainge was transferred to Ballyhaunis, but returned to Ballinlough in 1920, where he did intelligence work. By August of 1921, he was Head of Intelligence for No. 2 Brigade in the 2nd Western Division. During the Civil War he took an active role with the Anti-Treaty faction. His group captured four armed men at Ballinlough in July 1922, after which he drove them to Castlebar for detention. He was later arrested by Col. Pat Madden of the National Army, and detained until the general release in 1923

John Kinley took part in the **attack on the RIC patrol at Strokestown** in January 1921

Jack Knight (Quartermaster of the Glenamaddy Battalion) which was part of No. 2 Brigade in the 2nd Western Division under Brigade Commander Gerald O'Connor. In 1921 he became part of the ASU formed with the Tuam Battalion

Bartholomew Lally (Clooneenbaun, Fuerty) Quartermaster for "A" Coy., Cloverhill Coy. in the 2nd Battalion South Roscommon

Bernard Lally (Rahara Coy.) 4th Battalion South Roscommon

John Lally 1st Lieutenant of the Glinsk Coy. in the Glenamaddy Battalion. Although located in Co. Galway, this Battalion was incorporated into No. 2 Brigade, 2nd Western Division with Gerald O'Connor, former O/C of the 1st Battalion South Roscommon, serving as Brigade Commandant

Michael Lally (Rahara Coy.) 4th Battalion South Roscommon

Thomas Lally (Rahara Coy.) 4th Battalion South Roscommon, served as the 1st Lieutenant of the Company

Bridget Lane (Four Roads) later the wife of Patrick Gallagher, member of the Cumann na mBan, active in Harry Boland's South Roscommon election of 1918

Thomas Joe Lane (Cuilnakeava, Four Roads) a member of the Tisrara Company in the 4th Battalion South Roscommon

James Lannon (Bumlin, Scramogue) Captain of Scramogue Coy. in the 3rd Battalion North Roscommon. Lannon and Sean Leavy used to go on "let's discourage men from joining the RIC" runs. At one such meeting, the potential enlistee was sprayed with shotgun pellets. Dr. Dudley Forde of Strokestown treated the man, and thus knew the circumstances under which he received the peppering wounds. Fearing certain discovery, Leavy decided to go on the run, but Lannon declined because his mother was ill. He was soon arrested on charges of arms possession (which he did have but which the RIC could not not find — the revolver was hidden in a rick of hay).* Lannon was sent to Longford Barracks, and then shipped to Wormwood Scrubbs. His mother died while he was in prison. After the Truce he joined the Free State Army. He later returned to farming near Ashbrook. Died 2 November 1967

*Ciaran Leavy, interview by author, Scramogue, 29 June 2002.

John Lannon (Cloonylyons, Strokestown) a member of the Carniska Coy., 3rd Battalion North Roscommon

Michael Lannon (Doon, Strokestown) 3rd Battalion North Roscommon. Took part in the **Castlenode Confrontation** in November 1920

Charley Lardner (Ballaghaderreen) one of the first members of the Ballaghaderreen Coy. in the East Mayo Brigade

James Larkin (Ardmore, Donamon) a member of "E" Coy. in the 2nd Battalion South Roscommon

Joseph Larkin (Ardmore, Donamon) a member of "E" Coy. in the 2nd Battalion South Roscommon. Took part in the **raid on the military train at Ballymoe** in June 1920

Michael J. Larkin (Boyle) 1st Battalion North Roscommon. He was an officer in the Active Service Unit (Flying Column) of North Roscommon, and served as Chief of Chemistry. He was also the Quartermaster for the Column. Arrested near Ballaghaderreen on 25 August 1922 (along with a dozen other Anti-Treaty men) because he was suspected of participating in the **demolition of the Knockvicar and Cootehall Bridges** on 14 August. After the War he emigrated to Australia

Thomas Larkin (Killina Coy.) 2nd Battalion North Roscommon. He was one of the first members of the Company when it formed in August of 1917

Thomas Larkin (Knockskehan, Lecarrow) St. John's Coy. in the 4th Battalion South Roscommon. He was with his Company when **O'Brien's residence was burned down** — an action deemed necessary because the house was thought to be soon taken over by the British. He participated in the **destruction of Ballybay Bridge**. During the Truce he became a member of a special service unit

Joseph Lavender (Scramogue, Strokestown) a member of the Scramogue Coy., 3rd Battalion North Roscommon. Participated in the acquisition of rifles gained from deserting soldiers. His house was burned during the War

Michael Lavery took part in the **attack on the RIC patrol at Strokestown** in January 1921

Andy Lavin (Creevagh, Ballyfarnon) 4th Battalion North Roscommon. Organised Companies in the Ballyfarnon area. He served as Adjutant for the North Roscommon Brigade. Lavin joined the IRB in 1908, and was later Head Centre for the West. He was also a founding member of the Gaelic League, sitting on its executive board from 1909-1916. When the Dáil loan was floated in early 1919, Lavin became the chief collecting agent in the area. He resigned the position of Adjutant in December when he transferred to the engineering phase of operations. He was on the first Sinn Féin Council in Roscommon, and became the Chairman of the County Council in 1920-21. Lavin was interned in Sligo Gaol for a period during the War. After the hostilities ceased, he resumed his school teaching career in Dublin. From 1923 to 1927, he served as the TD for Roscommon for the Cumann na Gaelheal party. He also served as the Director of the Educational Building Society. Died 1959

Bernard V. Lavin (Ballinlough) first Sinn Féin County Council

Dominick Lavin (Callow, Frenchpark) Breedogue Coy. in the 1st Battalion North Roscommon

Rev. Fr. Thomas Lavin, a native of Cloonfower, Castlerea. Curate in Ruskey from 1911 to 1920, and the parish priest of Tulsk until his death in 1939. He was a noted preacher and supporter of the Gaelic League and Sinn Féin. He took the Pro-Treaty side following the Truce. He was an uncle to Rev. Dr. Thomas Lavin whose poem appears in the sidebar

T. J. Lavin (Fairymount) first Sinn Féin County Council

Tommy Lavin (Ballyfarnon) 4th Battalion North Roscommon. Joined the Volunteers in February 1917 when Andy Lavin (a relative) came to Ballyfarnon to organise a Company. He also joined the IRB, having been taken in by Pat Madden. Participated in the **march on Lord Kingston's lands** near Arigna in March 1919. Took part in the **burning of Ballyfarnon Barracks** on Easter Saturday night, and in various raids for arms. In November of 1920, he was appointed O/C of the Ballyfarnon Company, and, when Tom Moran was arrested, Lavin was promoted to the Vice O/C of the 4th Battalion. Blocked roads leading to Lord French's residence at Drumdoe House, raided the mails at Ballyfermoy and the post office at Ballyfarnon, which precipitated the chain of

Memory, 1916
by Rev. Dr. Thomas J. Lavin, Ph.D. (N.U.I.)
(printed in the *Roscommon Herald*
centennial edition)

To-night the starts are shinning bright
Above the city fair —
And neon-lights do pierce the night
A-twinkling through the air!

Now all O'Connell Street is bright,
As bright it was before —
When skies did blaze with freedom's light
That Easter time of yore!

And back across the years I fly,
Borne fast on mem'ry's wing,
To springtime in the long gone by
When Irish hearts did sing!

Yes, hearts did sing and pulses throbbed —
When neon-lights were few!
And old men of the Fenians sobbed
Because of dreams come true!

For Dublin's sky was pierced with light —
Symbolic of a faith reborn!
And fires were lit that Easter night
That ushered in Eternal morn!

And onward marched this nation old
To glorious freedom's goal —
It head held high, its step now bold!
The master of its soul!

Sean Leavy, O/C of the 3rd Battalion North Roscommon.

Peter Ledwith, Athlone Brigade.

events leading to the **Keadue Ambush**. He escorted Michael Dockery out of the area after the attack had taken place. He suffered some debilitating wounds when he was experimenting with GHQ grenades obtained from the Boyle Battalion. He was in a field at Kilmactranny while "in the act of priming one of the grenades by inserting and screwing home the igniter." The bomb exploded, blowing off his right hand. Local people took him by cart to Sligo Hospital, where he awoke to find that the police had surrounded the building, and he was under arrest. He subsequently served time in George V Hospital in Dublin and Mountjoy. He was forever deaf in his right ear, and the side of his face was permanently injured. He was released just before Christmas 1921. He later married the girl who worked in the Ballyfarnon Post Office who had been assisting the IRA. He moved to Ballytore, County Kildare, where he worked, of all places, in the post office

John Lawe (Ballyfeeny, Kilglass) a member of the Kilglass Coy. in the 3rd Battalion North Roscommon

Patrick Lawlor 1st Battalion (Castlerea) South Roscommon

Thomas Leary (Foughil, Castlerea) Trien Coy., 1st Battalion South Roscommon

Peter Leavy (native of Treanacreeve, Scramogue, Strokestown) 2nd Battalion North Roscommon, brother of Sean. Served as the First Lieutenant for "E" Company

Sean Leavy (native of Treanacreeve, Scramogue, Strokestown) O/C 3rd Battalion North Roscommon, joined the Volunteers at Ruskey in early 1917 when Joe McGuinness was campaigning for election as well as recruiting for the IRA. A year later he joined the IRB. Leavy organised a Company in Scramogue. He raided the mail cars several times in the closing months of 1920. He took part in the **attack on the RIC patrol at Strokestown** in January 1921. In his home, the plans were finalised for the **ambush at Scramogue**. Leavy and his friend, Jim Lannon, used to pay visits to potential enlistees of the RIC. Shotgun pellets were part and parcel of their prepared "speech." After a few of these visits (which came to the attention of Dr. Dudley Forde of Strokestown who had to treat the resulting injuries to the would-be recruits), Leavy decided the heat was on, and he had to go on the run. He was part of the group of men who met Rita Lengehan and gave her a sizable sum of money to transport to the guard in Boyle Barracks who had aided in the escape of Michael Dockery. After the Truce he joined the National Army, serving as a First Lieutenant. In October of 1922, he had the dubious honour of arresting some former colleagues (Sean Birmingham and George Tanner). After the War he became the Sheriff of Offaly in 1925. He also was involved with law enforcement in Limerick. Additional employment included ganger for the Land Commission, auctioneer, grocery store and pub owner in Scramogue. He died in March 1981, and is buried in the Scramogue Cemetery

Peter Ledwith (Lagan, Moate, County Westmeath) his Company worked in conjunction with the Volunteers in the Athlone Brigade. He was a member of the IRB, and fought in the Four Courts garrison during Easter Week. As a consequence, he was interned in Frongoch, the infamous "Irish University"

John Leech (Ballaghaderreen) one of the first members of the Ballaghaderreen Coy. in the East Mayo Brigade, a native of Kilkelly

Michael J. Leech (Ballymoe, Galway) was in charge of engineering for No. 2 Brigade, 2nd Western Division. He joined the engineering staff of Roscommon County Council in 1917, and retired in 1951 as Assistant County Engineer. Died 1960

Anthony Leneghan (Lenehan) Castlerea teacher in charge of dispatches for No. 2 Brigade in the 2nd Western division

Jack Leneghan (Lenehan) (Ashforth) Lenehan's in Hillstreet served as a clearing house for ammunition, guns, and dispatches in the northern area. His was also a safe house in which the boys on the run could count on food and shelter

John Leneghan (Rathallen, Croghan) 5th Battalion North Roscommon. He was a member of the Anti-Treaty Active Service Unit of North Roscommon

John Leneghan (Legan, Elphin) 2nd Battalion North Roscommon. Served as the Captain of Aughrim Company. Participated in the **attack on the Elphin patrol** 5 January 1921. He was interned during part of the War

Hubert Leneghan (Lenehan) (Ashforth) Adjutant for the 5th Battalion North Roscommon. Leneghan's in Hillstreet served as a clearing house for ammunition and dispatches in the northern area. He was the brother of Jack and Rita. After the Truce he joined the National Army

Rita Leneghan (Lenehan) (Ashforth) sister of John, and Hubert. Member of the Cumann na mBan, who began working with the IRA in 1919. She carried dispatches, and typed correspondence to GHQ. Firearms were left in her care in a dugout, and, when necessity demanded, she scouted an area in preparation for an ambush. Her home at Ashforth was ever open to men on the run. She was on duty the day of the **Fourmilehouse Ambush**, the **attack on Elphin Barracks** in February 1921, and the evening before **Scramogue**. She helped with the **rescue of Michael Dockery from Boyle Barracks** by conveying, under orders from Martin Fallon, the funds necessary (£300) to pay Corporal Meadlarklan. She was ordered to go to Boyle, where she was to get in touch with IRA officers who would position her in a safe house. She did so, and was staying on the Crescent the morning Dockery escaped. The owners of the house alerted her that the military were looking for strangers in town. At that moment, she noticed the soldiers coming towards the house. She dashed out the door, ran to the Boyle Station, where she boarded the first outgoing train possible — one headed to Dromod. From there she travelled eight miles to the place where Martin Fallon, Sean Leavy, and Michael Duignan were waiting for her with the money. She then travelled to the location where the transfer of funds was scheduled to take place, and proceeded to hand over the cash. After that incident, her home was often raided; consequently, she stayed the weeks before the Truce in the O'Connor home in Scramogue. After the War she married a Duignan and moved to Dublin

George Lenehan (Borefield, Strokestown) Kiltrustan Coy. in the 3rd Battalion North Roscommon

Bernard (Brian) Lenihan (Leneghan) (Lisbaun, Kiltoom) Captain of Kiltoom Coy. in the 4th Battalion South Roscommon. He was on the run for several years while his home serve as a safe house for other Volunteers. Black and Tans were so sure of his home being a haven for "rebels" that they broke in one evening and dragged his mother all around the kitchen by her hair. Their brutality was to no avail! Brian attempted to negotiate a hand-over of the Kiltoom Barracks to the Volunteers, but was thwarted when Constable Potter was shot and killed at the Knockcroghery Railway Crossing in August 1920. He took the Anti-Treaty side during the Civil War, but left the ranks early in the struggle. He was disgusted with the activities of the Republicans. Stopping trains and stealing food was not his idea of fighting for Ireland.* He left for Dublin, where he became a building contractor. Died in 1986, and is buried in Glasnevin Cemetery

Gloria Hogan,daughter of Brian, interview by author, Boyle, 6 August 2004.

John Lenihan (Leneghan) (Lisbaun, Kiltoom) 4th Battalion South Roscommon, brother of Brian, Michael, and Thomas. After the War he ran the family farm

Bernard (Brian) Lenihan, Capt.of Kiltoom Company
PHOTO COURTESY OF BRIAN LENIHAN

Michael Lenihan of Lisbaun, Kiltoom,
PHOTO COURTESY OF BRIAN LENIHAN

Thomas Lenihan of Kiltoom

James Lennon, Athlone Brigade

Patrick C. Lennon, Strokestown

Tom Lennon, Athlone Brigade

Michael Lenihan (Killina Coy.) 2nd Battalion North Roscommon. He was one of the first members of the Company when it formed in August of 1917

Michael Lenihan (Leneghan) (Lisbaun, Kiltoom) 4th Battalion South Roscommon, brother of Brian, John, and Thomas. After the War he became a stonemason in Curraghboy, Athlone (see photo on page 351)

Thomas Lenihan (Leneghan) (Lisbaun, Kiltoom) 4th Battalion South Roscommon, brother of Brian, John, and Michael. After the War he followed his brother to Dublin, where he worked as a plasterer

Ellen Lennon (Crannagh, Summerhill, Athlone) mother of four sons in the Republican movement. She had her house burned to the ground by the Tans in November 1920

James Lennon (Crannagh, Summerhill, Athlone) 3rd Battalion Athlone Brigade, one of four brothers involved in the Republican movement, charter member of The O'Rahilly Sinn Féin Club of Summerhill, arrested in 1919. He became an "invited guest" at Mountjoy, where he took part in a hunger strike

John Lennon (Crannagh, Summerhill, Athlone) 3rd Battalion Athlone Brigade, brother of Jim, Tom, and Paddy. He too was arrested in 1919, and sent to Ballykinlar Internment Camp in County Down. Lennon was released and **present for an attempted ambush of policemen** on the Athlone/Ballinasloe Road the day before the Cornafulla Ambush in February 1921

Michael Lennon (Ballygar Coy.) was considered part of 4th Battalion South Roscommon when the Divisional structure was implemented

Michael Lennon (Rooskagh, Bealnamullia) 3rd Battalion Athlone Brigade. Lennon drilled with his Company, trained to use firearms, took an active part in the General Election of 1918, attended Battalion meetings, and worked with the Republican Police force at disputed farmland in Bealnamullia and Clongowna. He was with a group of Volunteers that seized ammunition from an airplane that made a forced landing at Keelogues in 1919. Took part in the **burning of the Barracks at Bealnamullia**, mobilised for an **attack on Cloonark Barracks**, and **attempted an ambush at Curraghaleen** in October 1920. Near Truce time he guarded the ASU Headquarters in the area, **destroyed the bridge at Millbrook**, blocked roads at Millbrook and Monksland, harboured and aided escaped prisoners. During the Truce he trained at Greenfield, Donamon, and Falty, in addition to collecting funds to aid the Volunteers and attending the Arbitration Courts

Patrick C. Lennon (Elphin Street, Strokestown) a member of the Killina Coy., 2nd Battalion North Roscommon. Lennon was one of the founding members of the Company when it formed in 1917. He was active in the Strokestown branch of the Gaelic League, and was a founding member of the National Athletic Cycling Association. Died in 1964

Patrick Lennon (Crannagh, Summerhill, Athlone) youngest of four brothers, all of whom were involved in the Republican movement. He was the only one of the four to permanently evade capture. According to Paddy Kenny, who was interviewed in 2002, "Paddy Lennon was the most important man in the area." Lennon joined the local Company of the IRA in late 1917. He drilled with his comrades, worked extensively in the 1918 election, made slugs for shotguns, raided for arms, collected for the Dáil loan, and **burned the Bealnamullia Barracks** on Easter Saturday night in 1920. He blocked roads, cut communication lines, and helped destroy the bridge on the main Athlone/Ballinasloe road at Summerhill. Lennon provided security and food for the Flying Column when it was billeted in his area. His house was burned as a reprisal for the attack on Constable Doyle on 31 October 1920

Thomas Lennon (Blackstown, Cornafulla, Athlone) 3rd Battalion Athlone Brigade, served as secretary to the Father Flanagan Sinn Féin Club

Tom Lennon (Crannagh, Summerhill, Athlone) 3rd Battalion Athlone Brigade, also a charter member of the local Sinn Féin Club, arrested with his brother Jim in April 1919, and sent to His Majesty's boarding house at Mountjoy, where he participated in a hunger strike. Later emigrated to America

John Leonard (Ballintubber) was arrested during the Civil War for Anti-Treaty activities, and taken to Athlone on 28 November 1922, and then transferred to Mountjoy in January

Michael Leonard (Corbally, Donamon) 2nd Battalion South Roscommon, brother of Patrick. Took part in the **raid on the military train at Ballymoe** in June 1920. When the Western Division was formed, he volunteered to serve with the Oran Battalion Flying Column. He later emigrated to the United States of America

Patrick Leonard (Corbally, Donamon) a member of "E" Coy in the 2nd Battalion South Roscommon, brother of Michael. Took part in the **raid on the military train at Ballymoe** in June 1920

Tim Leonard (Boyle) Tim was taken into the IRB by Alec McCabe in February 1915

Tom Leonard (Kennyborough) Ballintubber Coy., 2nd Battalion South Roscommon, who, on 6 January 1921, narrowly escaped a Black and Tan bullet by foolishly sleeping in his own home (it was January and COLD in the haggards of hay!) He escaped with William Cunnane, but their third companion, Pat Durr, was not so lucky. Three month before that time, Tom had participated in the **attack on Frenchpark Barracks**

William Leonard (Ballintubber Coy.) 2nd Battalion South Roscommon

Arthur Leyland (Bridge Street, Boyle) 1st Battalion North Roscommon, a member of the Volunteers before the Rising

Joseph Leyland (Cloonfad, Cootehall, Boyle) 5th Battalion North Roscommon, joined the IRA in 1917 and was appointed Captain of his Company. Participated in the **attempted attack on the Carrick-on-Shannon Station Guard** in September 1918. Took part in the **attack and capture of Leitrim Barracks** in May 1920. In September he took part in the **attempted capture of the Carrick-on Shannon** military post, the holdup of RIC men between Leitrim and Drumshanbo, and commanded a raid on the sheriff's house in Leitrim, which yielded two shotguns and two revolvers, but not without a twenty-five minute firefight. He was arrested in early 1921 and interned until the following December. He returned to his area and reorganised his Company (on the Anti-Treaty side) in 1922, and was present at the **attack of Drumshanbo Barracks** in September 1922. He headed a Company of men in the **attack on Ballinamore Barracks** on 31 January 1923. He was also a member of the attack party on a Free State patrol between Carrick-on-Shannon and Drumshanbo

Austin Loftus (2nd Lieutenant) of Granlahan Coy. which was part of the 2nd Battalion, No. 2 Brigade in the 2nd Western Division. He emigrated to the United States

John Loftus served as 1st Lieutenant of Granlahan Coy. which was part of the 2nd Battalion, No. 2 Brigade in the 2nd Western Division Coy. His Company consisted of about twenty-five members in April of 1922. He emigrated to the United States

Michael Loftus (Rathnallog) Ballinagare Coy., 1st Battalion South Roscommon. Died at an early age

James Logan (Carricknaughton, Drum, Athlone) brother of John, was arrested during the Civil War, and taken to Athlone on 3 March 1923. He was released a few weeks later

John Logan (Carricknaughton, Drum, Athlone) was arrested during the Civil War, and taken to Athlone on 3 March 1923. He was released soon after

Patrick Logan (Clonown, Athlone) arrested 7 November 1922, and taken to Athlone a week later, where he was immediately released

Thomas Logan (Carricknaughton, Drum, Athlone) was arrested with his brothers during the Civil War, and taken to Athlone on 3 March 1923. All three were released three weeks later

Andrew Lohan (Ballygar Coy.) served as Adjutant of the Company which was considered part of 4th Battalion South Roscommon when the Divisional structure was implemented

Joseph Lohan (Moher, Strokestown) a member of the Carniska Coy., 3rd Battalion North Roscommon. After the War, emigrated to the United States

Patrick Lohan (Ballygar Coy.) 4th Battalion South Roscommon

another Patrick Lohan (Ballygar Coy.) which was considered part of 4th Battalion South Roscommon when the Divisional structure was implemented

Sean Lohan (Ballygar Coy.) was considered part of 4th Battalion South Roscommon. Sean was the Commanding Officer of Ballygar Company

Thomas Lohan (Tonamaddy, Kilbegnet) served as 1st Lieutenant of Kilbegnet Coy. in the Glenamaddy Battalion. Although located in Co. Galway, this Battalion was incorporated into No. 2 Brigade in the 2nd Western Division with Gerald O'Connor, former O/C of the 1st Battalion South Roscommon, serving as the Brigade Commandant. Most of the Company joined the Free State Army during the Civil War

Tom Lohan (Granny, Ballinameen, Boyle) 1st Battalion North Roscommon, aided in Jim Molloy's **escape from Boyle Barracks**

John Lough (Ballinlig, Knockcroghery) 4th Battalion South Roscommon. The Knockcroghery Company was formed in 1917 with Patrick Kelly serving as Captain. Lough drilled with the Volunteers, and attended practice battles at Taughmaconnell overseen by Ernie O'Malley in the summer of 1918. Participated in the South Roscommon election of 1918, and the **burning of Lecarrow Barracks**. Lough was a member of a party of Volunteers that succeeded in raiding a private home in St. John's that resulted in a Volunteer being very seriously wounded — needing medical attention in Dublin. He, along with the rest of his Company, **guarded the village of Knockcroghery** from reprisal on 15 August 1920 — a reprisal precipitated by British Forces being fired upon on Lough Ree. Lough also spent many hours going house to house collecting the IRA levy

Harry Loughran (Ballyfeeny, Kilglass, Strokestown) a member of the Kilglass Company in the 3rd Battalion North Roscommon

John "Jack" Loughran (Clooneen, Kilglass, Strokestown) Captain of the Kilglass Company in the 3rd Battalion North Roscommon, brother of Tommy. Jack took part in the **Clooneenhartland cattle raid** in 1919. In February 1921 he accompanied Mike Toolan on an all-night bicycle trip to Ballinameen (a distance of eighteen miles) to obtain two rifles from Jack Roche, and bring them back to the Battalion area for safe keeping. Before that evening, Loughran had never handled a military rifle.* He took part in cutting the road from Ballyfeeny to Scramogue in preparation for the **Scramogue Ambush**. He took the Anti-Treaty side during the Civil War, and was arrested on 8 September 1922, and taken to Athlone on 14 November 1922. After the War he emigrated to New York, where he went into the grocery business

*_An Old Soldier's Memories_ by Tommy Loughran, p. 263.

Jim Lowe (Ballinvoher, Mantua) 2nd Battalion North Roscommon. Participated in the **attack on the Elphin Dispensary** 13 December 1920, and the **attack on**

Tommy Loughran (Clooneen, Kilglass, Strokestown) a member of the Kilglass Company in the 3rd Battalion North Roscommon. Loughran spent the early years of the War in Dublin involved with the Volunteers. In August 1917, he joined Sinn Féin while working in Dun Laoghaire. He returned to Kilglass, Strokestown in April 1918, and became active there. As a reprisal for the attack in Strokestown on 5 January 1921 (in which he did not participate), he was arrested and beaten so badly "his teeth were broken and he spat out fragments, blood flowed from his mouth and nose and his eyes started to close."* Although he was never tried, he was imprisoned in Roscommon Gaol, and later transferred to Athlone. He was released on 7 February 1921. Loughran took part in cutting the road from Ballyfeeny to Scramogue in preparation for the **Scramogue Ambush**. He emigrated to the United States, where he worked as an air pollution officer for the city of Boston. In his later years, Tommy wrote an unpublished history of his participation in the Black and Tan War. His delightfully written manuscript, _An Old Soldier's Memories_, is quoted numerous times throughout the text of this book

*_The Parish of Kilglass, Slatta, Rooskey_ by Liam Coyle, p.139

Elphin Barracks 11 February 1921. After the War he emigrated to England

John Lowe (Croghan) in 1922 he served as the 2nd Lieutenant for Drumlion Company. Emigrated to America, where his job skills included making "hooch" during Prohibition. He eventually returned to Ireland, and lived near Frenchpark

Thomas Lowe (Croghan) Captain of Drumlion Company in the 5th Battalion North Roscommon. He was a member of the Anti-Treaty Active Service Unit (Flying Column) of North Roscommon. After the War he emigrated to England

Larry Lowry 2nd Lieutenant of the Clonberne Coy. in the Glenamaddy Battalion. Although located in Co. Galway, this Battalion was incorporated into No. 2 Brigade, 2nd Western Division with Gerald O'Connor, former O/C of the 1st Battalion South Roscommon, serving as Brigade Commandant

John Joe Luby (Corracreigh, Clooneyquinn) a member of the Killina Coy., 2nd Battalion North Roscommon. He was one of the first members of the Company when it formed in August of 1917

Stephen Luby (Cloonfad Coy.) 1st Battalion South Roscommon. Attended training camps during the Truce. His home served as the HQ for "F" Company in the 2nd Battalion, No. 2 Brigade, 2nd Western Division during the post-Truce times

Thomas Luby (Corracreigh, Clooneyquinn) Killina Coy. in the 2nd Battalion North Roscommon. He was one of the first members of the Company when it formed in August of 1917

Joseph Lunt (Ballybride) a member of "A" Coy. in the 2nd Battalion South Roscommon

James Lynagh (Granahan Dillon, Curraghroe, Strokestown) Captain of Curraghroe Company in the 3rd Battalion North Roscommon. He joined the Volunteers in 1917, attended weekly meetings, and was on parade during the South Longford election at Longford town, Killashee, Clondra, and Lanesboro. He was also active in the South Roscommon election. Took part in the armed raid of intended RIC recruits at Cloontuskert. Participated in the **burning of Scramogue Barracks**, was on protective duty at Kilgefin after the Fourmilehouse Ambush, and kidnapped two British soldiers. He was in charge of a section of men at the **Scramogue Ambush**. Lynagh took part in the **attack on Tarmonbarry Barracks** in January 1921, and after Scramogue sought out the spy who had given information about the participants of that attack. Lynagh was also with the men who **attacked the Tarmonbarry Barracks** in July 1921. He served with the ASU continuously until the Truce. Due to ill health incurred from sleeping in damp dugouts, he did not participate in the Civil War. After the War, he became a cattle dealer

Jim Lynam (Cuiltygower, Ballyfarnon) 4th Battalion North Roscommon. He and his brother, Tom, took part in the **raid on the Ballyfarnon Post Office** in March 1921 — the operation that began the chain of events leading to the **Keadue Ambush**

Thomas Lynam (Cuiltygower, Ballyfarnon) 4th Captain of Ballyfarnon Company in the 4th Battalion North Roscommon. He and his brother took part in the **raid on the Ballyfarnon Post Office** in March 1921 — the operation that began the chain of events leading to the **Keadue Ambush**. After the War he emigrated to the United States

Dominick Lynch (Loughglynn) 1st Battalion South Roscommon. Dispatch carrier. After the hostilities, he farmed his land, and became involved in local politics, serving as the Secretary of the Loughglynn Fianna Fáil *cumann* in 1928

George Lynch (Drumlion area) in the 4th Battalion North Roscommon. Served as a Judge in the Sinn Féin Courts. He later became State Solicitor for Sligo-Leitrim

James Lynch (Annsfield, Baylough, Athlone) gave his permission to the Volunteers to use his out-farm at Crannagh, Drum in south Roscommon to hold meetings, and eventually to become an active training base*

*_Drum and Its Hinterland_ by Edward Egan, p. 288.

Mrs. James Lynch became an active member of the Cumann na mBan Club of Summerhill, Drum, Athlone

John Lynch (Cleaheen, Cootehall) served as the Quartermaster for the Arigna Coy. in the 4th Battalion North Roscommon

Joseph Lynch (Ardkeenan, Drum, Athlone) 3rd Battalion Athlone Brigade

Larry Lynch (Clongowna, Bealnamullia) 3rd Battalion Athlone Brigade

Michael Lynch (Carrowkeel, Elphin) Creeve Coy., 2nd Battalion North Roscommon. Joined the IRA in April 1919. Blocked roads, carried dispatches, present at the **burning of Hillstreet Barracks**, the **attack on Elphin patrol** on 5 January 1921, and scouted the town of Elphin before the **attack on the Elphin Barracks** a month later. Arrested on 19 March 1921, and detained in Elphin, Strokestown (where he was badly beaten), and Longford Barracks until the last week of April 1921. Participated in the **attempted ambush a police patrol at Smithhill** in May. During the Truce he attended Cloonshee training camp, and went to Ballyoughter to learn revolver and hand grenade techniques

Peter Lynch (Toberpatrick, Strokestown) Quartermaster for Kiltrustan Company in the 3rd Battalion North Roscommon. Joined the Volunteers in 1917, and a year later performed scout duty while Ernie O'Malley was in the county organising the Companies. Aside from raiding for arms, parading, and attending weekly meetings, he was appointed the organiser for the boycott of the RIC. He participated in the **burning of Gallstown Barracks**, conveyed rifles and ammunition from Drumsna Railway Station to Strokestown, and acted as a summons server for the Republican Courts in the area. He participated in the **attack on Strokestown** 6 January 1921, blocked roads for the **attack on Elphin Barracks** in February, and was present at **Scramogue**. From April to May of 1921, he served as Quartermaster of the Company, and was in charge of collecting and caring for arms. During the Truce he spent time in the training camps engaged in the manufacture of munitions, and learning methods of preparing dugouts, all the while storing and caring for the Company arms. Taking an Anti-Treaty stand, he organised a Company in Kiltrustan area, and was appointed the Captain. Lynch was a member of the ASU and on active service when he was arrested by the Free State forces in January 1923. He escaped from custody, and went on the run until the cease-fire, after which he organised a local Sinn Féin Club, and was appointed the director of elections in the parish

Pat Lynch (Flannerys & Co., Boyle) 1st Battalion North Roscommon. He was arrested after ordering Boyle shops to stay closed after the death of hunger striker Terence MacSwiney. Pat was a member of the Active Service Unit (Flying Column) of North Roscommon. After the War he emigrated to the United States of America

Thomas Lynch (Lisnamucklagh) Dysart Coy., 4th Battalion South Roscommon. Joined the Company in 1917. Attended parades, received instructions under Ernie O'Malley, helped in the 1918 election. He was appointed to work with the Republican Police, and participated in the work involved in the Belfast boycott. Took part in raiding for arms, raiding the mails between Ballyforan and Thomas Street, and blocking roads between Ballyforan and Four Roads/Dysart and Taughmaconnell. He made dugouts, and fashioned ammunition. He helped prepare for an ambush of an RIC lorry which came along the road on the 3rd of each month. That month, however, the lorry failed to appear. Took part in the **ambush at Rahara**. During the Truce he attended training camps at Ballygar, Ballinaheglish, and Donamon. During the Civil War he took the Anti-Treaty side, and, along with his Company, assisted the Flying Column, helped escaped prisoners, carried dispatches, and blocked roads at Dysart and Ballyforan on five different occasions. He served under the command of Captain John Gately

Tim Lynch (Knocknanool, Brideswell, Athlone) Bealnamullia Coy. in the 3rd Battalion Athlone Brigade. Lynch drilled with his Company, trained to use firearms, took an active part in the General Election of 1918, attended Battalion meetings, worked with the Republican Police force at disputed farmland in Bealnamullia and Clongowna. He was with a group of Volunteers that seized ammunition from an airplane that made a forced landing at Keelogues in 1919. Took part in the **burning of the Barracks at Bealnamullia**, mobilised for an **attack on Cloonark Barracks**, and **attempted an ambush at Curraghaleen** in October 1920. Near Truce time he guarded the ASU Headquarters in the area, **destroyed the bridge at Millbrook**, blocked roads at Millbrook and Monksland, harboured and aided escaped prisoners. During the Truce he trained at Greenfield, Donamon, and Falty, in addition to collecting funds to aid the Volunteers and attending the Arbitration Courts. Lynch served under the command of Captain William Fallon

James Lyons (Mullaghalusky, Keadue) Keadue Company Captain in the 4th Battalion North Roscommon. After the War he became a small farmer. He never married. He died in the 1990s, and is buried in Kilronan Cemetery

John Lyons (Ballygar Coy.) was considered part of 4th Battalion South Roscommon when the Divisional structure was implemented

Patrick Lyons (Ballinlough Coy.) 1st Battalion South Roscommon. Took part in the **attempted ambush at Coshlieve** in July 1920, the **attempted attack on the Castlerea Station Guard** that same month, and the **burning of Ballinlough Barracks** 14 September 1920. During the Truce he attended the training camp at Hermitage

Patrick Lyons (Culliagh, Scramogue) 3rd Battalion North Roscommon, brother of Thomas. Joined the Volunteers in 1918. He was arrested in 1921, and released by mistake. He later joined the Garda Síochána, and was stationed in Clonaslee, Laois. Died in the 1980s, and is buried in Co. Laois

Thomas Lyons (Ballinlough Coy.) 1st Battalion South Roscommon. Served as Quartermaster for the Company. Took part in the **attempted ambush at Coshlieve** in July 1920, the **attempted attack on the Castlerea Station Guard** that same month, and the **burning of the Barracks at Ballinlough** 14 September 1920

Thomas Lyons (Culliagh, Scramogue) 3rd Battalion North Roscommon, brother of Patrick. Thomas was involved in a clash with the RIC, and performed good routine work for the organisation. He later became a farmer. Died 1978, and buried in Bumlin Cemetery

Thomas Lyons of Culliagh, Scramogue.

Harold McBrien (Drumduff, Ballintogher, Co. Sligo) joined the Volunteer movement in 1914. The organisation died away in the area, but was resurrected in 1917 when he and fourteen others formed the nucleus of a small Company of which he was the Captain. At the end of 1919, the Battalion O/C was arrested, and McBrien was selected to fill his position. During the Civil War he fought with the Arigna Flying Column. After the conflict, he married Michael and Seamus Cull's sister, Annie, and became a farmer. He lived a mile from the turn near Ballintogher. He died at age eighty-four and is buried in Sligo

Michael McBrien (Carrigallen) 4th Battalion North Roscommon. He deserted from the Free State Army, and became a member of the Arigna Column, where he served as Adjutant during the Civil War. Captured in the spring of 1923, and sentenced to death. He escaped on the morning of his scheduled execution, and remained on the run for five years until February of 1928 when he was re-arrested but "probably let go."* Emigrated to America

*The IRA in the Twilight Years by Uinseann MacEoin p. 482.

Alec McCabe (Keash, Co. Sligo) born in 1885 at Keash near Ballymote, was a primary teacher in Killybegs before the War. He joined the Volunteers in 1913. Sworn into the IRB by Sean McDermott, and a member of the Supreme Council of the IRB for Connaught. In preparation for the 1916 Easter Rising, he had obtained maps of the Sligo coastline in order to determine a suitable landing place for arms. (He chose

50th Anniversary of the Rising of 1916. Left to right: Joe McDavitt, Jimmy Moran, Pat Brennan, Alec McCabe, Frank Shouldice, Henry Feely, Micheál O'Callaghan, Paddy McGarry and ------.

Aughries.) Upon reading about Roger Casement's arrest, he travelled to Dublin, where, on Easter Saturday night, he met with Joseph Plunkett, Padraig Pearse, Tom Clarke, James Connolly, and Sean McDermott in a house on the corner of Hardwicke Place. Here McCabe was told that despite the countermanding order of Eoin MacNeill, the Rising would proceed on Monday. He was ordered back to Sligo.* McCabe mustered a few Volunteers who tried to draw the RIC out of their barracks in Tubbercurry, but the Volunteers had no luck. They cut telephone and telegraph wires and broke railway lines, but still there was no discernible RIC response to such actions. No guns and no orders from Dublin kept McCabe from staging any kind of significant outbreak in the Roscommon/Sligo area. He became very active in south Sligo, where he merged land reform with the Sinn Féin platform. He was the officer in charge of the **Rockingham Raid**, imprisoned in Mountjoy, and later in the Curragh, where he taught Irish classes. He was arrested and incarcerated in Mountjoy, where he went on a ten day hunger strike in April 1920. McCabe became a Pro-Treaty participant in the **Battle of Boyle**, and commanded troops in the Ballymote to Ballaghaderreen area during the years 1922 and 1923. He became a member of the Dáil in 1918, but resigned his seat in October 1924 because of the "Army Mutiny" affair. He returned to teaching in Dublin, and in 1935 founded the Educational Building Society to provide mortgage finance to teachers. He was Secretary and Managing Director of the Society until he retired in 1970. He died in 1972

*Alec McCabe Volunteer Witness Statement to the Bureau of Military History, p. 3-4.

John McCann (Doogara, Ballaghaderreen) one of the first members of the Ballaghaderreen Coy. in the East Mayo Brigade. Died in the 1918 influenza epidemic, and is buried in the old cemetery opposite the fair green in the town

Patrick McCarthy (Loughglynn Coy.) 1st Battalion South Roscommon. Took part in the **burning of the RIC Barracks at Loughglynn**. When the Western Division was formed, he volunteered to serve with the Oran Battalion Flying Column. During the Civil War he was a member of the Anti-Treaty garrison stationed at Clonalis House before it was attacked by the Free State forces in July 1922. He also participated in the **attack at Castlerea** in November 1922. Later emigrated to Cheshire, England

John McCarthy (Cloonycarran More, Strokestown) Carniska Coy., 3rd Battalion

Michael McCarthy (Castlebar) in charge of Accounts and Records for No. 2 Battalion, 2nd Brigade in the 2nd Western Division

Bernie Joe McConville (Mullagh, Ruskey) a member of the Kilglass Company in the 3rd Battalion North Roscommon

James McConville (Mullagh, Ruskey) a member of the Kilglass Company in the 3rd Battalion North Roscommon

Michael McConville (Mullagh, Ruskey) a member of the Kilglass Company in the 3rd Battalion North Roscommon, brother of Bernie and James

Agnes McCormack (Drumraney, Co. Westmeath) member of Cumann na mBan

Anthony McCormack (Tonlagee, Tang, Co. Westmeath) Captain of Tang Coy. in the Athlone Brigade. Joined the IRA in Athlone in 1914. He, along with sixty other Volunteers, headed to Shannonbridge on Easter Sunday 1916. Their orders were to hold Shannonbridge until men sent by Liam Mellows arrived. Halfway there, however, they received Eoin MacNeill's countermanding order. They halted their progress, and returned to the Coosan area to await further orders (which never came). McCormack was arrested on the following Tuesday, but was released shortly thereafter. In 1919 he was made Captain of the Company which numbered thirty-two. Participated in the **burning of Littletown Barracks** Easter weekend 1920. He was captured on 5 January 1921, sent to Athlone, and in February was transferred to Ballykinlar Camp in County Down, where he remained until the general release in December 1921. During the Civil War he took the Anti-Treaty side, and fought with the Flying Column. He was present at the **Ambush at Glasson** in August 1922. McCormack was arrested on 5 December of 1922 — found in Hoares public house in Ballymore. After firing on a patrol of eight National soldiers, he had taken refuge in the chimney, where he was discovered with a serious wound right above his ankle. His revolver and Lee Enfield rifle were confiscated as well as his ammo. McCormack was sent to the Curragh Hospital. After the War he went into the wholesale egg exporting business. Because of his former Republican stand, he entered the business under an assumed name. Ironically, he used to supply eggs to the National Army Barracks throughout the country. Later he inherited the Gap House pub and grocery business in Moate, and began a new career. Anthony had the use of only one leg because of the actions of one man in December 1922 — that man was Vincent McKeon, brother of the famous Sean McKeon (MacEoin). After thirty years, Anthony was reconciled with his shooter through the efforts of Anthony's brother — and what better place to mend fences than in the Three Jolly Pigeons Pub?* Anthony died in January 1998, and is buried in Tubberclair Cemetery

*Seamus McCormack, author interview, Three Jolly Pigeons Pub, Athlone, 13 August 2004.

Bernard McCormack (Drumraney, Athlone, Co. Westmeath) brother of Sean, and Michael, took part in the Howth gun running affair in Dublin. He fought in the College of Surgeons during Easter Week 1916. Arrested after the Rising, and sent to Frongoch. Died in 1919 from the wounds that he had received in the Dublin rebellion. His name is inscribed on the IRA monument in Athlone town

Claire McCormack (Drumraney, Co. Westmeath) member of Cumann na mBan

Edward McCormack (Carrowkeel and Chapel Street, Elphin) Creeve Coy. in the 2nd Battalion North Roscommon

Joe McCormack (Cortober, Carrick-on-Shannon) O/C of 5th Battalion North Roscommon, a member of the first Sinn Féin County Council in Roscommon. He was a native of Moate, Co. Westmeath, who worked as a railway clerk. Joe was the drill instructor of Drumlion Company and later its Captain. He accompanied Sean Connolly when the latter came to North Roscommon to organise the Companies. Joe was made the Battalion O/C, but was taken away from this position in order to work full time with the County Council as Paymaster. He was arrested in 1921 at Croghan, and became a prisoner at Boyle Barracks and Mountjoy. Later joined the Free State Army as an officer. Died in the 1920s

John (Sean) McCormack (Drumraney, Athlone, Co. Westmeath) brother of Bernard and Michael, a member of the IRB, and tireless organiser in Counties Westmeath and Kings (Meath). He was the Vice O/C of the Athlone Brigade in 1918, but was replaced in 1920 by Con Costello. After the War he lived in Drumcondra, Dublin. Died in the 1960s, and is buried in Glasnevin

John McCormack (Largan, Kiltrustan, Strokestown) 1st Lieutenant of Kiltrustan Company in the 3rd Battalion North Roscommon

Michael McCormack (Drumraney, Athlone, Co. Westmeath) joined the IRB in 1907, and attended meetings in Athlone and Tullamore. He was later appointed Head Centre in Drumraney. A Company of Volunteers was organised in Drumraney in 1914. He was arrested after the Rising, and sent to Wakefield on 13 May, and placed in solitary confinement for three weeks, where he was served very little food and forced to lay on bare boards. Released in mid-June 1916. Took part in the Joe McGuinness election in Longford. In 1918 he was appointed the Battalion Adjutant. Took part in the general election, and acted as the Receiver for Dáil loan funds (which he handed over to Mr. Robbins of Lake House, Moate, who in turn took them to Michael Collins). Participated in the **attempted attack on Ballymore Barracks** in March 1920, and the **burning of Moyvore and Meaghra Barracks** on Easter Saturday 1920. Volunteered for the Flying Column, but was told instead to keep the Battalion area strong and prepared. He made a list of friendly houses where men on the run could be safe, and constructed dugouts for arms and men. Michael became a member of the Westmeath Council in June 1920. He was arrested on 14 April 1921, along with his brother Patrick, and David Daly. Taken to Ballymore Barracks for identification and finally to Athlone, where he was coated with blood, eggs, and dust (a sorry sight indeed!) Later transferred

Bernard "Barney" McCormack.
PHOTO COURTESY OF DERRYGLAD FOLK MUSEUM CURRAGHBOY, ATHLONE

Michael McCormack.
PHOTO COURTESY OF BRIAN MCCORMACK

to the Curragh, from which he was released on 10 December 1921. After the War he farmed his land and ran a small business. Died 1971, and is buried in the new Drumraney Cemetery

Pat McCormack (Corgarrow, Strokestown) the first Captain of Kilglass Company in the 3rd Battalion North Roscommon

Patrick McCormack (Ballyglass Upper) near Ballinaheglish, a member of "B" Coy., in the 2nd Battalion South Roscommon. Dispatch rider. When the Western Division was formed, Pat was placed in charge of scouting and dispatch work for the 3rd Battalion, No. 2 Brigade. He also volunteered to serve with the Oran Battalion Flying Column. After the War he served on the Dublin Metropolitan Police Force

Patrick McCormack (Drumkeeran, Co. Leitrim) worked as a saddler with John McKenna on Elphin Street in Boyle, and was a member of the 1st Battalion North Roscommon

Thomas McCormack (Drumraney, Athlone, Co. Westmeath).

Thomas McCormack (Drumraney, Athlone, Co. Westmeath) was working in Dublin at the time of the Rising. Took part in the Howth gun running affair in Dublin, and also participated in the rebellion itself, fighting with the Volunteers at St. Stephen's Green. He was wounded in that action, but managed to escape deportation. He returned to Drumraney, where he later farmed the land. Died in 1979, and buried in Drumraney Cemetery

Thomas McCormack (Ballaghaderreen) arrested after the Rising, and sentenced to Lewes Prison on 20 May 1916. He was later transferred to Glasgow Jail, and finally to "The Irish University," Frongoch

Thomas McCormack (Mountdruid, Ballinagare) served as the 1st Lieutenant of his Company in the 1st Battalion South Roscommon. McCormack took part in the **destruction of local barracks**, enforcement of the Belfast boycott, and collection of monies for the Dáil loan. Participated in the **attempted attack on Kilmurray Military Camp** in June, the **attempted attack on the Castlerea Station Guard** in July, and the **attack on Frenchpark Barracks** 2 October 1920. McCormack became a member of the Active Service Unit formed in Castlerea in January 1921. He also served as Captain of the Ballinagare Coy. in February of 1922. During the Truce he attended the Company and Battalion training camps specialising in dispatch, scouting, and intelligence work. He took the Republican side during the Civil War, and participated in attacks against Free State forces **at Ballinagare** in July 1922 and **Castlerea** in November 1922

Thomas McCormack (Clooncunny, Killina, Elphin) 2nd Battalion North Roscommon. He was one of the founding members of the Killina Company when it formed in 1917

Thomas McCormack (Lisnalegan, Ballinaheglish) a member of "B" Coy. in the 2nd Battalion South Roscommon

William McCormack (Lisnalegan, Ballinaheglish) a member of "B" Coy. in the 2nd Battalion South Roscommon, brother of Pat and Thomas

Dominick McCoy (Tullaghanmore, Ballaghaderreen) during the Civil War he took the Anti-Treaty side, and fought against the Free State troopers. He was arrested and sent to Athlone on 14 November 1922, but escaped a month later

Michael McCoy (Captain of Cloonfree Coy.) 3rd Battalion North Roscommon. Organised a party of men to transport three severely burned Volunteers to the Strokestown Workhouse Hospital after the torching of the Strokestown Bridewell in July 1920

Alfred McCrann (Loughglynn Coy.) 1st Battalion South Roscommon, a native of Coolmeen, Elphin. A draper by trade, he was arrested after the Rising for his Sinn Féin sympathies, and sent to Wakefield on 13 May. He was released a few days later. He served as Captain of "H" Company, 2nd Battalion, No. 2 Brigade of the 2nd Western Division. His home served as the HQ for "F" Company during the post-Truce times. He later joined the Free State Army. He owned a shop and dance hall in Lanesboro

Peter McCrann (Drumsna) 5th Battalion North Roscommon. He worked in conjunction with Mick McLoughlin. McCrann was a member of the ASU taking the Anti-Treaty side and fighting against the Free State troopers. He was arrested 28 August 1922, and sent to Athlone on 14 November 1922. Emigrated to the USA

Stephen McCrann (Athlone) served a Judge for the Sinn Féin Courts

Hugh McDermott (Cloonfower, Tarmonbarry) 3rd Battalion North Roscommon. Joined the IRA in 1917, and participated in drilling and raiding for arms in those early years. When the War activities began heating up, he took part in the **attack on Tarmonbarry Barracks** in 1920 armed with a double-barreled shotgun, and stood guard for men blocking the roads for the **Scramogue Ambush**. During the Civil War he was arrested in July of 1922 for Anti-Treaty activities, but escaped to fight another day. He attacked the Free State forces at **Walshe's big bog** between Tarmon and Strokestown, the **Ruskey Barracks** in March of 1923, and exchanged fire with the National troops at **Lake Forbes** that same month

David McDermott (Mantua, Castlerea) joined the IRB in 1917. His Company, under Michael Rushe, drilled openly and marched in force before the Crown troops to demonstrate resistance to conscription. Perfomed dispatch work, raided for arms (he succeeded in collecting seventeen guns), constructed dugouts, and stored arms for the Volunteers. He officially joined the IRA in 1919. Present at the **attack on Elphin Barracks** on 11 February 1921, and the **attack on Frenchpark Barracks** in June of that year. During the Civil War he was present at the **Battle of Boyle** in July 1922, came under fire of Free State troopers in Elphin, but continued support for the Anti-Treaty Flying Column

James McDermott (Ballybeg, Strokestown) a member of Carniska Coy., 3rd Battalion North Roscommon. A Jimmy McDermott was present at the **Fourmilehouse Ambush** on 12 October 1920

James McDermott (Cloghran, County Dublin) a member of "E" Coy. in the 3rd Battalion South Roscommon, worked at Ballybeg, Strokestown. He became a member of Pat Madden's Flying Column. He was present at the **Scramogue Ambush**. After the War he moved to Dublin, where he died in October 1975. Buried in Glasnevin Cemetery

These two James McDermotts may be one and the same man

James McDermott a member of "A" Coy. in the 2nd Battalion South Roscommon. When the Western Division was formed, he volunteered to serve with the Oran Battalion Flying Column. After the War he emigrated to England

John McDermott (Carrowkeel, Elphin) a member of Creeve Coy., 2nd Battalion North Roscommon, arrested in 1920 for intercepting mail at the Elphin Post Office, "guest" at Mountjoy until after the Truce was signed

John McDermott (Ballyglass, Cloontuskert) a member of "E" Coy., 3rd Battalion South Roscommon. A member of Pat Madden's Flying Column. Many, but not all, of the members of the Kilgefin Company participated in the **Fourmilehouse Ambush** on 12 October 1920. John was present at the **Scramogue Ambush**. Later in life became a stonemason

John McDermott (Aghamuck, next to Kilgefin Cemetery) After the War he became a farmer. He is buried in Kilgefin Cemetery

John McDermott When the 2nd Western Division was formed, John McDermott became the Head of Chemistry

John McDermott (**Sean**) was the 1st Lieutenant of Castlerea Coy. when the Western Division was formed

John McDermott (Cootehall, Boyle) during the Civil War he took the Anti-Treaty side, and fought against the Free State troopers. He was arrested 8 August 1922, and sent to Athlone on 2 September. He was later transferred to Mountjoy in January, and finally to Tintown II on 20 February 1923

John J. McDermott (Cloontimullan, Kilteevan) a member of the Kilteevan Company in the 3rd Battalion South Roscommon

John J. McDermott (Crossna) during the Civil War he took the Anti-Treaty side, and was arrested. He was sent to Tintown A, and released on 18 December 1923

John M. McDermott North Roscommon Brigade. Arrested late 1920, but released in December. His beating was so severe that he suffered from mental illness throughout his lifetime

Joseph McDermott Quartermaster for Dromboylan Company in the 5th Battalion North Roscommon

Katie McDermott, who was reared in Ballybeg, Strokestown, was a member of Cumann na mBan

Luke McDermott (Aghamuck, Kilgefin) brother of John, a member of Kilgefin Company in the 3rd Battalion South Roscommon. After the War he emigrated to the United States, but later returned to Ireland, and settled in Strokestown. Died in the 1970s, and buried in Strokestown Cemetery

Mary McDermott (Cartron, Kilrooskey, Kilgefin) ran a safe house which was raided on numerous occasions. Bullet holes dotted the dining room walls long after the War. On one occasion, she kept the Tans at bay with a pitchfork while the boys went down the back stairs. Ireland has never known a more fierce fighter!

Old I.R.A. reunion dinner
(left to right): Pat Gibbons, Peter Collins, Michael McDermott, and Dick Simons.

PHOTO COURTESY OF EAMONN DUFFY

Michael McDermott a member of "E" Coy. in the 3rd Battalion South Roscommon

Michael McDermott of Corker, Tulsk drove the Anti-Treaty men around during the Civil War. He was the man behind the wheel during the raids on the post offices

Michael McDermott (Castlerea) arrested during the Civil War for Anti-Treaty activities, and taken to Newbridge. He was released on 19 December 1923

Michael McDermott a member of "B" Coy. in the 2nd Battalion South Roscommon. Present at **Fourmilehouse Ambush**. After the War he emigrated to Long Island, New York

McDermott Brothers who lived near Summerhill, Drum in the south of Roscommon. They helped to dismantle the keystone from the arch of the bridge across the Cross River in April 1920

Mrs. McDermott of Moyne was "very good to the lads"

Paddy McDermott (Cootehall Coy.) 5th Battalion North Roscommon Brigade. After the War he became a farmer

Paddy McDermott (Annaghmore, Kilteevan) sound and steady oarsman, who ferried doctors to the island of Incheneagh to tend to wounded Volunteers

Patrick McDermott (Enfield, Ballintubber) 2nd Battalion South Roscommon

Patrick McDermott (Kilteevan Coy.) 3rd Battalion South Roscommon

Patrick McDermott (Ballinagare Coy.) 1st Battalion South Roscommon. Emigrated to the United States

Peter McDermott (Ballinamore, Co. Leitrim) was beaten so severely that "his jaw looked like pulp." Incarcerated in Boyle Barracks. After the War he served with the Garda Síochána in Fermoy

Roger McDermott (Aghaderry, Loughglynn) ran a safe house near the Woodlands of Loughglynn

S. McDermott served as the 1st Lieutenant of Castlerea Coy. in April 1922

Stephen McDermott (Tully, Ballinagare) Quartermaster of the First Battalion South Roscommon. Participated in the **destruction of vacant barracks** in 1920, the **attempted attack on Kilmurray Military Camp** in June 1920, the **attack on Frenchpark Barracks** 2 October 1920, **attempted attacks at Castlerea** in January 1921, the **attempted ambush at Cloonsheever** in March 1921, and the **attack on**

Stephen McDermott in a childhood photo.

PHOTO COURTESY OF SEAN RAFTERY

the military in Castlerea 7 April 1921. At the age of nineteen, he was shot in The **Woodlands of Loughglynn** (19 April 1921), and buried in Ballinagare Cemetery. A monument to him was erected in the field where he was killed. His name is inscribed on the tablets at the Shankill Monument near Elphin

Stephen McDermott (Carrowgarve, Castlerea) a member of Lisliddy Coy., 1st Battalion South Roscommon. McDermott attended the training camps during the Truce period. He later emigrated to England

Thomas J. McDermott (Cartron, Kilgefin) a member of "E" Coy., 3rd Battalion South Roscommon. Many, but not all, of the members of the Kilgefin Company participated in the **Fourmilehouse Ambush** on 12 October 1920. After the hostilities ceases, he emigrated to America

Thomas McDermott 2nd Battalion North Roscommon

Thomas McDermott (Pollymount, Scramogue) a member of the Carniska Coy., 3rd Battalion North Roscommon

Thomas McDermott (Breedogue) 1st Battalion North Roscommon

Thomas McDermott (Ballinagare Coy.) 1st Battalion South Roscommon. Helped to enforce the Belfast boycott in the area

Thomas McDermott served as a member of "A" Coy. in the 2nd Battalion South Roscommon. He died before the 1940s

Thomas McDermott (Donamon) 2nd Battalion South Roscommon

Thomas McDermott (Cloonfower, Tarmonbarry) a member of the Tarmonbarry Coy. of the 3rd Battalion North Roscommon. Took part in the **Levins Gate encounter** with the RIC, the **attempted ambush in Tarmonbarry** in 1920, the **attack on the RIC patrol at Strokestown** in January 1921, and the **attempted ambush of a patrol at Tarmonbarry** in February 1921

Willie McDermott (Carrowkeel, Elphin) 2nd Battalion North Roscommon, Creeve Company. In 1920 he was arrested for intercepting mail at the Elphin Post Office. He participated in the **attack on the Elphin patrol** 5 January 1921, and the **attack on Elphin Barracks** 11 February 1921. Arrested and sent to Mountjoy Hotel, where he signed the "guestbook" (autograph book owned by James Feely) on 27 September 1921

Joe McDevitt (McDavitt), a native of Kilcar, Co. Donegal, active in the Sligo area during the Black and Tan War. Took part in the aborted attack on a convoy at the Sligo Railway Station in October 1920, and was arrested a month later on 20 November. A prisoner in Mountjoy who, in 1921, signed an autograph book belonging to James Feely. During the Civil War he headed a Flying Column which operated in south Sligo, Mayo, and north Roscommon. He was captured in September 1922 in Irishtown. From 1950, he worked as an insurance manager in Roscommon town. He died in 1968 (photo on page 357)

Bridie McDonagh (Ballinagare) member of the Cumann na mBan

Charles McDonagh (Ballaghaderreen) was active with Volunteers in the Liverpool area in 1920-21. During the Civil War he took the Anti-Treaty side, and fought against the Free State troopers. He was arrested 28 August 1922, and sent to Athlone on 2 September. He was transferred to Mountjoy, and finally to Tintown II on 20 February 1923

Jack McDonagh (Captain of Kilbegnet Coy.) in the Glenamaddy Battalion. Although located in Co. Galway, this Battalion was incorporated into No. 2 Brigade of the 2nd Western Division with Gerald O'Connor, former O/C of South Roscommon, serving as Brigade Commandant. His home was used as the headquarters of "E" Company. McDonagh's Company numbered sixty-four after the Truce. He later joined the Free State Army. After the War he became a farmer. Buried in Kilbegnet Cemetery

James McDonagh (Station Rd., Castlerea) during the Civil War he took the Anti-Treaty side, and fought against the Free State. He was arrested 7 August 1922, and sent to Athlone on 2 September 1922

Jimmy McDonagh (Boyle) 1st Battalion North Roscommon, a member of the Volunteers since before the Easter Rising

John McDonagh (Glinsk) his home served as the headquarters of Glinsk Company, which was part of the Glenamaddy Battalion after the Divisions were formed. The Brigade was commanded by Gerald O'Connor, former O/C of 1st Battalion South Roscommon

John McDonagh (Ballygar Coy.) was considered part of 4th Battalion South Roscommon when the Divisional structure was implemented

Mark McDonagh (Ballinagare Coy.) 1st Battalion South Roscommon. In July 1922 Mark was serving as the Company's 2nd Lieutenant. During the Civil War he became a member of the Anti-Treaty Active Service Unit of the 1st Battalion South. He later emigrated to the United States

Patrick McDonagh (Ballinagare Coy.) 1st Battalion South Roscommon. Participated in enforcing the Belfast boycott. His house was searched in reprisal for the attack on Frenchpark Barracks in October 1920. He, however, was not to be found because he had moved to Dublin where he worked in a lumber yard. Sensing the danger of the times, his family felt that he should emigrate, so they sold the family cow in order to purchase his fare.* In May 1921 he had emigrated to New York, where his stepmother had relations

*Robert McDonagh, grandson of Patrick, correspondence to author, 19 April 2004.

Patrick McDonagh (Donamon) a member of St. John's Coy. in the 4th Battalion South Roscommon. McDonagh drilled with the Volunteers two nights a week — Tuesdays and Thursdays. He participated with his Company at the sham battles for training purposes in the summer of 1918 under Ernie O'Malley at Lysterfield, Taughmaconnell, and Churchboro

Thomas McDonagh (Tibohine) Captain in the South Sligo Brigade, killed in the **Ambush at Ratra** 1 September 1920, buried Teampoll Ronain Cemetery. According to Jim Hunt, McDonagh was born in America, but reared by his Granny in Cloonloo. "He was intelligent and he was a fine cut of a man."* McDonagh died when he was but twenty years old. His name is inscribed on the Shankill Monument near Elphin

*Jim Hunt interview, UCD Archives, Ernie O'Malley Papers, No. 131.

John McDonnell (Killastalliff, Kilglass, Strokestown) a member of Kilglass Coy. in the 3rd Battalion North Roscommon, brother of Patrick. McDonnell was one of the Volunteers guarding a Republican Court in April 1920 at Kilglass Chapel when a party of RIC from Ruskey happened by, and shots were exchanged for twenty minutes. He also took part in the **attack near Ruskey village** on 5 July 1921

John James McDonnell (Carrowmore) Dysart Coy., 4th Battalion South Roscommon, brother of Martin. He served as Adjutant for the Company which he joined in 1917. Attended parades, received instructions under Ernie O'Malley, and helped in the 1918 election. He was appointed to work with the Republican Police, and participated in the work involved in the Belfast boycott. Raided the mails from the Curraghboy Coy. that had been put into the Dysart Post Office. Raided the home of an RIC man, made him promise to give up his job, and burned all the papers in his possession. Took part in raiding for arms, raiding the mails between Ballyforan and Thomas Street, blocking roads between Ballyforan and Four Roads/Dysart and Taughmaconnell, and making dugouts. He helped prepare for an ambush of an RIC lorry which came along the road on the 3rd of each month. That month, however, the lorry failed to appear. During the Truce he attended officers' training classes at Rahara three evenings a week, and a camp at Ballygar. He also attended the camps at Ballinaheglish and Donamon. During the Civil War, he, along with his Company, assisted the Anti-Treaty Flying Column, helped escaped prisoners, carried dispatches, and blocked roads at Dysart and Ballyforan on five different occasions

John McDonnell 2nd Lieutenant of the Glinsk Coy. in the Glenamaddy Battalion. Although located in Co. Galway, this Battalion was incorporated into No. 2 Brigade, 2nd Western Division with Gerald O'Connor, former O/C of 1st Battalion South Roscommon, serving as its Commandant

Martin McDonnell (Carrowmore) Dysart Coy., 4th Battalion South Roscommon. Martin served as the first Captain of Dysart Coy. He joined the Company in 1917. Attended parades, received instructions under Ernie O'Malley

Michael McDonnell (Killoy, Lecarrow) 4th Battalion South Roscommon. McDonnell was a member of the Knockcroghery Company which formed in 1917 with Patrick Kelly serving as Captain. McDonnell went house to house canvassing for signatures to the plebiscite for independence. He drilled with the Volunteers, and attended the sham battles at Taughmaconnell overseen by Ernie O'Malley in the summer of 1918. Participated in the South Roscommon election of 1918, and the County Council election

Michael McDonnell (Ballaghaderreen) one of the first members of the Ballaghaderreen Coy. in the East Mayo Brigade

Michael McDonnell (Castlerea) during the Civil War he took the Anti-Treaty side, and fought against the Free State. He was sent to Newbridge, and finally released on 19 December 1923

Mike "Joe" McDonnell (Ballaghaderreen) one of the first members of the Ballaghaderreen Coy. in the East Mayo Brigade

Patrick McDonnell (Killastalliff, Kilglass, Strokestown) is listed in official papers as the 2nd Lieutenant for Kilglass Company in the 3rd Battalion North Roscommon. McDonnell was one of the Volunteers guarding a Republican Court in April 1920 at Kilglass Chapel when a party of RIC from Ruskey happened by and twenty minutes worth of shots were exchanged. He also took part in the **attack near Ruskey village** on 5 July 1921

William McDonnell (Feevagh) Dysart Coy., 4th Battalion South Roscommon. Joined the Company in 1919. Drilled with his Company, and performed dispatch work. He was appointed to work with the Republican Police

Margaret McGann (Trilacroghan, Kilgefin) member of the Cumann na mBan

Beasie McGarry (Garrow, Boyle) sister of Jim and Paddy, member of the Cumann na mBan

Sean MacEoin (Ballinalee, Longford) "The Blacksmith of Ballinalee," who, along with Sean Connolly, organised the first Volunteer Company in Ballinalee. He later became the O/C of an aggressive Flying Column in Longford. He was captured and imprisoned and not released until August of 1921, when Michael Collins insisted that he be given his freedom before good-faith negotiations could begin on the Treaty. He joined the Free State Army, took over the Longford and Athlone Barracks from the British, and became the Head Officer of the Western Command centered in Athlone during the Civil War. MacEoin was appointed Army Chief of Staff in 1928, and was elected as Longford TD for Fine Gael in 1929. He served as Minister for Justice from 1948 to 1954, and as Minister for Defence from 1954 to 1957. He stood unsuccessfully in the Presidential elections of 1945 and 1959. He retired from politics in 1965, and died in July 1973

Jim McGarry (Garrow, Boyle) 1st Battalion North Roscommon, brother of Roger. One of the original members of the Boyle Coy. in the 1st Battalion North Roscommon

Maisie McGarry (Ballymagrine, Tarmonbarry) during the War for Independence, she brought a supply of guns by cart from Ruskey to Tarmonbarry

Mary Kate McGarry (Garrow, Boyle) sister of Jim, Paddy, Beasie and Roger, member of the Cumann na mBan

Michael "Del" McGarry (Ballaghaderreen) one of the first members of the Ballaghaderreen Coy. in the East Mayo Brigade

Michael McGarry (Derryquirk, Tulsk) 2nd Battalion North Roscommon. McGarry, Tom Connor, Seamus Ryan, Thomas Tiernan, and Joe Kelly of Rathcroghan raided the homes of two informers. The Volunteers knew of the men's spying because of mail seized and censored by Thomas Brady, the Battalion Intelligence Officer. During the raid, each spy managed to grab a revolver and shoot himself free of the Volunteers. Both men hid out in the RIC Barracks in Roscommon town until Truce time. McGarry was later arrested and interned until 1922. He took the Anti-Treaty side in the Civil War, and was re-arrested and kept in prison until the end of 1923. After the War he emigrated to Mount Vernon, New York

Paddy McGarry (Garrow, Boyle) 1st Battalion North Roscommon. He was taken into the IRB by Alec McCabe in February 1915. A member of the Volunteers since before the Rising. Listed in the GHQ papers in the UCD Archives as the Second Lieutenant of Doon Company

Roger McGarry (Garrow, Boyle) 1st Battalion North Roscommon, a member of the Volunteers before the Rising

Thomas McGarry (Tibohine) arrested during the Civil War on 7 August 1922, and taken to Athlone on 2 September 1922

Joseph McGauran (Cloonfower, Tarmonbarry) a member of Tarmonbarry Coy. in the 3rd Battalion North Roscommon

Peter McGearty (Derreenine, Keadue) on 3 February 1923, he and four other members of the Anti-Treaty Arigna Flying Column were arrested by a cycling patrol from Boyle. He was taken to Athlone on that same day

Edward McGee (Abbey St., Athlone) arrested during the Civil War on 9 July 1922, and taken to Athlone on 2 September 1922

Daniel McGeever (Ballaghaderreen) arrested during the Civil War and taken to Newbridge, where he was held until 18 December 1923

Thomas McGiff (Drumraney, Athlone, County Westmeath) fought with the Athlone Brigade, and served as the 2nd Battalion Commandant during the Civil War. Took part in the **raid on Ballinacaragy village**, Longford, on 16 December 1922. He was quite happy with the Treaty terms and was stationed in Custume Barracks when his wife, Agnes McCormack, encouraged him to come out of the Barracks and keep fighting for the Republic.* He often frequented the Doyle house in Littleton, Glasson. The National troops surrounded it on 20 September 1923, but he made a miraculous escape. His freedom was not long lasting, however, as he was captured at Bishopstown (six miles from Ballymore) on 19 November. He had escaped through a back window of Mrs. McCormack's house, but was captured 500 yards from the dwelling. He was sent to Athlone on 20 March 1923. He moved to Garrisker Moyvalley, Co. Kildare after the War, died in the late 1940s, and is buried in the old Drumraney Cemetery. Michael McCormack, Adjutant of the Drumraney Battalion during the War for Independence, described McGiff as such: "it was a great pity that Commandant McGiff was not of mature years at an earlier date (in the war). He was endowed with plenty of energy and initiative and was of a very high standard of intelligence and, although at this time was still merely a boy, he had a wealth of common sense. Had he been old enough to have been Battalion Commander earlier, things would have been different in our Battalion area."**

*Clare Whelan, daughter of Thomas McGiff. Interview by author, Dublin, 1 September 2004.
**Michael McCormack Volunteer Witness Statement to the Bureau of Military History 1913-1921, p. 32.

___ **McGeoghan** took part in the **attack on the Carrick-on-Shannon Courthouse** in September 1920

Daniel McGiff (see Westmeath Section of Surrounding Volunteers)

William McGill (Dunmore Coy. in Galway) part of No. 2 Brigade, 2nd Western Division. He was arrested after the Rising, and, when released, helped to form the Dunmore Company of Volunteers, which in its infancy numbered about twenty-five. He also organised the Dunmore Sinn Féin Club

Patrick McGlackin (Emlagh, Castleplunkett) Pat was a member of "B" Coy., 2nd Battalion South Roscommon under the command of Captain Jack Ryan. After the War he became a farmer

James McGlynn (Kilnamanagh, Frenchpark) in 1922 he served as 2nd Lieutenant of Breedogue Company in the 1st Battalion North Roscommon

James P. McGlynn (Ballymargrine, Tarmonbarry) a member of the Tarmonbarry Coy. in the 3rd Battalion North Roscommon. Took part in the **attempted attack at Tarmonbarry** in 1920

James Patrick McGlynn (Lavagh, Ruskey) a member of the Kilglass Company in the 3rd Battalion North Roscommon

William McGlynn (Knockcroghery Coy.) 4th Battalion South Roscommon. He was member of the Company as of 11 July 1921. He later moved to Dublin

John McGoldrick (Cloonybrien, Cootehall) listed in the GHQ papers in the UCD Archives as the 2nd Lieutenant for the Cootehall Company in the 5th Battalion North Roscommon

Richard McGough (Tuam) cellmate of Michael Dockery and Jack Glancy at Boyle Barracks in 1921, after having been arrested in Monasteraden for taking control of a train at Kilfree Junction in south Sligo to aid in an **attack on**

Ballaghaderreen Barracks. While in Mountjoy, he penned a verse about Sean MacEoin in a fellow prisoner's diary:

> "Long may you live, Leinster's hero
> Is a nation's prayer for thee:
> You are Ireland's pride and glory,
> Sean McKeon of Ballinalee."*

*The Blacksmith of Ballinalee by Padraic O'Farrell, p. 64.

James (Seamus) McGovern, a member of Fuerty Coy., appointed 2nd Batt. South Adjutant in 1921 when Ned Hegarty left that position to become Chief of the Republican Police. He, along with James Keegan, Joseph Belton, Pat Conboy, Tom Mannion, James Kenny, and Patrick Farrell captured a Tan during the War for Independence. Joined the Free State Army. Later emigrated to England

Thomas "Joe" McGovern (Willsgrove, Ballintubber) a member of "F" Coy. in the 3rd Battalion, No. 2 Brigade of the 2nd Western Division. Took part in the **raid on the military train at Ballymoe** in June 1920

George McGowan is listed as the Captain of Ruskey Company in the 3rd Battalion North Roscommon as of July 1921

Jim McGowan (Lack, Whitehall, Tarmonbarry) a member of Tarmonbarry Coy., 3rd Battalion North Roscommon

Joe McGowan of Portahard, Frenchpark was arrested during the Civil War on 8 August 1922 for Anti-Treaty activities, and taken to Athlone on 2 September. He was transferred to Mountjoy in January, and later to Tintown B. He was released on 7 December 1923. He was a brother of Johnnie (below)

John McGowan (Kye, Elphin) 2nd Battalion North Roscommon. Joined the IRA in 1919 and spent many of his days drilling, attending meetings, and carrying dispatches. Took part in the **burning of the Hillstreet Barracks, attempted ambush of RIC patrol between Strokestown and Elphin** in July 1920, **ambush of Elphin police patrol** on 5 January 1921, blocked roads for the **attack on Elphin Barracks**, and **waited in ambush at Smithhill** in May. A day before the Truce, he travelled to Mullooly's in Kiltrustan, armed with bombs and guns for the anticipated **ambush at Lavally**

John McGowan (Boyle) Connaught Ranger, who took part in the Indian Mutiny in 1920. Sentenced to ten years penal servitude in Maidstone Prison. Later joined the Garda Síochána. In 1940, helped set up the Local Defence Force

John McGowan (Lack, Whitehall, Tarmonbarry) a member of the Tarmonbarry Coy. in the 3rd Battalion North Roscommon

John McGowan (Kilmactrumy) arrested during the Civil War, and taken to Athlone on 7 March 1923

Johnnie McGowan (Portahard, Frenchpark) Captain of Tibohine Volunteer Company, which was part of the 4th Battalion of the East Mayo Brigade. Shot by the Tans in December 1920 in the home of Pat Dwyer, buried in the cemetery near Tibohine Church. (RIC reports from Roscommon town written by the District Inspector claim 15 December as the date. The National Graves Association claims 23 December. A hand-written account of events scripted by a Volunteer later in his life* claims that 20 December was the fatal day.) Name inscribed on the Shankill Monument near Elphin

*Pat Mullooly, private papers.

Thomas McGowan (Tarmonbarry) shot dead at his home on 6 July 1921. According to Sean Leavy's Volunteer Witness Statement (p. 23), the cause of his death had its roots in a family feud rather than an official Volunteer action

William McGowan (Castlerea) First Battalion South Roscommon

John McGrath (Ballyoughter, Elphin) 2nd Battalion North Roscommon. Second Lieutenant for Company "E" (Elphin). McGrath did dispatch work, helped organise Sinn Féin Clubs, collected for the Dáil loan, helped with Sinn Féin Courts, trenched roads for ambushes, and worked on the Republican Police force. He was arrested in February 1921, and interned until 9 December 1921.

He was not an active participant in the Civil War

Pat McGrath (Carrowreagh, Ballinagare) 1st Battalion South Roscommon

John McGreevey (Carrick-on-Shannon) part of the South Leitrim Brigade. Took part in **attacks at Garadice, Eslin, Fenagh** and other localities in Leitrim. When the Divisional structure came into being in 1921, these areas were transferred to No. 3 Brigade, 3rd Western Division under Pat Brennan

Owen McGreevey (Ballaghaderreen) during the Civil War he took the Anti-Treaty side, and fought against the Free State troopers. He was arrested 28 August 1922, and sent to Athlone on 2 September 1922

Patrick McGreevey (Lisheenanierin, Kilbride) 3rd Battalion South Roscommon

Frank McGuinness of Cloonmore, Tarmonbarry, proprietor of two drapery shops in Longford town, active on the political scene since the late 1880s. Having grown impatient "by the existence of home rule in theory but not in practice,"* he supported his brother Joe's involvement with the Easter Rising, and visited him in Dublin. Upon his return to Longford, Frank was himself arrested and sent to Wakefield Prison, where he spent only two weeks. He served as president of the South Longford district Republican Court. When his brother Joe died after being elected TD, Frank was selected to serve in his place for Longford/Westmeath. Frank served as the Quartermaster for the 3rd Battalion North area during the Civil War. He was also a member of the Anti-Treaty ASU.** In 1925, he was elected to the Senate, where he was a member for nine years. He died 30 November 1934

County Longford and the Irish Revolution by Marie Coleman, p. 43.
**Pat Brennan Papers*, private collection.

Joe McGuinness of Cloonmore, Tarmonbarry. Towards the end of the nineteenth century, he travelled to New York, where he became involved with the Gaelic League. He returned to Ireland in 1902, and helped establish a branch of the league in Longford town.* He moved to Dublin, where he took part in the Easter Rebellion. His company occupied the Four Courts. He was subsequently arrested and incarcerated in Portland Gaol. Released in the general amnesty of 1917, he was elected in a Longford bye election in May 1917, and re-elected in the General Electon of 1918. (The famous slogan, "Put him in to get him out" became the battle cry for numerous young Sinn Féiners in the bye election in Longford.) Re-arrested in 1918 for his defiance to conscription, and placed in Lewes Gaol. He was again incarcerated in January 1921, and held until after the Truce. McGuinness was not to live long enough, however, to see the results of his sacrifices. Weakened by years of imprisonment, he succumbed to pneumonia on 30 May 1922

County Longford and the Irish Revolution by Marie Coleman, p. 50.

Liza McGuinness (Cloonmore, Tarmonbarry) member of the Cumann na mBan. Sister of Frank and Joe. She died in February 1919. Her funeral was well attended by many friends as well as Volunteers from the area (see sidebar)

Peter McGuinness (Corraun) a member of Tarmonbarry Coy., 3rd Battalion North Roscommon

Francis McGuire (Maguire) (Carrowphadeen, Lecarrow) St. John's Coy. in the 4th Battalion South Roscommon. When the Company first formed in 1917, Maguire was its first 2nd Lieutenant. He later was promoted to 1st Lieutenant. He drilled with other Volunteers two nights a week — Tuesdays and Thursdays, and worked with the Republican Courts. He worked in the 1918 election, and his Company, now under the command of Patrick Grady, participated in the sham battles for training purposes under Ernie O'Malley at Lysterfield, Taughmaconnell, and Churchboro. Maguire examined the mails that were taken off the Kiltoom train. He, along with seventeen other men from the Company, participated in the **attempted ambush at Kilmurray Military Camp** in June 1920. He constructed dugouts, took part in several raids for arms, blocked roads, and was involved with the **blowing up of Ballybay Road Bridge**

John McGuire (Ballyfeeny, Strokestown) a member of the Kilglass Company in the 3rd Battalion North Roscommon

Michael (John) McGuire (Ballymote, Sligo) a member of the IRB. He, along with Batty Keaney, drove down in February 1918 from Ballymote with Alec McCabe

Cloonmore, Tarmonbarry
5-2-'19

D Capa,
Please accept and convey to the members of your Volunteer Company the best thanks of my mother and myself for your courtesy and kindness in attending my sister's funeral on Saturday the 1st. Though of course I do not regard your kindness in any way as a personal compliment I assure you it has been a source of the greatest consolation to us all in our great affliction and the honour done to her remains by the Volunteers will ever be most gratefully remembered by all our friends and relatives.

Yours Sincerely,
Frank McGuinness

and met the Roscommon Volunteers at the first Rockingham gate on the Carrick Road. Took part in the **Rockingham Raid**. He later emigrated to America

Michael McGuire (Policeman) for the Glenamaddy Battalion. When the Division structure for the Army was implemented throughout the country, this Battalion became part of No. 2 Brigade, 2nd Western Division under the command of Gerald O'Connor of Lisacul, Brigade O/C

Walter McGuire (Fairbanks, Strokestown) a member of the Kilglass Company in the 3rd Battalion North Roscommon. Arrested for Anti-Treaty activities during the Civil War on 28 August 1922, and sent to Athlone on 2 September 1922. Afterwards, he served as a Fianna Fáil member of Roscommon County Council from 1942 to 1974

William McGuire (Ballyfeeny, Strokestown) a member of the Kilglass Company in the 3rd Battalion North Roscommon, brother of Walter

William McHenry was the manager of the creamery in Croghan. He helped construct the bombs made by the Roche brothers

Michael McHugh (Crunkill, Ruskey) a member of the Kilglass Company in the 3rd Battalion North Roscommon

Patrick McHugh (Tonroe, Kingsland, Boyle) Quartermaster for the Breedogue Company in the 1st Battalion North Roscommon

Tom McKenna (either Giddaun or Cartronaglogh, Keadue) 4th Battalion North Roscommon, arrested on charges of murder of RIC constables at Keadue, "guest" at Boyle Barracks and Mountjoy. Released in January of 1922. Active with the Anti-Treaty Arigna Flying Column during the Civil War. McKenna, along with his comrades Cull, Cullen, Gannon, and Tymon, were immortalised in the poem "Arigna's Green Vale" (by American emigrant Michael Daly)

John McKeon (Knockroe, Croghan) 5th Battalion North Roscommon, brother of Patrick. Joined the Volunteers in 1920. Raided for arms, did dispatch work, made dugouts, and blocked and trenched roads the night before the **attack on Elphin Barracks**. During the Truce he attended Rockville training camp. He joined the Free State Army, but his heart wasn't committed to it. He acted as informer for the IRA, and finally deserted with others, bringing with him supplies and guns. In November 1922, he joined the Active Service Unit of North Roscommon. He remained on the run until the spring of 1924, after which he emigrated to Brooklyn, New York

Joseph McKeon (Ballagh) Rahara Coy., 4th Battalion South Roscommon. Joseph took part in the Civil War on the Anti-Treaty side, blocking ballast trains, and collecting gelignite for use in mines

M. McKeon a member of a Mayo Company, who became part of an Active Service Unit for the 3rd Brigade, 2nd Western Division. He, along with John Snee, Tom Regan, P. Behan, Mick Duffy, and M. Hunt, spent the first months after the Truce sniping at B-Specials along the six-county Border. He was part of the group of Anti-Treaty men who **attacked the Boyle Barracks** in July 1922 during the Civil War

Patrick McKeon (Knockroe, Croghan) a member of the Volunteers preceding the Rising. Served as the Captain of Croghan Company in the 5th Battalion North Roscommon. When the 3rd Western Division was formed, McKeon became the Quartermaster for the 4th Battalion. He was a member of the Anti-Treaty Active Service Unit (Flying Column) of North Roscommon during the Civil War. In 1924 he was arrested for

Shankill Monument Committee: Patrick O'Connell, Patrick McKeon, Sean Owens: Joint Treasurers. Joe O'Kelly, Secretary.

PHOTO COURTESY OF DERMOTT MULLOOLY

possession of firearms and ammo. He would not accept bail. He was charged, but escaped from custody. He was later recaptured and lodged in Sligo Gaol. McKeon was one of the founding members of the Elphin Monument Committee, whose work resulted in the erection of the impressive memorial at Shankill

T. McKeon (Boyle) 1st Battalion North Roscommon, a member of the Volunteers since before the Easter Rising

Christopher "Kit" McKeown led an Anti-Treaty Flying Column during the Civil War in the Athlone area. Killed in Moate on 12 November 1922. His name is inscribed on the Athlone IRA Memorial (see Surrounding Volunteers page 469)

Frank McLoughlin (Corralara, Kilmore) 5th Battalion North Roscommon, brother of Michael ("Mick"). He fought with the Volunteers during the War. After the fighting had ceased, he emigrated to the United States, where he joined the American army. He fought in the Pacific during World War II, where he was the only man to make it off an island alive. He returned to Ireland in later years, and is buried in Kilmore Cemetery

Jimmy McLoughlin (Boyle) 1st Battalion North Roscommon, a member of the Volunteers since before the Rising

Joseph McLoughlin (Ballyfarnon) deserted from the Free State Army at Boyle Barracks in September 1922. McLoughlin fought with the Anti-Treaty Arigna Flying Column, and was arrested on 4 September 1923 in Drumsna

Martin McLoughlin (Ballinameen) arrested for his Anti-Treaty activities during the Civil War on 21 July 1922, and taken to Athlone on 2 September

Michael "Mick" McLoughlin (Corralara, Kilmore) served as the Vice O/C of the 5th Battalion North Roscommon, and was a member of Kilmore Coy. McLoughlin worked for the railroad as a signalman, and he made good use of his connections. "He took all the dispatches for HQ and forwarded them to Dublin via the guards on the train."* Took part in the **attempted disarming of the military guard at Carrick-on-Shannon Station** in September 1918, the **attack on the Carrick-on-Shannon Courthouse** in September 1920, and the **attack on the Boyle Barracks** during the Civil War. When Divisions were formed, he became a member of the Third Western Divisional Staff. He was also a member of the Anti-Treaty Active Service Unit of North Roscommon during the Civil War. Emigrated to New York, where he was shot dead in 1931 by a bandit who attempted to raid the store where he was the manager. He was buried in Kilmore Cemetery

*Jack Glancy Volunteer Witness Statement to the Bureau of Military History 1913-21, p. 4.

Michael McLoughlin (Ballymore, Lackan, Strokestown) Carniska Coy. in the 3rd Battalion North Roscommon. After the War he became a farmer. Died 1980

Owen McLoughlin (Errironagh, Rockingham, Boyle) 1st Battalion North Roscommon. He was a member of the Anti-Treaty Active Service Unit (Flying Column) of North Roscommon during the Civil War. He had earlier deserted from the National Army when he was stationed in Boyle Barracks in September 1922. After the War he emigrated to England

Patrick McLoughlin (Seltannaveeny, Arigna) Captain of Arigna Company in the 4th Battalion North Roscommon. He, Jim and Tom Lynham, and Tommy Lavin raided the Ballyfarnon Post Office in March 1921 — the operation that began the chain of events leading to the **Keadue Ambush**. He chose not to be a participant in the Civil War. After the hostilities he farmed his land, and became a stone mason. Died 1960, and buried in Arigna Cemetery

Ed McManus (Drum Coy.) 3rd Battalion Athlone Brigade

John McManus (Crossna Coy.) 4th Battalion North Roscommon, served as the 2nd Lieutenant

John McManus (Ballyfeeny, Strokestown) a member of Kilglass Coy. in the 3rd Battalion North Roscommon. Took part in Anti-Treaty activities during the Civil War, and was arrested on 29 August 1922, and interned in Athlone on 2 September 1922. He was later transferred to Tintown A, where he secured his release on 10 January 1923

Michael McManus served as the Quartermaster for the Ballyfarnon Company in the 4th Battalion North Roscommon. Emigrated to the United States

Patrick McLoughlin, 4th Battalion North Roscommon.

Patrick McManus 2nd Lieutenant of Ballyfarnon Company in the 4th Battalion North Roscommon

Tom McManus (Drum Coy.) 3rd Battalion Athlone Brigade

Margaret McNally (Elphin) member of the Cumann na mBan, who carried dispatches in the tire of her bicycle. She would slice a hole in the inner tube, insert the message, then patch the inner tube, pump up the tire, and cycle on her way

Patrick McNally (Elphin) 2nd Battalion North Roscommon, joined the Volunteers when he was eighteen years old. Took part in five prepared ambushes. After the War he emigrated to Detroit, Michigan

Thomas McNally (Tulsk) 2nd Battalion North Roscommon. Listed in the GHQ papers in the UCD Archives as the First Lieutenant of Tulsk Company. After the War he emigrated to the United States

John P. McNamara (Woodfield, Knockvicar, Boyle) served as the 2nd Lieutenant of the Crossna Company, which was part of the 4th Battalion North Roscommon

Joseph McNamara (Rockfield, Donamon) a member of "A" Coy. (Cloverhill) in the 2nd Battalion South Roscommon

Michael J. McNamara (Culliagh, Scramogue, Strokestown) joined the Volunteers in 1917. He was involved in a skirmish with the RIC as early as 1918, whereupon he was sentenced to fourteen months. He was released in time to participate in an **attack at Tarmonbarry** in December 1920. He was arrested a few days after that attack, and released in 1921. All those prison walls did not stifle his desire to free Ireland. He returned to active duty, and was again arrested in 1922, during which year he served as the Captain for "C" Company in the 3rd Battalion North Roscommon. He was a member of an Anti-Treaty Flying Column in North Roscommon. He was nabbed by the Free State forces on 6 September 1922. Taken to Athlone in November

Packie McNamara (Lack, Whitehall, Tarmonbarry) a member of Tarmonbarry Coy., 3rd Battalion North Roscommon

Pat McNamara (Culliagh, Scramogue, Strokestown) 3rd Battalion North Roscommon, brother of Michael. McNamara was an escapee through the Brady tunnel at the Curragh in September 1921

Brian McNeill, son of Professor Eoin McNeill who countermanded the Easter Rising order, and was Education Minister in the Free State Government from 1922 to 1925. Brian was a trainer in the Mantua camp for members of the North Roscommon Brigade. He took the Anti-Treaty side in the Civil War. In November 1921, he and another officer from GHQ were sent to Sligo as a first step towards setting up a Divisional structure within the area. McNeill was killed in action in County Sligo 20 September 1922. He was part of the *Ballinalee's* armoured car crew, who abandoned the vehicle and attempted to escape up over Benbulben Mountain. He and four others were executed after they surrendered to the Free State troops. He is buried in Dublin (a tragic example of father and son being on opposite sides during a bitter war)

James McNeill (Milltown) a member of the Curraghboy Coy. in the 4th Battalion South Roscommon. From 1917-March 1919 did organisational work, practiced scouting procedures and military exercises during a visit by Sean Connolly, did police duty during the South Roscommon election. Enforced the Dáil decrees. There were a total of twenty arms raids conducted within the Company area, and another fifteen raids outside the vicinity, and performed in conjunction with other Companies of the Battalion. McNeill took part in those actions. McNeill was one of two selected men from the Company who were, for a time, attached to the Brigade Active

James McNeill, Curraghboy Company
PHOTO COURTESY OF EDWARD EGAN OF CURRAGHBOY

Service Unit. The entire Company participated in the arrest and confinement of a suspected spy. That man was tried by court-martial and eventually executed — an action which prompted the arrest of ten members of the Company on 5 January 1921. Another five men were arrested in March. McNeill escaped the dragnet. He raided houses of persons sympathetic with the enemy, and took part in the preparations for the **attack on Ballygar Barracks**. After the War he became a farm labourer. Died 3 July 1972, and is buried in the new Kiltoom Cemetery

William McNeill (Athleague village) a member of the Athleague Coy., 3rd Battalion South Roscommon, 1st Lieutenant of the Company

James McNulty (Tully, Gortaganny, Loughglynn) Ballinlough Coy., 1st Battalion South Roscommon, participated in the **attempted attack on the Castlerea Station Guard** in July 1920, the **burning of Loughglynn Barracks**, and the **burning of Ballinlough Barracks** on 14 September 1920. He also took part in the **attempted ambush at Lisacul** (in conjunction with the East Mayo men) in May 1921. During the Truce McNulty attended training camps at Kilkerrin and Erritt, specialising in first aid. His home served as the headquarters for Anti-Treaty "J" Company during the post-Truce times

John Patrick McPhillips of Ballaghaderreen

John Patrick McPhillips (Church St., Ballaghaderreen) one of the first members of the Ballaghaderreen Company in the East Mayo Brigade. He used to travel by bicycle to Tom Campbell's home in Church St., Swinford and to the *Roscommon Herald* office of Jasper Tully in Boyle. Messages included the advertisements for upcoming meetings, and the Sinn Féin Club notes. John guarded the ballot boxes during the 1918 election. He moved to Liverpool in 1919, and became active with the Volunteers there — collecting and shipping arms across the Irish Sea, and burning the houses of Black and Tans stationed in Ireland. He was arrested after a night spent in sabotaging communications ("convicted" by the presence of buttercups petals in the cuffs of his pants).* Sentenced to six years in Dartmoor. "He was released after eighteen months, on 14 February 1922, after Michael Collins travelled to London and confronted Prime Minister David Lloyd George personally with a demand that the small group of IRA in Dartmoor be released as called for in the Treaty. Lloyd George had claimed that prisoners arrested and convicted on The Mainland (Great Britain) were not covered by the Treaty. Collins won and so the men were freed to a huge welcome."** John was then assigned to the Coastal Service with the Free State forces. He later moved to Flushing, New York, where he wrote several long and detailed articles about his days in the Volunteer movement, and had them published in *The Western People* in 1964. He died in 1969

*The Western People, "Convicted by Buttercup Petals," by John McPhillips, 15 August 1964.
**William McPhillips, son of John, correspondence with author, 29 July 2004.

Michael James McPhillips (Church St., Ballaghaderreen) brother of John Patrick, also a member of the East Mayo Brigade. He and his brother, Jack, sailed across the Irish Sea and settled in Liverpool, where they worked for the Volunteer movement — collecting and shipping guns, and burning the houses of Black and Tans who were stationed in Ireland.* He was arrested on the same night as his brother, and sent to Kilmainham, and ultimately to Ballykinlar. Michael took the Pro-Treaty side during the Civil War, and was captured and interned by Anti-Treaty Republican forces. He never recovered from the treatment he received at that time. He died in 1943

*The Western People, "Mayo's Fighting Story The IRA in Liverpool." by Jack McPhillips. 25 July 1964.

James McWilliams (born in Elphin) 2nd Battalion North Roscommon. A member of the Church of Ireland, and the son of a RIC constable, he became a dispatch rider, and was arrested in November of 1920. He was sent to Elphin Barracks, Strokestown, and finally to Roscommon Gaol, where he spent four months. Emigrated in 1921 to England, and finally to the United States, where he became a successful businessman in Baltimore, Maryland. He owned and operated the Maxalea nursery

Robert McWilliams (born in Elphin) brother of James, 2nd Battalion North Roscommon. He too was a dispatch rider. He was arrested in November of 1920, and sent to Elphin Barracks, Strokestown, and Roscommon Gaol, where he spent four months sleeping on a metal box with a flimsy blanket for warmth. He left Ireland in 1921 on the advice of his commanding officer, who noted that he and his brother were marked men. He finally settled in Sykesville, Maryland, married a farmer's daughter, and reared a family

Joseph Macken (Lisdillure) Drum Coy., Athlone Brigade. A member of Father Flanagan's Sinn Féin Club

Malachy Macken (Lisdillure) Drum Company, brother of Joseph, Tom, and Michael

Michael Macken (Lisdillure) Drum Coy., 3rd Battalion Athlone Brigade. His home was burned on 1 November 1920 as a reprisal for the attack on Constable Doyle

Tom Macken (Lisdillure) Drum Coy., 3rd Battalion Athlone Brigade, and also a member of Father Flanagan's Sinn Féin Club

B. Madden (Lisacul) Company Captain in the 4th Battalion East Mayo Brigade (which included parts of west Roscommon)

Pat Macken (Castlepollard, Co. Westmeath) served as a Judge in the Athlone Sinn Féin Courts, and as Quartermaster for the Athlone Brigade. A member of the Athlone Flying Column. Participated in the **ambush at Parkwood** in County Westmeath in September 1920, and the **attempted ambush of a convoy on the Athlone-Ballinasloe-Galway Road** in October. During the Civil War he took the Anti-Treaty side, and was arrested and held in Custume Barracks in Athlone. Life behind bars was brief! He escaped in July 1922, and was on hand to participate in the **Ambush at Glasson** on 25 August 1922. He was recaptured on 16 September 1922, along with John Shortle of Baylin, Athlone. After the War he moved to Longford. (See Surrounding Volunteers, Westmeath section page 469)

Daniel Madden (Cloonylyons, Strokestown) 1st Lieutenant in Carniska Company in the 3rd Battalion North Roscommon. Joined the Volunteers in 1917. Took part in the **Walpole incident** in November 1920, the **attack on a patrol at Strokestown** in January 1921 armed with a revolver, and the **Scramogue Ambush** armed with a shotgun. He attended the Mantua training camp during the Truce. After the War he joined the Garda Síochána, and was stationed in Fermoy, Co. Cork

Frank Madden (Ballyfeeny, Strokestown) a member of the Kilglass Company in the 3rd Battalion North Roscommon

Frank (Dan) Madden (Ballagh) 3rd Battalion South Roscommon, Kilgefin Company, brother of Pat, a member of the IRB as well as the Flying Column. Participated in the **Fourmilehouse Ambush** on 12 October 1920. Arrested after the ambush, and became a guest of the English military at Athlone detention barracks, where he became the leader of the prisoners in the cell block. Quoting from Tommy Loughran's book, *An Old Soldier's Memories*, "Dan was about twenty-three, tall, slender, well built and handsome, with a neat brown moustache. He not only looked like a leader but had the courage to act like one. Being chosen by acclamation, Dan lost no time in presenting the prisoners' demands to Colonel Lambert."* Later he was transferred to Dartmoor in England, which he lamented was completely "lice infested." There was no prison the Irish dreaded more than Dartmoor. As described by Padraig O'Fathaigh from Galway, the prison was "built in a wild desolate mountain moor. During five days out of seven it is enveloped in a thick fog and the other two days raining (perhaps) with a stinging East Wind."** Madden remained in custody until the end of the Tan War. After hostilities ceased, he became an insurance agent. In 1939, when both Pat Madden and his wife died, Dan took charge of rearing one of the six children of Pat. Died 10 March 1982, and buried in Derrane Cemetery

*p. 241.
**Irish Narratives Padraig O'Fathaigh's War of Independence Recollections of a Galway Gaelic Leaguer p. 40.

Frank (Dan) Madden, Kilgefin Company, 3rd Battalion South Roscommon.

PHOTO COURTESY OF KATE BRENNAN

Lena Madden (Ballagh area) member of Cumann na mBan

M. J. Madden (Lisalway, Castlerea) served as Quartermaster for "C" Coy. in the 2nd Battalion South Roscommon

Michael Madden (Cloonylyons, Strokestown) a member of the Carniska Coy., 3rd Battalion North Roscommon, brother of Daniel. Joined the IRA in 1917. Attended weekly drills, took part in collecting funds for conscription resistance, stood duty at Aughnadarry polling booth during the North Roscommon election. Present at the **burning of Fourmilehouse Barracks**, and assisted in the **Fourmilehouse ambush**. Performed scout duty for the **attack on the Strokestown patrol** in January 1921, and blocked roads in preparation for **Scramogue Ambush**. He was arrested shortly after Scramogue and taken to Longford, where he was badly beaten, but fortunately let go. After the War he emigrated to New York

1922 photograph.
Back row, left to right: — Finnigan from Longford; — Brodrick from Ballinsloe, Galway; and (unknown).
Front row, left to right: Pat Mullooly from Kiltrustan, Strokestown; Pat Madden from Ballagh; John Neary, Bangor, Erris

PHOTO COURTESY OF DERMOTT MULLOOLY

PHOTO RESTORATION BY LEW THORNE

Pat Madden (native of Ballagh, Kilgefin, Roscommon) 3rd Battalion South Roscommon. Madden served in the British Army. When the Kilgefin Company formed in March of 1917, he became its first Captain. He moved to Dublin, where he remained active in the Volunteer movement during 1917-18. He attended an underground officer's school to study the techniques of guerilla fighting. The studies involved taking part in raids and ambushes carried out by the Dublin units.* He was arrested for illegal drilling in a hall in York Street, and served eighteen months in Belfast. While in gaol, he took part in the prison hunger strike for political status organised by Austin Stack. He returned to Roscommon, and assisted in forming the 3rd Battalion South Roscommon, having the wisdom to recruit ex-British soldiers into the IRA (a practice that was frowned on by some). Madden was appointed Battalion Commandant, as well as being a member of the IRB and Head Centre for the county. He participated in actions at **Lanesboro**, **the Moneen Ambush** in July 1920, the **Fourmilehouse Ambush** in October 1920, the **shootout at Castlenode** in November 1920, the **attack on Elphin Barracks** in February 1921, **Scramogue Ambush** in March, the **attack at Kilrooskey** in May, and the **attack on Frenchpark RIC Barracks** in June. According to his obituary in the Roscommon newspaper, Madden more than once donned the garb of the enemy to infiltrate their ranks and seek out their intent. The Tans' khaki pants would, after the Treaty, give way to the uniform of a colonel in the Free State Army. He saved Michael Kilroy, a prominent Anti-Treaty fighter from Mayo, from being shot after Kilroy had been captured in Mayo.** Madden took part in the Army Mutiny of 1924, after which he resigned his commission and became active in the formation of the National Association of the Old IRA with the aim of reconciling former comrades who took opposing sides in the Civil War. He married Rose Kenny in whose home the Flying Column was formed (the Glebe in Ballagh). Together they started a family. Tragically, at the birth of the sixth child, his wife died. Fighting the British was infinitely easier than facing the future without his wife and with six hungry mouths to feed. The stress became too great*** and Pat died 18 October 1939 of lung cancer. He is buried in Derrane Cemetery

*An Old Soldier's Memories by Tommy Loughran, p. 207.
**Gerald Davis interview, Ernie O'Malley Papers, UCD Archives, No. 137.
*** Bernadette Kilmartin, daughter of Pat Madden, interview by author, January 2001.

Death and Funeral of Mr. Pat Madden
National Manifestation of Sorrow

Eloquently touching was the tribute paid to the memory of one who had played a noble and inspiring part in the sad drama of Ireland's struggle for freedom in the final and sad scenes of conveying home to his native county and laying to rest the remains of the late Commandant, Pat Madden, who passed away after a short illness in Mercers Hospital, Dublin, on Thursday, 19th.

Eldest son of the late Mr. Edward Madden and the late Mrs. Madden of Ballagh, Kilrooskey, the deceased had been living in Dublin for some years. The news of his death came unexpectedly to most of his friends, as he had been enjoying good health until recently. The announcement caused hurt, one might say, in every part of Ireland for so widely known was the name of Pat Madden through his prominence in the National movement that national sorrow was evoked by his passing away. Particularly and poignant is his death by reason of the fact that his beloved wife only predeceased him a short twelve months to the great loss sustained by demise has been added the crushing __ by the death of a kind paternal guardian over a loving family of six young children. Such are the inscrutable wise ways of Providence in vale of sorrow, and no more single expression of heartfelt sympathy has been aroused by the death of one __ long time as that evoked amongst __who knew this big hearted Irishman. In his personal associations he was the soul of cheerfulness and good nature. Few, if any, there were with whom he became acquainted in private life that could help becoming impressed by his pleasing and lovable personality behind which was sheltered outstanding qualities of heart, mind, and character that marked him out as a big man amongst men. His Company was always a pleasure and his big soulful character was always a material in — in getting to the heart of people. Behind those qualities lay a reverence and forcefulness of purpose that moulded him into a real man of action. The part that such qualities were able to play in the unforgettable episodes of the National movement in the country are now well known. He was one of those whose magnanimity of thought, patriotic instinct, heroic heart, and forgetfulness of selfish devotion placed him at a critical stage of our country's story to embark with his fellow men to strike at oppression and subterfuge and weld themselves into an insuppressible and unconquerable entity with a common and urgent interest. He saw from the history of the past and in the hard inexorable school of experience — the experience of a demoralized people crushed by weight of callous, uncompromising Empire, that sacrifices would have to be made to shake off the terrible shackles of Imperial rule.

With the spirited and invincible recalcitrance of Celtic nature he embarked on the road of patriotic endeavor at a time when the outlook was nothing but of risk and danger and when the chances of any success seemed hopeless.

By the Chiefs of the Volunteer movement he was specially selected for many important undertakings in the work of organising the young men of his native county and his energy, courage, and zeal in that capacity were successfully applied in consolidating a virile organisation locally.

Soldierly Qualities

Defying the machination of the British secret service, he carried on drilling and secret manoeuvrs under the very eyes of the police and his sound soldierly attributes, quickness of thought and calm judgment, which afterwards were subjected to such supreme tests, were used to great effect in the upbuilding of a military machine and radiating confidence and hope in ranks of the Volunteers. But, it was in the rage of battle, during a long and anxious period of strife, that these fine qualities outshone in splendid heroism. His great courage and cool presence of mind in moments of imminent danger were phenomenal. His carrying out of acts of daring would fill a volume to recount, for more than once did he place himself in khaki disguise in the actual midst of the enemy, who were offering a price for his capture, for the purpose of carrying though some objective which would otherwise be regarded as part of the impossible. Amongst his early concentrations was the organisation of a Volunteer Company in his native parish which afterwards become the most active unit in the Tan War.

In 1918, when drilling Volunteers in a house in York Street, Dublin, he was arrested by the British Forces, and sentenced to six months' imprisonment in Belfast Jail. He took part in the famous prison fight for political status under Austin Stack in the same year. On his release after hunger strike, he returned to his native county and assisted in forming the Third Batt., South Roscommon Brigade, and was appointed its Commandant. Early in 1920 he was appointed O/C of the South Roscommon Flying Column. Under his command the column carried out ambushes on the British Forces at Lanesboro, Kilrooskey and Castlenode,

Fourmilehouse, Scramogue, and attacks on Elphin and Frenchpark R.I.C. Stations. After the treaty, Mr. Madden held the rank of Colonel in the Free State Army, and was a member of the GHQ Inspection Staff. He took a prominent part in what is now called the "Army Mutiny" of 1924, following which he resigned his commission.

Immediately after his resignation he strove to bring about a reconciliation between the forces split by the treaty and Civil War.

With that end in view he, with Simon Donnelly and a number of other prominent Republicans, sought to reorganise the old I.R.A., irrespective of which side they took during the Civil War, for the completion of the work which they began in 1916, and helped to form the National Association of Old I.R.A., of the Executive Council, of which he was a member. Although he held on with unswerving and undiminished tenacity and with undaunted sincerity to his views, his entire demeanor never savoured of rancour or bitterness. Once he believed he was right he took his stand accordingly. He deplored the circumstances of the fratricidal strife that put his old comrades in arms against each other, and with clearness of thought that so often characterised his actions he was one of the first to see the futility of that ever to be regretted internecine holocaust.

Quoted from Pat Madden's obituary notice in *The Roscommon Herald* 28 October 1939

Peter Madden (Roscommon Coy.) 3rd Battalion South Roscommon

Thomas Madden (Carrowgarve, Tulsk) 2nd Battalion South Roscommon. Participated in the **raid on the military train at Ballymoe** in June 1920, the **attack on Frenchpark Barracks** 2 October 1920, and the **ambush at Southpark, Castlerea** 10 July 1921

Tom Madden, 3rd Battalion
South Roscommon.

Tom Madden (Ballagh, Kilgefin, Roscommon) Lieutenant in "E" Coy., 3rd Battalion South Roscommon, brother of Pat and Dan, a member of the Flying Column. Many, but not all, of the members of the Kilgefin Company participated in the **Fourmilehouse Ambush** on 12 October 1920. Tom was present at the **Scramogue Ambush** in March 1921. In the 1950s, he was interviewed by Ernie O'Malley. His words are included in the papers of that author in the UCD Archives. Tom became a small farmer in Ballagh, and died 1 September 1977. Buried in Derrane Cemetery

William Madden (Kilrooan, Loughglynn) a farmer by trade who served as a Judge in the Sinn Féin Courts

William Madden (Ballyfeeny, Strokestown) a member of the Kilglass Company in the 3rd Battalion North Roscommon

Francis Maguire (McGuire) (Carrowphadeen, Lecarrow) 4th Battalion South Roscommon. Took over the position of 1st Lieutenant for the St. John's Coy. when Patrick Grady was promoted to the rank of Captain. Maguire drilled with other Volunteers two nights a week — Tuesdays and Thursdays, worked with the Republican Courts, and participated in the 1918 election. He and his Company, under the command of Captain Patrick Grady, participated in the sham battles for training purposes under Ernie O'Malley at Lysterfield, Taughmaconnell, and Churchboro in the summer of 1918. He took part in the **attempted ambush at Kilmurray Military Camp** in June 1920, and the **raiding of the mail train at Kiltoom**. Maguire blocked roads, constructed dugouts, and took part in the **blowing up of Ballybay Road Bridge**

John Maguire (Hodson Bay) a member of the Kiltoom Coy. in the 4th Battalion South Roscommon

Paddy Maguire (Aghadad, Castlecoote) ran a safe house

Frank Mahon (Captain) of Glenamaddy Coy. Although located in Co. Galway, this Company was incorporated into No. 2 Brigade of the 2nd Western Division with Gerald O'Connor, former O/C of the 1st Battalion South Roscommon, serving as as Brigade Commandant. Mahon was Captain in 1920, and was replaced by Pat Treacy up until Truce time. After the Truce Mahon again assumed the duties of Captain

George Mahon (Ballaghaderreen) was arrested during the Civil War on 24 November 1922, and released the next month

John Mahon (Ballaghaderreen) arrested during the Civil War, and taken to Tintown. Released on 18 December 1923

John Mahon (Captain) Clonberne Company was part of the Glenamaddy Battalion, which was incorporated into No. 2 Brigade, 2nd Western Division with Gerald O'Connor, former O/C of the 1st Battalion South Roscommon, serving as Brigade Commandant. Mahon's Company numbered fifty-eight in the autumn of 1921

John Mahon (Annagh, Castlerea) a member of Trien Coy., 1st Battalion South Roscommon

John Mahon (Emlaghnagree, Donamon) a member of "E" Coy. in the 2nd Battalion South Roscommon. Took part in the **raid on the military train at Ballymoe** in June 1920

Michael Mahon (Drumshanbo) part of the South Leitrim Brigade. Participated in the **attempted attack on the Carrick-on-Shannon Station Guard** in September 1918. Took part in the **attack and capture of Leitrim Barracks** in May 1920, and the **attempted attack on the Carrick-on-Shannon military post** September 1920. Participated in **attacks at Garadice, Eslin, Fenagh**. Was present at the **attack on Drumshanbo Barracks** in September of 1922, and the **attack of Ballinamore Barracks** in February 1923

M. Mahon (Ballaghaderreen) one of the first members of the Ballaghaderreen Coy. in the East Mayo Brigade

Owen Mahon (Southpark, Castlerea) 1st Battalion South Roscommon. Present at Pat Glynn's Memorial Service in 1970

Patrick Mahon (Ballaghaderreen) one of the first members of the Ballaghaderreen Coy. in the East Mayo Brigade. He took an active part in the Civil War, and was arrested the same day as Tom. He was taken to Athlone 14 November 1922

Tom Mahon (Carrigeen, Ballinameen) 1st Battalion North Roscommon. He was a member of the Active Service Unit formed in North Roscommon during the Civil War

Tom Mahon of Ballaghaderreen was arrested for Anti-Treaty activities during the Civil War on 8 September 1922, and sent to Athlone a month later

Pat Maleady (Mulleady) (Cloontuskert village) 1st Lieutenant of Cloontuskert Coy. in the 3rd Battalion South Roscommon. A member of Pat Madden's Flying Column. Present at the **shootout at Castlenode** in November 1920, and the **Scramogue Ambush** in March 1921. After the War he emigrated to the USA

Peter Maleady (Mulleady) (Cloontuskert village) a member of the Cloontuskert Coy. in the 3rd Battalion South Roscommon

James Maloney (Glenamaddy Battalion Commandant) which was part of No. 2 Brigade, 2nd Western Division under Brigade O/C Gerald O'Connor. In 1921 Maloney became part of the ASU formed with the Tuam Battalion area

M. A. Mangan (doctor) head of first aid for No. 2 Brigade, 2nd Western Division

Margaret Mangan (Loughglynn) set an example for her four daughters. She solidly supported the young men who came to her home "on the run." Daughters Mary, Bridgie, Annie, and Ellie learned their lessons well. Mary Kate Mangan was active in support of the fighters in the Donegal area. Bridgie made the tricolour flags that draped the caskets of Sean Bergin and Stephen McDermott after the two were killed in The Woodlands of Loughglynn. Ellie Mangan worked at E. J. McDermott's in Castlerea, and was said to have been engaged to Sean Bergin. Ellie died of a sorrow-ladened heart at the age of twenty-four. Bridgie and Annie Mangan emigrated to America

Frank Manning (Ruskey, Dromod, Leitrim) Barnacoola Coy., 5th Battalion, No. 3 Brigade, 3rd Western Division. Manning fought with the Anti-Treaty Arigna Flying Column during the Civil War

George Manning (Chapel St., Athlone) Adjutant for the Athlone Battalion in 1918, and later appointed Adjutant for the Athlone Brigade. Took part in the **raid on the Athlone Excise Office** in May 1920. He, along with other men from the Athlone Battalion, participated in the **attempted capture of the Riverstown RIC Barracks** in County Westmeath. He also was with the party who **trailed Sergeant Craddock** in Athlone on 22 August 1920. A member of the Athlone Anti-Treaty Flying Column. He later died from wounds received during the Civil War. His name is inscribed on the IRA Memorial in Athlone

Denis Mannion (Barry Beg, The Hill of Berries) 3rd Battalion Athlone Brigade. Actively involved with the Volunteers during the Tan War. He and his brother, Thomas, were sent to the Curragh. Before his capture, Denis did not sleep at home for twelve months, but rather lived in the bog with "a wagon cover for a roof."* Kate Dooley fed him and his comrades all those months. On the same night that he participated in the **burning of Bealnamullia Barracks**, he simply crossed the bog, then put a torch to the **Kiltoom Barracks**. While on the run, he hid in bed between the two Kenny sisters (one of whom served as a nurse on Quaker Island). The Kennys lived in Curraghboy. When the Black and Tans opened the bedroom door, one Tan hollered to the other, "Nothing here but a bunch of women — too many to be of much use to us!"** In quieter times, he hid out on Hare Island, on which a family named Duffy lived. While there, word came that a British patrol was due to search the island. Seamus O'Meara, the Brigade Commandant, sent word to the men to organise an ambush, which they did by positioning themselves on each side of the Shannon. During the Civil War he took the Republican side. Arrested on 23 September 1922 along with his brother

Denis Mannion, The Hill of Berries

The Mannion family
Back row, left to right: Tom, John, Vergil, and Denis with their parents seated in the front row

PHOTO COURTESY OF SISTER CLARE AND SADIE FEELY

and several comrades, and taken to Athlone on 14 November

*Sister Clare and Sadie Feely, interview by author, The Hill of Berries, County Roscommon, 11 November 2003.
**Sister Clare Feely, interview by author, Dublin, Ireland, 31 August 1994.

Emmett Mannion (The Hill of Berries) Judge in the Sinn Féin Courts

James Mannion a member of "C" Coy. in the 2nd Battalion South Roscommon. After the War he emigrated to the United States

James Mannion (Cartron Coote, Kilteevan) arrested for Anti-Treaty activities during the Civil War, and taken to Athlone on 25 January 1923

James Mannion (St. Francis Terrace, Athlone) a member of the 1st Battalion Athlone Brigade, participated in the **burning of Brawney Barracks and Moydrum Castle**

James Mannion (Cullen, Cartron, Kiltoom) arrested for Anti-Treaty activities during the Civil War, and taken to Tintown A. Released 22 December 1923

John Mannion (Ballyglass, Ballinagare) a member of "C" Coy. in the 2nd Battalion South Roscommon. Participated in the **raid on the military train at Ballymoe** in June 1920, the **attack on Frenchpark Barracks** 2 October 1920, and the **ambush at Southpark, Castlerea** 10 July 1921. When the Western Division was formed, he volunteered to serve with the Oran Battalion Flying Column. After the War he became a farmer. Died 6 October 1963, and is buried in Rathmoyle, Kilmurray

John Mannion (Barry Beg, The Hill of Berries) part of the 3rd Battalion Athlone Brigade. Brother of Denis and Thomas, actively involved with the Volunteers during the Tan War, which kept him on the run. He was arrested and confined in Athlone, from which he escaped, along with Joe Grenham. They hid out in Curraghmore, barely two miles away from his home

Martin Mannion (Captain of the Dunmore Coy.) Glenamaddy Battalion, brother of Thomas, who became part of an ASU formed with the Tuam Brigade. He also served as the Adjutant of the Glenamaddy Battalion. He was wounded in April 1921. Attended the Cloonkeen training camp during the Truce. He served as the Quartermaster for No. 2 Brigade, 2nd Western Division

Matt Mannion (Barry Beg, The Hill of Berries, Kiltoom) 3rd Battalion Athlone Brigade, brother of Thomas and William

"May" Mannion (Arigna area) fought with Ned Bofin's Anti-Treaty Flying Column during the Civil War. Arrested by troops from Ballyfarnon on 20 May 1923

Michael Mannion (Caher, Castlerea) a member of Trien Coy., 1st Battalion South Roscommon. Took part in the **attempted ambush at Coshlieve** in July 1920, and attended the Hermitage and Erritt training camps during the Truce. He later emigrated to England

Michael Mannion (Kilterna) Captain of the Kilterna Coy., which was part of the 1st Battalion, No. 2 Brigade. Although located in County Galway, this Battalion was part of No. 2 Brigade, 2nd Western Division with Gerald O'Connor, former O/C of the 1st Battalion South Roscommon, serving as Brigade Commandant. Michael's Company numbered forty-six after the Truce

Michael Mannion (Coolteige, Kilbride Coy.) 3rd Battalion South Roscommon

Emmett Mannion, The Hill of Berries Judge in the Sinn Féin Courts

PHOTO COURTESY OF SISTER CLARE AND SADIE FEELY

Patrick Mannion (Tobervaddy, Fuerty) a member of "D" Coy. in the 2nd Battalion South Roscommon

Patrick Mannion (Mannon) (Cloonmore, Whitehall, Tarmonbarry) a member of Tarmonbarry Coy. in the 3rd Battalion North Roscommon

Thomas Mannion (Aghadad, Fuerty) 2nd Battalion South Roscommon. Republican Police. When the 2nd Western Division was formed, Thomas served as the Lieutenant in charge of engineering for the 3rd Battalion, No. 2 Brigade, 2nd Western Division. He, along with James Keegan, Joseph Belton, Seamus McGovern, Pat Conboy, James Kenny, and Patrick Farrell captured a Tan during the War for Independence

Thomas Mannion (Brackloon, Dunmore) joined the Dunmore Company, which was organised by three released Rising prisoners: Thomas Kilgarriff, William McGill, and Michael Ronane. He became Captain of the Dunmore Coy., Glenamaddy Battalion, No. 2 Brigade, 2nd Western Division under Brigade Commander Gerald O'Connor. Joined the Volunteers in 1916. In 1921 he became part of the ASU formed with the Tuam Battalion area. His Company numbered fifty-three after the Truce

Thomas Mannion (Barry Beg, The Hill of Berries, Kiltoom) 3rd Battalion Athlone Brigade. Took part in the **raid on the Athlone Excise Office** in May 1920. Actively involved in many "rebel" activities during the Tan War. There is some confusion as to his exact arrest date during the Civil War. An incident related in Vergil Mannion's book, A Life Recalled, states that Bill Ganley and Thomas Mannion were caught in an open field behind the Mannion house and arrested by Free State soldiers in August.* The arrest date for Thomas Mannion found in the Military Archives is 17 September 1922. Bill Ganley has an arrest date of 17 July 1922. Mannion, who had been wounded in the back while attempting to outrun the soldiers, was shipped to Athlone on 14 November and transferred to Mountjoy on 10 January 1923

*pp. 38-39.

Thomas "Toby" Mannion (Barry Beg, The Hill of Berries, Kiltoom) 3rd Battalion Athlone Brigade, cousin of the other Thomas Mannion of The Hill of Berries. "He (Toby) and Tommy Martin were often seen in The Berries with guns slinging from hip and shoulder; they were continually on the move."* Dressed as a courting couple, he and Martin disarmed the double sentries on the Hall Bridge leading westward out of Athlone, and often harassed the troops travelling the Roscommon/Athlone Road.** He took the Anti-Treaty side during the Civil War, and was arrested on 26 March 1923 for carrying dum dum bullets and an incriminating document. He was sent to Athlone, where he was detained until he escaped with Commandant Tom Maguire and several others on 10 June 1923. He was shot by the Free State troops 14 August 1923 on a side lane off the main Athlone Road at The Hill of Berries. He died two weeks later. Buried in Kiltoom old cemetery. During the funeral oration, which was given by Commandant Tom Maguire, a convoy of lorries was seen approaching the cemetery. Johnny Kilcline grabbed Tom Maguire's sleeve and the two made their way to Upper Ardmullan to a safe house. While the graveyard had been ringed with steel and men scattered to avoid capture, Toby Mannion lay peacefully in his grave. His troubles were now over, and his torch passed to a new generation of fighters. His name is inscribed on the Shankill Monument near Elphin and the IRA Monument in Athlone. A Celtic cross in his memory also stands on the Athlone Road near the place where he was shot

*A Life Recalled by Vergil Mannion O.F.M. p. 38. ** Ibid. p. 44.

William Mannion (Barry Beg, The Hill of Berries, Kiltoom) 3rd Battalion, Athlone Brigade. During the Civil War he took the Republican side. After sniping at the Athlone Barracks, he was arrested on 23 September 1922, along with his brother Denis, Ned Dowling, Tom Martin, Bernard Martin, and — Finneran (all members of the Athlone Flying Column). He was taken to Athlone on 14 November 1922. He secured his released on 20 March 1923

William Mannion (Glenvela, Lisalway, Castlerea) a member of "C" Coy in the 2nd Battalion South Roscommon. Participated in the **raid on the military train at Ballymoe** in June 1920, the **attack on Frenchpark Barracks** 2 October 1920, and

William Mannion, Lisalway, Castlerea.

the **ambush at Southpark**, **Castlerea** 10 July 1921. After the War he became a farmer. Died 22 March 1986, and buried Rathmoyle, Kilmurray

Patrick Mara (Carrownolan, Kiltoom) a member of the Kiltoom Coy., 4th Battalion South Roscommon. After the War he became a carpenter. Died in the late 1970s, and buried in the new Kiltoom Cemetery

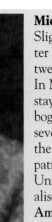

Michael J. Marren (Mount Irwin, Gurteen, Co. Sligo) O/C of the Ballymote Battalion, a carpenter by trade. He, along with Jim Hunt, had ten to twelve men permanently under their command. In May of 1920, Marren and Thady McGowan stayed up all night fashioning a fake coffin for a bogus funeral cortege the next morning. Sixty to seventy Volunteers were to act as mourners while the funeral procession wound its way to a police patrol escorting explosives from a local quarry. Unfortunately, the police patrol never materialised. On 1 September 1920, he took part in the **Ambush at Ratra**, and in January 1921 he was in charge of **attacking military personnel on a train at Kilfree Junction**. He also participated in the **attack on the RIC barracks at Collooney** in March 1921. Marren, along with Alec McCabe and Thady McGowan, made the bomb which was supposed to have blown a hole in the wall during the **attack on Ballaghaderreen Barracks** in February 1921. He was overzealous! Four weeks later, when the bomb was hauled out of town to be detonated in a bog, the explosion rumbled windows four miles away.* Marren made a few miraculous escapes during the Tan War. In July 1920, he and Jim Hunt were visiting Companies around Tubbercurry in Co. Sligo. They returned to Marren's at Mount Irwin and were sound asleep in an upstairs bedroom (fully armed with grenades) when, at daybreak, the house was surrounded. They both got away unscathed. They returned to the home shortly after this altercation to remove the arms dump. They and two other Volunteers were again accosted by the military, and again made a daring escape. His charmed life ended, however, on the day the Truce was signed. He drowned while sunbathing at Strandhill. His funeral was a great display of strength for the IRA in Sligo. Two thousand people along with eleven priests celebrated his Solemn Requiem Mass**

*Jim Hunt interview, Ernie O'Malley Papers, UCD Archives, No. 133.
**The Aftermath of Revolution Sligo 1921-1923 by Michael Farry, p. 18.

Albert "Bertie" Martin (Ballinagare village) joined the Free State Army when the split came in the IRA. He occupied Boyle Barracks in July 1922. He later joined the Garda Síochána

Bernard Martin (St. Mary's Terrace, Athlone) worked with other Anti-Treaty Volunteers in the Athlone area during the Civil War, and was arrested on 5 September 1922, and taken to Athlone, from which he escaped on 28 October 1922

Bernard Martin (Barry Beg, The Hill of Berries, Kiltoom) took the Anti-Treaty side in the Civil War, and was arrested on 23 September 1922, along with the Mannion brothers and his own brother, Tom. Bernard was sent to Athlone on 14 November 1922

Bill Martin (Bushfield, Ballinaheglish) 2nd Battalion South Roscommon

Brian Martin Adjutant for the Drumraney Battalion. Moved to Lower Abbey Street Dublin after War

Charlie Martin (Ballindoon, Ballyfarnon) 4th Battalion North Roscommon, severely beaten and taken to Boyle Barracks

Ed Martin (St. Mary's Terrace, Athlone) a clerk by trade, arrested after the Rising and sent to Wakefield Jail in England on 13 May. He was transferred to a former German prisoner-of-war camp in Wales. The place later earned the affectionate title of "The Irish University," and is commonly known as Frongoch

James Martin (Ballinagare village) a member of Ballinagare Coy., 1st Battalion South Roscommon. Martin drilled with his fellow Volunteers, collected for the Dáil loan, and enforced the Belfast boycott. He participated in the **destruction of vacant barracks** in 1920, and the **attack on Frenchpark RIC Barracks** 2 October 1920. After the War he became a postman. He was present in 1970 at the memorial for Pat Glynn who had died fifty years earlier in the burning of Ballinlough Barracks

James Martin (Knockcroghery Coy.) 4th Battalion South Roscommon. The Company was formed in 1917 with Patrick Kelly serving as Captain. During the Truce Martin was appointed to a special service unit. He took an active role on the Anti-Treaty side during the Civil War. He helped construct the heavy mines used to **blow up the Kellybrook railway bridge**. He participated in **derailing the Kiltoom train**, collecting gelignite for the making of bombs, and raiding an ex-policeman's house and serving him with notice to leave the county. Martin died at a young age from an accident in the Lecarrow quarry

James Martin (Barry Beg, The Hill of Berries, Kiltoom) 4th Battalion South Roscommon. Martin was Captain of The Berries Company, and in March/April of 1921 was appointed the Vice O/C of the Athlone Brigade. During the Civil War he took the Anti-Treaty side, and participated in the **Ambush at Glasson** in August 1922. He was later captured, along with Thomas Mannion and Thomas Muldoon of The Hill of Berries, and taken to Athlone on 26 March 1923. At the time of his arrest, he was unarmed, but carrying dum dum bullets and revolver ammunition. Emigrated to Boston after War

John Joe Martin (Ballinagare village) Ballinagare Coy., 1st Battalion South Roscommon. John worked in Dublin, and was involved in the Transport Strike in 1913. He returned to Roscommon to help organise for the IRA. Participated in the **attack on Frenchpark RIC Barracks** 2 October 1920. His house was burned by the Tans. By August of 1921, he was in charge of first aid for No. 2 Brigade in the 2nd Western Division. He took no active part in the Civil War. John later qualified as a doctor and worked in County Wexford. Died in September 1953. Buried in Kildavin Cemetery, Bunclody, Co. Wexford

John Martin delivered a recruitment speech at the corner of the old Drum Cemetery in early 1917. Two Sinn Féin Clubs were subsequently formed as a result of his encouragement

May Martin (Boyle) member of the Cumann na mBan

Michael Martin (Barry Beg, The Hill of Berries, Kiltoom) brother of James. Arrested for Anti-Treaty activities, and incarcerated in Mountjoy in January 1923. After the War he farmed the land

Michael Martin (Clooncashel More, Kilgefin) member of "E." Coy., 3rd Battalion South Roscommon. Many, but not all, of the members of the Kilgefin Company participated in the **Fourmilehouse Ambush** on 12 October 1920

Mrs. Martin (Ballinagare) mother of Albert, James, and John, member of the Cumann na mBan

Paddy Martin (Longnamuck, Gailey, Knockcroghery) 4th Battalion South Roscommon. The Company was formed in 1917 with Patrick Kelly serving as Captain. Martin drilled with the Volunteers, and attended practice battles at Taughmaconnell overseen by Ernie O'Malley in the summer of 1918. Participated in the South Roscommon election of 1918, and the County Council election. He was one of eight Volunteers who succeeded in raiding sixteen different homes and collecting about as many shotguns. He also helped collect the IRA levy

Pat Martin, pub proprietor in Ballinagare village, father of Albert, James, and John, whose house had its front portions blown away by the police on the evening of the Frenchpark Barracks attack (2 October 1920)

Thomas Martin (Cartron, Kiltoom) St. John's Coy. in the 4th Battalion South Roscommon, served as Quartermaster for the Coy. When the Company first formed in 1917, Martin drilled with other Volunteers two nights a week — Tuesdays and Thursdays, worked in the 1918 election, and collected the IRA levy. He also blocked roads in the area, and participated in **raiding the mail car of the train stopped at Kiltoom**. Martin was present at the **burning of O'Brien's house** — a residence the Volunteers thought was soon to be taken over by the British Forces

Tom Martin (Barry Beg, The Hill of Berries, Kiltoom) he and Toby Mannion "were often seen in The Berries with guns slinging from hip and shoulder; they were continually on the move."* Dressed as a courting couple, he and Mannion disarmed the double sentries on the Hall Bridge leading westward out of Athlone, and often harassed the troops travelling the Roscommon/Athlone Road. During the Truce he attended the Battalion camp at Drinaun, Galway. Martin took the

John Joe Martin, Ballinagare Company
PHOTO COURTESY OF JOHN MARTIN

Anti-Treaty side during the Civil War, and was arrested with his brother, Bernard, and the Mannion brothers on 23 September 1922, and taken to Athlone in November. He escaped on 27 January 1923, but was subsequently re-arrested on 26 March 1923. After the War he emigrated to Boston
*_A Life Recalled_ by Vergil Mannion O.F.M. p. 38.

Tom Martin (Fostra, Crossna, Boyle) Vice O/C for the 4th Battalion, North Roscommon Brigade. He fought with the Anti-Treaty Arigna Flying Column during the Civil War

William Martin (Bushfield, Ballinaheglish) a member of "B" Coy. in the 2nd Battalion South Roscommon. He was present at the **Fourmilehouse Ambush**

William Martin (Barry Beg, The Hill of Berries, Kiltoom) Kiltoom Coy. in the 4th Battalion South Roscommon

William Martin (Cloonfad, Castlerea) 1st Lieutenant of the Castlerea Coy. as of February 1922

Bertie Mason (Bawn Street, Strokestown) a member of Strokestown Coy., 3rd Battalion North Roscommon, brother of Tom. Arrested in 1918 and became a prisoner at Sligo Gaol. After the Fourmilehouse Ambush, Captain Peake threatened Mason and his brother, Tommie, with execution unless they left the area immediately (neither had any connection to the ambush). After the split in the IRA in 1922, Bertie was in charge of a group of Republicans who occupied the Boyle Barracks. When the Free State troops took over from them, the Anti-Treatyites booby-trapped the building. What Bertie didn't know was that his brother, Tommie, was a member of the Free State forces who would enter the barracks. Tommie was nearly killed in a subsequent explosion. Another unusual family connection is exemplified in his father's line of work. He was a member of the Church of Ireland, who worked as a gamekeeper on the Mahon estate. During the Civil War Bertie took the Anti-Treaty side, and was arrested by the Free State troopers, and sent to Tintown A where he was released on 18 December 1923

Tommie Mason, Strokestown Company.

PHOTO COURTESY OF JOHN KELLY
OF MUCKINAGH, STROKESTOWN

Tommie Mason (Bawn Street, Strokestown) a member of Strokestown Coy., who also served as the Adjutant of 3rd Battalion North Roscommon. He was arrested in 1918, and became a guest of the British in Sligo Gaol. Tommie joined the Volunteers while still in his teens. After the Fourmilehouse Ambush, Captain Peake threatened Mason and his brother, Bertie, with execution unless they left the area immediately. Tommie had been the Battalion commander, but upon his having to go on the run, Liam O'Doherty took his place. Tommie became a member of the Flying Column in the 3rd Battalion North area. While cleaning his gun at the home of Mr. Duignan, a teacher in Slatta National School, he was shot in the ankle and subsequently captured. He later joined the Free State Army, and nearly lost his life due to his brother's actions (see above). After the War Tommie returned to Strokestown, where he was known as a gifted vocalist. He died in 1965, and is buried in the new cemetery in Strokestown. The IRA firing party at his funeral was headed by Luke Duffy

B. Masterson Pro-Treaty Captain in Athlone, who led a raid by boat on Quaker Island in Lough Ree on 22 November 1922 when Matt Davis and nine other Anti-Treatyites were captured

Rev. Fr. Patrick J. Mattimoe, C.C. (Dangan, Kilmore) active supporter in the 1917 bye election of Count Plunkett

James Maxwell took part in the **attack on the Carrick-on-Shannon Courthouse** in September 1920

Michael Maxwell (Peak, Kilcorkey, Castlerea) a member of the Ballinagare Company, 1st Battalion South Roscommon. Helped to enforce the Belfast boycott in his area

Pat Maye (Carrowmore, Croghan) executive of Sinn Féin in North Roscommon. Born in 1880, Pat joined the Volunteers, and took over many of the responsibilities of Quartermaster for the area. He was arrested while attending a meeting in

Croghan, and subsequently became a prisoner in Boyle Military Barracks. One Sunday morning the Black and Tans paid a surprise visit to church. According to his sister-in-law, she saw Pat a few yards away from her, but when she looked again a moment later, he had disappeared. She never understood what he had done with himself. And Pat never told.* Participated in the **burning of Croghan Barracks**. He took no part in the Civil War. After the War he married, and worked a farm outside Croghan village. Died 1950s. Buried in Killappoge Cemetery in Croghan

*Denis Maye, *nephew of Pat, correspondence with author, Coogee Sydney New South Wales, Australia*

Corporal George Meadlarklan, guard at Boyle Barracks, who helped James Molloy and Michael Dockery escape by unlocking their cells. Molloy had escaped earlier, but on the evening of 15 June 1921, Meadlarklan unlocked the cell door of Michael Dockery as well as that of Jack Glancy. Shortly thereafter, a Sergeant passed by, and noticed the locks had been left open. He then secured the locks on both cells. Later that night, Meadlarklan returned to Dockery's cell and, finding it was tightly secured, used his bayonet to pry open the lock. In doing so, he broke off the tip of his bayonet* (which is how he was found out the next day). Meadlarklan never had the opportunity to jimmy the lock of Jack Glancy. The following day, upon careful inquiries by the District Inspector of the Boyle RIC, Meadlarklan was suspected of treachery and was removed to England, where he served a year in detention at Colchester Barracks. Upon his release, he married a local Boyle woman (Winifred Neary), and moved to London, where he remained a few years before returning to Ireland and enlisting in the newly formed Irish Army, where he attained the rank of Sergeant. According to his family, he was given a small farm at Ballytrasna (just south of Boyle) in recognition of his "services to Ireland." This last statement is somewhat in conflict with the private diary of Brigade Commander Pat Brennan, the pension application of Rita Leneghan, and the Witness Statement of Jack Glancy, all of whom claim that Meadlarklan was paid for his assistance in the gaol break. It is possible that although money was unquestionably given to Meadlarklan, he used those funds to pay other constables (including the guard in the guardroom).** Paid or unpaid, Meadlarklan contributed to the success of Roscommon's war effort and to the legacy of great Irish music. How so? The son of James Molloy is the flute player for the internationally renowned Irish band known as The Chieftains. Meadlarklan returned to England in the 1950s, died in 1958, and is buried in London

*Tony McAlister, *grandson of George Meadlarklan, correspondence with author, 6 September 2004.*
**B. Wickins, *daughter of George Meadlarklan, correspondence with author, 21 September 2004.*

Jeremiah Mee (Carrick-on-Shannon) arrested 31 August 1922, and taken to Athlone in September

Michael Mee (Curry, Curraghboy) 4th Battalion South Roscommon, older brother of Dick. Escaped through the Brady tunnel in September 1921

Dick Mee (Curry, Curraghboy) the third Captain of the Curraghboy Coy., 4th Battalion South Roscommon. From 1917-March 1919 did organisational work, drilled, attended lectures and instruction given by Ernie O'Malley, and performed police duty during the South Roscommon election (guard duty at polling booths and escorting ballot boxes to counting centres). He was one of a group of Volunteers who raided the private homes of three men — two of whom had joined and one who was about to join the RIC. Not surprisingly, these men decided on another vocation! About twenty raids for arms and ammunition were conducted within the Company area, and another fifteen raids were outside the immediate vicinity and performed in conjunction with other Companies of the Battalion. In one of those raids, Mee, along with William Murray, and members of an adjoining Company confiscated two revolvers, a shotgun, and ammunition, but were fired upon. One of the other men was wounded. Participated in the **attempted attack on Kilmurray Camp** in June 1920, but action was called off. Made preparations to ambush a police party conveying military equipment from Athlone to Ballyforan. Again action called off. Performed police duty in relation to enforcement of Dáil decrees. Participated in the **attempted attack on a military lorry at Knockcroghery** in January 1921, and **attempted attack on Ballygar RIC Barracks**. Prevented jurors and litigants from attending British Courts, and raided the mails. Manufactured ammunition, and constructed dumps for its storage. The entire Company participated in the arrest and confinement of a suspected spy. That man was tried by court-martial and eventually executed — an action which prompted the arrest of ten members of the Company in January. Mee escaped the dragnet until March, during which time he raided the houses of persons associated with the enemy. He was one of the men who escaped through the Brady tunnel at the Curragh in September 1921. After the War he moved to Trim, Co. Meath

Peter Melinn, Quartermaster for the Athlone Brigade in 1918.

Seamus Melinn of Athlone fought in Dublin during the Rising.

Eugene Melvin, Lisonuffy, Strokestown

Thomas Mee (Derryhippoo, Creggs) a member of Fuerty Coy. in the 2nd Battalion South Roscommon. He later emigrated to the United States

Darby Meehan (Boherroe, Elphin) was the Vice O/C of the 5th Battalion North Roscommon, brother of Patrick

Michael Meehan (Kilyclogher, Co. Leitrim) arrested in March of 1923, and taken to Newbridge, where he secured his release on 22 December 1923

Patrick Meehan (Boherroe, Elphin) according to the GHQ papers in the UCD Archives, Patrick served as the 2nd Lieutenant for Croghan Company

John Melia (Cloonfad, Ballinlough) Lieutenant in charge of scouting and dispatches for the 1st Battalion, No. 2 Brigade, 2nd Western Division under Gerald O'Connor, Brigade O/C

Joseph Melinn (Mardyke, Athlone) was employed in Tralee. He attended the national convention of Irish Volunteers on 25 October 1914, where he represented "B" Coy. of Kerry. Austin Stack, Joe, and several other officers met at the Rink in Tralee to finalise plans for their part in the Easter Rising. Melinn was arrested 8 May 1916, and charged with "being engaged in a conspiracy to land German arms in this country." For his efforts, he was housed in the county gaol in Ballymullen, Tralee, but eventually found his way to Frongoch, affectionately known as "The Irish University." In 1919 when the Volunteers were reorganised in Kerry, Melinn was appointed the deputy to Paddy Cahill, Brigadier of Kerry No. 1 Brigade

Peter Melinn (Mardyke, Athlone) brother of Joseph. During Easter week, he was with a party of men who headed for Shannonbridge ready to defend it until Roger Casement's rifles arrived. Halfway there, the men received the countermanding order and returned to Coosan. Soon after, he was arrested, and shipped across the Irish Sea, where he was interned in Wakefield Prison on 2 June 1916. He was later transferred to a former German prisoner-of-war camp in Wales known as Frongoch. In 1918 Peter became the Quartermaster for the Athlone Brigade, which included parts of the extreme south of County Roscommon. He served as the Head Centre of the IRB in Athlone until the Truce. After the War he worked in the wholesale egg business on Mardyke St. Due to the severe conditions of life on the run during the Wars, Peter died at a young age in 1930, and is buried in Cornamagh Cemetery, Athlone

Seamus Melinn (Mardyke, Athlone) fought in Dublin during the Rising. Arrested and sentenced to death, which was later reduced to penal servitude for life. Fortunately, he was released in June 1917 after the Longford Sinn Féin victory of McGuinness

John Mellin (Malynn) (Carrowkeel) a member of the Rahara Coy., 4th Battalion South Roscommon

Eugene Melvin (Lisonuffy, Strokestown) Carniska Coy. in the 3rd Battalion North Roscommon. Served as an outpost in the **Castlenode Confrontation** in November 1920. He also worked with the Sinn Féin police during the Truce. He returned to farming after the War, and died in 1985. Buried in Lisonuffy Cemetery

Edward Mengher (St. John's Road, Carrick-on-Shannon) incarcerated during the Civil War in Tintown A. Released on 18 December 1923

John Miley (Ballyglass, Knockcroghery) 4th Battalion South Roscommon. Knockcroghery Coy. was formed in 1917 with Patrick Kelly serving as Captain. Miley drilled with the Volunteers, and attended practice battles at Taughmaconnell overseen by Ernie O'Malley in the summer of 1918. Participated in the General Election of 1918. Miley took part in a raid on two hostile houses in Rahara. He, along with nine other Volunteers, arrested and tried a man for firing at and wounding a fellow Volunteer. The man's punishment — weeks of isolation in Cloverhill before returning to his family. Miley emigrated to the United States

Thomas Miley (Kilmore, Athleague) a member of the Tisrara Coy., 4th Battalion South Roscommon

Charlie Minogue (Strokestown Coy.) 3rd Battalion North Roscommon, arrested in 1918, and placed in Sligo Gaol. He then spent ten months in Crumlin Road Jail in Belfast. Died 19 May 1962

B. Mitchell served as the 2nd Lieutenant of Castlerea Coy. in April 1922

Herbert Mitchell (Coosan area) was very instrumental in reorganising the Volunteer Companies in 1917

Martin Mockler (Castleplunkett Coy.) in the 2nd Battalion South Roscommon. When the Western Division was formed, he volunteered to serve with the Oran Battalion Flying Column. After the War he emigrated to Cleveland, Ohio

Ed Moffatt (Drumboylan, Leitrim) 2nd Lieutenant for Drumboylan Company in the 5th Battalion North Roscommon. In autumn of 1920, the Volunteers spent the morning hours examining the correspondence they had just taken from the mail car at Ballyfermoy, lolled around Moffatt's house during the mid-day, then returned again to raid the same mail car they had hit in the early morning. They returned the sack of morning mail to the driver as they relieved him of the evening post. (Nothing of great importance was found!)

Matt Moffatt (Crunkill, Ruskey) a member of the Kilglass Company in the 3rd Battalion North Roscommon

Michael Moffatt (Moffitt) (Ballaghaderreen area) organiser of Volunteer Companies

Patrick Moffatt (Cloonsheever, Castlerea) Ballintubber Coy., 2nd Battalion South Roscommon. Took part in the **attack on Frenchpark Barracks** 2 October 1920. After the War he became a farmer. Buried in Cloonard Cemetery

James Molloy (Ballymote) Captain of the Ballymote Company, County Sligo, wounded and captured during an attack on a police patrol in Ballymote town in May 1921. He was taken to Boyle Barracks, where he was in custody at the same time as Michael Dockery and Jack Glancy. He escaped later that month with the aid of Roscommon Volunteers by shinnying down a rope thrown out of the wash-house window anchored by John Downes of Ballaghaderreen. Previous to his capture, he had taken part in the **Ratra Ambush** on 1 September 1920, the **attack on the RIC patrol** at Strokestown on 5 January 1921, and, after his escape, he continued his activities by attacking the **RIC Barracks at Tarmonbarry** in July 1921. He was arrested during the Civil War on 13 August 1922 for his Anti-Treaty activities, and taken to Athlone in September. Molloy was transferred to Mountjoy on 10 January 1923. After the War he lived in Ballaghaderreen, where he worked for the Roscommon County Council. He was a well respected musician (see George Meadlarklan p. 383). Buried at Carracastle in 1980

Joseph Molloy (Cryanstown, Knockvicar) fatally shot by the Tans 28 March 1921 in a field near his home after the Keadue Ambush. His crime: failing to halt. According to the Gerald O'Connor Papers, he was only thirteen years old (fifteen according to Canon Tonra's *History of Ardcarne*). His name is inscribed on the Shankill Monument near Elphin

James Moloney (Vicar Street, Tuam) O/C of the Glenamaddy Battalion, a member of the Flying Column. After the Truce he served as the Vice Commandant of No. 2 Brigade in the 2nd Western Division

Frank Monaghan (Gallowstown) Roscommon Coy., 3rd Battalion South Roscommon. After the War he worked with the County Council. Died 22 August 1969, and buried in St. Coman's Cemetery, Roscommon town

John Monaghan (Cornalee) Curraghboy Coy., 4th Battalion South Roscommon. During the Civil War, he raided homes of ex-RIC men who were ordered to leave the country, blocked roads at Whitepark intending to delay troop movements, guarded two shopkeepers' premises who were being victimised by local hooligans.

James Molloy, Captain of Ballymote Company.

PHOTO COURTESY OF MATT MOLLOY

He raided homes of National Army officers in order to secure arms and equipment, and escorted prisoner through Cornalee in the spring/summer of 1923

Michael Monaghan (Carrowntober, Glenamaddy) County Galway. Monaghan's home became the headquarters of the Kilkerrin Coy. Located in Co. Galway, this Company was part of the Glenamaddy Battalion which was incorporated into No. 2 Brigade, 2nd Western Division with Gerald O'Connor, former O/C of the 1st Battalion South Roscommon, serving as Brigade Commandant

Peter Monaghan (Ballagh, Kilgefin) 3rd Battalion South Roscommon. Many, but not all, of the members of the Kilgefin Company participated in the **Fourmilehouse Ambush** on 12 October 1920

Tim Monaghan (Gallowstown) 3rd Battalion South Roscommon, Company Captain. In his youth, he committed the "treasonous act" of climbing up the flag-pole at Roscommon town and replacing the Union Jack with the tricolour. He was a member of Pat Madden's Flying Column. After the War he emigrated to America, but returned to Ireland in the 1970s. Died 1976 and buried in St. Coman's Cemetery, Roscommon town

James Monds (Knockmurry, Castlerea) although not a Volunteer, he was a sympathiser who belonged to the Church of Ireland. According to Paddy Concannon, resident of Knockmurry, Castlerea, Monds was targeted as a result of a dispute with the Tans over local fowl.* He had also been active in land agitation, including the cattle drive on Cotton's farm. His political allegiance was questioned when, one Sunday morning, when "God Save the Queen" was being sung robustly in the local church, he had walked out in disgust.** Monds was taken from his home 6 April 1921, and shot for refusing to give information about the Volunteers. He was the father of six children. Buried in the Church of Ireland Cemetery in Castlerea. His name is inscribed on the Shankill Monument near Elphin

Paddy Concannon, resident of Knockmurry, Castlerea, interview by author, 14 August 2004.
**Sean Raftery, nephew of Luke, interview by author, Valeview Castlerea, 16 April 2004.*

George Moohan (Ballaghaderreen) during the Civil War he was arrested for Anti-Treaty activities on 8 September 1922. Sent to Athlone two months later

M. Moore (Carrick-on-Shannon) Quartermaster 5th Battalion North Roscommon

Peter Moore 2nd Lieutenant of the Glenamaddy Coy. in the Glenamaddy Battalion. This Battalion was incorporated into No. 2 Brigade of the 2nd Western Division with Gerald O'Connor, former O/C of the 1st Battalion South Roscommon, serving as Brigade Commandant

Jack (John) Moran (Ballinlough) First Captain of the Ballinlough Company in the 1st Battalion South Roscommon. Participated in the **raid for petrol at Ballinlough Station** in June 1920, the **attempted ambush at Coshlieve** in July 1920, the **attempted attack on the Castlerea Station Guard** that same month, and the **burning of the Ballinlough barracks** 14 September 1920, after which he went on the run, first to Killunagher, then northward to Doogary, Aghamore, where he stayed with family members. After the War he became a member of the Garda Síochána. He worked in Ballinasloe as an inspector of weights and measures. In 1932 he toured America with the Mayo footballers. Died early in life in 1942 (due to hardships suffered in the War). Buried in the Ballyhaunis friary

James Moran (Lavallyroe, Cloonfad, Ballyhaunis, Co. Mayo) a member of the Cloonfad Coy. in the 1st Battalion South Roscommon. Moran gave continuous service from June 1921 to April 1923. He participated in the **destruction of vacant barracks** in 1920, and took part in the **disarming of two British soldiers at Cloonfad** in May 1921. He served as the 2nd Lieutenant of Cloonfad Coy. in April 1922. During the Civil War he took the Anti-Treaty side. Moran evaded arrest **under fire at Ballinross** in October 1922, and took part in the **attack at Castlerea** in November. After the War he used to organise reunions of the old

Jack (John) Moran, Captain of Ballinlough Company.

IRA men. He became a rates collector for the Roscommon County Council. Died in late 1970s, and is buried in St. Coman's Cemetery

James Moran When the 2nd Western Division was formed, a James Moran served as Director of Training for the 3rd Battalion, No. 2 Brigade. After the War he emigrated to the United States of America

James Moran (St. Patrick's Terrace, Roscommon) a member of Fuerty Coy. in the 2nd Battalion South Roscommon

Jim Moran (Crossna, Boyle) brother of Paddy, Joseph, and Tom. Fought with the Anti-Treaty Arigna Flying Column during the Civil War. Present at the **attack on Ballinamore Barracks** on 31 January 1923. He was arrested along with four other members of the Arigna Flying Column by a cycling patrol from Boyle. He was taken to Athlone on 3 February 1923. After the War he became a commercial traveller. Died 1984, and buried in Ardcarne Cemetery (also see photo page 388)

John Moran (Sheervagh, Ballinameen, Boyle) 1st Battalion North Roscommon. Served as the Brigade scout. Helped with the **escape** of Michael Dockery **from Boyle Barracks**, and the **attack on Frenchpark Barracks** in June 1921. He was a member of the Anti-Treaty Active Service Unit (Flying Column) during the Civil War commanded by Pat Brennan

Jim, Tom, Joe, and Batty Moran from Crossna, Boyle
PHOTO COURTESY OF MAY MORAN

John Moran (Culleenaghamore, Kilglass) a member of the Slatta Coy. in the 3rd Battalion North Roscommon. Aided in the capture of an RIC man

John Moran (Lisnagroagh, Fuerty, Roscommon) a member of "D" Coy. in the 2nd Battalion South Roscommon

John Moran (Kinnitty, Kilbride) a member of Kilbride Company, 3rd Battalion South Roscommon

Joseph Moran (Crossna, Boyle) brother of Paddy, Jim, and Tom. Fought with the Anti-Treaty Arigna Flying Column, and was arrested during the Civil War on 8 September 1922, and sent to Athlone in November. During the War for Independence, he had hidden with Larry O'Hara in the attic of O'Hara's Cootehall cottage. After the War he emigrated to England, and worked as an electrician in Lancashire. He served with the British Forces during World War II on the Isle of Wright. Joseph returned to Ireland and lived in Crossna, where he died in 1972. Buried in Ardcarne Cemetery

Liam Moran (Dunmore, Galway) served as the Director of Chemistry for the 1st Battalion, No. 2 Brigade in the 2nd Western Division. Although located in Galway, this Battalion was joined with 1st Roscommon South Battalion in the 2nd Western Division. Moran later relocated to Enniscorthy, Wexford

Luke Moran (Drumahard, Drumboylan, Boyle) served as Captain of Drumboylan Company in the 5th Battalion North Roscommon, brother of Tom and Michael

Malachy Moran (Coolatober, Ballyforan) Dysart Coy., 4th Battalion South Roscommon. Joined the Company in 1917. He attended parades, received instructions under Ernie O'Malley, helped in the 1918 General Election, was appointed to work with the Republican Police and also took part in raiding for arms

Mathew "Mattie" Moran (Morahan) (Falmore, Ballinagare) 1st Battalion South Roscommon. Drilled with his fellow Volunteers, collected for the Dáil loan, enforced the Belfast boycott, and took part in the **destruction of vacant barracks** in 1920, the **attempted attack at Kilmurray Military Camp** in June, the **attempted attack on the Castlerea Station Guard** in July 1920, the **attack on Frenchpark Barracks** 2 October 1920, and several attempted ambushes in Castlerea in January 1921. He was the Company Captain at the time of the Truce, when he attended the Company and Battalion training camps, specialising in dispatch, scouting, and intelligence work. During the Civil War Morahan fought against the Free State troopers at the **attack at Ballinagare** in July 1922

Michael Moran (Moher, Strokestown) Carniska Coy. in the 3rd Battalion North Roscommon. After the War he became a farmer. Died 1985

Michael Moran (Carrowduff, Ballymacurley) 2nd Battalion South Roscommon. Present at **Fourmilehouse Ambush** on 12 October 1920

Michael Moran (Drumahard, Drumboylan, Boyle) served as the Adjutant for Dromboylan Company in the 5th Battalion North Roscommon, brother of Tom

Paddy, Annie, and Jim Moran of Crossna, Boyle
PHOTO COURTESY OF MAY MORAN

Patrick "Paddy" Moran (born in Crossna, Boyle) fought in Jacob's factory during the Rising of 1916, and as a consequence, was sent to Knutsford, Wormwood Scrubbs, and the "Irish University," Frongoch. Following the general release, he was back in Dublin, shipping arms to the Volunteers, and serving as the Captain of "D" Company in the 2nd Battalion, Dublin Brigade. His family home sheltered Sean Connolly when the latter was sent from Longford to Roscommon to organise the Volunteers. Moran was caught in the roundup after "Bloody Sunday" at Croke Park. As a prisoner at Kilmainham, he gave up his spot in the escape party with Ernie O'Malley because he knew that he was innocent of the charges filed against him and thought he could prove it. He was convicted anyway and hanged on the single most deadly day in Mountjoy's history. On 14 March 1921 six men were executed, Moran being one of the casualties. The men were hanged in pairs beginning at 6 a.m. His remains resided in Mountjoy for eighty years. A patriotic finale to Moran's personal drama finally played out on 14 October, 2001. He, along with nine other men, were given a state funeral and re-interred in Glasnevin Cemetery in Dublin. His name is inscribed on the Shankill Monument near Elphin

Patrick Moran (Ardeevin, Castleplunkett) a member of "C" Coy. in the 2nd Battalion South Roscommon. Took part in the **ambush at Southpark, Castlerea** 10 July 1921

Patrick Moran (Clooncunny, Elphin) (Killina Coy.) 2nd Battalion North Roscommon. He was one of the first members of the Company when it formed in August of 1917. He drilled with his Company every Tuesday evening — generally at Ball Alley House. Moran took part in the **attack on the Tarmonbarry patrol** in January 1921 armed with a shotgun, **Scramogue Ambush**, and the **attack on the Tarmonbarry Barracks** in July 1921. He was a member of the Anti-Treaty Active Service Unit (Flying Column) during the Civil War formed in North Roscommon. He was most reliable in transporting men and material across the Shannon. He later emigrated to England

Stanley Moran (Roscommon Coy.) 3rd Battalion South Roscommon

Terence Moran (Creggancor, Castlerea) Adjutant for Trien Company, 1st Battalion South Roscommon. Took part in the **attempted ambush at Coshlieve** in July 1920, and the **attempted ambush of RIC patrol near Ballymoe** in May 1921. Attended the Hermitage training camp during the Truce. He later emigrated to England

Thomas Moran (Gortacarnan, Rahara) 4th Battalion South Roscommon

Thomas Moran (Creggancor, Castlerea) Trien Coy., 1st Battalion South Roscommon, brother of Terence

Tom Moran (Crossna, Boyle) O/C of the 4th Battalion North Roscommon, brother of Paddy, Jim, and Joe. Tom was arrested 1 February 1921, and interned at Boyle and Athlone Military Barracks. He was sent to the Curragh Internment Camp, from which he escaped through the Brady tunnel in September 1921. He returned home to fight in the Civil War on the Anti-Treaty side. After the War he became a small farmer. Tom married late in life in 1941. He died in 1969 and is buried in Killeelan Cemetery (see photo on page 387)

Tom Moran (Drumahard, Drumboylan, Leitrim) according to the GHQ papers in the UCD Archives, Tom served as the 1st Lieutenant for "E" Company in the 5th Battalion North Roscommon

Michael Morgan (Breeole) Dysart Coy., 4th Battalion South Roscommon. Joined the Company in 1917. Attended parades, received instructions under Ernie O'Malley, helped in the 1918 election. He was appointed to work with the Republican Police, and took part in raiding for arms. He also raided an RIC man's home, warned him to quit his job, and burned all the papers found in the constable's possession. Ironically, Morgan later joined the Garda Síochána

John Morley (Ballyfeeny, Strokestown) a member of the Kilglass Company in the 3rd Battalion North Roscommon

John F. Morley (Main Street, Ballaghaderreen) Vice O/C of 4th Battalion East Mayo Brigade (which incorporated Companies in west Roscommon). A member of the IRB, who travelled to Dublin to fight in the Rising.* Arrested after the surrender, and, on 20 May 1916, was sentenced to Lewes Detention Barracks. He was later transferred to "The Irish University," Frongoch

*Jim Hunt interview, Ernie O'Malley Papers, UCD Archives, No.133.

Joseph Morley (Main St., Ballaghaderreen) was arrested for Anti-Treaty activities during the Civil War on 8 September 1922, and sent to Athlone on 14 November. He was transferred to the Curragh on 24 November. He was released a few days later on 9 December. Evidently he did not correct his rebel ways. Joe was re-arrested and taken to Athlone on 22 March 1923

Mary Morley (Main St., Ballaghaderreen) sister of John and Joseph, member of the Cumann na mBan

John Morris (Cloonshannagh) a member of the Tarmonbarry Coy. of the 3rd Battalion North Roscommon

Joseph Morrissey (Athlone) part of a unit of Westmeath Volunteers who operated in conjunction with the South Roscommon men. Killed 20 February 1921. His name is inscribed on the IRA Monument in Athlone town

Paddy Morrissey (O/C of Anti-Treaty Column in Coosan, County Westmeath.) The Column included three officers and about twenty men. Morrissey served as a delegate to the outlawed Convention in March 1922. He visited Sean MacEoin in Custume Barracks, and, during a disagreement, MacEoin stripped Morrissey of his Sam Browne belt — a humiliation not soon forgotten. After the War, Morrissey moved to Dublin

J. J. Muldoon (Island Upper, Donamon) a member of "E" Coy. in the 3rd Battalion, No. 2 Brigade, 2nd Western Division

P. J. Muldoon (Island Upper, Donamon) 2nd Battalion South Roscommon. Brother of J.J. Served as 2nd Lieutenant of the Company

Thomas Muldoon (Island Upper, Donamon) 1st Lieutenant of "E" Coy. in the 2nd Battalion South Roscommon. Took part in the **raid on the military train at Ballymoe** in June 1920. He later joined the Free State Army

Thomas Muldoon (Bealnamullia) 3rd Battalion Athlone Brigade. Muldoon drilled with his Company, trained to use firearms, took an active part in the General Election of 1918, attended Battalion meetings, worked with the Republican Police force at disputed farmland in Bealnamullia and Clongowna. He was with a group of Volunteers that seized ammunition from an airplane that made a forced landing at Keelogues in 1919. Took part in the **burning of the Barracks at Bealnamullia**, mobilised for an **attack on Cloonark Barracks**, and **attempted an ambush at Curraghaleen** in October 1920. Near Truce time, he guarded the ASU Headquarters in the area, **destroyed the bridge at Millbrook**, blocked roads at Millbrook and Monksland, harboured and aided escaped prisoners. During the Truce, he trained at Greenfield, Donamon, and Falty, in addition to collecting funds to aid the Volunteers and attending the Arbitration Courts

Thomas Muldoon (Bogganfin, The Hill of Berries, Kiltoom) 4th Battalion South Roscommon. During the Civil War he took the Anti-Treaty side, and was arrested on 26 March 1923, along with Vice O/C of the Athlone Brigade, James Martin, and Thomas Mannion, and sent to Athlone on 26 March 1923

Sergeant Muleady, a Roscommon police officer, who doubled as a sympathetic patriot, and saved the home of this author's great-uncle and aunt from being torched

Francis Mulherin (Tullynaha, Arigna) 4th Battalion North Roscommon. Fought with the Anti-Treaty Arigna Flying Column during the Civil War, and was captured by the Free State, along with Tom Beirne, on 4 September 1923. He later joined the Garda Síochána, and was stationed around the Dublin area

James Mulhern (Cornamucklagh, Ballinagare) a member of the Ballinagare Coy., 1st Battalion South Roscommon

Thomas Mulick (Corbally, Elphin) served as the Lieutenant, and, in January of 1921, the Captain of Aughrim Company in the 2nd Battalion North Roscommon. Canvassed for Count Plunkett's election, did dispatch work, resisted enemy baton charges in connection with a local farm dispute — a resistance that cost him a month in gaol. Participated in the **attempted attack on the Carrick-on-Shannon Station Guards** in September 1920, the **burning of Croghan and Hillstreet Barracks**, was a member of an ambush party at **Aughamon** on 20 September 1920, and served as a guard for the **attack on Elphin Barracks**. One of his more unusual duties included arresting local men for refusing to loan the IRA their implements for road blocking operations. He was a member of the Active Service Unit of North Roscommon

John Mullaly (Toberdan, Lecarrow) St. John's Coy., 4th Battalion South Roscommon, served as the Adjutant of the Company. When the Company first formed in 1917, Johnny Kilcline was the first Adjutant. When Kilcline moved to another position, Mullally replaced him. He drilled with other Volunteers two nights a week — Tuesdays and Thursdays, and worked with the Republican Courts. In 1918 his Company, now under the command of Patrick Grady, participated in the sham battles for training purposes under Ernie O'Malley at Lysterfield, Taughmaconnell, and Churchboro. He worked in the General Election of 1918, blocked roads, collected the IRA levy, and constructed dugouts. Mullally raided for arms — on one occasion being with the other raiding party the same night as the raid on Feehily's house in which Joseph Kearney was severely wounded in the stomach. He, along with a dozen other members of his Company, took part in the **attempted ambush at Clooncraff** under the command of Pat Madden, and the **attempted ambush at Kilmurray Military Camp** in June of 1920, which combined men from the 1st, 2nd, some 3rd, and 4th Battalions South. He participated in the **raiding of the mail car at Kiltoom Station**. He was present at the **burning of O'Brien's house** — an operation deemed necessary because the British Forces were thought to be soon taking over the residence. He was also engaged in **blowing up the Ballybay Road Bridge**. During the Truce he became a member of the special service unit

Patrick Mullaly (Toberdan, Lecarrow) a member of the St. John's Coy. in the 4th Battalion South Roscommon, brother of John. When the Company first formed in 1917, Patrick drilled with other Volunteers two nights a week — Tuesdays and Thursdays, and worked with the Republican Courts. In 1918 his Company, now under the command of Patrick Grady, participated in the sham battles for training purposes under Ernie O'Malley at Lysterfield, Taughmaconnell, and Churchboro. He worked in the 1918 election, blocked roads, and constructed dugouts. Mullally collected and transported gelignite for the Company engineer. He took part in the **attempted ambush at Kilmurray Military Camp** in June 1920. He raided for arms — on one occasion being with the other raiding party the same night as the raid on Feehily's house in which Joseph Kearney was severely wounded in the stomach. He was present at the **burning of O'Brien's house** — an operation deemed necessary because the British Forces were thought to be soon taking over the residence. During the Truce he became a member of the newly formed special service unit

Edward Mullan (Corrastoona Beg, Donamon) a member of "E" Coy. in the 2nd Battalion South Roscommon. He was arrested for Anti-Treaty activities during the Civil War on 25 August 1922

Dominick Mullaney (Cloonkeen, Cootehall) workman for the O'Haras in Cootehall, arrested in a raid of their house May 1921, released the next day

James Mullaney (Ballyfarnon Coy.) 4th Battalion North Roscommon, served as the 2nd Lieutenant of the Company in late 1920

Mrs. Mullaney (Runnamoat, Ballinaheglish) sister of Frank Simons, member of Cumann na mBan

John J. (Sean) Mullaney (Barnard St., Athlone) arrested after the Rising and sent to Wakefield on 13 May, but released within a few weeks. Member of the 1st Committee of the Midland Volunteers

Rev. Richard Mullaney, C.C. a native of Rinn, Ardcarne, Boyle, who was stationed in Lisacul. Active supporter of Count Plunkett in the bye election of 1917

William Mullaney (Culleenaghamore, Kilglass, Strokestown) prisoner in

John J. (Sean) Mullaney, Athlone.

the Demesne House at Strokestown at the time of the Scramogue Ambush. Although not a participant, he was severely beaten in revenge. Sent to Longford and Athlone Barracks, and eventually to the Curragh Prison Camp, where he spent seven weeks in a sick bed before being medically discharged

John Mullarkey (Ballinross, Cloonfad, Ballinlough) 1st Battalion South Roscommon. Participated in the **destruction of vacant barracks** in 1920, and took part in the **disarming of two British soldiers at Cloonfad** in May 1921. Mullarkey took the Anti-Treaty side in the Civil War, and fought the government troops **at Ballinross** in October 1922, and a month later **at Castlerea**

Thomas Mullarkey (Ballinross, Cloonfad, Ballinlough) 1st Battalion South Roscommon. Participated in the **destruction of vacant barracks** in 1920, the **disarming of two British soldiers at Cloonfad** in May 1921. He, like his brother, took the Anti-Treaty side in the Civil War, and attacked the Free State soldiers **at Ballinross** in October 1922, and, a month later, **at Castlerea**

Patrick Mulleady (see Patrick Maleady)

Patrick J. Mulleague (Cornamucklagh Falmore, Ballinagare) 1st Battalion South Roscommon. Attended the Company training camp during the Truce, and specialised in scouting, intelligence work, and dispatch work. Also participated in the Anti-Treaty **attack at Ballinagare** in July 1922 during the Civil War

Edward Mullen (Ballaghaderreen) one of the first members of the Ballaghaderreen Coy. in the East Mayo Brigade. Captured during the Civil War for Anti-Treaty activities on 25 August 1922

Bernie Mulligan (Ballaghaderreen) one of the first members of the Ballaghaderreen Coy. in the East Mayo Brigade

Bill Mulligan (Coolnafarna, Ballyhaunis, Co. Mayo) Intelligence Officer of the 3rd Battalion South Roscommon. Born in Cooltacker, Fairymount in the parish of Kilgefin, Mulligan served as the Intelligence Officer for Pat Madden's Company. His meticulous intelligence work was invaluable in planning and executing attacks. His part was so deftly played that many of the rank-and-file did not know of his involvement with the Volunteers until after the War. Many, but not all, of the members of the Kilgefin Company participated in the **Fourmilehouse Ambush** on 12 October 1920. Mulligan was present at **Scramogue**. He accompanied the body of John Scally from Incheneagh Island to its temporary burial site in Kilteevan Cemetery. After the Truce he joined the National Army, and served in Mayo/Galway area with the rank of Captain. When the guns fell silent, Mulligan became a school teacher, and later a principal in Ballyhaunis, Co. Mayo. Mulligan gave the oration at the funeral of Luke Duffy in 1971. He followed his

Bill Mulligan, Intelligence Officer for the 3rd Battalion South

Excerpts from the Graveside Oration of Bill Mulligan delivered by Eamonn Duffy, son of Luke Duffy, on 23 September 1990

Bill Mulligan was born in the parish of Kilgefin, County Roscommon, just a short mile from my home. He was reared in the townland of Fairymount overlooking Ballagh Church, and just beside my mother's home.

It was in this area that he first became involved with the Nationalist cause. He joined the local Volunteer company, known as "E" Company, 3rd Battalion, South Roscommon Brigade, then commanded by the late Pat Madden. Bill was appointed Intelligence Officer, and so tight was the security of the unit that it was not until after the truce that the rank-and-file of the Company were aware of his involvement. He was involved with the officers of the company in the planning of all the major engagements including the Scramogue ambush during that period. His intense knowledge of the countryside and the people was invaluable to the officers of the company. My father (Luke Duffy) often recounted for me the immense asset that Bill's Intelligence work was to the company.

After the Truce he joined the National Army and served in the Mayo/Galway area with the rank of Captain where he gained the respect of friend and foe alike.

Bill's teaching career began after he left the army. His first post was in his native Ballagh School. He moved to the Ballyhaunis area shortly afterwards where he had a distinguished career as principal here in Ballyhaunis until his retirement some 25 years ago.

He was instrumental in starting the Scout movement in Ballyhaunis and did tremendous work for youth organisations in the town.

A distinguished mathematician, he taught his pupils accountancy methods in a practical way of buying and selling livestock — a subject always dear to his heart.

Bill never forgot his old friends in the Kilgefin company. He made it his duty to visit them at every opportunity that arose and was sure to be there to pay his last respects on their passing. He was, as far as I am aware, the last survivor of that noble band. How many times have I heard him say the final words at the graveside of his comrades? It was only last year at the funeral of my aunt that he asked me to take him to visit the only other remaining survivor, Paddy Tiernan. The two old men sat reminiscing for over an hour and parted promising to meet shortly for further talks of bygone days. Unfortunately this never happened as Paddy died very shortly afterwards.

The freedom that we enjoy today is the result of the sacrifices of men like Bill Mulligan and Paddy Tiernan. Their existence in bog dugouts and on islands in Lough Ree leave us to wonder how they survived so long.

A true and loyal son of Ireland, Bill stood by his principles to the last and never compromised his position. He was proud to remind the younger generation of the history of his time....

friend to the grave nineteen years later at which time Luke Duffy's son, Eamonn, returned the honour by giving Mulligan's oration (23 September 1990). He is buried in Ballyhaunis Cemetery

Jack Mulligan (Ballaghaderreen) he was one of the first members of the Ballaghaderreen Coy. in the East Mayo Brigade

Martin Mulligan (Clooncrane, Creggs) during the Civil War he took the Anti-Treaty side. He was arrested, and sent to Athlone on 30 March 1923

Patrick Mulligan (Ballindrumlea, Southpark, Castlerea) 1st Battalion South Roscommon. Participated in the **destruction of vacant barracks** in 1920, the **attempted attack on Kilmurray Military Camp** in June 1920, the **capture of enemy stores at Ballymoe** in June 1920, the **raid and capture of military equipment at Ballymoe** September 1920, the **attack on Frenchpark Barracks** 2 October 1920, the **attempted ambushes at Castlerea and Frenchpark** in January 1921, and the **ambush at Southpark, Castlerea** 10 July 1921. He was a member of the Active Service Unit formed in January of 1921. During the Truce he attended the Company training camp. He took the Anti-Treaty side in the Civil War, and participated in the **burning of the train at Clooncundra** and **attack at Castlerea** in November 1922

Thomas Mulligan (Lisnagavragh, Four Roads) Tisrara Coy., 4th Battalion South Roscommon, served as the 2nd Lieutenant of the Company

Edward Mullin (Clooneenbaun, Fuerty) Cloverhill Coy., served as 2nd Lieutenant of the Company in the 2nd Battalion South Roscommon. After the War he emigrated to the United States

Joseph Mullin (Clooneenbaun, Fuerty) Cloverhill Coy. in the 2nd Battalion South Roscommon, brother of Thomas and Edward

Thomas Mullin (Clooneenbaun, Fuerty) a member of Cloverhill Coy. in the 2nd Battalion South Roscommon. After the War he emigrated to the America

James Mullooly (Lissacarrow, Fuerty) a member of "A" Coy. in the 2nd Battalion South Roscommon. Participated in the **raid on the military train at Ballymoe** in June 1920. After the War he took an active part in forming Fianna Fáil in the county. He was on hand to welcome de Valera to Roscommon town on 19 June 1926

John Mullooly (Clooneenbaun, Fuerty) a member of "A" Coy. in the 2nd Battalion South Roscommon. After the War he emigrated to the United States

Joseph Mullooly (Cams) served as 1st Lieutenant of "A" Coy. in the 2nd Battalion South Roscommon. Participated in the **raid on the military train at Ballymoe** in June 1920

Michael Mullooly (Luggs, Kiltrustan, Strokestown) brother of Pat, joined the IRB in 1916. He served as the 2nd Lieutenant of the first Kiltrustan Company formed in 1917. He was shot on 24 March 1921 in the garden of his own home in reprisal for the **Scramogue Ambush** (although he was not present for that fight). Buried Kiltrustan cemetery. Name inscribed on the tablets in front of the Shankill Monument near Elphin

Pat Mullooly (Luggs, Kiltrustan, Strokestown) Quartermaster for the North Roscommon Brigade and later for the Third Western Division. Helped to form the Kiltrustan Company in 1917. When Ernie O'Malley came to Roscommon to organise the men in 1918, he stayed in Mullooly's home for a fortnight. Mullooly left for Dublin, where he found employment, attended IRB meetings, and came in contact with Diarmuid O'Hegarty, Sean Connolly, and Michael Collins, who personally ordered him back to North Roscommon to serve as the Quartermaster for the Brigade. He was given two stones of gelignite with which to begin his new career, and put on a train headed west at Broadstone Station. Participated in the **attempted attack on the Carrick-on-Shannon Station Guard** in September 1918. Pat took part in the **attempted attack on a Tarmonbarry patrol** in early February

Michael Mullooly

Kiltrustan now is wrapped in gloom
at the death of a hero brave.
Mullooly bold has met his doom,
and now lies in his grave.

Once more we feel the tyrant's hand
that crushed this warrior gay.
May God forgive the Saxon band
that came the road that day.

His house was soon surrounded
by a cowardly, murderous gang,
And Michael's life was ended
by a coward's shot that rang.

He fell beside his homestead dear
where happy hours spent he,
where often careless childhood cheers,
he prayed for Ireland free.

For days and years he fought and prayed
to right his native land.
But now, alas, the price is paid
by a hero's death so grand.

His glory rolls from shore to shore
although he sleeps in clay.
The price of all his deed will soar
and live from day to day.

As Commandant of our Irish ranks
and a hero of the corps,
he nobly died, God rest his soul.
We ne'er shall see him more.

So now farewell, oh a long farewell
to a hero brave and true.
T'was in the prime of life you fell
for the cause of Róisín Dubh.

1921, and happened upon the **attack on Elphin Barracks**. He served guard duty on Sean Owen's house for days thereafter in case of reprisal. (Owens was the O/C of the local Battalion.) Mullooly was captured after the **Scramogue Ambush**, and severely beaten (even whipped with a "cat-o-nine-tails"). He was sentenced to imprisonment, but escaped from Athlone Barracks hospital, where he had been taken as a result of a skin rash — made worse by his rubbing sulfur into the wounded area. By jumping out of a two-story window and using various ladders to scale the different walls, he dashed to freedom. He hid out in Pat Mee's house in Curraghboy, where a nurse from Brideswell looked in on him and tended to an injured foot. He returned to the Strokestown area, where he organised an attempted ambush several days before the Truce. After the War he entered the Free State Army, where he was attached to the Headquarters Staff. Mullooly took part in the Army Mutiny of 1924. He, along with Pat and Dan Madden, Luke Duffy, Frank Simons, and John and Josie Gibbons took nine rifles out of the guard-room of the Roscommon Barracks, and hid them in the cave under Rooaun Lake. Ever the devoted Republican, when polling day in 1927 came, Mullooly went to the office of *Roscommon Herald* editor, Jasper Tully, and "impressed" on Tully's ribcage the wisdom of printing a "politically correct" account of election goings-on. Died 17 April 1977, and buried in the new cemetery in Strokestown

Pat Mullooly, Quartermaster for the North Roscommon Brigade.

Jack Mulrennan (Kiltymaine, Lisacul) along with his brothers, Seamus and Patrick, frequented Ballaghaderreen, where the three often encouraged the local men to organise and train

James (Seamus) Mulrennan was born in Kiltymaine, Lisacul. 1st Battalion South Roscommon Brigade. Wounded by the British Forces on 27 March 1921 while evading arrest at Kilmovee, Mayo. Seamus and his brother, Patrick, were tradesmen who knew about building structures and what it took to demolish them. In preparation for **an attack on Ballaghaderreen Barracks**, they both conferred with Jim Hunt regarding the weak points of the building.

Patrick Mulrennan born in Kiltymaine, Lisacul, brother of Seamus, 1st Battalion South Roscommon Brigade. He was incarcerated for Anti-Treaty activities in Connolly Barracks in Longford in August of 1922, and attempted to go with Joe Baker (O/C of the West Mayo ASU) and Tom Scanlon (of Sligo town) when the two made an attempt to escape. Baker talked Mulrennan out of making the attempt, citing that two had a better chance of escaping than did three. (It was a decision Baker was to regret for a lifetime.)* Mulrennan was shot looking out the window of his cell** (by Tony Lawlor***) while a prisoner in Pump Square, Athlone on 6 October.**** He is buried in Cuiltyboe Cemetery. His name appears alongside his kinsman on the tablets in front of the Shankill Monument

*<u>My Stand for Freedom</u> by Joe Baker, p. 52.
**<u>My Stand for Freedom</u> by Joe Baker p. 56.
***Intelligence Papers of the Western Command dated 6 October 1922.
****Interestingly, both the above-mentioned Intelligence Papers and Michael Hopkinson's <u>Green Against Green</u> (p. 216) claim 6 October as the death date. Yet the tombstone inscription of Patrick Mulrennan bears the date 3 November 1922.

During the Civil War Seamus took the Anti-Treaty side, and became the commander of an East Mayo Flying Column. He was killed by the Free State troops near Derrynacarthy 14 October 1922. Buried in Cuiltyboe Cemetery near Loughglynn. His name is inscribed on the Shankill Monument near Elphin

Sonnie Mulrennan (Ballygate, Whitehall) a member of Tarmonbarry Coy., 3rd Battalion North Roscommon

Andrew Mulrooney (Falmore, Ballinagare) drilled with his Company, participated in the destruction of local barracks, enforced the Belfast boycott, and served as the Quartermaster for his Company. He took part in the **destruction of vacant barracks** in 1920, the **attempted attack on the Kilmurray Military Camp** in June, the **attempted attack on the Castlerea Station Guard** in July, the **attack on Frenchpark RIC Barracks** 2 October 1920, and several attempted ambushes in Castlerea in January 1921. Andrew was a member of the Active Service Unit formed in Castlerea in January 1921. During the Truce he attended the Company and Battalion training camps, specialising in dispatch, scouting, and intelligence work. He took the Anti-Treaty side during the Civil War, and fought against the government troops at the **attack at Ballinagare** in July 1922, and the **attack on the military at Castlerea** in November 1922

James Mulrooney (Ballygar Coy.) was considered part of 4th Battalion South Roscommon when the Divisional structure was implemented

Michael Mulrooney (Falmore, Ballinagare) brother of Andrew and Patrick. Michael participated in the **attack on Frenchpark RIC Barracks** 2 October 1920, and became a member of the Active Service Unit formed in Castlea in January 1921. He also was present at several **attempted ambushes in Castlerea** that same month. During the Truce he attended the Company and Battalion training camps, specialising in dispatch, scouting, and intelligence work. He took the Anti-Treaty side during the Civil War, and fought the Free State troops at the **attack at Ballinagare** in July 1922

Patrick Mulrooney (Falmore, Ballinagare) drilled with his Company, participated in the **destruction of the local barracks**, and the Belfast boycott. Took part in the **attempted attack on Kilmurray Military Camp** in June, the **attempted attack on the Castlerea Station Guard** in July, the **attack on Frenchpark RIC Barracks** 2 October 1920, and several attempted ambushes in Castlerea in January 1921. Patrick served as a member of the Active Service Unit formed in Castlea in January 1921. During the Truce he, too, attended the Company and Battalion training camp, specialising in dispatch, scouting, and intelligence work. He, along with his brothers, took the Republican side during the Civil War, and fought the government troops at **Ballinagare** in July 1922

William Mulrooney (Tully, Ballygar) was considered part of 4th Battalion South Roscommon when the Divisional structure was implemented. Served as the Quartermaster of the Ballygar Company during the Black and Tan War, and fought in south Roscommon with the Anti-Treaty Flying Column during the Civil War. He was arrested on 30 March 1923, and sent to Athlone. He was later transferred to the Curragh, where he joined a hunger strike that eventually forced his release*

*_Ballygar — Just for the Record_ by Matt Nolan, p. 24.

Brian Mulvihill (Coosan) a member of the Athlone Brigade. Took part in the **raid on the Athlone Excise Office** in May 1920, and was **with the party who shot Sergeant Craddock** in Athlone on 22 August 1920. During the Civil War he took the Anti-Treaty side, and fought with the Flying Column at the **Ambush at Glasson** in August 1922. He was arrested and sent to Athlone in December 1922. In 1924, he was in charge of the IRA Honour Guard that escorted the bodies of the executed Republicans from Custume Barracks. For his efforts, he was arrested but released that day. Mulvihill had been trained as a printer in _The Athlone Printing Works_. After the War he married and moved to Sligo, where he worked as a printer for _The Sligo Champion_ for many years. Died 10 October 1979

Daisy Mulvihill (Coosan) a member of the Cumann na mBan

John Mulvihill (Ballymacfarrane, Donamon) a member of "E" Coy. of the 2nd Battalion South Roscommon

Lillie Mulvihill (Athlone area) a member of Cumann na mBan

Patrick Mulvihill (Edenan, Shankill, Elphin) took part in the **attack on Elphin Barracks** 11 February 1921. He later emigrated to New York

Thomas Mulvihill (Ballynahowna, Ballinagare) 1st Battalion South Roscommon

Bob Murphy (Stonetown, Glenamaddy) County Galway. 1st Battalion, No. 2 Brigade in the 2nd Western Division. No. 2 Brigade was commanded by Gerald O'Connor, formerly the O/C of the 1st Battalion South Roscommon. Murphy's home was used as the headquarters of "I" Company as well as Battalion headquarters (see Surrounding Volunteers - Galway section)

Frank Murphy took part in the robbery of the Dublin-Sligo mail train

George Murphy (Tonycurneen, Scramogue, Strokestown) a member of the Scramogue Company of the North Roscommon Brigade, brother of Jack. After the

Brian Mulvihill, Athlone Brigade.

PHOTO COURTESY OF PATRICK MURRAY

George Murphy, Scramogue Company.

PHOTO COURTESY
OF MARY GALLAGHER

War he joined the Garda Síochána, where he served in the Detective Branch and later as a regular policeman. He retired in 1964, and died eleven years later. Buried in Kilcolman Cemetery, Ballaghaderreen

J. Murphy (Loughglynn Coy.) 1st Battalion South Roscommon. After the War he emigrated to the USA

James Murphy (Treanacreeve, Scramogue, Strokestown) 3rd Battalion North Roscommon Brigade. He served as an Adjutant for the Battalion. On the day of **Scramogue Ambush**, he and Captain Jack Murphy and Sean Leavy were hard at work making a dugout to sleep in that night. The three had spent the morning at the ambush site. Participated in the **attack on Tarmonbarry patrol**. Later emigrated to the USA

John "Jack" Murphy (Tonycurneen, Scramogue, Strokestown) Captain of "C" Company in the 3rd Battalion North Roscommon. He was the brother of George, who was also a member of the Company. He took part in the **attack on the RIC patrol at Strokestown** in January 1921, and participated in **Ambush at Scramogue**, where he was positioned behind a hedge where he could well observe the road to Strokestown through a slit in the foliage. His was the job of reporting to Pat Madden the enemy's approach. His home was a drop spot for dispatches (carried by Brian Connors of Ballinameen). After the War he became a farmer. Died in the 1980s

Malachy Murphy (Sheehaun, Kilgefin, Roscommon) served as a scout for the Kilgefin Coy., 3rd Battalion South Roscommon. After the War he became a farmer. Died 1999

Michael Murphy (Ballyclare, Cloontuskert) a member of Cloontuskert Company, 3rd Battalion South Roscommon

Michael Murphy (Carnagh East, St. John's, Lecarrow) 4th Battalion South Roscommon, brother of Tom, William, and Hubert. Murphy worked in the 1918 elections, drilled with his fellow Volunteers, and participated in the sham battles overseen by Ernie O'Malley in the summer of 1918. He raided for arms, enforced the Belfast boycott, and collected gelignite on several occasions. He **stopped and raided the train at Kiltoom**, took part in the **attempted ambush at Clooncraff**, and the **attempted ambush at Kilmurray Military Camp** in June 1920. Took part in the **burning of O'Brien's house** — a residence thought to be soon taken over by the British. At Truce time he became a member of the special service unit. Murphy took part in the Civil War on the Anti-Treaty side, making mines that **blew up the Kellybrook and Curry Railway Bridges**, blocking the trains, and raiding for transport. He was arrested and interned in the Curragh. Died 1959, and buried in St. John's Cemetery

The William and Mariah Murphy family of Carnagh East, St. John's, Lecarrow,

Hubert Murphy (Carnagh East, St. John's, Lecarrow) in the 4th Battalion South Roscommon. Third Captain of St. John's Coy. Murphy paraded two nights a week with other Volunteers. He worked with the Republican Courts, served summons, and patrolled the public houses. In 1918 his Company, then under the command of Patrick Grady, participated in the sham battles for training purposes under Ernie O'Malley at Lysterfield, Taughmaconnell, and Churchboro. He worked in the 1918 election, and constructed dugouts in the area. Murphy raided for arms on at least eight different occasions, worked in connection with the Belfast boycott, collected gelignite as well as less lethal monies for the Defence Fund and IRA levy, manufactured ammunition (two lbs. of powder the first night,) and stopped and **raided the train at Kiltoom**. He, along with other members of his Company, took part in the **attempted ambush at Clooncraff** under the command of Pat Madden, and the **attempted ambush at Kilmurray Military Camp** in June 1920. He participated in the **burning of O'Brien's house** — a home thought to be soon taken over by the British Forces. He organised and commanded the party that **blew up the Ballymurray and Ballybay Road Bridges**, and was the only member of St. John's Company to participate in the **ambush at Ballygar**. He evaded capture when his home was broken into by the Tans in June 1921. During the Truce he attended the Brigade camp at Ballinaheglish for a week of officers' training, went to the officers' camp at Donamon for two weeks, and was a delegate to Commandant Tom Maguire's Review at Ballygar. All the while, he also served in the Courts at Culleen. Murphy commanded the special service unit formed during this time. He was arrested some time later, and taken to the Curragh, where he became one of the noted escapees through the Brady tunnel in September 1921. After the hostilities, he worked in the stone quarry in Lecarrow. Died 1970, and buried in Gailey Cemetery

PHOTO COURTESY OF TONY MURPHY

John "Jack" Murphy
Captain of Scramogue Company

PHOTO COURTESY
OF EUGENE MURPHY

Thomas Murphy, St. John's Company.

had eight sons, four of whom were deeply involved in the Volunteer movement — Hubert, Thomas, Michael, and William. The parents were the healers of many local lads — using potions made with herbs and poteen. They had been evicted from good land around Carnagh, and given some very rocky real estate in St. John's. They turned their energies instead to freeing Ireland

Thomas Murphy (Carnagh East, St. John's, Lecarrow) a member of St. John's Coy. in the 4th Battalion South Roscommon. Murphy paraded with his Company, and participated in the sham battles for training purposes under Ernie O'Malley at Lysterfield, Taughmaconnell, and Churchboro. He worked in the General Election of 1918, constructed dugouts in the area, and collected funds for the IRA Levy. Participated in a raid for arms the same night that Volunteer Kearney was severely wounded in the stomach. He was not in Kearney's party, however, but headed in another direction with a different group of Volunteers on another raid. He, along with twelve other men from his Company, took part in the **attempted ambush at Clooncraff** under the command of Pat Madden, the **burning of O'Brien's house**, and the **blowing up of Ballybay Road Bridge**. In 1921 the Tans broke into his house, took rifle butts to his face, and dragged him off to the barracks. They brought him back to his mother to die, but Mrs. Murphy had other plans. Unsure whether he would ever heal, she spent weeks nursing her son back to health. The scarring on his face, however, was with him until his death in 1966. After the War he worked in a sawmill near the Moycannon Castle. He is buried in St John's Cemetery

William Murphy (Carnagh East, St. John's, Lecarrow) 4th Battalion South Roscommon. Murphy paraded with other Volunteers several nights a week, worked with the Republican Courts, and served as a Policeman. He participated in the sham battles for training purposes under Ernie O'Malley at Lysterfield, Taughmaconnell, and Churchboro. He worked in the 1918 election, and constructed dugouts in the area. Murphy raided for arms many times — on one occasion securing three shotguns. He was also active in a raiding party the night Joseph Kearney was severely wounded in the stomach, although Murphy was not with Kearney's party, but headed in the opposite direction. Murphy worked in connection with the Belfast boycott. He collected gelignite on several occasions, and, along with other men from his Company, **stopped and raided the train for mail at Kiltoom**. He also took part in the **attempted ambush at Clooncraff** under the command of Pat Madden (O/C of the 3rd Battalion South), and the **attempted ambush at Kilmurray Military Camp** in June of 1920. After the War he became a farmer. He died in the 1950s, and is buried in the St. John's Cemetery

Becky Murray (Quarry Lane, Boyle) sister of Joseph, Cumann na mBan member

Bridie Murray (Quarry Lane, Boyle) sister of Joseph, was an active member of the Cumann na mBan from 1918 to 1924. Bridie served as Treasurer of the Boyle Branch. She carried dispatches, performed all typing work in connection with the RIC and the Belfast boycott, took part in providing benefits for prisoners by secret collections. Her typing was done in the wee hours of the morning so as to avoid detection, and her typewriter and files were hidden in a secret office. She sometimes transferred arms on her person when it was impossible for the IRA men to get guns where they needed to be. During the Civil War she was on duty for the Anti-Treaty fighters at the first aid station during **the Battle at Boyle**, and did indeed transfer some of the arms herself during the conflict. She sometimes directed Anti-Treaty men through the area who were from other parts of the country. Her place of business was raided, and carbon copies of her notes were seized. She was arrested and later released, and ordered not to leave town. Despite all this scrutiny, she kept the lines of communication open between the Brigade and the Western Division staff, carried dispatches, delivered foodstuffs to men on the run, and harboured the Active Service Unit. After the War, Bridie married a McDonald, and moved to County Cavan

Frank Murray (Knockcroghery Coy.) 4th Battalion South Roscommon

Frank Murray (Baylough, Athlone) Captain of "D" Company, 1st Midland Division. During the War he was on the run, but found time to serve as the officer in charge of policing in the Sinn Fein Courts. After the War he became an executive in the Athlone Woolen Mills. Died 1953, and buried in Cornamagh Cemetery, Athlone

James Murray (Derrinlurg, Mt. Talbot) Tisrara Coy., 4th Battalion South Roscommon

James Murray (Clooncraff, Kilteevan) 3rd Battalion South Roscommon

James Murray (Drum Coy.) 3rd Battalion Athlone Brigade

James Murray (Rahara Coy.) 4th Battalion South Roscommon

John Murray (Kilteevan Coy.) 3rd Battalion South Roscommon

John Murray (Gortnacloy, Mantua, Elphin) 2nd Battalion North Roscommon. Murray joined the IRA in November 1916. Served as the Company Intelligence Officer. He carried dispatches, raided for arms, participated in the **burning of Ballinameen Barracks** Easter Saturday night 1920, the **attack on the RIC patrol at the Elphin Dispensary** 13 December 1920, and the **attack on the RIC Barracks in Elphin** 11 February 1921, after which he was present in Ballyroddy to meet expected reprisals by the Crown Forces for the attack on their barracks at Elphin. He was also present at the **attack on a patrol at the Deanery** on 23 March 1921, as well as the **burning of Frenchpark Barracks and Courthouse** in June 1921. John was promoted to Brigade Intelligence Officer in October 1920, and served in that position until May of 1921, when he was given the position of Brigade Chemist. He became competent in making the cart box mines, wallflowers, cheddars, and other types of bombs used by the Battalion

John Murray, National soldier, was killed in Athlone 10 October 1922

John Murray (St. Columbus Terrace, Athlone) 1st Battalion Athlone Brigade. During the Civil War he took the Anti-Treaty side, and was arrested 30 July 1922, and sent to Athlone on 2 September 1922

Joseph Murray (Ballymartin, Kilglass, Strokestown) a member of the Kilglass Company in the 3rd Battalion North Roscommon

Joseph (Josie) Murray (Quarry Lane, Boyle) 1st Battalion North Roscommon, brother of Richard and Phil. Josie doubled as an IRA Intelligence Officer while serving in the RIC. He is among the Boyle Volunteers who posed for a picture in front of the Boyle Barracks the day the British troops finally left town for good (see page 199). Died 1987, and buried in Assylin Cemetery near Boyle

Margaret Murray (Taylorstown, Drum, Athlone) was a member of the Summerhill branch of the Cumann na mBan

Marian Murray (Quarry Lane, Boyle) sister of Joseph, member Cumann na mBan

Mary Murray (Clooncraff, Kilteevan) took into her home many men on the run

Michael Murray (Clooneragh, Strokestown) a member of Carniska Coy., 3rd Battalion North Roscommon

Patrick Murray (Ballymagrine, Tarmonbarry) a member of the Curraghroe Coy. of the 3rd Battalion North Roscommon. He joined the IRA in 1917, and took part in the General Election in South Longford. Ten times he raided for arms, took part in the **attack on Tarmonbarry patrol** in January 1921, where he was armed with a double barrel shotgun. He served under arms as a guard to the men who were blocking roads for the **Scramogue Ambush**. He attended the Battalion

Frank Murray (Baylough, Athlone), Captain of "D" Company, 1st Midland Division.

PHOTO COURTESY OF PATRICK MURRAY

training camps during the Truce, after which he took the Republican side in the Civil War. Murray **fired on Free State troopers** in a lorry between Tarmonbarry and Strokestown, took part in the **attack on Ruskey Barracks** in March 1923, and was with the attacking party at **Lakes Forbes**

Patrick Murray (Fuerty) 2nd Battalion South Roscommon. Lived in the small village of Muff. After the War he became a farmer. He died in the 1980s, and is buried in Fuerty Cemetery

Patrick Murray (Manor, Tulsk, Castlerea) 1st Lieutenant of Company "C" in the 2nd Battalion North Roscommon. He joined the Volunteers in 1917, and worked under Capt. Patrick Collins of Killina Coy. until the Tulsk Company was formed in 1918 under Captain Mick Neary. In 1920 he was arrested and sent to Galway Gaol for refusing to recognise the British Courts. When he returned to Roscommon, he continued his work blocking roads, raiding mail cars, and **burning the Tulsk Barracks**. He blocked roads in preparation for the **attack on Elphin Barracks** in February 1921, but was arrested in April for attempting to shoot a spy. He was court-martialled and imprisoned in the Curragh until the general release. On the day of the outbreak of Civil War, Murray had his own private crisis to concern him — he had to go to Dublin for an operation, after which his Anti-Treaty activities were limited to dispatch work

Patrick Murray (Muff, Fuerty) a member of "D" Coy. in the 2nd Battalion South Roscommon

Peter Murray (Upper Irishtown, Athlone) a weaver by trade, he was arrested after the Rising and sent to Wakefield on 13 May, but released a few days later

Phil Murray (Quarry Lane, Boyle) Battalion Adjutant, brother of Richard and Josie. Murray was arrested 17 March 1920, and became a prisoner of Boyle Barracks and the Curragh camp. He was released in time to see the British evacuate Boyle. He was a member of the Anti-Treaty Active Service Unit (Flying Column) of North Roscommon during the Civil War. He later became a member of the Local Defence Force in 1941. He was a carpenter by trade

Richard Murray (Quarry Lane, Boyle) 1st Battalion North Roscommon, brother of Phil and Josie. Murray was appointed chief armourer of the 1st Battalion — a position which entailed constant maintenance of guns, repairing of ones confiscated in raids, and reloading shotgun cartridges with scrap iron and buckshot. Dangerous enough work, but more so because his house and forge overlooked Boyle Workhouse, and was a constant target of Tan raids. In 1920 he participated in raids for arms, and ambushes on enemy patrols. He escorted escaped prisoners to safety, as well as delivered dispatches throughout the area on the "All Red Route." He also participated in the arrest, imprisonment, and deportation of criminals found guilty by the Sinn Féin Courts. During the Truce he attended a full course of training at the Battalion camp, as well as organised an intensive training for the Fianna boys. During the Civil War he went on the run, and was a member of the Anti-Treaty Active Service Unit (Flying Column) of North Roscommon. He was present at the **attack on Boyle Barracks** 1 July 1922. Three weeks later on 22 July, he was in a house with thirteen other men under the leadership of Pat Brennan, who had just taken another small group to tea, when the house was surrounded. Murray was wounded, and found temporary shelter in a sympathiser's home, where he was arrested eight days later. Sent to Boyle Barracks, Athlone (2 September), Mountjoy (10 January 1923), and eventually to Tintown Camp at the Curragh. He was finally released on 18 December 1923. No more poignant words than his own can describe what Murray gave to the cause: "...my work for the IRA was so heavy from 1919 onwards that I had to completely neglect my means of livelihood and when eventually released from jail, my health was undermined, my foot where wounded periodically breaking into a running sore, so that even now (in 1940) I am not fit to undertake the ordinary work of my trade." Murray is buried in Assylin Cemetery near Boyle

Stephen Murray (Cloonsellan, Kiltevan) 3rd Battalion South Roscommon. A member of Kilteevan Company as well as Pat Madden's Flying Column

Thomas Murray (Cagglebeg, Fourmilehouse) joined the IRA in 1917, and became the 1st Lieutenant of "A" Company (Carniska) in the 3rd Battalion North Roscommon. Murray collected funds, raided for arms, and was in charge of ten men who raided the house of a British Army Captain and confiscated four Webley revolvers, three automatic pistols, and a quantity of ammunition. The 1918 election found him standing guard at the Aughnadarry polling booth. He took part in the **burning of the Fourmilehouse Barracks**. He was appointed Chairman of the Parish Court in his area. Murray was with the Volunteers who staged the **attack on the RIC patrol at Strokestown** 6 January 1921, and served as an armed outpost for the **Scramogue**

Ambush. He was appointed District Justice in the Strokestown area. During the Civil War Murray did intelligence work for the Anti-Treaty side until the cease-fire. In 1928, he became the secretary of a Fianna Fáil Club at Fourmilehouse. He worked as a farmer, and Land Commission foreman. Died 1973, and buried in Lisonuffy Cemetery

Thomas Murray (Clooncraff, Kilteevan) a member of Kilteevan Coy., 3rd Battalion South Roscommon

Tom Murray (Cloonillan, Drum, Athlone) a member of Drum Coy., 3rd Battalion Athlone Brigade. He took the Oath of Allegiance to the Sinn Féin Party at the Ardkeenan House, the local Volunteer gathering point*

*Drum and Its Hinterland by Edward Egan, p. 301.

Una "Sis" Murray (Boyle) born in Elphin, married Josie Murray, and moved to Boyle. She remained an avid Republican all of her life, dying after her 90th birthday. She entertained this author in her home in Rathgar, Dublin, where she shared photos, told stories of her youth, and relived the days of the Tan War. Died 27 April 1997, and buried next to her dear Josie in Assylin Cemetery, Boyle

Author with Una "Sis" Murray.
PHOTO COURTESY OF LEW THORNE

William Murray (Curry) a member of the Curraghboy Coy. in the 4th Battalion South Roscommon. From 1917-March 1919 did organisational work, drilled, performed scouting duties, attended lectures and instruction given by Ernie O'Malley, manufactured ammunition, and performed police duty during the South Roscommon election (guard duty at polling booths and escorting ballot boxes to counting centres). Helped with Dáil Courts when necessity required their convening. Murray was one of a group of Volunteers who raided the private homes of three men — two of whom had joined and one who was about to join the RIC. Not surprisingly, these men had a change of heart! Murray participated in other arms raids — twenty raids were conducted within the Company area, and another fifteen raids were outside the immediate area and performed in conjunction with other Companies of the Battalion. He also raided the premises of a court messenger to the British Courts, and seized books and documents relating to same. Murray was involved in the raid of a local landlord in which Joseph Kearney of Knockcroghery Coy. was severely wounded. He participated in the **attempted attack on Kilmurray Camp** in June 1920, which was called off the very night of the proposed action, the **attempted ambush at Clooncraff**, the **attempted attack on military lorry at Knockcroghery** in January 1921, and **attempted attack on Ballygar RIC Barracks**. Prevented jurors and litigants from attending British Courts, and raided the mails. Constructed dumps for storage of manufactured arms. The entire Company participated in the arrest and confinement of a suspected spy. That man was tried by court-martial and eventually executed — an action which prompted the arrest of ten members of the Company on 5 January 1921, including Murray. He was beaten and taken to Athlone Barracks, and incarcerated in a cell with no bed for three months. Later transferred to Mountjoy and finally, in the last days of June, shipped to Wormwood Scrubbs and Pentonville Prisons in England. Released 11 January 1922, but he did not mend his ways. He returned home, and became active in organising a Company that resisted the Treaty. He also attempted to join an Active Service Unit that would fight in the north of Ireland. During the Civil War he raided homes of ex-RIC men, **derailed a train at Kiltoom**, blocked roads, and generally tried to harass the Free State troops wherever he found them. Murray worked with the Active Service Unit in south Roscommon as well as neighbouring counties. He held the rank of Battalion Adjutant during this period. He was arrested on 18 August 1922, and transferred to Athlone on 2 September 1922, but later escaped

Matthew Murtagh (Dooneen, Ballinameen) a member of Doon Coy., 1st Battalion North Roscommon. Took part in the **attack on Frenchpark Barracks and Courthouse** in June 1921. He later emigrated to New York City

Peter Murtagh (Corlis, Castleplunkett) a member of Moor Coy. in the 1st Battalion South Roscommon. Participated in the **destruction of vacant barracks** in 1920, the **attempted attack on Kilmurray Military Camp** in June 1920, the **capture of enemy stores at Ballymoe** June 1920, the raid and **capture of military equipment at Ballymoe** September 1920, the **attack on the Frenchpark RIC Barracks** 2 October 1920, the **attempted ambushes at Castlerea** and **Frenchpark** in January 1921, and the **ambush at Southpark, Castlerea** 10 July 1921. During the Truce he attended the Company training camp, and specialised in intelligence, scouting, and dispatch work. He took the Anti-Treaty side in the Civil War, and took part in the **attack at Castlerea**, and the **burning of the train at Clooncundra** during November 1922. After the War he became an engineer for Roscommon County Council. He was present for the Pat Glynn Memorial Service held in Loughglynn in 1970. Also present for 1973 reunion of Old I.R.A. men. Murtagh died 2 August 1979, and is buried in Baslick Cemetery

Thomas Murtagh (Carrowncully, Ballinameen) 1st Battalion North Roscommon. Member of the ASU, present for the **attack on Elphin Barracks**, and the **attack on Frenchpark Barracks and Courthouse** in June 1921. Trenched roads, carried dispatches, escorted prisoners from Ballinameen to Clooncunny, and stole the typewriter from the Boyle Railway Station. Served as Sergeant of the Republican Police at Ballinameen. He also lost his job as a road ganger for a long period of time due to his activities in the struggle. He worked as a farmer, and finally secured a job with the Roscommon County Council. He died in 1970, and is buried in the St. Attracta Church Cemetery in Ballinameen

Tim Murtagh (Carrowncully, Ballinameen) 1st Battalion North Roscommon, brother of Thomas. Blocked roads, performed a lot of dispatch work, helped to confiscated a typewriter from the Boyle Railway Station, raided for arms, collected for the Dáil loan, and participated in the **attack on Frenchpark Barracks** in June 1921

Richard Nally (The Square, Castlerea) a member of Castlerea Coy. in the 1st Battalion South Roscommon. A saddler by trade, he became a "guest" of the British Empire at Ballykinlar Internment Camp during the years 1920-21

Bernard "Brian" Nangle (Mongagh, Curraghroe) joined "B" Company, 3rd Battalion North Roscommon in 1917, and was appointed its Captain. Drilled his men, and had them on duty for the North Roscommon and South Longford elections, where he paraded them at Clondra, Longford town, and Lanesboro. Nangle was in charge of the Company during the South Roscommon election. Nangle attended the classes for officers given by Ernie O'Malley at Michael Green's home in Kilglass in the summer of 1918. Because he forcibly removed a party of RIC from a Sinn Féin dance, he was resented and targeted. Nangle was forced to go on the run. Although he could not remain at home, duty did not allow him to leave his Battalion area. He lived in a dugout set up by the Curraghroe Company. He often used the Curraghroe bog as his training ground for weapons instruction. Nangle was in charge of the armed party that raided an **RIC recruitment meeting** at Cloontuskert in 1919, and the Company of men who destroyed **Scramogue Barracks**. He was also in charge of a group of men who stood guard duty around the Kilgefin area after the Fourmilehouse Ambush. Nangle was appointed Battalion Adjutant in October 1920. The fol-

Ballykinlar Internment Camp
Irish Republican Prisoners 1920-21
Hut 31 "A" Company, No. 1 Camp
First Row: Raymond Kelly, R. O'Farrell, Tom Dunning, Pat Dinan, James Kelly
Second Row: Richard Nally*, Pat Fannon**, Michael Geary, Thomas Hancock, John Walsh, Francis V. Quinn, John Dolan, Thomas O'Brien
Third Row: P. Hannelly***, Chris Rock****, William Byrne, Patrick Franklin, Michael Leonard, Michael O'Doherty, Daniel Morrissey
Fourth Row: John Cassidy**, John O'Connor, Patrick McDermott, Thomas Hoban

*Richard Nally was a harness maker in the Castlerea area who was interred for part of the War. Patrick Vaughan spoke of Dick Nally many times in interviews with the author. After the War, Nally returned to Castlerea and resumed his trade.
**Pat Fannon and John Cassidy were from Castlerea.
***Paddy Hannelly was the 1st Lieutenant of Castlerea Company.
****In Micheál O'Callaghan's *For Ireland and Freedom*, his brother Colm notes in "Boyhood Reflections" at the end of the book that a "Christy Rock" of Castlerea sounded the Last Post for a memorial service in honour of John Vaughan and Ned Shannon.

lowing year he commanded the **attack on the Tarmonbarry patrol** on 5 January 1921, and was in charge of a group of men who blocked the roads between Strokestown and Elphin on the night of the **attack on the barracks at Elphin** on 11 February. He was also present at the **ambush at Scramogue** a month later. While he and other men were escorting one of the prisoners from that ambush, he was captured and given an horrendous beating — one which left him with an unrecognisable face. Sentenced to fifteen years, he became a "guest" of His Majesty at Roscommon and Athlone Barracks, the Curragh, and finally Mountjoy. Upon his release on 22 January 1922, Brian rejoined his Company, and became a member of the Anti-Treaty ASU (Flying Column) of North Roscommon, while continuing to serve as the O/C of the 3rd Battalion North. During the Civil War he was in charge of men felling trees, cutting roads, and generally harassing the Free State troops. He was in command of a Company of men who **attacked the Ruskey Barracks** in December 1922 when Frank O'Donoghue was shot (and later died of his wounds). He also destroyed military cars positioned at Curraghroe. All this activity stirred up attention, and he was targeted again for prison in January 1923, when he was sent to the Curragh until September 1923. After the War he became active in politics, securing a Sinn Féin seat on the Roscommon County Council in 1925. He also ran successfully as an Independent Republican candidate in 1934 and 1945

Pat Nangle When the 2nd Western Division was formed, Pat served as the Head of Signaling for the 3rd Battalion, No. 2 Brigade. He later emigrated to the USA

Bernard Naughton (Ardlaghleenbeg, Ballymacurley) brother of Ned, a member of "B" in the 2nd Battalion South Roscommon. His home served as the headquarters for "B" Company during post-Truce times. After the War he worked for the Land Commission, and as a farmer. He is buried at Southwark Cathedral grounds in Sussex, England

Denis Naughton (Ardkeenan, Drum) 3rd Battalion Athlone Brigade. Served as 1st Lieutenant of Drum Company

Edward Naughton (Ardmullan) Curraghboy Coy. in the 4th Battalion South Roscommon. Arrested by Free State troops for his Anti-Treaty activities, and detained for a time

Edward "Ned" Naughton (Ardlaghleenbeg, Ballymacurley) brother of Bernard. Ned served as 1st Lieutenant of "B" Coy., 2nd Battalion South Roscommon. The cottage his parents owned hosted Brigade meetings for two and half years. Present at **Fourmilehouse Ambush**. After the War Ned was part of a group of musicians who used to play for the house dances in the area. Died in the 1950s, and buried in Oran Cemetery

Ginger Naughton (Blackstown, Cornafulla) Drum Coy. area, a member of Father Flanagan's Sinn Féin Club

John Naughton (Ballygar Coy.) was considered part of 4th Battalion South Roscommon when the Divisional structure was implemented. He lived in Drum, Athlone. He was arrested during the Civil War on 7 April 1923 in possession of a book relating to dugouts and Anti-Treaty operations in the area

Michael Naughton (Fearagh, Knockcroghery) 4th Battalion South Roscommon. The Company was formed in 1917 with Patrick Kelly serving as Captain. Naughton drilled with the Volunteers, and attended practice battles at Taughmaconnell overseen by Ernie O'Malley in the summer of 1918. Participated in the South Roscommon election of 1918, the County Council election, and the **burning of Lecarrow Barracks**. Naughton was present at the **burning of a home in Milltown, Curraghboy (O'Briens)** — a residence thought to be soon taken over by the British military. He was also one of a very few men who guarded a suspected spy

John Naughton (Carrownderry, Kiltoom) St. John's Coy., 4th Battalion South Roscommon. Naughton took part in the Civil War on the Anti-Treaty side, making and setting the mines that **blew up the Kellybrook Bridge**. He later emigrated to the United States

Michael Naughton (Ballygar Coy.) was considered part of 4th Battalion South Roscommon when the Divisional structure was implemented. He lived in Drum,

Athlone, and was a member of Father Flanagan's Sinn Féin Club

Michael Naughton (Glanduff, Kiltoom) a member of the St. John's Coy. in the 4th Battalion South Roscommon. He drilled with other Volunteers two nights a week — Tuesdays and Thursdays, and worked in the 1918 General Election

Michael Naughton 2nd Lieutenant of the Kilkerrin Coy. in the Glenamaddy Battalion. Located in County Galway, this Battalion was incorporated into No. 2 Brigade, 2nd Western Division with Gerald O'Connor, former O/C of the 1st Battalion South Roscommon, serving as Brigade Commandant

Paddy Naughton (Knockcroghery Coy.) 4th Battalion South Roscommon. The Company was formed in 1917 with Patrick Kelly serving as Captain. Naughton drilled with the Volunteers, and attended practice battles at Taughmaconnell overseen by Ernie O'Malley in the summer of 1918. Participated in the South Roscommon election of 1918, and the County Council election. He later emigrated to the United States

Patrick Naughton (Glanduff, Kiltoom) St. John's Coy., 4th Battalion South Roscommon. He worked in the election of 1918

Thomas Naughton (Fearagh, Knockcroghery) 4th Battalion South Roscommon. The Company was formed in 1917 with Patrick Kelly serving as Captain. Naughton drilled with the Volunteers, and attended the sham battles at Taughmaconnell overseen by Ernie O'Malley in the summer of 1918. He went house to house canvassing for signatures to the plebiscite for independence. Participated in the South Roscommon election of 1918, the County Council election, and the **burning of Lecarrow Barracks**. Naughton was a member of a party of Volunteers that succeeded in raiding two homes accessible only by boat from Lough Ree — and this in broad daylight! He, along with the rest of his Company, **guarded the village of Knockcroghery** from reprisal on 15 August 1920 — a reprisal precipitated by British Forces being fired upon on Lough Ree. Naughton and others of his Company participated in an **attempted ambush at Clooncraff** — an operation under the command of Pat Madden. Naughton was one of a few men who were entrusted with important dispatches during this time. He, and eight other Volunteers, **stopped a goods train at Ballymurray Railway Station** and removed over twenty bags of mail which were subsequently censored. Naughton and his Company attempted an **ambush at Scrine** — an action that did not take place owing to the fact that the lorry did not return by the expected route. He served as an outpost on the Roscommon side at the attempt to **blow up the Curry and Ballymurray bridges**, and was present at the attempt to blow up the **bridge at Farnaseer**. He blocked roads, and was present at the **burning of a house in Milltown, Curraghboy (O'Brien's)** — a home the Volunteers thought was soon to be occupied by British Forces. During the Truce he was assigned to a special service unit. At the time of the IRA Army split, was one of five men responsible for the Trojan work of reorganising the Company

Patrick Naughton (Tisrara Coy.) 4th Battalion South Roscommon

Patrick Naughton (Ballygar Coy.) His Company was considered part of 4th Battalion South Roscommon when the Divisional structure was implemented

another Patrick Naughton (Ballygar Coy.) 4th Battalion South Roscommon

William Naughton (Blackstown, Cornafulla) Drum Coy., 3rd Battalion Athlone Brigade, a member of Father Flanagan's Sinn Féin Club. He had to cut short his Mass attendance on 6 February 1920 when he left Drum Church earlier than the last amen via the sacristy door. Seems the Tans were rumbling down the road in their lorry on their way to raiding the church

Edward Neary (Knockhall, Ruskey) a member of the Kilglass Company in the 3rd Battalion North Roscommon

Edward Neary (Buckill, Tibohine) a member of the Ballinagare Coy., 1st Battalion South Roscommon. Died at an early age

James Neary (Clooncullan, Elphin) Killina Coy., 2nd Battalion North Roscommon. He was one of the first members of the Company when it formed in August of 1917

Jim Neary (Ardmore, Breedogue, Ballinameen) 2nd Lieutenant in "D" Company of the 1st Battalion North Roscommon. He was on the North Roscommon Sinn Féin Executive. Arrested while attending a meeting in Croghan, and imprisoned in Boyle Barracks. After the War he joined the Garda Síochána, and was stationed in Cork

Michael Neary (Athleague Coy.) 3rd Battalion South Roscommon, served as the 2nd Lieutenant of the Company

Michael "Mick" Neary (Sroove, Tulsk) 2nd Battalion North Roscommon. He joined the IRA in 1917 in Killina Coy. under Captain Patrick Collins. The following year, he was appointed the Captain of "C" Coy. (Tulsk). Neary was trained in the use of firearms and did dispatch work, raided the mails, stopped locals from attending the British Courts, and blocked roads. He was arrested in January 1921, beaten and released, only to be re-arrested the following month. He took part in the capture of two suspected spies in April, but was again arrested when he came home to see his dying father. Neary was taken to Roscommon Gaol, where he was tortured for three weeks, then handed over to the military, tried by court-martial, and sentenced to fifteen years. He was released in January 1922, and immediately reported for duty. He was present at the **Battle of Boyle** in July, but, due to ill health, had to return home. He was arrested for his Anti-Treaty activities on 8 September, and sent to Longford, Mullingar, and finally Athlone, where he remained until November 1922. When he was released, he came home to Roscommon, and worked with the Anti-Treatyites, remaining on call until the cease-fire

Michael "Mick" Neary, Sroove, Tulsk.

PHOTO COURTESY MICHAEL LENNON

Peter Neary (Clooncullane, Elphin) Killina Coy., 2nd Battalion North Roscommon. He was one of the first members of the Company when it formed in August of 1917

Tommy Neary In December 1922 he, along the thirteen other Anti-Treatyites, attacked the Free State troops at the Chapel Gate in the village of Ballintubber. A five-hour fire fight ensued, after which the attackers retreated to Corner House, Frenchpark. Neary was severely wounded, and taken to Athlone hospital on 2 December 1922

P. J. Neary (Ardleckna, Aughrim) was a member of the IRB from October 1916 onward. He carried dispatches and munitions (once from Drumsna Station,) took part in the **burning of Hillstreet Barracks**, assisted in the North Roscommon election of Count Plunkett, served as the unpaid secretary of North Roscommon *comhairle ceanntair* as well as the secretary of Aughrim Cumann Sinn Féin for the same period. He loaned his voice to the Republican cause as a public speaker in Roscommon as well as Leitrim, an activity that earned him a stay in gaol. Neary acted as Judge in the District as well as Parish Courts. He also served on the first Sinn Féin County Council of which he was Vice Chairman. After the War he became the author of hundreds of poems, generally on patriotic topics. They were published in *Old Moore's Almanac*, *The Irish Packet*, *The Irish Homestead*, *Roscommon Messenger*, *Roscommon Herald*, and *Leitrim Observer*. He also acted as the local press correspondent for several local and national newspapers

Frank Nelson (Corry, Kilgefin) a member of Kilgefin Company in the 3rd Battalion South Roscommon. Many, but not all, of the Kilgefin Company were present at the **Fourmilehouse Ambush** in October 1920

James Nelson (Aghaclogher) Kilgefin Coy., 3rd Battalion South Roscommon. A stonemason by trade. During the Sinn Féin election in Kilrooskey in 1918, a local Redmondite became so anxious and vexed by the Volunteer fever that he broke three out of four prongs on his newly purchased hay fork over the head of Nelson! Nelson was an active member of the Kilgefin Company. He was present at the **Fourmilehouse Ambush** as well as the **Scramogue Ambush**. He was on guard duty in May 1921 at Kilrooskey when a firefight erupted between Tans and local Volunteers, resulting in the death of one policeman. During the Truce he attended the training camp near Slieve Bawn. He later joined the Free State Army. After the War one of his many activities included playing fiddle for the local house dances. Died in 1980, and buried in the Oran Cemetery

Andrew Nevin, the first 3rd Battalion Adjutant of North Roscommon

Tom Nevin (Kilgefin Coy.) 3rd Battalion South Roscommon

William Newcomber (a native of Athlone) and a National Army soldier, who was killed in a firefight on 6 March 1923 during the Civil War at The Three Jolly Pigeons pub on the road to Ballymahon

Henry Nicholl (Drumlion, Dromod) was arrested for Anti-Treaty activities during the Civil War, and sent to Dundalk. He wasn't released until 18 January 1924

William Nickolson (Cornafulla, Athlone) his house was burned as a reprisal for the Cornafulla ambush, and his neighbour's (Naughton) rick of hay was torched

Thomas Nohilly (Adjutant of the Tuam Battalion) who became part of an ASU formed with the Glenamaddy Battalion. That Battalion was part of No. 2 Brigade, 2nd Western Division under Brigade O/C Gerald O'Connor

Ann and Ellen Nolan (Bridge Street, Boyle) owned a drapery shop on the crescent in Boyle, and ran a safe house

John Nolan (Derreenadouglas, Crossna, Boyle) Captain of Crossna Company in the 4th Battalion North Roscommon. Arrested 16 February 1921, and taken to Boyle

John Nolan (Tully, Ballygar) when the Divisional structure was put in place, south Galway was grouped with parts of south Roscommon and became part of the 4th Battalion South Roscommon. He took the Anti-Treaty side during the Civil War, and was arrested and sent to Athlone on 30 March 1923

Roger Nolan (Ballygar Coy.) arrested during the Civil War. He was sent to the Curragh, where he went on hunger strike to obtain his release*

*_Ballygar — Just for the Record,_ by Matt Nolan. p. 24.

Tom Nolan (Ballygar Coy.) was considered part of 4th Battalion South Roscommon when the Divisional structure was implemented

another Tom Nolan of Ballygar Coy. in Galway

Jim Noonan (The Lodge, Ballytoohey, Tarmonbarry) a member of Tarmonbarry Coy., 3rd Battalion North Roscommon

Pat Noonan (Captain) of Williamstown Coy. in the Glenamaddy Battalion. Located in County Galway, this Battalion was incorporated into No. 2 Brigade, 2nd Western Division, with Gerald O'Connor serving as Brigade Commandant. Noonan's Company numbered forty-six after the Truce, and his home was used as the headquarters of "C" Company

Tom Noonan Quartermaster of the Athlone Brigade

Charles Noone (Moher, Lackan, Strokestown) 3rd Battalion North Roscommon. Present for the **attack on the Tarmonbarry patrol** in January 1921, **Scramogue Ambush**, and returned to the **Tarmonbarry Barracks** for another try in July 1921

Michael Noone (Carrowntoosan, Tulsk) a member of "C" Coy. in the 2nd Battalion South Roscommon. Participated in the **raid on the military train at Ballymoe** in June 1920, the **attack on Frenchpark Barracks** 2 October 1920, and the **ambush at Southpark, Castlerea** 10 July 1921. His home used to be a hideout for the Volunteers. (According to an August 2004 interview with Sean Raftery of Valeview, Lisalway,) one evening the Black and Tans, who were coming from the Tulsk side, converged on the house, and shot at it from behind a hedge. All the Volunteers ran out the back and scattered. After a few days, they regrouped, and found that one of their number was not with them. On further investigation, they discovered that this man had been wounded and subsequently bled to death. They quietly buried him in a vacant house in Tonroe underneath the floorboards. After the War, Noone became a farmer. Buried in Tulsk

Dominick Noone (Errisuane, Loughglynn) 1st Battalion South Roscommon. Participated in the **destruction of vacant barracks** in 1920, and the **attempted attacks at Castlerea and Frenchpark** in January 1921. He also took part in the special service training (intelligence, scouting, dispatch work) during the Truce

James Noone a member of "A" Coy. in the 2nd Battalion South Roscommon. He later emigrated to the United States

James Noone Captain of Ballyfarnon Company

Michael Noone (Finnor, Croghan, Boyle) Quartermaster for the 5th Battalion North Roscommon, brother of Tom. He was interned during the War

Tom Noone (Finnor, Croghan, Boyle) 5th Battalion North Roscommon. He was a member of the ASU in North Roscommon. He later emigrated to Australia

Walter Noone (Cagglefortyacres, Strokestown) Carniska Coy. in the 3rd Battalion North Roscommon

Jamesy Nugent (Cloonfad, Ruskey) 3rd Battalion North Roscommon, who saved Matthew Egan's life by mediating differences of opinion between the Volunteers (who thought Egan was an informer) and Egan who claimed neutrality

John Nugent (native of Cloonfad, Ruskey) Quartermaster for Ruskey Company in the 3rd Battalion North Roscommon. He was a member of the Active Service Unit of North Roscommon. Arrested during the Civil War for Anti-Treaty activity on 28 August 1922, and taken to Athlone on 2 September 1922

Lawrence Nugent (native of Cloonfad, Ruskey) in charge of the premises in Dublin used for the distribution of the "Irish Bulletin" — the official news sheet of Dáil Éireann in 1920-21

Terence Nugent (Cloonfad, Ruskey) 1st Lieutenant of Ruskey Coy., 3rd Batt. North Roscommon, brother of John, Jamesy, and Lawrence. Emigrated to USA

William Nugent (Slattagh More, Ruskey) a member of Kilglass Coy. in the 3rd Battalion North Roscommon. William joined Slatta Company in 1918. He took part in raiding for arms, the **cattle raid at Clooneenhartland** in January 1919, and served as an outpost for the **Scramogue Ambush**. During the Civil War he fought on the Republican side at Kilglass in September and Ruskey in January 1923

Francis O'Beirne (Carrowmurragh, Kiltoom) brother of Tom. He held a heart filled with regret over the turn of events after the Treaty. When the hostilities ceased, he farmed his land. Died 1945, and buried in Kiltoom Cemetery

Reverend Martin O'Beirne C.C. (native of Aughrim) active supporter of Count Plunkett during the 1917 election. He became vice president of the Sinn Féin Club founded in Crossna in 1917. Fr. Michael O'Flanagan served as its president

Rev. Fr. Michael O'Beirne. C.C. (Loughglynn) of Kilglass, Strokestown. Active supporter of Count Plunkett in the 1917 bye election

Thomas O'Beirne (Carrowmurragh, Kiltoom) 4th Battalion South Roscommon, served as the Quarter-master for the Kiltoom Coy. After the War he farmed his land for but a few years before dying in 1926. He is buried in the old Kiltoom Cemetery

Arthur O'Brien (Baylin, Athlone)

Henry "Harry" O'Brien (2nd from the left, back row). Harry was Captain of the Coosan Company, Athlone Brigade.

PHOTO COURTESY OF DECLAN GRIFFIN

arrested during the Civil War for Anti-Treaty activities on 5 July 1922, and taken to Athlone on 2 September

Henry "Harry" O'Brien (Strand St., Athlone) Captain of the Coosan Company in the Athlone Battalion. O'Brien joined the IRA Company in Ballykeeran in 1913, and accompanied other Volunteers towards Shannonbridge on Easter Sunday 1916 ready to take part in the uprising. In 1918 he drilled with his Company, collected funds, and worked in the general election. He was present at the **Parkwood ambush**. O'Brien and James Tormey were having tea at the Royal Hotel in Athlone in 1920, when they were spotted by the Auxiliaries, who had just entered the premises "generally the worse for drink." Both men exited through the back door, and starting walking through the town northeasterly and parallel to the Main Street. As they neared Maguire's pub, one of the Auxies tapped Tormey on the shoulder saying, "We want you, big fellow."* Tormey dived in the door of the pub, O'Brien shot the Tan who threatened to capture Tormey, and, by running down around the south side of town and crossing the Shannon, made good his own escape. He was a member of the Flying Column, frequently travelling back and forth across the Shannon attempting ambushes in both County Westmeath and County Roscommon. During the time that he was on the run, he often stayed in the Clonown area. Not wishing to keep bothering the local people for food, he

Loughlin "Lolly" O'Brien,
First Captain Curraghboy Coy.

Seamus "Jimmy" O'Brien and his
wife Eilis Elliott.

Michael O'Callaghan.

often went into the barns and ate the pig swill. This did lasting damage to his stomach.** Even in his last years, when he went to visit Ned Dowling in Dublin, he would often request a glass of water in which to dissolve the baking soda that he perpetually carried with him.*** During the Civil War he eventually took the Anti-Treaty side, and participated in the **Ambush at Glasson** in August 1922. Arrested 27 September 1923 near Summerhill, Drum

*Henry (Harry) O'Brien Volunteer Witness Statement to Bureau of Military History, p. 13.
** Donal O'Brien, son of Harry, interview by author, 5 August 2004, Athlone.
***Peggy Dowling Naughton, daughter of Ned, interview by author, 23 August 2004, Dublin.

Jimmie O'Brien (Behy, Crossna, Boyle) Captain of the Crossna Company, and later promoted to O/C of the 4th Battalion North Roscommon. He was present at the **Keadue Ambush** on 22 March 1921. After the formation of the Division, this Battalion was transferred to another Brigade. O'Brien fought with the Anti-Treaty Arigna Flying Column during the Civil War, and participated in the **demolition of the Knockvicar and Cootehall bridges** on 14 August 1922, and the **attack on Ballinamore Barracks** on 31 January 1923. Emigrated to Dearborn, Michigan

John O'Brien (Upper Irishtown, Athlone) a clerk by trade. During Easter week, he was with a party of men who headed for Shannonbridge ready to defend it until Roger Casement's rifles arrived. Halfway there, the men received the counter-manding order and returned to Coosan. Soon after, he was arrested, and sent to Wakefield on 13 May, but was released a few days later

John O'Brien (Annagh, Castlerea) a member of Trien Coy., 1st Battalion South Roscommon. Served as the 2nd Lieutenant of the Company. Took part in the **attempted ambush at Coshlieve** in July 1920, and attended the Hermitage train-ing camp during the Truce. O'Brien took the Anti-Treaty side during the Civil War, and participated in the **attack at Ballinlough** in July 1922

Loughlin "Lolly" O'Brien (Milltown) the first Captain of the Curraghboy Coy. in the 4th Battalion South Roscommon. From 1917-March 1919 did organisational work, drilled, performed scouting duties, attended lectures and instructions given by Ernie O'Malley, and raided for arms. Before the War he had played Gaelic foot-ball with his local team in Curraghboy. O'Brien was an epileptic in an age when few medications were available. He died at a young age in 1928, and is buried in Cornamagh Cemetery

Michael O'Brien had joined the Free State Army, but soon became discouraged and disgusted with its methods. He deserted the army, and joined the Arigna Flying Column during the Civil War. He was arrested and condemned to death, but escaped in February of 1923. Still active in Republican causes, he was again arrested in 1928

Seamus (Jimmy) O'Brien (Ballykeeran, Athlone) a tailor by trade, he col-lected guns to be used locally for the Easter Rising. He was arrested, and sent to Wakefield on 13 May 1916. After spending several months in gaol, he returned to Athlone, where he and his brother, Harry, were active during the Black and Tan War. He took no military part in the Civil War. Died in 1961, and is buried in Cornamagh Cemetery

Tom O'Brien ran a safe house in the Loughglynn area

Tom O'Brien, son of Tom, dispatch rider for the 1st Batt. South Roscom-mon. After the War became a carpenter. Died 1997, buried in Ballinagare

Michael O'Callaghan (Cloonboniffe) a member of the IRB and a school teacher, whose home served as the meeting place for the IRA. Through Michael's efforts the Vaughan brothers, Pat and John, were sworn into the Volunteer movement. He also harboured Sean Bergin in early 1921 when the latter had contracted pneumonia. O'Callaghan's involvement did not go unnoticed by the local RIC. A receipt for clothing purchased in O'Callaghan's name was found on the body of Sean Bergin who had been shot in the Woodlands of Loughglynn. O'Callaghan was subsequently apprehended while shopping in Castlerea. He was incarcerated in Athlone Barracks when he heard the news of Sean Bergin's demise. Michael was the father of Micheál O'Callaghan, former editor of the *Roscommon Herald* and author of *For Ireland and Freedom*, an invaluable resource book from which some of the names of the Roscommon Volunteers were taken (see page 482). Michael died in 1942, and is buried in Castlerea Cemetery

Michael John O'Connell (Sraduff, Taughmaconnell) Captain of Taughmaconnell Company in the 3rd Battalion Athlone Brigade, in whose home Pat Mullooly hid after his escape from the Athlone Barracks hospital in May 1921. Michael was arrested for Anti-Treaty activities during the Civil War on 23 February 1923, taken to Athlone Barracks, and released on 26 March 1923. After the War he farmed his land. Michael died in 1943. Buried in Taughmaconnell Cemetery

Annie O'Connor on the left with two other unidentified women.

Annie O'Connor (Church Street, Athlone) was born in Derevan, a townland of Tumbeagh in Co. Offaly. She worked as a dressmaker in Athlone, and became a member of Cumann na mBan in 1915. She worked on the Parliamentary election, participated in drilling, took classes in first aid, collected money for the purpose of resisting conscription, and helped to organise dances. In April 1919, she was sent to Galway to form a new branch of Cumann na mBan, of which she became the first president. From October 1919 onward, Annie became more involved in the military work of the Volunteers. She carried dispatches, did intelligence work, scouted (armed) for the **attempted ambush at Clonown**, took two wounded ASU men into her home and organised medical treatment for them. Annie also became a special courier for the Brigade area, carrying revolvers, ammunition, bomb detonators, electrical cables, and batteries from Dublin via train. She bought and secured a rifle and ammunition from a British soldier stationed at Athlone, and carried them through town in broad daylight. During the Civil War Annie continued her work with the Anti-Treaty forces, serving as a member of the firing squad over Christy McKeon and Toby Mannion's grave, catering to men of the ASU, and scouting for them armed with a revolver. She also transported bombs and explosives used by the men. After the War she married Edward Dowling, Captain of "A" Company, and moved to Dublin. Died in April 1937

Frank O'Connor (Coosan) Co. Westmeath. O'Connor joined the Irish Volunteers around July 1914 and the IRB early in 1917. During Easter week, he was with a party of men who headed for Shannonbridge ready to defend it until an envoy from Liam Mellows arrived. Halfway there, the men received the countermanding order, and returned to Coosan. Soon after, he was arrested and sent to prison. Upon his release, he came to The O'Rahilly Sinn Féin Club near Drum in south Roscommon, and trained the new recruits to the IRA. The men were instructed in foot drill and the use of arms, although oftentimes there were precious few arms with which to practice. O'Connor commanded the **burning of Brawny Barracks** in Irishtown, Athlone in April 1920, took part in the **raid on the Athlone Excise Office** in May, the **attack on a boatload of soldiers on the Shannon** in September, and the **attempted attack on Captain Tully** from Athlone. He also participated in the **burning of Moydrum Castle** in July 1921. During the Civil War he took the Anti-Treaty side, and fought with the Flying Column at the **Ambush at Glasson** in August 1922. He was arrested on 7 March 1923 by Commandant Garrahan accompanied by Captain Gibbons and forty-six other troopers

Gerald O'Connor (Loughglynn) 1st Battalion Commandant, later appointed No. 2 Brigade Commandant in the 2nd Western Division. Took part in the **capture of a Black and Tan** at Ballinagare in June 1920, the **destruction of vacant barracks** in 1920, the **attempted attack on the Castlerea Station Guard** in July 1920, the **attack on Frenchpark Barracks** 2 October 1920,

Gerald O'Connor, 1st Battalion South Roscommon. Later No. 2 Brigade O/C.

attempted ambush at **Cloonsheever** March 1921, and served in the covering party for the **attack on the military at Castlerea** 7 April 1921. Participated in the **attempted ambush at Loughglynn** in April 1921. In May, O'Connor was part of an ambush party waiting **at Lisacul** (an action taken in conjunction with the East Mayo men). He also participated in the **attempted ambush of an RIC patrol near Ballymoe**. O'Connor rescued Toby Scally, who was wounded in the shootout in the Woodlands of Loughglynn in April. On one occasion, O'Connor hid in the home of Thomas Hester in Aughaderry. When the Tans knocked on the door, the lady of the house quickly put O'Connor under the child's mattress, laying the infant on top, and, upon the Tan's entry into the house, warned them not to disturb her child who was gravely ill. The ruse worked!* He gave the "Cease and Desist" order on the lawn of the Clonalis House after the Truce was signed, urging the assembled Volunteers to go home, not to engage in hostilities against fellow Irishmen, and to let the politicians settle the issues. In response to those words, many in the South Roscommon Brigade did not actively participate in the Civil War. After the War he became a schoolteacher by profession. He was a Fianna Fáil member of Roscommon County Council from 1934 to 1942. O'Connor kept meticulous notes about men and engagements, because, in the 1930s and 1940s, the pensions of IRA men depended on his verification of their involvement. He diligently protected those notes, and bequeathed them to the son of one of his comrades — someone he knew would treasure them. (The author referred to these comprehensive notes in compiling this Volunteer list.) O'Connor persistently fought for his men's financial well-being during the 1940s and 1950s. There are hundreds of letters which he wrote verifying actions, and asking the government officials to review specific cases. He was a leader whom the Volunteers greatly respected. He felt likewise for his men. Gerald O'Conner died in 1972, and is buried in Lisacul Cemetery

Denis O'Connor, son of Gerald, interview by author, Dublin, 20 October 2003.

John O'Connor (Gallagh, Cloontuskert, Roscommon) Captain of Cloontuskert Company, 3rd Battalion South Roscommon. O'Connor worked with the Knockcroghery Company when they **held up a goods train** carrying mail. The train was stopped at Ballymurray by using a red light as a signal. When the train slowed, Volunteers boarded and seized twenty bags of mail. He was severely wounded in the Cloontymullen **mine explosion on the Lanesboro-Roscommon Road**. O'Connor spent two months on Incheneagh Island in Lough Ree recuperating from those wounds. After the War he returned to his home, where he resided until his death in the 1970s. Buried in Cloontuskert Cemetery

Joseph F. O'Connor (Carrowkeel, Fourmilehouse, Roscommon) was a messenger boy during the War. At Truce time, he attended a camp at Runnamoat House, where he studied Morse Code and flag signalling. During the Civil War he fought for the Anti-Treaty cause in County Mayo, where he was captured. He escaped on route to Athlone, and found refuge in a cousin's house in Curraghboy. He later went to Kilteevan to an uncle's house, where he remained "in seclusion for four months"* until the end of the War. Joe emigrated to New York, became a engineer on sailing vessels, and finally a businessman. On one of his frequent trips to Ireland, he noticed the slow progress of the building of the Elphin IRA monument, and offered to help raise funds. He was as good as his word. Over $3500 was delivered to the organising committee from his area of New York   *An Irish Civil War Exile by J. F. O'Connor, p. 15.*

Luke O'Connor (Church Street, Roscommon) 3rd Battalion South Roscommon

Martin O'Connor (Church Street, Strokestown) a member of the Strokestown Coy., 3rd Batt. North Roscommon. His involvement in the attempt to **burn down the Courthouse in Strokestown** in the summer of 1920 resulted in his being seriously burned. He had to spend weeks in a Dublin hospital recuperating. Martin returned to Roscommon, and hid out in the Curraghroe area, recovering sufficiently to participate in the **Scramogue Ambush** in March of 1921. Incarcerated in Athlone during the spring of 1921. After the War he became a District Court Clerk. Died in 1988. Buried in Tulsk Cemetery

Paddy O'Connor (Athlone) provided the music for dances given by the Summerhill Cumann na mBan club. Proceeds went to support the Volunteer movement

Patrick O'Connor (Ashbrook, Strokestown) Lieutenant in the local Company. Attempted to join Sean Connolly's attack party on a Tan patrol from Ruskey in early February 1921, but his commanding officer failed to rendezvous. He took part in cutting the road from Ballyfeeny to Scramogue in preparation for the **Scramogue Ambush**

Ted O'Connor (Ballindollaghan [Knox], Castleplunkett) 2nd Battalion South Roscommon

Thomas J. O'Connor (Ballyglass, Castleplunkett) 2nd Battalion South Roscommon

William O'Connor (Kilgarve, Ruskey) a member of the Kilglass Company in the 3rd Battalion North Roscommon

Mrs. Lena O'Doherty, wife of Liam, one of the Sharkey sisters of Strokestown, Captain of the Strokestown branch of the Cumann na mBan, arrested after the Scramogue Ambush

M. O'Doherty was a member of the 1918 Sinn Féin election committee in South Roscommon

Seamus O'Doherty a native of Derry City, who was a sales representative for a Dublin publishing house. Director of Elections for Count Plunkett during the momentous year of 1917

Dominick O'Donnell of Boghtaduff, Ballaghaderreen, East Mayo Brigade

Liam (William) O'Doherty (a native of Dungloe, Co. Donegal, who had a shop in Elphin) O/C of the 3rd Battalion North Roscommon. He was the first person to try to organise a small Company of men around the Strokestown area in early 1917. He aided Sean MacEoin in his defense of Ballinalee in County Longford, arrested in 1918, and became a prisoner at Sligo Gaol. Took part in the **Fourmilehouse Ambush** 12 October 1920, the **shootout at Castlenode** in November 1920, the **attack at Elphin Dispensary** 13 December 1920, the **attack on the RIC patrol at Strokestown** in January 1921, and the **attack on Elphin Barracks** 11 February of that same year. After numerous sweeps of the area by a mixed force of RIC and Tans, O'Doherty was captured on 20 February. He was beaten with fists, burned on his thighs and chest with a hot poker, and kept in solitary confinement for a week. His future lodging accommodations included stints in Longford, Athlone, and the Curragh, where he contracted a nasty case of scabies. He was again arrested during the Civil War, and on 5 December 1922 was incarcerated in Athlone. In January of 1923, he was transferred to Mountjoy. In the 1950s O'Doherty was interviewed by Ernie O'Malley, and his words are preserved in the Ernie O'Malley Papers in the UCD Archives

Manus O'Donnell (Boghtaduff, Ballaghaderreen) one of the first members of the Ballaghaderreen Coy. in the East Mayo Brigade, a coach builder by trade

Rev. Michael O'Donnell (a native of Castleplunkett and curate in Castlerea) who would walk to Castleplunkett from Castlerea to give warning of the Tans' approach

Tom O'Donnell, Adjutant of the Gurteen Battalion, County Sligo and later a TD

Frank O'Donoghue (Northyard, Kilglass, Strokestown) served as the Vice O/C of the 3rd Battalion North after the 3rd Western Division was formed. He was a member of the Anti-Treaty Active Service Unit of North Roscommon during the Civil War. He was wounded in Ruskey by the Free State forces, died (according to one source)* in the Curragh Military Hospital on 13 December 1922. According to Padraic O'Farrell's book, *Who's Who in the Irish War for Independence and Civil War*, O'Donoghue breathed his last at Athlone,** but according to *The IRA in the Twilight Years* by Uinseann MacEoin,*** O'Donoghue died of his wounds on Quaker Island in Lough Ree. He is buried in Kilglass Cemetery, where, in 1973, a monument was dedicated in his honour. His name is inscribed on the tablets in front of the Shankill Monument near Elphin

Pat Mullooly, Quartermaster of the North Roscommon Brigade, Private Papers.
**p. 221.*
***p. 91.*

James (Seamus) L. O'Donovan born in Castleview, Roscommon town. O'Donovan obtained a Master of Science degree from UCD, which he put to good use as Director of Chemicals for the IRA from December 1920 to July 1921. He was imprisoned in Mountjoy and Kilmainham, where he participated in a hunger-strike. Released but re-arrested and incarcerated in Newbridge, Co. Kildare, from which he escaped. O'Donovan experimented with explosives, and invented the

"Irish Wallflower" and "Irish Cheddar" devices.* After the War he worked in the head office of E.S.B., founded a literary/political magazine, and worked with Sean Russell on his scheme to bomb London. He married Mary Barry, sister of Kevin, and spent many years of his later life working on a biography of the martyred young man. Died 1979**

*<u>Who's Who in the Irish War of Independence and Civil War 1916-1923</u> by Padraic O'Farrell, p. 79. **<u>The IRA in the Twilight Years</u> by Uinseann MacEoin, pp. 879-880.

Evangela O'Dowd (Graffoge, Scramogue, Strokestown) joined the Cumann na mBan at the end of 1917 when Brigid O'Mullane first came to Roscommon to organise. She originally joined the Strokestown Company, but later formed a branch at Northyard. In the spring of 1920, she conveyed a bag containing revolvers, a Mills bomb, detonators etc. from Strokestown to her home in Graffoge on the orders of Liam O'Doherty. On several occasions, she was entrusted with storing and guarding revolvers in County Roscommon as well as in Longford. One of her more intriguing adventures was travelling to Dublin (on the orders of Sean Leavy) to convey a message to Liam O'Doherty, who was then in Mountjoy Prison. On Easter Saturday night 1921 during a raid on McGuinness's shop in Longford, she concealed a Webley revolver, an automatic, and box of bullets (which had been purchased from a Black and Tan earlier in the evening), and took them to Belton's shop where she hid them in a bag of oats. (One wonders if the guns ever functioned after such submersion?) She also acted as intermediary between post office officials and the IRA, taking and delivering police messages in code to the IRA. She later moved to North Circular Road, Dublin

Leo O'Dowd (Graffoge, Scramogue, Strokestown) brother of Patrick and Evangela. Arrested during the Civil War on 6 September 1922, and taken to Athlone on 14 November 1922

Patrick J. O'Dowd (Graffoge, Scramogue, Strokestown) 3rd Battalion North Roscommon, brother of Leo and Evangela, chief medical officer for the Third Western Division. He participated in the **attack on the Elphin Dispensary** on 13 December 1920, and the **attack on Elphin Barracks** 11 February 1921. After the War he served as the Chairman of Elphin *comhairle ceanntair*, and head medical officer in Elphin Dispensary District. In 1927 he became the president of the Official Fianna Fáil Board for North Roscommon, and served as a TD for Fianna Fáil from 1927-1932 and from 1933 to 1937. He moved his practice to Cabra, Dublin in 1932. He was captain of the Irish Bridge team

Sergeant Patrick O'Dowd of the RIC, who saved the town of Ballaghaderreen from flames by his protestations against the Tans to the English military. He was soon forced to resign from the force

James O'Farrell (Castlemosshill, Ballaghaderreen) arrested during the Civil War for Anti-Treaty activities. Taken to Athlone 28 January 1923

Sean O'Farrell (Dromard, Dromod, Co. Leitrim) when the 3rd Western Division was formed, he became the O/C of the 5th Battalion. All of South Leitrim was attached to the former North Roscommon Brigade. Sean was a member of the ASU of North Roscommon commanded by Pat Brennan. Sean became a TD for the Sinn Féin party, and was arrested on 7 December 1925 in connection with an arms dump. His father and three brothers were also arrested for the same reason

Sean O'Farrell Adjutant of the Athlone Brigade

Rev. Michael O'Flanagan (Cloonfower, Castlerea) whose father used to gather the youth of the countryside around him, and relate stories of the old Fenians. Father O'Flanagan served as a curate in Roscommon town and Crossna, gave the oration at the lying-in-state of O'Donovan Rossa, travelled in America for the Gaelic League, shipped arms to Ireland, was partly responsible for the union of Arthur Griffith's Sinn Féin and the Republican movements, served as the vice president of Sinn Féin, and spoke the first words in the historic Irish Dáil. He was stripped of his privileges by the Catholic hierarchy, who did not approve of his Republican activities. After the War he spent his last days transcribing the John O'Donovan papers of the 1830s, and penning a history of County Roscommon, which is written entirely in Irish and housed in the National Library. Died 7

Members of the First Dáil.
First row: Laurence Ginnell, Michael Collins, Cathal Brugha, Arthur Griffith, Eamon de Valera, Count Plunkett, Eoin McNeill, William T. Cosgrave, Ernest Blythe
Second row: P. J. Moloney, Terence MacSwiney, Richard Mulcahy, Joseph O'Doherty, Pierce McCann, Seamus Dolan, Joe McGuinness, Patrick O'Keeffe, Michael Staines, Joe McGrath, Bryan Cusack, Liam de Róiste, Michael Colivet, and Father Michael O'Flanagan
Third row: Peter Ward, Alec McCabe, Desmond Fitzgerald, Joseph McSweeney, Richard Hayes, Conor Collins, Pádraic O'Maille, Seamus O'Mara, Brian O'Higgins, Seamus Bourke, Kevin O'Higgins
Fourth row: Joseph McDonagh, Sean MacEntee
Fifth row: Piaras Béaslaí, Robert Barton, Peter Paul Galligan
Sixth row: Philip Shanahan, Sean Etchingham

PHOTO COURTESY OF GEAROID O'BRIEN, HEAD LIBRARIAN, ATHLONE LIBRARY   NAMES COURTESY OF ALBERT SIGGINS

August 1942, and is buried in the Republican plot in Glasnevin Cemetery. A small pebble from his gravesite is prominently displayed in this author's home in Oregon. Great men and their deeds live on!

Thomas O'Flynn (Carrownamaddy, Elphin) Adjutant for Creeve Company in the 2nd Battalion North Roscommon. After the War he joined the Garda Síochána, and was stationed in Banagher, Co. Offaly

William O'Flynn (Carrownamaddy, Elphin) a member of Creeve Company in the 2nd Battalion North Roscommon. Served as a Judge in the Republican Courts

Bartley O'Gara (Ballaghaderreen) arrested after the 1916 Rising and sent to Lewes Gaol. He was later His Majesty's guest at Glasgow Prison. He ended his post-Rising visit to the bigger isle with a stint in Frongoch, "The Irish University." Before the rebellion, he was a drapier's assistant in Elphin

John O'Gara (Cloonlyons, Strokestown) a member of the Carniska Coy., 3rd Battalion North Roscommon

Michael O'Gara (Lisacul, Ballaghaderreen) arrested during the Civil War for Anti-Treaty activities, and released on 23 February 1923

Rev. Michael O'Flanagan with the Roscommon Camogie team.

PHOTO COURTESY OF ALBERT SIGGINS

Sean O'Gara (Sheepwalk, Frenchpark) listed in the GHQ papers in the UCD Archives as the Captain of the Frenchpark Company. This group was disbanded shortly after it was formed and incorporated into other units

Thomas O'Gara (Ballaghaderreen) after the Rising he was sent to England, where he ended his incarceration at "The Irish University," Frongoch

James O'Grady (Rinnagan, St. John's, Athlone) a member of St. John's Coy. in the 4th Battalion South Roscommon

Johnny O'Grady (Ballymacurley, Ballinaheglish) cousin to Michael. Served as a member of the Republican Police. After the War he became a farmer. Buried in Oran Cemetery

Michael O'Grady (Ballymacurley, Ballinaheglish) Captain of Ballinaheglish Coy. in the 2nd Battalion South Roscommon, friend and confidant to Ned Hegarty. Present at **Fourmilehouse Ambush**. When the Western Division was formed, he volunteered to serve with the Oran Battalion Flying Column. After the War he worked as a tradesman. Buried in Oran Cemetery

T. O'Grady (Castlemore, Ballaghaderreen) arrested during the Civil War for Anti-Treaty activities, and taken to Mountjoy, Tintown II on 20 February 1923, transferred to Tintown A, and finally released on 18 December 1923

(left to right) Larry Joe O'Hara, Sean Leavy, Jack Fryer, Laurence O'Hara, and Michael Cox

Larry Joe O'Hara (Donald's Hill, Cloongreaghan, Cootehall) 5th Battalion North Roscommon, captured 16 May 1921 along with Michael Dockery and Jack Glancy and taken to Boyle Barracks, where he serenaded the prisoners on the night of Jim Molloy's escape. Molloy was a Captain in the South Sligo Brigade. O'Hara was later sent to Mountjoy

Michael O'Hara (Donald's Hill, Cloongreaghan, Cootehall) a member of Cootehall Company in the 5th Battalion North Roscommon. He was arrested on 16 May 1921, beaten, and then taken to the Boyle Barracks

Mrs. O'Hara of Ballymacurley, Ballinaheglish welcomed Luke Duffy, Pat Madden, and Sean Bergin into her home in January 1921 after they had escaped the roundup at Martin Ganley's house in Loughglynn. The men had travelled fifteen miles that day, and greatly appreciated Mrs. O'Hara's warm meal and warmer beds

Nan O'Hara, sister of Michael and Larry Joe, who lived next door to the Cootehall Church. She oftentimes aided her brothers in the fight. On the night her brother Willie was arrested with Jack Glancy and Michael Dockery in May 1921, she attempted to hide the rifles that they had brought into the pub. Unfortunately, she didn't have sufficient time to conceal them, and when they were confiscated, the markings on one of the rifles were recognised as belonging to Constable Dowling, who had been killed in the Keadue Ambush

P. O'Hara 2nd Lieutenant of the Castlerea Coy. as of February 1922

Paddy O'Hara (Croghan area) 5th Battalion North Roscommon

Peter O'Hara (Tinacarra, Boyle) 1st Battalion North Roscommon, a member of the Volunteers since before the Rising

Tom F. O'Hara (Ballaghaderreen) 4th Battalion East Mayo Brigade, arrested for his Sinn Féin sympathies after the Rising, prisoner at Lewes and Glasgow Gaols. At the time of the Rising, he was a shop assistant. He was a native of Ballina. In 1919 Tom was appointed to serve as the Republican Court Judge

Willie O'Hara (Cloongreaghan, Cootehall) 5th Battalion North Roscommon, brother of Larry Joe. Taken prisoner 16 May 1921 along with Michael Dockery and Jack Glancy, and sent to Boyle Barracks and Mountjoy. After the War,

William became active in Fianna Fáil politics, serving as vice president of the official board for North Roscommon in 1927

Christopher O'Keeffe (Ballinaheglish Coy.) 2nd Battalion South Roscommon. After the War he emigrated to England

Bridget O'Leary (Farranykelly, Castlecoote) harboured men on the run

Ernie O'Malley a native of Castlebar, Co. Mayo. Volunteer organiser on a national scale, whose mother was a Roscommon woman (the former Miss Marion Kearney of Cloonroughan, Castlerea). Active in organising Roscommon recruits. He arrived in South Roscommon in the summer of 1918, and helped reorganise the units to make them more efficient. While on the run, he lived, for a time, with Luke Dempsey in Grange, north of Boyle, as well as with Matt Davis in Kilteevan in south Roscommon. O'Malley was present at the **Battle of the Four Courts**, took the Anti-Treaty side, and became the Commandant of the 2nd Southern Division during the Civil War. He also served as the Acting Assistant Chief of Staff for the IRA. He was apprehended in November 1922 by Free State troops while hiding in a closet, where he was riddled with bullets. O'Malley spent months recuperating before setting sail for America. There he began his classic novel about Ireland's fight, *On Another Man's Wounds*. He married in the States, but returned to the Emerald Isle, where he authored several more books on the War — *The Singing Flame*, and *Raids and Rallies*. In the 1950s, O'Malley travelled around Ireland interviewing men who had fought in the War. His papers are dutifully preserved in the UCD Archives. Ernie O'Malley died on 25 March 1957

James O'Neill (Culleenanory, Curraghroe, Strokestown) 3rd Battalion North Roscommon, brother of Michael. Took part in the **attack on the Tarmonbarry patrol** in January 1921, **Scramogue Ambush**, and the **attack on the Tarmonbarry Barracks** in July 1921

Michael O'Neill (Culleenanory, Curraghroe, Strokestown) 3rd Battalion North Roscommon, brother of James. Took part in the **attack on the Tarmonbarry patrol** in January 1921, served as an outpost for the **Scramogue Ambush**, and was present for the **attack on the Tarmonbarry Barracks** in July 1921

Father O'Reilly, who was stationed near Tang, County Westmeath, helped start the local IRA Company, and procured arms (twelve rifles and some .303 ammunition) for the Volunteers' march to Shannonbridge on Easter Sunday 1916

Dan O'Rourke (Tarmon, Castlerea) Born in Tents, Lough Allen, Co. Leitrim, O'Rourke trained as a national school teacher at De La Salle College in Waterford. He moved to Castlerea in 1911. During the first years of the War, O'Rourke served as the O/C of the South Roscommon Brigade from 1918 until February of 1921. He was instrumental in starting up various Companies throughout the area. He often came to give instruction to the new recruits. He acted as a scout at the **disarming of the military at Tarmon Cross** in June 1920, participated in the **destruction of vacant barracks**

Seamus O'Meara (Connaught St., Athlone) first joined the Volunteers in 1914 at Drogheda, where he was apprenticed in the victualling business. Upon orders from his employer, he resigned shortly thereafter. When the split in the Redmond Volunteer movement came, nearly every member of the Company pledged his support to John Redmond. Another Irish Volunteer Company was formed in September 1915, and O'Meara, despite the objections of his boss, joined that Company of about a dozen men. In early March 1916, he also became a member of the IRB. He returned to Athlone on 11 April 1917, and participated in the Longford election. In 1918 O'Meara was appointed the Brigade O/C — a Brigade that encompassed south Roscommon and parts of Westmeath. He was arrested on 12 July 1919 and incarcerated for three months in Mountjoy. When he walked out the gates of the prison, he was re-arrested and taken to the Bridewell, and fined 3£ for destruction of government property (he took part in the Mountjoy Gaol smashup). He was again appointed the O/C of the Athlone Brigade, was re-arrested in April 1920, and sent to Galway Gaol. Upon his return to Athlone, he ordered the destruction of all not-yet-burned barracks, and a **raid on the Athlone Excise Office**, which he personally led. He took part in the **attack on Streamstown Barracks** in July 1920, and also was with the party who **killed Sergeant Craddock** in Athlone on 22 August 1920. O'Meara joined the men of the Flying Column, who waited in ambush in both County Westmeath and Roscommon for police patrols. He was with a party of men on the Ballinasloe/Galway Road the day before the Cornafulla Ambush in February 1921. Frustrated by the lack of successful campaigns against the enemy, he resigned his position as O/C of the Brigade in late March/early April. Con Costello was appointed in his stead. He attended the training camp at Drumraney in County Westmeath, after which he resigned from the Volunteer movement, and returned to his business in Athlone

Dan O'Rourke (Tarmon, Castlerea)

in 1920, the **attempted attack on the Castlerea Station Guard** in July 1920, and the **attack on Frenchpark Barracks** 2 October 1920. On 22 November, O'Rourke narrowly escaped capture at Tarmon School when he shoved Capt. McKay aside and dashed for safety across the fields. He made his way to Leitrim, where he stayed with relatives for a time. He remained on the run, frequently hiding out in the cottages of Ballinaheglish[2] and Knockcroghery,[3] and the home of Michael Kilroe in Corigh near the Galway border.[4] He was replaced as commanding officer in February 1921 — a position to which Frank Simons was appointed. (Gerald O'Connor also assumed some of the obligations of that position.) He refused to accept an appointment in August 1921 as Adjutant of the 2nd Western Division. O'Rourke was advised by General Headquarters not to attend the Army Convention in March of 1922.[5] He eventually resigned from the IRA.[6] As a member of the Dáil, he voted for the Treaty with reluctance, but became an adherent to the Anti-Treaty side from 8 December 1922. After the War he became an able administrator for many county activities: member of the first Sinn Féin Council in Roscommon, Chairman of the County Council (for many years), and National President of the Gaelic Athletic Association. He held the Fianna Fáil seat in the Dáil for a number of years. Dan O'Rourke died on 4 August 1968, and is buried in the Castlerea Cemetery

1. Tarmon Centennial Magazine, *"Tarmon and the War for Independence"* by Sister Elizabeth and Maura Flynn, p. 22.
2. Mick Concannon, Ballymacurley. Interview by author, 21 August 1994.
3. Michael Breheny, Knockcroghery. Interview by author, 22 June 2002.
4. Michael Kilroe, Ballybride, Roscommon. Interview by author, 12 October 1998.
5. Michael Collins Papers, Military Archives, Ref. No. A/0365, Group VII, Item viii.
6. Gerald O'Connor Papers

Michael O'Rourke (Carrick-on-Shannon) arrested for Anti-Treaty activities during the Civil War, but escaped from Newbridge

Patrick O'Rourke (Cloncowley, Drumlish, Co. Longford) a member of the 5th Battalion in the 3rd Western Division. Fought with the Anti-Treaty Active Service Unit of North Roscommon during the Civil War

Peter O'Rourke (Abbeytown, Boyle) 1st Battalion North Roscommon. In 1916 he was arrested after the Rising and sent to Wandsworth Prison. He was soon released. He was re-arrested after ordering Boyle shopkeepers to keep their doors closed after the death of hunger striker Terence MacSwiney

James Oates (Gardentown) a member of Cloontuskert Coy., 3rd Battalion South Roscommon. First Sinn Féin Council in Roscommon. He, along with John Scally of Portnahinch, rowed the body of another Volunteer, John Scally, from Incheneagh Island to Clooneigh, from whence it was born to a secret grave in Kilteevan graveyard. John had died from wounds received in the Lanesboro-Roscommon mine accident

Patrick Oates (Cartronaglogh, Keadue) was arrested during the Civil War on 28 August 1922 for Anti-Treaty activities, and taken to Athlone on 2 September 1922. He was released on 10 March 1923

Joseph Patrick "J. P." Owens (Lismehy, Strokestown) a member of Carniska Coy. in the 3rd Battalion North Roscommon, served as a dispatch rider. He emigrated to the United States, but later returned to his native land, dying in 1974. He is buried in Lisonuffy Cemetery

Liam Owens (Lismacool, Elphin) arrested for Anti-Treaty activities during the Civil War, and taken to Athlone on 16 April 1923

Patrick Owens (Glenvela, Castleplunkett) a member of "C" Coy. in the 2nd Battalion South Roscommon. Took part in the **attack on Frenchpark Barracks** 2 October 1920. Later emigrated to the United States

Sean Owens (Ballyroddy, Elphin) 2nd Battalion North Roscommon Intelligence Officer. Sean joined the IRB the first week of February 1917. He drilled and

Joseph Patrick "J.P." Owens, Lismehy, Strokestown.

trained twice weekly, being appointed 2nd Lieutenant of the Company at this time. A year later, he was appointed Captain of the Company, a position he held until September 1918, when he was advanced to the Battalion staff. He participated in the **burning of the Ballinameen Barracks**, the **burning of the Tulsk Barracks**, the **attack on the Elphin Dispensary** on 13 December 1920, where his revolver and a few hand grenades proved handy. With revolver, cable, and battery in hand, he charged into the **attack on Elphin Barracks** on 11 February 1921, and took part in the **attack on the RIC patrol at the Deanery**. He also participated in the **burning of Barracks and Courthouse in Frenchpark** in June 1921, armed only with a shotgun. In between actions, he blocked and cut roads on several occasions, and **raided the mail car at Tulsk and Killina**. During the Truce he attended the training camp at Glenasmole House in County Wicklow, as well as the local camps at Mantua and Cloonshee. In March he was present at the IRA convention held in Dublin as a representative of the Brigade. Sean was on duty in Boyle Military Barracks in April, and was present at the **Battle of Boyle** on 1 July 1922. He was a member of the Anti-Treaty Active Service Unit formed in North Roscommon during the Civil War. He took part in the **attack on the Free State troops at Boyle Railway Bridge** in November, **the attack on government troops in Strokestown** in December, the capture of government officers on the Boyle/Carrick-on-Shannon Road in February, and the **attack at Caldra** in March. His luck ran out on 11 April 1923 when he was brought to Boyle, then Athlone, and finally shipped off to the Curragh, where he participated in a hunger strike in October and November of 1923. His final days behind bars were spent at Sligo Gaol, from which he was released on 11 March 1924. Sean was interviewed in the 1950s by Ernie O'Malley, and his responses are recorded in the Ernie O'Malley Papers in the archives of UCD. He devoted a considerable amount of time and energy to collecting funds and arranging for the erection of the Shankill IRA Monument. Died 1978 and is buried in the Shankill graveyard

Sean Owens. Intelligence Officer 2nd Battalion North Roscommon.
PHOTO COURTESY OF GERALD OWENS

James Padian (Culleenaghmore, Kilglass, Strokestown) served as the 2nd Lieutenant for Slatta Company in the 3rd Battalion North Roscommon. He was a member of the ASU of North Roscommon. Arrested 11 January 1923

Tom Padian (Slatta, Kilglass, Strokestown) a member of Slatta Company in the 3rd Battalion North Roscommon. Took part in the **attack near Ruskey village** on 5 July 1921

Mollie Parker (Aghamuck) Kilgefin parish, a member of Cumann na mBan. Died 1972

Thomas Page (Cloonconra, Castlerea) a member of Trien Coy., 1st Battalion South Roscommon. Took part in the **attempted ambush at Coshlieve** in July 1920, and the **attempted ambush of an RIC patrol near Ballymoe** in May 1921. Blocked roads and scouted on the day Inspector King was shot in Castlerea. Attended the old Castlerea Barracks training camp during the Truce, where he specialised in scouting and dispatch work. Emigrated to the USA

William Parsons (Polredmond, Williamstown, Co. Galway) Located in County Galway, this Company was part of the Glenamaddy Battalion which was incorporated into No. 2 Brigade, 2nd Western Division. Gerald O'Connor, former O/C of the 1st Battalion South Roscommon, served as Brigade Commandant. Parson's home was used as the headquarters of "J" Company

Felix Partridge (Ballaghaderreen) brother of William, carpenter by trade, who worked at Duff's Carpentry. He and Michael Farrell constructed the platform on which the great Anti-Conscription debate took place in Ballaghaderreen on 5 May 1918. Utilising no machinery but a supreme supply of know-how, the two men used sixty empty Guinness half-barrels, a large number of heavy planks and some light timber. The platform was as solid as the foundation of a house!*

The Western People, "Service in Ballaghaderreen," by Jack McPhillips, 19 September 1964.

William Partridge (native of Ballaghaderreen) Captain in the Irish Citizen Army, took part in the 1916 Rising, sentenced to twelve years imprisonment. He served time in Dartmoor Prison, but was released early due to illness, and returned to Ballaghaderreen where he died in the home of his brothers and sisters on 26 July

1917. A large contingent of the Citizen Army came from Dublin to provide escort to Partridge's remains. The funeral oration was given by Countess Markievicz, and the local Volunteer Company under the command of Frank Shouldice and a Company from West Clare under the command of Michael Brennan formed the honour guard. Buried Kilcolman Cemetery

Mick Pender (Athlone) during the Civil War he took the Anti-Treaty side, and participated in the **Ambush at Glasson** in August 1922. He, and James Martin of The Hill of Berries, Kiltoom, led the Anti-Treaty forces which generally operated on the west side of the Shannon. He escaped twice from Custume Barracks in Athlone (once on 11 June 1923), but was captured again on 27 September 1923 at Cornalie (twelve miles from Athlone). After the War he emigrated

James Pettit (Carrigeen, Ballinameen, Boyle) listed in the GHQ papers in the UCD Archives as the 1st Lieutenant of "C" Company in the 1st Battalion North Roscommon. He was taken into the IRB by Alec McCabe in February 1915. He attended parades, protected IRA officers' homes, collected for the Dáil loan, and was present at the **attack on Frenchpark Barracks and Courthouse** in June 1921

Liam Pilkington a native of Sligo town. Termed "the fighting saint" by his men.* A member of the Volunteers since 1913. He was the Head of the IRB for Sligo, Leitrim, and Roscommon. He held meetings of the IRB at the Rockingham Arms Hotel in Boyle. O/C of the Sligo Brigade in 1917 when J.J. (Ginger) O'Connell was transferred to GHQ. He led the Volunteers who laid an **ambush at Moneygold**, near Grange, on 25 October 1920, and the **attack the Collooney Barracks** in March 1921. Served as Commandant of the 3rd Western Division, which included North Roscommon, Sligo, Leitrim, and parts of County Mayo. Head of the Anti-Treaty forces at Boyle during the Civil War. Pilkington, Michael Kilroy of West Mayo, and Thomas Maguire were the three Anti-Treaty commanders whose men were active in the west of Ireland. He was captured in August 1923 and imprisoned. After the War he joined the Redemptorist Order, and ordained a priest in 1931. He later served as a missionary in Africa**

*_The Singing Flame_ by Ernie O'Malley, p. 50.
**_Memoirs of Constable Jeremiah Mee, R.I.C._, edited by J. Anthony Gaughan, p. 129.

Charles Pinkman (Carrick, Keshcarrigan, Co. Leitrim) served on the Brigade staff when the 3rd Western Division was formed. He was the Intelligence Officer for South Leitrim

Count George Noble Plunkett, a Dublin intellectual, who became the Director of the National Museum and a member of the Society for the Preservation of the Irish Language, a precursor to the Gaelic League. Plunkett's two sons were involved in the Rising, and the elderly Count came to Boyle, Roscommon, in 1917 to stand in the bye election that became a milestone in Irish history. The Count became the first Sinn Féin candidate to proclaim the obsoleteness of the British Parliamentary system in Irish affairs. To honour his memory, in 1973 the old District Hospital and workhouse of Boyle were levelled only to be replaced by a facility for the elderly residents and terminally ill of the area. The facility's title — The Plunkett Home

George Plunkett, son of Count Plunkett, brother of executed Joseph Plunkett, who was a signer of the 1916 Irish Proclamation. George was an organiser for the IRB, who was arrested as a result of the **Rockingham Raid**. Sent to Mountjoy. He was shipped to Lewes Prison in England, where he participated in Irish classes being given to prisoners as they exercised in the yard. He also wrote for a one-issue Irish manuscript journal published at the prison. He often hid in Roscommon cottages on his travels for organising the fighting men. After the War he became a farmer near Dundalk. He died at an early age in an accident

John Pole a member of Castleplunkett Coy., 2nd Battalion South Roscommon

John Powell (Rathkineely, Ballinagare) a member of "C" Coy. in the 2nd Battalion South Roscommon. Took part in the **raid on the military train at Ballymoe** in June 1920, the **attack on Frenchpark Barracks** 2 October 1920, and **ambush at Southpark, Castlerea** 10 July 1921

John Pryal (Elphin) 2nd Battalion North Roscommon. He was the first Captain for the "E" Company (Elphin). Raided for arms and equipment, and carried dispatches on the Red Route, but was arrested in June 1918, and imprisoned in Belfast and Sligo Gaols until December 1918. Upon his release, he continued his Volunteer activities and again came to the attention of the authorities. He was

Liam Pilkington, O/C 3rd Western Division of the Anti-Treaty forces.

again arrested in January 1921, and detained at Boyle, Athlone, and the Curragh until the following December. During the Civil War he took the Anti-Treaty side, and was present at the **Battle of Boyle**, serving as a Red Cross worker. By 1940 Pryal was living in Knocknafushoga, Croghan

Bernie Quigley (Roscommon Coy.) 3rd Battalion South Roscommon

Brian Quigley (Ardkeel, Roscommon) a member of Roscommon Coy., 3rd Battalion South Roscommon. Served as the 2nd Lieutenant for the Company

John Quigley (Newtown, Roscommon) a member of Kilteevan Coy., 3rd Battalion South Roscommon, brother of Michael and William

Johnny Quigley (Ardkeel, Roscommon) a member of Roscommon Coy., 3rd Battalion South Roscommon, brother of Brian, Martin, and Patrick

Martin Quigley (Ardkeel, Roscommon) a member of Roscommon Coy., 3rd Battalion South Roscommon, brother of Johnny, Patrick, and Brian

Michael Quigley (Newtown, Roscommon) a member of Kilteevan Coy., 3rd Battalion South Roscommon, brother of John and William

Michael Quigley (Knockcroghery village) a member of Knockcroghery Coy., 4th Battalion South Roscommon. The Knockcroghery Company was formed in 1917 under the leadership of Patrick Kelly. Quigley drilled and paraded with the Volunteers, and attended the practice battles at Taughmaconnell in the summer of 1918 overseen by Ernie O'Malley. Participated in the South Roscommon election of 1918, and, along with his Company in conjunction with Kilteevan Company, took part in the **attempted ambush at Clooncraff**. He raided numerous houses for arms —

Jim Quigley (Rathconnor, Fourmilehouse) O/C of the 2nd Battalion South Roscommon. According to the Luke Duffy Papers, Jim was one of two crucial Volunteers in the Ballinaheglish area. Quigley became interested in the Volunteer movement through his association with the GAA. His home was raided after the 1916 Rebellion — perhaps, he speculated, because he was well acquainted with Liam Mellows.* Quigley was sworn into the IRA in 1917 by Sean Hyde, along with Jack Brennan of Carrowkeel, Fuerty. Quigley became somewhat of an organiser himself and soon commanded more than fifty men from his area. He helped plan the **attempted attack on Kilmurray Military Camp** in June 1920. He was part of an aborted raid in Castlerea in which the Volunteers boarded a train in Donamon and headed to Castlerea. At the same time, however, the Tans were arriving en-masse at the train's destination point. A prearranged signal from a Volunteer along the rail line alerted the men that something was awry at the other end of the tracks. They "jumped ship" and avoided capture. He loaned Pat Madden four rifles, which were used in the **Fourmilehouse Ambush**, and served as a outpost for that operation. On 21 March 1921, John Breheny of Knockcroghery was hiding out at Quigley's in Rathconnor in the 2nd Battalion area, where he had no doubt gone for a Brigade meeting. A knock was heard on the door of the main house, but Breheny, Quigley, John Gibbons, and a brother of John Conroy were sleeping in an out building. After ten minutes of flurry in the main house, the Tans left, unknowingly abandoning the four Volunteers who had been silently watching the goings-on from the safe vantage point of an adjacent building. Arrested during the Civil War for Anti-Treaty activities on 20 September 1922, and taken to Athlone on 14 November. He was transferred to Tintown A, and finally released on 18 December 1923. After the War Quigley played football for Kilbride. He moved to Sandpark, Tulsk, where he worked as a stockmaster and for the Land Commission. Died 1958. Buried in Oran Cemetery

Jim Quigley Volunteer Witness Statement to the Bureau of Military History 1913-21 p. 1

PHOTO COURTESY OF PAULINE GARVEY

many in the St John's area. Took part in the **attempted attack at Kilmurray Camp** — an action that was cancelled the very night of the proposed assault. In January 1921 he was a member of the party that **attempted an attack** on a group of military about eighteen strong **at Knockcroghery**. He later emigrated to the United States

Patrick Quigley (Ardkeel, Roscommon) member of Roscommon Coy., 3rd Battalion South Roscommon, brother of Martin, Johnny, and Brian

Thomas Quigley (Main St., Castlerea) arrested during the Civil War for Anti-Treaty activities on 21 July 1922, and taken to Athlone on 2 September 1922

Fr. Tim Quigley (Rathconnor, Fourmilehouse) brother of Jim, a trustworthy and dependable Volunteer (according to the Luke Duffy Papers). After the War, Tim was ordained a priest, and served as the pastor of Fourmilehouse Church. Father Tim was four times the Senior Golf Champion of Ireland. He completed fifty years of sacred ministry before God called him home on 6 November 1975. Buried beside the Fourmilehouse Church

William Quigley (Newtown, Roscommon) member of Kilteevan Coy., 3rd Battalion South Roscommon, brother of Michael and John

Frank Quinn (Killattimoriarty, Kilgefin, Roscommon) a member of the Kilgefin Coy., 3rd Battalion South Roscommon, brother of Martin

Jack Quinn (Carrick-on-Shannon) of the South Leitrim Brigade was a member of the Active Service Unit of North Roscommon commanded by Pat Brennan. He later moved to Waterford

Jack Quinn (Lecarrow, Elphin) a member of Creeve Coy., 2nd Battalion North Roscommon. Served as the Company Intelligence Officer

Joe Quinn (Ballaghaderreen) one of the first members of the Ballaghaderreen Coy. in the East Mayo Brigade

John Quinn (Emlaghkeadew, Fuerty) a member of Fuerty Coy. in the 2nd Battalion South Roscommon, brother of Michael

John Quinn (Cootehall Street, Boyle) 1st Battalion North Roscommon, a member of the Volunteers since before the Rising

Johnnie Quinn (Cloonfower, Castlerea) 1st Battalion South Roscommon, a member of John Vaughan's Cloonboniffe Company. After the War he emigrated to England

Martin Quinn (Willsgrove) Ballintubber Coy. Served as Quartermaster for the Company. Took part in the **attack on Frenchpark Barracks** 2 October 1920

Martin Quinn (Killattimoriarty, Kilgefin) a member of the Kilgefin Company in the 3rd Battalion South Roscommon Brigade. Many, but not all, of the members of that Company participated in the **Fourmilehouse Ambush** on 12 October 1920

Michael Quinn (Fairymount, Kilgefin) An ex-British soldier, who served as an Intelligence Officer for the area. He was so adept at his job that many in the Battalion did not know that he was associated with the Volunteers. He mixed freely with the police, and was unafraid to pass along what he had gained from their conversation. He alerted the IRA officers regarding the British army's new policy of planting mines in the trenches that had been dug across the roads as a blockade or, at least, an impediment to tender travel. (Annie —, who worked in Grealy's Hotel in Roscommon town, saw an open notebook on the table showing mining operations on the Lanesboro/Roscommon Road.) She alerted Quinn who sounded the alarm to Luke Duffy, who in turn passed it along to his men. It came too late or went unheeded by the four men who were wounded on that road when a Mills bomb with its pin extracted blew up

Michael Quinn was in charge of armour for the 3rd Battalion, No. 2 Brigade in the 2nd Western Division. He later emigrated to America

Michael Quinn (Castleplunkett Coy.) 2nd Battalion South Roscommon. After the War he emigrated to the United States

Michael Quinn (Emlaghkeadew, Fuerty) a member of "D" Coy. in the 2nd Battalion South Roscommon, brother of John

Michael Quinn (Kildaree, Williamstown) 1st Lieutenant of Polredmond Coy. in the Glenamaddy Battalion. Located in Co. Galway, this Battalion was incorporated into No. 2 Brigade, 2nd Western Division with Gerald O'Connor, former O/C of the 1st Battalion South Roscommon, serving as Brigade Commandant

Peter Quinn (Erritt, Gortaganny, Castlerea) 1st Battalion South Roscommon. Participated in the **capture of arms at the Castlerea Barracks** in April 1920, the **attempted attack on the Castlerea Station Guard** in July 1920, the **burning of Loughglynn Barracks** as well as the **burning of the Barracks at Ballinlough** 14 September 1920. He also took part in the **attempted ambush at Lisacul** (in conjunction with the East Mayo men) in May 1921. During the Truce he attended the Battalion training camp specialising in engineering

T. Quinn a member of the Granlahan Coy. in the Castlerea Battalion in July 1922

Thomas Quinn (Donamon) 2nd Battalion South Roscommon

Thomas Quinn (Newtown) Kiltoom Coy., 4th Battalion South Roscommon

John Rabbit (Cloonbard, Castleplunkett) a member of Moor Coy., 1st Battalion South Roscommon. Took part in the **attempted attack on Kilmurray Military Camp** in June 1920, the **attack on the Frenchpark Barracks** 2 October 1920, and the **attempted attacks at Castlerea** and **Frenchpark** in January 1921. During the Truce he attended the Company training camp and specialised in intelligence, scouting, and dispatch work. He took the Anti-Treaty side in the Civil War, and participated in the **burning of the train at Clooncundra** in November 1922. John later became a member of the Garda Síochána in Wexford

Owen Rabbit (Cloonbard, Castleplunkett) a member of Moor Coy. in the 1st Battalion South Roscommon, brother of John. Took part in the **attempted attack on Kilmurray Military Camp** in June 1920, the **attack on the Frenchpark Barracks** 2 October 1920, and **attempted attacks at Castlerea** and **Frenchpark** in January 1921. After the War Owen emigrated to Manchester, England

Roger Rabbit (Rabbitte) (Lissyconnor, Dunmore) joined the Volunteers in 1917, and became the 1st Lieutenant of Kilterna Company in County Galway. He drilled with his comrades, raided for arms in 1920 by going to the Polredmond and Williamstown districts where he would be unknown. He also collected money for the Dáil loan. He later became the Captain of Kilterna Coy., and served as Vice Commandant (post-Truce) of the 1st Battalion, No. 2 Brigade in the 2nd Western Division. The 1st Battalion was part of the Brigade commanded by Gerald O'Connor, formerly O/C of the 1st Battalion South Roscommon. Rabbit's home was used as the headquarters of "B" Company

James Rafferty (Castle Street, Roscommon) Kilbride Coy., 3rd Battalion South Roscommon, brother of John. Joined the Free State Army, and later in life owned a shop beside the Royal Hotel in Roscommon town

John Rafferty (Castle Street, Roscommon) a member of Kilbride Coy., 3rd Battalion South Roscommon, brother of James. Became an officer in the Free State Army. In 1922 he was the officer in charge of a garrison of twenty-five Free State soldiers who took over the Ballygar Barracks. Later in life he managed the Royal Hotel in Roscommon town. Buried in St. Coman's Cemetery

Dominick Raftery (Ballindollaghan, Castleplunkett) a member of the Castleplunkett Company in the 2nd Battalion South Roscommon

Frank Raftery (Rafferty) (Cloverhill) a member of "A" Coy. in the 2nd Battalion South Roscommon, brother of John and Patrick

George Raftery First Lieutenant of Fairymount Company in the 1st Battalion North Roscommon

John Raftery (Rafferty) (Cloverhill) a member of "A" Coy. in the 2nd Battalion South Roscommon, brother of Patrick and Frank. After the War he emigrated to New Jersey

Luke Raftery (Cloonbard, Lisalway, Castlerea) served as Captain of Castleplunkett Company in the 2nd Battalion South Roscommon. He participated in the **raid on the military train at Ballymoe** in June 1920, the **attack on Frenchpark Barracks** 2 October 1920, and the **ambush at Southpark, Castlerea** 10 July 1921. When the Western Division was formed, he volunteered to serve with the Oran Battalion Flying Column. After the War he lived in Bohagh near Castlerea, where he farmed the land. Died 22 April 1960, and buried in Ballintubber Cemetery

Pat Raftery (Cloonelt, Castlerea) a member of John Vaughan's Cloonboniffe Company, a blacksmith by trade, in whose shop the Volunteers used to make pellets and load them with bits of nails for use in shotguns

Patrick Raftery (Rafferty) (Cloverhill) a member of "A" Coy. in the 2nd Battalion South Roscommon, brother of John and Frank. During the Civil War he fought on the Anti-Treaty side, and was arrested on 21 July 1922, and taken to Athlone two months later. By November he was a free man

Luke Raftery, Captain of Castleplunkett Company.

PHOTO COURTESY OF SEAN RAFTERY

Thomas Raftery (Taughnarragh, Cloonboniffe, Castlerea) 1st Battalion South Roscommon, Participated in the **destruction of vacant barracks** in 1920, the **capture of arms from the Castlerea RIC Barracks** in April 1920, the **raid for petrol at Ballinlough Station** in June 1920, the **attempted ambush at Coshlieve** in July 1920, the **attempted attack on the Castlerea Station Guard** in July 1920, and the **attack on Frenchpark Barracks** 2 October 1920. He also took part in the **attempted attacks at Castlerea** and **Frenchpark** in January 1921, and served in the covering party for the **attack on the military at Castlerea** 7 April 1921. That same month he participated in the **attempted ambush at Loughglynn**, and the **attempted ambush of an RIC patrol near Ballymoe**. During the month of May, he joined with East Mayo Volunteers in an **attempted ambush at Lisacul**. Raftery died at a young age

William Raftery (Kilbride Coy.) 3rd Battalion South Roscommon. Died 15 April 1961

William Raftery (Cloonbard, Lisalway, Castlerea) a member of the Castleplunkett Coy., 2nd Battalion South Roscommon, brother of Luke

Frank Ramsey (Barrybeg, The Hill of Berries) a member of the Kiltoom Coy. in the 4th Battalion South Roscommon, brother of Robert

Robert Ramsey (Barrybeg, The Hill of Berries) a member of the Kiltoom Coy. in the 4th Battalion South Roscommon. Took part in the **raid on the Athlone Excise Tax office** in May 1920

James Rattigan (Killina Coy.) in the 2nd Battalion North Roscommon. After the conscription crisis ended, Rattigan faded out of the Volunteer movement. He was considered too old to be an active soldier

John Rattigan (Culliagh, Scramogue, Strokestown) 3rd Battalion North Roscommon

Sean Rattigan (Patrick Street, Athlone) scouted the town in August 1920 for the whereabouts of Sgt. Craddock. Imprisoned in Athlone Barracks in March of 1921

William Rattigan (Rhatligan) (Cloonfad Coy.) 1st Battalion South Roscommon. Attended the training camps during the Truce. He participated on the Anti-Treaty side in the **attack at Ballinagare** during the Civil War in July 1922. He later emigrated to the United States

Edward Reaney (Emlaghbeg, Donamon) 2nd Battalion South Roscommon, Quartermaster for the Company. Took part in the **raid on the military train at Ballymoe** in June 1920

Tom Reaney (Emlaghbeg, Donamon) 2nd Battalion South Roscommon, Adjutant for the Company, brother of Edward and William

William Reaney (Emlaghbeg, Donamon) a member of "E" Coy., 2nd Battalion South Roscommon, brother of Edward and Tom

Patrick Reddington (Rackans, Curraghboy, Athlone) a member of Curraghboy Coy. in the 4th Battalion South Roscommon. From 1917-March 1919 did organisational work, drilled with the men, performed scouting duties, paraded with his fellow Volunteers during a visit to the area by Sean Connolly, performed police duty during the South Roscommon election and in conjunction with enforcement of Dáil decrees. Reddington served as scout for a raid on the private homes of three men — two of whom had joined and one who was about to join the RIC. Not surprisingly, those men opted for a different career! Reddington raided for arms, his own closet being the first target — he gave up his own gun to be used by the Company. He participated in arms raids — twenty raids were conducted within the Company area, and another fifteen raids were outside the immediate vicinity and performed in conjunction with other Companies of the Battalion. He took part in a special raid for arms in the Kiltoom area. Participated in the **attempted attack on Kilmurray Camp** in June 1920, an operation that was called off the night of the intended attack. Prevented jurors from attending the British Courts, and held periodic meetings of Dáil Courts when necessity arose. Manufactured ammunition and constructed dugouts for storage of same. Raided the mails and the premises of a court messenger to the British Courts — whereupon books and documents were seized. Reddington served as a scout on the night of the **attempted ambush of a military lorry at Knockcroghery** in January 1921. The entire Company participated in the arrest and confinement of a suspected spy. That man was tried by court-martial and eventually executed — an action which prompted the arrest of ten members of the Company on 5 January 1921 including Reddington. He was beaten and taken to Athlone Barracks, and incarcerated in a cell with no bed for three months. Later transferred to Mountjoy and finally, in the last days of June, he was shipped across the waters to Wormwood Scrubbs and Pentonville Prisons in England. Released 11 January 1922, whereupon he returned to Curraghboy and rejoined his Company with the intent of resisting the Treaty. He raided homes of ex-RIC men who were ordered to leave the country, blocked roads at Whitepark, Curraghboy, Lysterfield, and Lisbaun, intending to delay troop movements, and guarded two shopkeepers' premises who were being victimised by local hooligans. He was arrested by the Free State troops, but detained for only a short time. He, along with other men, prevented the sheriff's bailiffs from evicting Mrs. Faynes of Curraghboy from her home. During the time of the Civil War, Reddington served as the 1st Lieutenant of the Company. After the War he farmed his land in Curraghboy

Tom Reddington (Ballygar Coy.) was considered part of 4th Battalion South Roscommon when the Divisional structure was implemented. He served as the 1st Lieutenant of the Company

Patrick Redican (Clooncraff, Hillstreet) in 1922 he served on the Anti-Treaty side as the 1st Lieutenant of "D" Company in the newly formed 4th Battalion of the 3rd Western Division

Jack Regan (Rathmoyle, Kilmurray, Castlerea) 2nd Battalion South Roscommon. Was present for Pat's Glynn's Memorial Service in 1970

John Regan (Castleplunkett Coy.) 2nd Battalion South Roscommon

Michael Regan (Cartron Coote, Kilteevan) a member of Kilteevan Coy., 3rd Battalion South Roscommon

Michael Regan When the Western Division was formed, he volunteered to serve with the Castlerea Battalion Flying Column

Patrick Regan (Mullaghlusky, Keadue) 2nd Lieutenant of Keadue Company in the 4th Battalion North Roscommon

Patrick Regan (Strokestown) a member of the IRB, who had planned to join up with Liam Mellows in Galway at Athenry in 1916. The confusion of countermanding orders during the Rising, however, kept him home. Operated a Strokestown pub

Peter Regan (Lack) Tarmonbarry Coy., 3rd Batt. North Roscommon

Scottie Regan (Keadue) 4th Battalion North Roscommon, chief accomplice of Jim Brady, who dug the "Brady tunnel" out from the Curragh Camp in September 1921

Batty Reid (Tawnyneden, Boyle) 1st Battalion North Roscommon, assisted in Jim Molloy's **escape from Boyle Barracks**. Listed in the GHQ papers of the UCD Archives as the First Lieutenant of "A" Company

Frank Reilly (Corramagrine, Whitehall, Tarmonbarry) a member of the Tarmonbarry Coy., 3rd Battalion North Roscommon. Took part in the **attack on Tarmonbarry**

Tom Regan (Mount Delvin, Cloonfad, Ballyhaunis, Co. Mayo) Company Captain, 1st Battalion (Castlerea) South Roscommon Brigade. Participated in the **destruction of vacant barracks** in 1920, and took part in the **disarming of two British soldiers at Cloonfad** in May 1921. He was a member of the Flying Column which trained in the camp in the Swinford area after the Truce in 1921. There he specialised in intelligence, scouting, and dispatch work. Regan took an active role in the Civil War, becoming part of an Anti-Treaty Active Service Unit whose other members included Mick Duffy, John Snee, M. McKeon, P. Behan, and M. Hunt. Regan spent time up along the six-county Border sniping at the B-Specials. He also participated in the **attack on Boyle Barracks** 1 July 1922, the **attack at Castlerea and Ballinagare** in July 1922, and the **attack at Castlerea** in November 1922. After the Civil War, he joined the National Army in 1940, and, while stationed at Custume Barracks in Athlone, won a shooting competition organised by the Western Command. He was equally accurate with a rifle or shotgun. He later moved to Ballybane, Galway City where he died. He was buried with full military honours complete with a tricolour and firing party from Renmore Barracks, Galway

PHOTO COURTESY OF PAT VAUGHAN

Barracks in 1920, served as an outpost at **Scramogue**, and, during the Civil War, was present for the **attack on Free State forces at Lake Forbes** in March 1923

"Birdie" Reynolds (Mullagh, Ruskey) a member of the Kilglass Company in the 3rd Battalion North Roscommon

Brigid Reynolds (Coosan, Co. Westmeath) served as the Captain of the Cumann na mBan in the Coosan area

Dominick Reynolds (Ballyglass, Ballinaheglish) a member of Ballinaheglish Coy. in the 2nd Battalion South Roscommon

George Reynolds (Knockhall, Ruskey) a member of the Kilglass Company in the 3rd Battalion North Roscommon. During the Civil War he was arrested on 8 September 1922 for Anti-Treaty activities, and taken to Athlone 14 November

James Reynolds (Kiltultogue, Ballinaheglish) a member of the Ballinaheglish Coy. in the 2nd Battalion South Roscommon, brother of Paddy and Tom. Later in life he became a member of the Garda Síochána

John Reynolds (Lisnalegan, Ballinaheglish) a member of "B" Coy. in the 2nd Battalion South Roscommon

John Reynolds (Ballykilcline, Ruskey) a member of the Kilglass Company in the 3rd Battalion North Roscommon

Michael Reynolds (Lisnalegan, Ballinaheglish) member of Ballinaheglish Coy. in the 2nd Battalion South Roscommon

Michael Reynolds (Ballykilcline, Ruskey) a member of the Kilglass Company in the 3rd Battalion North Roscommon

Paddy Reynolds (Kiltultogue, Ballinaheglish) a member of the Ballinaheglish Coy. in the 2nd Battalion South Roscommon, brother of James and Tom. Dispatch rider who, on one occasion on the way to Donamon, saw the Tans approaching, and put the dispatches in his mouth and fell into the drain. Regarding him as a drunken fool, the Tans laughingly passed him by. He acted as a scout and lookout for the **Fourmilehouse Ambush**. When the Western Division was formed, he volunteered to serve with the Oran Battalion Flying Column. Later emigrated to New York

Patrick Reynolds (Coolmeen, Elphin) 2nd Battalion North Roscommon, Creeve Coy. Although involved with the Volunteers since 1917, Patrick was officially sworn in on 19 June 1919. He drilled with his men, raided for arms, and helped in the organisation of Sinn Féin Clubs. Engaged in the **burning of Hillstreet Barracks, ambush of Elphin RIC** on 5 January 1921, and the **attack on Elphin Barracks** 11 February 1921. Served as the supply officer for camps in the area during the Truce. Arrested on 13 July 1922, and detained in Athlone Military Barracks for several weeks. Died in the 1930s

Thomas Reynolds (Kiltultogue, Ballinaheglish) brother of James and Paddy. When the Western Division was formed, he served as 2nd Lieutenant of "B" Coy., 2nd Battalion South Roscommon. Emigrated to the United States

Thomas Reynolds (Knockhall, Ruskey) a member of the Kilglass Company in the 3rd Battalion North Roscommon

Thomas Roarke (Cloverhill Coy.) 2nd Battalion South Roscommon

Edward Robinson (Kilnamanagh, Ballinameen) Captain of Breedogue Company in the 1st Battalion North Roscommon

John J. Robinson (Moneenbog, Tarmonbarry) Captain of Ruskey Coy. in the 3rd Battalion North Roscommon. Organised and trained sixty-five men from 1917-1918. Did house to house canvassing for the pleblecite for complete independence, raided the Shannon boats for petrol (and sank a few), raided at Drews Wood for arms, and the mails between Ruskey and Dromod. Constructed dugouts, collected for Dáil loan, and was forced to go on the run on 29 September 1920. Robinson participated in the **Scramogue Ambush** in March 1921, and the **attack on Tarmonbarry Barracks** in early July. During the Truce he attended camps at Strokestown and Mantua, where he contracted a nasty case of scabies. In February

John J. Robinson, Captain of Ruskey Coy.

1922 he **took over the Ruskey Barracks** from the RIC, which he held until May of that year. During the ensuing Civil War, he took the Anti-Treaty side, and assisted Jack Healy's Flying Column by supplying food, clothing, and ammunition. He also sniped at the Ruskey military station. "On Christmas Day of 1922, broken in mind and body," he came home

Celia Roche (Carrowcully, Ballinameen), mother of Jack and Michael. Her home was the headquarters of Sean Connolly when he first came to North Roscommon to organise the Volunteer Companies. She **sheltered Jim Molloy after his escape from Boyle Barracks**, and her property was the site of a dugout used by men on the run. Her home was often raided by the Tans (and for good reason). She and her sons made the cartbox mines used in numerous operations. Celia was quick-thinking as well as hard working. During one raid by the Tans who were looking for her sons, the mines were lying on the bed for all to see. She quickly flipped up the blankets and covered them! She died 9 March 1959, and is buried in Elphin Cemetery

John Roche (Bogganfin, Athlone) served with the Bealnamullia Coy., 3rd Battalion Athlone Brigade during the Civil War. He harassed the Free State troopers by blocking roads at Larkfield and Bealnamullia, assisting the Flying Column at blocking a road near Curraghboy, aiding prisoners to escape and join their various units, storing and transporting arms and explosives when and where required by the Flying Column, and serving as an outpost guard for the Column to ensure their safety. He was arrested on 18 November 1922, and sent to Athlone. He was released three months later on 23 February 1923

John "Jack" Roche (Carrowcully) Ballinameen Coy. in the 1st Battalion North Roscommon, whose home always provided a meal and shelter for Volunteers on the run, including Sean Connolly who came from Longford to organise the Roscommon men. Jack was a blacksmith by trade, who used those skills to make cartbox mines for the Volunteers. Took part in the **attack on the Elphin Dispensary** on 13 December 1920, the **attack on Elphin Barracks** 11 February 1921, and the **attack on the patrol at the Deanery** 23 March 1921. He was burned as a result of the **torching of the Barracks and Courthouse at Frenchpark** in June 1921. When the Civil War swept over Roscommon, he was a member of the North Roscommon Anti-Treaty Active Service Unit (Flying Column), and also worked with the Arigna Flying Column. He was arrested, along with John Kelly, while bicycling at Rathallen Crossroads at 3:30 a.m. on 3 August 1923. After the War he emigrated to Buffalo, New York, where he worked as a bricklayer until his retirement. Died 1 March 1982, and buried in Buffalo

Michael Roche (Carrowcully) Ballinameen Coy. in the 1st Battalion North Roscommon, brother of Jack. He too was a blacksmith, who constructed bombs for the Volunteers. He took part in the **attack on Frenchpark Barracks and Courthouse** in June 1921. Michael joined the Free State Army, but deserted with barracks' equipment in tow. He became a member of the Anti-Treaty Active Service Unit during the Civil War, and was its chief armourer. He spent part of the Civil War in north Roscommon and the Sligo hills fighting the Free State forces. He was arrested and interned. After the War he moved to Thurles, where he owned a sweetshop. Died 14 October 1967, and buried in Thurles, Co. Tipperary

Christy Rock (Castlerea) 1st Battalion South Roscommon. Interned for his Sinn Féin sympathies. His image is included along with other prisoners in a picture taken at Ballykinlar Camp in County Down (see page 400). He sounded the Last Post at the Memorial Mass for John Vaughan and Ned Shannon, who were killed in Cloonsuck in June 1921

Edward Roddy (Ballindollaghan, Castleplunkett) a member of Castleplunkett Coy., 2nd Battalion South Roscommon

Rev. James Roddy (Breedogue) a member of the Sinn Féin Executive in North Roscommon. Father Roddy served as a curate in Strokestown (1918-1919),

Celia Roche.
PHOTO COURTESY OF CATHERINE KEARNS

John "Jack" Roche, Ballinameen.
PHOTO COURTESY OF CATHERINE KEARNS

Michael Roche, Ballinameen.
PHOTO COURTESY OF CATHERINE KEARNS

Breedogue in Ballinameen parish (1919-1920), and Geevagh, Co. Sligo (1921-1928). He acted as the receiving agent in Strokestown for the funds collected when the Dáil loan was floated. While stationed at Breedogue, he was arrested at a meeting in Croghan in November 1920, tried and court-martialled, and held in Boyle Military Barracks for several weeks. During the Civil War Father Roddy was instrumental in negotiating a cease-fire for a meeting held in Ballyfarnon on 6 August 1922 between Flying Column leaders Ned Bofin and Harold McBrien and the Free State Commandants Mitchell and Andy Lavin. Unfortunately, the meeting did not prove successful. Father Roddy later served in Riverstown parish until his death in 1953

Luke Roddy (Clooneybrennan, Elphin) 2nd Battalion North Roscommon. Participated in the **attack on Elphin Barracks** 11 February 1921, and the **attack on the patrol at the Deanery** on 23 March 1921

Michael Roddy (Cloonsreane, Strokestown) North Roscommon Brigade. Served as Adjutant for "C" Company. Participated in the **attack on Elphin Barracks** 11 February 1921

P. Roddy (Ballindollaghan, Castleplunkett) a member of the Castleplunkett Coy., 2nd Battalion South Roscommon, brother of Edward

Pat Roddy (Finisclin, Ballinameen) is listed as the Quartermaster for "D" Company (Breedogue) in the 1st Battalion North Roscommon

Patrick Roddy (Drumnalasson, Ballaghaderreen) one of the first members of the Ballaghaderreen Coy. in the East Mayo Brigade. During the Civil War he was arrested for hiding Anti-Treaty men, and taken to Athlone on 31 March 1923. After the War he became a farmer in Creevy. Roddy attended the Pat Glynn Memorial Service in Loughglynn in 1971. Died 1987, buried in Lisacul Cemetery

Thomas Roddy (Lisacul) during the Civil War he fought on the Anti-Treaty side, and was arrested and sent to Athlone on 15 March 1923. At the time of his capture, he was accompanied by E. Colligan of Belfast, a Lewis gunner in Frank Carty's Column in Sligo

Dominick Rogers (Cornamaddy, Ballymurray, Roscommon) 4th Battalion South Roscommon, brother of Tom. The Company was formed in 1917 with Patrick Kelly serving as Captain. Rogers drilled with the Volunteers, and attended practice battles at Taughmaconnell overseen by Ernie O'Malley in the summer of 1918. Participated in the South Roscommon election of 1918. He, along with the rest of his Company, **guarded the village of Knockcroghery from reprisal on 15 August 1920** — a reprisal precipitated by British Forces being fired upon on Lough Ree. He also participated in the **attempted ambush of a military lorry in Knockcroghery** in January 1921

Dominick Rogers (Runnamoat, Ballinaheglish) 2nd Battalion South, in whose home many Republican Courts and Brigade meetings were held. The cottage was owned by the Naughton family. After the War he became a postman in the Ballinaheglish area

James Rogers (Cloonfad Coy.) 1st Battalion South. Participated in the **destruction of vacant barracks** in 1920, and attended training camps during the Truce

Joe Rogers (Loughglynn) 1st Battalion South Roscommon Brigade. Served with the Loughglynn Coy. from April 1918 to July 1922. Arrested and interned at the Curragh. After the War he emigrated to Cleveland, Ohio

John Rogers (Ardnamullagh, Ballintubber) a member of "F" Coy. in the 2nd Battalion, No. 2 Brigade in the 2nd Western Division. Took part in the **attack on Frenchpark Barracks** 2 October 1920

John Rogers (Cordrummon, Kiltrustan, Strokestown) a member of the Kiltrustan Coy. in the 3rd Battalion North Roscommon

Patrick Rogers (Ballinlough Coy.) 1st Battalion South Roscommon

Tom Rogers (Loughglynn) served as the first drill instructor of the Loughglynn Company in 1917. He had been a member of the British Army

Tom Rogers (Cornamaddy, Ballymurray, Roscommon) Knockcroghery Coy., 4th Battalion South Roscommon. The Knockcroghery Coy. was formed in 1917 under the leadership of Patrick Kelly of Culleen, Lecarrow. Rogers paraded with the

Volunteers and participated in the weekly drills. He participated in the sham battles overseen by Ernie O'Malley at Taughmaconnell in the summer of 1918. He also participated in the South Roscommon election of 1918, served as an armed escort for bank officials taking sums of money to fairs in Knockcroghery, and was present at the **burning of Lecarrow Barracks**. He raided many houses for arms. On one occasion, the daylight raid of an ex-RIC man succeeded in yielding a shotgun, revolver, and, best of all, an RIC uniform. On another occasion, he was with the party that raided two hostile houses in the Rahara district in which one of the Volunteers was slightly wounded. On another raid, the Volunteers were one step ahead of the RIC who, a few hours later, visited the same houses to collect the same guns. Took part in the **attempted attack at Kilmurray Camp** in June 1920, and the **attempted attack at Clooncraff** under the command of Pat Madden. Rogers was one of ten Volunteers who arrested, tried, and sentenced a local man for firing at and wounding a Volunteer. He, along with the rest of his Company, **guarded the village of Knockcroghery** from reprisal on 15 August 1920 — a reprisal precipitated by British Forces being fired upon on Lough Ree. Rogers took part in the **attempted attack** on a party of military about eighteen strong **at Knockcroghery** in January 1921, and the **attempted ambush at Scrine**. He collected the IRA levy from the local people. Rogers also assisted in destroying a wagonload of Northern Ireland mill goods at Roscommon Railway Station. He took part in the attempt to **blow up the bridge at Farnaseer**, and the **burning of O'Brien's home in Curraghboy** — a house the Company feared would soon be occupied by British Forces. Rogers was one of a few men entrusted with carrying important dispatches during this time. After the Truce, he was appointed to a special services unit

Thomas Rouane (Corglass, Keadue) 4th Battalion North Roscommon

Knox Roughneen (Kiltimagh, Mayo) was part of the group of Anti-Treaty men who **took over the Boyle Barracks** at the start of the Civil War. He was wounded on 1 July attempting to attack the Boyle workhouse, and was imprisoned in Connolly Barracks in Longford

Michael Ronan (Dunmore Coy. in Galway) was arrested after the Rising in 1916, and, when released, helped to form the Dunmore Company of Volunteers of which he served as Captain for a time. He also organised the Dunmore Sinn Féin Club. Dunmore Coy. became part of No. 2 Brigade, 2nd Western Division

William Roundtree (Rowntree) (Main St., Castlerea) during the Civil War he fought on the Anti-Treaty side, and was arrested 21 July 1922, and sent to Athlone on 2 September 1922

Michael Rourke (Carrick-on-Shannon) during the Civil War he fought on the Anti-Treaty side, and was sent to Athlone on 14 November 1922

Patrick Rourke (Ballyboughan, Roscommon) a member of the 1918 Sinn Féin election committee for South Roscommon

Thomas Rourke (O'Rourke) (Tonlegee, Fourmilehouse) a member of Cloverhill Coy. in the 2nd Battalion South Roscommon

William Rourke (Emlaghyroyin, Donamon) a member of "E" Coy. in the 2nd Battalion South Roscommon

Michael Rushe (Ballymurry, Mantua, Elphin) joined the IRA on 20 January 1917. He attended meetings, assisted in the Count Plunkett election, and raided for arms and ammunition. He was one of eight officers selected for advanced training in the use of firearms. He then taught the new recruits the fundamentals of loading, firing, and caring for a gun. He always had a stash of rifles and shotguns stored at his house for Volunteer use. Rushe was on armed outpost duty for the **attack on Elphin Barracks** on 11 February 1921, as well as the **attack on Frenchpark Courthouse** in June of that year. He attended the Cloonshee training camp for a week, did police duty in the Battalion area, and assisted in enforcing the boycott of Belfast banks and goods. During the Civil War he **attacked a group of Free State troops headed to Boyle** on 2 July. In October of 1922, he came under fire delivering dispatches to the Active Service Unit. During all this time, he faithfully stored and kept clean the guns and ammunition hidden in his home

Bernard Ryan (Annaghmacoolen, Cloone, Co. Leitrim) was on the staff of the 5th Battalion in the 3rd Western Division. He worked in conjunction with Pat Brennan and the North Roscommon Brigade Staff

Eugene Ryan (Blackfallow, Crossna, Boyle) 4th Battalion North Roscommon

James Ryan (Rathmoyle, Lisalway, Castleplunkett) a member of the Castleplunkett Coy., 2nd Battalion South Roscommon, brother of John

PHOTO COURTESY OF SEAN RAFTERY
PHOTO RESTORATION BY LEW THORNE

John Ryan (Rathmoyle, Lisalway, Castleplunkett) Captain of Castleplunkett Company in the 2nd Battalion South Roscommon, arrested after the 1916 Easter Rising and sent to Lewes Gaol. Upon release, he returned home to participate as Vice O/C of the Battalion. He took part in the **raid on the military train at Ballymoe** in June 1920, the **attack on Frenchpark Barracks** 2 October 1920, and the **ambush at Southpark, Castlerea** 10 July 1921. He also volunteered to serve with the Oran Battalion Flying Column. While on the run, he continued to attend Mass at Kilmurray Church. One Sunday the Black and Tans surrounded the chapel, arrested John, and began questioning him. The local landlord and sheriff, Colonel Irwin, walked confidently up to the Tans and ordered that John be set free. He was!* On 4 September 1922, he, along with Paddy Devaney and William Kellegher, broke into shops in Frenchpark and commandeered boots and whiskey — both soothing remedies for cold Irish nights! Later he emigrated to Leeds, England, but returned to Ireland, where he lived in Tarmon. He is buried in Castlerea Cemetery

Sean Raftery, interview by author, Valeview, Lisalway, 14 August 2004.

Martin Ryan Vice Commandant of the Glenamaddy Battalion, which was part of No. 2 Brigade, 2nd Western Division under Brigade O/C Gerald O'Connor. In 1921 Martin became part of the ASU formed with the Tuam Battalion area

Patrick Ryan (Cremully, Athleague) a member of the Athleague Company in the 3rd Battalion South Roscommon

Patrick J. Ryan (Ballaghaderreen town) Head Centre for the IRB, arrested after the 1916 Rising, and sent to Lewes Gaol on 20 May 1916. He ended his visit to the bigger isle with a stint in Frongoch, "The Irish University"

Seamus Ryan (Bridge Street, Strokestown) joined the Irish Volunteers the first year of their formation. His job entailed travelling, so he remained unattached to a particular Company until 1917, when he took up residence in Strokestown and formed the Strokestown Company. At a meeting in Croghan in early 1918, Seamus was elected the Brigade Commandant. He was arrested in October 1918, and imprisoned in Galway Gaol until May 1919. He made all the arrangements for the Brigade for the **burning of vacant barracks** throughout the area on Easter morning 1920. He also made arrangements for the **burning of income tax papers** in May 1920, as well as other vacant barracks outside his specific area. He travelled to Dublin on numerous occasions to negotiate the purchase of arms for the area. Due to ill health and the demands of his travelling job, he resigned his position in January 1921, whereupon Michael Dockery, at a meeting in Hillstreet at the end of that month, was elected Brigadier of North Roscommon. Seamus was selected as Vice O/C of the Brigade, and held that position until he resigned in August 1921. He participated in the **Strokestown Ambush** in January 1921. Through his instigation, the bomb-making workshop in Ballinameen was established. After the Truce he took the Anti-Treaty side in the Civil War, and continued to serve as Intelligence Officer. Seamus was again arrested in December 1922, and detained for a few days at Boyle before being released. He was on the first Sinn Féin Council. After the War he became the treasurer of Elphin Fianna Fáil *comhairle ceanntair* in 1926

Tommy Ryan (Quartermaster of the Glenamaddy Battalion) which was part of No. 2 Brigade, 2nd Western Division. In 1921 he became part of the ASU formed with the Tuam Battalion area

— Ryan (Ballinameen) 1st Battalion North Roscommon. Drill instructor in the Boyle area

William Ryan 2nd Lieutenant of the Kilcroan Coy. in the Glenamaddy Battalion. Located in Co. Galway, this Battalion was incorporated into the No. 2 Brigade, 2nd Western Division with Gerald O'Connor, former O/C of the 1st Battalion South Roscommon, serving as Brigade Commandant. Ryan's home was used as the headquarters of "D" Company

Fr. Edward Ryans (Aghabehy, Arigna) his father was the manager of the Arigna Mining Company, while his brother, Vincent, served as a member of the Arigna Flying Column. Fr. Ryans worked with the Column and aided them. Captured by the Free State on 31 March 1923 at Knockranny House in Keadue. After the cease-fire, Father's sympathies remained with the Anti-Treaty men. He was arrested in July 1925 in connection with an arms dump, and re-arrested again in the autumn of that same year. Father later emigrated to Scotland

Vincent Ryans (Knockranny House) Vice O/C of the 4th Battalion North Roscommon, brother of Father Ryans, a member of the Arigna Anti-Treaty Flying Column during the Civil War. He participated in the **demolition of the Knockvicar and Cootehall Bridges** on 14 August 1922

Albert Ryder (Cornaseer) Kiltoom Coy. in the 4th Battalion South Roscommon. Ryder was wounded in an **ambush of Crown Forces at Cloonark** on Ballinasloe Rd.

Jack Ryder, Quartermaster of Carniska Coy.
PHOTO COURTESY OF HENRY OWENS

Jack Ryder (Cloonlyons, Strokestown) listed in the GHQ papers in the UCD Archives as the Quartermaster of Carniska Company in the 3rd Battalion North Roscommon. After the War he became a farmer. Died 1977

Michael Ryder (Cloonlyons, Strokestown) a member of the Carniska Coy., 3rd Battalion North Roscommon, brother of Jack

Joe Satchwell (Termon Beg, Castlerea) 1st Lieutenant of Moor Coy. in the 1st Battalion South Roscommon. Participated in the **attack on the Frenchpark Barracks** 2 October 1920, the **attempted ambushes at Castlerea** and **Frenchpark** in January 1921, the **attempted ambush at Cloonsheever** in March 1921, and the **attempted ambush at Loughglynn** in April 1921. He was a member of the Active Service Unit formed in January of 1921. A former British soldier who was taken prisoner during the shootout at **The Woodlands of Loughglynn**, he was placed in Athlone Barracks, where he was recognised by Mr. Morris as a former member of the British Army, and thus was saved from more severe punishment. Sentenced to fifteen years. Died 30 April 1974. Buried Castlerea Cemetery

Joe Satchwell, Moor Coy., Castlerea.

Tom Satchwell (Cloonbard, Kilmurray, Castlerea) Moor Coy., 1st Battalion South Roscommon. Participated in the **destruction of vacant barracks** in 1920, the **attempted attack on Kilmurray Military Camp** in June 1920, the **attack on the Frenchpark Barracks** 2 October 1920, the **attempted ambushes at Castlerea** and **Frenchpark** in January 1921, and served in the covering party in the **attack on the military at Castlerea** 7 April 1921. He was a member of the Active Service Unit formed in January of 1921. He took the Anti-Treaty side in the Civil War, and participated in the **burning of the train at Clooncundra** in November 1922, and the **attack at Castlerea**. He was present for the Pat Glynn Memorial Service at Loughglynn Church in 1970

Patrick Saul (Tobervaddy, Fuerty) a member of "D" (Fuerty) Coy. in the 2nd Battalion South Roscommon

Patrick Scahill (Kilmurray, Lisalway, Castlerea) Castleplunkett Coy., 2nd Battalion South Roscommon. Participated in the **raid on the military train at Ballymoe** in June 1920, the **attack on Frenchpark Barracks** 2 October 1920, and the **ambush at Southpark, Castlerea** 10 July 1921. As an older man, he suffered ill health due to the wet cold nights in which he had to sleep out during those years in the early 1920s.* Died 1 March 1957

*Sean Raftery, resident of Lisalway, correspondence with author, 7 January 2005.

Patrick Scahill, Castleplunkett Coy.
PHOTO COURTESY OF SEAN RAFTERY

John Scally (Gallagh, Cloontuskert, Ballyleague) 2nd Lieutenant of Cloontuskert Coy. in 3rd Battalion South Roscommon. Died as a result of the **Lanesboro-**

Roscommon Landmine Operation. After the explosion at Cloontymullen, he was taken to a safe house on Incheneagh Island in Lough Ree, where he failed to notify the attending doctor, Dr. Dudley Forde of Strokestown, that he had a slight scratch. He later died of blood poisoning on 21 May 1921. Buried secretly in Kilteevan Cemetery. After the Truce he was re-interred in Cloontuskert Abbey Cemetery. A Celtic cross monument to his memory was erected and dedicated in 1934 at Beechwood. His name appears on the tablets in front of the Shankill Monument near Elphin

John Scally (Portnahinch, Cloontuskert, Ballyleague) who, in May 1921, rowed the body of another Volunteer of the same name from Incheneagh Island to Clooneigh, where the casket was quietly born to Kilteevan graveyard

Michael Scally (Cloonfree, Strokestown) Company Captain in the 3rd Battalion North Roscommon, brother of Stephen

Michael Scally (Carrowbehy, Gortaganny, Loughglynn) Ballinlough Coy., 1st Battalion South Roscommon. Participated in the **attempted ambush at Coshlieve** in July 1920, the **attempted attack on the Castlerea Station Guard** in July 1920, the **burning of the barracks at Loughglynn**, and the **burning of the Ballinlough Barracks** 14 September 1920. He also took part in the **attempted ambush at Lisacul** (in conjunction with the East Mayo men) in May 1921. During the Truce he attended the Battalion training camp specialising in dispatch work. He died before the 1940s

Paddy Scally (Ross Lane, Boyle) Connaught Ranger, who took part in the Indian Mutiny of 1920. Sentenced to ten years penal servitude in Maidstone Prison. Later joined the Garda Síochána

Peter Scally (Balytoohey) a member of Tarmonbarry Coy., 3rd Battalion North Roscommon

Stephen Scally (Cloonfree, Strokestown) 3rd Battalion North Roscommon. Scally joined the IRB in August 1916, and, a year later, the Volunteers, where he was attached to "J" Coy. He attended weekly meetings, raided for arms, and did duty at polling booths during the 1918 election. He served as the 2nd Lieutenant of the Cloonfree Company. In June 1920, he spent six days and nights with his Company making preparations for an **attack on Tulsk Barracks** (which was unexpectedly vacated before the attack could take place). Took part in the **attempt to burn down the Bridewell at Strokestown** in July 1920, an action which resulted in his being severely burned. His injuries required an eleven week stay in the hospital, but he left before he was fully recovered in order to continue his military duties. Those activities resulted in his being arrested on 22 December 1920, and sentenced to ten years in Mountjoy, Wormwood Scrubbs, and Dartmoor Prisons. He was released in the general amnesty on 18 January 1922, but bore the scars of his Strokestown Courthouse misadventure for life

Thomas "Toby" Scally (Driney, Loughglynn) a member of the 1st Battalion South Roscommon Flying Column. He, along with Ned Shannon and Patrick McCarthy, **burned the RIC Barracks at Loughglynn**. He participated in the **attack on the Frenchpark Barracks** 2 October 1920. He was part of the **ambush party at Lisacul** in May — an action taken in conjunction with the East Mayo Brigade men. Toby was wounded in the **battle of The Woodlands of Loughglynn**, after which he limped to Crean's house in

---

Oration for Toby Scally

Given by Commandant Gerald O'Connor
22 February 1971

Before we leave here, my comrades of the Old IRA have asked me to speak on their behalf about the man we have buried and the character he was. I have known Toby all my life and can speak intimately of some of the aspects of his character which made him liked and respected by all.

Toby joined the National Volunteer Army in 1913. When these divided at the outbreak of the First World War, he followed the Irish Volunteers led by Padraig Pearse. In 1919 the members of this body took an oath of allegiance to the Republic proclaimed by the first Dáil Éireann and from then on they were known as the IRA. Toby served in this army until he was taken prisoner in 1923. He was held a prisoner until the end of the Civil War and after taking part in a long hunger strike he was released in 1924 and returned home. Soon after he was offered a job as postman in Loughglynn which he accepted and held until he retired a few years ago.

Toby was not the wild gunman type that some may have imagined. He was an honest, kindly soul with a very good sense of humour which always made him good company. He never spoke harshly of anybody and I never heard an ugly word from his lips.

He was by nature the soldier type — he thought like a soldier, he acted like a soldier, and, quite unconsciously, he had the carriage and measured step of a well-trained army man. When the Civil War broke out, some of us resigned from the IRA rather than become involved, but for Toby there was no crisis of conscience. His simple reasoning was that he had sworn an oath to defend the Republic against all enemies — foreign and domestic, and this he did while he was able.

We must leave his body now to moulder in the grave, but surely "his soul will go marching on" to join the gallant Company of comrades who have gone before him. To his sisters and relatives we tender our sympathy, and pray that his soul and the souls of all the faithful departed may rest in peace.

Go ndéanaidh Dia trócaire ar a anam.

Moyne, and was then taken to Reilly Gallagher's cottage. Dr. Clarke attended to
his wounds. Toby was also a member of the Republican Police force in the
Loughglynn area. When the split in the IRA came, he fought with the Anti-
Treaty forces in County Mayo during the Civil War, where he served with Seamus
Mulrennan's Flying Column. Toby took part in the **attack at Ballinagare** in July
1922, the **burning of the train at Clooncundra**, and **attack at Castlerea** in
November 1922. He was arrested in 1923 by the Free State troops, and interned in
Castlebar, where he went on hunger strike for eighteen days. Later sent to
Mountjoy. He was released on 18 December 1923. His gun, which was the symbol
of resistance to British rule, was smuggled to America by Pat Vaughan of
Cloonsuck after the War, but later returned to Ireland, where it now hangs on the
wall of Hell's Kitchen pub in Castlerea. After the War Toby became a postman.
He died 20 February 1971, and is buried in Cuiltyboe Cemetery near Loughglynn

William Scally (Willsgrove) Ballintubber Coy. in the 2nd Battalion South
Roscommon. Took part in the **attack on Frenchpark Barracks** 2 October 1920.
After the War he farmed his land. Died 10 April 1968, and buried in Ballintubber
Cemetery

Andrew Scanlon (Ballinderry, Fourmilehouse) a member of the Kilbride Coy., 3rd
Battalion South Roscommon

John Scanlon (Quarry Lane, Boyle) 1st Battalion North Roscommon. He was
taken into the IRB by Alec McCabe in February 1915. A member of the
Volunteers before the Rising

Michael Scanlon, sentenced after the *'conacre take over'* in Boyle, active in land
agitation

Pat Scanlon (Drumfin, Ballymote, Co. Sligo) Adjutant of the 1st Battalion North Roscommon. After the 3rd Western Division was formed (joining Sligo, North Roscommon, and Leitrim into a larger military unit), Scanlon served in the same capacity (Adjutant for the 1st Battalion). He was interned in 1922

Sean Scanlon (Athlone) Captain of the Athlone Company, who trained his men in 1918 in the Coosan area. In 1918 he was appointed the Vice O/C of the Athlone Battalion

Tom Scanlon (Carrickbanagher, Ballymote) a member of the ASU in Sligo during the Civil War. Sniped along the Border until March 1922 when his unit was recalled. **Burned Sligo Barracks** in July 1922. He captured an armoured car in the **Rockwood Ambush** of 13 July. Scanlon was arrested 18 July 1922. He was finally released on 21 December 1923

Bridget Seery (Cloonillan, Drum, Athlone) sister of Tom, a member of the Summerhill Cumann na mBan club in South Roscommon

Michael Seery (Seary) (Walderstown, Athlone) during the Civil War he took the Anti-Treaty side. Arrested on 8 August 1922 and sent to Athlone on 2 September

Tom Seery (Cloonillan, Drum, Athlone) a member of Drum Coy., 3rd Battalion Athlone Brigade. He took the Oath of Allegiance to the Sinn Féin party at the Ardkeenan House, the local Volunteer gathering point*

*_Drum and Its Hinterland_ by Edward Egan, p. 301.

James Shallow (Tonlegee, Fourmilehouse, Roscommon) served as Quartermaster of "A" Coy. (Cloverhill) in the 2nd Battalion South Roscommon

Patrick Shallow (Tonlegee, Fourmilehouse, Roscommon) a member of the Cloverhill Coy., 2nd Battalion South Roscommon, brother of James

James Shally (Cloverhill Coy.) 2nd Battalion South Roscommon

Patrick Shanagher (Willsgrove, Ballintubber) a member of "F" Coy., 2nd Battalion South Roscommon

Thomas Shanagher (Corbally West, Creeve, Elphin) 2nd Battalion North Roscommon. Served as 2nd Lieut. for "F" Company (Aughrim)

Edward Shanley (Knockhall, Ruskey) member of Kilglass Company in the 3rd Battalion North Roscommon. Took part in the **attack near Ruskey village** on 5 July 1921. During the Civil War he was arrested for Anti-Treaty activities on 6 September 1922. Sent to Athlone on 14 November. Released a few days later

Patrick Shanley (Knockhall, Ruskey) a member of the Kilglass Company in the 3rd Battalion North Roscommon. Took part in the **attack near Ruskey village** on 5 July 1921. During the Civil War he took the Anti-Treaty side, and was arrested with his brother, Edward, on 6 September 1922, and sent to Athlone on 14 November 1922

Thomas Shanley (Knockhall, Ruskey) a member of the Kilglass Company in the 3rd Battalion North Roscommon, brother of Patrick and Edward

Thomas Shanley (Clooneagh, Dromod, Leitrim) O/C of the 5th Battalion, which was attached to North Roscommon as part of the 3rd Brigade, 3rd Western Division. He took the Anti-Treaty side during the Civil War, and was arrested on 5 March 1923 in Ruskey. His unit had attacked the barracks and had the Civic Guards out on the street with all their kits. The Guards were in the process of being stripped of their uniforms, when a cycling patrol of National soldiers, under the command of Captain Lenehan, happened upon the scene. Shanley was badly wounded in the ensuing gunfight, and Captain Lenehan received a slight wound in the knee. Shanley was shipped to Athlone on 26 September 1922. After the War he became a rate collector in Co. Leitrim

Edward "Ned" Shannon (Aghaderry, Loughglynn) 1st Battalion South Roscommon. Participated in the **attempted attack on Kilmurray Camp** in June 1920. He, along with Toby Scally and Patrick McCarthy, **burned the RIC barracks at Loughglynn** in early September 1920. He also participated in the

Monument at Loughglynn.

destruction of other vacant barracks during that year, the **raid for petrol at Ballinlough Station** in June 1920, the **attack on Frenchpark Barracks** 2 October 1920, the **attempted attacks on Castlerea** and **Frenchpark** in January 1921, and the **attempted ambush at Cloonsheever** in March. April 1921 was an eventful month for Ned. He was part of the covering party in the **attack on the military in Castlerea** on 7 April, was present for the **attempted ambush at Loughglynn**, and assisted Toby Scally in his escape from **the Woodlands of Loughglynn** on 19 April. The next month Shannon participated in the **attempted ambush at Lisacul** (in conjunction with the East Mayo men), and the **attempted ambush of RIC patrol near Ballymoe**. He was killed by the Tans at the Vaughan house in the village of Cloonsuck on 22 June 1921. Buried Kilruane Cemetery, Lisacul. Name inscribed on the tablets in front of the Shankill Monument near Elphin, as well as the Monument at Loughglynn

John Shannon (Brackloon, Castlerea) Moor Coy., 1st Battalion South Roscommon. Joined the Company in 1918, and became a member of the Active Service Unit formed in January of 1921. He drilled with his Company, and enforced the Belfast boycott. Participated in the **destruction of vacant barracks** in 1920, the **attempted attack on Kilmurray Military Camp** in June 1920, **attack on Frenchpark Barracks** 2 October 1920, the **attempted ambushes at Castlerea** and the successful **attack at Castlerea** in January 1921, the **attempted ambush at Cloonsheever** in March, the **attempted ambush at Loughglynn** in April 1921, the **attempted ambush at Lisacul** in May 1921 (in conjunction with the East Mayo Brigade), the **attempted ambush of RIC patrol near Ballymoe** that same month, and the successful **ambush at Southpark, Castlerea** 10 July 1921. Civil War record includes **attack at Ballinagare** in July 1922, **attack on Free State forces at Castlerea** in November 1922, and the **burning of the train at Clooncundra** during that same month. He later emigrated to Manchester, England

Michael Shannon (Lissaphuca, Tulsk) 2nd Battalion North Roscommon. Listed in the GHQ papers in the UCD Archives as the Quartermaster of Tulsk Company

Pat Shannon (Aghaderry, Loughglynn) brother of Ned and Pete, a member of the 1st Battalion South Roscommon Brigade. He was sent to the Castlerea garrison with the message that the RIC were responsible for his brother's near death condition in the Connor house in Aghadrestan, and the British military should be responsible for hospital care. His efforts saved his brother's life

(above left) Gerald O'Connor unveiling a memorial plaque honouring John Vaughan and Ned Shannon.

(above) The Monument at Loughglynn, on which is written:
"In affectionate memory of
Patrick Glynn
Michael Carty
Ned Shannon
Michael Glavey
Michael Keane
Stephen McDermott
Sean Bergin
John Vaughan
Paddy Flynn
Patrick Conry
That died in the fight for the Irish Republic
1920-21"

Pete Shannon (Aghaderry, Loughglynn) 1st Battalion South Roscommon. Shot 2 June 1921 by the Tans at the home of the O'Connors in Aghadrestan. He was later taken to Athlone Hospital, where seven bullets were extracted from his body. An eighth bullet had pierced his jaw and vocal chords — an injury which caused him to speak with a distinctively raspy voice for the rest of his life. He was sentenced to fifteen years penal servitude, and sent to Mountjoy Prison, where he remained until January 1922. After the War he became a Rate Collector with the Roscommon County Council. Died in the 1970s. Buried in Kilruane Cemetery, Lisacul

The Shannon Family (of Aghaderry, Loughglynn) who spent the summer of 1921 in an out building because the Crown Forces had burned their house to the ground. Three of their sons were active Volunteers

Tommy Shannon (Oldtown, Ballinameen, Boyle) 1st Battalion North Roscommon. He was a member of the Anti-Treaty Active Service Unit (Flying Column) during the Civil War. He died before 1940

Lena Sharkey (Drinaun, Strokestown) sister of Una. See Mrs. Lena O'Doherty

Patrick Sharkey (Liserpool, Ballaghaderreen) during the Civil War he took the Anti-Treaty side. Captured on 14 September 1922. He was sent to Athlone 14 November

Peter Sharkey (Edmondstown, Ballaghaderreen, Co. Mayo) was a member of Monasteraden Coy. in Mayo. He was fired upon in September 1922 by Anti-Treaty Forces who had ordered him out of town because he had sided with the Free State government. As a result of this attack, Sharkey was badly wounded

Thomas Sharkey (Ballaghaderreen) one of the first members of the Ballaghaderreen Coy. in the East Mayo Brigade, a coach builder by trade

Thomas Sharkey (Ballinadure, Roscommon) during the Civil War he took the Anti-Treaty side, and was arrested on 13 July 1922 and sent to Athlone on 14 November 1922. Thomas was transferred to Newbridge; released on 19 December 1923

Rev. Canon Timothy Sharkey (Boyle) who warned the Volunteers in November 1920 that a raid was to occur in the Ballinameen area. As a result of such warning, James Stephen Brennan of Boyle escaped the dragnet

Una Sharkey (Drinaun, Strokestown) along with her sister Lena, owned a shop in Strokestown, where she ardently championed the Volunteer cause. Una was the Brigade O/C for the entire North Roscommon region of Cumann na mBan. Because the Sharkey sisters sold Republican song sheets, their goods were confiscated by the military authorities. Una was interned three times under the Defence of the Realm Act. She held the chair position on Strokestown District Council and Board of Guardians, and was an ex-officio member of Roscommon County Council from 1920 to 1925

Edward "Ned" Shaughnessy (Corbohill, Strokestown) a member of Carniska Coy., 3rd Battalion North Roscommon

John Shaughnessy (Killerr, Ballintubber) Ballintubber Company, 2nd Battalion South Roscommon

Joseph Shaughnessy (Ballymoe) served as 1st Lieutenant of Williamstown Coy. in the Glenamaddy Battalion. Williamstown Coy. was part of No. 2 Brigade, 2nd Western Division with Gerald O'Connor, former O/C of the 1st Battalion South, serving as Brigade Commandant. His Company consisted of thirty members in April of 1922

Martin Shaughnessy (Ballymacurley, Ballinaheglish) member of "B" Coy., 2nd Battalion South Roscommon. Served as a Republican Policeman. After the War he emigrated to the USA. Ned Hegarty, his neighbour and comrade, was the last man in the area to shake his hand before the long voyage

Hugh Sheerin (Sherin) Captain of the Moate Company in the Athlone Brigade

John Sheerin (Sheeran) (Tawnytaskin, Boyle) Vice O/C of the 1st Battalion North Roscommon, Captain of Doon Company. He was taken into the IRB by Alec McCabe in February 1915. John was a member of the Active Service Unit of North Roscommon. He took part in the **Rockingham Raid**, and the **Hopkins**

Raid in Strokestown in mid-February 1921. During the Civil War he took the Anti-Treaty side, and participated in the **demolition of the Knockvicar and Cootehall Bridges** on 14 August 1922. After the War he became a farmer

Joseph Sheerin (The Warren, Boyle) 1st Company in the 1st Battalion North Roscommon Brigade. Later in life became the postmaster. Buried in the Assylin Cemetery in Boyle

Michael Sheerin (Doon, Boyle) Adjutant for Doon Company in the 1st Battalion North Roscommon Brigade

Patrick "Packie" Sheerin (Sherran) (Ardsallagh, Boyle) Doon Company, a member of the original committee to put forth Count Plunkett's name on the North Roscommon ballot. He was taken into the IRB by Alec McCabe in February 1915. Patrick took part in the **Rockingham Raid**, sentenced after **'conacre take-over' in Boyle**. After the War he became a farmer

Tom Shevlin, who originally came from Carrickmacross, Co. Monaghan, became the Strokestown Company Captain in the 3rd Battalion North Roscommon. He was convicted of illegal drilling, and served part of his term in Sligo Gaol. He returned to the area after completing his sentence, and resumed his Volunteer activities. After the Fourmilehouse Ambush, Captain Peake threatened Shevlin with execution unless he left the area immediately (Shevlin had no connection to the ambush). Shevlin locked up his footwear business, only to find that on fair day, 19 October, the Auxiliaries had looted his shop. He remained on the run until the Truce was signed. Died 4 July 1969, and is buried in New Strokestown Cemetery

James Shiel (Cagglestack, Strokestown) the second Company Captain of Carniska Coy. in the 3rd Battalion North Roscommon. Shiel joined the IRA in 1917. He took part in the North Roscommon and Longford elections, paraded twice weekly with his men, and collected arms. Jim's was an "excellent Company," according to Bill Doherty as recorded in the Ernie O'Malley Papers. He participated in a "meeting" to dissuade a man from joining the RIC, and, without British approval, did some "investigation" of British tax papers at Ballyfarnon. Took part in the **destruction of the Ballinderry Barracks**, and, armed with a revolver, the **Castlenode shootout** in November 1920. He participated in the **attack on the Strokestown patrol** in January 1921, where he was in charge of ten men. He secured a shotgun for his part in the **Ambush at Scramogue**, and the **attempted ambush at Tarmonbarry**. In 1922 he became a member of the Garda Síochána, and was stationed in Williamstown, Co. Galway. He retired to Strokestown where, after his death on 24 April 1984, his remains were taken to Strokestown Cemetery

John Shiel (Drinagh, Curraghroe, Strokestown) member of "B" Company in the 3rd Battalion North Roscommon, a carpenter by trade

Martin Shiel (Cagglestack, Strokestown) a member of the Carniska Coy. in the 3rd Battalion North Roscommon, brother of Jim. Took part in the North Roscommon and South Longford elections, attended Company parades, collected funds, carried dispatches. Took part in the **destruction of Ballinderry Barracks**, assisted at Sinn Féin Courts, and was present at the **Castlenode shootout** in November 1920. Served on outpost duty for the **attack at Strokestown** on 6 January 1921 and the **Scramogue Ambush**. After the War he became a farmer. Died 16 February 1966, and buried in Lisonuffy Cemetery

Patrick Shiel (Drinagh, Curraghroe, Strokestown) 2nd Lieutenant of "B" Coy. in the 3rd Battalion North Roscommon, brother of Peter and John. When he first joined the IRA, he participated in drills and local parades as well as duty parades during election time in Longford town, Killashee, Cloondra, and Lanesboro. In 1918 he acted as guard at the polling booth in Ballyleague. He helped to **burn Scramogue Barracks** on 3 April 1920. A month earlier, on 10 March 1920, he had raided the intended RIC recruitment meeting at Cloontuskert. Participated in the **ambush at Drinagh** on 20 July 1920, did protective duty in the Kilgefin area

James Shiel, 2nd Captain of the Carniska Company.

PHOTO COURTESY OF JOHN AND ELIZABETH GREENE

the night of the Fourmilehouse Ambush, present at the **attack at Tarmonbarry** 5 January, the **attempted ambush at Tarmonbarry** on 5 February 1921 (where he and the rest of the men lay in ambush for eighteen hours), and the **attempted ambush** laid for RIC **at Knockhall, Ruskey** in March 1921. He ventured farther afield in collecting arms at Killashee and Racline in Longford. He was a member of the Flying Column in North Roscommon, but was arrested in March 1921 in connection with securing arms for the Scramogue Ambush. He was interned until the general release, after which he returned to rebel deeds

Peter Shiel (Drinagh, Curraghroe, Strokestown) reared in Egan's at Ballybeg, Strokestown. He joined the IRA in 1918 as a member of Carniska Coy. Shiel was present at the **attack at Walpole's** in Castlenode in November 1920, armed with a shotgun, and the **Scramogue Ambush**. Also took part in the prepared ambushes at Tarmonbarry and the **attack on the Barracks in Tarmonbarry** in July 1921. He was a member of the Active Service Unit in charge of the arms dump. Imprisoned in Boyle Barracks. Later joined the Garda Síochána and was stationed in Ennis, County Clare. He retired early in order to manage an insurance company in Athlone. He died 1 September 1983, and is buried in Cornamagh Cemetery in Athlone

Tessie Shiel (Cagglestack, Strokestown) sister of James and Martin, member of Cumann na mBan. She emigrated to the USA in 1925 and married there. She later returned to Ireland in 1966, and is buried in the Strokestown Cemetery

William Shiel (Curraghroe) 1st Lieutenant of "B" (Curraghroe) Company in the 3rd Battalion North Roscommon, took part in the **attack on the RIC patrol at Strokestown** in January 1921. He also commanded the shotgun unit of men at the **attack on the Tarmonbarry patrol** in early July 1921

Johnny Shine (Drum Coy.) a member of Father Flanagan's Sinn Féin Club. After the War he became a farmer and worked for the Land Commission. He was a Fianna Fáil activist

Jolly Shine (Athlone) in the dark of night, he rowed the boat that held James Tormey's body across the Shannon to Clonmacnoise for burial

Peter Shine (Cunny, Clonown) provided a cot to shelter James Tormey's body after he had been killed at the ambush of Cornafulla

Thomas Shine (Rooskagh, Bealnamullia) 3rd Battalion Athlone Brigade. Shine drilled with his Company, trained to use firearms, took an active part in the General Election of 1918, attended Battalion meetings, worked with the Republican Police force at disputed farmland in Bealnamullia and Clongowna. He was with a group of Volunteers that seized ammunition from an airplane that made a forced landing at Keelogues in 1919. Took part in the **burning of the Barracks at Bealnamullia**, mobilised for an **attack on Cloonark Barracks**, and **attempted an ambush at Curraghaleen** in October 1920. Near Truce time he guarded the ASU Headquarters in the area, **destroyed the bridge at Millbrook**, blocked roads at Millbrook and Monksland, harboured and aided escaped prisoners. During the Truce he trained at Greenfield, Donamon, and Falty, in addition to collecting funds to aid the Volunteers and attending the Arbitration Courts

Willie Shine (Drum Coy.) a member of Father Flanagan's Sinn Féin Club

James Shivan (Crossna, Boyle) 5th Battalion North Roscommon

Bertie Shouldice (Ballaghaderreen) one of the first members of the Ballaghaderreen Coy. in the East Mayo Brigade. He was taken prisoner after the Rising, and sent to Lewes Gaol in England. Later he was transferred to "The Irish University", Frongoch. He was a brother of Frank and Jack

Frank Shouldice (Ballaghaderreen) worked in the British Civil Service in Dublin before the Rising. He was a member of the Four Courts garrison during The Rebellion. New cottages in Dublin were being built between Church Street and Beresford Street, and those positions were held by Volunteers under Seamus Ryan.

Tessie Shiel, member of Cumann na mBan.

PHOTO COURTESY OF JOHN AND ELIZABETH GREENE

William Shiel, Curraghroe Company.

PHOTO COURTESY OF JOHN AND ELIZABETH GREENE

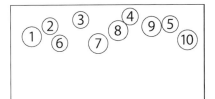

Survivors of the 1916 Easter Rising.
1st Battalion, Four Courts and McKnight garrison.
Photo taken in 1964.

1. John O'Connor, 2. Tom Shearer, 3. Frank
Shouldice, 4. Maurice Collins, 5. Eamon Morkan, 6.
Mick Flannagan, 7. Pierce Beaslai, 8. Jack Shouldice,
9. Fianan Lynch, 10. Mrs. Morkan.

Frank Shouldice.

Frank and a small group manned the Malthouse that backed up next to Jameson's distillery. As a result of his actions, the British sent him to Stafford Detention Barracks. He was later transferred to Frongoch, where he played many an outstanding football game with the camp team. Shouldice was released in the general amnesty of 1917, but did not mend his rebel ways. He was re-arrested and jailed in Usk Prison in Wales, from which he, along with George Geraghty of Roscommon town, made a daring escape. In 1919 he was arrested for leading the local Ballaghaderreen Company in a march on the big ranches. By 1920 he was again a prisoner, this time at Boyle Barracks, where he was re-sentenced to two years. He was transferred to Mountjoy, where he was incarcerated in 1921. He did not participate in the Civil War. After the hostilities, he joined the Irish Civil Service in Dublin. Died 1974, and buried in Glasnevin Cemetery

Jack Shouldice (Ballaghaderreen) was working in London in 1901 when he was sworn into the IRB by either Sam Maguire or J. B. Mulcahy.* He joined the Volunteers at the Rotunda meeting in Dublin in November 1913. Along with Edward Daly serving as Captain and Diamund O'Hegarty acting as 2nd Lieutenant, Shouldice was elected 1st Lieutenant of "F" Company, 1st Battalion.

He was informed in early April of plans for the Rising. The orders and counter-orders of the day caused "complete disorganisation," but he decided to parade at Colmcille Hall on Easter Monday morning with about a quarter of his men. He was ordered to "hold and fortify the crossing at North King Street and Church Street...." Jack was taken to Kilmainham Gaol, where he occupied the same cell which the executed men, Eamonn Ceannt and Michael Mallin, had just vacated. He was sentenced to death for his part in the Rising, but his sentence was commuted to five years penal servitude, and he was shipped to Dartmoor. He was released in the amnesty of 1917. After the War he became the Secretary of the Leinster GAA. (He had been a member of the All-Ireland winning Dublin GAA football team of 1908.) Died 1965, and buried in Glasnevin Cemetery

J. F. Shouldice Volunteer Witness Statement to the Bureau of Military History 1913-1921, p. 1.

Annie Simons (Carrowmoneen, Kilgefin, Roscommon) sister of Frank and Dick. Member of Cumann na mBan

Dick Simons (Carrowmoneen, Kilgefin, Roscommon) 3rd Battalion South Roscommon, brother of Frank, Michael, and Tom. He was known as "quite a jolly man." A member of Pat Madden's Flying Column. Many, but not all, of the members of the Kilgefin Company participated in the **Fourmilehouse Ambush** on 12 October 1920. Dick was present at the **Scramogue Ambush** in March 1921. After the War he became a small farmer. Died 22 November 1980, and buried in Kilgefin Cemetery

Frank Simons, Adjutant of 3rd Battalion South Roscommon.

PHOTO COURTESY OF FRANK SIMONS

Frank Simons (Carrowmoneen, Kilgefin, Roscommon) Adjutant of 3rd Battalion South Roscommon, and member of the 3rd Battalion Flying Column. Frank was one of the founding members of the Kilgefin Company which formed in March 1917. At that time the Company was attached to the Longford area. He worked closely with the Longford Volunteers and gravitated towards action near the Shannon River. Frank was a member of the Irish Republican Brotherhood, which he joined on 31 March 1915. (Pat Madden was Head Centre for the county, and meetings were held usually after Battalion Council gatherings.) When the Brigade structure was organised in late 1919, Simons was elected its Adjutant. When Jim Breheny of Portrunny, Vice O/C of the Brigade, was arrested in January of 1921, Simons was appointed to fill his position. In order to avoid capture, Simons slept for a full year in the house of Frank Nelson in Aghaclogher at the foot of Slieve Bawn.* Simons participated in the **destruction of the income tax records** in Roscommon town in late 1919, **ambush at Moneen** in July 1920, **Fourmilehouse Ambush** in October 1920, the **Castlenode shootout** in November 1920, and the **Scramogue Ambush** in March 1921. In February or March 1921, Simons received a letter purported to be from Dan O'Rourke, asking him to take over the responsibilities of the South Roscommon Brigade because O'Rourke planned to leave the area for an indefinite period of time. Simons and Pat Madden were suspicious of the note, because it had been delivered by a non-IRA man, who had gotten it from another non-member of the organisation.**

He aided the escapees from the Curragh Prison Camp in September 1921. Joined the Free State Army after the Truce and rose to the rank of Colonel. He was the officer in charge of Intelligence operations for the Free State in Galway, Mayo and Roscommon during the Civil War. He later became a Collector of Taxes for Co. Mayo. Simons was one of several Roscommon men interviewed in the 1950s by author Ernie O'Malley. Simons' words are included in the papers of O'Malley in the UCD Archives. Died 14 April 1982, and buried in St. Coman's Cemetery in Roscommon town

Seamus Nelson, interview by author, 11 November 2003, Roscommon town.
**Frank Simons, taped interview with James McCormick, summer of 1973, Roscommon town.*

Michael Simons (Carrowmoneen, Kilgefin, Roscommon) a member of "E" Coy., 3rd Battalion South Roscommon, brother of Frank, Tom, and Dick. After the War he emigrated to New York. Died in 1975

Tom Simons (Carrowmoneen, Kilgefin, Roscommon) brother of Dick, Tom and Frank. After the War moved to Dublin, where he was employed in the Civil Service. Died 16 December 1981, and is buried in Deans Grange Cemetery in that city

Edward Simpson (Ardakillan, Strokestown) 2nd Battalion North Roscommon. Listed in the GHQ papers in the UCD Archives as the O/C of Tulsk Company

Patrick Simpson (Clooncullane, Strokestown) a member of Tulsk Coy. in the 2nd Battalion North Roscommon Brigade. He served as Adjutant as well as local Intelligence Officer

Graham Sinnott member of the 1918 Sinn Féin election committee in South Roscommon. Local auctioneer who, along with Fr. O'Flanagan, helped to establish a land court in Roscommon. In 1919 a joint meeting of Sinn Féin executives assembled at Roscommon to orchestrate official policy towards land agitation in the county. Sinnott reported to the Dáil on 20 May 1920 regarding the tendency of some small farmers to join in cattle drives waving the Sinn Féin banner for the sole purpose of obtaining more land. Sinnott claimed that their devotion to political principle was limited to the amount of acreage they could extract from the "spoils"

John Sinnott served as Adjutant for the 3rd Battalion South before Frank Simons took over that position

Patrick J. Skeffington (Derrycashel, Crossna, Boyle) was a prisoner in Mountjoy in 1921 when he wrote the following words:

> **In Memory of the Mountjoy Martyrs**
>
> God give you rest, brave comrades.
> God grant you peace today.
> Yours was the work right hard to do,
> To mark out Freedom's Way.
>
> You did your best — sleep among the Bless'd,
> Then Justice held its sway.
> Adding another debt which we'll pay back yet,
> In our own Republican way.

Captain Skelly, Free State officer, who was killed in action 2 July 1922 during the **Battle for Boyle Barracks**

Peter Skelly (Balytoohey, Tarmonbarry) a member of Tarmonbarry Coy. in the 3rd Battalion North Roscommon

John Slein (Sheegorey, Boyle) a member of Doon Coy. in the 1st Battalion North Roscommon. Listed in the GHQ papers in the UCD Archives as the First Lieutenant of Doon Company. Took part in the raid at Farrell's. Also raided for arms and petrol. After the War joined the Garda Síochána and moved to Dublin

Patrick Sloan (Mount Temple, County Westmeath) Volunteers from South Westmeath and South Roscommon operated as a unit in the Athlone Brigade. He was interned during the War, and, as he walked towards a perimeter fence at Ballykinlar Interment Camp in County Down, he was shot by a

Edward Simpson, O/C of Tulsk Company, 2nd Battalion North Roscommon.
PHOTO COURTESY OF MICHAEL LENNON

IN COMMEMORATION

To those members of the
IRISH · REPUBLICAN · ARMY
ATHLONE · BRIGADE,

1916 · 1921

who gave their lives
in action against
BRITISH CROWN FORCES.

KILLED IN ACTION:

SEAN COSTELLOE I·V · JAMES TORMEY
JOSEPH TORMEY · JOHN CARTY
PATRICK SLOANE · GEORGE ADAMSON
DICK BERTLES · TOM HUGHES
CHRISTOPHER McKEOWN
SEAMUS FINN · MICHAEL BANNON
JOHN BLANEY · JOE MORRISSEY
TOM (TOBY) MANNION

DIED FROM WOUNDS AND HARDSHIPS:

GEORGE MANNING · MICHAEL CAFFEY
BRIAN CAFFEY · SEAN CALVIN
BERNARD McCORMACK I·V
JOE CUNNINGHAM

Inscription on the Athlone Monument.
PHOTO COURTESY OF LEW THORNE

sentry. Died 14 January 1921, and is buried in Drumraney Cemetery, Co. Westmeath. His name is inscribed on the Athlone IRA Monument

James Slyman (Trien Coy.) 1st Battalion South Roscommon

Jim Smith (Boyle) 1st Battalion North Roscommon, a member of the Volunteers since before the Rising

Owen Smith (Glenamaddy) Smith, along with other 4th Battalion South Roscommon men, broke into Mount Talbot 7 April 1922 and threatened the owner. Talbot and wife lived through the night, but packed up their belongings and headed for Dublin the next day

Pat Joe Smith (Ballyboughan, Roscommon) arrested after the 1916 Rising for his Sinn Féin sympathies and sent to Wakefield on 13 May 1916. He was later transferred to the great "Irish University," Frongoch, in Wales. He returned to Roscommon and continued his activities with the Roscommon Coy., 3rd Battalion South Roscommon. Later in life he ran a hotel and funeral business in Roscommon town

Andrew Smyth (Heathfield, Castleplunkett) a member of "C" Coy. in the 2nd Battalion South Roscommon. Andrew climbed the flagpole at Kilmurray and put up the tricolour. His activities came to the attention of the Black and Tans, who visited the fourth house on the LEFT of Kilmurray Road. No Andy! Smith actually lived in the fourth house on the RIGHT. When Smith saw the Tans paying a visit to the neighbours, he made a quick getaway. The Tans, realising their mistake, returned to the correct house, but Andy was long gone. His house, however, was not. It was burned! Took part in the **ambush at Tarmon Cross** in June 1920, and the **attack on Frenchpark Barracks** 2 October 1920. After the War he emigrated to Chicago

Edward Smyth (Cloonlaughnan, Mt. Talbot) a member of the Tisrara Company in the 4th Battalion South Roscommon

Hubert Smyth (Cloonkeen, Castlerea) a member of Trien Coy., 1st Battalion South Roscommon

Jack Smyth (Ballygar Coy.) which was considered part of 4th Battalion South Roscommon when the Divisional structure was implemented

James Smyth (Castleplunkett Coy.) 2nd Battalion South Roscommon. Participated in the **raid on the military train at Ballymoe** in June 1920, the **attack on Frenchpark Barracks** 2 October 1920, and the **ambush at Southpark, Castlerea** 10 July 1921. Later emigrated to the United States

Michael Smyth (Ballygar Coy.) Ballygar Compay was considered part of 4th Battalion South Roscommon when the Divisional structure was implemented

Owen Smyth (Ballygar Coy.) when the Divisional structure was put in place, south Galway was grouped with parts of south Roscommon and became part of the 4th Battalion South Roscommon

Thomas Smyth (Cloonerra, Strokestown) a member of Carniska Coy., 3rd Battalion North Roscommon. Joined the IRA in 1917, and participated in collection of funds to resist conscription. He was at his post at Aughnadarry polling booth during the South Roscommon elections. Smith participated in the **destruction of the RIC barracks at Fourmilehouse**, was in charge of a section blocking roads on the morning of the **Fourmilehouse ambush** in October 1920, participated in the **attack on Strokestown patrol** in January 1921, and assisted in the **Scramogue Ambush**. After the War he emigrated to Brooklyn, New York

John Snee born in Barcull, Kilkelly, Co. Mayo. He was sworn into the IRA in 1920 by Sean Welsh in a field in Kilkelly near the present-day Knock Airport. He, along with Tom Regan, M. Hunt, P. Behan, Mick Duffy, and M. McKeon, became part of the Brigade Active Service Unit. During the months after the Truce, he and his cohorts spent their time sniping at the B-Specials along the six county Border. He participated in the Anti-Treaty **attack on Boyle Barracks**, but his luck

Andrew Smyth,
Castleplunkett Company
2nd Battalion South Roscommon.

ran out on 7 July 1922. He was in a house with thirteen other men under the leadership of Pat Brennan. Brennan had just taken another small group to tea, when the house in which Snee was hiding was surrounded. (Another of the captured men was Richie Murray, brother of Josie Murray of the Boyle Battalion.) Snee was sent to Boyle Barracks, Connolly Barracks in Longford, Custume Barracks in Athlone on 14 November 1922, and finally to No. 2 Tintown Internment Camp at the Curragh. He was not released until November 1923. Two months later he emigrated to England, then, on 19 February 1926, sailed for the United States. He returned to Ireland in 1963, where he farmed, and owned or worked in pubs. John was one of five men on this list who was personally interviewed by this author (in 1997). He spent his last days in Lucan Lodge Nursing Home, and died at the age of 100 on 29 May 2002

John Snee in 1997 with author
PHOTO COURTESY OF LEW THORNE

Peter Spalding (Tarmonbarry Coy.) "D" Company, 3rd Battalion North Roscommon. Joined the IRA in 1917. He served as an outpost for the **Scramogue Ambush**. After the War he moved to New York

John Spellman (Cornaglia, Boyle) 1st Battalion North Roscommon

John Spellman (Callow, Frenchpark) in 1922 he served as 1st Lieutenant of "D" Company (Breedogue) in the 1st Battalion North Roscommon

Mary Kate Spellman (Ballaghaderreen) member of the Cumann na mBan, sister of Patrick

Michael Spellman (Lisserdrea, Boyle) 1st Battalion North Roscommon

Patrick Spellman (Knockavroe, Boyle) 1st Battalion North Roscommon. Took part in the **Rockingham Raid**. Later emigrated to England

Patrick Spellman (Church St., Ballaghaderreen) during the Civil War he was arrested for Anti-Treaty activities on 28 August 1922 and taken to Athlone the first part of September. He was released two months later in November, but found his way back to Custume Barracks again in April of 1923

Roger Spellman (Killeenboy, Kilteevan) a member of Kilteevan Company in the 3rd Battalion South Roscommon

Tom Spellman (Ballaghaderreen) one of the first members of the Ballaghaderreen Coy. in the East Mayo Brigade

Liam Staines (Ballinagare) some neighbours claim he died of injuries suffered in the 1916 Rising. Padraic O'Farrell claims in *Who's Who in the Irish War for Independence and Civil War 1916-1923* that he was killed 2 November 1918.* He was the son of an RIC constable
* p. 119.

John Stanley (Emlaghyroyin, Donamon) a member of "E" Coy. of the 2nd Battalion South Roscommon. Took part in the **raid on the military train at Ballymoe** in June 1920

John Staunton (Meeltraun, Cloonfad) a member of the Cloonfad Company, 1st Battalion South Roscommon. Attended the training camps during the Truce. Later emigrated to America

Patrick Staunton (Ardkeel, Roscommon) a member of Cloverhill Coy. in the 2nd Battalion South Roscommon

John Stephens (Capt. of Kilkerrin Coy.) located in Co. Galway, this Company was incorporated into No. 2 Brigade of the 2nd Western Division, with Gerald O'Connor, former O/C of the 1st Battalion South Roscommon, serving as Brigade Commander

Luke Stephens (Tromaun, Athleague) a member of the Athleague Coy., 3rd Battalion South Roscommon, brother of Michael

Michael Stephens (Tromaun, Athleague) Athleague Coy., 3rd Battalion South Roscommon

James Stewart (Clooneen, Kilglass, Strokestown) a member of the Kilglass Company in the 3rd Battalion North Roscommon

Joseph Stewart (Clooneen, Kilglass, Strokestown) a member of the Kilglass Company in the 3rd Battalion North Roscommon. Took part in cutting the road from Ballyfeeny to Scramogue in preparation for the **Scramogue Ambush**

John Stoneham (Castlecoote, Roscommon) during the Civil War he took the Anti-Treaty side, and was arrested and sent to Newbridge, from which he was released on 22 December 1923

John Stroker (Ardmagree, Kilteevan) a member of Kilteevan Coy., 3rd Battalion South Roscommon

John Stroker (Kilteevan Coy.) 3rd Battalion South Roscommon

William Stroker (Kilteevan Coy.) 3rd Battalion South Roscommon

James Swanick (Mountain Upper, Ballinlough) a member of Trien Coy., 1st Battalion South Roscommon

Francis Sweeney served on the Brigade Staff when the 3rd Western Division was formed. After the War he moved to Drumcondra, Dublin

James Sweeney (Corbo, Derrane, Roscommon) a member of Kilbride Coy., 3rd Battalion South Roscommon

Owen Sweeney (Clonbruske, Athlone) a farmer by trade, he was arrested after the Rising and sent to Wakefield on 13 May, but was released within a few days. He was again arrested by the British in May 1919

George Tanner, Strokestown.
3rd Battalion North Roscommon.

George Tanner (Elphin Street, Strokestown) served as the 1st Lieutenant of "I" Company in the 3rd Battalion North Roscommon. George joined the Volunteers in 1918. He carried dispatches, raided income tax offices, participated in the **attack at Walpole's** in November 1920, **attack on RIC in Strokestown** on 6 January 1921, and commandeered transport for men on the run. In the months prior to the Truce, he assisted in providing clothing for British soldiers who had deserted out of the Strokestown demesne. He was fired upon by an RIC man in Elphin while sitting in a taxi cab with James Feely and a driver named Hunt. Tanner was arrested, beaten, and taken to Richmond Hospital in Dublin, where a bullet fragment remained festering in his right hand. During the Civil War he cut communication lines and telephone wires, and raided for transport. He was arrested for Anti-Treaty activities 1 October 1922 in Strokestown by former comrade, Sean Leavy, and detained in Ruskey and Athlone before being released six months later. Died November 1966, and buried in Strokestown Cemetery

"Mickey" Tansey (Boyle area) 1st Battalion North Roscommon, a member of the Volunteers since before the Rising. He later moved to Co. Kildare

Owen Tansey (Commandant of the Gurteen Battalion, Sligo Brigade) died in the influenza epidemic of 1918. He was a member of the IRB

Thomas Tarney Brigade Adjutant for No. 2 Brigade, 2nd Western Division under Brigade O/C Gerald O'Connor. In 1921 he became part of the ASU formed with the Tuam Battalion area

Michael Tarpey (Trien Coy.) 1st Battalion South Roscommon

Michael Tarpey (Ballygar Coy.) when the Divisional structure was put in place, south Galway was grouped with parts of south Roscommon and became part of the 4th Battalion South Roscommon

John Tennant (Lisnahoon, Knockcroghery) 4th Battalion South Roscommon. A member of the Fianna, who, as a young lad, helped his brothers Michael and Pat with the guns

Michael Tennant (Lisnahoon, Knockcroghery) 4th Battalion South Roscommon. Knockcroghery Coy. was formed in 1917 with Patrick Kelly serving as Captain. Tennant drilled with the Volunteers, and attended practice battles at Taughmaconnell overseen by Ernie O'Malley in the summer of 1918. He also participated in the 1918 South Roscommon election. He was mobilised with his Company for the **attempted attack at Kilmurray Camp** — an action that was cancelled the very night of the proposed action. Tennant also was a part of the **attempted ambush at Clooncraff**, an operation under the command of Pat Madden. He, along with the rest of his Company, **guarded the village of Knockcroghery** from reprisal on 15 August 1920, a reprisal precipitated by British Forces being fired upon on Lough Ree. Tennant raided for arms. Sixteen such raids were carried out, yielding about as many shotguns. One such venture took him to several houses accessible only by boat from Lough Ree — and this in broad daylight! He and Joseph Kearney held up two enemy soldiers and robbed them of their dispatches. Tennant and seven other Volunteers also held up the evening mail train from Dublin. He participated in the **proposed attack on the Castlerea Station Guard**, and the **ambush at Knockcroghery Station** in which one policeman lost his life. He was also with his Company in an **attempted ambush of a military party** eighteen strong **at Knockcroghery** in January 1921. Along with other members of his Company, he assembled for an **ambush at Scrine**, an ambush that was thwarted when the lorry failed to pass. He took part on 14 May in the **burning of O'Brien's house in Curraghboy**, a home that the Volunteers feared was about to be taken over by British Forces. On 1 July he, along with five other men from the Company, attacked the **RIC Barracks at Ballygar**. During the Truce Tennant served as a delegate to Commandant Tom Maguire's review of troops at Ballygar, and was appointed to a special service unit. Throughout the Tan War, Tennant was actively involved in manufacturing weapons. He made a considerable number of fuse bombs, but not without mishap. On one occasion, he blew off some of his fingers. He also broke into the Crofton's vault and stole one of the lead-lined coffins, which he melted down and formed into bullets. After the split in the IRA, he joined the Free State Army. Later in life he became a postman (minus a few appendages). He died of a heart attack at the railroad station in Knockcroghery, where years before he had been with the party that shot RIC Constable William Potter on 26 August 1920. He is buried in St. Coman's Cemetery, Roscommon

Stephen Thewlis (Cloonsellan, Kilteevan) a member of Kilteevan Coy., 3rd Battalion South Roscommon

James Thompson (Timanagh, Ballintubber) a member of Ballintubber Coy., 2nd Battalion South Roscommon

Brighid Lyons Thornton Born at Moneenacully, Scramogue, Strokestown, she attended University College Galway, where she entered

Pat Tennant (Lisnahoon, Knockcroghery) 4th Battalion South Roscommon, brother of John and Michael. He served as the 2nd Lieutenant of the Company, which took active form in 1917. Tennant paraded with the Volunteers and participated in Battalion mobilisations and exercises held at Scregg, Barnacullen, and Churchboro, Knockcroghery. Attended practice battles at Taughmaconnell overseen by Ernie O'Malley in the summer of 1918. Tennant was with a group of Volunteers who visited six intended recruits to the RIC, and dissuaded them from joining the force. Participated in the South Roscommon election of 1918, and served as an armed escort for bank officials taking sums of money to fairs in Knockcroghery. He worked with the Police Force in the Sinn Féin Courts, and acted as enforcer of Sinn Féin rules regarding public houses. Participated in the **burning of Lecarrow Barracks**, and the **attempted ambush at Clooncraff**. Raided for arms numerous times, including a house of an ex-RIC man in which four guns, one revolver, and a quantity of ammunition were captured. Tennant participated in a raid with the St. John's Company in which a Volunteer was so severely wounded he had to be treated in a Dublin hospital. Tennant helped to censor letters taken from a Knockcroghery postman, and correspondence secured from the evening mail train from Dublin. Took part in the **attempted attack at Kilmurray Camp** in June 1920 — an action that was cancelled due to a spy alerting the British. He also took part in an **attempted capture of an enemy dispatch van**, **attempted ambush of two RIC constables at Lecarrow**, and the **ambush of two constables at Knockcroghery Railway Station** on 26 August 1920. Tennant participated in a holdup of a goods train at Ballymurray whereby twenty bags of mail were confiscated and subsequently censored. He also took part in the **attempted attack on a party of military** about eighteen strong **at Knockcroghery** in January 1921. Later that month, Tom Kelly and Jim Breheny were sleeping in a cock of hay near Kelly's home when the all-clear signal (a sheet put out in the yard) was given for Kelly and Breheny to enter the house for breakfast. Patrick arrived shortly afterwards with an urgent dispatch, but, before anything was done about it, two lorries arrived with troops that surrounded the house. All three men were immediately captured. Quoting from Tommy Loughran's unpublished manuscript, "The Tans who captured Pat Tennant bent him over a fence, pulled down his pants and whipped him on the bare buttocks with a piece of rope. They inflicted such damage that Pat had to sleep face down for several weeks."[*] He was taken to Athlone and later to the Curragh, from which he escaped through the Brady tunnel in September 1921. Tennant later joined the Free State Army, and became a career officer, rising to the rank of Captain. He is buried in Dublin

An Old Soldier's Memories, by Tommy Loughran, p. 243.

Jim Tiernam, Captain of Kilgefin Coy.,
3rd Battalion South Roscommon.

Paddy Tiernan, member of Pat Madden's
Flying Column, 3rd Battalion South
Roscommon.

Pat Tiernan, member of Kilgefin Coy.
3rd Battalion South Roscommon.

into medical studies. She accompanied her uncle Frank McGuinness of Longford (brother of Joe of "Put him in to get him out" fame) to Dublin, where she saw first-hand the rebellion in the Four Courts. She was imprisoned at Kilmainham Jail for two weeks before resuming her studies in Galway, where she organised a branch of the Cumann na mBan among her classmates. Brighid also accompanied Michael Collins on a visit to the bedside of Sean MacEoin in St. Bricin's Hospital in Dublin. After the Truce she joined the Free State Army as a medical officer, the first Irish woman to receive a commission in the Irish Army. She resigned in 1924 with the rank of Commandant. She went on to work in the public health service in Kildare, Cork, and Dublin. She was one of nine persons interviewed and filmed by Kenneth Griffith and Timothy O'Grady for their documentary and subsequent 1998 book, *Curious Journey—An Oral History of Ireland's Unfinished Revolution*

Jim Tiernan (Ballincurry, Kilgefin, Roscommon) Captain of Kilgefin Company of the 3rd Battalion South Roscommon, secured guns from Dublin. A member of Pat Madden's Flying Column. Jim was a widow's son, who was stopped from joining the British Army by Constable Lambert of Beechwood Barracks. The policeman told him that farmers were needed for England's war effort far more than another soldier in the field. Besides, Jim already had a brother serving in the war. Jim stayed in Ireland, became a member of the IRB, and fought the British on home ground. Many, but not all, of the members of the Kilgefin Company participated in the **Fourmilehouse Ambush** on 12 October 1920. He was present at the **Castlenode shootout** in November 1920, and **Scramogue Ambush** in March 1921. After the War he emigrated to America, but later returned to his homeland. Died 28 September 1979, and is buried in Kilgefin Cemetery

Michael Tiernan (Main St., Castlerea) a member of 1st Battalion South Roscommon

Michael Tiernan (Cregga, Strokestown) Kiltrustan Coy. in the 3rd Battalion North Roscommon. He, along with Tom Brady and Tim Caulfield, served as far outposts for the **Scramogue Ambush**

Paddy Tiernan (Sheehaun, Kilgefin, Roscommon) nicknamed "The Man in the Moon" of the 3rd Battalion South Roscommon was a member of Pat Madden's Flying Column, and took part in the **Fourmilehouse and Scramogue Ambushes**, and the **attack at Moneen**. After the roundup near Slieve Bawn, Tiernan ran for two solid days to escape capture. After the War he married but had no children. He lived on his land and died 16 July 1988. Buried in Derrane Cemetery

Pat Tiernan (Gortyleane, Kilrooskey) a member of Kilgefin Coy. in the 3rd Battalion South Roscommon. Many, but not all, of the members of the Kilgefin Company participated in the **Fourmilehouse Ambush** on 12 October 1920. Pat served as a scout during the War, after which he emigrated to New York. He stayed in the States for ten years, but returned to his native land of Gortyleane, where he remained until his death on 31 December 1984. He is buried in Kilgefin Cemetery

Patrick Tiernan (Clooneen, Kilglass, Strokestown) a member of the Kilglass Company in the 3rd Battalion North Roscommon

Thomas Tiernan (Derryquirk, Tulsk) a member of Tulsk Coy., 2nd Battalion North Roscommon. Tiernan, Michael McGarry, Tom Connor, Seamus Ryan, and Joe Kelly of Rathcroghan raided the homes of two informers. The attack party knew of the men's spying because of mail seized and censored by Thomas Brady, the Battalion Intelligence Officer. During the raid, each spy managed to grab a revolver and shoot himself free of the Volunteers. Both men hid out in the RIC Barracks in Roscommon town until Truce time. Tiernan was later arrested and interned until 1922. He took the Anti-Treaty side in the Civil War, and was re-arrested and kept in prison until the end of 1923. After the War he emigrated to Mount Vernon, New York

James Tighe (Cloontuskert Coy.) 2nd Lieutenant, 3rd Battalion North Roscommon. After the War he emigrated to the United States

John Tighe (Drumlion, Carrick-on-Shannon) 1st Lieutenant for Drumlion Company in the 5th Battalion North Roscommon

Martin Tighe (Levallyroe, Ballyhaunis) a member of the Cloonfad Coy. Took part in the **disarming of a Black and Tan at Cloonfad** in May 1921

Michael Tighe (Cortober, Carrick-on-Shannon) during the Civil War he took the Anti-Treaty side, and was captured on 8 August 1922 and sent to Athlone on 14 November 1922. Tighe was transferred to Tintown II on 20 February 1923

John Timothy (Rabradagh, Donamon) a member of "E" Coy. in the 2nd Battalion South Roscommon

Thomas Tobin served as the Adjutant for the Ballyfarnon Company in the 4th Battalion North Roscommon. During the Civil War he took the Anti-Treaty side, and was arrested and sent to Tintown A. He was released at Christmas time 1923. After the War he emigrated to the United States

Henry Tivnan began his defiance to British rule in his youth. He, along with Henry Feely, Addie Hayes, and Willie Devine, climbed the flagpole outside the home of the local British Army recruiter in Boyle. He and the other boys burned the Union Jack outside the door of the recruiter's home. He was never apprehended for this stunt! He later emigrated to the United States

John Tonry (Sheehaun, Kilgefin, Roscommon) a member of "E" Coy., 3rd Battalion South Roscommon. John served as an enforcer for Volunteer policies in the area. Many, but not all, of the members of the Kilgefin Company participated in the **Fourmilehouse Ambush** on 12 October 1920. After the War he emigrated to the United States

James Toolan (Scramogue) during the Civil War he took the Anti-Treaty side, and was arrested on 14 September 1922 and sent to Athlone on 11 November 1922. He was released at the first of the year on 11 January 1923

John Joseph Toolan (Killina, Clooneyquinn) Killina Coy. in the 2nd Battalion North Roscommon. He was one of the first members of the Company when it formed in August of 1917. He served as Quartermaster for the 2nd Battalion North Roscommon

Michael Toolan (Drumman More, Kilglass, Strokestown) a member of the Kilglass Company in the 3rd Battalion North Roscommon, brother of Pat. He accompanied Jack Loughran on an all-night bicycle trip to Ballinameen (a distance of eighteen miles) to obtain two rifles from Jack Roche, and bring them back to the Battalion area for safe keeping. Before that evening, Toolan had never handled a military rifle.* He took part in cutting the road from Ballyfeeny to Scramogue in preparation for the **Scramogue Ambush**

*An Old Soldier's Memories by Tommy Loughran, p. 263.

Miss Toolan (a native of Clooneyquinn, Elphin) telegraphist at the Castlerea Post Office, intelligence gatherer for the Volunteers. Arrested and sentenced to years of penal servitude

Pat Toolan (Drumman More, Kilglass, Strokestown) a member of the Kilglass Company in the 3rd Battalion North Roscommon. He took part in cutting the road from Ballyfeeny to Scramogue in preparation for the **Scramogue Ambush**. Days after the ambush, he stood guard at Loughran's cottage while James Murphy, Martin Fallon, and Sean Leavy slept inside. After the War he emigrated to New York, where he was accidentally killed on a subway in 1929

James Tormey (Moneen, Moate, County Westmeath) James had been in the British Army during the early years of World War I. He brought very useful methods of instruction and knowledge of drill and tactics to his Company, which he joined in 1918. In April 1920 Tormey was incarcerated in Galway Gaol. After his release, he led the raiding party at the **Faheran ambush** on 19 October 1920. In preparation for the **capture of the Streamstown RIC Barracks** in County Westmeath in July 1920, Tormey and Con Costello waylaid several RIC men on

James Tormey. Moate Co. Westmeath. Leader of the Athlone Flying Column

PHOTO COURTESY OF JOE TORMEY

(far left) Original design for the Athlone Monument.

(left) The finished monument.

(below) A crowd scene at the dedication of the Athlone Monument.

PHOTOS COURTESY OF JOAN O'BRIEN

their way to Mass. They took the policemen to a nearby farmhouse, where they relieved them of their uniforms and weapons. They exited the house, and began to blend into the crowd walking away from church. Meanwhile, to the ever suspicious eyes of the local RIC constables, strange men were reported in the area, and, worse yet, the Volunteers were parading in full view. All this activity alerted the policemen that something was astir. When Tormey and Costello arrived at the barracks door dressed in the borrowed uniforms, Tormey saved Costello from death by grabbing him and yanking him away from the doorway just before a grenade hurled by the RIC from a upstairs dummy loophole exploded in front of them. Tormey was also with the party who **killed Sergeant Craddock** in Athlone on 22 August 1920. In the autumn of 1920, Tormey was appointed O/C of the Athlone Flying Column. He participated in the **ambush at Parkwood** in County Westmeath. On 4 November 1920, he and Henry O'Brien were having tea at the Royal Hotel in Athlone, when they were spotted by the Auxiliaries who had just entered the premises "generally the worse for drink." Both men exited through the back door and starting walking through the town northeasterly and parallel to the main thoroughfare. As they neared Maguire's pub, one of the Auxiliaries tapped Tormey on the shoulder saying, "We want you, big fellow."* Tormey dived in the door of the pub. O'Brien shot the Auxiliary who threatened to capture Tormey. By running down around the south side of town and crossing the Shannon, O'Brien evaded his captors. Meanwhile, Maguire's pub was soon surrounded by the military, who decided to burn the place down around Tormey. By mingling with other workers who by now were carrying goods from the premises in order to rescue them from the flames, Tormey made a miraculous escape. His luck did not hold. Tormey was killed in the **Ambush at Cornafulla**, 2 February 1921, and secretly buried at the Cemetery of the Seven Churches at Clonmacnoise. Later re-interred in Mount Temple Cemetery, where his brother's fresh grave lay alongside his own. His name is inscribed on the tablets in front of the Shankill and Athlone Monuments

Joe Tormey (Moneen, Moate, Count Westmeath) brother of James, captured in 1920, and shot by an over-anxious sentry on 14 January 1921 while a prisoner at Ballykinlar Internment Camp in County Down. Buried alongside his brother, James, in Mt. Temple Cemetery. His name is also inscribed on the tablets in front of the Shankill and Athlone Monuments

Joseph Towey (Main St., Ballaghaderreen) during the Civil War he took the Anti-Treaty side, and was arrested on 18 September 1922. He was sent to Athlone on 14 November 1922. He was released a month later

Mary Towey (Ballaghaderreen) member of the Cumann na mBan

T. Towey (Ballaghaderreen) one of the first members of the Ballaghaderreen Coy. in the East Mayo Brigade

Frank Treacy (Cloonfree Coy.) 3rd Battalion North Roscommon. Took part in the **attempt to burn down the Bridewell at Strokestown** in July 1920

John Treacy (Ballinturly, Fuerty) brother of Joseph, Nora, and Patrick

Joseph Treacy (Ballinturly, Fuerty, Roscommon) brother of John, Nora, and Patrick. 1st Lieutenant of the Dunmore Coy. in the Glenamaddy Battalion, which was part of No. 2 Brigade, 2nd Western Division, with Gerald O'Connor, former O/C of the 1st Battalion South Roscommon, serving as Brigade Commandant

Nora Treacy (Ballinturly, Fuerty, Roscommon) sister of John, Patrick, and Joseph, member of Cumann na mBan

Pat Treacy (Ballinturly, Fuerty, Roscommon) brother of John, Joseph, and Nora. After the War he emigrated to Massachusetts and went into the insurance business

Patrick Treacy (Kilteevan Coy.) 3rd Battalion South Roscommon. A giant of a man, who became the Quartermaster for the Battalion. After the War he farmed his land and is buried in the Kilteevan Cemetery

Patrick Treacy (Captain of the Glenamaddy Coy.) Glenamaddy Battalion. His Company was part of No. 2 Brigade, 2nd Western Division. Gerald O'Connor, former O/C for the 1st Battalion South Roscommon, was the Brigade Commander. Treacy joined the ASU formed with the Tuam Battalion. He also served as the Adjutant for the 1st Battalion

Thomas Treacy (Cootehall) during the Civil War he took the Anti-Treaty side, and fought with the Arigna Flying Column. He and several of his comrades (Jim Moran, Frank Barlow, J. Doyle, and Peter McGearty) were arrested and sent to Athlone on 3 February 1923

Frederick Tremble (Ardmore, Donamon) a member of "E" Coy. in the 2nd Battalion South Roscommon. Took part in the **raid on the military train at Ballymoe** in June 1920. Served as Battalion Intelligence Officer when the 2nd Western Division was formed. His home served as the headquarters for "E" Company during the post-Truce times. He later joined the Free State Army

J. Tremble (Ardmore, Donamon) a member of "E" Company in the 2nd Battalion South Roscommon, brother of Frederick

Joe Trimble (Ballaghaderreen) arrested after the Rising for his Sinn Féin sympathies and sent to Lewes Detention Barracks on the 20 May 1916. He was later transferred to Glasgow Prison and finally to "The Irish University," Frongoch, from which he was released at the general amnesty of 1917

Cissie Tully (Newtownflood, Drum, Athlone) president of the Cumann na mBan club at Summerhill, Athlone, sister of Tom and Maggie

Hubert Tully (Clooneyquinn, Tulsk) foreman at Galway Railway Station, killed 11 May 1921. Buried Kilcooley Cemetery, Tulsk. Name inscribed on the Shankill Monument near Elphin

Tom Tully, 3rd Battalion
Athlone Brigade.

PHOTO COURTESY OF EDWARD EGAN, DRUM, ATHLONE

Patrick "Paddy" Tymon, Arigna Coy.
4th Battalion North Roscommon.

PHOTO COURTESY OF NABLA KANE
RESTORATION BY DAVE DERBY

Mrs. Ellen Vaughan.
Cloonsuck, Cloonboniffe, Castlerea

PHOTO COURTESY OF PAT VAUGHAN

Maggie Tully (Newtownflood, Drum, Athlone) sister of Cissie, also a member of the Cumann na mBan club of Summerhill

The Tully Family (Newtownflood, Drum, Athlone) who provided a safe house for many men on the run

Tom Tully (Newtownflood, Drum, Athlone) 3rd Battalion Athlone Brigade, charter member of The O'Rahilly Sinn Féin Club. Tom acted as lookout while the Crannagh River Bridge was being dismantled. He, along with other member of the Summerhill Company, returned to Cornafulla the night of the ambush. Their intent: to rescue the body of their dead comrade, James Tormey. Tom survived the War years and many after that. He lived past his eighty-ninth birthday

William Tully a member of Cloverhill Coy., 2nd Battalion South Roscommon. After the War he emigrated to the USA

Henry Tumulty (Curryroe, Drum) a member of Drum Coy., 3rd Battalion Athlone Brigade. He took the Oath of Allegiance to the Sinn Féin party at the Ardkeenan House, the local Volunteer gathering point*

*Drum and Its Hinterland by Edward Egan, p. 301.

Malachy Tumulty (Curryroe, Drum) 3rd Battalion Athlone Brigade, brother of Henry. He also took the Oath of Allegiance to the Sinn Féin party at the Ardkeenan House

Hugh Tuohy (Ballaghaderreen) one of the first members of the Ballaghaderreen Coy. in the East Mayo Brigade

Patrick Tuohy served as the drill instructor of the Ballaghaderreen Company

James Turbitt (Ross Lane, Boyle) 1st Battalion North Roscommon. He was taken into the IRB by Alec McCabe in February 1915. Took part in the **Rockingham Raid**, after which he was arrested and sent to Mountjoy, where he participated in the hunger strike organised by Austin Stack. After his release he became Chief of the Republican Police in North Roscommon, and was on the Staff of the 3rd Western Division

Kathleen Turbitt (Ross Lane, Boyle) active member of the Cumann na mBan, sister of James

Michael Tymon (Knockadryan, Arigna) 4th Battalion North Roscommon Brigade

Patrick "Paddy" Tymon (Knockadryan, Arigna) served as the 2nd Lieutenant for Arigna Company in the 4th Battalion North Roscommon. Tymon was involved in many skirmishes with the Free State troops, including the **attack on Drumshanbo Barracks** in September 1922, where he stood shoulder to shoulder with James Kelly and Michael Mahon. He was killed when the Free State troopers exploded a Mills bomb at the entrance of a dugout in the Arigna riverbank in which he was hiding on 27 February 1923. Patrick's father, John, had the sad duty of making the coffin for his son as well as that of Seamus Cull who was killed with him. Tymon is buried in the Arigna Cemetery. His name is inscribed on the tablets in front of the Shankill Monument near Elphin. On 19 September 1999, a memorial was dedicated to Patrick and his co-patriot, Seamus Cull. The memorial stands above the dugout where they met their deaths, and was sponsored by the Roscommon County Commemorative Committee (see photo on page 164)

Mrs. Ellen Vaughan (Cloonsuck, Cloonboniffe, Castlerea) mother of several Volunteer sons, who opened her door to many a man on the run. After the Tans had killed her son John in the field in back of her home, she received a crashing blow to the head from one of those men. After the War she remained on the farm where she died in the late 1950s

John Vaughan (Cloonsuck, Cloonboniffe, Castlerea) Captain of Cloonboniffe Company, 1st Battalion South Roscommon. Participated in the **destruction of vacant barracks** in 1920. He, along with Ned Shannon, was betrayed by a spy, who informed the Crown Forces of his whereabouts. He was shot at his home in the village of Cloonsuck 22 June 1921. Buried Castlerea Cemetery. His name appears on the tablets in front of the Shankill Monument near Elphin. A memorial bell tower was erected in his honour outside the Cloonboniffe Church

Patrick Vaughan (Cloonsuck, Cloonboniffe, Castlerea) brother of John and Tom, Intelligence Officer for South Roscommon, worker in the Connolly Hotel in Castlerea, who smuggled guns, ammunition, and petrol to the Volunteers. Emigrated to America in the early 1920s, and became the proprietor of Vaughan's Tavern in Boston, where used to hang a number of Lee-Enfield rifles fired during the Tan War, which he had smuggled to the States. The author spoke personally with Pat on many occasions. At the time, Patrick was a ninety-four-year-old resident of Boston, Massachusetts, whose keen mind and sharp wit added much to the first-hand material this author was able to obtain. He died in February 1997 loving Ireland as dearly as he had loved her in his youth

Tom Vaughan (Cloonsuck, Cloonboniffe, Castlerea) 1st Battalion South Roscommon, brother of John and Patrick. Participated in the **destruction of vacant barracks** in 1920, the **capture of arms from the Castlerea Barracks** in April 1920, the **raid for petrol at Ballinlough Station** in June 1920, and served as scout for the **capture of enemy stores at Ballymoe** that same month. Tom was also with the attack parties at the **attempted ambush at Coshlieve** in July 1920, the **attempted attack on the Castlerea Station Guard**, and **the raid and capture of military equipment at Ballymoe** September 1920. He blocked roads in preparation for the **attack on Frenchpark Barracks** 2 October 1920. In 1921, Tom became even more involved in Volunteer activity. He took part in the **attempted attacks at Castlerea** and **Frenchpark** in January 1921, and served in the covering party for the **attack on the military at Castlerea** 7 April 1921. Tom participated in the **attempted ambush at Loughglynn**, and the **attempted ambush of an RIC patrol near Ballymoe** in April 1921. During the month of May, he joined with other Volunteers in an **attempted ambush at Lisacul** in conjunction with the East Mayo men. During the Truce he attended the Battalion training camps. Tom was arrested by the Tans at his home in the village of Cloonsuck June 1921 after an engagement in which his brother, John, lost his life. Tom was beaten so severely (his ear drums were ruptured) that mental illness plagued him throughout his life. He did not, however, quit fighting the British! He took part during the Civil War on the Anti-Treaty side in the **attack at Ballinagare** in July 1922. After the War he returned to farming the land at Cloonsuck. Died June 1977, and buried in Castlerea Cemetery

Frank Vesey (Aghawerriny, Kilgefin, Roscommon) a member of "E" Coy., 3rd Battalion South Roscommon, brother of Larry. Many, but not all, of the members of the Kilgefin Company participated in the **Fourmilehouse Ambush** on 12 October 1920. Died 24 December 1976. Buried in Kilgefin Cemetery

James Vesey (Cloonlumney, Ballaghaderreen) during the Civil War he took the Anti-Treaty side. Arrested 6 September 1922 and sent to Athlone 14 November

Larry Vesey (Aghawerriny, Kilgefin, Roscommon) a member of "E" Coy., 3rd Battalion South Roscommon. Some, but not all, of the members of the Kilgefin Company participated in the **Fourmilehouse Ambush** on 12 October 1920. Larry was the brother of Frank

Michael Vesey (Ballindollaghan, Castleplunkett) a member of Castleplunkett Coy. in the 2nd Battalion South Roscommon

Martin Vizard (Mountain Upper, Ballinlough) a member of Trien Coy., 1st Battalion South Roscommon

John Waldron (Trien Coy.) 1st Battalion South Roscommon

John Waldron (Curry, Kiltoom, Athlone) served as the Quartermaster of Curraghboy Coy. in the 4th Battalion South Roscommon, brother of Patrick. From 1917-March 1919 did organisational work, drilled, and performed scouting duties. Attended lectures and instructions given by Ernie O'Malley during his tour

John Vaughan, Captain of Cloonboniffe Coy. 1st Battalion South Roscommon.
PHOTO COURTESY OF PAT VAUGHAN
PHOTO RESTORATION BY LEW THORNE

Patrick Vaughan. Cloonboniffe Coy.
PHOTO COURTESY OF PATRICK VAUGHAN
PHOTO RESTORATION BY LEW THORNE

Tom Vaughan, Cloonboniffe Coy. brother of John and Patrick
PHOTO COURTESY OF SEAN VAUGHAN

of the Battalion area. Performed police duty during the South Roscommon election and in conjunction with enforcement of Dáil decrees. Raided for arms. About twenty raids for arms were conducted within the Company area, and another fifteen raids were outside the immediate area and performed in cooperation with other Companies of the Battalion. Waldron was in those raiding parties. He also raided the premises of a court messenger to the British Courts, and seized books and documents relating to same. Participated in the **attempted attack on Kilmurray Camp** in June 1920, an operation that was called off the night of the intended attack. Prevented jurors from attending the British Courts, and held periodic meetings of Dáil Courts when necessity arose. Manufactured ammunition, and raided the mails. The entire Company took part in the arrest and confinement of a suspected spy. That man was tried by court-martial and eventually executed — action which prompted the arrest of ten members of the Company in January including Waldron. He was taken to Athlone Barracks and incarcerated in a cell with no bed. Three months later he was transferred to Mountjoy and finally, in the last days of June, shipped to Wormwood Scrubbs and Pentonville Prisons in England. Released 11 January 1922, whereupon he returned to Curraghboy and rejoined his Company with the intent of resisting the Treaty. He raided homes of ex-RIC men, blocked roads at Whitepark, Lisbrook, and Bredagh intending to delay troop movements, guarded two shopkeepers' premises who were being victimised by local hooligans, and generally harassed the Pro-Treaty soldiers

Michael Waldron (Ballinlough Coy.) 1st Battalion South Roscommon. Participated in the **burning of the Ballinlough Barracks** 14 September 1920. Later emigrated to New Jersey

Patrick Waldron (Curry, Kiltoom, Athlone) a member of Curraghboy Coy., 4th Battalion South Roscommon. From 1917-March 1919 did organisational work, drilled with the men, paraded during a visit to the area by Sean Connolly, did police duty during the South Roscommon election and in conjunction with enforcement of Dáil decrees. Waldron took part in over twenty raids for arms. He also raided the premises of a court messenger to the British Courts, and seized books and documents. Manufactured ammunition and constructed dugouts for storage of same. The entire Company participated in the arrest and confinement of a suspected spy. That man was tried by court-martial and eventually executed — an action which prompted the arrest of ten members of the Company on 5 January 1921 including Waldron. He was severely thrashed and taken to Athlone Barracks and incarcerated in a cell with no bed. Three months later he was transferred to Mountjoy and finally, in the last days of June, he was shipped across the waters to Wormwood Scrubbs and Pentonville Prisons in England. Tom Hales from Cork was his commanding officer in prison. He participated in a hunger strike while incarcerated, and was held in leg irons and shirtjacket. Released 11 January 1922, whereupon he returned to Curraghboy and rejoined his Company with the intent of resisting the Treaty. He raided homes of ex-RIC men, blocked roads at Curraghboy and Lysterfield hoping to delay troop movements, and generally harassed the Pro-Treaty soldiers along with his brother, John

Tom Waldron (Ballindrimley, Castlerea) Moor Coy., 1st Battalion South Roscommon. Took part in the **attack on Frenchpark Barracks** 2 October 1920. He was arrested in January 1921, and interned until December 1921. Present at Pat Glynn's Memorial Service in 1970

Francis Wallace (Clerragh, Fairymount, Castlerea) 2nd Lieutenant in "F" Coy. of the 1st Battalion South Roscommon

James Wallace (Carrick, Ballinlough) a member of Ballinlough Coy., 1st Battalion South Roscommon. Participated in the **raid for petrol at Ballinlough Station** in June 1920, the **attempted ambush at Coshlieve** in July 1920 and the **attempted attack on the Castlerea Station Guard** that same month, and the **burning of the Ballinlough Barracks** 14 September 1920. During the Truce he attended the Battalion training camp specialising in intelligence work

Gerald Walsh (Knockhall, Ruskey) a member of the Kilglass Company in the 3rd Battalion North Roscommon

Jamsey Walsh (Boyle) 1st Battalion North Roscommon, a member of the Volunteers since before the Rising

John Walsh (Killeenboy, Kilteevan) a member of Kilteevan Coy., 3rd Battalion South Roscommon

Martin Walsh (Lieutenant) in charge of Intelligence for the 1st Battalion, No. 2 Brigade. When the 2nd Western Division was formed, this area of Galway was grouped with parts of Roscommon and formed into a new military unit. Gerald O'Connor, former O/C of the 1st Battalion South Roscommon, became Commander of this Brigade

Michael J. Walsh (Cloonshannagh, Tarmonbarry) a member of the Tarmonbarry Coy. of the 3rd Battalion North Roscommon, brother of Patrick. During the years of 1917 and 1918, Walsh drilled with his Company, raided for arms, and enforced the Belfast boycott. He was present at the **attack on Tarmonbarry Barracks** in November 1920, **Scramogue Ambush**, and **attacks at Whitehall, Balytoohey** and **Ruskey**. During the Civil War he fired on a Free State lorry at Tarmonbarry, **attacked the Ruskey and Tarmonbarry Barracks**, and shot at a Free State patrol in Ruskey — an action in which one of the Volunteers was wounded. He was arrested in 1922 and imprisoned in Athlone until he was released two months later

Patrick Walsh (Knockhall, Ruskey) a member of the Kilglass Company in the 3rd Battalion North Roscommon

Patrick Walsh (Culleenaghmore, Kilglass) a member of Slatta Coy., 3rd Battalion North Roscommon. He took part in the **raid on** Walpole's land in **Clooneenhartland** in the spring of 1919

Thomas Walsh a member of the Flying Column of South Roscommon during the Civil War under the command of Matt Davis. Along with Davis and several others, he was captured in a raid on Quaker Island in Lough Ree on 22 November 1922

Patrick Walsh (Cloonshannagh, Tarmonbarry) a member of "D" Company in the 3rd Battalion North Roscommon. Walsh joined the IRA in 1917. He attended weekly meetings, took part in the North Roscommon and South Longford elections, raided boats on the Shannon for petrol and ammunition, did dispatch work, blocked roads for the **attack on Tarmonbarry Barracks** in 1920, assisted at the **Scramogue Ambush**, and **attempted ambushes at Balytoohey, Whitehall, Ruskey**, and the **attack on Tarmonbarry Barracks**. He also served with the military police up until the Civil War. In 1922 he reorganised the Company as an Anti-Treaty unit, and was appointed its Captain. During the Civil War he blocked roads, made an **unsuccessful attack on Ruskey Barracks**, commandeered boats on the Shannon, and carried out attacks on Free State troops in the Company area. He was a member of the ASU of North Roscommon. He was arrested and imprisoned at Athlone, but upon his release, returned to his old ways, and **attacked the Free State troops at Lake Forbes**

John Ward (Ballydooley, Oran) a member of "E" Coy. (Donamon) in the 2nd Battalion South Roscommon. Participated in the **raid on the military train at Ballymoe** in June 1920

Michael Ward (Green Street, Boyle) received dispatches from altar boy Joe Martin regarding escape plans from Boyle Barracks for Jim Molloy and Michael Dockery. Ward, in turn, passed the dispatches on to Pat Delahunty, Intelligence Officer

Michael Ward (Turla, Ballymoe) 1st Battalion South Roscommon. A member of the Active Service Unit from April 1920 to the Truce. He participated in the **destruction of the Glenamaddy Workhouse**

Thomas Ward (Ballyfeeny, Strokestown) a member of the Kilglass Company in the 3rd Battalion North Roscommon

William Ward Vice O/C of the 5th Battalion North Roscommon, arrested in the summer of 1920 and replaced by Jack Glancy

Michael Warde (Boyle) owner of the Princess Hotel, a member of the first Sinn Féin County Council in Roscommon. Arrested while attending a meeting in Croghan, and imprisoned in Boyle Barracks

Michael Warren (Rathmore, Kiltrustan, Strokestown) 3rd Battalion North Roscommon. In 1918 he replaced Pat Mullooly as Captain of the Kiltrustan Coy.

Edward Watson (Kilnasillagh, Kilgefin, Roscommon) a member of "E" Coy., 3rd Battalion South Roscommon. Many, but not all, of the members of the Kilgefin Company participated in the **Fourmilehouse Ambush** on 12 October 1920. After the War he became a postman in Lanesboro. Died in the 1970s, and buried in Cloontuskert Abbey

Hubert "Bert" Watson (Carrownderry, Kiltoom, Athlone) St. John's Coy., 4th Battalion South Roscommon. When the Company first formed in 1917, Watson drilled with other Volunteers two nights a week — Tuesdays and Thursdays, and worked as a Republican Policeman with the Republican Courts. Watson raided for arms many times. He was included in every raid taken on by the Company. He was present at the raid on Feehily's house in which Joseph Kearney was severely wounded in the stomach. Active in enforcing the Belfast boycott, he collected monies for the Defence Fund and IRA levy, and also more lethal gelignite. He, Johnny Kilcline, and Dan Kerrigan stopped two postmen and raided their mails for suspicious letters. He and eight other members of his Company stopped a **train at Kiltoom and raided the mail car**. He took part in the **attempted ambush at Clooncraff** under the command of Pat Madden, and the **attempted ambush at Kilmurray Military Camp** in June 1920. He was captured by the British, but released after the Truce, whereupon he returned to the area and became a member of the special service unit. Watson took an active role in the Civil War. He **blew up the Kellybrook and Curry Railway Bridges**, blocked ballast trains, collected gelignite, and served as the caretaker for such, and helped assemble the heavy mines used locally. Watson was also a crack shot. After the War he became a farmer. A man of fantastic memory, he oftentimes played the leading roles in local plays — on more than one occasion being accused of "re-writing Shakespeare." He died in the late 1970s, and is buried in Kiltoom Cemetery

John Watson (Lismoyle, Curraghboy, Athlone) a member of Curraghboy Coy., 4th Battalion South Roscommon. From 1917-March 1919 did organisational work, drilled with the men, paraded during a visit to the area by Sean Connolly, did police duty during the South Roscommon election and in conjunction with enforcement of Dáil decrees. Watson was with a group of Volunteers who raided the private homes of three men — two of whom had joined and one who was about to join the RIC. Not surprisingly, these men decided to pursue other interests! There were a total of twenty arms raids conducted within the Company area, and another fifteen raids were outside the immediate vicinity and performed in conjunction with other Companies of the Battalion. Watson took part in those actions and, in addition, prevented jurors from attending the British Courts. Manufactured ammunition and constructed dugouts for storage of same. Seven or eight mail cars were robbed during this time, and Watson was part of the attacking party. The entire Company participated in the arrest and confinement of a suspected spy. That man was tried by court-martial and eventually executed — an action which prompted the arrest of ten members of the Company on 5 January 1921. Watson raided homes of persons sympathetic to the enemy, and prepared for an attack on Ballygar Barracks in which he was unable to participate because he was arrested in March 1921

Larry Watson (Kilmocolmock, Drum, Athlone) a member of the Father O'Flanagan Sinn Féin Club, brother of Pat

Pat Watson (Kilmocolmock, Drum, Athlone) Vice O/C of 3rd Battalion of the Athlone Brigade. He also served as Captain of the Drum Company. After the War he was dispirited by the results, and although he joined the National Army in which he served for a number of years, he was, according to his daughter Frankie, "broken in health and spirit." Died 28 December 1955, and buried in Drum Cemetery

Edward "Ned" Weir (Carrowbaun, Ballintubber), active in land agitation, killed by the Tans 1 July 1921. They dragged him from his home and left his body in a nearby field. He was buried in Ballintubber Cemetery. His name is inscribed on the tablets in front of the Shankill Monument near Elphin

James Whelan (Ardmullan, Curraghboy, Athlone) Curraghboy Coy., 4th Battalion South Roscommon. Whelan was part of the Anti-Treaty Flying Column during the Civil War that travelled over south Roscommon, neighbouring Galway, and sometimes Westmeath and Longford. Activities include **derailing a train at Kiltoom**, blocking roads at Whitepark, cutting telegraph lines, **attacking Free State troops at Mount Talbot**, and general harassment of Free State troops

Pat Whelan (Carrick-on-Shannon) an officer in the South Leitrim Brigade under Bernard Sweeney. Took part in actions at **Garadice, Eslin, Fenagh, Ranthogue and Kesh***

**Who's Who in the Irish War of Independence and Civil War 1916-1923*, by Padraic O'Farrell p. 97.

Pat Watson. Vice O/C of the 3rd Battalion Athlone Brigade

PHOTO COURTESY OF FRANKIE WATSON

John White (Clooncah, Castlerea) served as Quartermaster for Trien Coy. in the 1st Battalion South Roscommon, a member of the Flying Column. White took part in operations in conjunction with the East Mayo Brigade, including the attempted ambush at Coshlieve in July 1920. He also participated in the attempted ambush of RIC patrol near Ballymoe in May 1921. He attended the Cloonkeen, Castlerea, Erritt, Swinford, and Runnamoat training camps during the Truce

John White (Boyle) 1st Battalion North Roscommon

Richard Wilkinson (Ballykilcline, Kilglass, Strokestown) Adjutant for Ruskey Company in the 3rd Battalion North Roscommon, acted as Republican Judge in the Kilglass area

Michael Winston (Carrick, Ballinlough) Captain of Ballinlough Coy., 1st Battalion South Roscommon. Member of the Flying Column. Participated in the **raid for petrol at Ballinlough** in June 1920, the **attempted ambush at Coshlieve** in July 1920, the **attempted attack on the Castlerea Station Guard** that same month, and the **burning of the Ballinlough Barracks** on 14 September 1920. During the Truce he attended the training camps at Erritt, Donamon, Swinford, and Castlerea. He later joined the Free State Army

Patrick Winston (Ballinlough Coy.) 1st Battalion South Roscommon. Participated in the **raid for petrol at Ballinlough** in June 1920, the **attempted ambush at Coshlieve** in July 1920, the **attempted attack on the Castlerea Station Guard** during that same month, and the **burning of the Ballinlough Barracks** 14 September 1920. During the Truce he attended the Battalion training camp specialising in first aid

Francis Wynne (Rattinagh, Kilglass, Strokestown) a member of the Kiltrustan Coy. in the 3rd Battalion North Roscommon

Patrick Wynne (Killeenboy, Kilteevan) a lad of sixteen, who was killed by the Tans on 9 May 1921 when they entered his home, and he tried to escape from the officers by scooting into an adjoining room. His is the last name on the list inscribed on the tablets in front of the Shankill Monument near Elphin

Patrick Wynne (Green Street, Boyle) a member of the first Boyle Coy. in the 1st Battalion North Roscommon

Patrick Wynne, a native of Ballinaheglish, who joined the British Army and served as a drummer boy in the Boer War. Upon his return to Ireland, he connected with the Volunteers and trained members of the Rahara Coy. in south Roscommon. A small man in stature, his walk was erect and his mind sharp. He joined the Free State Army, and upon release, returned to the Rahara area and worked as a farm labourer. He died in the 1980s

Roll of Honour Memorial at Shankill.
A listing of Volunteers from Roscommon who died in the War for Independence and Civil War.

PHOTO COURTESY OF LEW THORNE

Peter Wynne (Killeenboy, Kilteevan) brother of Patrick, arrested at his home and taken to the town of Roscommon, where he was beaten by the Tans in the spring of 1921. He was later released

William Wynne (Drumman Beg, Ruskey) a member of the Kilglass Company in the 3rd Battalion North Roscommon

PART IV

A GLIMPSE AT THE VOLUNTEERS OF THE SURROUNDING AREAS

GALWAY

Dublin County had the largest contingent of men captured and imprisoned after the Easter Rising. Galway County had the second largest group. There were 322 Galway men incarcerated in Frongoch alone.

North Galway Brigade Staff:
O/C Con Fogarty IRB, Patrick Dunleavy
Vice O/C Michael Moran
Adjutant: Joe Cooney, Thomas Tarmay
Quartermaster: Patrick Conway

Members of the North Galway Flying Column formed in January 1921:
O/C Patrick Dunleavy, Brigade Commandant and Column leader
Brigade Adjutant Thomas Tarmay
Brigade Q/M Patrick Conway
James Maloney O/C of Glenamaddy Battalion
Martin Ryan Vice O/C of Glenamaddy Battalion
Jack Knight, Quartermaster of Glenamaddy Battalion
Martin Mannion, Captain of Dunmore Coy., Glenamaddy Battalion
Thomas Dunleavy, brother of Patrick, Commandant of Glenamaddy Battalion
Thomas Nohilly, Adjutant of Tuam Battalion
Thomas Ryan, Quartermaster of Tuam Battalion
Thomas Mannion, Captain of Dunmore Coy., Glenamaddy Battalion
Brian Cunniffe, Captain of Kilkerrin Coy., Glenamaddy Battalion
Timothy Dunleavy, Captain of Barnaderg Coy., Tuam Battalion
Thomas Feerick Captain of Milltown Coy., Tuam Battalion
Peter Brennan, Milltown Coy., Tuam Battalion
Pat Treacy, Captain of Glenamaddy Coy., Glenamaddy Battalion
John J. Ryan, Tom Kilgarriff, Peter Burke, Patrick Walshe, John McCormack, Dan McCormack, Martin Slattery, Willie Feeney, Patrick McHugh

Killed in Action:
P. Cunnane, Sean Maguire, Martin Burke (Bourke), Stephen Joyce, Seamus O'Maille, Sean Newell, Hubert Collins, Martin Moylan, Michael Monaghan

There were two Battalions in the North Galway Brigade, Tuam and Glenamaddy Battalion
(which became, in 1921, part of No. 2 Brigade, 2nd Western Division with Gerald O'Connor of Roscommon serving as Brigade O/C)

Glenamaddy Battalion Staff:
O/C James Moloney
Vice O/C Martin Ryan
Quartermaster: Jack Knight
Adjutant: Martin Mannion, Pat Treacy
Commandant: Thomas Dunleavy
Medical Officer: Dr. Mangan
Chief of Police: Tom Concannon
Intelligence Officer: M. J. Walshe
Head of Signals: Martin Conagh
Policemen: Michael McGuire, Patrick Glennon

Headquarters: Bob Murphy, Stonetown, Glenamaddy
Meetings held monthly at Ballinastack
Active Service Unit formed in February 1921

Company Captains in the Glenamaddy Battalion
The Lieutenants and headquarters are listed as of July 1922:
Dunmore Capt. Michael Ronan and Thomas Mannion
    1st Lieutenant Joseph Treacy 2nd Lieutenant M. Gannon
    Headquarters: Martin Gannon, Ballintise
Kiltevna Capt. John Higgins, Roger Rabbitte (to the Truce) and Michael Mannion (Post Truce)
    1st Lieutenant Roger Rabbitte then Michael Mannion
    2nd Lieutenant Michael Mannion then James Costello
    Headquarters: Roger Rabbitte, Kiltevna
Williamstown Capt. Patrick Noonan
    1st Lieutenant Joe Shaughnessey 2nd Lieutenant J. Connor
    Headquarters: Patrick Noonan, Williamstown
Kilcroan Capt. John Hanley
    1st Lieutenant John Burke 2nd Lieutenant William Ryan
    Headquarters: William Ryan, Kilcroan
Glinsk Capt. Thomas Burke
    1st Lieutenant John Lally 2nd Lieutenant John McDonnell
    Headquarters: John McDonagh, Glinsk
Kilbegnet Capt. John McDonagh
    1st Lieutenant Thomas Lohan 2nd Lieutenant James Keane
    Headquarters: John McDonagh, Kilbegnet
Kilkerrin Capt. John Stephens (to July 1920), Brian Cunniffe
    1st Lieutenant Peter Collins 2nd Lieutenant Michael Naughton
    Headquarters: Michael Monaghan, Carrantubber
Clonberne Capt. John Mahon
    1st Lieutenant Tom Geraghty 2nd Lieutenant Larry Loury
    Headquarters: Dan Connolly (Matt), Lerhin, Clonberne
Glenamaddy Capt. Frank Mahon (from October 1920), Pat Treacy (to the Truce),
    Frank Mahon (Post Truce)
    1st Lieutenant John Jeffers 2nd Lieutenant Peter Moore
    Headquarters: Bob Murphy, Stonetown, Glenamaddy
Polredmond Capt. John Glennon
    1st Lieutenant Michael Quinn 2nd Lieutenant David Geraghty
    Headquarters: William Parsons, Polredmond, Williamstown

Tuam Battalion included ten Companies:
A Battalion was first organised in Tuam in 1917
O/C John P. Connolly, Con Fogarty
Adjutant: John J. Waldron
In late 1920/early 1921, following the arrest of Con Fogarty, Brigade Commander Patrick
Dunleavy named a new staff. He appointed the following officers for the Tuam Battalion:
O/C Thomas Dunleavy
Vice O/C Peter McHugh
Quartermaster: Thomas Ryan
In Charge of Police: James Burke
Adjutant: Sean O'Neill then Tom Nohilly in March 1921

Companies
Barnabeg Captain Tim Dunleavy
Tuam Captain Patrick Colleran
Sylane Captain Patrick McHugh
Corofin Captain Willie Feeney
Gardenfield Captain Martin Higgins
Milltown Captain Tom Feerick
Belmont Captain Thomas Hannon
Abbeyknockmoy Captain John Fleming
Kilconly Captain Frank Cunningham
Cortoon Captain Thomas Wilson

South Galway Brigade Staff

O/C Seamus Murphy
Pat Callanan
Engineer: John Kelly of Kilnadeena Coy.

Loughrea Battalion Staff

O/C Lawrence Burke (in March/April 1921 promoted to O/C of the Southeast Brigade)
Adjutant: James Flynn
Quartermaster: Martin Nevin
Patrick Coy

Companies included:

Clostoken O/C Patrick Coy and Patrick Connaughton
Kilmore O/C Edward Burke
Kilnadeena O/C Lawrence Kelly

Other Battalions included:

Mountbellew O/C John Hafferty
Athenry O/C Gilbert Morrissey
Gort O/C John Fahy
Ardrahan Vice O/C Peter Howley
Portumna
Ballinasloe
Oftentimes these Battalions worked independently of each other. In the spring of 1921, the Loughrea Battalion became associated with Michael Brennan's command in County Clare.

South Galway Brigade Structure Post Truce

Ballygar Company

Sean Lohan was the O/C of Ballygar Coy. That Company worked in conjunction with men from the extreme south of County Roscommon. In the years after the War, it was considered by the Department of Defence as part of the South Roscommon Brigade. Other officers in the Company included:
1st Lieutenant: John Kilroy
2nd Lieutenants: John Fitzmaurice and William Mulrooney
Adjutant: Andrew Lohan
Quartermaster: William Mulrooney
During the Civil War, Martin Kelly became the Officer in command
Commandant: Joseph Stankard
Vice O/C Jack Fahy
Quartermaster: Dan Ryan
Chief of Police: Padraig Kilkelly   *Intelligence Officer*: Padraig O'Fathaigh

Flying Column of West Connemara

Quoted from *Civil War in Connaught* by Nollaig O'Gadhra
O/C Peter Joseph McDonnell. Members: C. Breen, R. Joyce, G. Staunton, G. Bartley, J. King, M. Conneely, M. Conroy, Jack Feehan, J. Mannion, J. Conneely, J. King, P. Bartley, J. Dundass, Patrick Wallace, W. King, Peter Wallace, T. Madden, J. C. King, D. Keane, and T. Coyne,

Notes about Galway Volunteers

Louis Darcy was a student at the College of Surgeons in Dublin when he volunteered to "go down to the country" and organise Companies. His family was very pro-British, and when they discovered his activities, they threw him out of his house.* He became the O/C of Headford Battalion, and, as the result of an informer, was shot at Oranmore, Galway on 25 March 1921.** Buried in Clydagh Cemetery. This is the British version of his demise: "...in October of the same year (1920), the Police were able to lay their hands on large quantities of explosives and ammunition in the house of Lewis (Louis) Darcy, and, later on, information was received that he was about to leave by train for Dublin, disguised as a labourer. The Police arrived at the railway station at the same time as he did. He was arrested and, whilst being transported back to Galway in a lorry, attempted to escape and, by one of the extraordinary decrees of fate, met his death on the same spot where, a few weeks previously, he had brutally murdered a Police Sergeant. Thus died one of the most astute criminals in the West of Ireland."***
Gerald Davis Volunteer Witness Statement to Bureau of Military History 1913-21, p. 8.
**Who's Who in the Irish War of Independence and Civil War 1916-1923 by Padraic O'Farrell, p. 25.*
***British Intelligence in Ireland 1920-21, edited by Peter Hart, p. 77.*

Con Fogarty, O/C of the Galway Brigade, arrested in February 1921 and sent to Tuam workhouse, Galway Gaol, and the Curragh, from which he was released December 1921. When Patrick Dunleavy resigned his position as O/C of the Brigade, Fogarty (who was a member of the IRB) took his place. The Civil War found him commanding Anti-Treaty troops in Tuam, where he lived in the barracks after it had been handed over by the British. He was captured on 9 September 1922 and imprisoned in Athlone

Martin Hynes active with Liam Mellows during Easter Week and imprisoned in Frongoch

Patrick Coy was an officer in Clostoken Coy., then on the Battalion Staff, and finally promoted to the Southeast Galway Brigade staff. He was killed in action in Kerry during the Civil War

Jack Keogh leader of Anti-Treatyites in South Galway, was captured in September 1923 near Ballinasloe

The Loughnane Brothers from Owenbristy near Gort, Co. Galway, were arrested at their home, taken to Gort RIC Barracks, where they were beaten unmercifully. Their bodies were found eleven days later in a nearby pond by a neighbour who had "seen" their bodies in a dream. Their remains were waked at Hynes Barn and services were held at Kinvara Church*

(Padraig O'Fathaigh's War of Independence Recollections of a Galway Gaelic Leaguer p. 64-65.)

Patrick Kilkelly (Kinvara, near Gort in Co. Galway) worked as a language instructor assisted by Willie Hynes. He taught in Abbey Ballinakill and Woodford. He became a member of the Gort District Council and therefore a member of the County Council. During the Civil War, he was selected to head a Flying Column (that included men from Ballaghaderreen) that attacked Renmore Barracks. Captured in August 1922

Dan McCormack of Milltown, member of the Flying Column, escaped from military custody in Claremorris on 10 February 1923. He died 15 August 1929 from the wounds he received in the attack on Headford Barracks on 9 April 1923

Larry Lardner was elected to the Supreme Council of the IRB in 1917

Colm O'Gaora, Brigadier of the 4th Battalion in Connemara. "He and his men endured lack of clothing and provisions during a severe campaign" during the Civil War*

**Who's Who in the Irish War of Independence and Civil War 1916-1923*, p. 184.*

On Easter Sunday night in 1916, there was a general mobilisation of the Tuam IRB circle at Connolly's forge, Galway Road. Arrangements had been made to halt a train outside Tuam Station and convey all the men to Mayode Castle, Athenry. There was great confusion as to orders and counter-commands. All participants simply went home

Men of the 2nd Western Division who are buried in the Republican plot at Donaghpatrick located in Caherlistrane, Headford, Co. Galway:

Captain Martin Burke (Bourke), Manusflynn, Caherlistrane, Co. Galway
Captain Stephen Joyce, Caherlistrane, Co. Galway
Captain Michael Walsh, Caherlistrane, Co. Galway
Volunteer Hubert Collins, Kilkeel, Headford
Commdt. Frank Cunnane, Kilcoona, Headford
Lieut. Sean Maguire, Cross, Cong
Lieut. John Newall (Newell), Cloghanover, Headford
Vol. Martin Moylan, Farmerstown, Annaghadown, Co. Galway
Vol. Seamus O'Malley, Oughterard

Liam Mellows, born in Lancashire and raised in Galway and Wexford. He organised the only substantial activities outside Dublin during Easter Week. A Sinn Féin TD for Meath and Galway, he was later executed by the Free State government in December 1922

All Galway in 1917 was one Brigade with Seamus Murphy serving as Comdt. Sean Broderick was Quartermaster and Mattie Niland was the Adjutant

Liam O'Briain fought in Dublin during Easter Week. He became a Frongoch graduate, who served as Republican Judge for Galway/Connemara

Frank O'Heidin (Athenry) Captain of the local Company, incarcerated in Frongoch in 1916, later wrote articles for 'An Phoblacht' regarding Liam Mellows and Galway's part in the Rising*

Frongoch University of Revolution by Sean Mahony. p. 226.

Tom Glennon of Polredmond (a resigned RIC man) and Patrick Quigley of Glinsk became the first two Republican Policemen in Glenamaddy just after the Truce

Fr. James Fergus, C.C. of Glenamaddy, was a real friend to the Volunteers, giving spiritual consolation to all who approached him

Fr. William Rattigan C.C. of Kilkerrin was also a great sympathiser with the cause

Padraig O'Fathaigh was an IRB member and Republican loan officer for South and East Galway. Served as the Intelligence Officer for the South Galway Brigade after the Truce

Colm O'Geary was the Republican loan officer for Connemara

Timeline for Tuam area during the Civil War 1922:

15 July — take over of Tuam Barracks by Republican forces

25 July — Free State Army enters Tuam

9 September — Free State ambushed near Tuam. Volunteer Walsh KIA. Volunteer Cooney wounded

20 September — Republicans attack town of Tuam, making prisoner of every Free State soldier to be found. They withdraw at 2 a.m. with confiscated supplies

30 September — Another raid by Republicans on Tuam

18 November — Free State troops ambushed on way to Galway from Tuam

22 November — Still another raid by Republicans on Tuam. They set fire to the workhouse and commandeer supplies

30 December — Free State troops from Tuam and Ballinrobe operating in Headford area **captured nine prisoners.** Several of those men were executed in January 1923 in Athlone

Excerpted from Nollaig O'Gadhra's book _Civil War in Connaught 1922-1923_:

On 19 February, a raid at Cluid occurred. Eighteen Republicans were captured, six of whom would be executed* two months later in Tuam. The prisoners included: John Newell* (Headford); Pat Farragher (Kilmaine, Co. Mayo); Michael Joyce (Headford); James Craddock (Headford); Martin Moylan* (Farmerstown, Annaghdown); Patrick Jennings (Milltown); Thomas Madden (Caherlistrane); Edward Dooley (Headford); Michael Sweeney (Seefin, Claremorris); Batty Canavan (Mossfort); John Hession (Turlane, Caherlistrane); Michael Connolly (Hollymount, Co. Mayo); Michael Monaghan* (Headford); Francis Cunnane* (Headford); Sean (John) Maguire* (Cross, Cong); Joseph Collins (Kilkeel, Headford); Peter Brennan (Milltown); and Seamus O'Malley* (Oughterard).

A Sampling of Galway internees during the Civil War:

Name	Place of Residence	Gaol
James Burke	Tuam	Athlone & Mountjoy
Martin Burke (Bourke)	Caherlistrane (executed by Free State)	Athlone
William Burns	Ballinasloe	Athlone
Patrick J. Byrne	Cappataggle, Ballinasloe	Athlone
Patrick Carty	Ballinasloe	Galway & Tintown II
Martin Coleman	Ballaghall, Ballygar	Athlone& Stone Park
Stephen Coleman	Shannonbridge, Ballinasloe	Athlone
Thomas Collins	Menlough, Ballinasloe	Athlone & Tintown II
Daniel Connelly	Ballinasloe	Athlone
Patrick Connolly	Ballinderren	Galway & Tintown II
Patrick Coyne	Glenamaddy	Athlone & Mountjoy & Tintown
Patrick Coyne	Ballinasloe	Athlone & Mountjoy & Tintown
Patrick Dolan	Abbey, Loughrea	Galway
Michael Donnell	Soran, Ballinasloe	Athlone
James Downey	Ahascragh, Ballinasloe	Athlone
Patrick Farraher	Lough Mask, Ballinasloe	Athlone
Benjamin Fitzpatrick	Dunlo St., Ballinasloe	Maryborough
Michael Flanagan	Hollymount, Ballinasloe	Tintown
Daniel Gauquin	Fairfield, Ahascragh, Ballinasloe	Athlone
David Gauquin	Fairfield, Ahascragh, Ballinasloe	Athlone
Michael Geraghty	Glenamaddy	Athlone
Thomas Gilmore	Ballinasloe	Athlone
Thomas Glynn	Glenmaddy	Athlone
James Hanagh	Newcastle, Ballinasloe	Athlone
Sean Hanley	Ballygar	Athlone
John Harrington	Ballinasloe	Athlone
John Hill	Menlough, Ballinasloe	Athlone
Michael Hynes	Ballinasloe Aughrim	Athlone
Thomas Jennings	Cappataggle, Ballinasloe	Galway
Jack Keogh	captured September 1923	
Patrick Kilgannon	Mount Bellew	Athlone
Patrick McDonnell	Cleaghmore, Ballinasloe	Athlone
James Manning	Abbey, Ballinasloe	Galway
Martin Mannion	Menlough, Ballinasloe	Athlone
Michael Mannion	Aughrim, Ballinasloe	

Henry Mariner	Gavaveen, Ballinasloe	Athlone
Thomas Marron	Eskerpost, Ballinasloe	Athlone
Patrick Moclair	Kilure, Ahascragh	Galway
John Moloney	Greenage, Craughwell	Tintown II
John Mooloney	Craughwell	Galway
Thomas Mulraun	Kiltulla	Galway
Michael Mulvey	Cloniff, Ballinasloe	Athlone
Andrew Murphy	Ahascragh, Ballinasloe	Athlone
William Murphy	Ahascragh, Ballinasloe	Athlone
John Murray	Dunmore	Galway
Pat Murray	Clonfert, Ballinasloe	Galway
Michael Newell	Craughwell	Galway
Pat Norton	Clonlyon, Ballygar	Athlone
George Nugent	Aughrim, Ballinasloe	Athlone
James O'Keefe	Craughwell	Dundalk
Jerry O'Keefe	Craughwell	Galway
Patrick O'Keefe	Craughwell	Dundalk
John Rafferty	Glenamaddy	Athlone
Michael Rankiss	Castlegar	Athlone
Martin Regan	Loughrea	Athlone
Patrick Reilly	Kilmanagh	Athlone
John Ryan	Attimany, Loughrea	Galway/Curragh
Joseph Ryan	Attimany, Loughrea	Dundalk
Thomas Ryan	Killimor, Ballinasloe	Galway
Patrick Ryan	Attimany, Loughrea	Dundalk
Joseph Sammon	Renvyle, Tully	Athlone
William Scully	Annaghdown	Galway
Owen Smith	Caltra, Ballinasloe	Athlone
Martin Sullivan	Rosmuck	Athlone
James Treacy	Mount Bellew, Ballinasloe	Athlone
Joe Walsh	Taylor's Hill, Galway City	Galway
John Walsh	Attimany, Loughrea	Galway
Martin Walsh	The West	Galway
Michael Walsh	Attimany, Loughrea	Galway

LEITRIM

Internees in Frongoch after the Easter Rising:
Bernard Maguire (Glenfarne)
John Daly (Manorhamilton)
James Dolan (Manorhamilton)
Thomas McElgunn (Manorhamilton)
Thomas O'Loughlin (Manorhamilton)

South Leitrim Brigade Officers
O/C David (Edward) O'Brien (of Mohill), Sean Mitchell (Cloone, Co. Leitrim), Bernard Sweeney of Ballinamore
Vice O/C Henry McKeon (IRB)
Adjutant: Joseph Beirne, Eugene Kilkenny in March 1921
Quartermaster: Patrick Tiernan
Intelligence Officer: Charles Pinkman

Battalions:

1st Battalion Officers — Cloone O/C Bernard McGowan
Adjutant: Michael Baxter
Intelligence Officer: Patrick McGovern

2nd Battalion — Ballinamore
First O/C Packy Flynn
Vice O/C Michael Bohem
Adjutant: Francis McGowan
Intelligence Officer: Thomas Bohan

Quartermaster: Terence Boyle
Drilling Instructor: Ambrose Conway (an ex-British soldier)

Companies of the 2nd Battalion:
Aughnasheelin
Aughawilliam
Ballinamore
Cromlin (O/C Packy McTeague)
Corraleehan
Fenagh
Ballinamore whose first Captain was John William O'Beirne
    (Paddy Logan of Mohill was also instrumental in starting the Company.) Originally the
    Company numbered 40-50 members. Redmonite sympathies ran high in that area. In 1919,
    Bernard Sweeney became the Company Captain. Adjutant Joseph Barnes
    1st Lieutenant Michael Mulligan
Arms dump for the 2nd Battalion was in the boiler house in the Convent grounds in
Ballinamore. Later in the War, the arms were divided up among the Companies

3rd Battalion — Carrick-on-Shannon

4th Battalion — (Drumkeeran and Manorhamilton were not organised until after the Truce)

5th Battalion Staff
O/C Sean O'Farrell of Dromard, Dromod; Thomas Shanley of Clooneagh, Dromod
Vice O/C Thomas McKeon (emigrated to New York)
Quartermaster: James Canning of Tooma, Cloone
Intelligence Officer: Patrick McGovern (later emigrated to New York)
Adjutant: John J. Cooney of Aughnaglace, Cloone, Mohill
John Charles Keegan who later emigrated to California
Patrick O'Rourke of Cloncowley, Drumlish, Co. Longford
Bernard Ryan of Annaghmacoolen, Cloone

Companies of the 5th Battalion
Aughavas — Capt. Peter McIntyre
    Annaduff
    Ballinamore
Barnacoola — Capt. Patrick Keville
    Carrick-on-Shannon
    Carrigallen
Cloone — Capt. Frank Maguire
Cornageeha — Capt. J. McGarry
    Cromlin
Drumela, Newtowngore — Capt. J. Lee
    Drumsna
Drumreilly — Capt. Brian McEnroy
    Eslin
Fearglass — Capt. — Kirwan
    Gortletteragh
    Gorvagh
    Kilclare
Kiltubrid South — Capt. Harry McKeon, Patrick Pinkman (for a few days), then Charles Pinkman
    Mohill

Companies attached to North Roscommon Brigade as of 7 January 1922
    Aughawilliam
    Aughnasheelin
    Corraleehan
    Fenagh

J. J. Cooney, Adjutant of the 5th Battalion
COURTESY OF SARAH COONEY CONEFREY

Activities:
Derived from Bernard Sweeney's Volunteer Witness Statement to the Bureau of Military History:
    In July 1918, about 200 Leitrim men travelled to South Cavan to help keep order during the
bye election when Arthur Griffith was contesting on the Sinn Féin ticket
    Leitrim Volunteers stood guard duty and protected the ballot boxes in Carrick-on-Shannon
during in November 1918 election

Barracks at Fenagh, Garadice, Eslin, Kesh, Keshcarrigan, Rantogue, Cloone burned Easter Saturday in 1920

Masonic Hall in Ballinamore burned in mid-1920

Courthouse in Ballinamore burned in October 1920

RIC burned some private premises at Drumsna and Johnstown Bridge in November 1920

The ASU was formed in December 1920. The first O/C was Michael Gahigan who was replaced by Charles McGoohan. Sean Mitchell then took charge. Originally about 10-12 men, headquartered in the Aughnasheelin area

Attempted ambush at Edentenny in January 1921. RIC was a no-show!

In February 1921, Sean Connolly, IRA organiser from Longford, arrived and spent his time with the Column. An ambush was attempted at Fenagh. The lorries failed to appear. In March, another ambush was attempted on the main road from Ruskey to Carrick-on-Shannon. The whole affair was called off when the mine placed in the road "disintegrated." The materials used — cement and gravel — were of inferior quality. No mine resulted in no ambush and a long trudge home for the Column.

At Eslin Bridge (about four and a half miles west of Mohill), the larger Column split up and headed in smaller units to various destinations. Sean Connolly went with the Column headed towards Ballinamore. Members of that Column included: Bernard Sweeney, Andy McPartland, Michael Baxter (Clerk for Ballinamore Railway Station)*, Joseph O'Beirne (Clerk for Ballinamore Railway Station)*, John Joseph O'Reilly (Miskawn, Aughnasheelin)*, Seamus Wrynn (Tarmon, Ballinamore), John Hunt, and John Joseph Reilly (Derrinkeher, Aughnasheelin)*

All killed, along with Sean Connolly, at Selton Hill on 11 March 1921

After Selton Hill, the Column basically fell part. Captain Paddy Morrissey (from the Athlone area) was sent to reorganise it. As to the informers, whose wagging tongues resulted in the demise of the Column at Selton Hill — one informer, William Lattimer, was shot! Notices went out which stated that if Crown activities occurred in the area, many lives would be forfeited and every Protestant house would be burned. There were no reprisals!* The other informer, Dr. Pentland (Dr. Pringle claims Bernard Sweeney), managed to get out of the country, but was killed by being crushed to death against a wall in London

Charles Pinkman Volunteer Witness Statement to the Bureau of Military History 1913-21.

Notes about Leitrim Volunteers

In 1918, there were a few Companies organised in Leitrim, but, as yet, no Battalion structure existed. Near the end of 1919, **Eugene Kilkenny** and several others, dressed in British Army uniforms, and went around collecting arms from the local people. They had no trouble augmenting the Volunteers' meagre supply

"Unknown destinations": many were located along the Cavan/Leitrim border, while others were in the mountain area on the north Leitrim side

Fr. Ryan served as a Judge in the Sinn Féin Courts

Cumann na mBan: Captain Bridget McNabola (fifteen girls in the branch near **Kiltubrid South**) Secretary Kathleen McGee, Treasurer Bridget Flynn

Intelligence agents: Miss Nangle in the Mohill Post Office

Jim Sheerin in the Post Office at Carrick-on-Shannon

Three RIC contacts (Carrick-on-Shannon, Mohill, Ballinamore) would warn the Volunteers of impending raids and roundups

Two Duignan brothers from Annaduff (Thomas and William) were arrested in August of 1922 and sent to Athlone on the same day, 14 November 1922

A Sampling of Leitrim Civil War Internees:

Name	Place of Residence	Gaol
Charles Canning	Aughnalee, Cloone	Athlone
James Cassidy	Clooneagh, Dromod	Athlone
Patrick Creighton	Ballinamore	Athlone
Michael Curren	Mohill	Athlone
Tom Duignan	Mullagh Annaduff	Athlone
William Duignan	Mullagh Annaduff	Athlone
Patrick Ferguson	Ballinamore	Athlone
John Gallagher	Ballinamore	Athlone
Brian Gilgunn	Manorhamilton	Sligo
John Kerrigan	Mullinabreen	Athlone
John Kelly	Lullinclay	Athlone
John Kenney	Carrigallen	Athlone

James Loughrane	Ballinamore	Athlone/Tintown "A"
John McAllister	Dromahair	Tintown "A"
Michael McCabe	Carrigallen	Tintown "A"
Lawrence McDermott	Kiltyclogher	Athlone
Joe McGloin	Tullaghan	Newbridge
Lawrence McGovern	Lough Ryan	Athlone
Charles McGowan	Unshinagh, Ballinamore	Athlone
Michael McGowan	Glenade	Newbridge
Quintus McGriskin	Kiltyclogher	Sligo
Michael McIntyre	Callan, Mohill	Athlone
James McKeon	Drumbad, Ballinamore	Athlone
Tommy McKeon	Rengowna, Dromod	Athlone
Michael McKiernan	Tooman, Cloone	Athlone
John McLoughlin	Ballinamore	Sligo
John McLoughlin	Largydonnell	Newbridge
Patrick McLoughlin (McToughlin)	Ross, Manorhamilton	Athlone
James McManus	Drunnrig, Ballinamore	Athlone
Ber. McMorrow	Largydonnell	Newbridge
Michael McMorrow	Briscloonagh	Athlone
Patrick McNulty	Lawley	Newbridge
Patrick McTiernan	Monagh	Sligo
Patrick Martin	Ballinamore	Athlone
James Meehan	Carraflough, Ballinamore	Athlone
Michael Meehan	Kiltyclogher	Newbridge
Michael Mulligan	Ballinamore	Athlone
Arthur Murphy	Drumderry, Ballinamore	Athlone
Hugh Rynne	Spencer Harbour	Athlone & Tintown "A"
Pat Shanley	Ballinamore	Athlone
Joseph Thomas	Rooskey, Mohill	Athlone
Michael Thomas	Townard, Mohill	Athlone
Thomas Walsh	Kilmacurl, Manorhamilton	Athlone
Charles Wilson	Carrigallen	Athlone

LONGFORD

Originally one Battalion in the Athlone Brigade but eventually became a separate Brigade

Organisers:

Tom Reddington was a technical school teacher, whose profession demanded that he travel. He helped organise Longford and served as the Comdt. of Longford Brigade with Sean MacEoin acting as Vice O/C.

In 1913, Dr. Brian Cusack, James Flood, and others helped to organise the Volunteers in Granard. After the split in the movement caused by John Redmond, the Volunteers died out in the area.

Easter Week — John Cawley (IRB Head Centre) and Paul Cusack, brother of Brian, set out for Dublin on Easter Tuesday. They got no nearer than Lucan when they were arrested and eventually sent to Frongoch. Upon their release, they again set about organising the county. Sean Connolly and Sean MacEoin also played key roles in assembling a viable fighting force. It is no accident that most of the activity against the Crown Forces during the War for Independence in County Longford occurred around Ballinalee and Granard.

The first meeting to re-establish a North Longford Volunteer group was held in Cusack's house in July 1917. Those present: Michael Collins, Sean Connolly, Sean MacEoin, James Flood, Paul Cusack, John Cawley, and Tom Reddington, who later became the Brigade O/C.

1918 Brigade Staff
O/C Tom Reddington
Quartermaster: Ned Cooney
Adjutant: James Flood
A year later, Sean Connolly was serving as *Vice O/C*, but when Reddington's wife became ill, he left the Brigade area and Connolly became acting O/C.

North Longford Battalion
O/C Sean MacEoin
Vice O/C Sean Connolly, Sean Murphy of Granard
Adjutant: Sean Duffy

Eventually there were five Battalions in the county:
1. Colmcille
2. Ballinalee
3. Granard
4. Ardagh and Longford
5. Lanesboro and Rathcline

Companies in the North Longford Battalion included:
Edgeworthstown (Mostrim), Killoe, Mullinalaughta, Drumlish, Ballinamuck, Colmcille, Dromard and Ballinalee (formed at Eastertime 1917 by Sean Connolly and Sean MacEoin). "Later on Granard, Finea and Street replaced Drumlish, Dromard and Ballinamuck, and the unit was designated the First Battalion."*

(*<u>The Blacksmith of Ballinalee</u> by Padraic O'Farrell, p. 23.)

Key Intelligence Gatherers:
Miss Cooney and Miss Madden of the Longford town post office
Miss Skeffington, daughter of the station master in Longford
Miss May Maguire, Main Street, Longford

Brigade Officers:
Sean MacEoin, "The Blacksmith of Ballinalee," gave the British many a headache in and around his native parish. He became the Head Officer of the Free State Western Command centered in Athlone during the Civil War, and then proceeded to give many an Anti-Treaty man a severe migraine

Michael Francis Heslin was Adjutant of the Longford Brigade

Frank Davis QM for the Longford Brigade. Active in raiding for arms at Ballinamuck, Longford and Drumlish

Thomas Kelleher (Clonbroney, Co. Longford) orderly to the Longford Brigade O/C. While on his way to Roscommon accompanying the machine gun instructor, he was killed by Auxiliaries at Drumlish in May 1921*

*<u>Who's Who in the Irish War of Independence and Civil War 1916-1923</u>, by Padraic O'Farrell, p. 50.

James Savage Intelligence Officer for the Longford Brigade. He was incarcerated in the Ballykinlar Camp in 1921

Battalion and Company Officers:
Sean Duffy Adjutant of the Longford Battalion — the "up Duffy" misidentification at Scramogue, Strokestown, County Roscommon. Attacked the barracks at Drumlish, Edgeworthstown, Ballinamuck, and participated in the Clonfin Ambush 2 February 1921*

*<u>Who's Who in the Irish War of Independence and Civil War 1916-1923</u> by Padraic O'Farrell, p. 30.

Michael Mulligan (Clonfin) O/C of the Granard Coy. suggested and participated in the successful ambush of Clonfin on 2 February 1921

John O'Sullivan IO for Longford. Took part in an ambush on the Black and Tans in April 1921 in Fallon's tailor shop

The North Longford Flying Column:
Extracted from Marie Coleman's <u>County Longford and the Irish Revolution 1910-1923</u> p. 226.
Thomas Brady, James Brady, Patrick Callaghan, Seamus Conway, Patrick Cooke, Frank Davis, Sean Duffy, Thomas Early, Seamus Farrelly, Patrick Finnegan, Larry Geraghty, Michael Gormley, Michael F. Heslin, Hugh Hourican, Jack Hughes, Michael Kenny, Patrick Lynch, John McDowell, Sean MacEoin, Frank Martin, John Moore, Michael Mulligan, Michael F. Reynolds, Sean Sexton, Jim Sheerin, Michael Treacy, Ned Tynan

A complete listing of the Longford Volunteers and members of Cumann na mBan appears in Marie Coleman's book, <u>County Longford and the Irish Revolution 1910-1923</u>, pages 227-239.

MAYO

After Easter Week 1916, the Volunteers in the area were very quiet. In 1917 a reorganisation took place. The county was divided into four spheres of action — North, South, East, and West.

First All-County Mayo Brigade Officers:
O/C Michael HcHugh
Vice O/C John Hoban
Quartermaster: Michael Kilroy, Newport
Adjutant: Dick Walsh, Balla

Staff:
Representing North Mayo: Patrick Hegarty
Tom Ruane, Vice O/C for East Mayo
Sean Corcoran, Vice O/C from Kiltimagh and
Thomas Ruane (Kiltimagh) Vice O/C for West Mayo
Tom Derrig (Westport) representing South Mayo
Ned Moane (Westport)
Liam Forde (Ballaghaderreen)

North Mayo Brigade had 22 Companies some of which were:
(Quoted from Patrick Hegarty's Volunteer Witness Statement)
The first officers of the **Lahardane Company**:
   O/C Charles Flynn
   1st Lieutenant: William Barrett
   2nd Lieutenant: Patrick Hegarty
   Adjutant: Patrick Hale
   Quartermaster: Pat Carney
   Drill Sergeant: Jimmy Jennings, ex-British soldier
   Members: *O/C* Sean Corcoran, Patrick Hegarty, Edward Hegarty, Sean Hegarty, Pat Joe Marley, Mike Marley, Mike Waters, Michael Gallagher, Martin Flanagan, Martin Gallagher, Martin McNeely, P. McNeely, Pat Kelly, Edward Flanagan, Bernie Brennan

Ballina Company: Tom Ruane, Joe Ruane, Frank Jordan, Alfie, Tucky and Vin Colleary, Joe Doherty, Patrick Ruttledge, Martin McGrath, Pappy Forde, — McHale, Davy Ryder, the three musketeers: Paddy Coleman, Crimp Grimes and Chuddy Conway (known as Gultha-Gultha), Frank Flynn, John Moylett, Murty Gilmartin, John Moran, — McCawley, and Pat Cosgrave

Bonnyconlan Company: Tom Loftus (one-time Brigade O/C), Pat and Tom Andrew, Scally Mallon, Pat Lafferty, Pat Lawrence, Seamus Kilcullen (O/C Brigade at the time of the Truce and after), Tony Kilcullen, Matt Kilcawley, Tom Kilcawley, the brothers Gildea, J. Burke (Enniscrone), M. M. Tolan, Denis Tuffy, Denis Sheeran, Tom Finnerty, S. Kavanagh, Michael John Hanly, Tom Coen, Ned Hannon, Ted Kilgallon, Jack Bryon, John Gallagher (Lakefield), J. J. Brogan, Morrison and James — (of Knockmore) who were both killed in action, Tom Burke, E. Browne, Jack Finerty, William Jennings, James Boyle, William Doherty and Dr. Ferran of Foxford, Tom and Mick Harte, Paddy Bourke of Ballycastle, Dr. Crowley, Dr. Madden, Anthony Farrell, Michael O'Connor, E. Nealon (killed in action), Sean Langan, — Kelly of Belderrig, Michael Kelly, Michael Keaveney (Company Captain), Alex Boyd, Pat Boyd, John Barrett of Crossmolina, Mick Mulherin, Michael Mulderrig, Joe Sharkey, Andy McNeely (one of the first in Crossmolina), J. J. Leonard, Martin Harte, Michael Reilly, Pat Kelly, Pat Maycock, John Joe Browne (Mellows), the Moloney Brothers, J. Burke, Pat Coleman, Pat Loftus, and Pat Corcoran

Erris Company: Seamus and Tom Kilroy, Sean Munnelly, Mick Lavelle, P. Carabine, Tom Murphy, John Neary, John and M. Reilly, Dr. Gaughan and his brother Mick. There were four Collins brothers and their wonderful mother who spent six months in gaol, Padraig McAndrew (an old timer), and Tom McAndrew who served on the County Council

Ballycroy Company included Brian Corrigan, — Sweeney, Louis Cleary and his aunts

Crossmolina Company commanded by James Flynn

The 1st Battalion Flying Column was commanded by Seamus Kilcullen and Matt Kilcawley

South Mayo Brigade: *O/C* Tom Maguire
Known members of the South Mayo Flying Column:
(Quoted from Ruairí O'Bradáigh's *Dílseacht*)
Tom Maguire (Commandant), Martin Flannery, Jim Duffy, Terry O'Brien, John Collins, Tom Lally, John McGing, Tom Cavanaugh, Seamus Burke, Michael Shaughnessy, Michael Corliss, Michael O'Brien, Tom Carney, Patrick Gibbons, — Murphy, Paddy Maye, Michael Costello, John Ferguson

East Mayo Flying Column
(Quoted from *Memories of an Old Man* by John Snee)
Known members pre-Truce: John Snee of Barcull, Kilkelly, Pat and Ned Costello from Culmore, Mickey Hunt from Stonepark, Tim Duffy and W. Conboy from Falleighter
Known members Civil War: John Snee, Tom Regan, Mickey Hunt, P. Behan, M. Duffy, and M. McKeon, Seamus and Patrick Mulrennan, Liam Forde, Jack Creaton, Toby Scally, Robert King. P. MacEnri served as Assistant Adjutant

The "Men of the West" Column was commanded by Michael Kilroy. He was a member of the IRB, and Commandant of the 4th Western Division. Captured 12 September 1922 and imprisoned in Athlone and Mountjoy. Before his capture, he was very active during both the Tan War and the Civil War, but thankfully was saved from being killed on the orders of Pat Madden of Roscommon.

Members of his column: Edward Moane (Vice O/C of the Brigade), John Gibbons (Adjutant), Tom Ketterick (Quartermaster), Joe Walsh, P. J. Cannon, P. Lambert, J. Kelly, J. Doherty, Broddie Malone, J. Rush, Joe Ring, M. Naughton, J. Hogan, J. Hearney, D. Simmon, J. Keane, J. Connolly, R. Joyce, P. McNamara, Willie Malone, G. Gavin, T. Heavey, John Duffy, J. McDonagh, P. Kelly, J. Moran, Jimmy Flaherty, B. Cryan, M. Staunton, and Dr. J. A. Madden

West Mayo Flying Column commanded by Joe Baker
(Quoted from *My Stand for Freedom* by Joe Baker)
Members: Frank Chambers (Shramore, Newport), Patrick Chambers (Shramore, Newport), Patrick Chambers (of Derrybrock, Newport), John Clarke (Tiernaur, Newport), Patrick Cleary (Glenhest, Newport), James Collins (Drummin, Westport), Patrick Conway (Skirdagh, Newport), Thomas Corcoran (Altamont Street, Westport), Joseph Corr (Newport), Patrick Cummins (Kilmeena, Westport), James Doyle (Westport Rd., Castlebar), Patrick Fergus (Ardagh, Carrowmore, Westport), James Gavin (The Bakery, Castlebar), Edward Gibbons (Rossinrubble, Newport), Larkin Heavey (Carrowbaun, Westport), P. Henneghan (Ballyheane, Castlebar), Michael Horan (Newport), James Jordan (Glenhest, Newport), John Judge (Owenwee, Westport), Patrick Keane (Sand Hill, Tiernaur, Newport), Patrick Keane (Glenhest, Newport), "Sonny" Kearns (Liscarney, Westport), Henry Latter (Castlebar), Thomas Lavelle (Burrishoole, Newport), Michael McDonnell (Skirdagh, Newport), Alfred McMenamin (Glenhest, Newport), — McMenamin (Shramore, Newport), Tom McMenamin (Newport), John McNea (Arda, Carrowmore, Westport), John Maloney (Skirdagh, Newport), James Moran (Callowbrack, Newport), George Mulvaney (Brownes Drapers, Shop Street, Westport), Robert Nelis (Quay Rd., Westport), Patrick O'Boyle (Glenhest, Newport), Peter O'Malley (Fair Green, Westport), John Philbin (Castlebar), Michael Ryder (Castlebar Road, Westport), Joseph Sherry (Mill Street, Westport), Michael Staunton (Mill Street, Westport), John Tierney (Castlebar)

Notes about Mayo Volunteers
The **East Mayo Brigade** was commanded by **Sean Corcoran.** Sean was arrested after the Rising and sent to Wandsworth on 13 May 1916 and eventually incarcerated at Frongoch. He was the O/C of the party that burned the Ballacorick Barracks at Eastertide 1920. Corcoran was killed in action at Crossard, Tooreen, Ballyhaunis in April of 1921
Richard Walsh Balla, Co. Mayo, the original Adjutant for the Mayo Brigade. He served as arms procurer in England. Once, on a visit to Liverpool, he was walking with Sean Mór Lynchehan to his lodging. (Mór Lynchehan had formerly lived in Achill Sound.) Walsh was stopped by a policeman and questioned. Another policeman happened upon the scene and vouched for Walsh, even though he was a stranger, because his friend (Mór Lynchehan) worked on the Liverpool docks. Walsh left the next day with the guns for which he had travelled across the Irish Sea. He was a member of the IRB and IRA. Arrested and placed in the condemned cell row at Galway Gaol in April 1923. He shared a cell with Joe Baker, O/C of a West Mayo Flying Column
Conor Maguire (Cong) helped draft the constitution and rules for the Republican Courts and organised them in the South Mayo area. He was elected chairman of the first Republican County Mayo Council

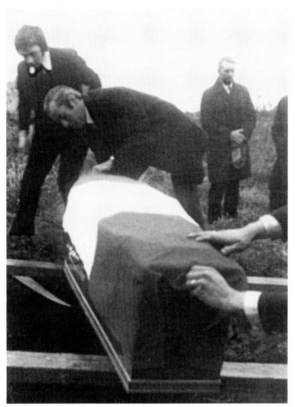

Bartley Hegarty's funeral.

A Noteworthy Family

from Enniscoe, Crossmolina, Ballina, Co. Mayo:

Patrick Hegarty, the first 2nd Lieutenant of the Lahardane Company, who later became an organiser for Mayo and Sligo. He was sworn into the IRB by Michael Kilroy. In March 1918, Patrick was arrested for illegal drilling and sent to Crumlin Road Jail, where he came in contact with many of the leaders of the movement including Austin Stack, Terence MacSwiney, and Seamus Robinson of Tipperary. He helped plan the attack on Ballacorick Barracks in April 1920. (His brother Edward, Sean Corcoran, and Tom Loftus were in charge of the main body of men.) Patrick served on the Brigade staff as well as being selected as a member of the Mayo Co. Council in late 1920. He attended the first Republican Council meeting

Martin Hegarty, eldest of the family, was arrested by the Tans at his home and taken to

Patrick Hegarty.

Cecelia Hegarty.

Castlebar and Sligo Gaols. He was released several weeks later

Edward Hegarty, one of the first members of the Lahardane Company, took part in the attack on Ballacorick Barracks in April 1920. He was killed during the Civil War in 1922 at Glenhest on the road from Castlebar to Belmullet. A monument to his memory stands by that road. He lies in the family plot in the Kilmurray Churchyard

Bartley "Bart" Hegarty, a twin of Sean, and member of the Lahardane Coy., went on to become the O/C of No. 2 North Mayo Brigade Active Service Unit from 1921 through the Civil War. He also fought with the West Mayo and Connemara men during that time. After the War, he emigrated to Canada, returned to Ireland, and later settled in England. He never married. Died 9 October 1973 and is buried in Kilmurray Cemetery

The **father of the family** was beaten so severely by the Tans in late 1920 that he died seven weeks later

Sean Hegarty, a member of the Lahardane Coy., took part in the attack on the Ballacorick Barracks in April 1920. He was arrested by the Tans, taken outside his house some distance away, his moustache pulled out and every hair on his head extracted with a pair of pliers, then beaten and kicked to the ground. His head swelled to three times its normal size and he died some time later

Cecelia Hegarty, the sister, was dragged along a gravel road on her bare knees and beaten. The injury to her knees set the stage for rheumatoid arthritis, which crippled her in later years and left her unable to leave a wheel chair. Died 1946

Nell Hegarty, the keeper of the trust, who later married a Jordan, settled on the home place, and took care of her aging brothers who returned to Ireland

Diarmuid Crowley a member of the Republican Supreme Court 1920. Helped draft the constitution and rules for the Republican Courts. Arrested at Ballina, Co. Mayo in 1921

Felix Murray (Ballyhaunis) a van salesman by trade, was shot in Mount Devlin during the Civil War on 25 November 1922

John Grealy (Shanwalla, Aghamore) QM of Ballyhaunis Battalion, East Mayo Brigade. Took possession of Boyle Barracks in the spring of 1922 from the Pro-Treaty men. Headed a Flying Column along with — Mullen that centered around the Kilgariff and Kilkenny areas. There were around 75 members of the Column whose armament included a Lewis and Thompson submachine gun. He was arrested in October of 1922

Monument to Edward Hegarty

Tomas Mac Camhthaoil helped draft the constitution and rules for the Republican Courts and organised them in the East Mayo area

Tom Maguire O/C of the South Mayo Brigade during the Black and Tan War and Anti-Treaty commander of the South Mayo Flying Column operating in Ballinrobe area and beyond. He became the O/C of the 2nd Western Division IRA. Last surviving member of the Second Dáil and the longest-living man to hold the rank of Commandant General in the Irish Republican Army of 1921. Died 5 July 1993

Michael J. O'Brien Neale Coy., Mayo was the Adjutant of the South Mayo Brigade. He was KIA at Tourmakeady

P. J. Ruttledge (Ballina) of Westport, Co. Mayo was prominent in organising Republican Courts in North Mayo. He also served as a TD. He visited The O'Rahilly House in Sligo during the Civil War in pursuit of an armoured car to aid operations in his own area

Thomas Murray served as the Medical Officer for the East Mayo Brigade

Larry McGovern and his sister **Tillie** of Newfield, Newport, Co. Mayo were both battered by angry Tans who knocked all their teeth out of their heads

The Western People "West Mayo's Fighting Story" as told by Anthony Lavelle. 16 May 1964. p. 8.

Tom Derrig of High Street, Westport became the first 1st Lieutenant of the University College Galway Company in October 1917. He was later the O/C of the West Mayo Brigade in September 1920. His leadership, however, did not last long. He was arrested in January and replaced by Michael Kilroy. He later became the Minister for Education in de Valera's government of the 1940s

Joe Ring became the Westport Battalion O/C in September 1920. He later formed the Westport Active Service Unit with Broddie Malone as Vice O/C. Because of the successful ambush at Carrowkennedy, Ring's home was burned to the ground. He joined the National Army and was killed in an ambush at Bonnyconlan, Ballina in September 1922

A Sampling of Mayo Internees during the Civil War:

Name	Place of Residence	Gaol
John Barrett	Breaffy, Castlebar	Athlone
Patrick Carroll	Ballinacurry, Kiltimagh	Athlone & Stone Park
Patrick Concannon	Ballygowan, Claremorris	Athlone & Tintown II
Patrick Coleman	Ballina	Athlone
James Deacy	Thornhill, Kiltimagh	Athlone/Mountjoy
Martin Devaney	Brackloon, Ballyhaunis	Athlone
Timothy Duffy	Kilkelly, Ballyhaunis	Athlone
Andrew Egan	Aughmore, Ballyhaunis	Stone Park
John Fallon	Castlebar	
John Finn	Holywell, Ballyhaunis	Maryborough
Patrick Freeman	Aughmore, Ballyhaunis	Athlone & Mountjoy & Tintown II
John Freyne	Aughmore, Ballyhaunis	Athlone
James Flynn	Grange, Crossmolina	Athlone
Patrick Galvin	Knockbagha, Ballyhaunis	Tintown
Martin Geraghty	Kiltimagh	Athlone
John Gordon	Crossard, Tooreen, Ballyhaunis	Athlone
Michael Harkin	Natantee, Ballyhaunis	Athlone
Peter Hopkins	Ballyhaunis	Athlone
Michael Hughes	Ballyhaunis	Athlone
Thomas Hunt	Kilkenny, Ballyhaunis	Mountjoy
John Kennsey	Crosscra, Ballyhaunis	Stone Park
Patrick King	Hollyhill, Ballyhaunis	Athlone
Martin Kirrane	Bekan, Ballyhaunis	Athlone
Bernard Lyons	Bekan, Ballyhaunis	Athlone
John Lyons	Taughboy, Ballyhaunis	Athlone
James McCarthy	Castlebar	Mountjoy/Tintown II
John McCarthy	Newline, Castlebar	Athlone
William McCarthy	Newline, Castlebar	Athlone
John McCormack	Castlebar	Athlone
Patrick McCormack	Castlebar	Athlone
Bernard McDonagh	Tucker St., Castlebar	Mountjoy/Tintown II
John McGeever	Main St., Charlestown	Athlone
Patrick McGuinne	Brogher, Charlestown	Tintown "B"
John McIntyre	Charlestown	Athlone/Tintown "B"

Michael McIntyre	Sinnagh, Charlestown	Athlone/Tintown II, Mountjoy
Patrick McIntyre	Sinnagh, Charlestown	Newbridge
Paddy McKetrick	Tucker St., Castlebar	Athlone
Henry McNicholson	Carranhane, Kiltimagh	Athlone/Mountjoy
Thomas McNicholson	Treenaghleragh, Kiltimagh	Athlone/Mountjoy/Tintown "B"
James Maloney	Kiltimagh	Hare Park
Larry Monaghan	Castle St., Castlebar	Athlone
Thomas Moran	Linenhall Street, Castlebar	Athlone
Patrick Moran	Charlestown	Athlone
Martin Morley	Bekan, Ballyhaunis	Athlone & Tintown "A"
Michael Morris	Drumarra, Ballyhaunis	Athlone
John Morrissey	Crossard, Ballyhaunis	Mountjoy & Tintown
John Mullaly	Kiltimagh	Tintown "A"
Michael Mullen	Breaffy, Castlebar	Athlone
Patrick Mullins	Lurganboy, Ballyhaunis	Mountjoy
Patrick Murtagh	Sangana, Charlestown	Hare Park
Michael Nolan	Ballyhaunis	Tintown "A"
Pat Noonan	Charlestown	Athlone
John Payton	Charlestown	Mountjoy & Tintown "A" and Tintown II
Edward Rattigan	Kilbrnan, Ballinrobe	Athlone
Michael Rattigan	Kilbrnan, Ballinrobe	Athlone
Thomas Rochford	Kiltimagh	Tintown "A"
Jim Rush	Kiltimagh	Escaped
John P. Sammon	Louisbragh, Castlebar	Athlone/ Tintown "A"
Daniel Sheehy	Kiltimagh	Athlone
Edward Sheridin	Cashlough, Ballinrobe	Athlone
George Smith	Spencer Lee, Castlebar	Mountjoy/Newbridge
James Staunton	Breaffy, Castlebar	Athlone
Luke Taylor	Aughmore, Ballyhaunis	Athlone/Newbridge
John Tierney	David's Terrace, Castlebar	Athlone
Frank Waldron	Adraig, Ballyhaunis	Athlone
Luke Waldron	Bekan, Ballyhaunis	Athlone
Patrick Waldron	Globe St., Ballinrobe	Athlone
James Walsh	Knockglass, Ballinrobe	Athlone

SLIGO

Alec McCabe "the best known Sinn Féiner in the county."* Member of the IRB and early organiser in Sligo. He was arrested in November 1915 at the Sligo Station in possession of explosives. He was dismissed from his teaching position because of his Volunteer activities. (His photo and bio are included with Roscommon men.)
*_The Aftermath of Revolution Sligo 1921-23_ by Michael Farry

Brigade Staff:

O/C of the 3rd Western Division Liam Pilkington (included with Roscommon men)
Vice O/C of the Sligo Brigade Henry Brehony was captured 28 July 1922. He escaped from
 Athlone Barracks in September, but was killed 16 February 1923
Quartermaster: for the 3rd Western Division Charles Gildea, member of the Tubbercurry Battalion,
 organised the raid on the National Bank in Sligo when £2000 was taken
Michael Nevins, manager of Connolly's licensed premise, served as the _Intelligence Officer_ of a
 Sligo Company. He was later appointed the Brigade _Intelligence Officer_. After the War, he
 became the Mayor of Sligo

There were eight Battalions in Sligo:

Ballintogher area Battalion
O/C Charlie Timoney, then Harold McBrien

Companies and eventual strength:

Organised in 1917 Ballintogher — 50
Capt. Harold McBrien, then Capt. Michael Mulligan
1st Lieutenant Ned Mulrooney
2nd Lieutenant Paddy Coleman

In **1918** four more Companies came into existence:
Dromahair, Co. Leitrim — 30 — Capt. Charles Canning
Newtownmanor — 80 — Capt. Charles Timoney
Killorga
Killavoggy, Co. Leitrim — 64 — Capt. Patrick Hannon
In **1919** two more Companies formed
Ballingar, Dromahair, Co. Leitrim — 40 — Capt. Thomas O'Connor
Greaghafarna, Dromahair, Co. Leitrim — 84 — Capt. Patrick O'Rourke
In 1920 one more Company was added
Gleen — 30 — Capt. John Owens

Tubbercurry Battalion
Frank Carty O/C, commander of the Flying Column during the Civil War. Served as a TD and as a member of Sligo County Council. (See Roscommon Volunteer listing)

Grange Battalion
Seamus Devins O/C. Incarcerated in Dartmoor in 1921. Active as a Republican Brigadier in the Civil War. He became the O/C of the North Sligo Brigade when the Divisions were formed. Killed on Benbulben Mountain 20 September 1922
Eugene Gilbride Captain of Grange Coy.
Willie Devins Quartermaster of Grange Coy.

Collooney Battalion
Frank O'Beirne O/C of Collooney Battalion and Vice O/C of Frank Carty's Column, fought with the Anti-Treaty forces in Collooney in mid-July 1922 before being captured at a house supposedly offering sanctuary close to the Southern Railway Station. (Included with Roscommon Volunteer Listing beginning on page 200.)
Andy Conway Captain of Cliffoney Coy.
Paddy Branley Captain of Glencar Coy.
Ned Bofin Captain of Rosses Point (included with listing of Roscommon men)

Gurteen Battalion
After Owen Tansey died in the flu epidemic of 1918, **Jim Hunt** became the O/C of the Battalion. (Included with Roscommon Volunteer Listing beginning on page 200.)
James Dwyer Vice O/C
Thomas O'Donnell was the Adjutant. (He was also extremely active in the organisation and control of the Sinn Féin Courts.)
Joe Finnegan Quartermaster

There were five Companies within this Battalion:
Gurteen, Cloonloo, Killaraght, Monasteraden, Towinadden. Later a Company in Edmondstown was formed

Ballymote Battalion
Michael Marren O/C (included with Roscommon listing)
Thady McGowan Adjutant
Josie Hannon Quartermaster

Companies:
Ballymote, Keash, Culfadda, Kilavil, Bunninadden, Emlaghnaghton, Kilcreevan, Ballinafad and Derroon. All key members of these Companies were IRB men.

Notes about Sligo Volunteers
Patrick Hegarty of Mayo came into the Gurteen, Sligo area to organise the Dáil loan
James Kearns, Anti-Treaty commander, held Westport in July 1922 for the Anti-Treaty side until a large contingent of government troops landed
Linda Kearns was arrested for driving Volunteers and supplies on 20 November 1920 to an attack on Frenchpark Auxiliaries headquarters. Seamus Devins, O/C of the Brigade, was also captured with her. Sentenced to ten years imprisonment*
* Padraic O'Farrell in his book Who's Who in the Irish War of Independence and Civil War 1916-1923 claims that the date was April 1921 (p. 49). Proinnsios O'Duigneain in Linda Kearns A Revolutionary Irish Woman claims 20 November 1920
J. J. "Ginger" O'Connell, who once served in the United States military, used to give classes and lectures in the Sinn Féin Hall in Sligo. He became the Assistant Director (later Director) of Training for the Volunteers in 1920. Helped plan the Customs House assault. He was kidnapped by Anti-Treaty forces — an action that was a significant factor in the decision to attack the Four Courts

John Kennedy of Castlerea purchased rifles for the Tubbercurry Company to be used for Easter Week. Those guns were never fired in 1916

Charles Gildea joined the IRA in late 1914 or early 1915 and helped organise Companies. He was taken into the IRB by Alec McCabe in July 1915. He was captured on 28 February 1921, and taken to Sligo Gaol from which he escaped on 29 June with the help of warder, Joseph Henry

On **Easter Saturday** Keash Barracks and Temple House were burned. A month later, Ballinafad and Mullaghroe Barracks went up in flames

Michael J. Marren was in charge of the attack on the military in the train at Kilfree Junction in January 1921 (he is included with the Roscommon Volunteer listing on page 380)

Martin Savage (Streamstown, Ballisodare) Fought in Dublin during the Rising

Tom Duignan (Deignan) O/C of the 5th Battalion, had a plan for capturing the Ballintogher Barracks in 1920. He would dress as a Sergeant in the British Army and be accompanied by Ned Bofin who would also be costumed in an army uniform. The whole scheme came to naught because the barracks was vacated by the police before the plan could be implemented

— Duignan and Harold McBrien attempted an ambush of a police patrol at Five Cross Roads, Cloonkeevy, Tubbercurry. No luck

Joe McDevitt (McDavitt) concocted a scheme whereby the Sligo Railway Station would be taken over in October 1920. That plan also found its way into the dustbin

In March 1921, **Harry Brehony, Tom Duignan and Liam Pilkington** headed up an operation targeted with capturing the Collooney Barracks

Peculiar Facts: By January 1923, Sligo had two Garda stations that were occupied with the new police force. Roscommon had six

WESTMEATH

Command Structure of Athlone Brigade — (see Roscommon Volunteer Listing on pages 208-209)

In August 1920, County Westmeath was reorganised. The 2nd Brigade included:
1st Battalion — Mullingar —
O/C Michael McCoy
2nd Battalion — Loughnavalley
3rd — Kinnegad/Milltownpass
4th — Castlepollard

Athlone Brigade Men Interned after the Rising:
George Amos (Athlone)
John Elliott (Tubberclair)
Gilbert Hughes (Coosan)
Sean Hurley (Athlone)
Michael McCormack (Drumraney)
Edward Martin (Athlone)
Peadar Melinn (Athlone)
Sean Mullaney (Barnett St., Athlone)
Peter Murray (Athlone)
Seamus O'Brien (Athlone)
Owen Sweeney (Clonbrusk)

Training camp at Coosan in 1915.

First row: (left to right) Mr. Spillane, J. Green, Donal O'Buckley, William Mullins, Michael Cremins, Michael Brennan

Second row: Peter Mellin, Dick Fitzgerald J. Burke, J.J. O'Connell, Paul Galligan, Larry Lardener, Terence MacSwiney, and Michael Kerins

PHOTO COURTESY OF PATRICK MELINN

Names Inscribed on the IRA Monument in Athlone

Died during the Wars:

Sean Costello	Joseph Tormey	James Tormey
John Carty	Patrick Sloan	George Adamson
Dick Bertles	Christopher McKeown	Tom Hughes
Tom "Toby" Mannion	Michael Bannon	John Blaney
Joe Morrissey	Seamus Finn	

Died as a result of wounds incurred during the Wars:

Bernard "Brian" Gaffey	Michael Gaffey	Sean Galvin
Bernard McCormack	Joe Cunningham	George Manning

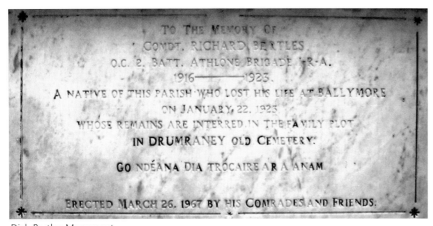

Dick Bertles Monument.

PHOTO COURTESY OF LEW THORNE

Notes about Westmeath Volunteers

Diarmuid O'Hegarty and **Ernie O'Malley** came to this area to organise a Brigade. O'Malley gave classes in Athlone during the winter of 1918. The curriculum included: drill, musketry, Morse Code, map reading, and talks on guerilla tactics

Battalions first formed and initial organisers:

Athlone — Sean Hurley

Mullingar — David Burke resigned as O/C and shortly thereafter James McGuire returned from Liverpool and took on the task

Seamus Murphy served as Adjutant

Terry Smyth acted as Quartermaster assisted by Tom Lennon of the Athlone Brigade

Castlepollard — Joseph Kennedy

Herbert Mitchell and Sean Mullaney were instrumental in reorganizing Companies around the Coosan area

Peadar Bracken Tullamore. Member of the IRB, took part in the Rising in Dublin in April 1916. He returned to Drumraney, Westmeath and met with other officers in the home of John McCormack, where plans for local units' participation were laid down. Marching on Shannonbridge was not carried out due to the countermanding order. Bracken was arrested and held in Athlone, Richmond Barracks in Dublin, and finally shipped across the Irish Sea. He was placed on GHQ staff in 1920. Bracken helped to organise the Republican Courts in Longford/Westmeath

Joseph "Paddy" Daly was a train engine driver stationed in Athlone. His sister Katy was a very active member of Cumann na mBan. When the prisoners were incarcerated in the Curragh in 1921, Katy would send in a load of turf. "The turf was the most useful thing we could receive as our supply of coal and cooking facilities were very restricted; sometimes it was lunch-time when the last of the breakfast was cooked."*

*Michael McCoy Volunteer Witness Statement, Bureau of Military History 1913-21, p. 38.

Patrick Sloan of Mount Temple and **Joe Tormey** of Moate were both killed at Ballykinlar Internment Camp on 14 January 1921 by an over-anxious sentry. Both names are included on the Athlone IRA Monument

Joseph Cunningham, president of the local Dáil Court, was assaulted and injured by masked men in Westmeath 23 August 1920. He was left permanently damaged due to that thrashing. His name is inscribed on the Athlone IRA Monument

Michael and Patrick Carty of Tubberclair Coy. were wanted men. The Black and Tans once paid a visit to their home, and, when they couldn't find the Volunteers, tore the place to shreds. Michael later emigrated to Canada and then to New York, where he worked for the Metropolitan Transit Company. He was active in the Hibernians in Manhattan, and served as the Grand Marshall of the St. Patrick's Day parade in that city. Later in life he returned to Ireland. He died in Athlone and is buried in the Tubberclair Parish Cemetery

Volunteer Seamus Finn was killed in the ambush near Auburn on 2 November 1920 on the Athlone/Longford Road. He was very young (about sixteen) and told to stay home, but failed to obey. His name is inscribed on the Athlone IRA Monument. There is also a memorial to him at the site of the ambush

John Carty died during the Civil War in Headford, Co. Galway on 9 April 1923

— Fitzpatrick IRA officer in charge of the Royal Hotel in Athlone when George Adamson was killed by a sniper's bullet. He surrendered to Sean MacEoin in disgust

Edward (Kruger) Farrell of Coosan was the man who had secretly taken rifles to Shannonbridge in anticipation of the Rising

Drumraney Company held a vote to decide which side the Volunteers would support in the Redmondite split in 1914. Sixteen declared for John Redmond, but seventeen for the Eoin McNeill faction. The majority voters got to retain possession of the eight rifles in the Company's arsenal (five had been obtained after the Howth gun running incident in Dublin. Three had been sent down by Thomas Clarke, one of the signers of the Poblacht na H Éireann)

Simon Grennan was the first O/C of Moate Company

Father O'Reilly organised a Company of Volunteers in Tang in 1914 and bought five Lee Enfield rifles for them

The **parish priest in Tobber** acted as the agent for the Dáil loan

Father Casey served as a Judge in the Sinn Féin Courts in the Drumraney area

Seamus Finn monument.

PHOTO COURTESY OF LEW THORNE

Many Volunteers and members of Cumann na mBan in the Athlone area emigrated after the War:
John Lennon (Boston), Brian Costello, Sean Costello (Chicago), Mick Carty, Joe Kennedy (New York), James and Tommy Martin (Boston), Davy Curley (Brooklyn, New York), Mick Pender, and Mary and Betty O'Reilly (Bristol, England)

Thomas Keenan acted as Judge in the Sinn Féin Courts in the Tang area

Anthony McCormack and **Dick Bertles** paid a visit to Colonel King-Harman at his residence at Newcastle, Ballymahon. Their mission: to collect the levy that had been assessed on King-Harman's property by the IRA. After a few scuffles and tussles with a hidden revolver, the Colonel unwillingly paid his fair share

John Coghlan of Tang was the Intelligence Officer for the Anti-Treatyites during the Civil War. He was arrested on 23 October 1922

Christopher "Kit" McKeon (McKeown), officer in the Flying Column, was killed in action in Moate on a Sunday morning, 13 November 1922. His name is inscribed on the Athlone IRA Monument

Peter Benson was an engine driver for the Great Southern & Western Railroad. He was a tried and true dependable dispatch carrier

Unfriendly territory: Athlone, Tullamore, and Mullingar had a huge presence of British military. The local population was hostile to the Volunteers — mainly because there was a preponderance of war wives receiving money from the British Army. "Their only fear was that the war would come to a sudden end."* Irishtown in Athlone was particularly ill disposed
Volunteer Witness Statement of David Daly, O/C of Athlone Battalion, p. 5.

Four Anti-Treatyites were arrested on 8 August 1922 after an ambush at Tang: Daniel McGiff, — Moran, — Canells, and — McLynn

The Ambush at Glasson on 25 August 1922 was carried out by the Flying Column. Members included: Thomas McGiff (Drumraney), Anthony McCormack (Tang), Pat Macken (Castlepollard), Mick Pender (Athlone), James Martin (The Hill of Berries), John Galvin (Carrick), Frank O'Connor (Coosan), Brian Mulvihill (Coosan), Paddy Golden (Coosan), Thomas Berry (Tubberclair), Jack Costello (Crosswood), Jack Kelly (Mt. Temple), Paddy Fitzpatrick and his brother from Cornamaddy, Bertie Gaynor (Tullywood), Harry O'Brien (Athlone), James Fox (Athlone), Ned Dowling (Athlone), and Simon Mulvihill (Coosan). They were assisted by Michael Finneran (Glasson), James Casey (Killenure), Tim McCann (Portlick), Pat Killian (Glasson), Paddy Cunningham (Killenure), Ned Flynn (Kilkenny West), Michael Tinn (Tonagh), Tom Heslin (Littletown), L. Corrigan (Kilfaughney), Pat Keegan (Tubberclair), and Willie Keegan of Tubberclair

Mick (top) and Pat Carty of Tubberclair
COURTESY OF ANN ROHAN VETTER

Note: Records from individual prisons were collated after the Civil War and entered into two large ledgers that are now housed in the Military Archives at Cathal Brugha Barracks. Unfortunately, not all prisoner names were entered into the two summary books. Thus, it may be that inadvertently, some men's names do not appear on this listing below. Only the names of men who resided close to the Athlone Brigade area were included. Those who lived further east and north, were omitted from this Westmeath listing.

The dates entered below are written in European style, i.e., October 20, 1922 is written as 20/10/22.

Prisoners	Place of Residence	Arrest & Incarceration Dates
John Balfe	Glynwood, Athlone	Arrested 8/11/22 and released 18/11/22
Patrick Berry	Moneen, Moate	Arrested 29/7/22. Taken to Athlone 2/9/22. Transferred to Mountjoy on 10/1/23
Patrick Birmingham	Mt. Temple, Moate	Incarcerated in Athlone 22/2/23
Patrick Bracken	Castletown, Ballycumber, Co. Offaly	Arrested 4/7/22 and taken to Athlone two months later
William Brown	Clara, Co. Offaly	Arrested 13/7/22 and taken to Athlone two months later
Joe Carrigan	Moate	Sent to Tintown II on 20/2/23
John Carroll	Main St., Moate	Sent to Mountjoy 10/1/2
Could be same man:		
Jack Carty	Ballinakill, Glasson, Athlone.	Detained in Mountjoy transferred to Tintown II 20/2/23
John Carty	Glasson, Athlone	Incarcerated in Athlone on 29/11/22 and sent to Mountjoy on 10 January 1923
Gerald Carthy	Drumraney	Arrested 11/7/22. Taken to Athlone on 2/9/22 then transferred to Mountjoy on 10/1/23
John Carville	Main St., Moate	Sent to Tintown II on 20/2/23
James Cassels	Ballycloughduff, Moate	Arrested 25/7/22 and taken to Athlone on 2/9/22. In January of 1923 he was transferred to Mountjoy
Dan Claffey	Moate	Incarcerated Athlone 5/4/23

Michael Claffey	Tullybane, Moate	Incarcerated Athlone 6/3/23
Thomas Claffey	Faherin, Moate	Imprisoned Athlone 27/11/22
George Cosgrave	St. Columbus, Athlone	Arrested 30/7/22 and incarcerated in Athlone 2/9/22. Transferred to Mountjoy 10/1/23 and sent to Tintown II on 20/2/23
Thomas Cullen	Drumraney, Moate	Arrested 11/7/22 and sent to Athlone two months later. He was transferred to Mountjoy 10 January 1923
J. Cunningham	Glasson, Athlone	Incarcerated Athlone 2/9/22
William Cunningham	Cartroncoragh, Drumraney	Arrested 17 April 1923
Prisoners	**Place of Residence**	**Arrest & Incarceration Dates**
John Daly	Moate	Arrested 28/9/22 and sent to Athlone on 14 November. He was transferred to Mountjoy in January 1923
Malachy Daly	Moate	Incarcerated in Maryborough (Portlaoise) 19/8/22 and sent to Tintown II on 22/2/23
M. Daly	Moate	Incarcerated in Wellington 12/8/22
Patrick Donlan	Littletown, The Pigeons Athlone	Incarcerated in Athlone 3/3/23
Andrew Donoghue	Ballincock, Mount Temple	Arrested 26/9/22 and taken to Athlone on 14/11/22. He was transferred to Mountjoy on 10/1/23
Thomas Donoghue	The Pigeons, Athlone	Arrested 11/7/22 and sent to Athlone two months later. He was transferred to Mountjoy on 10/1/23 and in February was transferred to Tintown II at the Curragh
James Doolan	Annagh, Ballykeeran, Athlone	Arrested 18/7/22 and sent to Athlone on 2/9/22
Patrick Doolan	Annagh, Glasson, Athlone	Incarcerated on 11/12/22 in Athlone and sent to Mountjoy on 10/1/23
James Dorrington	Moate	Arrested 28/7/22 and sent to Athlone on 2 September 1922
Edward "Ned" Dowling	Capt. of "A" Coy. (see Roscommon Listing)	
		Arrested 23 September 1922 in a roundup in the Kiltoom area
James Duffy	Creeve, Baylin Athlone	Arrested and interned in Athlone 2/9/22
Joseph Edwards	Ballyscarvin, Moate	Arrested 16/11/22 and sent to Athlone on 25/11/22. He was transferred to Tintown on 20/2/23
Francis Egan	Faheran, Moate	Interned in Athlone on 27/11/22
Joseph Egan	Cartrons, Moate	Arrested 26/10/22 and taken to Athlone on 14/11/22 where he was immediately released
Martin Egan	Clerhane Quarry, Shanonbridge, Co. Offaly	Mountjoy 29/1/23
Thomas Erwin	Tullywood, Baylin, Athlone	Arrested 9/7/22 and sent to Athlone on 2/9/22
Pat Farrell	Coosan, Athlone (see details in Roscommon Volunteer Listing)	
John Farrelly	Grangemore, Killucan	Arrested 23/9/22 and sent to Mullingar on 6/10/22. Later transferred to Dundalk 14/11/22
John Fay	Stonestown, Delvin	Incarcerated in Newbridge 7/9/22
Michael Finn	Glasson, Athlone	Incarcerated Athlone 14/2/23
Michael Finneran	Glasson, Athlone	Arrested 31/8/22 and sent to Athlone a month later
Francis Fitzpatrick	Ballykeeran, Athlone	Incarcerated in Athlone 15/2/23
Patrick Fitzpatrick	Ballykeeran, Athlone	Incarcerated in Athlone 2/3/23
Martin Flannery	Aughicale, Shannonbridge, Co. Offaly	Athlone
Edward Flynn	Kilkenny West, Glasson	Incarcerated in Athlone 18/12/22 and sent to Mountjoy a month later. He was transferred to Tintown on 20/2/23
John Flynn	Shurock, Moate	Arrested 29/7/22 and sent to Athlone 2/9/22
Michael Flynn	Killkenny West, Glasson	Incarcerated Athlone 14/3/23
William Flynn	Fore, Castlepollard	Newbridge 7/9/22
John Fox	Tang	Arrested 13/7/22 and sent to Athlone in November. He was soon released
Michael Fox	Dalivan	Incarcerated in Newbridge 20/12/22
Sean Galvin	Carricknaughton, Athlone	Arrested and incarcerated in Athlone 21/4/23. He later died of the wounds inflicted during the war. His name is included on the IRA monument in Athlone
William Ganley	The Pigeons, Athlone	Arrested 1/11/22 and sent to Athlone. He was released 13/11/22 but was again behind bars in Athlone by March of 1923
James Gavin	Ballymore, Moate	Incarcerated in Tintown II on 20/2/23
James Gaynor	Macken, Mount Temple	Arrested 1/11/22 and taken to Athlone on the 14th
William Geraghty	Ballymore, Moate	Taken to Athlone on 10/12/22 and transferred to Tintown II 20/2/23. He was admitted to the hospital there in March
Joe Groarke	Tully, The Pigeons, Athlone	Incarcerated Athlone 3/3/23
Tom Irwin	Tully, Baylin, Athlone	Incarcerated in Mountjoy on 10/1/23 and sent to Tintown a month later
John Joyce	Mount Temple, Moate	Arrested 29/7/22 and taken to on 2/9/22

Thomas Kearney	Ballymore, Moate	Arrested and incarcerated in Athlone on 6/12/22
James Keegan	Drumraney, Moate	Incarcerated in Athlone /11/22
Michael Keges	Moate	Arrested 31/8/22 and sent to Athlone on 2/9/22
B. Kelly	Tullybane, Mt. Temple	Taken to Athlone on 2/9/22
William Kenaghan	Rosemount, Moate	Taken to Athlone on 20/3/23
James Kerrigan	Drumraney, Moate	Arrested 29/7/22, sent to Athlone, and released on 19 December 1922
Joseph Kerrigan	Drumraney, Moate	Arrested 29/7/22 and sent to Athlone 2/9/22. He was transferred to Mountjoy on 10/1/23

Prisoners	Place of Residence	Arrest & Incarceration Dates
John Kilduff	Glasson, Athlone	Arrested 9/10/22 and sent to Athlone 14/11/22. He was soon released
Patrick Killian	Glasson, Athlone	Arrested 1/11/22 and sent to Athlone 14/11/22. He was released shortly there after
Kiernan Kilmartin	Cushla, Monksland, Athlone	Arrested 10/7/22 and sent to Athlone 2/9/22
James McCann	Kilfaughny, Kilkenny West	Sent to Athlone on 3/3/23
John McCann	Cartrontroy, The Pidgeons, Athlone	Sent to Athlone 3/3/23
Patrick McCarthy	Boher, Athlone	Athlone
Anthony McCormack	Capt. of Tang Coy. (see Roscommon listing)	
		Arrested on 5/12/22 at Ballymore. Hoares' public house was searched. McCormack was found in a chimney seriously wounded in the leg. Also a revolver, Lee Enfield rifle and ammo recovered. He was admitted to the Curragh Hospital on 5/12/22
James McCormack	Tonlegee, Tang	Arrested 29/9/22, sent to Athlone two months later. He escaped the night before he was scheduled to be shot. He was later arrested and spent eleven months in the Curragh*

*Seamus McCormack, son of James. Interview by author, Tang, Athlone. 13 August 2004.

James McCormack	Stonestown, Castlepollard	Incarcerated during the Civil War at Gorman Camp on 8/9/22. Released 19/12/23
John McCormack	Moate	Arrested 28/7/22 and taken to Athlone in September. He was transferred to Mountjoy 10/1/23 and finally to Tintown II on 20/2/23
Martin McCormack	Castlepollard	Arrested 13/7/22 and sent to Athlone on 14/11/22
Michael McCormack	Stonestown, Castlepollard	Sent to Mountjoy, then transferred to Tintown II on 20/2/23
Michael McCormack	Ardbough, Moate	Arrested 8/8/22 and sent to Athlone 2/9. At the first of the year on 10/1/23 he was transferred to Mountjoy
Patrick McCormack	Drumraney, Moate	Arrested 28/7/22 and taken to Athlone in September. He was transferred to Mountjoy in January and finally shipped to II on 20/2/23
Thomas McCourt	Stranmullen	Taken to Mountjoy on 4/2/23 released a month later
James McDermott	Tang	Arrested 29/7/22 and taken to Athlone on 2/9/22
James McDermott	Kilcaner, Drumraney	Incarcerated in Mountjoy on 10/1/23
Daniel McGiff	Drumraney, Moate	Arrested at Tang 8/8/22 and taken to Athlone on 2/9/22
Thomas McGiff	(see Roscommon listing)	O/C of 2nd Battalion, Athlone Brigade captured escaping from Mrs. McCormack's house in Bishopstown on 17 November 1923
Frank McGuinness	Kilbeggan	Taken to Maryboro on 14/8/22
John McLynn	Ballycloughduff, Moate	Arrested on 29/9/22 and taken to Athlone on 14/11/22
Pat Macken,	QM Athlone Brigade	captured on 16 September 1922 (See Roscommon Listing)
Tom Maguire	Castlepollard	Arrested 8/11/22 and eventually taken to Mountjoy on 30/1/23. Sent to the Curragh 27/11/22
Joseph Mallayne	Loonebeg, Drumraney	Arrested 17 April 1923
T. Malynn	Ballycloughduff, Moate	Incarcerated in Athlone /9/22 and sent to Mountjoy on 10/1/23
Patrick May	Kilkerran, Castlepollard	Arrested 5/9/22 and sent to Athlone on 9/11. January of the next year found him incarcerated in Mountjoy
Timothy Molyneux	Ballycloughduff, Moate	Arrested 25/7/22 and taken to Athlone in September
James Moran	Drumraney	Arrested 25 July 1922 and sent to Athlone on 2 September
Brian Mulvihill	Coosan	Sent to Athlone 9/12/22 (See Roscommon men listing)
Joseph Murphy	Ballycomoyle, Castlepollard	Arrested and sent to Newbridge on 20/12/22
Matt Murphy	Robinstown, Castlepollard	Sent to Gorman Camp on 8/9/22 and transferred to Maryboro on 18/12/22. He was released on 20/12/23
Michael Murphy	Ballycomoyle, Castlepollard	Arrested and taken to Newbridge on 18/12/22. He was released on 23/3/23
Thomas Murphy	Ballycomoyle, Castlepollard	Sent to Newbridge 20/12/22
Thomas Murray	Castlepollard	Arrested 21/12/22 and released shortly afterwards on 2/1/23
Hugh Murtagh	Drumraney, Moate	Arrested 8/8/22 and sent to Athlone on 2/9/22. He was transferred to Mountjoy on 10/1/23
James Nea	Castlepollard	Taken to Newbridge 7/9/22

Frank Neilan	Towneagh Rd., Castlepollard	Arrested and taken to Mountjoy, then transferred to Tintown II on 20/2/23
Arthur O'Brien	Baylin, Athlone	Arrested on 5/7/22 and taken to Athlone on 2/9/22
Michael O'Brien	Rossmore, Moate	Incarcerated in Athlone on 2/9/22
John Quist	Kilkenny West, Athlone	Arrested on 9/8/22 and taken to Athlone on 2/9/22
Joseph Quist	Kilkenny West, Glasson, Athlone.	Sent to Athlone on 8/12/22 and released two months later
Michael Reilly	Drumcree, Delvin	Sent to Gormanstown Camp on 8/9/22 and released on Christmas Eve 1922
Michael Sammon	Kilkenny West, Glasson.	Arrested 3/7/22 and sent to Athlone on 2/9/22
Larry Savage	Streamstown, Moate	Arrested 30/7/22 and sent to Athlone on 2/9/22
Michael Seary	Corr, Walderstown, Athlone	Arrested 8/8/22 and taken to Athlone 2/9/22

Prisoners	Place of Residence	Arrest & Incarceration Dates
Hugh Sheerin	Jamestown, Castletown	Sent to Athlone on 2/9/22
James Shiel	Castlepollard	Sent to Gormans Camp on 8/9/22
Thomas Shields	Rathowen	Taken to Athlone on 2/9/22 and shipped to Tintown II on 20/2/23. He was finally released on 16/4/23
John Shortle	Baylin, Athlone	Captured on 16/9/22 along with Pat Macken and taken to Athlone on 14/11/22
John Smyth	Carduff, Dangan, Co. Offaly	Arrested 26/9/22 and sent to Mullingar on 6/10/22 where he was admitted to the hospital. Transferred to Dundalk on 5/11/22
David Tormey	Monea, Moate	Arrested on 11/9/22 and sent to Athlone from which he escaped on 24 October 1922
John Tumeety	(Tumeely) Maldra	Arrested and taken to Athlone on 3/3/23
Thomas Walsh	Rathowen	Arrested 7/7/22 and taken to Athlone in September
Patrick Ward	Annagh, Ballykeeran, Athlone	Arrested on 18/7/22 and sent to Athlone on 2/9/22. He was transferred to Tintown II on 20/2/23

The vision for which all Volunteers fought ---the back side of the British Army leaving Ireland.
The above photo was taken in Athlone, February 1922.

BIBLIOGRAPHY

Books:
Abbott, Richard. *Police Casualties in Ireland 1919-1922.* Dublin: Mercier Press. 2000.
Adams, Gerry. *The Politics of Irish Freedom.* Dingle, Co. Kerry: Brandon Book Publishers Ltd. 1986.
   Before the Dawn An Autobiography. New York: William Morrow and Company. 1996.
Andrews, C. S. *Dublin Made Me.* Dublin: The Mercier Press. 1979.
Augusteijn, Joost. *From Public Defiance to Guerilla Warfare.* Academisch Proefschrift. University of Amsterdam. 1994.
Baker, Joe. *My Stand For Freedom.* Westport: Westport Historical Society. 1988.
Barrett, J. J. *In the Name of the Game.* Bray, County Wicklow: The Dub Press. 1997.
Barry, General Tom. *Guerilla Days in Ireland.* Cork: The Mercier Press Limited. 1955.
Bell, J Bowyer. *The Secret Army The IRA.* Dublin: Poolbeg Press. 1997.
Bowers, Claude G. *The Irish Orators A History of Ireland's Fight For Freedom.* Indianapolis: The Bobbs-Merrill Company. 1916.
Breen, Dan. *My Fight for Irish Freedom.* Dublin: Anvil Books. 1993.
Brennan, Michael. *The War in Clare 1911-1921.* Dublin: Four Courts Press. 1980.
Carey, Tim. *Mountjoy The Story of a Prison.* Doughcloyne Wilton Cork: The Collins Press. 2000.
Carroll, Denis. *They have fooled you again Miceál O'Flannagáin Priest, Republican, Social Critic.* Dublin: The Columbia Press. 1993.
Clonown: The History, Traditions and Culture of a South Roscommon Community. Clonown Community Centre. 1989.
Coffey, Martin F. (Compiler and Editor) *Roscommon — past and present.* Dublin: Professional Publications. 1961.
Coleman, Marie. *County Longford and the Irish Revolution.* Dublin: Irish Academic Press. 2003.
Collins, Michael. *The Path to Freedom.* Boulder, Colorado: Roberts Rinehart Publishers. 1996.
Colum, Padraic. *Ourselves Alone! The Story of Arthur Griffith and the Origins of the Irish Free State.* New York: Crown Publishers Inc. 1959.
Coogan, Timothy Patrick. *Ireland Since the Rising.* London: Frederick A. Praeger, Publisher. 1966.
   Eamon De Valera. New York: Harper Perennial. 1996.
   Michael Collins. London: Arrow Books Limited. 1991.
   The I.R.A. London: Praeger Publishers. 1970.
   Disillusioned Decades Ireland 1966-87. Dublin: Gill and Macmillan. 1987.
   The IRA A History: Niwot, Colorado: Roberts Rinehart Publishers. 1993.
Coyle, Albert (transcriber and annotator). *Evidence on Conditions in Ireland.* Washington, D. C. Bliss Building. 1921.
Coyle, Liam. *A Parish History of Kilglass, Slatta, Ruskey.* Boyle: *The Roscommon Herald.* 1994.
Cumann na Poblachta Review. Commemorative Booklet on the occasion of 70th Anniversary of First Dáil 21st January 1919. Tullamore, Co. Offaly: Kearns, Printers. 1989.
Devoy, John. *Recollections of an Irish Rebel.* New York: Charles P. Young Company. 1929.
Dockery, Martin J. *Lost in Translation Vietnam A Combat Advisor's Story.* New York: Ballantine Books. 2003.
Dublin Castle Historical background and Guide. Dublin, Ireland: Office of Public Works.
Dwyer, T. Ryle. *Tans, Terror and Troubles.* Dublin: Mercier Press. 2001.
Earl of Longford and Thomas P. O'Neill. *Eamon de Valera A Biography.* Boston: Houghton Mifflin Co. 1971.
Egan, Edward (editor). *Drum and its Hinterland.* Athlone: Alfa Print Limited. 2003.
Elliott, Marianne. *Wolfe Tone.* London: Yale University Press. 1989.
Evans, E. Estyn, Kathleen Hughes, Roger Stalley, Brian de Breffny, Rosemary Ffolliot, Anne Crookshank, Gearoid O'Tuathaigh, Phillip L. Marcus, Jeanne Sheehy, William V. Shannon, Kevin B. Nowlan. *The Irish World.* New York: Harrison House/ Harry N. Abrams, Inc. 1986.
Fanning, Ronan. *Independent Ireland.* Dublin: Helicon Limited. 1983.

Farry, Michael. *The Aftermath of Revolution Sligo 1921-23*. Dublin: University College Dublin Press. 2000.

Fitzgerald, Desmond. *Memoirs of Desmond Fitzgerald 1913-1916*. London: Routledge & Kegan Paul. 1968.

Fitzgibbon, Constantine. *The Life and Times of Eamon de Valera*. New York: Macmillan Publishing Co., Inc. 1973.

Foley, Mark. *Nobody's Business: Aspects of County Roscommon Politics 1925-1931*. Masters Thesis, Dept. of Modern History, National University of Ireland, Maynooth. 1999.

Griffith, Kenneth and Timothy O'Grady. *Curious Journey An Oral History of Ireland's Unfinished Revolution*. Dublin: Mercier Press. 1998.

Harkness, David. *Northern Ireland since 1920*. Dublin: Helicon Limited. 1983.

Harnett, Mossie. *Victory and Woe*. Dublin: University College Dublin Press. 2002.

Hart, Peter. *The I.R.A. & Its Enemies*. Oxford, England: Oxford University Press. 1999.

   British Intelligence in Ireland 1920-21 The Final Reports. Cork University Press. 2002.

Hayes-McCoy (editor). *The Irish at War*. Cork: Mercier Press. 1964.

Healy, Paul. *God Save All Here*. Roscommon town: Paul Healy. 1999.

Hopkinson, Michael (editor). *Frank Henderson's Easter Rising Recollections of a Dublin Volunteer*. Cork City: Cork University Press. 1998.

   Green Against Green. Dublin: Gill and Macmillan. 1988.

Iris leabar na Feise Moire Rat Cruacain. Baile ata cliat: clobuailte. 1924.

Jennett, Sean. *Connacht*. London: Faber & Faber Limited. 1970.

Jordan, Anthony. *Sean MacBride*. Dublin: Blackwater Press. 1993.

Keneally, Thomas. *The Great Shame*. London: Vintage. 1999.

Keogh, Dermot. *Twentieth-Century Ireland*. Dublin: Gill & Macmillan. 1994.

Kilteevan. Edited by Hazel A. Ryan. Published by Kilteevan School Board of Management. 1997.

Links. Creggs, County Galway, Ireland: The Kilbegnet-Ballinakill Historical Society. 1991.

Litton, Helen. *The Irish Civil War An Illustrated History*. Dublin: Wolfhound Press Ltd. 1997.

Luddy, Maria. *Hanna Sheehy Skeffington*. Dublin: Historical Association of Ireland. Series No. 5. 1995.

McDermott, Vera. *The Woodlands of Loughglynn*. Mrs. CV Brookes 2 The Manor House, Thorner, near Leeds England. 1998.

MacDowell, Vincent. *Michael Collins and The Brotherhood*. Dublin: Ashfield Press. 1997.

MacEoin, Uinseann. *The IRA in the Twilight Years. 1923-1948*. Dublin: Argenta Publications. 1997.

MacManus, Seumas. *The Story of the Irish Race*. Old Greenwich, Connecticut: The Devin-Adair Company. 1921.

McGowan, Joe. *Constance Markievicz*. Mullaghmore, Co. Sligo: Constance Markievicz Committee. 2003

Magan, William. *The Story of Ireland*. Shaftesbury, Dorset: Element Books Limited. 2000.

Maher, Helen. *Roscommon Authors*. Roscommon. 1978.

Maher, Jim. *Harry Boland*. Boulder, Colorado: Mercier Press. 1998.

Mattimoe, Cyril. *North Roscommon — its people and past*. Boyle, Ireland: *Roscommon Herald*. 1992.

Martin, F. X. *The Irish Volunteers 1913-1915*. Dublin: James Duffy & Co. Ltd. 1963.

Maye, Brian. *Arthur Griffith*. Dublin: Griffith College Publications. 1997.

Moody, T. W. and F. X. Martin. *The Course of Irish History*. Dublin: Mercier Press. 1994.

Moylurg Writers, Boyle. *Boyle — The Origins, the Buildings, the Times*. Boyle, Roscommon: *Roscommon Herald* Printers. 1988.

Moylurg Writers, Boyle. *Boyle — Its People, Its Times Past and Present Vol. 2*. Boyle, Roscommon: *Roscommon Herald* Printers. 1993.

Murphy, Charles. *Heritage of Ireland*. New York: Crescent Books. 1991.

Murphy, Jeremiah. *When Youth Was Mine. A Memoir of Kerry 1902-1925*. Dublin, Ireland: Mentor Press. 1998.

Neeson, Eoin. *The Civil War 1922-1923*. Dublin, Ireland: Poolbeg Press Ltd. 1989.

   Birth of a Republic. Dublin: Prestige Books. 1998.

Neligan, David. *The Spy in the Castle*. London: MacGibbon & Kee Limited. 1968.

Nolan, Matt. *Ballygar — Just for the Record*. Crigean Press. 2004.

Nolan, William editor. *The Shaping of Ireland*. Cork: The Mercier Press. 1986.

O'Ballance, Edgar. *Terror in Ireland*. Novato, California: Presidio Press. 1981.

O'Callaghan, Micheál. *For Ireland and Freedom*. Boyle, County Roscommon, Ireland: *Roscommon Herald*. 1991.

O'Connor, Father Dominic O. M. Cap., *A Brief History of the Diocese of Baker City*. Baker, Oregon: Ryder Brothers. 1930.

O'Connor, Frank. *The Big Fellow*. Dublin: Clonmore & Reynolds Ltd. 1965.

   An Only Child. New York: Alfred A. Knopf, Inc. 1961.

O'Connor, J. F. *An Irish Civil War Exile*. New York: Vantage Press, Inc. 1988.

O'Donoghue, Florence. *No Other Law*. Dublin: Anvil Books. 1986.

O'Donovan, Donal. *Kevin Barry and His Time*. Dublin: The Glendale Press Ltd. 1989.

O'Duigneain, Proinnsios. *Linda Kearns A Revolutionary Woman*. Manorhamilton, Co. Leitrim, Ireland: Drumlin Publications. 2002.

O'Farrell, Padraic. *The Blacksmith of Ballinalee*. Mullingar, Ireland: Uisneach Press. 1993.

  Who's Who in the Irish War of Independence and Civil War 1916-1923. Dublin: The Lilliput Press. 1997.

O'Fathaigh, Padraig. *Padraig O'Fathaigh's War of Independence Recollections of a Galway Gaelic Leaguer*. Cork: Cork University Press. 2000.

O'Gadhra, Nollaig. *Civil War in Connaught*. Dublin: Mercier Press. 1999.

O'Hegarty, P. S. *The Victory of Sinn Fein*. Dublin: University College Dublin Press. 1998.

O'Leary, John. *Recollections of Fenians and Fenianism*. Shannon: Irish University Press. 1969.

O'Mahony, Sean. *Frongoch University of Revolution*. Killiney, Co. Dublin: FDR Teoranta. 1995.

O'Malley, Ernie. *On Another Man's Wound*. Dublin: Anvil Books. 1994.

  Raids and Rallies. Dublin: Anvil Books. 1982.

  The Singing Flame. Dublin: Anvil Books. 1978.

O'Sullivan, Donal J. *The Irish Constabularies*. Brandon (an imprint of Mount Eagle Publications Ltd.) 1999.

Pinkman, John A. *In the Legion of the Vanguard*. Boulder, Colorado: Mercier Press. 1998.

Rossa, O'Donovan. *Irish Rebels in English Prisons*. Dingle, Co. Kerry: Brandon Books Publishers Ltd. 1991.

Ryan, Meda. *The Day Michael Collins Was Shot*. Dublin: Poolbeg Press Ltd. 1997.

Snee, John. *Memories of an Old Man 1910-1986*. Published privately. 1986.

Stone, Msgr. William S. *A Cross in the Middle of Nowhere*. Bend, Oregon: Maverick Publishers. 1993.

Tarmon National School Centenary, 1890-1990. Martin Lavin editor. Boyle: *Roscommon Herald*. 1990.

Travers, Pauric. *Settlements and Divisions Ireland 1870-1922*. Dublin: Helicon Limited. 1988.

Twohig, Patrick J. *Green Tears for Hecuba*. Ballincollig, Co. Cork: Tower Books. 1994.

  The Dark Secret of BealnaBlath. Ballincollig, Co. Cork, Ireland: Tower Books. 1991.

Valiulis, Maryann Gialanella. *Portrait of a Revolutionary General Richard Mulcahy and the Founding of the Irish Free State*. Lexington, Kentucky: The University Press of Kentucky. 1992.

Warfield, Derek. *Irish Songster of the American Civil War*. P. O. Box 747 Kilcock, County Kildare, Ireland.

White, Robert. *Provisional Irish Republicans An Oral and Interpretive History*. Westport, Connecticut: Greenwood Press. 1993

With the IRA in the Fight for Freedom 1919 to the Truce. Tralee: *The Kerryman*. 1955.

Younger, Calton. *A State of Disunion Four Studies: Arthur Griffith, Michael Collins, James Craig, Eamon de Valera*. London: Frederick Muller Ltd. 1972.

  Ireland's Civil War. Great Britain: Fontana Press. 1990.

1916 Rebellion Handbook. Dublin: The Mourne River Press. 1998

Interviews:

Banahan, Eileen. Daughter of Michael Collins of Kilgefin Coy., 3rd Battalion South Roscommon. Interview by author. 18 and 20 November 2000. Ballagh and Roscommon town, Ireland.

Beattie, Frank. Son of Pat Beattie, Capt. of Rahara Coy. Interview by author. 23 and 26 June 2002. Rahara and Roscommon town. Also 14 November 2003 Roscommon town.

Beirne, Rose. Interview by author. 22 August 1993, 12 August 1995, 21 September 1997, and 25 June 2002. Ballinaheglish, County Roscommon, Ireland.

Bergin, Patrick. Nephew of Sean Bergin. Interview by author. 24 August 1994. Roscommon town, Ireland.

Bergin, Sheila. Half-sister of Sean Bergin. Interview by author. 5 November 2003. Nenagh, Co. Tipperary.

Boland, Michael. Longtime resident of Ballinaheglish. Interview by author. 11 October 1998. Bushfield, Ballinaheglish.

Bosco, Sister. Former resident of Ballinaheglish. Interview by author. 29 September 1997, and 25 June 2002. Tulla, Co. Clare and Carrowduff, Ballymacurley, Co. Roscommon.

Breheny, Michael John. Interview by author. 22 June 2002. Knockcroghery, Co. Roscommon.

Brennan, Maeve. Daughter of Jack Brennan, Vice O/C of the South Roscommon Brigade. Interview by author. 3 November 2003, Salthill, Galway.

Brennan, Mary. Daughter of Dan Madden of Kilgefin Coy., 3rd Battalion South Roscommon. Interview by author. 18 and 23 November 2000. Ballagh and Roscommon town, Co. Roscommon, Ireland.

Brennan, Matty. Nephew of Jack Brennan, Vice O/C of the South Roscommon Brigade. Interview by author. 30 October 2003. Fuerty, Co. Roscommon.

Brennan, Paraic. Grandson of Pat Brennan, O/C of the North Roscommon Brigade during the Civil War. Interview by author. 17 June 2002; 13 November 2003. Ballytrasna, Boyle, Co. Roscommon.

Brown, Sean. Proprietor of Hell's Kitchen. Interview by author. 24 November 2000; 8 November 2003. Castlerea, Co. Roscommon.

Campion, Elizabeth. Wife of Ned Campion. Interview by author. 13 August 1995. Castlerea, Ireland.

Carroll, Mary. Daughter of Tom Murphy of Kiltoom. Interview by author. 1 November 2003. Glanduff, Kiltoom, Ireland.

Conboy, Tony. Teacher and local historian. Interview by author. 24 September 1997, 9 October 1998, 17 November 2000, 17 and 26 June 2002. Boyle, Co. Roscommon. Also numerous correspondences.

Concannon, Mick. Resident of Ballinaheglish. Interview by author. 18 August 1993 and 21 August 1994. Ballinaheglish, Co. Roscommon, Ireland.

Concannon, Paddy. Resident of Knockmurry, Castlerea. Interview by author. 14 August 2004. Knockmurry, Castlerea.

Connolly, Michael. Resident of Ballinaheglish. Interview by author. 19 November 2000. Ballinaheglish, Co. Roscommon.

Cooney, Patrick. Resident of Garnafailagh, Athlone, nephew of Sean MacEoin. Correspondence 28 December 1995.

Costello, Sean. Son of Sean Costello of Castlerea. Correspondence 17 February 2004 from Dublin.

Crawley, Eamonn. Correspondence 17 February 2004 from Aughaloor, Loughglynn.

Cullen, Gerry of Perth, Australia. Nephew of Josie and Michael Cullen. Correspondence 31 October; 3, 10, 11, 14 and 21 November 2004.

Derby, David. Grandson of Tom Derby. Boyle. Correspondence 17, 18, 27 September 2003. Also interview by author. 2 November 2003. Roscommon town.

Dorr, Rita. Sister of Jim Dorr. Correspondence from Dublin. 15 November 2000.

Dowd, John. Lifetime resident of County Roscommon. Interview by author. 18 November 1992 and 22 August 1994. Castleplunkett, Roscommon.

Dowling, Eamonn, son of Edward. Correspondence 3 and 27 Feb. 2004. Interview by author. 23 August 2004. Dublin.

Duffy, Eamonn. Son of Luke Duffy, Vice O/C of the 3rd Battalion South Roscommon. Interview by author. 22 November 2000. Ennis, Clare. Also correspondence 8 November 1999 and 10 January 2000.

Duignan, Hugh. Correspondence 29 September 2003.

Duignan, James. Nephew of Patrick Duignan. Correspondence 1 October 2003.

Duignan, Jerry. Son of Patrick Duignan of Kilfaughna, Knockvicar. Interview by author. 27 September, 2004. Rinn, Carrick-on-Shannon.

Egan, Edward. Author and historian, Drum, Athlone. Interview by author 29 October 2003. Drum, Co. Roscommon. Also written correspondence. 30 April 2001; 10 and 30 May 2002; 11 December 2002; and 20 January 2003.

Egan, Tom. Interview by author. 29 October 2003. Bealnamullia, Co. Roscommon.

Feely, Barry. Son of Henry Feely of the 1st Battalion North Roscommon. Interview by author. 25 September 1997 in Roscommon town, 9 October 1998 in Boyle, and 17 June 2002 in Doon, Boyle.

Feely, Sister Clare. Niece of Toby Mannion. Interview by author. 31 August 1994 in Dublin, Ireland. Also 11 November 2003 at The Hill of Berries, Athlone.

Feely, Sadie. Niece of Toby Mannion. Interview by author. 11 November 2003. The Hill of Berries, Athlone.

Finneran, Charlie. Derryglad Folk Museum. Interview by author. 6 August 2004. Curraghboy, Athlone.

Fitzmaurice, Michael. Former editor of the *Roscommon Association Yearbook*. Interview by author. 7 August 1999 and 29 June 2002 in Dublin, Ireland. Also correspondence 28 March 1998; 14 May 1999; and 29 September 1999.

Fitzmaurice, Patrick. Correspondence 27 December 2002 from Oranmore, Co. Galway.

Flannery, Barry. Descendant of Tom Flannery. Correspondence 27 November 2004.

Foddy, Kiernan. Descendant of a member of the North Mayo Brigade. Correspondence 20, 24, 25 June and 31 July 2003.

Foley, Pierce. Son of Martin Foley, Captain of the Cloonboniffe Coy. Interview by author. 29 May 2002 and 19 October 2003. Dublin, Ireland.

Gacquin, William. Teacher and local historian. Curraghboy, Athlone. Correspondence 11 and 31 May 2003.

Gallagher, Mary. Daughter of George Murphy. Interview by author. 23 October 2003. Ballaghaderreen, Ireland.

Galvin, John. Oldest living Volunteer of the South Roscommon Brigade when interviewed at the age of 104. Interview by author. 16 September 1997. Ballygar Nursing Home. Ballygar, County Galway.

Garvey, Pauline. Daughter of Jim Quigley, O/C of the 2nd Battalion South Roscommon. Interview by author. 24 November 2000. Glenamaddy, Co. Galway.

Gilleese, Mrs. Linda. Lifetime member of Our Lady of Angels Catholic Church in Hermiston, Oregon U.S.A. Interview by author. 8 September 1998. Hermiston, Oregon.

Greene, John and Elizabeth. Son and daughter-in-law of Michael Greene, Capt. of Kilglass Coy. Interview by author. 11 and 14 November 2003. Roscommon town.

Griffin, Declan. Descendant of Seamus O'Brien of Athlone. Ballykeeran, Athlone. Correspondence 14, 15, 17, 22 July 2004.

Harney, Tom. Son of Tom Harney of Drum Coy. Interview by author 22 and 23 June 2002; 29 October, and 16 November 2003. Kiltoom, Co. Roscommon.

Hegarty, Joe and Annie. Nephew and niece of Michael Hegarty of Cloonboniffe Coy. Interview by author. 28 June 2002. Clooncundra, Castlerea.

Hester, John. Longtime resident of County Roscommon. Interview by author. 21 August 1993; 27 August 1994; 26 September 1997; 10 October 1998; 17 August 1999; 15 August 2004. Lanesboro, Co. Longford, Ireland.

Hevican, Joe and Kathleen. Son and daughter-in-law of Michael Thomas Hevican, Capt. of Gortaganny Coy. Interview by author. 28 June 2002. Carrowbehy, Castlerea. Also correspondence 19 October 2001.

Hevican, Patrick. Long-time resident of Roscommon County. Interview by author. 13 November 1992. Runnabracken, Donamon, Co. Roscommon, Ireland.

Hogan, Gloria. Daughter of Brian Lenihan. Interview by author. 6 August 2004. Boyle.

Irvine, Jim. Leitrim historian. Correspondence 18, 19, 21, 26 June 2003.

Jordan, Mary and Seamus. Niece and nephew of Patrick Hegarty of Mayo. Interview by author. 23 January 2005. Enniscoe, Crossmolina, Ballina. Co. Mayo, Ireland.

Kearns, Catherine. Niece of Michael and Jack Roche. Carrowcully, Ballinameen. Correspondence 29 October 2003. Also interview by author 31 October 2003. Carrowcully, Ballinameen.

Keating, Father Bernard. O. F. M. Cap. Parish priest in Redmond, Oregon, former resident of Dublin. Interview by author. 13 June 1996. Redmond, Oregon, USA.

Kelly, Anthony. Son of John Kelly of Ballinameen. Correspondence 1 March 2004 from Roscrea, Co. Tipperary.

Kelly, Father Evangelist O. F. M. Cap. Pastor of St. Francis of Assisi Church, Bend, Oregon. Interview by author. 10 June 1996. Also written correspondence.

Kelly, John. Son of John Kelly of Muckinagh, Kilglass. Interview by author. 15 November 2003. Muckinagh, Kilglass.

Kenny, Patrick. Dispatch rider and lookout for Drum Coy. Interview by author assisted by Tom Harney. 24 June 2002. Drum, Athlone.

Kenny, Willie. Resident of Carrick, Kiltoom. Interview by author. 23 June 2002. Kiltoom, Co. Roscommon.

Kerrigan, John. Historian in Roscommon town. Interview by author. 20, 21, 24 August 1994; 10, 11 August 1995; 15, 16 September 1997; 10 October 1998. Roscommon town, Ireland.

Kilcline, John. Son of Johnny Kilcline, Vice O/C of the 4th Battalion South. Interview by author. 2 May and 26 October 2003 in Roscommon town; 1 November 2003 Corrigeen, Knockcroghery, Co. Roscommon. Also correspondence December 2003.

Kilcline, Tom. Son of Johnny Kilcline, Vice O/C of the 4th Battalion South. Interview by author. 1 November 2003 Corrigeen, Knockcroghery, Co. Roscommon.

Kilmartin, Bernadette. Daughter of Pat Madden, O/C of the 3rd Battalion South Roscommon. Interview by author. 20 January 2001. London, England.

Kilroe, Michael. Former dispatch rider for the IRA during the Tan War. Interview by author. 12 October 1998. Ballybride near Roscommon town.

Leavy, Ciaran. Son of Sean Leavy, O/C of the 3rd Battalion North Roscommon. Interview by author. 27 and 29 June 2002, and 5 August 2004. Roscommon town and Scramogue, Co. Roscommon.

Leneghan, Michael and Kathleen. Nephew and niece of James Flanagan of Rockingham. Interview by author. 13 November 2003. The Bawn, Cootehall, Co. Roscommon.

Lennon, Michael. Editor of *Roscommon Life*. Interview by author. 10 November 2003, 4 August 2004 Roscommon town, and 24 August 2004 Dublin. Also numerous e-mail contacts from the years 2001-2004.

Lyons, Michael Joseph. Resident of Portrunny, County Roscommon. Interview by author. 17 August 1999.

McAlister, Tony. Grandson of Corporal George Meadlarklan. Correspondence 6 September 2004.

McCormack, Brian. Son of Michael. Interview by author. 13 August 2004. Drumraney, Westmeath.

McCormack, Seamus. Relative of Anthony McCormack. Interview by author. 13 August 2004. Drumraney, Westmeath.

McHugh, Anna. Resident of Ballybane, County Galway. Interview by author. 5 October 1998 and 18 August 1999.

McLoughlin, Frank. Son of Patrick McLoughlin, Capt. of Arigna Coy. Interview by author. 16 November 2000. Arigna, County Roscommon.

McManus, Margaret. Niece of Seamus and Michael Cull, daughter of Owen. Interview by author. 17 June 2002. Arigna, Co. Roscommon.

McPhillips, William. Son of John Patrick of Ballaghaderreen. Long Island, New York. Correspondence 29 July 2004.

Maloney, Tom. Longtime resident of Aghaderry, Loughglynn. Interview by author. 8 October 1998, 18 August 1999, and 28 June 2002. Loughglynn, County Roscommon.

Martin, John. Resident of Ballinagare. Interview by author. 14 August 2004. Ballinagare, Co. Roscommon.

Maye, Denis. Nephew of Pat Maye of Croghan. Correspondence 17 August 2001 and 29 November 2001 from Coogee, New South Wales, Australia.

Melinn, Patrick. Son of Seamus Melinn. Interview by author. 13 August 2004. Athlone.

Moran, May. Niece of Paddy Moran. Interview by author. 25 August 2004. Dublin, Ireland.

Moran, Seamus. Son of Jack Moran, O/C of Ballinlough Coy. in 1920. Interview by author. 19 August 1999. Waterford town, Ireland.

Morrissey, Tom. Resident of Ballinaheglish, County Roscommon. Interview by author. 18 August 1993; 11 August 1995. Ballinaheglish, Co. Roscommon, Ireland.

Mulligan, Rev. Bertram K. Historian for the Capuchin Order. Interview by author. 26 February 1999. Also written correspondence 2 March 1999. Burlingame, California, USA.

Mullooly, Dermott. Son of Patrick Mullooly, Quartermaster for the North Roscommon Brigade. Interview by author. 20 June and 27 June 2002. Kiltrustan, Strokestown, Ireland.

Murphy, Tony. Son of Hubert. Interview by author. 4 August 2004. Roscommon town.

Murray, Jimmy. Captain of the 1943 Roscommon Football Team that won the All Ireland. Interview by author. 24 September 1997; 22 November 2000; 11 November 2003. Knockcroghery, Co. Roscommon. Written correspondence 26 April 1998. Telephone interview 19 September 2002.

Murray, Mrs. Una (Sis). Wife of Josie and former resident of Boyle. Interview by author. 21 August 1995. Dublin, Ireland.

Nelson, Seamus. Lifelong resident of County Roscommon and son of James Nelson of the Kilgefin Coy. Interview by author. 19 and 21 August 1993; 29 August 1994; 11 October 1998; 16 August 1999; 25 November 2000; 27 June 2002; and 11 November 2003. Ballinaheglish and Roscommon town, Ireland. Also numerous correspondences.

Nolan, Tom. Solicitor and researcher from Athlone. Multiple personal correspondences throughout July, August, and September 2003.

O'Brádaigh, Ruairí (Peter Roger Casement Brady). Resident of Roscommon town. President of Republican Sinn Féin. Interview by author. 26 August 1994; 25 September 1997; 6 November 2003. Roscommon town, Ireland. Also correspondence 22 October 1996.

O'Brien, Donal. Son of Harry O'Brien. Interview by author. 5 August 2004. Athlone.

O'Brien, Gearóid. Head Librarian at Athlone Library. Interview by author. 6 August 2004. Athlone.

O'Brien, Joan. Daughter of Harry O'Brien. Interview by author. 18 August 2004. Athlone.

O'Callaghan, Colm. Brother of Micheál O'Callaghan, who was the author of *For Ireland and Freedom*. Interview by author. 26 August 1994 and 24 November 2000. Roscommon town, Ireland.

O'Connor, Denis. Son of Gerald O'Connor, O/C of the 1st Battalion, South Roscommon Brigade. Interview by author. 20 June 2002 Roscommon town, and 20 October 2003 Dublin, Ireland.

O'Flanagan, Sr. M. Niece of Father Michael O'Flanagan. Correspondence 20 February 2004.

O'Keefe, Maureen. Daughter of Tom Devaney. Interview by author. 25 November 2000. Aughakilmore, Ballinalee, County Longford.

O'Rourke, Lilly. Daughter-in-law of Dan O'Rourke, second O/C of the South Roscommon Brigade 1917-1921. Interview by author. 22 August 1993 and 13 August 1995. Castlerea, County Roscommon.

Owens, Gerald. Nephew of Sean Owens. Correspondence 7 January 2004 from Ashford, Co. Wicklow.

Owens, Henry. Local historian. Interview by author. 19 August 1999 in Lismehy, Strokestown; 28 October 2003, 6 November and 15 November 2003. Roscommon town.

Raftery, Sean. Nephew of Luke Raftery of Lisalway. Interview by author. 16 April 2004; 10 and 14 August 2004. Also correspondence 7 January 2005. Valeview, Castlerea.

Reynolds, Marina. Interview by author. 12 November 2003. Strokestown, Co. Roscommon.

Satchwell, Thomas. Son of Joe Satchwell of the 1st Battalion South Roscommon. Interview by author. 22 and 23 August 1994. Cloonkeen, Castlerea.

Sheridan, Catherine. Niece of Jim Breheny. Correspondence 20 September 2002 and 19 November 2002.

Shiel, Seamus. Son of Jim Shiel. Interview by author. 31 October 2003. Roscommon town.

Siggins, Albert. Former curator of Roscommon Museum. Interview by author. 26 August 1994; 29 August 1995; 15 September 1997. Roscommon town, Ireland. Correspondence 17 September 1996 and September 1999. Also numerous e-mail correspondences in 2004 and 2005.

Simons, Frank. Son of Frank Simons, Adjutant for the 3rd Battalion South Roscommon. Interview by author. 22 August 1995, and 28 May 2002. Dublin, Ireland.

Snee, John. One of the last survivors of the East Mayo Brigade, who fought with the Anti-Treaty side in 1922-23. Interview by author. 16 September 1997. Lucan, Co. Dublin.

Staunton, Ema. Daughter of Matt Davis, Quartermaster of the South Roscommon Brigade. Interview by author. 8 November 2003. Ballaghaderreen, Co. Roscommon.

Tanner, Helen. Relative of George Tanner. Interview by author. 12 November 2003. Strokestown, Co. Roscommon.

Tarpey, Frank and Rita. Owners of Tarpey's Travel. Interview by author. 18 June 2002. Boyle, Co. Roscommon.

Tiernan, Patrick. Nephew of Tommy Loughran. Interview by author. 15 November 2003. Kilglass, Co. Roscommon.

Toolan Kathleen and Alan. Daughter and grandson of Michael Duignan. Interview by author. 26 October 2003.
    Roscommon town.
Tormey, Joe. Nephew of Jim and Joe Tormey. Interview by author. 13 August 2004. Athlone.
Vaughan, Patrick. Brother of John Vaughan of Cloonsuck. Resident of Boston, Mass. Interview by author. 8 January, 10
    February, 23 March, 10 April, 10 September, 27 December of 1995. Also 9 January, 4 June, 11 October of 1996.
    Boston, Massachusetts.
Ward, Mick. Resident of Castlerea. Interview by author. 22 August 1994. Castlerea, County Roscommon.
Watson, Frankie. Teacher and historian, daughter of Pat Watson of Drum. Interview by author. 13 November 2003.
    Cootehall, Co. Roscommon. Also correspondence in 1997, 1 April 2000, and 24 December 2004.
Whelan, Clare. Daughter of Thomas McGiff. Interview by author. 1 September 2004. Dublin, Ireland.
Wickins, B. Daughter of George Meadlarklan. Correspondence 21 September 2004.

Newspapers and Periodicals:

Boston Globe Magazine. 1 May 1966.
Dwyer, Ryle. *The Kerryman*, article on Tom McEllistrim. 19 August 1994.
Roscommon Association Dublin Yearbook 1986. Vol. 7. Dublin: Avelbury Limited (Publishers). 1986.
Roscommon Association Dublin Yearbook 1987. Vol. 8. Dublin: Avelbury Limited (Publishers). 1987.
Roscommon Association Dublin Yearbook 1994. Vol. 16. Dublin: Avelbury Limited (Publishers). 1994.
Roscommon Association Dublin Yearbook 1996. Vol. 17. Dublin: Avelbury Limited (Publishers). 1996.
Roscommon Association Dublin Yearbook 1997. Vol. 18. Dublin: Avelbury Limited (Publishers). 1997.
Roscommon Herald "Incidents in County Roscommon" 15 May 1920 p. 1.
Roscommon Herald "Last Tribute to Roscommon Man who Fought for Irish Freedom." 28 October 1939.
Roscommon Historical and Archaeological Society Journal. Vol. 1. Boyle, Ireland. *Roscommon Herald*. 1986.
Roscommon Historical and Archaeological Society Journal. Vol. 2 Boyle, Ireland. *Roscommon Herald*. 1988.
Roscommon Historical and Archaeological Society Journal. Vol. 3. Boyle, Ireland. *Roscommon Herald*. 1990.
Roscommon Historical and Archaeological Society Journal. Vol. 4. Boyle, Ireland. *Roscommon Herald*. 1992.
Roscommon Historical and Archaeological Society Journal. Vol. 5. Boyle, Ireland. *Roscommon Herald*. 1994.
Roscommon Historical and Archaeological Society Journal. Vol. 6. Boyle, Ireland. *Roscommon Herald*. 1996.
Roscommon — past and present. The Roscommon Men's Association, Dublin. Dublin: Professional Publications. 1961.
Saoirse Irish Freedom, The Voice of Irish Republicanism. December 1996. p. 6.
Roscommon Champion. "Memorial to Cull Brothers Unveiled in Arigna." 29 September 1999.
The Western People
    "West Mayo's Fighting Story," by Anthony Lavelle, 16 May 1964.
    "The Burnings in Liverpool," by Henry Coyle, 27 June 1964.
    "The IRA in Liverpool," by John McPhillips, 25 July 1964.
    "Convicted by Buttercup Petals," by John McPhillips, 15 August 1964.
    "More Liverpool Exploits by IRA Recalled," by Bat Keaney, 5 September 1964.
    "Solitary Confinement in Dartmoor!" by John McPhillips, 12 September 1964.
    "Service in Ballaghaderreen," by John McPhillips, 19 September 1964.
    "With the IRA in Dartmoor," by Bat Keaney, 26 September 1964.
    "Mayo's Fighting Story — The IRA in Liverpool," as told by Anthony Lavelle.

Displays:

County Roscommon Museum, Roscommon town

Private Papers:

Pat Brennan Papers, private collection.
Gerald O'Connor Papers, private collection.
War of Independence (1919-1921) An Account by Thomas Cunningham of Gortfree. Written in 1978.
Summary of Activities of Companies in the 4th Battalion South, written by Company commanders and co-signed by Tom
    Kelly, Battalion O/C.
Handwritten listing of members by Captain Michael Greene of Kilglass Company.
Handwritten listing of members of Carniska Company by Captain Jim Shiel.
Summary Papers of William Fallon of Bealnamullia Coy., Athlone Brigade.
(Partial) summary papers of Pat Conboy of the Athleague Coy.
Listing of Kiltoom Company supplied by Liam Mannion of The Hill of Berries.
An Old Soldier's Memories by Tommy Loughran (unpublished).

Public Papers:
Mulcahy Papers, University College Dublin Archives.
Ernie O'Malley Papers, University College Dublin Archives.
Intelligence Reports of the Western Command, Bureau of Military History, Cathal Brugha Barracks, Dublin.
Civil War Internees Log, Military Archives, Cathal Brugha Barracks, Dublin.

Audio Tapes:
Denis Mannion, of The Hill of Berries, Athlone, taped in 1987, and transcribed by Sister Clare Feely.
Frank Simons, Acting O/C of the South Roscommon Brigade at the time of the Truce, interview by James McCormick,
   MA candidate at Loyola University in Chicago, Illinois. Summer of 1973, Roscommon town.

Other Sources:
IRA Pension List supplied by Mr. Eddie Fitzgerald, Pensions Administration Section, Department of Defence, Renmore,
   Galway.

Sources Specific to the Volunteer Listings:
Books:
This author owes an enormous debt of gratitude to Micheál O'Callaghan whose book, *For Ireland and Freedom*, provided a sound and secure foundation on which to build the Roscommon Volunteer Listing of names.

Micheál O'Callaghan, author of *For Ireland and Freedom*,
former editor of the *Roscommon Herald*
PHOTO COURTESY OF COLM O'CALLAGHAN

Names of men in the south of the county were dutifully
   recorded in Edward Egan's book, *Drum and its
   Hinterland*, published in 2003.
The Aftermath of Revolution Sligo 1921-23 by Michael
   Farry helped to clarify specific actions and people
   involved in the Sligo area.
Some names and dates were derived from Padraic
   O'Farrell's book, *Who's Who in the Irish War of
   Independence and Civil War 1916-1923*.
The 1916 Rebellion Handbook, first printed in 1916 by *Weekly Irish Times*, later published by Mourne River Press in 1998,
   provided names and dates for persons arrested after the Rising.
A few names were found in Ernie O'Malley's book, *Raids and Rallies*.
Nollaig O'Gadhra's *Civil War in Connaught 1922-1923* supplied information about Galway happenings and personnel.
Other Volunteer names were derived from *Clonown The History, Traditions and Culture of a South Roscommon Community*,
   published by the Clonown Community Centre in 1989.
Seamus O'Donovan's biography was found in *The IRA in the Twilight Years 1923-1948* by Uinseann MacEoin.
John Thomas Carley's 1922-1923 whereabouts are known by examining Denise Kleinrichert's *Argenta*.
Roscommon prisoners who were interned at Frongoch were recorded by Sean O'Mahony in his book, *Frongoch University
   of Revolution*.
Members of the Longford Flying Column were quoted from Marie Coleman's book, *County Longford and the Irish Revolution
   1910-1923*.
Mayo Flying Column members were obtained from Ruairí O'Bradáigh's book, *Dílseacht*.
West Mayo personnel were found in *My Stand for Freedom* by Joe Baker.
Some Longford activities and personnel were obtained from Padraic O'Farrell's book, *The Blacksmith of Ballinalee*.
Linda Kearns's activities were found in Proinnsios O'Duigneain's book, *Linda Kearns A Revolutionary Irish Woman*.
Private Collections:
Precise dates, specific actions, and names of participants in the 1st Battalion South area were found in the Gerald
   O'Connor Papers, which are held in a private collection.
Precise dates, engagements, and names of participants in the north of the county were found in the Pat Brennan Papers
   held in a private collection.
Other names were obtained from the Luke Duffy Papers, which were held by his son, Eamonn, of Ennis, Co. Clare.

Volunteer Witness Statements:
A wide variety of actions and personnel were described in the Volunteer Witness Statements. These formal summaries were made to the Bureau of Military History in the 1950s, and are now open for public reading at the National Archives in Dublin. Statements from the following Roscommon men were examined:

Thomas Brady, Intelligence Officer for 2nd Battalion North
Thomas (Con) Costello, Vice O/C Athlone Brigade
Tom Crawley, Vice O/C 1st Battalion South
Gerald Davis, 3rd Battalion South and "C" Coy. in Dublin
Matt Davis, Quartermaster for the South Roscommon Brigade
Jim Dorr, O/C 5th Battalion North
John Duffy, RIC, Roscommon town
Luke Duffy, Vice O/C 3rd Battalion South
Martin Fallon, O/C of the Flying Column in the 3rd Battalion North
James Feely, O/C 1st Battalion North
Jack Glancy, Adjutant of the North Roscommon Brigade
John Haran, (Frenchpark Coy.)
Andy Keavney, 1st Battalion South
John Kelly, (Cloontuskert Coy.)
Tom Kelly, O/C 4th Battalion South
Tommy Lavin, Vice O/C 4th Battalion North
Sean Leavy, O/C 3rd Battalion North
Patrick Lennon, Summerhill Coy., Athlone Brigade
Pat Mullooly, Quartermaster North Roscommon Brigade
Seamus O'Meara, O/C Athlone Brigade
Jim Quigley, O/C 2nd Battalion South
Stephen Scally (Cloonfree Coy.), 3rd Battalion North
Jack Shouldice, Ballaghaderreen, participant in the Easter Rising
Frank Simons, Adjutant of the 3rd Battalion South

Volunteer Witness Statements of men in the surrounding counties were also examined:
Patrick Connaughton, Capt. of Closetoken Coy. in Co. Galway
David Daly, O/C 2nd Battalion, Athlone Brigade
Patrick Dunleavy, O/C of North Galway Brigade and Column leader, Co. Galway
Martin Fahy, Galway Brigade Engineer
James Flood, Adjutant for the Longford Brigade
Con Fogarty, O/C of the North Galway Brigade
Charles Gildea, Quartermaster for the 3rd Western Division, Co. Sligo
Patrick Hegarty, Brigade Staff of North Mayo
Jim Hunt, O/C Gurteen Battalion, Co. Sligo
Eugene Kilkenny (Leitrim)
Harold McBrien, Captain of Ballintogher Coy., Co. Sligo
Alec McCabe, O/C of the 3rd Western Division
Anthony McCormack, Capt. of Tang Coy., Athlone Brigade
Michael McCormack, Tang, Coy., Athlone Brigade
Michael McCoy, Mullingar, Co. Westmeath
Thady McGowan, Co. Sligo
Harry O'Brien, Capt. of Coosan Coy., Athlone Brigade
Frank O'Connor, Capt. of Coosan Coy., Athlone Brigade
Charles Pinkman, Intelligence Officer for Leitrim Brigade
Roger Rabbitte, Captain of Kiltevna Coy., Co. Galway
Bernard Sweeney, O/C South Leitrim Brigade
Pat Treacy, member of the Galway Flying Column

INDEX

Flynn, Francis (Tarmon, Castlerea) 49, 64, 66, 68, 114, 206, 295

Flynn, Frank (member of Ballina Coy., Co. Mayo) 463

Flynn, James (Adjutant Loughrea Batt.) 455

Flynn, James (Kilteevan Coy.) 295

Flynn, James (Crossmolina Coy., Co. Mayo) 463, 466

Flynn, Jimmy (Ballyforan) 295

Flynn, John (Shurock, Moate) 472

Flynn, John (Killina Coy.) 295

Flynn, John (Trien Coy.) 295

Flynn, John "Jack" (Cloonree, Castlerea) 66, 89, 158, 245, 290, photo of 295, 302, 312

Flynn, Johnny (Ballyforan) 295

Flynn, Joseph (Curraghboy Coy.) 295

Flynn, Joseph (Ruskey Coy.) 295

Flynn, Martin (Trien Coy.) 65, 296

Flynn, Matthew (Tisrara Coy.) 296

Flynn, Michael (Kilteevan Coy.) 296

Flynn, Michael (Carrick, Ballinlough) 64, 65, 296

Flynn, Michael (Kilkenny West, Glasson) 472

Flynn, Packy (O/C Ballinamore Batt.) 458

Flynn, Patrick "Paddy" (Tarmon, Castlerea) 57, 64, 65, 66, 68, 180, 206, 296, 431

Flynn, Patrick (Ballyforan) 207, 209, 296

Flynn, Patrick (Ballymartin, Strokestown) 296

Flynn, Patrick (Deerpark, Boyle) 296

Flynn, Stephen (Arigna Flying Column) 141, 296

Flynn, Thomas (Ballymartin, Strokestown) 296

Flynn, Thomas (Castle Street, Roscommon town) 296

Flynn, Thomas (Grange, Fourmilehouse) 296

Flynn, William (Fore, Castlepollard) 472

Flynn's Cottage (Taughmaconnell) 296

Fogarty, Con (O/C North Galway Brigade) 150, 193, 453, 454, 456

Foley, Edward (Knockcroghery Coy.) 23, 64, 296

Foley, Martin (Cloonboniffe area) 32, 64, 65, 66, 67, 68, 89, 112, 130, 157, 206, photo of 295, photo of 297, 302, 312

Foley, Martin (RIC constable) 110

Foley, Michael (Carrick-on-Shannon area) 297

Foley, Thomas (Ballaghaderreen) 149, 151, 297

Forde, Dr. Dudley (Strokestown) 40, 112

Forde, Joseph (QM Fairymount Coy.) 297

Forde, Liam (Lisacul, Mayo Brigade staff) 145, 188, 297, 463, 464

Forde, Pappy (member of Ballina Coy., Co. Mayo) 463

Forde, Pat (Moor Coy.) 64, 298

Foresters' Hall, Athlone 43

Forgney, Co. Longford 163

Forsyth, Jack (Ballaghaderreen) 298

Four Courts (Dublin) 9, 10, 13, 82, 127, occupation of 129, photo of 131, 132, 135, 156, 186, 187

Four Roads 185

Fourmilehouse 21, 35, 50, 51, 52, 54, 56, 66, 77, 85, 110, 129, 146, 170, 178, 179, 180, 193

Fourmilehouse Ambush 50, 51, 52, 54, 56, 66

Fox, James (Athlone) 131, 158, 208, 298, 471

Fox, James "Jim" (Kilgefin Coy.) 66, 298

Fox, John (Tang Co., Westmeath) 472

Fox, Michael (Dalivan, Co. Westmeath) 472

Fox, Michael (Kilteevan Coy.) 298

Fox, Owen (Moor Coy.) 64, 66, 68, 89, 298

Fox, Pat (Kilteevan Coy.) 298

Foxford, Co. Mayo 188

Franklin, Patrick (prisoner at Ballykinlar Camp) 400

Frayne (Frain), Lily (Drumman More, Ruskey) 298

Frayne, Michael (Knockhall, Ruskey) 298

Frayne, Patrick (Castleard, Ballaghaderreen) 298

Free State 38, 54, 55, 61, 62, 118, 121, 125, 126, 129, 131, 132, 133, 136, 137, 138, 139, 140, 141, 142, 145, 146, 147, 148, 149, 150, 151, 152, 153, 154, 155, 156, 158, 159, 160, 161, 162, 163, 164, 165, 166, 167, 168, 169, 172, 186, 187, 188, 189, 190, 191, 192, 193, 194, 195, 196, 198

Free State Army 118, 125, 126, 129

Freehily, Paddy (Highlake, Ballymacurley) 274, photo of 298

Freeman, Michael (Loughglynn) 298

Freeman, Patrick (Aughmore, Ballyhaunis) 466

Freeman's Journal 82, 124

Frehill, Michael (Castleplunkett) 298

French, A. G. (Kilmore) 298

French, Allen (Drumsna) 298

Frenchpark 5, 13, 15, courthouse 38, 44, 45, barracks 49, barracks 56, 57, 59, barracks 65, 68, 70, 89, 98, 106, 110, 113, 120, 129, 146, 149, 155, 167, 168, 169, 170, 177, 179, 180, 181, 183, 184, 185, 188, 194, 195, 197

Freyne, — (Ballymurray) 299

Freyne, John (Aughmore, Ballyhaunis) 466

Freyne, Michael (Cloonmaul, Loughglynn) 64, 66, 71, 89, 112, 298

Freyne, Ned (Cloonmaul, Loughglynn) 299, 312

Frizelle, Constable 84

Frongoch Internment Camp 10, 12, 82, 177

Fryar, John (Clooneybrien, Cootehall) 299, photo of 412

Fuerty 10, 59, 159, 182, 184

Fullard, Michael (Roscommon town) 299

G

Gacquin, Denis (Capt. Dysart Coy.) 120, 207, 299

Gacquin, Michael (Tisrara Coy.) 299

Gaelic Athletic Association (GAA) 6, 25

Gaelic League 6, 25, 62, 177, 178

Gaffey, Ann (Summerhill) 299

Gaffey, Bernard "Barney" (Garrynagowna) 16, 34, 47, 75, 76, 89, 99, 209, photo of 299, 469

Gaffey, Edward (Correal, Four Roads) 299

Gaffey, Jack (Drum Coy.) 299

Gaffey, John (Cregganmeen, Castlerea) 299

Gaffey, Joseph (Kiltoom Coy.) 299

Gaffey, Mary (Summerhill) 299

Gaffey, Michael (Cregganmeen, Castlerea) 299

Gaffey, Michael (Athlone area) 300, 469

Gaffey, Paddy (Garrynagowna) 300

Gaffey, Thomas (Cregganmeen, Castlerea) 300

Gaffney, Bartley (Keadue) 141, 300

Gaffney, John (executed in Dublin) 155

Gaffney, Michael (Keadue) 141, 300

Gaffney, Patrick (Keadue) 141, 300

Gaffney, Patrick (Geevagh, Arigna) 300

Gaffney, Seamus (Arigna Flying Column) 141

Gaffney, Thomas (Keadue) 141, 300

Gaffney, Thomas (Derreenatawy, Crossna) 85, 300

Gaherty, John T. (Clooncrim, Ballinlough) 65, 300

Gaherty, Michael (Clooncrim, Ballinlough) 65, 300

Gahigan, Michael (Leitrim) 460

Gallagher, Andrew 68

Gallagher, Charles 300

Gallagher, Constable Francis 51

Gallagher, Francis (RIC constable) 110

Gallagher, Hugh (Bealnamullia) 300

Gallagher, James (Kilteevan Coy.) 300

Gallagher, Jim (Ballaghaderreen) 300

Gallagher, John (Bonnyconlan Coy., Co. Mayo) 463

Gallagher, John (Ballinamore) 460

Gallagher, Martin (Ruskey) 301, 463

Gallagher, Mary (Ballaghaderreen) 201

Gallagher, Michael (Knockhall, Ruskey) 301, 463

Gallagher, Miss (Gate House, Frenchpark) 146, 300

Gallagher, Patrick (Curraghboy Coy.) 65, 66, 88, 130, 133, 301

Gallagher, Reilly (Loughglynn area) 301

Gallagher, Tom (Tibohine) 301

Gallagher, Tom (Carton, Ballaghaderreen) 301

Galligan, Sergeant 28, 39, 43, 44

Galvin, Joe (Cloonlaughnan, Mount Talbot) 116, photo of 117, 118, 128, 207, 211, 288, photo of 301

Galvin, John (Cloonlaughnan, Mount Talbot) 131, 158, photo of 301, 471

Galvin, Nellie (Summerhill, Athlone) 302

Galvin, Patrick (Ballyhaunis) 466

Galvin, Sean (Carricknaughton) 302, 469, 472

Galway 32, 38, 46, 61, 63, 74, 77, 81, 96, 100, 109, 110, 112, 125, 130, 133, 140, 142, 144, 145, 148, 150, 152, 153, 158, 160, 164, 168, 169, 170, 171, 181, 184, 185, 187, 188, 190, 192, 193, 194, 195, 196, 197, 198, 453, 455, 456, 457, 458, 464, 466, 470

  North Galway Brigade 81, 193

  North Galway Brigade Staff 453

  South Galway Brigade Staff 455

  South Galway Brigade Structure Post Truce 455

  Galway Companies (strength of) 140

Gandon, James 129

Ganley, Bill (The Hill of Berries) 302

Ganley, Francis (Newtown, Whitehall) 302

Ganley, John (Willsgrove, Ballintubber) 65, 302

Ganley, John (Cloonmaul, Loughglynn) 64, 302

Ganley, Martin (Cloonmaul, Loughglynn) 64, 65, 66, 67, 68, 71, 79, 89, 105, 106, 112, 181, 206, 213, 228, 245, 246, 247, 299, 302, 312

Ganley, William (The Pigeons, Athlone) 472

Gannon, Bernard "Barney" 25, 30, 84, 85, 90, 141, 203, 302, 303

Gannon, Charles (East Mayo Brigade) 170, 303

Gannon, Francis "Frank" (Kilbarry, Ruskey) 130, 303

Gannon, Jim (Cloontuskert Coy.) 95, 303

Gannon, John (Tarmonbarry Coy.) 303

Gannon, Joseph (Rodeen, Hillstreet, Drumsna) 303

Gannon, Martin (Dunmore Company) 303, 454

Gannon, Patrick Joseph (Carrow, Elphin) 89, 303

Garda Síochána (Civic Guard) 32, 38, 166, 186

Gardiner, Frank (Ruane, Kilglass) 303

Gardiner, Michael (Ruane, Kilglass) 303

Gardiner, Thomas (Ruane, Kilglass) 303

Garrahan, Capt. 166, 167, 190

Garrahan, J. (Ballaghaderreen) 303

Garrahan, Jim 303

Garrahan, Joe (Cloonbony, Fourmilehouse) 303

Garrahan, Michael (Cloonbony, Fourmilehouse) 303

Garrahan, Patrick (Strokestown area) 88, 303

Garrahan, Peter (Gortlustia, Scramogue) 303

Garrick, Eugene (Aghagad, Fuerty) 303

Garrick, John (Aghagad, Fuerty) 303

Garrynagowna 34, 46, 74, 75, 76

Garvin, Luke (Cloontogher, Kilteevan) 304

Garvin, William (Cloontogher, Kilteevan) 304

Gately, John (Feevagh, Dysart) 120, 207, 304

Gately, John (Bredagh, Dysart) 120, 304

Gately, Thomas (Feevagh, Dysart) photo of 304

Gately (Gatley), Peter (Monksland) 304

Gaughan, Dr. (Erris Coy., Co. Mayo) 463

Gaughan, Mick (Erris Coy., Co. Mayo) 463

Gauquin, Daniel (Fairfield, Ahascragh, Ballinasloe) 457

Gauquin, David (Fairfield, Ahascragh, Ballinasloe) 457

Gavican, Bernard (Erra, Clondra, Co. Longford) 88, 90, 113, 304

Gavigan, Annie Joe (Ballylugnagon, Boyle) 304

Gavigan, May (Ballylugnagon, Boyle) 304

Gavigan, Thomas (Ballylugnagon, Boyle) 304

Gavin, G. (member of Michael Kilroy's Flying Column in West Mayo) 464

Gavin, George (Abbeytown, Roscommon) 304

Gavin, James (Carrick-on-Shannon) 304

Gavin, James (Castlebar) (Joe Baker's West Mayo ASU) 464

Gavin, James (Ballymore, Moate) 472

Gavin, John (Kiltoom Coy.) 305

Gavin, Kate (Clonown, Athlone) 305

Gavin, Tim (Racecourse, Ballymurray) 305

Gaynor, Bertie (Tullywood, Co. Westmeath) 131, 158, 471

Gaynor, James (Macken, Mount Temple) 472

Gaynor, Matt (Roscommon Coy.) 305

Gaynor, Patrick J. (Kilglass, Strokestown) 305

Gearty, Michael (Tarmonbarry Coy.) 90, 305

Gearty, Rev. Roderick (Strokestown) 305

Gearty, William J. (Tarmonbarry Coy.) 305

Geary, Michael (prisoner at Ballykinlar Camp) 400

Geevagh 146, 190

General Election of 1918 22, 25

General Headquarters (GHQ) Dublin 32, 35, 36, 38, 39, 42, 43, 48, 53, 54, 59, 61, 63, 67, 71, 79, 88, 94, 108, 109, 117, 119, 123, 124, 132

Genoy, Michael (Kilbride Coy.) 305

Genoy, Patrick (Ballinaheglish Coy.) 305

Geoghan Barracks 151

Geoghan, Mrs. 305

Geoghegan Barracks 190

Geoghegan, Denis (Carniska Coy.) 305

Geoghegan, John Joe (Thomas Street) 305

Geoghegan, Michael 198, 305

Geoghegan, Patrick (Ballaghaderreen) 305

Geoghegan, Theobald (Thomas Street) 305

George, David Lloyd 5, 68, 121, 122, 131, 135, 178, 180

Geraghty, David (Polredmond Coy., Galway) 305, 454

Geraghty, George (Roscommon town) 10, 68, photo of 306, 307

Geraghty, Jack (Roscommon town) 306

Geraghty, James (Knockcroghery) 64, 306

Geraghty, Larry (North Longford Flying Column) 462

Geraghty, Martin (Kiltimagh, Co. Mayo) 466

Geraghty, Michael (Glenamaddy) 457

Geraghty, Michael (Corramagrine, Whitehall) 307

Geraghty, Michael (Kilcash, Rahara) 306

Geraghty, Tom (Clonberne Coy.) 307, 454

Geraghty, Tom (Kilcash, Rahara) 89, 307

Geraghty, William (Ballymore, Moate) 472

Geveran, Patrick (Monksland) 307

Gibbons, Anne (Clooncagh, Strokestown) 307

Gibbons, Edward (member of Joe Baker's Flying Column in Mayo) 464

Gibbons, Elizabeth "Lizette" (Clooncagh, Strokestown) photo of 307

Gibbons, Helen (Ballincurry, Kilgefin) 307

Gibbons, John (Roscommon town) 307

Gibbons, John (member of Michael Kilroy's Flying Column) 464

Gibbons, John (Aghamuck, Ballagh) 52, 58, 66, 77, 86, 88, 90, 207, 219, 239, 307

Gibbons, Joseph "Josie" (Aghamuck, Ballagh) 66, 308

Gibbons, Michael (Clooncagh, Strokestown) 52, 66, 88, 90, photo of 308

Gibbons, Pat (Clooncagh, Strokestown) 66, 308, 362

Gibbons, Patrick (member of Tom Maguire's Flying Column in south Mayo) 464

Gibbons, Tom (Ballaghaderreen) 308

Giblin, Daniel (Ballymoylin, Kilglass) 308

Giblin, Edward "Ned" (Kilglass Coy.) 308

Giblin, Hugh (Drumman Beg, Ruskey) 130, 150, 308

Giblin, Patrick (Drumman Beg, Ruskey) 130, 150, 308

Gilboy, Thomas (Arigna Flying Column) 141

Gilbride, Eugene (Grange Coy., Sligo) 468

Gilchrist, Michael (Ballycummin, Kilmore) 308

Gilchrist, Pat (Ballycummin, Kilmore) 308

Gilchrist, William (Ballycummin, Kilmore) 308

Gildea, Charles (Sligo) 78, 467, 469

Gildea brothers (Bonnyconlan Coy., Co. Mayo) 463

Gilgunn, Brian (Manorhamilton) 460

Gilhooley, Michael (Arigna) 308

Gilhooly, Patrick (Arigna) 309

Gill, Ann (sister of Pat) 47

Gill, John (Corlara, Kilmore) 309

Gill, Lieutenant 164

Gill, Michael (Strokestown) 66, 87, 88, 90, photo of 309

Gill, Pat (Kilmore) 47, 179, 309

Gill, Tom (Castleplunkett Coy.) 309

Gillane, Joseph (Athleague) 309

Gilleran, Bernard (Kinitty, Kilbride) 309

Gilleran, James (Clooncraff, Kilteevan) 309

Gilleran, John Joe (Clooncraff, Kilteevan) 309

Kilcommons, Patrick (Tisrara Coy.) 345

Kilcloghan, Elphin 27

Kilcorkey Cemetery 107

Kilcourse, John (Ballaghaderreen) 345

Kilcourse, Tom (Ballaghaderreen) 345

Kilcourse, William "Billy" (Ballaghaderreen) 345

Kilcullen, Seamus (Bonnyconlan Coy., Co. Mayo) 463

Kilcullen, Tony (Bonnyconlan Coy., Co. Mayo) 463

Kildare County 81, 117, 131, 160

Kildea, John (Lawrence) (Clonoghil, Taughmaconnell) 165, 345

Kilduff, Edward (Roscommon town) 346

Kilduff, John (Glasson, Athlone) 473

Kilfaughna, Knockvicar, Boyle 141, 173

Kilfaughney, Athlone 131, 158

Kilfree 98, 155, 156, 180, 181, 191, 192, 193

Kilgallon, P. (Boyle) 346

Kilgallon, Ted (Bonnyconlan Coy., Co. Mayo) 463

Kilgannon, Patrick (Mountbellew, Co. Galway) 457

Kilgarrif, Thomas (Dunmore, Co. Galway) 346, 453

Kilgarvan 156, 164, 193, 196

Kilgefin 85, 87, church 95, 129, 181

Kilgefin Company 50, 51, 53, 66, 94

Kilglass Company members opening end sheets, 31, 85

Kilglass 16, 31, 35, 61, 66, Company 85, 90, 99, 178, 192, 193

Kilkelly, Co. Mayo 189, 194

Kilkelly, Patrick (Pro-Treaty soldier KIA) 152

Kilkelly, Patrick (Kinvara, Galway) 455, 456

Kilkenny West, Co. Westmeath 131, 158, 194

Kilkenny, Eugene (South Leitrim Brigade Staff) 458, 460

Kilkenny, Tom (Castleplunkett Coy.) 346

Kilkerrin, Glenamaddy 119

Killalea, Martin (Doon, Boyle) 29, 103, 130, 144, 202, 204, 346

Killasser, Co. Mayo 38, 141, 187

Killeen, Co. Galway 190

Killian, Edward "Ned" (Mihanboy, Drum) 346

Killian, James (Clooncraff, Kilteevan) photo of 346

Killian, James (Mihanboy, Drum) 346

Killian, John (Mihanboy, Drum) 209, 346

Killian, John (Kellybrook, Knockcroghery) 346

Killian, Luke (Cruit, Knockcroghery) 186, 346

Killian, Pat (Glasson, Athlone) 131, 158, 471, 473

Killian, Thomas (Cloonsellan, Kilteevan) 346

Killilea, Martin "Mattie" (Ballygar Coy.) 346

Killina Company 78

Killian Family of Incheneagh Island 112

Killoe, Longford 170

Killogeenaghan crossroads 169

Killorgan, Granard, Co. Longford 170

Kilmaine, Co. Mayo 153

Kilmainham Gaol 10, 18, 81, 82, 96, 129, 155

Kilmartin, John (Roscommon Coy.) 290, photo of 312, 346

Kilmartin, Kiernan (Monksland, Athlone) 473

Kilmartin, Maudie (Summerhill) 346

Kilmartin, William (Roscommon town) 28, 72, 347

Kilmaryal (Mantua) Church 100, 182, 184

Kilmore 21, 30, 35, 105, 130, barracks 168, 169, 178, 179, 182, 192, 193, 197, barracks 198

Kilmovee, Co. Mayo 162

Kilmulkin, Co. Offaly 153

Kilmurray Military Camp 36-37, 179

Kilowmy, John (Roscommon Coy.) 347

Kilroe, John (Cooly, Fuerty) 347

Kilroe, Michael (Cooly, Fuerty) 66, photo of 347

Kilronan ambush 83-84, 164, 171, 183

Kilrooskey 52, 87, 94, 101, 110, 162, 169, 184, 185, 194, 198

Kilroy, Edward (KIA Charlestown, Co. Mayo) 193

Kilroy, James (Ballygar Coy.) 347

Kilroy, John (Ballygar Coy.) 347, 455

Kilroy, Malachy (Toberdan, St. John's) 60, 65, 130, 347

Kilroy, Michael (Flying Column leader in west Mayo) 123, 125, 132, 138, 144, 147, 192, 463, 464, 465, 466

Kilroy, Seamus (Erris Coy., Co. Mayo) 463

Kilroy, Tom (Drum) 347

Kilroy, Tom (South Leitrim) 130

Kilroy, Tom (Erris Coy., Co. Mayo) 463

Kilteevan 22, 23, Company 52, Company 61, 73, 81, Company 85, cemetery 95, 125, 130, 146, 181, 184, 190, 192

Kiltimagh, Co. Mayo 136, 141, 144, 162, 169, 188, 194

Kiltoom 28, barracks 39, 43, barracks and Company 44, 72, 101, 118, 130, 145, 148, 154, 155, train derailed 158, 162, 163, 164, 169, 172, 188, 189, 190, raid on 191, 192, 194, 195, 196, 197, 198

Kiltrustan 15, 16, 22, 24, Company 85, 88, Company 90, 183

Kiltyclogher 148, 190

King-Harman family of Rockingham 14, 19, 22, 81

King-Harman, Col. 471

King, Andrew (Shankill, Elphin) 347

King, George (Kilglass) 347

King, Inspector James (Castlerea) 67, 111, 112, 119, 186

King, J. (West Connemara Flying Column) 455

King, J. (West Connemara Flying Column) 455

King, J. C. (West Connemara Flying Column) 455

King, John (Stonepark, Roscommon) 347

King, Patrick (Hollyhill, Ballyhaunis) 466

King, Robert (Figh, Lisacul) 64, 66, 347, 464

King, W. (West Connemara Flying Column) 455

Kinley, John (Strokestown area) 88, 348

Kinnegad 189

Kirwan, — (Fearglass Coy., Co. Leitrim) 459

Knight, — (Longford Flying Column leader) 167

Knight, Jack (QM Glenamaddy Batt.) 348, 453

Knockcroghery 5, 20, 21, 22, 23, 24, 27, 33, 42, 43, 44, 59, 60, 61, 64, 65, 66, 70, 72, 89, 96, 103, photo of 104, 105, 108, 110, 118, 120, 125, 130, 145, 155, 156, 158, 162, 170, 177, 179, 180, 181, 182, 183, 185, 191, 192, 193, 194

Knockcroghery Company 15, 42, 65, 66, 89

Knockhall, Ruskey 85

Knockmealdown mountains 167

Knockranny House 141, 166, 196

Knockroe 130, 179

Knockvicar 81, 83, 85, 141, 145, bridge demolition 158, 173, 188

Knutsford Prison 82

Kyne, Martin (Caherlistrane, Co. Galway) 197

L

Lackamore Wood 110

Lackan, Strokestown 27, 189

Lafferty, Pat (Bonnyconlan Coy., Co. Mayo) 463

Laide, Richard (Co. Kerry) 24

Lainge, Christopher (Castlerea area) 157, 348

Lake Forbes 195

Lakeview 38, 156, 192

Lally, Bartholomew (Fuerty) 348

Lally, Bernard (Rahara Coy.) 348

Lally, John (Glinsk Coy., Co. Galway) 348

Lally, Michael (Rahara Coy.) 348

Lally, Stephen (Connaught Ranger) 38

Lally, Thomas (Rahara Coy.) 348

Lall, Tom (South Mayo Flying Column) 188, 464

Lambert, Col. 91, 104, 108, 185

Lambert, P. (Michael Kilroy's "Men of the West" Flying Column) 464

Land Commission 31

Land League 12, wars 16, 31

Lane, Bridget (Four Roads) 348

Lane, Thomas Joe (Four Roads) 348

Lanesboro, Longford 23, 41, 42, 70, 85, 87, 95, 108, bank robbery 128, 148, 179, 181, 184, 186, 188, barracks 189 and 193

Langan, Sean (Bonnyconlan Coy., Co. Mayo) 463

Langan, Thomas (National Army soldier KIA) 190

Lannon, James (Bumlin, Scramogue) 202, 348

Lannon, John (Strokestown) 348

Lannon, Michael (Strokestown) 66, 348

Lynch, Dominick (Loughglynn) 355
Lynch, Fianan (Dublin) 435
Lynch, George (Drumlion area) 355
Lynch, Jack (Connaught Ranger) 38, 39
Lynch, Jack (Beal a Ghleanna, Cork) 24
Lynch, James (Baylough, Athlone) 208, 355
Lynch, Mrs. James (Baylough, Athlone) 355
Lynch, John (Cootehall) 24, 203, 355
Lynch, Joseph (Drum, Athlone) 356
Lynch, Larry (Bealnamullia) 356
Lynch, Liam (O/C Republican forces in Civil War) 15, 81, 123, 128, 131, 133, 155, 167, 197
Lynch, Michael (Carrowkeel, Elphin) 89, 113, 356
Lynch, Paddy "Kid" (Boyle) 130, 356
Lynch, Patrick (North Longford Flying Column) 462
Lynch, Peter (Strokestown) 88, 89, 90, 130, 356
Lynch, Thomas (Dysart Coy.) 120, 356
Lynch, Tim (Bealnamullia Coy.) 356
Lynchehan, Sean Mór (Achill Sound) 464
Lynn, John (Donamon footballer) 274
Lynn, W. H. (Ballyfarnon) 119
Lynnott, John (Connaught Ranger) 38
Lyons, Bernard (Ballyhaunis) 466
Lyons, James (Pro-Treaty soldier KIA) 153
Lyons, James (Keadue) 203, 357
Lyons, John (Ballyhaunis) 466
Lyons, John (musician) 84
Lyons, John (Ballygar Coy.) 357
Lyons, Patrick (Ballinlough Coy.) 65, 357
Lyons, Patrick (Culliagh, Scramogue) 357
Lyons, Thomas (Culliagh, Scramogue) photo of 357
Lyons, Thomas (Ballinlough) 65, 357
Lyonstown 91, 183
Lysterfield 22

M

MacNeill, Brian (IRA organiser) (Adjutant 3rd Western Division) 119, 132, 148, 190, 371
MacNeill, Eoin (Dublin) 4, 6, 8, 17, 119
MacSweeney, Patrick (prisoner at Tintown) 161
MacSwiney, Mary (sister of Terence) 123
MacSwiney, Terence (Cork) 10, photo of 180, 465, photo of 469
McAllister, John (Dromahair) 461
McAllister, Private 144
McAndrew, Padraig (Erris Coy., Co. Mayo) 463
McAndrew, Tom (Mayo County Council) 463
McArdle, Sergeant Peter J. (stationed at Strokestown) 69, 110, 181
McBreen, J. (Arigna Flying Column) 141, 169, 198
McBrien, Harold (Capt. Ballintogher Coy., Co. Sligo) 138, 141, 142, 144, 146, 188, 357, 467, 469

McBrien, Michael (Carrigallen, Co. Leitrim) (Arigna Flying Column) 141, 357
McCabe, Alec (Keash, Co. Sligo) 7, 8, 16, 18, 19, 29, 78, 137, 145, 162, 182, 188, 319, 326, 329, 335, 346, 353, photo of 357, 467, 469
McCabe, Michael (Carrigallen, Co. Leitrim) 461
McCaffrey, Hugh (Pro-Treaty soldier KIA) 153
McCann, James (Kilkenny West, Co. Westmeath) 473
McCann, John (Ballaghaderreen) 358
McCann, John (The Pigeons, Athlone) 473
McCann, Tim (Portlick, Co. Westmeath) 131, 158, 471
McCarthy, Constable (KIA at Ratra) 45
McCarthy, James (Castlebar) 466
McCarthy, John (Castlebar) 466
McCarthy, John (Carniska Coy.) 358
McCarthy, Martin (RIC constable) 110
McCarthy, Michael (Castlebar) 358
McCarthy, Patrick (Loughglynn Coy.) 130, 158, 358
McCarthy, Patrick (Boher, Athlone) 473
McCarthy, William (Castlebar) 466
McCausland, Marcus 31
McCawley, — (Ballina Coy., Co. Mayo) 149, 463
McComgary, Briged (Tintown prisoner) 159
McConville, Bernie Joe (Mullagh, Ruskey) 358
McConville, James (Mullagh, Ruskey) 358
McConville, Michael (Mullagh, Ruskey) 358
McCormack, Agnes (Drumraney) 358, 366
McCormack, Anthony (Tonlagee, Tang, Co. Westmeath) 22, 29, 64, 65, 131, 158, 192, 208, 358, 471, 473
McCormack, Bernard (Drumraney) photo of 359, 469
McCormack, Claire (Drumraney) 359
McCormack, Dan (North Galway Flying Column) 196, 453, 456
McCormack, Edward (Creeve Coy.) 359
McCormack, James (Tonlagee, Tang, Co. Westmeath) 473
McCormack, James (Castlepollard, Co. Westmeath) 473
McCormack, Joe (Cortober, Carrick-on-Shannon) 203, 359
McCormack, John (North Galway Flying Column) 453
McCormack, John (Drumraney) 18, 208, 209, 359, 470, 473
McCormack, John (Castlebar) 466
McCormack, John (Kiltrustan, Strokestown) 359
McCormack, Martin (Castlepollard, Co. Westmeath) 473
McCormack, Michael (Stonetown, Castlepollard) 473
McCormack, Michael (Ardbough, Moate) 473

McCormack, Michael (Drumraney, Athlone, Co. Westmeath) 11, 65, 208, photo of 359, 366, 469
McCormack, Patrick (Drumraney, Athlone, Co. Westmeath) 473
McCormack, Patrick (Castlebar) 466
McCormack, Patrick (Corgarrow, Strokestown) 203, 360
McCormack, Patrick (Ballyglass Upper, Ballinaheglish Coy.) 130, 360
McCormack, Patrick (Drumkeeran, Co. Leitrim) 360
McCormack, Sean (Glasson, Athlone, Pro-Treaty soldier KIA) 145, 152
McCormack, Thomas (RIC constable) 111
McCormack, Thomas (Ballaghaderreen) 11, 360
McCormack, Thomas (Clooncunny, Killina, Elphin) 360
McCormack, Thomas (Drumraney, Athlone, Co. Westmeath) photo of 360
McCormack, Thomas (Lisnalegan, Ballinaheglish) 360
McCormack, Thomas (Mountdruid, Ballinagare) 64, 65, 66, 67, 89, 157, 158, 360
McCormack, William (Lisnalegan, Ballinaheglish) 360
McCormick, James (American interviewer) 115, 123, 132, 135, 145, 269
McCourt, Thomas (Stanmullen, Co. Westmeath) 473
McCoy, Dominick (Tullaghanmore, Ballaghaderreen) 360
McCoy, Michael (Cloonfree Coy.) 40, 203, 360
McCoy, Michael (O/C Mullingar Batt.) 469, 470
McCrann, Alfred (Loughglynn Coy.) 10, 360
McCrann, Patrick (organising committee Shankill Monument) 200
McCrann, Peter (Drumsna) 130, 361
McCrann, Stephen (Athlone) 361
McDermott Brothers (Summerhill, Drum) 362
McDermott Michael (Corker, Tulsk) 362
McDermott, David (Mantua) 89, 113, 157, 361
McDermott, Hugh (Cloonfower, Tarmonbarry) 90, 361
McDermott, James (Cloverhill Coy.) 130, 361
the following two James McDermotts may be the same man
McDermott, James (Ballybeg, Strokestown) 66, 361
McDermott, James (Kilgefin Coy.) 52, 66, 90, 361
McDermott, James (Tang, Co. Westmeath) 473
McDermott, James (Kilcaner, Drumraney) 473
McDermott, John (2nd Western Division) 361
McDermott, John (Aghamuck, Kilgefin) 361

McGrath, Joe (Dublin) 13
McGrath, John (Ballyoughter, Elphin) 367
McGrath, Martin (Ballina Coy., Co. Mayo) 463
McGrath, Pat (Ballinagare) 368
McGreevey (McGreevy), John (Carrick-on-Shannon) 368
McGreevey, Owen (Ballaghaderreen) 368
McGreevey, Patrick (Kilbride) 368
McGreevy, Tommy (Ballinaheglish) 142, 143
McGriskin, Quintus (Kiltyclogher, Leitrim) 461
McGuinn, James (KIA Co. Sligo) 194
McGuinn, Martin (KIA Co. Sligo) 196
McGuinne, Patrick (Charlestown) 466
McGuinness, Frank (Cloonmore, Tarmonbarry) 130, 204, 368
McGuinness, Frank (Kilbeggan) 473
McGuinness, Joe (Cloonmore, Tarmonbarry) 15, 17, 25, 178, 181, 359, 368
McGuinness, Liza (Cloonmore, Tarmonbarry) 368
McGuinness, P. J. (Justice for District Court) 55
McGuinness, Peter (Tarmonbarry Coy.) 368
McGuire (Maguire), Francis (St. John's Coy.) 65, 368
McGuire, James (Mullingar) 470
McGuire, John (Kilglass Coy.) 368
McGuire, Michael (Glenamaddy) 369, 453
McGuire, Michael (John) (Ballymote, Sligo) 29, 368
McGuire, Walter (Kilglass Coy.) 290, 369
McGuire, William (Ballyfeeny, Strokestown) 369
McGurk, RIC Constable 332
McHale, — (Ballina Coy., Co. Mayo) 463
McHenry, William (Croghan area) 369
McHugh, Michael (Crunkill, Ruskey) 369
McHugh, Patrick (Capt. Kiltevna Coy., Co. Galway) 453, 454
McHugh, Patrick (Kingsland, Boyle) 369
McHugh, Peter (Vice O/C Tuam Batt.) 454
McIntyre, John (Charlestown) 466
McIntyre, Michael (Sinnagh, Charlestown) 461, 467
McIntyre, Patrick (Sinnagh, Charlestown) 467
McIntyre, Peter (Aughavas Coy., Co. Leitrim) 459
McKay, Captain 57
McKelvey, Joe 156, 193
McKenna, Tom (Keadue) 85, 141, 165, 369
McKeon (McKeown), Christopher "Kit" 144, 191, 370, 469, 471
McKeon, Harry (Kiltubrid South, Co. Leitrim) 458, 459
McKeon, James (Ballinamore) 461
McKeon, John (Knockroe, Croghan) 89, 130, 369
McKeon, Joseph (Rahara Coy.) 130, 369
McKeon, M. (East Mayo ASU) 157, 369, 464

McKeon, Patrick (Knockroe, Croghan) 130, 200, 203, 204, 369
McKeon, T. (Boyle) 370
McKeon, Thomas (Vice O/C 5th Batt. North) 203, 459, 461
McKetrick, Paddy (Castlebar) 467
McKiernan, Michael (Tooman, Cloone) 461
McLoughlin, Frank (Kilmore) 370
McLoughlin, J. (Arigna Flying Column) 141, 171, 198
McLoughlin, J. (Pro-Treaty soldier KIA) 152
McLoughlin, Jimmy (Boyle) 370
McLoughlin, John (Ballinamore) 461
McLoughlin, John (Largydonnell, Leitrim) 461
McLoughlin, Joseph (Ballyfarnon) 141, 149, 370
McLoughlin, Martin (Ballinameen) 370
McLoughlin, Michael (Lackan, Strokestown) 370
McLoughlin, Michael "Mick" (Corralara, Kilmore) 24, 25, 30, 47, 70, 130, 145, 191, 203, 370
McLoughlin, Owen (Rockingham, Boyle) 130, 149, 370
McLoughlin, Patrick (Capt. Arigna Coy.) 84, 90, 203, photo of 370
McLoughlin, Patrick (McToughlin) (Ross, Manorhamilton) 461
McLynn, — (Moate, Co. Westmeath) 471
McLynn, John (Ballycloughduff, Moate) 473
McManmy, John (Gurteen Batt., Co. Sligo) 44
McManus, Ed (Drum Coy.) 370
McManus, James (Ballinamore) 461
McManus, John (Crossna Coy.) 370
McManus, John (Ballyfeeny, Strokestown) 370
McManus, Margaret Cull 172
McManus, Michael (QM Ballyfarnon Coy.) 370
McManus, Michael (Pro-Treaty soldier KIA) 153, 194
McManus, Patrick (Ballyfarnon) 371
McManus, Tom (Drum Coy.) 371
McMenamin, — (Shramore, Newport) (Joe Baker's West Mayo ASU) 464
McMenamin, Alfred (Joe Baker's West Mayo ASU) 464
McMenamin, Tom (Joe Baker's West Mayo ASU) 464
McMorrow, Ber. (Largydonnell, Co. Leitrim) 461
McMorrow, Michael (Briscloonagh, Co. Leitrim) 461
McNabola, Bridget (Capt. Cumann na mBan Kiltubrid South, Leitrim) 460
McNally, Margaret (Cumann na mBan in Elphin) 371
McNally, Patrick (Elphin) 371
McNally, Thomas (Tulsk) 371
McNamara, John P. (Knockvicar, Boyle) 371
McNamara, Joseph (Rockfield, Donamon) 371

McNamara, Matthew (Pro-Treaty soldier KIA) 153
McNamara, Michael J. (Culliagh, Scramogue) 130, 371
McNamara, P. (Michael Kilroy's "Men of the West" Flying Column) 464
McNamara, Packie (Tarmonbarry Coy.) 371
McNamara, Pat (Culliagh, Scramogue) 118, 371
McNea, John (Joe Baker's West Mayo ASU) 464
McNeely, Andy (Bonnyconlan Coy., Co. Mayo) 463
McNeely, Martin (Lahardane Coy., Co. Mayo) 463
McNeely, P. (Lahardane Coy., Co. Mayo) 463
McNeill, James (Milltown, Curraghboy) photo of 371
McNeill, William (Athleague) 372
McNicholson, Henry (Carranhane, Kiltimagh) 467
McNicholson, Thomas (Treenaghleragh, Kiltimagh) 467
McNulty, James (Gortaganny, Loughglynn) 64, 65, 372
McNulty, Patrick (Lawley, Leitrim) 461
McPartland, Andy (Leitrim ASU) 460
McPhillips, John Patrick (Ballaghaderreen) x, photo of 372
McPhillips, Michael James (Ballaghaderreen) 372
McSweeney, Dan Thady (Beal a Ghleanna, Cork) 24
McTeague, Packy (O/C Cromlin Coy., Co Leitrim) 459
McTiernan, Patrick (Monagh, Sligo) 461
McWilliams, James (Elphin) 372
McWilliams, Robert (Elphin) 373
MacBride, John (native of Mayo involved in the Easter Rising) 201
MacDowell, Vincent (author) 121, 133, 143
MacEnri, P. (East Mayo Flying Column) 464
MacEoin, Sean (Longford) 48, 121, 125, 127, 135, 137, 144, 146, 147, 153, 158, 167, 187, 190, 365, 366, 389, 461, 462, 470
MacEoin, Uinseann (author) 172
MacHenry, William (Ballinameen area) 61
Macken, Constable 41, 42, 47, 101
Macken, James (Ballinalee, Co. Longford) 170
Macken, Joseph (Drum Coy.) 373
Macken, Malachy (Drum Coy.) 373
Macken, Michael (Drum Coy.) 373
Macken, Pat (Castlepollard, Co. Westmeath) 47, 131, 144, 150, 158, 189, 208, 209, 373, 471, 473, 474
Macken, Tom (Drum Coy.) 373
Madden, B. (Lisacul) 209, 373
Madden, Daniel (Cloonylyons, Strokestown) 373
Madden, Dr. (Bonnyconlan Coy., Co. Mayo) 463

Martin, Tom (Fostra, Crossna, Boyle) 141, 203, 382
Martin, William (Barry Beg, The Hill of Berries, Kiltoom) 382
Martin, William (Bushfield, Ballinaheglish) 66, 382
Martin, William (Cloonfad, Castlerea) 382
Mary St. Headquarters 117
Mason, Bertie (Strokestown Coy.) 382
Mason, Tommie (Strokestown Coy.) 34, 202, 215, photo of 382
Massbrook House 189
Masterson, B. (Captain in the National Army) 382
Mattimoe, Rev. Fr. Patrick J. (Kilmore) 382
Maxwell, James (Carrick-on-Shannon area) 382
Maxwell, Michael (Peak, Kilcorkey, Castlerea) 382
May, Patrick (Kilkerran, Castlepollard) 473
Maycock, Pat (Bonnyconlan Coy., Co. Mayo) 463
Maye, Paddy (Tom Maguire's Flying Column) 464
Maye, Pat (Carrowmore, Croghan) 382
Maynooth 100, 152
Mayo 77, 78, 80, 83, 119, 123, 124, 125, 132, 135, 136, 138, 141, 144, 145, 146, 147, 149, 152, 153, 155, 156, 157, 158, 160, 161, 162, 164, 169, 170, 183, 185, 187, 188, 189, 190, 191, 192, 193, 194, 197, 457, 463, 464, 465, 466, 468
  North Mayo Brigade 187
  South Mayo Brigade 464, 466
  South Mayo Flying Column 464, 466
  1st Battalion Flying Column 463
  First All-County Brigade 463
  East Mayo Brigade 78, 96, 119, 183
  East Mayo Column 136, 144, 145, 188, 190, 464
  West Mayo Flying Column 138, 147, 464
  Mayo Internees during the Civil War 466
Meadlarklan, Corporal George (stationed at Boyle) 19, 37, 102, 103, 113, 383
Meath County 46
Meagher, Thomas Francis 8
Mee, Dick (Curraghboy Coy.) 65, 73, 89, 118, 133, 171, 207, 263, 383
Mee, Jeremiah (Carrick-on-Shannon) 383
Mee, Michael (Curry, Curraghboy) 383
Mee, Thomas (Derryhippo, Creggs) 384
Meehan, Darby (Boherroe, Elphin) 203, 384
Meehan, James (Ballinamore) 461
Meehan, Michael (Kilyclogher, Co. Leitrim) 384, 461
Meehan, Patrick (Boherroe, Elphin) 384
Melia, John (Cloonfad, Ballinlough) 384
Melinn, Joseph (Mardyke, Athlone) 384
Melinn, Peadar (Peter) (QM Athlone Brigade) 11, 18, 209, photo of 384, 469
Melinn, Seamus (Mardyke, Athlone) photo of 384

Mellin, John (Rahara Coy.) 384
Mellows, Liam 8, 9, 23, 131, photo of 156, 160, 193, 456
Melvin, Eugene (Lisonuffy, Strokestown) 66, photo of 384
Middleton, Earl of 86
Miley, John (Knockcroghery) 384
Miley, Thomas (Athleague) 385
Millbank Prison 4
Milltown 184, 185
Minogue, Charlie (Strokestown Coy.) 385
Miranda, John (Connaught Ranger) 37
Mitchell, B. (Castlerea Coy.) 385
Mitchell, Commandant (National Army) 142, 151, 196
Mitchell, Herbert (Coosan) 385, 470
Mitchell, Sean (O/C Leitrim ASU) 458, 460
Moane, Edward (Michael Kilroy's "Men of the West" Flying Column) 463, 464
Moate, Co. Westmeath 18, 27, Battalion 42, 46, 105, 145, 156, 165, 169, 170, 181, 189, 191, 193, 194, 195, 196, 198
Mockler, Martin (Castleplunkett Coy.) 130, 385
Mockmoyne, Boyle 15, 178
Moclair, Patrick (Ahascragh, Galway) 458
Moffatt, Ed (Drumboylan, Leitrim) 385
Moffatt, Matt (Crunkill, Ruskey) 385
Moffatt (Moffitt), Michael (Ballaghaderreen area) 385
Moffatt, Patrick (Cloonsheever, Castlerea) 66, 385
Mohill 81, 150, 151, 154, 190, 191, 192, 194, 196, 197
Mohill Barracks 151, 154, 162, 190, 191, 192, 194, 197
Molloy, James (Capt. Ballymote Coy., Co. Sligo) 37, 38, 44, 88, 101, 113, 184, 198, 383, photo of 385
Molloy, Joseph (Cryanstown, Knockvicar) 83, 85, 91, 183, 385
Moloney brothers (Bonnyconlan Coy., Co. Mayo) 463
Moloney, James (Tuam) 385, 453
Moloney, John (Craughwell, Galway) 458
Molyneux, Sir Capel 128
Molyneux, Timothy (Ballycloughduff, Moate) 473
Monaghan County football team 123
Monaghan, Frank (Roscommon Coy.) 385
Monaghan, John (Curraghboy Coy.) 57, 66, 130, 385
Monaghan, Larry (Castlebar) 467
Monaghan, Michael (Clooneen, Headford) 197
Monaghan, Michael (Glenamaddy) 386, 453, 454, 457
Monaghan, Peter (Ballagh, Kilgefin) 66, 386
Monaghan, Tim (Gallowstown, Roscommon) 52, 207, 386
Monasteraden 98
Monastevan 160

Monds, James (Knockmurry, Castlerea) 91, 183, 386
Moneen 41, 101, 179
Moohan, George (Ballaghaderreen) 386
Mooloney, John (Craughwell, Galway) 458
Moor Company 33, 65, 68, 83, 110, 140
Moore, John (North Longford Flying Column) 462
Moore, M. (Carrick-on-Shannon) 203, 386
Moore, Peter (Glenamaddy) 386, 454
Moore, Thomas (Pro-Treaty soldier KIA) 153
Moore, Col. M. 179
Moran, — (Tang) 471
Moran, Annie (Crossna) photo of 388
Moran, Bartley (Crossna) 80
Moran, Batty (Crossna) photo of 387
Moran, Bridget (Crossna) 80
Moran, Constables 119
Moran, J. (Michael Kilroy's "Men of the West" Flying Column) 464
Moran, "Jack" (John) (Capt. Ballinlough Coy.) 68, 206, photo of 386
Moran, James (Joe Baker's West Mayo ASU) 464
Moran, James (Drumraney) 473
Moran, James (Lavallyroe, Cloonfad, Ballyhaunis, Co. Mayo) 112, 158, 386
Moran, James (3rd Batt., No. 2 Brigade, 2nd Western Division) 387
Moran, James (St. Patrick's Terrace, Roscommon) 387
Moran, Jim (Crossna) 141, 165, 194, 357, photo of 387, photo of 388
Moran, John (Culleenaghamore, Kilglass) 387
Moran, John (Kinnitty, Kilbride) 387
Moran, John (Lisnagroagh, Fuerty, Roscommon) 387
Moran, John (Sheervagh, Ballinameen, Boyle) 387
Moran, John (Ballina Coy., Co. Mayo) 463
Moran, Joseph (Crossna) photo of 387
Moran, Liam (Dunmore, Galway) 387
Moran, Luke (Drumboylan, Boyle) 203, 387
Moran, Malachy (Coolatober, Ballyforan) 387
Moran (Morahan), Mathew "Mattie" (Falmore, Ballinagare) 64, 65, 66, 89, 157, 387
Moran, Michael (Vice O/C North Galway Brigade) 453
Moran, Michael (Carrowduff, Ballymacurley) 388
Moran, Michael (Drumahard, Drumboylan, Boyle) 388
Moran, Michael (Moher, Strokestown) 388
Moran, P. (Pro-Treaty soldier KIA) 152
Moran, Paddy (Crossna) 80- 83, photo of 81, 89, 96, 141, 182, photo of 388
Moran, Patrick (Charlestown) 467
Moran, Patrick (Ardeevin, Castleplunkett) 114, 388
Moran, Patrick (Clooncunny, Elphin) (Killina Coy.) 63, 88, 90, 113, 130, 388

Murphy, James (Scramogue) 88, 90, 202, 395
Murphy, Jeremiah (author) xx, 30, 133, 172
Murphy, John "Jack" (Scramogue) 88, 90, 202, photo of 395
Murphy, Joseph (Castlepollard) 473
Murphy, Liam (Tintown prisoner) 117
Murphy, Malachy (Kilgefin) 395
Murphy, Matt (Robinstown, Castlepollard) 473
Murphy, Michael (Castlepollard) 473
Murphy, Michael (Ballyclare, Cloontuskert) 395
Murphy, Michael (Carnagh East, St. John's, Lecarrow) 65, 395
Murphy, Patrick (Pro-Treaty soldier KIA) 153
Murphy, Seamus (O/C South Galway Brigade) 455, 456, 470
Murphy, Sean (Granard, Longford) 462
Murphy, Thomas (St. John's Coy.) 101, photo of 396
Murphy, Thomas (Castlepollard) 473
Murphy, Tom (Erris Coy., Co. Mayo) 463
Murphy, William (St. John's Coy.) 65, 89, 396
Murphy, William (Ahascragh, Ballinasloe) 458
Murphy, William and Mariah (Carnagh East, St. John's) 395
Murray, Becky (Quarry Lane, Boyle) 396
Murray, Bridie (Quarry Lane, Boyle) 20, 119, 136, 396
Murray, Felix (Ballyhaunis) 465
Murray, Frank (Baylough, Athlone) photo of 397
Murray, Frank (Knockcroghery Coy.) 397
Murray, James (Clooncraff, Kilteevan) 397
Murray, James (Drum Coy.) 397
Murray, James (Derrinlurg, Mt. Talbot) 397
Murray, James (Rahara Coy.) 397
Murray, John (Dunmore, Co. Galway) 458
Murray, John (National soldier) 397
Murray, John (Pro-Treaty soldier KIA) 153
Murray, John (Gortnacloy, Mantua, Elphin) 61, 63, 89, 98, 113, 190, 202, 397
Murray, John (Kilteevan Coy.) 397
Murray, John (St. Columbus Terrace, Athlone) 397
Murray, Joseph (Ballymartin, Kilglass, Strokestown) 397
Murray, Joseph (Josie) (Quarry Lane, Boyle) 199, 231, 397
Murray, Kathleen (Ballyduff, Strokestown) 87
Murray, M. (Kilbride Coy.) 207
Murray, Margaret (Taylorstown, Drum, Athlone) 397
Murray, Marian (Quarry Lane, Boyle) 397
Murray, Mary (Clooncraff, Kilteevan) 397
Murray, Michael (Clooneragh, Strokestown) 397
Murray, Pat (Ballinasloe) 458
Murray, Patrick (Ballymagrine, Tarmonbarry) 88, 90, 158, 397
Murray, Patrick (Manor, Tulsk, Castlerea) 89, 398

Murray, Patrick (Muff, Fuerty) 398
Murray, Patrick (Fuerty) 398
Murray, Peter (Athlone) 11, 398, 469
Murray, Phil (Quarry Lane, Boyle) 102, 130, 199, 202, 204, 398
Murray, Richard (Quarry Lane, Boyle) 130, 157, 199, 398
Murray, Stephen (Kilteevan Coy.) 52, 398
Murray, Thomas (Justice for District Court) 55
Murray, Thomas (Castlepollard) 473
Murray, Thomas (Clooncraff, Kilteevan) 399
Murray, Thomas (Cagglebeg, Fourmilehouse) 88, 90, 207, 209, 398, 466
Murray, Tom (Drum, Athlone) 399
Murray, Una "Sis" (Elphin) 29, photo of 399
Murray, William (Curry, Curraghboy) 65, 88, 130, 133, 158, 383, 399
Murtagh, Hugh (Drumraney, Moate) 473
Murtagh, Matthew (Dooneen, Ballinameen) 113, 399
Murtagh, Patrick (Glasson) 145
Murtagh, Patrick (Sangana, Charlestown) 467
Murtagh, Peter (Corlis, Castlerea) 64, 66, 68, 89, 114, 158, 290, 312, 400
Murtagh, Thomas (Carrowcully, Ballinameen) 89, 113, 400
Murtagh, Tim (Carrowcully, Ballinameen) 113, 400

N

Nally, Richard (Castlerea) 400
Nangle, Bernard "Brian" (Mongagh, Curraghroe) 68, 77, 85, 87, 88, 89, 90, 130, 158, 202, 204, 216, 400
Nangle, Miss (Mohill) 460
Nangle, Pat 401
Nation 2
National Army Brigade Staff in Athlone photo of 147
National Army Reorganisation 144
Naughton, Bernard (Ballymacurley) 401
Naughton, Denis (Ardkeena, Drum) 401
Naughton, Edward (Ardmullan, Curraghboy) 401
Naughton, Edward "Ned" (Ballymacurley) 66, 401
Naughton, Ginger (Cornafulla) 401
Naughton, John (Ballygar Coy.) 196, 401
Naughton, John (Carrownderry, Kiltoom) 130, 401
Naughton, M. (Michael Kilroy's Flying Column) 464
Naughton, Michael (Ballygar Coy.) 401
Naughton, Michael (Glanduff, Kiltoom) 46, 402
Naughton, Michael (Fearagh, Knockcroghery) 130, 401
Naughton, Michael (Kilkerrin Coy.) 402, 454
Naughton, Paddy (Knockcroghery Coy.) 402
Naughton, Patrick (Ballygar Coy.) 402
Naughton, Patrick (Ballygar Coy.) 402
Naughton, Patrick (Glanduff, Kiltoom) 402

Naughton, Patrick (Tisrara Coy.) 402
Naughton, Thomas (Fearagh, Knockcroghery) 64, 130, 402
Naughton, William (Cornafulla) 402
Nea, James (Castlepollard) 473
Nealon, E. (Bonnyconlan Coy., Co. Mayo) 463
Neary, Edward (Buckill, Tibohine) 402
Neary, Edward (Knockhall, Ruskey) 402
Neary, Frank (Pro-Treaty soldier KIA) 153, 188
Neary, James (Clooncullan, Elphin) 402
Neary, Jim (Breedogue, Ballinameen) 402
Neary, John (Erris Coy., Co. Mayo) 463
Neary, Michael (Athleague Coy.) 402
Neary, Michael "Mick" (Sroove, Tulsk) 89, 157, 202, photo of 403
Neary, P. J. (Aughrim) 403
Neary, Peter (Clooncullane, Elphin) 403
Neary, Tommy 155, 192, 403
Neeson, Eoin (author) 21, 24, 124, 133, 168
Neilan, Frank (Castlepollard) 474
Neligan, David (author) 18
Nelis, Robert (Joe Baker's West Mayo ASU) 464
Nelson, Frank (Kilgefin Coy.) 403
Nelson, James (Kilgefin Coy.) 90, 101, 403
Nelson, Seamus (Ballymacurley) 86, 90
Nenagh, Tipperary 92, 93, 100, 112
Nevin, Andy 15, 202, 403
Nevin, Martin (QM Loughrea Batt.) 455
Nevin, Tom (Kilgefin Coy.) 403
Nevins, Michael (Sligo Brigade staff) 467
New York Nation (American newspaper) 107
Newcomber, William (Pro-Treaty soldier KIA) 153, 166, 195, 403
Newell, John (Sean) (Winefort, Headford) 197, 453, 456, 457
Newell, Michael (Adjutant 3rd Batt. North) 458
Newport 138, 152, 153, 154
Newtowncashel 190
Nicholl, Henry (Drumlion, Dromod) 403
Nickolson, William (Cornafulla) 403
Niland, Mattie (Adjutant of Galway Brigade in 1917) 456
Nohilly, Thomas (Adjutant of Tuam Battalion) 403, 404, 453, 454
Nolan, Ann and Ellen (Boyle) 404
Nolan, John (Tully, Ballygar) 130, 166, 196, 404
Nolan, John (Derreenadouglas, Crossna, Boyle) 203, 404
Nolan, Michael (Ballyhaunis) 467
Nolan, Roger (Ballygar Coy.) 404
Nolan, Tom (Ballygar Coy.) 404
Nolan, Tom (Ballygar Coy.) 404
Noonan, Jim (Tarmonbarry Coy.) 404
Noonan, Pat (Capt. Williamstown Coy., Co. Galway) 404, 454
Noonan, Pat (Charlestown) (prisoner in Athlone during Civil War) 467

Roddy, Luke (Clooneybrennan, Elphin) 89, 424

Roddy, Michael (Strokestown) 89, 424

Roddy, P. (Castleplunkett) 424

Roddy, Pat (Breedogue Coy.) 424

Roddy, Patrick (Ballaghaderreen) 166, 312, 424

Roddy, Thomas (Lisacul) 166, 196, 424

Rogers, Dominick (Cornamaddy, Ballymurray, Roscommon) 89, 424

Rogers, Dominick (Runnamoat, Ballinaheglish) xxi, 206, 424

Rogers, James (Cloonfad) 424

Rogers, Joe (Loughglynn) 424

Rogers, John (Ardnamullagh, Ballintubber) 65, 424

Rogers, John (Cordrummon, Kiltrustan, Strokestown) 424

Rogers, Patrick (Ballinlough) 424

Rogers, Tom (Cornamaddy, Ballymurray, Roscommon) 89, 424

Rogers, Tom (Loughglynn) 424

Ronan, Michael (Capt. Dunmore Coy., Co. Galway) 425, 454

Rooney, William 3, 4

Roper, Esther 18

Rosbeg, Westport, Co. Mayo 80

Roscommon:

Barracks 73, 77, 88, 188, 198

County Council 8

County Museum 159

Roscommon Herald 25, 55, 62, 83, 93, 112, 123, 133, 149, 172

Roscommon town 5, 28, 29, 38, 39, 43, 50, 51, 52, 53, 56, 62, 71, 72, 73, 77, 79, 85, 90, 94, 95, 96, 108, 112, 113, 117, 118, 119, 123, 132, 135, 136, 145, 147, 155, 177, 178, 179, 180, 183, photo of 184, 188, 189, 192, 193, 198, photo of 265 and 288, 312

bye election of 1917 12, 13, 14

Brigades, Battalions, and Flying Columns see **Battalions and Brigades**

Rosemount Company 43

Rossa, O'Donovan xx, 4, photo of funeral 6, 177

Rouane, Thomas (Keadue) 425

Roughneen, Knox (East Mayo ASU) 136, 425

Round, Harold "Sammy" (RIC constable) 103, 111, 185

Roundtree (Rowntree), William (Castlerea) 425

Rourke, Michael (Carrick-on-Shannon) 425

Rourke, Patrick (Ballyboughan, Roscommon) 425

Rourke, Thomas (Fourmilehouse) 425

Rourke, William (Donamon) 425

Royal Irish Constabulary (RIC) 15, 23, 24, 25, 28, 32, 33, 34, 35, 36, 37, 38, 39, 41, 42, 43, 44, 45, 46, 47, 49, 51, 55, 56, 59, 63, 64, 65, 67, 69, 70, 72, 73, 74, 76, 77, 79, 80, 81, 83, 84, 88

92, 94, 95, 96, 97, 98, 100, 101, 104, 107, 108, 109, 110, 112, 113, 119, 120, 133

Ruane, Joe (Ballina Coy., Co. Mayo) 463

Ruane, Thomas (Ballina Coy., Co. Mayo) 463

Runnamoat, Ballinaheglish 118, 119, 184, 186

Rush, J. (Michael Kilroy's "Men of the West" Flying Column) 464

Rush, Jim (Kiltimagh) 467

Rush, Thomas (Lisacul) 185

Rushe, Michael (Ballymurry, Mantua) 89, 113, 425

Ruskey 15, 16, 19, 48, Company 56, 66, 70, 76, 79, 85, 87, 94, 110, 141, 150, 155, 158, 166, 179, 180, 181, 182, 183, 185, 186, 189, 191, 193, 194, 195, 196

Ruskey Barracks 70, 79, 141, 180

Russell, Sean 123

Ruttledge, Patrick J. (Ballina Coy., Co. Mayo) 144, 463, 466

Ryan, Bernard (Annaghmacoolen, Cloone, Leitrim) 203, 426, 459

Ryan, Dan (Quartermaster South Galway Brigade) 455

Ryan, Eugene (Crossna) 426

Ryan, Father (Lanesboro) 23

Ryan, James (Castleplunkett Coy.) 426

Ryan, John (Castleplunkett Coy.) 64, 65, 114, 130, 149, 207, 228, 270, photo of 426

Ryan, John (Attimany, Loughrea) 458

Ryan, John J. (North Galway Flying Column) 453

Ryan, Joseph (Attimany, Loughrea) 458

Ryan, Martin (Vice O/C Glenamaddy Batt.) 426, 453

Ryan, Meda (author) 143

Ryan, Patrick (Athleague) 426

Ryan, Patrick (Attimany, Loughrea) 458

Ryan, Patrick J. (Ballaghaderreen) 11, 426

Ryan, Seamus (Strokestown) 15, 48, 88, 89, 202, 204, 426

Ryan, Thomas (QM Glenamaddy Battalion) 426, 453, 454

Ryan, Thomas (Attimany, Loughrea) 458

Ryan, William (Kilcroan Coy.) 427, 454

Ryans, Father Edward (Knockranny House) 141, 166, 196, 427

Ryans, Vincent (Arigna Flying Column) 141, 158, 196, 427

Ryder, Albert (Kiltoom Coy.) 427

Ryder, Davy (member of Ballina Coy., Co. Mayo) 463

Ryder, Jack (Carniska Coy.) photo of 427

Ryder, Michael (Strokestown) 427

Ryder, Michael (Joe Baker's West Mayo ASU) 464

Rynne, Hugh (Spencer Harbour, Leitrim) 461

S

Sacred Heart Parish, Roscommon town 62

Sammon, John P. (Castlebar) 467

Sammon, Joseph (Renvyle, Tully, Galway) 458

Sammon, Michael (Kilkenny West) 474

Sampey, Henry 47

Sandfield, Knockcroghery 61, 64, 65, 130, 158

Satchwell, Joe (Moor Coy.) 66, 67, 89, 93, 112, 290, photo of 295, 302, 312, photo of 427

Satchwell, Tom (Moor Coy.) 64, 66, 68, 89, 158, photo of 312, 427

Satchwell, Tom (RIC constable) 110

Saul, Patrick (Fuerty) 427

Savage, James (IO Longford Brigade) 462

Savage, Larry (Streamstown, Moate) 160, 474

Savage, Martin (Streamstown, Ballisodare) 469

Scahill, Patrick (Lisalway) 64, 65, 114, photo of 427

Scally, John (Gallagh, Cloontuskert, Ballyleague) 95, 427

Scally, John (Portnahinch, Cloontuskert, Ballyleague) 428

Scally, Michael (Capt. of Cloonfree Coy.) 203, 428

Scally, Michael (Carrowbehy, Gortaganny, Loughglynn) 64, 65, 428

Scally, Paddy (Connaught Ranger) 38, 428

Scally, Peter (Tarmonbarry Coy.) 428

Scally, Stephen (Cloonfree, Strokestown) 40, 41, 65, 428

Scally, Thomas "Toby" (Loughglynn) gun of 59, 67, 93, 112, 157, 158, 428, photo of 429, 430, 431, 464

Scally, William (Ballintubber Coy.) 66, 429

Scanlon, Andrew (Fourmilehouse) 429

Scanlon, Francis (prisoner in Boyle Barracks) 162

Scanlon, John (Boyle) 429

Scanlon, Michael (Boyle) 429

Scanlon, Pat (Ballymote, Co. Sligo) 430

Scanlon, Sean (Vice O/C Athlone Battalion) 17, 208, 430

Scanlon, Tom (Sligo) 133, 150, 157, 189, 430

Scardaun crossroads 170

Scottish Borderers 117

Scramogue 15, 22, 34, 35, 55, River 58, 83, 85, 87, 88, Company 90, 91, 96, 99, 105, 110, 129, 158, 178, 180, 183

Scramogue Ambush 34, 85, 87, 88, 90, 96, 99, 105, 110, 183

Scully, William (Annaghdown, Galway) 458

Seanad Éireann 54

Seery, Bridget (Cloonillan, Drum) 430

Seery, Michael (Walderstown, Athlone) 208, 430, 474

Seery, Tom (Cloonillan, Drum) 430

Seiry, Michael (prisoner at Tintown) 162

Selton Hill, Leitrim 116

Sexton, Sean (North Longford Flying Column) 462

Shallow, James (Fourmilehouse) 430

Shallow, Patrick (Fourmilehouse) 430

Shallow, William (Connaught Ranger) 38

Shally, James (2nd Batt. South) 328, 430

Shally, Peter (footballer) 274

Smyth, Owen (Ballygar Coy.) 438
Smyth, Terry (Mullingar) 470
Smyth, Thomas (Strokestown) 66, 88, 90, 438
Snee, John (Kilkelly, Co. Mayo) photo of 119, 157, 201, 212, 241, 438, photo of 439, 464
Soloheadbeg, Tipperary 24, 109, 178
Southgate, George (RIC constable) 111
Southpark, Castlerea 15, 33, 110, 114, 179, 186
Spalding, Peter (Tarmonbarry Coy.) 90, 439
Spellman, John (Breedogue Coy.) 189, 439
Spellman, John (Cornaglia, Boyle) 199, 439
Spellman, Mary Kate (Ballaghaderreen) 439
Spellman, Michael (Boyle) 199, 439
Spellman, Patrick (Church St., Ballaghaderreen) 197, 439
Spellman, Patrick (Knockavroe, Boyle) 29, 439
Spellman, Roger (Kilteevan) 439
Spellman, Tom (Ballaghaderreen) 439
St. Croan's Catholic Church (Ballymoe) 38, 39
St. John's area 23, 24, 104, 185
St. John's Company 60, 65, 66, 125
Stafford, Sir Thomas 18, 19
Staines, Liam (Ballinagare) 439
Staines, Michael (General Headquarters Quartermaster) 16, 59
Stankard, Joseph (O/C South Galway Brigade) 455
Stanley, John (Donamon) 64, 439
Staunton, G. (Flying Column West Connemara) 455
Staunton, James (Castlebar) 467
Staunton, John (Cloonfad) 439
Staunton, M. (Michael Kilroy's "Men of the West" Flying Column) 464
Staunton, Michael (Joe Baker's West Mayo ASU) 464
Staunton, Patrick (Ardkeel, Roscommon) 439
Stenson, Patrick (KIA Co. Sligo) 196
Stephens, James (IRB organiser) 3, 4
Stephens, John (Kilkerrin Coy., Co. Galway) 439, 454
Stephens, Luke (Athleague) 439
Stephens, Michael (Athleague) 439
Stewardstown, Co. Tyrone 156
Stewart, James (Kilglass) 439
Stewart, Joseph (Kilglass) 90, 440
Stoneham, John (Castlecoote) 440
Strabane, Co. Tyrone 51
Streamstown RIC Barracks 42, 179
Stroker, John (Kilteevan Coy.) 440
Stroker, John (Ardmagree, Kilteevan) 440
Stroker, William (Kilteevan Coy.) 440
Strokestown 7, 13, 15, 16, 22, 25, 27, 31, 34, 38, (burning of courthouse) 40, 41, 50, 51, 55, 59, 66, 68, 69, 76, 80, 83, 85, 86, 87, (attack at) 88, 89, 90, 94, 107, 108, 110, 118, 126, 137, 155, 156, (attack at) 165, 167, 168, 169, 170, 178, (burning of courthouse) 179, 180, 181, 182, 183, 186, 189,

190, 191, 192, 193, 194, 195, 197, 198
Strokestown Democrat 51, 66, 83, 89
Suck River 103
Sullivan, Charles (Pro-Treaty soldier KIA) 153
Summary of Armament 120
Summerhill, Athlone 18, 23, 27, 32, 47, 62, 73, 74, 178
Summerhill College 73
Surrender of all Republican forces 187
Swan, Lt. 195
Swanick, James (Ballinlough) 440
Swanlinbar, Co. Cavan 110
Sweeney, — (Ballycroy Coy., Co. Mayo)
Sweeney, Bernard (O/C South Leitrim Brigade) 116, 132, 150, 458, 459, 460
Sweeney, Francis (3rd Western Division Staff) 440
Sweeney, James (Derrane, Roscommon) 440
Sweeney, Joe (National Army Commandant in Donegal) 135
Sweeney, John (Pro-Treaty soldier KIA) 137, 153, 187
Sweeney, Michael (Claremorris) 457
Sweeney, Owen (Clonbruske, Athlone) 11, 440, 469
Swinford 119, 141, 149, 152, 153, 157, 162, 187, 189, 190, 194
Swinford Barracks 38, 141, 149, 157, 187, 189, 190

T
Tadhg, Twomey (Beal a Ghleanna, Cork) 24
Taghshinney, Co. Longford 170
Talbot, W. John 128, 186
Tang, Co. Westmeath 35, 65, 131, 144, 156, 158, 163, 178, 188, 189, 192, 193
Tanner, George (Strokestown) 66, 88, photo of 440
Tanner, J. 27
Tanning, Sgt. 97
Tansey, "Mickey" (Boyle area) 440
Tansey, Owen (Gurteen Battalion, Co. Sligo) 440, 468
Tarmay, Thomas (North Galway Flying Column) 453
Tarmon 33, 54, river 57, 66, 91, 110, 179, 180, 183, 185, 186
Tarmon Cross 33, 179
Tarmonbarry 15, 19, 63, 68, 70, 76, 85, patrol 88, 94, 106, 107, 113, 129, 158, 180, 181, 182, 183, 186
Tarmonbarry Barracks 68, attack at 113, 180, 181
Tarney, Thomas (Galway) 440
Tarpey, Michael (Ballygar Coy.) 440
Tarpey, Michael (Trien Coy.) 440
Taughmaconnell 18, 22, 99, Company 165, 195, 196
Taylor, Luke (Ballyhaunis) 467
Teeling, Frank (Dublin) 82

Tennant, John (Lisnahoon, Knockcroghery) 440
Tennant, Lt. 86
Tennant, Michael (Lisnahoon, Knockcroghery) 42, 64, 65, 89, 440
Tennant, Patrick (Lisnahoon, Knockcroghery) 61, 64, 65, 89, 118, 441
The Hill of Berries 131, 150, 158, 162, 166, 167, 170, 171, 194, 196, 197
The Shan Van Vocht 4
Thewlis, Stephen (Cloonsellan, Kilteevan) 441
Thomas, Joseph (Mohill) 461
Thomas, Michael (Mohill) 461
Thomastown 46, 47, 163, 165, 195
Thompson, James (Ballintubber) 441
Thornton, Brighid Lyons 441
Three Jolly Pigeons public house 166, 195
Tibohine 45, Company 63, 64, 83
Tibohine Church 45, 64
Tiernan, Jim (Ballincurry, Kilgefin) 52, 58, 66, 90, 207, photo of 442
Tiernan, Michael (Cregga, Strokestown) 90, 442
Tiernan, Michael (Main St., Castlerea) 442
Tiernan, Paddy (Sheehaun, Kilgefin) 21, 41, 50, 52, 66, 90, 278, photo of 442
Tiernan, Pat (Gortyleane, Kilrooskey) 66, photo of 442
Tiernan, Patrick (Clooneen, Kilglass) 442
Tiernan, Patrick (Quartermaster of South Leitrim Brigade) 458
Tiernan, Thomas (Pro-Treaty soldier KIA) 153
Tiernan, Thomas (Derryquirk, Tulsk) 89, 442
Tierney, David (Moate) 189
Tierney, John (Castlebar) (Joe Baker's West Mayo ASU) 464, 467
Tighe, James (Cloontuskert Coy.) 443
Tighe, John (Drumlion, Carrick-on-Shannon) 443
Tighe, Martin (Ballyhaunis) 112, 443
Tighe, Michael (Cortober, Carrick-on-Shannon) 443
Timoney, Charles (Newtownmanor, Co. Sligo) 467, 468
Timothy, John (Donamon) 443
Tinn, Michael (Tonagh, Co. Westmeath) 131, 158, 471
Tinnacarra 178
Tintown Internment Camp 159, 160, 161, 162, 169
Tintown Diary (prisoner diary) 159 through 169
Tipperary County 24, 118, 125, 178, 196
Tisrara 5, 177
Tivnan, Henry (Boyle) 443
Tobin, Thomas (Ballyfarnon) 443
Tolan, Francis (Mayo) 196
Tolan, M. M. (Bonnyconlan Coy., Co. Mayo) 463
Tonagh 131, 158
Tonry, John (Kilgefin) 66, 443

ABOUT THE AUTHOR

Kathleen Hegarty Thorne was born in Kansas City, Missouri, close to the location where her emigrant grandfather from Ballinaheglish, County Roscommon, had settled. She graduated from Avila College and obtained master's degrees from the University of Missouri at Kansas City and the University of Oregon in Eugene, Oregon, where she currently resides with her husband, Lew. Kathleen has previously authored two historical works, *The Story of Starlight Theatre*, a chronicle of the birth and development of the second largest outdoor theatre in the United States, and *The Trail Tribune*, a compendium of vignettes about people and events at both ends of the Oregon Trail.

In 1992 Kathleen travelled to County Roscommon to seek her Irish roots and research family records. She found, instead, the whisperings of neighbours regarding her family's involvement in the War for Independence, and a forgotten gravesite in the old Ballinderry Cemetery. And thus her quest began.

MICHAEL O'CONNELL

STEPHEN McDERMOTT

I · R · A
ERECTED TO THE MEMORY
DERMOT JAMES TORMEY
BRIG·GEORGE ADAMSON
VOL· JOSEPH TORMEY
E·VOL·PATRICK SLOANE
ALL OF ATHLONE BRIGADE
WHO GAVE THEIR LIVES FOR THE
THIRTY TWO COUNTY REPUBLIC
IN 1921 & 1922
TORMEY BROTHERS & ADAMSON
INTERRED IN M·T·TEMPLE CEMETERY
SLOANE IN DRUMRANEY
I PEACE I MEASS NA LFLANN
SO RAIB ACA AR NEAMH
R · I · P
ERECTED BY FORMER
COMRADES OF I · R · A·

IN LOVING MEMORY OF
JOSEPH FALLON
CAPPAGH
DIED 10TH OCT. 1977
AGED 78 YEARS
HIS WIFE ELLEN
DIED 29TH AUGUST 2002
AGED 88 YEARS

In Loving Memory of
MARTIN SHIEL
Cagglestack
died 16 Feb. 1966 aged 77 yrs.
his wife NORA
died 11 Aug. 2001 aged 92 yrs.
their son MATTHEW
died 13 Nov. 2002
Interred in Boston U.S.A.

R. I. P.

IN LOVING MEMORY OF
PATRICK J TIERNAN
SHEEANE CURRAGHROE
DIED 16TH JULY 1988

R. I. P.

ERECTED BY HIS WIFE KATHLEEN

EDWARD "NED" HEGARTY

THEY FOVE
THEIR DAUGHTER
THEIR SON EDW

IN
LOVING MEMORY OF
JAMES TIERNAN
BALLINCURRY
DIED 28TH SEPT 1979
AGED 84 YEARS
HIS WIFE LENA
DIED 9TH AUG. 1979 AGED 77 YEARS
THEIR DAUGHTER MONA
DIED 11TH JULY 1934 AGED 3 YEARS

R. I. P.